Proceedings

1999 IEEE International Conference on
Information Visualization

An International Conference on Computer Visualization & Graphics

Proceedings

1999 IEEE International Conference on
Information Visualization

An International Conference on Computer Visualization & Graphics

14-16 July 1999
London, England

Edited by
E. Banissi, F. Khosrowshahi, M. Sarfraz, E. Tatham, and A. Ursyn

Convened by
GraphicsLink

Supported by
Visualisation & Graphics Research Unit (VGRU), South Bank University, UK
Intelligent CAD Laboratory, Pontificia Universidade Catolica do Rio De Janeiro, Brazil
Computer Graphics & Modelling Group, DMU Milton Keynes, UK
Information and Computer Science Department, KFUPM, SA
The Augmented Reality Research Group, The Open University, UK
School of Construction, South Bank University, UK
Faculty of Architecture and Town Planning, Technion, Israel
Department of Visual Art, University of Northern Colorado, USA

IEEE
COMPUTER
SOCIETY

Los Alamitos, California
Washington • Brussels • Tokyo

IEEE Computer Society Order Number PR00210
ISBN 0-7695-0210-5
ISBN 0-7695-0212-1 (microfiche)
Library of Congress Number 99-61704
ISSN 1093-9547

Additional copies may be ordered from:

IEEE Computer Society
Customer Service Center
10662 Los Vaqueros Circle
P.O. Box 3014
Los Alamitos, CA 90720-1314
Tel: + 1-714-821-8380
Fax: + 1-714-821-4641
E-mail: cs.books@computer.org

IEEE Service Center
445 Hoes Lane
P.O. Box 1331
Piscataway, NJ 08855-1331
Tel: + 1-732-981-0060
Fax: + 1-732-981-9667
mis.custserv@computer.org

IEEE Computer Society
Asia/Pacific Office
Watanabe Building,
1-4-2 Minami-Aoyama
Minato-ku, Tokyo 107-0062 JAPAN
Tel: + 81-3-3408-3118
Fax: + 81-3-3408-3553
tokyo.ofc@computer.org

Editorial production by Danielle C. Martin

Cover art production by Alex Torres

Printed in the United States of America by The Printing House

Table of Contents
1999 International Conference on Information Visualization (IV'99)

⌇ Session 1-1: Information Visualization
Chair: Mark W. McK. Bannatyne, Purdue University, USA

Keynote Lecture

*Mikael Jern, Linköping University, Sweden and Director of EC Commission
Affairs Advanced Visual Systems, Denmark*

Keynote Lecture

*Brian A. Barsky, University of California at Berkeley, USA and
The Hong Kong University of Science and Technology, HK*

⌇ Session 1-2: Information Visualization
Chair: Yuhua Luo, University of Balearic Islands, Spain

A. Rossi and M. Varga

C. Chen and L. Carr

Y. Gong, G. Proietti, and D. LaRose

⌇ Session 1-3: Augmented and Virtual Reality in Training
Chair: Eric W. Tatham, The Open University, UK

A. Boud, D. Haniff, C. Baber, and S. Steiner

J. Watson, D. Taylor, and S. Lockwood

V. Geroimenko and M. Phillips

Session 3-7: Applied Visualization
Chair: Rivka Oxman, Technion, Israel

Keynote Lecture

Preface

Scholars of computer science have a determination and a vision to push the application of computing to new frontiers. In many new applications, the aim is to use computers to help us visualize and this has brought visualization and graphics to the fore within computer science. It is part of the current revolution in "Seeing Aids" that searches for simplicity, the hiding of complexity, or the highlighting of ambiguity in data motivate new and exciting forms of visual language. Information Visualization, although a fairly recent area of focus, has a multidisciplinary and long lasting impact. For this reason, IV series intends to promote this domain of activity by drawing on the expertise of practitioners from a range of disciplines.

Information Visualization 1999 (IV'99) is the third conference on information visualization techniques and application that aims to bring together scientists and artists from of a variety of backgrounds to present, review and update the latest work related to visualization of computer-based information. We were encouraged by the success of the previous events and by the outstanding originality and diversity of the intellectual thought brought to bear by the conference's contributors.

This year, IV'99 once again aims to resonate the scope of the evolving spectra of computer Visualization and Graphics with a spotlight on Information Visualization. Joining us in this endeavor are over 100 researchers who will share a chapter of their efforts with their fellows. Together, the papers collected here reflect the vibrant state of Information Visualization research and, bringing together researchers from around the world, has allowed us to assess and address the scope of this field from a much wider perspective. Each contributor to this conference has indeed added a fresh view, challenged our beliefs and progressed our adventure in innovation. I am grateful to each for sharing their valuable work with us.

With the hope that this conference will widen our awareness of knowledge, we welcome you to IV'99.

Acknowledgement

I am deeply indebted to all contributors to this conference and all the referees for their infinite patience and cogent reviews of papers, who helped us with their expertise and thoughtful advice and consequently made this event a truly joint project. I would like to extend my sincere thanks to our keynote speakers: Professor Brian A. Barsky, Professor Mikael Jern and Dr. Ghassan Aouad. My special thanks to all the Program, Organizing and Liaison committees:

PROGRAM COMMITTEE:

Professor Arie Kaufman, *USA*

Dr. Mikael Jern, *DK*

Dr. Mark W.McK. Bannatyne, *USA*

Dr. Ken W Brodlie, *UK*

Dr. Ebad Banissi, *UK*

Dr. Farzad Khosrowshahi, *UK*

Professor Yuhua Luo, *Spain*

Professor Michael L.V. Pitteway, *UK*

Professor Vladimir Prokhorov, *Russia*

Mr. John Risch, *USA*

Professor Przemyslaw Rokita, *Poland*

Professor Hassan Said, *Malaysia*

Professor Nadia Magnenat Thalmann, *Switzerland*

Dr. Leonardo Traversoni, *Mexico*

Dr. Keith Unsworth, *New Zealand*

Dr. Wenping Wang, *Hong Kong*

Dr. Gordon Clapworthy, *UK*

Dr. Muhammad Sarfraz, *KFUM, SA*

ORGANIZING & LIAISON COMMITTEE:

Symposium on Augmented and Virtual Reality, AVR'99

Eric Tatham, The Augmented Reality Research Group, *The Open University, UK*

Symposium on Design Visualization, D-vis'99 — Liaison

Rivka Oxman, *Technion, Israel*

Digital Typography'99 Liaison

Fiaz Hussain, *De-Montfort University*

Computer Animation & Special Effects'99 Liaison

Marcelo Dreux, ICAD, *Brazil*

Information Visualization'99 Liaison

Ebad Banissi, *VGRU, SBU*

Computer Aided Geometric Design-CAGD'99 Liaison

Muhammad Sarfraz, *KFUM, SA*

Visualization in Construction & Architecture'99 Liaison

Farzad Khosrowshahi, *SBU*

Symposium and Gallery of Digital Art (D-ART'99) Liaison

Anna Ursyn, *University of Northern Colorado*

Multimedia'99 Liaison

Fiaz Hussain, *De-Montfort University*

Tutorial Liaison

Frank Devai, *VGRU, SBU*

Technical Programme Organizer

Ahmad Aljamali, *VGRU, SBU*

Local Organizational Liaison

Anita D'Pour, *GraphicsLink, UK*

The conference event and the Proceedings are the work of many members of the Program Committee, the Organizing Committee, all the other Reviewers, Technical members and Administrative team and, most importantly, the contributors to whom we remain beholden in every sense of the word.

Finally, I would offer my sincere thanks to Ms Anita D'Pour of GraphicsLink for her continuos effort in preparing, organizing and handling of the conference's administration. My appreciation to Danielle Martin and Regina Spencer Sipple and the IEEE publishing team for their patience, professionalism and high standard of editorial production of the Proceedings.

Ebad Banissi

Session 1-1

Information Visualization

Chair
Mark W. McK. Bannatyne
Purdue University, USA

Visual Intelligence Turning Data into Knowledge

Mikael Jern
Advanced Visual Systems Denmark

ABSTRACT

In an intensely competitive global business environment, companies compete for advantage on many fronts, including the area of information technology. Companies that exploit their business data effectively can gain important insight into markets, and respond to the constantly changing needs of customers. Consider how often business data is generated: every time we make a credit card purchase, use a mobile telephone, and conduct many other of our daily tasks, potentially valuable data is created. Data is both plentiful and available. The challenge, and the opportunity for creating competitive advantage, is successfully identifying relevant information in massive repositories of raw, transactional data. In the *information age*, lack of data is rarely a problem.

In contrast, it is increasingly common to encounter problems for which all the necessary data is potentially available to make a complete assessment of the risks, and hence to reach an optimum solution. Mapping the data through to timely, quality decisions has never been harder.

Answering the call is a new realm of data exploration tools called ***Visual Intelligence***. This is a process that provides revolutionary technology to address the challenge of discovering and exploiting information. For innovative companies, powerful Visual Intelligence applications are improving their decision-making capabilities by performing spatial and multivariate visual data analysis and providing rapid access to comprehensible information. This paper examines the issue faced by most business - how to turn data into powerful business knowledge, and make this knowledge accessible to persons who rely on it. The role of Information Visualization techniques and the Visual User Interface in the overall Visual Intelligence process is assessed.

The Visual Intelligence tools introduce a brand new opportunity for decision-makers. It brings open and customizable visual data mining tools to their desktop. Advanced visualization methods provide an easy to use and economic way to build qualitative knowledge.

The integration of Data Warehousing, Information Visualization, Web and new Visual Interaction techniques will change and expand the paradigms of current work of humans using computers. Visual Intelligence will improve visual communication that takes place in all elements of the user interface and provide decreased time-to-enlightenment.

VISUAL INTELLIGENCE – TURNING DATA INTO KNOWLEDGE

Mikael Jern
Advanced Visual Systems and Linkoping University
E-mail: mikael@avs.dk

ABSTRACT

Visual Intelligence is a process that provides information visualization technology to address the challenge of discovering and exploiting information. For innovative companies, Visual Intelligence applications are improving their decision-making capabilities by performing spatial and multivariate visual data analysis and providing rapid access to comprehensible information. This paper examines the issue faced by most business - how to turn data into understandable business knowledge, and make this knowledge accessible to persons who rely on it. The role of information visualization techniques and the Visual User Interface (VUI) in the overall Visual Intelligence process is assessed.

The integration of Data Warehousing, Information Visualization, Web and new Visual Interaction techniques will change and expand the paradigms of current work of humans using computers. Visual Intelligence will improve visual communication that takes place in all elements of the user interface and provide decreased *"time-to-enlightenment"*.

CHALLENGES

The evolution in information visualization is presenting many technological challenges, but perhaps the greatest challenge is in retaining the intimate involvement and understanding of the end user. The traditional interfaces of mouse, keyboard and screens of text allow us to work *on* the desktop computer, while information visualization truly enables us to work *with* the desktop computer. There are major challenges in providing the perfect information visualization tools that will change and expand the paradigms of current work of humans using computers.

The **first challenge** is *locating and retrieving the relevant data*, from a data world which is growing in size, but is also declining in average information content.. Our ability, however, to consume information is largely unchanged. Tools will be required to *navigate* efficiently to retrieve specific data, to *explore* data surrounding a topic of general interest, and effortlessly *browse* the wider data world.

The **second challenge** is *understanding the complexity*, i.e. the conversion of appropriate data to relevant information. This can be achieved by maintaining a high level of human involvement and participation in the processing and analysis of data through visual interaction with the data analysis process. Information visualization retains our involvement and understanding, and ensures that we do not generate abstract solutions that are divorced from the original problem. Consider the simple example of regression analysis to fit a straight line. Seeing the points and regression line in the same graph provides an immediate understanding of the process. We can easily spot weaknesses in the interpretation.

The **third challenge** of information visualization techniques is to *find interfaces and display formats* that maximize information content in applications without introducing corresponding levels of application complexity. Visual tools, in addition to representing information, can act to simplify an application's user interface, and by so doing, contribute to the application's acceptance on the business desktop.

The **fourth challenge** is in effectively *communication a vision*, such that it is accurately shared and understood by a wider and less specialist audience. Web-based information visualization tools will provide solutions.

Although advanced data mining techniques are available, they often appear as inaccessible "black box" solutions with a poor user interface and cannot be changed by the users. The **final challenge** is to provide "*open*" and "*customizable*" visualization tools to better integrate the visual user interface with the data mining process. These tools must comply with an industry-standard architecture, such as DCOM/ActiveX or Java.

VISUAL INTELLIGENCE

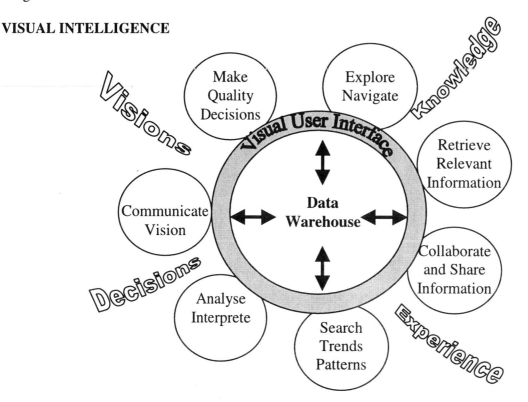

Figure 1: Conversion of data to informed decisions and shared knowledge in the overall Visual Intelligence process provided by a set of Tasks (circles).

Important features of the Visual Intelligence Process:

1. Full integration with the data warehouse or spreadsheet process by which data is brought together and stored in a multidimensional data structure.
2. A set of Information Visualization tasks which may be undertaken by the user.
3. Different categories of users who impose different goals on the process.
4. Visual User Interface layer with support for both local and network interaction – "Thin" and "Fat" client scenarios.
5. Web-based component architecture (DCOM/ActiveX or Java).
6. Tight integration between data and visualization supporting "drill-down" features.
7. Customizable and user friendly solutions instead of inaccessible "black boxes"
8. Sharing of increased knowledge though better "communication" tools

ROLE FOR VISUALIZATION

The fundamental purpose of any visualization is to communicate information to users. Visualization sits at the interface between what machines are good at (data information) and what people are good at (Knowledge, Experience). The overall objective of visual communication that takes place in all phases of a Visual Intelligence process is to provide decreased ***"time-to-enlightenment"***.

Visualization is the glue within the Visual Intelligence process and the user will be able to navigate within this process. The visualization tasks enables data analysts to fast analyze large quantities of information (millions of entities), aiding quick understanding of data distributions and rapid detection of patterns. This activity "*explore*" naturally takes place before the detailed specific analysis "*understanding complexity*", which may employ statistical and data mining tools. Finally, visualization is a powerful tool to "*communicate*" and "*navigate*" through the results of a Visual Intelligence process.

Exploration

Visualization components combine the use of industry standard component technology with advanced multidimensional data visualization. More important the VUI capabilities provide tight integration with the underlying data repository. This integration includes "drilldown" features that enable you to get back to the real, underlying data, while working with the visual tasks. It is important at the outset that a "user interface" is not only a screen design but also a ***method of interacting with the data warehouse and its data***.

VISUAL EXPLORATION

In this scenario, visualization techniques are used to rapidly scan through the large quantities of data enabling the user to visually search for patterns and relationships. The user will discover relationships without prior knowledge of what is interesting and important information. The aim is to directly engage the user in the Visual Intelligence process using visualization as a discovery tool, and as much as possible bring the

user into "direct" association with the data. Visualization will present the data landscape in a natural and intuitive form, making full use of the human capacity to absorb and interact with complex images, far beyond typical directory structures or screens of text and numbers.

Visual exploration tools are:

- Integrated with data storage and data analysis (data warehouse, Excel,..)
- Fast and interactive but easy-to-use
- Natural and intuitive visual interface
- Meaningful spatial relationship through 3D geographic visualization
- Multi-dimensional data analysis, filtering, segmentation, pattern identification
- Programmed to "*look for something interesting*"
- Open and Customizable

A concept demonstrator has been developed funded by an EC project CONTENTS using the Advanced Visual Systems' OpenViz DCOM/ActiveX components (visualization and visual interaction) and Microsoft's Visual Basic (user interface) to illustrate the use of an interactive visual interface for exploring data in a standard Excel Spreadsheet.

Demonstrator: EXCEL Visualizer

The "customizable" visualization component in figure 2, is an example of the VUI technique serving as the visual front-end to any Excel application. The user explores various aspects of multidimensional data using a 3D glyph visualization paradigm with value-based filtering and data "drill-down". The selected data to be viewed is automatically transferred from Excel to the embedded visualization component.

There are three important roles for visualization in the Visual Intelligence process:

- **Explore** (What-if, interaction, drill-down, VUI, integration, open tools)
- **Understanding Complexity** (visual tools integrated with analysis process)
- **Communicate and Navigate** (Descriptive Visualization, Collaboration, Web)

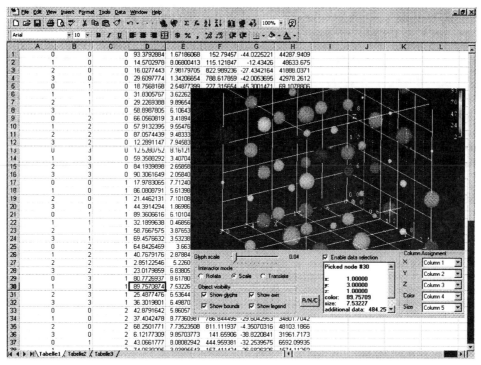

Figure 2: The 3D glyph visualization is implemented as an ActiveX DCOM component, fully integrated with Excel. Rows and columns are selected and highlighted in an Excel spreadsheet. Data can easily be selected, viewed, edited, added or deleted. With a simple mouse-click, the user has selected a "sphere" representing data in row 30 of the spreadsheet.

UNDERSTANDING COMPLEXITY

Understanding the complexity, i.e. the conversion of appropriate data to relevant information represents is another important role for visualization. This means maintaining a high level of human involvement and participation in the processing and analysis of data through visual interaction. While data mining typically relies on numerical techniques such as statistics to uncover relationships and patterns in large data warehouses, visual tools incorporates the power of an additional analysis tool; the human eye. There are many parallels with the initial "exploring" of data, in that the overall goal is summarization and compression of data without significant loss of content.

Although sophisticated data mining tools is available, they can often appear as inaccessible "black boxes" to the user. Moreover, response to the output ranges from blind trust and acceptance because of expert status of the data mining package, through to skeptical distrust because the underlying techniques are invisible and poorly understood. Integrating visual tools with the data

modelling and analysis tools will retain the human involvement and understanding.

Direct-manipulation Visual User Interface tools provide intuitive and interactive user interfaces that maximize information content. Users not only view data, but also explore what they see. Picking or drilling down operations are used to return summary information, launch additional queries into the data store, and propagate the applications interface components with particular information, thus promoting the process of information discovery.

AVS's open Java and DCOM component architectures represent the framework for integrated visualization and VUI tools within the scope of a Visual Intelligence process. Furthermore, these tools provide a sophisticated data model that can represent all types of, and dimensions of, data. The tools can easily operate on data from various sources, including operational databases and data warehouses, dynamic data feeds, and files out put from other applications. The visualization tools can integrate diverse data sources and analytical processes in a single Visual Intelligence process.

"Understanding Complexity" tools are:

- Integrated with data storage and data analysis (database, data warehouse, etc)
- Intuitive and interactive visual interface - Visual User Interface
- Direct engagement of the user – immediate, continuous feedback
- Computation steering of the data analysis process
- Open and Customizable

COMMUNICATION

The final role of Visualization is in effectively communicating a vision, such that it is accurately shared and understood by the audience. This seemingly easy task can employ an entire marketing department in defining and conveying the features of a service. It is unlikely that the business managers and IT specialists will be able to find a common language for their discussions, but a common expression could be possible in a three dimensional visual representation.

Communication tools support the ability to draw the users focus to the key relationships already discovered and deliver enough information and in the right context for effective decision making. By preparing and presenting the data graphically, the user can uncover properties of the data and quickly and easily detect patterns or deviations from expected results. He or she can get a picture of "what the data is trying to tell him/her", and then perhaps confirm the observations with other statistical analysis.

Visual Intelligence allows the user to focus on what is important, but it's critical to have immediate access to the detail data behind the summary data. Detail data should be available to help provide the rationale for discovered trends.

Web-based technology provides the framework for a superior navigation tool through the Visual Intelligence process.

Communication tools are:

- Delivering the right information in an appropriate context
- 2D and 3D *Descriptive* Visualization tools
- Open and Customizable graphs
- Annotation, layout, axes, color map, text
- Animation supported on any variable
- GIF, TIFF, VRML formats
- Collaborative or Web-based visualization – "Thin" and "Fat" visualization clients

The Communication role can be thought of as the last step in a Visual Intelligence process, but the same visual tools may assume different roles in the process.

"SMART" DOCUMENTS FOR WEB-ENABLED COLLABORATION

With the increasing use of Microsoft's electronic documents (Office 97), distributed by Internet and Intranet, the opportunity to provide easy-to-use, advanced interactive 3D visualization techniques within electronic documents on the powerful PC desktop has become possible. Open and customizable visualization components allow the author of a report to distribute the relevant electronic information coupled with an embedded data analysis-viewer "smartdoc", which allows the recipients to interactively examine the data in the same way as the original analyst. Instead of being a dumb document, the "smartdoc" would be a complete data exploration application through which a reader could, via embedded ActiveX visualization/analysis components, explore the data underlying the report. Instead of being a static summary document the report becomes much more like a very natural interface or portal onto the data.

To embed the new assembled visualization ActiveX component into a Word97 document, simply import the ActiveX control into your Word97 document like any GIF or TIFF file and add interactive 3D visualization to your electronic document. This document can then be transmitted to colleagues over the network. The ActiveX components reside locally on your PC and must only be downloaded and installed once on your local PC.

CONCLUSION

The ability of businesses to collect data has outpaced their ability to analyze it. As data repositories grow larger, applications that can process this data become increasingly important. Visual Intelligence is emerging as an essential technique for exploiting the information content of multidimensional databases, and this technique is revolutionizing the functionality of business desktop applications. Visual Intelligence tools developed within the European Project CONTENTS provide capabilities which are key to the information discovery process.

- Data structures for accurately modeling complex business and warehouse data.
- Information rich, interactive visual representations of highly multivariate data.
- Web-based component architecture (DCOM/ActiveX or Java).
- Tight integration between data and visualization supporting "drill-down" features.
- Customizable and user friendly solutions instead of inaccessible "black boxes".
- Sharing of increased knowledge though powerful communication tools.

About the European ESPRIT Project CONTENTS – Start 1 January, 1999

The objective of the CONTENTS Project is to develop customisable Application Components for the interactive visual analysis of data on powerful PC platforms. The data of interest are large multivariate data sets (engineering, medical and commercial) generated by simulation / modelling / measurement running in a distributed and heterogeneous environment (including NT-based Intel parallel processor and suitable UNIX platforms). The components will be based on the emerging industry standard ActiveX/DCOM architecture, and will be properly "bridged" towards CORBA based architectures, for multi-platform portability and compatibility.

These Interactive Visualisation Components will be embedded within electronic documents, allowing the author of a report to distribute the relevant electronic information coupled with an embedded High Performance data analysis-viewer "smartdoc", which allows the recipients to interactively examine the data in the same way as the original analyst. Instead of being a dumb document, the "smartdoc" will be a complete data exploration application through which a reader can, via embedded High Performance visualisation / analysis components explore the data underlying the report.

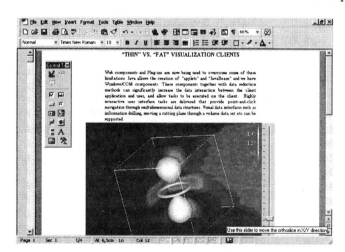

Figure 3: Example of a "Smart" Document – interactive 3D visualization embedded in a standard Word97 document. "Smart" documents provides solutions to the Visual Intelligence process and contribute to the application's acceptance on the business desktop.

The OPTICAL Project:
OPtics and Topography Involving the Cornea And Lens

Brian A. Barsky
University of California, Berkeley

ABSTRACT

The OPTICAL project is a multidisciplinary effort in the Computer Science, Division and School of Optometry. "OPTICAL" is an acronym for "OPtics and Topography Involving the Cornea And Lens". This project is concerned with the measurement, modeling, reconstruction, and visualization of the shape of the human cornea.

The cornea is the clear fibrous tissue forming the front surface of the eye. Its shape is very important in determining visual acuity. The shape is also important for fitting contact lenses and performing corneal refractive surgery.

To recover the shape of the cornea, clinicians use one of several commercially available corneal topography instruments known as videokeratographs. These devices project a pattern onto the cornea and record the reflected image. The image is then analyzed to recover the shape information.

We have developed a new analysis algorithm that has several advantages compared to current approaches: it is more accurate, it directly recovers position of the cornea, and it produces a continuous map over the entire surface. To develop this algorithm, we have assimilated ideas from a variety of fields, including ray-tracing (computer graphics and optics), smooth B-spline surfaces (geometric modeling) and simulation.

This algorithm for accurately measuring the cornea is an essential first step in the scientific visualization of corneal topography. After measuring the shape of the cornea, it is important to be able to display the results in a manner that highlights the important features of the surface and is understandable to viewers with a wide variety of backgrounds. We have developed new scientific visualization approaches which overcome some of the shortcomings of the displays used in current corneal topography instruments.

Session 1-2

Information Visualization

Chair

Yuhua Luo

University of Balearic Islands, Spain

Visualisation of Massive Retrieved Newsfeeds in Interactive 3D

Adrian M. Rossi and Margaret Varga

DERA Malvern, St Andrews Rd, Malvern, WORCS WR14 3PS
Email: arossi@dera.gov.uk, varga@dera.gov.uk

Abstract

This report describes work carried out under the Automatic Information Retrieval project at DERA, in building a 4D landscape (a TextScape*) which acts as a graphical user interface (GUI) to the DERA-OKAPI search engine. Traditionally search engines present a 2D visual interface (usually a Windows-Icons-Menus-Pointer (WIMP) interface) to the user. Key words are entered and the 'hits' are displayed usually in a list form. Unfortunately the number of documents retrieved is often overwhelming and a significant amount of time is still required to read abstracts and sections of documents in order to determine if they are relevant, even after the search engine has performed relevance ranking. The challenge is how to improve on this. We propose to render the information most immediately required onto the visual attributes of a 3D landscape. Shape, colour and size can then project the information that is sought, and mining the object hierarchy visually returns information more rapidly.*

Keywords: Information Visualisation, Search Engine, Graphical User Interface

I. Introduction

This report describes work carried out under the Automatic Information Retrieval (AIR) project in applying 4D Information Visualisation technology to improving the interface between a human user and the DERA-Okapi search engine.

Section II briefly summarises the 4D visualisation process, so that the reader has an established framework with which to understand the tasks which need to be carried out. Section III gives an overview of the functionality of the DERA-Okapi newsfeed search engine. Section IV applies the data visualisation process to the DERA-Okapi interface in order to demonstrate how 4D technology greatly enhances a user's ability to extract the relevant articles they require over DERA-Okapi's traditional 2D graphical user interface (GUI). Section V concludes with a screenshot of the 4D *TextScape* and a brief functional description.

II. Creating a 4D visualisation

The steps which we follow in order to create our 3D landscape are described in [1]. There are essentially four stages: (I) Data Collection; (II) Geometric Modelling; (III) Rendering; and, (IV) Architecture Design, but they are not necessarily applied only once. The process is more iterative in nature whereby several cycles through the four stages could easily be justified, or even necessary. In fact, if the data source is a live feed then every time new data arrives,

the process is executed dynamically by the visualisation system in order to rebuild the landscape.

III. The DERA-OKAPI information retrieval demonstrator

DERA-Okapi is an experimental information routing system, developed as an alternative to the present available Boolean systems. It aims to provide an interactive application where the user can guide the search according to the relevance of terms and/or phrases of interest to the user. The DERA-Okapi is different to other text-based search engines because it is able to search continuous data sources, such as newsfeeds.

To initiate a search a minimum of three terms must be entered; these terms become the Keywords or Key-phrases that the DERA–Okapi search engine uses. Once enough terms have been entered the *Search Database* option becomes available. The results of a search are then displayed in the *Document Hit List* window. Information about each document is summarised in a green bar, which when double-clicked will open the document. The actual content of the document is summarised underneath the green bar.

The potential relevance of both the document and its contents is determined by the system. However, after the user has chosen some relevant documents (at least three must be selected) DERA-Okapi generates a more specific search *profile* from the most common terms among the

0-7695-0210-5/99 $10.00 © 1999 IEEE

documents selected. A profile is a list of *Keywords* or *Keyphrases* which DERA-Okapi will use to rank documents it retrieves from the database for relevance. An initial profile is defined by DERA- Okapi, but the user can save a search and load this new updated profile using the options menu. The user can then initiate a more detailed search using the new profile or can change the profile by adding and removing terms from the generated list.

The current DERA-Okapi window is divided into four panes. Pane A, labelled *Query Terms*, contains the current active profile. Pane B, initially empty, will contain a list of Keywords which have been rejected for use within future searches by the user. As previously mentioned, pane C, labelled *Document Hitlist*, will contain a list of the most relevant retrieved documents matching the search criteria. Finally, Pane D lists the documents which the user has decided to retain from the search.

The search of the database is refined by a weighting of the search data, which helps rank the retrieved documents in an order of relevance. The frequency of the term in both the database and the documents is taken into account. If a term only occurs in a few documents and with a high frequency in those documents, then it would have a high relevance. The ranking of the document would increase if the same number of terms were found in a short document as in a document of a longer length i.e. *normalisation* is performed.

When DERA-Okapi has completed searching the database for the most relevant newsfeeds, the retrieved documents are summarised in the Document Hit list window. The search terms are listed with the word count of their occurrence within the document in brackets next to each of them. The user is then able to choose whether the document is relevant or not using the three option buttons available: 'FULL DOCUMENT RELEVANT', 'PASSAGE ONLY RELEVANT', and 'NOT RELEVANT' and hence retain those they consider most relevant.

IV. Applying the data visualisation process

A. Geometric modelling

(i) Data Analysis

Clearly the objective in any text search is to locate as quickly as possible all available documents on the topic of interest. and to this end it is up to the human user to determine which *key words* best reflect the topic of the article or report which is to be retrieved and pass this to the search engine. With respect to our application, there are two main problems with this: (1) there may be documents sharing the same key words but discussing very different topics and (2) the user may not come up with the most effective keywords at first, resulting in a suboptimal search path to the most relevant documents, assuming they are located at all. Both of these are a result of the fact that concepts can not easily be represented by a few key words and it is keywords, not concepts, which computers understand.

An immediate practical solution to (2) is that used by DERA-Okapi; make the search process an iterative one and have the search engine generate possible key words for selection or rejection by the user (thus creating the keyword profile). The search is then repeatedly refined until only a manageable number of documents remain. Through the generation of an increasingly large set of relevant key words the hope is that in the limit the topic is well-captured. Of course this does not alleviate (1) as the reading of some part of the documents retrieved must still be carried out.

So, this solution does not remove the need for the user to examine the context of the keywords for document relevance. It may suffice to examine the title of the document; on the other hand it may be necessary to delve deeper into other data components such as the *contextual sentence, paragraph,* or *passage* (i.e. the body of text in the which the key words reside), the *contextual section titles* (if they exist), or ultimately, and least desirably, into the *whole document.*

A first step then in building an effective 4D visualisation is to specify the information which the user wants to extract from it. This may imply more than just identification; one might prioritise these data components and place them in an *accessibility hierarchy* so that the most readily available data is also the most important or the most likely to be required early on in the data mining process.

Other textual constructs which may give rapid understanding of the topics covered in the document are the *Abstract, Executive Summary* or even the *Introduction.* If these components exist within the documents in the database one is searching then the next step is to order them on the basis of most-likely-to-reveal-a-document's-subject to the least-likely-to-reveal-a-document's-subject. Intuitively we can assert that the longer it takes to assimilate the information within the component the better the reader's understanding of the concepts covered in the document. Ultimately if the user reads the whole document from cover to cover they will have the maximum degree of comprehension of the document's content and hence can make the most informed decision as to whether to keep it. This is also the task which takes the greatest amount of time. At the other extreme knowing the sentence in which the key word resides gives only a marginally better picture of the topics covered in the document.

Despite the subjective nature of deciding which constructs reveal the most about a document in the smallest amount of time, a decision must be made. Nevertheless we can sidestep the issue by building configurability into the user interface so that the user is left to make this decision. This has the added advantage of allowing the application to be customised for a particular document database, e.g. for newsfeeds consisting of short articles with little internal structure or for journal papers which obey strict formatting rules, and can hence be assumed to have an abstract, for example.

For our purposes the exact ordering is irrelevant; our task is to map the components at the top of the hierarchy to the most quickly accessible graphical entities within our visualisation. Nevertheless, for the sake of providing a concrete demonstration of the design process we assume the database we are inspecting consists of newsfeeds (e.g. *Reuters*) and hence are short articles with little internal structure. The fundamental constructs for determining relevance are those provided within DERA-Okapi: *Key Word(s)* (or *Hit Words;* we use the two terms interchangeably), *Document Label, Document Title, Contextual Sentence, Contextual Passage* and *Whole Document.*

So far we have discussed only the raw data which is available immediately within the retrieved documents. We have yet to consider derived information, or *meta-data*. This is information which can be obtained by performing some statistical or mathematical analysis on the raw data. In DERA-Okapi this includes *Key Word Frequency* (the number of key words per total number of words in the article) and *Document Word Length* (self-explanatory). The former quantity provides insight into the depth of the discussion of a particular topic as one can identify when there is only a passing reference to a chosen key word. The latter yields some feeling for whether the document is likely to provide sufficient information on the topic required; the user may feel that a very short article is unlikely to contain an in-depth discussion on the topic.

One further piece of meta-data proves useful; *KeyWord Position.* This is the position of the KeyWord from the beginning of the document, in words. Such information gives a feel for whether the Hitword is clustered around only a few passages, and is hence not the focus of the article, or whether it is distributed uniformly throughout the article.

The next step is to prioritise these components. Figure 1 shows the data layers ranging from 'immediately accessible' to those requiring several levels of data mining. Each subsequent layer requires one further action by the user for access to it, e.g. *brushing* or *selection.* (The exact details of the architecture which was developed will be discussed in Section C)

(ii) Mapping the Data onto Selected Visual Primitives

Having identified the data components which we will need to visualise we proceed to map them onto the eight possible visual primitives: *Shape, Position, Size, Colour, Motion, Brightness, Texture, Orientation* based on their resolution.

The most readily accessible information – *Document Label, Keyword Label,* and *Keyword count* – will be immediately visible without user interaction being required. *Keyword Count* was mapped onto *Size* - the height of a 3D bar. This allows preattentive recognition of the documents which hold the greatest number of Hit Words. Both *Document Label* and *Keyword Label* are shown on the axes as 2D text in the *x-y* plane. The *Document Length* is mapped onto *Size-* the length of a line. The remaining variables are accessed through pop-up 2D Text Boxes. *KeyWord Position* is mapped onto another of the very high resolution primitives, *position* in 3D space. This is an obvious and natural mapping and this should almost always be exploited. The actual numerical value is also available in a pop-up 2D Text Box.

(iii) Symmetry Issues

We have chosen a rectilinear symmetry and a Cartesian co-ordinate system (we discuss the CityScape visualisation technique and the other graphical objects in our visualisation in Section B) and deviate from using boxes and the like only when a change of symmetry needs to reflect a different kind of information. This is an attempt to avoid distracting the viewer with irrelevant visual cues.

B. Rendering the data

(i) Extending the Cityscape Technique

The visualisation design we produced is based on the CityScape technique. It consists of a grid lying in the *x-y* plane upon which 3D bars ('*boxes*') live. The *x*-axis represents the documents and the *y*-axis lists the current keywords which have been generated or entered by the user. The height of the boxes is proportional to the Keyword Count and the actual numerical value can be seen by comparison with the *z*-axis labels.

Because a plain CityScape plot would only use one-eighth of the available 3D space (i.e. one quadrant) the technique was extended so that the region beneath the plot also serves a purpose. Hence we distinguish the positive *z*-axis (showing KeyWord Count) from the negative *z*-axis showing Document Length (in words). A second grid is constructed for visual orientation at some fixed position beneath the first. In our prototype this value is 1000 Word-units.

Denote the space above the grid as *Alpha-space* and that beneath as *Beta-space*. Then Alpha-space is occupied by the Cityscape visualisation discussed above and Beta-space is filled with a new visual entity which we can call *Threaded Tiles*. This consists of a series of regularly sized, square tiles threaded together on a common axis which extends down from the centre of the CityScape square. This axis has a length equal to the length of the document it represents. Each tile is equally thick in the *z*-direction and represents the Key Word which can be found in the document. The position of the tile along the negative *z*-axis from the ground plane (the *x-y* plane which contains the origin and on which the CityScape rests) indicates the position of the Key Word within the document. In this way clustering of Key Words within an article is immediately evident.

Of the remaining passive visual variables only *Colour* is actively used. The choice of colour is made so as to clearly distinguish each visual entity from the other. For this reason the Document Labels are in Dark Blue, the Key Word Labels are in Red and the Boxes are in Yellow so that it stands out against the grey background.

For the sake of continuity, the Threaded Tiles are coloured Gold; visually close to yellow, thus giving the impression that the CityScape Boxes transform into the Threaded Tiles. Since the height of the Boxes is equal to the number of Key Words within the document and there are exactly this number of Tiles in the corresponding Beta-space object, this is a natural transformation, which will not

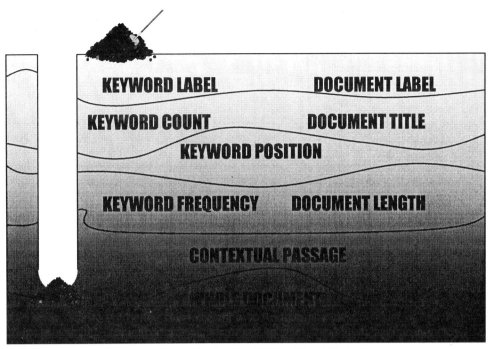

Figure 1: Access hierarchy for the DERA-Okapi Data Components

confuse the viewer. The question of how each datoid[1] is created and manipulated is the subject of the next section. The Threaded Tiles are terminated with a Purple Sphere. This helps the eye to make comparisons between the lengths of various documents by clearly delineating the end of each Thread. Interaction with the ball yields further information and again this is a part of the *Architecture Design* phase.

So far we have described the key graphical components which make up TextScape. The remaining visual components are more traditional and belong to the GUI design phase; a task which falls within the final stage of the visualisation process, Architecture Design.

C. Architecture design

(i) The Datoids

For future reference we name the various views in the 3D scene. The 3D Boxes in Alpha-space which form the TextScape and represent the Key Word Counts of each Hit Word against each Document we refer to as *Alpha Boxes*. The Beta-space tiles representing the position of each word within a document we have previously dubbed *Threaded Tiles*. The spherical datoid which terminates the thread passing through each Threaded Tiles view is a *Termi-Ball*.

In addition to adding interaction to existing visual elements we introduce a purely UI datoid; 3D Buttons which we call *Buttoids*. They are the equivalent 3D version of standard 2D GUI buttons found in most API's. They are spheres which when selected provide additional

information to the user while visually they contract to half-radius size and turn black. There is one Buttoid for each document and for each Key Word and they are situated adjacent to the corresponding document and word labels in the *x-y* plane. These buttons provide an upper-level, immediate access to the retrieved document text and key word contexts thus bypassing any incremental data mining. Of course, this is also the most time-consuming method for determining relevance but the option must be there for the user. They are described in more detail below. The Buttoids along the Document axis we will call *Buttoids-D* and those along the Key Word axis, *Buttoids-K*.

(ii) Interactivity

In3D implements several of the most important user interaction mechanisms within its 3D environment; we make use of two of these – *Selection* and *Brushing*.

Brushing is the where the mouse pointer is moved over a view in the scene and a pop-up 2D text panel appears, displaying information somehow connected to the graphical entity which has been brushed. *Selection* is where additionally the left mouse button is pressed once. There is also *Double-Selection* (two left-mouse clicks in rapid succession) but we have not implemented this feature. Selection and brushing have been implemented on all scene datoids.

Brushing on the Alpha-boxes opens a overlay 2D text box which lists the name of the document, the Key Word and the Key Word Count for this Key Word within the document. Selecting an Alpha-box creates a Threaded Tiles view for that document and Key Word combination, extending down into Beta-space. A secondary effect is to set the height of the Alpha-box to zero, thus reducing cluttering in Alpha-space. The user can use this mechanism

---

[1] Datoid is an abbreviation of 'data solid' and refers to any 3D object which represents data in some way, analogous to a point on a graph in 2D space, for example.

to temporarily remove boxes from the TextScape to increase visibility of the remaining boxes. Selecting the base square of the Alpha-box (also the top of the Threaded Tiles at this point since it is visible) reverses the process, recreating the Alpha-box and making invisible the Threaded Tiles.

Brushing on a particular tile will pop-up an overlay text box showing the Key Word, the document and the position of the word which is given by counting the number of words from the beginning of the text. Selecting a tile will open-up a text panel overlay (using the class *TextPanel* from the Java Swing package). The panel shows the actual passage within which the Key Word resides; this data is read in dynamically from a text file in memory. Scroll-bars allow the user to see all the text and at the same time keeps the initial size of the text panel small. Selecting the same tile again closes the panel. Redundancy has been built-in in many places and in this case the text panel can also be closed using its Window's button in the top right hand corner of the panel.

The panel also contains a button at the bottom which is labelled 'Relevant'. When pressed the current passage is identified as being relevant and the details of the document selected are added to the DR pane with a '[P]' in front. The symbol [P] tells the user that only the passage containing that particular Key Word is relevant, not the whole document.

Brushing the Termi-ball creates an overlay listing the total length of the document in words and the name of the document. Selecting the Termi-ball opens a Text Panel with the *whole* document now visible within it. The button at the base of the panel selects the whole document for retention thus adding its details to the DR pane and placing an '[F]' in front of it.

The Buttoids-D can only be selected and when they are several things happen. The first is a visible indication that the buttoid has been selected – it turns black. The second is that the row of Alpha-boxes indicated by the document are shaded grey. The final event that is triggered is to add this document to a list of Documents Retained; hence the purpose of this button is to select documents which are of interest and keep them for future reference. The list resides in a 2D visual GUI component described in more detail in the next section.

The Buttoids-K are used to remove Key Words permanently from the search criteria. Selecting them adds the word to a list of Key Words removed. DERA-Okapi no longer uses this word in its search but it is necessary to keep a record of the words which have been removed to avoid introducing them again later in the iterative search procedure.

(iii) Designing the 2D GUI

As previously mentioned the Buttoids-K select KeyWords to be rejected (from the automatically generated set or from the set of user defined key words) and Buttoids-D select documents to be retained.

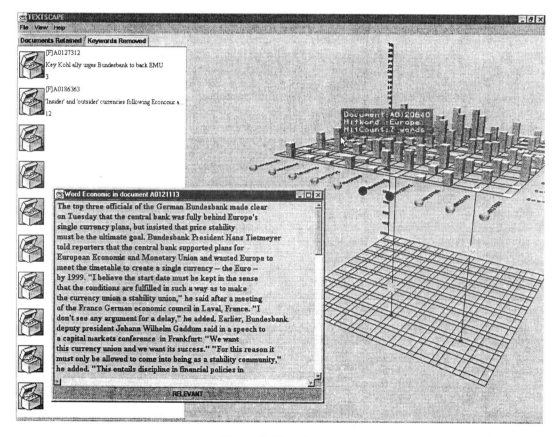

Figure 2 : TextScape

We have divided the screen up into two areas: the 3D window containing TextScape occupies approximately two thirds of the available real-estate on the right and the remaining space is taken up by two tabbed panes (from the Java Swing class *TabbedPane*). Selecting a tab will bring that pane to the foreground and obscures the second pane. The tabs are labelled with *Documents Retained* and *Key Words Removed* and we refer to these two lists or window panes as the DR and KR panes from now on.

In order to bypass the creation of Threaded Tiles, the user can select one of the Buttons-D. The corresponding document to be retained is then added to the DR window with an '[F]' indicating that the whole document is relevant. This avoids having to read or open the document at all before selecting it for retention. Similarly for the Buttons-K, the Key Word label is added to the KR pane when they are pressed.

So, to recap and summarise, to open only part of the document one must single-click an Alpha-box and create a Threaded Tiles view. Single-clicking on the Termi-ball for a particular article will add the item to the DR window with an '[F]' next to it. Single-clicking on a Tile will open a passage which shows the Keyword within its context. The 2D pop-up text panel contains a button for selecting the passage relevant option and this closes the window and adds the article to the DR pane with a '[P]' next to it. The icon for these documents is in a different colour from those where the whole document is relevant. A similar button on the pop-up text panel produced from clicking the Termiball selects the '[F]' option and adds it to the DR window. This has the same effect in other words as clicking the Buttons-D but additionally allows one to view and hence read the document beforehand.

V. Conclusions

Figure 2 is a complete screenshot of the TextScape environment, showing brushing behaviour and pop-up text displays of the underlying documents. The 3D engine and Java API (Application Programming Interface) for it are part of a product called In3D/Java© Developer's edition, from Visible Decisions Inc.

As much as possible we have attempted to design a user interface which is intuitive, straightforward, and retains those characteristics of traditional search engine UI's which users have found attractive.

Nevertheless, extensive testing of the usability of this system needs to be carried out and feedback incorporated into subsequent versions. It is possible to imagine (and the authors have) many other interactive extensions which could be incorporated into the visualisation and these will be the subject of future research efforts.

VI. Acknowledgements

This work was carried out as part of Technology Group 10 of the MoD Corporate Research Programme.

VII. References

[1]   **Rossi A.M.,** Fundamental Design Issues in 4D Information Visualisation, 1998 *(to be published in IEEE Computer Graphics & Applications)*

[2]   **Treisman A.**, "Preattentive processing in Vision", Computer Vision, Graphics and Image Processing, Vol. 31, 1985, pp.156-177,

[3]   **Bertin, Jacques**, "Graphics and Graphic Information Processing", translated by P.Berg and P.Scott, Berlin: William de Gruyter and Co.,1989

[4]   **Harrand V.J.** *et al* "Scientific Data Visualisation: A Formal Introduction to the Rendering and Geometric Modelling Aspects", Proc. of Supercomputing '90, IEEE Computer Science Press,1990 , pp. 12-16

[5]   **Keim, D.A. and Kriegel, H.**, "Visualization Techniques for Mining Large databases: A Comparison", IEEE Transactions and data Engineering,1996

[6]   **Tufte E.R**. "Envisioning Information", Graphics Press, Cheshire, Connecticut, 1990

[7]   **Young P.,** "Three Dimensional Information Visualisation", Computer Science Technical Report 12/96, Department of Computer Science, University of Durham, 1996

A Semantic-Centric Approach to Information Visualization

Chaomei Chen
Department of Information Systems & Computing
Brunel University
Uxbridge UB8 3PH, UK
Tel: +44 1895 203080
E-mail: chaomei.chen@brunel.ac.uk

Leslie Carr
Department of Electronics & Computer Science
Southampton University
Southampton SO17 1BJ, UK
Tel: +44 1703 594479
E-mail: L.Carr@ecs.soton.ac.uk

Abstract

A semantic-centric approach to information visualization is described in this paper. In contrast to the conventional document-centric approaches, the semantic-centric approach focuses on the intrinsic connectivity in an information space beyond the boundary of individual documents. The approach aims to visualize the profound interrelationships perceived by the scientific community through the literature. An application of this approach is demonstrated through an author co-citation analysis of the entire collection of the ACM Hypertext conference proceedings over the last decade. Sub-fields, or specialties, in the field of hypertext are visualized based on the results of a factor analysis of author co-citation patterns. Nine snapshots of annual author co-citation maps introduce a new way of knowledge discovering in an information space shaped by the contemporary literature.

Keywords: Visualisation for Knowledge Discovery, Citation Analysis, Visualisation of Literature

1 Introduction

Vannevar Bush [1] described a visionary device called Memex, in which all the information ever available to the mankind would be richly inter-connected. Users would be able to find relevant information and organize it into a thread, or a trail, for their own use. Information can be grouped together as trails to meet the need of users.

Maintaining the interconnectivity and accessibility of an information space is a crucial issue in a modern information society. According to Schatz [2], the next generation of information technology should transcend the boundary of documents and enable users to handle the semantics underlying these documents. Schatz and his collaborators have been experimenting with techniques for creating concept spaces using supercomputers based on bibliographic information obtained from several databases heavily used by computer scientists.

Approaching the accessibility issue from a different perspective, the Institute for Scientific Information (ISI), best known for its Science Citation Index (SCI), has been exploring the structure of scientific literature based on citation data embedded in scientific literature. ISI's work was originally motivated to break the barrier in subject indexing — by relying on the collective and accumulated views of researchers in a given discipline regarding what the most influential work is and what is likely to be the most fruitful research topic.

The pioneering work at ISI is known as the Atlas of Science [3], which was based on document co-citation patterns. Recently, ISI is increasingly interested in the applicability of visualisation technologies in revealing the structure of science [4, 5].

Author co-citation analysis (ACC) is an analytical method that has been traditionally used to identify interrelationships between pairs of authors. ACC uses authors as data points in the literature. The focus of ACA is on authors instead of articles or journals. author co-citation is a more rigorous grouping principle than that of typical subject indexing, because it depends on repeated statements of connectedness by citers with subject expertise [6]. It is believed that author co-citation can provide invaluable information about how authors, as domain experts, perceive the interconnectivity between published works. A sub-field may be identified by a group of researchers contributing to closely related themes and topics. Such sub-fields are also known as specialties.

18

In this paper, we introduce our work in incorporating visualization techniques into citation analysis so that the structure and evolution of the field of hypertext can be revealed through the groupings of the most influential authors. Our aim is to identify the most predominant specialties in the field of hypertext and to use author co-citation maps as a means of trailblazing the literature of hypertext.

2   Document versus Author Co-Citation

There are two types of co-citation relationships: one is based on documents and the other is based on authors. Document co-citation approaches focus on a finer granularity than author co-citation approaches — it is possible for analysts to track down the contribution of specific documents to a given field of research. Author co-citation approaches, on the other hand, have a major advantage over document co-citation approaches — forging intrinsic interconnectivity links that might be missing by a document-centric analysis.

Figure 1 illustrates how document co-citation counts are measured. Let us consider two articles: one is a classic citation of the WWW and the other presents MultiCard, an open hypermedia system.

> Berners-Lee, T., Caillau, R., Nielsen, H. & Secret, A. (1994) The World Wide Web, *Communications of the ACM* , 37(8), 76-82.

> Rizk, A. & Sauter, L. (1992) *Multicard: An open hypermedia System*, Proceedings of the European Conference on Hypermedia Technology (ECHT'92) (pp. 4-10), Milano, Italy, November 1992. ACM Press.

Between 1997 and 1998, the WWW paper has been cited by seven articles published in the ACM Hypertext conference proceedings, whereas the MultiCard paper has been cited by six articles. As shown in Figure 1, four articles cited the two papers together.

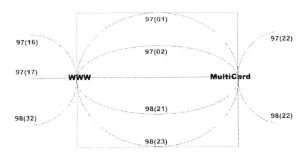

Figure 1. Document co-citations. The WWW paper and the MultiCard paper have been co-cited four times in the ACM Hypertext conference proceedings in 1997 and 1998.

The document co-citation counts have revealed the co-citation relationship between the WWW paper published in Communications of the ACM in 1994 and the MultiCard paper published in ECHT '94. However, instead of citing the WWW paper published in Communications of the ACM in 1994, three articles in the 1997 and 1998 proceedings have cited two earlier publications on the same topic of the WWW by Berners-Lee.

> Berners-Lee, T. (1992) World-Wide Web: An Information Infrastructure for High-Energy Physics, *Software Engineering, AI and Expert Systems for High Energy and Nuclear Physics*, La Londe-les-Maures, France. [98(16)]

> Berners-Lee, T. (1992) World-Wide Web: The Information Universe, *Electronic Networking: Research, Applications and Policy*, 1(2), 52-58. [98(16), 98(17), 98(32)]

An examination of the context of each citing suggests that these three articles are equivalent from citers' point of view, but a document co-citation analysis would treat these articles as different items and fail to recognize the fundamental connections among these three. The intrinsic connections among the citations of these articles may be lost.

One may argue that we should only take into account those articles that have been predominant in terms of their overall citation profile and weed out articles that turn out to be less influential. This is a document-centric view. From a semantic-centric view, articles that describe essentially the same concept should be tightly coupled with one another as they represent integral aspects of the same thought. What we need is instrumental information that can help us to uncover such implicit but profound connections.

Information visualization based on word frequencies and distribution patterns has been a unique research branch, especially originated from information retrieval applications. The changing patterns at the lexical level have been used to detect topical themes. Some intriguing visualization technologies have been developed over the past few years [7-9].

In our research, we are interested in visualization techniques that can handle the connectivity issue at a higher granularity so as to overcome some of the problems identified in the above example. Note that the name of Berners-Lee is associated with all the three WWW articles. In this case, his name more appropriately summarizes the nature of these citations. This suggests that, instead of focusing on individual documents, one could gain insights into the nature of citing behavior by shifting the focus to authors who have contributed to the literature.

Figure 2 illustrates a author co-citation network. In this example, Card and Robertson, who are well known for their work in information visualisation, have been cited through several different articles, including Cone Trees and the WebBook. Marchionini's work includes his book on information seeking and a popular article published in IEEE Computer. He is also a co-author of self-organized maps. Robertson and Marchionini have been co-cited by three articles in the ACM Hypertext conference proceedings in 1998. Author co-citation networks can be very complex. A visualisation method should reduce the complexity.

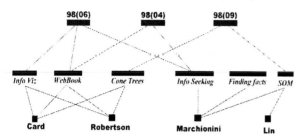

Figure 2. Author co-citations. Card and Marchionini have been co-cited three times in the ACM Hypertext conference proceedings in 1997 and 1998.

3 Author Co-Citation Analysis

White and McCain [6] used author co-citation analysis to map the field of information science. Their analysis included the top 120 authors ranked by citation counts based on 12 key journals in information science from 1972 through 1995. One of the most remarkable findings is that the field of information science consists of two major specialties with litter overlap between their memberships: experimental retrieval and citation analysis.

Multidimensional scaling techniques are typically used in author co-citation analysis as a means of depicting the underlying patterns between authors. However, author co-citation studies have been limited by the number of authors that one can map with multidimensional scaling facilities in the SPSS statistical package. For example, they had to limit the maximum number of authors within the capacity of the multidimensional scaling routines. In 1980s, the limit was 40 authors and in 1990s, this number is raised to 100 authors.

Author co-citation analysis provides an additional perspective to help us understand the dynamic structure of a field. The groupings of authors and research groups all provide clues to the value of their contribution to the development of the field. Therefore, we expect that author co-citation analysis, enhanced by visualization techniques, can play a significant part in helping people to make sense of the literature as a whole.

4 Methods

In a series of studies, we have been investigating the role of Pathfinder network scaling techniques in a virtual structure-generation methodology that can be used to reduce the excessive number of links and extract the most

salient structures from a range of proximity data [10]. In this paper, we introduce the latest results from our research in incorporating visualization techniques based on Pathfinder network scaling into author co-citation analysis.

Author citation and co-citation counts were obtained from a database covering all the articles published in the ACM Hypertext conference proceedings since 1989 up to 1998. In addition to full text articles, the data set also included data derived from short papers, especially for 1998 data. Author co-citation counts were computed for all the authors who were cited five times or more during the whole period. This selection criterion resulted in a pool of 367 authors for the entire period. In order to discover significant advances and trends in the history of the field, we applied the same methodology to the series of nine conference proceedings. We introduced a three-year sliding window scheme for these single-year visualizations. For year X, co-citation counts were calculated for authors who have been cited for five time or more in any year of the sliding window, i.e. year X-1, X, or X+1. This scheme provides a wider context for the author co-citation analysis in each single year.

Following [6], the raw co-citation counts were transformed into Pearson's correlation coefficients using the factor analysis on SPSS for Unix Release 6.1. These correlation coefficients were used to measure the proximity between authors' co-citation profiles. Self-citation counts were replaced with the mean co-citation counts for the same author.

Pearson's r was used as a measure of similarity between author pairs, because, according to [6], it registers the likeness in shape of their co-citation count profiles over all other authors in the set. Pearson correlation matrices were submitted to Pathfinder network scaling. The resultant Pathfinder network was modeled in VRML. An author co-citation map was then generated automatically. Hypertext reference links are provided in these VRML maps from the name of an author in the co-citation map to the corresponding bibliographical entry in a citation table maintained at Southampton University's Web server.

5 Results

Information visualization is an inter-disciplinary domain. Finding out the characteristics of visualization in hypertext may lead to additional insights into the spatial-semantic structure of the visualization. We summarize the major results in the following sections, including author co-citation maps based on the proceedings of 1998, a landscape view of the entire co-citation network, and a series of annual snapshots showing the major developments in the field.

5.1 Author Co-Citation Maps in 1998

Factor analysis of the author co-citation patterns has identified 18 underlying factors. The first 10 authors with the highest factor loading on each factor are shown in Table 1, including the accumulated percentage of variance explained by each factor.

Table 1. The first three factors in the 1998 data.

Factor 1		Factor 2		Factor 3	
22.6%		33.4%		42.2%	
Smith_J	0.89	Deerwester_S	0.74	Landauer_T	0.49
Nurnberg_P	0.87	Dumais_S	0.74	Golvchinsky_G	0.47
Schneider_E	0.87	Harshman_R	0.74	Richardson_J	0.45
McCracken_D	0.86	Shneiderman_B	0.73	McKnight_C	0.45
Schuler_W	0.86	Landauer_T	0.73	Dillon_A	0.45
Schutt_H	0.86	Chen_C	0.72	Hill_G	0.43
Trigg_R	0.85	Fairchild_K	0.67	Remde_J	0.42
Heath_I	0.85	Poltrock_S	0.67	Lochbaum_C	0.42
Streitz_N	0.85	Rivlin_E	0.63	Harman_D	0.42
Leggett_J	0.85	Marchionini_G	0.62	Gomez_L	0.42

Figure 3 shows an author co-citation map based on author co-citation patterns derived from the proceedings of 1998. It contains 259 authors. Citation indices over three periods are displayed as stacked bars to provide additional cues for understanding the implications of the overall structure. The higher the stacked bar, the more frequently the author has been cited in this sample of the literature. In Figure 4, we used the factor loading of the first three of the 18 factors extracted from the co-citation patterns to color the network. The first three factors together explain 42.2% of the variance. Color-coded nodes and links allow users to identify and distinguish authors from different specialties, or invisible colleges.

5.2   A Coherent View of Literature

Figure 5 is a screenshot of the visualization of the structure of the field of hypertext in terms of its most representative authors and the strongest co-citation paths among them. In this landscape view, generic contributions tend to gather towards the center, whereas unique and specific contributions tend to be placed towards the tips. This interpretation has been partially verified by the skyline of the landscape — periodical citation poles. A color-coded citation pole represents the citation counts for the corresponding author over three periods with the latest period on the top. As we can see from the screenshot, the height is gradually increasing as we move from the rim towards the center. The network structure is the union of all the possible minimal spanning trees. In this case study, it appears almost like a tree, with a few extra links, which implies that there are alternative shortest paths connecting two points in the network.

Figure 3. The author co-citation map in 1998 with citation indices displayed as stacked bars to provide additional cues for understanding the implications of the structure.

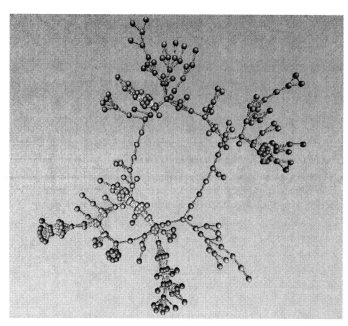

Figure 4. The author co-citation map in 1998 colored by the first three of the 39 factors identified in factor analysis. Predominant specialties in the field become apparent in the map.

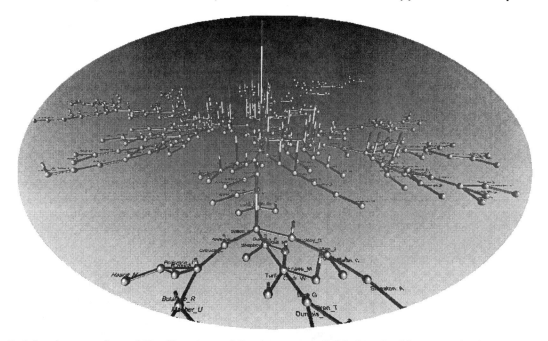

Figure 5. A landscape view of the literature of the hypertext field. Stacked bars vertical to the author co-citation network represent periodical citation index for corresponding authors.

At the beginning of this paper, we present an example of how the WWW paper and the MultiCard paper have been co-cited. Figure 6 highlights the local structure in the author co-citation map generated automatically from our semantic-centric approach. It shows that the authors of MultiCard, Rick and Sauter, have been placed in a strategically important position connecting a few clustering branches. The figure also shows that Berners-Lee and other co-authors of the WWW paper are grouped together with Berners-Lee in the center. By looking at who has made the co-citation one may obtain additional insights into who has painted this picture of the literature. In this example, all the citing papers address open hypermedia on the WWW.

6 DISCUSSIONS

We have generated a series author co-citation maps of the field of hypertext. These maps not only visualize the structure and evolution of the hypertext literature, but also provide a basis for researchers to understand the structure of the contemporary literature. The domain visualization essentially reflects the collective view of the community.

This literature mapping is based on the ACM Hypertext conference proceedings alone. Of course, there are many other forums for hypertext research and development. We plan to extend our literature mapping across several interrelated fields, such as the WWW conferences, the ACM SIGIR conferences on information retrieval, the ACM Digital Libraries conferences, and major journals in these fields. Cross-domain literature mapping is likely to reveal more insightful patterns than a single-domain literature mapping.

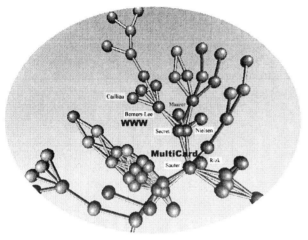

Figure 6. Shortest paths between the authors of the WWW paper and the MultiCard paper.

7 Conclusions

We have integrated visualization techniques into author co-citation analyses. We have used Pathfinder networks to layout our maps. These maps are different from the multidimensional scaling-based maps typically used in author co-citation analyses, such as [6]. Pathfinder networks can provide more accurate information about local structures than multidimensional scaling maps [11]. We found that the provision of explicit links in our maps made it easier to interpret interrelationships among different data points.

The value of this work is in its ability to thread through the literature and extract the most salient associations among authors who have made significant contributions to the field. Furthermore, author co-citation maps provide a means of identifying research fronts, i.e.

specialties in the field, and a visual aid of interpreting the results of citation analysis.

Using factor loading to color author co-citation maps provides additional insights into the dynamic structure of the field. To our knowledge, this visualization technique has not been applied to semantic-centric information visualization.

We expect that the semantic-centric approach will be valuable for synthesizing a field of study, optimizing the interconnectivity and accessibility of the literature to their learning and communication needs, and for developing engaging digital libraries and virtual environments.

Acknowledgements

This work was supported in part by the British research council EPSRC (Grant Number: GR/L61088).

References

[1]   V. Bush, "As we may think," *The Atlantic Monthly*, vol. 176, pp. 101-108, 1945.

[2]   B. R. Schatz, "Information retrieval in digital libraries: Bringing search to the net," *Science*, vol. 275, pp. 327-334, 1997.

[3]   ISI, *ISI atlas of science: Biochemistry and molecular biology, 1978/80*. Philadelphia, PA: Institute for Scientific Information, 1981.

[4]   E. Garfield, "Mapping the world of science," presented at the 150 Anniversary Meeting of the AAAS, Philadelphia, PA, 1998.

[5]   H. Small, "Update on science mapping: Creating large document spaces," *Scientometrics*, vol. 38, pp. 275-293, 1997.

[6]   H. D. White and K. W. McCain, "Visualizing a discipline: An author co-citation analysis of information science, 1972---1995," *Journal of the American Society for Information Science*, vol. 49, pp. 327-356, 1998.

[7]   B. Hetzler, P. Whitney, L. Martucci, and J. Thomas, "Multi-faceted insight through interoperable visual information analysis paradigms," presented at IEEE Information Visualization '98, 1998.

[8]   J. A. Wise Jr., J. J. Thomas, K. Pennock, D. Lantrip, M. Pottier, A. Schur, and V. Crow, "Visualizing the non-visual: Spatial analysis and interaction with information from text documents," presented at IEEE Symposium on Information Visualization '95, Atlanta, Georgia, USA, 1995.

[9]   H. Chen, T. D. Ng, J. Martinez, and B. R. Schatz, "A concept space approach to addressing the vocabulary problem in scientific information retrieval: An experiment on the Worm Community System," *Journal of the American Society for Information Science*, vol. 48, pp. 17-31, 1997.

[10]   C. Chen, "Visualising semantic spaces and author co-citation networks in digital libraries," *Information Processing and Management*, vol. 35, pp. 401-419, 1999.

[11]   R. W. Schvaneveldt, F. T. Durso, and D. W. Dearholt, "Network structures in proximity data," in *The Psychology of Learning and Motivation, 24*, G. Bower, Ed.: Academic Press, 1989, pp. 249-284.

A Robust Image Mosaicing Technique Capable of Creating Integrated Panoramas

Yihong Gong*   Guido Proietti†   David LaRose

Robotics Institute, Carnegie Mellon University
5000 Forbes Avenue, Pittsburgh, PA 15213, U.S.A.

Abstract

Existing featureless image mosaicing techniques do not pay enough attention to the robustness of the image registration process, and are not able to combine multiple video sequences into an integrated panoramic view. These problems have certainly restricted applications of the existing methods for large-scale panorama composition, video content overview and information visualization. In this paper, we propose a method that is able to create an integrated panoramic view for a virtual camera from multiple video sequences which each records a part of a vast scene. The method further enables the user to visualize the integrated panoramic view from an arbitrary viewpoint and orientation by altering the parameters of the virtual camera. To ensure a robust and accurate panoramic view synthesis from long video sequences, we attach a global positioning system (GPS) to the video camera, and utilize its output data to provide initial estimates for the camera's translational parameters, and to prevent the camera parameter recovery process from falling into spurious local minima. Our proposed method is not only suitable for video content overview, but also applicable to the areas of information visualization, team collaborations, disastrous rescues, etc. The experimental results demonstrate the effectiveness of the proposed method.

1. Introduction

Applications for image mosaicing techniques are becoming more and more common in computer graphics, computer vision, and multimedia systems. In the computer graphics domain, image mosaicing techniques have enabled cost-effective creation of virtual environments [1] and super-resolution images [2, 3]. In the computer vision field, these techniques have been exploited to extract 2-D textures and 3-D models of the target scenes [4, 5]. In the multimedia area, the same techniques have been used to create content overviews and visual indexes of digital video images [6].

Image mosaicing techniques can be mainly divided into two categories: feature-based methods, and featureless methods. Feature-based methods assume that feature correspondences between image pairs are available, and utilize these correspondences to find transforms which register the image pairs. A major difficulty of these methods is the acquisition and tracking of image features. Good features are often hand-selected, and reliability of feature tracking is often a problem due to image noise and occlusion. On the other hand, featureless methods discover transforms for image registration by minimizing a sum of squared difference (SSD) function that involves some parameters. Since featureless methods do not rely on explicit feature correspondences, they bear no problems associated with feature acquisition and tracking. However, methods in this category typically require that the change (translation, rotation, etc) from one image to another be small, and that good guesses for the parameters of the transform be given as initial values to the program. Moreover, since there is no guarantee that the parameter estimate process will definitely lead to the optimal solution even when the above requirements are met, special efforts must be made to prevent the parameter estimate process from falling into local minima.

Another important thing to be emphasized here is that both the existing feature-based and featureless image mosaicing methods can only create panoramic image from a single video sequence, and are not able to combine multiple video sequences into an integrated panoramic view. This limitation, in addition to the problems described above, has certainly restricted applications of the existing methods for large-scale panorama composition, video content overview and information visualization.

In this paper, we propose a featureless image mosaicing technique that is able to create an integrated panoramic view for a virtual camera from multiple video sequences which each records a part of a vast scene. The major contribution of this work includes: (1) The panoramic view is synthesized from multiple, independent video sequences, breaking the limitation of the existing image mosaicing techniques. (2) The panoramic view synthesis is seamlessly combined with the virtual environment creation. More specifically, each panoramic view is synthesized according to the virtual camera specified by the user, and can be visualized from an

---

*The author now works for NEC USA, C&C Reseach Laboratories. EMAIL: ygong@ccrl.sj.nec.com

†The author did this work when he was on leave from University of L'Aquila, Italy. EMAIL: proietti@univaq.it

arbitrary viewpoint and orientation by altering the parameters of the virtual camera. (3) To ensure a robust and accurate panoramic view synthesis from long video sequences, a global positioning system (GPS) is attached to the video camera, and its output data is utilized to provide initial estimates for the camera's translational parameters, and to prevent the camera parameter recovery process from falling into spurious local minima. We also develop a hardware GPS encoder/decoder that is able to encode/decode the GPS data into/from the audio track of the video camera. The GPS data acquisition, and the synchronization between the GPS data and the video frames are fully automated without the need of human assistance. Our proposed method is not only suitable for video content overview, but also applicable to the areas of information visualization, team collaborations, disastrous rescues, etc.

2. Related Work

Existing featureless image mosaicing techniques include cylindrical/spherical panoramas, affine transform-based panoramas, and projective transform-based panoramas. Cylindrical/spherical panoramas [1, 7] are commonly used by various commercial software products because of their ease of construction. However, this class of methods require the camera to be mounted on a leveled tripod, and allow only camera pan and tilt around the tripod. Because of these restrictions, the application domain of cylindrical/spherical panoramas is quite limited.

Affine transform-based panoramas [2, 8] are often used as an approximation to projective transform-based panoramas. Allowable camera motions include translations, change of focal length, and rotation about the optical axis. This class of methods provide adequate image registration if the camera does not pan and tilt excessively, and if the focal length is sufficiently large.

Projective transform-based panoramas[3, 9, 5] permit arbitrary camera motions. Methods in this category are able to register image sequences taken under any camera movements, such as translations, zooming, rotation about the optical axis, panning and tilting. The only constraint is that the target scene being recorded must be a planar scene so that no parallax exists. In practice, whenever the target scene is sufficiently remote from the camera, it can be approximated as a planar scene.

A genuine projective transform is represented by the following two equations:

$$x_{t+1} = \frac{m_0 x_t + m_1 y_t + m_2}{m_6 x_t + m_7 y_t + 1} \qquad (1)$$

$$y_{t+1} = \frac{m_3 x_t + m_4 y_t + m_5}{m_6 x_t + m_7 y_t + 1} \qquad (2)$$

where (x_t, y_t) and (x_{t+1}, y_{t+1}) denote a point in image I_t, and I_{t+1}, respectively, and $m_0, m_1, \ldots, m_7$ are 8 parameters that determine the projective transform. The image

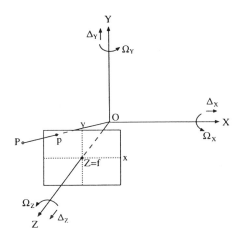

Figure 1. The world and the camera coordinate systems.

registration process is the process of discovering the 8 parameter set, which is achieved through an iterative process to minimize the following sum of squared difference (SSD) function:

$$SSD = \sum_{x_t, y_t} [I_{t+1}(x_{t+1}, y_{t+1}) - I_t(x_t, y_t)]^2 \qquad (3)$$

In order for the iterative minimization process to converge to the optical solution, the change (translation, rotation, etc) between I_t and I_{t+1} must be very small, and a good estimate of the 8 parameters must be given as the initial values to the program. As the 8 parameters do not correspond to physical movements of the camera, it is not an easy task to make a good guess for these parameters even when the physical camera motions are known. In an implementation reported in [5], the user has to bring each frame into the vicinity of its final position in the panoramic image, and the registration program starts from there to find the exact position of that frame. Moreover, as with other image mosaicing techniques, this method provides no means of combining multiple video sequences into an integrated panoramic view, and thus has a limited capability for the purpose of content overview and information visualization.

In this paper, we propose a projective transform-based panoramic view creation method which addresses the problems described above. The following sections provide the detailed descriptions.

3. Camera Parameter Estimation

Suppose the camera is placed at the origin O of the world coordinate system (X, Y, Z), and the image plane (x, y) is located at the focal length $Z = f$ (see Figure 1). The perspective projection of a scene point $P = (X, Y, Z)^t$ onto the image plane at a point $p = (x, y)^t$ is expressed by:

$$p = \begin{bmatrix} x \\ y \end{bmatrix} = \begin{bmatrix} \frac{X}{Z}f \\ \frac{Y}{Z}f \end{bmatrix} \qquad (4)$$

Suppose I_{t+1} and I_t are the two consecutive frames taken by a moving camera. The camera motion comprises two components: a translation $\Delta = (\Delta_X, \Delta_Y, \Delta_Z)$ and a rotation $\Omega = (\Omega_X, \Omega_Y, \Omega_Z)$. When the field of view is not very large (a planar scene) and the camera rotation is relatively small, each point (x_{t+1}, y_{t+1}) in frame I_{t+1} can be expressed as a transformed version of the corresponding point (x_t, y_t) in frame I_t [10]:

$$\begin{bmatrix} x_{t+1} \\ y_{t+1} \end{bmatrix} = \begin{bmatrix} x_t \\ y_t \end{bmatrix} + \frac{1}{Z} \begin{bmatrix} -f & 0 & x_t \\ 0 & -f & y_t \end{bmatrix} \begin{bmatrix} \Delta_X \\ \Delta_Y \\ \Delta_Z \end{bmatrix}$$
$$+ \begin{bmatrix} \frac{x_t y_t}{f} & \frac{-(f^2 + x_t^2)}{f} & y_t \\ \frac{(f^2 + x_t^2)}{f} & \frac{-x_t y_t}{f} & -x_t \end{bmatrix} \begin{bmatrix} \Omega_X \\ \Omega_Y \\ \Omega_Z \end{bmatrix} \quad (5)$$

where Z is the scene depth corresponding to image point (x_t, y_t). Based on the planar scene assumption, all the scene points (X, Y, Z) satisfy a plane equation:

$$Z = A + B \cdot X + C \cdot Y \quad (6)$$

By dividing both sides of Eq.(6) by Z, and replacing X, Y using Eq.(4), we have:

$$\frac{1}{Z} = \alpha + \beta \cdot x + \gamma \cdot y \quad (7)$$

In summary, the above projective transform consists of 9 parameters: 3 for camera translations, 3 for camera rotations, and 3 for the scene depth. The reason why we adopt Eq.(5) for panoramic view creation is because this projective transform model explicitly recovers the scene depth, which will enable us to project the resultant panoramic images into any specified camera coordinate systems, and hence will play a critical role in creating integrated panoramic view for a given virtual camera. Furthermore, as the remaining six parameters involved in this model correspond directly to physical camera movements, it becomes much easier for us to provide good guesses for the initial values of these parameters. Good guesses for the parameters give great impact in ensuring the parameter estimate process to converge to the optical solution.

Clearly, there is a scale ambiguity between $1/Z$ and Δ. More precisely, there is an unlimited number of combinations of $1/Z$ and Δ which produce the same displacement between (x_{t+1}, y_{t+1}) and (x_t, y_t). However, if correct values of Δ can be provided, the remaining 6 parameters will be uniquely determined.

In the image capturing process, We attach a GPS device to the camera to obtain the camera's approximate translations along the XYZ axes, and then use the GPS data to initialize Δ. The GPS data acquisition, and the synchronization between the GPS data and the video streams are fully automated by the hardware GPS encoder/decoder developed by us. Civilian GPS receivers are limited in accuracy to about several centimeters, and consequently it is

more appropriate to use the GPS data as a good guess for, rather than the final result of, the parameter set Δ.

In order to further address the local minimum problem of the iterative minimization process, we add three additional terms to the SSD function in Eq.(3):

$$SSD(\mathbf{m}) = \sum_{x_t, y_t} [I_{t+1}(x_t, y_t; \mathbf{m}) - I_t(x_t, y_t)]^2 +$$
$$\varphi \cdot \left\{ \left[\frac{\Delta_X - \Delta_X^{GPS}}{\sigma_X^{GPS}} \right]^2 + \left[\frac{\Delta_Y - \Delta_Y^{GPS}}{\sigma_Y^{GPS}} \right]^2 + \right.$$
$$\left. \left[\frac{\Delta_Z - \Delta_Z^{GPS}}{\sigma_Z^{GPS}} \right]^2 \right\} \quad (8)$$

where $\mathbf{m}$ is the 9-parameter set, $\Delta_X^{GPS}, \Delta_Y^{GPS}, \Delta_Z^{GPS}$ are the camera translations given by the GPS device, and $\sigma_X^{GPS}, \sigma_Y^{GPS}, \sigma_Z^{GPS}$ are the standard deviations of the corresponding camera translations, respectively. φ is the user provided confidence coefficient that specifies how much confidence should be given to the GPS data. Large values of φ will cause the final values of $\Delta_X, \Delta_Y, \Delta_Z$ to be close to $\Delta_X^{GPS}, \Delta_Y^{GPS}, \Delta_Z^{GPS}$, while small values of φ will have the opposite effect. Therefore, as a rule of thumb, φ should be given a value in proportion to the accuracy of the GPS output. Note that the first term of the above equation has exactly the same meaning of the right-hand side of Eq.(3), but is expressed in a different form. Because x_{t+1}, y_{t+1} are determined by x_t, y_t, and the 9-parameter set $\mathbf{m}$, $I_{t+1}(x_{t+1}, y_{t+1})$ can be also expressed as $I_{t+1}(x_t, y_t, \mathbf{m})$.

To perform the minimization of the SSD function, we use the Levenberg-Marquardt iterative non-linear minimization algorithm [11], which is known for its quick convergence in comparison to the direct gradient descent methods (the details of the method has to be omitted because of the space limitation).

To further increase the robustness and accuracy of the image registration, we have employed hierarchical registration and exact model acquisition in the registration process. In hierarchical registration, a multi-level Gaussian pyramid is created for each image in the sequence. Registration begins from the top level of the pyramid, using the most coarsely subsampled image pair. Parameters estimated from the top level are used to initialize parameter estimates at the subsequent (finer) level. The process continues down the pyramid until the bottom of the pyramid is reached. While this technique is not guaranteed to avoid the local minimum problem, it works well even when image pairs have relatively large displacements.

Exact model acquisition relates the parameters in Eq.(5) back to the parameters in Eq.(1) and Eq.(2), which represent the exact projective transform. Here we adopt the "four point method" proposed in [3] for relating the two parameter sets, which results in four easy to solve linear equations. The advantage of performing exact model acquisition is that the law of composition applies to the exact projective transform, so that we can project image I_i into the space of image I_1 using equation $\mathbf{A}_{ij}\mathbf{P}_j$ without sacrificing accuracy. Here, $\mathbf{A}_{ij}$ is the registration matrix that projects I_i into the space of I_j, and $\mathbf{P}_j$ is the global registration matrix that projects I_j into the space of image I_1.

In summary, the registration of the entire image sequence can be described as follows:

1. Set $i = 1$, $\mathbf{P}_1 = \mathbf{I}$. Input image i from the sequence.

2. Input image $i+1$, and register $i, i+1$ using hierarchical image pair registration as described above.

3. Relate the parameters obtained from Step 2 to the parameters of the exact projective transform using the exact model acquisition technique. This is equivalent to acquiring the registration matrix $\mathbf{A}_{i+1i}$.

4. Project image $i + 1$ to the space of image 1 using $\mathbf{A}_{i+1i}\mathbf{P}_i$. Set $\mathbf{P}_{i+1} = \mathbf{A}_{i+1i}\mathbf{P}_i$.

5. increment i by 1. If i reaches the end of the sequence, terminate the operation; otherwise, go to Step 2.

4. Integrated Panoramic View Creation

In the previous section, we proposed the robust panoramic image creation by employing GPS data. In this section, we move beyond the real panoramic view creation to create integrated panoramic view encompassing multiple video sequences for a given virtual camera.

The process of compositing an image sequence into a panoramic image is equivalent to projecting the rest of the images into the space of a reference image. The reference image could be the one that overlaps all other images, or could be just the first frame of the image sequence.

Suppose that a panoramic image Φ is created for the target scene, and the coordinate system of the reference image is known. Then, if the coordinate system for a virtual camera is specified, the panoramic image of this virtual camera can be obtained by transforming Φ into the virtual camera's coordinate system. The operation consists of the following steps:

1. Project all the pixels (x, y) of the panoramic image Φ back into the 3-D world coordinates (X, Y, Z):

$$\begin{cases} X = \frac{x \cdot Z}{f} = \frac{x}{f(\alpha + \beta \cdot x + \gamma \cdot y)} \\ Y = \frac{y \cdot Z}{f} = \frac{y}{f(\alpha + \beta \cdot x + \gamma \cdot y)} \\ Z = \frac{1}{f(\alpha + \beta \cdot x + \gamma \cdot y)} \end{cases} \quad (9)$$

where f is the focal length of the real camera, and α, β, γ are the parameters about the scene depth recovered by the proposed image registration method (see Section 3).

2. Transform (X, Y, Z) into the world coordinate system of the virtual camera:

$$\begin{bmatrix} X' \\ Y' \\ Z' \end{bmatrix} = \begin{bmatrix} m_{11} & m_{12} & m_{13} \\ m_{21} & m_{22} & m_{23} \\ m_{31} & m_{32} & m_{33} \end{bmatrix} \cdot \begin{bmatrix} X \\ Y \\ Z \end{bmatrix} \quad (10)$$

Since the world coordinate systems of both the reference image and the virtual camera are known, elements m_{ij} of the transform matrix $\mathbf{M}$ can be easily obtained.

3. Project (X', Y', Z') into the image plane of the virtual camera:

$$\begin{cases} x' = f'\frac{X'}{Z'} \\ y' = f'\frac{Y'}{Z'} \end{cases} \quad (11)$$

where f' is the focal length of the virtual camera.

In the above operation, we can analytically alter the parameters of the virtual camera to simulate a change of focal length or a 3-D displacement/rotation of the virtual camera. In this way, we can synthesize new panoramic views from an arbitrary position and orientation, just as a real walk through a 3-D space.

When there are multiple video sequences, we first create a real panorama for each sequence, and then project each of these real panoramas into the space of the virtual camera. The final result is an integrated large-scale panoramic image as if it was taken by the virtual camera. Theoretically, there is no limitation in the number of video sequences the proposed method can integrate, as long as there is an enough memory space in the computer. However, the video sequence must be closely related to each other (e.g., each sequence covers a part of the vast scene) in order to create a meaningful integrated panoramic view. This ability of integrating multiple panoramic images into a collaborative perspective not only considerably extends the content overview ability, but also enables members in a collaborative team to contribute and share their observations about the environment under investigation among themselves.

5. Results and Discussions

The proposed image mosaicing technique was implemented with C++, and was tested using three image sequences. The three sequences were taken by the same camera in different days and different locations. The camera was a SONY digital video camcorder which gives a 640×480 resolution and 30 FPS frame rate. A GPS antenna was attached to the video camera to obtain 3-D displacements of the camera. The GPS device was run in the differential mode, which gives up to one centimeter accuracy and five position updates per second. To synchronize between the video stream and the GPS data, the GPS output was encoded into the DTMF audio signals using a hardware encoder, and was recorded onto the audio track of the video tape. The

GPS data were then recovered by feeding the audio output from the video camera into a hardware DTMF decoder. Because the GPS data update rate is much lower than the video frame rate (5 vs 30), only the video frames that have corresponding GPS data were used for the creation of panoramic images. Our experiments have shown that this 5 FPS frame rate is sufficient for the proposed technique when the camera motion is not very fast.

Figure 2 shows the three panoramic images which were created using video sequences 1, 2, and 3, respectively. All of the panoramic images were fully automatically generated by the proposed method without any human intervention. Sequence 1 consists of more than 100 frames, while Sequence 2 and 3 were taken in a cloudy day with remarkable brightness variations. To let readers better understand the composition of each panoramic image as well as the brightness changes in the corresponding video sequence, image boundaries were deliberately left, and no post-processing was performed to smooth out the uneven brightness in the panoramic images. It is clear from the figure that the three panoramic images were all properly composited with no apparent errors.

For comparison, we implemented the image mosaicing method presented in [5], and tested it using the above three video sequences. This method uses the exact projective transform defined by Eq.(1),(2) in combination with hierarchical image pair registration. None of the three sequences were fully successfully registered by this method. Errors occurred when geometrical changes or brightness variations between image pairs were relatively large. When given a good guess for the parameter set, however, the method was able to properly register all the frames, and finally create correct panoramic images from these sequences.

Figure 3 shows three integrated panoramic images for a given virtual camera. These three images were created by projecting panoramic images (2) and (3) from Figure 2 into the coordinate system of the virtual camera, and by altering the orientation and zoom settings of the virtual camera. The angles of the optical axes of the reference frames of video sequences 2 and 3 (the first frame in each case) were measured during the video recording, which were horizontal, and were $60°$, $65°$ east from the north pole, respectively. The virtual camera was placed at a point around the middle of the gap between the video sequences 2 and 3, and its orientation and zoom settings were described in the caption of Figure 3. A blank in these results exists because video sequences 2 and 3 do not overlap each other, and no information for that part of the scene was captured. Sequence 1 was not projected into the synthesized panoramic images because it was taken miles away from the rest of the two sequences.

The above experimental results have demonstrated the effectiveness of the proposed method. This method is applicable to various application domains such as video content overview, information visualization, team collaborations, disastrous rescues, etc.

References

[1] S. E. Chen, "Quicktime VR – an image-based approach to virtual environment navigation," in *ACM Computer Graphics (SIGGRAPH'95)*, pp. 29–38, Aug. 1995.

[2] M. Irani and S. peleg, "Improving resolution by image registraion," in *Graphical Models and Image Processing*, May 1991.

[3] S. Mann and R. Picard, "The virtual bellows: A new perspective on the rigid planar patch," in *Technical Report 260, MIT Media Lab Perceptual Computing Section*, (Cambridge, MA), Jan. 1994.

[4] R. Szeliski and J. Coughlan, "Hierarchical spline-based image registration," in *IEEE Conference on Computer Vision and Pattern Recognition (CVPR'94)*, (Seattle), pp. 194–201, June 1994.

[5] R. Szeliski and S. Kang, "Direct method for visual scene reconstruction," in *IEEE Workshop on Representations of Visual Scenes*, (Cambridge, MA), June 1995.

[6] Y. Taniguchi, A. Akutsu, and Y. Tonomura, "PanoramaExcerpts: Extracting and packing panoramas for video browsing," in *ACM Multimedia'97*, (Seattle), Nov. 1997.

[7] L. McMillan and G. Bishop, "Plenoptic modeling: An image-based rendering system," in *ACM Computer Graphics (SIGGRAPH'95)*, pp. 39–46, Aug. 1995.

[8] J. Koenderink and A. van Doorn, "Affine structure from motion," *Journal of the Optical Society of America*, vol. 8, 1991.

[9] M. Irani, P. Anandan, and S. Hsu, "Mosaic based representations of video sequences and their applications," in *ICCV'95*, (Cambridge, MA), June 1995.

[10] J. Bergen, P. Anandan, K. Hanna, and R. Hingorani, "Hierarchical model-based motion estimation," in *Second European Conference on Computer Vision (ECCV'92)*, (Santa Margherita, Italy), May 1992.

[11] W. Press and et al., *Numerical Recipes in C: The Art of Scientific Computing*. Cambridge, England: Cambridge University Press, 2 ed., 1992.

Figure 2. Three panoramic images: (1) from sequence 1; (2) from sequence 2; (3) from sequence 3.

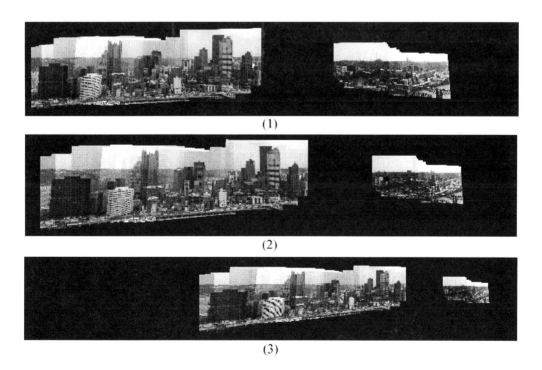

Figure 3. Three integrated panoramic images created using panoramic images (2) and (3) from Figure 2. The optical axes of the reference frames of video sequences 2 and 3 were horizontal, and were $60°$, $65°$ east from the north pole, respectively. The virtual camera was placed at a point around the middle of the gap between the two sequences. (1) Integrated panorama for a virtual camera with the optical axis $50°$ east from the north pole; (2) Integrated panorama for a virtual camera with the optical axis $60°$ east from the north pole; (3) Integrated panorama for a virtual camera with a smaller zoom setting, and with the optical axis $70°$ east from the north pole.

Augmented and Virtual Reality in Training

Chair

Eric W. Tatham

The Open University, UK

Virtual Reality and Augmented Reality as a Training Tool for Assembly Tasks

A.C. Boud, D.J. Haniff, C. Baber, and S.J. Steiner

The University of Birmingham
The School of Manufacturing and Mechanical Engineering
a.c.boud@bham.ac.uk

Abstract

In this paper we investigate whether Virtual Reality (VR) and Augmented Reality (AR) offer potential for the training of manual skills, such as for assembly tasks, in comparison to conventional media.

We present results from experiments that compare assembly completion times for a number of different conditions. We firstly investigate completion times for a task where participants can study an engineering drawing and an assembly plan and then conduct the task. We then investigate the task under various VR conditions and context-free AR.

We discuss the relative advantages and limitations of using VR and AR as training media for investigating assembly operations, and we present the results of our experimental work.

1. Introduction

In recent years, the terms virtual reality (VR) and augmented reality (AR) have each received a growing amount of interest and support that has seen the development of a number of different fields of investigation. However, although VR and AR rely on different technologies providing very different solutions, both technologies are often 'branded' in the same category. For example, Wilson [1] categorises AR as a form of VR, while Drascic and Milgram [2] describe VR and AR in terms of a 'reality-virtuality continuum', where AR is towards the real world end of the continuum and VR is at the opposite extreme.

VR can be defined as a three dimensional computer generated environment, updating in real time, and allowing human interaction through various input/output devices. By providing a variety of representations, e.g. 2D or 3D, desktop or immersive, VR can offer users the opportunity to explore virtual objects at levels of detail appropriate to the work activity.

AR can be defined as the *enhancement* of the real world by a virtual world, which subsequently provides additional information [3]. AR itself can then be classified into two types: computationally *context-free* and computationally *context-aware*. The context-free systems use a see-through head mounted display with the computer image projected in front of the user by a half-silvered mirror. The context-aware systems overlay graphics or other media onto a real image by sensing the context in which it finds itself. Context-aware AR can only be achieved through the use of computer-vision or electronic sensors. In comparison, VR simulates rather than supplements the real world.

There has been little discussion comparing these technologies, mainly due to the differing benefits offered by both of these disciplines. In this paper we do not seek to suggest one as the optimal method at the expense of the other, but rather wish to present the relative advantages of each technology. As a basis of evaluation, we have chosen to investigate the use of both technologies as a training tool for assembly tasks.

2. Assembly

Assembly requires the manipulation and joining of parts to form a whole [4]. In order to achieve the apparently simple goal of placing a peg in a hole, a number of factors need to be considered, such as reaching for and grasping the peg, determining the relative positions of peg and hole, transporting the peg towards the hole (aiming), and inserting the peg accurately [5]. Each of these actions requires differing levels of haptic and visual guidance. If multiple pegs are to be inserted into multiple holes, then further consideration of a higher order of cognitive activity, such as planning, is required.

If assembly can be considered to have such cognitive components, then we ought to be able to demonstrate a

32

 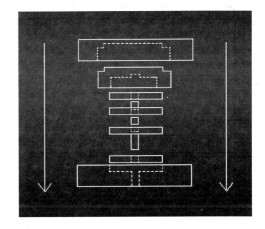

(a) **(b)**

Figure 1. Pictorial representation of the water pump assembly
(a) VR conditions (b) AR condition

learning period (during which assembly performance improves), and to observe the effect of the instruction format on the learning of the assembly task. Work on assembly in the 1960s as reviewed by Seymour [6], clearly showed learning periods in assembly work.

Baggett and Ehrenfeucht [7] demonstrated that the presentation of instructions via a video could improve performance of assembly operations. One group of participants viewed a video of each subassembly being put together (with no information regarding final build), while another group viewed a video of subassemblies being put together in the correct sequence. The hypothesis was that the latter would facilitate learning of the assembly sequence better than the former. However, there was a clear interaction between knowledge of the assembly and activity, and impact of the video; for participants with little prior experience, the subassemblies plus sequence video led to better performance, while for participants with assembly knowledge there was no difference in the effect of video. Thus, simply seeing the assemblies being built was sufficient for experienced participants to be able to develop assembly plans.

While the work of Baggett and Ehrenfeucht [7,8] suggest that dynamic representations, i.e., through video, present superior training media to static, i.e., through paper, their work does not allow any interaction between the participant and the assembled item. This study investigates whether the application of VR and AR to permit direct manipulation of assembly components would facilitate training in this activity.

3. Experimental Work

Information for an operator to conduct an assembly task is conventionally obtained from a combination of engineering drawings and written assembly procedures. The investigation at the University of Birmingham has sought to develop a VR system where an operator could visualise the construction of a product, and then perform the assembly operations in the virtual environment (VE) under a number of different conditions in order to evaluate the application of VR as a tool to improve assembly completion times, in this case for a water pump assembly.

We also present a context-free AR system that displays a static pictorial representation of the water pump's assembly sequence. For the purpose of this study, the issue of attaching and overlaying representations to objects is unimportant due to the measurement of performance in terms of carrying out the task without using the AR system. The AR system is only used for training. However, work is being carried out at the University of Birmingham to develop a computer vision-based, context-aware AR system so that further studies can be carried out; for example, comparing the performance between context-free and context-aware systems.

The aim of the experimentation is to investigate the immediate impact of a given format of media on task performance to operator training and post-training.

3.1 Subjects

Five groups of five participants were selected from the student body of the School. All participants were from an engineering background and were familiar with 2D engineering drawings and assembly plans. None of the subjects had any previous experience of VR or AR.

3.2. Equipment

The VR conditions were conducted on a Silicon Graphics Indigo[2] maximum impact workstation, using either a conventional '2D' mouse and monitor (Desktop), a '2D' mouse, monitor and CrystalEyes stereoscopic glasses (Stereoscopic), and a Virtual Research 'Vr4' HMD, a Polhemus Fastrak tracking system and a '3D' mouse (Immersive). The model was generated using 3D Studio Max. with Divisions' dVISE VR software, and was constructed from approximately 7k polygons, and maintained at approximately ≥ 20 fps (see figure 1(a)).

For the context-free AR condition a see-through, monocular, monochrome, head mounted display (HMD) developed by Seattle Sight was used. The HMD was connected to a Pentium PC running at a speed of 200 MHz. A 2D static engineering diagram was used to provide the augmentation for the user. The diagram had a white outline and a black background; the black background allowed the real world to be seen more clearly (see figure 1(b)).

3.3. Method

Participants were asked to assemble a water pump (consisting of 8 separate components) in the real world, after receiving information from either:

- Conventional 2D engineering drawings (Conventional)
- Desktop VR using a monitor and 2D mouse (Desktop)
- Desktop VR using stereoscopic glasses to provide a 3D images, but still using a 2D mouse (Stereoscopic)
- Immersive VR using a HMD and '3D' mouse (Immersive), and
- Context-free AR (AR)

To complete the assembly using conventional 2D drawings, each participant was shown an assembly plan and an engineering drawing of a water pump assembly, and then given 10 minutes to study the construction. The participant then assembled the water pump. Each task completion time was measured.

The VR participants were firstly given a brief introduction on how to use the VR software and opportunity experience the interaction techniques for each variation. The 2D engineering drawing was then given to the participant to study for 2 minutes in order to assess the correct sequences of assembly operations, whereby the participant could then investigate the assembly operation in the VE for the remaining 8 minutes. The participants then completed the assembly operations in the VE using one of the specific

interaction techniques, and were then asked to complete the assembly task on the water pump in the real world. The time taken to complete the assembly of the water pump was recorded in each case.

In the AR condition, participants were asked to don the headset and adjust the display to enable them to view the image clearly. Once the headset was correctly fitted, participants viewed the image on the screen to construct the pump. A maximum of 8 minutes was allotted to this task. The subjects were then asked to construct the pump without the AR system and the completion time was monitored.

3.4. Results

Figure 2 indicates that task completion times are longer when the participants train to assemble the water pump using the 2D drawing before assembling the real product, in comparison with the other conditions. There was a significant difference between the best VR condition and AR system (t=2.132, df=4, p <0.01). However, there are no significant findings between the different forms of VR interaction, although participants suggested that immersive VR was more 'intuitive', as they were able to manipulate 3D objects in 3D space.

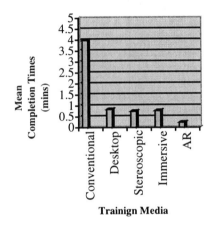

Figure 2. Comparison of total assembly completion time in the real world using different interaction techniques

The participants were asked for their opinions of both the VR and AR systems at the end of the experiments. From this, several issues were highlighted which may have contributed to the slower performance times in the VE in comparison to the real world. 8 out of the 20 users indicated that their control of the system was slow; 7 users indicated that the VR system limited the participant to conduct the task using only one hand. In the real world however, both hands would be used. Finally, 4 users indicated difficulty in selecting objects and 'reaching through' the computer generated components, as no haptic feedback was provided. In addition, for the AR condition the subjects were generally positive about the usefulness of the technology.

3.5. Discussion

One of the most important theories of skill acquisition stems from the work of Fitts [9], who suggested a three-stage development process. Initially, people learn the basic procedures and properties of the object. This is the cognitive stage. Secondly, the procedures and knowledge of the objects become 'chunked' into sequences of action. This is the associative stage. Finally, the sequences of actions are combined into a smooth pattern of activity. Each stage requires a decreasing level of overt conscious control, with the final stage representing 'skilled' activity.

It is proposed that assembly tasks completed using 2D drawings and assembly plans are based on the cognitive phase, where participants require a longer period of time to calculate the correct sequence of actions. Using VR to conduct the assembly tasks uses the cognitive and associative stages, where plans are developed to complete the tasks. VR and AR therefore ought to be superior for learning sequences.

However, assembly not only requires a learned sequence, but also a learned motor behaviour. VR participants were able to investigate assembly sequences through a number of VR conditions, before physically assembling the water pump. By enabling participants to investigate tasks at the level of detail appropriate to the work activity, VR offers improvements over conventional media.

The subjects in the AR system could construct the real life pump and simultaneously access the virtual information for guidance. The mapping between the training and the actual task is therefore more tightly coupled than for the other conditions. AR can therefore facilitate fast learning for simple assembly tasks, as the operator is able to conduct the actual task whilst referencing additional training material. In terms of Fitt's theory of skill acquisition, the AR system allowed the subject to cognize, chunk information and to become partially skilled by the use of augmentation while performing the training for the task. By the time the subject had to perform the real task, their skill level was starting to develop.

There are, however, problems that need to be addressed with both VR and AR. one of the main problems of VR technology is the lack of provision of haptic feedback, and this plays an important role when manipulating objects in VEs, especially for immersive applications. Although there are a number of commercially available devices, several limitations are still encountered. (See Burdea [10] for a review of force feedback technology for VR). Previous work by Boud et al., [11] has addressed this problem with the use of instrumented objects (IOs).

AR on the other hand, allows the user to have tactile feedback through the manipulation of the real objects. Additional virtual information supplements the user's knowledge by providing instructions in the same manner as a piece of paper. AR allows the user to attend to the set of instructions and the real world without having to refer to separate media, such as an instruction manual. Context-free and context-aware AR systems have been used in a variety of applications to provide support for the user. For example, Webster et al., [12] used AR to aid in the construction of architectural structures, and Feiner et al., [3] used an AR system to provide information on printer maintenance. However, AR systems have not been examined as a training tool where the user is expected to use the AR system to build up their knowledge of the task and then perform the task without the aid of the AR system.

With context-free AR, the user still needs to attend to an image at a specific focal length and then refocus on the real world [13]. The images can be merged using context-aware AR systems; however, problems such as registration between the virtual objects and the real objects needs to be overcome [14].

VR does however, have the advantage of separating the real world from the virtual world in terms of the accessibility of the real world objects. Hence, in a manufacturing environment, operators could be trained for an assembly operation during a product's design cycle, before a physical prototype has been manufactured. With AR, the physical objects need to be present in order for the subject to be trained; this is not the case for VR.

4. Conclusion

The VR and AR conditions were found to out-perform the 2D engineering drawing condition. The two types of realities therefore offer the advantage of improved performance for assembly training over the conventional approach of studying a 2D drawing and then being asked to perform the task. The VR conditions demonstrated that there were no significant differences between the VR technologies for this particular application, however, there was a significant difference between the best VR condition and the AR system. VR allows the user to manipulate objects without the use of the real objects and hence offers benefits in applications such as manufacturing, where operators can be trained to assemble a product before the product has been physically manufactured. In terms of training, VR is more flexible than AR in that the environment in which it can be used can be separated from the real environment. For example, in some cases it may not be practical to interact with the real objects due to their non-availability and their associated costs. However, AR does improve performance times as the training is conducted on the real objects.

Both AR and VR have relative merits for training purposes, but their use relies upon the particular application. Therefore before employing these technologies it is important to investigate the task to ensure the benefits offered by both technologies are maximised.

Acknowledgements

The work undertaken in this project would not have been possible without the invaluable assistance of Simon Batterbee, an undergraduate student in the School of Manufacturing and Mechanical Engineering (1994-1997).

References

[1] Wilson, J.R., "Virtual environments and ergonomics: needs and opportunities", *Ergonomics*, *40(10)*, 1998, pp. 1057-1077.

[2] Drascic and Milgram "Perceptual Issues in Augmented Reality", *SPIE Volume 2653: Stereoscopic Displays and Virtual Reality Systems III,* Ed. M.T. Bolas, S.S.Fisher, J.O. Merritt, Jan Jose, California, USA, January-February 1996, pp. 123-134.

[3] S. Feiner, B. MacIntyre, D. Seligmann, "Knowledge-based Augmented Reality", *Communications of the ACM*, 36(7), 1993, pp. 53-62.

[4] J.L. Nevins, and D.E. Whitney, "Assembly research", *Automatic, 16*, 1980, pp. 595-613.

[5] R.F. O'Connor, C. Baber, M. Musri, and H. Ekerol, "Identification, classification and management of errors in automated component assembly tasks", *International Journal of Production Research 31(8)* 1993, pp. 1853-1863.

[6] W.D. Seymour, *Industrial Skills*, London:Pitman. 1967.

[7] P. Baggett, and A. Ehrenfeucht, "Building physical and mental models in assembly tasks", *International Journal of Industrial Ergonomics, 7 (3),* 1991, pp. 217-227.

[8] P. Baggett, and A. Ehrenfeucht, "Conceptualizing in assembly tasks", *Human Factors 30(3),* 1988, pp. 269-284.

[9] P.M. Fitts, "The information capacity of the human motor system in controlling the amplitude of movement", *Journal of Experimental Psychology, 47,* 1954, pp. 381-391.

[10] G. Burdea, *Force and Touch Feedback for Virtual Reality*, Wiley-Interscience Publication, 1996.

[11] A.C. Boud, C. Baber, S.J. Steiner, "Virtual Reality: A Tool for Assembly", *Presence: Teleoperators and Virtual Environments.* In Press.

[12] A. Webster. S. Feiner, B. McIntyre, W. Mussie, and T. Krueger, "Augmented Reality in Architectural Construction, Inspection and Renovation", *Proceedings of ASCR Third Congress on Computing in Civil Engineering*, Anaheim, CA, June 17-19 1996, pp. 913-919.

[13] C. Baber, D. Haniff, L. Cooper, J. Knight, and B.A. Mellor, "Preliminary Investigations into the Human Factors of Wearable Computers", In Ed. H. Johnson, L. Nigay, & C. Roast, *People and Computers XIII*, Berlin: Springer-Verlag, 1998, pp.313-326.

[14] R.T. Azuma, "A Survey of Augmented Reality", *Presence: Teleoperators and Virtual Environments, MIT Press, 6,*(4), 1997, pp.355-385.

Visualisation of Data from an Intranet Training Systems using Virtual Reality Modelling Language (VRML)

J. Watson*, D. Taylor, S.Lockwood
Dept. Electronic and Electrical Engineering,
University of Huddersfield,
Queensgate,
Huddersfield,
HD1 3DH.

Abstract

This paper describes the design of a generic computer-based Training Information System (TIS) and visualisation of the data that it generates. Today's desktop training applications are delivered over the Internet to users who can exploit this flexibility and train when and where they like. However, the training manager or the author of the training material require a record of who has been trained, when they were trained and what kind of progress they made. The TIS co-ordinates this by remotely recording each training session, then sending a small summarising session database back to a central collection point for collation and subsequent analysis.

Because of the large amounts of data that this generates in large companies we are beginning to use Virtual Reality for analysis and presentation of training results. Described in this paper are the results from a session of monitored intranet training that was undertaken by approximately 60 students over a one week period.

Introduction

In today's cut-throat economic climate companies have to look more than ever for new ways of operating efficiently. When a company looks for ways of reducing its fixed expenditure it is inevitable that long-term investments such as the budget allocated for training will come under scrutiny first. So, as companies become leaner, and budgets become tighter, the money allocated for training becomes tighter. At the same time there is pressure to maintain a well-trained workforce and good ongoing training programmes are essential to the recruitment of well-qualified staff.

Computer Based Training (CBT) has now been proved, over several years and in many diverse applications, to be an extremely cost-effective way of training large numbers of people and is being examined increasingly by trainers and managers as a cost effective alternative to more traditional methods of instruction. In addition, today's company structures and work practices, where multinational companies have offices all over the world and many people hot-desk or work from home mean that computer-based instruction has many other additional advantages. For example, employees can train when they want, where they want and they can complete single modules using multiple sessions.

However, it is also extremely important for a company to maintain exact records of what training each of its employees has undergone and how well their employees have performed. This is especially so with the advent of new European legislation making companies more responsible than ever for maintaining up-to-date records of, for example, health and safety training records. A Management System can provide the instructor with numerous facilities, including selection of the most suitable instruction for a student at a particular time and the automatic testing of students both before and after instruction. The Management System creates a database to store information on the trainee learning process for each course and lesson [3]. The ability to automatically record and disseminate this type of training information is an essential ingredient of next generation computer-based training applications.

This paper describes a Training Information System (TIS), that has been developed by the University of Huddersfield and CBL Technology,

37

and visualisation of the vast amounts of data that it generates.

CBL Technology is the training division of Vega Group and the UK's largest bespoke computer-based training and multimedia/VR analysis, design and production company, currently employing 70 full-time development staff operating within an ISO 9001-registered quality system from offices in Derby and Bristol [5].

The TIS can monitor the usage of a particular training application by any number of users anywhere in the world and can be supplied on CDROM or actually run over the Internet. Each time a training session is completed anywhere on the on the internet, or the company intranet, a record is added to the training database which can be queried from anywhere on the network by anyone with access rights. The system provides a training manager with the ability track student progress in curricula and determine which training objectives have been met. Rapid technological change means that the number of courses that have to be introduced to such a system is always increasing. Its is therefore a challenge to introduce a way to display the vast amount of information contained in the training database in a simple, innovative, and easy to visualise manner, for perusal by the training manager. The human species have an array of very advanced brain functions at their disposal. These functions include the storing of information, the processing of new information (derived from internal or external resources) and, most importantly, the ability to analyse information and make informed decisions from it [1, chapter 1]. However, humans lack the ability to absorb, retain, and process, the vast amounts of ever increasing information that is available today. Such a task is more suited to a computer. The problem of a person reacting to this data is therefore one of communicating with such a computer. Virtual-reality is perhaps the solution in providing a way to manipulate and visualise vast quantities of data using intuitive man-machine interfaces. As a consequence, we are implementing Virtual Reality to facilitate visualisation of data and relationships between data elements. The use of Virtual Reality Modelling Language (VRML) [6] opens up numerous opportunities to use attributes which are far more palatable to the human brain than conventional methods of data visualisation. We are currently researching into the use of spatial awareness, time, shapes, and sounds to enhance the understanding of complex data structures. The use of Virtual Reality will allow training managers to instantly evaluate training effectiveness, employee proficiency and enable them to hunt down and contact subject matter experts when required. Using virtual reality to visualise data is not new. Virtual reality has been used for molecular modelling, astrophysics, engineering and large-scale environmental research [2 chapter 5]. There are also existing instances of where virtual reality has been implemented to visualise complex data; Virgilio, is a system that generates 3D visualisations of complex data objects [4].

Examples Of Usage

We have developed a Windows dynamic link library (DLL) of C++ functions that the creative CBT author can use to include additional monitoring facilities into training material without an in-depth knowledge of how they actually work. The system (figure 1) consists of two geographically separated sections. The 'Student' or 'Client' section consists of the CBT itself and the integrated monitoring and transmission system. This 'Student' section transmits information about student activities across a network medium (such as the Internet) to the 'Administrator' section. There is only one 'Administrator' section, but there could be thousands of instances of the 'Student' section. The 'Administrator' section collates all of the information it receives from each of the students into a single master database, and ultimately, into Virtual Reality Mark-up Language (VRML) code. The Training Manger is able to view the vast quantities of data such a system provides, summarised in an easy to explore virtual world.

Monitoring and Reporting

Within Authorware the author constructs an application by assembling icons on a flow-line. (figure 2)
Icons contain the objects that you include in the piece. Different types of icons contain different types of objects, such as graphics, text, sound, digital video movies, or a set of instructions.

Figure 1. Schematic of the Training Information System

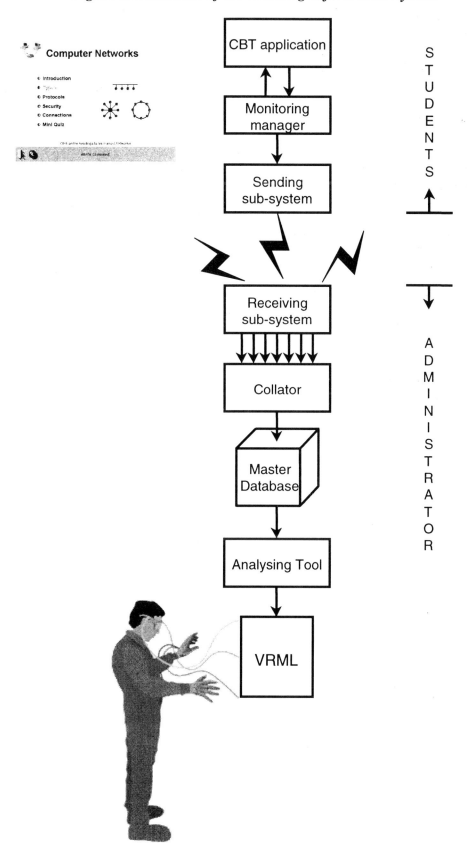

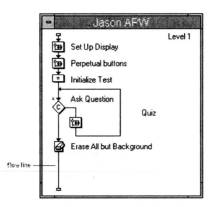

Figure 2. Example of an Authorware flow-line

The visual parts of the piece appear in the presentation window. This is where you arrange objects on screen and test-run the piece as you construct it.

The system implemented for monitoring user progress and performance is based on a single specially created Authorware icon which can be easily integrated into a CBT application and hence add monitoring functionality. By inserting the icon into the normal program flow and renaming it accordingly the icon will either automatically identify the host computer, manipulate databases or write information about a to a database of progress and performance records. All the monitoring functionality is accessed through the same generic Icon which has its functionality dictated by its title. This completely detaches the author from the inner workings of the icon's function and immediately defines the action of the icon at a glance. These monitoring functions have been implemented in this flexible and transparent manner so that an author can pass any information such as usage time, responses to questions, response times, navigation routes to the database. They utilise the Microsoft Open Database Connectivity (ODBC) facilities with Standard Query Language (SQL) calls to a database.

Although most databases created will be quite complex, figure 3 shows a simple example of some records created by the monitoring utilities described above:

The database comprises of several tables. The 'Details' table is standard to all databases created by the system and contains information about the source CBT, the session, the username of the student, the host name and IP address and also when the session started and finished. The remaining tables are specific to the CBT

application, their structure is standard and consistent but their content is dependant on how the author decides to implement monitoring in that particular application.

The Management Information System

Details						
CBTname	Session	Username	Host	Source	Start	Finish
Networks	0	Watson	161.12.6.23	Source	3-5-1999 1632	3-5-1999 1713

Types			
Session	Time Reported	Variable name	Variable Value
0	3-5-1999 1634	Question 1	Correct
0	3-5-1999 1638	Question 2	Incorrect
0	3-5-1999 1639	Question 3	Not attempted
0	3-5-1999 1645	Question 4	Correct
0	3-5-1999 1648	Visits	3/5

Protocols			
Session	Time Reported	Variable name	Variable Value
0	3-5-1999 1655	Question 1	Not attempted
0	3-5-1999 1657	Question 2	Incorrect
0	3-5-1999 1701	Visits	8/9

Figure 3. Example of a typical database records

The Management Information System (MIS) consists of collation system that brings together the individual session records into one single database so that it can be queried. The collation system accepts the 'session databases' that arrive over the Internet and determines their origin. If the collator system recognises that the database belongs to a CBT application its already aware of it simply merges the session data into that master CBT database. If the database is not recognised a new master CBT is created for that application.

Once a single database describing the use of the CBT application is constructed it can be queried to determine:

- What proportion of students have completed the module
- Whether anyone had any problems with the material
- Average training times
- Information as to when students find it convenient to use the material.

This information can be used by CBL as feedback into the development cycle or by a training manager/tutor to assess the success of the training.

Data Visualisation

In early 1999 we ran an experimental on-line training session for 60 students who are studying computer networks on the first year of a multimedia course at the University of Huddersfield (http://www.hud.ac.uk/schools/engineering/undgrad/mmvr/networks/cbt.htm).

At the request of the tutor this particular application firstly monitors:

- Who the student is
- When they accessed the application
- Where they accessed the application from

It records:

- How long the session lasted
- Which chapters/pages they visited
- How long they spent there
- Their response to tutorial questions delivered at the end of each section
- Their performance in an end of Module assessment

All of this data for all of the students therefore gets transmitted to a central collection point where it is collated into one large database. This database can of course be queried, but the results of the queries are often difficult to interpret. In the current phase of the project we are therefore looking at data visualisation in three dimensions. Since the whole project is Internet based, the obvious tool to do this with is VRML. Also a VRML description is a neutral ASCII text format file which we can easily generate automatically from the contents of a database. VRML also requires no compiler or specialist viewer and therefore requires no additional investment by the user.

As a consequence of the decision to use VRML, we have developed an application (written in C++/MFC) that examines the contents of the training database and automatically generates the VRML to represent the data. The VRML 'worlds' that the application generates can be placed directly onto a web-site for perusal by both students, and training managers, at any location. Currently, the system is able to represent the data in three different types of virtual worlds; The 'World of Colour', the 'World of Columns', and the 'World of Spheres' world. Various studies on database visualisation systems have been conducted, but they are proprietary systems aimed at their specific objectives and could not successfully integrate with training information systems (e.g., statistical data [7], medical data, document databases [8],[9],[10],[11]). Unlike these existing systems, our solution provides quick, light and flexible approach to data visualisation.

"The World of Colour"

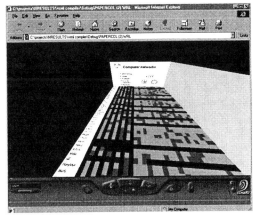

In this world, student responses to questions, and the extent of the content in each section they have viewed, are both represented by colour. If a student has visited a section it is demonstrated by a blue colour. The brighter the shade of blue, the more content the student actually viewed in that section. If a student has responded correctly to a question then the response is shown by the colour green. An incorrect response is indicated by the colour red. This method of data visualisation demonstrated the benefits of being able to visualise large amounts of data from different perspectives. If the user orientated themselves so that the Y axis was in front, data could be observed on individual student performance. However if the user orientated themselves so that the X axis was in front, data could be observed on overall acceptability of an individual question. This first attempt at data visualisation method did not employ many of the facilities that VR can offer to assist with data visualisation, (such as different shapes, size etc..).

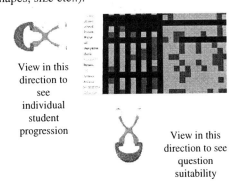

View in this direction to see individual student progression

View in this direction to see question suitability

"The World of Columns"

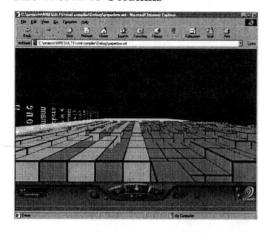

1In this world, student responses to questions, and the extent of the content in each section they have viewed, are represented by the height of the columns. The tall columns represent questions with which students had difficulty with. If a column is absent, then the student failed to visit that section of material, or answer that particular question. By orientating themselves correctly, the user is able absorb large amounts of information by performing a 'fly-by' over the field of columns. If the user flies over the terrain in one direction individual student performance can be assessed. Overall course suitability for the students can be assessed by flying over the terrain in the other. However, this visualisation method did prove to be problematic. If the columns were viewed close up, the use of height made overall evaluation of the whole scene difficult (the columns are not translucent, and the users vision of the remainder of the terrain would be blocked). However, if the user was sufficiently high enough, then it was difficult to keep track of which line of results (or course acceptability by students) was being viewed. We decided that the use of height, with this quantity of results hindered successful visualisation.

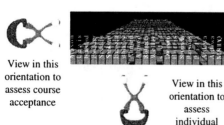

View in this orientation to assess course acceptance

View in this orientation to assess individual student progress

"The World of Spheres"

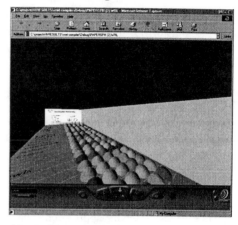

In this world, student activities and responses to all questions have be summarised into 5 autonomous chapters. Each chapter is represented by a sphere. As a consequence each student has 5 spheres that together represent his/her total training activity within the courseware. The size of a sphere represents the amount of content/lecture-material that the student viewed in that particular chapter. The colour of the sphere varies in shades between red and green depending on how well the student performed in the assessment linked with that particular chapter. If the student got all questions correct, the sphere is fully green, if the student got all questions incorrect, the sphere is fully red. This visualisation technique allows the training manager to make comparisons between students at a glance.

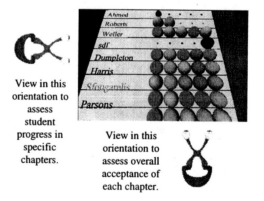

View in this orientation to assess student progress in specific chapters.

View in this orientation to assess overall acceptance of each chapter.

This technique also allows different categories of students to be easily distinguished between. For example:

Small green sphere:	Indicates a student who performed extremely well in the assessment, without consulting much lecturing material.
Large green sphere:	Indicates a student who performed extremely well in the assessment, and viewed all the lecture material.
Large red sphere:	Indicates a problem student who performed badly in the assessment, even after viewing all the lecture material.
Small red sphere:	Indicates a problem student who performed badly in the assessment, but did not bother with the lecture material.

The tutor is therefore primarily looking for any large red spheres that indicate that a student has not understood it.

Conclusions

The early stages of this project have demonstrated that traditional CBT can be much improved by exploiting computer network technology to improve delivery and turnaround times. It can also produce a far more attractive CBT product with superior functionality and many scheduling and monitoring applications, and perhaps "pay per view".

The facilities that can be offered reflect different learning and working practices that are now commonplace. This project was developed to provide a flexible solution to the challenging requirements of a training manager. The developed system allows any CBT application to be run by any user from a distributed WWW site, vastly easing the dissemination of their training material. In addition, the system automatically monitors what has which student has seen which material and when, along with any other necessary information that the training manger wants to record. These features, combined with the automatic generation of Virtual Worlds to facilitate visualisation of reported data provides both authors of training, and training managers with a complete solution for delivering, monitoring and tracking of activities in computer-based training.

Feedback from both the students (using the criteria in appendix a) and the group tutor was both positive and interesting. The most striking feedback was how negative some students felt about having their actions monitored to such an extent.

The use of the networked CBT and data visualisation has allowed the tutor to:

- Monitor attendance at the session
- Identify students who had trouble understanding the material
- Correlate marks for the written submissions with student" performance in and attendance at the CBT Session

At this stage, this project has not exploited the Virtual Environment to its full potential. The work completed so far is in early stages and does not benefit fully from using the interactivity that determines what is considered by some people as the only true Virtual Reality. Further work will explore interactivity between the Training Manager and the objects in the virtual worlds. In addition, the benefits from applying the use of characteristics such as shapes, sound, and Time (through animations) to represent data will be explored.

The proliferation of computer networks will continue to promote distance learning, virtual laboratories and people working from home bases. In these types of situations the functions which this project is creating are likely to play an essential co-ordinating role.

References

[1]   Philip Barker, Harry Yeates, *"Introducing computer assisted learning"*, Prentice/Hall, 1985.

[2]   Joshua Eddings, *"How Virtual Reality Works"*, Ziff-Davis Press, 1994

[3]   Roy Rada, *"Multimedia Education"* - Handbook of Internet and Multimedia Systems and Applications, CRC Press/IEEE Press, 1999

[4]   Antonio Massari , Lorenzo Saladini, Fabio Sisinni, Walter Napolitano, *"Virtual Reality Systems For Browsing Multimedia"* Handbook of Internet and Multimedia Systems and Applications, CRC Press/IEEE Press, 1999

[5]   *"CBL Technology Ltd."*, Promotional Material for CBL technology Ltd, January 1996

[6]   *"The Virtual Reality Modeling Language"* Version 2.0 Spec.http://vag.vrml.org/

VRML2.0/FINAL/spec/

[7]   L. Meo-Evoli, M. Rafenelli, F.L. Ricci, *"An Interface for the Direct Manipulation of Statistical Data"*, Journal of Visual Languages and Computing, 1994

[8]   M. Hemmje, *"A 3D Based User Interface for Information Retrieval Systems"*, Proceedings IEEE Workshop on Database Issues for Data Visualisation, Vol.871, Oct. 1994

[9]   U. Krohn, *"VINETA: Navigation through Virtual Information Spaces"* Proceedings Workshop on Advanced Visual Interfaces, 1996

[10]   B. A. Wilson, R. H. Fowler, W.A.L. Fowler, *"Integrating Query, Thesaurus, and Documents through a Common Visual Representation"*, Proceedings of the 14th Annual International ACM SIGIR conference on Research and Development in Information Retrieval, 1991

[11]   M. Chalmers, P. Chitson, *"Bead: Explorations in Information Exploration"*, Proceedings SIGIR'92, published as a special issue of SIGIR Forum, ACM Press, pp. 330-337

Multi-user VRML Environment for Teaching VRML: Immersive Collaborative Learning

Vladimir Geroimenko and Mike Phillips
School of Computing, University of Plymouth, Drake Circus, Plymouth, Devon PL4
8AA, UK
vladg@soc.plym.ac.uk
mikep@soc.plym.ac.uk

Abstract

VRML-based environments can be used very effectively for teaching a variety of online courses. This paper describes the development of an Internet-based collaborative learning environment in which VRML is not only the means but also the subject of teaching. Such a VRML environment is designed to assist and support employees of the 'New Media' industries enrolled on short courses run by the Interactive Media Group in the School of Computing, University of Plymouth.

This paper focuses on some key issues in the design of the VRML teaching environment and using it for real-time and on-demand course delivery. One of the most interesting issues is the experience of learning and teaching VRML while being within a VRML world. Such an immersive method of learning provides students with unique experiences and significantly increases the efficiency of the learning process.

1: Introduction

Distributed Virtual Environments can be used very effectively for teaching a variety of online courses and for supporting collaborative work [1, 2]. The main goal of our project was and is the development of an Internet-based collaborative learning environment in which VRML is not only the means but also the subject of teaching. Such a VRML environment is designed to assist and support employees of the 'New Media' industries (including; digital TV, Interactive Media developers, electronic publishing, Information Architects, etc) enrolled on short courses run by the Interactive Media Group in the School of Computing, University of Plymouth. The project will ultimately deliver a number of on-line VRML spaces/places and software tools that will allow participants to collaboratively create their own 'haptic' learning sub-environments within the overall architecture of the project.

2: The architecture of the virtual environment

This learning environment is a Web Site made up of pages which consist of the following three frames: a VRML browser frame for navigating through 3D virtual environments, a chat frame for text-based communication and a reference frame for representing VRML specifications and codes. Currently, we are developing three slightly different prototypes of the multi-user collaborative environment based on VNet, Sony and Blaxxun software. These software are different in terms of the quality of rendering, the availability of cross-platform versions, the richness of communication and navigation such as pre-programmed avatar gestures or text-to-speech chat window options, and so on. It is very difficult to say at this moment, which of the above versions will be preferred by students. Therefore, we have decided to make a usability test after all the working prototypes will be completed to choose the most appropriate version on the base of real-life practice.

The 'hub' of the OnLine Multi-user Learning Environment is inspired by and based on Bentham's architecture for the Panopticon. Jeremy Bentham's (1748-1832) 'Panopticon; or the Inspection House' (circa 1791, see [5]) was never build to serve its intended function. Within this virtual environment the 'fluid

45

architecture' of the 'Panopticon' becomes the perfect form to support a social learning interaction where the surveyors co-operatively survey themselves. At each level or module or the structure, each 'cell' in this Panopticon is a gateway to another 'place' where work can be done. Each layer of the building houses a module. Access to the modules is provided through the 'Core' which runs up through the centre of the 'building'. Here participants can register for a particular module, and have access to that layer of the building.

From the pedagogical and also technological point of view, there are two distinguishing areas within the 3D environment. The first area is a chain of spaces in which a variety of VRML nodes, scripts and other elements are represented and also grouped according to the similarity of their content into several tutorials. In other words, this space a unique 3D version of the VRML specifications where students can learn the basics of the language as well as they can come back to this session any time for reference. The second space offers opportunities for students to present their own VRML objects and environments. This part of the virtual world is highly changeable offering a flexible environment with significant creative potential.

3: 3D and 2D representation of the contents

The 3D representation of the VRML specification is one of the most difficult issues. It is quite obvious that there are no simple ways of translating this document from 2D format into 3D. Firstly, it is hardly possible to create a complete 3D version of the VRML specification because of a great deal of its logical and other "non-spatial" details. Secondly, a 3D space has its own logic. Therefore, to represent the VRML content adequately, one needs to create 3D objects, environments, animations and other spatial structures. It is impossible to do this just by coping the structure and logic of the appropriate text of the VRML specifications.

Of course, it depends on the logical complicity of the part of the VRML specification being converted into a 3D form. For example, the standard VRML building blocks, such as primitive shapes (box, cone, cylinder and sphere), are very easy to represent both in the 3D environment and in the 2D reference frame. To create a 3D model that would show how a specific type of sensors, interpolators or lights works is a more difficult task. This task is complicated mostly from a pedagogical (not technological) point of view: how to present 2D content in a 3D way that would show the essence of the subject matter in a clear visual form.

The pedagogical effectiveness of using the VRML environment depends on the extent to which the contents of the 3D environment and the 2D reference frame are mutually supplementary. That is, they must help students to understand each other's material represented through contrasting forms.

4: Immersive collaborative learning

This 3D online environment may be used in three ways. A teacher can use the environment to deliver real-time lectures and workshops that are, in terms of teacher-student communication, very similar to standard sessions in real-life classrooms. Secondly, a group of students can meet in this environment, without a teacher, to learn VRML together and to discuss some VRML related questions. Thirdly, any student can use this environment to teach himself or herself VRML.

Navigating through the virtual environment, students can experience most of the VRML nodes and samples as virtual objects and interact with them. For example, a group of students (represented by their avatars) can gather around a red cube, click on it to see its behaviour (rotation and changing colour), learn the appropriate VRML codes in the frame nearby and then discuss this sample with the teacher and/or each other.

In order to make our environment accessible from any ordinary computer, we have created it as Web-Based Desktop Virtual Reality. Of course, the sense of immersion in Desktop VR is not as strong that offered by head-mounted displays, but nevertheless it exists in a limited form [3, 4]. Students can feel themselves as part of a virtual environment (the sense of "being there") because of their active behaviour within the environment. When one navigates through the virtual space, to interact with virtual objects and to communicate with the avatars of other participants using familiar 'real world' processes (i.e. worrying constantly about your position in the space and synchronising your action with other people) a specific sense of immersion is developed. Our research shows that by being within the same world as interactive VRML objects, students are able to learn VRML materials much quicker and deeper than in a non-virtual learning situation.

5: Conclusions

We have found that the use of a specially created VRML environment to teach the VRML specifications provides students with the unique experience of immersive collaborative learning and significantly increases the efficiency of the learning process. The main problems connected with designing and creating such an environment are locating appropriate 'architectural' forms of space and representing information in a hybrid 3D/2D form.

6: References

[1] Frécon, E. and Nöu, A. Building distributed virtual environments to support collaborative work. *VRST '98. Proceedings of the ACM Symposium on Virtual reality software and technology* 1998, pp. 105-113.

[2] Neal, L. Virtual Classrooms and Communities. *GROUP '97. Proceedings of the international ACM SIGGROUP conference on Supporting group work: the integration challenge,* 1997, pp. 81 - 90.

[3] Robertson, G., Czerwinski, M. & van Dantzich, M. Immersion in Desktop Virtual Reality. *UIST '97. Proceedings of the 10th annual ACM symposium on User interface software and technology,* 1997, pp. 11-19.

[4] Steinke, G. Preparing Students to Communicate in a Virtual Environment. *SIGCPR '97. Proceedings of the 1997 conference on Computer personnel research,* p. 249.

[5] Bentham, J., *Works*, ed. Browning, IV, 1834 (The Bentham Collection University College London).

Session 1-4

Visualization in Construction

Chair
Dino Bouchlaghem
Loughborough University, UK

Designing a Computer-Aided-Learning application using multimedia to train inexperienced Building Surveyors in Building Pathology

M. Shelbourn,[1] G. Aouad,[1] M. Hoxley,[2]

1   Research Centre for the Built & Human Environment (BUHU), Time Research Institute, The University of Salford, United Kingdom
2   Division of Property & Construction Management, Business School, Staffordshire University, United Kingdom
Email – m.a.shelbourn@surveying.salford.ac.uk

ABSTRACT

Computer Aided / Assisted Learning (CAL) systems aim to provide learners with both a rich set of learning resources and tools to help them navigate through such structures. The advent of high quality graphics and multimedia has enabled learning styles that were previously impractical to be developed and supported by state of the art CAL systems. This paper will concentrate on how multimedia can be used as a Computer-Aided-Learning medium in training inexperienced Surveyors in Building Pathology.

Keywords Computer-Aided-Learning, Building Pathology, Multimedia, Virtual-Reality

1.0   Introduction

Multimedia technology is a powerful way of presenting information so that it can be easily navigated and easily understood. One of the reasons multimedia has gained popularity is because information that appeals to multiple senses is more easily assimilated and is generally more interesting than that presented in one format.

Multimedia provides the user of an application the freedom to view information at the touch of a button rather than searching through many texts and publications. The use of visual graphics, video, sound, animation, and small amounts of text mixed together provides more interesting viewing for the user.

The invention of multimedia has given application developers in all fields of life the opportunity to give more interesting ways of teaching the uninformed as well as the so-called well trained. This section describes how multimedia has influenced education, and shows some example applications.

"...I hate the idea that novels are not interactive. I've got 26 symbols and a handful of punctuation and I can create in your mind sounds and visions and people and scenery - and all this is specific to each individual..." [Pratchett 1991 pp. 12-18]

and,

"...our experience of life is multi-sensory...so multimedia is a highly appropriate way of presenting it" [Wilson 1994 pp. 219-228]

There have been many arguments about the usefulness of multimedia in education and whether its implementation is actually worth the expense and extra training that would accompany it. Of course multimedia could not be said to be the only answer to education and learning, but if properly implemented it can certainly help. Outlined in the next three sections are practical implementations of multimedia in education:

1. Creating multimedia projects.

Multimedia is particularly effective in schools. Potentially it develops not only student's knowledge but also their research and reasoning skills. Students work in-groups, thereby experiencing awareness of different viewpoints, flexibility and teamwork. They create multimedia databases that they know could be used by subsequent pupils, thereby developing their sense of responsibility and self worth.

50

2. Multimedia as a support to teaching.

Potentially a CD-ROM can store 550 Mb of data, which is equivalent to 300,000 pages of information in a book or 12 encyclopaedias. The advantage of the CD is that it presents it in a far more interesting fashion! Jonathan Butters and Charlotte Corke developed a CD at Liverpool John Moores University that describes and reflects upon the documenting of a major school-based development project on a CD-ROM. [Butters and Corke 1998] The project is called SISP (Supporting Innovation in Schools Project). This was a three-year project, which aimed to enhance the secondary school curriculum through the promotion of innovation and the development of creative skills, primarily in the Design and Technology subject area.

However, there are limitations on a multimedia tool such as a CD-ROM. Even though it can be described as interactive in that the user can pursue what he / she wants, it is not interactive at all, in that the most basic of educational questions, WHY?, may not be answerable. There is no knowledge of an information field beyond what is presented and there is no adaptation of presentation to the user and the user's knowledge base. Hence it must be used as a support tool for a teacher who, potentially, can fill in the blanks. As such it has great potential, holding student interest for longer and providing more information than the limited budgets of libraries can normally provide.

3. Multimedia as an alternative to teaching.

The third use of multimedia in education is potentially the most expensive and certainly the most difficult to obtain, however, when it works, it is most effective. A knowledge-based simulator developed at the University of Massachusetts for teaching about cardiac resuscitation provides spoken advice, Emergency Room (ER) sound and graphic representations of ECG (electrocardiograms), blood gases and vital signs. The student has one goal, to save the patient by implementing the correct procedure. The tutor, based on expert knowledge, grades student performance and even customises the problem according to a previous student's achievement. The students who have used the system have valued it as being equal to "working one on one with an ER physician." The system makes things a lot clearer than text, but it is obviously less daunting than working with real patients and facing potential lawsuits whilst techniques are perfected!

There is still along way to go before this kind of expert multimedia system can be implemented in all areas of education. With medicine, there are definite right and wrong responses that can be covered by expert knowledge; Building Surveying is far more vague.

2.0 Computer-Aided-Learning (CAL)

The first CAL program was developed in 1954, but it did not really become common place until the mid-sixties. In 1966 Patrick Suppes developed the first adaptive CAL program and predicted that it would "...change the face of education in a very short time." [Suppes 1966 p.215] It was not until the early 1980's when micro-technology made computers more affordable that they became more prominent in educational use. In 1981, Seymour Papert, author of LOGO, a programming language designed to help children learn geometry by "doing", declared that the "worksheet curriculum" could be confidently abandoned to allow "children's minds to develop through the exploration of computer simulated microworlds." [Papert 1981] By 1985, 80% of UK secondary schools and 95% of primary schools had some level of computing. [Jackson et al. 1986] A 1986 survey by Bleach [1986] concluded that, although generally welcomed by teacher's computers were little used, sometimes remaining idle for 80% of the available time, and certainly used significantly less than television in primary schools. The major affect reported by teachers was a change in the furniture. Despite their potential, the greatest use is still in automated practice and testing routines similar to established teaching techniques and CAL has produced a polarity of views among teachers.

The advent of high quality graphics and multimedia has heralded an increased research effort in this area. Learning styles that were previously impractical are now being developed and supported by state of the art CAL systems.

The basic assumption upon which most of the CAL tradition has been based is that the principles of programmed instruction or generative CAL provide an automation of the most essential step of giving the learner, at an appropriate moment, the next piece of information to learn or the next problem to try.

2.1 Computer-Aided-Learning – Existing in a Vacuum?

The design of CAL material often seems to proceed, and to be considered, far away from any consideration of where it will be used, by whom, and in what institutional context. This is perfectly acceptable as long as each application is to be seen as a specific local initiative, but it gives the lie to the grander claims that are made for CAL, such as Suppes's view that it could provide for every child:

"...the personal services of a tutor as well-informed as Aristotle..." [Suppes 1966]

and Reinhardt's claim that:

"...this generation of technology promises more than just an improvement in educational productivity: it may deliver a qualitative change in the nature of learning itself..." [Reinhardt 1995]

It is necessary to know where the technology is being, and is going to be, used. If it is to be brought by those who can afford it, in the form of "edutainment", or primarily by employers as part of their fine-tuning of their employee's skills, the effect will be very different to if it becomes a central part of mass compulsory education.

2.2 What are the Obstacles to the use of CAL?

The first and obvious obstacle is the lack of the necessary material resources. This lack of material resource becomes even more pressing when the revolution in CAL is seen as coming through networking, connection to other schools and to the Internet. Carol Twigg [1995] refers to "the installed base of telecommunications technology in the schools, 80% of which is obsolete."

The second and more serious obstacle is that the hardware is the simplest and least expensive of the problems. The Liberal Democrat spokesman may have promised "...a computer on every child's desk..." but that is meaningless. The computer is not a magic machine that works itself. Passey and Ridgway [1994] state the appropriate levels of human support have been grossly underestimated. Teachers will need a large amount of support if they are able to incorporate CAL properly into their practice, Passey and Ridgway suggest as much as 100 hours training per year may be the level required. There is little evidence that schools are prepared to expand the necessary time for training or expense of providing adequate ancillary support, especially given the increasing pressures from government requirements (National Curriculum, etc.)

The third obstacle is the present lack of very good educational software. Carol Twigg quotes Peter Drucker as saying that for nay new technology to be successful, it must do the job ten times better, [Twigg 1995] as for example word processing does over hand-drafting a document.

2.3 Is Education the place for CAL?

This brings a fourth and, possibly, the most crucial obstacle to the widespread use of CAL in primary, secondary and tertiary education. The promise that CAL holds out is that of individualised learning. Where does this fit into schools? As Seymour Papert says:

"In the 1980's...I caught myself telling school establishments and administrators that what I've got with this technology is what they need. Wow! It's not what they need at all. It's the kiss of death. It's the end of education as an organised entity - of the schools as we've known it....Is there any reason to believe that the school - with its structure of classroom, organisation by age, and so on - will exist in fifty years? [Papert, Grillos, Norman et al. 1994]

That is, the promise that CAL offers just does not fit in with education as it is presently organised as institutions. Therefore, bits of CAL will be bolted on to the present practice, to little effect, or, for CAL to work properly, policy changes for how education is to work must act as a pressure from outside the institutions themselves. These are political decisions as to the purposes and requirements of public education. They need to be addressed explicitly, unless the possibilities that CAL offer will wither on the stony ground of institutional incompatibility.

3.0 The Building Pathology CAL Application

Building Pathology is a term particularly associated with the field of Building Surveying. It simply means identifying faults / defects in buildings. This said, it has been difficult to train young inexperienced surveyors in this practice due to insurance and logistical problems of enabling a large group of students to visit a property where defects can be found. Many employers of young surveyors are now recruiting directly from higher education rather than traditional apprentice type applications. This means that the employers expect their new recruits to have a wider knowledge of surveying buildings than in previous years.

To overcome these problems a project is being devised, at the University of Salford, [Shelbourn, Aouad & Hoxley 1998] that enables young and inexperienced surveyors to gain skills in diagnosing defects in buildings without leaving the confines of a computer desk. The architecture of the system is shown below. The project incorporates a number of different fields of expertise that are outlined below.

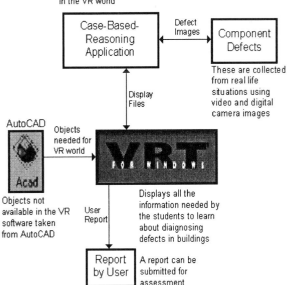

Figure 1 Architecture of the CAL application

3.1 Types of Survey

There are three reasons why a survey can be undertaken on a property. The first is required by a prospective purchaser of a property. There are four different types of survey available to the purchaser. These are outlined below.

1. Building Surveys

This survey is often called a "Structural" or "full" survey where a surveyor is expected to look at all "accessible areas" of the building without risking damage to the building or themselves. "All accessible areas" is defined as "areas from the ground, floors, fixed stairways or other vantage points. All hatches, access traps, manholes etc will be inspected if they can be safely reached." The report is individually hand crafted for each property, and lists how the building is constructed, what condition it is in, the reasons for any problems, and recommendations for current and future maintenance. If a specialist is required to further survey certain aspects of the property then they should also be included in the report.

2. Mortgage Valuation

This type of survey is often called a "Building Society Survey" and is only termed

a survey in the loosest of terms. The main purpose of a mortgage valuation is to assure the bank or building society who are lending the money that the building is good security for the amount wanting to be borrowed. The report will be no more than two pages, and gives a general idea of the condition of the property.

3. RICS Home Buyers Survey & Valuation

This survey is halfway between the two above. It is most suited to 20th century housing and flats. The report is more substantial than a mortgage valuation but not as detailed as a building survey. It mainly covers the current condition of the building, without giving advice on specialists required and maintenance to the property.

4. Single Issue Report

This type of survey is often asked for after a Building Survey has highlighted the need for a specialist's report to a specific problem with the property. The detail of the report is the same as a building survey, but only on the specialist requirements given.

The second reason for undertaking a survey on a property is to enable parties to agree the condition of a property when they are entering into a lease. There are two types of lease that are entered with each requiring different types of survey. These are outlined below:

1. Full Repairing & Insuring Lease

The responsibility of putting the building into full repair, and to give it back in full repair is that of the tenant regardless of the condition it was in when they took it. In order to understand the extent of this a Building Survey report is generally advised.

2. Schedule of Condition

A Schedule of Condition is needed where the lease require the tenants to hand back the property in a no worse condition from that when they took it. The report will not contain advice on reasons or remedies to problems, but details on cracks, dampness, weathering and so on.

The third reason for undertaking a survey is to enforce repairing clauses through a Schedule of Dilapidations. This is a report prepared by the landlord's surveyor describing the current condition of the building and setting out the work necessary to bring the building into repair.

The CAL application will be based solely on the Building Survey requirements, as this is the most common type of survey that an inexperienced surveyor is likely to undertake. Details on how to undertake such a survey will be included within the CAL application.

3.2 Building Defects

Perhaps the most recognised person within this field is Professor Malcolm Hollis, who is currently researching a number of topics at the University of Reading in the UK. He has made a number of educational videos and written countless texts on different ways to survey a property and diagnose defects within buildings. One of the major aspects of his work is testing the knowledge of surveyors that are currently practising within the industry. A good example of this was shown on a well-known television current affairs programme. Professor Hollis was asked to show how some surveyors were not carrying out their duty to members of the public when they were asked to survey a property. Professor Hollis spent nearly 4 hours in the property and highlighted at least 10 defects that would cause him concern. The programme secretly filmed three separate surveyors on their surveys of the same property and the results seen were quite startling! Only one of the three surveyors spent more than 1 hour in the property, with the least time spent being 55 min. All three surveyors were very poor in diagnosing the problems that Professor Hollis had highlighted. All of them only found 1 out of the 10 problems highlighted. No reason was actually given in the programme why this had occurred as the surveyors concerned were not given a chance to speak, so reasons for their not diagnosing the problems have to be second guessed. Perhaps one of the main reasons for this was inadequate training, another may be a busy schedule, etc. The main reason that the project is interested in is the lack of training was highlighted in the programme, hence the design and implementation of this system.

Professor Hollis's techniques will be the basis used in this application to help the users learn how to survey a building properly. His techniques are well publicised and the one to be used is taken from his book "Surveying Buildings". [Hollis 1992]

3.3 Information Technology - Virtual Reality

The use of Virtual-Reality in this project is very important as it gives the user a visual portrayal of a defect in a building. A typical 19th century property is used that has characteristic features such as bay windows and not so modern building techniques associated with it. The virtual environment is developed using the "Superscape - VRT" software. It is relatively easy to use with a number of different editors for the designer to use when developing their worlds.

The environment will show the property with tags on certain elements of the building. If a user clicks on these tags a number of defects will be shown to them highlighting the type of defect that may affect that element. The defects themselves are taken from real-life examples obtained from partnerships with local surveying practices. The photographs are taken using a digital camera so that they are in a format that can be easily recognised by the VR software. This reduces problems of scanning the photographs where quality of the picture can be reduced. The VR environment forms the main basis of the application, as this is the main view that the user has of the application.

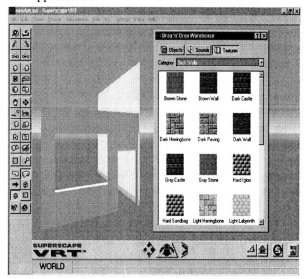

Figure 2 Screen shot showing the development of the VR world

The screen shot above is taken during the development of the building in the VR software. It shows the world with objects that make up the property, and the warehouse box that enables users to add objects, create and add sounds, and texture objects in the VR world.

3.4 Information Technology-Case-Based-Reasoning

The Case-Based-Reasoning software is programmed into the application to provide the different defects to be portrayed within the VR environment. Each individual defect is stored as a separate case within the software. As some defects are associated with others these provide the basis of specific cases. The CBR software can then show different case scenarios for the same element within the property. This means that the user does not get used to which particular element of the building has a defect associated with it, and so makes them concentrate every time they use the application.

This particular approach has been used on another CAL application within the University of Salford. A CAL application was developed using VR as the interface to identify whether or not different scaffolds on a property complied with current statutory requirements. [Oliveira et al. 1997] Each individual scaffold was saved a single case and when the application was loaded a new type of scaffold was portrayed within the VR environment for users to comment upon to see whether or not it complied with current statutory requirements. Some of the application's fundamental designs have been incorporated into the building pathology application.

4.0 Conclusions

This paper has described the fundamentals of multimedia technology. It has highlighted the advantages of how information technology and in particular multimedia can be used to produce educational training material in a wide variety of professional disciplines. The paper has described a brief history of the origins of Computer-Aided-Learning and when best to use such CAL systems has also been shown. Some advantages and disadvantages of CAL systems have been discussed, along with some of the debates that are common to implementing CAL systems.

The paper has shown in some detail how multimedia can be used in conjunction with other technologies to produce CAL training material in building pathology. It has shown information on surveying properties, how the defects for the application are gathered and recorded in the case-based-reasoning software. Finally it has shown how the development of the application has progressed, and how virtual reality will play a large part in this.

References

1. Bleach, P, (1986), The use of Computers in Primary Schools, University of Reading;
2. Butters, J and Corke, C (1998), Supporting Innovation in Schools Project –SISP-, Information & Visualisation Conference Proceedings, Southbank University, IEEE Computer Society, Los Alamitos, California;
3. Hollis, Malcolm, (1992), Surveying Buildings, 3rd edition, RICS Books, London, UK;
4. Jackson et al, (1986), A Survey of Microcomputer use and Provision in Primary Schools, Journal of Computer Assisted Learning, Issue 2;
5. Oliveira, L., Watson, I. and Retik, A., (1997), Case-based-reasoning in virtual reality: an application for training on inspection of scaffold structures, Dept of Surveying, Uni. of Salford;
6. Papert, S, (1981), Mindstorms - Children, Computers and Powerful Ideas, Harvester Press;
7. Papert, S, Grillos, J, Norman, D, et al, (Nov./Dec.1994), Transforming and Preserving Education (round table discussion), EduCom Review No. 29;
8. Passey, Don, and Ridgway, Jim, (February 1994), The Current Impact of Information Technology, Computer Education No. 76;
9. Pratchett, Terry, (1991), Amazing Possibilities, Educational Computing and Technology;
10. Reinhardt, Andy, (March 1995), New ways to Learn, Byte Issue 20;
11. Shelbourn, M et al, (1998), An Integrated Virtual Reality and Case-Based Reasoning Model for Training in Building Pathology, Information & Visualisation Conference Proceedings, Southbank University, IEEE Computer Society, Los Alamitos, California, p.44-49;
12. Suppes, P, (1966), The Uses of Computers in Education, Scientific American;
13. Twigg, Carol, (Jan./Feb.1995), Man Bites Dog, EduCom Review, No. 30, page 1;
14. Wilson, Martyn, (1994), Educational and Training Technology International, Vol. 31.

The Mathematics of Shape-Geometry Approach To The Analysis Of Curve Profile

Dr. Farzad Khosrowshahi, School of Construction, South Bank University, London, UK

Abstract

It has been previously shown that the visual approach to the analysis of the behaviour of growth patterns can provide a viable solution to the understanding of the physical behaviour of the subject matter. Also, it has been demonstrated that the shape of the profile can be defined in terms of a number of characteristics some of which are general for all profiles and others are specific to individual circumstances. These characteristics, referred to as shape-parameters, are used for the analysis of the profile. Also, they are used for construction of the profile that the phenomenon is likely to assume. The method was validated by applying it to construction project expenditure pattern forecasting and further validation was undertaken by the use of statistical technique, namely, Principal Component Analysis.

In this paper, the mathematics of the model is represented, whereby, for a given set of shape-parameters, the precise profile is mathematically generated.

Due to its complex nature, the problem is decomposed into separate modules each satisfying a number of requirements. The modules operate independently but when combined, the overall boundary requirements are also satisfied.

Keywords: Mathematical Models, Shape-Parameters, Curve Profile, Visualisation, Forecasting

Introduction

Often, the behaviour of a phenomenon, over time, is represented by means of a graph and analysed accordingly. The visual analysis of such graphs provides an insight into the behaviour of the subject matter. It has been previously demonstrated that the profile of many phenomenon displaying behaviour of growth, contains characteristics that are descriptive of the behaviour of the pattern (Khosrowshahi 1998). The work applied the concept to construction project expenditure pattern and showed that a forecast of expenditure pattern can be generated by constructing the shape of the pattern from which monthly valuation figures were derived. The parameters defining the shape consist of Peak time *(Xp)*, Peak cost *(Yp)*, Initial Slope *(ISLP)*, End Slope *(ESLP)*, Intensity *(INT)*, Distortion(s): [Position, duration, intensity and type].

As shown in Figure 1, It was noted that with these variables, the shape of project expenditure pattern could be constructed. Since the bahviour of construction expenditure pattern is one of, growth nature, the concept is applicable to all phenomenon displaying the behaviour of growth. Examples include human physical growth, population growth, and the growth and decay of radioactive isotopes.

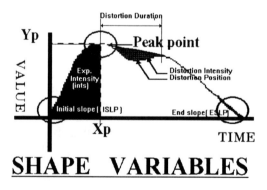

Figure 1. Shape Parameters

Having identified the parameters defining the shape of the profile, the next logical step was to acquire a mathematical expression, which, for a given set of values, for shape-parameters, generates the profile. The effort commenced by a thorough search among current expressions. These included growth models that were developed for particular applications and were tailor-made to the relevant data. These models proved to lack any use for subjects other than the one for which they were generated. Also, many general models representing growth patterns were examined. However, they tend to rely on simple exponential expressions which simulate only the underlying pattern of growth. All other efforts to find a suitable model from current expressions or indeed probability distribution functions (PDFs) were also unsuccessful. Subsequently, a new expression was developed.

This paper will introduce the mathematical expression which, on the one and, fulfills the objectives of the research for which it was developed - simulation of construction expenditure patterns. On the other hand, the expression is of adequate generic nature for it to be applied to other phenomenon displaying the behaviour of growth. These include several areas from various disciplines.

Requirements of the Mathematical Expression

For the expression to satisfy all requirements it has to comply with the following;

a. It must comply with the general characteristics of growth profile, as described by Khosrowshahi (1998).
b. It must comply with specific characteristics of the diversity of shape profiles (Khosrowshahi, 1998).
c. It must be independent of data [unlike methods such as regression, where data and the expression are integrated.
d. The parameters of the expression must be fully interpretable.

It was somewhat apparent that the incorporation of all requirements into one expression was a near-impossible task. To this end, the problem was divided into modules each represented by a separate mathematical expression. Therefore, each module was responsible for fulfilling a number of requirements relating to shape-parameters.

A precondition for the modular approach was that each module should operate independently from other modules, but their combination must satisfy the overall requirements without violating a single one. Also, each module should contain parameters

allowing full control over the behaviour of the variables that they generate. A brief description of each module is given below:

i. Control Module: this module is a single curve representing the underlying pattern of growth.

ii. Kurtosis Module: this module consists of two independent curves which adjust the initial and end slopes, as well as the curve-intensity (total sum of all values from the origin to the main peak point).

c. Distortion module: this module consists of one or more curves which simulate distortions of the underlying curve

Control Module

By its nature the control module should be able to reflect the properties of growth, hence, it is highly likely that its mathematical expression will assume an exponential form. Indeed, an attempt to develop a polynomial expression proved to be unsuccessful. Basically, the module is a two-phased single, smoothed, continuous and monotonic curve.

The control module is required to comply or control the following:

i. Comply with general conditions of growth profile.
ii. Full control over the position of the peak point on the X-axis.
iii. Full control over the position of the peak point on the Y-axis.
iv. With zero initial slope and with zero end slope.
v. With zero initial value and zero end value.

Since all modules are eventually superimposed, any alteration in the value of the parameters of any one module would alter the total area under the curve (or the total sum of all Y-values). Therefore, another responsibility of the control module was to make adjustments for the total area-requirement (total area under the periodic curve must be unity). Therefore,

vi. Full control over the area under the periodic curve (total sum of all Y-values).

Mathematical Expression for Control Module

It had been hoped that amongst all growth expressions or PDF's there could be at least one which would satisfy part or all of control module requirements. The search proved informative but unsuccessful. In the absence of an off-the-shelf model, a new mathematical expression needed to be developed. All attempts such as Polynomial fitting proved to be fruitless, subsequently, the focus was turned to exponential functions.

Due to the complexity of the model it was decided to generate / simulate the periodic pattern rather than cumulative pattern, thus requiring only one order of differentiation. In conjunction with the aforementioned requirements, the structure of the module had to satisfy the following;
1. $f(0) = 0$
2. $f(1) = 0$
3.   Contain a parameter for controlling X_p
4.   Contain a parameter for controlling Y_p
5.   Contain a parameter for controlling the area under the curve

Therefore, the model should be structured in such a way as to comply with *1* and *2* above and it should have three parameters each facilitating control over one of the specific requirements (*3, 4* and *5* above). As the result of extensive analysis of current expressions and through an evolutionary path, the following expression was developed;

$$Y_C = e^{bx^a(1-x)^d} - 1 \qquad (1)$$

Where, Y_c represents the periodic value as a proportion of unity and x is the proportion of period number over the number of periods. Here, $x(1-x)$ satisfies *1* and *2*, also, *3, 4* and *5* are implemented through a, b and d.

The derivative of (1) gives ➔

$$Y'_C = bx[b(1-x) - dx](1-x)^{d-1}e^{bx^a(1-x)^d}$$

For $Y'_c = 0$ at $X = X_p$ gives

$$x_p = \frac{a}{a+d} \qquad (2)$$

For $X = X_p$ gives

$$Y_p = e^{bX_p{}^a(1-X_p)^d} - 1 \qquad (3)$$

It is evident from equations *2* and *3* that both X_p and Y_p are expressed in terms of both a and b This implies that X_p and Y_p can not be independently controlled. In order to overcome this problem,

parameterisation is introduced: a and b are constant parameters as part of the equation, but also, a parameter can be a variable as a function of the constant parameter(s). This use of parameter is referred to as parameterisation (see Jeffery, 1985).

Let $X_p = R$ and $Y_p = Q$

Parametrisation of a and b in terms of R and Q yields the following equations;

$$a = \frac{dR}{1-R} \qquad b = \frac{Log(1+Q)}{R^a(1-R)^d}$$

Parameterisation of d proved to be an impossible task. Solution for d could not be obtained through fundamental theorem of calculus. Therefore, the only solution was by the use of numerical methods. To this end, an improvised method was adopted which used a series of iterations aiming for the solution by narrowing down the steps at each stage. Also, research has shown that the relationship between the value of d and total value can be represented by a polynomial. Therefore, in order to improve the speed of the operation, initially, the approximate position of the solution is determined by fitting a polynomial to the data.

The expression proved highly satisfactory: Figure 2, shows values of X_p ranging from 0.01 to 0.99 at increments of 0.05. It is evident that the module can generate profiles with extreme flexibility and sensitivity towards changes in the position of the peak point on the X-axis.

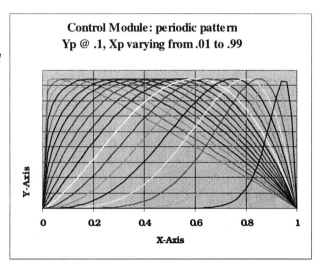

Figure 2. Control Module: full control over the position of Xp

Figure 3, shows a range of curves for varying values of Y_p. It is evident from the figure that the model is highly sensitive in reflecting Y_p on the profile. Again because it is mathematically defined, the accuracy is to the degree of complete precision.

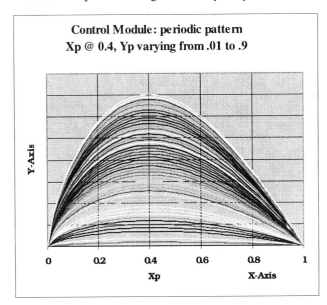

Control Module: periodic pattern
Xp @ 0.4, Yp varying from .01 to .9

Figure 3. Control Module: full control over the position of Yp

In Figure 3, the impact of changing Y_p on the total area has not been taken into account. This adjustment is carried out through parameter *d*. Figure 4, shows that for fixed values of X_p and Y_p, the total area (value) decreases with *d* and that the model is highly sensitive towards changes in *d*.

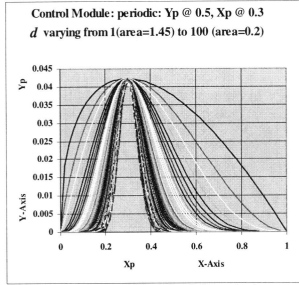

Control Module: periodic: Yp @ 0.5, Xp @ 0.3
***d* varying from 1(area=1.45) to 100 (area=0.2)**

Figure 4. Control Module: full control over the total sum of values- parameter *d*

Kurtosis Module

Basically, the kurtosis module controls the peaked-ness of the profile: how convex or concave the curve is. While the peak point conditions are satisfied by the control module and the distortion properties by the distortion module, the kurtosis module is responsible for the remaining shape-parameters. These consist of the following;

i.   Control over the value of the initial slope
ii.   Control over the value of the end slope
iii. Control over the value of curve-intensity (total values from the origin to the peak point).

The kurtosis module is a single curve consisting of two parts connected at the main peak point.

Mathematical Expression for Kurtosis Module

The simulation of the kurtosis module requires identification of the variables associated with the module. These are the initial slope *(IS)*, end slope *(ES)* and curve-intensity *(INT)*. Since this module is divided into two parts connected at the peak point, two separate curves are generated: the first curve starts from the origin to the peak point and the second curve starts from the end reversing towards the peak point. The general mathematical expressions for these parts are identical. They are based on a new polynomial expression that is developed from the first principal. Since there are five conditions, the degree of polynomial is selected as 4, with five parameters. The expression is given below;

$$Y_k = k(X) = a_1 X^4 + a_2 X^3 + a_3 X^2 + a_4 X^1 + a_5 \quad (4)$$

Where Y_k is the periodic values for kurtosis and X is the proportion of the period number over total kurtosis periods (*n* - origin to X_p or end to X_p). The conditions are as follows;

$$k(0) = 0,$$
$$k'(0) = g \text{ (where } g \text{ is the initial slope)}$$

For the two curves to meet smoothly at the peak point, their values and slopes must both be zero.

Hence, k(1) = 0 and k'(1) = 0

The curve-intensity h is measured as follows;

$$\sum_{i=0}^{i=Xp} Y_i = h = Na_1 + Ma_2 + La_3 + Ka_4 + \quad (5)$$

Where;

$$X_1{}^4 + X_2{}^4 + X_3{}^4 + \ldots X_n{}^4 = N$$
$$X_1{}^3 + X_2{}^3 + X_3{}^3 + \ldots X_n{}^3 - M$$
$$X_1{}^2 + X_2{}^2 + X_3{}^2 + \ldots X_n{}^2 = L$$
$$X_1{}^1 + X_2{}^1 + X_3{}^1 + \ldots X_n{}^1 = K$$

The above equations (4 and 5) are used to find the parameters a_1, a_2, a_3, a_4 and a_5 as follows;

$a_5 = 0$
$a_4 = g$ (initial/end slope)
$a_3 = [h + g (3M - 2N - K)] / (N + L - 2M)$
$a_2 = - (2a_3 + 3g)$
$a_1 = - (g + a_3 + a_2)$

Slope values can be measured numerically or, based on the percentile system, the slope values are grouped into categories namely, 'extremely low', 'low', 'moderate', 'high', 'very high' and 'extremely high'.

Figure 5, shows a number of curves with different initial slopes and curve-intensity.

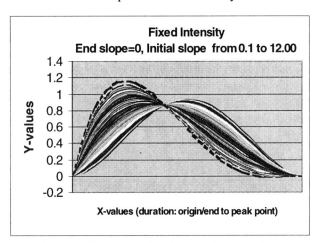

Fixed Intensity
End slope=0, Initial slope from 0.1 to 12.00

Figure 5. Kurtosis Module: full control over the value of initial slope.

Distortion Module

The work has relied on the basic assumption that the underlying pattern of growth is smooth and continuous. Any deviation from this is due to the introduction of events and 'abnormalities', the result of which is a distortion on the underlying pattern. For example, in construction projects, if the production rate is increased for fast track projects or if the rate is decreased due to weather conditions, then a distortion maybe generated. The size of the distortion can be significant enough to produce a trough and a bi-modality (secondary peak). A curve may have more than one distortion.

A distortion has a position of application, duration, type and intensity. The position of the trough is the position of the distortion and the distance between the successive peaks is the duration of the distortion. The type distortion can be Retarding (reducing the rate of change) or accelerating (increasing the rate of change). Also, a distortion has an intensity which is the sum of all distortion values, (Khosrowshahi, 1998).

Mathematical Expression for Distortion Module

The mathematics of distortion simulation is rather similar to that of kurtosis module. The main differences are due to different conditions and requirements. The mathematical expression for the distortion module - given below - is subject to the following five conditions suggesting that the degree of polynomial should be 4.

$d(0) = 0$ zero initial state
$d(1) = 0$ zero end state
$d'(0) = 0$ zero initial slope
$d'(1) = 0$ zero end slope
Total control over total value - distortion intensity I

(slopes are maintained at zero, in order not to interfere with kurtosis module)

$$Yd = d(x)$$
$$= a_1X_1 + a_2 X_2 + a_3 X_3 + a_4 X_4 + k \quad (6)$$

Where Y_d is the value of distortion at proportional period X and k is a constant.

Given the intensity of the distortion I, the following applies;

$$X_1{}_1{}^1 + X_2{}_2{}^1 + X_3{}_3{}^1 + \ldots X_n{}^1 = K$$
$$X_1{}_1{}^2 + X_2{}_2{}^2 + X_3{}_3{}^2 + \ldots X_n{}^2 = L$$
$$X_1{}_1{}^3 + X_2{}_2{}^3 + X_3{}_3{}^3 + \ldots X_n{}^3 = M$$
$$X_1{}_1{}^4 + X_2{}_2{}^4 + X_3{}_3{}^4 + \ldots X_n{}^4 = N$$

Then

$$a_1 K + a_2 L + a_3 M + a_4 N = I$$

The above are used to find the parameters $a1$, $a2$, $a3$ and $a4$ as follows;

$k = 0$

$a_1 = 0$

$a_2 = -(a_3 + a_4)$

$a_3 = -2a_4$

$a_4 = I / (N - 2M + 2L)$

The extreme flexibility of the distortion expression is demonstrated in Figure 6.

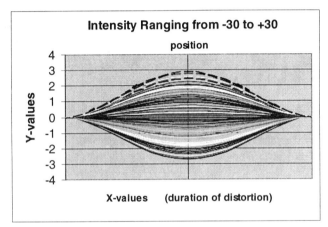

Figure 6. Distortion Module: full control over distortion's intensity.

Conclusion

This paper built on the product of a previous paper in which the significance of visual approach to the analysis of curve profiles was demonstrated. The earlier work had shown that the curve profile of time series data inherent features that describe the behaviour of the subject matter. Therefore, the work provided means for constructing the profile through identification of the parameters that define the shape of the profile, namely, the shape-parameters.

The aim of the current paper, was to identify the mathematical expression that would facilitate generation of the profile. Failing to find the required mathematical expression in whole or in part, a new set of mathematical expressions were subsequently developed consisting of three modules, namely, control module, kurtosis module and distortion module. Each module was responsible for satisfying a number of requirements. The expressions for the kurtosis and distortion modules were rather simple

and straightforward: both relied on fresh development of two 4-degree polynomial equations each complying with different requirements. The expression for the control module, however, proved rather challenging. Eventually, an exponential function consisting of three parameters satisfied all requirements of the module. The control over peak point co-ordinated and total area under the curve was facilitated through parameterisation. Subsequently, full control over the requirements was achieved.

The sensitivity of the model was measured, in terms of the behaviour of the curve in response to variations in the value of the shape-parameters and shown graphically.

References

Brandon, P. S. and Newton, S, (1986). Improving the forecast. Chartered Quantity Surveyor, may, pp. 24-7.

Gompertz, B., (1825), On the nature of the function expressive of the law of human mortality, Philosophical Transactions of the Royal Society, Vol. Xxxvi, 513-585.

Jeffery, Alan, (1985) Maths for engineers and scientists, Van Nostrand Ranhold, UK, p55.

Khosrowshahi, F. (1986), Database value/time related project information for construction projects, Interim report II, South Bank Polytechnic.

Khosrowshahi, F. (1996), Value profile analysis of construction projects, journal of financial management of property and construction, vol. 1, no. 1. Feb, 55-77.

Khosrowshahi, F., (1998), A visual approach to the analysis of curve profile: a case in construction industry, ProceedingsofInternational Conference on Information Visualisation, IV'98, IEEE, 321-326.

Preece and Baines (1978)

Rektorys, K.(1969), Survey of Applicable Mathematics.

Stone, R. (1980), Sigmoids, Bulletin of Applied Statistics, 7(1), pp. 59 - 119.

SIMULATED SITE VISITS
A 4D multimedia database for the study of architectural construction.

Clare Newton

Faculty of Architecture, Building & Planning
University of Melbourne
Melbourne, Victoria, 3205
Australia
c.newton@architecture.unimelb.edu.au

Abstract

Architectural designs are translated into buildings using the documentation language. Gaps invariably exist between what is documented and what is built. Once a building is complete, its construction is largely concealed and it becomes difficult to compare the drawn details with the built details. This difficulty is compounded by the abstract nature of traditional architects' orthographic drawings.

A multimedia relational database titled 'Simulated Site Visits' (SSV), developed by Clare Newton and Jonathan Finkelstein at the University of Melbourne, records the process of constructing buildings. The structure and layout of SSV facilitates comparisons across media and helps to shift the focus onto the connections and gaps between a building and its representation.

The development of SSV has been funded because of its potential as a teaching aid for architecture and building students. This paper will outline teaching implications of this form of multimedia intertwined with a discussion of the research potential.

1. Background

Simulated Site Visits has been developed within rapidly changing architecture and construction industries. Architects and builders are exploiting new forms of representation and communication made possible with computer and internet developments. At the same time, the construction industry is in a state of flux as new light weight materials and new construction methods become available.

Robin Evans argued that architects have to assume there is a uniform space between the drawing and the building through which meaning can glide unchanged. He called this a 'suspension of critical disbelief (which) is necessary in order for architects to perform their task at all' (1997, p154). There is another possibility: a form of reverberation may be perceived between architecture as idea, and architecture in its

realized form. Just as language translation can result in shifts and development of meaning, so can translations between media. By studying its representation, the object may take on new meaning and visa versa. The documentation process and its relationship to construction warrants further research

2. The SSV program

Simulated Site Visits is an Oracle relational database designed to be deliverable over the Internet. Resources such as photographs, Quicktime movies, drawings and computer models are stored with date, time and location information so viewers can visit and tour through building construction sites.

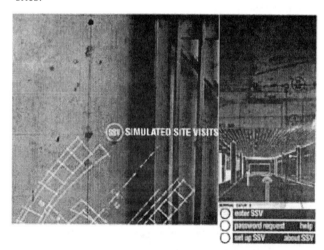

(fig1) Simulated site visits

A challenge in the design of SSV has been to ensure viewers can find information without getting lost in time or space. Simulated Site Visits uses virtual reality VRML models for orienting the viewer along with a time scale which dates the site visit.

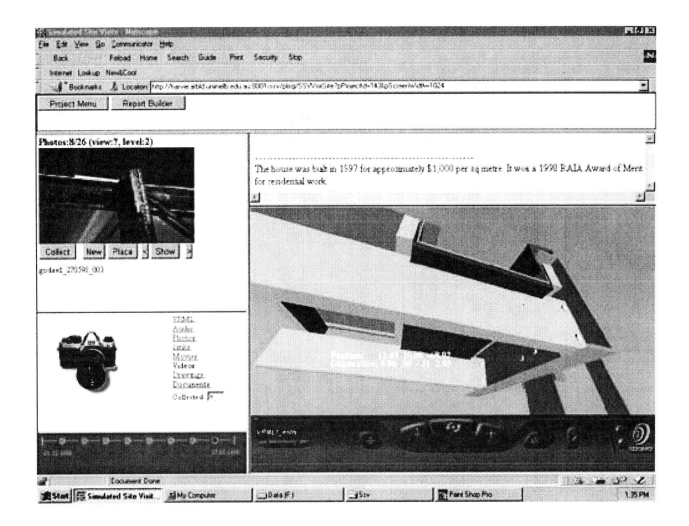

(fig2) Interface Screen

3. The interface screen

Note the time scale in the lower left of the screen in Figure 2. Icons floating within the VRML model indicate the resources available for that site visit date. The viewer can click on the icon and the database will search for and display the detail or photograph indicated.

The navigational screen (Fig 2) contains five areas. On the right is a display window where VRML models have icons showing where photographs, detail drawings and other resources like Quicktime movies are located. Above this is a short description. On the left, above the time scale, is a list of resources which controls what is displayed in the preview

window in the top left of the screen. The 'Place' button locates the resource from the preview window to the larger window. Alternatively, the 'Show Me' button directs the VRML to rotate to the same view as the resource. Resources are grouped according to site visit dates.

4. The use of SSV for teaching

Extra funding has been received to further refine the graphics and structure of SSV. Part of the programming brief for this second stage is to allow records to be linked with back and next arrows. This is useful for building construction procedures such the installation of a window or the placing of pre-cast concrete panels.

This second stage of development of Simulated Site Visits is focussed on the needs of students learning about changing construction techniques. These developments are being funded with both Commonwealth Government and University grants. They have been loosely gathered together under the title of 'Pathways into a Maze'.

Students need to understand the first principles of construction within the context of a changing industry. One of the best ways for students to learn about current construction techniques is by visiting construction sites but there is a Catch 22. Unless students have some basic site skills, building sites are confusing and intimidating. Even second and third year students are reluctant to ask building supervisors questions for fear of appearing ignorant.

The analogy of a Street Directory is a useful way to understand how the Pathways program relates to the city of SSV with its network of information in which students need skills to avoid becoming lost. Pathways into a Maze consists of Signposted Pathways to direct students; Spot the Difference tasks to study the links and gaps between contract documents and their built form; Scavenger Hunts to develop students' skills in using a search aid and a Street Directory to assist with navigation. The story board illustrated in Figure 4 illustrates these ideas.

The teaching strategies of critical observation followed by creative imitation help students to undertake the transition from knowledge of first principles as presented in lecture to applied knowledge. Pathways allows students to critically observe the transformation of working drawings into building. When they attempt to document their own designs, they have access to precedents which they can creatively imitate.

Pathways into a Maze is designed to enable students to make sense of the activities on sites and to develop their knowledge and skills of observation so they can undertake independent site visits. Pathways in conjunction with SSV will give students access to information about the construction industry which is not readily available from any other source.

5. Learning outcomes

SSV allows more open ended exploration by students; access to current and complex case studies rather than idealized construction environments; supplementation of existing studio learning with tutors as mentors and a review of information at each student's own pace and access to information when the need it.

It is intended that SSV will be largely stocked with work by students which will be entered into a holding pen for authorization by a staff member. Students, in an assignment shared between construction and computing subjects, have been developing 3D computer models from architects' working drawings. Layers are allocated according to the order in which elements are installed. This enables

short movies to be developed in which details are constructed or layers peeled from completed buildings.

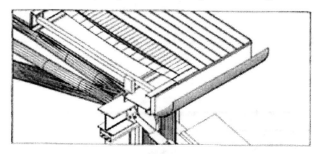

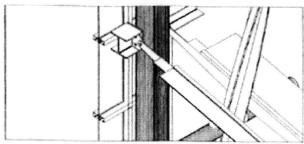

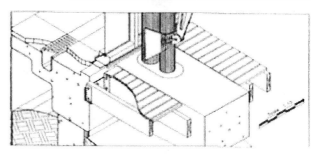

(fig3) **Computer** **model** **by** **a** **3rd** **year** **architecture** **student**

6. Evaluation and limitations

SSV works well on local networks but slower international networks are less ideal. The aim was for the Oracle database to be Internet deliverable to a world wide audience. Until networks are faster we will develop CD based options to partially overcome this problem. Development of the database has proved more difficult and expensive than anticipated. The search tool which was intended to be a part of the 1997 Stage One is only now being developed as part of Stage Two because of budget limitations. The difficulties of orienting the viewer in large scale construction environments have not been fully resolved.

The use of computer models drawn by students from architects' working drawings with layers to represent time, is a rich addition to the site photographs which was not entirely anticipated in 1997.

7. Exploring gaps

In architecture, what you see is often different to what you get. The Schroder house appears to be concrete but is a hybrid layered construction (Ford 1990). Mies van der Rohe used steel representations of structure over concrete framed buildings. Our perception of a building is often at odds with the construction reality, particularly as changes in the construction industry result in more lightweight and layered construction techniques. Once a building is completed its construction process is, to a large extent, lost except for the memory contained within the contract documentation set.

It is within the context of these ambiguities of representation and our lost construction knowledge, that we have developed Simulated Site Visits. SSV records the translation processes which occur between architectural documentation drawings and their built form.

Construction detailing is part of the design process. Because students have not experienced their ideas being built, it is sometimes difficult for them to comprehend the shifts in meaning that can develop as architects grapple with the pragmatic constraints of building within an environment of regulations, budget, client expectations and construction considerations.

There is an understandable desire for architects to reduce the gaps which exist between a building and how it is represented in the construction documents. Differences are, of course, likely to result in cost variations. But there is another, more positive possibility. Just as language translation can result in shifts and development of meaning, so can translations between media. By studying its drawings, an object does take on new meaning and visa versa. Architects can celebrate the shifts in meaning which exist between built forms and their representations.

Drawings are translated into buildings via the construction process but the complex and messy construction process is normally concealed once a building is complete. Some architects design remnants of the construction process into buildings revealing to the occupants the construction complexity.

For students, a surprising paradox exists between architectural drawings and construction. Refined and minimalist details are typically more expensive and difficult to build even though they use less materials than details which contain a hierarchy of layers. Structurally expressive buildings which appear lean are often more difficult to build than layered architecture with applied cladding.

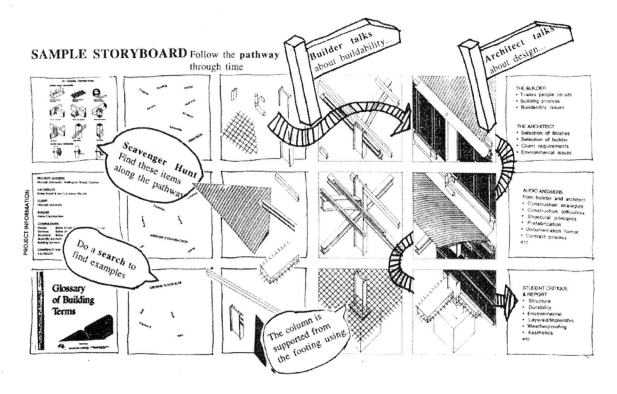

(fig 4) Storyboard for Pathways into a Maze

8. Conclusion

The development of SSV was funded as a teaching aid for architecture and building students learning about construction. It allows students to view photographs of buildings under construction and compare them with drawings. SSV provides a computer environment in which students can undertake archaeological digs through lost construction environments. Layers can be peeled from buildings to show the hidden structure behind.

By studying the translation of drawings into buildings, the documentation and construction processes can be understood as not simply dull instrumental phases but as vital components of the design process which have scope for further exploration.

REFERENCES

[1] Blau, Eve & Kaufmann, Edward, *Architecture and its image : four centuries of architectural representation*, MIT Press, Mass., 1989.

[2] Bolton, Richard, *The Contest of Meaning: critical histories of photography*, MIT Press, Mass., 1989.

[3] Earnshaw, R. A., M. A. Gigante et al., eds. *Virtual reality systems*, Academic Press, London, 1993.

[4] Evans, Robin, *Translations from drawing to building and other essays*, London : Architectural Association, 1997.

[5] Evans, Robin, *The projective cast : architecture and its three geometries*, Cambridge, Mass., MIT Press, c1995.

[6] Fausch, Deborah, 'Towards "An architecture of our time"' in Fausch, D., Singley, P., El-Khoury, R., & Efrat, Z., eds. *Architecture in Fashion*, Princeton Architectural Press, New York, 1994.

[7] Finkestein, Jonathan, '4D multimedia datascapes: The SSV program', in Banissi, E., Khowsrowshahi, F. & Sarfraz, M. *1998 IEEE Conference on Information Visualisation*, IEEE Computer Society, Los Almitos, Claifornia, 1988.

[8] Ford, Edward R., *The details of modern architecture*, Vols 1 & 2, MIT Press, Mass., 1990<1996>

[9] Mitchell, William J., *The Logic of Architecture: Design, computation and cognition*, MIT Press, London, 1990

[10] Porter, Tom, *The Architect's Eye, Visualisation and depiction in space of architecture*, E & FN Spoon, London, 1997.

[11] Sekula, Alan, 'The Body and the Archive', *The Contest of Meaning*, edited by Richard Bolton, MIT Press, Mass., 1989

[12] Wexelblat, A., ed. *Virtual reality: applications and explorations*, Academic Publishers Professional, Boston.

Session 1-5

Information Visualization

Chair

M.L.V. Pitteway

Brunel University, UK

A Volumetric Approach to Visualize Holographic Reconstructions

Matthias König, Joachim Böttger, Oliver Deussen, and Thomas Strothotte
Department of Simulation and Computer Graphics
Otto-von-Guericke University of Magdeburg
Universitätsplatz 2, D-39106 Magdeburg, Germany
{koenig|jboettge|deussen|tstr}@isg.cs.uni-magdeburg.de

Abstract

In synthetic holography, the emphasis has been on numerical simulation methods for the recording and reconstruction processes, but methods to visualize the calculated results are yet underdeveloped. We show how volume slicing and volume rendering using a threshold for translucency can be applied to synthetic holography. Results of the three-dimensional visualization of the reconstruction are presented, thereby illustrating the usefulness of the threshold operator.

Keywords: Scientific visualization, synthetic holography, reconstruction.

1 Introduction and motivation

In synthetic holography, a number of methods and tools for computing holograms and holographic images exist. These tools are commonly used for calculating the diffraction properties of holograms. The visualization of the reconstruction in depth is not the primary task of such programs, although two-dimensional reconstructions are usually performed. Tools specialized in visualizing three-dimensional holographic reconstructions are missing. In this work we describe such a tool and show that it allows a better spatial understanding of the holographic reconstruction and circumvents the time-consuming and material-wasting optical verification of synthetic holograms.

The reconstruction of a two-dimensional object like a thin plate which is parallel to the hologram plane appears sharp only at a distinct distance to the hologram. If this distance is known, a two-dimensional visualization is sufficient. The visualization of a three-dimensional object poses new challenges: parts of the object appear sharp at a specific distance where other parts appear blurred. To discover the shape of the reconstructed object, it is necessary to find the sharp parts and to visualize them in a three-dimensional view.

In this paper we approach the visualization of holographic reconstruction using three-dimensional volumetric methods. We will show that volume slicing helps to find focus points and that volume rendering using a threshold operator for translucency exposes the shape of the object in three dimensions.

The paper is organized as follows: First, we briefly discuss optical and synthetic holography. Then we exemplify related work and explain our approach to simulate and visualize the hologram reconstruction. We discuss results and close with an outline of future work.

2 Optical and synthetical holography

Holography is a method for three-dimensional imaging of objects. Dennis Gabor presented holography for the first time in 1948 [5].

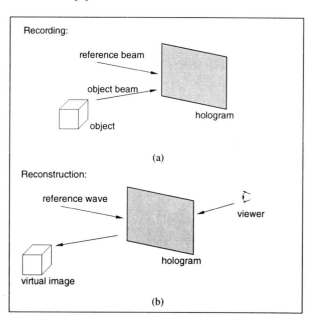

Figure 1: Recording (a) and reconstruction (b)

As illustrated in Figure 1 holography is a two-step process. In the recording step a coherent light wave is split in two beams. One beam illuminates the object to be imaged, the other beam — called reference wave — hits directly the holographic plate. The waves reflected by the object are called object wave. The interference pattern of object wave and reference wave is recorded on the holographic plate and constitutes the hologram (see Figure 1(a)).

In the reconstruction step, the hologram (suitably processed) is illuminated with another reference wave. The reference wave is diffracted by the interference pattern of the hologram. Part of the diffracted wave is an identical copy of the object wave of the recorded object. Looking at the hologram, the viewer gets the impression of a three-dimensional object, the virtual image (Figure 1(b)).

In synthetic holography, the optical processes are (partially) replaced by numerical calculations performed by the computer.

To record a synthetic hologram, the object and the reference wave are described by their physical properties. For each object point the amplitude and phase of the emitted light is given in the form of a data set. With this description various methods for calculating the interference pattern of the hologram exist (e.g. [4] [10]). The computed hologram can either be transferred to a holographic film which is reconstructed optically in an experimental setup or be reconstructed synthetically.

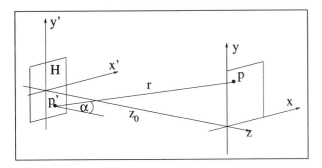

Figure 2: Presumed geometric relationship between object and hologram H for solving the Kirchhoff diffraction integral

For synthetical reconstruction, the hologram is given as two-dimensional complex valued field. Additionally the parameters of the reference wave are given. The illumination of the hologram with the reference wave is simulated by evaluation of the Kirchhoff diffraction integral (cf. [7]),

$$U(p) = \frac{1}{i\lambda} \int_S u_0(p') \frac{exp(ikr)}{r} \cos(\alpha) ds. \qquad (1)$$

or its approximations (see Figure 2). Here, $U(p)$ is the electric field strength at the point p. $U(p)$ yields from the field strength $u_0(p')$ contributed from each point p' of the hologram plate H, λ is the wavelength, r the distance between p and p' and α the angle between $p' - p$ and the incident illumination wave. The intensity of $U(p)$ constitutes the image of the reconstructed object.

3 Related work

Programs like the optical cad system DigiOpt [1] and ImageH [12] compute two-dimensional visualizations of holographic reconstructions. This is done by calculating the amplitude and phase of each point p in a plane parallel to the hologram in distance z_0 by evaluating Eq. 1. The intensity of each point in this plane results in an image.

If the hologram displays a two-dimensional object, this reconstructed object will focus only in a distinct depth which equals to the distance of the object at recording time. For all other distances the object will be blurred. Figure 3 shows a hologram and two images of reconstruction in different depths.

For three-dimensional objects recorded in the hologram, only the points belonging to the object will appear sharp in a reconstruction plane. Other tools developed for optical design are not much advanced.

For educational purposes, The Optics Project (TOP) points out the possibilities of three-dimensional visualization in optics [3]. TOP provides interactive visualization of fundamentals of optics, e.g. Fresnel diffraction of a single and a double slit, but provides no volume visualization of hologram reconstruction.

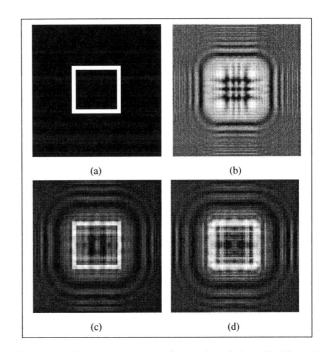

Figure 3: Example of a two-dimensional visualization of hologram reconstruction: (a) original object (b) hologram, (c) sharp reconstruction focusing the object, and (d) blurred reconstruction

4 Visualization of hologram reconstruction

The three-dimensional interactive visualization of the holographic reconstruction is performed by computing a volumetric data set; the difficulty to overcome, as indicated above, is the blurring effect. This is done by calculating a set of two-dimensional images parallel to the hologram using the Fresnel transform

$$U(x,y) = \frac{exp(ikz)}{i\lambda z} \int \int_{-\infty}^{\infty} u_0(x',y')$$
$$\times exp(\frac{ik}{2z}((x-x')^2 + (y-y')^2))\,dx'dy' \qquad (2)$$

that approximates the Kirchhoff diffraction integral, where z runs from the chosen z_s to z_e in steps of length dz. These images are combined to form a volumetric data set (see Figure 4).

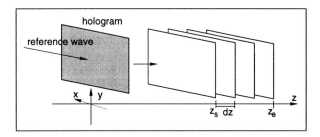

Figure 4: Calculation of the volumetric data set

The data set consists of scalar intensity values depending on their position in space. We normalize the data and map the intensities to 256 grey values. Various volume visualization techniques are applicable to the data space [9] [6]. To visualize the holographic reconstruction, we found volume slicing and volume rendering to be appropriate methods.

Interactive volume slicing offers good possibilities to identify the foci of the reconstructed image. In this way we achieve impressions of the object coded in the hologram. Our system provides three views exhibiting the intensity of the electric field on each slicing plane and one view displaying the cutting planes in three dimensions to enforce the impression of the reconstruction. The cutting planes are moved interactively through the volume data set.

Volume rendering provides the employment of translucency. Therefore, we defined a threshold operator that determines what is transparent and what is opaque.

The techniques described above are implemented in C++ on Silicon Graphics workstations. For the three-dimensional volume visualization we use the graphics libraries OpenGL [8] and VTK [11]. By using graphics hardware supporting three-dimensional textures [2] we obtain a speed-up for the rendering process.

Calculation of the volumetric data set and its visualization are separated in different modules. The calculation module runs as a server process on a single machine, the visualization modules can run as a client process on different computers (see Figure 5). Each client process sends an

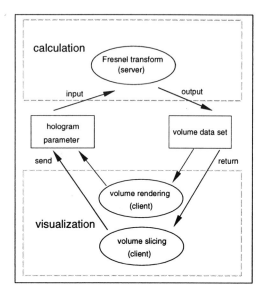

Figure 5: Architecture of the software

image depicting the hologram and a parameter set needed for computing the volumetric data set to the server. The parameter set contains hologram resolution, start and end distance and the step value for the calculation of the Fresnel transforms (see Figure 4: z_s, z_e and dz). The server program computes the Fresnel transforms and returns the requested volume data to the client. Now the client is able to interactively display the data set.

5 Results

In Figures 6–9 we show reconstruction results of two holograms, one displaying a rectangle which is parallel to the hologram plane, the other displaying a line in three-dimensional space. In both cases the hologram consisted of 128x128 points, the calculated volumetric data sets consisted of 128x128 pixels and 64 layers. On an SGI Onyx2 with two processors, the computation of the data sets requires ten minutes each, the volume visualization is performed in real-time.

In the first case a rectangle was placed in a far distance compared to its extensions. Figure 6 illustrates volume slicing through the intensity field which was generated as described in Section 4.

The upper left part of Figure 6 shows a cutting plane which is parallel to the hologram plane. The chosen distance equals the distance of the object during recording, so the result is a sharp reconstruction.

The upper right and the lower left parts of Figure 6 show slices which are perpendicular to the hologram plane. Here, the focus plane of the object becomes apparent through the focus of the two beams. The small white lines drawn above the cutting planes help positioning them in space.

In the lower right part of Figure 6 a three-dimensional representation of the slices is shown.

Figure 7 depicts volume rendering of the reconstruction field. Figures 7(a) – 7(c) show the same volume, while increasing the translucency threshold. By this variation the structure of the reconstructed rectangle becomes visible.

The figures demonstrate the optical effect of a wide focus area. The reconstructed object seems to have a spatial extension in the third dimension. This results from the far distance to the hologram plane during recording.

The reconstruction of a line inclined in space is demonstrated in Figure 8. The line is composed of a number of points. Here, the cutting planes are positioned in a way that the focus area of the points is perceived. The upper right part shows a slice through all points of the line.

The effect of an alteration of the transparency threshold for displaying the intensity field is shown in Figure 9. Again, the reconstruction of the points becomes visible. In Figure 9(c) the positions of the different points in space can be detected.

6 Conclusion and future work

In this paper, we applied volume visualization techniques like volume slicing and rendering to holographic recon structions. The results shown in Section 5 demonstrate the usefulness of these techniques during exploration of holographic reconstructions. In contrast to the so far used two-dimensional techniques, the user is able to detect spatial patterns, like focus planes, directly.

In the future we will apply further techniques for volume visualizing to hologram reconstructions. This includes more sophisticated methods to tune the visualization like choosing the translucency threshold automatically. This is needed to remove the blurring effect. The resulting reconstruction will then be saved as a set of points in three-dimensional space. This will enable subsequent post-processing steps that help for example optimizing the holograms.

An application of our methods for the visualization of holographic recording and reconstruction is prepared for educational purposes. The interactivity of our approach should be able to help understanding the physical background of holography. Future work will investigate such possibilities.

References

[1] H. Aagedal, S. Teiwes, and T. Beth. Design of paraxial diffractive elements with the cad system digiopt. In I. Cindrich and S. H. Lee, editors, *Diffractive and Holographic Optics Technology III, Proc. SPIE 2404*, pages 50–58. SPIE, 1995.

[2] K. Akeley. RealityEngine graphics. *Computer Graphics*, 27:109–116, August 1993.

[3] D. C. Banks, J. T. Foley, K. N. Vidimce, and M. Kiu. Instructional software for visualizing optical phenomena. In *Proc. IEEE Visualization*, pages 447–450. IEEE, 1997.

[4] O. Bryngdahl and F. Wyrowski. Digital holography – computer-generated holograms. *Progress in Optics*, 28:1–86, 1990.

[5] D. Gabor. A new microscopic principle. *Nature*, 161:777–778, 1948.

[6] R.S. Gallagher, editor. *Computer Visualization - Graphics Techniques and Engineering Analysis*. CRC Press, Boca Raton, Florida, 1995.

[7] J. W. Goodman. *Introduction to Fourier Optics*. McGraw-Hill, New York, 2nd edition, 1968.

[8] J. Neider, T. Davis, and M. Woo. *OpenGL Programming Guide: The Official Guide to Learning OpenGL*. Addison-Wesley, 1993.

[9] G. M. Nielson. Modeling and visualizing volumetric and surface-on-surface data. In *Focus on Scientific Visualization*. Springer-Verlag, Berlin-Heidelberg-New-York, 1993.

[10] A. Ritter, J. Böttger, O. Deussen, M. König, and Th. Strothotte. Hardware-based rendering of full-parallax synthetic holograms. *Applied Optics*, 38(8):1364–1369, 1999.

[11] W. J. Schroeder, K. M. Martin, and W. E. Lorensen. *The Visualization Toolkit*. Prentice-Hall, Englewood Cliffs, New Jersey, 1988.

[12] E. Zhang. *Computer Holography: Theory, Algorithms, and Realization*. PhD thesis, Ruprecht-Karls-Universität Heidelberg, 1995.

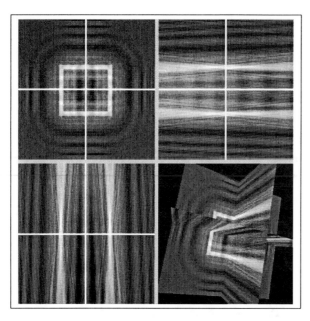

Figure 6: Three-dimensional visualization of a holographic reconstruction by three orthogonal cutting planes through the intensity field and their spatial arrangement.

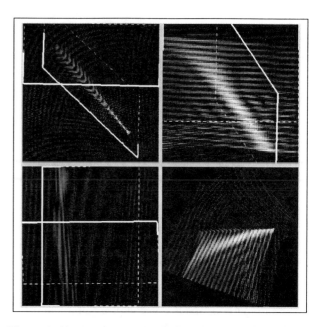

Figure 8: Non-orthogonal cutting planes through the intensity field of a reconstructed line. In this case the line was assembled out of a number of points.

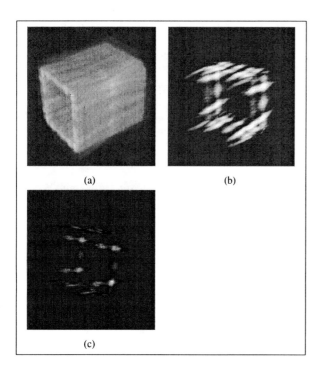

(a)   (b)

(c)

Figure 7: Volume rendering the intensity field of a hologram reconstruction with increasing translucency threshold: (a) low threshold, (b) and (c) higher thresholds.

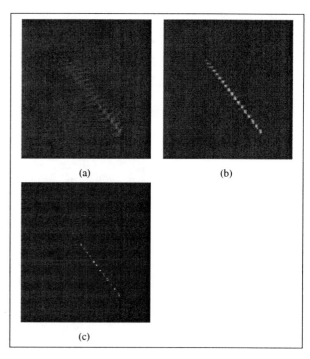

(a)   (b)

(c)

Figure 9: Increasing the transparency threshold of the intensity field enables identifying the object coded in a hologram. Using a high threshold causes only the focus points to remain.

Organizing and Visualizing Related Work Events on Personal Information Management Systems

Akira ABETA

Department of Computer Science and
Electronics Kyushu Institute of Technology
680-4 Kawazu, Iizuka, Fukuoka, 820,Japan.
Kyushu Hitachi Maxell Ltd.
4680 Ikata, Houjou,Tagawa, Fukuoka, Japan
abeta@macross.cse.kyutech.ac.jp

Kaoru SATOH and Ken'ichi KAKIZAKI

Department of Computer Science and
Electronics Kyushu Institute of Technology
680-4 Kawazu, Iizuka, Fukuoka, 820,Japan.
kakizaki@cse.kyutech.ac.jp
satoh@cse.kyutech.ac.jp

Abstract

This paper proposes a method to automatically organize and visualize related work events as a work-project structure. This is accomplished by accumulating and analyzing the target event and time of the user's operations such as registrations and references on a Personal Information Management system (PIM). Our processes for organization are : (1) extracting relations between events from the records of user's reference operations using balloon-help function, (2) intensifying the relations between events during interaction with the user by visualizing the relations and presenting them to the user, (3) making connections between events based on the extracted relations. Our visualization method represents the organized work events as connected graphs in which nodes and arcs indicate events and relations between events, and in which the intensity of the relation is represented with arcs of width in proportion to the intensity. Furthermore, in order to visualize a structure of collaboration among several users, our visualization method places each user's connected graph on the side planes of a three-dimensional multi-angular prism.

1. Introduction

In order to improve the process of work projects, it has become important that we analyze how to perform our work project such as the details and timing. This paper proposes a method that visualizes a user's work-project structure by organizing related work events during a user's ordinary use of a PIM [1,2].

In a PIM, a work project consists of some detailed tasks that are called "events". Users input the events of our work and update them in progress. The sum of these inputs and modifications may, in fact, represent the process of a work project. From this viewpoint, we propose a method that

automatically extracts relations between events by analyzing the records of user's operations and organizes related work events based on the relations.

When recording the user's reference operations, the user is usually just viewing events on his or her calendar without involving input device operations, so determining the user target event and time of reference is difficult. In order to record the user's reference behavior, we introduced a balloon-help function (as the solid ellipse in Fig.1) for support of reference to detail information of an event. We ran a trial prototype PIM with this function, and confirmed [3] that our method can record a user's reference actions efficiently.

In this paper, we outline the method for organizing and visualizing related work events, and discuss the results of trials with the prototype PIM. This visualization method represents the organized related work events using a two-dimensional connected graph that indicates events with nodes and relations between events with links. Furthermore, in order to visualize collaboration among some users, we use a three-dimensional connected graph. This places each user's connected graph on the side planes of a three-dimensional multi-angular prism. We discuss actual collaboration among the users in these trials using a sample view drawn by our method.

2. Schedules as process of work projects

2.1. Problem

Fig.1 shows a calendar view on an ordinary PIM. A PIM user inputs events such as appointments and tasks in the calendar view, and will refer to this information as needed. Events for a work project are relations among them. But an ordinary PIM just shows the individual events on a calendar and doesn't manage the relations between events. Therefore it is impossible to present the user a structure of a work project including the relations between events.

2.2. Relations between events on a PIM

A PIM user imagines the relations between events shown as connecting solid or dotted lines on the calendar in Fig.1, thus the user grasps the process of work projects from the information of the PIM. Our ideal PIM should discern the user's understanding of relations and group related work events to produce a PERT diagram [4] like that of Fig.1. Our PIM should also return the structure of the work project including relations between events so that the user can analyze the user's own work projects.

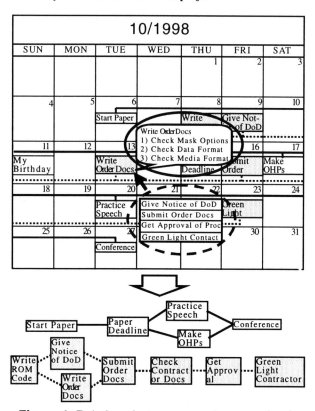

Figure 1. Relations between events on a calendar.

2.3. Relations between events in user's actions

During confirmation of event schedules, a user's changes of eye point or instructions by mouse are performed based on relations between events as the user understands them. We believe that the user signals relations between events in the way he or she uses the PIM. We frame a hypothesis as follow.

- Hypothesis: Users make sequential references to related work events frequently.

Based on this hypothesis, we extract relations between events and organize related work events.

3. Organizing related work events

3.1. Extracting relations between events based on sequential references

In our ideal PIM, users can easily make sequential references to events on their calendar with the balloon-help function (as shown solid ellipse in Fig.1). Therefore, our method can get many records of a user's sequential operations. Based on our hypothesis, we think that users frequently make sequential references to events of a work project. A user may occasionally make only a single sequential reference, but we find the relation between events when the user frequently makes sequential references to those events. Therefore, we extract relations between two events by calculating the frequency of sequential reference operations between their events.

When the duration between two operations is shorter than a certain value, we regard the two operations to events as a sequential operation. Then, as shown in Fig.2, the duration between two operations doesn't include duration of operations.

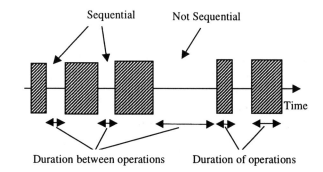

Figure 2 Detecting sequential operations.

3.2. Grouping related work events

Our method groups related work events by connecting events when the value for relations between events is high.

We explain our method for grouping related work events by using graph theory [5] in Fig.3. It shows a time-sequential series of events registered on the PIM. In this figure, the small circles and the number of each circle indicate events and the number of each event. When a value for a relation between two events is higher than our chosen value, they are connected by an arc. So, as shown in Fig.3 (a), we get a disconnected graph, which can isolate some connected components. These connected components allow us to make groups of related work events. Furthermore, we identify which groups are work projects as distinct from individual events (such as Fig.3(a) events No.3 and No.10-11) by deleting isolated circles and connected components of circles with less than our chosen value (Fig.3(b)).

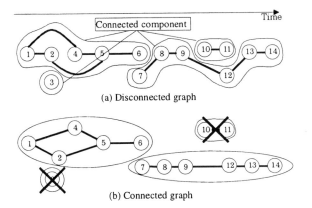

(a) Disconnected graph

(b) Connected graph

Figure 3 Process of grouping related work events.

4. Support of user's sequential references and intensifying the organization of work events

Users' sequential references are either:
- References to related events, or
- References to unrelated events.

There are events for work projects and individual events in a calendar. So, there are sometimes sequential references to unrelated events in records of reference extracted by analyzing records of sequential references using balloon-help. That is, groups of events extracted by our method may include unrelated events. In order to organize related work events correctly, our method needs a mechanism to sort out related work events from unrelated events. Therefore, we introduce a function that supports a user's reference only to related work events.

4.1. Related-reference-support function

When a user clicks an event on his or her calendar with reference to the target event, our PIM shows a list box for events related to the target event as shown by the broken ellipse in Fig.1. In addition, when the user selects the event out of the list, this function automatically moves the user's mouse pointer to the event that the user chose.

Using this function, the user can check a list-box which concentrates related work events that may be scattered all over the calendar. So, the user comes to make many sequential references to related work events spontaneously.

4.2. Creating the related event list

The related event list function needs to show the event that the user intends to refer to next. In addition, it is desirable that the user can easily find the event on the list. Our method assigns a value of relation between two events to

indicate the frequency of sequential references to the events. So, when this value is high, a user frequently made sequential references to their events. The user would frequently make sequential references to their events in the future. Therefore, our method lists events where the value of relation against the target event is high, and indicates in order of the value in the related event list. This makes the user easily find the event to refer to from the list.

4.3. Encouraging sequential references

When the related event which the user intends to next refer to is registered in same month, the user can easily refer to the related event without turning a leaf on the user's calendar. On the other hand, when the related event is registered in another month, the user can't refer it without such operations. In additions, when the user doesn't grasp where the target event is registered, the user has to seek for it through each month. So, the user is discouraged from referencing the related work event.

Using the related-reference-support function, a user can check related work events in the list box including events registered in other months of those events. Therefore, this function encourages the user to make sequential references that the user had hesitated to make, and our method can obtain relations between events registered in other month with high accuracy.

5. Evaluation

5.1. The trials

In order to confirm the efficiency of our method, we developed our prototype PIM, and held a trial with 6 persons. In order to evaluate separately the efficiency of the balloon-help function (shown as solid circle in Fig.4) and the related-reference-support function (shown as broken circle in Fig.4), we first held a two-month trial of the prototype PIM with the balloon-help function. Next, a one-month trial, adding the related-reference-support function, was held.

The users could register, change, and refer to events on the calendar view (shown in Fig.4). Using a detailed window for the information of an event, the users could input and refer to the information such as necessary resources and noteworthy points for an event. Alternatively, users could refer to the same information using our balloon-help function. Our system recorded the target events and reference times by balloon-help.

Figure 4. Calendar view of the prototype PIM.

5.2. Evaluation of the relation based on sequential references--verification of hypothesis

During this trial, for all users, we regarded two operations as being sequential when the interval between the user's two operations was less than twenty seconds. We adopted this value for the interval because it resulted in the best correspondence to the groups of truly related work events as the user intended.

5.2.1. Efficiency of the balloon-help function

In order to verify our hypothesis, we evaluate whether the users made correctly sequential references to related work events. Table 1 for first two months trial shows the number of the sequential references to events which the users understand to be related or unrelated to particular work projects.

In the case of the three users A, B and C, the frequency of sequential references to related work events which they understand was very high. But, in the case of the three users D, E and F, the frequency of sequential references to related work events was very low.

We interviewed them on this result. The first three users said that they made sequential references to related work events as they used our PIM for practical use while managing their work projects. In this case, we confirmed that our hypothesis is useful. We heard from the last three users that they only used our PIM within the set time as their duty in our trial, not for meaningful work. Our hypothesis is less useful in such cases.

Table 1 Frequency of sequential operations(1st trial).

Users	A	B	C	D	E	F
Related sequential references	293	288	53	110	45	10
	88%	90%	76%	38%	49%	42%
Unrelated sequential references	39	32	17	175	47	14
	12%	10%	24%	62%	51%	58%
All sequential references	332	320	70	285	92	24

5.2.2. Efficiency of related-reference-support function

Table 2 for next a month trial shows the results of the same type evaluation as shown in Table 1. As shown in Table 2, they made about twice the frequency of sequential references compared to the first trial period. In addition, it is apparent that they made sequential references to related work events more as well.

Therefore, we confirmed that this function encouraged users to make sequential references to related work events, and our hypothesis becomes useful against all users.

Table 2 Frequency of sequential operations(2nd trial).

Users	A	B	C	D	E	F
Related sequential references	619	649	191	425	193	230
	90%	91%	80%	61%	61%	69%
Unrelated sequential references	67	69	49	269	124	102
	10%	9%	20%	39%	39%	31%
All sequential references	686	718	240	694	317	332

5.3. Evaluation of the method organizing related work events

5.3.1. The method for evaluation of the grouping results

We asked the users to group their events manually, and to compare and verify the groups made by them with the groups extracted by our system.

When an event is contained in our system-extracted group and also appears in the same group which the user identified manually, we say that our system correctly grouped the event. If a event contained in our system-extracted group isn't contained in his group, we say that our system incorrectly grouped the event. Conversely, if the event contained in his group isn't contained in our system-extracted group, we say that our system-extracted group was short of the event.

Fig.5 shows a sample view when our prototype PIM connected related work events based on relations between events. For all users in these trials, our method connected events when values for relations between events were higher than three.

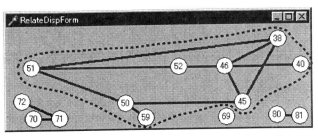

Figure 5 Sample view of disconnected graph.

5.3.2. The evaluation of the grouping results

Table 3 shows the grouping results for the three users A, B and C. Our method could put their events in each correct group - as high as 80 percent of the total events, and improve all ratio for the three users. Therefore, we confirmed that our method can correctly group related work events for the three users A, B and C who used the PIM for their actual work scheduling.

Table 3 Grouping results against each user.

Users	A	B	C	A,B and C
Manually grouped by user	10	5	5	20
Groups identified by user	9	4	3	16
All events	77	46	65	188
Events correct by PIM	68	37	47	152(81%)
Events incorrect by PIM	9	9	18	36(19%)
Events short by PIM	9	5	8	22(12%)

6. Visualization of the organized work events

6.1. Presentation of the organized work events including relations between events

It is important that our method presents the user with related work events as a work-project structure representing by a connected graph including relations between events. In our grouping results, there were some cases in which our method incorrectly linked events of some work projects to another work project. Fig.6 shows a sample of such connected graphs. In Fig.6, our PIM made the group including the events of two works as "Write international conference paper" in the solid frame (1) and " English Lesson " in the solid frame (2). We interviewed the user on this result. We found that because he had his paper for the international conference corrected by his English teacher, there were some relations between some events of "Write international conference paper" and some events of "English Lesson " (as shown two arrows in Fig.6). In real work projects, there are sometimes weak relations among the events of different work projects, so we simply can't separate their events.

The broken frame in Fig.6 was a subproject of "Write

international conference paper" such he surveyed books for reference of his paper and arranged them, and introduced them at a meeting. In this case, by looking such connected lines between those events, we can find that here No.122 : "Write paper" branched off from the main project and he did No.134 : "Survey books for reference", No.136 : "Make documents of books for reference" and No.135 : "Introduce of books for reference", and understand a series of events for the subproject.

Thus, in such cases that our method grouped events of some work projects as a group of a work project, users can determine their events for two different work projects or for the subprojects in one main project and understand the individual relations between events of each work projects by presenting them with a connected graph including relations between events. Therefore, we believe that a user may learn how to perform a work project by examining and comparing their own connected graph with an experienced worker's.

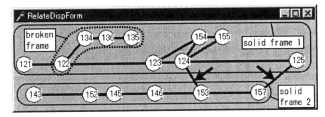

Figure 6 Sample view of connected graph.

6.2. Representing intensity of relations between events

Fig.7 shows a sample view of our PIM connecting events in proportion to the value of relations between events. A wide connection line indicates that a user frequently made sequential references to events. So, we believe that these wide connection lines, such as those from No.46: "Practical speech" to No.40: "Presentation" and from No.51: "Write paper" to No.38: "Paper deadline" in Fig.7, are critical. So, our method may allow users to visually understand the degree of importance of relations between events.

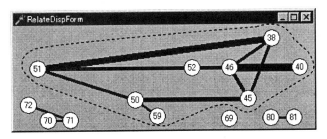

Figure 7 Indicating the strength of relations.

7. Representing a structure of collaboration among group members

These trials included some cooperation among some users. So, we represent their cooperation using connected graphs. When our method shows a work project by a single user, it can represent the spread of the work project using a two-dimensional connected graph. On the other hand, when our method shows a work project among several members, it needs to show multiple two-dimensional connected graphs for them. Therefore, it is difficult for our method to represent the structure of cooperation on a two-dimensional plane. In order to solve this problem, our visualization method represents the structure of cooperation among group members as three-dimensional graphs in three-dimensional space.

7.1. Three-dimensional graphic representation

Using direction of depth, nodes can be placed in a 3D space more than on a two-dimensional plane. In addition, nodes can always be assigned to positions such that no arcs intersect, when the viewpoint can be moved so that the arcs no longer appear to intersect. Furthermore, the perspective view makes nodes nearer the viewpoint appear larger, helping the user to examine local neighborhoods more effectively. SemNet [6], used to visualize a large knowledge bases, is a pioneer using three-dimensions graphics to indicate graph structure. There are Perspective Wall [7]and FSN[8] using perspective view.

7.2. Three-dimensional connected graph representing method

Our 3D connected graph representing method indicates :
● an event as a ball (sphere).
● a relation between events as a stick (cylinder).
● a value of relation as a thickness of a stick (cylinder).

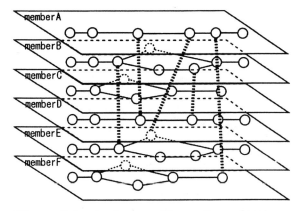

Figure 8 Layer display of three-dimensional connected graph.

In SemNet, K. M. Fairchild clarified some basic problems in three-dimensional visualization. One of these is three-dimensional layout of elements. The problem is that users can't grasp the structure of information, because it is too complex when each element of information is randomly assigned to a position. But the events on our PIM are placed based on their execution dates, and each member's connected graph is given a semitransparent plane as a guide. In this way, our method deal effectively with this problem.

In Fig.8, a method that stacks a plane for each member's graph is shown. However, it is difficult to grasp connections between members (such as A and B) because the planes of other members interfere with their connections as shown bold broken lines in Fig.8.

7.3. Use of a multi-angular prism

In order to show each member's graphs, our visualization method uses a three-dimensional multi-angular prism with multiple side planes. For example, when we show the structure of cooperation among six co-workers, as shown in Fig.9, our method provides a semitransparent multi-angular prism with six side planes to place each worker's three-dimensional graph on one side plane. The method takes the time axis from one side base to the other side base, and puts balls for events in date order of the events. The method shows sticks between the balls for relations between events. In addition, the method shows arcs for relations between events of different workers as broken lines in Fig.9. Using this method, when showing connections between members, the arcs for the connections don't go through other members' planes. Therefore, the method can indicate the connections more clearly than the layer display method.

One more of the problems in visualization referenced by Fairchild are that users often get lost their position and viewpoint in three-dimensional space when they explore. As concerning this problem, using our method, users can easily grasp a time axis by a spindle of the multi-angular prism, and their position and viewpoint by shape of the multi-angular prism.

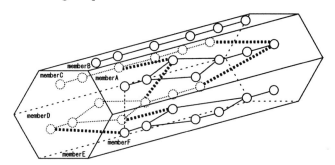

Figure 9 Side-plane display of three-dimensional connected graph.

7.4. Representing attributes of graphs using the dimensions of side planes

When analyzing the process of a work project, it is important that we grasp not only time-schedules but also labor-hours or costs of the tasks. Our method can show such information in each member's graph by assigning side-plane dimensions in proportion to the value for the information. Then, indicating this information as the dimensions of side planes, we can visually grasp the degree of each worker's contribution (labor-hours or costs) just by looking at the size of the graph.

7.5. A example view of three-dimensional connected graph

We developed a function that outputs VRML graphs for the users' related work events organized by our method. We can view the VRML graphs with a web browser (as shown in Fig.10). This allows users to grasp connections between members from the various angles by operating the browser interactively. Fig.10 shows when users see the connected graph from inside to future on time axis. Thus, we can explore the connected graph of the work project among users from inside or outside of the multi-angular prism.

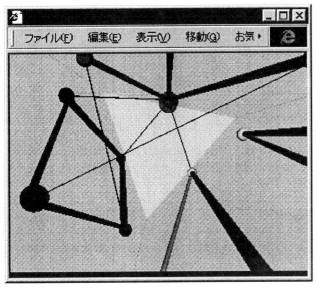

Figure 10 A sample view in a WWW browser.

In order to discuss cooperation among three users in these trials, we use our visualization method. Our method outputs the VRML code for the connected graphs of the three users. We can view them with a web browser as shown in Fig.11 or Fig.12.

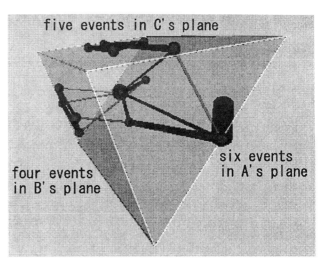

five events in C's plane

four events in B's plane

six events in A's plane

Figure 11 Difference in size of side planes in proportion to the number of events.

In Fig.12, member A performed "conference presentation", and members B and C helped him with the work project. First, we'll discuss each user's connected graph. Our method shows the value of relations between events as a thickness of the stick, so we can visually grasp the strength of relations between events. For example, the stick between member A's "OHPs deadline" and "conference" is thick, so we can see that the relation between their events are tight. Because the sticks between member B's "help to make videos" and "conference", between member B's "help to make OHPs" and "conference", and between member C's " help to make OHPs" and "conference" are thick, we confirmed that member B and C cooperated with member A in "conference", in order to finish the OHPs or videos for member A by the date of the conference.

Next, we discuss the connections between members. In Fig.12, when the three users registered the same title events, for example "conference", we connected solid lines between them. In addition, based on the relations between other members that we found in interviews with the three users, we connected member A's "make OHPs" and member C's "make OHPs", between member A's "practice presentation" and member B's: "practice presentation", between member A's: "make videos" and member B's: "help to make videos", and between member A's: "OHPs deadline" and member B's: "help to make OHPs". As shown in Fig.12, we can understand the cooperation among three members in order to support member A's work project of "conference" by interactively exploring the VRML browser.

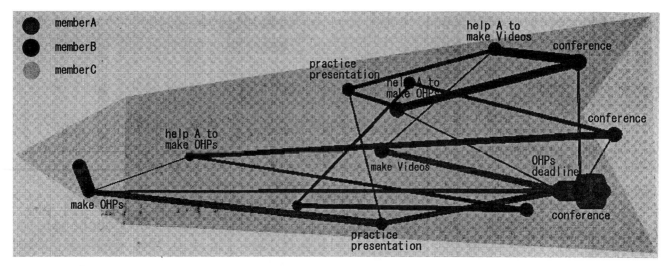

Figure 12 3D connected graph for the structure of collaboration.

Therefore, we believe that we can use our method as a tool to analyze the structure of cooperation among co-workers in detail. Because users can explore and grasp a structure of relations between a user's events and between co-workers' events, they can use our PIM as a tool to understand how they may perform a work project.

Fig.11 illustrates the difference in the size of side planes for three members. In this figure, the number of each member's events is substituted for labor-hours. As shown in Fig.11, A's side plane is largest. We can visually grasp the degree of his contribution against all labor-hours needed for the work project.

8. Conclusions

In this paper, we presented a method that automatically extracts relation between events by analyzing sequential references from user's operations records, and organizes related work events based on the relations between events. We also showed a method that visualizes the organized work events as a user's work-project structure. We have developed a prototype PIM and tested it. We confirmed that our method can automatically organize related work events as a connected graph including relations between events. In addition, we visualized actual collaboration among three users in the trials using three-dimensional connected graphs on multiple side planes of a multi-angular prism. We confirmed that our method is useful for examining collaboration among users. Hereafter, we will redesign and develop our system so that users may interactively explore the structure of their work projects.

References

[1] Lotus Development Corporation: *Organizer Users Guide*, (1995).

[2] Now Software, Inc: Now Up To Date -- Reference Manual, Version2.1, Seiwa Systems, Ltd. (1991). (in Japanese)

[3] Abeta, A. and Kakizaki, K.: Operation Record based Work Events Grouping Method for Personal Information Management System, *Proc.COMPSAC98*, IEEE, pp. 548-555 (1998).

[4] Sekine,T.: *PERT-CPM*, Nikkagiren (1965). (in Japanese)

[5] Ore, Oystein. and Wilson, R.: Graphs And Their, The Mathematical Association of America, (1990).

[6] Fairchild, K. M., Poltrock, S. E. and Furnas, G. W. : SemNet : Three-dimensional graphic representation of large knowledge bases, In R. Guindon (ed.): Cognitive Science And Its Applications For Human-Computer Interaction, pp.201-233, Lawrence Erlbaum Associates, (1988).

[7] Mackinlay, J. D., Robertson, G. G. and Card, S. K.: The perspective wall: Detail and context smoothly integrated, *Proc. ACM CHI'91*, pp.173-179 (1991).

[8] Silicon Graphics, Inc. : *FSN: File System Navigator*, online manual, (1992).

The User's View Level of the GOQL Graphical Query Language

Euclid Keramopoulos[1], Philippos Pouyioutas[2], Tasos Ptohos[1]

Abstract

The paper addresses issues related to the design of a graphical query mechanism that can act as an interface to any Object-Oriented Data Base System (OODBS), in general, and the Object Model of ODMG 2.0, in particular. In the paper, a brief literature survey of related work is given, and an analysis methodology that allows the evaluation of such languages is proposed. Moreover, the User's View level of a new graphical query language, namely GOQL (Graphical Object Query Language), for ODMG 2.0 is presented. The User's View level provides a graphical schema that does not contain any of the perplexing details of an object-oriented database schema, and it also provides a foundation for a graphical interface that can supports ad-hoc queries for object-oriented database applications. Herein we illustrate, using an example, the User's View level of GOQL.

1. Introduction

The evolution of database query languages during the last thirty years is strongly related to the evolution of database models and database systems. In the early days, i.e. the file processing systems era, the manipulation of data stored in such systems depended on programs written in some third generation programming language. Similar imperative languages were also used for querying the hierarchical and network database systems that followed the file processing systems. The introduction of relational database systems proved a major leap forward in the design/use of query languages as it led to the development and use of declarative query languages.

The development of *declarative* query languages, such as QUEL and SQL, meant that users were able to query a system by describing *what* they wanted rather than *how* to get what they wanted. The declarative nature of these languages made them easier, for the end-user, to use and understand; moreover, it allowed them to be established as "user friendly" query languages suitable for both expert and naive users. *Tabular* query languages, that were based on the QBE paradigm [24], were also proposed for relational database systems. In a tabular language, such as DBase-IV and Paradox, a *skeleton* (structure) of the required tables is displayed on the user's screen; users can usually express their queries by checkmarking projected attributes, inserting selection criteria in the appropriate attributes, and performing any join operations by inserting common *example variables* in the join attributes.

Recent developments in database systems have resulted in the appearance of object-oriented databases, which also support the use of declarative query languages. The SQL-like object-oriented query language of the ODMG 2.0 [5], namely OQL, has been widely accepted as the standard in the field. However, OQL is much richer than the current SQL/92 standard [11] both in terms of the data structures and the operators it supports, as it caters for the support of complex object structures and the object-oriented features of object-oriented databases; furthermore, the language "avoids" the SQL problem of *joining* tables because traversing data over simple *navigational paths* replaces the need for joins.

Recent advances in the use of graphical interfaces and the successful introduction of the Graphical User Interfaces (GUIs) by a number of vendors, such as Apple and Microsoft, have also led to the development of a number of graphical programming languages, such Visual C++ and Visual Basic. The popularity of graphical programming languages might be attributed to users' perception that these languages are easier to use and learn compared to textual languages, mainly because users are freed by the perplexing details of the constructs of textual languages.

The phenomenal success of graphical programming languages combined with researchers' drive to provide casual database users with an interface that will allow these users to pose ad-hoc queries, led to the development of a number of graphical interfaces for various database systems. Typically, such interfaces allow queries to be

---

[1] School of Informatics & MT, University of North London, 166-220 Holloway Rd, London N7 8DB, UK.
[2] School of Computing, Intercollege, 46 Makedonitissas Ave., P.O. Box 24005, Nicosia 1700, CYPRUS.

visualised and be represented diagrammatically or graphically rather than in some obscure code.

In this paper, in Section 2 we critically review most of the recently proposed graphical query languages, whereas in Section 3 we propose an analysis methodology that allows the evaluation and comparative study of such languages. In Section 4, firstly we outline some of the features that GOQL offers, and secondly we introduce a database that we will be using in the remainder of this paper. In Section 5 we present (and illustrate, with the use of the example database) the graphical database schema that GOQL utilizes in order to represent an object-oriented database schema. The proposed graphical schema, which is called the *User's View*, allows the representation of all the perplexing details of any object-oriented database schema and yet it makes these details simpler for the naive user to understand and use. We conclude, in Section 6, by discussing our current and future work and the implementation of the proposed language.

2. Critical Review of Related Work

The importance of graphical interfaces to the database field has been reflected by the number of graphical query languages that have appeared in the literature during the last decade. Each of these interfaces caters more or less for the needs of database users by providing them with a variety of features that allow them to interface with an underlying database in a graphical way. Here we review most of these graphical query languages.

PICASSO [14] is one of the first graphical query languages proposed and provides an interface for the universal relation database system System/U; KIVIEW [17] is a browser interface for object-oriented databases. PASTA-3 [15] provides a graphical user interface, similar to the interface of GQL [22], for the KB2 knowledge database system.

QBD* [1,2] is a graphical user interface which supports most of the relational algebra primitives. One of the innovative characteristics of QBD* is that it introduces abstraction to simplify the representation of the database schema. QBD* is claimed to be a user-friendly graphical query language, however, users have to go through a series of rather complex steps to formulate even the simplest of queries; finally, QBD* does not support the use of universal/existential quantifiers and the Boolean operator *not*.

GOOD [21] was built based on the idea of perceiving a database instance as a graph; the language allowed users to express queries visually by graphs that were built from components of a scheme graph. G-Log [20] also builds on the representation power of graphs but a prolog-like interface is utilised to express queries on an object-oriented schema. Although innovative, we feel that G-Log's prolog-like interface can alienate most users, as to express even the simplest of queries prolog rules have to be used.

OOQBE [23] is based on the QBE paradigm and it provides a form-based graphical interface for the KIWIS knowledge base management system. DOODLE [7] is a visual browser that provides an interface that allows end-users to display database contents using arbitrary pictures. SMARTIE [25] is another graphical browser that uses a set of visual display methods to display data stored using the ITASCA Distributed Object Database Management System.

AMAZE [3] provides a 3D interface to represent data and to express queries on an object-oriented database. The fact that the language supports only arithmetic/logical expressions, i.e. no support is provided for set operators, aggregate functions, existential/universal quantifiers and recursion, casts doubts on the expressiveness of the language. Moreover, we are sceptical about the possible benefits of a 3D interface because we feel that the process of navigating through the schema/data maze might be overwhelming for the user.

Both GQL [22] and Visualizer Query for Windows [10] utilise the Entity-Relationship (E-R) Model and allow users (a) to perceive data and the relationships between these data in terms of an E-R Diagram and (b) to perform graphical queries on that E-R Diagram. Business Objects [4] provide users with an interface that allows a database to be perceived as a set of meaningful objects, which are constructed from various tables and which incorporate and encapsulate "join" relationships; based on this set, queries can be expressed in a diagrammatic and graphical way.

SUPER [9] is a generic interface, which can provide support for queries in both relational and object-oriented databases. It is based on the ERC+ data model, which is an enhancement of the E-R Model designed to support complex objects and object identity. OdeView [8] is based on the Ode object-oriented database system and is influenced by the QBE paradigm [24].

Gql [19] is a powerful query language based on the functional data model. It allows graphical queries to be expressed on a functional database schema, it is at least as expressive as relational algebra and relational calculus and it supports queries that contain aggregate functions, simple arithmetic expressions and nesting of results.

GOMI [12] is based on the object-oriented database model, and provides users with a powerful graphical interface for data manipulation and data definition. We believe that GOMI is not intuitive for naive users as (a) it utilises mathematical symbols to provide a visual representation of operators, and (b) its graphical queries reflect the underlying object-oriented database, which a naive user might not understand; finally a major drawback of GOMI is that it does not support method invocation, and thus, it deprives expert users from using the full expressive potential of the underlying model.

Kaleidoquery [18] is based on a filter flow-oriented visual model that provides a 3D interface for data stored in an object-oriented database. The language is ODMG 2.0 compliant and consistent with OQL; however, we feel that the 3D interface might suffer from the same problems as that of AMAZE, and the filter flow-oriented visual model uses a limited number of metaphors, the semantics of which might be restrictive.

Quiver [6] seems to be a rather promising graphical query language for the object-oriented model, and it provides an interesting interface to formulate graphical queries; however, from the published work, it looks as if its design is in its early stages. Thus, for example, it is not clear, how the database schema looks like or whether the language supports/will support the set of operators, that are usually provided by the other query languages. Based on the published work the language does not support negation, set operators, existential/universal quantifiers, etc.

3. An Analysis/Evaluation Methodology

It is apparent that each of the above-discussed languages addresses a variety of topics and issues, and if we were to embark on a comparative study of these languages it would be necessary to adopt an analysis methodology. The methodology we are proposing builds on an analysis methodology used in [16] to evaluate conventional query languages. Our methodology modifies and enhances this methodology with features and characteristics that apply to the graphical query languages case. The features/criteria that we have used are as follows:

- the **underlying data model** that is supported by the graphical query language - the underlying model is rather important as graphical languages are interfaces to the data structures and the querying mechanism that the underlying model provides; for example, OODBMSs provide a much richer data definition and querying mechanism;
- the **functionality** available to user, i.e. whether a language allows retrieval, update, and/or other organisational /data definition functions;
- the **language interface**, - the type of interface affects the structural appearance of a language; furthermore,

a graphical language with a textual interface is not so user-friendly, whereas a 3D interface might be too overwhelming for some types of users;
- the levels of **user expertise** supported; users have been categorised as:
  - *casual* or *naive* users, i.e. untrained users,
  - *skilled* frequent users, i.e. users who although have access to a database they do not have much knowledge of computer systems in general, and
  - *expert* users, i.e. professional database programmers;
- the **expressiveness**, i.e. whether a language supports any/all of the following features:
  - predicates,
  - complex Boolean expressions and set operations (union, intersection, difference),
  - arithmetic expressions,
  - existential and universal quantification,
  - aggregate functions (count, max, min, sum, avg),
  - the Group-by operator,
  - recursion;
- the support of **methods**; although this characteristic is applicable only to object-oriented databases, it has been included because it represents an important feature of a model that is used as the underlying database in a high proportion of the reviewed languages;
- the **colour** support; despite a number of problems related to the use of colour (colour aesthetics are subjective, some people are colour blind), it can be used to effectively emphasise, differentiate, or order important elements, or to code quantitatively values.

The table, in Figure 1, contains a comparative study of most of the above surveyed graphical query languages using the criteria laid out above and is based on information that can be found in the literature.

4. An Overview of GOQL

The language GOQL has been designed to address the needs of naive users; thus, the provided interface hides and encapsulates some features of the underlying database and represents some others using metaphors. The language is based on the object model of the ODMG 2.0 and it provides a graphical querying mechanism. Because there is a direct correspondence between the features of GOQL and OQL (GOQL supports all the features of OQL), the language can be used as an alternative graphical interface to OQL. Thus, GOQL allows users to express graphically queries ranging from simplistic ones to rather complicated ones. Among the features provided/supported by the language are: the support of a 2D colour interface, the use/support of methods, predicates, boolean & set operators, arithmetic expressions existential/universal quantifiers, aggregate functions, group by and sort operators, functions, and subqueries.

In the remainder of the paper we present the User's View level of GOQL, through which users pose ad-hoc queries using our graphical query language. The User's View level of GOQL is presented through a database schema example. The database schema used is called *HOSPITAL*. The database is assumed to contain information about patients, surgeons and operating theatres. Figure 2, contains the schema definition of the HOSPITAL database expressed in ODL, the data definition language of ODMG 2.0.

Features		PICASSO	Pasta-3	QBD*	G-Log	OOQBE	AMAZE	SUPER	Ode View	Gql	GOMI	Kaleidoquery	Quiver
Data Model	Relational	✓	✓	✓				✓					
	Object-Oriented				✓	✓	✓		✓		✓	✓	✓
	Functional									✓			
Functionality	Retrieval	✓	✓	✓	✓	✓	✓	✓	✓	✓	✓	✓	✓
	Update		✓					✓	✓		✓		
	Organisational		✓					✓	✓		✓		
Language Form	2D	✓	✓	✓	✓	✓		✓		✓	✓		✓
	3D						✓					✓	
	Textual								✓				
User Type	Naive						✓			✓			✓
	Skilled	✓	✓	✓					✓		✓	✓	
	Expert				✓	✓		✓					
Expressivity	Predicates	✓	✓	✓	✓	✓	✓	✓	✓	✓	✓	✓	
	Boolean & Set Operators	✓	✓	✓	✓	✓	✓	✓	✓	✓	✓	✓	
	Arithmetic Expressions	✓	✓	✓	✓	✓	✓	✓	✓	✓	✓	✓	✓
	Existential/Universal Quantifiers	✓	✓		✓	✓		?		✓	✓	✓	
	Aggregate Functions	✓	✓	✓	✓	✓		✓	✓	✓	✓	✓	✓
	Group-by Operator	✓	✓	✓	✓			?		✓	?	✓	
	Recursion		✓		✓								
Methods	Yes								✓				✓
	No				✓	✓	✓				✓	?	
	Not applicable	✓	✓	✓				✓		✓			
Colour	Black & White	✓	✓	✓		✓		✓	✓	✓	✓		
	Colourful				✓		✓					✓	✓

Figure 1

```
Class Person {
  attribute string Name;
  attribute string Address;
  attribute string Tel_no;
  attribute date DoB;
  attribute string Sex;
  unsigned short Age ();
};

Class Surgeon extends Person {
  attribute string Staff_no;
  attribute float Salary;
  relationship set <Operation> Performs_op
    inverse Operation::Performed_by;
  relationship set <Private_Patient> Treats
    inverse Private_Patient::Treated_by;
  float Tax ();
};

Class Private_Patient extends Patient{
  relationship Surgeon Treated_by
    inverse Surgeon ::Treats;
};
```

```
Class Patient extends Person {
  attribute char Blood_gp;
  relationship set<Operation> Undergoes
    inverse Operation::Performed_on;
};

Class Operation {
  attribute date Op_date;
  attribute string Type;
  relationship Theatre Located_in
    inverse Theatre::Holds;
  relationship Surgeon Performed_by
    inverse Surgeon::Performs_op;
  relationship Patient Performed_on
    inverse Patient::Undergoes;
};

Class Theatre {
  attribute short Theatre_no;
  relationship set <Operation> Holds
    inverse Operation::Located_in;
  attribute set <string> Room;
};
```

Figure 2

5. The User's View Level of GOQL

The graphical representation of the schema of the underlying database has been utilised by most of the graphical interfaces that appeared in the literature. The presence of a graphical database schema is rather important as it provides a basis upon which graphical queries can be expressed. Thus, this graphical representation of the schema must provide for the various features supported by the underlying data model.

Other graphical interfaces have chosen to represent explicitly every feature of the underlying database schema; e.g. in [12] class hierarchies, subtyping, object relationships, and methods are explicitly represented. However, such representations can be rather confusing to naive users, because they contain details which should not be of their concern.

The graphical representation of the underlying database schema, that GOQL provides, is called *User's View* (UV). A UV allows the representation of all the features of the underlying ODMG 2.0 object model; however, it hides from users most of the perplexing details, such as methods, hierarchies, relationships. In particular, a UV (a) does not distinguish between methods and attributes; (b) does not explicitly support the representation of *is-a* hierarchies, but instead it allows properties inherited by a subclass to be explicitly represented in that subclass as properties of the corresponding class table; (c) utilises a number of desktop metaphors that allow the representation of the other features of the object model. In Figure 3, the UV of the HOSPITAL database is given.

The UV is generated from the stored metadata of the underlying database schema, and it is comprised by a number of named **class tables**; each of these class tables is named by the name of the class it represents, and it contains a list of all the attributes, relationships and methods of that particular class and all its superclasses; the types of the properties of a class are hidden. The desktop metaphors that we use in a UV are the following:

- **Folders** are used to represent relationships, and they are linked to the row of a class table that is named by the relationship they represent, e.g. the "Operation" folder is linked to the "Undergoes_op" row of the class table "Patient".

- **Briefcases** are used to represent a relationship between a class and its superclasses; i.e. briefcases are linked to the row of a class table that is named by the particular relationship. A briefcase can be either "shut", in which case it is named with the name of the most general superclass, or "open". An "opened" briefcase reveals a number of folders/shut briefcases that are immediate subclasses of the class that gives the name to the briefcase, e.g. the "Performed_on" property of the "Operation" class table.

- **Paper-clips** are used to represent collections; they appear on the right hand side of a class table row that is named by a collection type, e.g. in the "Theatre" class table the "Room" row is a collection of strings, whereas the "Holds" row represents a collection of "Operation". The UV does not distinguish between the different types of collections.

- **Disks** are used to represent parameters of a method or a function.

- **Envelopes** are used to represent properties that have a complex internal structure, i.e. properties defined as `struct` constructs in the underlying object model, and they are placed on the right hand side of a class table row.

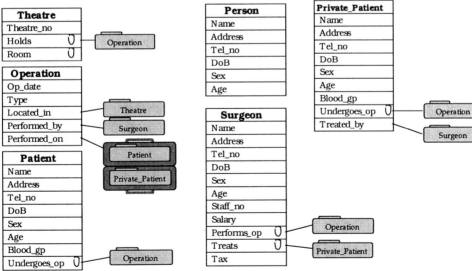

Figure 3

6. Conclusions

In this paper we have reviewed and evaluated most of the graphical interfaces that have appeared in the literature during the last decade. We have also presented, using an example, the User's View level of GOQL which can be used as a graphical interface to OQL. We believe that the proposed interface supported by GOQL is the "simplest" interface amongst those supported by the various other proposed query languages. We are currently engaged in a detailed evaluation exercise. The database schema example presented in this paper will be mapped to the corresponding graphical representation schema of each of the discussed query languages. All these graphical schemas will be given to a group of users to compare and evaluate. The results of this comparison study will be presented in a forthcoming paper.

We are also currently implementing, using Tcl/Tk, on an O_2 OODBMS the design of the GOQL User's View level and the query constructs of the language. We are at the same time working on the formal specification of the language's semantics.

7. References

1. Angelaccio M., Catarci T. & Santucci G., 1990a: QBD*: A Graphical Query Language with Recursion. In *IEEE Transaction on Software Engineering*, Vol. 16, No 10, pp. 1150-1163.
2. Angelaccio M., Catarci T. & Santucci G, 1990b: Query by Diagram*: A Fully Visual Query System. In *Journal of Visual Languages and Computing*, Vol. 1, pp. 255-273.
3. Boyle J., Fothergrill J.E. & Gray P.M.D., 1994: Design of a 3D User Interface to a Database. *Proceedings of 2nd International Workshop on Interfaces to Databases,* Vol. 2, pp. 127-142.
4. Business Objects Ltd, 1995: Business Objects.
5. Cattell R.G.G. & Barry D.K. (Eds.), 1997: *The Object Database Standard: ODMG 2.0.* Morgan Kaufmann Publishers.
6. Chavda M. & Wood P. T., 1998: Towards an ODMG-Compliant Visual Object Query Language. In *Proceedings of the 23rd VLDB Conference*, Athens (Greece), August, pp. 456-465
7. Cruz I., 1992: DOODLE: A Visual Language for Object-Oriented Databases. In *ACM SIGMOD,* No. 5, pp. 71-80.
8. Dar S., Gehani N.H., Jagadish H.V. & Srinivasan J., 1995: Queries in an Object-Oriented Graphical Interface. In *Journal of Visual Languages and Computing*, Vol. 6, pp. 27-52.
9. Dennebouy Y., Andersson M., Auddino A., Dupont Y., Fontana E., Gentile M. & Spaccapietra S., 1995: SUPER: Visual Interfaces for Object + Relationship Data Models.
   In *Journal of Visual Languages and Computing*, Vol. 5, pp. 73-99.
10. IBM-ASTRAC Ltd, 1995: Visualizer Query for Windows (VQ/W).
11. International Standards Organisation, 1992: *ISO/IEC 9075:1992(E) Information technology - Database language - SQL.*
12. Jun Y.S. & Yoo S.I., 1995. GOMI: A Graphical User Interface for Object-Oriented Databases. In *Proceedings of International Conference on Object-Oriented Interface Systems (OOIS),* pp. 238-251.
13. Keramopoulos, E., Pouyioutas, P. & Sadler, C. 1997. GOQL, a Graphical Query Language for Object-Oriented Database Systems. In *Proceedings of the Third Basque International Workshop on Information Technology (BIWIT'97):* Data Management Systems, Biarritz (France), July 2-4, pp. 35-45.
14. Kim, H., Korth, H.F. & Silverschatz, A., 1988: PICASSO: A Graphical Query Language. In *Software-Practice and Experience*, Vol. 18, No 3, 169-203.
15. Kuntz, M. & Melchert, R. 1989: Pasta-3's Graphical Query Language: Direct Manipulation, Co-operative Queries, Full Expressive Power. *Proceedings of the 15th International Conference on Very Large Databases*, pp. 97-105.
16. McDonald N.H. & McNally J., 1982: Query Language Feature Analysis by Usability. In *Computer Languages*, Vol. 7, pp. 103-124.
17. Motro A., D'atri A. & Tarantino L., 1988: The Design of KEVIEW: An Object-Oriented Browser. In *Journal of Expert Database Systems*, pp. 107-131.
18. Murray N., Paton N. & Goble C., 1998: Kaleidoquery: A Visual Query Language for Object Databases. *Proceedings of the 4th IFIP Working Conference on Visual Database Systems - VDB 4.*
19. Papantonakis A., & King, P.J.H., 1995: Gql, a Declarative Graphical Query Language Based on the Functional Data Model. In *Journal of Visual Languages and Computing*, Vol. 6, No 1, pp. 3-25.
20. Paredaens J., Peelman P. & Tanca L., 1991: G-Log, A Declarative Graphical Query Language. In *Proceedings of the 2nd International Conference on Deductive and Object-Oriented Databases*, pp. 108-128.
21. Paredaens J., Van den Bussche J., Andries M., Gemis M., Gyssens M. & Thyssens I., 1992: An Overview of GOOD. In *ACM SIGMOD Record*, Vol. 21, No. 1, pp. 25-31.
22. SOFT TOOLRACK LTD, 1995: GQL (Graphical Query Language).
23. Staes F., Tarantino L. & Tiems A., 1991: A Graphical Query Languages for Object Oriented Databases. In *Proceedings of the IEEE workshop on Visual Languages*, pp. 205-210.
24. Zloof M. M., 1975. Query By Example. In Proceedings of the AFIPS Conference, Vol 44, pp. 431-438.
25. Zoeller R. & Barry D, 1992: Dynamic Self-Configuring Methods for Graphical Presentation of ODBMS Objects. IEEE, pp. 136-143.

Visualization

Chair
James L. Mohler
Purdue University, USA

Continuous Field Visualization with Multi-Resolution Textures

Ian Curington

Advanced Visual Systems Ltd.
Hanworth Lane, Chertsey, Surrey KT16 9JX, U.K .
ianc@avs.com

Abstract

A method of using a texture mapping approach to color scales is described, for the purpose of visualizing continuous field scalar quantities. The technique is most appropriate where high gradients are present in the data, or where geometric surfaces are projected to significant screen area. The use of texture mapping takes advantage of widely available 3D display systems for interactive visualization system design. The technique yields a significant reduction in visualization artifacts caused by color interpolation. Multiple resolution textures are shown to improve visualizations of high dynamic range data.

Key words: Interpolation, Color, Visualization, Texture

1. Introduction

When continuous field numerical data is presented in a visualization system as a continuously varying color, artifacts can be introduced due to color interpolation in the display system. A technique is described using texture map color in the visualization display, especially suitable where small non-linear regions in the data must be highlighted, or where the data contains sharp gradients. The characteristics of the artifacts caused by color are discussed first, followed by an explanation and example of the texture color map technique.

2. Gouraud Shading

The common technique of Gouraud shading, used by many 3D rendering systems, computes shading and color information at discreet points, generally at the vertices of polygonal objects [5]. Once the color assignment has taken place, the graphics system displays the object by performing linear interpolation of the color across each face of each polygon. Although highly efficient, the technique ignores variations in the data or the lighting environment during interpolation, and simply blends the vertex colors across the faces. As shown in figure 1, the well-known artifact of "Mach Banding" occurs where a curved surface under a directional light source appears to have dark bands or discontinuities in the surface shading. If the surface color is derived from continuous numerical data, as is the case in visualization systems, the bands appear to be contour discontinuities. While more sophisticated lighting models can eliminate the banding effect due to shading, it cannot correct for color interpolation effects when the color is derived from numerical data.

3. RBG Color Interpolation

Most visualization systems contain operators to map data values to color. These operators are typically yield smooth contours, and are used to represent continuous field data. Color map systems are used to specify such mapping, such as blue for

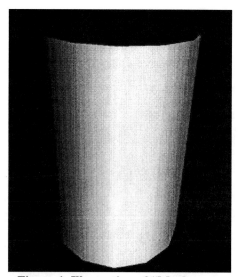

Figure 1. Illustration of "Mach Banding" effect in Gouraud shading.

a low value, and red for a high value. When applied to data on geometry (meshes), data values are known only at discreet points on the geometry. Using continuous color maps, smooth changes in color are displayed between available data points. The way in which the color is smoothed, or interpolated between the points can have a dramatic effect on the interpretation of the underlying data [2]. At best these factors display an approximation of the data, with a possibility of completely hiding important features in the data, and at worst create misleading artifacts in the visualizations [4].

In many systems, the data values are sampled and converted to color values, typically (Red, Green, Blue) triplets at each node or vertex of the geometry. During display, interpolation is left to the underlying display system, which then interpolates intermediate values by blending the two colors using low precision color interpolation.

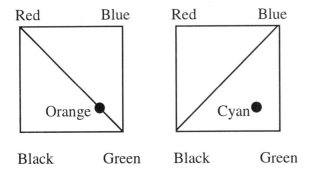

Figure 2. Triangulation effect on interpolation.

Triangulation can also affect color interpolation. In the illustration, the color of a point may change from orange to cyan under different triangulation directions. The more fundamental problem is that colors specified in the color map may be omitted completely. If two adjacent data points have the colors Red and Blue, color interpolation will generate Purple at the half-way point. If the values are at extreme ends of the color map, and the color map has Green at the center point of the scale, then Green would be the expected color, not Purple. Even when color space interpolation is desired, the problems with using an RGB are well known, and alternative color space models are available [3], but rarely implemented by display system vendors.

If the color map resolution matches the data value resolution, and the data variation across each facet of the model is very low or close to the resolution of the color map, then the color interpolation

method is adequate and few errors will be observed. The highest chance of artifact generation occurs when the data gradient is high over individual facets, and relates the data range over significant portions of the color map.

4. Texture Display

A solution to this situation is to use a 1-dimensional texture mapping technique. Texture mapping is an advanced graphics technique that has become available on almost all graphics systems through its popular use in games such as Doom, Quake, and Tomb Raider. Texture mapping is also well supported through software interfaces such as *OpenGL* and *Direct3D*. Instead of passing pre-sampled colors to the display, parametric texture coordinates are passed, along with an RGB texture image. Interpolation is then performed directly on the texture coordinates (using floating point arithmetic), which are used to look up color values from the reference image. Pixel color assignment is indirect, using the color image as a lookup table. Textures have also been used to represent vector fields, or more complex feature display of scalar fields [1].

Using the same color map structure as used in Gouraud shading as the reference image, the same color map information may be passed to the display. Display update times may be slightly slower, since more operations are performed, and more data must be processed by the display system, however this is a small price to pay to achieve interpolation accuracy. Interpolation can now show much more detail in the original data, and show subtle variations that are completely lost using the usual color interpolation. Users can specify an order of magnitude higher resolution color maps, and the entire color map can be displayed between two adjacent data points if needed.

Since many texture display systems need a square image structure, a 1-dimensional color-map is placed down the diagonal of the image. A color map pattern is easily sketched using a paint program to create a color map image. As so many image handling tools exist, our prototype uses standard TIFF images. Interactive performance of this technique has been verified on systems ranging from a small laptop PC to a Silicon Graphics immersive virtual reality environment.

5. Applications of Texture based Color Maps

This texture based color map technique has been implemented as a filter module in the visualization framework AVS/Express. The filter takes any geometric mesh with scalar node data, and replaces it with a mesh with UV texture coordinate data. The mapping matches the range of the input data, so that all positions on a texture image source containing color map values may be used. The texture image source is intended as a single dimensional color table source, with values sampled along the primary diagonal. Because the technique is a direct replacement for the color interpolation technique, no additional user defined parameters need to be specified.

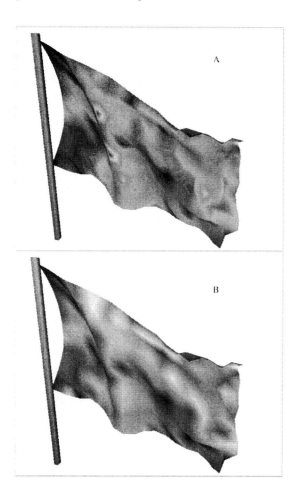

Figure 3. Flag forces shown using (A) texture based color map, and (B) color interplation with Gouraud shading. Note the yellow ring in A is missing in B.

The differences in detail presented in the visualization can easily be seen in the following comparison. In the bottom model (B), the data is displayed using a standard color hue range from low to high, with blue as the lowest color, and red the highest. In the upper model (A), the same colors are used as the texture based color map. Much more data variation detail is shown in the upper model than the lower, using the texture based color map technique. The model is of a 3D finite element analysis of a flag under windy conditions, with resultant force magnitude values displayed as color. Near the central crease, two bright red spots indicate the highest forces. In the top model (A), the red spots are surrounded by yellow, the next color in table. In the lower model, color interpolation skips over these values, so the yellow rings are missing.

Multi-resolution texture images are used where the data contains important information in different numerical ranges. In this case a special image is assembled with regions defined with independent color scales that will allow differentiation of the numeric ranges present in the data. In this way wide dynamic range data can be interpreted in the visualization system. The following example shows a geologic structure with simulated oil reservoir attribute values placed on the geometry using the multi-resolution texture map color technique. Such detail is normally lost using color interpolation.

6. Conclusion

A technique is described to reduce visual artifacts due to color interpolation using a texture map display technique. The method is suitable for a wide range of numerical data visualization problems, and is especially suited to widely available hardware, and where high data gradients must be shown accurately. The software developed for the research presented in this paper is available at the International AVS Center site, http://www.iavsc.org .

7. References

[1] Roger Crawfis and Michael Allison, **"A Scientific Visualization Synthesizer"**, Proceedings of Visualization '91, IEEE Press, 1991

[2] Richard S. Gallagher, **"Computer Visualization: graphics techniques for scientific and engineering analysis"**, CRC Press, 1995

[3] Roy Hall, **"Illumination and color in computer generated imagery"**, Springer-Verlag, 1989

[4] Terry Hewitt, Manchester Visualization Centre, Personal Communication, 1999

[5] William Newman and Robert Sproull, **"Principles of interactive computer graphics"**, McGraw-Hill 1979

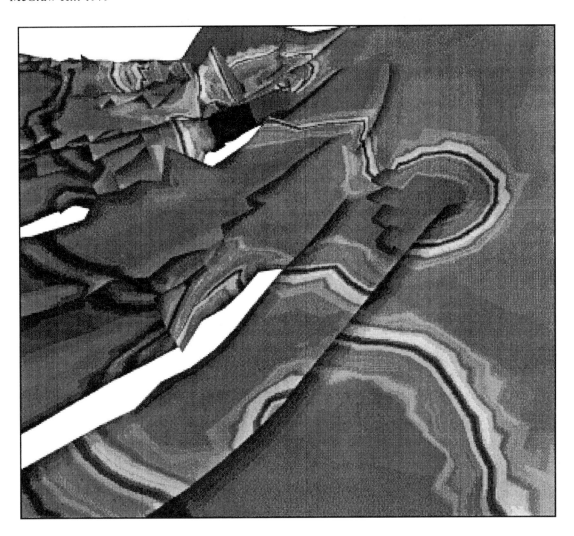

Figure 4. Geologic structure showing oil reservoir properties, using multi-resolution texture. (*Data Courtesy of Schlumberger Geoquest*)

3D Ray-Tracing on PC Networks using TCP/IP

T. D. Scott, V. F. Fusco and R. S. Ferguson

High Frequency Electronics Laboratory
School of Electrical and Electronic Engineering
The Queen's University of Belfast, N. Ireland UK BT7 1NN

Tel: +44 (0) 1232-274087 Fax: +44 (0) 1232-667023

Email: t.scott@ee.qub.ac.uk, v.fusco@ee.qub.ac.uk, r.ferguson@ee.qub.ac.uk

Index terms:

3-D Ray Tracing, Distributed Computing, TCP/IP.

Abstract

This paper presents a 3D graphics rendering algorithm for photo realistic ray tracing operating over a network of personal computers. The implementation incorporates partitioning methodologies for both memory and workload to achieve efficient execution on a distributed personal computer, PC, network. Experimental results that compare algorithm efficiency in dual processor machines and TCP/IP networks with respect to execution on a single processor are discussed.

Introduction

In the field of 3D computer graphics the technique of Ray-Tracing has long been used to synthesize photo realistic pictures from a mathematical description of the subjects that are to appear in the image. The form that this description takes will depend on the complexity of the subject material, i.e. the description of the content of the image. For example a sphere is defined by its origin and radius, a requirement of only 4 floating point numbers. On the other hand the object depicted in Figure 1 is specified by a planar faceted approximation of over 20,000 triangular shapes, approximately 90,000 floating point numbers 1.5Mb in additional data storage is required for image maps and surface textures.

For a highly detailed scene the Z-buffer algorithm [1] will generate images (termed 'rendering the scene') at video frames rates of 30 time per second while it could take ray tracing procedures many minutes if not hours to achieve only a slightly better quality picture. The independence between pixels comprising the scene make ray tracing algorithms ideal candidates for implementation in a multi-processor or distributed processor computing environment. In an ideal scenario with infinite BW communications between processors a linear improvement in speed of execution might be expected.

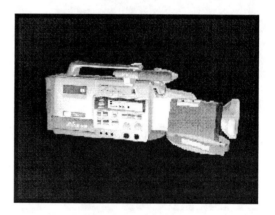

Figure 1. Planar faceted scene.

Personal computers with more than two processors are uncommon, so a cost-effective solution to realizing a multiprocessor computing environment is to harness the CPU power of desktop PCs connected together by a local area network or wide area network (LAN or WAN). An added benefit derived from this approach is the large distributed memory subsequently available. In such a distributed computing environment, processors can work concurrently on different sub-domains (in this paper these are designated as scanlines) of the overall problem, communicating with each other only when necessary. However to achieve maximum efficiency with this approach redesign of the ray-tracing algorithm is an essential prerequisite.

In this paper we present an implementation of a 3D Ray tracing algorithm which can be configured to execute in a number of threads. The threads of execution can be deployed in single machine, multi-processor, or, single client multiple server network environments. The implementation discussed here incorporates new partitioning methodologies for both memory and workload to achieve efficient execution. Experimental results that compare algorithm efficiency in a dual processor machine and a range of network configurations relative to performance on a single processor using the TCP/IP protocol discussed. Some comments on the relative merits of TCP/IP and MPI message passing protocols are described briefly.

Ray Tracing on Distributed Network

In the Client-Server model, communication generally takes the form of a request message from the Client who is requesting to the Server that work is to be done. The Server then does the work and sends back the result, usually, there are many Servers using a small number of Clients.

In, the dynamic method used here individual PC processors are assigned to single scanlines each scanline represents a 2-D slice through the scene being traced. This method is similar to Kay and Greenberg's [2] concept, except in our case, each task is a single scan line rather than groups of scanlines. For each of the scanlines to be transmitted across the network to the Server, TCP/IP is used since windows based operating systems readily support this protocol. The algorithm is an extension of Hue's[3] approach and incorporates, load balancing i.e. each processor is used as effectively as every other processor. This means that in the ideal case, each processor has exactly the same amount of work to do and will finish its work at the same time as the others in the network thereby removing processor latency. In our work this is achieved by polling client tasks and relocating slower processors (slowed due to multiple users bidding for computer resources) onto faster available machines (i.e. less heavily used processors). Load balance solutions can be, (I)

static assignment of large tasks, or, (ii) dynamic assignment of smaller tasks.

In this work adaptability with respect to the number of processors is included allowing flexibility in the dynamic adjustment of workload. Thus if a fast machine finishes before all ray tracing is complete the workload is reassigned to the fastest latent machine on the network, however, if there are only three scanlines left to complete the current task, then the Client will not split the workload, as any computational advantage would be negligible due to re-assignment, reallocation, network overhead penalties incurred.

Network Implementation
TCP/IP Header

Each of the scanlines to be transmitted across the network is divided into eight segments. The TCP/IP header must be present during each and every transmission across the network. The TCP/IP header is shown in Figure 2 each element of this header is defined in [5].

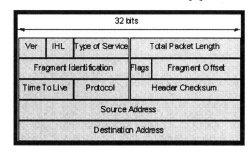

Figure 2. TCP/IP Header.

Each scanline is considered to be the smallest problem allowed. To allow transmission across a network, the scanlines where divided into 8 segments. The first 7 packets of a scanline are 256 bytes long and the last one 128 bytes long. The reason for this, is to keep the amount of data sent over the network as small as possible. At first glance this would appear arbitrary, however each scanline is 1920 bytes in size. Dividing this by 256 bytes, yields the result above.

An algorithm was written to divide up the workload just before they are dispatched to a Server for rendering. When received by the Server(s), the scanlines are assembled before the rendering process begins. Scanline Segments are given tags T1 to T8, from which both the Client and Server know in which order to reassemble the scanline.

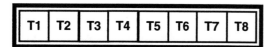

| T1 | T2 | T3 | T4 | T5 | T6 | T7 | T8 |

Figure 3. Order of tags in the re-assembly of a scanline.

The re-assembly of the scanlines follows the format shown in Figure 3. During network rendering it was noted that some of the packets where missing from the final image. Figure 4, shows this effect in the form of white lines appearing in the image. To eliminate these from occurring, retransmission of missed packets must take place.

Figure 4. Missed Packets from network Rendered scene.

The reason for the occurrence this problem is that the UDP (User Datagram Protocol) client algorithm [5] provides unreliable datagram delivery. While a simplistic UDP client can work well on local networks that exhibit low loss, low delay, and no packet reordering, this algorithm may not work effectively across a complex LAN or WAN. To work in LAN or WAN environment, a client must implement reliability through timeout and retransmission. It must also handle the problems of duplicate or out-of-order packets. Adding reliability can be difficult, and requires expertise in protocol design.

Due to the unreliability of the UDP transmission, scanline data retransmission had to be implemented to ensure that the complete scene is received by the Server. In our work if the Client does not receive a packet from a Server, the Client sends a status command to the Server to retransmit the missed packet. In general it is only necessary to execute this error correction process either when the Client detects the packet is corrupted, or when it is missing. Retransmission occurs when the Client sends an error status message to the appropriate Client, i.e. the Client first checks if there are any missing packets with the use of tags, the Client then performs a numeric check on the scanline segments received.

Results

With the software philosophy described above it is possible to predict the relative speedup obtained by operating on a network as the number of processors is increased. The total time for one picture to be traced is the time from generation of the first ray to the time at which the last return packet is added into the frame buffer. For a small number of processors the computation time will be dominated by the total amount of processing to be done by the busiest processor. If however the number of processors are large (greater than the total number of rays, for example) then the time will be dominated by the transit time for the longest ray.

Equation 1 was used to calculate the speedup of the system using a Dual processor system relative to a single processor system. Using different test scenes, the average percentage speedup performance for the dual multiprocessor system varied from 70% to 85%.

$$Dual\ Speedup = \frac{(Single - Dual)}{Single} \qquad (1)$$

Equation 2 shows how speedup is normally determined. The time used by 1 processor for program execution is divided by the time used P processors for execution. The speedup is an indication of the effective number of processors utilized [4].

$$Multiprocessor\ Speedup = \frac{T_1(1)}{T_P(P)} \qquad (2)$$

Since the conditions in any computational environment are far from ideal, the results will be below that of ideal due to problems such as: network contention, memory and processor latency, scheduling, synchronization and code modification and overhead due to adaptation will most certainly have an affect on the performance of the distributed computation. This observation leads to the conclusion that simple scenes are not worth ray tracing across the network. To do so would involve the network overhead, which would slow the ray tracing down rather than speed it up.

In order to test the networked version of the distributed Ray tracing algorithm, the number of available processors were increased by one each time the experiment was run, and the time taken to ray trace the scene in Figure 4 was recorded. From Table 1, for the test scene in Figure 4 (640X480 Pixels) the speedup varied linearly with the available number of processors.

Network contention refers to the slowdown involved when more than one message attempts to use the same switch node at the same time. The amount of time taken to serve a given request will increase as more messages enter the network since it may take longer to find a free network pathway in this situation. Latency and/or communication costs are factored out of the times. Equation 3 shows the formula for switching contention(SC), here superscript i refers to the particular task i undergoing computation. T is time, P is the number of processors [4].

$$SC = \frac{\sum_{i=1}^{\#TASKS} \left[T(P)^i - T(1)^i \right]}{T_P * P} \qquad (3)$$

For the example given in Table 1 for 5 processors switch contention accounts for 6.5% of the decrease in processor run time from the ideal situation. In addition the cost of transferring these messages across the network is the communication overhead. In our work we use a 100MB Ethernet to interconnect the PCs in the network.

NUMBER OF PROCESSORS	TIME IN (S)	MEASURED SPEEDUP
1	1300	
2	1015	1.4
3	510	2.6
4	370	3.5
5	275	4.7

Table 1. Measured speedup.

This overhead factor is derived by measuring the total number of bytes transferred in the system. Using the data for block transfer time for this number of bytes can be defined [4], in Equation 4. Taking into account that each message is a maximum of 256 bytes long, the total

communication overhead is derived, T_{bt} is the cost per byte transferred, T_{SETUP} is the time setup cost for the message. When computed for the example here, communication overhead(CO) accounts for 17% of decrease in processor run time from the ideal situation, this when added to the switch contention overhead accounts for the speedup differential between ideal linear speedup and measured results.

$$CO\% = \frac{\left(\frac{\#bytes}{256} * T_{SETUP} \right) + \left(\#bytes * T_{bt} \right)}{T_p * P} \qquad (4)$$

TCP/IP Versus WinMPICH

WinMPICH the version of MPI for PC's from the engineering research center at Mississippi State University is derived from the Unix version MPICH for use with Microsoft Windows NT platforms [6]. WinMPICH allows processes to communicate with each other through shared memory or over a network. (WinSock)TCP/IP [7] and WinMPICH exhibit similar performance characteristics for message length(Bytes) from 1 to 1k, thereafter, as the message length increases WinMPICH is superior in terms of transfer speed . However in our work the data packets are 256 Bytes therefore WinMPICH will not offer a significant advantage over TCP/IP in this repect.

Conclusions

In this paper, we have described a distributed PC processor scheme for 3D ray tracing. The approach presented efficiently exploits all of the distributed resources available with this type of arrangement e.g., computation, storage and communication resources. For a network rendering scenario, we observed that the more processors the nearer the theoretical maximum speedup was achieved bar communication overheads, latency, etc. For example it was shown in the dual processor case a speedup of 1.8 is usually achieved and for a five networked processor system 4.7 was achieved using the scanline methodology as adopted for algorithm design in this work.
The technique given here is portable since it relies on TCP/IP message passing and can be used on any network of PC's supporting this protocol.

Acknowledgements

This work was performed under EPSRC contract GR/L23215.

References

[1]   Alan Watt: "Three-Dimensional Computer Graphics," Addison-Wesley Publishing Company, 1989, ISBN 0-201-154420.

[2]   D.S. Kay, and D. Greenberg, "Transparency for Computer Synthesized Images," SIGGRAPH 1979, p158-164.

[3]   Hu, M.-C. and Foley, J.D. "Parallel Processing Approaches to Hidden-Surface Removal in Image Space." Computers & Graphics 9, 3 (1985) pp.303-317.

[4]   S. Witman 1992, "Multiprocessor Methods for Computer Graphics Rendering", (pub: Jones and Bartlett Publishers, London), ISBN 0-86720-229-7.

[5]   TCP/IP client – server programing and applications, COMER STEVENS, PHIPE, 1989, ISBN 0-13-261348-4.

[6]   Marker Baker, "MPI on NT: The Current Status and Performance of the Available Environments", P64, Recent Advances in Parallel Virtual Machine and Message Passing Interface, 5th European PVM/MPI Users' Group Meeting Liverpool, UK, September 1998 Proceedings, Springer, 3-540-65041-5

[7]   Martain Hall, Mark Towfiq, Geoff Arnold, David Treadwell, Henry Sanders, "Windows Sockets, An Open Interface for Network Programming under Microsoft Windows", Version 1.1, 20th January 1993.

Multi-Modal Verification of Patient Positioning in Radiotherapy.

P.A. Graham, B. Thompson, J. Stratford, R.I. MacKay, C.J. Moore and P.J. Sharrock
North Western Medical Physics, Christie Hospital, Manchester, UK

Abstract

Conformal radiotherapy uses multi-leaf collimation to customise radiation dose fields to the three-dimensional shape of the target tumour. Its effectiveness is governed by the precision of dose delivery achieved using a few coplanar tattoo markers. During a course of treatment, the patient's body surface profile fluctuates causing the reference skin tattoo markers to move and hence, without the ability to verify target position, the precision of pre-treatment set-ups will degrade, often significantly.

Cross-modal patient set-up verification software has been developed which allows the user to examine images from various modalities. All imaging modalities available can be used to collectively define anatomical landmarks, outlined on a representative reference image in order to verify radiation field placement using anterior and lateral pre-treatment portal images. This software is presently being used within a national clinical trial for recording the field placement error observed daily at pre-treatment.

1. Introduction

Radiotherapy is an established clinical option for the treatment of localised tumours[1]. As the dose prescribed is fractionally delivered over many days, the effectiveness of any treatment is governed by the daily precision of patient set-up. Since the advent of conformal plans which reduce beam margins, greater emphasis is placed on the precision and coherence of target volume definitions[2]. Consequently, treatments are becoming more intricate and require many verification checks in order to ensure that the dose prescribed and that delivered to the tumour are consistent[3].

Conventional pre-treatment set-ups attempt to re-create a patient orientation on the treatment couch that is identical to that planned from the computed tomography (CT) scan. Immobilisation[4] and fiducial marking[5] techniques have been used in conjunction with portal imaging[6] in order to improve the precision of patient set-up. Patient immobilisation using custom mouldings fail to account for any daily shape changes in the patient's body surface. Surgically implanted fiducial markers are invasive, costly and can migrate, causing problems when portal imaging is used to confirm patient set-up. Tumour target movement data compiled both from simulations[7] and the clinical study of repeat CT scans[8] have been incorporated into conformal treatment plans[9].

Within many treatment room environments, electronic portal imaging is the only reliable source of verification for target tumour position. Due to the inherent poor contrast at treatment energies, the soft tissue definition within these images is severely limited to the extent that only bony landmarks or tissue/air boundaries can be used reliably. Hence, verification of the tumour target position can only be assumed by moving the patient on the treatment couch until corresponding landmarks in the portal image agree with those in a pre-treatment image[10]. Every modal image has inherent limitations associated with it that are unique to the imaging system used and ultimately define the detail that is visible. It is because of these limitations that any modal image considered in isolation, can not be used as a panacea for landmark comparisons.

Cross-modal patient set-up verification software has been developed which offers a more flexible image environment for performing anatomical landmark comparisons. This design allows the user to examine images from various modalities that include: Simulator Films, Digitally Reconstructed Radiographs, Scan Projection Radiographs, CT Slice and Mega-voltage (treatment room) images. Inter-comparisons may be performed on any available patient image set, by using the mouse to move previously drawn landmark graphics on a reference image, to their corresponding position in a verification image. Comparisons of this nature, can only be performed using this utility if the image scale and treatment isocentre/patient tattoo reference marker coordinates are known. Using this utility, decisions regarding which landmark features are to be outlined, may be formulated collectively by the inter-comparison of all of the patient images that are available to the user. Pre-treatment patient set-ups are performed by comparing visible landmark features in the Mega-voltage portal image with the corresponding features defined by the landmark graphics on a representative reference image.

In addition to recording the field placement error, this utility stores all information regarding the images used and the landmark graphics drawn during patient set-up. Essential image 'pre-load' data is permanently recorded and includes the treatment isocentre/tattoo marker coordinates, image pixel scales/magnification, and windowing values. By accessing such information, this utility can re-create precisely, the image platform on which a patient pre-treatment set-up was performed so that the field placement errors that were observed can themselves be analysed.

2. Loading Patient Image

All images are held within a patient database which is structured so that the directory-tree pathname catalogues information specific to the identity of each image. This format uniquely catalogues modal images under the dates of capture and imaging source. The user can interactively negotiate this database in order to access any patient image and its associated treatment information. It should be noted that images can only be compared if their view perspective and patient code are identical. Comparisons may only be performed on images in which the treatment isocentre reference coordinates and pixel scale are known.

Using this utility, the user first selects an image and treatment file from the patient database menu and then identifies the isocentre/tattoo marker reference location. When the reference marker has been identified, the image is automatically re-positioned so that the treatment isocentre lies at the centre of the display window. The pixel scales are either computed by positioning a box graphic over a visible scale grid of known dimensions or, assigned directly from the treatment file data. Rotations can also be performed in order to counter image twist that has been introduced by any digitisation equipment. When an image has been viewed, all of the data concerning the compulsory pre-load procedure are stored in an associated file. When available, this file can be accessed and the image data automatically loaded from the display menu.

During the image load process, the modal comparison software displays all previously stored landmark graphics associated with the image in the same format. This type of landmark recall facilitates the autonomous transfer of all reference graphics to the opposite window image. The functionality of cross-modal image comparison software is concerned with the speedy verification of patient set-up using images captured pre-treatment. Many of the design features incorporated, specifically address the speed issue of field placement verification which must not impede patient throughput.

The visual appearance of patient images can be altered in order to enhance those regions of anatomical detail that can act as a source of landmarks. Windowing techniques are commonly used whereby the user can interactively alter the width/level values and hence the dynamic range of information contained. Alternatively, magnification of the patient image assists in revealing previously obscured detail for those instances where the images are small and contain large amounts of information. Introducing dark borders allows the user to eliminate image glare and also improve the results of windowing. By clipping the image dimensions it is possible to eliminate unwanted detail and reduce the screen space occupied when this software utility is used with other packages.

2.1 Drawing Landmark Graphics

Within images, anatomical landmarks can be outlined using the mouse either 'free-hand', in line segments, or marked with a 'cross' icon. A number of menu options are available within this utility which reverse any outlining mistakes, close line segment structures and abort the draw process. The process of landmark outlining is initiated by a mouse button action that does not require any menus and is terminated by a similar 'double-click' procedure. For the purpose of indicating the position of landmark sites without recording their profile, the user can place 'cross-shaped' icon markers. These 'cross-shaped' markers are used to indicate landmark position either for verification speed or, to record the site location only, when profile is unimportant. All landmark identifiers are drawn in colour so that they are easily discernible from the patient image background.

When the landmark profiles/markers have been drawn, they can be individually re-classified into groups and/or stored to file. The consequences of group classification apply mainly to movement processes whereby performing any 'Click-n-drag' translation or rotation operation on a landmark profile/marker will also apply to all members of the same group. Group status is assigned by first using the mouse to individually select the appropriate landmark graphics and then invoking the relevant menu option. By default, all landmark profiles/markers may be universally grouped without prior selection.

All of the landmark graphics drawn may be stored with the request window background patient image. However, patient set-ups automatically default all landmark storage requests so that they are associated with the 'reference' image. All stored landmark graphics associated with a patient image are immediately displayed when initially loaded from the database, illustration 1. 'Power icons', displayed with the patient information (at the top of the image), allow the user to recall stored landmarks without 're-loading' the patient image. When landmark graphics are 'recalled', the group membership of identical graphics already displayed are re-configured in order to agree with those stored.

2.2 Treatment Isocentre Verification

The position of the treatment isocentre, defined when loading the patient image, can be verified and altered interactively if required. Verification of the treatment isocentre position can be performed by superimposing the multi-leaf collimator (MLC) prescription graphic over the patient image. The treatment isocentre is symbolised by a unique graphic which is a representation of that projected by the optical set-up component of the treatment machine. When the MLC prescription graphic is superimposed on the patient image, the user can perform a 'Click-n-Grab' mouse operation on the treatment isocentre icon and interactively re-position it. As the isocentre icon graphic is moved, the MLC prescription moves also, in order to maintain their relative positions. Finally, the isocentre coordinates held within the data file associated with the patient image are revised with the new values when the 'shift' operation is concluded.

Patient images in which skin tattoo markers provide the only source of reference are verified immediately they are loaded. During the load procedure, verification of the previously identified tattoo marker position is facilitated by superimposing orthogonal line graphics over the image which intersect precisely at this location. If necessary, the user is able to interactively re-position the intersection point correctly on the tattoo marker. Upon confirmation,

the image is then automatically shifted so that the location of the treatment isocentre is positioned at the center of the display window.

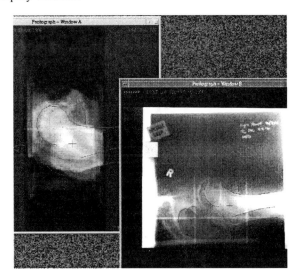

Illustration 1

Inter-comparisons performed between a DRR and Simulator Film reference image in order to derive a set of collective landmark features.

3. Placement Error Evaluation

Any individual landmark or landmark group can either be translated and/or rotated interactively using the mouse. The re-alignment speed of the landmark graphic over the corresponding feature in the none-reference patient image can be optimised by minimising the use of screen menus. As such, for the most common of placement operations, that of translation, the user simply performs a 'Click-n-Grab' operation on the landmark of interest. Moving a constituent landmark of a user defined group results in all members being moved.

When any landmark graphic is moved, the component distances are computed and displayed in the information summary window. Distances moved are also displayed in an abbreviated form at a location relative to the landmark graphic position within the pantograph window. Both forms of information presented are continually updated as the graphic is moved.

Assistance is provided in the form of an additional display window appearing above the landmark graphic being moved (screen space permitting) enabling the user to perform image feature/landmark graphic alignments with greater speed. Within this utility window, which is horizontally partitioned, the respective regions of interest containing the corresponding patient image background and landmark graphics are displayed, illustration 2.

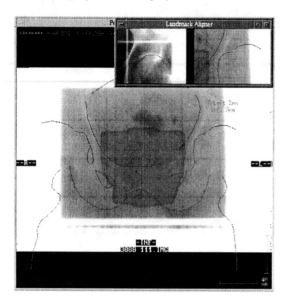

Illustration 2

The Alignment Window presents the user with a region of interest display of both the reference and set-up images within the same field of view.

The alignment window places both regions of interest (containing the appropriate landmark pair - one from each pantograph window) within the same field of view. As the landmark is moved, the corresponding viewing port of the alignment window is updated. The illusion of movement is created by laterally shifting the patient image beneath the landmark graphic which effectively remains stationary within the view port window. This window appears above the landmark graphic being moved only if there is enough vertical screen space available (after a specified margin has been introduced so that the window does not obscure the user's view of that graphic). If there is not enough screen space available, then this type of alignment window is not created.

There are two types of rotation that can be applied to the patient image landmark feature/graphic combination. One involves rotation of the patient image beneath the graphic and the alternative involves rotating the landmark profile in isolation. Re-orientating the patient image about the isocentre is equivalent to rotating the treatment head within which the MLC equipment is housed. Rotation of the landmark graphic is, by default, performed about the treatment isocentre. Although the user may re-position the centre of rotation, no combinations of rotations about different centres are permitted. This over-complicates the field placement issue by introducing too many variables.

Rotations of the landmark graphic or patient image can be interactively previewed. This utility allows the user to observe the relative angular displacement between patient image feature/landmark graphic combination by mouse action alone, without formally invoking the request. This prevents the unnecessary repeat-application of rotation transforms from introducing perturbations as a result of rounding errors. Rotations are invoked by positioning the mouse cursor away from the landmark graphic, but still within the pantograph window, and performing a 'Click-n-Drag' operation. All rotation angles are rounded to the nearest half-degree and the value is displayed at the position previously occupied by the rotation centre icon.

Landmark graphic rotations can be performed about a centre of rotation that can be interactively re-positioned by the user. By default, the rotation centre is coincident with the treatment isocentre for every landmark graphic drawn. A non-zero degree rotation applied to a landmark will automatically inhibit any further movements of the rotation centre. Only when the landmark graphic has a zero degree rotation with respect to the corresponding reference graphic in the opposite pantograph window, can the rotation centre be re-positioned. When rotation mode operations are being performed, the landmark graphic can also be translated. Whilst in this mode of operation, all translation distances are communicated to the user in the format standard previously described.

3.1 Recording Field Placement Errors

When a landmark graphic has been suitably positioned so that it agrees closely with the corresponding feature in the patient image, the user can then establish a transform in addition to recording the field placement error, illustration 3. Fixing a transform establishes a mathematical link between the image features in both pantograph windows. When fixed, the mathematical transform is applied to all subsequent landmarks during the autonomous transfer of coordinates between patient images. The fixed intra-image transform establishes an instant link between both patient images so that corresponding features can be related. Transforms, like the landmark graphics drawn, can only be registered for those images having the same patient identity code and a consistent view perspective.

Establishing a mathematical transform link between a combination of images, which constitute a patient set-up, will invoke an administrative request for patient specific treatment details, illustration 4. The details requested, cover all aspects which are both universal and specific to the patient's treatment. First presented/requested are treatment details which catalogue/record the prescribing clinician's initials, the energy, dose and number of fractions together with any appropriate comments.

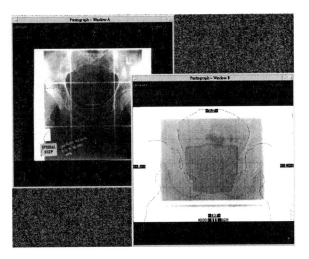

Illustration 3

Pre-treatment set-up using the collective landmark features available to all reference images re-aligned within the MVI image.

Treatment details are followed by a request for fraction specific details which are specific to the pre-treatment set-up. The user is presented with a brief summary of the field placement error for the view orientation and an entry request is made for the 'source-to-skin distances' for all field angles. Finally an administrative request is made for the initials of the radiographer performing the set-up and the treatment machine id. The fraction number, treatment date and patient/image details are automatically recorded.

No treatment details can be recorded unless a password is entered by the user. This restricts access and prevents the user from accidentally over-writing previously stored

data. When pre-treatment set-up data has been recorded, the patient images and landmark graphics used are 'write-locked' so that future amendments will be inhibited. If the landmark graphics used have not been previously stored, the software will automatically first store them and then 'write-lock' the data. When a patient's treatment has finished, the user can 'write-protect' the field placement data to prevent its accidental erasure, by password entry. This ensures data preservation and does not prohibit the user from future access for post-treatment analysis.

Illustration 4

Patient set-up information is requested in the formats shown. This information is stored with the prescription data in the patient database.

3.2 Field Placement Analysis

For any patient image inter-comparisons, the user can interactively perform on-screen ruler measurements using the 'power icon' utility, where necessary. Measurements of landmark features and anatomical distances from those reference points can be simply performed by a 'Click-n-Grab' mouse operation. By positioning the mouse cursor near the image feature and without moving any landmark graphics in the vicinity, a 'Click-n-Grab' mouse operation will invoke the ruler utility. It appears as a flexible line graphic whose 'start point' is coincident with the location at which the initial 'Click' operation occurred and has a magnitude/direction which is directly controlled by the mouse.

As the ruler is flexibly adjusted to register the distance being measured, the length of the graphic is evaluated in millimetres using the pixel-scale, and displayed vertically above the center. For those instances when the accidental movement of a landmark graphic or isocentre re-location could occur, the user can invoke the 'FRZ' power icon. This icon 'halts' the functionality of the inter-comparison software and all possible actions which are likely to occur during this type of measurement.

4. Discussion

Many of the extensive design features incorporated in this verification software utility have been developed under close consultation with treatment radiographers. This package is at present being used within a national MRC clinical trial (RT01 - organised by the Royal Marsden Hospital, London) in order to record the field placement errors that are observed daily at pre-treatment. All imaging modalities currently available to the hospital are used in order to define those collective landmark features that will be outlined on a representative reference image in order to verify radiation field placement using anterior and lateral pre-treatment portal images. Multi-leaf collimator graphics are superimposed in order to permit the verification of radiation field edge patterns and correctly locate the treatment isocentre. Speed and operator 'ease-of-use' are priority features that have influenced the design, with many of the common functions being initiated without the use of menus or complex mouse actions. When pre-treatment information has been recorded for a patient over a course of treatment, the user has the facility to reflectively examine the data and movie through the Mega-voltage images captured at each fraction. The data recorded by this utility can also be accessed in order to assess the robustness of a treatment plan given the field placement error recorded for a particular fraction. Using biological modelling, the consequences of a simulated treatment plan that incorporated the field placement error recorded can be invoked in order to compute the effects on the quality of treatment if the patient pre-treatment set-up remained unaltered.

5. References

[1] Hanks G E, "External Beam Radiation Treatment for Prostate Cancer: Still the Gold Standard", Oncology, Vol. 6, pp79-89, 1992.

[2] Ketting C H, Austin-Seymour M, Kalet I, Unger J, Hummel S and Jacky J, "Consistency of Three-dimensional Planning Target Volumes Across Physicians and Institutions", Int. J. Radiation Oncology Biol. Phys., Vol. 37, No. 2, pp445-453, 1997.

[3] Withers H, Taylor J and Maciejewski B, "Treatment Volume and Tissue Tolerance", Int. J. Radiation Oncology Biol. Phys., Vol. 14, pp751-759, 1988.

[4] Verhey L, Goitein M, McNulty P, Munzenrider J and Suit H, "Precise Positioning of Patients for Radiation Therapy", Int. J. Radiation Oncology Biol. Phys., Vol. 8, pp289-294, 1982.

[5] Grusell E, Montelius A, Russell K, Blomquist E, Pellettieri A, Mostrom U and Jakobsson P, "Patient Positioning for Fractionated Precision Radiation Treatment of Targets in the Head using Fiducial Markers", Radiotherapy and Oncology, Vol. 33, pp68-72, 1994.

[6] Gilhuijs K, Drukker K, Touw A, Van De Ven P and Van Herk M, "Interactive Three Dimensional Inspection of Patient Setup in Radiation Therapy using Digital Portal Images and Computed Tomography Data", Int. J. Radiation Oncology Biol. Phys., Vol. 34, No. 4, pp873-885, 1996.

[7] Killoran J, Kooy H, Gladstone D, Welte F and Beard C, "A Numerical Simulation of Organ Motion and Daily Setup Uncertainties: Implications for Radiation Therapy", Int. J. Radiation Oncology Biol. Phys., Vol. 37, No. 1, pp213-221, 1997.

[8] Van Herk M, Bruce A, Guus Kroes A, Shouman T, Touw A and Lebesque I, "Quantification of Organ Motion During Conformal Radiotherapy of the Prostate by Three Dimensional Image Registration", Int. J. Radiation Oncology Biol. Phys., Vol. 33, No. 5, pp1311-1320, 1995.

[9] Mageras G, Kutcher G, Leibel S, Zelefsky M, Melian E, Mohan R and Fuks Z, "A method of Incorporating Organ Motion Uncertainties into Three-Dimensional Conformal Treatment Plans", Int. J. Radiation Oncology Biol. Phys., Vol. 35, No. 2, pp333-342, 1996.

[10] Bieri S, Miralbell R, Nouet P, Delorme H and Rouzaud M, "Reproducibility of Conformal Radiation Therapy in Localised Carcinoma of the Prostate without Rigid Immobilisation", Radiotherapy and Oncology, Vol. 38, pp223-230, 1996.

6. Acknowledgements

This work has been funded by the EC Framework IV BIOMED 2 programme, project INFOCUS, contract number BMH4-CT95-0567. Special recognition is given to resident radiographers: Beverly Thompson and Julia Stratford at Christie Hospital for their assistance in the design of this software utility.

Visualization in Construction

Chair
Farzad Khosrowshahi
South Bank University, UK

Visualization and Information: A Building Design Perspective

Jennifer Whyte, Dino Bouchlaghem, Tony Thorpe
Department of Civil and Building Engineering
Loughborough University, UK
J.K.Whyte@lboro.ac.uk

Abstract

Virtual reality (VR) packages offer good visualization capabilities but inadequate facilities for either internal data management or data exchange with other packages. The potential usefulness of VR packages for industrial and business applications is limited by their lack of support for the manipulation of specialist information. Their generic nature cannot retain the complex semantics and syntax of industrial information. Within the iterative process of building design and visualization, support is required for construction industry data, which is ordered in a complex and domain specific manner. Improved transfer of data from specialist building design tools to virtual reality has been investigated in previous research, but in this paper it is argued that data transfer is not enough. Virtual reality techniques need to become available within the specialist buildings design tools and alter the interface to such applications.

1. Introduction

In design applications visualization is not an end in itself. The process of design and visualization should be iterative, with changes made as a result of insights gained through visualization propagated into the next version of the design. The iterative nature of this process requires adequate software support and thought processes should not be interrupted by a requirement to translate the design concepts into software terms for visualization [1].

The design of the urban environment involves many interested parties. These parties, who start with different understandings, include professionals such as engineers, architects, and planners and non-specialists such as clients and local residents. Collaborative building design requires a shared understanding to be reached between all of the interested parties.

Virtual reality packages offer good visualization capabilities that can facilitate shared understanding across interdisciplinary groups. However they have inadequate facilities for both internal information management and data exchange with other packages [2]. The potential usefulness of VR packages for industrial and business applications is limited by their incapacity to support manipulation of specialist information. Within building design tools, construction industry data is ordered in a complex and domain specific manner. Support is required for this information in VR, but the generic nature of VR packages cannot retain the complex semantics and syntax of such industrial information. The utility of VR for consensus building between different parties within the iterative process of building design and visualization cannot be realised without adequate information management.

In this paper the particular benefits of virtual reality in terms of building visualization and the challenges of information management for building design are considered. The generic nature of virtual reality packages is contrasted with the highly specialised nature of building design packages.

2. Visualization Capabilities

2.1 How is Virtual Reality Different?

Virtual reality models are interactive 3D models that can be experienced in real-time[1]. The term virtual reality is similar to, and sometimes used synonymously with visual simulation, digital mock-up, virtual prototyping, walk/flythrough, and 4D CAD.

The work undertaken by the authors of this paper concerns the use of PC-based virtual reality models by building designers. High-end immersive virtual reality systems with high visual fidelity and hardware peripherals for haptic and audio feedback are not considered necessary for virtual reality as defined above. Rather it is

---

[1] Optimal real-time interaction is not always attainable. Optimal interaction requires a frame rate of 60 frames a second combined with a system latency, in responding to user's actions, of 50 milliseconds. A minimum requirement for interaction is described as 10 frames per second with a latency, or control lag, of 0.1 seconds [3].

Fig. 1. A VR model offers dynamic interaction.

the interactive and real-time (or near real-time) nature of virtual reality models that makes them of particular interest and distinguishes their use from that of other visualization techniques.

Other visualization techniques, such as rendered images and animations of architectural models can be produced from within computer aided design (CAD) and modelling packages but do not provide real-time interaction. These images and animations show the context, materials and shadows of the proposed building and can be aesthetically so convincing as to be termed photo-realistic. They have the advantage that they are easily understood by both different kinds of building professionals and non-professionals. Produced using techniques like ray tracing, radiosity, parametric animation, and panoramas, they can take a long time to render and are static or predefined.

Like the images and animations described above, virtual reality offers the advantage of easy comprehension by both different kinds of building professionals and by non-professionals. The level of visual realism in desktop VR models is not as high as that attainable in static images or predefined animations and panoramas, as techniques such as radiosity rendering are too computationally intensive to be undertaken in real-time. VR is different from other visualization techniques in that it offers the capacity to dynamically interact with a realistic model of a building in a manner that is not predetermined. The dynamic nature of VR models allows the comprehension of spatial aspects of the proposed building development that are important in the understanding of architectural intent. Realism may be more than graphical and real world behaviours may be simulated leading to applications of VR for the detection of collisions, and the simulation of climatic conditions.

The authors see VR models as particularly valuable for collaborative discussion of design. For this function it has been found that when models are too highly realistically detailed they intimidate users from changing them or lead to the impression that all decisions have been

made and therefore the only choices are the complete rejection or acceptance of the modelled proposal [4]. VR is particularly useful for interdisciplinary collaboration as it provides both a degree of realism that allows easy comprehension and the possibility of interaction.

3. Information Management

3.1 Within Building Design Tools

The most common computer-aided design (CAD) tools used in the construction industry today have little in-built intelligence, and deal with graphical/mathematical entities such as two-dimensional lines. Their interface has been severely criticised as clumsy and un-user friendly [1] requiring the user to translate the architectural concepts into software terms.

Latest versions of popular CAD packages offer a degree of abstraction from software concepts to higher-level architectural entities. There are special customised libraries of routines available as add-ons to the basic packages to allow the automation of common activities and increase the productivity of AEC (architecture, engineering and construction) specialists such as the housing designer designing timber frame buildings or the civil engineer involved in road layout. Such CAD packages contain large libraries of parametric building parts, such as doors, windows, and structural components, which are used to organise building assembly and material information. These library components contain 2D and 3D representations of the building part that can be substituted in the different viewpoints. Thus the user can design in 2D using the library of components, and automatically generate a 3D model, or design in 3D, and extract plans, and sections.

The graphical user interface (GUI) in the latest versions of CAD packages has also been refined and real-time pan and zoom facilities have been added to aid navigation around the drawing. These dynamic navigation tools enhance the user's ability to interact with the software. Visualisation techniques such as fast ray tracing, reflection, refraction, transparency, translucency, radiosity, photomatching and shadow effects can be used to produce more realistic images either in the package or in modelling packages that import their native format.

It has been predicted that advanced building design tools will become semantically richer [5]. It is possible that such tools will be based on Industry Foundation Classes (IFCs). These are a common set of intelligent building design objects that have been developed by an industry driven standardisation initiative concentrating on building construction, the International Alliance for

Interoperability (IAI). These IFCs use inheritance as a means of reusing and elaborating data and methods within the different classes. The intelligent building design objects represent architectural components and encapsulate information about their attributes and the methods needed for their manipulation. However for such objects to be used in VR, they must also encapsulate information about their behaviours, for example a representation of a door must contain information, not just of what material it is made of and what it is fixed to but also of how it opens.

3.2 Within VR tools

VR has been developed out of advanced simulations and computer graphics techniques and even the more high-level user-friendly packages, which do not require extensive programming, use concepts that are unfamiliar to the building designer. The visualization is not static, but is dynamic and for large data sets generating dynamic images requires considerable computational effort. With limited computer power, there is a trade off between the amount of information processed and the speed of navigation. Many features of information management within VR packages are concerned with optimising the model to achieve real-time navigation. This is achieved by reducing the information to be processed and hence the computational effort required during each simulation loop. Model optimisation is not satisfactorily dealt with entirely automatically by the software and, instead of leaving the user to concentrate on their domain-specific task, requires of the user some consideration of computing techniques. Thus instead of dealing with purely architectural entities, the building designer using a VR package finds themself dealing with lower-level concepts such as polygons, nodes, bounding boxes, and scene-graphs.

In a VR model, information is typically organised hierarchically in an acyclic scene graph. The scene graph is structured in a tree-like manner, with nodes attached together from top to bottom and the root node representing the top point, as shown in **Figure 1**. Nodes may include content such as geometries or lights. Nodes inherit the translations and orientations of their parent nodes and pass on their own translation and orientation to their children nodes. The scene graph traversal order is important, as this is the order in which the scene is rendered. In VR packages such as WTK this is in a top to bottom, left to right order [6]. Thus in Figure 1, the light node will affect the geometry node 3, but not the nodes 1 and 2.

The scene graph is used to facilitate spatial culling. The part of the model being viewed is determined and geometry and effects are selectively loaded and rendered, with unseen geometry and effects being culled to increase performance.

Geometric simplification is also used to reduce computational effort through the use of levels of detail (LODs) and the use of texture mapped predefined or primitive solids.

- Special switching nodes provide distant dependant levels of detail (LODs), replacing complex geometry with simpler geometry at a sufficient distance from the viewpoint for the eye not to perceive the loss of detail. This substitution of simpler geometry frees up memory and system resources.

- Simple predefined objects, such as spheres, cubes and cylinders, can be used together with texture maps to simplify the amount of geometric data in a model. Predefined geometries more efficient than custom geometries. For example in the Virtual Reality Modelling Language (VRML) a model built out of primitive shapes will run significantly faster than one built using the customised indexed face set command.

Virtual reality technologies are developing and becoming out-dated fast. The non-proprietary VR format VRML was made an international standard for 3D (VRML'97 - ISO/IEC DIS 14772-1) and formed a basic generic VR functionality. However browsers for this format are no longer supported and have become open-source. At present both VRML and the proprietary PC-based VR systems are based on Open GL or Direct 3D Application Programming Interfaces (APIs), however technologies such as Java 3D and Fahrenheit might become increasingly important.

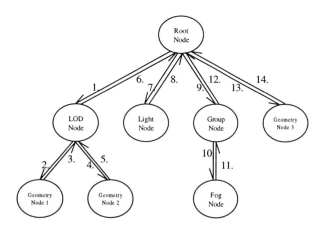

Fig. 2. An Acyclic Scene Graph, showing the scene graph traversal order.

3.3 Data Transfer

Data transfer between CAD and VR is neither easy nor reliable [7][8]. The transfer of data has normally been unidirectional or "downstream" [2]. Data can be passed from CAD to VR but the retrieval of data from the visualization has not been successfully implemented. Significant operator intervention and interpretation of the available data can also be involved in the creation of a suitable VR model from CAD data.

Many CAD and 3D modeling packages now export to VRML and/or have native formats that can be imported directly by VR packages. However commercial or in-built translators often produce large or inaccurate VR models due to the problems of translating the syntactic and semantic structure of CAD data into VR. Specific problems are encountered with 1) the use of optimised geometries and instances, 2) the different scales and alignments used in CAD and VR, and 3) the determination of the orientation of polygons, or faces within the VR world.

1) Commercial and in-built translators often do not create data optimised for the VR world, and the resultant simulations run unacceptably slowly. Primative shapes are not used, for example the conversion of simple shape such as a cube from 3D Studio into VRML creates a form based on VRML's indexed face sets, which requires more computational effort than the in-built primitive shape. Instances are not recognised, so instead of the geometry for one window being created and duplicated fifty times on a uniform facade, the geometry is created fifty times, greatly increasing the file size.

2) CAD packages use a world base co-ordinate system – with X and Y describing the ground plane and Z describing the height, but VR uses a differently oriented co-ordinate system with X and Y describing a vertical plane and Z describing depth as shown in **Figure 3**. Translators between CAD and VR packages use a transformation matrix to correctly orientate the resultant geometry, but these are not reliable. VR models imported into the same scene from different sources often have to be scaled, for example the CAD data relating to buildings may have been based on a unit of 1mm, whilst the terrain data may assume a unit size of 1m.

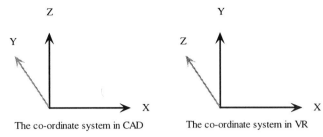

The co-ordinate system in CAD   The co-ordinate system in VR

Fig 3. Different Co-ordinate systems in CAD and VR

3) The orientation of polygons is important in VR for back face rejection. The front side of the polygon is that for which the vertices are ordered counter-clockwise. In CAD there is no necessity to create the vertices of shapes in a particular order. Hence when CAD files are translated into VR, the orientation of the polygons is random, and unordered. The degree of accuracy in VR is also not as great as in CAD (Bourdakis, 1997) and hence two faces that are within 0.6mm may be taken to be co-existing in the same space when the model is translated into VR. These problems lead to difficulty with the rendering.

Manually solving these problems or 'tweaking' VR models leads to a decline in productivity. Better data transfer from CAD to VR was advocated in previous work by the authors, and three methods of facilitating the rapid creation of virtual environments through managed data transfer have been identified for use in different circumstances [2]. These methods are the creation of a library of parts, simple translation and the use of a central database.

4. Generic VR tools

At present most virtual reality packages are generic tools for the visualization of data within many different application areas, from the interactive games and entertainment market, to data visualization and industrial applications in the engineering disciplines. This generic nature of the VR tools leads to difficulties within highly specialised application areas such as construction.

5. Research at Loughborough University

As part of ongoing research at Loughborough University, VR models of housing developments have been created in the commercially available generic VR packages, **Figures 1 & 4**, using different VR technologies

Fig 4. VR Model assembled in a Generic VR Tool, using CAD housetype data, and site layout data

and modelling techniques [9]. These VR models have been demonstrated to construction professionals involved in housebuilding and feedback has been gained concerning the potential use of such models.

From this work, the importance of improving visualisation without dramatically reducing productivity has been noted. The professionals interviewed were concerned about the time consuming nature of the modelling process.

The unfamiliar nature of the graphical user interface of the VR package, the lack of internal support for construction data, and the lack of sophisticated tools for model creation and modification have been identified as problems.

1) The interfaces to VR tools are unfamiliar to the building designer and are not customised to automate tasks that are frequently carried out by them. This leads to a reduction in user productivity, as the building designer spends time learning to interact with the software through an unfamiliar interface and dealing with unfamiliar software concepts.

2) There is a lack of internal support for the complex and domain specific manner in which construction industry data is ordered. There is no internal support for architectural entities and their attributes within the VR package. Construction data in the VR package is represented by geometries and can be interacted with only in terms of these geometries and their faces, rather than as intelligent architectural components. As discussed in the previous section, this translation of data from CAD leads to the re-entering, translating and re-ordering of construction industry data to suite the VR package and this is a non- value added activity for a company, reducing user productivity and limiting the commercial potential of VR.

3) The tools provided for model creation and modification in VR packages are not as sophisticated as those provided in CAD packages as the production of construction and architectural models has not been the main objective of the programmers who have developed VR packages. At present building designers tend to design in CAD packages and then translate the file into . VR for visualisation. Changes made in the VR model cannot be unproblematically propagated back into the CAD model.

Generic virtual reality packages do not allow the integration of modelling and visualization nor do they have the domain specific functionality that the industry or business user requires.

6. Construction Industry Requirements

They require VR tools that can provide the benefits of advanced visualisation, without reducing productivity. Features identified during this research, which are required of VR tools for building design and visualization, are:

1) A familiar interface – at present specialist skills are required for operating VR software, building professionals would like to interact with VR models that use construction industry conventions and the familiar metaphors (eg. drag and drop) used by common windows software.

2) Internal support for construction industry data – building professionals would like to move and place architectural components rather than deal with polygons, geometries, nodes etc.

3) Sophisticated tools for model creation and modification - housebuilders are constantly modifying designs. They would like to be able to change design interactively in the VR environment.

At present VR packages do not have the sophisticated tools for the selection and creation of architectural entities that exist in CAD, and the process of designing in VR is clumsy and time consuming

7. Lessons from other industries

Within process and manufacturing engineering the need for specialist VR tools has been recognised [10]. In these application areas vendors are beginning to provide virtual reality packages containing sophisticated in-built domain-specific design and information management functions, or forming alliances with specialist CAD providers. Products have been developed that use a central database to provide the range of functionality that is normally found in seperate CAD and VR packages. The integration of CAD and VR functionality into one design tool seems likely to continue as the VR company, Division, has been sold to Parametric Technology Corporation, makers of Pro/Engineer; a CAD package specialised in the manufacturing industry [11].

By combining the information management capabilities of CAD packages with the visualization capabilities of VR, the next generation of building design tool could be born. Virtual reality techniques can be used to provide another view on the architectural model from within the CAD package.

8. Conclusions

The requirements of construction industry users of VR cannot be accommodated in generic VR packages. At present the construction industry information and information management facilities are in one package whilst the visualization techniques are only available in another package. Translation between the two packages is unsatisfactory and changes made as a result of the visualization in VR cannot be easily propagated back into the design data held in CAD.

Support is needed for the complex semantics and syntax of specialised construction industry information during the visualization phase, as interdisciplinary groups using VR for collaborative design need to interact with architectural components rather than geometries and faces.

For use in the iterative process of design and construction, virtual reality techniques need to become available within the specialist building design tools and alter the interface to such applications. This has already begun to happen in the process and manufacturing industries.

9. Further Work

Work is currently focussed on the use of desktop VR within the housebuilding industry. The industrial potential of VR within this sector and the type of VR representation that best facilitates collaborative design are being investigated.

10. References

[1] S. Johnson, "What's in a representation, why do we care, and what does it mean? Examining evidence from psychology", *Automation in Construction*, Vol. 8 No 1, 1998, pp 15 – 24.

[2] J. Whyte, N. Bouchlaghem and A. Thorpe, "The Promise and Problems of Implementing Virtual Reality in Construction Practice", *Proceedings of CIB W78, The life-cycle of Construction IT innovations: technology transfer from research to practice* Stockholm, 3-5 June 1998.

[3] L.J. Rosenblum, and R.A. Cross, "The Challenge of Virtual Reality", in ed. Earnshaw, R., Vince, J., Jones, Huw. *Visualization & Modeling*, Academic Press, 1997.

[4] J. Counsell, B. Phillips, "The Tower of London Computer Models", *Proceedings of the IEEE International Conference on Information Visualisation (IV'97)*, London, England, 27-29 August 1997.

[5] C. Eastmann, "Future Development of Applications in Architecture and Construction", *ISFAA-97 - Information Sources for AEC Applications.* Available at http://sage.alphawest.net.au/~ausstep/aec-libraries/w1-reference/eastman.html, 1997.

[6] WorldToolKit Reference Manual, Release 8, Sense 8,California, 1998.

[7] V. Bourdakis, "The Future of VRML on Large Urban Models", *Proceedings of VR-SIG'97*, Brunel, 1 November 1997, pp 55-61.

[8] M. Alshawi, "Integrating CAD and Virtual Reality in Construction", *Conference on VR and Rapid Prototyping in Engineering*, EPSRC, Salford, 1995.

[9] J. Whyte, N. Bouchlaghem, and A. Thorpe, "Visualising Residential Development using Desktop Virtual Reality", *Proceedings of the IEEE International Conference on Information Visualisation (IV'98)* London, 29-31 July 1998.

[10] D. Fanguy, Oral presentation at the UKVRForum meeting, Cambridge, 8 March 1999.

[11] Parametric Technology Corp. "Parametric Technology Corp. Completes Acquisition of Division Group plc" http://www.ptc.com/   (Division -http://www.division.co.uk)

Visualisation of Unbuilt Buildings in their Landscape

Rob Howard and Ernst Petersen,
Graphic Communications, Technical University of Denmark
rh@gk.dtu.dk

Abstract

Computer modelling can provide better information on building projects presented in two dimensional drawings but never built. A cemetery project in Denmark was formed as a solid model in its sloping landscape using Softimage. Boolean operations were used to position walls at a given height above the terrain. More accurate still and video images were made and compared with original sketches.

1. Introduction

There are many unbuilt designs by famous architects which were presented too inadequately to be fully understood. We now have visualisation techniques which can use the published data on these designs to explain such buildings more fully with multiple 3D views and animation.

One such project was submitted by the Finnish architect, Alvar Aalto, to a competition in Denmark in 1951. It was unsuccessful but the Graphic Communications group at the Technical University of Denmark has now modelled the design and discovered that one of the drawings was rather imaginitive. Nowadays more precise information is expected and it is possible to submit computer models, which competition juries can explore to obtain more complete and accurate information.

The computer techniques employed by DTU are well established ones but involved modelling a building, positioning it on an accurate site model with landscape features to show the design. SoftImage was used on a Silicon Graphics Indigo 2 and, both still and animated views of the building in its landscape, were produced.

2. The Lyngby cemetery

The Kommune of Lyngby Taarbaek in Denmark ran a competition for the design of a cemetery chapel and its surrounding graveyard in 1951. One of the entrants was the famous Finnish architect, Alvar Aalto, working with local architect, J J Baruel. He was awarded second prize for the chapel but was not in the first three for the landscape. The winning design, by Henrik Iversen and Harald Plum, was built and now occupies the more level area on the south side of the site.

On the north side of the site are two shallow valleys which form an attractive landscape in the relatively flat Danish countryside. The choice of the winning design may have been influenced by a wish to keep these valleys in their natural state, as grassland with wild flowers.

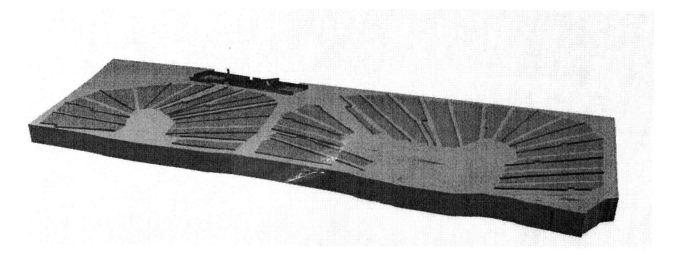

Figure 1. View of chapel and graveyard from above

110

Aalto's design opted to use the tops of the valleys for placing the graves in wedge-shaped areas defined by walls running down into the valleys, and to provide channels for the supply of water for flowers left at the graves.

The chapel building he placed at the top of one of the valleys. A sketch of his proposal for the graveyard seen from below shows a romantic view of steeply sloping hills with planting leading up to the graveyard area and the chapel.[1] Figure 2.

Figure 2. Sketch by Alvar Aalto of his design for Lyngby cemetery

Figure 3. View of model from the same direction showing actual slopes

Did he ever visit the site? The steepness of the slope indicated in his sketch is more reminiscent of an Italian hill town than the unspectacular Danish landscape. It shows the graves, typically placed between hedges, sheltered by walls with extensive planting. We can now model the

buildings from his drawings and the site from surveys, and provide more topologically accurate images of how his design would have appeared, but without the planting. Figures 1, 3, 4.

3. The techniques used

Ernst Petersen has worked on integrating video with models of unbuilt objects looking particularly at how to compensate pictures taken from a car for the movement of the camera. He modelled the Aalto design mainly using the program SoftImage installed on a Silicon Graphics Indy workstation. The process of modelling was divided into three elements: the ground, the graveyard walls and the chapel building. At the end the models were put together, placing the walls and the building at the locations shown in the Aalto drawings. The background materials for the model were copies of drawings and a video, made by DTU, of the original wooden model kept at the Department of Building in the town hall of Lyngby-Taarbaek.

Placed on the hard disk the bitmap file was converted in a two-stage operation into a vector file and then into splines in the three-dimensional space in SoftImage. Within this space the contours were combined into pairs and made into solids. Each solid's top face represents a one metre step and shows the surface of the ground. Together these surfaces show the entire terrain.

A series of selected still views was obtained from the video of the wooden model for comparison with the digital model during the process of virtual building. The first phase, the ground, consisted of several steps. First reproduction of the contours of the site through manual drawing, then scanning this drawing into the computer.

The positions of the graveyard walls were found by means of tracing contours. The map showing the entire site with contours, building and walls was scanned into the computer. The bitmap image generated was redrawn to show only the boundaries of the site and the profiles of the walls. These profiles and boundaries were converted into splines by the 3D program using an autotrace function. Once traced, the splines were put beneath the ground model in wireframe mode and scaled to fit the model. Walls were placed at each profile and scaled to their individual lengths. There was little published information about the walls but their height was set at two meters above ground level, stepping down half a metre at each one metre contour and between each pair of contours using Boolean operations to fix the heights above the ground.

Figure 4. View of chapel across a valley showing walls dividing graveyard area

The building plan was similarly scanned and the wall structure copied by digital drawing. This copy was edge traced and converted into splines in the 3D-program. The spline structure served as the outline on which the walls were placed. The walls were made out of solids scaled to fit the length and width of the outline beneath. There was no indication of heights from the scanned drawings, so a baseline had to be found. The overall length of the building was known to be 155 meters from dimensions on the drawing. A base line of the building's total length was divided by 155 and a one metre base line found. With this tool the building heights taken from the drawings were transferred to the model. The vertical location of the model was fixed by adjusting the relative heights of the model so that marks on the walls, measured to be where the walls meet the ground, intersected with the contours.

The areas of the graves, normally separated by low hedges in Denmark, were indicated in a darker colour, and these too give an indication of the site surface which, in gently sloping areas, can be difficult to represent in computer models. The contrast between the model view, Figure 3, and the original competition sketch, Figure 2, even allowing for the simpler presentation in the model, is quite significant. The animated views, which are accessible on the DTU web site, [4], showing what would be seen when walking up from the valleys, through the graveyard, towards the chapel, provide even more information about what the experience of moving through this design might have been like.

4. Computer models allow better understanding of design

If Aalto had had the computer tools available today, he could have made a more accurate submission and we might now have a landmark building on the site. There are other such models being produced to reconstruct historic buildings or archaeological work as well as the unbuilt designs of modern architects. Students of architecture at MIT have also modelled famous buildings including photo realistic images of Aalto's competition entry for a church centre in Zurich Alstetten, Switzerland, by Andrzej Zarzycki   http://www.gis.net/~zarzycki/aalto.html   [2] Virtual libraries of both built and unbuilt buildings are being created and can be viewed over the Internet. Figure 5

Figure 5. Photorealistic view of interior of Aalto church in Zurich by Andrzej Zarzycki

Architects have been known to distort views of their buildings or, at least, to present only the most favourable views. If computer models are submitted in future, then competition juries, local planning authorities and the public, would have the ability to view them from any position and gain a fuller understanding of the design.

Many of the most sensitive buildings are in an urban context where relationships to existing buildings are important. For example the competition for Paternoster square next to St Paul's cathedral in London involved each of the shortlisted entrants in setting up computer models of the surrounding area. Municipalities could supply such models as the context within which a design proposal is to be presented. This would require a standard co-ordinate system and a defined relationship to the mapping grid. Such a standard, which may emerge from Geographical Information Systems work, would allow models of parts of a city to be combined into a model of the whole city, to be maintained by the municipality.

At present such models in the UK have been produced by universities using student labour for such cities as Bath [3] Figure 6, Glasgow and Edinburgh, but each uses a different approach.

Figure 6. Bath model - Centre for Advanced Studies in Architecture, Bath University

5. Conclusions

In the case of Aalto's design for Lyngby cemetery, there was an abcence of contextual information and what might have become a landmark building was never built, although the cemetery that exists is also good. Nowadays landmark buildings have enormous value to cities. You have only to look at Sydney Opera House, designed by a Danish architect and engineer, and now a symbol for the whole of Australia. More recently Frank Gehry's Guggenheim Museum at Bilbao has boosted the reputation of that city enormously.

With such dramatic forms and famous architects there is bound to be controversy, and good presentation of design using computer models, visualisation and video montage will inform such discussions. Very often the complex forms which occur in landscape can only be presented in models. These can be shown as still images, animations or virtual reality and can promote the place where the buildings are located. But who, outside Denmark, has heard of Lyngby?

Acknowledgements

The authors would like to thank Lyngby Taarbaek Kommune for copies of competition drawings and access to the model of the Lyngby cemetery chapel, and the Alvar Aalto Foundation in Helsinki for copies of sketch drawings.

References

[1] Fleig, Karl. (1996) *Alvar Aalto works and projects.* Editorial Gustavo Gili, Barcelona

[2] Zarzycki, Andrzej. *Zurich church model. Web site* http://www.gis.net/~zarzycki/aalto.html

[3] Centre for Advanced Architectural Studies, University of Bath. *Web site* www.bath.ac.uk/Centres/CASA/

[4] Technical University of Denmark, Department of Planning, *Web site for Itbyg* www.ifp/~it/itforsk/

A Role for VRML as a Multimedia Backbone in Interpreting Cultural Heritage Sites.

John Counsell, Nada Brkljac
Faculty of the Built Environment
University of the West of England, Bristol. Frenchay Campus,
Coldharbour Lane, Bristol, BS16 1QY, U.K.

Abstract

This paper appraises the role of Virtual reality modelling language (VRML) based 3D computer based models of Historic Environments in increasing access for and assisting the understanding of the general public. It is argued that VRML based 3D models and linked media create a low cost easy to use and intuitively accessible interface through which transient or casual users can retrieve information or experience narrative. The same data collation and modelling process can also assist conservation professionals in their tasks. Criteria are discussed for determining when it is more appropriate to model rather than use photographic techniques in the light of the commonly expressed fear in conservation circles that vicarious presentations may dominate genuine historical experience. Developments are identified which may assist in improving ease of use and understanding by visitors on and off-site.

1: Introduction

Interpretation of heritage sites is seen as a specialised form of education. Interpretation is revelation based upon information, 'not what you can do with history but what history does to you'. [Barzun J]. The dimensions of discovery are the ways by which we measure the world around us, testing one against another. 'Interpretation' is a process involved in every dimension, and it is arguable that it is not the *communication* process that we take it to be, but the activity of *opinion-making*.' [Machin A. 1986]. Heritage organisations perceive a need to entertain visitors but at the same time to convince them of the value of conservation of that heritage, to sustain the case for conservation in the minds of the public who directly or indirectly fund it. While originally cultural heritage sites were shrines, needing no interpretation for their educated or informed visitors, now that oral tradition has diminished and there is not a preponderance of informed fellow visitors, interpretation needs to be formalised. [Freeman Tilden 1957]

The question of when it is appropriate to model instead of or in addition to experiencing first hand is central to this paper. The Grand Canyon is cited in support of the argument that some sites do not require any visitor interpretation, (which does not however preclude the need for informed professional understanding), and that such interpretation is increasingly required the more foreign the view is to the visitors' experience. [HMSO 1975].

Fig 1-Tower Model in VRML with Associated WWW Page

There is a perceptible tension currently between the need to swiftly enlighten the diverse range of visitors to cultural heritage sites and an increasing risk of trivialisation. It is argued here that a digital spatial information system is an effective way of organising and accessing diverse data for which location is an important aspect. Where the spatial information relates to a complex three-dimensional structure a three-dimensional model however abstract is created within the information system. The group of potential users becomes increasingly wider the more immediately recognisable and credible the model appears. Transient or occasional users of such systems need an interface that is intuitive and easy to use through which to retrieve information or experience a narrative. It is argued that Multiple Media linked to VRML 3D models takes a further step towards this goal. *(figures 1 & 2)*

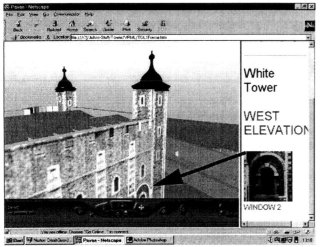

Fig 2 - Close Up of White Tower, Cupolas imported from CAD, WWW page invoked by touch sensor mapped onto Geometry using Pavan within Mapinfo GIS.

2: Interpretation

Finch distinguishes between primary and secondary levels of interpretation. Primary Interpretation is defined as that of the conservator or archaeologist, the professionals' view, in order to reconstruct either hypothetically (through drawings or models) or in 3D actuality. Secondary Interpretation is defined as for the edification or education of the public. [Finch JM. 1982]. Other professionals engaged with cultural heritage sites also deploy Primary Interpretation to assist in their understanding of the site. For example conservation maintenance management is made more difficult by the accelerated wear and tear exerted by the visitors who partially or wholly fund it. Visitor management is used and Visitor Centres are created to channel visitors away from fragile and easily damaged areas. Visitor centres can also convey a briefing or preparatory function. "Off-site interpretation may or may not succeed in arousing in its audience a wish to conserve an area but it will almost certainly arouse a desire to go and see it." [HMSO. 1975]. Sharpe for example further divides Secondary Interpretation into either edification or education. [Sharpe GW. 1976]. *Edification* can be termed 'sound-bytes' for capturing fleeting visitor interest, whereas *education* has been defined as conservation education in more depth. VRML Models may be particularly useful for off-site interpretation.

The Primary Interpretation identified above can be further sub-divided between personal experience and group activity. Personal experience involves examining and comparing source data in order to gain new insights. This is in many ways similar to the examination and comparison of information from a variety of sources which underpins the personal process of conceptual design in buildings. If the data is digital but in diverse formats and databases then a single unified interface will ease that process. A group that is engaged in the same process uses media in addition to support and record their common understanding. This need becomes greater the more asynchronous and less interactive the exchange becomes. One example of this form of activity is in the group project work undertaken in schools prior to and following a visit to the actual site. Many heritage sites now provide information and study packs for schools for this purpose. It is significant that Historic Royal Palaces for example have an education team and that at many National Trust and English Heritage sites there is a room set aside for on site project work with school parties with props for study and role play.

There is now an increasing demand for the case-study recording of the design and realisation process of building projects in general which is similar to the Educational aspect of Secondary Interpretation defined above. Such recording is of paramount importance in the field of conservation of historic buildings and environments to guide and inform future conservation. The material gained in this way can be interpreted to provide a detective story narrative.

Washburne and Wagner argued that 'visitors found messages organised into comprehensive stories or concepts tied together by central themes to be more interesting than unrelated facts and identification of objects.' [Washburne RP & Wagner JA. 1972]. Many heritage sites now use museum staff members in historic costumes to enact scenarios using genuine museum artefacts or props to interpret family lifestyle, community linkages and historic themes. Research indicates that visitors learn and retain significantly more from participating in this form of dramatic pageant. [Hayward NG & Larkin JW. 1983].

There is a fear in conservation circles that this causes the genuine historic evidence to become secondary to the theatrical experience. For the Society for the Preservation of Ancient Buildings (SPAB) their secretary wrote that 'The Society doesn't really get involved in questions of interpretation and presentation, so we don't have any formal policies other than indirectly (e.g. that later layers of history should not be destroyed merely to give access to earlier ones etc; or where plaster has been removed from a wall, revealing information about early masonry construction, this should be recorded but plaster should then be reapplied). Fairly obviously we don't approve of the "restoration" of historic buildings to some earlier form for educational purposes, and computers clearly have a role. If we have any philosophy at all I suppose it is that presentation should always be secondary to the historic fabric, and that may well mean that important things of interest will not be visible other than by photograph, video, model etc.' [Venning P. 1995]. In fact much of the interpretation of historic buildings and sites involves drawing attention to hidden or inaccessible features where modelling may greatly assist understanding.

3: Selection of Appropriate Media

Binks et al state that for non-specialist visitors the aim is to give them an overall picture, to explain what is happening, what is being revealed, and what its significance is. For repeat visitors it is necessary to also explain what has changed since the last visit. They add that the interpretation will need to be presented at a variety of depths. They suggest that themes and stories presented in a logical sequence relating to route from the human angle, which are participatory, which explain the detective story, effectively provide living history for the visitor. [Binks et al. 1988]. Other research has also shown that animated and interactive exhibits are more valuable than static presentations. 'Above-expected interest was shown in the dynamic, animated, or changing presentations represented by movies, changing lighting, and audio sequences.... all the sequences with less-than-expected interest involved flatwork, suggesting a greater preference for three-dimensional presentations'. [Washburne RP & Wagner JA 1972]. Sharpe uses this research to argue that an interpretative audience prefers those interpretative media which are most closely associated with entertainment, and that the dichotomy of education and entertainment parallels that of inertness and animation. He also records that participation increases retention and that multimedia is necessary to cater for a variety of levels of information. Visitors in fact are discouraged by reading while looking at objects and prefer an audio commentary. [Sharpe GW. 1976]. The HMSO guide adds that the medium chosen to communicate the message should avoid dominance of any other media used, gain visitor interest and establish rapport. They also endorse interactive participation as particularly important for younger children and advocate self-paced material that enables an appropriate pace for the casual visitor. They define the task as helping visitors to 'imagine accurately' while producing a conservationist response. They infer that the chosen approach should obtain feedback by testing the recall of the visitor and that a conservationist response is produced. [HMSO. 1975].

While firsthand experience of parts of heritage sites is possible for many visitors there are problems of access for the disabled and the elderly. Howell argues that if we consider people in our profile who have perceptual problems then an analogue within the CAD system can be used, with careful consideration, to present that part of the building which cannot otherwise be perceived. 'In any event much of the understanding of any interior or piece of environment has to be conveyed in words. I have to say that a description of a cathedral by, say, Willis or le Duc are often brilliant analogues. It is almost inevitable that words will have to accompany the visualisations and auralisations... the words... could be transcribed into signing alongside a picture or subtitles provided for the deaf or hard of hearing.' [Howell P. 1995]. Other parts of these sites are often temporarily or permanently closed to the public. While Finch states that the public are as interested in the process of restoration as in the restored artefact itself, it is precisely during the process of restoration that the site may be too vulnerable or too unsafe to allow general access. [Finch JM. 1982]. Equally some parts of sites may not normally be accessible at all to professionals either for similar reasons of health and safety. In addition when carrying out maintenance or repair it is necessary to consider the location of and the risk to below ground or otherwise concealed remains. Sites are large and those responsible for their care cannot at all times experience them at first-hand, nor can all those who wish to know more about them. The National Trust for example owns over 900 properties. They define their properties as fragile and beautiful and at the same time physically and historically complex. This is described as often making them hard for visitors to understand and rendering much of the information about them difficult to access. Archives and libraries are generally not available to the public because they are so fragile. They have sought various means using multimedia and visitor centres to both overcome these barriers to access and to convey a clear overview and sense of context to the visitor prior to entering a maze of rooms and corridors.

4: Tasks which may be supported by a model

It is necessary to distinguish between those conservation tasks that relate directly to preservation of the fabric and those that a model might equally well support. It is also necessary to determine when photographic images will serve and when only a model will perform the necessary tasks, (although arguably VRML can be used to integrate both 3D model and photograph in one environment).

Finch classifies seven cases of increasing intervention in heritage sites. [Finch JM, 1982]. Preservation is the first, which may only involve restraint rather than any direct action. The second, restoration, restores a previous condition. The third, conservation and consolidation, involves using new materials and tools, whereas the fourth, reconstitution, consists of partial re-building using traditional materials and skills. The fifth is adaptive re-use, such as placing a new roof on a ruin in order to use it in a way it was not used originally. In the five cases above the significant elements remain. Therefore photographs, digital images or 3D scans may serve for 'off-site' interpretation. A digital model would similarly serve as an adjunct in the same sense as a visitor centre acts in a preparatory or briefing role. It would however also enable concealed aspects to be demonstrated and act as one interface to the process of maintaining and accessing records relating to the site. Case six consists of reconstruction, of vanished buildings by creation of a surrogate in the original context. It is noteworthy that the 'first-rate' building is more likely to be preserved than the 'sixth-rate' buildings that may have formed its original setting.

The Museum of London Archaeological Service use 3D CAD to understand and extrapolate from the excavated portions of sites such as London's Roman Amphitheatre, to model their interpretation of the complete original structure, thereby recreating buildings or forms that no longer exist. [MOLAS 1995]. Case seven is replication, the creation of a duplicate, which coexists with the original, often for reasons of the fragile nature of the original. In both reconstruction and replication a model is built, which may or may not be full size and as fully detailed as the original, depending on the need. With accelerating use of the WWW it is increasingly used for narrative using a mix of media, for interaction, for testing recall, for monitoring user reactions and providing a context sensitive response. Now that Virtual Reality (VR) is increasingly technically possible it is possible to consider a digital alternative to a physical model, which can also serve the information needs expressed above. Such has happened with first the creation of Lascaux II as a full-size physical model of the original cave system which has been followed by the more recent scanning and modelling of a VR version showing bitmap images of the prehistoric cave paintings in interactive context.

5: Further Development

This paper argues that the perceived advantages of VRML for construction in general are equally applicable to heritage sites and that additional value can be obtained, because of the special nature of heritage sites and the need for interpretation. VRML is a useful adjunct to firsthand experience for Secondary Interpretation, providing a multi-layered capacity for both edification and conservation education. While the attention span of the visitor to the heritage site or visitor centre may be fleeting this does not necessarily apply to a remotely accessed digital model with related information. Such a model may be explored at a variety of levels of understanding.

Equally the understanding gained from Primary Interpretation needs to be shared between professionals working within conservation. The physical and historical complexity of heritage sites is held to be better modelled in 3D than 2D to ensure commonality of understanding between all those engaged in its care. WWW Browsers and VRML plug-ins are affordable and accessible from all desktops. VRML '97 is now an ISO Standard and a useful non-proprietary neutral 3D format in which to record information about the hidden or inaccessible parts of heritage sites.

Further work is necessary to enable all these aspirations to be met by digital modelling. Thompson argues that "The best basis for understanding a ruin is therefore a wide knowledge of other structures of the same period, whether ruined or not, since the mind is consciously or unconsciously making comparisons, and the larger the stock on which it is possible to draw, the more reliable the result is likely to be." [Thompson MW, 1981]. This broad understanding can only be gained asynchronously by first hand experience at present. Linked digital models could well improve this process. For this to be effective a critical mass of heritage sites need to become available which meet the same standards and support the same classification systems so that they can be interactively linked and browsed to provide this broad understanding. Similar significant elements need to be classified similarly so that they can be inter-linked. Standards for scale of model and matching levels of detail need to be agreed and established.

Sharpe stated that "in early writings there was an element of interpretation when the writer passed on his or her impressions or observations to the recipient, the reader, who may never have been near the feature being interpreted. In present day interpretation we work more closely with the feature itself, are in direct contact with the recipient, and have a variety of media to rely on.". [Sharpe GW. 1976]. This direct contact of the guide with the recipient would not apply so readily to a digital model. Yet it may also be of interest to compare the views of such as Pevsner with those of others who do not agree. A WWW based digital model could support a palimpsest of commentaries linked together. Different representations and commentary trails can be mapped onto the same model of the cultural heritage site, in a similar manner to mapping shifting political boundaries onto a less mutable physical relief map. To serve such data in the most flexible way development is needed to supply not just WWW pages on demand but frames on demand which show the requested contrasting views.

Other recent research at UWE based upon the hands-on science exhibits at the Bristol Exploratory has been testing cellular phone and active badge based means of delivering context sensitive audio commentary to visitors using the interactive exhibits. [Heard P et al, ESS Faculty,

UWE]. There is scope for considering portable versions of some of the information held which could be delivered in this manner as a direct complement to first-hand experience. The Digital model would in this sense become one easily used point of access to a digital archive, an integrative repository from which such information is served. There is a need for an improved feedback tool that monitors use and amends delivery to suit the individual. An interactive system is potentially capable of doing so and one aspect of the use of active badges at the Exploratory is to cue the system to deliver material appropriate to the object of focus and the length of time spent examining it.

6: Conclusion

Provided that it is widely available on the WWW and readily updated the model can serve as an off-site preparatory and briefing tool. One particular such need is to improve accessibility for the handicapped, permitting them to explore a model in order to plan an accessible route to points of interest, and where this is not possible to at least vicariously experience the otherwise inaccessible. However such a model does not have to be complete in all respects to be useful. It may suffice to model either the most significant points to meet visitor interpretation needs, or to model on a project specific basis over time, which would build from one case study to the next. Either would lead to building a comprehensive model through accretion. Standards would need to be defined to enable a grid of different levels of detail focusing on areas of interest, while still giving an overview and a context for the remainder.

WWW Browsers can be used to deliver interactive linked multimedia showing historic environments. This is capable of arrangement on demand to suit the diverse retrieval requirements of the professional. It is also capable of being of use to the professional in explaining interactively to colleagues or for recording that explanation to form the basis of an edited narrative for visitors. More work is required on tools and server applications. Tools are required that enable the interactive explanation to be developed into a script or storyboard for a narrative, while retaining multi-level links through case-studies to primary source data. Server applications are required that serve on-demand frames of associated VRML and WWW pages.

Acknowledgements

This work has been partly funded through the National Creative Technology Initiative of the ESRC in the UK.

References

Jean Barzun quoted by Freeman Tilden, 'Interpreting our Heritage', University of N. Carolina Press 1957.
Machin A. 1986.'Changing the Viewpoint' in Heritage Interpretation, 1986, Winter 34, pp 4-5.
Freeman Tilden, 1957. 'Interpreting our Heritage', University of N. Carolina Press.
HMSO 1975. 'Guide to Countryside Interpretation Part 1, Principles of Countryside Interpretation and Interpretative Planning', published by HMSO.
Finch JM, 1982.'Curatorial Management of the Built World', McGraw Hill.
Sharpe GW, (Ed).1976. 'Interpreting the Environment', J Wiley & Sons inc.
Washburne RP & Wagner JA, 1972. 'Evaluating Visitor Response to Exhibit Content' in Curator 1972, XV 3 pp 248-254).
Hayward NG, Larkin JW, 1983. 'Evaluating Visitor Experiences...' in Museum Studies Journal 1983 Fall 1 2.
Venning P, 1995, Secretary to the SPAB, in letter to the author.
MOLAS. 1995. The Museum of London Archaeological Service Annual Report for 1994.
Thompson MW, 1981, 'Ruins, their preservation and display', British Museum Press.
Binks G, Dyke J, Dagnall P, 1988, 'Visitors Welcome, A Manual on the Presentation and Interpretation of Archaeological Excavations', published by HMSO.
Howell P, 1995, 'Perception, Disability and the Conservation Element', in Journal of Architectural Conservation, No 2 July 1995 pp 63-77.
[Heard P et al, ESS Faculty, UWE].

Session 1-8

Augmented and Virtual Reality

Chair

Paul Graham

Christie Hospital NHS Trust, UK

Virtual Lunar Landscapes for Testing Vision-Guided Lunar Landers

Dr Stephen M. Parkes & Mr Iain Martin,
Applied Computing, University of Dundee,
DUNDEE, DD1 4HN, SCOTLAND, UK
Tel: +44 1382 345194, Fax: +44 1382 345509,
email: sparkes@computing.dundee.ac.uk, imartin@computing.dundee.ac.uk

Abstract

Virtual reality techniques are being used to support the development of unmanned space-probes intended to land on other planets in the solar system. These planetary landers will operate autonomously during landing and will use vision for navigation and guidance down to a safe landing spot. Suitable vision techniques have been developed but must be extensively tested on realistic test surfaces. A system (LunarSim) for producing realistic simulations of heavily cratered planetary surfaces has been developed to support exhaustive testing of vision guidance software.

This paper begins by describing the reasons for developing a realistic simulation of the lunar surface. The techniques that have been used to produce models of impact craters are then described. A description of the LunarSim software is provided and an example is presented of an image sequence produced using LunarSim. Finally a summary of related current and future work is given.

1. Introduction

The European Space Agency (ESA) has studied several possible missions to the moon using intelligent unmanned landers [1,8]. Previous manned and unmanned missions have landed in broad, relatively safe areas to minimise the risk of damage during landing. Manned missions with the capability of landing close to a required target landing spot, avoiding boulders and other hazards, have been limited by the need to minimise the risk to astronauts on-board the lander. Unmanned missions have not had sufficient computing capability to permit accurate surface relative navigation and obstacle avoidance. Advances in spacecraft on-board processing technology [2,3] have made autonomous or semi-autonomous vision-based lander guidance feasible. This means that unmanned missions to specific sites of scientific interest in potentially hazardous areas can be considered.

Landing on the moon, close to a predetermined target landing spot, in an area of rough terrain, is a difficult task. Accurate navigation relative to the lunar surface is necessary, together with the detection of possible hazards like boulders, small craters or steep slopes. The ESA (European Space Agency) 3D Planetary Modelling study [4] demonstrated the feasibility of using vision for the guidance of planetary landers. Extensive testing of these intelligent vision guidance algorithms is essential if they are to be able to cope with the full range of possible surface conditions that could be experienced during a landing.

The problem is that only relatively poor information about the detailed surface morphology of other planets is available. The moon, for example, has been extensively mapped to a resolution of some 200m by NASA's Clementine mission [5]. This is inadequate for a vision based lander which must detect and avoid boulders and craters as small as 0.5m across. Some form of simulation or mock-up of the planet's surface is necessary to support the development of the vision based guidance algorithms. This must be based on known information about the surface morphology and must be convincingly realistic.

During the ESA 3D Planetary Modelling Study the vision guidance algorithms developed were tested using a robotic frame to move a camera above a 2m x 1m physical mock-up of the lunar surface. This physical simulation was appropriate for demonstrating the feasibility of vision based guidance and navigation but proved inflexible when more exhaustive testing was required to show that the vision system was robust and able to cope with many different but similar surface conditions. Several problems soon became apparent with the use of physical modelling on its own:-

- **Illumination:** It is difficult to simulate low sun elevation angles with a physical model illuminated by a lamp.
- **Calibration:** To test the vision algorithms used it is necessary to have a digital elevation model representing the physical model. This requires careful measurement of the surface. The robotic frame also requires calibration.
- **Inflexibility:** To ensure that the computer vision algorithms are robust they must be tested on many different lunar surface models. Physical models cannot be altered very easily and each new model has to be hand made.
- **Scale and Resolution:** A physical model can only cover a limited area. Scaling the model is restricted by manufacturing constraints and by the camera used. For example a 2m x 2m physical model with a 0.5m feature scaled to say 2mm would represent an area of just 500m x 500m.
- **Cost:** Producing a physical model and calibrating it and the robotic frame are time consuming activities. The robotic frame is expensive.

The LunarSim project at the University of Dundee has developed and is continuing to develop computer models of the lunar surface which can overcome the difficulties with physical models. These models are for use in support of computer vision for autonomous, semi-autonomous and operator-guided planetary landing systems.

The required output from a computer simulation of the lunar surface is an image of the surface taken from a camera on a lander at a particular position and orientation relative to the surface. Virtual reality techniques can be used to produce the image from the simulated surface and to model Sun and Earth illumination.

Compared to physical modelling the LunarSim software is readily able to simulate low illumination angles, does not require calibration, is extremely flexible

(lunar surfaces can be generated or modified at the touch of a button), and is of low cost.

2. Realistic crater models

Virtual reality and computer graphics techniques for producing images from a surface model are well developed. The main difficulty is in producing a convincing lunar surface model, ideally the simulated images should be indistinguishable from the real thing.

The crater models combine idealised mathematical impact crater models with fractal techniques to produce a realistic appearance to the craters. The crater bowl, rim and ejecta-blanket are simulated.

2.1 Simple crater model

The simple crater model consists of two main functions, a crater bowl and an ejecta blanket, which meet at the crater rim, as shown in figure 1.

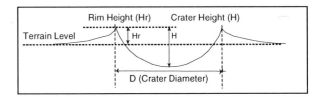

Figure 1: Basic Crater Model

The depth of the crater, H, is given by
$$H = 0.196 \cdot D^{1.01}$$
and the height of the crater rim above the surrounding terrain by
$$H_r = 0.036 \cdot D^{1.014}$$
where D is the rim peak-to-peak crater diameter [6].

The height at any point in the simple crater model is described as separate functions for the bowl and the ejecta blanket. Each is defined as a function of radius from the centre of the crater. Larger craters (commonly called complex craters) are less bowl shaped with flatter bases and may have central peaks or peak rings.

$$BowlHeight = 4.H.(radius/D) + H_r - H$$

$$EjectaHeight = 0.14 \left(\frac{D}{2}\right)^{0.74} \cdot \left(\frac{D}{2.radius}\right)^3$$

The crater bowl is placed onto a plane which describes the average inclination of the terrain on which the crater is to be added. The ejecta blanket is added to the existing terrain and a fractal terrain (with varying fractal parameters as a function of radius) is overlaid over the whole theoretical model to give added realism to the crater.

2.2 Adding the crater model to the terrain

The area of terrain onto which the crater bowl is to be added is first smoothed into a plane. This plane is calculated by averaging height values around the rim of the crater. When a meteorite impacts a surface the energy released is so large that the original surface is obliterated.

The ejecta blanket results from debris thrown out after the impact and extends for a distance of D/2 from the crater rim. The ejecta blanket is superimposed onto the top of the original terrain. A linear fix is added to the crater bowl to points greater than a given radius (varied fractally around 0.7 radius) which seamlessly matches the height of the rim and plane to the height of the rim and the underlying terrain. This has the duel effect of allowing the crater rim to take characteristics from the terrain and also to give substance to the crater walls. A similar linear fix is added to the ejecta to match the maximum height of the ejecta to the crater rim and the minimum height to the terrain at the edge of the ejecta along a radius from the centre.

2.3 Fractal regions of the crater.

To add realism to the "ideal" crater, a fractal surface, created using random mid-point displacement, is superimposed onto the smooth crater. Different fractal regions are defined as a function of radius from the crater centre. These regions have different values for Fractal Number and Height Factor, which control the roughness of the fractal surface. This allows the "roughness" of the different areas of the crater (i.e. floor, wall, ejecta blanket) to be varied. In real images the ejecta blanket appears highly fractal around the rim of the crater smoothing off the further it is from the crater rim. To simulate this the ejecta blanket region is set to be highly fractal, but the amplitude of this region of the fractal surface is decreased linearly to zero from the rim to the edge of the ejecta region.

2.4 Summary of crater model

The complete models for the crater bowl and ejecta blanket are illustrated in figures 2 and 3 respectively.

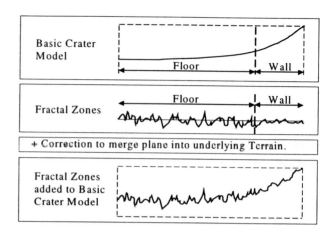

Figure 2: Crater Bowl Model

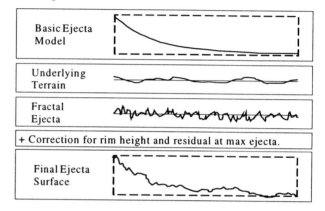

Figure 3: Summary of Ejecta Blanket Model

2.5 Ageing craters

The above simple crater model produces craters with sharp rim edges. This is appropriate for recently formed craters but subsequent geological activity or further impact cratering can cause the rim to collapse, resulting in a more rounded crater rim. To allow for craters with rims of varying roundness the theoretical underlying model was altered by the addition of two parameterised polynomials. One parameter *alpha* controls the "roundness" of the crater rim. A quadratic is defined which matches the height and gradient of the basic bowl model (at a point *alpha* radius in from the rim), to the height and gradient of at the crater rim (gradient on the rim is zero). A cubic is defined which matches the basic ejecta model (at a point *alpha* radius away from the rim) by height and gradient, to the crater rim by height and gradient. By varying *alpha,* craters of different apparent age can be created with older craters appearing more rounded than younger ones.

2.6 Crater size density-distribution

For meteorite impact craters to appear realistic on a surface the crater size density distribution must be correct as well as the individual crater models i.e. there must be many more small craters than there are large ones. The crater size density distribution varies across the lunar surface and has been measured in many areas [6]. The general form of the crater size density distribution is given by

$$N_{cum} = cD^{-b}$$

where N_{cum} is the cumulative number distribution per unit area, D is the crater diameter, and b and c are constants. When b = 2 the constant c becomes dimensionless. Measurement of crater size density on the moon has provided a typical value for b of 1.8.

3. LunarSim software

Using the LunarSim software, a lunar surface model is built by simulating impact cratering on an initial terrain model. A predefined surface (e.g. an existing digital elevation model) or a fractal surface may be used as the initial terrain model. Craters are placed on the terrain either manually via a graphical user interface, or randomly according to a user defined crater size-density distribution based on actual lunar crater size-density studies [6].

The positions and sizes of a set of craters can be stored separately from the elevation model in a text file known as a crater file. This means the same set of craters can be added to different terrain surfaces and also allows crater files to be edited using a text editor if required. Craters are defined in LunarSim in real scale (metres) and a small text file related to each output image is created which contains the image scale and other information.

The sun is modelled as an area light source, its size and distance from the surface are set to appropriate values for the moon. The output image is ray-traced using the POV-Ray ray-tracing software[7] to simulate an image taken by a camera fixed to a spacecraft. The spacecraft is defined in terms of position (x,y,z) and attitude (pitch, yaw, roll). The camera controls the picture to be taken; its attributes being field of view, image quality and output file size/type. The output images can be types tga, bmp, ppm or png.

Crater files can be produced interactively on top of a background image. This feature allows LunarSim to generate a realistic lander test environment, based on a proposed landing site. A lunar image is first loaded into LunarSim and then used as a background to help define the size and position of any large or distinctive craters. LunarSim can then randomly generate additional smaller craters according to a size-density distribution related to the landing area. This crater file could then be added to different terrain models, resulting in a set of realistic test models, which represent a particular region of the moon.

4. Example images

Figure 4 is an example of a real image taken by the Clementine mission [5]. Figure 5 is an example of an image of a similar area produced by LunarSim. Figure 6 is a close up of the centre portion of the simulated terrain used in Figure 5.

Figure 4: Real Lunar Image

Figure 5: Simulated Lunar Image

Figure 6: Close-Up Simulated Image

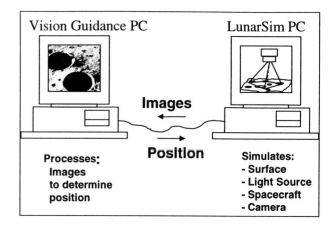

Figure 7: LunarSim with Vision Guidance Computer

5. Current and Future work

Effort, to date, has concentrated on producing realistic impact crater models and in providing a simple but versatile user interface for the creation of cratered landscapes. The visualisation of the terrain model produced is done with the POV-Ray ray tracing program [7], which means that the image frame rate is very low. Current work is focussed on improving the speed of image generation through the use of Direct3D and on improving the terrain model by adding boulders to the simulation. The realistic simulation of large impact craters (over 10km diameter) which have a different form to the smaller "simple" craters is also being studied.

The complete test system will consist of two independent computers as shown in figure 7. One computer will run the LunarSim software (representing the "camera" onboard the spacecraft) and will produce images of the lunar surface. The other computer will run the vision guidance software (representing the spacecraft "flight" system). The LunarSim PC produces an image of the simulated surface as seen from the initial position of the lander (unknown to the vision guidance software). This image is passed to the vision guidance PC to process, which uses it to determine the spacecraft's position. The LunarSim PC will then simulate the motion of the spacecraft and take the next picture from the spacecraft's new position. This system provides a versatile test environment for developing intelligent vision guidance software.

As well as testing vision-based lander guidance algorithms the LunarSim software can be used for testing vision-based rover navigation and path planning algorithms. Other applications may include different planetary surfaces, asteroids and comets.

6. Conclusion

Virtual reality has been used to simulate the surface of the moon and has many advantages over alternative methods of simulating the unknown surfaces of various planetary bodies. Realism is vital for the range of space applications, which include the evaluation and development of vision-based guidance and navigation control systems for planetary landers. The LunarSim system provides a convenient and versatile means of generating realistic simulations of the surface of the moon.

7. Acknowledgements

The Authors would like to acknowledge the support of ESA for the LunarSim study, ESA Contract No. 12821/98/NL/MV, on which this paper is based. The assistance of Patrick Plancke, the ESA study technical manager, has been appreciated.

8. References

[1] EuroMoon Core Team, "EuroMoon Mission Feasibility Study Report, ESA (Draft Report). Edited by G. Scoon Mission Implementation Manager, ESTEC.

[2] S.M. Parkes, DSP (Demanding Space-based Processing!): the Path Behind and the Road Ahead, DSP'98, 6th International Workshop on Digital Signal Processing

Techniques for Space Applications, ESTEC, Noordwijk, The Netherlands, 23-25 September 1998, ESA publication no. WPP-144, paper 4.1.

[3] S.M. Parkes, "On-Board Processing: Cheaper, Faster, Better,", 32nd ESLAB Symposium, ESTEC NoordWijk, The Netherlands, 15-18 September 1998, ESA publication SP-423.

[4] Paar G, Parkes SM, Classen HJ, "3D Planetary Modelling Study Final Report" ESTEC contract 9195/90/NL/SF, Joanneum Research 1996.

[5] Regeon, P., Lynn, P., Johnson, M., and Chapman, J. "The Clementine Lunar Orbiter", 20th International Symposium on Space Technology and Science, Gifu, Japan, 19-25 May 1996. (Images available at http://www.nrl.navy.mil/clementine/)

[6] Melosh, H.J. "Impact Cratering – A Geologic Process", Oxford University Press, 1989, ISBN 0-19-510463-3.

[7] http://www.povray.org

[8] EuroMoon 2000: A plan for a European Lunar South Pole Expedition, December 1996. ESA Publications Division, c/o ESTEC, Noordwijk, 2200 AG The Netherlands, ESA Publication BR-122, ISBN 92-9092-428-4.

Optical Occlusion and Shadows in a 'See-through' Augmented Reality Display

Eric W Tatham

Augmented Reality Research Group
Faculty of Mathematics and Computing
The Open University
Walton Hall
Milton Keynes, MK7 6AA
UK
Tel. +44 (0)1908 655098
Fax. +44 (0)1908 652140
Email e.w.tatham@open.ac.uk

Abstract

As distinct from virtual reality, which seeks to immerse the user in a fully synthetic world, computer-augmented reality systems supplement sensory input with computer-generated information. The principle has, for a number of years, been employed in the head-up display systems used by military pilots and usually comprises an optical display arrangement based on part-silvered mirrors that reflect computer graphics into the eye in such a way that they appear superimposed on the real-world view. Compositing real and virtual worlds offers many new and exciting possibilities but also presents some significant challenges, particularly with respect to applications for which the real and virtual elements need to be integrated convincingly. Unfortunately, the inherent difficulties are compounded further in situations where a direct, unpixellated view of the real world is desired, since current optical systems do not allow real-virtual occlusion, nor a number of other essential visual interactions. This paper presents a generic model of augmented reality as a context for discussion, and then describes a simple but effective technique for providing a significant degree of control over the visual compositing of real and virtual worlds.

Superimposing electronic graphics on our view of the real world is a familiar feature of SLR (Single Lens Reflex) cameras that typically present exposure and other information superimposed over the photographer's view through the lens. It is evident that there is further potential in using such an arrangement for providing visual information adaptable to given situations and, indeed, this was exploited by Knowlton [7] in 1977 when he developed a system that visually superimposed computer displays onto an input device. The purpose was to allow users to interact with a real physical keyboard whilst also providing flexibility of function by optically superimposing alternative labels onto the keys. In this way, the same physical keyboard could be endowed with the appearance of a typewriter, a calculator or a telephone operator's console.

The essential generic components of such a computer-augmented reality system are illustrated in figure 1. Perceptual stimuli from the real environment are augmented by computer generated elements to provide a composite perceptual experience. Depending on the system's purpose, it is normally necessary for the synthetic elements to be harmonised in some way with the real. Usually, this will require that the synthesising computer have access to information about pertinent aspects of the world, such as; world geometry, user position and orientation, illumination, or physical object and atmospheric properties. For simplicity the model shows the augmentation system as external to the user's environment. Although this generic model is intended to be applicable for all kinds of other stimuli, such as augmentation of a real environment with computer-generated music, it is primarily real-virtual visual integration on which many new applications depend.

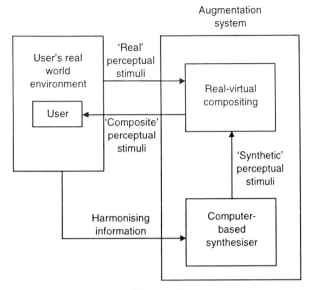

Augmentation
system

User's real
world
environment

User

'Real'
perceptual
stimuli

'Composite'
perceptual
stimuli

Real-virtual
compositing

'Synthetic'
perceptual
stimuli

Harmonising
information

Computer-
based
synthesiser

Figure 1

A wide range of possibilities exist for usefully augmenting reality and includes; assistance for manufacturing and maintenance [4,5], medical imaging [3], annotating the real world [11], training [8], collaborative working [10]. However, a number of teleoperation of robots [9], design visualization [1] and technical problems need to be resolved if the promise of augmented reality is to find fruition. Almost all potential applications depend on the acquisition and utilisation of appropriate harmonising information, and this often presents a significant hurdle. For example, accurate spatial and temporal registration of computer graphics onto a real scene remains crucial to the success of most applications, especially those providing manufacturing or surgical guidance. Whereas small tracking inaccuracies may not be noticeable in an immersive virtual reality system, even very small angular errors in detecting the orientation of an augmented reality headset can result in a large displacement in the registration of the graphics. Ultimately, more accurate methods of position and orientation tracking are required, as well as effective methods of tracking over larger distances. Further registration problems can occur due to latency between changes in the real scene and the corresponding computer graphics update, as the graphics almost inevitably lag behind. The total delay is caused by the period it takes for the tracker subsystem to take its measurements and the time for the corresponding images to appear on the display devices. Not surprisingly, these problems provide the focus for much of the current research effort [2], but seamless visual integration of real and virtual worlds also depends on

effective simulation of other factors [6]. It is of fundamental importance in conveying a convincing perception of depth that, where appropriate, real objects appear in front of virtual, occluding parts that cannot be seen, and that virtual objects be suitably interposed before real. Achieving such interpositioning is obviously dependent on the availability of knowledge concerning the depth of real-world objects. However, occlusion is just the tip of a much larger iceberg of interactions that need to be resolved if convincing integration is to be realised. For example, virtual objects placed in a real environment should be expected to appear as if lit by the light sources that exist in reality. In turn, but less tractable, is the case where the virtual object is itself a light source that would be expected to illuminate the real environment. In practice, almost all objects will reflect some light that will add to the illumination of nearby objects; thus some of the colour from a red virtual object would appear to bleed into a real matt white surface on which it is placed, and vice-versa. Glossy or mirrored surfaces in reality should reflect appropriately placed virtual objects, and the real should be reflected in the virtual. Real shadows may fall across virtual objects and virtual shadows across real objects. Reality should appear refracted through transparent graphics, and virtual objects refracted by the real. In addition, atmospheric effects such as fog, smoke or heat haze should affect the appearance of virtual objects in the same way as they do real.

There is little doubt that acquisition and utilisation of appropriate harmonising information present the most pressing challenges for augmented reality researchers. However, consideration of the required visual interaction effects exposes an inherent limitation associated with current augmented reality display hardware in its ability to achieve effective real-virtual compositing. In Knowlton's system the compositing was achieved by reflecting the computer graphics in a semi-transparent mirror that was positioned over the keyboard at a strategic angle, and it is this same principle that is employed, although greater freedom of movement obtained, by current see-through, head-mounted displays; see figure 2.

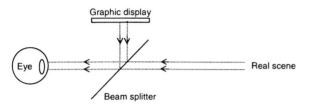

Figure 2

A similar visual effect, but at the expense of stereopsis, is obtained by presenting the computer graphics to just one eye whilst leaving the other eye free to view the real scene directly so that the task of superimposition of the two components is left for the brain to complete. Unfortunately, both arrangements produce an overlaid image that is transparent and ghost-like, providing no control over light from the real world and precluding the possibility of occluding real objects by the virtual. An alternative compositing technique that overcomes this particular problem, and is often used, is to key computer graphic elements into a video image of the real scene. However, such an arrangement requires head-mounted cameras, pixellates the real-world view and, in the event of hardware failure, obscures the user's vision.

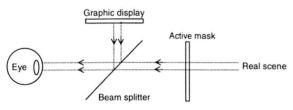

Figure 3

In order to retain the direct-view advantages of a see-through augmented reality display while also providing occlusion and other desired visual interaction effects, a modified hardware set-up is proposed. The basic alteration to existing displays is very simple but effective and is illustrated in figure 3. It is based on the introduction of an active filter capable of masking portions of the real scene. In the illustrated

arrangement, a computer-generated image is viewed by reflection in a part-silvered mirror as before. However, the real world is now viewed, not only through the mirror, but also via a transparent active panel that is placed along the viewer's line of sight. The computer display and transparent panel image are both spatially registered and temporally synchronised, with the transparent element acting as an active mask selectively reducing the intensity of light from the world that reaches the viewer's eye. On the other hand, the reflected image selectively increases the light reaching the eye. This arrangement allows for significant flexibility and control as it is now possible to both reduce and increase the intensity and colour of light reaching the viewer from selected areas of a scene.

Using the transparent display element to create an opaque mask and the reflected element to display the superimposed graphic object allows virtual entities to visually occlude a real background. The active mask can also be used to generate areas of neutral density that reduce light received from selected portions of the real world enabling the simulation of virtual shadows within a real scene. The left-hand image in figure 4, showing a shaded sphere with black background, is reflected into the eye by the beam splitter (see figure 3) while the shadow image with transparent background, shown on the right in the figure, is displayed as the active mask. These images combine to form one of the frames for an animated sequence in which the virtual sphere orbits a real Lego™ pillar. The sphere occludes its real background and appears to cast its shadow on reality as it moves. Figure 5 shows a single frame from the video sequence. Figure 6 is a photograph taken directly through the display to show a real finger inserted through a virtual torus. Besides producing occlusion and shadow effects, using an active colour mask colour permits selective filtering of areas of real world colour. Thus, employing such a mask facilitates production of any desired colour bleeding or illumination effects.

Although the illustrations in this article have been produced, for convenience, using a LCD panel as the active mask, this is not ideal since such panels introduce limiting attenuation and distortion. Fortunately, there are possible alternative methods of realising the required active masking and these form the subject of the author's current research effort. Promising designs that dispense entirely with the need for an active transparent panel, as well as obviating the requirement for a part-silvered mirror, are likely to be based on the use of spatial light modulator devices. Whatever the hardware used for implementation, the principle of incorporating active masking, as outlined in this paper, overcomes many of the inherent limitations of current see-through displays. Such a technique provides a degree of control that could help enable computer-augmented reality to fulfil its promise of becoming a highly versatile tool for the future.

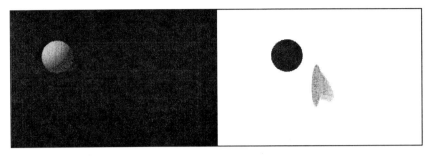

Figure 4

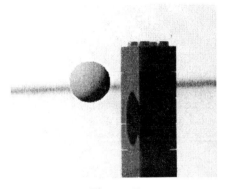

Figure 5

Figure 6

Acknowledgements

The ideas described in this paper arose as a result of work supported by the author's former employer; Coventry University, UK. Thanks are also due to R. Kalawsky of Loughborough University and N.Godwin, K. Monk and R.Newman all of Coventry University.

References

1. Ahlers, K., Kramer, A., Breen, D., Chevalier, P.Y., Crampton, C., Rose, E., Tuceryan, M. Whitaker, R., and Greer, D. Distributed Augmented Reality for Collaborative Design Applications. Proc. Eurographics '95 Conf., (Maastricht, Netherlands, August 1995), 3-14.
2. Azuma, R. Tracking Requirements for Augmented Reality. Communications of the ACM, Vol. 36 (7), (July 1993), 50-51.
3. Bajura, M., Fuchs, H., and Ohbuchi, R. Merging Virtual Objects with the Real World: Seeing Ultrasound Imagery within the Patient, Computer Graphics, 26 (2), (1992), 203-210.
4. Caudell, T., and Mizell, D. Augmented reality: An Application of Heads-up Display Technology to Manual Manufacturing Processes, Proc. Hawaii Int. Conf. System Sciences, (January 1992), 659-669.
5. Feiner, S., MacIntyre, B., and Seligmann, D. Annotating the Real World with Knowledge-Based Graphics on a See-through Head-mounted Display, Proc. Graphics Interface 1992, Canadian Info. Proc. Soc, (1992), 78-85.
6. Kalawsky, R.S. and Tatham, E.W. Effects of Spatial and Temporal Mis-registration in Augmented Virtual Environments, Proc. of the 16th Annual Conference of Eurographics, UK, Leeds, (March 1998), 127-134.
7. Knowlton, K. Computer Displays Optically Superimposed on Input Devices, The Bell Syst, Tech. Journal, 56 (3), (March 1977), 367-383.
8. Metzger, P.J. Adding Reality to the Virtual, Proc. IEEE Virtual Reality Annual Int. Symp., (Seattle, WA, September 1993), 7-13.
9. Milgram, P., Drascic, D., Grodski, J., Restogi, A., Zhai, S., and Zhou, C. Merging Real and Virtual Worlds, Proc of IMAGINA '95, (Monte Carlo, February1995), 218-230.
10. Rekimoto, Jun. TransVision: A Hand-held Augmented Reality System for Collaborative Design. Sony Computer Science Laboratory Inc., Takanawa Muse Building, 3-14-13 Higashi-Gotanda, Shinagawa-ku, Tokyo 141, Japan, (1996).
11. Rose, E., Breen, D., Ahlers, K., Crampton, C., Tuceryan, M., Whitaker, R., and Greer, D. Annotating Real-world Objects using Augmented Reality, Proc. of Computer Graphics: Developments in Virtual Environments International 95, (June 1995), 357-370.

Footnote: Lego™ is a trademark of the Lego Group.

Old Theories, New Technologies: Cumulative Clutter Effects Using Augmented Reality

A.W. Stedmon[Φ1], R. S. Kalawsky[±], K. Hill[±], & C.A. Cook[Φ]
[Φ]Centre for Human Sciences, Defence Evaluation and Research Agency, UK
[±]Advanced VR Research Centre, Loughborough University, UK
[1]Author for correspondence: astedmon@mail.dera.gov.uk

Abstract

This paper investigates human cognitive performance when information is presented via Augmented Reality (AR) and overlaid upon a primary display. Initial results support traditional experimental paradigms of human memory [1] and comprehension of information [2], and have been used to compare AR and standard display formats when used in isolation. Results from these experiments provide a fundamental baseline for cognitive performance with a see-through AR headset. Furthermore the results lay the foundations for more comprehensive trials later in the research programme when the display formats are combined to provide a full AR facility. Consideration is given to the specific effects of cumulative clutter and two experiments are outlined that investigate the effects on target identification. Although the data are still being analysed, further consideration is given to key points addressed in the experimental design. Details of a dedicated website are provided where information will be consolidated and provide a basis for developing guidelines for the future development and application of AR technology.

1: Introduction

The DERA Centre for Human Sciences (CHS) is evaluating the potential of AR for providing operator feedback in a future Advanced Embedded Training (AET) system for the Royal Navy. Whilst the main focus of the work addresses issues relating to embedded training and on-line feedback provision [3], another aspect of the research is concerned with investigating the cognitive ergonomics of AR technology and human information processing issues that may arise through its use.

Although AR concepts have been around since the 1950s, the technology and its application is still in its infancy. Indeed, research into the human factors issues surrounding the use of AR systems is very limited and so far no formal guidelines have been found for any application of AR technology.

For the purposes of the research detailed in this paper, AR is defined as supplementary visual information overlaid on the real-world environment by the use of a see-through head-set. Although this is by far the most common definition of AR, 'augmenting reality' can be performed in a number of ways and through various sensory mechanisms such as tactile and even olfactory systems [4].

Within the present research programme at DERA, a number of non-technical issues are being investigated, focusing on potential psychological limitations of AR technology. The difference between the majority of existing AR applications and the research reported here, is that the AR display is not being used to supplement the conventional real-world environment, but to overlay another visual display unit (VDU) to support Naval tactical training and feedback provision. Overlaying one synthetic image upon another, however, may exacerbate any processing difficulties for the user, since the fusion of two synthetic images may create an unacceptable cognitive load. If the perceptual load placed upon the user is too great, it is unlikely that AR will prove to be an effective support to learning. Trade-offs may therefore need to be made between the complexity of the primary visual environment and the amount of information that can be provided by a supplementary AR display. Of particular interest, therefore, are any excessive human information processing demands which may be associated with the use of AR.

This paper summarises the progress, to date, of work carried out in association with the Advanced VR Research Centre (AVRRC) at Loughborough University. An experimental programme has been developed to investigate issues of human cognitive processing in an AR environment and particular attention is focused on the effects of cumulative clutter between an AR and primary display format.

2: Progress to date

A preliminary series of trials (Series 1) have been carried out with four experiments to assess the viability of an AR headset as display format. These experiments have incorporated traditional experimental paradigms to test out AR technology against a conventional VDU format. Experiments 1.1 and 1.2 were based on paradigms to test short-term memory (STM) and comprehension of single text or graphics information, based on the work of [1], [5] and [6], provided by either an AR or a standard primary display format.

In addition a further trial was conducted (experiment 1.3) to investigate the comprehension and analysis of simple prose [2], [7]; and learning effects for hieroglyphics (experiment 1.4), [2].

These latter experiments were developed on the basis that AR technology might be exploited to offer feedback in a text based, simple sentence format or even perhaps through the use of simple icons. The hieroglyphics represented a real symbol set with which the participants were unlikely to be familiar but could be assessed for implicit meaning and learning effects throughout the experimental trials.

This first series of experiments were conducted by using the primary and AR display formats in isolation. This provided baseline data for both AR and standard display systems alone, before they were combined in a full AR facility.

The overall results illustrated that there was no significant difference between the performance scores whether the stimuli were presented on a conventional VDU or AR headset.

Further to these results, specific measures of memory for text and graphics (experiments 1.1 and 1.2), comprehension (experiment 1.3) and learning effects (experiment 1.4) were analysed, and supported the paradigms upon which they were tested. In addition subjective measures were analysed and comparisons across the sexes were carried out. A full account of these results is presented in [8].

As there were no significant differences in the performance scores between the display formats in these initial trials, this laid important foundations for more comprehensive trials which are due to be conducted later

in the research programme. Had significant differences in the performance scores become apparent at this stage then a more detailed investigation into why one display format out-performed the other would need to have been carried out. Furthermore, in such circumstances the results could have had far reaching implications for the design and use of AR systems in the future and their impact on user cognition. What the results showed, however, was that the AR display format performed as well as a more conventional display format (i.e. VDU).

From the results of Series 1, a second series of experiments was developed which concentrated on cumulative clutter effects when the two display formats were combined and overlaid in a true AR facility.

3: Cumulative clutter effects

The Series 2 experiments (2.1 and 2.2), detailed below, build upon the findings of Series 1, combining information presented on a primary display format (VDU) and AR headset and setting it within a target identification task to assess clutter effects.

In a training application, the use of an AR display could introduce a number of undesirable effects that could lead to a decrement in performance and training effectiveness with the primary display. For instance, the presence of additional visual stimuli, or clutter, on the AR display may increase the difficulty of successfully completing a visual search task on the primary display. Alternatively, a high density of information on the primary display may make it difficult to detect and comprehend information presented on the AR display.

These experiments were designed to evaluate any perceptual interference on the primary display caused by information presented on the AR display. In order to address these issues, it was necessary to vary a range of display parameters that were expected to impair performance on the primary display task, such as obscuration and clutter effects caused by overlaying a primary display with AR information.

Display clutter is the interference of information on a display when too much information is presented at once [9]. This may be caused by too much, or different types of, information being presented at the same time, that saturates the display and overwhelms the operator's cognitive abilities; or it may be that information is presented or updated at such a rate that it overlays other information, causing obscuration effects.

Although clutter can be controlled for with various automatic and manual de-cluttering techniques, the AR environment, by its very nature, assumes that synthetic images can be overlaid over the real world to 'augment' the operator's capabilities. At some point, however, this augmentation may well prove to hinder, rather than help, user performance.

4: Experiment 2.1

The aim of the first experiment was to determine the extent to which clutter (non-targets) interfered with a visual search task. This first set of trials was carried out again using the display formats in isolation so that comparative analyses could be carried out in experiment 2.2. As such, the task was performed either entirely on the primary display (with the AR headset worn but turned off) or entirely on the AR display (with the primary display behind but turned off). It was hypothesised that the presence of additional visual stimuli, or clutter, would increase the difficulty of successfully completing a visual search task and also, from the Series 1 data, that there would not be a difference in performance between the primary and AR display formats.

A dominant effect on search time is the number of elements to be searched because the search is usually serial and the more items to be scanned, the longer the search time [10], [11].

The target identification task was a visual searching task where a target had to be located amongst a group of non-targets. Clutter, in the form of non-targets was displayed in order to make the visual search task more complex and relevant to monitoring tactical information and searching for potential threats in a military role.

4.1: Participants

The same 16 participants were employed throughout Series 1 and Series 2. This was done in order to overcome any initial novelty effects caused by using the AR head-set and to ensure that exposure to the AR display progressed at a uniform rate. All participants had normal, or corrected to normal, vision, and no prior experience of AR. In addition, equal numbers of male and female participants were employed so that the results could be generalised for both sexes. All trials and stimuli were counterbalanced to eliminate any experimental artifacts or practice, learning or fatigue effects.

4.2: Apparatus

Stimuli were generated using Microsoft PowerPoint on standard PC hardware and the AR display was provided by Virtual I-O 'I-Glasses' and Sony 'Glasstron' Systems operating in see-through mode. Special modifications to the optics on the Sony 'Glasstron'

device were undertaken to increase the transmission of primary display information through the head-set. Without these modifications the primary display would have been more difficult to see the primary display through the AR head-set, and may have confounded the experimental results.

4.3: Design

A mixed design was employed and three independent variables were manipulated throughout the trials:

- display format with 2 levels: primary or AR;
- clutter density with 4 levels: 26, 52, 78 or 104 non-targets;
- target characteristics with 3 levels: colour, shape and size.

Each of the target characteristics had three further levels as shown in the table below.

Target	Level 1	Level 2	Level 3
Colour	RED	GREEN	BLUE
Shape	CIRCLE	TRIANGLE	DIAMOND
Size	SMALL	MEDIUM	LARGE

Table 1: Target Characteristics

The combination of target characteristics allowed for 27 discrete targets to be tested on each display format and in each clutter condition. The mixed design allowed for a within-subjects comparison of display format, and a between-subjects comparison of density of clutter. The design also allowed for comparison of target dimensions in different levels of clutter and for different display formats.

There were four levels of clutter with one target stimulus item: low (26 non-targets), medium (52 non-targets), high (78 non-targets) and very high (104 non-targets). The dependent variables were the time taken to locate the target correctly on the display and subjective measures for display format preference.

4.4: Procedure

The participants were briefed on the overall aim of the experiment and asked to sign a consent form. They then underwent Baylie Lovie [12] optometric tests of visual acuity to ensure that they all had normal, or corrected to normal, 6/6 (20/20) vision.

Participants sat 1m in front of the primary display on a fixed seat, in a normal sitting position, with the AR headset fitted. Depending on the experimental condition the AR display was either active or inactive, but still worn at all times.

The participants were instructed that they would be required to carry out a visual search task in which a target was to be located amongst a group of non-targets. A description of the target was given which matched the characteristics of only one target shape on the display amongst the clutter items.

When the participant had successfully located the target they pressed the spacebar on the keyboard to stop the timer. For each of the two display format levels there were 108 trials and participants underwent the same procedure for each.

At the end of each trial participants were presented with their performance score indicating the number of correct responses as a percentage across all trials and their response times for detecting the target stimulus.

Before leaving the trials, participants filled out a questionnaire detailing their subjective opinions about the display formats, and were paid for their participation.

5: Experiment 2.2

The aim of this experiment was to determine to what extent, if any, information displayed on the AR display affected task performance on the primary display. It was hypothesised that, apart from visual obscuration effects, there would be a reduction in the performance of the primary display task, indicated by either an increase in the response time data and/or accuracy of target detection.

This experiment followed the same design as experiment 2.1. On this occasion, however, the primary and AR display formats were combined to provide a true AR facility in order to test the experimental hypothesis. The participants were therefore instructed that the target could be presented on either display, so both displays had to be searched in order to perform the task.

The combinations of stimuli were set at two levels which reflected the low (26 non-targets) and medium (52 non-targets) clutter levels in experiment 2.1. However, by combining the displays the cumulative clutter total represented the high level condition (78 non-targets) in Experiment 2.1. Both levels of clutter were shown on the AR and the primary displays as detailed in the table below, with the target stimulus randomly presented on either the primary display or the AR headset.

Condition	Primary	AR	Target
1	52	26	AR Display
2	26	52	AR Display
3	52	26	Primary Display
4	26	52	Primary Display

Table 2: Clutter Combinations and Display Formats

6: Discussion

At the time of going to print, the formal analyses of the experimental data for 2.1 and 2.2 are due to be carried out.

Experiment 2.1 data will provide the baseline comparative data for experiment 2.2 and as such it is not anticipated that there will be any significant differences in the performance data between the two display formats. Indeed, the data from the initial experiments of Series 1 would support this, illustrating that performance data for the AR display format was not significantly different to a conventional VDU format.

Based on the number of non-target items to be searched in identifying the target stimulus, it is anticipated that as the number of non-targets increases performance data will show significant effects. Response time is expected to increase significantly as the clutter density increased and response accuracy may also have suffered, as the clutter became more apparent.

Experiment 2.2 data offers the opportunity to scrutinise performance in more detail. In this experiment the performance data are not expected to be significantly different from each other as all conditions represented a cumulative total of high clutter density (78 non targets). If any difference in the performance data exists then this will be due to how the information was combined across the two display formats and would highlight difficulties in searching for targets on one display rather than another. For example, searching a primary display 'through' AR clutter may be more difficult than searching an AR display with primary display clutter, because in the former case the information may have been harder to discriminate.

From the combinations of information density on the two display formats (as illustrated in Table 2) a simple comparison can be made to investigate the cumulative clutter effects. Experiment 2.2 data can be compared to the high clutter density data (78 non-targets) in both the primary display clutter and AR display clutter in experiment 2.1. This will show if performance is either enhanced or undermined through the use of AR overlaid on a primary display. Furthermore the baseline data from experiment 2.1, will also show to what extent performance has been affected in the combined display formats of experiment 2.2 by illustrating if this is significantly different from the single display data.

Subjective data collected in these experiments will also enable analyses and correlations of display format preference and task performance to be carried out, as well as attitudes to AR technology in general. It is anticipated that participants might prefer the AR display to the primary display as a medium for augmentation and that this will be reflected in a significant relationship for display type and performance, especially in later experiments. However, it may also be found that aspects of visual performance such as image accommodation and image convergence may undermine the subjective acceptance of AR technology. If this is the case, then until these underlying technological issues are resolved, the potential of AR may be limited.

Further analysis of the results will aim to determine any relationship between objective performance measures and subjective preference measures of the two displays. Any correlations of particular attitudes the participants had towards the AR display or conventional VDU display may then have implications for how such systems are implemented in the future and ultimately combined.

A number of further human factors issues relating to the use of AR technology and its impact in human cognition are to be addressed in subsequent phases of this programme. These will include: information content and density; cognitive workload; attention effects; symbology characteristics; and the overlaying of text and graphics combinations.

In supporting the main DERA research programme, the findings from these experiments will provide a valuable insight into the fundamental cognitive ergonomics of using AR technology. This research will be used to support recommendations to be made to the Royal Navy on the future use of AR in Advanced Embedded Training systems.

7: AR website

As the potential of AR technology is being realised and the technology becomes ever cheaper and sophisticated, results from this research will underpin the development of generic guidelines for the use of AR in many other applications. Outside of the potential use for AR technology in the military domain (for training, simulation, and tactical decision support systems) commercial and domestic sectors are already looking to exploit AR technology by enhancing activities in construction, maintenance, medicine, education and entertainment. To this end, and so that information regarding human factors issues of AR is freely available and can be consolidated, a dedicated website is being developed at the following site:

<http://sgi-hursk.lboro.ac.uk/~avrrc/AR.html>.

8: Acknowledgements

This work was carried out as part of Technology Group 5 of the MoD Corporate Research Programme. Any views expressed in this paper are those of the authors and do not necessarily represent those of DERA.

9: References

[1] Miller, G.A. (1956). The Magical Number Seven, Plus or Minus Two: Some Limits on Our Capacity for Processing Information. *The Psychological Review,* 63(2).

[2] Wickens, C.D. (1992). Engineering Psychology and Human Performance. 2nd Edition. Harper Collins. New York.

[3] O'Shea, A., Cook, C.A., Young, A.L. (1999). Providing On-line Feedback in an Advanced Training System: Initial Work. *Proceedings of Occupational Psychology Conference,* Blackpool 5-7 January, 1999.

[4] Croft, D., & Craig, I. (1998). Facilitating Inventiveness - Context Orientation (Sense of Smell). DERA Report, DERA/CHS3/3.6/7/1.

[5] Paivio, A., Yuille J.C., and Madigan, S.A. (1968). Concreteness, Imagery and Meaningfulness Values for 925 Nouns. *Journal of Experimental Psychology Monograph Supplement,* 76(1), part 2.

[6] Dukes, W.F. & Bastion, J. (1966). Recall of Abstract and Concrete Words Equated on Meaningfulness. *Journal of verbal Learning and verbal Behaviour,* 5, 455-458.

[7] Tinker, M.A. (1955). Prolonged Reading Tasks in Visual Research. *Journal of Applied Psychology,* 39(6), 444-446.

[8] Stedmon, A.W., Hill, K. Kalawsky, R.S. & Cook.C.A. (in print). Old Theories, New Technologies: Comprehension and Retention Issues in Augmented Reality Systems. In,

Proceedings of the 43rd Annual Meeting of the Human Factors and Ergonomics Society, Texas, Sept 27-Oct 1, 1999.

[9] Stedmon, A.W. & Selcon, S.J. (1997). An Evaluation of the Effectiveness of Alternative Launch Success Zone Formats in Tactical Pilot Decision-Making. In, D. Harris (Ed). *Engineering Psychology and Cognitive Ergonomics – Vol. 1.* Ashgate, 1997.

[10] Drury, C.G., & Clement, M.R.. (1978). The Effect of Area, Density and Number of Background Characters on Visual Search. *Human Factors.* 20 (5), 597-602.

[11] Mocharnuk, J.B. (1978). Visual Target Acquisition and Ocular Scanning Performance. *Human Factors.* 20(5), 611-631.

[12] Bailey, I.L. & Lovie, J.E. (1976). New Design Principles for Visual Acuity Letter Charts. *American Journal Optom Physiol Opt*, 53, 740-745.

Session 1-9

Graphical Modelling

Chair
Muhammad Sarfraz
KFUPM, SA

Smooth Rational Motion of a Rigid Triangle in $\mathbb{R}^3$

Farzana S. Chaudhry
Oxford University Computing Laboratory
Wolfson Building Parks Road
OX1 3QD Oxford UK
E-mail: Farzana.Chaudhry@comlab.ox.ac.uk

Stephen A Cameron
Oxford University Computing Laboratory
Wolfson Building Parks Road
OX1 3QD Oxford UK
E-mail: Stephen.Cameron@comlab.ox.ac.uk

Abstract

Using rational motions it is possible to apply many fundamental Bézier spline (or B-spline) techniques to the designs of motion. This paper develops and tests a simple automatic algorithm for representing C^1 smooth motion of a rigid triangle $\triangle$ in $\mathbb{R}^3$, by means of piecewise parametric rational curves of degree $2m/2m$ for some m, when measurements of the positions of the vertices of the triangle $\triangle$ at a sequence of times t_i, $i = 0, 1, \ldots, n$, in $\mathbb{R}^3$ are given. The method presented in this paper can be applied to various problems in computer animation as well as in robotics.

Keywords: rigid triangle, translation, rotation, quaternion, orthogonal matrix, motion, smooth, rational Bézier splines, interpolation, fixed distance

1. Introduction

Mathematicians and computer scientists have developed geometric algorithms and methods for problems in computer graphics and computer aided design [2], [3]. There has been, however, no merging of the two fields, Kinematics and Computer Aided Geometric Design. During the last several years, it has become apparent that the methods of computer aided geometric design provide elegant tools for various tasks in computer graphics, robotics and kinematics, especially for the design of rigid body motions [11]. Shoemake [15] was among the first to develop Bézier methods for motion design. He developed a spherical generalization of the de Casteljau-algorithm to interpolate rotations using normalized quaternion curves. The idea was extended by Ge and Ravani [4]. They modified the algorithm in [15] by generalizing the subdivision algorithm of Bernstein-Bézier curve. Kim and Nam [10] gave a method to smoothly interpolate a given sequence of solid orientations using circular blending quaternion curves. These methods are computationally more efficient than other methods, however they have many limitations in terms of flexibility.

In order to apply CAGD-methods to kinematical problems, it therefore seems to be essential to restrict to motions with only rational point trajectories [7]. Ge and Ravani [5] was were first who applied rational splines to motion design, using dual quaternions. A de Casteljau-like algorithm is formulated, but the influence of the weights of the control points (which are dual numbers!) is very complex. Jüttler [7] formulated a more general version of polynomial interpolation. The trajectories of the moving objects are rational Bézier curves. He then extend his results [8] for the construction of rational tensor-product representations of sweeping surfaces with a kinematic net of parametric lines. Jüttler and Wagner [9] derived the algorithms to represent the motion as rational B-splines curves. Horsch and Jüttler [6] described an algorithm for interpolation of positions by a rational spline motion. In all these (rational motion) algorithms are given for the construction of rotational rational curves, translational part are considered to be splines curves. rotational and translational curves are computed separately, which is computationally expensive. One of the principal demands on the result of such a design process is that the motion should be rational [13], i.e all the marked points on a rigid body has rational trajectories, but these motions are not rational in general.

Motivated by these facts, I shall present these spline curves in such a way that it meet the constraints (interpolation and distance constraints), imposed on them and are smooth. I shall then give the method to compute the rotational and the translational curve as rational interpolants having the same common denominator. Consequently all the moving points on a rigid body have rational interpolants and also keep the distance apart for all t.

2. Description of Problem

From a number of observations of the position and orientation of a moving rigid triangle $\triangle$ in space (see Figure 1), suppose positions of its three vertices, $\mathbf{a}_i$, $\mathbf{x}_i$, $\mathbf{y}_i \in \mathbb{R}^3$, are recorded at some instants t_i, $i = 0, 1, \ldots, n$. Smooth functions $\mathbf{a}(t)$, $\mathbf{x}(t)$, $\mathbf{y}(t)$ are required to fit the data in some sense and to maintain some length relationship between these smooth fuctions $\forall\ t$.

Our goal here is to give the method for the construction

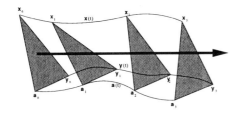

Figure 1. Motion of a rigid triangle given a number of its positions and orientations.

of rational curves $\mathbf{x}(t)$ and $\mathbf{y}(t)$ with denominator $w(t)$ and some degree m. Then the method for defining the rational curve $\mathbf{a}(t)$ of the same degree m and with the same denominator $w(t)$ will be given such that for all $t \in [t_0\ , t_n]$

$$\|\mathbf{x}(t) - \mathbf{a}(t)\| = l_1, \quad \|\mathbf{y}(t) - \mathbf{a}(t)\| = l_2, \quad \|\mathbf{y}(t) - \mathbf{x}(t)\| = l_3.$$

3. General Position of any Point of a Moving Triangle

The general position of a typical point $\hat{\mathbf{x}}(\hat{t})$ of the rigid triangle $\triangle$ at time $\hat{t}$ with respect to another point $\hat{\mathbf{a}}(\hat{t})$ of triangle at time $\hat{t}$, can be given by combining a translation of points $\hat{\mathbf{a}}(\hat{t})$ from its initial position to its final position with a rotation about some axis.

$$\hat{\mathbf{x}}(\hat{t}) \quad = \quad \hat{\mathbf{a}}(\hat{t}) + \mathbf{R}(\hat{t})(\hat{\mathbf{x}}(\hat{t}_0) - \hat{\mathbf{a}}(\hat{t}_0)) \qquad (1)$$

where $\mathbf{R}(\hat{t})$ is a matrix representing the rotation of the triangle $\triangle$ between time $\hat{t}_0$ and $\hat{t}$.

4. Quaternion Description of Rotation Matrix

Given the elements of a unit quaternion, $Q = [q_0, q_1, q_2, q_3]$, we can obtain the elements of the rotation matrix $\mathbf{R}$, corresponding to Q [14] as: $\hat{w}\mathbf{R}(q_0, q_1, q_2, q_3) =$

$$\begin{pmatrix} q_0^2 + q_1^2 - q_2^2 - q_3^2 & 2(q_1q_2 - q_0q_3) & 2(q_1q_3 + q_0q_2) \\ 2(q_1q_2 + q_0q_3) & q_0^2 - q_1^2 + q_2^2 - q_3^2 & 2(q_2q_3 - q_0q_1) \\ 2(q_1q_3 - q_0q_2) & 2(q_2q_3 + q_0q_1) & q_0^2 - q_1^2 - q_2^2 + q_3^2 \end{pmatrix}$$

where $\hat{w} = q_0^2 + q_1^2 + q_2^2 + q_3^2$. Assume that Q (i.e. every coordinate q_0, q_1, q_2, q_3 of Q) is a spline function of some degree $m \geq 1$ in $\hat{t}$. Then we can see that the elements of $\mathbf{R}$ are rational spline functions of degree $2m/2m$ with common denominator $\hat{w}(t) = q_0^2 + q_1^2 + q_2^2 + q_3^2$.
Let $\hat{\mathbf{a}}(\hat{t})$ too be a rational spline function of the same degree $2m/2m$ with same denominator $\hat{w}(\hat{t})$, then every $\hat{\mathbf{x}}(\hat{t}) = \hat{\mathbf{a}}(\hat{t}) + \mathbf{R}(\hat{t})\left(\hat{\mathbf{x}}(\hat{t}_0) - \hat{\mathbf{a}}(\hat{t}_0)\right)$ will likewise trace out a parametric rational spline curve as $\hat{t}$ varies

5. C^0 Smooth Rational Motions

We are left with the problem of constructing smooth spline curves.
Let, the curves traced out by the vertices of the moving triangle, be denoted by $\mathbf{a}(t)$, $\mathbf{x}(t)$, $\mathbf{y}(t)$ and let $\mathbf{a}(t)$, $\mathbf{x}(t)$, $\mathbf{y}(t)$ are interpolating the points $\mathbf{a}_i$, $\mathbf{x}_i$, $\mathbf{y}_i$ at t_i; $i = 0, 1, \ldots, n$. Assume that one of the curves, say $\mathbf{a}(t)$, represents the translation of the moving rigid triangle. Let $Q_i = [\alpha_i, \beta_i, \gamma_i, \delta_i] = [\cos\frac{\phi_i}{2}, \sin\frac{\phi_i}{2}\mathbf{n}_i]$ be the unit quaternion, represents the rotation of the triangle at instant t_i, when it is displaced from the first position to its ith position, where ϕ_i is the angle of rotation and $\mathbf{n}_i \in \mathbb{R}^3$ is a unit vector in the direction of the axis of rotation through $\mathbf{a}(t_i)$. Let $\alpha(t)$, $\beta(t)$, $\gamma(t)$ and $\delta(t)$ be piecewise spline functions interpolating α_i, β_i, γ_i and δ_i respectively for all i and let $\alpha_i(\theta_i)$, $\beta_i(\theta_i)$, $\gamma_i(\theta_i)$ and $\delta_i(\theta_i)$ be the ith segments of piecewise parametric spline functions $\alpha(t)$, $\beta(t)$, $\gamma(t)$ and $\delta(t)$ respectively, where $\theta_i = \frac{t-t_i}{t_{i+1}-t_i}$ is the local parameter for the ith segments. We arrange the spline functions $\alpha_i(\theta_i)$, $\beta_i(\theta_i)$, $\gamma_i(\theta_i)$ and $\delta_i(\theta_i)$ such that for $k = i, i+1$

$$\alpha_i(t_k) = \alpha_k, \ \beta_i(t_k) = \beta_k, \ \gamma_i(t_k) = \gamma_k, \ \delta_i(t_k) = \delta_k.$$

The simplest way to achieve this is take $\alpha_i(\theta_i)$, $\beta_i(\theta_i)$, $\gamma_i(\theta_i)$ and $\delta_i(\theta_i)$ linear in θ_i. Let

$$\begin{aligned} \alpha_i(\theta_i) &= (1-\theta_i)\alpha_i + \theta_i\alpha_{i+1} : & t &\in [t_i, t_{i+1}], \\ \beta_i(\theta_i) &= (1-\theta_i)\beta_i + \theta_i\beta_{i+1} : & t &\in [t_i, t_{i+1}], \\ \gamma_i(\theta_i) &= (1-\theta_i)\gamma_i + \theta_i\gamma_{i+1} : & t &\in [t_i, t_{i+1}], \\ \delta_i(\theta_i) &= (1-\theta_i)\delta_i + \theta_i\delta_{i+1} : & t &\in [t_i, t_{i+1}]. \end{aligned}$$

Then $\alpha(t)$, $\beta(t)$, $\gamma(t)$ and $\delta(t)$ are C^0 linear spline curves. Thus every entry in $\mathbf{R}(\alpha(t), \beta(t), \gamma(t), \delta(t))$ is a C^0 piecewise Bernstein-Bézier rational quadratic spline in t with denominator $w(t) = \alpha^2(t) + \beta^2(t) + \gamma^2(t) + \delta^2(t)$. Consequently $\mathbf{x}(t) - \mathbf{a}(t) = \mathbf{R}(t)(\mathbf{x}(t_0) - \mathbf{a}(t_0))$ and $\mathbf{y}(t) - \mathbf{a}(t) = \mathbf{R}(t)(\mathbf{y}(t_0) - \mathbf{a}(t_0))$ are $C^0[t_0, t_n]$ piecewise rational quadratic splines with denominator $w(t)$. As $Q_i = [\alpha_i, \beta_i, \gamma_i, \delta_i]$ is a unit quaternion, therefore

$$\begin{aligned} w(t_i) &= \alpha^2(t_i) + \beta^2(t_i) + \gamma^2(t_i) + \delta^2(t_i) \\ &= \alpha_i^2 + \beta_i^2 + \gamma_i^2 + \delta_i^2 = 1. \end{aligned}$$

Let $\mathbf{a}_i(t)$, $\mathbf{x}_i(t)$, $\mathbf{y}_i(t)$ and $w_i(t)$ be the ith segments of $\mathbf{a}(t)$, $\mathbf{x}(t)$, $\mathbf{y}(t)$ and $w(t)$ respectively then

$$\mathbf{x}_i(t) - \mathbf{a}_i(t) = \mathbf{R}(\alpha_i(t), \beta_i(t), \gamma_i(t), \delta_i(t))(\mathbf{x}_0 - \mathbf{a}_0) \quad (2)$$

$$\mathbf{y}_i(t) - \mathbf{a}_i(t) = \mathbf{R}(\alpha_i(t), \beta_i(t), \gamma_i(t), \delta_i(t))(\mathbf{y}_0 - \mathbf{a}_0). \quad (3)$$

are piecewise rational quadratic splines. If we write these rational quadratic splines in a Bernstein-Bézier form as

$$w_i(t) = B_0^2(\theta_i) + \zeta_i B_1^2(\theta_i) + B_2^2(\theta_i) \quad (4)$$

$$\mathbf{x}_i(t) - \mathbf{a}_i(t) = \mathbf{o}_{i_0}^x B_0^2(\theta_i) + \mathbf{o}_{i_1}^x \xi_i B_1^2(\theta_i) + \mathbf{o}_{i_2}^x B_2^2(\theta_i) \quad (5)$$

$$\mathbf{y}_i(t) - \mathbf{a}_i(t) = \mathbf{o}_{i_0}^y B_0^2(\theta_i) + \mathbf{o}_{i_1}^y \xi_i B_1^2(\theta_i) + \mathbf{o}_{i_2}^y B_2^2(\theta_i) \quad (6)$$

where $B_k^2(\theta_i) = \begin{pmatrix} 2 \\ k \end{pmatrix} (1-\theta_i)^{2-k}\theta_i^k$, the quadratic Bernstein polynomials, the weight $\xi_i = \alpha_i\alpha_{i+1} + \beta_i\beta_{i+1} + \gamma_i\gamma_{i+1} + \delta_i\delta_{i+1}$ and the control points $\mathbf{o}_{i_j}^x$, $\mathbf{o}_{i_j}^y \in \mathbb{R}^3$, $j = 0, 1, 2$ can easily be compute by comparing the coefficients of (5) and (6) with that of (2) and (3).

Corresponding rational quadratic spline $\mathbf{a}_i(t)$, the ith segment of $\mathbf{a}(t)$, in a Bernstein-Bézier form with denominator $w_i(t)$ as defined above, having the following properties $\mathbf{a}_i(t_i) = \mathbf{a}_i$, $\mathbf{a}_i(t_{i+1}) = \mathbf{a}_{i+1}$, $\mathbf{a}_i'(t_i) = \mathbf{d}_i^{(1)}$ for $i = 0, 1, \dots, n-1$ can easily be derived as

$$\mathbf{a}_i(t) = \frac{B_0^2(\theta_i)\mathbf{a}_i + \xi_i(\mathbf{a}_i + \frac{h_i\mathbf{d}_i^{(1)}}{2\xi_i})B_1^2(\theta_i) + \mathbf{a}_{i+1}B_2^2(\theta_i)}{B_0^2(\theta_i) + \xi_i B_1^2(\theta_i) + B_2^2(\theta_i)}$$

such that $\mathbf{a}_{i-1}(t_i) = \mathbf{a}_i(t_i)$; $i = 1, 2, \dots, n-1$. Thus $\mathbf{a}(t)$ defined above is $C^0[t_0, t_n]$.

If $\xi_i = 0$ for any i, the middle control points of $\mathbf{a}_i(t)$, $\mathbf{x}_i(t)$ and $\mathbf{y}_i(t)$ are at infinity for that i. To cope with this situation we adopt the same stragty as adopted in [12].

Since $\mathbf{x}(t) - \mathbf{a}(t)$ and $\mathbf{y}(t) - \mathbf{a}(t)$ are C^0 and $\mathbf{a}(t)$ is C^0, so $\mathbf{x}(t) = (\mathbf{x}(t) - \mathbf{a}(t)) + \mathbf{a}(t)$ and $\mathbf{y}(t) = (\mathbf{y}(t) - \mathbf{a}(t)) + \mathbf{a}(t)$, being the sum of two C^0 curves, are $C^0[t_0, t_n]$.

6. Computation of Rotation

For this it is enough to compute the unit quaternion $Q_i = [\alpha_i, \beta_i, \gamma_i, \delta_i] = [\cos\frac{\phi_i}{2}, \sin\frac{\phi_i}{2}\mathbf{n}_i]$ at each parameter t_i, where $\mathbf{n}_i$ is the unit vector in the direction of the axis of rotation and ϕ_i, the angle of rotation. i.e. Determination of the unit vector bn_i and the Angle of Rotation ϕ_i for each i is enough.

Let the non-colinear vertices P_1, P_2, P_3 of a triangle $\triangle$ be situated at the points A_0, B_0, C_0 at parameter t_0 and at the points A_i, B_i, C_i; $i = 1, \dots, n$ after the ith displacement at parameter t_i. We assume that the position vectors $\mathbf{a}_i$, $\mathbf{x}_i$, $\mathbf{y}_i$ of these points A_i, B_i, C_i; $i = 0, 1, \dots, n$ are anyhow known values with respect to some coordinate system with origin at O.

First all vertices undergo a translation $\mathbf{d}_i = \mathbf{a}_i - \mathbf{a}_0$ from

their positions OA_0, OB_0, OC_0, the vertex P_1 reaches its position A_i, $i = 1, \dots, n$. Other two vertices P_2, P_3 will move to points, whose position vectors with respect to O are equal to $\hat{B}_i = OB_0 + d_i$, $\hat{C}_i = OC_0 + \mathbf{d}_i$ respectively. Then we displace the triangle from its intermediate position to its final position, keeping vertix P_1 fixed to its position $OA_i = OA_0 + \mathbf{d}_i = \mathbf{a}_i$.

Let axis of rotation be the directed line A_iN through A_i,

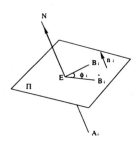

Figure 2.

perpendicular to planes $A_i\hat{B}_iB_i$, Figure 2 (also perpendicular to the plane $A_i\hat{C}_iC_i$ and ϕ_i be the angle of rotation. The plane through $\hat{B}_i$ with A_iN as normal is labelled Π: it meets the axis A_iN in the point E. In order to define the rotation we draw the circle, centre E, radius $E\hat{B}_i$ that lies in the plane Π. The vector $A_i\hat{B}_i$, when rotated from $\hat{B}_i$ to B_i about the axis A_iN, moves along the circumference of this circle and $\phi_i = \angle\hat{B}_iEB_i$ (also $\phi_i = \angle\hat{C}_iEC_i$).

Theorem 1 *Let $A_i\hat{B}_i = \mathbf{s}_2$, be the position vector with respect to A_i of the vertice P_2 before the rotation, and $A_iB_i = \mathbf{s}_1$, its position vector after the rotation then*

$$\mathbf{s}_1 - \mathbf{s}_2 = \tan\frac{\theta_i}{2}\mathbf{n}_i \times (\mathbf{s}_2 + \mathbf{s}_1), \quad (7)$$

where $\mathbf{n}_i$ is a unit vector in the direction of given axis of rotation A_iN and ϕ_i is the given angle of rotation.

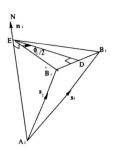

Figure 3. Displacement.

142

Proof:- Let D be the midpoint of $\hat{B}_iB_i$ (see Figure3), then $\hat{B}_iB_i$ is perpendicular to $\underline{ED}$ and also perpendicular to $\mathbf{n}_i$ and hence we have, using the definition of the vector product, that $\hat{B}_iB_i = \alpha\mathbf{n}_i \times \underline{ED}$, where α is some scalar to be determined. Comparing magnitudes yields the following equation for α:

$$2|\underline{\hat{B}_iD}| = |\hat{B}_iB_i| = \alpha|\mathbf{n}_i||\underline{ED}|\sin\frac{\pi}{2} = \alpha|\mathbf{n}_i||\underline{ED}|$$

Alternatively $\alpha = 2|\hat{B}_iD|/|\underline{ED}| = 2\tan\frac{\phi_i}{2}$.

$$\underline{\hat{B}_iB_i} = 2\tan\frac{\phi_i}{2}\mathbf{n}_i \times \underline{ED} = 2\tan\frac{\phi_i}{2}\mathbf{n}_i \times (\underline{A_iD} - \underline{A_iE})$$

as $\mathbf{n}_i$ and $\underline{A_iE}$ are parallel and $\underline{A_iD} = \frac{1}{2}(\mathbf{s}_1 + \mathbf{s}_2)$ so that $\mathbf{s}_1 - \mathbf{s}_2 = \tan\frac{\phi_i}{2}\mathbf{n} \times (\mathbf{s}_1 + \mathbf{s}_2)$, as required. $\square$

By choosing the sense of $\mathbf{n}_i$ to be the same as that of $\tan\frac{\phi_i}{2}\mathbf{n}_i$, take ϕ_i to be in the range 0 to π. For $\phi_i = \pi$ as $\tan\frac{\phi_i}{2}$ is infinite. This value of ϕ will be considered separately. Other rotations obtained by adding or subtracting multiples of 2π from this value (of ϕ) produce the same effect on the particle and may therefore be referred to as equivalent rotations.

In order to make use of the results contained in the proof of Theorem 1 it is necessary for A_i to be the origin for position vectors of B_i, $\hat{B}_i$, C_i and $\hat{C}_i$. We have

$$A_i\hat{B}_i = \mathbf{x}_0 - \mathbf{a}_0, \qquad A_iB_i = \mathbf{x}_i - \mathbf{a}_i$$
$$A_i\hat{C}_i = \mathbf{y}_0 - \mathbf{a}_0, \qquad A_iC_i = \mathbf{y}_i - \mathbf{a}_i.$$

Observing that axis of rotation is perpendicular to both $\hat{B}B_i$ and $\hat{C}C_i$ so it must be proportional to the vector $\hat{B}B_i \times \hat{C}C_i$. Therefore, take the unit vector $\mathbf{n}_i$ as

$$\mathbf{n}_i = \frac{(\mathbf{x}_i - \mathbf{a}_i - \overline{\mathbf{x}_0 - \mathbf{a}_0}) \times (\mathbf{y}_i - \mathbf{a}_i - \overline{\mathbf{y}_0 - \mathbf{a}_0})}{|(\mathbf{x}_i - \mathbf{a}_i - \overline{\mathbf{x}_0 - \mathbf{a}_0}) \times (\mathbf{y}_i - \mathbf{a}_i - \overline{\mathbf{y}_0 - \mathbf{a}_0})|} \quad (8)$$

provided that $|(\mathbf{x}_i - \mathbf{a}_i - \overline{\mathbf{x}_0 - \mathbf{a}_0}) \times (\mathbf{y}_i - \mathbf{a}_i - \overline{\mathbf{y}_0 - \mathbf{a}_0}))|$ is non-zero.

Replace $\mathbf{s}_2$ by $A_i\hat{B}_i = \mathbf{x}_0 - \mathbf{a}_0$ and $\mathbf{s}_1$ by $A_iB_i = \mathbf{x}_i - \mathbf{a}_i$, and substitute $\mathbf{n}_i$ in the Theorem 1, using $(\mathbf{c} \times \mathbf{b}) \times \mathbf{a} = (\mathbf{c} \cdot \mathbf{a})\mathbf{b} - (\mathbf{b} \cdot \mathbf{a})\mathbf{c}$ from vector analysis and the fact that $(\mathbf{x}_i - \mathbf{a}_i - \overline{\mathbf{x}_0 - \mathbf{a}_0}) \cdot (\mathbf{x}_i - \mathbf{a}_i + \overline{\mathbf{x}_0 - \mathbf{a}_0}) = 0$, then comparing both the sides we have

$$\tan\frac{\phi_i}{2} = \frac{|(\mathbf{x}_i - \mathbf{a}_i - \overline{\mathbf{x}_0 - \mathbf{a}_0}) \times (\mathbf{y}_i - \mathbf{a}_i - \overline{\mathbf{y}_0 - \mathbf{a}_0})|}{(\overline{\mathbf{y}_0 - \mathbf{a}_0} - \mathbf{y}_i - \mathbf{a}_i) \cdot (\mathbf{x}_i - \mathbf{a}_i + \overline{\mathbf{x}_0 - \mathbf{a}_0})}$$

which will give us the value of ϕ_i.

If $|(\mathbf{x}_i - \mathbf{a}_i - \overline{\mathbf{x}_0 - \mathbf{a}_0}) \times (\mathbf{y}_i - \mathbf{a}_i - \overline{\mathbf{y}_0 - \mathbf{a}_0})|$ is a zero for any i then either $(\mathbf{x}_i - \mathbf{a}_i - \overline{\mathbf{x}_0 - \mathbf{a}_0})$ or $(\mathbf{y}_i - \mathbf{a}_i - \overline{\mathbf{y}_0 - \mathbf{a}_0})$ or both are zero or both parallel to eachother for that value of i.

In case of pure translation, both $(\mathbf{x}_i - \mathbf{a}_i - \overline{\mathbf{x}_0 - \mathbf{a}_0})$ and $(\mathbf{y}_i - \mathbf{a}_i - \overline{\mathbf{y}_0 - \mathbf{a}_0})$ will be zero. Therefore $\phi_i = 0$ and

$$Q_i = [\cos\frac{\phi_i}{2}, \sin\frac{\phi_i}{2}\mathbf{n}_i] = [1, 0, 0, 0].$$

If one of them say $(\mathbf{x}_i - \mathbf{a}_i - \overline{\mathbf{x}_0 - \mathbf{a}_0})$ is zero then the points A_i and B_i will be fixed after translation $\mathbf{d}_i$, so we take A_iB_i as axis of rotation.

If both $(\mathbf{x}_i - \mathbf{a}_i - \overline{\mathbf{x}_0 - \mathbf{a}_0})$ and $(\mathbf{y}_i - \mathbf{a}_i - \overline{\mathbf{y}_0 - \mathbf{a}_0})$ are parallel to each other for any i then the rotation is of amount π about an axis parallel to the vectors $(\mathbf{x}_i - \mathbf{a}_i + \overline{\mathbf{x}_0 - \mathbf{a}_0})$ or $(\mathbf{y}_i - \mathbf{a}_i + \overline{\mathbf{y}_0 - \mathbf{a}_0})$.

For $i = 0$ the values of α_0, β_0, γ_0 and δ_0 are yet to choose. We choose $[\alpha_0, \beta_0, \gamma_0, \delta_0] = [1, 0, 0, 0]$ such that $\mathbf{R}(t_0)$ is a unit matrix.

The main disadvantage of using quaternions is that their 2-to-1 correspondence with rotations necessitates a preprocessing step, to choose whether the plus or minus quaternion is the appropriate one to use. Keep Q_0 fixed then choose the sign of Q_i; $i = 1, \ldots, n$ such that

$$\alpha_{i-1}\alpha_i + \beta_{i-1}\beta_i + \gamma_{i-1}\gamma_i + \delta_{i-1}\delta_i > 0; \ i = 1, \ldots, n. \quad (9)$$

An example for C^0 smooth rational motion of a rigid triangle in $\mathbb{R}^3$ is given in Figure 4.

7. C^1 Smooth Rational Motions

To improve the smoothness we increase the degree of $\alpha_i(\theta_i)$, $\beta_i(\theta_i)$, $\gamma_i(\theta_i)$ and $\delta_i(\theta_i)$ to quadratic. Let

$$\begin{aligned}
\alpha_i(\theta_i) &= (1-\theta_i)^2\alpha_i + 2\mu_i(1-\theta_i)\theta_i + \theta_i^2\alpha_{i+1} \\
\beta_i(\theta_i) &= (1-\theta_i)^2\beta_i + 2\nu_i(1-\theta_i)\theta_i + \theta_i^2\beta_{i+1} \\
\gamma_i(\theta_i) &= (1-\theta_i)^2\gamma_i + 2\eta_i(1-\theta_i)\theta_i + \theta_i^2\gamma_{i+1} \\
\delta_i(\theta_i) &= (1-\theta_i)^2\delta_i + 2\lambda_i(1-\theta_i)\theta_i + \theta_i^2\delta_{i+1}
\end{aligned}$$

where μ_i, ν_i, η_i and λ_i are chosen by imposing the following constraints

$$\begin{aligned}
\alpha_{i-1}(t_i) &= \alpha_i(t_i), & \alpha'_{i-1}(t_i) &= \alpha'_i(t_i) & (10) \\
\beta_{i-1}(t_i) &= \beta_i(t_i), & \beta'_{i-1}(t_i) &= \beta'_i(t_i) & (11) \\
\gamma_{i-1}(t_i) &= \gamma_i(t_i), & \gamma'_{i-1}(t_i) &= \gamma'_i(t_i) & (12) \\
\delta_{i-1}(t_i) &= \delta_i(t_i), & \delta'_{i-1}(t_i &= \delta'_i(t_i). & (13)
\end{aligned}$$

The constraints (10)–(13) give the following system of 'consistency equations'

$$h_{i-1}\mu_i + h_i\mu_{i-1} = (h_i + h_{i-1})\alpha_i : \ i = 1, \ldots, n-1 \ (14)$$
$$h_{i-1}\nu_i + h_i\nu_{i-1} = (h_i + h_{i-1})\beta_i : \ i = 1, \ldots, n-1 \ (15)$$
$$h_{i-1}\eta_i + h_i\eta_{i-1} = (h_i + h_{i-1})\gamma_i : \ i = 1, \ldots, n-1 \ (16)$$
$$h_{i-1}\lambda_i + h_i\lambda_{i-1} = (h_i + h_{i-1})\delta_i : \ i = 1, \ldots, n-1 \ (17)$$

To solve these systems (14)–(17) with n variables and $n-1$ equations, we need one extra condition for each system. For simplicity, assume that μ_0, ν_0, η_0 and λ_0 (or μ_{n-1}, ν_{n-1}, η_{n-1} and λ_{n-1}) are given as end conditions. If we suppose that

$$\alpha''_0(t_0) = 0 = \beta''_0(t_0) = \gamma''_0(t_0) = \delta''_0(t_0), \quad (18)$$

$$\eta_0 = \frac{1}{2}(\gamma_0 + \gamma_1), \qquad \eta_i = \gamma_i + \frac{h_i}{h_{i-1}}(\gamma_i - \eta_{i-1})$$

$$\lambda_0 = \frac{1}{2}(\delta_0 + \delta_1), \qquad \lambda_i = \delta_i + \frac{h_i}{h_{i-1}}(\delta_i - \lambda_{i-1}).$$

If we suppose that

$$\alpha''_{n-1}(t_n) = 0 = \beta''_{n-1}(t_n) = \gamma''_{n-1}(t_n) = \delta''_{n-1}(t_n), \quad (19)$$

then $\mu_i, \nu_i, \eta_i, \delta_i : i = n-1, n-2, \ldots, 0$ are

$$\mu_{n-1} = \frac{1}{2}(\alpha_{n-1} + \alpha_n), \qquad \mu_{i-1} = \alpha_i + \frac{h_{i-1}}{h_i}(\alpha_i - \mu_i)$$

$$\nu_{n-1} = \frac{1}{2}(\beta_{n-1} + \beta_n), \qquad \nu_{i-1} = \beta_i + \frac{h_{i-1}}{h_i}(\beta_i - \nu_i)$$

$$\eta_{n-1} = \frac{1}{2}(\gamma_{n-1} + \gamma_n), \qquad \eta_{i-1} = \gamma_i + \frac{h_{i-1}}{h_i}(\gamma_i - \eta_i)$$

$$\lambda_{n-1} = \frac{1}{2}(\delta_{n-1} + \delta_n), \qquad \lambda_{i-1} = \delta_i + \frac{h_{i-1}}{h_i}(\delta_i - \lambda_i).$$

For these values of μ_i, ν_i, η_i and λ_i, $\alpha(t)$, $\beta(t)$, $\gamma(t)$, and $\delta(t)$, are C^1 piecewise quadratic splines and so $w(t)$ is a C^1 piecewise quartic spline. Thus every entry in $\mathbf{R}(t)$ is a C^1 piecewise rational quartic spline. Consequently $\mathbf{x}(t) - \mathbf{a}(t) = R(t)(\mathbf{x}_0 - \mathbf{a}_0)$, and $\mathbf{y}(t) - \mathbf{a}(t) = R(t)(\mathbf{y}_0 - \mathbf{a}_0)$ are C^1 piecewise quartic rational splines with common denominator $w(t)$.

If we write the ith segments, $\mathbf{x}_i(t) - \mathbf{a}_i(t)$ and $\mathbf{y}_i(t) - \mathbf{a}_i(t)$ of rational quartic splines $\mathbf{x}(t) - \mathbf{a}(t)$ and $\mathbf{y}(t) - \mathbf{a}(t)$ respectively, in a Bernstein-Bézier form as

$$w_i(t) = \sum_{k=0}^{4} \xi_{i_k} B_k^4(\theta_i)$$

$$\mathbf{x}_i(t) - \mathbf{a}_i(t) = \sum_{k=0}^{4} \xi_{i_k} \mathbf{o}_{i_k}^x B_k^4(\theta_i)$$

$$\mathbf{y}_i(t) - \mathbf{a}_i(t) = \sum_{k=0}^{4} \xi_{i_k} \mathbf{o}_{i_k}^y B_k^4(\theta_i) \quad (20)$$

with the quartic Bernstein polynomials $B_k^4(\theta_i)$ in θ_i. Then weights $\xi_{i_0} = 1 = \xi_{i_4}$ and ξ_{i_k}, $k = 1, 2, 3$ are

$$\xi_{i_1} = \alpha_i \mu_i + \beta_i \nu_i + \gamma_i \eta_i + \delta_i \lambda_i$$

$$\xi_{i_2} = \frac{2}{3}(\mu_i^2 + \nu_i^2 + \eta_i^2 + \lambda_i^2)$$

$$+ \frac{1}{3}(\alpha_i \alpha_{i+1} + \beta_i \beta_{i+1} + \gamma_i \gamma_{i+1} + \delta_i \delta_{i+1})$$

$$\xi_{i_3} = \mu_i \alpha_{i+1} + \nu_i \beta_{i+1} + \eta_i \gamma_{i+1} + \lambda_i \delta_{i+1}$$

and the expression for the Bézier points $\mathbf{o}_{i_k}^x$, $\mathbf{o}_{i_k}^y \in \mathbb{R}^3$, $k = 0, \ldots, 4$ can be found by comparing the coefficients.

Let $\mathbf{a}_i(t)$ too be a Bernstein-Bézier rational quartic curve

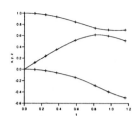

(a) Three independent curves drawn by the vertex represents the translation curve.

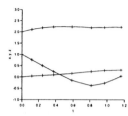

(b) Three independent curves drawn by one of the other two vertices.

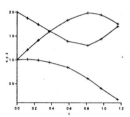

(c) Three independent curves drawn by the third vertex.

(d) Curves drawn by the three vertices of triangle.

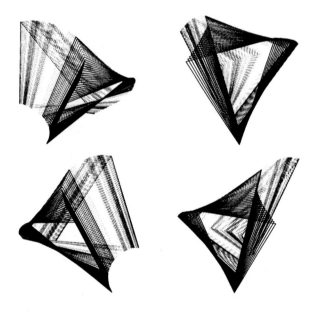

Figure 4. C^0 smooth motion of a rigid triangle from different angles of observation.

then $\mu_i, \nu_i, \eta_i, \delta_i : i = 0, 1, \ldots, n-1$ are

$$\mu_0 = \frac{1}{2}(\alpha_0 + \alpha_1), \qquad \mu_i = \alpha_i + \frac{h_i}{h_{i-1}}(\alpha_i - \mu_{i-1})$$

$$\nu_0 = \frac{1}{2}(\beta_0 + \beta_1), \qquad \nu_i = \beta_i + \frac{h_i}{h_{i-1}}(\beta_i - \nu_{i-1})$$

with same denominator $w_i(t)$

$$\mathbf{a}_i(t) = \frac{\sum_{k=0}^4 \xi_{i_k} \mathbf{c}_{i_k}^{(1)} B_k^4(\theta_i)}{\sum_{k=0}^4 \xi_{i_k} B_k^4(\theta_i)};$$

where weights ξ_{i_k}, $k = 0, \ldots, 4$ are same as defined above. Imposing the following conditions $\mathbf{a}_i(t_i) = \mathbf{a}_i$, $\mathbf{a}_i(t_{i+1}) = \mathbf{a}_{i+1}$, $\mathbf{a}_i'(t_i) = \mathbf{d}_i^{(1)}$, $\mathbf{a}_i'(t_{i+1}) = \mathbf{d}_{i+1}^{(1)}$, $\mathbf{a}_i''(t_i) = \mathbf{d}_i^{(2)}$, we can found the Bézier points $\mathbf{c}_{i_k}$, $k = 0, \ldots, 4$ as

$$\mathbf{c}_{i_0}^{(1)} = \mathbf{a}_i, \ \mathbf{c}_{i_1}^{(1)} = \mathbf{a}_i + \frac{h_i \mathbf{d}_i^{(1)}}{4\xi_{i_1}}$$

$$\mathbf{c}_{i_2}^{(1)} = \mathbf{a}_i + \frac{(4\xi_{i_1} - 1)h_i \mathbf{d}_i^{(1)}}{6\xi_{i_2}} + \frac{h_i^2 \mathbf{d}_i^{(2)}}{12\xi_{i_2}}$$

$$\mathbf{c}_{i_3}^{(1)} = \mathbf{a}_{i+1} - \frac{h_i \mathbf{d}_{i+1}^{(1)}}{4\xi_{i_3}}, \ \mathbf{c}_{i_4}^{(1)} = \mathbf{a}_{i+1}.$$

Then $a_{i-1}(t_i) = \mathbf{a}_i(t_i)$, $\mathbf{a}_{i-1}'(t_i) = \mathbf{a}_i'(t_i)$; $\forall \ i$ is $C^1[t_0, t_n]$.

Since $\mathbf{x}(t) - \mathbf{a}(t)$ and $\mathbf{y}(t) - \mathbf{a}(t)$ are C^1 and $\mathbf{a}(t)$ is C^1, so $\mathbf{x}(t)$ and $\mathbf{y}(t)$, where $\mathbf{x}(t) = (\mathbf{x}(t) - \mathbf{a}(t)) + \mathbf{a}(t)$ and $\mathbf{y}(t) = (\mathbf{y}(t) - \mathbf{a}(t)) + \mathbf{a}(t)$, being the sum of two C^1 curves, are $C^1[t_0, t_n]$.

The parametric values t_i are unknown to us. We either choose unit parametrization or estimate them from the given data (list of different possibilities can be found in the literature [7]).

Figure 6. C^1 **smooth motion of a rigid triangle from different angles of observation using end conditions (19) on** t_n.

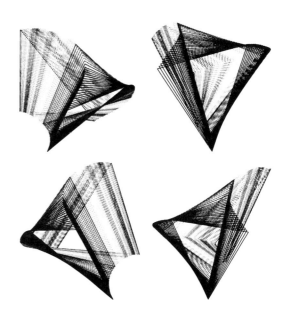

Figure 7. C^1 **smooth motion of a rigid triangle from different angles of observation using end conditions (18) on** t_0.

Figure 5. C^1 **smooth motion of a rigid triangle from different angles of observation using end conditions (18) on** t_0.

8. Conclusion

We have derived a new algorithm of automatic construction of C^1 smooth piecewise quartic rational curves,

Figure 8. C^1 smooth motion of a rigid triangle from different angles of observation using end conditions (19) on t_n.

through each vertex of triangle. The resulting curves are passing through the given data points, are smooth and also keep the fixed distance between any two of these curve. The algorithem can be used for the motion of any rigid body, because the position of any rigid body can be found exactly if positions of its any three non-colinear points are known. The method is simple to use, simple to implement, robust, computationally efficient and cheap. We present a few numerical examples (see Figure 5–Figure 8) to show that the resulting rational motions of the rigid triangle in $\mathbb{R}^3$ is smooth and natural-looking. These examples shows that our algorithm is good enough for practical use, but there are much that can be still be done to improve our algorithms.

References

[1] F. S. Chaudhry and D. C. Handscomb, *(1997), Smooth Motion of a Rigid Body in 2D and 3D, in Proceedings International Conference on Information Visualization IV'97, IEEE Computer Society, 205–210.*

[2] G. Farin, *(1993), Curves and Surfaces for Computer Aided Geometric Design (3rd edition) Academic Press, Boston.*

[3] I. D. Faux and M. J. Pratt, *(1981), Computational Geometry for Design and Manufacture, Ellis Horwood, London.*

[4] Q. J. Ge and B. Ravani, *(1994), Geometric Construction of Bézier Motions, ASME Journal of Mechanical Design, Vol. 116, 749–755.*

[5] Q. J. Ge and B. Ravani, *(1994), Computer Aided Geometric of Motion Interpolants, ASME Journal of Mechanical Design, Vol. 116, 756–762.*

[6] T. Horsch and B. Jüttler, *(1998), Cartesian Spline Interpolation for Industrial Robots, Computer-Aided Design, Vol. 30(3), 169–178.*

[7] B. Jüttler, *(1994), Visualization of Moving Objects Using Dual Quaternion Curves, Computers & Graphics, Vol. 18(3), 315–326.*

[8] B. Jüttler, *(1995), Spatial Rational Motions and their Application in Computer Aided Geometric Design, Mathematical Methods for Curves and Surfaces, M. Dæhlen, T. Lyche and L. L. Schumaker (eds.), 271–280.*

[9] B. Jüttler and M. G. Wagner, *(1996), Computer-Aided Design with Spatial Rational B-Spline Motions, ASME Journal of Mechanical Design, Vol. 118, 193–201*

[10] M. S. Kim and K. W. Nam, *(1995), Interpolating Solid Orientations with Circular Blending Quaternion Curves, Computer-Aided Design, Vol. 27(5), 385–398.*

[11] B. L.MacCarthy, C. S. Syan and M. C. Browne, *(1993), Spline in Motion – An Introduction to MODUS and some Unsolved Approximation Problems, Numerical Algorithms, Vol. 5, 41–49.*

[12] L. Piegl, *(1987), On use of Infinite Control Points in CAGD, Computer Aided Geometric Design, Vol. 4, 155–166.*

[13] O. Röschel, *(1998), Rational Motion Design—a Survey, Computer-Aided Design, Vol. 30(3), 169–178.*

[14] E. Salamin, *(1979), Application of Quaternions to Computation With Rotations, Stanford AI Lab. Internal Working Paper, On the World-Wide Web at ftp://ftp.netcom.com/pub/hb/hbaker/quaternion /stanfordaiwp79-salamin.ps.gz (also .dvi.gz).*

[15] K. Shoemake, *(1985), Animating Rotation with Quaternion Curves, Computer Graphics, Vol. 19(3), 245-254.*

The Delaunay Constrained Triangulation :
The Delaunay Stable Algorithms

L. Rognant*, J.M. Chassery**, S. Goze*, J.G Planès*

(*)Alcatel Space Industries,
26 av. J.F. Champollion B.P. 1187
31037 Toulouse Cedex - FRANCE
tel: 33 (5) 34 35 69 50
Loic.Rognant@space.alcatel.fr

(**)TIMC/IMAG
(Institut d'Informatique et de Mathématiques appliquées de Grenoble)
Institut Albert Bonniot
Université Joseph Fourier - Grenoble
38706 La Tronche Cedex - FRANCE

Abstract

The Delaunay triangulation is well known for its use in geometric design. A derived version of this structure, the Delaunay constrained triangulation, takes into account the triangular mesh problem in presence of rectilinear constraints.

The Delaunay constrained triangulation is very useful for CAD, topography and mapping and in finite element analysis. This technique is still developing. We present a taxonomy of this geometric structure. First we describe the different tools used to introduce the problem. Then we introduce the different approaches highlighting various points of view of the problem.

We will focus on the Delaunay stable methods. A Delaunay stable method preserves the Delaunay nature of the constrained triangulation. Each method is detailed by its algorithms, performances, and properties. For instance we show how these methods approximate the generalised Voronoï diagram of the configuration.

The Delaunay stable algorithms are used for 2.5D DEM design. The aim of this work is to demonstrate that the use of topographic constraints in a regular DEM without adding new points preserves the terrain shape. So the resulting DEM can be more easily interpreted because its realism is preserved and the mesh still owns all the Delaunay triangulation properties.

Keywords : Delaunay triangulation, Delaunay constrained triangulation, surface model, Delaunay stable algorithm, DEM application.

1. Introduction

After the presentation of the Delaunay constrained triangulation problem, we define tools to describe the working area and the algorithm behaviour classification. Then we expose the different approaches, from the basic redefinition of the problem to full preserving methods. Among them, the Delaunay stable methods are detailed with the algorithmie description.

Finally, we use these stable algorithms to improve and maintain at the lowest cost the DEM realism during the resampling process.

2. The problem

The problem of the constrained triangulation is to make appear a constraint graph described by constraint edges. Each constraint edge is then a part of triangles. We will use the Delaunay triangular structure. Let's define the constraint elements.

Definition 2.1 (The constraints field)
The constraint field C_{ont} is the set of all the constraint edges, having no intersections except with other vertices or edges at their ends.

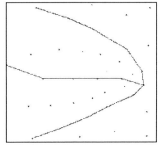

Figure 2.1 Example of data and Constraint field

Definition 2.2 (Polygon triangulation)
The triangulation of a polygon is performed by

looking at its defining elements separately as constraint edges.

2.1 Tools and definitions

Definition 2.3 (Delaunay compliant edge)

A Delaunay compliant edge is an edge for which the insertion of its extremities in the Delaunay triangulation makes sure the appearance of the edge as a Delaunay edge.

Definition 2.4 (The constraint tube)

The tube of a constraint edge e in the triangulation T(s) is the set of triangles of T which are directly crossed by the edge.

$$t_u(e) = \{triangles \ t \in T | t \cap e \neq \emptyset\}$$

This area is the limit of the direct triangulation impact of the constraint incorporing methods. This helps to keep the local aspect of the Delaunay triangulation (Markovian behaviour).

Definition 2.5 (Exact verification of a constraint field)

A triangulation T verifies exactly a constraint field if each element of C_{ont} appears as element of the triangulation..

So we can define a first class of incorporing methods :

The constraint forcing method :

The principle of this method is to modify the direct neighbourhood triangulation to avoid the constraint crossing edges without modifying the constraint edge.

Definition 2.6 (Poor verification of a constraint field)

A triangulation T verifies poorly a constraint field if each element of C_{ont} appears as it is or as a partition in the triangulation.

This leads to the second class of incorporing methods.

The constraint breaking method :

The constraint breaking principle is to transform the constraint edge by partitioning it into Delaunay compliant edges. The corresponding algorithms are mainly Delaunay stable.

Definition 2.7(Delaunay stable incorporing method)

A constraint incorporing method in a Delaunay triangulation is said to be stable if the resulting triangulation is still a Delaunay triangulation.

Proposition 2.1 (Delaunay unstable method)

A constraint incorporing method in a Delaunay triangulation is said to be Delaunay unstable if the result is a triangulation respecting no longer the empty circle criterion.

2.2 Semantics

The difference between the stable and unstable methods can be translated in their naming manner.

It has to be stressed that the Delaunay Constrained Triangulation (DCT) is different from the Constrained Delaunay Triangulation (CDT). The CDT are produced by Delaunay unstable methods. On the contrary, DCT are

the result of a Delaunay stable algorithm.

3. Delaunay triangulation under constraint

The principle is to redefine the building criterion of the Delaunay triangulation. So, we define the constrained empty circle criterion taking into account the graph of visibility of the configuration. The constraint field is exactly verified because the edge integrity is preserved.

Definition 3.1 (mutual visibility)

Two vertices Vi and Vj are mutually visible if no constraint edge crosses their linking segment.

Definition 3.2 (Constraint empty circle criterion)

A triangle t(vi,vj,vk) of T respects the constraint empty circle if and only if there is no other vertex v of T such :

- *v is contained in the circumscribed circle to t.*
- *v is not visible from the three vertices vi,vj,vk at the same time.*

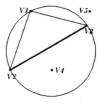

Figure 3.1: The constraint empty circle criterion (v2,v3 is a constraint edge)

Definition 3.3 (The Delaunay triangulation under constraint)

A triangulation is a Delaunay triangulation under constraint if all the triangles respect the constrained empty circle criteria.

So the defined triangulation contains the constraint graph as part of itself. The constraint field is exactly verified.

The Voronoï diagram is redefined too and it has been proved that the duality between the constrained Voronoï diagram and the Delaunay triangulation under constraint still exists.

Definition 3.4 (Constraint Euclidean distance)

If d(v,v') is the euclidean distance from v to v' the constrained euclidean distance by the constraint field is defined by:

$$d_{C_{ont}}(v,v') = \begin{cases} d_{C_{ont}}(v,v') \ if \ v \ and \ v' \ are \ mutually \ visible \\ \infty \end{cases}$$

Definition 3.5 (Constrained Voronoï diagram)

The constrained Voronoï diagram of C_{ont} is defined as the set of the cVOR cells. The plan is partitioned into constrained Voronoï cells where each area is defined by:

$$cVOR(v_i) = \left\{ v \in \Re^2 \middle| \begin{matrix} d_{c_{ont}}(v,v_i) < \infty \ and \\ d_{c_{ont}}(v,v_i) < d_{c_{ont}}(v,v_j) \ \forall v_j \in V \end{matrix} \right\}$$

4. The unstable methods

First we compute the Delaunay triangulation of the vertices and the constraint extremities. Then we incorporate the missing constraint edges. The main principle is to retriangulate the constraint edge's tube while preserving the edge integrity. So, the resulting triangulation verifies exactly the constraint field but is no more of Delaunay type.

Both sides of the edge are processed separately. Lots oft methods are proposed using the same theorem guaranteeing an existing solution to the problem.

Theorem 4.1(triangulation without internal points) [5]

For each area whose boundary is a simple non crossed polygonal lines, there exists a triangulation without internal points.

Algorithms are based on edge swapping on each side of the constraint edge. Basic methods test every solution while elegant methods swap the edges at random, so exploiting the finite size of the problem to converge to a solution.

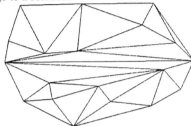

Figure 4.1 The Delaunay unstable forcing method

5. The stable methods

The Delaunay stable methods are based on the breaking method building new Delaunay compliant edges. The resulting triangulation is Delaunay type but verifies poorly the constraint field.

5.1 Densification

This method states that the constraint doesn't appear in the triangulation, because its sampling doesn't fit the neighbourhood. This method presented in [8] analyses the constraint tube to compute an adapted sampling distance to discretise the constraint edge.

Proposition 5.1 (Sampling distance)

Let $d(v,e)$ be the distance between a tube vertex and the constraint edge.

So, the best sampling distance for this set is :

$$P(e,T) = 2 * \min_{\forall v_i \in t_u(e)} d(v_i, e)$$

Theorem 5.1 (Edge incorporation by densification)

The partition of a constraint edge with the sampling distance $P(e,T)$ makes the edge Delaunay compliant.

Proof : The constraint edge doesn't appear in the triangulation because it doesn't fulfill the empty circle criterion . The new edges respect it because the circles, whose diameter they are, contain no other vertices. So we are sure that the partitioned edges are Delaunay compliant. ❏

5.2 Dichotomy

this method uses the classic principle of splitting the constraint edges until all the new edges are Delaunay compliant.

Theorem 5.2 (Edge incorporation by dichotomy)

It always exists an edge partition by dichotomy leading to Delaunay compliant edges.

Proof : the convergence is guaranteed by the densification method. There is a step from which all the edge sizes are below the densification distance which has been defined previously. So they are Delaunay compliant. ❏

5.3 The perpendicular projection

Each vertex of the tube is orthogonally projected on the constraint edge.

Theorem 5.3 (Incorporation by orthogonal tube projection)

The discretisation of a constraint edge by inserting all the orthogonal projections of the tube vertices makes it Delaunay compliant.

(short) **Proof** : The insertion of the orthogonal projection on the constraint edge disturb the empty circle criterion for the tube triangles. So, step by step, from the start to the end of the constraint edge we split it into Delaunay compliant edges. ❏

Proposition 5.2 (Arc cost)

The cost of arcs for the incorporation of an edge with the orthogonal projections is directly related to the edge tube configuration.

$$\text{cost} = Card(t_u(e)) + 1$$

5.4 The intersection incorporation

We split the constraint edge by inserting all the intersections between the tube and its corresponding constraint edge.

Theorem 5.4 (Tube-constraint intersections incorporation)

The partition of a constraint edge by inserting all the intersections between the edge and its tube triangulation makes it Delaunay compliant.

Proof : Each intersecting edge belongs to two Delaunay circles. So, inserting the intersection point disturbs the Delaunay criterion and produces a Delaunay compliant edge. ❏

Proposition 5.3(Arcs cost)

The cost in arcs of inserting the tube-edge intersection method depends on the tube configuration:

$$\text{cost} = Card(t_u(e))$$

5.5 The impact on Voronoï diagram

Stable methods produce Delaunay triangulations. So these DCT still have the Voronoï diagram as dual diagram.

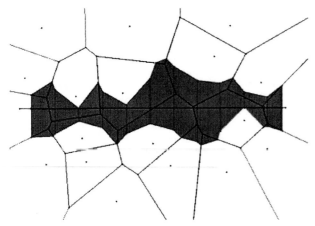

Figure 5.1 Impact of the densification method on the Voronoï diagram

In Figure 5.1, we notice the trace of the new Voronoï diagram after incorporation over the original one. Its typical shape shows the approximation of the generalised Voronoï diagram corresponding to the constraint edge. The quality of the approximation depends on the partition distance (Theorem 5.5).

We present the required principles to define the generalised Voronoï diagram. So we can check the link between the DCT related Voronoï diagram and the generalised Voronoï diagram.

Definition 5.1 (Objects)

Points, open segments and open polygons are considered as simple elements. An object is a set of simple elements.

Definition 5.2 (Generalised Voronoï diagram)

The generalised Voronoï diagram is the nearest neighbourhood cell partition of a set of objects.

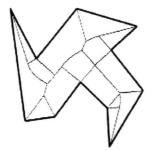

Figure 5.2 : Sample of the generalised Voronoï diagram for a polygon interior.

The "classic" Voronoï diagram is called the punctual Voronoï diagram dealing with vertices. In Figure 5.2 we can see that the generalised Voronoï diagram is made of arcs and parabola sections.

Theorem 5.5 (Convergence of the punctual diagram to the generalised Voronoï diagram)[1]

Let S be a set of objects and S(h) be a discretisation of S. The punctual Voronoï diagram of S(h) converges to the generalised Voronoï diagram of S when the discretisation step decreases to 0.

Theorem 5.6 (The Voronoï diagram associated to the

Delaunay stable methods)

The Voronoï diagram corresponding to the triangulation made by Delaunay stable methods is a punctual approximation of the generalised Voronoï diagram of the configuration.

5.6 Performance analysis

The performance analysis is conducted in two ways. First we use subjective criteria to compare the methods. Then we evaluate quantitatively the gains over ten different configurations.

Definition 5.3 (Certitude of an incorporation method)

the method certitude evaluates how this method progresses at each step toward the solution : i.e. the appearance of the constraint in the Delaunay triangulation.

The densification is a reliable method but it costs a lot. The orthogonal projection or intersection insertion methods are also reliable and improve the arcs cost because it is directly related to the tube configuration. The dichotomy method offers the lowest cost of arcs but we can not predict the final cost.

Method	Certitude	Arcs cost
Densification	+	-
Orthogonal	+	+/-
Intersections	+	+/-
Dichotomy	-	+

Table 1 : Certitude/Cost

Method	Arcs Cost
densification	$f(distance(t_u(e),e)$
dichotomy	-
orthogonal projection	$= Card(t_u(e))+1$
intersections	$= Card(t_u(e))$

Table 2 : Bound of the arcs cost for the Delaunay stable methods

The following table shows the average cost of new arcs computed over ten different configuration.

Method	nb arcs	Gain			
		dens.	ortho.	inters.	dicho.
dens.	104,00		-209,52%	-219,02%	-336,97%
ortho.	33,60	67,69%		-3,07%	-41,18%
inters.	32,60	68,65%	2,98%		-36,97%
dicho.	23,80	77,12%	29,17%	26,99%	

Tableau 1: Average arcs gains over 10 various configurations

5.7 Example

We present the behaviour of the different Delaunay stable algorithms on the same configuration. In the following figure we have:
1. The original configuration.
2. The Densification method.
3. The dichotomy method.

4. The orthogonal projection method.

5. The intersection method.

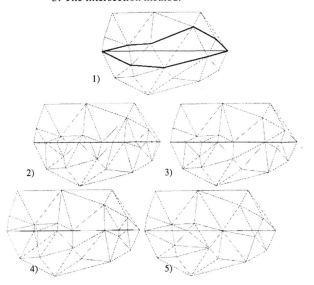

Figure 5.3

The bold line in the first vignette outlines the constraint edge tube boundary. Figure 5.1 is the associated Voronoï diagram to this configuration for the densification method.

6. Application for DEM

6.1 The DEM design

Rippa in [7] shows that the Delaunay triangulation minimises the flexion energy of the mesh. So the Delaunay triangulation provides the best approximating surface reconstruction. This property is very useful for terrain surface from a set of scattered data. Moreover, the duality of the Delaunay triangulation with the Voronoï diagram offers a lot of new perspectives for exploiting the DEM For instance in [8], the Voronoï cells are used to extend the ground roughness measured at different points. So the 2D Delaunay triangulation is used to build a 2.5D surface.

Those properties lead us to look for a constrained Delaunay triangulation preserving its nature and so its properties. So we used the developed algorithms to design the DEM and improve its realism.

The constraints lines describe topographic lines (ridges, valleys) which help to sketch the final DEM

6.2 The resampling problem

The problem of regular DEM is that their sampling method misses topographic features whose size is below the sampling rate distance. We want to improve those DEM by using a triangular Design and incorporating the missed topographic constraints before resampling.

Definition 6.1 (topographic link)

A topographic link is a constraint edge linking two points which belong to the same terrain feature and are mutually visible (for instance two points in the same river).

A topographic link doesn't costs anything because the information needed along the edge for its incorporation is interpolated from the height of its extremities.

6.3 Application

In this example we take a regular mesh over the terrain. Its sampling rate has missed the valley. So when resampling is performed to a better scale, the valley is no longer seen. It is quite a problem for hydrologic computation or when piloting a vehicle.

Figure 8.1 presents the three strategies we developed to improve the DEM realism. The first one is the classic method resampling the grid to make another grid. The second adds topographic links and in the last we correct (move) a few points before adding topographic links.

The Figure 8.2 shows the results of these strategies. We can verify the appearance of the main valley whereas the secondary valley is still missing. In the best method both valleys are well described for a very low cost (1.25% of the whole DEM points are modified).

7. Conclusion and outlooks

We have shown that we have the choice between different philosophies for constraining the Delaunay triangulation. This is summarised in Table 3 .

We have especially described Delaunay stable methods which preserve the Delaunay nature of the resulting triangulation and keep the duality with the Voronoï diagram. The cost of these methods can be evaluated and bounded.

So we are no more limited by the design algorithm to exploit the mesh information.

We have presented a practical application for the DEM resampling. It shows that for a very low cost the Delaunay constrained triangulation can improve the DEM realism and preserves it along the resampling process.

8. References

[1] Bertin E., *Diagrammes de Voronoï 2D et 3D: application en analyse d'images*, Ph.D thesis, TIMC - IMAG, Université Joseph Fourier - Grenoble 1, pp. 163, 1994

[2] Chew L. P., "Constrained Delaunay Triangulations" *Algorithmica*, vol. 4, no. 1, pp. 97-108, 1989

[3] De Floriani L., Falcidieno B., and Pienovi C., "Delaunay-based representation of surfaces defined over arbitrarily shaped domains" *Computer vision, graphics and image processing*, vol. 32, pp. 127-140, 1985

[4] Edelsbrunner , H., "Algorithms in combinatorial geometry" Springer Verlag, 1988

[5] George P. L. and Borouchaki H., "Triangulation de Delaunay et maillage - application aux éléments finis" Hermès, 1997

[6] Preparata F.P. and Shamos M.I., "Computational geometry - An introduction" Springer Verlag, 1985

[7] Rippa S., "Minimal roughness of the Delaunay triangulation" Computer Geometric Design, vol. 7, pp. 489-497, 1990

[8] Rognant L., Modélisation et risques naturels, M. S. thesis, DEA de mathématiques appliquées, TIMC-IMAG-Université Joseph Fourier de Grenoble, pp. 86, 24 1994

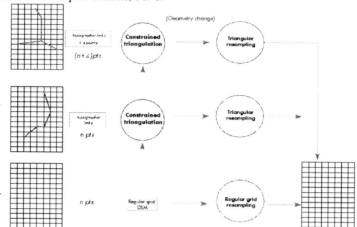

Figure 8.1 The different strategies for DEM resampling

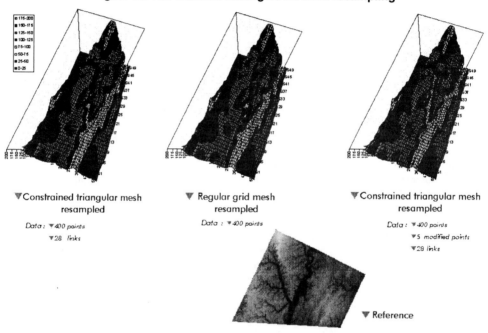

▼Constrained triangular mesh resampled

Data : ▼400 points
　　　　▼28 links

▼ Regular grid mesh resampled

Data : ▼400 points

▼Constrained triangular mesh resampled

Data : ▼400 points
　　　　▼5 modified points
　　　　▼28 links

▼ Reference

Figure 8.2 The result of the resampling process using different strategies

Triangulation			Dual diagram	Elements
Name	Delaunay Nature	Verification of C_{ont}		
Punctual Delaunay Triangulation	o	-	punctual Voronoï	points
Delaunay Triangulation under constraint	n	exact	constrained Voronoï	points, arcs
-	-	-	generalised Voronoï	points, arcs, polygons
constrained Delaunay Triangulation (unstable) - CDT	n	exact	-	points, arcs
Delaunay constrained Triangulation (stable) - DCT	o	poor	punctual approximation of the generalised Voronoï diagram	points, arcs

Table 3 Summary of the different approaches of the constrained Delaunay

An Overview of Triangulation Algorithms for Simple Polygons

Marko Lamot
Hermes Softlab, Kardeljeva 100, 2000 Maribor, Slovenia

Borut Zalik
Faculty of Electrical Engineering and Computer Sciences, Smetanova 17, 2000 Maribor, Slovenia

Abstract

Decomposing simple polygon into simpler components is one of the basic tasks in computational geometry and its applications. The most important simple polygon decomposition is triangulation. Different techniques for triangulating simple polygon were designed. The first part of the paper is an overview of triangulation algorithms based on diagonal inserting. In the second part we present algorithms based on Delaunay triangulation. The basic ideas and approach for each algorithm are presented in this paper. The last part of the paper some representative algorithm by its efficiency are compared.

1. Introduction

Polygons are very convenient for computer representation of the boundary of the objects from the real world. Because polygons can be very complex (can include a few thousand vertices, may be concave and may include nested holes), there is many times the need to decompose the polygons into simpler components which can be easily and faster handled. There are many ideas how to perform this decomposition. Planar polygons can be, for example, decomposed into triangles, convex parts, trapezoids or even star-shaped polygons. Computing the triangulation of a polygon is a fundamental algorithm in computational geometry. It also seems to be the most investigated partitioning method. In computer graphics, polygon triangulation algorithms are widely used for tessellating curved geometries, such as those described by spline.

The paper gives a brief summary of existing triangulation techniques and comparison between them. We will try to cover all techniques for triangulating simple polygons. It is organized into five sections. The second chapter introduces the fundamental terminology, in the third chapter a diagonal inserting algorithms are considered. Fourth section explains the constrained Delaunay triangulation, together with the approaches which introduce Steiner points. The last fifth section contains the comparison of mentioned triangulation methods. For each algorithm, the basic idea and worst time complexity estimation is given. The quality of triangulation is also considered.

2. Background

Every simple polygon P (polygons with edges crossing only in its endpoints) with n vertices has a triangulation. The key for proving of existence of triangulation is the fact that every polygon has a diagonal which exists if the polygon has at least one convex vertex. We can conclude that [17]:
- every polygon has at least one strictly convex vertex,
- every polygon with $n = 4$ vertices has diagonal,
- every polygon P of n vertices may be partitioned into triangles by adding the diagonals.

There is a large number of different ways how to triangulate a given polygon. All these possibilities have in common that the number of diagonals is $n - 3$ and the number of the triangles being generated is $n - 2$. See for details and proofs in [17].

Following the fact of existence of diagonal a basic triangulation algorithm can be constructed as follows: find a diagonal, cut the polygon into two pieces, and recurs each. Finding diagonals is simple application which repeats until all diagonals of polygon are determined. For every edge e of the polygon not incident to either end of the potential diagonal s, see if e intersects s. As soon as an intersection is detected, it is known that s is not a diagonal. If no polygon edge intersects s, then s is a diagonal.

Such direct approach is too inefficient (it takes $O(n^4)$ time) and therefore many authors proposed much faster triangulation algorithms.

As mentioned above, there is a large number of different ways how to triangulate a given polygon (see figure 1). For some applications it is essential that the minimum interior angle of a triangle of the computed triangulation is as large as possible what defines a quality measure. The way that algorithm triangulates a simple polygon is dependent on technique used in algorithm. In figure 1a, for example, the triangulation can be considered as a low quality, because there exist a lot sliver triangles. The algorithms based on Delaunay triangulation ensure better quality triangulation (figure 1b). The quality can be significantly improved by using so-called Steiner's points (figure 1c).

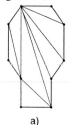  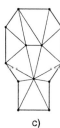

a)   b)   c)

Figure 1: a) Low quality triangulation; b) High quality triangulation; c) Triangulation with Steiner's Points

It is also important into which class of the polygons the input polygon can be classified. It has been shown that monotone polygons, star-shaped polygons, spiral polygons, L-convex polygons, edge visible polygons, intersection-free polygons, palm-shaped polygons and anthropomorphic polygons can be triangulated in linear time [13].

3. Polygon triangulation algorithms based on diagonal inserting

History of polygon triangulation algorithms begins in the year 1911 [14]. That year Lennes proposed an "algorithm" which works by recursively inserting diagonals between pairs of vertices of P and runs in $O(n^2)$ time. At that time mathematicians have been interested in constructive proofs of existence of triangulation for simple polygons. Since then, this type of algorithm reappeared in many papers and books. Inductive proof for existence of triangulation was proposed by Meisters [16]. He proposed an ear searching method and then cutting them off. Vertex v_i of simple polygon P is a principal vertex if no other vertex of P lies in the interior of the triangle v_{i-1}, v_i, v_{i+1} or in the interior of diagonal v_{i-1}, v_{i+1}. A principal vertex v_i of simple polygon P is an ear if the diagonal v_{i-1}, v_{i+1} lies entirely in P. We say that two ears v_i, v_j are non-overlapping if interior $[v_{i-1}, v_i, v_{i+1}] \cap [v_{j-1}, v_j, v_{j+1}] = 0$.

Meisters proved another theorem: except for triangles every simple polygon P has at least two non-overlapping ears [16]. A direct implementation of this idea leads to a complexity of $O(n^3)$. But in 1990 it was discovered that prune and search technique finds an ear in the linear time [11]. It is based on the following observation: a good subpolygon P_1 of a simple polygon P is a subpolygon whose boundary differs from that of P in at most one edge. The basic observation here is that a good subpolygon P_1 has at least one proper ear. Strategy now is as follows: split polygon P of n vertices into two subpolygons in $O(n)$ time

such that one of these subpolygons is a good subpolygon with at most $\lfloor n/2 \rfloor + 1$ vertices. Each subpolygon is then solved recursively. The worst case running time of the algorithm is $T(n) = cn + T(\lfloor n/2 \rfloor + 1)$, where c is a constant. This recurrence has solution $T(n) \in O(n)$. That leads to implementation of Meisters's algorithm with the complexity of $O(n^2)$:

Garey, Johnson, Preparata and Tarjan proposed a divide and conquer algorithm which first broke $O(n^2)$ complexity [10]. Algorithm runs in $O(n \log n)$ time. Their approach includes two steps: the first one decomposes simple polygon into monotone sub-polygons in $O(n \log n)$. The second step triangulates these monotone sub-polygons what can be done in a linear time. Different divide and conquer approach by Chazelle also achieves $O(n \log n)$ running time. Very complicated data structures are used in Tarjan and Van Wyk algorithm that runs in $O(n \log \log n)$ time. However, the same complexity was introduced by Kirkpatrik using simple data structures.

Next improve of speed were algorithms with time complexity $O(n \log^* n)$. Such algorithms were not just faster but also simpler to implement. They all have in common a randomized ("Las Vegas") approach. The most well-know algorithm has been suggested by Seidel [19]. His algorithm runs in practice almost in linear time for the majority of simple polygons. The algorithm has three steps: trapezoidal decomposition of polygon, determination of monotone polygon's chains, and finally, the triangulation of these monotone polygon's chains. The efficiency of Seidel's algorithm is achieved by very efficient trapezoidal decomposition: first a random permutation of edges is determined and then these edges are inserted incrementally into trapezoidal decomposition. With two corresponding structures containing current decomposition and search structure presented algorithm runs in $O(n \log^* n)$ time.

Some researchers designed adaptive algorithms that run fast in many situations. Hertel and Mehlhorn described a sweep-line based algorithm that runs faster the fewer reflex vertices it has [12]. Algorithm's running time is $O(n + r \log r)$ where r denotes the number of reflex vertices of P.

Chazelle and Incerpi also presented an algorithm which time complexity depends on shape of the polygon [4]. They describe a triangulation algorithm that runs in $O(n \log s)$ time where $s < n$. The quantity s measures the sinuosity of the polygon representing how many times the polygon's boundary alternates between complete spirals of opposite orientation. In practice, quantity s is very small or a constant even for very winding polygons. Consider the motion of a straight line $L[v_i, v_{i+1}]$ passing through edge v_i, v_{i+1} where $0 < i < n$. Every time L reaches the vertical position in a clockwise (counter-clockwise) manner we decrement (increment) a winding counter by one. L is spiraling (anti- spiraling) if the winding counter is never decremented (incremented) twice in succession. A new polygonal chain is restarted only when the previous chain ceases to be spiraling or anti-spiraling.

Toussaint proposed in [20] another adaptive algorithm which runs in $O(n(1+t_0))$; $t_0 < n$. The quantity t_0 measures the shape-complexity of the triangulation delivered by the algorithm. More precisely, t_0 is the number of triangles contained in the triangulation obtained that share zero edges with the input polygon. The algorithm runs in $O(n^2)$ worst case, but for several classes of polygons it runs in the linear time. The algorithm is very simple to implement because it does not require sorting or the use of balanced tree structures.

Kong, Everett and Toussaint algorithm is based on the Graham scan. The Graham scan is a fundamental backtracking technique in computational geometry. In [13] it is shown how to use the Graham scan for triangulating simple polygon in $O(kn)$ time where $k - 1$ is the number of concave vertices in P. Although the worst case of the algorithm is $O(n^2)$, it is easy to implement and therefore is useful in practice.

Finally, in 1991 Chazelle presented $O(n)$ worst-case algorithm [5]. Basic idea is in deterministic algorithm, which computes structure, called visibility map. This structure is a generalization of a trapezoidalization (horizontal chords towards both sides of each vertex in a polygonal chain are drown). His algorithm mimics merge sort. The polygon of n vertices is partitioned into chains of with $n/2$ vertices, and these into chains of $n/4$ vertices, and so on. The visibility map of a chain is found by merging the maps of its subchains. This takes actually at most $O(n \log n)$ time. But Chazelle improves process by dividing it into two phases. The first phase includes computing coarse approximations of the visibility maps. This visibility maps are coarse enough that merging can be accomplished in linear time. A second phase refines the coarse map into a complete visibility map also in linear time. A triangulation is then produced from the trapezoidation defined by the visibility map. The algorithm has a lot of details and therefore remains open to find a simple and fast algorithm for triangulating a polygon in the linear time.

Table 1 shows all algorithms presented above and is expanded table presented in [17]. Algorithms are grouped by time complexity.

4. Polygon triangulation algorithms based on Delaunay triangulation

Triangulation of the monotone polygons can also be achieved by well-known Delaunay triangulation of a set of points (figure 2a). Namely, the vertices of polygon can be considered as individual input points in the plane. When computing the Delaunay triangulation we have to consider that some line segments (edges of polygon) must exists at the output. That problem is known as a constrained Delaunay triangulation (CDT).

Let V be a set of points in the plane and L set of non-intersecting line segments having their extreme vertices at points of V. The pair $G = (V, L)$ defines constraint graph.

Two vertices $P_i P_j \in V$ are said to be mutually visible if either segment $P_i P_j$ does not intersect any constraint segment or $P_i P_j$ is a subsegment of a constraint segment of L.

Now the visibility graph of G is pair $G_v = (V_v, E_v)$; $V_v = V$ and $E_v = \{(P_i, P_j) \mid P_i, P_j \in V_v$ and P_i, P_j are mutually visible with respect to set $L\}$ (see figure 2b).

An edge in E_v joins a pair of mutually visible points of V with respect to all straight-line segments belonging to L.

Time complexity	Author	Year	Technique/Algorithm
$O(n^2)$	Lennes	1911	Recursive diagonal insertion
$O(n^3)$	Meisters	1975	Ear cutting
$O(n^2)$	ElGindy, Everett, Toussaint	1990	Prune and search
$O(n \log n)$	Garey, Johnson, Preparata, Tarjan	1978	Decomp. into monotone polygons
$O(n \log n)$	Chazelle	1982	Divide and conquer
$O(n + r \log r)$	Hertel & Mehlhorn	1983	Sweep – line
$O(n \log s)$	Chazelle & Incerpi	1983	-
$O(n (1 + t_0))$	Toussaint	1988	-
$O(kn)$	Kong, Everett, Toussaint	1990	Graham scan
$O(n \log \log n)$	Tarjan, Van Wyk	1987	-
$O(n \log \log n)$	Kirkpatrik	1990	-
$O(n \log^* n)$	Clarkson, Tarjan, Van Wyk	1989	Randomized incremental
$O(n \log^* n)$	Kirkpatrik, Klawe, Tarjan	1990	Using bounded integer coordinates
$O(n \log^* n)$	Seidel	1990	Randomized incremental
$O(n)$	Chazelle	1990	-

Table 1: Algorithms for computing triangulation of simple polygon.

So, a triangulation of V constrained by L is defined as a graph $T(V; L) = (V_t, E_t)$; $V_t = V$ and E_t is a maximal subset of $E_v \cup L$ such that $L \subseteq E_t$, and no two edges of E_t intersect, except at their endpoints.

Figure 2: a) Empty circle property; b) Visibility map; c) Constrained Delaunay triangulation

A CDT $T(V; L)$ of set of points V with respect to a set of straight-line segments L is a constrained triangulation of V in which the circumcircle of each triangle t of T does not contain in its interior any other vertex P of T which is visible from the three vertices of t. (see figure 2c) Another characterisation of CDT is given by the empty circle property: a triangle t in a constrained triangulation T is a Delaunay triangle if there does not exists any other vertex of T inside the circumcircle of t and visible from all three vertices of t (see figure 2a). See details in [9].

Triangulation of simple polygon can be in generally computed as follows: first step computes CDT of edges of simple polygon and second step removes triangles which are in exterior of simple polygon. The information that input is simple polygon (not just general constraint graph) could be useful in step one and therefore algorithms for building a CDT can be subdivided into two groups: algorithms for computing the CDT when the constraint graph is a simple polygon and algorithms for computing a CDT for general constraint graph.

4.1 Constrained Delaunay triangulation algorithms for simple polygons

Lewis and Robinson describe an $O(n^2)$ algorithm based on divide-and-conquer approach with internal points [15]. The boundary polygon is recursively subdivided into almost equally sized subpolygons that are separately triangulated together with their internal points. The resulting triangulation is then optimize d to produce CDT.

A recursive $O(n^2)$ algorithm for CDT based on visibility approach is described by Floriani [8]. The algorithm computes the visibility graph of the vertices of the simple polygon Q in $O(n^2)$ time and the Voronoi diagram of set of its vertices in $O(n \log n)$. The resulting Delaunay triangulation is built by joining each vertex Q of P to those vertices that are both visible from Q and Voronoi neighbours of Q.

Another $O(n \log n)$ algorithm describe Lee and Lin [9]. Algorithm is based on Chazelle's polygon cutting theorem. Chazelle has shown that for any simple polygon P with n

vertices, two vertices t_1 and t_2 of P can be found in linear time such that segment $t_1 t_2$ is completely internal to P. Each of the two simple subpolygons resulting from the cut of P by $t_1 t_2$ has at least $n/3$ vertices. Lee's and Lin's algorithm subdivides the given polygon Q into two subpolygons Q_l and Q_r and recursively computes the constrained Delaunay triangulations T_l and T_r. The resulting triangulation T of Q is obtained by merging T_l and T_r. They proposed also similar algorithm for general constraint graph which runs in $O(n^2)$ time.

4.2 Constrained Delaunay triangulation algorithms for general constraint graphs

Chew describes an $O(n \log n)$ algorithm for the CDT based on the divide-and-conquer approach. The constraint graph $G = (V, L)$ is assumed to be contained in a rectangle, which is subdivided into vertical strips [6]. In each strip there is exactly one vertex. The CDT is computed for each strip and adjacent strips are recursively merged together. After last merge we got final CDT which is CDT for input graph. The major problem here is merging such strips that contains edges which crosses some strip having no endpoint in it.

Algorithm for computing CDT which includes pre-processing on the constraint segments is proposed by Boissonnat [3]. By pre-processing CDT problem is transformed into standard Delaunay problem on set of points. The idea is to modify the input data by adding points lying on the constraint segments in such a way that resulting Delaunay triangulation is guaranteed to contain such segments. Constraint segment e is a Delaunay edge if the circle having e as diameter does not intersect any other constraint segment. If the circle attached to e intersect some other segment, then e is split into a finite number of subsegments such that none of the circles attached to those segments intersect any constraint. When two constraint segments intersect at an endpoint, one new point is inserted into both segments. The circumcircle of the triangle defined by the common endpoint and by the two new points does not intersect any other constraint segment. This algorithm takes at most $O(n \log n)$ time and generates at most $O(n)$ additional points.

All mentioned algorithms for CDT demand that all points are defined at the beginning of triangulation. Algorithm proposed by Floriani and Puppo [9] resolves CDT problem by incrementally updating CDT as new points and constraints are added. The problem of incrementally building of CDT is reduced to the following three subproblems: computation of an initial triangulation of the domain, insertion of a point, insertion of a straight-line segment.

An initial triangulation of the domain can be obtained by different approaches. For example, we can determine a triangle or rectangle (made of two triangles) which contains the whole domain. In the following incrementally points and line segments are inserted. After each insertion we got new CDT which has more elements than the previous one. After inserting last point or line segment, the bounding triangle is removed. Algorithm runs at most in O(ln^2) where n is number of points and l number of straight-line segments in final CDT.

4.3 Delaunay refinement algorithms

Finally we have to mention the algorithms which cares also about the quality of triangulation. That is the algorithms allow to determine the minimum interior angle of triangles in outputting triangulation. Generally, that feature is possible only if the use of so-called Steiner points is allowed. In that case the number of output triangles is increased regarding the minimum number of triangles in output triangulation. In other words, we want to provide shape guarantee (minimum interior angle is as high as possible) with minimum size triangles in output triangulation (size guarantee).

One of such techniques of triangulation points and line segments is Delaunay refinement technique. Chew presented a Delaunay refinement algorithm that triangulates a given polygon into a mesh. In mesh all triangles are between 30° and 120°. The algorithm produces a uniform mesh to obtain all triangles of the roughly the same size [7].

Ruppert extended Chew's work [18] by giving an algorithm such that all triangles in the output have angles between π – 2a. Parameter a can be chosen between 0° and 20°. The triangulation maintained here is a Delaunay triangulation set of points which is computed at the beginning. Vertices for Delaunay triangulation are in that case endpoints of segments and possible isolated vertices. After computing Delaunay triangulation, vertices are added for two reasons: to improve triangle shape, and to insure that all input segments are presented in Delaunay triangulation. Two basic operations in the algorithm are: splitting of a segment by adding a vertex at its midpoint, and splitting of a triangle with a vertex at its circumcenter. In each case, the new vertex is added to set of vertices. When a segment is split, it is replaced in set of segments by two subsegments. Such algorithms runs in O(M^2) time, where M is number of vertices at the output, but in practice are very fast.

Some other algorithms which give shape guarantees are available. They are more complicated to implement and are not based on Delaunay triangulation. They use such structures as grids and quadtrees. See details in algorithm presented by Baker, Grosse and Rafferty [1] and algorithm presented by Bern, Eppstein and Gilbert [2].

Table 2 shows algorithms for computing triangulation of simple polygon based on Delaunay triangulation. First part of the table shows constrained Delaunay triangulation algorithm, last two lines shows Delaunay refinement algorithms. First part of the table shows algorithms based on Delaunay triangulation without use of Steiner points and second part shows algorithms with use of Steiner points. Parameter M is in that case the number of outputting points.

Time com.	Author	Year	Input
O(n^2)	Lewis, Robinson	1979	Simple polygon
O($n \log n$)	Floriani	1985	Simple polygon
O($n \log n$)	Lee, Lin	1980	Simple polygon
O(n^2)	Lee, Lin	1980	General
O($n \log n$)	Chew	1987	General
O($n \log n$)	Boissonnat	1988	General
O(ln^2)	Floriani, Puppo	1992	General
O(M^2)	Chew	1989	Simple polygon
O(M^2)	Ruppert	1994	General

Table 2: Delaunay based triangulation algorithms

5. Properties of some polygon triangulating algorithms

The issue of this chapter is to briefly show the basic properties of triangulation algorithms and difference between them. In that matter we will take some algorithms for triangulating a simple polygon described above.

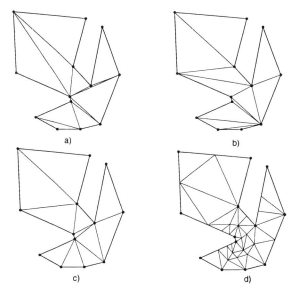

Figure 3: a) Ear cutting; b) Randomized incremental c) Constrained Delaunay triangulation; d) Delaunay refinement

We will try to compare its properties despite sometimes is obvious that difference is present because of different issues of selected algorithms. We will compare attributes as quality of triangulation, asymptotical running time, and the possibility of triangulating polygons with holes. We will rely on each algorithm definitions.

We compared the following algorithms: Meister's ear cutting algorithm [16], Seidel's randomized incremental algorithm [19], constrained Delaunay triangulation [9], Ruppert's Delaunay refinement algorithm [18].

Algorithms based on Delaunay triangulation provides the triangulation with the highest quality of output triangles. Delaunay refinement algorithms are in that way the most quality algorithms because they ensure that the minimum interior angle is as high as possible. Of course, that is possible only with the use of Steiner's points.

Figure 3 shows an example how all four algorithms actually triangulate simple polygon. For that matter we extended the example in [18] with additional triangulations. In figure 3a we can see that ear cutting provides the lowest quality. A better triangulation is provided by randomized incremental algorithm (see figure 3b). Those two algorithms have no mechanism of ensuring quality and therefore is understandable why this low quality. The highest quality (with no using of Steiner's points) provides constrained Delaunay triangulation, but

there is impossible to avoid some sliver triangles what we can see in figure 3c. If the Steiner's points are allowed the quality of obtained triangulation is ensured (see figure 3d for Ruppert's Delaunay refinement algorithm).

All algorithms provide triangulating polygons with holes except ear cutting. Ear cutting is designed as recursive algorithm which cuts off ears and therefore can not detect holes. Seidel's randomized incremental algorithm actually wasn't expected to triangulate holes at the beginning but the extension for holes is very simple because of structure of the algorithm. The less problems with holes has Delaunay based algorithms, because in basic inputs for those algorithms are line-segments in the plane. So after triangulation the triangles from holes are removed.

For all four algorithms is known that they are rather simple to implement regarding to other algorithms in the same category. If we look at the worst case time complexity of these algorithms we notice that Seidel's randomized incremental gives us the best results.

If we have to choose from among those four algorithms we will take Seidel's randomized algorithms if we want very fast algorithm. If we need quality in the first place, then we will take Ruppert's Delaunay refinement algorithm. If we need quality but we don't want Steiner's points then perhaps the best choose will be Constrained Delaunay triangulation algorithm.

References

[1]   Baker, B., Grosse, E., and Rafferty C. S., *Nonobtuse triangulation of polygons*. Disc. and Comp. Geom., Vol. 3, 1988, pp. 147-168.

[2]   Bern, M., Eppstein, D., and Gilbert, J. R., *Provably good mesh generation*. In Proceedings of the 31st Annual Symposium on Foundation of Computer Science, 1990, pp. 231-241 IEEE. To apear in J. Comp. System Science.

[3]   Boissonnat, J.D., *Shape reconstruction from planar cross sections*, Comp. Vision Graphics Image Process., Vol. 44, 1988, pp. 1-29.

[4]   Chazelle, B., Incerpi, J., *Triangulation and shape complexity*, ACM Transactions on Graphics, Vol. 3, 1984, pp. 135-152.

[5]   Chazelle, B., *Triangulating a simple polygon in linear time*, Disc. Comp. Geom. 6, 1991, pp. 485-524.

[6]   Chew, L. P., *Constrained Delaunay triangulation*, in Proceedings, Third ACM Symposium on Computational Geometry, Waterloo, June, 1987, pp. 216-222.

[7]   Chew, L. P., *Guaranteed - quality triangular meshes*, Technical report, Cornell University, No. TR-89-983, 1989.

[8]   De Floriani, L., Falcidieno, B. and Pienovi, C., *A Delaunay-based representation of surfaces defined over arbitrarily-shaped domains*, Comput. Vision Graphics Image Process. 32, 1985, pp. 127-140.

[9]   De Floriani, L. and Puppo, E., *An On-Line Algorithm for Constrained Delaunay Triangulation*, Graphical Models and Image Processing, Vol. 54, No. 3, 1992, pp. 290-300.

[10] Garey, M.R., Johnson, D.S., Preparata, F.P. and Tarjan, R.E., *Triangulating a simple polygon*, Inform. Process., Lett. 7, 1978, pp. 175-180.

[11] ElGindy, H., Everett, H. and Toussaint, G. T., *Slicing an ear in linear time*, Pattern Recognition Letters, Vol. 14, 1993, pp. 719-722.

[12] Hertel, S., Mehlhorn, K., *Fast triangulation of simple polygons*, Proc. FCT, LNCS 158, 1983, pp. 207-215.

[13] Kong, X., Everett, H., Toussaint, G. T., *The Graham scan triangulates simple polygons*, Pattern Recognition Letters, Vol. 11, 1990, pp. 713-716, http: //cgm.cs.mcgill.ca/-godfried/research/triangulations.html.

[14] Lennes, N. J., *Theorems on the simple finite polygon and polyhedron*, American Journal of Mathematics, Vol. 33, 1911, pp. 37-62.

[15] Lewis, B.A., Robinson J. S., *Triangulating of planar regions with applications*, Comput. J., Vol. 4, No. 21, 1979, pp. 324-332.

[16] Meisters, G. H., *Polygons have ears*, American Mathematical Monthly, Vol. 82, June/July, 1975, pp. 648-651.

[17] O'Rourke, J., *Computational Geometry in C*, Cambridge University, Press, 1994, pp. 1-65.

[18] Ruppert, J., *A Delaunay Refinemt Algorithm for Quality 2-Dimensional Mesh Generation*, NASA Arnes Research Center, Submission to Journal of Algorithms, 1994, http://jit.arc.nasa.gov/nas/abs.html.

[19] Seidel, R., *A simple and fast incremental randomized algorithm for computing trapezoidal decompositions and for triangulating polygons*, Computational Geometry: Theory and Applications, Vol. 1, No. 1, 1991, pp. 51-64.

[20] Toussaint, G. T., *Efficient triangulation of simple polygons*, The Visual Computer, Vol. 7, No. 3, 1991, pp. 280-295.

Session 1-10

Visualization in Construction

Chair
Farzad Khosrowshahi
South Bank University, UK

Enhancement of Decision Support Process in Road Administration Domain with the Use of GIS Technology

Nenad Čuš Babič, Danijel Rebolj
Faculty of Civil Engineering
University of Maribor
Nenad@Computer.org

Cveto Gregorc
OMEGA Consult
Cveto.Gregorc@OMEGAconsult.si

Abstract

In recent years, geographic information systems and spatial database technology are fast spreading across the tight circles of experts, working in the fields of geography and geodesy. In the first wave, GIS functions have been built into engineering applications, which were not just GIS centered (as for example road design, emission calculation, building site-plan etc.). The use has been accelerated through the component technology, which simplifies the insertion of GIS components into a variety of applications - including administration.

In the article we describe the upgrading of the business information system of the Slovenian road administration, where the basic applications user interfaces were enriched with a specialized GIS component, which enables a fast and clear (geo)graphical view of the data about the selected part of the road network. The simplicity of using this intelligent digital map (as we could name this specialized component) makes it possible to effectively and clearly display the relevant information, which is so necessary in the process of decision making. Besides, there is no need to leave the application the user is familiar with.

1. Introduction

This article describes a component named GeoPIS. With this component it is possible to visualise geographic and attributive data from Road database (BCP) which is used by Slovenian road administration. The component is an upgrade of their business information system, which includes BCP, by adding geographic dimension. Geographical data can significantly improve understanding of road attributive data and information searching. The component can also be used in other information systems that use BCP.

Geography is essential attribute of a road. In business information system, data about current state of road sections, events and planned activities are connected to road network through unique road section ID and offset. From this data several reports about state of the road sections can be generated with standard SQL. As an example, you can get report about car accidents on selected road sections or report with index of road surface state on selected road sections. Such reports are a base for road section's reconstruction planning process. However, tabular data are some times hard to follow. If we want to check correlation between road surface state index and car accidents on a road section, this is not easy to figure out from tabular data. Geographic information significantly increases the value of attribute data. When same example is displayed on a map, correlation is immediately evident. Therefore, in road administration department has been using parallel GIS system. Custom maps have been prepared on demand. Nevertheless, this solution has several deficiencies. To name just two of them, as a rule decision-makers do not use sophisticated GIS tools and data stored in business database and spatial database are not connected. Every time when map is to be rendered, it is necessary to import current data. Therefore, we decided to implement a component, which will enable decision-makers to work with geographic data from environments they are familiar with and which will connect spatial and business database.

GeoPIS is an ActiveX component and can easily be used in any program environment that supports this standard. For example, it is possible to include GeoPIS into MS Access database or MS Word document or MS Excel spreadsheet. Also, you can incorporate the component into Visual Basic application. Application communicates with the component through well-defined interface of properties and methods. Principal tasks of the component are graphical representation of road network on the specified area and visualisation of an attribute from a table related to or included in the BCP database.

GeoPIS can also communicate with Road life-cycle environment RO (Rebolj 1998). This environment includes methods for Road body model (MCT) data manipulation such as: perspective 3D visualisation of a road section (Rebolj et.al. 1998), emission calculation and visualisation (Rebolj 1995, Rebolj et. al. 1997), tracking of land acquisition process (Kovacic and Rebolj 1997) etc. Direct connection to detailed constructional data of the selected road section defined by MCT is provided through the road network presented in GeoPIS.

2. System architecture

Geographical road section network is a foundation for GeoPIS operation. This network is stored into spatial database. At this moment, it is possible to use ARC/INFO cover or Arc/View shape format. Every road section has to be labelled with a unique identifier that enables connectivity with relational database.

Two additional thematic layers from spatial database are handled in special way. These are municipals layer and road companies layer (maintainers of roads). You can add some additional thematic layers like terrain raster for example, to variegate a map.

attributes of the tables are optional. Two sorts of tables are foreseen. These are:

1. Tables, which attributes are valid for whole road section. For example, these are road width, traffic flow, etc. On a map, attribute value is displayed as a line. Width of the line depends on attribute value and selected scale.

2. Tables, which attributes are valid on a part of the road section (bridges for example). These records must have defined start and end stationary of the object. These objects are displayed as lines of different width on a road section and cover the road section partially. As previously, width of the line depends on attribute value and selected scale.

GeoPIS is directly accessing attributive data in relational database. This is possible after specifying database location, table and attribute name.

User activates the component with a set of road sections identifiers. The component displays attribute values for selected road sections in a form of dynamic segments on a map. The map is zoomed to the selection. User can add or remove road section to/from selection. On exit the component returns modified selection.

Methods and properties of GeoPIS are described in further detail in a separate section (Interface description).

Constructional data of a road section are stored in Road life cycle RO database in a form defined by Road body model (MCT). In this database, there is no road section identifier, but project name instead. Therefore, this identifier can not be used as a key for accessing the data. We implemented an interface module to overcome

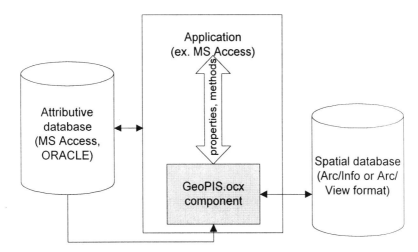

Figure 1. Component integration with other parts of the information system

In attributive database, existence of unique road section identifier has to be provided in the tables. Other

this discrepancy.

3. Component design

GeoPIS is developed in Visual Basic RAD environment, and it is compiled to ActiveX component. Further information about component technology reader can find elsewhere (Krajnc et. al. 1997). User interface includes main window with a map and a couple of dialog boxes. On the main window, central component is digital map form ESRI MapObjects (ESRI 1996).

4. Interface description

GeoPIS is 32 bit ActiveX component. Programmers can use this component in various development environments on Windows 95, 98 or NT platform. In most of development environments, the component is imported to some kind of a component toolbar. From this toolbar, programmer drags the component to a form from

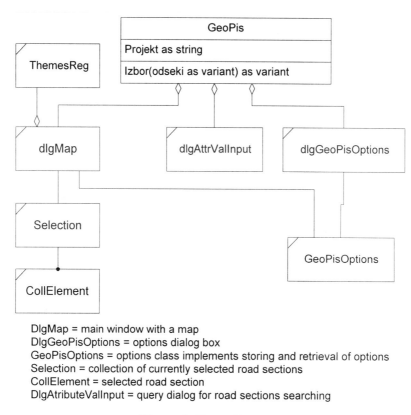

DlgMap = main window with a map
DlgGeoPisOptions = options dialog box
GeoPisOptions = options class implements storing and retrieval of options
Selection = collection of currently selected road sections
CollElement = selected road section
DlgAtributeValInput = query dialog for road sections searching

Figure 2 Class diagram

Functionality of GeoPIS is designed to support specific BCP environment. Also general GIS functionality of MapObjects is preserved. GeoPIS integrates objects presented in the following class diagram (Figure 2).

From implementation viewpoint, some of these classes are implemented as class modules and some of them as components (controls in Visual Basic jargon). Main window is dlgMap. This window displays digital map at GeoPIS activation. Other windows are displayed on user request.

User activates GeoPIS functionality in two ways. End user calls functions through user interface menus and toolbars. All functions can also be called programmatically when incorporating the component into some application.

where this component is going to be used and adjust component properties at design time (Figure 3).

Also, programmer can interact with the component programmatically. Adjustments made in a code will override design time settings, of course. More about methods and properties of GeoPIS reader can find in GeoPIS user manual (Rebolj and Čuš-Babič 1998).

In current version GeoPIS component itself is invisible at runtime and has to be activated in event handler of some other component (button for example). On activation, component displays modal window. In the future, we are planing to modify the component in a way to be visible at runtime. This will enable inclusion of the interactive map in a document (like MS Chart for example).

GeoPIS is activated with method GeoPIS.Izbor where desired selection of road sections is passed as an argument. Main window with a map showing current selection is displayed (Figure 4).

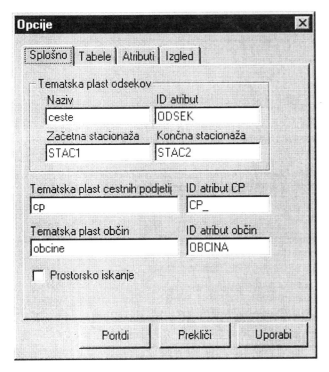

Figure 3 Options dialog

User can add some road section to the current selection or remove selected road sections from selection. User can also interactively modify konponent properties through options dialog. Properties and selection changes are propagated to program code.

Functionality of GeoPIS can be reached interactively through three toolbars: general, selection and attributes. General toolbar aggregates general GIS functionality:

- Show entire map
- Adding and removing of thematic layers
- Copy the map to clipboard
- Print the map
- Display Options dialog (Figure 3)
- Confirm selection changes and exit
- Reject selection changes and exit

On Selection toolbar user can choose from different kinds of selection methods like single road section selection, selection by municipality, etc.

From Attribute toolbar user can turn attribute rendering on and off, refresh display, change attribute displayed on the map and change scale for attribute rendering.

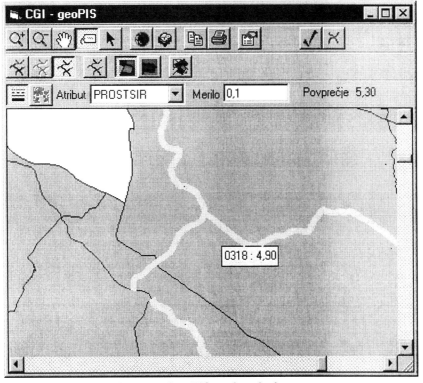

Figure 4 GeoPIS main window

5. Example of GeoPis usage

As mentioned above, GeoPIS can be used in any application, which supports ActiveX components. One of these environments is MS office. In the following

6. Conclusion

In this article, we presented essential features of GeoPIS component. During short period of use, users

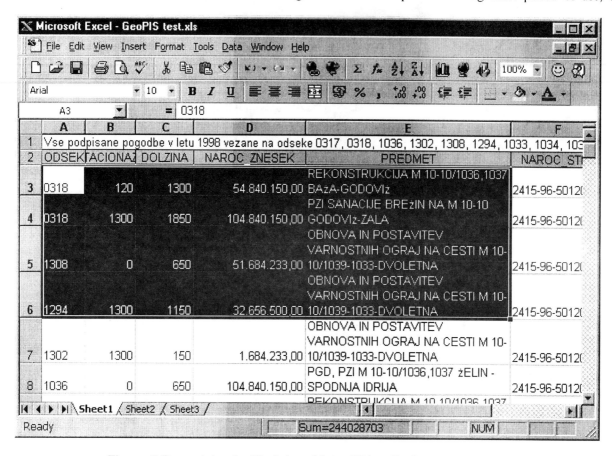

Figure 5 Spreadsheet with data, which will be displayed on a map

example, we used the component in MS Excell spreadsheet.

This spreadsheet contained financial data about road section maintenance (Figure 5). We added GeoPIS to the spreadsheet and set basic properties.

In this example, our source of attributes was not a database. The component also enables rendering of values passed to it on activation as parameters coupled with road section identifications. Since all the data are in the spreadsheet we simply past them to the component. To do that, we wrote a procedure in Excel VB for applications. User selects data about desired road sections in spreadsheet and activates the component. Result of this action is new window with map containing selected road sections (Figure 6).

Like in this example, users can also apply the component easily in other environments. This enables geographical display of data from various sources.

reported that geography dimension is important information for them. This new dimension significantly raises the level of decision support process quality. Also the use of component technology proved to be suitable decision for this kind of software because it is possible to use the component in various interactive environments. This resulted in component application for the tasks not anticipated at the beginning. In the future, we expect users will find this component even more useful when they start to build custom applications.

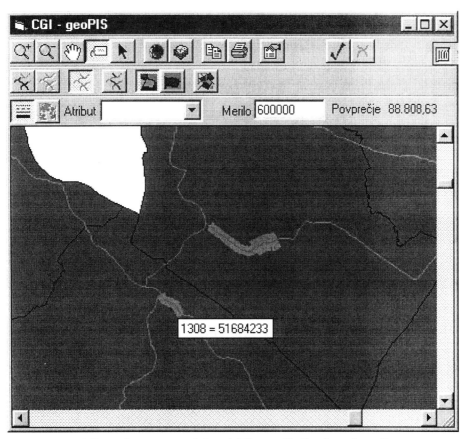

Figure 6 Data from spreadsheet (Figure 5) displayed on the map

12. References

[1] A.B. Smith, C.D. Jones, and E.F. Roberts, "Article Title", *Journal*, Publisher, Location, Date, pp. 1-10.

[2] Jones, C.D., A.B. Smith, and E.F. Roberts, *Book Title*, Publisher, Location, Date.

[1] ESRI, *Building Applications with MapObjects*, Environmental Systems Research Institute (ESRI), Inc., Redlands, 1996

[2] Kovačič, B., Rebolj, D., "Uporabnost programskega okolja RO za urejanje lastninskih razmerij pri gradnji cest.", *Geodetski vestnik*, Zveza geodetov Slovenije, let. 41, št. 3, 1997, str. 211-217

[3] Krajnc, M., Krajnc, A., Kline, A., "Komponentna tehnologija – nadgradnja objektne tehnologije.", *Objektna tehnologija v Sloveniji OTS'97*, Univerza v Mariboru, Maribor-SI, 1997, pp. 43-51.

[4] Rebolj, D., "Simulacija škodljivih emisij prometa s pomočjo dinamičnega emisijskega modela", *Zbornik četrtega mednarodnega posvetovanja Komunalna energetika*, Univerza v Mariboru, Maribor-SI, 1995, pp. C/135-143

[5] Rebolj, D., Sturm, P. in Hausberger, S., "Dinamično določanje in vizualizacija onesnaženja, ki ga povzroča cestni promet", *Zbornik šestega mednarodnega posvetovanja Komunalna energetika*, Univerza v Mariboru, Maribor-SI, 1997, pp. C/71-80

[6] Rebolj, D., "Integrated information system supporting road design, evaluation and construction", *Computer-Aided Civil and Infrastructure Engineering*, Blackwell Publishers, MA, Vol. 13, 1998, pp. 179-187

[7] Rebolj, D., Čuš-Babič, N. in Tibaut, A., "Automatic visualization of the road design", *Proceedings of the 77th Annual meeting of the Transportation Research Board*, Washington D.C., 1998, CD-ROM

[8] Rebolj, D. in Čuš-Babič, N., *Programska komponenta GeoPIS 1.1. Navodila za uporabo*, Fakulteta za gradbeništvo, 1998, Maribor.

APPLICATION OF COLLABORATIVE SUPPORTED FRAME ACCURATE ANIMATION FOR BRIDGE CONSTRUCTION PROJECT

Fukuchi, Yoshihiko, Ph.D
Konoike Construction Co., Ltd.
3-6-1 Kitakyuhoji-machi, Chuo-ku, Osaka 541-0057, Japan
TEL:06-244-3674,FAX:06-244-3632
E-Mail: yfukuchi@alum.mit.edu

Hirai, Yujiro
Kumamoto Prefecture
6-18-1 Suizenji, Kumamoto 862-8570, Japan
TEL:096-384-1591
E-Mail:yujiro_hirai@email.msn.com

Kobayashi, Ichiro, Dr. of Eng.
Kumamoto University
2-39-1 Kurokami, Kumamoto 860-8555, Japan
TEL:096-342-3536,FAX:096-342-3507
E-Mail:ponts@gpo.kumamoto-u.ac.jp

Hoshino, Yuji
Kumamoto University
2-39-1 Kurokami, Kumamoto 860-8555, Japan
E-Mail:hoshino@gpo.kumamoto-u.ac.jp

Yamamoto Kazuhiro
Ministry of Construction, Government of Japan
1-19-32 Okaya, Otsu 520-2122, Japan
TEL:077-545-5675, FAX:077-543-5340
E-Mail:y-kazu@mx.biwa.ne.jp

Abstract

During a civil engineering construction process many types of professionals are involved, such as engineers, constructors, designers, clients and so forth. To provide mutual understanding among construction workers and unify their ideas is necessary the creation of an effective presentation. In addition, the construction process have to work relatively in harmony with the situation of the construction site. Moreover, the use of Computer Graphics (CG) can help to visualize clearly sequences of the construction process, simulate changes in the execution of the project and make it possible to be carried out smoothly before the construction begins. The paper introduces the application of Frame Accurate Animation (FAA) as an important implement for the construction management. Also explains the use of FAA in an illustrative example of the Sashiki Bridge (provisional name) construction project in Kumamoto. Our main expectation is for the work environmental become more cooperative, efficient and safely.

Key words: Collaborative Work, Frame Accurate Animation (FAA), Presentation

of CALS/EC in the construction business area. CG Animation (CGA) is one of these types of information technology, and has been reported with many practical uses on design drawing processes. The authors has applied Frame Accurate Animation (FAA), one of the CGA technologies, on different sequences of several construction projects so far, and distilled the application requirements and issues as follows:

(1) purposes of use and objects were not clear during the use of FAA;

(2) according to each purpose of the applications, FAA was not well expressed; and

(3) specific role and usage of FAA were not well informed to the evaluators.

In this research, FAA reproduces construction sites' condition, attempting to support the construction collaboratively. The possible usage of FAA during the construction process as a presentation tool has been observed through our second pilot project, Sashiki (provisional name) Bridge, the first extra-dosed bridge in Kyushu region in Japan, introducing the concept of the collaborative supported FAA application for construction management practice.

1. Introduction

In phases of the public investment process, the construction work has to be shared and subdivided among construction workers. For this reason, exchanging design drawings, ideas and information about the construction project becomes not so simple to be done. The positive use of information technology can be observed trough the introduction

2. Presentation of Construction Process with FAA

By using FAA during the construction process, two specific forms of the use have been verified. They are presentation and simulation. Whether it is presentation or simulation depends on the exact purpose of the usage. Strictly saying, however, users can adopt simulation as a tool to make presentation.

Table-1 Usage of Collaborative Supported FAA

	Main Objective	Tender	Planning	Management
For Engineer	Explanation (Confirmation, Consensus Making)	To decide construction method and sequence for tender price estimation	To help examine construction planning; To examine alternatives for change order; for example construction method construction schedule site layout	
For Worker	Explanation (Confirmation, Instruction)		To instruct work conditions for subs; To instruct construction activity; for example safety instruction coaching traffic control	
For Client	Persuasion (Recognition, Suggestion)	VE Proposal Technological Promotion	To get agreement on change order To propose plan in VE tender To get agreement for construction plan To inform construction plan	
For Local Community	Persuasion (Understanding, Agreement)		To publicize construction activity for example site surroundings from start to finish completion status construction outline construction method environmental impact To mitigate complaint	

Depending on each specific purpose of the use, FAA scenarios must be created for the effective presentation. In this paper, the presentation with FAA for expediting communication during the construction management process is called "Collaborative Supported FAA."

As the FAA application impacts so many people related in public works, applications of Collaborative Supported FAA have to be categorized, and subjects and purposes have to be made clear to obtain an effective presentation. According to Kunishima, important matters and issues on the construction management process and its condition can be observed. Examples of specific uses of the Collaborative Supported FAA have been illustrated. Three main processes of the use are considered as follows: (1) acceptance of an order, (2) construction work planning, and (3) construction management. In each stage of the construction process stated above,

audiences are specified and considered:. They are engineers, construction workers, clients, and local community. The Table-1 explains each position of the use. Engineers can use Collaborative Supported FAA when they seek authorization or confirmation to execute his task.

In the phase of acquiring orders, the first step engineers involve in the construction project, engineers have to make a proposal in tenders with value engineering, promoting in-house technologies. In the phase of construction, thanks to the FAA's persuasiveness, the construction work sequences can be understood without enough construction management expertise or the presence of an expert. Therefore, a group of technical workers and engineers are able to carefully and easily analyze the construction work plan, making a successful decision in studying proposals of construction work plans.

The Table-1 also presents the possibility of

FAA applications in decision making process in proposals for the client. Clients expect to hedge risks and get their project done faster. To let the local community go through the construction work plan and construction site management processes enables collaborative relationship between engineers and local community. Moreover, it is necessary to give details of construction management process to all construction workers. Thus, FAA provides the capacity to explain the contents of the construction work process, gives safely directions to the workers, and allows engineers to share data and information with others.

3. Collaborative Supported Frame Accurate Animation:

To make Collaborative Supported FAA, the following two points should be considered. They are entire reproduction of construction site and visualization of the model creation content. Entire reproduction of the construction site is very important for simulation. Forecasting construction site condition is also very important during the construction process. Collaborative Supported FAA can be expressed in two dimensions. They are spatial expression, which provides enlargement, reduction, and visual effects, and temporal expression, which is flexibility of time scale. Collaborative Supported FAA enables to reproduce both huge amount of information such as whole construction site surroundings and detail expression such as re-bars arrangement depending on the specific size of enlargement and reduction at the same time. Collaborative Supported FAA also makes it possible

to visualize impossible situations as if it were in reality, simulating virtual conditions inside of the structure that a naked eye can not observe. In terms of the flexibility of time scale, Collaborative Supported FAA reproduces not only the whole work schedule from the beginning to the completion of the construction work activities but also certain complicated work schedules. Thus, what Collaborative Supported FAA can realize and forecast is summarized as follows; (1) condition and relative position of the structure through the spatial expression, and (2) construction process and any relevant activities to the work through temporal expression. Moreover, the advantage of using Collaborative Supported FAA is the faithful reproduction of the construction site circumstances and is the ability to forecast the construction site condition precisely.

Repeating a series of still images makes collaborative Supported FAA. In this way, the project participants can visualize construction in three dimensions and different sequences of the construction process by just turning on and off. Also, selecting a certain frame of the animation can easily print out a still image.

AutoCAD r14J and 3DStudioVIZ 1.0J were used for the modeling and each FAA's still frames, and both are from Autodesk Inc. Director 5.0J, a MACROMEDIA product, was used to script each command of action. CD-ROM was used for the distribution of Collaborative Supported FAA.

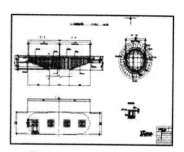

Figure 1. The CAD drawing

Figure 2. Study of Arrangements

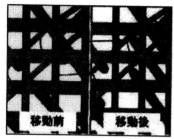

Figure 3. Re-Arrangement of a Pier

4. Case Studies

Sashiki Bridge (provisional name) is situated at Ashikita area in Kumamoto Prefecture, Japan. The bridge is being constructed as the second route in a wide agricultural area of Ashikita (alias: Orange Belt). Details of the Sashiki Bridge construction project can be observed as follows:

Description: Construction of 3 clear span extra-dosed pre-stressed concrete bridge;

Length of main span: 225m,

Width of Bridge: 9.25m - 12.25m

Duration of Work: March, 1998 ~ November, 2000 (Estimated Completion)

The agricultural road projects of the second route in the wide agricultural area of Ashikita intend to improve the circulation and transportation systems of the district. The district of Ashikita is a prosperous area in the southernmost Kumamoto Prefecture. The project aims at the development and stability of the agricultural work by improving logistics access. The extension of the road is around 25km, and the road system is called the Orange Belt. The Orange Belt will be alternative route for the Route 3.

The construction process of the Sashiki Bridge, the first extra-dosed bridge in Kyushu region, was relatively unfamiliar. The extra-dosed bridge has the normal girder bridge structure whose upper floor slab is arranged with pre-stressed cables to support the diagonal member arranged outside of the slab. The structure is an alternative solution to make use of pre-stressed concrete in the main girder and to stand the bending moment. Applications of Collaborative Supported FAA are illustrated as follows.

(1) Simulation of Re-bar Arrangements of a Pier

FAA visualized the re-bar arrangements of a bridge pier and helped site engineers for examining better installation processes. The animation was used to facilitate communication with re-bar placers and site engineers, allowing them to examine various ways of the re-bar arrangements. In general, re-bar arrangements of the bridge pier were designed independently among its base, column and beam. (Figure-1) Through regular designing process, the thickness of re-bars in the same part such as a base or column is taken into account although not taking others parts into consideration. Therefore, the re-bars of each part are always interfered each other. In this situation, site engineers usually redesign re-bar arrangements beforehand, and redraw re-bar arrangement drawings before making decisions in changing positions, cutting or reinforcement

Figure 4. Overall Construction Schedule

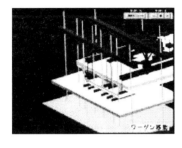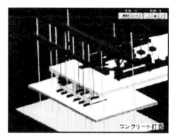

Figure-5   Simulation of Cantilever Erection System

However, the engineer often find the presence of re-bars interfered each other at the actual construction site, only to find that the re-arrangement is needed. For this reason, the engineers decided to place all re-bars of three parts altogether in advance on the computer to see where the interference was observed and how they can re-arrange them. (Figure-2) Then, they re-arranged interfered re-bars so as to interfere with each other (Figure-3).

the project intuitively. For local community, it can be used to improve the image of the construction project. Thus, in this specific application, the FAA was created with the function of the bridge structure turned on or off, showing the major work schedule from start to completion (Figure-4). Through the application, the whole process of the project including the geographical features was visualized. The objects created for this application can be used for other FAA applications.

(2) Overall Construction Schedule

It's important for project participants, such as engineers, workers, clients and local community, to grasp the whole process of the project in the earlier stage of the construction. For example, the FAA can be used for the engineers to support the rational construction planning by grasping the whole story of

(3) Simulation of Cantilever Erection System

The Figure-5 shows the erection process of moving wargen in Cantilever System. The FAA can be used for the working explanation and for pointing out the dangerous part in education for inexperienced workers. Captions in each figure help understand the

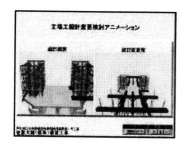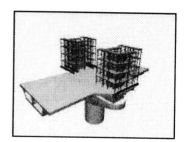

Figure 6. Change Order Approval for Main Tower

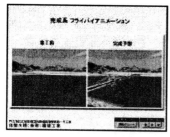

Figure 7. Completed Animation   Figure 8. The view of a car   Figure 9. CG Photo-Montage

complicated erection process. It may not be effective for well skilled workers, but the complex construction which is difficult to grasp a situation only from the information of the still images.

(4) Change Order Approval for Main Tower

For explanation of changing scheme on construction sequence of the main tower and cantilever construction, FAA was created by showing both original and changed designs side by side. (Figure-6) On the process of the main tower construction, constructing main tower in advance and construct cantilevers later was the original sequence. However, engineers decided to change the order. In the proposed alternative plan, three blocks of cantilevers have to be erected before the main tower construction begins for ease of working. It would be

critical if engineers found any problem on the construction site with everything set up, such as working space shortage. FAA should be used to rehearse several site layout of construction by comparing the working space in advance.

(5) Completed Structure and CG Photo-Montage:

It seems important for residents what kind of structure is going to build and how the view changes rather than the way of construction. So the animation was made which have several viewpoints such as from the sky, ship, and car. (Figure-7, 8) The contractor has to improve the image for residents, because their cooperation is needed to carry forward the construction. For example, to explain the outline of construction, it is considered that all of the processes and the completed structures help enhance their understanding. Furthermore, it is possible to use CG photomontage. A cut of animation scenes is combined with a site photo. (Figure-9)

5. Conclusion

In this paper, authors tried to help support construction management process by reproducing the construction site and virtually performing construction activities on the computer, proposing Collaborative Supported Frame Accurate Animation. Case studies on an actual bridge construction project in Sashiki have been performed and the results from the studies have been examined. Through the case studies, the evaluation method for the Collaborative Supported FAA application in construction projects found to be necessary not only by the cost and the period of production but by some other performance evaluators such as the value chain analysis method which can expect synergy of each application.

In this research, designers mainly produced the data of FAA. It will, however, be important for clients such as the Ministry of Construction in Japan, to deal with FAA by themselves since the keyword "Accountability" has been look at to carry out their duties and to explain how the public works projects are needed.

References

[1] The Ministry of Construction's internet site, http://www.moc.co.jp, 1999.4.

[2] Fukuchi, Yoshihiko et al., "SERIES OF APPLICATIONS OF COMPUTER GRAPHICS FOR A DAM CONSTRUCTION SITE MANAGEMENT AND SITE SURROUNDINGS", First International Conference on New information Technologies for Decision Marking in Civil Engineering,Volume2,pp.1209-1216,1998.

[3] Kunishima, Masahiko et al., "The Philosophy of Construction Management.", Sankai-dou, 1994.

The visualisation of building data in VR-DIS.

M.K.D. Coomans and H.J.P. Timmermans
Eindhoven University of Technology, Faculty of Architecture, Building and Planning
PO BOX 513,Mail station 20, 5600MB Eindhoven, The Netherlands

Abstract

The VR-DIS system is a design application for the Building and Construction industry (VR-DIS stands for Virtual Reality - Design Information System). The user interface is characterised by a mixed representation of the task domain. A pictorial representation of the appearance of the building is combined with a visualisation of the formal description of the design. The latter visualisation is worked out as a highly interactive 3D graph in which relation types are mapped on distinct planar directions and the browsing history is visualised in the third dimension. We discuss the theoretical foundations of the interface as a whole and those of the developed 3D graph.

1 Introduction

Design tasks, in particular architectural design tasks, have been found hard to support by means of computers. We point out two reasons. One reason is that design decisions are stored in subsequent graphic representations. Graphic representations are a generally acknowledged medium through which the architect develops the design [1]. Design representations are instrumental to both visual reasoning (idea generation) and evaluation. In the conceptualisation phase of the design process designers typically use sketches. Sketches are quick and easy, and support visual reasoning [2]. The current graphical computer systems lack this "perceptual interactivity" of the sketch. To support design evaluation, many aspects of the design (appearance, costs, physical behaviour, etc.) can currently be simulated in dedicated computer applications. Unfortunately, this split-up into unrelated applications results in different, unrelated data presentations and faulty mutual feed-back functionality.

A second reason is that the design objects provided by conventional CAD systems do not reflect the designer's thinking. The designer's elements are task specific and differ between individuals. Moreover, during a particular design process, these elements of design are not static but are invariably subject to change [3]. Design is a problem solving process that requires the computer to handle the information in a dynamic way.

VR-DIS is a research project in which possible solutions for these problems are investigated. VR-DIS stands for Virtual Reality - Design Information System. Key characteristics are information modelling using features, and Virtual Reality (VR) user interfaces. Feature based information handling is expected to provide a bridge between the user's dynamic design concepts, and the information storage capabilities of the computer. The medium of Virtual Reality is expected to constitute the medium through which successful multi-aspect visualisations can be offered, and with which an intuitive and quick interaction method can be developed.

This paper discusses the theoretical grounds of the developed visualisations. We discuss in detail the notion of mixed representation interfaces, and the 3D graph drawing that has been developed for browsing the feature data model.

2 Virtual Reality user interface

The VR-DIS user interface has a direct manipulation style because of the general performance advantage of such interfaces in design applications [4]. With VR technology, the direct manipulation style can better be worked out than with conventional GUI technology. VR establishes a virtual environment that appears 'natural' to the user. He can grab and manipulate through the natural movements of his hand or head. As a result, the user experiences immersion which leads to a much higher level of engagement [5].

VR as a User Interface is expected to replace many of the existing techniques due to the (added) possibilities [6]. In particular in the architectural environment the challenge lies in developing a new work environment in which the design process can take place [7].

Unlike conventional windows and mouse interfaces, VR has yet to evolve a dominant interaction paradigm. Currently, the design of a VR user interface requires the design of both the data visualisation and the interaction method. In this paper though, we focus on the visualisation part of the VR-DIS interface.

Figure 1: Virtual visit to the Tajmahal (a) and a planned office (b). [8]

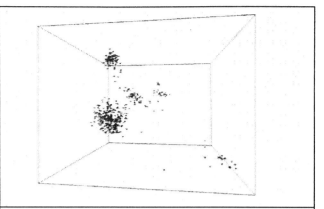

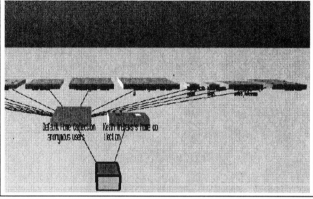

Figure 2: 3D Abstract data visualisations: (a) 3D starfield representation [9], (b) information landscape [10].

The visualisations found in other VR applications can roughly be divided in two categories: visualisations of inherently spatial data , and visualisations of abstract data using a spatial metaphor. The first form of VR-visualisations can present an architectural or mechanical site with a high level of verisimilitude. It provides visual access on the working place to sites that really exist, that are disappeared, or that will exist in the future. Figure 1 shows examples of the usage of VR in that way . It is the most common application of VR technology.

VR can also be used to communicate abstract information. Visuals presented by these VR applications include 3D chart and starfield representations, information landscapes (e.g. city methaphor), and 3D graph drawings. See figure 2.

A unique property of the VR-DIS user interface is that it combines two visualisations of both categories in a single interface. There combination is based on the notion of mixed-representations.

3 Mixed representations

VR-DIS is set up to compile all disciplines that are involved in an architectural or urban design process. As a result, VR-DIS will handle information of many different kinds: geometry data, lay-out data, appearance data, stability data, hydro-thermal data, cost information, ageing data, organisational data for the building process, and so on. What kind of representation can present all these different kinds of data? Clearly, a visualisation of the appearance of the building is insufficient.

UI modality analysis distinguishes between two types of interface representations: linguistic and non-linguistic representations (e.g. [12]). In cognitive psychology, an analogue distinction is made between verbal and pictorial mental representations. For VR-DIS, both types of representations seem equally relevant. Some data can best be communicated verbally (e.g. names, labels), other data can best be communicated in a pictorial way (e.g. appearance characteristics).

Because the VR-DIS system deals with such a hybrid set of data, a single representation can not visualise all data. A combination of a verbal and pictorial representation is required. (See also [13])

The interface representation of VR-DIS is a combination of two views: the "feature" view and the scale-model view. The feature view is a spatially structured verbal representation of the data structure that underlies the VR-DIS system. This data structure is organised in "features", hence the name. (See also later.)

The scale-model view is a pictorial representation of the design information, based on the physical appearance of the designed building. This view will feature a high level of verisimilitude.

In [4], the authors discuss four demands for a successful integration of multiple views. The feature and the scale-model representations of the VR-DIS system are integrated on the basis of these four demands. The most important aspects are the following.

1. Supplementary representations: the features display exact numbers (e.g. "width = 5.20m" and "thermal performance has been estimated at 67K"). The scale-model will only visualise a selection of these numbers in qualitative way (e.g. dimensions are presented as such; thermal performance could be visualised by a colour in the range from red (badly isolated) to blue (well isolated).) On top of that, the scale-model provides a means to evaluate the spatial experience of the designed spaces.

2. Integration in one view: while navigating through the scale-model, the user will be able to point out an object (i.e. a building part) and ask for the features that described that object. The demanded features will appear in a frame near the object. The frame with the feature representations is itself an object that behaves similarly to other objects of the scale-model.

3. Consistency: the consistency will be maintained between the representations of the task data. For example, the dimensions of an object in the scale-model will always correspond with the numbers that can be read from the dimension features of that object.

4. Mutually referring: the frames in which features appear will be visually connected to the scale-model object. The objects in the scale-model and the corresponding features in the frames will always be simultaneously highlighted. When a feature is touched (pointed out) or grabbed (selected), both the feature and the scale-model object will be highlighted, and vice versa. Finally, when a property of either an object or a feature is modified by manipulating a particular handle or hot-spot, then all the handles and hot-spots of the other representation with which the same result could be

obtained, will also be highlighted during the execution of the operation. Figure 3 shows the set-up of the interface. The features are visible in the frame in the front ; the scale model is visible in the background.

Figure 3 also shows the flying mouse with the red virtual pen with which the user can grab, relocate, and activate features in the feature view and building parts in the scale model view. The whole interface is worked out as "fish tank VR" system in which the perspective distortion of the image on the screen is in real time updated according to the viewer's head position in front of the screen. Details of the interaction and control characteristics of the interface are described in [13].

4 Designing by features

The VR-DIS system applies an innovative information modelling technique: Feature Based Design. This techniques has evolved from Feature Based Modelling that originates in the disciplines of mechanical engineering and industrial design. Van Leeuwen [3] has transported the design-by-Features approach to the context of architectural design.

In this architectural form of Feature Based Design, feature types can represent any physical or abstract concept involved in the design process: space, function, costs, safety, comfort, form, … . In a design project, one feature-instance might represent a particular wall, another might represent the building as a whole, yet another feature might represent the principal's demand that the meeting room should be "comfortable". The designers can make instances of predefined feature-types, but they can also define new types, reflecting the precise design concepts they have in mind.

Features are linked together forming feature models. A single feature model stores all information related to a particular design project. There are two main predefined relation types between features: composition relations, and specification relations. All other possible relations are termed "associations". Examples of associations are: "is supported by" (a beam supported by a column), "is accessible by" (the building by the road), and so on. As with the feature types, the designer can add his own kinds of relations if he feels that's appropriate. Features can be linked together on both the type and the instance level. Type level relations are used to form complex feature types, to be stored in a feature library. Instance level relations are used to describe the relations between the feature instances of a design project at hand.

The cost of the great flexibility and extensibility of this data model is that it lacks almost any structure. While designing with the VR-DIS system, feature models grow that are not ordered in any strict predefined way: no hierarchy, no matrix structure, no list structure. Feature models are just (chaotic) relational data structures, consisting of features that are of an extensible list of types,

Figure 3: VR-DIS interface

and mutually connected by relations which are decompositions, specifications, or other types of relations. On top of this, in real design projects feature models can grow as large as (presumably) 10 to 100.000 features. It is clear that the flexibility, the extensibility, and the scale of the feature models constitute high demands for the representation through which the feature models are communicated to the user.

5 The Feature View

Relational data sets are currently typically displayed either in table format or in 2D graphical layouts. Tables can display lists of object-relation-object sets in a very efficient way and are very readable at the same time. The disadvantage of tables is that they do not very well support the discovery of implicit data structuring.

Graphical layouts do provide a much better insight in the structure of the data sets. Object clustering and relation sequences can much easier by denoted. The drawback of graphs is that they are often less efficient in screen area usage.

The most used graphical layout format is the "treeview" (figure 4a) which is suited for hierarchical data sets. It's screen efficiency is close to that of tables. Non-hierarchical (cross linked) data sets can best be visualised in graph layouts (figure 4b). Graph layouts are

badly supported by software developed tools. This has resulted in the inappropriate usage of treeviews in many applications, showing the data at hand only fragmentally.

In VR-DIS, we have chosen to visualise the feature models as interactive 3D graphs. We discuss subsequently the visualisation of single features and their relations, and the interactive graph drawing technique.

A feature is visualised as shown in figure 5. Each feature consists of a front plate and a rectangular area behind it. The front-plate features a textual representation of the feature's name and type. The rectangular area behind the front-plate represents the content of the feature. This area is subdivided in a left and a right half.

The left half represents the content that has been defined on the type level. In the case of a primitive ("simple") feature type, the content is something like a number, or a string. Such a primitive content is represented by a 3D icon. In the case of a complex feature type, the content is constituted by all the components (cf. component relations). In this case, the left half of the content area is filled with small visualisations of all the features that have been defined as components at the type level.

The right half of the content area represents the content that has been defined on the instance level. For all feature types, this area is filled with the visualisation of the components that have been added at the instance level.

When a feature has specification relations, those specifications are hidden in a drawer that is connected to the bottom of the front-plate. The drawer has a left type-level part, and a right instance-level part. The drawer can be opened by pulling the handle downwards. When the drawer is opened, all features appear that specificy the central feature (see figure 6). The specification relations

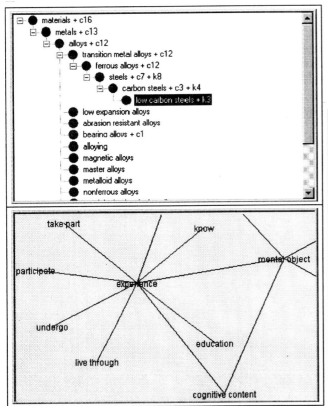

Figure 4: Graph layouts: (a) a treeview, (b) 2D graph.

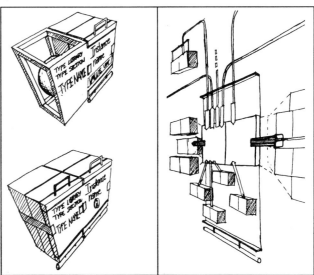

Figure 5: A Simple and a Complex Feature, in initial state   **Figure 6: A Complex Feature, in exploded state**

themselves are visualised by arrows with an overprint of the relation's name. The top of the front-plate features a similar drawer that hides all associations of the feature. It can be opened in a similar manner.

Because the front-plate hides most of the component-features, those component features can be pulled to the side of the front-plate. When pulled to the side, the components are visualised similar to the specifications and associations: the component-relations are visualised as bands with an overprint of the relation's name.

Specifications, association, and components each appear in specific directions relative to the parent feature. This systematic grouping eases the "reading" of features. It also eases feature browsing because we can map users' input gestures to these directions: pointing the 3D input device to the right indicates that one wants to manipulate user defined compositions, pointing to the left refers to type defined compositions, etc.

Since we are dealing with large data-sets, only a small subset of the information at hand is drawn at once. Therefore, an interactive graph drawing technique is needed such that the user can specify subsequent steps from which part of the graph he/she wants to see more. Eades and Graham have both [14] [15] proposed an interactive drawing techniques for the visualisation of very large graphs. Both produce 2D images in which child-nodes are placed on circles around parent nodes. The spatial distribution of the child nodes around their parent depends on the number of the children's children, and on the browsing history (= which "uncle" and "nephew" nodes that have been looked at before). This layout mechanism makes the technique difficult to apply for feature models. We already organised child features around their parent on the basis of the type of their relation. Eades' and Graham's layout mechanisms suppose only one relation type. Their layout mechanisms cannot be superimposed on our's because the two would interfere and result in an unreadable graph.

In VR-DIS, we have chosen to visualise the browsing history in the third dimension. When a feature's relations are visualised, the feature first moves to a new transparent plane that is laid on top. Recursive requests for more detail results in multiple display layers. This mechanism has been inspired by Lieberman's multiple translucent layering technique [16]. We have designed a specific virtual tool through which this browsing process can take place. We refer to this tool as the "feature box".

When starting, the feature box looks just like a real closed box. The box represents the whole feature model of a specific design project. The box can be opened, after which a pyramidal area lights up. In the enlightened pyramid, the shell of a sphere emerges concentric around the box. The shell is orthogonally subdivided in a number of rectangular fields. In each field, a single feature and its directly related features can appear.

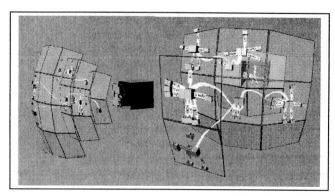

Figure 7: Feature Tool.

The user can formulate type and name based queries to retrieve a first feature from the database. When this feature has components, specifications, and/or associations, they can appear around the original feature, all within a single field of the feature box's shell. The related features are shown smaller than the central feature. When the designer asks such a related, small feature to explode its relations, then it will first move to a new empty field of its own. This new field will be located at a shell that's concentric around the previous shell, but with a bigger radius. While moving to the new field, the relations to the features on the original field stay intact: arrows and bands are bend to S-like shapes. In this new field, the feature can then explode its own related features. These will again appear around their parent, unless the relation goes to a feature that is already visible on any of the other fields of the feature box. In that later case, the related feature stays where it is, and is connected by a bent arrow or band.

6 Experimental Evaluation

The described design of the feature view is based upon 5 main thesis. The first 3 relate to the feature visualisation :

1. Positioning features onto fixed locations in the 3D graph would improve the user's data retrieval performance (=landmark effect). This characteristic is exploited in so called information landscapes. We postulate that the same effect is achieved when a second representation is mixed with the feature view (the scale model view) that provides fixed locations for a minority of the data objects present in the feature view (the geometry features only).

2. Mapping relation types onto fixed directions in the (3D) representation would improve their distinguishability, and thus the user's data retrieval performance. We postulate that a similar performance advantage is achieved when only the end sections of the relations have fixed directions and the rest is allowed to bend into S-like shapes.

3. We postulate that animating events like features appearing, hiding, being deleted, … will improve the

learnability, decrease the error rate, and improve the user's subjective satisfaction.

The following 2 relate to the control of the interaction with the feature set:

4. We postulate that a more efficient set of user commands for manipulating 3D graphs can be developed for a flying 3D mouse then for a conventional 2D mouse.

5. We postulate that using a "Fish tank VR" set up (coupling head motion with the perspective distortion) decreases the user's error rate when working with the designed feature tool.

Most of the theoretical grounds for these theses were visualisation were described in previous sections. There validity is currently experimentally being verified. The experiment involves about 50 test persons. The conducted experiment has a fractional factorial design, allowing the measurement of the main effects of the 5 postulates, as well as their interaction effect with the size of the database at hand (a 6th factor).

7   Conclusion

We have presented the information visualisation in the VR-DIS system. Because the VR-DIS system deals with a hybrid set of data, it requires a combination of a descriptive and a pictorial representation: the feature view and the scale model view. There integration is worked out on the basis of the four demands: complementarity, integration, consistency, and mutual reference.

The descriptive feature view presents the architectural design data as a 3D graph. In this graph, relation types are mapped on distinct planar directions and the browsing history is visualised in the third dimension. A tool composed of spherical transparent layers has been designed to facilitate the browsing process.

Further we discussed the 3d graph browsing tool that has been developed for the visualisation of feature models. This tool is expected to facilitate working with large relation datasets. It supports user extendable data units, and dynamic data models.

References

[1] Achten, H.H. (1997). Generic representations - Knowledge representation for architectural design. G. Ang, L. Hendriks, P. Nicholson and M. Prins (eds.) 1997. *Journal of Architectural Management 13*

[2] Goldschmidt (1994) On Visual Design Thinking: the vis kids of architecture, *Design Studies*, vol. 15, pp. 158-174.

[3] J.P. van Leeuwen and H. Wagter, "Architectural Design-by-Features", in CAAD futures 1997. Proceedings of the 7th International Conference on Computer Aided Architectural Design Futures, Munich, 4-6 August 1997, Junge, Richard (ed.), Kluwer Academic Publishers, Dordrecht, p. 97-115

[4] M.K.D. Coomans and H.H. Achten (1998) Mixed Task Domain Representation in VR-DIS. Proceedings of the 3rd Asia-Pacific Conference on Human Computer Interaction, APCHI'98, Shonan village Center, Japan, July 15-17, 1998.

[5] Smets, G.J.F. (1992) Designing for telepresence: the interdependence of movement and visual perception implemented, in IFAC Man-Machine Systems, the Hague, The Netherlands, 1992, pp. 169-175

[6] W. Bauer, H.J. Bullinger, and A. Rössler, "Virtual Reality – the Ultimative Interface?", in Symbiosis of Human and Artifact, Y. Anzai, K. Ogawa, and H. Mori (eds.), Elsevier Science B.V., 1995, P.587-596

[7] B. de Vries, "VR-DIS research program", internal report, Eindhoven University of Technology, 1998. An extract of the report can be , http://www.ds.arch.tue.nl/Research/program/

[8] Design presentations developed by Calibre BV, The Netherlands, http://www.calibre.tue.nl/

[9] Starlight, by Pacific Northwest National Laboratory, http://multimedia.pnl.gov:2080/showcase/?it_cont ent/starlight.node

[10] 3D Information Landscape, by Institute for Information Processing and Computer Supported New Media, Graz University of Technology, http://www2.iicm.edu/

[12] N.O.Bernsen, "A toolbox of output modalities", the Amodeus-II WWW-site at http://www.mrc-apu.cam.ac.uk/ amodeus/, 1995.

[13] M.K.D. Coomans, "A Virtual Reality User Interface for a Design Information System", Tom De Paepe (ed.), Journal for the Integrated Study of Artificial Intelligence, Cognitive Science and Applied Epistimology, vol 15 n°4, 1998.

[14] Eades, P., F. Cohen and M.L. Huang (1997) Online Animated Graph Drawing for Web Navigation. G. Goos, J. Hartmanis and J. van Leeuwen (eds.) 1997. Graph drawing, Proceedings of the 5th International Symposium on Graph Drawing, GD'97, held in Rome, Italy, Sept. 18-20, 1997. Springer-Verlag, Berlin, pp. 330-335.

[15] Graham, J.W. (1997) NicheWorks – Interactive Visualization of Very Large Graphs, G. Goos, J. Hartmanis and J. van Leeuwen (eds.) 1997. Graph drawing, Proceedings of the 5th International Symposium, GD'97, held in Rome, Italy, Sept. 18-20, 1997. Springer-Verlag, Berlin, pp. 403-414.

[16] Lieberman H. (1994) Powers of Ten Thousand: Navigating in Large Information Spaces. Proceedings of the ACM Symposium on User Interface Software and Technology, 1994. p.15-16

Information Visualization

Chair
Ian Curington
Advanced Visual Systems, UK

Visualizing Real Estate Property Information on the Web

Theodore Hong
Department of Computing
Imperial College of Science, Technology and Medicine
180 Queen's Gate, London SW7 2BZ, United Kingdom
t.hong@doc.ic.ac.uk

Abstract

We have designed and are implementing a system called ReV (Real estate Visualiser) for exploring real estate property listings on the world-wide web. Given the large number of different websites providing listings, each with its own presentation format, and the high-dimensionality of the property space itself, it is difficult to obtain a comprehensive single view of property data on the web. ReV addresses this problem by using grammar induction techniques to automatically learn to parse pages from new websites and collate all of their listings together. It them visualizes this listing data using a map-based color-coding technique. This work draws together a number of strands from the fields of information visualization, machine learning, and database integration. We also hypothesize that ReV will be adaptable to inducing structures from other types of web data.

1. Introduction

The rapid growth in data of all kinds stored in computerized form is bringing a surge of interest in visualization and analysis techniques to interpret the raw data. But while most efforts have been focused on analyzing fielded static databases, we are now seeing information increasingly being provided on a substantial scale through the dynamic medium of the web. In the web context, existing methods of information retrieval have largely emphasized keyword-based searching (e.g. Harvest [4] and WebCrawler [11]), but this approach neglects the possibility of fielding within web documents, treating them simply as unstructured text collections.

An alternative approach is to exploit the markup structure of HTML to enable more sophisticated methods of information extraction and visualization. Many web documents, particularly those generated by query scripts, can be considered as *semistructured* data sources: that is, sources containing data which is fielded but not constrained by a global schema (for an overview, see e.g. [1, 5]). Documents such as on-line product catalogs or real estate listings fall into this category, for example. In these documents, patterns in the HTML markup such as a hierarchical or repeating layout can be used as hints to automatically tag data fields and extract them to a structured format, rather than simply treating the page data as a set of keywords. This allows us to apply established techniques of visualization and analysis in the new setting of the web. We describe a system for web visualization which we are building, called ReV (Real estate Visualizer).

2. Extracting real estate data with ReV

ReV is designed to explore the domain of real estate property listings on the web. There are a large number of competing sources of listings in operation, each with its own unique presentation format, making it difficult to obtain a comprehensive single view of the information available. Furthermore, since there are a multitude of variables which affect the price and desirability of a property, the data space is inherently high-dimensional and cannot easily be visualized. ReV addresses these problems with two main features. First, it provides an extensible way to easily and automatically add new data sources to the system. Given a new website, it sends a few typical queries to obtain samples of the web pages that the source returns. Grammar induction is applied to these pages, to look for regularities in their layout that might be used to parse them into fields. When combined with a few domain-specific heuristics to semantically identify the field contents, together with some manual tweaking if necessary, this yields a wrapper which ReV can use to extract fielded listing data from the new source. (In fact, since very little domain-specific knowledge is

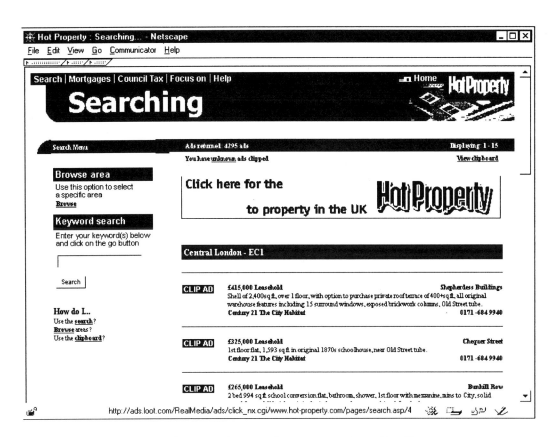

Figure 1. Typical result page from a search on Hot Property.

used, we hypothesize that ReV can be easily adapted to parse other types of web data as well.) Second, once wrappers for each of the data sources have been constructed, ReV is able to issue unified queries that merge search results from all sources. These combined results are then presented to the user in an intuitive, navigable form. Specific details on the visualization used by ReV are given in section 3, below.

2.1. Real estate data sources

A quick web search turns up some twenty-odd sites carrying property listings within Greater London. Hot Property (http://www.hot-property.com) is a typical example. Figure 1 shows a partial screenshot of a result page from a property search on Hot Property, which carries over four thousand London listings in total. The page is structured with a header, a left column containing instructions, a right column with listings, and a footer (not shown). To the eye, it is easy to segment the right column into individual listings, but when looking only at the source HTML it is not so obvious. However, by analyzing the structure of the HTML, ReV is able to

discover the repeated pattern of an image ("Clip Ad") followed by two strong fields, free text, then two more strong fields, and deduces that each of these repetitions constitutes an instance of a listing. Given this information, ReV can examine the particular instances and (by applying some heuristics) determine that, for example, the first strong field contains the price while the second contains the address. It can then generate a parser to search for that particular markup pattern and extract the price and address fields from any Hot Property page.

2.2. Grammar induction algorithm

The task of deriving a parse based on a sample HTML page can be formulated as a grammar induction problem. In this type of problem, the objective is to infer a formal language from a finite sample set. The result should be a derived grammar which is a consistent generalization of the given set of positive examples (and possibly some negative ones). Machine learning techniques have in the past been used for grammar induction tasks such as segmenting unmarked letter sequences into words [14], identifying semantic units in C code fragments [9], and generating a grammar for a document containing dictionary entries [3]. In the ReV context, we are given as input an HTML document containing a set of property listings, and would like to induce a general grammar describing its structure. From this grammar, we can later identify rules as corresponding to particular data fields of interest and create wrappers to extract them.

ReV determines a grammar based on a stylized version of the web page being examined. Attributes are stripped from HTML tags, so that all tags of the same type (e.g. anchor start tags) are considered indistinguishable tokens. Free text occurring between tags is also reduced to a single token simply indicating the presence of text. This is so that structural patterns can be detected despite varying content. For example, two different occurrences of a listing footer giving contact information:

```
<hr><a href="mailto:sales@a.com">
Company A</a>

<hr><a href="mailto:help@b.com">
Company B</a>
```

would both reduce to the stylized version:

```
<hr><a>text</a>
```

To the stylized page we apply a modified version of Wolff's induction algorithm [14]. First, a single start rule is created whose expansion is the entire document. ReV scans the document, counting the occurrences of each digraph within it, where a digraph is a pair of adjacent tokens. If any digraph count exceeds a given threshold (currently ten occurrences), it is considered significant and a corresponding new grammar rule is created. All occurrences of that digraph are then replaced with the rule token, and ReV discards its counts and scans the document again from the beginning. This process continues until no further digraphs exceeding the threshold are found.

We make one exception and specify that rules should not be formed from identical pairs. This prevents an exact repetition such as AAAAAAAA from being subsumed into a rule, since we actually expect such a sequence to occur (as when A corresponds to an entire listing) and would like to see it clearly.

At this point, no rule is more than two tokens long. Longer patterns in the input will be transformed into a cascade of rules. For example, if the sequence `<hr><a>text</a>` occurred as a frequent pattern, it would become the rule token C, where:

```
C -> B </a>
B -> A text
A -> <hr> <a>
```

To flatten this cascade, we specify that if a rule is referenced fewer than a certain number of times (currently five), it is dropped from the grammar and expanded inline wherever it is referenced. Repeated application of this requirement gives first:

```
C -> B </a>
B -> <hr> <a> text
```

and then:

```
C -> <hr> <a> text </a>
```

(assuming that rules A and B are not referenced elsewhere. We may now recognize the cascade as having concealed a pattern four tokens long. In addition to flattening cascades, this modification also ensures that rules created accidentally and without explanatory power are dropped.

2.3. Application of the algorithm

When the induction algorithm is applied to the Hot Property page from Figure 1, we obtain the grammar shown in Figure 2. (Some rules have been omitted for space reasons. Also, for clarity, nested rules have been expanded and are indicated by parentheses.) The rule corresponding to a single listing may be easily identified as 57, which is the largest rule and occurs in a long repeated block in the input (rule 0). From this rule, ReV scans the page searching for occurrences of the pattern, `<a><img></a>...<font><strong><a></a>text </strong></font></td><td><font><strong> text</strong>`...etc., and extracts the text fields in it. In this particular instance, we obtain records such as those shown in Figure 3.

Heuristics are then applied to determine what each field represents semantically – for example, the first field contains a pound sign and numbers and is likely to be the price, while the last field contains eleven digits beginning with the London exchange code 0171 and is probably a contact telephone number. Some post-processing may also be necessary to find further features of interest within the long description that usually accompanies a listing (here, the number of bedrooms, for example). Finally, if a postcode can be determined, either by matching a street name against a postcode database or by direct recognition of a postcode field, a cross-reference is created linking to supplementary information about the area (such as school quality or transport accessibility).

```
0:  !-- base !doctype html head meta meta meta title text /title /head body  9  9 map area
    area area area area /map  6  map area /map  11  15  16  13  59  22  6  6 12  6  59  10
    /table  16  9  text  22  26  59  26  9  6  26  20  60  22  text  13  text  22  9  12
    17  form input input input /strong /font  13  9  9  12  img br text  25 23  23  13  9
    12  12  input  13  input  23  13  br text  20  17  br 18  27  25  font text br  27  25
    font text br  27  25  font  27  13  input /form  23  22  11  15  16  22  9  9  20  22
    20  23  13  9  17  text a strong  18  /a 18  /font  22  25  23  23  5  9  5 36  22  12
    12  11  15  13  4  26  26  20  13  20  60  13  9  59  23  60  10  tr td  57  57  57  57
    57  57  57  57  57  57  57  57  57  57  36  /td td table tr td  17  a /a  18  /font /td
    td  20  /td /tr tr td font  27  /td /tr tr td  20  /td td  20  /td /tr /table /td /tr
    tr td div table tr td img /td /tr /table /td /tr  13  font img img  36  36  /font  23
    10  15  13  text  22  text  13  6  26  9  17  text a strong  18  /a  18  /font  22  25
    23  60  13  59  13  text  22  text  60  60  10  /table  16  /body
1:  text text td
2:  img img /td
4:  text text tr text td
5:  table table (text tr text td)
6:  img img /td text td
7:  text text /tr
    ...
32: table table tr td)
33: /td /td td ((font strong) (text /strong) /font)
34: /table /table /td /tr tr td
36: a a img /a
38: /a /a (text /strong) /font
39: font font (text /font)
56: (a img /a) (a img /a) /td td table tr td (font strong) a /a (text /strong) /font /td td
    ((font strong) (text /strong) /font) /td /tr tr td font (text /font) /td /tr tr td
    ((font strong) (text /strong) /font) /td td ((font strong) (text /strong) /font) /td
    /tr /table /td /tr tr td div table tr td img /td /tr
57: (a img /a) (a img /a) /td td table tr td (font strong) a /a (text /strong) /font /td td
    ((font strong) (text /strong) /font) /td /tr tr td font (text /font) /td /tr tr td
    ((font strong) (text /strong) /font) /td td ((font strong) (text /strong) /font) /td
    /tr /table /td /tr tr td div table tr td img /td /tr /table /td /tr tr td
58: font font img
59: font font img /font
60: (/td text /tr) (/td text /tr) (text /table text) /div
```

Figure 2. Grammar induced from the Hot Property result page.

£215,000	St Johns Square	2 bed loft style apartment, stripped wooden floors throughout, balcony, fully fitted kitchen with integrated appliances, en-suite shower room.	Tower Properties	0171-613 3311
£186,500	Pemberton House	1 bed ground floor apartment, kitchen appliances included, private square, feature fireplaces, new development, between Chancery Lane and Blackfriars station.	Carringtons	0171-247 4002

Figure 3. Some records extracted using the grammar from Figure 2.

3. Visualizing real estate data

Visualisation in the ReV system is to be geographically-based. The main mode of presentation envisioned is through a map displaying an overview of all properties known to the system, shown as colored points. The user will be able to set ranges for each of the major property attributes, such as price, number of bedrooms, school quality, etc., which will toggle the display of only those listings matching the conjunction of all requested attributes. One attribute can be chosen as the primary attribute, which will be shown by using a rainbow spectrum to color-code the points appearing – yellow (brightest) for listings in the center of the specified range, fading out to darker blues and reds at the high and low ends, respectively. This gives an overall view at a glance of the geographical trend in that attribute. By adjusting the various ranges chosen and seeing listings appear, disappear, and change color, the user can quickly follow trends up and down and observe the interaction among the different attributes. Selecting an individual point will bring up a detailed display for that listing.

4. Related work

Work on integrating data from different websites has been carried out by a number of researchers. Krulwich's BargainFinder [8] was able to scan product listings and prices from a set of on-line web stores and place them into a unified ordered table. However, it was not extensible, as it was based entirely on hand-coded wrappers which needed to be tailored specifically to each source site.

ShopBot [7] went a step further by defining a set of heuristics which could be used to automatically parse pages from new sites and extract prices, although the heuristics used were quite specific to parsing on-line store pages. In our system, much greater emphasis is placed on the post-processing and visualisation phase which makes the output useful, vis-a-vis the initial collation phase. Further, we add extra value to the output by cross-referencing it against additional external data sources.

The Stanford TSIMMIS project [6] is another system aimed at integrating web data sources; however, its main focus is on query planning and reasoning about source capabilities rather than information extraction, which is again performed by hand-coded wrappers.

Lorel [2] is a query language for semistructured data which attempts to give a SQL-like semantics to the world-wide web, but does not cover the issues of fielding the data in the first place or of visualizing the results afterwards. WebSQL [10] enhances simple keyword searching with facilities for expressing hyperlink

relationships between documents, but this link structure is at the meta-document level and does not examine the internal structure of the documents themselves.

The proposed visualization concept is similar to that of HomeFinder [13], but differs from it in two important respects. First, while HomeFinder used only fictitious data, this system draws data from real, current listings which are continually being updated. Secondly, HomeFinder showed points only as either matching or not matching the criteria given and did not show any differentiation between listings. It was necessary to slide a range up and down and watch points appearing and disappearing in order to detect trends, whereas we show that time-resolved process in a single snapshot by using gradations of color.

5. Conclusion

We have designed and are currently implementing ReV, a real estate visualization system for the world-wide web. ReV brings together a number of previously disparate ideas from the fields of information visualization, machine learning, and database integration. It provides an extensible means of collating a high-dimensional space of property listings from a number of data sources and visualizing it for the user in an intuitive and navigable way. Additionally, the front-end grammar induction component of the system contains very little that is domain-specific, making it adaptable to inducing structures from other types of web data.

Acknowledgements

The author acknowledges the support of the Marshall Aid Commemoration Commission. This material is based upon work supported under a National Science Foundation Graduate Fellowship.

References

[1] Abiteboul, Serge, "Querying semi-structured data," in Database Theory, 6th International Conference (ICDT '97), Delphi, Greece, 1-18. London: Springer (1997).

[2] Abiteboul, Serge, Dallan Quass, Jason McHugh, Jennifer Widom, and Janet Wiener, "The Lorel query language for semistructured data," Journal on Digital Libraries **1** (1). (1996).

[3] Ahonen, Helena and Heikki Mannila, "Forming grammars for structured documents: an application of grammatical inference," in Grammatical Inference and Applications, 2nd International Colloquium (ICGI '94), Alicante, Spain, 153-167. London: Springer-Verlag (1994).

[4] Bowman, C. Mic, Peter Danzig, Darren Hardy, Udi Manber, and Michael Schwartz, "The Harvest information discovery and access system," Computer Networks **28** (1-2), 119-126 (1995).

[5] Buneman, Peter, "Semistructured data," in Proceedings of the 16th ACM SIGACT—SIGMOD—SIGART Symposium on Principles of Database Systems (PODS '97), 117-121. New York: ACM Press (1997).

[6] Chawathe, Sudarshan, Hector Garcia-Molina, Joachim Hammer, Kelly Ireland, Yannis Papakonstantinou, Jeffrey Ullman, and Jennifer Widom, "The TSIMMIS project: integration of heterogenous information sources," in Proceedings of the 10th Meeting of the Information Processing Society of Japan (IPSJ '94), 7-18. (1994).

[7] Doorenbos, Robert, Oren Etzioni, Daniel Weld, "A scalable comparison-shopping agent for the world-wide web," in Proceedings of the First International Conference on Autonomous Agents (Agents '97), Marina del Rey, CA, USA, 39-48. New York: ACM Press (1997).

[8] Krulwich, Bruce, "The BargainFinder agent: comparison price shopping on the Internet," in Bots and Other Internet Beasties, ed. by Joseph Williams. Indianapolis, IN (USA): Sams Publishing (1996).

[9] Nevill-Manning, Craig and Ian Witten, "Inferring lexical and grammatical structure from sequences," in Compression and Complexity of Sequences (Sequences '97), Positano, Salerno, Italy. Los Alamitos, CA (USA): IEEE Computer Society (1997).

[10] Mendelzon, Alberto, George Mihaila, and Tova Milo, "Querying the world wide web," in Conference on Parallel and Distributed Information Systems (PDIS '96), Miami Beach, FL, USA, 80-91. (1996).

[11] Pinkerton, Brian, "Finding what people want: experiences with the WebCrawler," in Proceedings of the Second World Wide Web Conference, Chicago, IL, USA. (1994).

[12] Stolcke, Andreas and Stephen Omohundro, "Inducing probabilistic grammars by Bayesian model merging," Grammatical Inference and Applications, 2nd International Colloquium (ICGI '94), Alicante, Spain, 106-118. London: Springer-Verlag (1994).

[13] Williamson, Christopher and Ben Shneiderman, "The dynamic HomeFinder: evaluating dynamic queries in a real-estate information exploration system," in International Conference on Research and Development in Information Retrieval (SIGIR '92), Copenhagen, Denmark, 338-346. New York: ACM Press (1992).

[14] Wolff, J.G., "The discovery of segments in natural language," British Journal of Psychology **68**, 97-106 (1977).

A Design, Simulation and Visualization Environment for Object-Oriented Mechanical and Multi-Domain Models in Modelica

Vadim Engelson, Håkan Larsson, Peter Fritzson
Linköping University, Sweden

E-mail: {vaden,x98hakla,petfr}@ida.liu.se

Abstract

The complexity of mechanical and multi-domain simulation models is rapidly increasing. Therefore new methods and standards are needed for model design. A new language, Modelica, has been proposed by an international design committee as a standard, object-oriented, equation-based language suitable for description of the dynamics of systems containing mechanical, electrical, chemical and other types of components. However, it is complicated to describe the system models in textual form whereas CAD systems are convenient tools for this purpose. We have designed an environment that supports the translation from CAD models to standard Modelica notation. This notation is then used for simulation and visualization. Assembly information is extracted from the CAD models, from which a Modelica model is generated. By solving equations expressed in Modelica, the system is simulated. A 3D visualization tool based on OpenGL visualizes expected and actual model behavior, as well as additional parameters. The environment has been applied for robot and flight simulation.

Keywords: CAD, SolidWorks, Mechanical modeling, Simulation, Animation, Visualization, Modeling languages, Modelica, OpenGL .

1. Background

The use of computer simulation in industry is rapidly increasing. Simulation is typically used to optimize product properties and to reduce product development cost and time to market. Whereas in the past it was considered sufficient to simulate subsystems separately, the current trend is to simulate increasingly complex physical systems composed of subsystems from multiple domains such as mechanical, electric, hydraulic, thermodynamic, and control system components.

A new language called Modelica [5, 4, 10, 11] for hierarchical physical modeling is developed through an international effort. Modelica 1.1 was announced in December 1998. It is an object-oriented language for modeling of physical systems for the purpose of efficient simulation. The language unifies and generalizes previous object-oriented modeling languages. Compared with the widespread simulation languages available today this language offers three important advances: 1) non-causal modeling based on differential and algebraic equations; 2) multidomain modeling capability, i.e. it is possible to combine electrical, mechanical, thermodynamic, hydraulic etc. model components within the same application model; 3) a general type system that unifies object-orientation, multiple inheritance, and templates within a single class construct.

Modelica is a standard notation which is used for standard domain libraries and for applications that use these libraries. Tools and environments are built to comply with this standard.

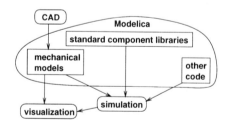

Figure 1. Structure of the integrated environment.

The structure of the environment is shown in Figure 1. Section 2 gives an introduction to the Modelica language and its standard libraries for electrical and mechanical modeling. Section 3 describes the CAD tool we use and translation from CAD models to the standard Modelica notation. Sections 4 and 5 describe simulation and visualization issues.

2. Modelica Language

2.1. Simple Electric Circuit

As an introduction to Modelica we will present a model of a simple electrical circuit. Our goal is to describe features of universal Modelica standard notation, which can be used in applications in various domains (such as electrical, mechanical or chemical). A detailed description of this example can be found in [5, 10]. The system can be broken into a set of connected electrical standard components.

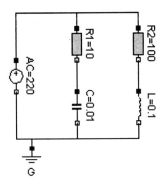

Figure 2. Sample circuit structure in Modelica graphical notation.

Assume that the sample model (Figure 2) consists of a voltage source, two resistors, an inductor, a capacitor and a ground point. Models of such components are available in Modelica standard class libraries for electrical components.

A declaration like the one below specifies R1 to be an instance (i.e. an object) of standard library class `Resistor` and sets the default value of the resistance, R, to 10 (i.e. `R1.R` is 10).

```
Resistor R1(R=10);
```

A Modelica description of the complete circuit appears as follows:

```
class circuit
  Resistor  R1(R=10);
  Capacitor C(C=0.01);
  Resistor  R2(R=100);
  Inductor  L(L=0.1);
  VsourceAC AC;
  Ground    G;
equation
connect(AC.p,R1.p);  connect(R1.n,C.p);
connect(C.n,AC.n);   connect(R1.p,R2.p);
connect(R2.n,L.p);   connect(L.n,C.n);
connect(AC.n,G.p);
end circuit;
```

A composite model like the circuit model described above specifies the system topology, i.e. the components and the connections between the components. The connections specify interactions between the components.

The components (`Resistor`, `Capacitor`, etc.) are subclasses derived from the class `TwoPin` which in turn contains two `Pin` objects:

```
class Voltage = Real;
class Current = Real;

connector Pin
  Voltage  v;
  flow Current i;
end Pin;

class TwoPin
  Pin p, n; //positive and negative pin
  Voltage v;
  Current i;
equation
  v = p.v - n.v; //voltage difference
  p.i = - n.i; //current going inside via two pins
  i = p.i;
end TwoPin;
```

A connection statement `connect(Pin1,Pin2)`, with `Pin1` and `Pin2` of connector class `Pin`, connects the two pins so that they form one node. This implies an equality for v and flow balance for i, namely: `Pin1.v = Pin2.v` and `Pin1.i + Pin2.i = 0` .

Modelica and its standard libraries for electrical models provide short, clear, extensible and concise notation for such models.

During system simulation the variables i and v evolve as functions of time. The solver of algebraic and differential equations computes the values of all variables in the model for all simulation time steps.

2.2. Implementation of Model Simulation

Instances of classes in a model, including equations, are translated into flat set of equations, constants and variables. After flattening, all the equations are sorted in order of data dependence.

The symbolic solver/simplifier performs a number of algebraic transformations to simplify the dependencies between the variables. It can also solve a system of differential equations if it has a symbolic solution. Finally, C code is generated which is linked with a numeric solver. As the result a function of time (t), e.g. $R2.v(t)$ can be computed for a time interval $[t_0, t_1]$ and displayed as a graph or saved in a file. This data presentation is the final result of system simulation.

2.3. Mechanical System Modeling in Modelica

To facilitate mechanical system modeling there exists a standard Modelica class library for modeling multi body mechanical systems (MBS) [9, 13], i.e., systems of rigid bodies connected to each other with certain degrees of freedom.

A model that uses MBS consists of an inertial system (instance of class `Inertial`), joints (instances of classes `RevoluteS` or `PrismaticS`), massless bars (class `Bar`) and bodies (class `Body`) with mass. The objects are connected together with the Modelica `connect` statement.

The `Inertial` object defines the global coordinate system and the gravitational force. All other objects are in some way connected to this object, either directly or through other objects.

The use of the MBS library can be represented by a double pendulum example (see Figure 3):

```
class Pendulum
  Real L = 0.5;
  Inertial I;
  Body P1(rCM={L/2,0,0});
  Body P2(rCM={L/2,0,0});
  RevoluteS rev1(n={0, 0, 1});
  RevoluteS rev2(n={0, 0, 1});
  Bar arm(r={L, 0, 0});
equation
  connect(I.b,     rev1.a);
  connect(rev1.b,  P2.a);
  connect(rev1.b,  arm.a);
  connect(arm.b,   rev2.a);
  connect(rev2.b,  P1.a);
end Pendulum;
```

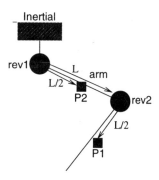

Figure 3. Logical presentation of the pendulum.

The instances of Modelica classes (such as P1, P2, rev1 etc.) have attributes that can be modified. For instance, `Body` has attributes that define mass, inertia tensor

and location of center of mass relative to the local coordinate system (`rCM`). Instances of `RevoluteS` (revolute joint) have an attribute n that define direction of rotation axis. Instances of `PrismaticS` (prismatic joint) have an attribute that specify direction of allowed translation. For a `Bar` the coordinates of its end are specified as r.

The classes of the MBS library have connectors called a and b, of type `MBSCut`. A **connect** statements usually connects two `MBSCut`s attached to two different instances. This specifies equality of rotation, position, velocity and acceleration. It also specifies that there is a balance for force and torque between the connectors.

Every MBS class contains differential equations that specify relations between rotation, positions and forces at its connectors a and b.

During system simulation all equalities, balances and differential equations are solved and the values of all the numeric items are computed for each time step.

There are 70 other classes in the MBS library (for bodies and joints) and 30 classes in drive train library (for motors and other mechanical elements).

3. CAD Tools

In order to simplify design of mechanical Modelica models, CAD tools can be utilized. The system used in our project is SolidWorks[16].

SolidWorks uses the concept of parts and assemblies. Each solid component (a rigid body) is modeled as a separate *part* document.

In the *assembly* document these parts are put together to form a complete model. Each part model can also occur more than once in the assembly.

The *assembly* document defines the mobility between the parts of an assembly. Between two parts, several so called *mates* are connected, each adding some constraint to the mobility between the parts.

A part consist of entities, such as planes, faces, edges, axes and points. A mate connects two entities from different parts. There exist several mate types. The most typical are *coincident* (all the points of one entity are inside another entity) or *parallel* (it keeps entities parallel to each other).

Two parts can be connected by one, two or more mates. Some combinations of mates are valid, some are not. Invalid combinations of mates are rejected by SolidWorks automatically. In [7] we analyze valid sets of mates between pairs of parts and translate them to corresponding sets of Modelica joints. There are similar concepts for parts, assemblies and mates in other 3D CAD tools, e.g. [19].

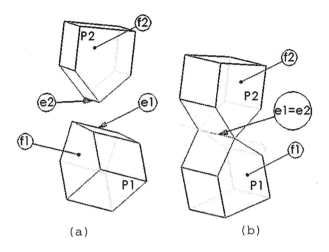

(a)   (b)

Figure 4. Parts and their mates specification before (a) and after (b) adjustment according to the mates.

3.1. Example

The example (Figure 4(a)) describes a fragment of the pendulum model. The part P1 has front face (f1) and upper edge (e1). The part P2 has the front face (f2) and bottom edge (e2). There is a mate M_1 that specifies that planes of f1 and f2 are coincident. The mate M_2 specifies that the edges e1 and e2 are coincident. The Solid-Works system analyzes the mates and adjusts positions of the parts (Figure 4(b)). The system automatically rejects invalid mate combinations. Our translator [7] finds that there is a joint with one rotational degree of freedom between the parts P1 and P2, and calculates the position and orientation of the rotation axis. This pair of mates corresponds to an instance of class RevoluteS from Modelica MBS library with attached Body instance.

3.2. Modelica Model

Each SolidWorks assembly consists of a set of parts, and it stores a set of mates. All these are validated and translated to a set of Modelica MBS class instances and appropriate *connections* between them. Mass, position of center of mass and inertia tensor are extracted from the corresponding part documents by SolidWorks. The result of a Modelica model simulation is position, rotation, velocity, acceleration and other physical properties of each Body as functions of time during the simulated time period.

4. Translation and simulation

Figure 5 represents components of the environment needed for visualization. Our translator from SolidWorks to

Modelica takes information about the mates and produces a corresponding set of Modelica class instances with connections between them. The mass and inertia tensors for each part are computed by SolidWorks. These are extracted and used in Modelica model. Geometry information is saved in a separate STL [17] file for each part.

By default the gravity force is applied to the mechanical model. Usually this is not enough for simulation. All external forces that are applied to the bodies, as well as motor forces that are applied to revolute and prismatic joints should be specified. This is done outside the SolidWorks model by adding code for new class instances to the Modelica model.

A control subsystem that controls the forces according to a certain plan (mission) can be written in Modelica. If necessary, external code in C can be added to the model.

When a Modelica model is simulated, the position, orientation, velocity and acceleration for each part (Body instance) is computed. For Modelica simulation we use the Dymola tool with Modelica support[3].

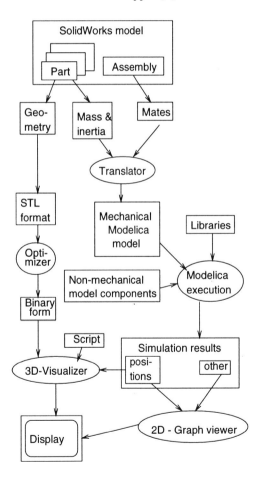

Figure 5. The path from SolidWorks model to dynamic system visualization.

191

5. Visualization

The integrated environment includes a visualizer that provides online dynamic display of the assembly (during simulation) or offline (based on saved state information for each time step).

The STL format[17] is a very simple format suitable for visualization. All surfaces are divided into triangles and the the coordinates of the triangle vertices, as well as normal vectors of the triangles, are listed in the STL-file.

The visualizer loads the corresponding STL file for each part and optimizes it for rendering. After that, rendering is performed by OpenGL [8] library functions. During optimization the vertices positioned very close are merged together. Optimized STL code is stored in a binary file for future use.

The user of the visualizer can alternatively utilize the pop-up menu system, keyboard shortcuts, or a command string in order to control various options. We found that the following options (that can be turned on and off) should be available, and we have implemented them.

— Rotating the camera in 2 degrees of freedom (DOF), moving the camera in 3 DOF, zooming in and out.

— Using perspective and orthographic projection.

— Display of a part as a wire-frame, filled with certain color, using a lighting model with certain light sources, or hiding a certain part.

— Display of an application-specific landscape, for instance, road for car simulation, or a runway surrounded by hilly landscape for flight simulation. Such a landscape can be created as a SolidWorks assembly that does not move, or directly in C using OpenGL.

— Display of planned trajectory (mission) of some parts.

— Display of actual trajectory of some parts.

— Display of origin and coordinate axes (local for bodies and global one) as well as grid lines.

— Display pseudo-shadow. The pseudo-shadow is not depending of light at all. We found that for flight simulation it is convenient to display a projection of vehicle and trajectory on the ground plane.

— Synchronization of animation with machine clock.

— Starting, stopping, continuing animation, stepping forward and backward.

— Targeting camera center of view on a particular part, so that camera follows the part all the time.

— Rotating camera together with the target part.

The integrated system has been used for modeling industry robot behavior as well as helicopter flight simulation (Figure 6). We have designed a robot and helicopter control models and performed design optimization for the control system [18, 15]. The helicopter is designed in SolidWorks and consists of 10 parts, 4 revolute and 2 prismatic joints.

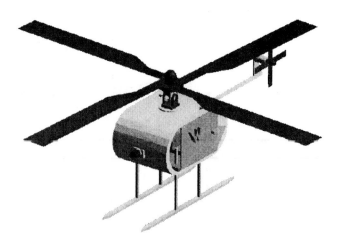

Figure 6. Helicopter dynamic visualization.

It is possible to export the visualization to the 3D Studio MAX [1] (to create and save movies) and MultiGen[12] on SGI (to design Virtual Reality applications).

6. Related Work

Our approach has similarities to the Working Model 3D tool [19]. This tool permits construction of a mechanical model with joints (free and motor-controlled), springs, dampers and ropes. It also has built-in collision detection options. Working Model 3D can import assemblies from SolidWorks.

However Working Model 3D is a *closed* system and user-defined control code can be used there in a very limited way. On the contrary in Modelica we specify arbitrary control algorithms for mechanical and mechatronic models. Working Model 3D is limited to certain types of mechanical systems, whereas Modelica supports general multi-domain modeling.

Similar mechanical simulation features are available in some other advanced CAD tools.

7. Future work

7.1. Using STEP/EXPRESS for Contact Computation

STEP (Standard for the Exchange of Product data)[6, 14] is an international standard for data exchange. It includes a language called *EXPRESS*, that can be used for exchanging advanced geometric information between CAD/CAM systems. This is an advanced file format where the geometry of the solids is represented in a more mathematical way than in STL. This format could be useful when calculating points of contact between parts or if a representation of the part geometry on closed form was to be included in the Modelica model.

7.2. True Multidomain Applications

Modelica is suitable for multiple application domains. Components from several domains (mechanical, electrical, hydraulic simulation) can be used within the same Modelica model. For instance, electrical components can be combined with mechanical components in the model. The electrical parts can be written by hand, or designed using a block-oriented editor, or extracted from an electric CAD system. The generated Modelica code for electrical components in combination with a mechanical design tool produces a multidomain Modelica model.

8. Conclusions

An integrated environment for simulation of multidomain models has been implemented using Modelica as a standard model representation. The user can work with arbitrary SolidWorks models, extend the corresponding Modelica model in various ways, and analyze the simulation results in high performance visualization environment. A complex model such as a pendulum consisting of seven bars can be created in ten minutes. It is simulated 5-7 times faster than corresponding model in Working Model 3D [19]. The helicopter and industrial robot models [18, 15] were successfully designed and simulated.

9. Acknowledgments

The Modelica definition has been developed by the Eurosim Modelica technical committee [10] under the leadership of Hilding Elmqvist (Dynasim AB, Lund, Sweden). The work has been supported by the Wallenberg foundation as part of the WITAS project [18].

References

[1] *3D Studio Max*, Autodesk Inc., http://www.ktx.com

[2] *Cult 3D Home Page*, Cycore AB, http://www.cykar.se

[3] *Dymola Home Page*, Dynasim AB, http://www.dynasim.se

[4] H. Elmqvist, S. E. Mattsson. Modelica – The Next Generation Modeling Language – An International Design Effort. In *Proceedings of First World Congress of System Simulation*, Singapore, September 1–3 1997.

[5] P. Fritzson, V. Engelson, Modelica – A Unified Object-Oriented Language for System Modeling and Simulation, In *Proc. of Eur. Conf. on Object-Oriented Progr. (ECOOP98)*, Brussels, July 20–24, 1998.

[6] *ISO 10303, Industrial Automation Systems and Integration - Product Data Representation and Exchange*, ISO TC 184/SC4, 1992.

[7] H. Larson, *Translation of 3D CAD models to Modelica*, Master Thesis, IDA, Linköping Univ., Sweden, April 1999.

[8] J. Leech, *OpenGL Web Site*, http://reality.sgi.com/opengl

[9] S.E. Mattsson, H. Elmqvist, M. Otter, Physical system modeling with Modelica, *Control Engineering Practice*, 1998, vol. 6, pp. 501–510.

[10] *Modelica WWW site*, Modelica Group, http://www.modelica.org

[11] *Modelica activities in PELAB*, PELAB Group, Linköping University, http://www.ida.liu.se/˜pelab/modelica

[12] *Multigen*, OpenFlight section, MultiGen-Paradigm, Inc., http://www.multigen.com

[13] M. Otter, *Objektorientierte Modellierung mechatronischer Systeme am Beispiel geregelter Roboter*. Dissertation, Fortschrittberichte VDI, Reihe 20, Nr. 147, 1995.

[14] J. Owen, *STEP – An Introduction*, Information Geometers Ltd., 1993, ISBN 1-874728-04-6.

[15] J. Parmar, *Modeling Autonomous Helicopters using Modelica*, Master Thesis, IDA, Linköping Univ., Sweden, To appear in June 1999.

[16] *SolidWorks*, SolidWorks Corporation, http://www.solidworks.com

[17] *StereoLithography Interface Specification*, 3D Systems, Inc., Valencia, CA 91355. Available via http://www.vr.clemson.edu/credo/rp.html.

[18] WITAS group, *The Wallenberg Laboratory for Research on Information Technology and Autonomous Systems*, Linköping University, http://www.ida.liu.se/ext/witas

[19] *Working Model*, MSC.Working Knowledge, http://www.krev.com

Video Composition by Spatiotemporal Object Segmentation, 3D-Structure and Tracking

Ebroul Izquierdo and Mohammed Ghanbari

Department of Electronic Systems Engineering, University of Essex
Colchester, CO4 3SQ, United Kingdom

Fig. 1: Integration of video objects in a computer generated world.

Abstract

In this paper a stereo vision based system for composition of natural and computer generated images is presented. The system focuses on the solution of four essential tasks in computer vision: disparity estimation, object segmentation, modeling and tracking. These tasks are performed in direct interaction with each other using novel and available multiview analysis techniques and standard computer graphics algorithms. The system is assessed by processing natural video sequences. Selected results are reported in the paper.

1 Introduction

Manipulation, composition and integration of natural video with computer generated environments is essential in a large variety of advanced computer vision applications. This process not only requires accurate registration between the video objects and the synthesized environment, but also the extraction of single objects from video sequences representing complex scenes. In this context advanced technologies for mixing and enhancing views of the real world with computer generated environments have to be capable of segmenting natural images and tracking single video objects. Currently, there exists a large collection of application domains for these key technologies including: entertainment, education, medical imaging, augmented reality, immersive telepresence, etc.

In this paper a stereo vision based system for composition of natural and computer generated images is presented. In Fig. 1 an example of integration of segmented stereoscopic video objects and computer generated worlds is outlined. The presented system focuses on the solution of four essential tasks in computer vision: disparity estimation, object segmentation, modeling and tracking. To deal with the first and second tasks a strategy is used in which segmentation and disparity estimation interact in a recursive process providing a robust recognition of physical objects present in the scene and at the same time improving an initial displacement field. Initial displacement fields are obtained by applying the estimator introduced in [4]. An advanced technique based on nonlinear diffusion is used for object segmentation. In this approach initial disparity fields are used to define the conduction coefficients in the nonlinear diffusion process. Finally, the initial displacement fields are refined using segment information.

The third task addressed in the presented system is concerned with the extraction of 3D structure from single objects in an unrestricted environment and the efficient modeling of their surfaces. To cope with this task we exploit some well-established algorithms from both computer vision and computer graphics, improving and combining them with new strategies. The goal is to extract the 3D structure of single objects present in natural scenes and to give a compact and efficient representation of them, keeping computational cost low. The basic idea of the technique presented is to use feature points and relevant edges in the images as nodes and edges of an initial 2D wire-grid. Starting from this initial 2D model the final 3D wireframe is generated by fitting the 2D model to a previously recovered depth map of the object. Depth is estimated by triangulation, using refined disparity fields and camera parameters.

Two different objectives are challenged in the tracking task: to establish temporal consistency in the generated model and to maintain accurate registration between the real and computer generated environments when they are integrated. Establishing temporal consistency means that nodes of the wireframes have to follow the natural optical flow of the analyzed sequence. Maintaining accurate registration between the real and computer generated environments means that the background must remain aligned with the 3D-orientation and perspective of the real objects. This goals are achieved by tracking the nodes of the mesh from frame to frame as long as the same faces of the object of concern are visible. When a new part of the object becomes visible or occluded, the wireframe is again initialized taking into account the nodes that remain visible and expanding the mesh in order to cover the new object face.

The paper is organised as follows. Next section describes the used techniques for combined disparity estimation and segmentation. In section 3 the methods used for 3D Modelling are described. Section 4 is concerned with tracking task. Selected results obtained by processing natural video sequences are reported at the end of each section. The paper closes with a summary and conclusions in section 5.

2 Disparity-Driven Object Segmentation

Object segmentation in computer vision consists of extraction of the shape of physical objects projected onto the image plane, ignoring edges due to texture inside the object borders. In most cases the extraction of segment masks with physical meaning cannot be carried out without additional information about the structure or the dynamic of the scene. For this reason robust systems for object segmentation should addresses different image processing tasks. In the proposed method object segmentation is carried out by combining initial disparity estimates with an advanced nonlinear diffusion technique for accurate segmentation. The segmentation results are then used to refine the initial disparity estimates. To obtain initial disparity fields, we basically use the hierarchical block-matching method introduced by Izquierdo [4]. This estimator is based on a hierarchical approach in two levels. In the first level, global displacements are estimated and used as potential displacements in the second level. This scheme copes with arbitrary disparity ranges and performs very robustly even in the case of low correlation between the left and right image areas. More detailed description of this estimator and the assessment of its performance by several computer simulations is given [4]. In the image at the left of Fig. 2 the initial disparity field corresponding to the first frame pair of the sequence JARDIN is displayed. The original stereoscopic images are shown in Fig. 1.

To extract masks of physical objects, we introduce a technique based on nonlinear diffusion. In the context of image segmentation, it is known that the nonlinear diffusion paradigm leads to impressive results clearly outperforming well-established filters like the canny operator [2]. The nonlinear diffusion model for image segmentation was introduced by Perona and Malik [5] and extended by several other authors [1, 3]. In this technique averaging is inhibited at the image edges and the diffusion velocity is controlled by the magnitude of the gradient intensity. Within the nonlinear diffusion process a set of images $I(x, y, t)$ is generated, with $I(x, y, 0)$ as the original image and t as scale parameter, by applying the parabolic diffusion equation

$$I_t = \nabla \cdot [c(x, y, t)\nabla I] = div(c(x, y, t)\nabla I) . \quad (1)$$

If c is chosen as a suitable function of the image edges, the diffusion process should tend to a piece-wise constant solution representing a simplified image with sharp boundaries. Using the diffusion equation (1) with $c(x, y, t) = f(\|\nabla I(x, y, t)\|^2)$, a set of simplified images is

generated. Different choices for f are proposed in the literature. In our work we use

$$f(w) = A/(1 + \frac{w}{B}) \quad (2)$$

as proposed in [5]. Note that the so-defined equation is of type forward parabolic if the image gradient is smaller than $\sqrt{B}$, otherwise it is of type backward parabolic. That is, the used model smoothes regions where the gradient is smaller than $\sqrt{B}$ but enhances edges with gradient larger than $\sqrt{B}$. Fig. 3 shows the nonlinear diffused image obtained when the left first image of the sequence JARDIN is taken as initial condition in the model.

To smooth edges due to texture inside of object contours, we introduce an extended diffusion model in

Fig. 2: Initial disparity field estimated by hierarchical block-matching (left); and enhanced disparity field estimated after segmentation (right).

which the conduction coefficient is also modulated by the disparity field. The main idea behind this approach is to control the diffusion process according to the variations in the disparity. This strategy has been inspired from the fact that image areas with smooth disparity variation probably represent a single physical object of the scene, thus edges in these regions are due to texture and should be smoothed. It is expected that the solution to the modified nonlinear model tends to a piece-wise constant function representing a simplified image with sharp boundaries. In contrast to the solution of the conventional Perona-Malik model, in the solution of the proposed model each image region with constant intensity should correspond to a physical object in the scene.

The degree of smoothness $\varsigma(z)$ of the disparity field at any sampling position $z=(x, y)$ is obtained by measuring the variance of the disparity vectors inside a small observation window W centered at z:

$$\varsigma(z) = \sigma_{z,W}^2 = \sqrt{(\sigma_x^2)^2 + (\sigma_y^2)^2} , \text{ where } (\sigma_x^2) \text{ and } (\sigma_y^2)$$

are the variances of the horizontal and vertical components of the disparity vectors inside the window W.

The conduction coefficient c in (1) is now defined as function of a ς-weighted image gradient $\|\nabla I\|_\varsigma$. That is the magnitude of the image gradient is weighted at each sampling position by the local disparity variance $\sigma_{z,W}^2$. Let σ_{max}^2 be the maximal variance of the considered disparity field and $g:[0, \sigma_{max}^2] \to [0,1]$ be any increasing function satisfying the two conditions $g(0)=0$ and $g(\sigma_{max}^2)=1$. Then we define $\|\nabla I\|_\varsigma^2 = g(\sigma_{z,W}^2).\|\nabla I\|^2$. Obviously, there are several choices for the control function g. The results reported in this paper have been obtained by choosing

$$g(v) = \begin{cases} (v/\sigma_{max}^2)^2 & \text{if } v \le C \\ 1 & \text{else} \end{cases}$$

where $C \in (0,1)$ is a threshold modulating the influence of ς in the diffusion process. Applying the parabolic diffusion equation (1) with $c(x,y,t) = f(\|\nabla I(x,y,t)\|_\sigma^2)$ and f as the Perona-Malik function (2), an iterative disparity-driven diffusion process is carried out. Fig. 3 shows the result obtained by applying this technique to the sequence JARDIN.

Fig. 3: Smoothed image by nonlinear diffusion using the Perona-Malik model (left); and disparity-dependent nonlinear diffusion (right).

To finish interaction process between disparity estimation and segmentation, the initial disparity field is improved by matching along the object contour and considering only intensity information corresponding to the foreground objects. The field shown at the right hand side of Fig. 2 correspond to the improved disparity field, estimated by block-matching but using segmentation results.

3   3D Modelling

Efficient and flexible modelling of arbitrary 3D objects from stereoscopic views is carried out using the results of previous processing. The main goal is the generation of spatially-optimised and temporally-consistent models which properly reflect the geometrical surface characteristics of the objects. The basic idea of the techniques presented is to use feature points, relevant edges and abrupt variations in the disparity map as nodes and edges of the wire grid. The method is adaptive in the sense that an initial rough surface approximation is progressively refined at the locations where the triangular patches do not approximate the surface accurately. The approximation error is measured according to the distance of the model to the object surface taking into account the reliability of the depth estimated from disparity and camera parameters.

3.1 Generation of a 2D model by constrained Delaunay triangulation

To generate a wireframe model approximating the object surface, a complete set of surface characteristics reflecting relevant object features is initially estimated. In this process three different features are considered: Piece-wise linear approximation of image edges (denoted by Λ in the sequel), *edgeness* and *cornerness*. These features are then used to constrain the position of nodes and edges of the model. To obtain meshes with nodes regularly distributed over the non-uniform object areas, the object is split into rectangular blocks of moderate size. For each block that does not intersect a feature, the point which is most clearly distinguished from its neighbors is also considered as a candidate for the mesh nodes. Let us denote the set of feature points and lines representing object surface characteristics as $SC = \Phi \cup \Lambda$, where Φ is the set of relevant image points and corners. Moreover let E be the set of end points and vertices of the polygonal lines Λ. The generation of the projection in the image plane of an initial surface approximation constrained to the surface characteristics leads to a 2D triangulation constrained to SC. There are different ways to triangulate a 2D object. We are interested in a locally optimal triangulation T in the sense given by the *goodness* property $g(T)$ introduced by Lawson [6]. Here $g(T)$ is defined as function of the minimum interior angles of each triangle of T.

In order to obtain a local optimal triangulation in the sense of $g(T)$, we first construct the Delaunay triangulation of all points belonging to $\Phi \cup E$. After that, the remaining lines of Λ that are not edges of the Delaunay triangulation are inserted in T. The resulting constrained Delaunay triangulation is then locally optimized according to the *goodness* property $g(T)$.

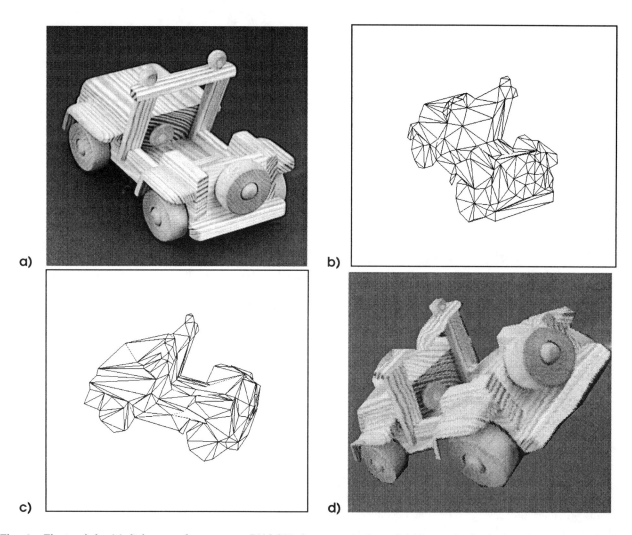

Fig. 4: First original left frame of sequence BUGGY a); generated model b); tracked wireframes corresponding to the twelfth frame; and perspectively views obtained by rendering the 3D model after texture mapping.

3.2 Generation of the 3D model

Depth maps are estimated for each segmented object using previously estimated disparities and camera parameters The accuracy of depth estimation is improved by averaging corresponding depth values of independently estimated depth maps, taking into account the reliability of the disparity estimates. In the averaging process, different combinations of disparity fields are considered, e.g., using four cameras with optical axes converging to a common point and lying on the same plane, a total of 12 disparity fields can be estimated using all possible image combinations. In this case, 12 depth values may be calculated for each sampling position. Ideally, all depth values should coincide, but due to occlusions, matching errors, sampling perturbations, noise, etc., these values differ in practice.

Assigning the depth value to each node of the 2D wire grid an initial wireframe is obtained. Next, a local adaptive refinement procedure is performed in order to generate a polyhedral approximation of the object surface within a preset error tolerance. The approximation error is estimated independently for each triangular patch by measuring the distance between the depth map and the initial wireframe. If the error is greater than a given threshold, the model is refined locally around this patch. The refinement is performed by selecting the point in the triangular patch that gives the worst approximation and inserting it as a new node in the 3D triangulation. In order to compute the approximation error of a given triangular patch a partition of the image domain is defined. A weighted Euclidean distance between the triangular patch and the depth map is used as error estimate. The weights are calculated in proportion to the reliability of the disparity vectors used to estimate depth. The reliability measure is defined as a linear combination of two different criteria. The first one is based on the disparity-uniqueness constraint. The second is derived from the analysis of the curvature of the correlation surface obtained during the matching process.

4 Tracking

Once a wireframe is available for the first frame pair, its mesh nodes are tracked by analyzing the natural optical flow of the video sequence. The motion of the nodes is accurately estimated from frame to frame as long as the same faces of the object concerned are visible. When a new part of the object becomes visible or occluded, the wireframe is again initialized taking into account the nodes that remain visible and expanding the mesh in order to cover the new object face. The motion estimation is based on a model in which each motion vector inside any object is represented as the sum of a global motion vector and a local motion vector. The global motion is calculated by applying a parameter model and a robust statistical regression approach. The local motion is estimated from the global motion parameters and accurate matching. Outliers are simultaneously detected by applying a strategy which combines the local and global motion estimates with their reliability. Fig 4 shows results obtained by applying

the modeling and tracking techniques to the stereoscopic sequence BUGGY. In Fig 4a the segmented foreground object corresponding to the first left frame is shown. The wireframe generated for this object is shown in Fig. 4b. Fig. 4c shows the tracked wireframe corresponding to the twelfth frame. A perspectively different view of the object, obtained by rendering the 3D model after texture mapping, is displayed in Fig. 4d.

5 Summary and Conclusions

A complete framework for stereoscopic image analysis and synthesis has been introduced. The main challenges targeted in this work are the segmentation of video objects and the efficient modeling of their 3D surfaces. These goals are reached by combining advanced multiview analysis techniques with some standard computer graphics algorithms. Applications of the presented system include manipulation and integration of natural video with computer generated worlds. Selected results obtained by processing natural video sequences are reported in the paper. Experimental results demonstrate that the objectives challenged in the work can be achieved by the proposed system.

Acknowledgment This work was supported by the Virtual Centre of Excellence in Digital Broadcasting and Multimedia Technology Ltd., U.K.

References

[1] L. Alvarez, P. L. Lions and J. M. Morel, "Image Selective Smoothing and Edge Detection by Nonlinear Diffusion. II", *SIAM J. Numer. Anal.*, Vol. 29, No. 3, 1992, pp. 845-866.

[2] J. Canny, "A Computational Approach to Edge Detection", *IEEE Transaction on Pattern Analysis and Machine Intelligence*, Vol. PAMI-8, No. 6, 1986, pp. 679-697.

[3] F. Catté, P. L. Lions, J. M. Morel and T. Coll, "Image Selective Smoothing and Edge Detection by Nonlinear Diffusion I", *SIAM J. Numer. Anal.*, vol. 29, no. 1, 1992, pp. 182-193.

[4] E. Izquierdo, "Stereo matching for enhanced telepresence in 3D-videocommunications", *IEEE Transaction on Circuits and Systems for Video Technology, Special issue on Multimedia Technology, Systems and Applications*, vol. 7, no. 4, Aug. 1997, pp. 629-643.

[5] P. Perona and J. Malik, "Scale Space and Edge Detection Using Anisotropic Diffusion", *Proc. IEEE Comput. Soc. Workshop on Comput. Vision*, 1987, pp. 16-22.

[6] C. L. Lawson, "Software for C1 surface interpolation", *In Rice J. R. Ed. Mathematical software III*, Academic Press, pp. 161-164, 1977.

Display Models for Visualization

Jonathan C. Roberts
Computing Laboratory,
University of Kent at Canterbury,
England, UK, CT2 7NF

J.C.Roberts@ukc.ac.uk

Abstract

Models for visualization are important, helping the developer and user to understand the visualization process; to follow the connections and the data paths through the system; and to reference and compare the functionality and the limitations of different systems or techniques.

Display models specifically classify the data by what type of output can be created.

Jacques Bertin [2] described a symbolic reference model that he used to describe images and displays. In this paper we review his and other 'display orientated models' describing important aspects of these methods and ideas. We then translate Bertin's scheme into an algebraic form as a method to describe visualizations.

Keywords: Visualization models, Display models, Bertin's semiology.

1. Introduction

There are many diverse data types, data storage methods, system configurations and dimensions all with different names, terminology and models applied to them. A classification model allows systems, data and algorithms to be grouped and compared.

Display models classify the information by what type of output may be created. In this paper we present different display models including Bertin's model. Indeed, Bertin's display model [1, 2] describes many 'image space' components with a graphical method for representing the "Utilization of the Image Space" and it is possible to transfer this method into an algebraic form. Thus, within this paper we also present one such algebraic scheme and use it to describe different visualization techniques.

Visualization is an issue that has been addressed by many researchers but there is currently no standard model for visualization, whether for the visualization system, flow of data or display aspects. A commonly adopted model, describing the visualization flow, is the *dataflow* model (Upson [15], and Haber and McNabb [7]), this is a good general model and is used in many visualization systems, for example, AVS [15], IBM Data Explorer [11] and IRIS Explorer [8].

Within this paper we focus on the 'display methods' of visualization. In the following sections we provide a review of many 'display models', then extend Bertins method into an algebraic form.

2. Data and Dimensionality

Earnshaw and Wiseman [6] provide a general "Data and Display Dimensionality" classification scheme that organises current output representation techniques by comparing the output primitives dimension with the dimension of the data.

Collins [5] extends Earnshaw and Wiseman's model (Table 1) to include the data types of Scalar (S), Vector (V) and Tensor (T). The Table includes multiple display examples; some of these are explained below:

Attribute Mapping maps attributes to a surface, using colours and textures.

Colour Maps are formed by mapping colour, from the range of the data values, onto a 2D image.

Dot Surfaces are surfaces that are made from points.

Glyphs represent symbols that change in appearance depending on the values and position within the data, and can depict values, vectors and tensors.

Height Fields are generated from creating a height (terrain) at each point on two dimensional data.

Moreover, Bertin specifically presents a display categorization.

Display	Dimensionality of the Data			
Dimension	1D	2D	3D	nD
0D	Points	Scatter Plots(S,M)	3D Scatter Plots(S, M) Tri-Scatter Plot(S) Dot Surfaces(S)	
1D	Lines / Curves(S)	Contour Maps(S)	Vector Arrows(V)/ Streamlines(V)	
2D	–	Height Fields(S) Colour Maps(S)	Tiled Surfaces(S) Ribbons(V)	Attribute mapping (S,M)
3D	–	–	Solid (S)/ Volume Modelling (S)	Glyph (T) icon (M)
Scalar(S), Vector(V), Tensor(T), Multivariate(M)				

Table 1. Examples classified by Data and Display Dimensions, after Earnshaw/Wiseman [6]

3. Bertin's Display Primitive Model

Bertin [1, 2] describes a display primitive classification model dividing the output primitives into four categories:

Diagrams including bar charts, scatter plots, histograms and schematics.

Networks including trees and path connections.

Maps including geographical maps and diagrams in which the positions are constrained by a "real life" object. Often maps incur a non-uniform projection (that must be understood when reading the map); for example, the spherical surface of the Earth is often mapped onto a flat two dimensional geographical map.

Symbols including signs and icons.

Bertin splits these into components that represent the dimensions of the output primitive, with each output primitive split into three categories of either *point*, *line* or *area*. He designates a level of *organization* to each primitive. A primitive can therefore be:

Associative ($\equiv$) where any object can be immediately isolated as belonging to the same category, and each object can be considered as *similar*.

Selective ($\neq$) where each object can be grouped into a category *differenced* by this variable (forming families).

Ordered (O) that allows each element to be grouped into an order of scale.

Quantitative (Q) where each element can be compared to be greater or less than another element. This includes values as percentages and logarithms.

This classification model allows the inclusion of methods such as pie diagrams, bar charts, scatter plots and three dimensional isosurface diagrams. Bertin classifies the output display method as an icon, using lines, arcs and arrows (Figure 1). The Diagrams, Networks, Maps and Symbols are represented by how they 'utilize' the image space, whether circular or linear, and this is represented in Figure 1 as "Utilization of the Image Space".

3.1. Display technique Catalogs

Lohse et al [10], with many volunteers, have classified multiple visualization representations. Subjects sorted the visual representations into clusters of objects, from which a hierarchical tree diagram was created. The clusters formed groups of graphs, tables, maps, diagrams, icons and network charts; using similar classifications to Bertin [2]. A scatter plot, of icons to networks (on one axis) against graphs, tables to maps and diagrams (on the other axis) was generated.

4. Bertin's Symbolic Schema

We extend Bertin's representation to include a Composite classification. This Composite category includes images that use multiple primitives, such as, a diagram of glyphs or a map (showing geometric information) with a network (showing connectivity information). Figure 5 shows some visualization techniques within Bertin's classification structure, however, the Organization of each component is not depicted in the diagram. This information can easily be included but the component of Organization often depends on the data being represented and on the method of representation. Figure 4 shows some examples with one particular Organization classification.

Bertin describes six representation methods, named *Retinal Variables*, of shape, orientation, colour, texture, value,

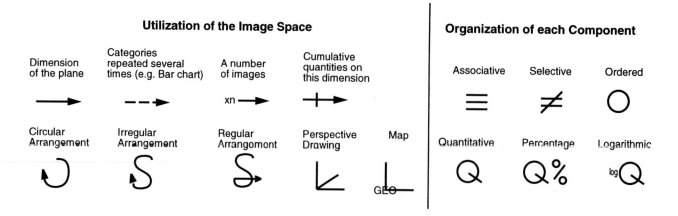

Figure 1. Graphical Classification Scheme, after Bertin

Utilization of the Image Space (within the figure)
- Dimension of the plane
- Categories repeated several times (e.g. Bar chart)
- A number of images — xn
- Cumulative quantities on this dimension
- Circular Arrangement
- Irregular Arrangement
- Regular Arrangomont
- Perspective Drawing
- Map

Organization of each Component (within the figure)
- Associative ≡
- Selective ≠
- Ordered O
- Quantitative Q
- Percentage Q%
- Logarithmic log Q

Figure 2. Retinal Variable Examples, after Bertin

(figure contents — columns: Point, Line, Area; rows: Shape, Orientation, Colour, Texture, Value, Size)

Figure 3. Retinal Variables, after Bertin

Retinal Variable	Point, Line or Area	≡	≠	O	Q
Shape	p,l,a	√			
Orientation	p	√	√		
	l	√	√		
	a	√			
Colour	p,l,a	√	√		
Texture	p,l,a	√	√	√	
Value	p,l,a		√	√	
Size	p,l,a		√	√	√
Planar Dimensions	–		√	√	√	√

≡ Associative, ≠ Selective, O Ordered, Q Quantitative

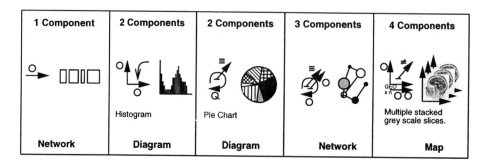

1 Component	2 Components	2 Components	3 Components	4 Components
		Pie Chart		Multiple stacked grey scale slices.
	Histogram			
Network	Diagram	Diagram	Network	Map

Figure 4. Output Classification Model with Component Organization, after Bertin

Object Classes	Operation Classes
scalar	identify
scalar field	locate
nominal	distinguish
direction	categorize
direction field	cluster
shape	distribution
position	rank
spatially extended object	compare
structure	within and between relations
	associate
	correlate

Table 2. Object and Operation Classes, after Wehrend and Lewis

size. Each variable can be classified using points, lines and areas. Figure 2 shows examples of the six retinal variables. Moreover, colour may be described by Hue, Saturation and Brightness, and attributes such as transparency, and animation may be added [9]. The level of organization can be compared with the retinal variables in classifications of point, line or area; this is shown, with the planar dimensions, in Table 3.

Wehrend and Lewis [16] generate a matrix of display techniques of 'Object Classes' against 'Operation Classes'. Object Classes are defined by the nature of the target domain, such as a scalar value and the shape of an object. The Operation Classes define the user's goal, whether to read off an actual value (Identify) or to compare two such values (Compare), for example. Table 2 lists the Object and Operation Classes. This 'catalog' of techniques does not hold information about the difference, similarity or merits of each technique, but can be used as a reference into techniques that are available.

4.1. Underlying Field Models

Brodlie [4] describes a classification model that "models the underlying field rather than the dimensionality and order of the sampled data", creating a conceptual model, Figure 6. He then describes a classification scheme that allows the underlying field and display to be classified with an algebraic expression. He splits the data into two cases of *ordinal (O)* and *nominal (N)* which describe order and no associated order, respectively. Scalar, Vector and Tensor details are referenced as S, V and T, that represent the type of the data, and are applied to the basic type (N or O) as superscripts. Independent variables are noted inside parenthesis and a range, or an aggregate, is labelled inside square brackets. The dimensions of each variable is noted as subscripts; positions in two dimensional space can be represented by O_2; sim-

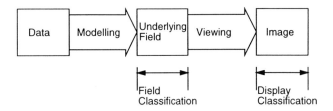

Figure 6. Underlying Field Visualization Process Model

Output Method	Field Classification	Display Classification
Histogram	$O^S(O_1)$	$O^S([O_1])$
Bar Chart	$O^S(N_1)$	$O^S(N_1)$
2D Contouring	$O^S(O_2)$	$O^S(O_1)$
Surface Rendering (from 3D data)	$O^S(O_3)$	$O^S(O_2)$
Volume Rendering	$O^S(O_3)$	$O^S(O_3)$
3D wind, arrow plot	$O^{V_3}(O_3)$	$O^{V_3}(O_3)$
Ordinal(O), Nominal(N), Scalar(S), Vector(V), Tensor(T) Dimensions 1, 2, 3 etc.,		

Table 3. Visualization Classification Examples, after Brodlie

ilarly the number of components of a Vector (V), such as two, is represented by V_2 and the components of a Tensor (each separated by colons), such as a three by three dimensional tensor, are represented by $T_{3:3}$. Some examples are described in Table 3.

Brodlie explains that this system allows the underlying data field and the display technique to be classified, but it does not classify multiple techniques. For example, "temperature over an aircraft wing, is a two dimensional subspace within three dimensional space".

4.2. Display Models for Automated Visualization Design

Some visualization systems automatically create the visualizations from a database of knowledge (metadata information) and user requirements. These tools classify the display variables to generate an appropriate visualization automatically.

The Vista tool [14], for example, creates appropriate visualizations by asking the user to preference each variable. Perception rules are applied to the variables such as "position is more effectively perceived than colour" and quantitative information is easier to perceive "by using geometry rather than colour". Vista divides the primitive visualiza-

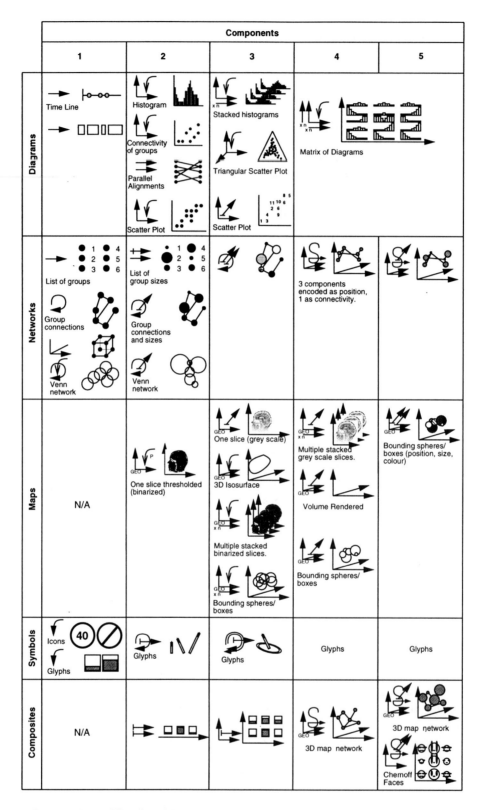

Figure 5. Output Classification Model, after Bertin, diagram representations by Roberts

tion techniques into Positional, Temporal and Retinal variables. Positional is divided further into one, two and three dimensions. Animation is used to depict the Temporal variables and the Retinal variables are divided (like Bertin) into colour, shape, size, orientation and texture.

Mackinlay [12] designed APT (A Presentation Tool), based on terminology from Bertin [2] and the effectiveness of visual perception from the work of Cleveland and McGill. Mackinlay composes complex presentations from simpler presentations, where each less complex presentation displays a subset of the overall information. The tool can create effective displays of bar charts, scatter plots and connected graphs.

Beshers and Feiner [3] discuss many other Automated Visualization Design tools.

5. Algebraic Extension to Bertin's Model

Bertin's model uses a graphical notation to describe the different display techniques. He encodes the type of the display, utilization of the image space and the organisation of the component. This classification scheme could be represented in algebraic notation. We propose one method to encode the type of the display and the utilisation of the image space. The organisation of the component depends on the data and the type of retinal variable used to display the component, so it is not encoded in this scheme.

5.1. Classifiers

We break, as before, the images into: Diagrams (D), Networks (N), Maps (M) and Symbols (S). Therefore D, N, M and S represent the classifiers. However within an image display some of the components are represented by the retinal variables (such as size, shape and colour). The classifiers are extended to include these Retinal Variables (R). The scheme encodes no distinction between the types of the retinal variables, but does encode the total amount of retinal variables used in a particular view. (See Classifier Quantity, section 5.2).

Multiple images, or multiple views [13], such as a matrix of histograms, are represented by Bertin with '$\times n$' symbols. Our scheme represents these by the letter X.

Symbols (including icons and glyphs) and Retinal variables can be explained as describing the same component. For example, a glyph, such as a temperature gauge, is represented by the retinal variable size. In some instances the reverse is also possible where, for example, every point in a diagram is represented by a circle symbol. Our scheme therefore overloads the retinal operator (R) to represent both retinal variables (R) and the symbol (S) classifiers. Moreover, the classifiers now only include D, N, M, X and R; i.e. S is excluded.

5.2. Classifier Quantity

Bertin represents each component as a single closed arrow, the total number of components therefore being calculated from the number of arrows in the graphical representation. We represent the number of components (for a particular classifier) as a power. A scatter plot diagram (of x component against a y component) could then be represented by D^2.

The total number of components for a particular display can be calculated by adding the powers together.

Moreover, if the Symbol (S) classifier was included (with the Retinal Variable R), the quantity classifier would need to represent zero components. The example of a temperature gauge (with the retinal variable size) could be represented by (the composite form of) $S^0 R^1$.

5.3. Utilization of the Image Space

Bertin describes the utilization of the image space in categories of: regular, irregular, circular and perspective arrangement; our scheme divides them similarly, and names them: r, i, c and p respectively.

The symbols, for example, do not easily fall under this classification as not having any particular arrangement; however, we represent the symbols under the irregular classification.

5.3.1. Expression Form

The algebraic expressions are formed from Classifiers and a 'Method of utilizing the image space' and a power represents the number of components for this classifier. For example, a circular network of objects depicting their connectivity with one retinal variable (representing the number of elements in the object) is represented by $N c^1 R^1$, the total amount of components being two.

Composite forms are generated by joining the single expressions together. Brackets are used to disambiguate the scope of the the multiple classifier X. For example a group of stacked grey scale slices (maps) can be represented by $X^1(M r^2 R^1)$.

6. Examples and Summary

Table 4 lists some display methods with their appropriate Algebraic notation; the algebraic display methods are taken from the schematics in Figure 5.

The algebraic form allows complicated displays to be described as composite groups of statements, but the scheme disregards information about the organization of each component (whether selective, ordered or associative). The origin of the data and the exact description of the display is not

Display Methods		
Type	Description	Algebraic Classification
D	Time Line Histogram Stacked Histogram Matrix of Histograms	Dr^1 Dr^2 X^1Dr^2 X^2Dr^2
N	List of Groups Circular Group Connections Venn Network List of Group and Sizes Network of Groups and Sizes Network of Groups, Sizes and Texture	Nr^1 Nc^1 Nr^1 Nr^1R^1 Nc^1R^1 Nc^1R^2
M	Binary Threshold Slice Grey level Slice Stacked, Grey level Slices Volume Rendering	Mr^2 Mr^2R^1 $X^1(Mr^2R^1)$ Mp^3R^1
S	Road Sign Temperature Gauge	R^1 R^1
C	Network with Size, inside 3D Map	$Mp^3Nr^1R^1$
D Diagrams, **N** Networks, **M** Maps, **S** Symbols, **C** Composites		

Table 4. Display Methods with Algebraic Classification

represented; for example, both an X-Ray image and a two dimensional slice (through *real-life* data) are represented as Mr^2R^1, both having a total of three components. However, the algebraic form provides a method to classify abstractions and visualizations.

6.1. Acknowledgements

I acknowledge Dr. Tim Hopkins and Dr. Steve Hill for their help.

References

[1] J. Bertin. *Graphics and graphic information-processing.* Walter de Gruyter, 1981. William J. Berg and Paul Scott (Translators).

[2] J. Bertin. *Semiology of Graphics, translation from Sémilogie graphique (1967).* The University of Winsonsin Press, 1983. William J. Berg (Translator).

[3] C. G. Beshers and S. K. Feiner. Automated design of data visualizations. In L. Rosenblum, R. A. Earnshaw, J. Encarnacao, H. Hagen, A. Kaufman, S. Klimenko, G. Nielson,

F. Post, and D. Thalmann, editors, *Scientific Visualization Advances and Challenges*, pages 87–102. IEEE Computer Society Press and Academic Press, 1994.

[4] K. Brodlie. A classification scheme for scientific visualization. In R. E. Earnshaw and D. Watson, editors, *Animation and Scientific Visualization – Tools and Applications*, pages 125–140. Academic Press, 1993.

[5] B. M. Collins. Data visualization — has it all been seen before? In R. E. Earnshaw and D. Watson, editors, *Animation and Scientific Visualization – Tools and Applications*, pages 3–28. Academic Press, 1992. 0-12-227745-7.

[6] R. A. Earnshaw and N. Wiseman. *An Introductory Guide to Scientific Visualization.* Springer-Verlag, 1992.

[7] R. B. Haber and D. A. McNabb. Visualization idioms: A conceptual model for scientific visualization systems. In B. Shriver, G. M. Nielson, and L. J. Rosenblum, editors, *Visualization in Scientific Computing*, pages 74–93. IEEE Computer Society Press, 1990.

[8] M.-A. Halse, D. Young, and L. McCormick. *IRIS Explorer User's Guide.* Silicon Graphics Computer Systems – Silicon Graphics Inc., 1992. (Document Number 007-1371-020).

[9] Karen R. Atkinson and Jonathan C. Roberts. Graphics and Visualization within Cross-Stitch. In *Eurographics UK 1999 Conference Proceedings*, 17th Annual Conference, pages 129–141, Eurographics UK, PO Box 38, Abington, Oxon, OX14 1PX, April 1999. (http://www.cs.ukc.ac.uk/people/staff/jcr/eguk99/index.html).

[10] J. Lohse, H. Rueter, K. Biolsi, and N. Walker. Classifying visual knowledge representations: A foundation for visualization research. In *Proceedings Visualization '90*, pages 131–138. IEEE Computer Society Press, 1990.

[11] B. Lucas, G. D. Abram, N. S. Collins, D. A. Epstein, D. L. Gresh, and K. P. McAuliffe. An architecture for a scientific visualization system. In *Proceedings Visualization '92*, pages 107–114. IEEE Computer Society Press, 1992.

[12] J. Mackinlay. Automating the design of graphical presentations of relational information. *ACM transactions on Graphics*, 5(2):110–141, 1986.

[13] J. C. Roberts. On Encouraging Multiple Views for Visualization. In E. Banissi, F. Khosrowshahi, and M. Sarfraz, editors, *IV'98 – Proceedings International Conference on Information Visualization*, pages 8–14. IEEE Computer Society, July 1998.

[14] H. Senay and E. Ignatius. A knowledge-based system for visualization design. *IEEE Computer Graphics and Applications*, 14(6):36–47, November 1994.

[15] C. Upson, T. Faulhaber, D. Kamins, D. Schlegel, D. Laidlaw, F. Vroom, R. Gurwitz, and A. van Dam. The application visualization system: A computational environment for scientific visualization. *IEEE Computer Graphics and Applications*, 9(4):30–42, 1989.

[16] S. Wehrend and C. Lewis. A problem-oriented classification of visualization techniques. In *Proceedings Visualization '90*, pages 139–143. IEEE Computer Society Press, 1990.

Session 2-2

Virtual Reality in
Construction

Chair

John Counsell

University of West England, UK

A Comparative Study of Environmental Cognition in a Real Environment and its VRML Simulation (Virtual Reality Modelling Language)

Ayman H. Mahmoud, Andrew Clayden, and Catherine Higgins
Department of Landscape, University of Sheffield

Abstract

This paper investigates the acquisition of environmental cognitive knowledge in a real world and its desktop VRML simulation. It focuses on the effect of design background and gender on spatial cognition in both displays. A post-test-only control-group design is used examine to what extent a desktop VRML simulation providse users with cognitive data that is comparable to real-world experience. Results indicate that there is a between-group agreement and disagreement depending on the typology of space. Participants using desktop VRML could provide cognitive distance estimations that are equivalent to their counterparts in real world. Design background did have a significant effect on spatial cognition in real world, however it did not show a remarkable effect in desktop VRML . Gender has effected heights' estimation in real world, however it did not show any effect in desktop VRML.

Introduction

The study that is reported in this paper considers evidence for the degree to which VRML (Virtual Reality Modelling Language) simulations provoke similar environmental cognitive responses to those experienced in the real environment. It describes an investigation of the validity of VRML simulations through analysis of independent preference reactions for a real landscape and its equivalent VRML representation.

Investigating Environmental Cognition

Environmental cognition can be defined as cognitive activity which enables the 'acquisition and representation of predominantly spatial information in real-world settings' [9,10,11,22]. Many environmental cognition studies have been conducted in outdoors-physical settings [9,19,26], however, these field-based studies have encountered empirical and analytical problems including the difficulty in maintaining enough control.

Kaplan & Kaplan [17,18] provided a cognitive model to study cognitive-based landscape preferences that rests on two main motivational properties including a need to understand one's surroundings and a need to engage with that environment. Understanding is determined by 'coherence' and 'legibility'. Coherence refers to the extent to which the environment is understood to be structured and harmonious. Legibility refers to the extent to which users can locate and orientate them within an environment. Engagement is defined by the Kaplans as the extent to which people are interested in a setting. Engagement is determined by 'complexity' and 'mystery' as predictors. Complexity is defined as the amount of diversity within a setting. Mystery refers to the extent to which an environment is experienced as offering opportunities for further exploration. Coherence and legibility accommodate understanding, whereas complexity and mystery engage users by introducing uncertainty and challenge to make a place interesting.

The study reported in this paper uses Kaplan & Kaplan's cognitive model to carry out a comparative study of cognitive experience of a digital and actual environment. Kaplan & Kaplan [17] suggest that environmental behaviour can be studied in both real and simulated settings.

In addition to using the Kaplan's cognitive model, this study also adapted Golledge & Stimson's [12] method for establishing cognitive ability to gauge distance. Cognitive distance describes " the relative spatial separation of objects in a cognitive map". [12:75]. There are indications that differences in people's ability to accurately judge distance are based on a number of factors. These factors include gender [20], the nature of the endpoints between which cognitive distances are estimated [24], and the nature and frequency of intervening barriers [21].

Environmental cognition in real and simulated landscapes

The validity of media used to simulate landscapes has been subject to a considerable number of investigations [1, 25]. Craik's [7] research indicated that there was a need to study the effects of different simulation media upon viewer's understanding of the environment which was being represented in the simulation. More recently Evans & Garling [10] argued that real-world settings differ from the stimuli used in most psychological investigations because real-world settings exhibit many extraneous factors on behavioural responses including variables such as weather conditions, and human activities taking place. Earlier Ittelson [15] indicated that real-world stimuli occur in a spatial and temporal context; that surrounds and engages people who interact with places in a dynamic way. These studies suggest the need for simulated environments that are capable of replicating some of the interactive, temporal and dynamic qualities of real-world settings. Recent studies have begun to provide evidence that virtual digital environments (VE) have the potential to replicate some of these "real world" qualities.

Virtual environments as simulated settings

Henry [14] sought to compare the performance of participants who navigated a real building and that of participants who navigated a low visual fidelity virtual model of the same building displayed using either a desktop VE or immersive VE. He found no significant differences between the three groups in terms of participants' directional accuracy when pointing to unseen locations.

Other studies suggested that spatial knowledge is developed more quickly in the real world than in VE and furthermore that spatial knowledge developed in a VE is less accurate than that developed in the real world. [23, 30, 31]

Cognitive distance in virtual environments has received some attention in recent literature. Turner & Turner [27] studied distance estimation in minimal virtual environments. They concluded that such virtual environments favour a "restricted Euclidean environment". Other researchers have studied the practical applications of VE technology for environmental planning and design. Hall [13] investigated the role of computer visualisation in planning control.

Vazquez, and Martin's, [28] comparative study of computer models and architectural scale models found that computer models were more flexible, less expensive, and easier to update than conventional models, demonstrating the potential advantages of VRML to professional practice.

VRML as a simulation technique

VRML is defined as "...a file format for describing 3D interactive worlds and objects..." [29]. It is important at this point to establish why VRML was selected as a simulation technique for this study.

The particular interest of this investigation is in the potential of VRML to facilitate wider design communication between professionals and users. VRML enables design practitioners to exploit existing software tools and to disseminate models via the Internet. This has implications for increasing participation in design processes. The study is concerned with investigating the validity of VRML in this context and in particular its ability to replicate "real world" environmental cognitive experience.

A recent review of the research literature on simulation of urban settings using virtual environments indicates that VRML has received increasing attention since 1995. Bourdakis [3] concluded that the limitation of VRML for large-scale models include design related and implementation related problems. Kaiser [16] investigated

limitations of desktop virtual environments. These limitations included a perceptual conflict as viewers of VRML environments are simultaneously aware of a two dimensional screen whilst experiencing a three dimensional environment. However, Bourdakis [3] studied aspects of representation rather than the behavioural responses of users. One aim of this study is to establish the validity of VRML simulations in representing real environments through the measurement of participants' cognitive responses.

Research Design

We chose to measure the Kaplans'[17] predictors of cognitive-based preference including legibility, coherence, mystery and complexity and Golledge & Stimson's [12] cognitive distance ability and compare participants responses for VRML and real landscapes. This part of our research was designed to explore the influence of the following variables: environmental display (i.e., real and VRML model), gender, and design background.

A post-test-only experimental design was employed [4, 6, 5], using two equivalent groups (control and experimental groups). The control group received a real-site experience, while the experimental group received a VRML experience. Post-test measurements of preference variables were observed.

The environmental setting was selected because of its potential to provide a cognitive experience, which would enable participants to respond to questions regarding cognitive-based preference and distance estimation.

Method

Participants

The sample consisted of 37 undergraduate and postgraduate students, 14 females and 23 males of which 14 have design background and 23 have non-design background. All participants were students at Sheffield University. The students participated in the investigation as volunteers. The sample was chosen using stratified probability sampling, from different sub-populations including different ethnic groups, different backgrounds, and different interest groups. The sample was assigned into two groups by stratified probability sampling including a control group (P.E., N=19 receiving no experimental treatment), and an experimental group (V.E., N=18 receiving experimental treatment).

Stimuli

The environmental display used in this investigation included two connected urban spaces within the Sheffield University Campus. The rationale of selecting the university campus is based on Danford & Willems [8] criteria. These criteria include its homogeneity of design; its relative isolation from external environments; accessibility and proximity for participants. The two connected spaces may be spatially classified into two different types of urban spaces including semi-enclosed urban space, and semi-open urban space.

The stimuli set for the control group (P.E.) was the actual environment of two connected urban spaces. The stimuli set for the experimental group (V.E.) was a VRML simulation model of the same urban spaces. The desktop V.E. system included hardware, software, and geometry database.

The VRML browser enabled participants to navigate through the model using a standard mouse in 6 degrees of freedom including 3-D movement, and 3-D rotational options. Participants could select movement and rotational options by clicking a number of buttons displayed at the bottom of the display monitor. They could move forward and backward, to left and to right, and up and down. Movement options included rotation about X, Y & Z-axes.

Procedure

The experiment was conducted during May 1998. P.E. participants received on-site guided group sessions (N= 5). Each percipient was provided with a data collection form, writing pad, a pencil/pen and an eraser. The data collection form included a brief introduction about the objectives of the test and summary of the procedure. Participants were asked to provide some of their personal data including gender, age group, their background, familiarity with the environmental display, and familiarity with using personal computers.

Participants received a guided on-site tour in which they were asked to spend 10 minutes in each of the two spaces to move around. In each of the two spaces, participants were asked to rate each of the four Kaplan & Kaplan's cognitive variables using 5 point rating scale ranging from 1 (not at all) to 5 (very much). The 'Coherence' was described as 'do the elements of the space fit together well and logically in harmony?'. 'Legibility' was characterised as 'how easy it is to find

one at a time in a lab-like environment, participants were provided with an office chair, a data collection form, a pencil/pen, an eraser, and a writing pad. They received 5-minute instructions on how to use the input device in navigating. Functions of the navigation buttons were demonstrated. They found difficulty at the very beginning but within few minutes, most of them mastered the navigation tools. They were asked to navigate in each of the two spaces for 10 minutes and rate each of the four Kaplan & Kaplan's cognitive variables using the same 5-point scale used in the P.E. case. The experience of the participants can be described as navigating through a real setting whilst looking through the viewfinder of a camera (170-cm above the ground level). Participants reported difficulties in navigation as they frequently "went through" walls because of a lack of "collision detection" in the VRML model. This problem could have been avoided using other VRML browsers but with the disadvantage of slower rendering rates, and longer response time.

Results

Cognitive data collected from both groups including Kaplan & Kaplan's cognitive variables rating scales and distance estimation was analysed descriptively by calculating the tendencies and dispersions of each variable. Between group agreements and disagreements are analysed using Independent Samples t-Test statistics.

Within Group responses

Results of Kaplan & Kaplan's cognitive variables are described in Table (1). Results show that participants in VRML saw the enclosed setting as more coherent ($M = 3.22$, $SD = 1.00$) than those who were in the control group ($M = 2.74$, $SD = 0.99$), however participants in control group saw the semi-open setting as more coherent ($M = 3.42$, $SD = 0.90$) than those who experienced it in VRML ($M = 2.94, SD = 0.87$).

	Space 1: Enclosed setting		Space 2: Semi-open setting	
	Control	*Experimental*	*Control*	*Experimental*
Coherence	2.7368 (0.9912)	3.2222 (1.0033)	3.4211 (0.9016)	2.9444 (0.8726)
Legibility	4.2105 (1.0317)	4.0000 (1.0290)	3.9474 (0.8481)	3.4444 (0.9218)
Complexity	2.7895 (0.9763)	2.3889 (0.6978)	3.4211 (1.3464)	3.2222 (0.9428)
Mystery	2.8421 (0.9582)	2.9444 (1.0556)	3.2632 (0.9912)	3.7222 (0.8948)

Table (1) Means and standard deviations (in parentheses) as a function of both sample group and space type.

your way around in this space?' 'Complexity' was illustrated as 'to what extent can the space be described as a complex space or containing a lot of elements (e.g., trees, fences, signs, etc.) of different kinds?'. 'Mystery' was presented as 'does the space promise more to be seen as you walk deeper into it?'. Participants were asked at the end of the in-site test to estimate both the distance of one element from a fixed standpoint, and the height of a particular element from the same standpoint.

V.E. participants were asked individually to perform the same task in a computer laboratory equipped with the Desktop V.E. system. Participants did the test

Results indicate that participants in VRML saw the horizontal distance longer ($M = 148.61$, $SD = 109.03$) than those who estimated it in the control setting ($M = 135.578$, $SD = 8.73$). However, VRML participants saw heights as lower ($M = 19.50$, $SD = 11.73$) than those who estimated it in the control setting ($M = 22.47$, $SD = 16.87$)

Between-Group Responses

The differential between-groups data were analysed on comparative basis using the Independent-Samples T- by examining the variance and mean difference of ratings for each preference variable between the two groups. Because it is desirable to reject the statistical null hypothesis of no significant differences between the response groups, it was considered more appropriate to report significance levels of $\rho \leq 0.150$ to minimise the risk of Type II error (i.e., rejecting a scientific hypothesis when it is true) [2: 159, 5: 393]

Kaplan & Kaplan's cognitive variables:

The result of t-test of independence showed that for the semi-enclosed space there was a significant difference between the ratings of both groups for the 'coherence' variable ($P < 0.150$). However, results reveal no significant difference between the two groups in other cognitive variables including 'legibility', 'complexity', and 'mystery' ($P > 0.150$).

On the other hand, in the semi-open space, results of the same statistical test indicate that there was a significant difference ($P < 0.150$) between ratings of the participants of both groups in 'coherence', 'legibility', and 'mystery'. Ratings for the 'complexity' variable showed no significant difference ($P > 0.150$).
Table (2) depicts F-test and t-test results.

group, results reveal no significant difference between estimations of both designers and non-designers ($P > 0.15$).

Effect of gender on cognitive distance
Table (2) illustrates that different genders in the experimental group did not show significant difference in exploration and understanding of the semi-enclosed ($P > 0.15$). However, in the control group there was a significant difference between genders in coherence variable ($P < 0.05$) and no significant differences in the other Kaplan & Kaplan's variables ($P > 0.15$). On the other hand, in the semi open space, both genders in the control group show significant difference in mystery ($P < 0.10$) and no significant difference in the case of any other variable. Males and females in the experimental group show significant difference in coherence ($P > 0.10$).

Independent samples t-test indicates that in distance estimation, there is no significant difference between males and females in the control group ($P > 0.15$) while a significant difference does exist between males and females in the experimental group ($P < 0.15$).

	Space 1: Enclosed setting		Space 2: Semi-open setting	
	Control	Experimental	Control	Experimental
Coherence	2.197 (0.042)***	1.344 (0.198)	0.489 (0.631)	-2.039 (0.058)**
Legibility	1.151 (0.266)	-0.918 (0.372)	-0.201 (0.843)	-0.222 (0.827)
Complexity	-1.221 (0.239)	-1.311 (0.208)	0.326 (0.748)	-0.603 (0.555)
Mystery	0.434 (0.670)	-0.638 (0.533)	1.989 (0.063)**	0.939 (0.362)

Table (2) Results of independent sample T-test (equality of means) and their significance (in parentheses) between males and females sub-groups
* $\rho \leq 0.150$ ** $\rho \leq 0.100$ *** $\rho \leq 0.050$

Distance and Height Estimations

Results of t-test of independence indicate no significant difference between the VRML group and the control group in distance estimation ($P > 0.150$) and height estimation ($P > 0.150$)

Effect of Design background on cognitive distance
Looking at the responses of both designers and non-designers sub-groups in the experimental group, we find that results suggest no significant difference between both sub-groups in Kaplan & Kaplan's variables ($P > 0.150$). This result tends to be consistent for both semi-enclosed and semi-open spaces. On the other hand, participants in the control group show some disagreements. Ratings for 'coherence' are significantly different between designers and non-designers ($P < 0.150$) in the semi-enclosed space, similarly, ratings for 'legibility' are significantly different ($P < 0.050$) in the case of semi-open space.

Results indicate that there is no significant difference in distance estimations between designers and non-designers sub-groups whether in control or experimental main groups ($P > 0.15$). Variances in distance estimations between both sub-groups were not significantly different ($P > 0.15$). For height estimations, results indicate a considerably high significant difference ($P < 0.001$) in measurements between designers and non-designers in the control group. For the experimental

Measurements of height estimation show very high significant difference in variances between males and females in both control and experimental groups ($P < 0.01$ & $P < 0.05$ respectively). There was a significant difference between height estimations of both males and females in the control group ($P < 0.15$), however this difference does not exist in the experimental group ($P > 0.15$).

Discussion

We have sought to investigate the extent to which desktop VRML could develop cognitive knowledge of the environmental display encountered compared with the real setting. For the semi-enclosed space, immediate understanding (coherence) of the stimuli seems to be significantly different between real VRML displays however inferred understanding (legibility) of the same space in real environment is not significantly different from the VRML. On the other hand, there was no significant difference between both environments whether in immediate (complexity) or inferred (mystery) explorations.

For the semi-open space, results imply that both immediate and inferred understanding of the display in real environment is different from VRML. Inferred exploration in both environments is different. Participants in VRML could develop immediate exploration cognitive learning that is no different from the participants in real environment.

In development of cognitive distance, it seems that the relative spatial separation of objects in a cognitive map of a real environment is not significantly different from a VRML model. Participants in VRML could provide cognitive distance estimations that are equivalent to their counterparts in real environments.

Environmental cognition of Designers v Non-designers

The second question was how different is the spatial cognition between designers and non-designers participating in both real and VRML experiences. This study reveals that in VRML, both designers and non-designers did not manifest major differences in their understanding and exploration, immediate or inferred, of both semi-enclosed and semi-open spaces. On the other hand, designers and non-designers in real environment show disagreement in their immediate understanding of the semi-enclosed space, and their inferred understanding of the semi-open space.

Our results imply that in real environment, non-designers' spatial understanding of horizontal separation between the two elements were not different from designers'. In VRML, results show that cognitive understanding of distances is not different between designers and non-designers. In cognitive understanding of heights, we can conclude that in the studied environmental display, there is a remarkable difference in understanding of both designers and non-designers. That difference does not exist in VRML where both designers and non-designers did not show a significant difference in their height estimations.

VRML in both the semi-enclosed and semi-open spaces. This study shows that for inferred exploration (i.e., mystery) in the semi-open space both genders show disagreement in the real environment and no noticeable disagreement in VRML. However, in the semi-enclosed space they did not show any remarkable disagreement whether in real environments or VRML.

For interpreting spatial relationships between elements in real environment and VRML, this investigation indicate that in the real environment, both genders did not agree on interpreting the vertical height of the element. In VRML, both genders could interpret the simulated height without disagreement; however, they did not interpret the distance without disagreement.

Spatial cognition in desktop VRML

Kaplan & Kaplan's model: Coherence, complexity, legibility and mystery:
Analysis of results, hence, indicates that VRML recorded a degree of success in providing immediate information for exploration independent on space type, however, it did not succeed in providing immediate information for understanding. Results demonstrate that VRML was successful enough to provide inferred information for both understanding (legibility) and exploration (mystery), however this success was not consistent regarding space type. Table (3)

Cognitive Distance
The second question we sought to answer is to see how experience in VRML could provide participants with enough information to decide the relative separation of

| | Space 1: Enclosed Space | | Space 2: Semi-Open Space | |
	Understanding	Exploration	Understanding	Exploration
Immediate	Coherence *	Complexity **	Coherence *	Complexity **
Inferred, predicted	Legibility **	Mystery **	Legibility *	Mystery *

Table (3) Projecting VRML simulation information on Kaplan & Kaplan (1989) preference matrix for both spaces (1 & 2)
Variables labelled with (**) illustrate consistent successful information provided by the VRML simulation.
Variables labelled with (*) illustrate non-successful information provided by the VRML simulation.

Environmental cognition of Males v Females

The third inquiry concerns the differences between spatial cognition of both males and females in the two environments. Our results show that in the semi-enclosed space, males and females had different immediate understanding of the space in the real environment, however both sub-groups did not show difference in VRML model. On the other hand, in the semi-open space, the opposite happened. Males and females did not show agreement in immediate understanding in the virtual environment, while their counterparts in real environment did. We have yet to do further analysis to establish the precise nature and significance of gender differences.

For inferred understanding (legibility) and immediate exploration (complexity) both genders did not show any disagreement whether in real environment or

objects in a cognitive map compared with real environment experience.

Conclusion

The implications of this study may highlight the potential of VRML as an environmental simulation technique for a number of reasons. The VRML model consistently provided immediate information for exploration of the two spaces in this study. This information was not significantly different from information obtained from experiencing the real environment. The VRML model provided information for both understanding and exploration for one of the two spaces. We may imply that the VRML simulation used in this investigation could be a valid environmental simulation technique with some limitations.

VRML could have considerable advantages. The potential of VRML as a simulation medium used in this study has the following characteristics:

1. As a simulation medium, it could control possible factors affecting the spatial cognition of a place.
2. It created a 3-D interactive virtual environment that – to some extent- replicates a sense of navigation through a real environment.
3. Participants have options that may not be available in reality (e.g., flying over) that provide new experience that may enhance their behavioural responses.
4. Being Internet-oriented, VRML files can be uploaded to and downloaded from the World Wide Web enhancing the possibility of social surveys.

VRML reported in this study shares other simulation media in the limitation of environmental encounter to visual experience only. The VRML technique used here has some particular limitations. This study is limited to two spatial categories only (i.e., enclosed and semi-open urban spaces) and a particular typology of spaces (spaces within a university campus). It lacks larger sample of landscapes from a variety of types. The population was limited to postgraduate and undergraduate university students. The accessible population for our study was restricted only to those who are familiar with personal computers. Finally results are affected by the limitations hardware and software configurations used in this study.

REFERENCES

1. Appleyard, D. (1977). Understanding Professional Media. In I. A. J. F. Wohlwill (Ed.), *Human Behavior and Environment: Advences in Theory and Research* (Vol. 2, pp. 43-88). New York: Plenum Press.
2. Blalock, H. M. (1972). *Social statistics (Revised edition).* Tokyo: McGraw Hill.
3. Bourdakis, V. (1997). The future of VRML on large urban models. *Proceedings of the 4th. UK Virtual Reality Special Interest Group Conference,* Uxbridge.
4. Campbell, D. T., & Stanley, J. C. (1963). *Experimental and quasi-experimental designs for research.* Chicago, IL: Rand McNally College Pub.
5. Christensen, L. B. (1994). *Experimental methodology (6th. ed.).* Boston, MA: Allyn & Bacon.
6. Cook, T. D., & Campbell, D. T. (1979). *Quasi-experimentation: Design &analysis issues for field settings.* Chicago, IL: Rand McNally College Pub.
7. Craik, K. H. (1968). The comprehension of the everyday physical environment. *American Institute of Planners, 34*(1), 27-37.
8. Danford, S., & Willems, E. P. (1975). Subjective responses to architectural displays: A question of validity. *Environment and Behavior, 7*(4), 486-516.
9. Evans, G. W. (1980). Environmental cognition. *Psychological Bulletin, 88*(2), 259-287.
10. Evans, G. W., & Garling, T. (1991). Environment, cognition, and action: The need for integration. In T. Garling & G. W. Evans (Eds.), *Environment, cognition, and action: An integrated approach* (pp. 3-13). New York: Plenum Press.
11. Golledge, R. G. (1987). Environmental cognition. In D. Stokols & I. Altman (Eds.), *Handbook of environmental psychology* (pp. 131-174). New York: Wiley.
12. Golledge, R. G., & Stimson, R. J. (1987). *Analytical behavioural geography.* London: Croom Helm.
13. Hall, A. (1996). Assessing the Role of Computer Visualization in Planning Control: A Recent Case Study. *Paper presented at the third Design and Decision Support Systems: Architecture and Urban Planning Conference,* Spa: Belgium.
14. Henry, D. (1992). Spatial perception in virtual environments: Evaluating an architectural application., *Unpublished master's thesis,* HITL, University of Washington, Washington, Seattle.
15. Ittleson, W. (1973). Environmental perception and contemporary perceptual theory. In W. Ittelson (Ed.), *Enviroment and cognition* (pp. 1-20). New York: Seminar.
16. Kaiser, M. K. (1996). High-power graphic computers for visual simulation: A real-time rendering revolution. *Behavior Research Methods: Instruments and Computers, 28*(2), 233-238.
17. Kaplan, R., & Kaplan, S. (1989). *The Experience of Nature: A Psychological Perspective.* New York: Cambridge University Press.
18. Kaplan, S., & Kaplan, R. (Eds.). (1982). *Humanscape: Environments for People.* Ann Arbor: Michigan: Ulrich's Books, Inc.
19. Kitchin, R. M. (1994). Cognitive maps: What are they and why study them? *Journal of Environmental Psychology, 14*(1), 1-19.
20. Lee, T. R. (1970). Perceived distance as a function of direction in the city. *Environment and Behavior, 2*(1), 40-51.
21. Lowrey, R. A. (1970). Distance concepts of urban residents. *Environment and Behavior, 2*(1), 52-73.
22. Moore, G. T. (1979). Knowing about environmental knowing: The current state of theory and research on environmental cognition. *Environment and Behavior, 11*(1), 33-70.
23. Ruddle, R. A., Payne, S. J., & Jones, D. M. (1997). Navigating buildings in desk-top virtual environments: Experimental investigations using extended navigational experience. *Journal of Experimental Psychology: Applied, 3*(2), 143-159.
24. Sadalla, E. K., & Staplin, L. J. (1980). The perception of traversed distance: Intersections. *Environment and Behavior, 12,* 167-182.
25. Shuttleworth, S. (1980). The use of photographs as an environment presentation medium in landscape studies. *Journal of Environmental Management, 11*(1), 61-76.
26. Siegel, A. W., & White, S. H. (1975). The Development of Spatial Representations of Large Scale Environments. In H. W. Reese (Ed.), *Advances in Child Development and Behavior* (Vol. 10,). New York: Academic Press.
27. Turner, P., & Turner, S. (1997). *Distance estimation in minimal environments.* Paper presented at the Proceedings of the 4th. UK Virtual Reality Special Interest Group Conference, Uxbridge.
28. Vazquez, J. A., & Martin, E. (1995). Computer models versus architectural scale models. In S. Hernandez & C. A. Brebbia (Eds.), *Visualization and Intelligent Design in Engineering and Architecture* (pp. 183-190). Southampton: Computational Mechanics Publications.
29. VRSIG. (1996). The Virtual Reality Modeling Language Specification. : http://vrml.sgi.com/moving-worlds/spec/index.html.
30. Wilson, P. N., & Foreman, N. (1993). Transfer of information from virtual to real space: Implications for people with physical disability, *Proceedings of the First Eurographics Workshop on Virtual Reality* (pp. 21-25). Aire-la-Ville, Switzerland: Eurographics Association.
31. Wilson, P. N., Foreman, N., & Tlauka, M. (1997). Transfer of spatial information from a virtual to a real environment. *Human Factors, 39*(4), 526-531.

Robotic 360° Photography for Virtual Site Visits

Qunhuan Mei and Robert Wing
Department of Civil Engineering, Imperial College, London SW7 2BU
q.mei@ic.ac.uk and r.wing@ic.ac.uk

Abstract

A robotic photographic method has been developed for use in outdoor locations such as construction sites, to provide 360° panoramic visual database material for representation of a virtual site, together with the software for authoring and delivery the material to users via the Internet. A portable digital photographic system thus built can take a 360° panorama photograph in digital form within minutes. The Java software package can present an image in an efficient and effective "video" style with full dynamic "hyperlink" support.

1. Introduction

The teaching of building construction related disciplines ideally requires the provision of visits to operational construction sites. Today, the time and expense that such visits demand, together with increasingly restrictive **HSE** regulations make it very difficult to provide actual site visits, and lecturers are resorting to use of conventional audio/visual materials, predominantly 35mm slides.

Virtual site visits using on-line delivery of the materials would provide a close simulation and affordable alternative to the real thing. In its simplest case the virtual site visit could take the form of video footage, but this would involve only passive student behaviour. An interactive system, teleoperated over the network or from a local server, would allow the student to move around the site according to his own commands; such operation is extremely desirable in its involvement of the student.

Ideally, a virtual site would consist of dozens of 360° panorama images, with "hyperlinks" built among them, so that student can go from one image/page to another through a "door"/button/hyperlink. Furthermore, as almost all images are 360° panoramas, when they are presented, continuous, endless and controllable panning and zooming functions would be expected.

The problems facing creation and presentation of the virtual site are:

- The lack of portable hardware support to be used indoor/outdoor for taking 360° panorama image files. Traditional manual 360° photography must be considered inefficient – it usually involves taking many pictures at pre-calculated angles, carefully slicing them into strips and then stitching them together using software to make complete 360° panorama pictures. Another approach uses spherical lenses to produce spherical panoramas (www.ipix.com) [1, 2]; these tend to produce large image files as they also include sky and/or ground; the system is generally good for interiors but poorer for outdoor sites. The image resolution varies considerably across the picture, and the use of film in

Fig. 1 - The hardware system

the process also limits the resolution and involves the extra task of scanning into a computer.

- Lack of effective Web authoring software support with dynamic hyperlink capability for 360° panorama images. Although there are a few commercial software packages available, such as Apple's **QTVR** (www.apple.com/quicktime) and **LivePicture** (www.livepicture.com), these either use movie formats, which produce very large source files (usually more than 400k for average viewing effect), or they require download of plug-in software, which needs extra effort and time. Futhermore, there is only minimal support for the variety of user interfaces needed to support different applications in the large panorama image domain.

To solve these two problems, a two-stage R&D plan was proposed:

(1). To construct a remote-controllable portable digital 360° panorama photographic system with pan and tilt functions using robotic principles. This involves panning and titling mechanisms, digitally indexed servo-motors, and a notebook computer, such that the 360° panorama image would be generated and transferred automatically into the computer. The image file format chosen was JPEG, as the file sizes and viewing effect are well matched to Internet applications. **Fig. 1** shows the prototype of the hardware system developed.

(2). To develop a "Panorama Web design" tool kit based on pure Java technology. The kit had to support automatic horizontal panning, together with support for dynamic hyperlink and various user interfaces. Java has a unique feature of "once written, runs anywhere". The size of a Java program is also negligible in comparison to the panorama images.

2. Portable digital panorama photographic system

Automated 360° panorama photography can be imagined as using a video camera seated on a stepping rotational device, catching a video frame after each step movement, extracting a narrow strip from each frame and then stitching these together to form a 360° panorama image.

Our 360° panorama imaging concept uses an area-scan CCD with image strip stitching, and thus differs the method which used for **line-scan** CCD cameras. The line-scan system has much higher resolution, is over-qualified for Web work, and is expensive (www.spheron.com). We

favour area-scan since the quality of the results is more suited for general Web use. Line-scan can be considered as a special case of area-scan. In our system, the video camera has been positioned with a 90 degree turn so that the better resolution appears in the vertical direction, i.e.utilising the longer axis of the frame.

A usual way to realise the controlled step rotation is by using a stepping motor with a dedicated logic controller. The problems with this are that, firstly, the stepping motor and its dedicated controller are quite costly; secondly, the mechanical connection between the motor and camera has to be custom designed, as does the tilting mechanism.

The decision was made to use an inexpensive off-the-shelf pan and tilt device as used for security camera applications. The device already had basic functions for both continuous panning and tilting, supported by two general-purpose D.C. control motors rather than stepper motors. Our first task was to realise the stepping movement control so that stepwise image- strip stitching could be realised. **Fig 2** shows a schematic diagram of the hardware system.

A PCMCIA frame grabber (24-bit colour) with resolution of 922x576 was used to catch video frames on

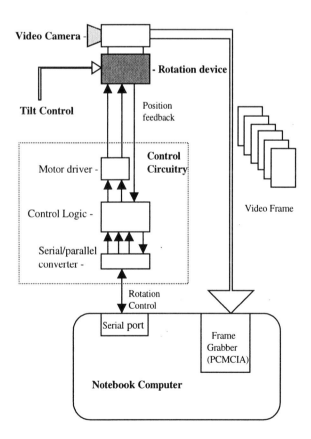

Fig. 2 – Schematic diagram of the system

215

Fig. 3 - A panorama image generated by the hardware system (5681x922 pixels – 6mm normal lens)

the fly. A narrow image strip was obtained from the frame and then stitched to make a full 360° digital image using C++ software. The number of horizontal pixels of the image is determined by the lens used. For a normal lens (6mm), about 5600 pixels will be generated in the horizontal direction. Fewer pixels in horizontal direction will be generated if a wide-angle lens is used, and vice versa. The vertical resolution is always 922 pixels.

The whole system is powered by two separate batteries, one for the video camera, and the other for the rotation device and logic control circuitry. Two batteries rather than one are used to isolate the camera from any power supply 'bounce' caused by digital switching.

The position feedback was realised using an opto-switch to monitor the position of the main drive shaft. When the horizontal drive shaft, to which is attached a small metal vane plate, completes a full turn, the opto-switch generates a pulse. This pulse stops the motor via control logic; additionally, it triggers the computer, signalling that the camera has made another step movement and another image strip can be stitched. The enhanced rotation device is capable of doing 300 steps maximum for a full 360° turn.

3. The software components of the hardware system

The hardware system is controlled by software written in **MSVC++5.0**. The current C++ system has the following main functions:

1. Control of rotation through a serial line by stepping either clockwise or anti-clockwise. Given starting and ending angles, the camera can be controlled to move in steps of 1.2° each.
2. Control of the frame grabber through the PCMCIA interface so that the image is grabbed and a strip is obtained.

3. Stitch image strips to make a complete panorama image in BMP format.

4. Turn the BMP file(s) into JPEG file(s) with chosen parameters from a dialogue menu.

The system can produce a 0~360° panorama image file directly into a notebook computer in 3~9 minutes. Using such a system, a normal 360° panorama image will be sized at about 5600 by 920 pixels, which is 15 MB in BMP or around 1MB in JPEG [**Fig 3**].

Considering the screen size of the computer display (say 1024x768) and typical network bandwidth, the image resolutions are considered more than adequate for Web applications.

4. Use of Java for 360° panorama viewing software

Once the 360° panorama images have been captured, we identified three choices to let the user view these special images:

(1) use of QTVR software to present the 360° panorama images
(2) use of other Panorama Viewing Plug-in software to view the image
(3) provision of a Java program (either applet or stand-alone application) to view the image.

The main difference between a normal and a panorama image is that the 360° panorama must have a perfect match between its start and end. This makes it possible for the 360° panorama image to be presented in a continuous panning mode.

One commercial software package suited to these images is QTVR from Apple Computer. It has an ideal video fashioned multifunction ability for image/model presentation, and can present a 360° panorama image in

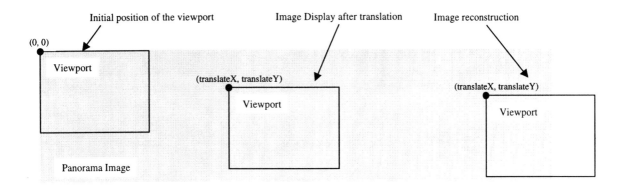

**Fig. 4 – Fast Panning using image translation when inside
and viewport image reconstruction when across the border**

an interactive video style. The problem of using QTVR for virtual construction site applications is its large image file size, as some intermediate frames have to be generated [3]. This is not ideal for this application, as the video file is slow to download, especially when the original image files are, say, more than 1M pixels.

Plug-in software packages can be very fast in their performance; they are usually platform dependent in order to be fully optimised. The disadvantage of using this approach is that it requires the first time user to download the platform-dependent plug-in software. The user interface creation has also to be confined to the capabilities available.

Java holds the claim that "written once, will run everywhere". Java programs are very small, secure and capable. It is an object-oriented and architecture-neutral language. The main advantage of using Java to present our panorama images is that the user/viewer has no need to download a plug-in, and it is also easier to program than other OO languages, such as C++. Also worth noticing is that Java's performance on panning/zooming 360° panorama images can be made as good as that done in any native language such as C++, since this involves mostly image operations, rather than intensive data processing. It can be seen that for presenting a 360° panorama image, Java is probably the best choice.

5. The principle of panning 360° panorama images

Java by default recognises two types of image: JPEG and GIF. Since GIF is only used for images of 8 bits colour, it was not suitable for our 24-bit colour Panorama project. Panning a 360° panorama image involves preparation of the data, timing, thread synchronisation, and user interface control. The major issue here is how image data

is prepared for panning. Other issues can be solved by Java programming directly.

As with any other programming language, there is no direct support in Java for automatic panning of a 360° panorama images. The default colour model for Java uses a single integer to describe each pixel, thus allowing 32 bits for a pixel's colour model. The bits are divided into four bytes: three for the familiar red (8 bits), green (8 bits) and blue (8 bits), which defines 24 bits colour; the fourth byte is used for "alpha", which defines the transparency of the pixel (0 for transparent; 255 for opaque).

An image is an array of pixels. Java has methods both for converting an image to an array of pixels and converting an array of pixels back to an image.

We have tried various ways to realise the panning of a 360° panorama image. The following three methods are found to be useful for image panning data preparation:

(1) Fast panning inside and reconstructing when across the border.
When the image is initially shown, it is displayed with its upper-left corner corresponding to the upper-left corner of the viewport. When the viewport is moved right inside the current image space [**Fig. 4**], a simple translation can realise panning. Whenever the viewport is moved across the image border, an extra image reconstruction sized for the viewport is carried out, which combines two parts from both the beginning and end of the image according the origin of the viewport. It is then displayed.

Using this method, panning is fast when the viewport is right inside the image space. The disadvantage is that an uncomfortable "wait" will occur when the panning position is outside the border of the 360° panorama image, since the reconstruction takes an amount of time proportional to the size of the viewport. In addition, the switch of image for display between normal

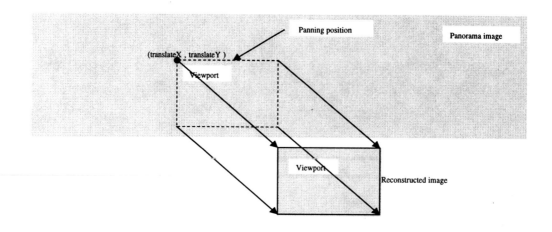

Fig. 5 - Constantly reconstructing the viewport image while panning

and the extra reconstructed one takes yet further time.

(2) Constantly reconstruction of the viewport image while panning

The logic underlying this method is to track the current viewport position inside the given image's space, constantly reconstruct an image out of the original one, then display it. **Fig. 5** shows the principle of this method.

The time spent on reconstruction of the image is proportional to the size of the viewport. The disadvantage is that there is an uncomfortable delay between each frame, so that the feeling of panning will not be "real video" as the reconstruction is data processing intensive, which takes a noticeable time and makes translation based on one pixel a time usually not possible.

However, this method has very good potential in functional panning where data intensive processing is necessary, such as perspective panning or other image processing panning where image reconstruction according to a specific algorithm is necessary.

(3) Reconstructing initially, then always fast panning.

It is worth noticing that almost all computers have an efficient way of copying a block of bits from memory onto the screen. As seen from method (1), if reconstruction of the image can be avoided when the viewport strides over two ends of the image, fast panning can be realised. The way to reach this objective is to reconstruct the original image before panning it. As shown in **Fig. 6**, the end part of the image has been extended by adding the initial section of the image that is proportional to the viewport size. When the viewport appears to stride over two ends of the original image, it can be viewed as still falling right inside the reconstructed image, so that no further reconstruction is necessary and fast panning can be realised.

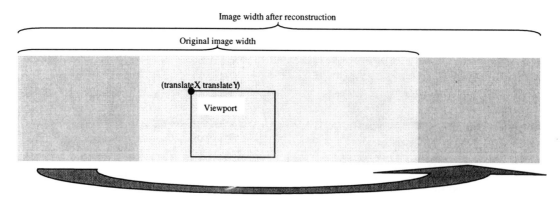

Fig. 6 – Extending image for fast panning

Using this method, the image display can be refreshed at a controllable rate of more than 30 frames per second. Even when the viewport size is as large as the screen (say 1024x768), real-time and controllable panning can still be realised. A screen sized viewport with panning 360° panorama image provides enough information to cover all the details of a scene from a construction site or any similar application.

Adding dynamic hyperlink ability, we can now build "hot spots" into the panning image, which enables the user to click on the "hot spot" during panning to go to next interesting "place".

Method (3) has been fully implemented in our JAVA software package, which is capable of doing real-time, photo-realistic, zoomable and interactive operations. An example is shown in **Fig. 7**. An initial test showed that to generate about 50 seconds of panning "video", with the original image sized at 1600x400, it needed a JPEG file sized at about 55kb when using Java panning software, whereas for a similar sized image, it needs about 400k when using Apple's QTVR. The size benefit is obvious considering today's congested network bandwidth.

6. Conclusion

It can be concluded that the method of robotic 360° photography for virtual site visits presented is pragmatic, in terms of its concept, approach and performance. The hardware system provides an easy, quick and effective way to capture surround scenes (0~360°). The JAVA software simply gives a normal image a "video" life, which shows an image with dynamic, stepless and real time appearance. It is also equipped with dynamic "hyperlink" ability, which extends that of the HTML, as HTML's image map can only be used for static images.

The whole process, from taking panorama images (0 ~ 360°) using the portable computer integrated panorama imaging system, to HTML scripting for selecting appropriate Java class file and setting up imageMaps and other parameters, etc, is streamlined, systematic, complete and straightforward. There is no third party software nor other process involved. Our future objective is to integrate the

system with a consumer digital camera and to include the perspective viewing function during image panning.

Ackowledgement: The authors gratefully acknowledge the financial assistance for this project provided by HEFCE under the JISC initiative (see http://www.jisc.ac.uk/

7. References

1. M. Yachida, "Omnidirectional Sensing and Combined Multple Sensing", Proceedings of the 1998 Workshop on Computer Vision for Virtual Reality Based Human Communications, IEEE.
2. S.K. Nayar, "Omnidirectional Vision", proceedings of the 1997 International Symposium on Robotics Research, Japan.
3. S. Chen, "QuickTime VR – An Image-Based Approach to Virtual Environment Navigation", Proceedings CD-ROM Computer Graphics SIGGRAPH 95, 6-11 August 1995, Los Angeles, California

Fig. 7 – An example of controlled panning and zooming, accessed from a hotspot (an elliptical button) inside a map image.

Finite State Automata as Form-Generation and Visualization Tools

Buthayna Eilouti
Ph.D. Candidate
College of Architecture and Urban Planning
The University of Michigan
(buthayna@umich.edu)

Emmanuel-George Vakalo
Ph.D., Chair
College of Architecture and Urban Planning
The University of Michigan
(egvakalo@umich.edu)

Abstract

Architects and other designers use diagrams to visualize the process of product analysis and synthesis. This paper outlines a new pictorial representation tool that helps designers visualize the process of composing and classifying their final products.

Finite State Automata (FSAs) are used in the context of formal languages as recognition devices. In this sense, they complement the synthetic device of linear grammars in the definition of regular languages. Using the paradigm of language for understanding the design process, FSAs can be developed to describe how basic shapes standing for elements or subsystems can be put together into meaningful subsystems or systems. They can classify different options for component grouping. Compared to flow charts, FSAs represent graphically a class of flow charts that share a set of predefined criteria. In addition, FSAs allow the representation of recursive as well as topological and spatial relations among components.

Finite State Automata

The mechanism of a finite automaton is based on reading an input symbol and then entering a new state determined by the transition function that maps a pair of current state and current input symbol into a new state. Finite automata can be deterministic or nondeterministic. The operation of the former is completely *determined* by their input. The operation on some of their input in the latter is probabilistic. In other words, on one input symbol a nondeterministic automaton can go to more than one state. Finite automata are represented graphically as state diagrams, where a circle signifies a state of string processing, and double circles signify final states, also known as states of string acceptance. Arcs are used to show the direction of string processing. The initial state where the process of string recognition begins is usually shown by a > symbol. To understand the concept, one can think of an elevator as a finite automaton. An elevator is initially in a static state (no movement). It can receive an order to move up one floor from where it is. The new floor where it stops is a new state. Depending on what order it receives (up or down, how many floors to skip), it takes the next step.

Finite State Automata in Form-Making

This paper will focus on form-making as a component of design. Please note that FSAs can be used in any design field to describe a sequence of element grouping.

It is possible to think of architectural compositions as families each sharing one or more characteristics. Each family may be defined as a formal language that shares a vocabulary of physical elements and its members are composed by applying a set of grammatical rules to the vocabulary elements.

Finite state automata can be borrowed from formal languages to be used in describing sets of geometric compositions that are geometrically and spatially alike. They provide tools for the graphic representation of architectural compositions. They describe how basic forms can be arranged. This entails what, and how many shapes are composed, as well as in which sequence they are aggregated. For example, the finite state automaton (FSA) shown in Figure 1. It describes a simple geometric composition. A composition that satisfies this FSA has to begin with one or more cubes or one cylinder, followed optionally, by any number of cylinders, followed, in turn, optionally by one cylinder or one cone. The composition can also consist of one cube, cylinder, or cone. It can also end with any number of cones.

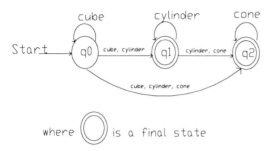

Figure 1: A Finite State Automaton for a Linear Composition

As a pictorial representation tool, FSA can be used to formulate exercises for beginning design students to train them in form-making. Some examples of such exercises are given below. However, the pedagogical is not the only application field of FSAs. They can also be used to classify families of compositions for the purposes of data organization and storage. For example, the DFSA (deterministic finite state automaton) shown in Figure 2 describes all compositions that begin with a cube followed (assuming a linear composition) by a cylinder; or a cube followed by a cylinder followed, in turn, by another cube.

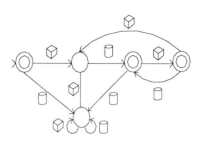

Figure 2: FSA for L= {{cube cylinder} or {cube cylinder cube}}*

One of the compositions that *satisfy* the FSA shown in Figure 2 is shown in Figure 3. This composition starts with the {cube cylinder cube} sub-composition, followed by another similar subcomposition, followed, in turn, by {cube cylinder} subcomposition. Following the sequence of masses in this composition in the FSA of Figure 2 leads from the start state to an acceptance state.

Figure 3: A Composition That Belongs to the FSA Defined in Figure 2

In contrast, the composition shown in Figure 4 will be *rejected* by the same FSA. Comparing the spatial relation of masses with the FSA in Figure 2 shows that this composition ends in a "nonacceptance" state.

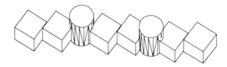

Figure 4: A Composition That Does Not Belong to the FSA Defined in Figure 2

Generating the FSA in Figure 4 can be thought of as an exercise in form generation or analysis. Another spatial composition exercise can be formulated as follows: construct a FSA that accepts only compositions that have exactly one occurrence of a given subcomposition {cube cube}. The FSA that satisfies the condition is shown in Figure 5.

Another exercise entails using FSA to summarize the description of a family of spatial compositions. It can be formulated as follows: Construct a FSA that describes a family of spatial compositions in which each cube is immediately preceded and immediately followed by a cylinder. The FSA shown in Figure 8 constitutes a solution to this problem.

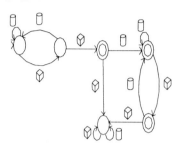

Figure 5: FSA That Accepts Only Compositions That Have Exactly One Occurrence of the Subcomposition { cube cube}

For the FSA described above one composition that would be accepted is shown in Figure 6. This composition has exactly one occurrence of the subcomposition { cube cube}.

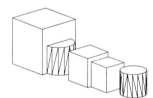

Figure 6: A Composition That Belongs to the FSA Defined in Figure 5

And a composition that would be rejected by the same FSA is shown in Figure 7, because it has two occurrences of the subcomposition {cube cube}.

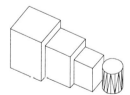

Figure 7: A Composition That Does Not Belong to the FSA Defined in Figure 5

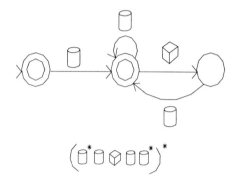

Figure 8: FSA for Compositions in Which Each Cube is Immediately Preceded and Immediately Followed by a Cylinder

The composition shown in Figure 9 would be rejected by the FSA illustrated in Figure 8. This composition includes a cube that is not immediately followed by a cylinder.

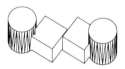

Figure 9: A Composition That Does Not Belong to the FSA Shown in Figure 8

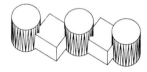

Figure 10: A Composition That Belongs to the FSA Shown in Figure 8

In contrast, the composition shown in Figure 10 would be accepted, because it satisfies the criterion of the FSA in Figure 8.

The FSAs in the previous examples assume linear compositions. To overcome their linearity and the lack of topological information, it is possible to extend the model to include "centralized" compositions. In the extended model, the possibility of describing multiple, as opposed to one, directions is introduced. The new directions include right, left, up, and down from the central element. A square is used to represent the start of the composition (i.e., the initial state). Circles represent other states. A shaded circle represents a state of acceptance or a final state. Figure 11 shows an example of the extended model.

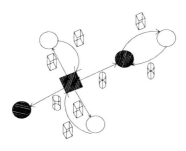

Figure 11: A Topological Version of a FSA

A composition that satisfies the FSA shown in Figure 11, is illustrated in Figure 12. In this composition, following each of the arrows in the FSA leads to an acceptance state.

Figure 12: A Composition That Belongs to the FSA Shown in Figure 11

The subcompositions {cube, cylinder} to the right, and {cube, cube} to the front and back of the central cylinder may be repeated as many times as desired. So, this FSA diagram can describe a family of compositions that satisfy some set of given criteria. Arguably, this FSA version is more flexible and powerful than the ones in the previous diagrams. This is due to the inclusion of thus multiple directions. Thus enabling the form-maker to derive central in addition to linear compositions.

Now, the FSA model can be extended even further to satisfy a broader spatial representation. As shown in Figure 13, nodes (or circles) can be established in all directions. The first arrow <u>from</u> the start shape defines the desired direction. According to the convention used in this paper, other arrows have to conform to the direction of the first.

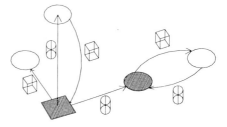

Figure 13: A Spatial Version of FSA

Figure 13 represents a compositional language where directions are important. In the *spatial state diagram* shown in this Figure, any composition that starts with a cylinder followed by a cube then a cylinder located to its right, and a cylinder followed by a cube above it is acceptable. A possible instance of this class of compositions is shown in Figure 14.

Figure 14: A Composition That Belongs to the FSA in Figure 13

Another instance appears in Figure 15.

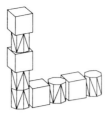

Figure 15: A Composition That Belongs to the FSA in Figure 13

Because the distances between objects are significant for their composition, numbers can be appended to the arcs of FSAs, to show the distance between two elements pairwise. Also, if crucial to the composition, dimensions, or ratios (e.g., x/y = 0.5) can be added to the image representing each element.

Conclusion

FSAs are tools used to represent pictorially families of strings in formal languages. This paper showed that they can be developed to derive and represent families of composition consisting of geometric elements. They represent topological relations among a set of elements or subsystems. They also describe the process of combining subsystems that can be used to form other systems or subsystems. In architectural form-making, they can be used to conduct massing studies. In this regard, they can be applied as a visualization tool in basic design courses as well as a classifying tool for buildings.

References:

[1] Aho, A.V., and J.D. Ullman, *The Theory of Parsing, Translation, and Compiling*, Prentice-Hall, Inc., Englewood Cliffs, New Jersey, 1972.

[2] Aho, A.V., R. Sethi, and J.D. Ullman, *Compilers, Principles, Techniques, and Tools*, Addison-Wesley Publishing Company, Reading, Massachusetts, 1986.

[3] Arnheim, R., *The Dynamics of Architectural Form*, The University of California Press, Berkeley, 1977.

[4] Arnheim, R., *Visual Thinking*, The University of California Press, Berkeley, 1960.

[5] Barwise, J., *Logical Reasoning With Diagrams*, Oxford University Press, New York , 1996.

[6] Harrison, M.A., *Introduction to Formal Language Theory,* Addison-Wesley Publishing Company, Massachusetts, 1978.

[7] Hopcroft, J. E., and J.D. Ullman, *Introduction to Automata Theory, Languages, and Computation*, Addison-Welsley Publishing Company, Reading, Massachusetts, 1979.

[8] A. Koutamanis, "The Future of Visual Design Representations in Architecture," in *Automation Based Creative Design: Research and Perspectives*, Elsevier Science B.V., New York, 1994, pp. 76-98.

[9] Linz, P., *An Introduction to Formal Languages and Automata,* Jones and Bartlett Publishers, Massachusetts, 1997.

[10] Marr, D., *Vision: A Computational Investigation Into the Human Representation and Processing of Visual Information*, W. H. Freeman, San Francisco, 1982

[11] Revesz, G. E., *Introduction to Formal Languages*, McGraw-Hill Book Company, New York, 1983.

[12] Salomaa, A., *Formal Languages*, Academic Press, New York, 1973.

[13] Schiffer, S. and S. Steele, *Cognition and Representation*, Westview Press, Boulder, 1988.

[14] Sheppard, S., *Visual Simulation: A User's Guide for Architects, Engineers, and Planners,* Van Nostrand Reinhold, New York, 1989.

Visualisation of Construction Costs and Techniques of Employment-Intensive Road Construction in Developing Areas

Filip L.M. Taylor Parkins and Robert T. McCutcheon
Department of Civil Engineering, University of the Witwatersrand

Abstract

Employment generation in the construction of economically efficient infrastructure can contribute to the alleviation of poverty. Practical Choice of Technique Analysis (COTA-P) is a tool that enables decision-makers to estimate the financial and socio-economic costs involved in a construction. COTA-P looks at the construction from an employment-intensive perspective, with the underlying idea to substitute as much labour for machines as is feasible, and to promote the use of local labour in underdeveloped and poor areas. COTA-P consists of a technical screening phase, a financial and socio-economical screening phase, and thirdly the monitoring and evaluation phase. Each phase analyses the possibility of the enhanced use of labour. COTA-P is programmed in a Windows 32-bit environment, and gives the user maximum user-friendliness, while allowing for extensive manipulation of the core variables and parameters, thus enabling the user to analyse various scenarios in a short time.

1: Introduction and conference context

Employment-intensive Construction takes a special place in the field of Civil Engineering, as it is primarily aimed at generating employment, alleviating poverty, equalising income inequalities and capacity building in historically, economically, politically or geographically disadvantaged communities. South Africa emerged from the apartheid era with a legacy of low economic growth, severe poverty especially in rural areas and among the black population, extreme income inequality by international standards, chronically high unemployment, a fragmented labour market, and due to apartheid's educational system, low skills and capacity among the black population - all linked to the threat of further social conflict [1]. Hence, employment-intensive construction methods have enormous potential in these areas.

It is exactly here that this research attempts to contribute; by critically developing and examining a socio-economic decision model that promotes the use of a high number of unemployed people in the construction industry during the construction and maintenance of both the existing infrastructure and the much needed new infrastructure.

This decision tool is called Practical Choice Of Technique Analysis, or COTA-P. The COTA-P tool attempts to improve and evaluate decisions made in the field of employment-intensive engineering, by comparing the construction of infrastructure, and especially roads, with different degrees of machine-intensity and labour-intensity. This makes COTA-P a unique tool, as it interactively analyses employment-intensive, development-orientated, road construction projects by means of high-tech tools such as customised computer database programs and choice of technique models.

2: Introduction to employment-intensive construction

From a theoretical perspective, supported by experience elsewhere in Africa, there are reasons for considering that properly structured programmes based on the use of employment-intensive methods, rather than conventional equipment-intensive technology, should be established. Such a programme would construct and maintain the required physical infrastructure, thus creating employment, skills and institutional capacities [2]. However, this mode of employment generation has to be socio-economically efficient to make best use of the scarce resources.

The origins of current interest in employment-intensive methods on a world-wide scale can be traced to the instigation of the World Employment Programme (WEP) by the International Labour Office (ILO) in Geneva in 1969. The objective of the WEP was to try to define an employment-oriented development strategy. Even though concern for employment remains a cornerstone of the employment-intensive programmes, other considerations strengthen the arguments for adopting an employment-intensive approach to public works. First are the modest development prospects confronting many developing countries, especially the majority in Sub-Saharan Africa. Second are the positive achievements with labour-based road works since the

WEP was launched. These achievements have shifted the debate from employment per se so that current employment-intensive projects and programmes embrace a multiplicity of objectives.

From the socio-economic viewpoint, an employment-intensive operation is generally known as an operation in which proportionately more labour is used than other production factors. Employment-intensive construction is defined as follows [2]:

The economically efficient employment of as great a proportion of labour as is technically feasible to produce as high a standard of construction demanded by the specification and allowed by the funding available.

Conventional, machine-intensive road construction is highly equipment-intensive, with generally only some 10 per cent of the total construction costs going to labour, while in employment-intensive rural road engineering up to 65 to 70 per cent of total construction costs could go to labour; i.e. more than 600% as much [3]. This is achieved largely through the creation of individual, community and institutional capacities by the establishment of large, carefully planned, long-term national programmes. Hence, Employment-Intensive Construction is the effective substitution of labour for equipment and results in a significant increase in employment opportunities per unit of expenditure (for example from 10% to 50%, as opposed to contractors who claim to be "employment-intensive", with a "40%" increase, meaning an increase from 10% to 14%).

To avoid confusion, Employment-Intensive Construction is not the use of large numbers of people on relatively unplanned emergency or relief projects to construct something of ill-defined quality and value; that is "labour-extensive" [2]. Labour-extensive construction emphasises the size of the labour force rather than the product or productivity.

Progress in productive employment generation is severely limited by engineers and planners who express reservations regarding the financial and socio-economic costing, product quality, time consumption and labour management of employment-intensive works by comparison with equipment-intensive construction methods. Although these assertions may be challenged from both a theoretical and practical perspective, these views are still widely held. Numerous practical and research projects have shown that employment-intensive construction is an option well worth considering under certain conditions. The World Bank carried out extensive studies and showed that employment-intensive projects can be technically feasible and economically efficient.

But, this research was a mammoth work [4,5] and cannot be easily repeated. However, this question of cost-competitiveness between employment-intensive and machine-intensive techniques cannot be ignored, because it is so often raised in debates. The majority of properly planned operations in South Africa has been cost-competitive and studies of work elsewhere in Africa have come to the same conclusion. Therefore, it has been necessary to develop a method to compare financial and socio-economic costs of using employment-intensive and machine-intensive construction methods.

3: Introduction to COTA

Since the early days of Cost Benefit Analysis (CBA), it has been a tool used in the analysis and choice of infrastructural construction projects. However, 'conventional' CBA does not contribute significantly to the analysis of the socio-economic effects of the reverse substitution of labour for equipment [6]. That is one of the reasons that the COTA methodology has been developed. COTA is a decision making tool that enables the user to identify the most suitable portions of the construction project or construction item where labour effectively could be substituted for equipment, and it enables policy and decision makers to assess the (socio-) economic costs and employment implications of such a substitution. COTA and COTA-P are partially based on earlier work by the ILO [7, 8, 9].

3.1: COTA Characteristics

1. COTA is a Decision-Making Tool
COTA was originally developed [10] as a decision path and computer spreadsheet model, to estimate and predict the financial and economic costs and employment implications of a theoretical employment-intensive constructed urban busroute with a Waterbound Macadam basecourse.

2. Incremental Approach to Increasing Labour-Intensity
Some types of public works, such as masonry stormwater and housing are traditionally highly employment-intensive. Thus employment-intensive construction of these types of work may be carried out without a prior period of technical development work, training, capacity building, and related institutional changes. However, other types of public works are conventionally built using highly mechanised construction techniques. In order to ensure high product quality and reasonable financial cost, employment-intensive construction of these types of works should be preceded by a process of technical development work (including the identification of appropriate designs), institutional change, training and

226

capacity building. Thus, the labour-intensity of the construction industry should be increased incrementally, while the capacity of the industry to build more and more types of public works using cost-effective employment-intensive techniques is developed [11].

3. COTA compares machine-intensive and employment-intensive projects

COTA enables employment-intensive costs (both financial and socio-economic) to be compared to machine-intensive costs. A decision regarding the use of labour in that particular project can then be taken. However, data about employment-intensive road construction projects in South Africa is often scarce and not consistently documented. Therefore, a calibration with international data is necessary to come to a realistic comparison with local machine-intensive construction projects.

4. Two Main Assumptions

The following two assumptions are crucial for the COT Analysis:

a. *Decision to build has been taken*

COTA does not provide decision support for the process of choosing *what* to build, *where* to build it, or *when* to build it. COTA helps decision-makers to decide about *how* to build the infrastructure, given variables and character of machines, labour and construction activities.

b. *No sacrifice in cost and/or quality*

Compared to machine-intensive construction, COTA assumes that it is possible to construct the employment-intensive infrastructure in the same time, for the same financial and socio-economic cost, and with the same quality of end product, but with a significantly increased generation of employment.

3.2: Problems with original COTA

Research on the first version of COTA revealed some important problems, withholding it from being applied in practical situations [12]. First of all, in terms of compatibility between users and computers, the original COTA was not very user-friendly. It was written in a Lotus 1-2-3 spreadsheet, and consisted of one large sheet, containing all the variables, formulas and results. Hence, it was hard for people other than the creator to understand it.

Therefore, this original version was hardly utilised by the people and organisations that could benefit from it, like policy and decision-makers in the field of civil construction. Until now (May 1999) COTA has been used only once, on a feasibility study for the rehabilitation of the National Route N1 between Matoks and Louis Trichardt [13].

Further use of COTA failed to materialise. In the authors' opinion, this is because of the poor userfriendliness, transparency and direct compatibility of COTA.

3.3: From COTA to COTA-P

So what is the main difference between the original COTA and the new COTA-P? COTA-P offers the user a practical, user-friendly and straightforward method to estimate, predict and monitor the financial and socio-economic costs involved in an infrastructural construction. This is achieved through a spreadsheet/database-like user interface for the Microsoft Windows® environment. This software will take the user through the decision steps of COTA, and requires merely more than mouse-clicks and the setting of some values for core variables. The results will then give an indication whether the project or construction item has an enhanced scope for the use of labour, or the substitution of labour for machinery.

3.4: Phases in COTA-P

COTA-P adopts the same phases in its decision path as the original COTA. These steps can be summarised as follows:

1. Technical Screening

After appropriate employment-intensive designs have been prepared for the construction, the physical

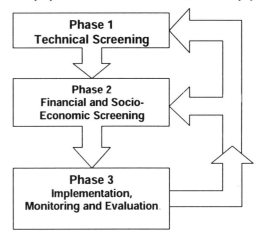

Figure 1 Phases in COTA-P

characteristics of each construction item will indicate whether it is possible to use employment-intensive construction techniques. If the employment-intensive methods meet the required standards, the result of this screening phase will be the most employment-intensive set of construction items, which are technically feasible.

2. Financial and Socio-Economic Screening

The decision rule gives the financial and socio-economic conditions that have to be fulfilled to pass employment-intensive construction methods. The next step in this phase is to calculate these financial costs and to establish the socio-economic feasibility of using employment-intensive techniques. Resulting from this second analysis is the most employment-intensive set of construction techniques, which is technically, financially and socio-economically feasible.

3. Implementation and Evaluation

The last phase in COTA-P provides the link between the short term (design and costing) and the long term (implementation, monitoring and evaluation), as the results of monitoring and evaluation could influence future analysis. This implies that the three parts of COTA-P are interrelated and iterative, as future analysis is informed by the results of past projects.

3.5: Data and calibration

The underlying data and parameters of COTA-P will be extracted both from international and local (South African) studies on employment-intensive road construction. The decision to focus on road construction is based on research by the National Economic Forum [3].

Table 1 Spending on labour as % of spending on labour, plant and materials [3]

Sector	Current Spending	Maximum Spending
Simple projects*	60-80%	60-80%
Low cost housing*	25-35%	30-40%
Social buildings*	20-30%	25-35%
Water reticulation	5-15%	25-35%
Stormwater	5-15%	40-50%
Sanitation	5-15%	25-35%
Roads	5-15%	30-80%
Dams	10-20%	50-80%
Railways	5-15%	20-30%
Forestry	25-35%	35-45%
Electrification	10-15%	12-17%
Small-scale agriculture-related infrastructure*	40-80%	40-80%

* These sectors are conventionally highly employment-intensive, and hence there is little potential for increasing labour intensity in these sectors

Table 1 shows that besides roads the several other sectors have an enhanced scope for the use of employment-intensive construction methods. These sectors are therefore also targeted by the Research Centre for Employment Creation in Construction, and the possibility of using COTA-P on them is under investigation.

Until now, COTA-P relies on the parameters that were used in the original COTA. An important step in the development of COTA-P for Windows is to analyse and where necessary update these data and parameters. Calibration of COTA-P will be done by analysing the original data and importing new data from other international and national projects. Projects that are used for extraction of new data and parameters are, inter alia:

1. South Africa: National Route N1 [14]
2. South Africa: Thukela Basin Project
3. Ghana Feeder Road Programme
4. Kenyan Rural Access Roads Programme
5. Malawian District Road Improvement
6. Botswana Maintenance Programme

4: Conclusions

This COTA-P version will be software independent from spreadsheet and database software and can be used on any computer working under a Windows 32-bit operating system.

The main benefits of COTA-P for Windows, maximum userfriendliness and maximum compatibility, combined with an as high as possible calculating speed, ensure that this version of COTA is an ideal instrument for policy-makers and decision-makers in the field of employment-intensive construction.

One of the problems that is currently under investigation, is the availability and relevance of reliable South African data and parameters. In order to get meaningful results from COTA-P, the underlying parameters should be as concrete as possible, and should not allow room for ambiguous interpretation.

Another important characteristic of COTA-P is that it is not the ultimate tendering tool or cash flow program. It is purely a decision tool to estimate, predict and monitor the use of labour (and its implications) in construction projects. It is developed to offer the user a practical and flexible decision-making tool that gives him relevant and realistic quantitative results rather than just some "guestimates".

5: References

1.   Standing, G, Sender, J et al, Restructuring the labour market: the South African challenge, ILO Country Review book, International Labour Office, Geneva, 1996
2.   McCutcheon, R T, Employment-intensive Construction in Sub-Saharan Africa, Habitat International, Vol 19, No 3, Elsevier Science Ltd, Great Britain, March 1995, pp 331-355
3.   NEF, Pre-investment investigation National Employment Creation Programme for the Provision of Public Infrastructure using Employment-intensive Methods, Report for the Technical Focus Group prepared for NEF, Technical Committee on Public Works Programme, South Africa, April 1994

4.   Coukis, B, et al, <u>Labor-based Construction Programs: A practical guide for Planning and Management</u>, IBRD/World Bank, Oxford University Press, United Kingdom, 1983

5.   World Bank, The Study of the Substitution of Labor and Equipment in Civil Construction, <u>Project Completion Report</u>, Transportation Department, IBRD/World Bank, Washington, USA, 1986

6.   McCutcheon, R T, Personal Communication, November 1996 - May 1999

7.   Costa, E, et al, <u>Guidelines for the Organisation of Special Labour Intensive Works Programmes</u>, International Labour Organisation (ILO), Geneva, Switzerland, 1976, pp iv-18

8.   Edmonds, G A, de Veen, J J, Technology Choice for the Construction and Maintenance of Roads, <u>Report CTP128</u>, ILO, Geneva, Switzerland, 1991, pp 14

9.   Garnier, P, <u>Introduction to Special Public Works Programmes</u>, ILO, Geneva, Switzerland, 1982

10.   Phillips, S D , Theoretical Analysis of Employment-intensive Construction of Waterbound Macadam Roads, <u>PhD thesis</u>, Wits, Faculty of Engineering, South Africa, August 1994

11.   Phillips, S D, Pintusewitz, C A, McCutcheon, R T, Choice of Technique Analysis, <u>presented at Regional Seminar on Labour-based Roadworks</u>, Wits, South Africa, 16-20 January 1995

12.   Taylor Parkins, F L M, Critical Analysis of the Practical Use of Choice of Technique as a Decision Tool for Labour-Intensive Construction Projects, <u>MSc thesis</u>, Twente University, Holland, 1997

13.   SARB, Report on the Choice of Technique Analysis for the Reconstruction between Matoks and Louis Trichardt, <u>Report on SAPR Project no. D05-000-15/7</u>, N1-27X, South Africa, January 1995

14.   SARB, The Rehabilitation of National Route N1-28 from Matoks to Louis Trichardt, <u>Report on contract no. SAPR N0128005/2</u>, Project Document, Volume 3, South Africa, July 1996

Computer Aided Geometric Design

Chair

Brian A. Barsky

University of California at Berkeley, USA

Conic Representation of a Rational Cubic Spline

Muhammad Sarfraz
Department of Information & Computer Science
King Fahd University of Petroleum and Minerals
KFUPM # 1510, Dhahran 31261
Saudi Arabia.
E-mail: `sarfraz@ccse.kfupm.edu.sa`

Zulfiqar Habib
National College of Textile Engineering
Faisalabad
Pakistan.
E-mail: `zulfiqar_habib@hotmail.com`

Abstract

A rational cubic spline, with on family of shape parameters, has been discussed with the view to its application in Computer Graphics. It incorporates both conic sections and parametric cubic curves as special cases. The parameters (weights), in the description of the spline curve can be used to modify the shape of the curve, locally and globally, at the knot intervals. The rational cubic spline attains parametric C^2 smoothness whereas the stitching of the conic segments preserves visually reasonable smoothness at the neighboring knots. The curve scheme is interpolatory and can plot parabolic, hyperbolic, elliptic, and circular splines independently as well as bits and pieces of a rational cubic spline.

1. Introduction

Piecewise rational cubic spline functions provide a powerful tool for designing of curves, surfaces and some analytic primitives such as conic sections that are widely used in engineering design and various Computer Graphics applications. These applications may be representing some font outline, round corner in an object, or it may be a smooth fit to a given data. Several segments of curves, to compose a desired curve outline, can have different mathematical descriptions. For example, a font "S" when designed, appears to have straight lines, conics, and cubics as essential parts of its outline. Single mathematical formulation for the precise definition of various types of geometry shapes is one of the major advantages of the rational cubic spline functions.

This research describes the parametric C^2 rational cubic spline representation possessing a family of shape control parameters. This family of shape parameters has been utilized to produce straight line segments, conics, and cubics. The presented curve scheme encompasses and extends the results in [1]. The features of maintaing some reasonable amount of continuity between conic and cubic arcs, estimated end derivatives, conic (circular, elliptical, parabolic, and hyperbolic) splines, and circular arcs for given radius or center, are further achievements in this research.

There are many schemes in the literature for shape control using cubic interpolants. For brevity, the reader is referred to [1-18]. In [1], a C^1 rational cubic spline with approximated derivatives at control points was used and continuity between conic and cubic arcs was not discussed. Intermediate point interpolation scheme and circular arcs presented in [3] are not practical as the space curves and exact circular arcs are not possible. In [6], end derivatives are based on the assumption of the user, which is not convenient. Moreover, the conics were not discussed at all. We have estimated most suitable end derivatives for more pleasing results. In [4], rational quadratic spline is used for circular spline. We are using very simple technique using rational cubic spline for the same circular spline. In addition, the scheme has the following properties which may lead to a more useful approach to curve and surface design in CAGD:

- The curve has C^2 continuity between the rational cubic arcs and G^1 continuity between cubic and conic arcs.
- Most suitable end derivatives are estimated.
- The scheme is local, i.e. shape control parameters will not significantly effect the adjacent parts of the design curve.
- Any part of the rational cubic spline can be made conic (with exact circle and ellipse) or straight line using the same interpolant.
- The method is most suitable for space curves and hence can be generalized to surfaces.

The distribution of the paper is as follows. A C^2 parametric rational cubic spline scheme, together with determination of tangents at the knot points, is considered in Section 2. Analysis of the designing curve has been made in Section 3. Conditions for conics and straight line segments are given in Section 4. This section also covers all types of circular arcs in space. In Section 5, we have presented a scheme to calculate end derivatives (tangents). The Section 6 concludes the paper.

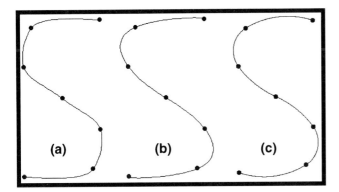

Figure 1. Spline curves with various end conditions: (a) with distance based derivatives, (b)-(c) with exact derivatives.

2. The Rational Cubic Spline

Let $F_i \in R^m$, $i = 0,1,....n$, be a given set of data points at the distinct knots $t_i \in R$. Also let $D_i \in R^m$, denote derivative values defined at the knots. Then a parametric C^1-piecewise rational cubic Hermite spline $P : R \to R^m$ is defined by:

$$P(t) \equiv P_i(t) = \frac{N_i(t)}{M_i(t)}, \ i = 0,1,....,n-1, \qquad (2.1)$$

where

$$N_i(t) = (1-\theta)^3 F_i + \theta(1-\theta)^2(\gamma_i +1)V_i$$
$$+ \theta^2(1-\theta)(\gamma_i +1)W_i + \theta^3 F_{i+1}$$

$$M_i(t) = (1-\theta)^2 + \theta(1-\theta)\gamma_i + \theta^2$$

$$\theta = (t-t_i)/h_i, \ h_i = t_{i+1} - t_i,$$

and

$$\left.\begin{array}{l} V_i = F_i + \dfrac{1}{1+\gamma_i} D_i, \\[3mm] W_i = F_{i+1} + \dfrac{1}{1+\gamma_i} D_{i+1}. \end{array}\right\} \qquad (2.2)$$

The choice of parameters $\gamma_i > -1$ ensures a strictly positive denominator in the rational cubic. Thus from Bernstein Bezier theory, the curve lies in the convex hull of the control points $\{F_i, \ V_i, \ W_i, \ F_{i+1} \}$ and is variation diminishing.

2.1. Estimation of Tangent Vectors

There are different choices of the tangent vectors D_i at F_i, which can be opted for practical implementation for the computation of a curve with specific amount of smoothness. For C^1 curve methods, some reasonable tangent approximation method can be used. The distance-based approximations are found reasonably good as far as pleasing smoothness is concerned. These tangent vectors D_i at F_i are defined as follows:

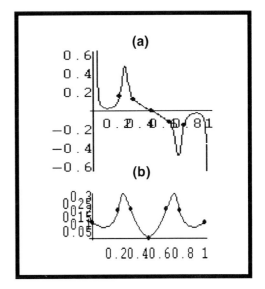

Figure 2. Curvature plots of Spline curves with exact derivatives: (a) with distance based end derivatives, (b) with conic compatible end derivatives.

For open curves, the end conditions are defined as:
$$\left.\begin{array}{l} D_0 = 2(F_1 - F_0)-(F_2 - F)/2, \\[2mm] D_n = 2(F_n - F_{n-1})-(F_n - F_{n-2})/2, \end{array}\right\} \qquad (2.3)$$
and the tangents at the interior knots, for $I = 1, 2, ..., n-1$, are given by:
$$D_i = a_i(F_i - F_{i-1})+(1 - a_i)(F_{i+1} - F_i) \qquad (2.4)$$
where
$$a_i = \frac{|F_{i+1} - F_i|}{|F_{i+1} - F_i|+|F_i - F_{i-1}|}, \ i = 0, ..., n.$$
For close curves, the end conditions are defined as:
$$F_{-1} = F_{n-1}, F_{n+1} = F_1,$$
and the tangents at the interior knots are same as in (2.4) but $i = 0, 1, ..., n$.

The experiments have shown that the use of the distance-based approximated derivatives, corresponding to any control polygon (open or closed), provides visually pleasing output. Figure 1(a) is the display of this derivative scheme for an "S" shaped data. For further details, the reader is referred to [1].

For a higher continuity than C^1, more complicated constraints are required to be fit. For example, for C^2 rational cubic spline, the constraints lead to a tridiagonal linear system of equations. This system is diagonally dominant and hence provides a unique solution. This system can be solved using some tridiagonal linear system solver like LU decomposition method. Their details are as follows:

C^1 constraints
$$P^{(1)}(t_i^+) = P^{(1)}(t_i^-), i = 1, ..., n.$$
give
$$D_i = \gamma_{i-1}(F_i - F_{i-1}) - D_{i-1},$$
and C^2 constraints
$$P^{(2)}(t_i^+) = P^{(2)}(t_i^-), i = 1,..,n-1.$$
lead to the following system of equations:
$$\left. \begin{array}{r} h_i D_i + (h_i(\gamma_{i-1}-1) + h_{i-1}(\gamma_i - 1)) + h_{i-1}D_{i+1} \\ = \gamma_{i-1}\Delta_i + \gamma_i\Delta_{i-1}, i = 1,..,n-1. \end{array} \right\} \quad (2.5)$$

For the need of practical results, exact derivatives may be computed from (2.5) together with the end conditions in (2.3). Figure 1(b) is the demonstration for this derivative scheme. The end conditions used here may not be appropriate for the objectives of this article. Therefore, a reasonable choice has been made in Section 5 which demonstrates the "S" shaped data in Figure 1(c). The difference can be seen in Figure 2 demonstrating curvature plots of Figures 1(b) and 1(c) in Figure 2(a) and 2(b) respectively.

3. Design Curve Analysis

The parameters γ_i are mainly meant to be used freely to control the shape of the curve. At the same time, for the convenient of the designer, it is also required that the ideal geometric properties of the curve are not lost. The geometric properties like variation diminishing, convex hull, and positivity are the ones which needed to be present in the description of the design curve.

- For the constraints, $\gamma_i \geq 0, \forall i$, it is very obvious that the rational cubic is characterized as of Bernstein Bezier form.
- Thus following the Bernstein Bezier theory, the piece of curve $P_i(t)$ lies in the convex hull of $\{F_i, V_i, W_i, F_{i+1}\}$
- It also follows the variation diminishing property within the convex hull. That is any straight line

crossing the control polygon of $\{F_i, V_i, W_i, F_{i+1}\}$ does not cross the curve more than its control polygon.

The parameters γ_i may be used to control the shape of the curve. For the practical implementation, we choose $\gamma_i \geq -1$. The *interval tension* properties are apparent for the rational Hermite form and are explained in the following subsections.

3.1. Interval Tension

The interval shape property is obvious from the following limit behaviour. That is, the increase in the shape parameter in any interval tightens the curve towards the line segment joined by the control points.

$$\lim_{\gamma_i \to 0} P(t) = (1 - \theta)F_i + \theta F_{i+1}$$

3.2. Global Tension

Applying the interval property above successively, the design curves converges to the control polygon as the derivatives, either being distance-based or computed from the system of equations, are bounded.

4. Conic and Linear Segments

Conic and straight line are the most important part in designing which can be achieved through rational cubic interpolant, so that we can use the same interpolant for all types of curves and surfaces. The procedure is as follows:

Let U_i be taken as the point of intersection of tangents at F_i and F_{i+1} (in case the tangents are parallel, U_i can be taken as the point where the arc is desired to be splitted, for example, it may be the inflection or the middle point, etc.)

$$\left. \begin{array}{l} V_i = \dfrac{F_i + \gamma_i U_i}{1 + \gamma_i}, \\ W_i = \dfrac{F_{i+1} + \gamma_i U_i}{1 + \gamma_i} \end{array} \right\} \quad (4.3)$$

For conic section properties and choice of shape parameters, the conic shape factor (sharpness parameter), for each piece of curve, is determined as follows:

$$k_i = \frac{1}{\gamma_i^2} \quad (4.4)$$

Various conics are recovered depending upon the nature of weights in (4.4). That is, the ith arc will be:
- parabolic if $\gamma_i = 2$

- hyperbolic if $\gamma_i > 2$
- elliptic if $\gamma_i < 2$
- straight line: $\gamma_i = 0$ (can be considered as a second method for straight line segment)
- circular if

$$\gamma_i = 2\cos\phi \qquad (4.5)$$

where ϕ is the angle between $F_{i+1} - F_i$ and $U_i - F_i$ and

$$U_i = F_i + \mu_i T_i \qquad (4.6)$$

where T_i is the unit vector along D_i and

$$\mu_i = \frac{(F_{i+1} - F_i)^2}{2(F_{i+1} - F_i).T_i} \qquad (4.7)$$

is determined by the condition

$$|U_i - F_i| = |U_i - F_{i+1}|$$

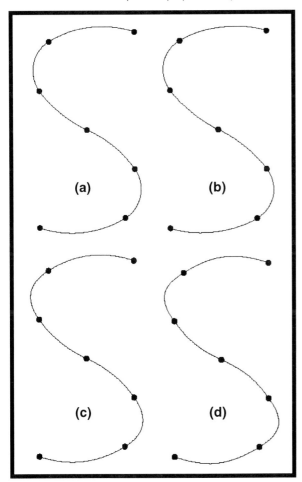

Figure 3. Spline curves: (a) Circular spline, (b) Elliptic spline, (c) Parabolic spline, (d) Hyperbolic spline.

Now we are imposing continuity conditions so that both segments can share same tangent direction at knot to ensure G^1 continuity. For this we are changing the

direction of exact derivatives with same magnitude. Thus, to preserve continuity at F_i, we take

$$D_i = \frac{|D_i|}{|U_i - F_i|}(U_i - F_i), \quad W_{i-1} = F_i - \frac{\beta_{i-1}}{\beta_{i-1} + \gamma_{i-1}}D_i \quad (4.8)$$

To achieve a straight line, one needs to replace U_i with F_{i+1}. Similarly, for continuity at F_{i+1}, we take

$$\left.\begin{array}{l} D_{i+1} = \dfrac{|D_{i+1}|}{|F_{i+1} - U_i|}(F_{i+1} - U_i), \\[2mm] V_{i+1} = F_{i+1} + \dfrac{\alpha_{i+1}}{\alpha_{i+1} + \gamma_{i+1}}D_{i+1} \end{array}\right\} \qquad (4.9)$$

and replacement of U_i with F_i leads to a straight line.

4.1. Circular Arc for Given Radius

Let r be the given radius of the circular arc such that

$$r > \frac{|F_{i+1} - F_i|}{2}$$

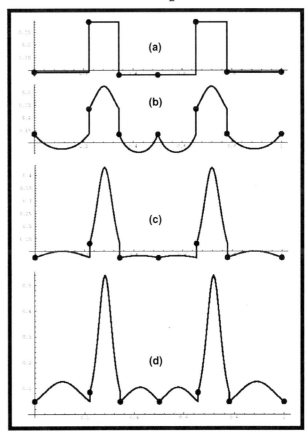

Figure 4. Curvature plots of Figure 3: (a) Circular spline, (b) Elliptic spline, (c) Parabolic spline, (d) Hyperbolic spline.

then center M can lie anywhere on the circle centred at

$$N = \frac{|F_i + F_{i+1}|}{2} \qquad (4.9)$$

and radius

$$b = \sqrt{r^2 - \left(\frac{|F_{i+1} - F_i|}{2}\right)^2} \qquad (4.10)$$

but we will prefer that it should lie on the plane passing through F_i, F_{i+1} and U_i', where U_i' is the intersection of D_i and D_{i+1}. Therefore circular arc should lie on the side of U_i'.

Let e_1 be the rotation of F_{i+1} about N through angle θ on the plane passing through F_i, F_{i+1} and U_i'. Where $\theta = 90^0$ for anti-clockwise rotation and $\theta = -90^0$ for clockwise rotation of circular arc. Now

$$e = \frac{e_1 - N}{|e_1 - N|}$$

is a unit vector passing through N and perpendicular to $F_{i+1} - F_i$. Then $M = N + be$ will be the center of the circular arc. Let ϕ be the angle between $N - M$ and $F_i - M$, therefore

$$\gamma_i = 2\cos\phi$$

Take $\phi = -\phi$ for anti clockwise rotation of circular arc. Let T' is the rotation of F_{i+1} by F_i through angle ϕ on the plane passing through F_i, F_{i+1} and U_i'. Then

$$T_i = \frac{T' - F_i}{|T' - F_i|}$$

is a unit tangent vector at F_i.

Now use equation (4.6) to find U_i, equation (4.3) to find control points V_i and W_i, equation (4.8) for continuity at F_i, equation (4.9) for continuity at F_{i+1} and finally use rational cubic interpolant in equation (2.1) for required circular arc. In this scheme, the radius r can be used as a shape control parameter.

4.2. Circular Arc for Given Centre

Let M be the given center of the circular arc such that

$$|M - F_i| = |F_{i+1} - M|$$

Let M' be the rotation of M by F_i through angle θ on the plane passing through F_i, F_{i+1} and M. Where $\theta = 90^0$ for clockwise rotation of circular arc and $\theta = -90^0$ for anti-clockwise rotation. Then

$$T_i = \frac{M' - F_i}{|M' - F_i|}$$

is a unit tangent vector at F_i. Let ϕ be the angle between $F_{i+1} - F_i$ and T_i, therefore

$$\gamma_i = 2\cos\phi$$

Now use equation (4.6) to find U_i, equation (4.3) to find control points V_i and W_i, equation (4.8) for continuity at F_i, equation (4.9) for continuity at F_{i+1} and finally use rational cubic interpolant in equation (2.1) for required circular arc.

5. End Conditions

A compatible choice, which is more appropriate for the curve scheme of this paper, is presented here. For tangent at first point, let θ_0 be the angle between $F_1 - F_0$ and $F_2 - F_0$. Take $\theta_0 = -\theta_0$ for anti-clockwise rotation of points F_0, F_1 and F_2. Let T_0 be the rotation of F_1 about F_0 through angle θ_0 on the plane passing through F_0, F_1 and F_2. Then

$$\left.\begin{array}{l} \mu_0 = \dfrac{(F_1 - F_0)^2}{2(F_1 - F_0).T_0}, \quad U_0 = F_0 + \mu_0 T_0, \\[2mm] V_0 = \dfrac{F_0 + 2U_0}{3}, \quad D_0 = 3(V_0 - F_0), \end{array}\right\} \qquad (5.1)$$

where μ_0 is determined by the condition

$$|U_0 - F_0| = |U_0 - F_1|$$

and V_0 & D_0 are taken from (4.1) & (2.2) respectively.

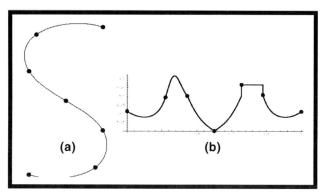

Figure 5. (a) Rational Cubic Spline with second last interval as circular arc piece, (b) the corresponding curvature plot.

Similarly for tangent at last point, let θ_n be the angle between $F_{n-1} - F_n$ and $F_{n-2} - F_n$. Take $\theta_n = -\theta_n$ for anti-clockwise rotation of points F_n, F_{n-1} and F_{n-2}. Let T_n be the rotation of F_{n-1} about F_n through angle θ_n on the plane passing through F_n, F_{n-1} and F_{n-2}. Then

$$\left.\begin{array}{l} \mu_{n-1} = \dfrac{(F_{n-1} - F_n)^2}{2(F_{n-1} - F_n).T_n}, \quad U_{n-1} = F_n + \mu_{n-1} T_n, \\[2mm] W_{n-1} = \dfrac{F_n + 2U_{n-1}}{3}, \quad D_n = 3(F_n - W_{n-1}), \end{array}\right\} \qquad (5.2)$$

where μ_{n-1} is determined by the condition

$$|U_{n-1} - F_n| = |U_{n-1} - F_{n-1}|$$

and W_{n-1} & D_n are taken from (4.1) & (2.2) respectively.

6. Demonstration

The demonstration in this section has used derivative end conditions of Section 5. Figure 3 contains a block of conic splines where Figure 3(a) is Circular spline, Figure 3(b) is Elliptic spline, Figure 3(c) is Parabolic spline, and Figure 3(d) is Hyperbolic spline. Figure 4 represents the corresponding curvature plots of the curves in Figure 3. The demonstration of a rational cubic spline when it contains conic segments is made in Figure 5. Figure 5(a) is a rational cubic spline with second last curve as circular spline, the corresponding curvature plot in Figure 5(b) verifies the result.

7. Conclusion and Future Work

We have described an interval controlled rational cubic interpolation scheme. The scheme offers a number of possible ways in which the shape of the corresponding curves may be altered by the users. It is therefore felt that such a scheme could be a useful addition to an interactive design package, with the user having enough control over the curve segments. The provision of the shape parameters, in the description of the piecewise rational functions, provides freedom to modify the shape in desirous regions in a stable manner.

The rational spline scheme is meant for parametric curves and is capable of designing plane as well as space curves. It is an interpolatory rational spline scheme enjoying all the ideal geometric properties. It has features to produce all types of conic curves in such a way that whole of the design curve may be produced as a circular, elliptic, parabolic, or a hyperbolic spline curve. In addition, the desired conic pieces may also be fitted within the rational cubic spline.

Overall smoothness of the rational cubic spline is C^2 whereas the conics are stitched with G^1 continuity. The curve scheme is extendable to surfaces and authors are lookng to publish it in a subsequent paper.

Some extra shape control parameters are also expected to be included to have some more degrees of freedom for designers. These shape parameters may be like point, interval, or biased shape control parameters used by various authors including Nielson, Foley, Barsky, Sarfraz, Gregory [13-18].

References

[1] M. Sarfraz, Z. Habib and M. Hussain, Piecewise Interpolation for Designing of Parametric Curves, Proceedings IEEE Conference on Information Visualization, IV'98, London, 1998, pp. 307-313.

[2] M. Sarfraz, M. Hussain, and Z. Habib, Local Convexity Preserving Rational Cubic Spline Curves, Proceedings IEEE Conference on Information Visualization, IV'97, London, 1997, pp. 211-218.

[3] M.A. Jamaludin, H.B. Said, and A.A. Majid, Shape Control of Parametric cubic curves, CAD/Graphics, China, 1995.

[4] J. Hoschek, Circular Splines, Computer-Aided Design, Vol 24, 1992, pp. 611-618.

[5] Gregory, J. A. and Sarfraz, M. (1990), A Rational Spline with Tension, Computer Aided Geometric Design, Vol. 7, 1-13.

[6] Gregory, J. A., Sarfraz, M., and Yuen, P.K. (1994), Interactive Curve Design using C^2 Rational Splines, Computers and Graphics, Vol. 18(2), 153-159.

[7] Sarfraz, M. (1993), Designing of Curves and Surfaces using Rational Cubics, Computers and Graphics, Vol. 17(5), 529-538.

[8] Sarfraz, M. (1995), Curves and Surfaces for CAD using C^2 Rational Cubic Splines, Engineering with Computers, Vol. 11(2), 94-102.

[9] Foley, T.A. (1989), Surface Interpolation with Tension Controls using Cardinal Bases, Computer Aided Geometric Design, Vol. (6), 97-109.

[10] Nielson, G.M. (1986), Rectangular v-splines, IEEE Computer Graphics and Applics. 6, 35-40.

[11] L. Piegl, and W. Tiller, The NURBS book, Springer, 1995.

[12] G. Farin, Curves and Surfaces for Computer Aided Geometric Design, Academic Press, 1988.

[13] G. Nielson, Rectangular Nu-splines, *IEEE Computer Graphics and Applications*, pp. 35-40, 1986.

[14] M. Sarfraz, Curves and Surfaces for CAD using C^2 Rational Cubic Splines, *Engineering with Computers*, Vol.11(2), pp. 94-102, 1995.

[15] T. A. Foley, Surface Interpolation with Tension Controls using Cardinal Bases, *Computer Aided Geometric Design*, Vol. 6, pp. 97-109, 1989.

[16] B. A. Barsky, *Computer Graphics and Geometric Modeling using Beta-Splines*, Springer-verlag, 1986.

[17] M. Sarfraz, Designing of Curves and Surfaces using Rational Cubics, *Computers and Graphics*, Vol. 17(5), pp. 529-538, 1993.

[18] M. Sarfraz, A Rational Cubic Spline with Biased, Point and Interval Tension, *Computers and Graphics*, Vol. 16, pp. 427-430, 1992.

Direct Manipulation of Surfaces using NURBS-Based Free-Form Deformations

Robert A Noble[1], Gordon J Clapworthy[2]

[1]Department of Mathematics & Computing, The Robert Gordon University,
St. Andrew's Street, Aberdeen, U.K.

[2]Department of Computer & Information Sciences, De Montfort University,
Hammerwood Gate, Kents Hill, Milton Keynes, MK7 6HP, U.K.

email : rn@scms.rgu.ac.uk, gc@dmu.ac.uk

Abstract

This paper demonstrates how NURBS-based Free-Form Deformations (NFFDs) can be used to generate and sculpt NURBS-based objects in a way that avoids many of the limitations of ordinary FFDs. A system is described in which the user interacts with the NFFD through a set of direct-acting tools, removing the need to manipulate the mesh directly. As the user applies the tools to the object, the NFFD is updated automatically. Objects are represented as isosurfaces of the NFFD volume, giving a good insight into the way an NFFD would deform a general object.

Keywords : free-form deformation, geometric modelling, parametric surfaces, NURBS, sculpting

1. Introduction

Much work has been done in recent years on methods which allow computer-based flexible objects to be modelled as if they were real models made of clay. The twisting and bending transformations of Barr [1] were a step in this direction, shaping tools were designed by Cobb [2] specifically for B-Spline surfaces and the free-form deformations (FFDs) of Sederberg & Parry [3] represented an important step forward, allowing objects to be deformed in a controlled and meaningful way.

This paper describes a technique which uses NURBS-based FFDs (NFFDs) to generate and sculpt such flexible objects. The technique avoids many of the limitations of ordinary FFDs, when used on NURBS-based objects.

Shaping flexible objects often has two phases, a general transformation to obtain a rough shape, followed by local transformations to add detail (Blanc & Guitton [4]). In our case, the two phases are the generation of an NFFD mesh, followed by the manipulation of the weights of the mesh. Only weight changes are considered since we wish to animate the object at a later stage by controlling the position of the mesh points.

The intention of the system is to present the user with a generic object (the general transform) which they can then sculpt locally to their required shape (the local transform). As such, the NFFD mesh is not designed to include specific local detail. However, analysis of the technique shows that the mesh can be adapted to represent tools which supply specific detail, in a manner similar to the Extended FFD (EFFD) of Coquillart [5].

2. Background to FFDs

A general method for deforming an object in a free-form manner is as follows. Firstly, define a volume enclosing the object; secondly, define a method of deforming the volume; and finally, make the object deform as part of the volume it occupies. For this approach to be useful there must be a simple and meaningful way of deforming the volume. This was provided by Sederberg & Parry [3] in their FFD technique by using a tricubic Bézier volume. This volume can be deformed by altering its control points, in an analogous manner to deforming a Bézier curve.

The FFD technique proceeds as follows:

1. Define a spline volume enclosing the object using a 3D control mesh and the 3 spline parameters (v, u, t).

2. Take a set of points (x_i, y_i, z_i) describing the embedded object and find their corresponding parametric coordinates (v_i, u_i, t_i).

3. Deform the volume by manipulating the control mesh.

4. Calculate the positions of the points describing the object in the deformed volume, using their parametric co-ordinates and the updated control-point positions.

In general, embedding the object as required in step 2 is an iterative process and hence slow, since the iso-parametric surfaces, v = constant etc., are spline surfaces. Sederberg & Parry [3] simplified step 2 by using a mesh in which all the control points P_{ijk} for a given i, j or k lay on a plane – the resulting isosurfaces were then planar.

Using parallelepipeds means that the range of volumes which can be constructed is very limited. EFFDs [5] overcame this by using tricubic Bézier volumes, each representing a basic FFD, but not necessarily having parallel faces. By careful design, continuity was maintained across adjacent volumes so that, for example, a cylinder was built of wedge-shaped volumes. Although more flexible as a deformation, embedding the object inside the volume demanded an iterative solution.

The basic FFD and the EFFD were complicated by the fact that joining two Bézier volumes imposes certain conditions on the control points if continuity is to be maintained. This problem is removed if the volume is defined by B-splines or NURBS, as in the system based on B-splines described by Hsu et al [6].

Lamousin & Waggenspack [7] describe a system of NFFDs based on a mesh built from rectangular parallelepipeds. Using NFFDs allows the whole object to be enclosed by a single mesh, with as many control points as the user requires, without continuity problems.

This system overcame the problem with FFDs that, in general, the deformation volume does not fill the whole mesh volume, by using multiple end knots. For a non-parallelepiped mesh however, even having multiple knots does not force the volume to fill the whole mesh, although the convex hull property means that it approximates it.

One example showed a leg enclosed in a rectangular mesh with 5×5×13 control points. The leg could be bent by moving groups of control points and shaped locally by changing appropriate weights. Whilst the NFFD mesh allowed the leg to be sculpted, there were 208 weights which could be adjusted, 99 of which were internal to the mesh and therefore difficult to access. Furthermore, the range of influence of some of the internal weights could include both the front and the back of the leg, making them unusable for deformation purposes.

Modelling packages such as Amapi 3D® allow a user to enclose an object in an FFD mesh and then manipulate the mesh. However, it is often difficult for a user to know what changes to make to the mesh to obtain the required results, particularly when weight changes are available. What they need is a method of defining the required

change and to have the system change the mesh appropriately, allowing direct manipulation of the object. Davis and Burton [8] presented an early result which moved in this direction by building an FFD system which allowed the user to bend, twist and taper an object.

Hsu et al. [6] took this further, allowing the user to select and move points on the object's surface using the mouse; the system calculated the changes required to the control points. A bust modelled from a sphere using a rectangular B-spline mesh had 20×20×20 control points. With 8,000 control points, 5,832 of which are internal, manual manipulation becomes almost impossible.

Hsu et. al. point out that the control lattice is not usually directly related to the object. Suppose, for example, one were trying to deform a leg which was already bent. Simply encasing it in a global rectangular control net would not be very helpful if the aim were to perform local deformations.

Finally, there is the question of how to represent the deformed object. Even if the original form is known analytically, the final form may not be easily represented. For example, Lasser [9] states that a rational Bézier surface of degree (L, M) deformed by a rational Bézier FFD of degree (l, m, n), results in rational Bézier surface of degree (rL, rM), where r = l + m + n. For a general surface, Coquillart [5] suggested using subdivision to maintain resolution. This may make it difficult to use the resulting surface in keyframe animation. For example, when animating an object, we wish to sculpt it using an FFD at the first key position, transform the result to the second key position, sculpt using an FFD again, etc.

This discussion has highlighted a number of potential difficulties of the FFD technique:

1. Maintaining object continuity is not trivial when using multiple Bézier volumes. B-splines or NURBS are to be preferred.

2. Embedding the object (step 2) is non-trivial for any but uniform parallelepiped meshes.

3. Internal control points may effect large parts of an object and hence be unsuitable for local deformations.

4. For parallelepiped meshes, the generated volume does not fill the mesh volume unless multiple knots are used. For non-parallelepiped meshes the volume is not filled, even with multiple knots.

5. Large meshes have many internal points which cannot easily be seen or used.

6. Tools are required to help the user sculpt the object, particularly with large meshes.

7. After applying an FFD, the surface does not generally have a known analytic description; its data description thus becomes increasingly complex.

Having discussed the problems relating to FFDs, the paper now proceeds as follows. In Section 3 we discuss our approach to free-form sculpting which avoids the above problems. Section 4 describes the direct acting tools which remove the need for the user to know how to manipulate the mesh. Section 5 then considers the effect of the NFFD on the total volume, as required for application to non-NURBS objects. Section 6 considers the results in the light of the problems outlined above and Section 7 outlines some future work.

3. The free-form sculpting system

The usual way to use FFDs is to start with an object, embed it in a mesh and then deform it. In our system, the NFFD mesh is defined first, creating the rough shape of the object as described below. The NFFD weights are then used to add local detail. This avoids many of the problems outlined in Section 2; it allows the mesh to be deformed in a structured manner and the process to be repeated to generate a series of key positions which can be used for coherent animation – Noble & Clapworthy [10].

As a first step, suppose we define an NFFD mesh, with no particular constraints on the positions of the control points, or the size of their weights. The volume defined by the mesh is given by Equation 1 and depends upon the three parameters v, u and t.

$$Q(v,u,t) = \frac{\sum\limits_{v=0}^{N_v-1}\sum\limits_{u=0}^{N_u-1}\sum\limits_{t=0}^{N_t-1} C_{vut} \cdot w_{vut} \cdot B_t^{k_t}(t) \cdot B_u^{k_u}(u) \cdot B_v^{k_v}(v)}{\sum\limits_{v=0}^{N_v-1}\sum\limits_{u=0}^{N_u-1}\sum\limits_{t=0}^{N_t-1} w_{vut} \cdot B_t^{k_t}(t) \cdot B_u^{k_u}(u) \cdot B_v^{k_v}(v)} \quad (1)$$

Setting $t = t_c$ = constant generates the isosurface which we use as our object. It is a NURBS surface in parameters u and v, defined by the control points and weights:

$$N_{vu} = \frac{\sum\limits_{t=0}^{k_t-1} w_{vut} \cdot B_t^{k_t}(t_c) \cdot C_{vut}}{w'_{vu}} \quad (2)$$

$$w'_{vu} = \sum\limits_{t=0}^{k_t-1} w_{vut} \cdot B_t^{k_t}(t_c) \quad (3)$$

For simplicity, we refer to the control points of the NFFD mesh, C_{vut}, as "C-points" and those of the NURBS surface, N_{vu}, as "N-points".

We use cubic NURBS with 4 C-points across the mesh ($k_t = 4$), arranged in two pairs. Only the inner two weights, w_1 and w_2, are varied, giving two active weights, one on each side of the surface.

From Eqn. (2), each N-point is on the straight line joining its corresponding C-points (2 double points). The initial mesh points are therefore placed as required to generate the rough shape of the object, there being no specific restriction on their positions. This allows the initial rough object to be produced by defining a suitable mesh and isosurface. Detail can then be added using the NFFD weights. The object is thereby automatically embedded in a suitable NFFD mesh for sculpting.

4. Direct acting sculpting tools

The technique of Section 3 overcomes the continuity and embedding problems described in Section 2. It also greatly reduces the number of internal control points and the range of their effect. The mesh is well suited to the object and, although the entire volume generated by the mesh is not entirely obvious, it can be made more so by using multiple knots in the t direction. The resulting sculpted object is known in analytical form from Eqn. (1), provided that there is a suitable way of performing the sculpting, which is the subject of this section.

Consider first a simplified situation in which the NFFD mesh is a simple rectangular array of points, with a planar isosurface, as shown in Fig. 1. Only every third set of control points is shown. The cubes represent the sizes of the adjustable weights at the control points shown.

Increasing a weight at a point moves all affected points within the volume towards that point, Piegl & Tiller [11]. In Fig. 1, an upper weight has been increased, thus pulling the surface up. A lower weight has been decreased, also pushing up the surface.

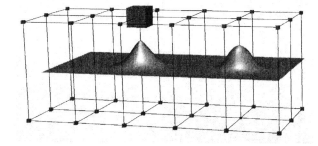

Figure 1 Sculpting by changing one NFFD weight

4.1 The three basic tools

This method introduces local detail, but both changes above produce upward bumps, one sharper, one rounder. This makes it difficult to sculpt the object by manipulating individual weights. Instead, three tools are supplied which change the weights in a controlled way to produce meaningful changes in shape, Noble & Clapworthy [10].

The *Hammer* tool changes the height of a peak without changing its shape – for positive mesh weights, the peak will always remain inside the mesh. The *Crimp* tool changes the shape of a peak, without altering its height (Fig. 2). Using this tool, sharpening increases the mesh weights until the profile of the peak becomes virtually triangular, while rounding decreases the weights – this is limited by the fact that the weights should not be allowed to become negative. The *Reset* tool resets the shape of the object at the indicated point by returning the weights to the values they had when the file was loaded. Thus, when objects are saved and reloaded for further sculpting, resetting restores the most recently-saved shape.

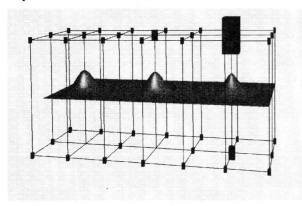

Figure 2 Changing the shape of the peak

The user applies the tools by pointing the cursor at the object and clicking the mouse left/right button to increase/decrease the effect – the system adjusts the weights appropriately. Hence, the user does not need to see the NFFD mesh, but can view the system as a set of tools, connected to the mouse, which act directly on the object.

4.2 Larger tools

The tools described above operate on only one row of the mesh (in the t-direction) and hence have a very localised effect on the object's shape. Larger versions of the tools can be defined by manipulating more than one row of the mesh at a time.

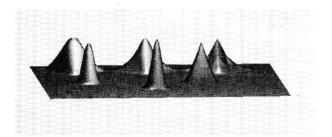

Fig. 3 Bumps produced by the various tools

The *Very Small* version affects one row, the *Small*, *Medium* and *Large* tools each affect an added ring of rows, centred on the point indicated by the mouse.

Fig. 3 shows the results of the *Very-Small* tool at the front and the *Medium* tool at the back. The central peak is from the *Hammer* tool alone, the left and right peaks show the effect of then applying the *Crimp* tool.

An object may be sculpted by applying the tools. Fig. 4 shows the result of trying to sculpt a smooth, horizontal ridge on the flat object. Those weights which have been changed to raise the ridge can be seen to be larger above the plane and smaller below the plane. Again, only every third row of control points is shown.

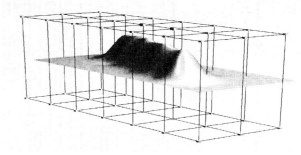

Fig. 4 The NFFD control net for the ridge

As shown in Fig. 2, each weight in the NFFD mesh produces a bump at a specific surface location. Constructing a ridge from such bumps produces an aliasing effect similar to drawing a line on a VDU with fixed pixel positions. To reduce this, the ridge in Fig. 4 was created using the *Small* tool, which affects both the indicated control point and the four control points connected to it. It is, in effect, "3 pixels wide". Detail was then added using the *Very Small* tool.

4.3 Application of the tools to other objects

The previous section illustrated the basic changes which can be achieved by varying the weights of an NFFD, using the direct-acting tools and a rectangular mesh. The tools can also be applied to objects created from other meshes. Their effect is similar (see Section 5), and since there are only two active mesh weights across the object, there are few hidden internal mesh points.

If the rectangular mesh of Fig. 1 is wrapped round an ellipse, the isosurface becomes an elliptical cylinder. The mesh now matches the shape of the object well. Each mesh weight can only affect the cylinder locally, so there is no danger that manipulations at an internal point will alter diametrically-opposite parts of the surface.

Were the cylinder to be embedded in the more usual rectangular NFFD mesh, sculpting would be much more difficult to accomplish. Further, to produce local detail, the mesh would require many control points across the cylinder, leading to a large number of internal points, some of which could affect diametrically-opposite parts of the cylinder simultaneously.

5. The effect on other isosurfaces

The system as described sculpts only the single isosurface. To apply it to a general embedded object, we need to know how it affects all the isosurfaces in the volume. The embedding process for an object relates points on the object to corresponding isosurfaces, the deformation of which determines the deformation of the object. This section considers how the tools affect all the isosurfaces and shows that the effects are predictable. The remaining figures each show five isosurfaces across the volume.

If uniform knots are used in the t direction, the volume generated by a rectangular mesh (Fig. 1) extends from $1/6^{th}$ to $5/6^{th}$ of the way across the mesh. Using multiple knots forces the volume to fill the whole mesh, with a less linear relationship between t and distance.

The relationship between the change in a weight and the movement of points in the volume is well known (Piegl & Tiller [11]). It is clear, both by experiment and analysis, that the effect on the volume of changing a weight is very similar for both uniform and multiple knots in the $1/6^{th}$ to $5/6^{th}$ region. The latter will also affect the whole of the volume, but the movement is very small there.

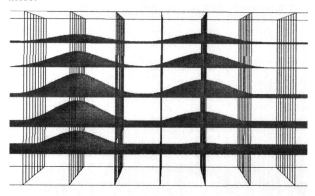

Fig. 5. Multiple isosurfaces, multiple knots

Fig. 5 shows the result of increasing an upper weight (left) and decreasing a lower one (right), using multiple knots. Five isosurfaces corresponding to equally spaced values of t, covering the 1/6 to 5/6 region, are chosen. Note how the left side is pulled towards the increasing weight and the right hand side pushed away from the decreasing one.

Fig. 6 shows the same thing as the left side of Fig. 5, but now the t values are uniformly spaced across the whole range of t. The vertical lines are lines on which u and v are constant and illustrate how these isolines are pulled towards the increasing weight. Note that the end points of these lines cannot move.

Fig. 6. Isolines pulled by an increased weight

The tools, when applied, have similar effects on all isosurfaces, with their effect moderated by the reducing effects of the mesh weights across the volume. Fig. 7, for example, shows the effect of the *Hammer* tool on a short elliptical cylinder (uniform knots). Here, the mesh has been wrapped around into an annular structure, with the t-direction being radial, Noble [12]..

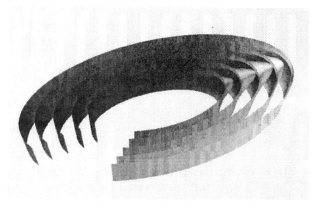

Fig. 7. The *Hammer* tool acting on an elliptical cylinder

6. Discussion

The system described here uses isosurfaces of an NFFD volume as the initial objects, which can then be sculpted as desired. This avoids many of the problems associated with normal FFDs, whilst at the same time giving a good insight into the behaviour of NFFDs under changes in weights.

We now discuss the advantages of this type of NFFD and then consider what can be learned for general objects.

Comparing the list of problems of Section 2 shows the following. Firstly, since the mesh defines the object as an isosurface, there is no continuity or embedding problem. Secondly, the mesh shape naturally matches the object shape. This is valuable where, for example, a cylinder is encased in a matching mesh, not a rectangular block each of whose weights has a different effect, according to how close to the cylinder it happens to be. Furthermore, the isosurface must remain within the volume, whatever the limits of the volume.

Thirdly, it does not have large numbers of internal weights which cannot be seen or accessed, but the tools provided mean that the user does not have to manipulate the mesh directly, anyway.

Fourthly, since each pair of active C-points affects only its own local part of the surface, there is no cross-coupling across an object. One side of a cylinder, for example, is not affected by the internal points of the mesh on the opposite side of the cylinder, however close the mesh points are to it. Even if the surface were a figure of eight, each weight would still only affect its own part.

Finally, the sculpted object is known in closed form, either by the mesh or as a NURBS surface.

Whilst NURBS can be sculpted directly, this NFFD approach has several advantages. Firstly, it allows direct-acting tools to be defined in a natural way, such that the user does not have to understand the workings of the NFFD. Secondly, since the object is defined by the mesh, it can be naturally incorporated into a key-frame animation system. The mesh weights allow it to be sculpted at given key positions; changing the mesh position allows a new key position to be defined and then sculpted and the continuity of the mesh between positions guarantees the resulting animation is coherent.

Thirdly, any NURBS surface can be imported into the system simply by creating an NFFD volume in which the surface is an isosurfaces. This is achieved by matching the mesh to the control points of the surface. This will be investigated in the next part of the project (see Section 7).

Fourthly, this approach gives a good insight into how such an NFFD would affect an embedded object which was not a NURBS surface. Section 5 showed how the tools have equivalent effects on different isosurfaces. A non-NURBS object can therefore be sculpted in a similar manner, once a suitable mesh is generated, provided that the embedding calculations can be performed.

7. Future work

The system has been implemented, as has an extended system which successfully addressed the aliasing problem

identified in Section 4.2, Noble [12]. However, the greater complexity of the extended system made it a less suitable vehicle on which to base the above discussion.

The tools included so far are relatively simple. Other types of tool could be developed to provide greater versatility of sculpting. User tests will be carried out to determine the precise functions that can best be added.

At present, we generate the object from the mesh. It is more usual to want to generate a mesh for a particular object. So, given a NURBS object, a method is required to generate a suitable NFFD mesh. Since the N-point lies on the line of the C-points, this becomes a question of finding a suitable method of generating the mesh to pass through the N-points. Work continues on this investigation

References

1. A.H. Barr, "Global and Local Deformations of Solid Primitives", Computer Graphics, Vol 18, No 3, pp 21-30, 1984

2. E.S. Cobb, "Design of Sculptured Surfaces using the B-Spline representation", *PhD Thesis*, University of Utah, 1984

3. T. Sederberg and S. Parry, "Free-Form Deformation of Solid Geometric Models", *Computer Graphics*, Vol 20, No 4, pp 151-160, 1986

4. C. Blanc and P. Guitton, "Surface Deformation by Normalized Operators", *Proc. 12th UK Eurographics Conf.*, Oxford, pp. 71-86, March 1994.

5. S. Coquillart, "Extended Free-Form Deformation: a Sculpturing Tool for 3D Geometric Modelling, *Computer Graphics*, Vol. 24, No 4, pp. 187-196, 1990

6. W.M. Hsu, J.F. Hughes and H. Kaufman, "Direct Manipulation of Free-Form Deformations", *Computer Graphics*, Vol. 26, No 2, pp. 177-184, 1992.

7. H.J. Lamousin and W.N. Waggenspack, "NURBS-Based Free-Form Deformations", *IEEE Computer Graphics & Applications*, pp 59-65, 1994

8. O.R. Davis and R.P. Burton, "Free-Form Deformation as an Interactive Modelling Tool", *Journal of Imaging Technology*, Vol. 17, No 4, pp. 181-187, 1991

9. D. Lasser, "Rational Tensor-Product Bézier Volumes", *Computers and Mathematics with Applications*, Vol 28, No 8, pp 49-62, 1994

10. R.A. Noble and G.J. Clapworthy "Improving Interactivity within a Virtual Sculpting Environment", *Information Visualization '98*, pp. 232-238, IEEE Computer Society Press, 1998

11. L. Piegl and W. Tiller, *The NURBS Book*, Springer-Verlag, 1995

12. R.A. Noble, "Intuitive Sculpting of Flexible Objects for Coherent Animation", *PhD Thesis*, De Montfort University, UK, 1998.

Optimal Linear Spline Approximation of Digitized Models

Bernd Hamann[1], Oliver Kreylos[1], Giuseppe Monno[2] and Antonio E. Uva[2]

[1]*Center for Image Processing and Integrated Computing (CIPIC)*
Department of Computer Science, University of California, Davis, USA
hamann@cs.ucdavis.edu, okreylos@gallagher.cipic.ucdavis.edu

[2]*Dipartimento di Progettazione e Produzione Industriale*
Politecnico di Bari, Bari, Italy
gmonno@poliba.it, uva@dppi.poliba.it

Abstract

In this paper we present a new technique for surface reconstruction of digitized models in three dimensions. Concerning this problem, we are given a data set in three-dimensional space, represented as a set of points without connectivity information, and the goal is to find, for a fixed number of vertices, a set of approximating triangles which minimize the error measured by the displacement from the given points.

Our method creates near-optimal linear spline approximations, using an iterative optimization scheme based on simulated annealing. The algorithm adapts the mesh to the data set and moves the triangles to enhance feature lines. At the end, we can use the approach to create a hierarchy of different resolutions for the model.

1. Introduction

Surface reconstruction is concerned with the extraction of shape information from point sets. Often, these point sets describe complex objects and are generated by scanning physical objects, by sampling other digital representations (e.g., contour functions), or by merging data from different sources. The result of this scanning process is usually a cloud of points at a very high resolution but without connectivity information. In order to utilize this data for actual modeling in a CAD system, it is important to reduce the amount of data significantly and determine a polygonal representation from the samples. Moreover, multiple approximation levels are often needed to allow rapid rendering and interactive exploration of massive data sets of this type. Surface reconstruction problems arise in a wide range of scientific and engineering applications, including reverse engineering, industrial design, geometric modeling, grid generation, and multiresolution rendering.

1.1. Related Work

Hoppe et al.[4] address the problem of reconstruction of surfaces using only the three-dimensional coordinates of the data points. Their method uses a "zero-set" approach to reconstruction, using the input points to create a signed distance function d, and then triangulating the isosurface d=0. They determine an approximate tangent plane at each sample point, using a least-squares approximation based on k neighbors. The isosurface is then generated using the marching cubes algorithm.

Amenta[14] directly uses a three-dimensional Voronoi diagram, and an associated Delaunay triangulation to generate certain "crust" triangles which are used in the final triangulation. The output of their algorithm is guaranteed to be topologically correct and convergent to the original surface as the sampling density increases.

Heckel et al.[2] introduce a surface reconstruction method that is based on cluster analysis. The reconstructed model is generated in two steps. First, an adaptive clustering method is applied to the data set, which yields a set of almost flat shapes, so-called tiles. Second, the gaps are eliminated between the tiles by using a constrained Delaunay triangulation, producing a valid geometrical and topological model. This method allows one to create a hierarchy of representations.

1.2. Our Approach

We present a new "optimal" (more precisely, near-optimal) method for the generation of surface triangulation. Our method exhibits the following characteristics:

• It requires only scattered points in the space, without connectivity information;

- it needs a minimal user-interaction for a general topology, none for particular topologies;
- it generates an optimal approximation of the surface, with a fixed number of vertices; and
- it produces a multiresolution approximation of the data, where the user can specify the number of vertices in the reconstruction.

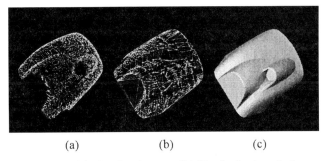

(a)   (b)   (c)

(a) The original point data set. (b) The final triangulation. (c) The shaded reconstructed model. The original data set consists of 37,594 sample points and the model has been reconstructed with 400 vertices.

Figure 1. Laser scan of a Ski-Doo hood.

The algorithm reconstructs a valid triangulated surface model in a three-step procedure:
- **Cutting** the data set in topological simple areas
- **Optimization** applied to all areas
- **Stitching** the shells together

2. Cutting Step

The core reconstruction algorithm treats the point cloud as a set of samples of a two-dimensional function f(x,y), where the samples are taken at random sites (x_i, y_i). If the original surface, or the surface we want to reconstruct, is not functional, the algorithm will deliver invalid results. This forces us to first find a mapping M from three-dimensional space (x,y,z) into two-dimensional parameter space (s, t) such that the mapping satisfies

$$(x, y, z) = M^{-1}(s, t, f(s, t))$$

for a function f. If we restrict ourselves to use orthogonal projections onto planes to define such a mapping, we have to find a plane the surface can be projected onto without self-overlap. If the model is too complex to find such a projection plane, we subdivide the model into smaller parts of simpler topology and provide different projection planes for the parts. To achieve this we first visualize the cloud of points. The user interacts with "cutting planes" subdividing the data set in sub-domains. Instead of cutting

planes we should more precisely say "half-spaces" since we visualize the planes and the oriented normals. All the points included in those half-spaces are mapped (using orthogonal projection) onto the respective planes. Since the result of this subdivision is quite hard to visualize, the convex hull of the projections on the plane is shown to a user. This subdivision phase is typically not necessary if we are given a set of laser scanned images. This type of device usually captures points as distance from a sensor and then geometrically evaluates the xyz-coordinates. For all the points coming from a single pass scan, we are sure to find one single orthogonal projection plane.

3. Optimization Step

For each of the sub-domains (where all the points are "functional" in the way described above), we apply our iterative optimization algorithm based on the principle of simulated annealing, see [8][9][10]. The core of this algorithm is a function that changes the current triangulation randomly in every iteration step. After each step, a distance between the triangulation and the original data set is calculated, and the current step is accepted or rejected based on the change of distance during the step. The main difference between simulated annealing algorithms and classic optimization algorithms is that a simulated annealing algorithm not only accepts "good" steps, but also accepts some steps that increase the distance.

The strategy to accept steps is borrowed from thermodynamics, where Boltzmann's law states that a change ΔE in internal energy of a body occurs with the probability:

$$p = e^{-\frac{\Delta E}{kT}}$$

where k is the Boltzmann constant, and T is the absolute temperature of the body. We use the same function here, replacing ΔE with the change in distance during a step and kT with an arbitrary value we nonetheless call "temperature." If ΔE is negative, meaning the step was a good step, we always accept it; in the other case, we accept it with the probability given by Boltzmann's law.

We then lower the value kT during the course of iteration to decrease the probability of accepting "bad" steps. In the end, when the temperature is almost zero, the algorithm proceeds like a classic optimization. The function decreasing the temperature over time is called "annealing schedule," and [1] presents a heuristic to create it. The benefit of allowing "bad" steps is, that such algorithms do not as easily get stuck at local minima as classic algorithms do. This is an important property for us, since we are dealing with problems typically having local minima in abundance, see Figure 2.

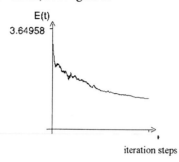

Figure 2. Typical error graph: general error behavior as a function of iteration steps.

The previous formula shows the effect of the temperature on the probability of accepting a bad step.

The user can define the number of vertices to be used in the triangular approximation of the sub-domains. The following pseudo-code summarizes the optimization algorithm, which is described in more detail in the following sections.

Algorithm 1: Optimal linear spline approximation.
Create initial configuration (vertex placement and connectivity);
Determine initial temperature and create annealing schedule;
While iteration is not finished
    {
    Change current configuration;
    Calculate change in error measure;
    Undo iteration if rejected by simulated annealing;
    }
Return current configuration;

3.1. Creating an Initial Configuration

To evaluate a reasonable initial configuration we start to determine the data set's convex hull by selecting all non-interior vertices; then we choose the rest of the vertices (according to the user-specified number) randomly from the original data set. A Delaunay triangulation of the initial vertices' sites defines the initial connectivity.

To define the annealing schedule, we first estimate the mean change in distance during the first iteration steps and set the initial temperature such, that an "expected bad" step is initially accepted with a probability of one half. Next, we lower the temperature in steps, leaving it constant for a fixed number of iterations and scaling it by a fixed factor afterwards.

3.2. Changing the Configuration

The simulated annealing algorithm's core is its iteration step. In principle, one can use any method to change the current configuration, but we have found out that the "split" approach, presented in Algorithm 2, works very well.

Algorithm 2: Changing the configuration.
*if(acceptWithProbability(**moveVertex**)) /*move a vertex*/*
    {
    Choose an interior vertex v;
    Estimate v's contribution vE to the error measure;
    *if(vE < **localMovementFactor** × E)*
        Move v globally;
    else
        Move v locally;
    if(moveVertex == 1) /* Vertex movements only?*/
        Restore Delaunay property;
    }
else /* swap an edge */
    {
    Choose a swappable edge e;
    Swap edge e;
    }

The constant ***moveVertex*** gives the probability of moving a vertex during an iteration step. If it is zero, the algorithm never moves vertices, but becomes a data-dependent triangulation algorithm as presented in [8]. If ***moveVertex*** is one, we only move vertices, and we decided to uphold the connectivity's Delaunay property throughout the iteration in this case. In all other cases the algorithm can either move a vertex or swap an edge, thereby optimizing both vertex placement and triangulation simultaneously. When moving a vertex, we use two different strategies:

- If the chosen vertex is located in a planar region of the surface, we move it **globally** to a random new position inside the point set's convex hull, see Figure 3.
- If the chosen Vertex is located in a high-curvature region of the surface, we move it **locally** to a random new position inside its platelet, see Figure 4.

We decide which strategy to use by estimating how much the chosen vertex contributes to the current distance. If this contribution is larger than a constant factor *localMovementFactor* times the distance, we move the vertex globally, otherwise, we move it locally.

By using global movements we ensure that vertices get driven away from nearly planar regions of a function during early stages of the iteration.

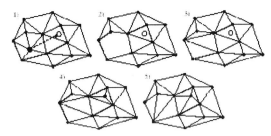

1) Initial state; 2) removing vertex; 3) filling hole; 4) inserting new vertex; 5) restoring Delaunay property.

Figure 3. Moving a vertex globally.

If the vertex is currently located in an important high-curvature region of the surface, we keep this vertex "in loco" and we try to move it to a better site inside its platelet. To move a vertex **locally**, we "slide" the vertex on the line from its old to its new site, dragging the edges connecting it to all surrounding vertices along. Whenever a surrounding simplex becomes degenerate during the vertex' motion, we swap one edge of the affected simplex before moving the vertex any further, see Figure 4.

1) Initial state; 2) swapping edge to prevent triangle T from becoming degenerate; 3) resulting state.

Figure 4. Moving a vertex locally.

In our case, the quality of a configuration depends on both vertex placement and connectivity. The output of this second step is a set of two-manifold shells, which correspond to the number of topological sub-domains the whole data set was subdivided into. Defining an increasing number of vertices, we can create a hierarchy of linear spline approximations, each one being a superset of all lower-resolution ones (Figure 6.)

4. Stitching Step

In this step we stitch together the boundaries of the shells to define a consistent model. We do not move the vertices of the shell boundaries to match, but we add a new set of fill-the-gap triangles. The input of the stitching algorithm consists of two boundaries, each of them described by a sequence of vertices and edges. To define

the boundaries we first project each point into the selected half-space onto the cutting plane. Then we calculate the convex hull boundary on the plane and afterwards map the segments back into three-dimensional space. The second boundary is evaluated with the same procedure with a few modifications for the unselected half-space. In this case not all the points participate in the definition of the convex hull.

The stitching algorithm is applied every time a cut is performed. In this way we already have two sets of points (and edges) to define a strip to be triangulated. We start from a random point and we find the closest point on the other boundary. Those two points define a new edge. For each vertex we maintain a flag indicating whether this vertex was already matched or not. We repeat this edge-creation step until all the vertices are matched. Then we scan the edge list to eliminate duplicates and we extract the fill-the-gap triangles (Figure 5.a.) When a new cut is performed over a previous subset, an edge of its boundary (defined by the previous cut) is hit by the cutting plane. This edge is preserved in the subsequent phase to ensure that this new fill-the-gap set will match exactly on the boundary (Figure 5.b.)

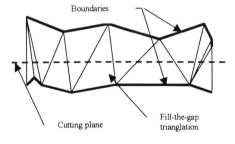

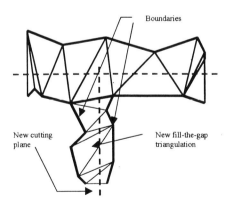

(a) First stitch. (b) subsequent stitch preserving the first triangulation.

Figure 5. Stitching two boundaries.

5. Results

This method has revealed to be very powerful with regard to error reduction. Concerning the Ski-Doo test case, after a few thousand iteration steps (requiring just a few seconds on an SGI Octane), we reduced the error to 40% of the initial configuration error (Delaunay triangulation). Figure 6 shows how the vertices move away from flat areas (large triangles) to converge towards the features of the model (high curvature, small triangles). The last example shows the reconstruction of a model with 2,000 vertices starting from a 1,2000 points data set (Figure 7).

6. Acknowledgements

This work was supported by various grants and contracts awarded to the University of California, Davis, and to the Politecnico di Bari, Italy, including the National Science Foundation under contract ACI 9624034 (CAREER Award), the Office of Naval Research under contract N00014-97-1-0222, the Army Research Office under contract ARO 36598-MA-RIP, the NASA Ames Research Center under contract NAG20-1216, the Lawrence Livermore National Laboratory under contract W-7405-ENG-48 (B-335358), the Department of Energy as part of the Accelerated Strategic Computing Initiative (ASCI) under contract W-7405-ENG-48, the North Atlantic Treaty Organization (NATO) under contract CRG. 971628, and the National Research Council (CNR), Italy. We also acknowledge the support of Silicon Graphics, Inc. We thank all members of the Visualization Thrust at the Center for Image Processing and Integrated Computing (CIPIC) at the University of California, Davis, and of the Dipartimento di Progettazione e Produzione Industriale, Politecnico di Bari, Italy, for their help.

7. References

[1] Kreylos, O., Hamann, B., "On simulated annealing and the construction of linear spline approximations for scattered data", *EUROGRAPHICS-IEEE TVCG Symposium on Visualization*, Vienna, Austria, May 1999 (to appear).

[2] Heckel, B., Uva, A. E., and Hamann, H., "Clustering-based generation of hierarchical surface models, " in: Wittenbrink, C. M. and Varshney, A., eds., Late Breaking Hot Topics Proceedings, *Visualization '98* (Research Triangle Park, North Carolina, October 1998), IEEE Computer Society Press, Los Alamitos, California, pp. 41-44.

[3] Bonneau, G. P., Hahmann, S. and Nielson, G. M., "BLaC-wavelets: A multiresolution analysis with non-nested spaces", in Yagel, R. and Nielson, G. M., eds., *Visualization '96* (1996), IEEE Computer Society Press, Los Alamitos, CA, pp. 43-48.

[4] Hoppe, H., DeRose, T., Duchamp, T., McDonald, J., and Stuetzle, W., "Surface reconstruction from unorganized points," in Computer Graphics (SIGGRAPH '92 Proceedings), pp. 71-78, 1992.

[5] Gieng, T. S., Hamann, B., Joy, K. I., Schussman, G. L. and Trotts, I. J., "Constructing hierarchies for triangle meshes", *IEEE Transactions on Visualization and Computer Graphics* 4(2) (1998), pp. 145-161.

[6] Hamann, B., "A data reduction scheme for triangulated surfaces", *Computer Aided Geometric Design* 11(2) (1994), pp. 197-214.

[7] Hamann, B., Jordan, B. J. and Wiley, D. A., "On a construction of a hierarchy of best linear spline approximations using repeated bisection", *IEEE Transactions on Visualization and Computer Graphics* 5(1) (1999).

[8] Schumaker, L. L. "Computing Optimal Triangulations Using Simulated Annealing", *Computer Aided Geometric Design* 10 (1993), pp. 329-345.

[9] Nielson, G. M., "Scattered data modeling", *IEEE Computer Graphics and Applications* 13(1) (1993), pp. 60-70.

[10] Press, W. H., Teukolsky, S. A., Vetterling, W.T., and Flannery, B. P., *Numerical Recipes in C*, 2nd ed. (1992), Cambridge University Press, Cambridge, MA.

[11] Barequet, G., Duncan, C.A., and Kumar, S., "RSVP: A geometric toolkit for controlled repair of solid models", *IEEE Trans. on Visualization and Computer Graphics* (TVCG), vol. 4 (2), pp. 162-177, April-June 1998.

[12] Barequet, G. and Sharir, M., "Filling gaps in the boundary of a polyhedron", *Computer Aided Geometric Design* 12(2), pp. 207-229, 1995.

[13] Gueziec, A., Taubin, G., Lazarus, F., Horn, W., "Converting Sets of Polygons to Manifold by Cutting and Stitching", in Yagel, R. and Nielson, G. M., eds., *Visualization '98* (1998), IEEE Computer Society Press, Los Alamitos, CA, pp. 43-48.

[14] Amenta, N., Bern, M., Kamvysselis, M., "A new Voronoi-based surface reconstruction algorithm", *Siggraph '98*, (1998), pp 415-421.

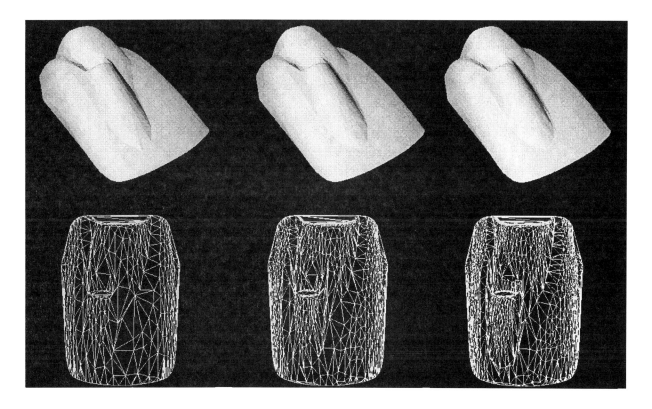

Figure 6. Multiresolution reconstructions using 400, 700, and 1000 vertices for the Ski-Doo data set.

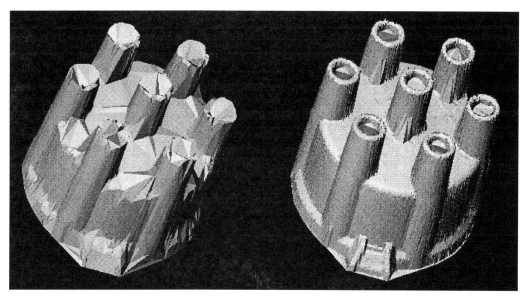

a) Randomly chosen points   b) After optimization step

Figure 7. Reconstruction of a mechanical part using 2,000 vertices for a 12,000 points data set.

Solving Geometric Constraints
by a Graph-Constructive Approach

Samy Ait-Aoudia, Brahim Hamid, Adel Moussaoui, Toufik Saadi
INI - Institut National de formation en Informatique
BP 68M - Oued Smar 16270 ALGIERS ALGERIA
Tel : 213 2 51 60 33
Fax : 213 2 51 61 56 Telex : 64531
E-mail : s_ait_aoudia@ini.dz, ini@ist.cerist.dz

Abstract

A geometric constraint solver is a major component of recent CAD systems. Graph constructive solvers are stemming from graph theory. In this paper, we describe a 2D constraint-based modeller that uses a graph constructive approach to solve systems of geometric constraints. The graph-based approach provides means for developing sound and efficient algorithms. We present a linear algorithm that solves a large subset of the rule and compass constructive problems. Methods for handling over- and under-constrained schemes are also given.
Key Words: *Computer aided design, constraints solving, geometric constraints, graph-based solver, over- and under-constrained schemes.*

1. Introduction

In CAD (Computer Aided Design), geometric modelling by constraints enables users to describe shapes by specifying a rough sketch and adding to it geometric constraints. The constraint solver derives automatically the geometric elements that are to be found. Typical constraints are : distance between two geometric elements (two points, a point and a line, two parallel lines), angle between two lines, tangency between a line and a circle or between two circles ...

Many resolution methods have been proposed for solving systems of geometric constraints. We classify the resolution methods in four broad categories : numerical, symbolic, rule-oriented and graph-constructive solvers.

Numerical methods (Newton-Raphson's iteration, homotopy, gaussian elimination and so on) are $O(n^3)$ or worse (see [1,2,3,4]). Most numerical methods have difficulties for handling over- and under-constrained schemes.

Symbolic methods (Gröbner bases, elimination with resultants) are typically exponential in time and space (see [5,6]). They can be used only for small systems. According to Lazard [7], computing the Gröbner bases of an irreducible system of degree two in ten unknowns is a hopeless case.

Rule-based solvers rely on the predicates formulation (see [8,9,10,11]). Although they provide a qualitative study of geometric constraints, the "huge" amount of computations needed (exhaustive searching and matching) make them inappropriate for real world applications.

Graph-constructive solvers are stemming from graph theory. They are based on an analysis of the structure of the constraint graph. The graph constructive approach provides means for developing sound and efficient algorithms (see [12,13,14]). Owen [15], Fudos and Hoffman [16], Lamure and Michelucci [17] give quadratic algorithms for solving constrained schemes.

In this paper, we describe a 2D constraint-based modeller that uses a graph constructive approach to solve systems of geometric constraints. We present a linear algorithm that solves a large subset of the rule and compass constructive problems. We also give efficient methods for isolating over- and under-constrained schemes.

This paper is organised as follows. The graph representation of the constraint problem is explained in section 2. We present in section 3, the core algorithm that handles structurally well-constrained problems. The phase for isolating over- and under-constrained schemes is given in section 4. We describe in section 5, our constraint-based modeller. Section 6 gives conclusions.

2. Constraints and graphs

2.1 Graph representation

Geometric modelling by constraints enables users to describe geometric elements such as points, lines, circles, line segments and circular arcs by a set of required relationships of distance, angle, incidence, tangency, parallelism and perpendicularity. With some pre-processing, the geometric elements are reduced to points and lines, and the constraints to those of distance and angle (see [18]).

We use an undirected graph G=(V,E) where |V|=n and |E|=m to represent the constraint problem. The geometric elements are represented by the graph nodes and the constraints are the graph edges. The edges are labelled with the values of the distance and angle dimensions.

Example 1 :

A dimensioning scheme defining a constraint problem is shown in figure 1. It involves six points and six lines. The constraints are six point-point distances, three line-line angles, twelve point-line implicit distances that are zero. The corresponding constraint graph is shown in figure 2. The unlabeled edges correspond to the implicit point-line distances.

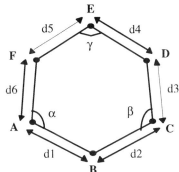

Figure 1. A constraint problem.

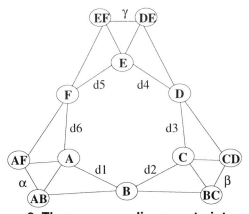

Figure 2. The corresponding constraint graph.

2.2 Graph structure analysis

Let us now give some definitions concerning the structural properties of the constraint graph.

Definition 1

A constraint graph G=(V,E) where |V|=n and |E|=m is structurally well-constrained if and only if m=2*n-3 and m' ≤ 2*n'-3 for any induced subgraph G'=(V',E') where |V'|=n' and |E'|=m' (see [19]).

Definition 2

A constraint graph G=(V,E) contains a structurally over-constrained part if there is an induced subgraph G'=(V',E') having more than 2*n'-3 edges.

Definition 3

A constraint graph G=(V,E) is structurally under-constrained if is not over-constrained and the number of edges is less than 2*n-3.

Note that a constraint graph can have over- and under-constrained parts. An example is shown in figure 3.

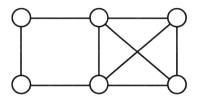

Figure 3. Over- and under-constrained parts.

The graph constructive approach uses only the structure of the constraint graph and forgets numerical informations. A constraint graph can be structurally well-constrained but numerically under constrained. The dimensioned scheme shown in figure 4 (left) is numerically under-constrained (the edges are labelled with distance arguments). Its corresponding constraint graph shown in figure 4 (right) is structurally well-constrained.

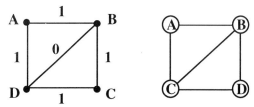

Figure 4. An under-constrained problem (left), and its associated constraint graph (right).

Nonetheless, with the graph constructive approach, such cases will be detected during the construction phase.

3. Solving the constraints

3.1. Basic clusters formation

The first phase of the algorithm is the formation of what we call "basic clusters". A cluster is a rigid geometric structure whose elements are known relatively to each other. A basic cluster is obtained by the algorithm given below. The nodes (geometric elements) and the edges (geometric constraints) are initially unmarked.

Algorithm :
1. Pick an unmarked edge (constraint) ;
   Mark the edge ;
   Pin the two geometric elements related by the constraint being marked ;
   Mark the two geometric elements to belong to a new basic cluster BCi
   (the two geometric elements are now known).
2. Repeat the following :
   if there is a geometric element with two unmarked constraints related to known elements
   then mark the two constraints ;
   mark the geometric element to belong to the basic cluster Bci ;
   place this element by a constructive step (this geometric element is now known).

The placement steps correspond to standardised geometric construction steps (place a point at given distances from two points, place a line at prescribed angle from another line through a point, …). When placing a geometric element, our solver uses some rules to choose the "best" solution. We assume that the constraint problem has been specified by a user-prepared sketch. The distance and angle arguments are signed quantities. The solution, automatically chosen, is the one that preserves the topological order given by the sketch. If these rules fail, the solutions are browsed and the user selects one of them.

To form all the basic clusters steps 1 and 2 are repeated until no unmarked edge can be found. The goal is to systematically "visit" all the edges of the constraint graph.. Step 2 uses a recursive procedure to form a basic cluster. During this step, we check the unmarked edges related to known elements of the basic cluster being considered to see if two of them lead to a same node. If so this node is added to the basic cluster and the edges marked. The first phase can be computed in linear time using a simple variation of depth first search. Each cluster is placed in a local co-ordinate system. Note that a geometric element can belong to several basic clusters.

Example 2 :
To illustrate the process, consider the constraint graph of figure 2. Three basic clusters are found C1, C2 and C3 (see figure 5). The geometric elements B, D and F belong each to two clusters : the point B to (C1,C3), the point D to (C2,C3) and the points F to (C1,C2).

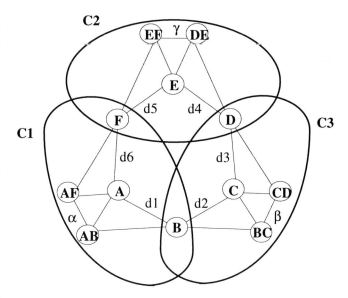

Figure 5. Clusters of the graph.

3.2. The skeleton of the constraint graph.

The second phase of the algorithm is to construct the skeleton of the constraint graph. The skeleton is a graph Gs=(Vs,Es) which is obtained by the algorithm given below.

Algorithm :
1. The nodes Vs of the skeleton are the nodes of the constraint graph that belong to several basic clusters (these nodes are marked with at least two basic clusters names).
2. The edges Es of the skeleton are obtained as follows :
   Es=∅;
   For each basic cluster Ci
   Do pick the nodes {N1,N2,…,Nj} of Ci that belong to Vs;
   triangulate the set {N1,N2,…,Nj} by doing:
   Add* edge (N1,N2) to Es;
   For k=3 to j
   Do Add* edges (Nk,Nk-1) and (Nk,Nk-2) to Es;

If an added edge (s,t) to Es is not a member of the initial set of constraints then we insert a "virtual" constraint whose value is easily determined because the nodes s and t belong to a rigid structure (a basic cluster).

The graph skeleton (of problems solved by our algorithm) is a basic cluster. All its nodes are placed in the plane. The skeleton can be empty if the constraint graph consist of only one basic cluster (the final configuration is then directly obtained).

Example 3 :

To better illustrate this phase, consider the constraint graph of figure 2. His skeleton is given in figure 6. All the edges of this skeleton are "virtual" constraints.

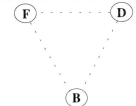

Figure 6. Skeleton of the previous constraint graph.

Example 4 :

Another constraint graph (the basic clusters are already formed) and its corresponding skeleton are shown in figure 7.

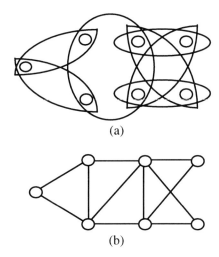

Figure 7. A constraint graph (a), and its corresponding skeleton (b).

3.3. Final computation phase

Once the nodes of the skeleton are placed (computed), each cluster is positioned relatively to the skeleton by computing the three required parameters (two transitional and one rotational). Note that each basic cluster share with the skeleton at least two nodes. The final scheme is then obtained.

Example 5 :

After placing the skeleton of the constraint graph given in figure 2, the three found basic clusters C1, C2 and C3 are positioned (rotated and translated) relatively to this skeleton (see figure 8).

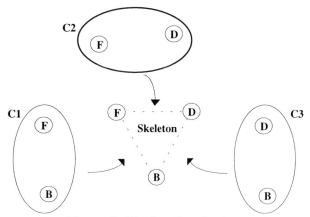

Figure 8. Placing the clusters.

4. Handling over- and under-constrained schemes

When designing, the first time, the sketch of a dimensioning scheme, the user often, over-constrains and under-constrains some geometric elements. Giving the following message "your constraint graph is over- or under-constrained" to the user when the graph contains more than 100 nodes is not sufficient. The "lazy" user (not only him) wants a message like "the point P_{99} is over-constrained and the line L_{24} is under constrained" so he can easily remove or add geometric constraints.

Detecting over- and under-constrained geometries in a constraint graph is an important part of a "good" constraint-based modeller.

By adding some extra checking to the algorithm of section 3.1, we can detect the extra-constraints in the same time bound. The extra-constraints are the constraints we shall remove so that the constraint graph will be well constrained. Before marking a constraint in step 1, we test if the two geometric elements related by this constraint belong to a same basic cluster. If so, the considered constraint is necessarily an extra-constraint (a basic cluster is a rigid geometric structure, so if we add another constraint between two of its nodes it become over-constrained). This constraint is removed and is not considered further.

Example 6 :

Consider the constraint graph given in figure 9 (left). We can have the marking shown in figure 9 (right). The crossed out edges belong to a basic cluster. The unmarked edge AC is the extra-constraint (the nodes A and C already belong to a basic cluster). Note that this marking is not unique.

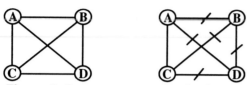

Figure 9. An over-constrained scheme.

Detecting under constrained schemes is a two steps process. First, we test the number of "links" between the basic clusters and the skeleton graph (we assume that the constraint graph is connected). A basic cluster B that is linked to the skeleton by one node N can move relatively to this skeleton. We must add a constraint, that do not involve the node N, between the cluster B and another cluster of the constraint graph so that the cluster B will be "firmly" attached (see example 7). In the second step, we form the basic clusters BCSi of the skeleton (if the skeleton is under-constrained we will have more than one basic cluster) and construct the meta-skeleton (skeleton of the initial skeleton). We then apply the first step to the BCSi and the meta-skeleton (see example 8).

Example 7 :

Consider the constraint-graph of figure 10. The basic clusters are : C1, C2, C3 and C4. In this example the skeleton is well-constrained.

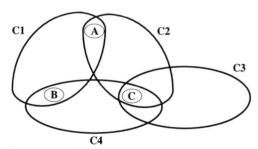

Figure 10. An under-constrained scheme.

The cluster C3 is linked to the skeleton by one node (the node C). We must add a constraint, that do not involve the node C, between the cluster C3 and another cluster (C1, C2 or C4) so that the entire configuration will be well constrained.

Example 8 :

Consider the skeleton graph given in figure 11.

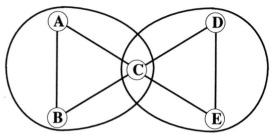

Figure 11. An under-constrained skeleton

This skeleton is under-constrained. The meta-skeleton is reduced to the node C. A constraint (that does not involve the node C) must be added between the two basic clusters of the skeleton so that it becomes well constrained.

5. A 2D constraint based modeller

We have implemented an experimental 2D constrained based modeller in C++ on an IBM PC compatible machine (CPU Pentium, 200 MHz and 32 Mo of RAM). The user creates points, lines, circles and specify constraints in an interactive way. The user can have directly the final solution (if there is one) of the constraint problem. He can also follow the resolution process step by step (clusters formation, visualisation of the skeleton). When the solver detect over- or under-constrained schemes, a message is delivered to the user showing him what he must do (adding or removing constraints between specified geometries).

For all configurations we have tested, our algorithm is faster than those of Owen[15] and Fudos [16]

A screen dump of a scheme solved by our algorithm is given in figure 12. This scheme involves seventeen circles, five points and four lines. The constraints are thirty one circle-circle distances, three line-circle distances and two point-circle distances that are zero, two point-point distances, three line-line angles, eight point-line implicit distances that are zero.

6. Conclusion

We have described and implemented a linear algorithm that solves a system of geometric constraints using a graph constructive approach. The class of configurations solved is a large subset of the rule and compass constructive problems. Over- and under-constrained schemes are also handled by this algorithm.

Our current interest is to extent the scope of the solver while keeping the same time bound for the core algorithm.

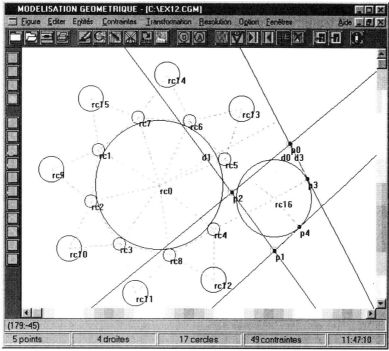

Figure 12. A screen dump of a constrained scheme

References

[1] D. Serrano. *Automatic Dimensioning in Design for Manufacturing.* Symposium on Solid Modeling Foundations and CAD/CAM Applications, 1991, pp. 379-386.

[2] E.L. Allgower and K. Georg. *Continuation and path following.* Acta Numerica, pages 1-64, 1993.

[3] A. Perez and D. Serrano. *Constraint base analysis tools for design.* Second Symposium on Solid Modeling Foundations and CAD/CAM Applications, Montreal Canada. May 93. pp. 281-290.

[4] H. Lamure and D. Michelucci. *Solving constraints by homotopy.* Symposium on Solid Modeling Foundations and CAD/CAM Applications. May 95. pp. 263-269.

[5] K. Kondo. *Algebraic method for manipulation of dimensional relationships in geometric models.* Computer Aided Design, 24 (3), pp. 141-147, March 1992.

[6] R. Anderl and R. Mendgen. *Parametric design and its impact on solid modeling applications.* Symposium on Solid Modeling and CAD/CAM Applic. May 95. pp. 1-12.

[7] D. Lazard. *Systems of algebraic equations : algorithms and complexity.* Rapport interne LITP 92.20, Mars 92.

[8] G. Sunde. *Specification of shape by dimensions and other geometric constraints.* Geometric modeling for CAD applications, pp. 199-213. North-Holland, IFIP, 1988.

[9] H. Suzuki, H. Ando and F. Kimura. *Variation of geometries based on a geometric-reasoning method.* Computer and Graphics, 14(2), pp. 211-224. 1990.

[10] P. Schreck. *Modélisation d'une figure géométrique adaptée aux problèmes de constructions.* Actes des journées GROPLAN'91, France 1991.

[11] A. Verroust, F. Schonek and D. Roller. *Rule-oriented method for parametrized computer-aided design.* Computer Aided Design, 24 (3), pp. 531-540, Oct. 1992.

[12] S. Ait-Aoudia, R. Jegou and D. Michelucci. *Reduction of constraint systems.* In Proceedings of Compugraphics, (Alvor, Portugal), pp. 83-92, 1993.

[13] W. Bouma, I. Fudos, C.M. Hoffman, J. Cai, R. Paige. *A geometric constraint solver.* Computer Aided Design, Vol. 27, No.6, June 1995, 487-501.

[14] I. Fudos. *Constraint solving for computer aided design.* Ph.D. Thesis, Dept. of Computer Science, Purdue University, Aug. 1995.

[15] J.C. Owen. *Algebraic Solution for Geometry from Dimensional Constraints.* Symposium on Solid Modeling Foundations and CAD/CAM Applications, 1991, pp. 397-407.

[16] I. Fudos, C.M. Hoffman. *A Graph-Constructive approach to Solving Systems of Geometric Constraints.* ACM Trans. on Graphics, Vol. 16, No. 2, April 1997, 179-216.

[17] H. Lamure and D. Michelucci. *Qualitative study of geometric constraints.* Geometric Constraint Solving and applications, B. Brüderlin and D. Roller editors, Springer-Verlag, 1998.

[18] I. Fudos. *Editable representation for 2D geometric design.* Master's thesis, Dept. of Computer Science, Purdue University, Dec. 1993.

[19] G. Laman. *On graphs and rigidity of plane skeletal structures.* Journal of Engineering Mathematics, vol. 4, num. 4, pp. 331-340, Oct. 1970.

Session 2-4

Design Visualization

Chair

Yuhua Luo

University of Balearic Islands, Spain

An Analysis of Architectural Visual Reasoning in Conceptual Sketching via Computational Sketch Analysis (CSA).

J. Mcfadzean, N.G.Cross and J.H.Johnson

The Open University, Department of Design & Innovation, Milton Keynes. MK7 6AA UK.

Abstract

Visual reasoning in design is facilitated by sketching. This research investigates how designers sketch, specifically analysing the physical details of mark making. It relates the graphical representations to the abstract cognitive processes of architectural design. A new form of protocol analysis has been developed using video and computer records of designers' sketching activity. The analysis of the resulting data compares the designer's retrospective commentary and interpretations of the sketching activity with the computer's record of that activity. The analysis will lead to a greater understanding of the relationships between 'Design Events' and 'Graphical Events' and thus how the notational activity of sketching supports the cognitive activity of conceptual design.

1. Introduction

Designers rely on sketching as a form of visual reasoning, especially in the early conceptual stages of the design process. Sketches clearly involve a complex interaction between external representation and cognition. Wiggins and Schon[25]; Akin[1][2] describe the need to sketch in order to conceptualise an architectural design problem space. Ullman, Wood and Craig[22] suggest that designers in general are especially notorious for not being able to think without making marks on paper. Sketches can be deconstructed in to lines, strokes and other marks[1]. The way in which the sketch is composed is defined here as the *graphical notation,* this includes both symbolic and non-symbolic externalisations. The ways in which marks are joined together to create forms is referred to in this paper as the *graphical notational language* of sketching.

---

[1] *Mark* is referred to here as the externalisation of a line, that is the movement from a point A to a point B, by a physical instrument i.e. a pen or pencil.

Protocol studies have been successfully used to analyse some aspects of design activity[3], but little research has been done to examine empirically the use of sketches during conceptual designing. One of the first studies to empirically examine sketches in relation to rational thought was carried out by Goldschmidt[12]. She found that design reasoning is characterised by the designers oscillation between two modes of thought: 'seeing as' which deals with figural arrangements and 'seeing that' which refers to non-figural issues that need to be resolved. Ellen Do[5][6] carried out three protocol analysis studies, which examined the verbal activity and more fundamentally the graphical notation of sketches. She examined 'what' designers draw, the kinds of shapes and symbols they use. The results indicated that designers share conventions in their use of symbols to represent objects, configurations, and functional concerns. Suwa and Tversky[20]; Suma Purcell and Gero[19] carried out protocol studies, with retrospective commentary. Their research found that sketches act as an external memory that can be inspected for visual cues relating to the identification of functional issues. These studies were instigated in order to elicit information about the graphical notation used by architectural designers during conceptual sketching.

This paper draws on the empirical evidence discussed above together with studies from design science[3] and cognitive psychology[8][9][11][14]. The research uses empirical studies of architectural design activity to develop a new computational method for the analysis of designers conceptual sketching activity.

This paper is based on a study designed to examine the representational mapping between the graphical notation used by designers in the early stages of conceptual designing and the cognitive systems that are activated whilst reasoning over a conceptual design problem space. The objective of the research is to understand how graphical notation is utilised as a problem resolution device and how it is used to define a design problem space.

This paper focuses on the analysis of cognitive processes, with specific emphasis on the use of sketching to aid visual and spatial reasoning. A secondary focal point of the paper is the sequential analysis of mark making generated during conceptual sketching.

2. Computational Sketch Analysis

'Computational Sketch Analysis' (CSA) for conceptual design has been developed in order to elicit graphical information at the micro level of sketching. Research carried out by McFadzean[16] has revealed that it is only by having a detailed computational representation of the design session that analysis can be carried out with objectivity and consistency. The results of past research have suggested that a more extensive and reliable data set can be extracted from computational experimental procedures[16]. For example, by using a computational approach, algorithms can be applied to the recorded design session that will extract quantitative data regarding:

a. The time spent drawing.
b. The time spent on each pencil mark.
c. The pressure of the pencil strokes.
d. The speed at which the marks are created.

The aim of the computational analytical approach is to record the generation of graphical notation used by designers in order to produce a rich source of data that allows the analysis of the use of graphical notation used in conceptual design. This allows the definition of a representation of the graphical notation used in sketching.

CSA consists of two functional pieces of software a *Data Collector* and a *Sketch Analyser*. The Data Collector captures and timestamps all the graphical data from the design session. The Sketch Analyser serves two functions. Firstly it acts as a record of the graphical notational activity which can be replayed to the designer retrospectively, for comments and analysis. Secondly the software is an analytical tool which builds graphical information structures in a hierarchical manner.

Because a stream of time-stamped co-ordinate data allows graphical events to be abstracted automatically CSA is a more appropriate method of data collection and analysis than previous methods of data collection for study of sketching activity. The new method of collecting data allows a rigorous and consistent analysis of the graphical notation used by designers.

3. Computational Sketching Analysis Experiment

The CSA experiment proposed four questions:

1. Can a predefined set of *Design Events*[2] account for the majority of the cognitive systems used in architectural problem solving?
2. Can *Design Events* be applied consistently to a designer's retrospective report of their conceptual design activity?
3. Can *Graphical Events*[3] be consistently and systematically identified in the architectural designers graphical notation?
4. Can the *Graphical Events* be systematically mapped to the Design Events?

The experimental set-up, shown in figure 1, is proposed to replicate a conventional sketching environment with additional facilities for data capture. A graphics tablet with plain or tracing paper overlay allows the designer to sketch normally.

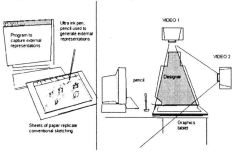

Figure 1. Apparatus set-up

There are two forms of data capture:

1. The Data Capture program collects and time-stamps the graphical data generated during a design session.
2. Video recorders capture the context of the design actions and verbalisations of the designers.

The data capture techniques and analyses of information throughout the design session are shown in Table 1

Five CSA experiments were undertaken using participants who were architects with between 2 and 20 years of professional experience. The experiments were all identical, lasting about one hour and consisted of two tasks; a design task and a retrospective report task. The

[2] *Design Events* are processes that manipulate chunks of information, representing important incidents that occur during the process of conceptual designing. Design Events are not considered to be mutually exclusive thus a chunk of information may have more than one Design Event attached to it.

[3] *Graphical Events* are processes that manipulate 'chunks' of graphical information that emerge out of the sketching activity.

Experimental procedure	Computer	Video 2	Video 3-retrospective analysis
3. Extract Data	Using the Sketch Analyser the experimenter investigates the graphical data for graphical events	Transcribe the video tape	Transcribe the video tape
4. Analyse	(Sketch Analyser) Automatic generation of graphical events	Investigate the tape for design events	Investigate the tape for design events

Table 1. The data capture and analysis procedures

design task asked the participants to design a smokers lodge (an outdoor shelter for smokers) for a University campus. Participants were given a design brief, after which they were taken to a site that could potentially house the lodge. On returning they were asked to produce conceptual designs, on an A3 graphics tablet and using a lead pencil on the paper provided. The task was recorded using the 'Data Collector'. Following the design task, the designers reviewed their sketching activity using the Sketch Analyser and they were asked to report on what they were thinking when they were generating the graphical notation.

A classification-encoding schema was derived from the design literature [7][18][21][10] and an initial interpretation of the retrospective report task, based on the idea of 'Design Events'. 'Design Events' are incidents that can be considered to be important because they change the state of the design problem space in a significant way. They are the verbalisations of cognitive operations that have taken place during the design process. Thus a set of 'Design Events' will not contain all verbal protocols; rather they are nominal data types that are associated with aspects of the designers verbalisations. An Example of a 'Design Event' is the use of sketches as an *External Memory Aid*. The classification-encoding schema suggests the following instance of such an event:

a. Exemplars are recalled from memory and either written or drawn so that they are stored as an external memory
b. The designer writes down a possible problem in order to deal with it later
c. The designer draws in order to aid recollection from memory.
d. The designer writes in order to visualise and record a concept.
e. The designer writes as a thought occurs.

A detailed discussion and analysis of Design Events is discussed by McFadzean, Cross and Johnson[17]. Nine Design Events define the classification-encoding schema:
1. External memory aid,
2. Emergence,
3. Requirements,

4. Abstraction of the Design Problem,
5. Reasoning,
6. Problem defining/ Resolving,
7. Reflection,
8. External Representations,
9. External visualisation Problems.

The results of the statistical analysis of the data, showed that the assessment of the participant's retrospective reports, in terms of the Design Events classification-encoding schema, allows a rigorous means by which to segment and encode verbal protocols. The approach also allows a rigorous and consistent analysis of architectural design activity and the use of visual and spatial reasoning in the early stages of conceptual designing[16]

4. Analysis of Visual and Spatial Reasoning

In the early stages of the design sessions the participants described a process of externalising symbolic information in order to place the design problem *in the mind*. From an analysis of the retrospective reports of all the participants, the process was one of externalising information in order to extract it from long-term memory. As demonstrated from the following quotes all participants set out the constraints, elaborated on elements of the brief, and on knowledge gained from other places.
[Participant 4]:
"Right well, firstly what's going on here is I'm writing down, in no particular order various thoughts that occur to me about the building, [in order] to try and sort of fix the thing in my mind. It's not the content it's the process that got me interested in it. [I jotted them down] to put them in my head. It was just a question of a sort of process of writing them down that sort of helps you clarify the things in your head."
[Participant 5]:
"Just to kind of remind myself of the context that I was going to be putting things into. I'm just trying to set the scene in my own head."

As has been previously suggested by Goldschmidt[12] at this point in the design process, there seems to be no logical sequence of decisions that stem from one another. In fact the participants seem to want to encourage non-linear thoughts that did not make the concepts concrete. [Participant 2]:

"I'm thinking about the main bits that are written in the text, about what is required. At this point [I was just drawing and writing] these icons so that I can refer back to them. I was thinking, or I think I had the pre-conception in my mind, [for] although you are trying to think really clearly and allow anything to spring into your mind it doesn't happen like that, because within seconds of anything unfortunately your brain has decided on things."

An analysis of the transcripts via the classification-encoding schema showed that the use of the Design Event - *External Memory aid* - was prevalent in the early stages of the design sessions and at this stage the use of graphical notation can be associated with non-linear reasoning within the design problem space. The results indicate that the representations generated to aid memory are used to influence the emergence of design in the following ways:

Emergence – The designer indicates that

a. A shape is derived from consideration of previously written text
b. By looking at a previously depicted shape a different or new shape emerges.
c. A Visual memory arises from text or a drawing.
d. 'A new' concept emerges out of the drawing or thinking about the text
e. A Shape arises from dimensions or structured reasoning

The results suggest that emergence is explicitly defined by the use and perception of graphical notation. This is in line with previous research carried out by Verstijnen[24]. Verstijnen found that sketching facilitates the perception of emergent properties that arise from changing the structure of an object. The research found that emergence was usually driven by the participants dissatisfaction with an aspect of the design. In these cases the graphical notation that was derived from emergence can be related to the participants verbalisations of the way in which the drawings were constructed. For example participants often used:

1. *re-representation* - the designer redraws a previously drawn visual element
2. *re-structuring* - the designer draws over existing lines or elements indicating important design features

Participant 5's reasoning, over an aspect of the design that was not considered to be satisfactory, resulted in the participant re-structuring and re-representing the design. This enabled the participant to make the transition from a conical shape to the emergence of two semi-circular arcs,

represented back-to-back. The participant's retrospective report of the reasoning is described below, along with the externalisations of their visual reasoning (Figure 2).

A. "A conical roof, a little round roof and light (Figure 2.1). I looked at it and I thought no that's too enclosing. You need a much more open form really... So then I started just thinking about how a curved form could be built (Figure 2.2). This sort of light... just little posts in the ground and then everything could be built of that. It's [about] visual affect, or was it [about] ventilation and opening? "

Q. You came up [here to the top of the page] and you've done these curves,

A. "Yes, I was trying to work out how I would put a roof over it (Figure 2.3). If I just had part of a curve then you have the problem of how do you...*(pause)*. You want some shelter from the rain and how do you hold that up? So I was trying to think of a sort of cantilever thing up here to see if I could hold it up like that."

Q. You wrote a comment on here, then you came down here and created a new representation.

A. "Yes, (Figure2.4) and it's similar to this one up here (Figure2.1). It's still really about that roof. I'm still worried about how I can economically hold that up because to do that it's actually quite expensive. Because it means things are hanging about in mid air like that."

A. "And the glaze roof at the top. And I'm going back (Figure2.4) and thinking about the form of it; what it will be. *(Pause)* And then I put the posts in there. It's the form I think I'm trying to sum really what I've been drawing here (Figure2.5), the thoughts that are going through my head"

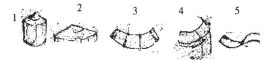

Figure 2. Graphical representations generated during participant 5's design session.

5. Eliciting Graphical Notation

The current research demonstrates new ways to describe and analyse the graphical notation of conceptual sketching. The 'Sketch Analyser' uses a representational schema to determine how sketches are constructed. The schema is derived from: Van Sommers[24] suggestion that drawings are constructed and constrained by a set of executive constraints, such as the preferred starting position and preferred stroke direction of a line, Ullman's, Wood and Craig[24] analysis of drawing and the results of observations from the authors early empirical research[16]. The lowest representation level is defined as types of *points(x)*. The next layer extracts the lines and trajectory information, in order to define sets of graphical notation. For example, 'a line set' may consist of the following object structures: *{linear_line(x), arc(x), circle(x), threaded_link(x), threaded_linear_line(x)}* (See Graph 1.) These lines then form sets of 'primitives' and sets of 'forms' that can be grouped together to produce sets of 'representations'.

Primitives=   *{corner(x),intersection(x),closed(x),*
                 recursive_link(x), open(x)}

Forms=   *{triangle(x),square(x),rectangle(x), polyhedron(x),*
               ∀x [(closed(x)]}

grouping=   *{proximity(x),distance(x),near(x),adjoining(x),*
               collinearity(x), linkage(x)}

$$representation = \{X | \sum_{n=1} \sum_{x=0} line\,(x_n\,)rajectory \quad \forall x\ grouping(\,X\,)$$

$$Sketch = \{X | \sum_{n=1} \sum_{x=0} line(x_n\,)rajectory\,\}\ or$$

$$\sum_{x=0}^{n} representation(x_n)$$

6. Graphical Notation

At present there is no formal description of graphical notation in conceptual designing. This makes it difficult to analyse with any precision how and what designers draw. It seems essential to determine via analysis of the graphical notation, whether differentiation can be made between non-iconic systems such as writing and numbering and iconic systems, in a way that will reflect perceptual constraints such as differentiation between shapes, elements, strings, and actions. For example, the difference in the spatial frequency of drawing, and writing allows the classification of a graphical text mark and a line drawing mark, permitting the separation of these marks from each other.

This aspect of the research investigates *how* designers sketch, specifically analysing the physical details of mark making and they marks are constructed to form sketch

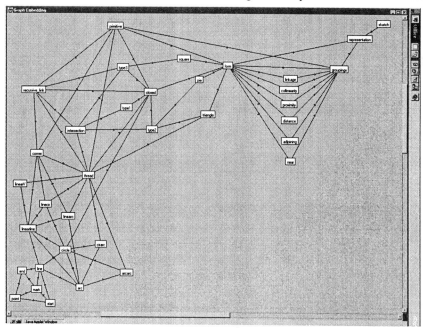

Graph 1. Graph diagram of the hierarchical structures that build up the sketch

A sketch may be constructed from 'all the lines on a sheet of paper' or equivalently 'the set of representations'. Graph 1 shows how the sketch is built up in a hierarchical manner.

representations (Graph 1). Figure 3a-3c shows the sequential analysis of sketches by a designer and the extraction of the order and context of the graphical notation and the extraction of single marks based on the 'representational schema' discussed above.

262

Figure 3a. Sketches by a designer

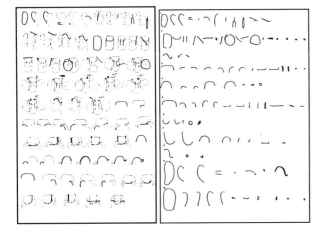

Figure 3b. Extracting representations, Figure 3c. Extraction of marks.

In this instance the deconstructing of the sketches activity revealed that the representational schema allows the perception of similar representations to be identified through rigorous analysis. For example, in Figure 3c line 4 and line 6 have similar constructional components and can be perceived as similar representations in Figure 3a. Thus we are able to trace the designers evolution of the conceptual design problem space and the designers visual reasoning over graphical notation of the external representations.

The participants of the CSA experiment used many different forms of mark making. Examples of the Sketch Analyser's records from a participant's design session are shown in Figure 4.

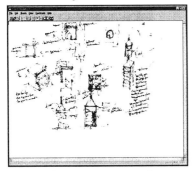

Figure 4. Graphical representations generated during a participants design session

From a literature review of the principle investigators in the field of drawing analysis[13][15][22][24] a graphical classification-encoding schema has been derived based on the salient principles that govern drawing. Examples of the taxonomy of salient graphical principles are presented in Table 2.

7. Mapping Notation and Cognition in Conceptual Design

Ullman, Wood and Craig[22] claim there is strong evidence to support the idea that drawings utilise cognitive chunks of information and that each drawing action represents a separate feature of the design. They assume that when the designer is generating graphical notation they are manipulating cognitive chunks. Ullman, Wood and Craig [22] proposed that this manipulation of information in a designer's head can only be studied through an analysis of his or her representation of these features as text written text, words, drawing or gestures.

The research presented in this paper maps the sketching of external representation with the abstract cognitive processes used in the early stages of architectural design. It is hypothesised that these mappings will allow the extraction of denotational sub-systems that relate the designers' mode of problem solving with the syntactic structure of the external representations. Thus showing that graphical notation in sketching is limited, constructed and constrained by the system of its intended use. An analysis of the mapping between Design Events and the Graphical Events addresses the question how does graphical notation enable us to understand the early stages of design? The overall aim of the research is to discover whether designers use a single notational language, inferring a general problem solving strategy or use multiple notational languages that may infer different problem solving strategies.

8. Conclusions

The evidence, from research in design science, design education and cognitive science suggest that sketching, within the design process, is a fundamental activity. It has been shown that sketching has properties that make it important in design. Understanding these complex aspects of design cognition requires rigorous methods of analysis of the graphical notational language of conceptual sketching. The research has suggested that visual reasoning and the ways in which it is aided by sketching activity needs more reliable methods of data capture and interpretation.

Graphical Principles	Types	Intentions
Marks	Non-iconic marks	Constraints, functional issues, problems
	Iconic marks	Used for recalling information used previously
		Copying a previously designed part over for detail
Graphical constraints	Starting position	
	Preferred stroke direction	
	Resisting anticipated embedding	
	Accretion	
Overdrawing	3 movements	
	Return overdraw	To extend the line
		(After a pause) recalling previous thoughts
	Overdrawing of faint lines	Global creation of drawing.
Drawing faintly		Possible used to draw to record
		Deliberate decision to use faint lines as a construction device
		Suggests a degree of caution
Tentativeness	Drawing faintly	As drawing faintly -as above
		Indecision
Non mark-marking, movements	Hovering	
	Moving towards and then away from the drawing area.	What to draw?
	Rehearsing an intended mark	Sizing / measuring

Table 2. A summary taxonomy of salient graphical principles

The research indicates that CSA as a method of data collection gives essential information, enabling new methods of 'sketch representation' to be developed. The CSA experimental results indicate that the application of the analytical methodology for the assessment of conceptual design activity provides a rigorous means by which to segment and encode graphical notation. The approach allows a consistent analysis of architectural design activity and the use of graphical notation in early conceptual design.

The research demonstrates the need for a notational language to be applied to graphical representations. The Data Collector and the Sketch Analyser address the following issues:

1. The extraction of non-symbolic information and the classification of this information into graphical units, based on knowledge of the graphical notation and cognitive processing of the information.

2. The appropriate development of a representation that can deal with;

- The represented sketch.
- The graphical notation of the sketch.
- The relationship between the concepts of the sketch and the facts inferred by the graphical notation.

A key suggestion of the paper is that designers sketching activity can be mapped to their cognitive processing of design information. This paper has suggested that CSA can be extended to construct a high level cognitive analysis, so that the designers evolution of the conceptual design problem space can be traced. However the method of CSA, used to determine how drawings map to the designers cognitive process needs more work. The mappings between the designers use of graphical notation and their cognitive processing of design information needs to be examined in closer detail. For example, the exact nature of the use of graphical notation to aid visual and spatial reasoning needs close scrutiny.

This research contributes towards design education and design science by gaining an insight into architectural design expertise, through its comprehensive understanding of the mapping between drawing, conceptualisation, cognition, and complex problem solving.

References

[1] Akin, O.:1993, Architects reasoning with structures and functions. *Environment and Planning B-planning and Design* 20(3), pp.273-294.

[2] Akin, O. and Lin, C.:1996, Design Protocol Data and Novel Design Decisions, *in* Cross, N., Christiaans, H. and Dorst, k.(eds), *Analysing Design Activity* , John Wiley & Sons Ltd., Chichester, pp. 35-63

[3] Clapin, H.:1998, *Visual Representation and Taxonomy*, proceedings of Visual Representation and Interpretation'98, Liverpool, Foresight Centre, Springer Verlag.

[4] Cross, N., Christiaans, H. and Dorst, K.(ed.):1996, *Analysing Design Activity*, John Wiley & Sons Ltd., Chichester.

[5] Do, E. and Gross, M.:1996, *Drawing as a Means to Design Reasoning*, Visual Representation, Reasoning and Interaction in Design Workshop notes, proceedings of Artificial Intelligence in Design'96, Stanford University.

[6] Do, E.:1995, *What's in a diagram that a computer should understand*? proceedings of The Global design Studio, CAAD Futures, National University of Singapore.

[7] Do, E. and Gross, M.:1997, *Thinking with Diagrams in Architectural Design*, proceedings of Thinking with Diagrams'97, University of Portsmouth.

[8] Do, E.:1998, *The Right Tool at the Right Time: Investigation of Freehand Drawing as an Interface to Knowledge Based Design Tools,* unpublished Ph.D, College of Architecture, Colorado, Georgia Institute of Technology..

[9] Ericsson, K. A. and H. A. Simon.:1993, *Protocol Analysis: verbal reports as data,* A Bradford book.

[10] Finke, R. A. and Slayton, K.:1988, Explorations of Creative Visual Synthesis in Mental Imagery, Memory & Cognition 16(3), pp.252 - 257.

[11] Finke, R. A.,Ward, T. and Smith.:1996, *Creative Cognition: Theory, Research and applications,* MIT Press.

[12] Fish, J.:1996, *How sketches work.,* unpublished Ph.D., Loughborough University of Technology.

[13] Goel, V.:1995, *Sketches of Thought,* Bradford Books.

[14] Goldschmidt, G.:1991, The dialects of Sketching, *Creativity of Research Journal* 4(2), pp.123-143.

[15] Jenkinson, L.:1990, *Architectural concepts design and drawing*, in Dept Architecture, unpublished M.Phil Thesis, University of Liverpool.

[16] Karniloff-Smith, A.:1995, *Beyond Modularity: A Developmental Perspective on Cognitive Science,* MIT Press.

[17] Mazijoglou, M., Scrivener, S. and Clark S.:1996, Representing Design Workshop Activity. .*in* Cross, N., Christiaans, H. and Dorst, k.(eds), *Analysing Design Activity*, John Wiley & Sons Ltd., Chichester, pp. 389-415

[18] McFadzean, J:1998, *Computational Support for Conceptual Sketching: An Analysis and Interpretation of the Graphical Notation of Visual Representations*, proceedings of Visual Representation and Interpretation'98, Liverpool, Foresight Centre, Springer Verlag.

[19] McFadzean, J., Cross, N. and Johnson, J.:1999, *Drawing and the Soliloquizing of Design Supposition.* proceedings of The 4th Design Thinking Research Symposium, MIT Press.

[20] Suwa, M., Gero, J. S. and Purcell, T. A.:1998a, *The roles of sketches in early design,* proceedings of the 20th Annual Conference of the Cognitive Science Society .

[21] Suwa, M., Purcell, T. and Gero, J.:1998b, Macroscopic Analysis of Design Processes based on a scheme for coding designers' cognitive actions, *Design Studies*, 19(4), pp.455-483.

[22] Suwa, M. and Tversky, B.:1997, What do architects and students perceive in their design sketches? A protocol analysis. *Design studies* 18(4), pp.385 - 403.

[23] Ullman, D.G.,Dietterich,T.G and Stauffer, L.A:1988,A Model of the Mechanical Design Process Based on Empirical Data, *AI EDAM* 2(1), pp.33-52.

[24] Ullman, D.G., Wood,S. and Craig,D.:1990, The Importance of Drawing in the Mechanical Design Process, *Computer & Graphics* 14(2), pp. 263-274.

[25] Van Sommers, P.:1984, *Drawing and Cognition,* Cambridge University Press, New York.

[26] Verstijnen, I.M.:1997, Sketches of Creative Discoveries: A psychological Inquiry into the role of Imagery and Sketching in creative Discovery Thesis Technische Universiteit Delft.

[27] Wiggins, G. and Schon, D.A.:1992, Kinds of Seeing and their Function in Designing, *Design Studies* 13(2), pp.135-156.

The Web as a Visual Design Medium

Dr. Rivka Oxman and Dr. Amnon Shabo
Faculty of Architecture and T.P.
Technion, Haifa, 3200, Israel.
e-mail: arrro01@technion.techunix.ac.il

ABSTRACT

One of the main problems of the web is its dominant textual characteristics. Since the natural way designers express their design ideas is in graphical form, accessing graphical information is a key issue. Since most of the design documents which are created today are products of CAD programs, our current research emphasis is upon indexing and retrieval of CAD documents on the WEB. In this paper we present an approach for the *utility and accessibility of* CAD-based design information. An approach for the use of CAD documents as a form of distributed case-based design resource on the web is proposed. Possibilities for employing case-based CAD as a theoretical foundation for building large design resource bases on the Web are presented.

Introduction

Despite the fact that the advancement of Web technology has contributed to a strong medium which assists the designer

particularly in the areas of information exchange and communication, it cannot yet be said to provide a design medium.

From a design point of view, the Web can currently be classified into three types of media.

a. The Web as an information medium

In its most common function, the Web is employed as an information medium, providing connectivity to, and representation of, information sources. Some common applications of *design information systems* are applications in product development, design resources etc.

Two. The web as a communication medium

266

Web applications which facilitate communication among individuals, members of distributed groups and teams exchanging information about design enhance the function of the Web as a communication medium. This facility is based on the use of Web tools for exchanging text, graphics, animation, or for running communications software in distributed computers. These types of applications have been employed in distributed design environments in which the members of the team located at different locations employed Internet technology as a medium to support communication and collaboration through sharing files.

c. The web as a social medium

As a result of enhancing communication between team members in distributed environments, the Web may now also be considered as a social medium. Designers can now meet in distributed and virtual environments and share their ideas and comments in real-time discussions. The content of design is built up by the team itself through the exploitation of tools such as interactive bulletin boards, discussion sessions, exchanges of graphical representations, collaboration protocols and personal images. These have contributed to interesting applications in various fields such as virtual design; virtual design studios; synchronic and asynchronic collaborative design, etc (Mitchell, 1995; Schmitt, 1988, Woo and Sasada, 1998). This class of medium involves intense information processing, immediate feedback and communicating knowledge in a simulation of face to face encounter.

Though these types of functionality through the Internet have rendered communication and distributed collaborations more effective, they have not resulted in fundamental changes in the way we actually do design. If one of the inherent characteristics of this new medium is the large volume of information which is available, how can we optimise the *utility for design* of Web-based information and how can we improve the *accessibility* of this information? With respect to these questions, we propose an approach to the use of CAD Case-Bases as a form of distributed design resource, and present certain of the possibilities for employing case-based CAD as a theoretical foundation for building large design resource bases in the Web. Furthermore, we exploit case-based technology as a basis for indexing and storage of design cases in a form which enhances the accessibility of design information.

2. Web - based design : accessing visual information

Vis-a-vis design information systems one of the main problems of the web is its dominant textual characteristics. The web does not yet support a graphical, or visual, environment the same way it supports a hypertextual environment for navigation and browsing. Since the natural way designers express their design ideas is in graphical form, accessing graphical information is a key issue. Therefor we should first consider the graphical properties of design information. What are its dominant graphical forms, how can they be represented, indexed, accessed and manipulated in the web? Since most of the design documents which are created today are products of CAD programs, our current research emphasis is upon these factors in distributed CAD documents.

CAD case-bases potentially provide a promising combination of CAD graphical files and case-based technology. Case-based reasoning has been adopted as a paradigm for design since it addresses various of the classical problems of knowledge representation, indexing and search. Current research and applications of web-technologies, systems for browsing, searching and sharing textual and graphical information share a high level of overlap with these key theoretical issues in case-based reasoning. The affinity of the web as a resource base and its relationship with case-based design has opened up possibilities of a new scale of design resource development. The web already functions as a large case-based system. Our work attempts to exploit these conditions by proposing a new format for design case representation which may be valid for the intrinsic characteristics of the web.

3. Distributed CAD Resources on the Web

We describe on-going research and development work on a CAD-based design case representation system that can provide a designer with relevant designs from a CAD-based design resource system in the web. The utility will work within a system which is based in the Internet and includes the following three modules: a repository of design cases (including CAD representations of cases), a Java designer's utility running on the client side, and a CAD program for local use.

In the following three sections we describe this system. In the first section we discuss certain issues related to the case-based factors; in the second section we discuss issues related to the CAD representation of cases, and finally, we present an integrative approach employing these as an integral system for a CAD case repository as a web-based design resource.

3.1 Representation in a design case-base

In prior research we have developed an approach to design case representation which is based on the theory of case-based reasoning (Kolodner, 1993). This approach to design case representation is intended to enhance the user's ability to efficiently search, access and exploit prior relevant designs. In this work (Oxman, 1994, 1997), we have attempted to identify the unique knowledge of design cases and have proposed a formalization of that knowledge. The representational formalism termed ICF (Issue-Concept-Form) represents chunks of case knowledge of design cases, and provides explicit linkages between the issues of a design problem, a particular solution concept and a related form description. As a representational formalism ICF was particularly suited to modelling designs. Furthermore, this formalism enhances textual search through semantic nets of issues and concepts in design domains. In order to assist in search and navigation among multiple cases in different locations on the web the ICF formalism has been implemented and enabled the sharing of design knowledge across the Web as well as the collaborative construction of "open design Web resources" which share this formalism.

If we define a case to be the entire design, then we have quite complex cases. However, if we define a case to be a particular component of a design, we then have designs represented by clusters of case components. In fact, we propose to take a layered case representation approach. On the one hand, we provide complete descriptions of the whole design, as well as descriptions of its separate components. The similarity measurement process can therefor be twofold: similarity processes at the component level are the basis for defining similarity at the complete case level.

These basic concepts are currently being realised in a CAD-based utility which uses the *multi-layered design case model*. Currently this model has three layers: the *project layer* which is an integrative layer providing a total representation and giving a cohesive framework to all documents related to a project; the *drawing layer* with graphical CAD representation of the entire design, and the *component (ICF) layer* with graphical CAD and textural representation of separate components of the drawing layer. In this lowest layer, we have proposed to make use of the ICF formalism and to expand it in order to integrate it with CAD drawings. Similarity measurements will take into account the similarity degree in each layer and will make use of a semantic network based on the ICF formalism.

At the highest, or project level, we can conceive of web-based project banks based upon CAD representation, but also supporting the ideational content of the component level. Thus we can underlay the graphical content of the CAD representation by the ideational content of issues and concepts. Using this formalism, a design case can be described by different issues of the design rationale which were addressed during its design. The project bank can also include the alternative representations which form part of the design history of the development of the design.

3.2 The CAD module

The model described in the previous section is based on the incorporation of CAD drawings within a design case representation. The design case is represented both by its graphical and its textural content. With respect to the graphical representation, we propose to use the internal representation of the drawings created by CAD programs. In order to accommodate the structure of our three-layered model, we are currently experimenting with CAD programs which have a component model for representing drawings. A component model is a model where each drawing consists of components and each component is a customisable object with a rich set of attributes from geometric attributes through functional attributes.

3.3 Integrating the modules into an Internet system

It is quite difficult for a single designer to store his/her own case base and, even in a large architect's office, the diversity of cases is limited. Therefore, it appears to be logical to use the Internet as the medium for interchanging cases and constructing case bases around the globe. The Java programming language will be used as the main vehicle for integrating the CAD program with a utility that makes use of the multi-layered case base. The effective performance of any CBR system depends much on the richness of the case base, the richness of each case, and more importantly, the diversity and number of cases. The way this could be done is as follows. The utility we are developing is a Java Applet running either within a CAD program such as MicroStation/J or in a Web browser such as Netscape. However, the case-bases with the actual repository of cases could be either local or on the Internet. When the utility starts a search for similar designs, it looks first into a local case-base (if any), and then proceeds to other case-bases on the net. In a crawling algorithm, the utility is looking for cases that satisfy a requirement for similarity beyond a certain threshold. The utility can access other case-bases only if it has the right privileges. Each designer or a designers' site develops their own case-base and can decide whether it is world- wide readable or perhaps restricted to certain users who certify the use of their case-base in exchange.

A central site, could hold an updated index of case-bases so that each running utility could know where the available case-bases are located. The priority of search and the creditability of different sites will be defined by each user. A user can decide, for example, to direct the utility to look for similar cases in various sites according to a certain priority, since the user attributes credit to these sites only and is not interested in other sites

4. Conclusions

The significance of new web technologies for the design potential of inter-activity with distributed CAD resources appears to be a major issue for the next generation of design resources in the web. How to use the Web as a design medium, and how to actually realise distributed design environments appear to us to be questions of great relevance. Solution for these issues can be based upon a case-based approach. We have described our work on the formalization of design case representations which integrates CAD representations with textural content. The future of web-based design repositories depends upon their utility. We have proposed that such design repositories must successfully integrate CAD representations with the information and data which underlies those drawings. This is, in fact, a general problem in CAD. The success of a web-based design resource will depend also on the power of the representational system. It is this combination of factors (graphical-textural interaction; powerful design representational systems) which can attract the collaboration of others. In the open system of the web, collaboration by emulation may be a way to large co-operative design resource bases.

Acknowledgments

The theoretical research and experimental implementations was supported by the German DFG grant. It was also supported by the Technion research fund. This paper is a modified version of a paper submitted to an ICED - 99 workshop on web-based design in Munich.

References

1. Rodger P. (ed) (1988) AID Workshop on Distributed Web-Based AI Design Tools, Lisbon, Portugal

2. Kolodner, J. (1993). Case Based Reasoning. Morgan Kaufmann Publishers, San Mateo, CA, .

3. Mitchell, W. (1995)"The Global Design Studio", in CAAD Futures 95, (eds. Milton and Robert T.) Singapore

4. Oxman Rivka E. (1994). "Precedents in Design: a Computational Model for the Organization of Precedent Knowledge" Design Studies, Vol. 15, No. 2, pp. 141 - 157

5. Oxman Rivka E. (1997). Shared Design Web-Space. International Journal of Design Computing.

6. Oxman Rivka E and Shabo A. (1999) Enabling the WEb as a design medium, in a workshop on web-based design in an International Conference on Engineering Design, ICED 99

7. Schmitt, G. (1988), Design and Construction as Computer-Augmented Intelligence Processes, in CAADRIA'98 Third International on CAAD Education, (eds T. Sasada, S. Yamaguchi, M. Morozumi, A. Kaga, R. Homma) Japan

Interaction with the Reorderable Matrix

Harri Siirtola
Human-Computer Interaction Group
Department of Computer Science
University of Tampere
P.O. Box 607
FIN-33101 Tampere, Finland
+358-40-5488700
hs@cs.uta.fi

Abstract

The Reorderable Matrix is a simple visualization method for quantitative tabular data. This paper examines how first-time users interact with the Reorderable Matrix and how well they perform a simple task of finding correlating attributes. Visualizing a set of data is a common task in various activities such as decision-making or opinion-forming. Typical situations are a person making business-related decisions, a doctor examining test results of a patient or an engineer making choices between different constructs. All these situations involve examining complex data interactions in a limited time. In this experiment the participants were interacting with the Reorderable Matrix for the first time and tried to find correlating attributes from an unfamiliar set of data.

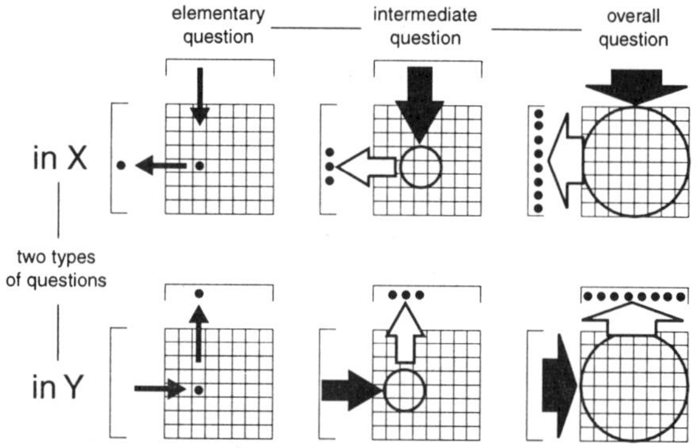

Figure 1. Three levels of information: elementary, intermediate and overall [1, p. 13].

1. Introduction

Jacques Bertin wrote a book called *Graphics and Graphic Information Processing* [1] over 30 years ago. In that book, he presents a method for studying a data matrix with an interactive visualization method called the *Reorderable Matrix* (also known as the *Permutation Matrix*). The basic idea is to replace numeric cell values with appropriately sized ink blobs and to allow the user to change the row and the column orders of the data matrix. Although this sounds trivial, it allows the user to explore the data set in surprisingly powerful ways.

The Reorderable Matrix is not generally implemented in commercial products, but it has been used in experimental tools (e.g. *VisuLab* [6] and *Table Lens* [4]) and it has inspired new visualization techniques (e.g. *Survey Plots* in *INSPECT* [3]).

Bertin's foundation is that *information is a relationship*. Graphical information processing is about revealing these relationships among data elements, data subsets or data sets. Visualization of a data set must be such that these three levels are retained. Fig. 1 illustrates how the Reorderable Matrix displays these three levels in graphical representation.

Reordering rows and columns allows us to see similarities and sets in the underlying data. Bertin claims that this is a natural characteristic of human vision and visual perception and does not require any special skills.

This paper describes the results of an experimental study in which the users interacted with the Reorderable Matrix. The idea was to introduce the Reorderable Matrix to persons who had no prior experience with it and to study how they would interact with it. Interaction was evaluated from the perspective of usability.

2. Reorderable Matrix

The Reorderable matrix is a simple interactive visualization artifact (IVA) for tabular data. It is the unifying concept throughout Bertin's work. This construction places multivariate data into a matrix with attributes along the x-axis and objects along the y-axis. Attributes can be defined in different domains and attributes can have different types (continuous, discrete, ordinal). Table 2 in the appendix presents a typical data matrix that can be visualized using the Reorderable Matrix. The visualization can be seen in Fig. 2.

Figure 2. Table 2 as a Reorderable Matrix.

Table 2 contains monthly data compiled from an imaginary hotel. The data contains various numbers describing the clientele, varying in nationality, profession and age to the average price of room and the average length of stay. Most of the numbers are percent figures, except for the average length of stay, the average price of rooms and the information if there was a convention during that month or not. The average length of stay is given in days and the average price of room is, presumably, given in the local currency. Hotel management would use this kind of data to design marketing, to define price structure, and to plan services offered for the customers.

On each row of the visualization the largest value (or values) is displayed with a completely black square and the smallest value (or values) is shown as an empty square. Values in between are shown as a black circle. The size of the circle is in proportion to the smallest and the largest value.

There are several variations on how to display a Reorderable Matrix. Bertin himself gave a few of them in his book

[1, pp. 23, 44, 80], and more have been proposed. One particularly interesting variation is to color-code the values below and above average with different colors [5].

2.1. Operations

Users can manipulate the Reorderable Matrix with four simple operations:

† Rows and columns can be dragged into a new position.

† Rows and columns can be sorted in an ascending or a descending order.

Dragging a row into a new position changes the order in which the attributes are listed. Sorting a column has the same effect. Likewise, dragging a column into a new position or sorting a row changes the order of columns.

3. An Empirical Study

Eleven participants (5 women, 6 men) were used in the study. All participants were fluent computer users and the majority of the participants had research interests related to user interfaces and usability. None of the participants had read Bertin's book, nor were familiar with Bertin's work in general.

3.1. Test setting

A simple implementation of the Reorderable Matrix was constructed as a standalone Java program. The program was instrumented to collect all events of interest and to log them with time-stamps with a resolution of one millisecond.

The user interface has simple controls. Dragging inside the Reorderable Matrix will move the row or column underneath. As a side-effect, it is also possible to drag a row and a column simultaneously. A mouse click just outside the matrix denotes a sort operation, depending on where the user clicked. Fig. 3 illustrates sorting a row into an ascending and a descending order.

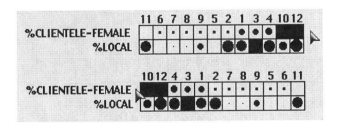

Figure 3. Sorting a row into ascending and a descending order.

The remaining controls are Undo and Redo, displayed as buttons with arrows pointing either backward or forward, and buttons that reset the matrix into its initial state. The initial state is defined by the order in the data file.

Figure 4. The user interface.

Fig. 4 also illustrates a situation where the matrix has been arranged row-wise according to column 1.

Data from Bertin's hotel example (Table 2) was used as test material. Table 3 at the end of this article contains the correlation matrix for Table 2.

The strongest correlation in Table 2 is the negative correlation between the percentage of tourists and the percentage of businessmen.

Fig. 5 illustrates how the Reorderable Matrix visualizes correlating objects. Strong correlation coefficients, having an absolute value close to 1.00, are quite easy to see, but weaker correlation is much harder to detect. The correlation coefficient for the pair % TOURISTS vs. % BUSINESS-MEN is ¡1.00, and the correlation coefficient for the pair % CLIENTELE FEMALE vs. % CLIENTS UNDER 20 is +0.81.

3.2. Procedure

Each participant saw the test matrix in numerical form, and the meaning of each attribute was explained to the participants. Participants had the chance to ask questions and

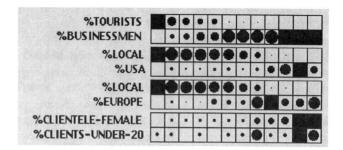

Figure 5. Correlation coefficients in the Reorderable Matrix.

to make sure they understood the data.

In the next step the test program was shown and the available operations were demonstrated. Again, the participants had the chance to ask questions and to try out briefly the features in the user interface.

The test task was formulated as follows: *"Try to find as many as possible correlating attributes in twenty minutes. Two attributes are correlating if one attribute's values have a rising or falling trend while the other attribute also has either a rising or a falling trend. As soon as you detect either a positive or a negative correlation, mention it, and move on. If you see anything else of interest, you may also mention it."*

While the participants examined the data with the Reorderable Matrix, the screen display was captured and the subjects' remarks were recorded. After a twenty minute test session, the participant was interviewed.

The test task corresponds to Bertin's levels two and three, answering intermediate and overall questions about the set of data. A typical intermediate level discovery from Table 2 was "there seems to be a negative correlation between the percentage of tourists and the percentage of businessmen". Likewise, a typical overall level finding was "the room price is at its lowest during summer".

4. Results

4.1. Interviews

Subjective user satisfaction was clearly positive. Only two of the participants announced that they didn't like to use this kind of interface, and doubted its general usefulness. On the other hand, the rest of the participants found the Reorderable Matrix to be *interesting*, *exciting* or otherwise positive.

Almost all of the participants said that the Reorderable Matrix was easy to use. The only operation difficult to grasp was the simultaneous moving of a row and a column. Most of the subjects left this feature unused, and those who used it, might have done so unintendedly. One exception was a participant who used this feature a lot and with success. He presumably had a good mental model for moving rows and columns simultaneously that the others lacked.

Some participants were worried that the lack of domain knowledge might have hindered their performance. They expressed this usually by saying that "I wish I had my own data to operate with". However, none of the participants had ever run a hotel, so this problem affected everyone.

The most common comment on the user interface was about visibility. The test program did not indicate where to click for the sort operations and during the drag operations there was no feedback. Because of the pre-test briefing, feedback was not considered a problem during tests. But clearly a proper feedback is needed for a high quality implementation.

Many of the participants mentioned grouping. They wished either to move rows as one group, or to color or highlight a group. The reason for this wish was that the data contained obvious groups, like the nationalities or age groups of the clientele. Since sorting moves rows into new positions, a differently colored or otherwise highlighted group would have stood out and made visual scanning more efficient.

4.2. Operation patterns

Program instrumentation shows that the participants can be classified into four categories according to the two most frequently used operations. Table 1 summarizes this data.

Category	Number of participants	Pattern
1	4	MOVE ROW / SORT ROW
2	3	SORT ROW / MOVE ROW
3	3	SORT ROW / SORT COLUMN
4	1	MOVE ROW / MOVE COLUMN

Table 1. Patterns in operation use.

The most common strategy was to sort the Reorderable Matrix along one of the rows, then move the similar or the contradicting rows to inspect the situation.

The participants in category 1 did more MOVE ROW-operations than SORT ROW-operations. These participants performed a sort operation and then took their time to arrange the visualization into a more readable setting. This approach is similar to the strategy that Bertin suggests in his book. However, the goal state of the arrangement varied.

In category 2 the participants used a similar tactic as in category 1, except that they did not use as much effort to arrange the matrix after the sort operation. Because of this, they performed more SORT ROW-operations than MOVE ROW-operations.

Participants in category 3 performed mainly sort operations, either horizontally or vertically, and used very little effort to arrange the matrix after sorting. They performed a sort operation, scanned the new state visually, and moved on.

One of the participants chose not to use sorting at all and preferred to arrange the matrix by hand.

4.3. Goal states

The goal state is the preferred arrangement of the Reorderable Matrix before reading it. For some of the participants, the goal state was simply the state produced by a sort operation. But far more common was to do some arranging before reading, as Table 1 shows.

Four distinct strategies were observed. The most common one was to keep the reference row as the top row. The reference row was moved up either before or after the sort operation. Two other strategies were to keep the reference row in the bottom, or somewhere near the center of the matrix. One of the participants had a unique strategy: instead of keeping the reference row stationary, he moved it through the matrix and looked for similar ones.

Those participants who kept the reference row in the middle of the matrix were more apt to read the visualization backwards, i.e., to build a black area and then see what happened to be on those rows.

4.4. Performance

In this experiment the overall performance was estimated by looking at the strengths of pair-wise correlations that were observed. Correlation coefficients having an absolute value above 0.7 were included, meaning that the coefficient of determination was about 50% of the total variation. In other words, this means that the independent variable explains about 50% of the total variation of the dependent variable.

Table 4 tabulates the highest correlation values in Table 3 and lists how many of them each participant was able to discover. On the average, the participants were able to find about one third of the strongest correlations, and about one half of the participants discovered the only $_{i}$ 1.00 correlation coefficient. This is not bad considering that the data was unfamiliar and that the test time was only twenty minutes. Also, looking at Table 4, it is apparent that finding the positive correlation values was easier than finding the negative ones.

The visualization in Fig. 6 summarizes the performance-oriented results. It displays the operation frequency data from the program log file, and the observation and the correlation data. Correlating objects are presented as the number of pairs found, as the sum of all correlation coefficients, and as the average strength of correlation coefficients found. The absolute values of the correlation coefficients were used in all computations.

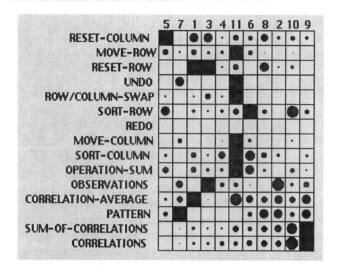

Figure 6. Test results as a Reorderable Matrix.

The interesting parts in Fig. 6 are the lower right and the upper left corners. As can be seen from the lower right corner, the participants who found the most correlating objects had also relatively high average correlation strength. All participants in this area used pattern 2 or pattern 3 in their operation. This seems to support the idea that careful reading is more productive than trying to produce the 'best' visualization for a given correlation.

5. Conclusions

The Reorderable Matrix is a simple and effective user interface to reveal relations in a set of data. Its strength lies in the fact that it takes advantage of the underused human visual system.

This study shows that the best strategy for a novice user to interpret a Reordable Matrix is to do a sort operation and then take some time to read the view. It seems that moving similar and complementary rows to their own groups is not worthwhile, although this was the approach that was originally recommended by Bertin [1, p. 38]. However, this

is only true for finding a pair of correlating attributes – for set-level discoveries such arranging is of course essential.

The Reorderable Matrix could be improved further by automating the arrangement after a sort operation, as Hinterberger has suggested [2]. If similar rows would move automatically next to each other, it would make the process faster and it would make harder to bypass the obvious dependencies.

Looking at the current state of the art in interactive visualization artifacts, it seems strange that the Reorderable Matrix is not widely used. It is simple to implement and most people learn to use it in a matter of minutes. The Reorderable Matrix visualization would be a nice feature for current spreadsheet programs, instead of those countless variations of static scatter, bar and pie charts.

6. Acknowledgements

I wish to thank my colleagues at the HCI Group and our students for participating in the experiment. This research was funded by a *TEKES (Technology Development Centre)* project on *Intelligent Management Information Systems (IMIS)*.

References

[1] J. Bertin. *Graphics and Graphic Information Processing.* Walter de Gruyter & Co., Berlin, 1981. (Originally *La graphique et le traitemente graphique de l'information*, 1967, translated in English by William J. Berg and Paul Scott).

[2] H. Hinterberger and C. Schmid. Reducing the influence of biased graphical perception with automatic permutation matrices. In *Proceedings of the Seventh Conference on the Scientific Use of Statistic-Software, SoftStat 93, Heidelberg.* Gustav Fischer Verlag, Stuttgart, Mar. 1993.

[3] H. Lohninger. Multivariate exploratory data analysis by means of INSPECT. In R. Moll, editor, *Software-Development in Chemistry*, volume 9, pages 91–98. GDCh, Frankfurt/Main, Germany, 1995. ISBN 3-924763-52-6.

[4] R. Rao and S. Card. The Table Lens: Merging graphical and symbolic representations in an interactive Focus+Context visualization for tabular data. In *Proceedings of CHI'94, Boston*, pages 318–322. ACM Press, 1994.

[5] C. Schmid and H. Hinterberger. Comparative multivariate visualization across conceptually different graphic displays. In *Proceedings of the Eight International Working Conference on Scientific and Statistical Database Management, SSDBM'94, Charlottesville, VA.* IEEE, Mar. 1994.

[6] C. Schmid and H. Hinterberger. VisuLab user's guide: User manual and tutorial. Technical report, Institute for Scientific Computing, ETH Zurich, Feb. 1995.

	1	2	3	4	5	6	7	8	9	10	11	12		
	26	21	26	28	20	20	20	20	20	40	15	40	1.	% CLIENTELE FEMALE
	69	70	77	71	37	36	39	39	55	60	68	72	2.	% CLIENTELE LOCAL
	7	6	3	6	23	14	19	14	9	6	8	8	3.	% CLIENTELE USA
	0	0	0	0	8	6	6	4	2	12	0	0	4.	% CLIENTELE SOUTH-AMERICA
	20	15	14	15	23	27	22	30	27	19	19	17	5.	% CLIENTELE EUROPE
	1	0	0	8	6	4	6	4	2	1	0	1	6.	% CLIENTELE M.EAST, AFRICA
	3	10	6	0	3	13	8	9	5	2	5	2	7.	% CLIENTELE ASIA
	78	80	85	86	85	87	70	76	87	85	87	80	8.	% BUSINESSMEN
	22	20	15	14	15	13	30	24	13	15	13	20	9.	% TOURISTS
	70	70	75	74	69	68	74	75	68	68	64	75	10.	% DIRECT RESERVATIONS
	20	18	19	17	27	27	19	19	26	27	21	15	11.	% AGENCY RESERVATIONS
	10	12	6	9	4	5	7	6	6	5	15	10	12.	% AIR CREWS
	2	2	4	2	2	1	1	2	2	4	2	5	13.	% CLIENTS UNDER 20 YEARS
	25	27	37	35	25	25	27	28	24	30	24	30	14.	% CLIENTS 20-35 YEARS
	48	49	42	48	54	55	53	51	55	46	55	43	15.	% CLIENTS 35-55 YEARS
	25	22	17	15	19	19	19	19	19	20	19	22	16.	% CLIENTS MORE THAN 55 YEARS
	163	167	166	174	152	155	145	170	157	174	165	158	17.	PRICE OF ROOMS
	1.65	1.71	1.65	1.91	1.9	2	1.54	1.60	1.73	1.82	1.66	1.44	18.	LENGTH OF STAY
	67	82	70	83	74	77	56	62	90	92	78	55	19.	% OCCUPANCY
				X	X	X			X	X	X	X	20.	CONVENTIONS

Table 2. The hotel example from Bertin's book [1].

	2.	3.	4.	5.	6.	7.	8.	9.	10.	11.	12.	13.	14.	15.	16.	17.	18.	19.	20.
1.	0,42	-0,42	0,18	-0,42	-0,18	-0,56	0,02	-0,02	0,33	0,33	-0,13	0,81	0,50	-0,78	0,19	0,34	-0,17	-0,02	0,23
2.		-0,89	-0,66	-0,83	-0,56	-0,48	0,24	-0,24	0,09	-0,54	0,61	0,59	0,50	-0,68	0,13	0,55	-0,29	0,15	-0,06
3.			0,52	0,52	0,62	0,25	-0,32	0,32	-0,03	0,36	-0,44	-0,52	-0,49	0,62	-0,07	-0,71	0,15	-0,34	0,07
4.				0,41	0,29	0,06	-0,01	0,01	-0,22	0,71	-0,68	-0,07	-0,19	0,24	-0,09	-0,16	0,39	0,21	0,25
5.					0,29	0,44	-0,12	0,12	-0,17	0,51	-0,48	-0,49	-0,61	0,68	0,02	-0,35	0,14	-0,07	0,08
6.						-0,09	-0,15	0,15	0,30	0,07	-0,42	-0,50	0,08	0,35	-0,53	-0,25	0,40	-0,11	0,18
7.							-0,21	0,21	-0,07	0,14	-0,10	-0,50	-0,32	0,40	0,05	-0,30	0,07	-0,13	-0,39
8.								-1,00	-0,54	0,49	-0,04	0,16	0,07	0,09	-0,37	0,32	0,64	0,73	0,71
9.									0,54	-0,49	0,04	-0,16	-0,07	-0,09	0,37	-0,32	-0,64	-0,73	-0,71
10.										-0,67	-0,23	0,30	0,67	-0,59	-0,18	0,03	-0,44	-0,62	-0,47
11.											-0,57	-0,26	-0,47	0,53	-0,07	-0,20	0,66	0,58	0,46
12.												0,01	-0,13	-0,04	0,30	0,23	-0,38	-0,06	-0,08
13.													0,54	-0,83	0,12	0,35	-0,39	-0,06	0,15
14.														-0,78	-0,04	0,49	-0,06	-0,06	-0,15
15.															-0,12	-0,46	0,37	0,21	0,25
16.																-0,14	-0,39	-0,25	-0,28
17.																	0,14	0,45	0,00
18.																		0,68	0,47
19.																			0,46

Table 3. Correlation matrix for Table 2.

1	2	3	4	5	6	7	8	9	10	11	Attributes	Corr. coeff.
x					x		x	x	x	x	% BUSINESSMEN – % TOURISTS	¡ 1:00
x										x	% CLIENTELE LOCAL – % CLIENTELE USA	¡ 0:89
										x	% CLIENTELE LOCAL – % CLIENTELE EUROPE	¡ 0:83
	x		x		x		x	x	x		% CLIENTELE FEMALE – % CLIENTS UNDER 20 YEARS	+0 :81
x											% CLIENTS UNDER 20 YEARS – % CLIENTS 35-55 YEARS	¡ 0:78
							x	x			% CLIENTELE FEMALE – % CLIENTS 35-55 YEARS	¡ 0:78
								x			% CLIENTS 20-35 YEARS – % CLIENTS 35-55 YEARS	¡ 0:78
	x										% BUSINESSMEN – % OCCUPANCY	+0 :73
											% TOURISTS – % OCCUPANCY	¡ 0:73
	x	x					x	x			% CLIENTELE SOUTH-AMERICA – % AGENCY RESERVATIONS	+0 :71
	x							x			% CLIENTELE USA – % PRICE OF ROOMS	¡ 0:71
x		x	x	x	x	x	x	x	x	x	% BUSINESSMEN – % CONVENTIONS	+0 :71
					x		x		x		% TOURISTS – % CONVENTIONS	¡ 0:71

Table 4. Highest correlation coefficients found by the participants.

Graphics & Visualization Fundamentals

Chair
Marcelo Dreux
PUC-Rio, Brazil

Triangle Mesh Compression for Fast Rendering[*]

Dong-Gyu Park, Yang-Soo Kim, Hwan-Gue Cho
Department of Computer Science, Pusan National University
Jang-Jun Dong, Keum-Jung Ku, Pusan, 609-735, Korea
e-mail : {dongupak,yskim,hgcho}@pearl.cs.pusan.ac.kr

Abstract

Modern GIS(Geographic Information System) application programs and simulation systems have to handle large datasets for rendering. Currently three dimensional rendering hardware are facing a memory bus bandwidth bottleneck problem at the graphics pipeline. One general solution for this problem is to compress the static three dimensional geometry in a preprocessing phase.

We present a new mesh compression/decompression algorithm for this application. Our compression algorithm breaks down a triangle mesh into a set of triangle strips and vertex chains. After decomposition, we encode vertex connectivity with entropy encoding. Our algorithm provides a 32% improvement in the compression ratio over existing "Generalized Triangle Mesh(GTM)" compression and supports parallel decompression. We also proposed a parallelogram prediction method for vertex coordinate compression.

1. Introduction

The volume of geometric models used in GIS and graphics applications is increasing. So many geometric datasets require a large amount of disk space. One main objective of geometric compression is to develop a fast and simple algorithm to handle those large geometric data. As the size of rendering data increases, a large amount of memory bus bandwidth is required for graphics display systems. We can see that rendering a 20 megabyte data model using a 30 Hz graphics display requires as much as 600 MB/sec of memory bus bandwidth. This transfer rate is beyond the capability of current low-cost graphics systems. So current three dimensional rendering hardware frequently face a memory bus bottleneck problem.

Compressing the static three dimensional geometric datasets through a pre-processing phase has been proposed

as a general solution of this problem. The geometric datasets are compressed and stored in main memory for real-time rendering, then they are sent to the rendering hardware for real-time decompression using a fast hardware decompressor[1]. For this rendering application, the hardware decompressor needs a fast and simple decoding algorithm.

"Generalized Triangle Mesh(GTM)" was first introduced by Deering, it consists of triangle strips and a mesh buffer to store the old vertices[2]. In GTM, interior vertices should be referenced twice to store the original triangle mesh. GTM has small queues(called mesh buffer) to reference old vertices in the triangle strip[2][3]. This technique needs $(1/8\lceil log_2(n)\rceil + 8)n$ bits to represent the connectivity information for a given triangle mesh[6]. Chow improved the performance of GTM using some heuristics[1].

Taubin have proposed an efficient method for geometric dataset compression using topological surgery[9]. He encoded total edge connectivity of the mesh about 2 bits per triangle. But this method needs a large amount of internal memory during decompression.

Touma proposed a new triangle mesh compression method created by exploiting triangle marching structure[10]. He uses a vertex connectivity code for compressing triangulation. The connectivity codes consists of "add", "split" and "merge". He encodes mesh connectivity as a list of vertex degrees in a special order, and this procedure requires a vertex stack to make the final triangles, where the edge connectivity is encoded by 1.5 bits/vertex.

Floriani has proposed a compression method based on shelling[8]. This method uses 2 bits for control codes, which are called "skip", "vertex", "left" and "right". He also proposed a progressive compression method in which the edge connectivity is encoded by 4.4 bits/vertex.

Gumhold has presented new compression algorithm which are fast enough for real time applications[5]. The connectivity is encoded about 1.7 bits/vertex and requires $10\sqrt{n}$ memory during compression and decompression.

Recently, Kim has proposed a new triangle mesh compression method based on Delaunay Triangulation[7]. The

[*]Authors wish to acknowledge the financial support of the Korea Research Foundation made in the Program Year 1999.

280

main feature of this compression method is that almost 90% of triangles are the same as in Delaunay triangulation.

Each compression method has trade-offs between compression ratio and compression/decompression time. Taubin, Floriani and Kim's methods need quite a long compression/decompression time. Since hardware decompressor supports only small register to store previous vertices, Taubin, Floriani, Kim, and Touma's algorithms will not satisfy real-time rendering constraints. So we will focus on Deering and Chow's method for real-time rendering[1].

2. Triangle strip decomposition

We define triangle strip T^i as a consecutive sequence of triangles $< t_0^i, t_1^i, \cdots, t_n^i >$ and vertex chain C^i as a consecutive sequence of vertices $< v_0^i, v_1^i, \cdots, v_n^i >$. In Figure 1, let $t_0 = \triangle(1, 6, 7)$, and $t_1 = \triangle(1, 2, 7)$, where $\triangle(v_i, v_j, v_k)$ denotes a triangle whose vertices are v_i, v_j, v_k. The triangle mesh M_o can be decomposed as a set of triangle strips $\{T^0, T^1, \cdots, T^n\}$.

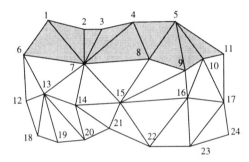

Figure 1. Triangle strip T^0 is constructed from a boundary vertex chain $< 1, 2, 3, 4, 5 >$. Also the second vertex chain is obtained from the first triangle strip.

Figure 1 shows the triangle strip construction step. The first triangle strip T^0 can be constructed from the first vertex chain $< 1, 2, 3, 4, 5 >$. All triangles in the first triangle strip T^0 are adjacent to the first vertex chain C^0. All triangles in T^0 are marked as "visited", and the second vertex chain $< 6, 7, 8, 9, 10, 11 >$ is obtained from T^0. We can make the next triangle strip T^1 from the second vertex chain C^1. This procedure continues till whole triangles are marked as "visited". Breaking down a triangle mesh into a set of triangle strips is very similar to the GTM algorithm and can be accomplished in linear time. A triangle strip can be made from a pair of vertex chains and edge connectivity information between those two vertex chains. Edge connectivity is represented by the degree of each vertex.

In Figure 1, vertex 6 has only one edge connection to the first vertex chain, vertex 7 has four edge connections.

We know that all vertices in a vertex chain are ordered by their adjacency. Therefore, vertex 6 is connected to vertex 1, vertex 7 is connected to vertex 1,2,3 and 4 in the first vertex chain. We restore vertex chains and degree of each vertex to reconstruct the triangle strips. One distinguishing difference with GTM is that our algorithm does not need to revisit the vertex chain to encode a triangle mesh. Table 1 shows the final encoding results of Figure 1.

vertex chain	vertex list	vertex degree
C^0	$< 1, 2, 3, 4, 5 >$	$< 0, 0, 0, 0, 0 >$
C^1	$< 6, 7, 8, 9, 10, 11 >$	$< 1, 4, 2, 1, 1, 1 >$
C^2	$< 12, 13, 14, 15, 16, 17 >$	$< 1, 2, 1, 3, 2, 2 >$
C^3	$< 18, 19, 20, 21, 22, 23, 24 >$	$< 2, 1, 2, 2, 2, 2, 1 >$

Table 1. Final encoding results of Figure 1.

2.1. Triangle strip encoding

We start with an arbitrary vertex from a given triangle mesh. Since the starting point has no connectivity to the previous vertex chain, the degree of starting vertex chain is 0. The next vertex chain is obtained from the starting vertex. We obtain the triangle strip from the previous vertex chain. The vertex degree is the number of connected edges between the current vertex and the previous vertex chain. The end of vertex chain has one dummy vertex for marking the end of vertex chain.

Because we only consider the edge connectivity between previous vertex chain and current vertex chain, the most common vertex degree of our algorithm is 2. Large number of vertex degree(e.g. 8,9,10) seldom appear in general meshes. The number of vertex degree has locality in our experiments, small degree numbers(e.g. 1,2,3) are about 95% of the total vertices. A sequence of vertex degrees is encoded with Huffman encoding to reduce disk storage[10]. After compression, mesh connectivity information can be broken down by ordered vertex set $\{v_0, v_1, \cdots, v_n\}$, and Huffman code $\{H(d(v_0)), H(d(v_1)), \cdots, H(d(v_n))\}$.

2.2. Decoding procedure

Here we will explain our decoding algorithm with small test data. Figure 2 shows an example of the decoding procedure.

Let C^k be a kth vertex chain and v_i^k be a ith vertex in C^k. The test data is encoded as a vertex chain $C^k = \{v_1^k, v_2^k, v_3^k, v_4^k\}$ and $C^{k-1} = \{v_1^{k-1}, v_2^{k-1}, v_3^{k-1}, v_4^{k-1}, v_5^{k-1}\}$, where $d(v_1^k) = 1$, $d(v_2^k) = 3$, $d(v_3^k) = 3$, and $d(v_4^k) = 1$. Triangle mesh is constructed from vertex chain C^k and previous vertex chain C^{k-1}.

The degree of vertex v_1^k is 1, so we can see that v_1^k has connection to v_1^{k-1}. We also know next vertex v_2^k is connected to v_1^k. This connectivity shows that vertex set $\{v_1^k, v_2^k, v_1^{k-1}\}$ consists of triangle T_1^{k-1}. The next vertex v_2^k has 3 edge connectivity to C^{k-1}. This fact tells us that v_2^k has connectivity to $v_1^{k-1}, v_2^{k-1}, v_3^{k-1}$ and the next vertex v_3^k. We can make triangles t_2^{k-1}, t_3^{k-1} and t_4^{k-1} from set of vertices $\{v_2^k, v_1^{k-1}, v_2^{k-1}\}$, $\{v_2^k, v_2^{k-1}, v_3^{k-1}\}$ and $\{v_2^k, v_3^{k-1}, v_3^k\}$.

At the end of the vertex chain, $d(v_4^k) =1$, but v_4^k does not have a following vertex. After making the final triangle, vertex chain C^k is assigned to the previous vertex chain and the next vertex chain C^{k+1} is constructed.

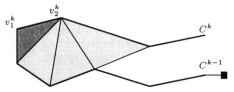

(a) Vertex v_1^k and v_2^k make 1 and 3 triangles, respectively.

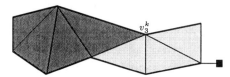

(b) d(v_3^k)=3, vertex v_3^k makes 3 triangles.

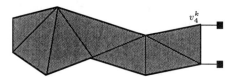

(c) d(v_4^k)=1, but v_4^k does not have following vertices.

Figure 2. A snapshot of decoding procedure.

Another advantage of our decompression method is that it supports parallel decompression. We can make a triangle strip from only two adjacent vertex chains.

Triangle strip T^{k-1} and T^k are made from vertex chain $\{C^{k-1}, C^k\}$ and $\{C^k, C^{k+1}\}$, respectively. Although C^k is referenced by T^{k-1} and T^k, vertices in C^{k-1}, C^k and C^{k+1} can be referenced independently. Therefore, triangles in T^{k-1} and T^k can be constructed using parallel algorithm.

3. Special cases: hole, pocket

In this section, we present some degenerated cases of our triangle strip algorithm and propose heuristics to improve the compression performance. We make a set of triangles

from the previous vertex chain. If one triangle strip has a pocket or hole, triangles in the next triangle strip are not adjacent to the current strip. So we have to handle these special cases. We define two degenerated cases of triangle strips.

- pocket - a set of triangles which are *not* isolated by vertex chain and not adjacent to the next vertex chain.

- hole - a set of triangles which are isolated by vertex chain.

If a pocket or hole is encoded in processing a vertex chain C^k, they must be marked to generate next triangle strip T^k, whose information is added to the current vertex. The basic assumption of our method is that all vertices in the vertex chain C^k and C^{k+1} are adjacent. But vertices in pockets and holes are not adjacent to the next vertex chain, and must be eliminated from current vertex chain.

If a pocket or hole is found, a skip code "S" and the number of vertices in a pocket or hole are inserted. If a vertex v_i in the current vertex chain C^k meets a skip code "S2", the set of vertices in C^k must be updated to a vertex chain $< \cdots, v_i, v_{i+3}, \cdots >$.

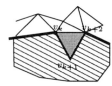 

(a) A triangle in the pocket can be constructed from skip code S1.

(b) Triangles in the pocket can be made from skip code(S2) and OP code C13.

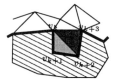

(c) Triangles in the pocket can be made from skip code(S2) and OP code C02.

(d) In this case, skip code S2 and OP code C12 cannot make any triangle.

Figure 3. A snapshot of skip code and OP code.

The triangles in the holes and pockets comprise about 10% of the total triangles, which are revisited after all of the triangles are made into a set of triangle strips. All vertices in these degenerated cases will be referenced twice in the mesh.

To achieve a high compression ratio, we must reduce this vertex reference in pockets and holes to improve compression performance. In our experiments, we found that more than 67% of pockets and holes have only one skip vertex. This example is shown in Figure 3 (a). Since vertex

v_k meets skip code S1, triangle $\triangle(v_k, v_{k+1}, v_{k+2})$ can be made using this implicit rule.

Furthermore, we find that more than 20% of pockets and holes have two skip vertices. If the vertex v_k meets skip code S2, there would be three kinds of degenerated cases. Figure 3 (b), (c) and (d) show all of the degenerated cases of skip code S2. Figure 3 (b) shows that two triangles $\triangle(v_k, v_{k+1}, v_{k+3})$ and $\triangle(v_{k+1}, v_{k+2}, v_{k+3})$ can be made from skip code and OP code C13. Also, Figure 3 (c) shows two triangles $\triangle(v_k, v_{k+1}, v_{k+2})$ and $\triangle(v_k, v_{k+2}, v_{k+3})$ can be made from skip code and OP code C02. In Figure 3 (d) skip code S2 meets OP code C12 and this kind of OP code cannot make additional triangles.

Additional OP codes are required for this description but significantly smaller than vertex references. Using those implicit rules, we can reduce revisited vertices.

Figure 4 shows an example of a run of our encoding algorithm.

4. Vertex coordinate compression

The vertices in triangle mesh have three coordinates information, normals and colors. The vertex compression technique was proposed by Deering[2].

The 8-bit exponent of 32-bit IEEE floating point numbers is used to represent the x, y, z coordinate. Deering proposed delta encoding to store the x, y, z coordinate. This compression is lossy but shows a good compression ratio by using data locality[2].

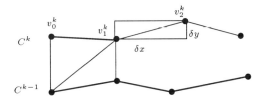

Figure 5. A snapshot of delta encoding.

Figure 5 shows an example of delta encoding. The vertex v_2^k in vertex chain C^k can be represented by the delta difference between v_1^k and v_2^k. The sum of difference value $(\delta x, \delta y, \delta z)$ and v_1^k is v_2^k. The delta difference between v_1^k and v_2^k is relatively small because they are neighborhood vertex in the same vertex chain C^k.

Taubin encoded the mesh vertex coordinates v_i by first quantizing the three vertex coordinates to a finite number of bits(8 bit is typical) by bounding the interval in which the coordinates lie[10]. The algorithm used a linear prediction scheme:

$$v_n = \epsilon(v_n) + P(\lambda, v_{n-1}, \ldots, v_{n-K})$$

The λ and the K are prediction parameters, and $v_{n-1}, \ldots, v_{n-K}$ are K ancestors of the vertex along the unique path to the vertex tree root.

Touma proposed a parallelogram prediction scheme. The method is based on their encoding scheme, using an "active list", whenever a new vertex is encoded, the existing triangle is used to predict the next vertex. He used a discrete "curvature" value to make a more accurate prediction value.

Our encoding scheme is similar to Touma's parallelogram rule. The basic assumption of our algorithm is that the curvature of a vertex chain C^k is very similar to the previous vertex chain C^{k-1} and next vertex chain C^{k+1}. Using this curvature, we can predict the coordinates of the next vertex.

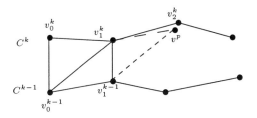

Figure 6. Parallelogram prediction.

Figure 6 shows our parallelogram prediction scheme. The next prediction position of a vertex v_1^k in vertex chain C^k is predicted by the parallelogram of a vertex v_0^{k-1} and the next vertex v_1^{k-1} in the previous vertex chain C^{k-1}. Using three vertices $\triangle(v_1^k, v_1^{k-1}, v_2^{k-1})$, we can predict the next vertex v_p using the parallelogram rule.

We measured the error value with three different methods. The experimental results show that the parallelogram rule gives 6%, 15% better prediction results compared with delta encoding and linear prediction, respectively.

5. Experiments

The experimental terrain data files were obtained from USGS(US Geographical Survey). The data were used by Garland for their experiments with the refinement algorithm in the SCAPE system[4]. The number of vertices in our test data is between 30,000 and 50,000.

Table 2 show the experimental results of our compression.

Table 3 shows our experimental results of decoding time. Execution time was obtained on an SGI O2 workstation, which has a MIPS R5000 180MHz single processor and 256MB of main memory. The test data are the same as in table 2. The experimental results show that over 1,466,996 faces are decoded in one second. Our decompression time outperforms the other compression algorithms. Compared with the Gumhold's algorithm, which was run on a similar

model	vertex	face	conn.(bits)	bits/vert.	bits/face
Ashby	50,000	99,468	302,904	6.05	3.04
Crater	50,000	99,472	310,912	6.21	3.13
GrandCa'n	50,000	99,697	310,120	6.20	3.11
Spokane-w	30,000	59,721	224,390	7.47	3.75
Yakima-e	50,000	99,637	341,720	6.83	3.42
Yakima-w	30,000	59,713	218,992	7.29	3.66

Table 2. Experimental results of the mesh compression.

model	face	decompression time(sec)		face/sec
		reading time	decoding time	
Ashby	99,468	3,13	0.070	1,420,971
Crater	99,472	3.32	0.079	1,259,139
GrandCa'n	99,697	3.22	0.059	1,689,780
Spokane-w	59,721	1.98	0.059	1,688,305
Yakima-e	99,637	3.26	0.070	1,261,228
Yakima-w	59,713	1.98	0.059	1,688,458

Table 3. Experimental results of decompression time. Our algorithm decodes average 1,466,996 faces per second and read average 30,299 faces per second from disk.

machine(O2 workstation), they decoded average 800,000 faces per second[8].

Figure 7 show the visualized results of Crater Lake. All test data were encoded and decoded on an SGI O2 workstation and visualized with Open Inventor library and Java3D, respectively.

6. Conclusions

We proposed a new algorithm for compressing/decompressing large triangle meshes for real-time rendering. Among the many existing triangle mesh compression methods, GTM is widely used for real-time rendering. Our algorithm gives a 32% improvement in the compression ratio over existing GTM algorithms for this application, and does not need any additional buffer during decompression. Moreover, our method supports linear time mesh compression and parallel decompression. We implemented an encoding algorithm on an SGI machine and visualized the results with Open Inventor and Java3D environments. Here we give some future works:

1. How to encode the holes and pockets efficiently.
2. To develop an algorithm for minimizing pockets and holes.

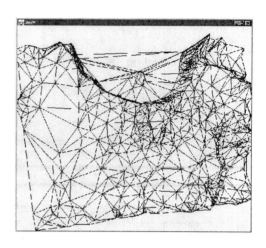

Figure 7. Terrain visualization using Java3D API(Crater Lake).

3. Implementation of the parallel decompression on parallel display hardware.

References

[1] M. Chow. Optimized geometry compression for realtime rendering. In *IEEE Visualization '97 Proc.*, pages 347–354, Oct. 1997.

[2] M. Deering. Geometry compression. In *SIGGRAPH '95 Proc.*, pages 13–20, Aug. 1995.

[3] F. Evans, S. Skiena, and A. Varshney. Optimizing triangle strips for fast rendering. In *IEEE Visualization '96 Proc.*, pages 319–326, 1996.

[4] M. Garland and P. S. Heckbert. Fast polygonal approximation of terrains and height fields. Technical report, CS Dept., Carnegie Mellon U., Sept. 1995.

[5] S. Gumhold and W. Straßer. Real time compression of triangle mesh connectivity. In *SIGGRAPH '98 Proc.*, pages 133–140, July 1998.

[6] H. Hoppe. Progressive meshes. In *SIGGRAPH '96 Proc.*, pages 99–108, Aug. 1996.

[7] S. Kim, Y. Kim, M. Cho, and H. Cho. A geometric compression algorithm for massive terrain data using delaunay triangulation. In *WSCG '99*, volume 1, pages 124–131, Feb. 1999.

[8] P. M. Leila De Floriani and E. Puppo. Compressing tins. In *ACM-GIS'98*, pages 130–145, Nov. 1998.

[9] G. Taubin and J. Rossignac. Geometric compression through topological surgery. Technical report, Research Report RC-20340, IBM Research Division, 1996.

[10] C. Touma and C. Gotsman. Triangle mesh compression. In *Proc. of Graphics Interface '98*, pages 26–34, 1998.

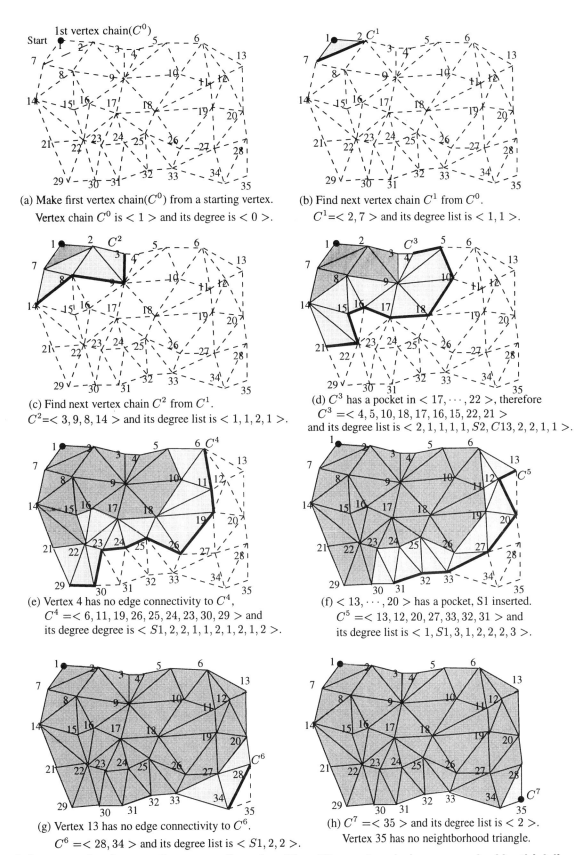

(a) Make first vertex chain(C^0) from a starting vertex. Vertex chain C^0 is $< 1 >$ and its degree is $< 0 >$.

(b) Find next vertex chain C^1 from C^0. $C^1 = < 2, 7 >$ and its degree list is $< 1, 1 >$.

(c) Find next vertex chain C^2 from C^1. $C^2 = < 3, 9, 8, 14 >$ and its degree list is $< 1, 1, 2, 1 >$.

(d) C^3 has a pocket in $< 17, \cdots, 22 >$, therefore $C^3 = < 4, 5, 10, 18, 17, 16, 15, 22, 21 >$ and its degree list is $< 2, 1, 1, 1, 1, S2, C13, 2, 2, 1, 1 >$.

(e) Vertex 4 has no edge connectivity to C^4, $C^4 = < 6, 11, 19, 26, 25, 24, 23, 30, 29 >$ and its degree degree is $< S1, 2, 2, 1, 1, 2, 1, 2, 1, 2 >$.

(f) $< 13, \cdots, 20 >$ has a pocket, S1 inserted. $C^5 = < 13, 12, 20, 27, 33, 32, 31 >$ and its degree list is $< 1, S1, 3, 1, 2, 2, 2, 3 >$.

(g) Vertex 13 has no edge connectivity to C^6. $C^6 = < 28, 34 >$ and its degree list is $< S1, 2, 2 >$.

(h) $C^7 = < 35 >$ and its degree list is $< 2 >$. Vertex 35 has no neightborhood triangle.

Figure 4. An example of a run of our encoding algorithm. The vertex chains are marked by thick lines and triangles already visited are filled.

Towards Fast Volume Visualisation on the WWW

Meleagros Krokos[1], Feng Dong[1,2], Gordon J. Clapworthy[1], J. Y. Shi[2]

[1]Department of Computer & Information Sciences, De Montfort University,
Milton Keynes MK7 6HP, United Kingdom.

[2]State Key Lab of CAD and CG, Zhejiang University,
Hangzhou, P. R. of China.
{melk, fdong, gc}@dmu.ac.uk

Abstract

The steady growth of the Internet has dramatically changed the way information is shared, and modern users expect near real-time delivery, high quality images together with in-depth navigation and exploration of 3D models. Multiresolution is a promising approach for fast distributed volume visualisation employing Levels-of-Detail. We review multiresolution algorithms and visualisation systems on the WWW. Our discussion is based on experience gained in the development of the IAEVA-II project funded by the European Commission. A new method for rapid data classification/rendering of multiresolution volumes, based on shear-warp factorisation, is described. We can change classification functions and data resolution during rendering without significant reduction in interactivity. A method for constructing multiresolution transfer functions for determining opacity is also investigated. Finally, future trends in developing WWW visualisation systems are discussed.

Keywords: volume visualisation, levels of detail (LoDs), multiresolution, computer graphics, Internet, component models.

1. Introduction

Nowadays, visualisation of volume datasets plays an important role in many diverse disciplines, Kaufman [1], and this is particularly true in medical visualisation.

Technologies for capturing volume datasets are becoming increasingly advanced and more widespread, resulting in an increase in both the number and the sizes of these datasets. The growth in the use of the Internet has dramatically changed the way in which data is stored and accessed; the Internet now provides excellent facilities for building reference libraries and for rapid dissemination of information.

Volume datasets are typically stored in large distributed databases that are maintained by one or more servers. Users browse through the datasets by accessing the databases through client systems, which can range from high-end graphics workstations to low-end PCs. When an appropriate dataset is identified, the subsequent visualisation typically requires high-quality rendering.

Volume-visualisation algorithms can produce stunning images of volume data, but execution times are generally slow because of the high computational complexity. If the user has access only to the computational power and storage capacity of the typical PC, the use of standard volume-visualisation techniques is impractical. Further, given the Internet's bandwidth limitations, the time required to download a typical dataset over standard communication lines is too long to be acceptable for general usage.

It is for these reasons that, to our knowledge, all the currently-available systems for visualising volume data are surface based.

The modern user has come to expect near real-time delivery, a high quality of the images rendered and to be able to perform in-depth navigation and exploration of the model. The availability of flexible and efficient 3D interaction significantly enhances the user's ability to identify and investigate regions of interest.

There is a clear conflict between, on one hand, the size of volume datasets, the transmission speeds on the Internet and the computational resources of the average user, and, on the other hand, the demands of an increasingly-sophisticated user population.

Progressive transmission of the data and progressive refinement of the image can overcome a number of the difficulties outlined above.

Progressive refinement of the image as the data comes in from the remote server is one way of enhancing interactivity, while still eventually rendering a high-quality image, Schroeder [2].

For progressive transmission, volume datasets are represented through continuous families of levels-of-detail (LoDs) datasets. On transmission at the coarsest resolution, a fundamental visualisation is presented to the user; as finer LODs are transmitted, the visualisation is gradually updated. Which resolutions are employed for viewing depend upon an acceptable balance between image quality and rendering speed.

Our paper reviews multiresolution algorithms and Internet visualisation systems employing multiresolution. The factors associated with design and implementation are identified. Our discussion is based on experience gained in the development of IAEVA-II, a project funded by the European Commission.

We also describe a new method for rapid data classification/rendering of multiresolution volumes, based on shear-warp factorisation; this enables the modification of classification functions and/or data resolution during rendering without significant reduction in interactivity. A method for constructing multiresolution transfer functions for determining opacity is also investigated.

The paper is organised as follows. Section 2 surveys approaches for constructing WWW-based volume visualisation systems, while Section 3 reviews the use of multiresolution in volume visualisation algorithms. System architectures and component models are described in Section 4. The IAEVA-II system and a multiresolution volume rendering and classification method are presented in Section 5, with concluding remarks and future trends appearing in Section 6.

2. Systems

This section reviews recently-proposed WWW-based volume-visualisation systems.

Trapp & Pagendarm [3] present a prototype flow-visualisation system in which users send data to a visualisation server, where visualisations are constructed and returned as VRML models. Plain ASCII text is used for communication between clients and server; this requires a very high network throughput and processing overhead. The geometric data produced by the server requires complete transmission to clients for viewing to commence, thus severely restricting interactivity.

Another interesting approach is VizWiz, Michaels & Bailey [4], in which users can load 2D or 3D datasets and visualise them interactively, using a number of standard scientific-visualisation techniques such as iso-

surfaces, cutting planes and elevation plots. Iso-surfaces are constructed using the Marching Cubes algorithm, Lorensen & Cline [5]. VizWiz is implemented in Java for platform independence. To compensate for performance limitations, simplified rendering, caching and a tool to control resolution are used. Nevertheless, this is not a truly multiresolution system, e.g. users cannot select the desired granularity.

Gueziec et al [6] outline a framework in three parts for progressive transmission of geometry: a process to generate multiple levels-of-detail (LoDs), a transmission process, and a suitable data structure for receiving and exploiting LoDs. This approach can employ any known vertex-clustering algorithm for polygon reduction. The LoDs are accessed on the fly by manipulating vertex indices. Smooth transitions (or geomorphs) are supported, and this approach complements existing compression schemes - volume datasets can be converted into the author's format following transmission in compressed form using any known algorithm.

A distributed volume visualisation system is described by Engel et al [7]; it is based on the concept of progressive iso-surfaces introduced by Grosso & Ertl [8]. The visualisation server generates multiresolution surface representations and transmits these progressively to clients. Coarse levels of resolution require low network throughput, thus enabling interactive visualisation rates. Refinement up to the highest level of resolution is possible, but it requires a longer network transmission. The system allows the unrestricted selection of granularity for viewing. Clients have to build VRML or Java3D scene graphs to allow switching between different levels of resolution. Although the authors discuss the possibility of applying the same methods to transmission of volume models, no implementation has yet been reported.

All the approaches described above are based on surface models. In contrast, Lippert et al [9] describe a method for volume compression/rendering, based on the wavelet splats of Lippert & Gross [10], which is designed for distributed applications. To achieve fast transmission over the network, a progressive compression scheme allows storage of RGB and intensity data on the server in terms of a bitstream. The clients carry out rendering immediately in the compression domain, i.e. full decompression is not necessary.

The limited memory requirements enable execution even on very low cost computers. Although fast rendering is offered, the images are of low quality (no depth information), so this method is more suited to use as a fast volume browser than as a high-accuracy visualisation tool.

As seen above, the majority of WWW-based volume visualisation systems are surface-based, offering various forms of multiresolution to improve Internet transmission times. To our knowledge, no full-scale volume-based systems exist apart from that developed by Lippert et al [9], which is seriously restricted by its low image quality.

In IAEVA II, we have developed methods for high-quality multiresolution rendering and data classification (see Section 5). We believe that the development of similar methods for distributed visualisation offers the best prospect for delivering real-time volume visualisation on the Internet.

3. Multiresolution

Multiresolution has attracted considerable attention over the last few years, and numerous articles have appeared addressing the problem of multiresolution volume rendering and/or modelling.

A general framework for the approximation of rendering integrals using multiresolution spaces was presented in Westermann [13]. After projecting into a pre-selected wavelet basis, many wavelet coefficients can be safely neglected without compromising accuracy, which dramatically reduces the amount of computer memory necessary for rendering.

Using a pyramidal volumetric representation, a progressive-refinement rendering algorithm called splatting was introduced by Laur & Hanrahan [11]. Depending upon the desired image quality, the splatting algorithm scans different pyramid levels in a back-to-front order.

Orthonormal wavelets are also useful for volume decomposition into a pyramidal representation. An approximate rendering equation solution is obtained either through spline functions, Gross et al [12], or by unifying Fourier-domain volume rendering and texture mapping, Lippert & Gross [10].

A promising class of volume-rendering algorithms factorises the viewing transformation into a 3D shear parallel to the data slices to form an intermediate distorted image; a 2D warp is subsequently applied, so as to form an undistorted final image.

Shear-warp factorisation and min-max octrees are used in Lacroute & Levoy [14] to encode spatial coherence in unclassified volumes. Near-interactive rendering rates are obtained with no significant quality loss, e.g. a 256^3 dataset is rendered in 1 sec on an SGI Indigo. However, min-max octree construction is computationally expensive, so a pre-processing step is necessary. Further, changing the resolution of datasets requires full rebuilding of the associated min-max octrees, which

makes this algorithm too slow for use in multiresolution volumetric rendering.

Recently, Yuting et al [15] introduced a volume-rendering method exerting shear-warp of the viewing transformation on multiresolution volume datasets.

However, none of the above methods address the problem of interactively changing resolution during the rendering process. In Section 5, we describe our method for achieving this, and also how to modify classification functions interactively. Our method also allows progressive transmission of volume datasets. On transmission at the coarsest resolution, a hierarchical structure is initially constructed; as finer LODs are transmitted, this structure is updated and displayed. Apart from new nodes, no previously constructed nodes need computing when a new LOD arrives.

4. Architectures

This section reviews the different architectures employed in the construction of WWW visualisation systems. These systems are based on the client-server model: users and service providers.

Different system architectures are obtained depending upon where the visualisation computation is performed, e.g. if visualisation is placed with the service providers, a server-based architecture is obtained. The advantage of such an architecture is that software distribution to clients, and maintenance and support for the many possible operating systems on remote clients, are no longer necessary.

However, as standard WWW browsers are static with no support for visual data manipulation, the visualisation interactivity then depends heavily upon the communications bandwidth. If this is low, and a number of clients simultaneously request updates, the server may become overloaded.

Java applets can be employed to overcome such limitations. They are automatically downloaded and allow processes to execute locally; applets and associated datasets must be downloaded whenever they are used. A large number of executables may need to be downloaded, and as demand for larger applets and datasets grows, significant downloading delays can be anticipated.

This problem is often addressed by loading visualisation components locally on clients. Typically these components run embedded within particular WWW browsers. The browser is aware of them and launches them automatically once data transfer terminates, so that data manipulation and rendering are performed locally. Using components also allows visualisation software and complex interfaces to be developed separately.

Developers are beginning to create components, rather than complete applications, in order to release themselves from their previous slow, expensive form of application development by building up a core of portable, reusable code. This will enable them, for example, quickly to attack new market opportunities.

Microsoft's Component Object Model (COM) allows developers to create autonomous software components that can be used without intimate knowledge of their contents [16]. Components perform specific tasks through well-defined interfaces. COM is a language- and platform-independent standard that allows communications among different objects using a common, agreed protocol.

ActiveX controls are a specific implementation in COM programming. They can be inserted into a Web page, an ActiveX-enabled application, or programming environments such as Visual C++ or Visual Basic.

There are two important aspects to developing ActiveX visualisation controls. Firstly, a well-specified interface has to be defined, the so-called properties of the ActiveX, e.g. an iso-surface number, transfer functions values, viewing attributes, etc. Components may then be combined using the COM aggregation mechanism. When using Visual Basic, for example, developers can assemble completely new ActiveX controls with customised interfaces by combining built-in controls with existing ActiveX controls through a few lines of code; this is a comparatively simple task and can be performed even by non-expert programmers.

The next step in the evolution of COM will be COM+, which will greatly simplify the coding required. COM objects will work more like C++ objects. Further, Distributed COM (DCOM) will allow components running on different machines to communicate as if they were located on the same machine.

JavaBeans is an alternative component model, developed by Sun [17]. JavaBeans enables developers to write reusable components once and run them on any platform using any architecture, thus benefitting from the platform-independent power of Java. This is in contrast to ActiveX which is essentially relevant only to an MS Windows/Intel x86 platform.

Beans are Java classes that can be manipulated in a visual builder tool and subsequently composed into an application. JavaBeans components can be used to build a range of solutions from full Java desktop applications to WWW-based applets. JavaBeans works with any network model including DCOM and CORBA. Further, the JavaBeans Bridge for ActiveX includes features to allow information to be exchanged between JavaBeans and ActiveX components.

The main advantage of implementing WWW visualisation systems using components is that they can significantly increase user interaction by supporting point and click navigation through complex volume datasets. IAEVA II currently employs ActiveX components, but our development is under constant review for incorporating the latest technologies.

5. IAEVA

The medical community is keen to support the creation of distributed multimedia databases on the WWW for disseminating important research and/or clinical information, and for education.

Anatomical information usually comes in the form of 2D radiological images, but 3D models developed from these can be extremely helpful in providing insights into the medical conditions displayed.

This is the background to the pilot project, *IAEVA*, which developed an integrated methodology for constructing organised WWW databases of 3D models of pathological human organs and providing relevant retrieval and manipulation mechanisms, Krokos et al [18]. The results of IAEVA are now being exploited by the development of *IAEVA-II* in which algorithms for accelerating the transmission and manipulation of 3D models over the Internet are included, and advanced educational tools are provided, Crudele et al [19].

IAEVA-II is designed as a WWW-based medical education system for standard PC configurations and Internet connections. Here, fast rendering and transmission are of the highest priority. Given the previously-described limitations of the Internet, it is not feasible, at present, to include full-scale volumetric rendering in a general service of the type of IAEVA-II.

Thus, current provision is limited to 3D surface models consisting of polygons produced from the Marching Cubes algorithm [5]. Depending upon the shape complexity of the anatomical structure under consideration, hundreds of thousands (or perhaps millions) of polygons are produced. Optimisation of rendering and transmission times for these large 3D models is achieved through multiresolution algorithms.

For a particular 3D model, a continuous range of Levels of Detail (LoDs) is captured. For rendering, different LoDs are displayed, depending upon the user's viewpoint and the particular interaction. For transmission, a coarse LoD is transmitted initially followed by a sequence of finer LoDs, so the quality of the model is upgraded incrementally. Interaction also takes place at the lower resolutions, which considerably improves the response of the system to user input.

Continued improvements in CPU power, PC graphics cards and communications technology are beginning to make it feasible to employ multiresolution methods for the incremental transmission of large datasets and for real-time volume visualisation on standard PCs.

We now briefly describe an algorithm developed within the IAEVA-II system, further details of which can be found in Dong et al [20]. The algorithm renders different volume resolutions through fast shear-warp factorisation. The main advantage of this approach is the ability to modify classification functions or data resolution during rendering without significant reduction in interactivity. This is achieved through newly-developed data structures, called multiresolution min-max octrees (MMMOs).

Definition: MMMO nodes contain minimum and maximum parameter values for sub-cubes of the volumetric dataset contained in different LoDs. At the root (depth 0), the min and max values correspond to 2×2×2 resolution, and are employed for determining opacity for the whole volumetric dataset. At depth 1, they correspond to 4×4×4 resolution. This process is repeated recursively until the finest resolution is reached.

Properties: MMMOs have the property that nodes at depth m are determined completely from the $m+1$ resolution of the associated multiresolution volumetric dataset; e.g. the root (depth 0) depends upon resolution 2×2×2, depth 1 nodes depend on resolution 4×4×4 etc. This offers the following advantages:

- MMMOs can represent multiresolution datasets uniquely, i.e. after modification of the resolution of the dataset, no MMMO change is needed
- on transmission of the coarsest resolution, an MMMO is initially constructed; as finer LoDs are transmitted, new nodes are inserted in the MMMO but none of the old nodes has to be updated when a new LOD arrives.

This scenario allows rapid browsing and display of complex volume models residing on distributed WWW databases; it is independent of the underlying hardware and speed of the network connections. Multiresolution transfer functions for deciding opacity of the MMMO nodes are also provided – details can be found in Dong et al [20].

6. Fast Volume Visualisation on the WWW

Most WWW volume-visualisation systems employ surface-based models because surfaces can be rendered and transmitted rapidly over the Internet.

However, if the models involved are complex, hundreds of thousands of polygons are necessary. To cope with this situation, most researchers concentrate on simplification and multiresolution algorithms to optimise rendering and Internet-transmission times.

However, surfaces do not convey the full information contained in volume datasets as they are obtained from the datasets by applying thresholding. Thus, there is a demand to develop WWW volume visualisation systems based on full-scale volume models.

Until now, using classical volume rendering algorithms in a stand-alone environment has required long execution times and specialised hardware. As mentioned above, technological developments have now made it feasible to consider delivering volume rendering across the Internet at speeds acceptable to the user.

Traditional approaches to volume rendering have required the complete volume dataset to be present before rendering commences. Given the bandwidth limitations of the Internet and the typically large sizes of volume datasets, it is not practical to transfer complete volume models due to very long transmission times. This situation is likely to remain in the near future, even with the planned satellite-based Internet connections.

Consequently it is imperative to develop new ways of modelling volume datasets. One way forward is through multiresolution representations for progressive transmission and interactive rendering. To our knowledge no systems currently exist that employ multiresolution volume models. Lippert et al [9] introduced such a system, but their approach lacks depth information and is thus restricted to X-ray-like images.

The architecture models of visualisation systems is another aspect in need of improvement. The traditional way of using a Web browser as a simple viewer is not suitable for rapid interaction. To this extent, the ultimate Web-base visualisation capabilities will be delivered through Web components.

Component-model technologies such as ActiveX from Microsoft and JavaBeans from SUN provide an important aspect of cyberspace in that they allow the creation of objects that behave similarly in different environments and on different computer platforms. This reflects the nature of the Web : a multitude of different machines connected together to exchange information.

Using visualisation components can speed up user interaction, especially if the client machine is of high specification. The local visualisation component can handle any special format used for multiresolution modelling. These visualisation components can be highly advanced, allowing sophisticated graphical visualisation.

Another aspect of using visualisation components is that the visualisation can be developed independently from the front-end interface, as long as it adheres to a prescribed communication protocol.

Future developers will distribute not only core visualisation components but also high-level components using other low-level components. Programming a specific application will just involve joining them together and adding any extra functionality that may be necessary.

This scenario will allow WWW visualisation to become more active and dynamic. Visualisation systems will be highly customisable and flexible; they will develop according to customer demand by adding extra local components for extra functionality or by modifying existing components.

IAEVA-II is a WWW-based medical education system for standard PC configurations and Internet connections. Given the bandwidth limitations of the Internet current provision is limited to 3D surface models.

Nevertheless, we have developed an approach using MMMOs based on shear-warp factorisation for achieving fast progressive volume transmission and rendering. This method allows easy modification of classification functions and/or data resolution during rendering without significant loss of interactivity.

We believe that developing similar methods and incorporating them into WWW-based visualisation systems such as IAEVA-II for addressing a wide audience will allow real-time volume visualisation to become a common experience to the average Internet user.

Acknowledgements

This research is supported by the European Commission under the project IAEVA II (An Internet Service for fast viewing and manipulation of 3D models of human pathologies, HC4009), and the Chinese National Natural Science Fund (No.69703004).

References

[1] A. Kaufman, W.E. Lorensen, H. Pfister, C. Silva and L. Sobierajski-Avila, "Advances in Volume Visualisation", *SIGGRAPH '98 Course Notes*, 1998

[2] W. Schroeder, "A Topology Modifying Progressive Decimation Algorithm", *Visualisation '97*, IEEE Press, pp 205-212, 1997

[3] J. Trapp and H. Pagendarm, "A Prototype for a WWW-based Visualisation Service", *Eurographics Workshop on Visualisation in Scientific Computing*, 1997

[4] C. Michaels and M. Bailey, "VizWiz: A Java Applet for Interactive 3D Scientific Visualisation on the Web", *Visualisation '97*, IEEE Press, pp. 261-267, 1997

[5] W.E. Lorensen and H.E. Cline, "Marching Cubes : a High-Resolution 3D Surface-Construction Algorithm", *Computer Graphics*, Vol. 21, No 4, pp 38-44, 1987

[6] A. Gueziec, G. Taubin, B. Horn and F. Lazarus, "A Framework for Streaming Geometry in VRML", *IEEE Computer Graphics & Applications*, pp 68-78, March-April, 1999

[7] K. Engel, R. Grosso and T. Ertl, "Progressive Iso-surfaces on the Web", *Visualisation '98, Late Breaking Hot Topics*, IEEE Press, 1998

[8] R. Grosso and T. Ertl, "Progressive Iso-Surface Extraction from Hierarchical 3D Meshes", *Computer Graphics Forum*, Vol. 17(3), pp 125-135, 1998

[9] L. Lippert, M. Gross and C. Kurmann, "Compression Domain Volume Rendering for Distributed Environments", *Computer Graphics Forum*, Vol. 16(3), pp. 95-107, 1997

[10] L. Lippert and M. Gross, "Fast Wavelet based Volume Rendering by Accumulation of Transparent Texture Maps", *Computer Graphics Forum*, Vol. 14(3), pp. 431-443, 1995

[11] D. Laur and P. Hanrahan, "Hierarchical Splatting: A Progressive Refinement Algorithm for Volume Rendering", *Proc. SIGGRAPH '91*, pp. 285-288, 1991

[12] M. Gross, L. Lippert, A. Dreger, and R. Koch, "A New Method to Approximate the Volume Rendering Equation Using Wavelet Bases and Piecewise Polynomials", *Computers & Graphics*, Vol. 19(1), pp. 47-62, 199

[13] R. Westermann, "A Multiresolution Framework for Volume Rendering", *1994 Symposium on Volume Visualization*, Washington, D.C., October 1994, pp 51-58

[14] P. Lacroute, and M. Levoy, "Fast Volume Rendering using a Shear-Warp Factorization of the Viewing Transformation", *Computer Graphics*, Vol. 28(3), July 1994, pp 451-458

[15] Y. Yuting, L. Feng and S. Soon, "Multiresolution Volume Rendering Based on Shear-Warp Factorisation", International Workshop on Volume Graphics, Swansea, United Kingdom, pp. 49-64, 1999

[16] http://msdn.microsoft.com/workshop/components/

[17] http://java.sun.com/beans/

[18] M. Krokos, G. J. Clapworthy, M. Crudele, G. Salcito and N. Vasilonikolidakis, "Organisation, Transmission, Manipulation of Pathogical Human Organs on the WWW", Medical Informatics Europe '97, *Technology and Informatics*, Vol. 43, IOS Press, pp. 99-103, 1997

[19] M. Crudele, G. J. Clapworthy, F. Dong, M. Krokos, N. Vasilonikolidakis and G. Salcito, "Accessing a WWW Reference Library of 3D Models of Pathological Organs to Support Medical Education", *Proc Medical Informatics Europe '99*, 1999 (accepted for presentation)

[20] F. Dong, M. Krokos, G. J. Clapworthy and J. Y. Shi, "Fast Multiresolution Volume Rendering and Data Classification using Multiresolution Min-Max Octrees", (submitted for publication)

Occlusion Culling
Using
Minimum Occluder Set and Opacity Map

Poon Chun Ho   Wenping Wang
Department of Computer Science and Information Systems
University of Hong Kong
{ chpoon | wenping } @csis.hku.hk

Abstract

The aim of occlusion culling is to cull away a significant amount of invisible primitives at different viewpoints. We present two algorithms to improve occlusion culling for a highly occluded virtual environment. The first algorithm is used in pre-processing stage. It considers the combined gain and cost of occluders to select an optimal set of occluders, called minimum occluder set, for each occludee. The second algorithm uses the improved opacity map and sparse depth map for efficient run-time overlap tests and depth tests, respectively. Without using pixel-wise comparison, this algorithm uses only three integer operations to perform an overlap test, and carry out a depth comparison sparsely. Both algorithms have been implemented and applied to test a model composed of about three hundred thousand polygons. Significant speedup in walkthroughs of the test model due to our algorithms has been observed.

1   Introduction

In many applications the demand for interactive display of complex geometric environments composed of millions of geometric primitives always outpaces the advance of the high-end graphics technology. These include interactive visualisation of architectural models and walkthrough of outdoor scenes. The models found in these applications normally have high depth complexity. An efficient algorithm for identification of hidden primitives is critical to interactive rendering, while pixel-level culling, such as hardware z-buffering, is no longer enough to determine visibility in real-time. An occlusion culling algorithm makes use of occlusion relation among the primitives of the model, and culls away a significant amount of invisible primitives at different viewpoints quickly, in order to achieve an interactive frame rate.

There are two stages in an occlusion culling algorithm: selection of occluders, which is usually off-line for a static environment, and actual invisible surface culling with occluders, which is a run-time operation for real time rendering.

In this paper, we present two new algorithms:
1. a novel method to select occluders with multiple criteria at pre-processing stage, using the idea of the *minimum occluder set* (MOS). The MOS of an occludee is the minimal set of primitives that occludes the occludee.
2. an efficient occlusion culling algorithm using the *opacity map* (OM) and *sparse depth map* (SDM), which are applied to the spatial hierarchy of the whole model at each frame at run-time.

Though we perform occluder selection using the minimum occluder set, the culling part makes no assumption about the model and occluders, and can therefore be carried out along with occluders selected with any other criteria.

We shall briefly discuss related work in the section 2. In the section 3, we present an overview of our occlusion culling approach. Details of the minimum occluder set algorithm and the occlusion culling algorithm using the opacity map and sparse depth map will be presented in sections 4 and 5, respectively. The result and analysis are given in section 6, and the paper concludes in section 7.

2   Related Work

Hidden surface removal is a fundamental problem of computer graphics. The conventional z-buffer algorithm is implemented in hardware or software [2, 3] that yields exact visibility information by pixel-wise comparison of depth values of every primitive.

The binary space partitioning (BSP) tree algorithm [6, 12], which refines the work in [13], determines visible primitives in a static environment from an arbitrary viewpoint. After building the BSP tree, one can have a linear query response of visibility sorting for the whole set of primitives.

Based on probabilistic geometry, an efficient and randomized algorithm for hidden surface removal is presented in [11]. Further research in computational geometry on randomized algorithms for maintaining a BSP tree for a dynamic model has been conducted [1, 16], which, however, does not lead to practical results.

The potentially visible set (PVS) [10, 15] is designed for indoor architectural walkthrough systems. It divides the entire model into cells, and computes cell-to-cell visibility at the pre-processing stage. Combined with a view cone, one can obtain a tight bound for the visible primitives (eye-to-cell visibility) at run-time.

For densely occluded scenes, hierarchical z-buffer visibility [7] is exploited to speedup the conventional depth value comparison during rasterization process. With z-pyramid, this method allows quick termination of depth comparison for the nodes of octree hierarchy far away from the viewpoint. It performs efficiently when is implemented in hardware. Hierarchical polygon tiling [8] combines z-pyramid to further reduce the rasterization time with triage coverage masks. It traverses the convex polygons in front-to-back order, and culls off polygons that are covered in image hierarchy.

The occlusion culling algorithm in [4, 5] computes the separating and supporting planes for each pair of occluders and the nodes of the model hierarchy. If the viewpoint is found inside the supporting frustum, then its corresponding node is considered as completely occluded. The algorithm takes the advantage that frustum is constant and has to be computed only once for static models. However, it is relatively computationally consuming, especially with a floating point implementation. Another occlusion culling algorithm [9] applies shadow frusta that are extended from the viewpoint, and uses several large occluders as bases, and then culls off object nodes which are inside the frusta. This approach is limited with the number and the shape of occluders. Later, the same authors proposed a visibility culling algorithm using hierarchical occlusion maps (HOM) [17]. Our approach is closely related to this work. The main innovations of HOM are occluder fusion and efficient usage of conventional hardware acceleration.

Recently, the problem of exact visibility sorting of geometric objects without the help of hardware z-buffer is addressed in [14]. Instead of using conventional 3D rendering, it produces a sequence of layered images from a set of geometric parts, and uses them to compose the final image. This approach does not demand fast 3D

graphics hardware, and relies mainly on general computation and 2D image operations.

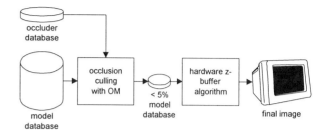

Figure 1: The occlusion culling algorithm using opacity map acts as a fast filter to cull away a large portion of hidden primitives in the model database.

3 Overview

We first divide the entire model into hierarchical bounding volume, by constraining that the leave nodes of the tree contain at most 256 primitives. Our approach makes use of occluders that are selected carefully in the pre-processing stage, to cull away a large portion of hidden nodes of the hierarchical bounding volume tree at run-time. Figure 1 shows the process flow of the rendering pipeline integrating this approach.

At the pre-processing stage, we construct the occluder database for certain grid points of the whole environment, using the minimum occluder set algorithm. The minimum occluder set is a minimal set of primitives that occlude one occludee. Note that an occludee may have several different minimum occluder sets. We compute the minimum occluder sets only for the occludees with more than 20 primitives. After grouping and sorting, the optimal set of occluders can be found out.

At the run-time, the algorithm performs the following tasks at each frame:

1. To query the occluder database, and retrieve the occluder list from the grid point nearest to the current viewpoint.
2. To render the retrieved occluders off-screen by conventional graphics hardware with frame and depth buffers. As we only need the image bitmap and depth value of the occluders, this rendering process is optimised by ignoring light and material setting. The resolution applied can be lower than the final display.
3. The resulting buffer contents are used to construct the opacity map and sparse depth map, respectively.

4. Using the opacity map and sparse depth map, we test recursively occlusion with the rectangular bounding box of the node's projected image. The occlusion culling consists of two dimensional overlap tests and depth comparisons. The two dimensional overlap test is enhanced by using only three integer additions or subtractions, while the depth comparison is carried out sparsely.

5. Finally, the nodes not culled in the occlusion culling step are regarded as conservatively visible and fed into the hardware z-buffer algorithm for exact visibility determination.

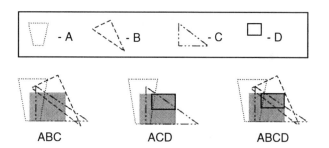

ABC   ACD   ABCD

Figure 2: The idea of MOS. The primitives and their labels are shown in the box above. The shaded rectangle is the image of an occludee. The left and middle figures show two MOS (ABC and ACD) of the same occludee, while the one on right shows the wrong selection for MOS, as either B or D is redundant.

4 Minimum Occluder Set Algorithm

The general occluder selection criteria involve four major properties of a primitive. They are the size or projected size, first-hit, redundancy and computation cost. The former two are typically used to determine good occluders. Note that a primitive with a large projected size may have low depth complexity and incomplete coverage, and that first-hit primitives usually form a super set of the optimal set. Moreover, these do not take into account the combined gain with its neighbour occluders.

We define the optimal set of occluders to be the set of primitives giving the maximum ratio of its culling percentage to its computation cost. As any single occluder selection criterion cannot give the combined culling percentage of the whole set of occluders, only a rough approximation can be expected. In contrast, our scheme tries to find out the minimum set of primitives that occlude an occludee, as shown in Figure 2. This means that it chooses a set of primitives at one time, instead of

picking only one primitive, which leads to more efficient elimination than occluders with incomplete coverage. With a suitable scoring scheme, we can find out the optimal set of occluders at a given viewpoint. The MOS algorithm has three major components: construction of occluder stack, generation of MOS for each occludee, and calculation of the score for each MOS. We pick the MOS with the highest score, and keep checking on redundancy.

4.1 Construction of Occluder Stack

For each occludee, an occluder stack is constructed to generate MOS for each occludee. It is a three dimensional array, with the rectangular base of the same size as the bounding box of the projected image of the occludee in the screen space. After depth sorting, if a primitive is in front of the occludee and covers some pixels of the occludee's projected image, the identifier of the primitive is pushed into the stack at the location of the covered pixels, as shown in Figure 3. With hardware graphics pipeline, the projected image of occludees and primitives can be found quickly.

Ideally, we would like to construct the occluder stack for all occludees. But it may need too much memory and time. In order to make it practical, the algorithm filters out the less significant occluders and occludees, such as tiny occluders and occludees containing only few primitives.

4.2 Generation of Minimum Occluder Set

After constructing the occluder stack, the algorithm first sorts the pixels of the occludee rectangular base, in ascending order of the number of primitives' identifier it contains, and builds up a table as shown in Figure 3. If there are pixels that are covered by no primitive, this occludee is regarded as visible and the search for this occludee's MOS stops. The first row of the combination table shows the number of primitives that cover different pixels. The first column indicates that there are pixels covered by only one primitive (A or C), while the second column indicates that there are some pixels covered by two primitives, and similar for the rest. In other words, one slot represents a group of pixels that are covered by the IDs (primitives) it contains.

A slot will be cancelled if any of its IDs has been picked to be in *intermediate MOS*. For example, if the primitive A is picked, all slots containing A will be cancelled. If all slots of combination table have been cancelled, the occludee is completely covered by the current MOS, which will be stored into MOS database. Thus, finding one MOS of an occludee is equivalent to finding one combination of primitives that cancel all the slots - the whole combination table. In order to find all MOSs of an occludee, an exhaustive search is carried out, for all the combination of primitives inside the table.

We run through the table from left to right, as it usually gives early termination. We simply pick the IDs of first column's slots as intermediate MOS, and cancel the associated slots. Then we concatenate the first IDs of the first remaining slot, and cancel the corresponding slots repeatedly. If the whole table is cancelled, we save this intermediate MOS in MOS database. Afterwards, we backtrack to the last concatenated ID's slot, remove the last ID from the intermediate MOS, recover the slots it cancelled, and try the next allowable ID in the same slot, and cancel the corresponding slots repeatedly, until we get another MOS. If there is no next allowable ID in the same slot, we backtrack further to the previous concatenated ID's slot, one step back at a time, until we find out all the MOSs. According to Figure 3, we first collect *A* and *C* as intermediate MOS. Then, only the third slot (*BD*) of second column remains. Hence, the MOSs of this example are *ABC* and *ACD*.

An upper bound on the complexity of an exhaustive search is $O(n!)$, where n is the number of different primitives of the table. Though it is run at pre-processing stage, shorter computation time is preferred. In practice, we usually do not need to compute all MOSs of each occludee; only the cheapest (in cost) portion of MOSs for each occludee will be kept. A pruning technique is applied to shorten the exhaustive search. If we find that the intermediate MOS already has higher cost compared with the ones inside the MOS database, we backtrack immediately. This leads to a quicker termination, and is a trade off for efficiency.

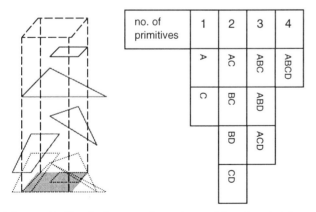

Figure 3: Occluder stack and combination table.

no. of primitives	1	2	3	4
	A	AC	ABC	ABCD
	C	BC	ABD	
		BD	ACD	
		CD		

4.3   Scoring and Selecting

Each MOS has its gain and cost. The gain is the number of occludees it occludes, and the cost is the computation time for processing the MOS during occlusion culling at run-time. The gain is found by grouping the identical MOSs of all occludees together. If an MOS S_1 is the superset of MOS S_2, the algorithm adds the gain of S_2 to S_1. This approach explores the effectiveness of occlusion fusion. The cost of MOS is usually the rendering cost, as the occlusion culling will render all the selected occluders at each frame at run-time. This value is approximated by the number and the total projected sizes of occluders that the MOS contains. The number of occluders increases geometric computation, while their image sizes affect the rasterization time. Combining the gain, cost and user preference, the algorithm assigns a score to each MOS.

After sorting, the algorithm collects the top portion of MOSs up to a user defined limit. In order to remove redundant occluders that are contained in more than one MOS, or even hidden by occluders with higher scores, the algorithm makes use of *ID rendering*, that is, to render the occluders into the frame buffer with their IDs for rasterization, instead of their colours. With ID rendering, the redundant or hidden occluders will not be found in the ID buffer. The algorithm overlays the ID rendering of each MOS to the previous ID buffer, and repeats until the number of selected occluders reaches the limit. The final set of optimal occluders for the whole scene from a fixed viewpoint is then extracted from the ID buffer. This process of selecting MOS is essentially repeated for all representative viewpoints in different directions.

5   Occlusion Culling

The occlusion culling consists of three parts. These are view frustum culling, overlap test with the opacity map, and depth comparison with the sparse depth map. The view frustum culling is the typical one to apply on the hierarchical bounding volume tree at first. It culls away the nodes falling outside the view frustum, but not those hidden by occluders. In the occlusion culling algorithm an occludee is occluded if (*a*) the bounding box of its projected image is completely covered by occluders' image; and (*b*) the nearest depth value of occludee is farther than the depth values of occluders. The overlap test and depth comparison are applied to check these two conditions. If a node passes through both tests, it is hidden by the selected occluders; otherwise, the occlusion culling continues for its children recursively.

The straight forward solution to the overlap test and depth comparison is by a pixel-wise test. But its computation cost is prohibitive for interactive display. In contrast, the opacity map needs only two integer additions and one subtraction to do the overlap test. The sparse depth map further simplifies depth comparison. In this section, the opacity map and sparse depth map, as well as their uses and features will be described.

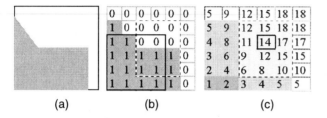

(a)   (b)   (c)

Figure 4: (a) The back buffer for rendering the occluders. The grey area is covered by all occluders. (b) The bitmap of the occluders. (c) The opacity map, and the shading showing the usage of opacity function.

5.1   Opacity Map

The opacity map is a two dimensional array of the scaled size of the final image, and stores the *opacity values* at each pixel. The *opacity value* of a pixel is the number of pixels , being covered by occluders and laying inside the rectangular area from lower left corner up to the pixel. In Figure 4, pre-selected occluders are rendered off-screen to produce the bitmap of the occluders' image. The bitmap is generated in the back buffer by graphics hardware. A 1 in the bitmap indicates that the pixel is covered by occluders, with 0 indicating not. The opacity value of the black box in (c) is equal to the number of 1's in the black bordered region in (b). The algorithm uses scan-line conversion to calculate the opacity values at each pixel. A row and column of zeros are added to eliminate the boundary cases during overlap test. For simplicity, we do not show them in the figure. As these zeros do not need to be updated, they are ignored at the construction phase of the opacity map. The resolution of the opacity map used for the model tested in this paper is 128×128, excluding the first row and column of zeros, while the displayed image resolution for the final images are 512×512 or 1024×1024. We feel that this is a good balance between the accuracy and computation time.

5.2   Overlap Test

The aim of the overlap test is to check whether the rectangular area of the projected image of an occludee is completely covered by occluders' images. In other words, it checks if the area of occludee's image is fulfilled by 1s in the bitmap. With the opacity map, this query can be done by *opacity function (OPF)*,

$OPF(x_1, x_2, y_1, y_2) =$
$Op(x_1, y_1) - Op(x_1, y_2) - Op(x_2, y_1) + Op(x_2, y_2)$

where $Op(s, t)$ means the opacity value at co-ordinates (s, t) in the opacity map, while the lower left corner of the opacity map has the co-ordinates $(1, 1)$. The OPF calculates the number of 1's in the rectangular region $(x_1 < x <= x_2, y_1 < y <= y_2)$ of the bitmap. Figure 4c shows the application of OPF to do overlap test for one occludee. The dash lines border the rectangular region $(2 < x <= 5, 1 < y <= 5)$, which is the occludee's projected image. The region has 12 pixels in total. Then, we calculate,

$OPF(2, 5, 1, 5)$
$= Op(2, 1) - Op(2, 5) - Op(5, 1) +$
$\quad Op(5, 5)$
$= 2 - 9 - 5 + 18$
$= 6$

It means that the occluders cover only 6 pixels inside this region. Compared with the region size (12 pixels), the occludee is not occluded by the occluders and therefore fails the overlap test.

Besides the benefit of occluder fusion, the opacity map allows the overlap test of one occludee to be done with only two additions and one subtraction. Moreover, two more modifications can be made to perform approximate overlap tests and adaptive overlap tests.

Approximate Overlap Test: For a highly dense scene composed of many tiny primitives, such as a bottle full of small stones, a certain tolerance can be added to the opacity function. This makes the overlap test ignore some holes of the occluders' image, and regard the almost entirely hidden nodes being occluded. Using the opacity map, this modification is easy to achieve.

Adaptive Overlap Test: In order to balance the computation time of the occlusion culling algorithm and rendering process, a *coverage ratio* threshold is used to trigger a stop signal to the recursive occlusion culling algorithm. The coverage ratio is the ratio of result of the opacity function of one occludee to its rectangular image size. If the occludee has a coverage ratio less than 0.2, the algorithm stops testing its descendants, as in this case the occluders cover too little area of the occludee and have low chance to completely cover the occludee's descendants. Consequently, those descendants are regarded as conservatively visible. The threshold will be adjusted according to the culling time, and prohibits the extra occlusion culling in the case where the rendering capacity is much larger than the number of primitives falling in the view frustum.

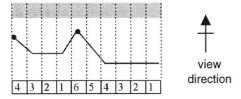

Figure 5: One row segment of the sparse depth map. It is the top view of an occludee (the grey rectangular box), and some occluders (the black lines). The two black dots mark the local farthest pixels (with the locally largest depth values) of this segment, called the peaks.

5.3   Sparse Depth Map

The sparse depth map is an auxiliary data structure of the depth map, which is generated at the same phase of off-screen rendering. The depth map is a two dimensional array recording the depth values (nearest) of the occluders. In a general approach, the depth comparison is carried out for every pixel the occludee covers. But there is depth coherence in the same row, especially in the case of the same occluder. In a row, the depth value varies in three modes, *near-to-far*, *far-to-near* or *still*; and this can be plotted as a line segment chart, where the line segment increases, decreases or keeps flat. With the chart, we locate the local peaks, which has the largest depth values locally, as shown in the Figure 5. The algorithm now only seeks the local peaks of the occluders, instead of every pixel. The sparse depth map is constructed to store the number of pixels apart from the nearest local peak to the right.

To construct the sparse depth map, the algorithm transverses the depth map from the upper right corner to the bottom left, row by row. An integer variable *step* is used to record the number of pixels that can be skipped. Ignoring the border case, it tests two consecutive (named *current* and *last*) pixels. If they are increasing or keeping still, the algorithm adds one to the *step* variable and saves it into *current* pixel of sparse depth map. Otherwise, if the previous test shows increasing and keeping still, the current pixel is the peak. It stores *step* plus one into the

peak pixel of the sparse depth map, and then resets the *step* to one.

To reduce the construction time of the sparse depth map, the algorithm does not compute the row of pixels that are covered by no occluders, because those rows will not be used for the depth comparison. As the sparse depth map exploits the pixel coherence, if the depth map varies from near-to-far and far-to-near alternatively each pixel, the sparse depth map will contain all 1s. This means there is no pixel that can be skipped, and the algorithm will test every pixel as the usual depth comparison. In this case, the sparse depth map should be disabled, in order to save the construction time. The resolutions of depth map and sparse depth map used in our tests are the same as the opacity map, i.e. 128×128.

5.4   Depth Comparison

The depth comparison uses both the depth map and sparse depth map. For an occludee, the algorithm finds the nearest depth value of its bounding volume. This simplifies the depth comparison, and also guarantees the correctness of the culling algorithm. The depth comparison is applied to the rectangular projected area of the occludee. It tests the depth from the bottom row to the top of the rectangular area. For one row, it first tests the depth value of the leftmost pixel. If the nearest depth value of the occludee is large than the pixel value of the depth map, it will test the next-jump pixel indicated in the sparse depth map. Otherwise, the occludee is in front of the occluder and the depth test fails and terminates.

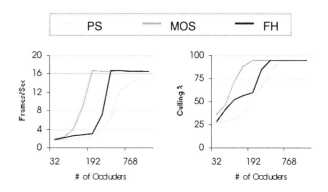

Figure 6: Frame rate and culling percentage of different occluder selection methods. *PS* stands for the criterion of projected size, *FH* stands for the criterion of first-hit.

6 Results and Analysis

We have implemented the above algorithms on a simple walkthrough system, which uses OpenGL and runs on SGI Max IMPACT workstation with R10000 CPU (200MHz) and 192 MB RAM. In this section, we demonstrate the performance of the minimum occluder set algorithm and occlusion culling using the opacity map. The test model is composed of thirty copies of a Chicago city model and contains 300,540 polygons in total. The whole environment uses one light and no texture. An overview of the test model is shown in Figure 11.

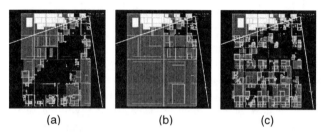

(a)   (b)   (c)

Figure 7: The top view of model. The light grey boxes are outside the view frustum, the dark grey boxes are culled by occluders and the black boxes are conservatively visible. From the left to right, the figures show the cases (a) projected size, (b) MOS and (c) first-hit criteria respectively.

6.1 MOS Algorithm

In the following tests, we compare the performances of different occluder selection criteria. They are the projected size, MOS, and first-hit. The experiment is carried out at a certain viewpoint that gives about 400 visible primitives in 512×512 resolution. For the criterion of projected size, we simply pick occluders in the descending order. For the first-hit criterion, we first find out all the visible primitives, and count the number of pixels covered by these primitives. Afterwards, we choose the occluders in the descending order. We record the frame rate and culling percentage, varying the maximum number of occluders used.

Figure 6 shows that the MOS algorithm needs 192 occluders to achieve the optimal culling percentage, about 94%. The criterion of first-hit uses about 384 occluders to reach the same culling percentage. The projected size criterion has about 93% culling with 512 occluders. The culling percentage of the projected size criterion has the slowest growth rate. Also, more occluders are used, more computation overhead is introduced for occlusion culling,

thus decreasing the frame rate shown in the tail part of the curve. The MOS algorithm uses a half of occluders as by the first-hit criterion to yield the optimal culling percentage, as it considers the combined gain and redundancy of primitives. These points are illustrated in Figure 7, which shows the top view of the whole model. The light grey boxes are nodes outside the view frustum, and the dark grey boxes are culled away by the occluders. These are the results when 192 occluders are used. Except in the MOS algorithm, the incomplete coverage caused by other two methods reduces the culling percentage, while the redundancy of occluders leads to increased overhead without improving culling ratio.

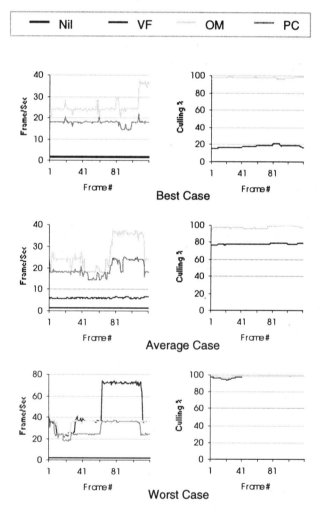

Figure 8: Performances of occlusion culling with different routes. Nil represents that no culling is applied. VF represents that view frustum culling is applied. OM represents that occlusion culling with opacity map and sparse depth map is applied. PC means occlusion culling with pixel-wise comparison.

6.2 Occlusion Culling

We have conducted two groups of tests for the occlusion culling. The first group is aimed to illustrate the speedup of occlusion culling with different depth complexities; and the second group shows performances and bottleneck at different resolutions.

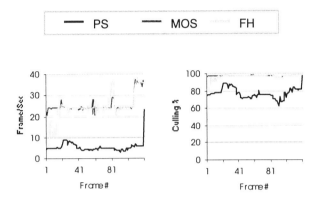

Figure 9: Performances of occlusion culling with different occluder selection criteria for the best case route. *PS*, *MOS* and *FH* **represent the criteria of projected-size, minimum occluder set and first-hit, respectively.**

Tests at Different Routes: The following three tests are carried out with the same Chicago model, but alone different routes. The three routes are located with different depth complexities, and classified as *best*, *average* and *worst* cases for the speedup. The tests use 64 occluders and have 512×512 resolution. The three routes have 120 frames each.

For the best case, the route starts at the lower left corner of the environment, and heads towards the center part. It has the highest depth complexity. The speedup of occlusion culling to view frustum is 14.6 and the average frame rate is 25.5. For the average case, the route is located at the center of the environment, the depth complexity is medium. It has the speedup of 4.4 and average frame rate of 26.7. For the worst case, the route is set at the upper right corner of the environment, with the viewer looking outwards. It has lowest depth complexity, and the speedup and average frame rate are 0.7 and 34.6, respectively. For reference, the frame rate of occlusion culling with pixel-wise comparison is also shown in Figure 8. It has the average frame rate of 17.7, 19.4 and 28.8 for the three routes, respectively.

According to Figure 8, the occlusion culling has adverse effect on the frame rate in the worst case. That is because the computation cost of view frustum culling is

lower than occlusion culling. If the environment has low depth complexity, occlusion culling causes overhead instead of profit to culling percentage.

Figure 9 shows the performance of occlusion culling using different occluder selection criteria for the best case route. The average frame rates for projected size and first-hit criteria are 5.4 and 24.5, relatively. The difference between MOS and first-hit criteria decreases progressively in the first twenty frames, and their performances are similar in the remaining frames. That is because the routes do not have too much visible primitives, so the superset of occluders (first-hit ones) converges to the optimal set after the first twenty frames.

Tests at Different Resolutions: The performance of occlusion culling using the opacity map is shown in Figure 10. The test is based on the best case route, using MOS. The two figures show the results of view frustum culling and occlusion culling at resolutions of 512×512, 768×768 and 1024×1024. The average frame rates are 25.6, 20.1 and 16.7 of the three ascending resolutions. As the sizes of opacity map and sparse depth map applied for three resolutions are the same, their culling percentages are constant. It is regarded as no change for the geometric computation. The drop in frame rate is caused by the rasterization of hardware rendering process, which is also the bottleneck of walkthrough system now. Although the frame rates of 768×768 and 1024×1024 resolutions are lower, we still have a speedup of 9.8 and 11.6 respectively.

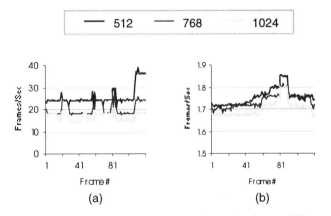

Figure 10: (a) Performances of occlusion culling using opacity map and MOS algorithm at different resolutions, 512×512, 768×768 and 1024×1024, (b) The result of view frustum.

7 Conclusions and Future Work

We have presented an occlusion culling algorithm (MOS algorithm) using the minimum occluder set and opacity map. Our algorithm results in significant speedup of the frame rate and a reduced number of occluders required. The speedup by occlusion culling is due to the use of the opacity map and sparse depth map. The opacity map needs only two integer additions and one subtraction to do the overlap test. The sparse depth map further simplifies depth comparison, by not using pixel-wise comparison. Moreover, the high culling percentage is achieved by the MOS algorithm, which takes into account the combined gain and redundancy of occluders. The occlusion culling algorithm makes no special assumption on occluders and models and is suitable for implementation on current graphics systems.

Further research includes the extension of the MOS algorithm to dynamic environments and integration with impostors for scalability. The MOS algorithm can be adapted to a dynamic model if the probability of dynamic occlusion is considered in the process of scoring. For an environment with a large number of visible primitives, we can apply impostors [18] for distant objects. Integration with impostors would make a walkthrough system into a semi-image-based VR system. Thus we would still have geometric data for nearby objects, which allows collision detection and interaction for the users, and the total number of primitives handled by graphics hardware is greatly reduced since distant primitives are represented as impostors.

Figure 11: A birdeye view of the test model, which is composed of thirty copies of a Chicago city model and contains 300,540 polygons in total.

8 Acknowledgements

We thank Mr. Cheng Kin Shing for his contributions and many discussions during the formative phase of this work.

9 References

1. P. K. Agarwal, L. J. Guibas, T. M. Murali and J. S. Vitter. Cylindrical Static and Kinetic Binary Space Partitions. *Computational Geometry '97*, pp. 39-48.
2. K. Akeley. RealityEngine Graphics. *SIGGRAPH '93*, pp. 109-116.
3. E. Catmull, A Subdivision Algorithm for Computer Display of Curved Surfaces. PhD thesis, University of Utah, 1974.
4. S. Coorg and S. Teller. Temporally Coherent Conservative Visibility. *Symposium on Computational Geometry 1996*, pp. 78-87.
5. S. Coorg and S. Teller. Real-time Occlusion Culling for Models with Large Occluders. *Symposium on Interactive 3D Graphics 1997*, pp. 83-90.
6. H. Fuchs, Z. M. Kedem, and B. F. Naylor. On Visible Surface Generation by A Priori Tree Structures. *SIGGRAPH '80*, pp. 124-133.
7. N. Greene, M. Kass and G. Miller. Hierarchical Z-Buffer Visibility. *SIGGRAPH '93*, pp. 231-238.
8. N. Greene. Hierarchical Polygon Tiling with Coverage Masks. *SIGGRAPH '96*, pp. 65-74.
9. T. Hudson, D. Manocha, J. Cohen, M. Lin, K. Hoff and H. Zhang. Accelerated Occlusion Culling using Shadow Frusta. *Computational Geometry '97*, pp. 1-10.
10. D. Luebke and C. Georges. Portals and Mirrors: Simple, Fast Evaluation of Potential Visible Sets. *Symposium on Interactive 3D Graphics, 199*, pp. 105-106.
11. K. Mulmuley. An Efficient Algorithm for Hidden Surface Removal. *SIGGRAPH '89*, pp. 379-388.
12. B. Naylor. Partitioning Tree image Representation and Generation from 3D Geometric Models. *Graphics Interface '92*, pp. 201-211.
13. R. Schumacker, B. Brand, M. Gilliland, and W. Sharp. Study for Applying Computer-Generated Images to Visual Simulation. *Technical Report AFHRL-TR-69-14. 1969.*
14. J. Snyder and J. Lengyel. Visibility Sorting and Compositing without Splitting for Image Layer Decomposition. *SIGGRAPH '98*, pp. 219-230.
15. S. Teller and C.H. Sequin. Visibility Pre-processing for Interactive Walkthroughs. *SIGGRAPH '91*, pp. 61-69.
16. E. Torres. Optimization of the Binary Space Partition Algorithm for the Visualization of Dynamic Scenes. *Eurographics '90*, pp. 507-518.
17. H. Zhang, D. Manocha, T. Hudson and K. E. Hoff III. Visibility Culling using Hierarchical Occlusion Maps. *SIGGRAPH '97*, pp. 77-88.
18. F. Sillion, G. Drettakis, B. Bodelet. Efficient Impostor Manipulation for Real-Time visualization of Urban Scenery. *Eurographics '97*, pp. 207-218.

Session 2-6

Computer Aided Geometric Design

Chair
M.L.V. Pitteway
Brunel University, UK

A Method for Deforming Polygonal Shapes into Smooth Spline Surface Models

Chiew-Lan Tai, Kia-Fock Loe[1], Brian A. Barsky[2], and Yim-Hung Chan
Department of Computer Science
The Hong Kong University of Science and Technology
Clear Water Bay, Kowloon, Hong Kong

Abstract

This paper describes a new spline formulation that supports deformation of polygonal shapes into smooth spline surface models. Once a polygonal shape with underlying rectangular topology is specified by the user, it is deformed into a smooth surface that interpolates all the polygonal vertices. The user can then modify the default smooth surface by increasing or decreasing the amount of deformation, either globally or locally. This is accomplished by interactively controlling the shape parameters associated with the polygonal vertices. This modeling paradigm is conceptually simple, and allows C^2 continuous surfaces to be easily designed, even by a novice user.

1. Introduction

Deformation from polygonal shapes to smooth surfaces is an attractive design tool since it relieves the user from the burden of having to first specify a large set of control points and then stitching complex patches together. This paper presents a new interpolating spline formulation that supports such a modeling paradigm. It only requires the user to manipulate quadrilaterals to design polygonal shapes which are then smoothed or deformed by controlling the shape parameters associated with the vertices. The resulting surface is C^2 continuous and interpolates the given vertices. The formulation allows sharp corners to be easily introduced without using multiple knots or multiple control points.

Our deformation formulation applies only to polygonal shapes of rectangular topology. Cylindrical or toroidal topology is also supported since they can be tiled by rectangular patches. The smoothing of polygonal shapes is achieved by combining a network of *singularly reparametrized bilinear patches*[12] with a piecewise

---

[1]Department of Computer Science, School of Computing, National University of Singapore, Lower Kent Ridge, Singapore 119260.

[2]On sabbatical leave from Computer Science Division, University of California, Berkeley, CA 94720-1776, U.S.A.

smooth surface to obtain a new surface that interpolates all the polygonal vertices. In addition to not needing to solve a system of equations to achieve interpolation, this approach has the advantages of having local tension shape parameters and being C^2 continuous.

2. Related work

Barr [2] introduced deformation operations for twisting, stretching, bending and tapering surfaces around a central axis. His work was followed by Sederberg and Parry's [13] more generalized deformation technique, called the Free-Form Deformation (FFD) method. The FFD method embeds the object to be deformed in a lattice of control vertices that defines a trivariate Bézier volume. Deformation is done by altering the lattice and recalculating the new positions of the points of the embedded object based on their unique parameter values. Several extended versions of FFDs have since been proposed, incorporating B-spline and NURBS trivariate volumes [11] and allowing lattices of arbitrary shape and topology [9]. Other more recent deformation techniques can be found in the comprehensive survey paper of Bechmann [4]. None of them, however, addresses deformation of polygonal shapes to smooth spline surfaces.

In addition to purely geometric deformation approaches, there are physics-based deformable models. A physics-based model employs elasticity theory to construct an energy functional, and calculates the model's shape directly by finding a minimum to the energy functional or by solving a set of differential equations [6, 16]. Physics-based models can most closely mimic the sculpting effect and their optimization algorithms automatically produce fair surfaces. However, they typically require intensive computations.

To produce curved surfaces from polygonal shapes, a traditional method is to round sharp corners and edges using parametric blending and filleting techniques [7, 8]. Parametric blends typically join the base surfaces with only C^1 continuity. Another method is to replace each face of a polyhedron by an algebraic surface patch. Bajaj and Ihm[1] replace each face of a triangulated polyhedron by a low degree (5 or 7) algebraic surface patch, which has independent degrees of freedom that provide local shape control. More recently, subdivision techniques [5, 10, 14] have emerged as a popular method for obtaining smooth surfaces from polygonal meshes; this is largely due to their elegance in supporting meshes of arbitrary topology and their relationship with multiresolution techniques like wavelets.

3. Singularly reparametrized line segment

A *singularly reparametrized* (SR) *line segment* is a line segment that possesses parametric derivative(s) equal to zero at each end. It is obtained by blending two endpoints with a *singular blending function*[12, 15]. A function $s(t)$, $t \in [0, 1]$, is called an mth-level singular blending function if

1. it is monotonically increasing from $s(0)=0$ to $s(1)=1$

2. its first to mth derivatives are equal to zero at $t = 0$ and $t = 1$; *i.e.*, $s^{(k)}(0) = s^{(k)}(1) = 0$ for $k = 1, ..., m$.

One possibility for an mth-level singular blending function is $s_1(t) = 1 - (1 - t^{m+1})^{m+1}$. A lower degree alternative for the same level can be developed as a special case, $s_2(t)$, of the Hermite polynomial [3]. In addition, for our purpose of formulating C^2 continuous splines, we note that the second-level singular blending function is sufficient. In this case of $m = 2$, $s_1(t) = 1 - (1 - t^3)^3$ and the Hermite polynomial is $s_2(t) = 10t^3 - 15t^4 + 6t^5$. Comparing $s_1(t)$ with $s_2(t)$, the latter has a lower degree but requires slightly more computation. For the remainder of this paper, we do not assume any specific $s(t)$ function, it can be any second- or higher level singular blending function.

Using a singular blending function $s(t)$, we can blend two adjacent points $\mathbf{V}_j$ and $\mathbf{V}_{j+1}$ to produce an SR line segment $\mathbf{L}_j(t)$; that is,

$$\mathbf{L}_j(t) = (1 - s(t))\mathbf{V}_j + s(t)\mathbf{V}_{j+1} \qquad t \in [0, 1] \quad (1)$$

which interpolates the two points as well as satisfies the following property

$$\mathbf{L}_j'(0) = \mathbf{L}_j'(1) = \mathbf{L}_j''(0) = \mathbf{L}_j''(1) = 0.$$

4. Singular blending

Given a C^2 continuous piecewise curve (comprising a sequence of curve segments), a sequence of SR line segments can be blended with it to create a new piecewise curve that preserves the continuity of the given curve. The blending introduces a parameter which can simulate the effect of tension. Denoting the given piecewise curve by $\mathbf{C}(t)$ and the sequence of SR line segments by $\mathbf{L}_j(t)$, $j = 1, ..., n$, then the new piecewise curve $\mathbf{Q}(t)$ is

$$\mathbf{Q}_j(t) = (1 - \alpha)\mathbf{C}_j(t) + \alpha\mathbf{L}_j(t), \qquad j = 1, ..., n \quad (2)$$

where $0 \leq \alpha \leq 1$. If the SR line segments are very different from the given piecewise curve $\mathbf{C}_j(t)$, then the parameter α simply indicates the blending proportions; however, if they are a linearized approximation of the given $\mathbf{C}(t)$, then α can simulate the tension effect. Since both $\mathbf{C}(t)$ and $\mathbf{L}_j(t)$, $j = 1, ..., n$, are C^2 continuous, thus the curve $\mathbf{Q}(t)$ must also be C^2.

Fig. 1(a) illustrates the concept of singular blending by blending a polygon $\mathbf{P}_1, \mathbf{P}_2, \mathbf{P}_3, \mathbf{P}_4$ with a smoothing unit circle $\mathbf{C}(t)$. In this case, the edges of the polygon are defined as SR line segments as specified in Eqn.(1) for $\mathbf{L}_j(t)$, $j = 1, ..., 4$, where $\mathbf{V}_i = \mathbf{P}_i$, $i = 1, ..., 4$, and the smoothing circle is defined by

$$\mathbf{C}_j(t) = (\cos \frac{2\pi(j - 1 + t)}{4}, \sin \frac{2\pi(j - 1 + t)}{4})$$

$t \in [0, 1]$, $j = 1, ..., 4$. By blending the polygon with the circle using Eqn.(2), we obtain a C^2 continuous closed curve $\mathbf{Q}(t)$ which can be interpreted as a deformed or smoothed version of the polygon.

When the smoothing curve $\mathbf{C}(t)$ does not interpolate the vertices of the polygon, as is the case in this example, the resulting curve $\mathbf{Q}(t)$ may bear little resemblance to the polygonal shape for low values of α, which could be undesirable. However, there is no reason to restrict the SR line segments to be the polygon edges. Instead, we will use the following more general approach. We will determine a new sequence of SR line segments $\mathbf{L}_j(t)$, $j = 1, ..., n$ such that when they are blended with the smoothing curve $\mathbf{C}(t)$, the resulting curve $\mathbf{Q}(t)$ will interpolate the polygon vertices.

This is shown in Fig. 1(b). Given the smoothing circle $\mathbf{C}(t)$, and the polygon $\mathbf{P}_1, \mathbf{P}_2, \mathbf{P}_3, \mathbf{P}_4$, we can find a new sequence of SR line segments $\mathbf{L}_j(t)$, $j = 1, ..., n$ which when blended with the smoothing circle produces the curve $\mathbf{Q}(t)$ that interpolates the polygon vertices.

This approach can be extended to smoothing polygonal surfaces. The smoothed surface will interpolate the polygon vertices and is thus guaranteed to resemble the polygonal shapes.

This is the central idea of our approach. The user first sketches the polygonal outline of the object to be modeled in terms of nonplanar quadrilaterals without regard to smoothness of the surface. The resulting smooth surface is guaranteed to interpolate all the polygon vertices. This provides an intuitive modeling approach for the user, and should be especially appropriate for novice designers. Our modeling system initializes the α value to a reasonable default value, such as 0.5. The user can then modify the default smooth surface by varying the α value. To provide further and more precise control over the shape, we also provide local tension parameters. This is described in the next section.

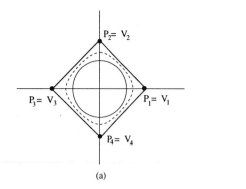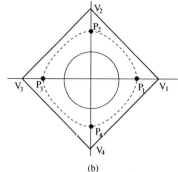

Figure 1. Blending a polygon with a smoothing circle.

5. Smoothing closed polygon

In the previous section, we gave an example of using a unit circle to smooth a closed polygon. For the technique to be a useful modeling tool, it must be improved in two ways.

First, to enable the user to adjust the tension locally at each joint, we need to generalize the constant α value in Eqn.(2) to a function of t. To provide local deformation control, we assign a local tension parameter α_j^* to each vertex $\mathbf{P}_j$, $j = 1, ..., n$ and then interpolate these tension parameters using the singular blending function:

$$\alpha_j(t) = (1 - s(t))\alpha_j^* + s(t)\alpha_{j+1}^* \qquad j = 1, ..., n. \quad (3)$$

By replacing the constant α value in Eqn.(2) by the tension function $\alpha_j(t)$, we obtain a locally deformable curve $\mathbf{Q}(t)$ as follows:

$$\mathbf{Q}_j(t) = (1 - \alpha_j(t))\mathbf{C}_j(t) + \alpha_j(t)\mathbf{L}_j(t) \quad j = 1, ..., n. \quad (4)$$

Second, we need to generalize the unit circle to a smoothing closed curve that is independent of the coordinate system and resembles the polygonal shape. We will use a B-spline to define the smoothing curve since the B-spline has many desirable geometric and computational properties.

Let $\{\mathbf{P}_1, ..., \mathbf{P}_n\}$ be the vertices of a given n-sided polygon and $\{\alpha_1^*, ..., \alpha_n^*\}$ be the set of corresponding tension parameters. Our approach first obtains a closed uniform cubic B-spline curve $\mathbf{C}_j(t)$ which *approximates* the given vertices. To produce the closed curve, three additional vertices $\mathbf{P}_0$, $\mathbf{P}_{n+1}$, and $\mathbf{P}_{n+2}$ are introduced, where

$$\mathbf{P}_0 = \mathbf{P}_n \qquad \mathbf{P}_{n+1} = \mathbf{P}_1 \qquad \mathbf{P}_{n+2} = \mathbf{P}_2.$$

Using $\mathbf{P}_j$, $j = 0, ..., n + 2$ as the control points of the B-spline curve, we obtain

$$\mathbf{C}_j(t) = N_0(t)\mathbf{P}_{j-1} + N_1(t)\mathbf{P}_j + N_2(t)\mathbf{P}_{j+1} + N_3(t)\mathbf{P}_{j+2} \quad (5)$$

where $j = 1, ..., n$ and $N_i(t)$, $i = 0, ..., 3$ are the cubic uniform B-spline basis functions [3].

Let $\{\mathbf{V}_1, ..., \mathbf{V}_n\}$ denote the unknown points that define the sequence of SR line segments $\mathbf{L}_j(t)$, $j = 1, ..., n$ to be blended with the B-spline curve obtained. The SR line segments that are determined must be such that the blended curve $\mathbf{Q}(t)$ in Eqn.(4) interpolates the polygon vertices. That is, we impose the following n constraints:

$$\mathbf{P}_j = \mathbf{Q}_j(0) \qquad j = 1, ..., n.$$

Substituting for $\mathbf{Q}_j(0)$ from Eqn (4),

$$\mathbf{P}_j = (1 - \alpha_j(0))\mathbf{C}_j(0) + \alpha_j(0)\mathbf{L}_j(0) \qquad j = 1, ..., n.$$

Substituting for $\alpha_j(0)$ from Eqn.(3) and for $\mathbf{L}_j(0)$ from Eqn.(1) yields

$$\mathbf{P}_j = (1 - \alpha_j^*)\mathbf{C}_j(0) + \alpha_j^*\mathbf{V}_j \qquad j = 1, ..., n.$$

Due to the linearity of the SR line segments, the points defining them are independent of each other and hence can be determined by simple computation. Solving Eqn.(5) for $\mathbf{V}_j$ yields:

$$\mathbf{V}_j = \mathbf{P}_j + \frac{1 - \alpha_j^*}{\alpha_j^*}(\mathbf{P}_j - \mathbf{C}_j(0)) \qquad j = 1, ..., n.$$

Note that the geometric interpretation of this equation is that when $\alpha_j^* = 1$, then $\mathbf{V}_j = \mathbf{P}_j$, and as α_j^* decreases to 0, $\mathbf{V}_j$ moves away from $\mathbf{P}_j$. When $\alpha_j^* = 0$, $\mathbf{V}_j$ is at infinity, implying no suitable SR line segments can be found. We therefore restrict the value of α_j^* to be in the range $(0, 1]$.

Since $\mathbf{L}_j(t)$, $\mathbf{C}_j(t)$, and $\alpha_j(t)$ are all C^2 continuous, the resulting curve in Eqn.(4) is clearly C^2 continuous. Differentiating Eqn.(4), we note that the end tangents are in the same directions as those in the B-spline counterpart, with the magnitudes scaled by $1 - \alpha_j^*$; that is,

$$\mathbf{Q}_{j-1}'(1) = (1 - \alpha_j^*)\mathbf{C}_{j-1}'(1) \text{ and } \mathbf{Q}_j'(0) = (1 - \alpha_j^*)\mathbf{C}_j'(0)$$

and since $\mathbf{C}'_{j-1}(1) = \mathbf{C}'_j(0)$, we have $\mathbf{Q}'_{j-1}(1) = \mathbf{Q}'_j(0)$.

When α^*_j approaches 1, the corresponding SR line segments that are determined are close to the given polygon. In addition, since the contribution of the SR line segments to the curve $\mathbf{Q}(t)$ is larger as α^*_j approaches unity, the resulting curve segments increasingly resemble the SR line segments and hence are more tensed. In the case when $\alpha^*_j = 1$ for all j, we obtain the given polygon.

Fig. 2 shows the effects of decreasing the tension parameters globally from 1 to 0.1. It illustrates the deformation of a square to rounder closed curves. To illustrate the local effect of tension parameters, Fig. 3 shows the same square with all vertices having $\alpha^*_j = 0.5$ except for the lower right one where the local tension parameter decreases from 1 to 0.25.

6 Smoothing open polygon

In the previous section, we have assumed that the given vertices $\{\mathbf{P}_1, ..., \mathbf{P}_n\}$ form a closed polygon. For the case where these vertices form an open polygon, the polygon must be smoothed by an open B-spline curve. Since the polygon has $n - 1$ segments, to obtain the same number of segments in the open uniform cubic B-spline curve, we introduce two phantom vertices $\mathbf{P}_0$, $\mathbf{P}_{n+1}$ where

$$\mathbf{P}_0 = 2\mathbf{P}_1 - \mathbf{P}_2 \quad \text{and} \quad \mathbf{P}_{n+1} = 2\mathbf{P}_n - \mathbf{P}_{n-1}.$$

The phantom vertices are chosen so that the B-spline curve $\mathbf{C}_j(t)$, $j = 1, ..., n - 1$ interpolates the endpoints $\mathbf{P}_1$ and $\mathbf{P}_n$ [3]. The interpolation constraints imposed on $\mathbf{Q}(t)$ then become

$$\mathbf{P}_j = \mathbf{Q}_j(0), j = 1, ..., n - 1 \quad \text{and} \quad \mathbf{P}_n = \mathbf{Q}_{n-1}(1).$$

Thus, the vertices of the SR line segments can be solved from

$$\mathbf{V}_1 = \mathbf{P}_1 \qquad \mathbf{V}_n = \mathbf{P}_n$$
$$\mathbf{V}_j = \mathbf{P}_j + \frac{1 - \alpha^*_j}{\alpha^*_j}(\mathbf{P}_j - \mathbf{C}_j(0)) \qquad j = 2, ..., n - 1.$$

7. Singularly reparametrized bilinear patch

Next, we will generalize the above idea from curve to surface design. We first introduce the *singularly reparametrized* (SR) *bilinear patch*, which is geometrically equivalent to a bilinear surface but has vanishing end derivatives. That is, an SR bilinear patch is defined by four vertices $\{\mathbf{V}_{i,j}, \mathbf{V}_{i,j+1}, \mathbf{V}_{i+1,j}, \mathbf{V}_{i+1,j+1}\}$:

$$\mathbf{L}_{i,j}(u,v) = (1-s(u))(1-s(v))\mathbf{V}_{i,j} + (1-s(u))s(v)\mathbf{V}_{i,j+1}$$
$$+ s(u)(1-s(v))\mathbf{V}_{i+1,j} + s(u)s(v)\mathbf{V}_{i+1,j+1} \quad (6)$$

Differentiating $\mathbf{L}_{i,j}(u,v)$ in Eqn.(6) and evaluating at $u = 0$, $u = 1$, $v = 0$, and $v = 1$, yields the following singular properties:

$$\partial_u\mathbf{L}_{i,j}(0,v) = \partial_u\mathbf{L}_{i,j}(1,v) = \partial_v\mathbf{L}_{i,j}(u,0) = \partial_v\mathbf{L}_{i,j}(u,1) = 0,$$
$$\partial_u^2\mathbf{L}_{i,j}(0,v) = \partial_u^2\mathbf{L}_{i,j}(1,v) = \partial_v^2\mathbf{L}_{i,j}(u,0) = \partial_v^2\mathbf{L}_{i,j}(u,1) = 0,$$
$$\partial_{uv}^2\mathbf{L}_{i,j}(0,v) = \partial_{uv}^2\mathbf{L}_{i,j}(1,v) = \partial_{uv}^2\mathbf{L}_{i,j}(u,0) = \partial_{uv}^2\mathbf{L}_{i,j}(u,1) = 0.$$

8. Smoothing polygonal surfaces

We now apply the idea to the smoothing of polygonal surfaces, in particular quadrilaterals. Let $\{\mathbf{P}_{i,j} : i = 1, ..., m; \ j = 1, ..., n\}$ be a network of vertices. Let $\{\alpha^*_{i,j} : i = 1, ..., m; \ j = 1, ..., n\}$ be the corresponding set of tension parameters, where $0 < \alpha^*_{i,j} \le 1$. The network can have a rectangular, cylindrical, or toroidal topology.

First, we assume that the network has a cylindrical topology, where i is the index in the closed direction and j is the index in the open-ended direction. That is, the network of vertices has $m \times (n - 1)$ quadrilaterals.

To obtain a B-spline surface $\mathbf{S}_{i,j}(u,v)$, $i = 1, ..., m$ and $j = 1, ..., n - 1$, from the network of vertices, we first introduce some additional points as in the case of curves. Analogous to handling open curves, we add two rows of phantom vertices $\mathbf{P}_{0,j}$ and $\mathbf{P}_{m+1,j}$ where $j = 1, ..., n$; that is,

$$\mathbf{P}_{0,j} = 2\mathbf{P}_{1,j} - \mathbf{P}_{2,j} \quad \text{and} \quad \mathbf{P}_{m+1,j} = 2\mathbf{P}_{m,j} - \mathbf{P}_{m-1,j}$$

$j = 1, ..., n$. Analogous to handling closed curves, we add three rows of vertices to wrap around the end vertices

$$\mathbf{P}_{i,0} = \mathbf{P}_{i,n} \qquad \mathbf{P}_{i,n+1} = \mathbf{P}_{i,1} \qquad \mathbf{P}_{i,n+2} = \mathbf{P}_{i,2}$$

$i = 0, ..., m + 1$. The B-spline surface is then

$$\mathbf{S}_{i,j}(u,v) = \sum_{p=0}^{3}\sum_{q=0}^{3} N_p(u)N_q(v)\mathbf{P}_{i+p-1,j+q-1} \quad (7)$$

$i = 1, ..., m; \ j = 1, ..., n - 1$. Let $\mathbf{L}_{i,j}(u,v)$, $i = 1, ..., m$, $j = 1, ..., n - 1$ be the unknown SR bilinear patches to be blended with the B-spline surface. The blended smooth surface is given by

$$\mathbf{Q}_{i,j}(u,v) = (1 - \alpha_{i,j}(u,v))\mathbf{S}_{i,j}(u,v) + \alpha_{i,j}(u,v)\mathbf{L}_{i,j}(u,v)$$
$$(8)$$

where

$$\alpha_{i,j}(u,v) = (1-s(u))(1-s(v))\alpha^*_{i,j} + (1-s(u))s(v)\alpha^*_{i,j+1}$$
$$+ s(u)(1-s(v))\alpha^*_{i+1,j} + s(u)s(v)\alpha^*_{i+1,j+1} \quad (9)$$

$i = 1, ..., m; \ j = 1, ..., n - 1$.

To find the points $\{\mathbf{V}_{i,j} : i = 1, ..., m; \ j = 1, ..., n\}$ that define the SR bilinear patches, we impose a set of constraints on $\mathbf{Q}(u,v)$ to interpolate the polygonal vertices:

$$\mathbf{P}_{i,j} = \mathbf{Q}_{i,j}(0,0) \qquad i = 1, ..., m; \ j = 1, ..., n - 1,$$
$$\mathbf{P}_{i,n} = \mathbf{Q}_{i,n-1}(0,1) \qquad i = 1, ..., m.$$

Figure 2. Decreasing the tension parameters globally from 1, 0.75, 0.5, 0.25 to 0.1.

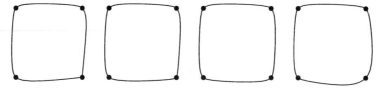

Figure 3. Decreasing the tension parameter locally (at the lower right vertex) from 1, 0.75, 0.5 to 0.25. All the other vertices have $\alpha_j^* = 0.5$.

Substituting for $\mathbf{Q}_{i,j}(0,0)$ and $\mathbf{Q}_{i,n-1}(0,1)$ from Eqn.(8), we have

$$\mathbf{P}_{i,j} = (1 - \alpha_{i,j}(0,0))\mathbf{S}_{i,j}(0,0) + \alpha_{i,j}(0,0)\mathbf{L}_{i,j}(0,0)$$
$$i = 1, ..., m; \; j = 1, ..., n-1,$$
$$\mathbf{P}_{i,n} = (1 - \alpha_{i,n-1}(0,1))\mathbf{S}_{i,n-1}(0,1)$$
$$+ \alpha_{i,n-1}(0,1)\mathbf{L}_{i,n-1}(0,1) \qquad i = 1, ..., m.$$

Substituting for $\alpha_{i,j}(0,0)$ and $\alpha_{i,n-1}(0,1)$ from Eqn.(9) and for $\mathbf{L}_{i,j}(0,0)$ and $\mathbf{L}_{i,n-1}(0,1)$ from Eqn.(6), we have

$$\mathbf{P}_{i,j} = (1 - \alpha_{i,j}^*)\mathbf{S}_{i,j}(0,0) + \alpha_{i,j}^*\mathbf{V}_{i,j}$$
$$i = 1, ..., m; \; j = 1, ..., n-1,$$
$$\mathbf{P}_{i,n} = (1 - \alpha_{i,n}^*)\mathbf{S}_{i,n-1}(0,1) + \alpha_{i,n}^*\mathbf{V}_{i,n}$$
$$i = 1, ..., m. \qquad (10)$$

Substituing $\mathbf{S}_{i,1}(0,0) = \mathbf{P}_{i,1}$ and $\mathbf{S}_{i,n-1}(0,1) = \mathbf{P}_{i,n}, i = 1, ..., m$, and simplifying yields

$$\mathbf{V}_{i,1} = \mathbf{P}_{i,1} \qquad \mathbf{V}_{i,n} = \mathbf{P}_{i,n} \qquad i = 1, ..., m.$$

The remaining $\mathbf{V}_{i,j}$ can be solved from Eqn.(10) as follows:

$$\mathbf{V}_{i,j} = \mathbf{P}_{i,j} + \frac{1 - \alpha_{i,j}^*}{\alpha_{i,j}^*}(\mathbf{P}_{i,j} - \mathbf{S}_{i,j}(0,0))$$

$i = 1, ..., m; \; j = 2, ..., n-1$. Note that the equations for computing $\mathbf{V}_{i,j}$ are very simple. The computation that is needed is much simpler than many surface interpolation approaches which require solving a system of linear equations.

We have assumed a cylindrical topology; the case of a rectangular topology can be handled in a similar way. Since both the u and v parametric directions are open-ended, we add two rows of phantom vertices in both directions. The points defining the $(m-1) \times (n-1)$ SR bilinear patches are

$$\mathbf{V}_{i,1} = \mathbf{P}_{i,1} \qquad \mathbf{V}_{i,n} = \mathbf{P}_{i,n} \qquad i = 1, ..., m,$$
$$\mathbf{V}_{1,j} = \mathbf{P}_{1,j} \qquad \mathbf{V}_{m,j} = \mathbf{P}_{m,j} \qquad j = 1, ..., n,$$
$$\mathbf{V}_{i,j} = \mathbf{P}_{i,j} + \frac{1 - \alpha_{i,j}^*}{\alpha_{i,j}^*}(\mathbf{P}_{i,j} - \mathbf{S}_{i,j}(0,0))$$
$$i = 2, ..., m-1; \; j = 2, ..., n-1.$$

9. Results

To illustrate the proposed modeling paradigm, we will now show how a vase can be modeled using our prototype system. The user first specifies a polygonal shape, as shown in Fig. 4(a). Our system then uses these vertices to define a smooth B-spline surface, which is shown in Fig. 4(b). This B-spline surface only approximates the polygonal shape. Next, the system assumes a global tension value of $\alpha = 0.5$, and determines a set of SR bilinear patches (Fig. 4(c)) to be blended with the B-spline surface to produce the smooth vase shown in Fig. 4(d). This smooth surface is C^2 continuous and interpolates all the given vertices (the black squares shown in the figure).

Fig. 5 and 6 show some possible ways of modifying the default shape ($\alpha = 0.5$) generated by the system. The leftmost vase in all these figures is the default shape. Fig. 5

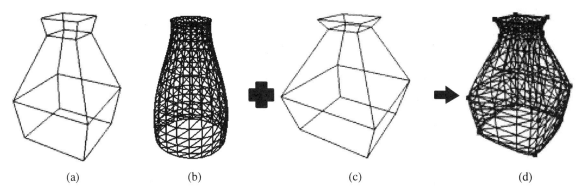

Figure 4. A user-input polygonal shape (a), then the B-spline surface (b) and the SR bilinear patches (c) are blended together using $\alpha = 0.5$ to generate vase (d). The black squares in (d) indicate the polygonal vertices in (a).

shows the effects of changing the tension parameters globally; the vase can be made to have sharper corners (Fig. 5(a)) or be rounder (Fig. 5(b)). The user can also modify the vase locally. Fig. 6 shows the effects of varying the tension parameters of those vertices in the third row.

10. Conclusion

We have presented a new spline formulation for deforming polygonal shapes to smooth surfaces. It is conceptually simple and easy to use even for novice users. The user needs only to specify a polygonal shape and then the modeling system will generate a default smooth surface interpolating all the polygonal vertices. The user can then modify the default smooth surface, either globally or locally, by changing the local tension parameters. The method is computationally simple, and guarantees C^2 continuity. The usefulness of this new modeling paradigm has been demonstrated by several modeling examples.

Acknowledgement

This work is partially supported by the Hong Kong RGC Grant DAG97/98.EG14.

References

[1] C. L. Bajaj and I. Ihm. Smoothing polyhedra using implicit algebraic splines. *ACM SIGGRAPH '92 Proceedings*, 26(2):79–87, 1992.

[2] A. H. Barr. Global and local deformations of solid primitives. *Computer Graphics*, 18(3):21–30, July 1984.

[3] R. H. Bartels, J. C. Beatty, and B. A. Barsky. *An introduction to splines for use in computer graphics and geometric modeling*. Morgan Kaufmann, San Francisco, 1987.

[4] D. Bechmann. Multidimensional free-form deformation tools. In *Eurographics '98 (State of The Art Report)*, pages 105–112, 1998.

[5] E. Catmull and J. Clark. Recursively generated B-spline surfaces on arbitrary topological meshes. *Computer-Aided Design*, 10(6):350–355, Nov. 1978.

[6] G. Celniker and D. Gossard. Deformable curve and surface finite-elements for free-form shape design. *Computer Graphics*, 25(4):257–266, 1991.

[7] H. Chiyokura and F. Kimura. Design of solids with free-form surfaces. *ACM SIGGRAPH '83 Proceedings*, pages 289–298, 1983.

[8] B. K. Choi and S. Y. Ju. Constant radius blending in surface modeling. *Computer-Aided Design*, 21:213–220, 1989.

[9] S. Coquillart. Extended free-form deformation: A sculpturing tool for 3D geometric modeling. *Computer Graphics*, 24(4):187–193, Aug. 1990.

[10] D. Doo and M. A. Sabin. Behaviour of recursive subdivision surfaces near extraordinary points. *Computer-Aided Design*, 10:356–360, 1978.

[11] W. M. Hsu, J. F. Hughes, and H. Kaufman. Direct manipulation of free-form deformations. *ACM SIGGRAPH '92 Proceedings*, 26(2):177–184, July 1992.

[12] K. F. Loe. αB-spline: a linear singular blending B-spline. *The Visual Computer*, 12:18–25, 1996.

[13] T. Sederberg and S. Parry. Free-form deformation of solid geometric models. *ACM SIGGRAPH '86 Proceedings*, 20(4):151–160, July 1986.

[14] T. W. Sederberg, J. Zheng, D. Sewell, and M. Sabin. Non-uniform recursive subdivision surfaces. *ACM SIGGRAPH Proceedings '98*, pages 387–394, 1998.

[15] C. L. Tai and K. F. Loe. α-spline: a C^2 continuous spline with weights and tension control. In A. Pasko, editor, *Shape Modeling International '99*, pages 138–143, Aizu-Wakamatsu, Japan, 1999. IEEE Computer Society Press.

[16] J. A. Thingvold and E. Cohen. Physical modeling with B-spline surfaces for interactive design and animation. *Computer Graphics*, 24(4):129–137, 1990.

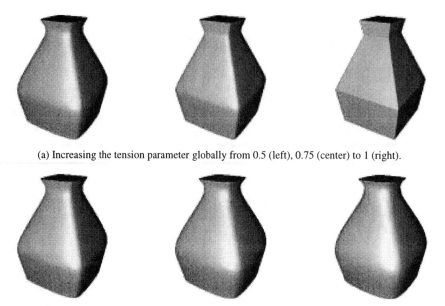

(a) Increasing the tension parameter globally from 0.5 (left), 0.75 (center) to 1 (right).

(b) Decreasing the tension parameter globally from 0.5 (left), 0.35 (center) to 0.25 (right).

Figure 5. Starting from the default shape ($\alpha = 0.5$), the vase can be modified to become either more tensed (a) or rounder (b).

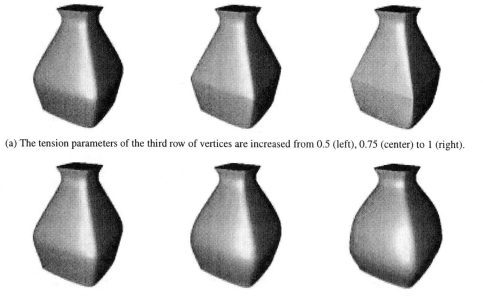

(a) The tension parameters of the third row of vertices are increased from 0.5 (left), 0.75 (center) to 1 (right).

(b) The tension parameter of the third row of vertices are decreased from 0.5 (left), 0.35 (center) to 0.25 (right).

Figure 6. Starting from the default shape ($\alpha = 0.5$), the lower part of the vase can be modified to become either more tensed (a) or rounder (b).

Signed Area of Sectors Between Spline Curves and the Origin

Kenji Ueda

Ricoh Company, Ltd.

ueda@src.ricoh.co.jp

Abstract

Formulas for representing the signed area of sectors between Bézier and B-spline curve segments and the origin are presented. The area is expressed by using the coordinates of the control points and coefficients calculated with the basis functions of the spline curves. Area-preserving deformations of the spline curves by moving the control points are also investigated.

1 Introduction

As the signed area between a curve and an axis is calculated by means of integration, the area bounded by polynomial curves can be calculated exactly. A formula for calculating the signed area between Bézier curves and an axis has been shown in [9]. The formula, which is based on the area of a trapezoid, has complicated coefficients.

We can also calculate the signed area of a sector between a curve and the origin. The method is based on the area of a triangle. By using the sector formula, the signed area between spline curves and the origin is given using a form with simpler coefficients.

In this paper, we present formulas representing the signed area of the sectors between polynomial spline curves and the origin. In Section 2, we give a general formula that calculates the areas between parametric curves and the origin. Section 3 shows Wronskian determinants for Bernstein and B-spline basis functions. The formulas for the sectors between Bézier and B-spline curves and the origin are presented in Section 4. We show some area-preserving deformations of spline curves on the basis of the formulas in Section 5.

2 Signed Area Defined by Spline Curve Segments

The signed area of the region bounded by a polygon with vertices $P_0, P_1, \cdots, P_n$ is calculated via

$$
\begin{aligned}
\Box(P_0, P_1, \cdots, P_n) &= \frac{1}{2} \sum_{k=0}^{n} P_k \times P_{k+1} \\
&= \frac{1}{2} \sum_{k=0}^{n} (x_k y_{k+1} - x_{k+1} y_k)\,, \quad (1)
\end{aligned}
$$

where $P_{n+1} = P_0$ [3]. As the signed area of the triangular region between the line segment $\overline{P_i P_j}$ and the origin $O = (0,0)$ is expressed as

$$
\triangle(O, P_i, P_j) = \frac{1}{2} P_i \times P_j\,, \qquad (2)
$$

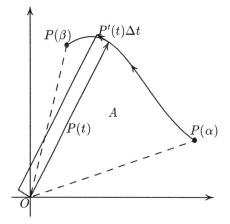

Figure 1: Signed area defined by a curve segment.

the area of the polygon is the sum of the signed areas of the triangles defined with the line segments of the polygon and the origin.

The area of a region bounded by curve segments is also obtained as the sum of the signed areas of the sectors between the curve segments and the origin. For a curve segment $P(t) = (x(t), y(t))$ with a parameter $t \in [\alpha, \beta]$, the area between the curve and the origin is calculated as follows.

The half of the parallelogram shown in Figure 1 is represented as

$$
\Delta A = \frac{1}{2}[P(t) \times (P'(t)\Delta t)] = \frac{1}{2}
\begin{vmatrix}
x(t) & y(t) \\
x'(t)\Delta t & y'(t)\Delta t
\end{vmatrix}.
\tag{3}
$$

The area A between the curve segment and the origin is calculated by integrating Equation (3) on the support of the curve.

$$
A = \lim_{\Delta t \to 0} \sum \Delta A = \frac{1}{2} \int_{\alpha}^{\beta} (x(t)\, y'(t) - y(t)\, x'(t))dt\,.
\tag{4}
$$

This formula is called Leibniz's sector formula.

By using basis functions $b_i(t)$, a spline curve $P(t)$ with control points $P_i = (x_i, y_i)$ is given by

$$
P(t) = (x(t), y(t)) = \left(\sum_{i=0}^{n} x_i b_i(t), \ \sum_{i=0}^{n} y_i b_i(t) \right). \tag{5}
$$

The derivative $P'(t)$ of the curve is also given by

$$P'(t) = (x'(t), y'(t)) = \left(\sum_{i=0}^{n} x_i b_i'(t), \sum_{i=0}^{n} y_i b_i'(t) \right).$$

$$(6)$$

Hence, the signed area A for the spline curves is expressed as

$$A = \int_{\alpha}^{\beta} \left\{ \sum_{i=0}^{n} \sum_{j=0}^{n} x_i y_j \frac{b_i(t) b_j'(t) - b_i'(t) b_j(t)}{2} \right\} dt$$

$$= \sum_{i=0}^{n} \sum_{j=0}^{n} x_i y_j \, a_{i,j}, \qquad (7)$$

where

$$a_{i,j} = \frac{1}{2} \int_{\alpha}^{\beta} [b_i(t) b_j'(t) - b_i'(t) b_j(t)] \, dt. \qquad (8)$$

As it is obvious that $a_{i,i} = 0$ and $a_{i,j} = -a_{j,i}$, the area A is represented as the weighted sum of the signed areas of the triangles defined by the origin and two control points chosen out of the control polygon.

$$A = \sum_{i=0}^{n-1} \sum_{j=i+1}^{n} (x_i y_j - x_j y_i) \, a_{i,j}$$

$$= \sum_{i=0}^{n-1} \sum_{j=i+1}^{n} 2 \triangle(O, P_i, P_j) \, a_{i,j}. \qquad (9)$$

For any affine transformation

$$g : (x, y) \mapsto (ax + by + e, \, cx + dy + f) \qquad (10)$$
$$(ad - bc \neq 0),$$

the triangular areas are scaled by a constant as

$$\frac{\triangle(g(O), g(P_i), g(P_j))}{\triangle(O, P_i, P_j)} = ad - bc. \qquad (11)$$

Therefore, the area of the region bounded by spline function is scaled with an affine transformation.

3 Wronskian Determinant

Suppose that $W(t)$ is defined as

$$W(t) = x(t) \, y'(t) - y(t) \, x'(t) = \left| \begin{array}{cc} x(t) & y(t) \\ y'(t) & x'(t) \end{array} \right|. \qquad (12)$$

This function $W(t)$ is called a Wronskian determinant and is the integrand in (4). The degree of $W_{i,j}(t)$ is $2n - 2$, if the functions $x(t)$ and $y(t)$ are of degree n. The signed area A is half of a definite integral of the Wronskian of the functions $x(t)$ and $y(t)$ defining a spline curve.

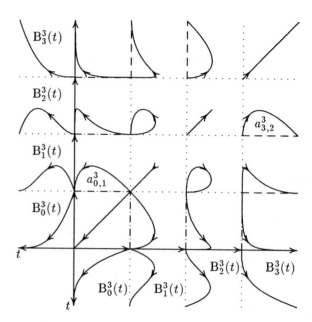

Figure 2: Curves defined by Bernstein basis functions.

On the other hand, the coefficients $a_{i,j}$ in (7) is also expressed as the integral of the Wronskian $w_{i,j}^n(t)$ of the basis functions $b_i(t)$ and $b_j(t)$,

$$w_{i,j}^n(t) = b_i(t) b_j'(t) - b_i'(t) b_j(t) = \left| \begin{array}{cc} b_i(t) & b_j(t) \\ b_i'(t) & b_j'(t) \end{array} \right|. \qquad (13)$$

This means that the coefficient $a_{i,j}$ are the areas for the curves $c_{i,j}(t) = (b_i(t), b_j(t))$.

3.1 Wronskian of Bernstein basis functions

When the curve $P(t)$ is a Bézier curve of degree n, the basis functions $b_i(t)$ are Bernstein basis functions $B_i^n(t)$.

$$b_i(t) = B_i^n(t) = \binom{n}{i} (1 - t)^{n-i} t^i. \qquad (14)$$

The Wronskians of Bernstein basis functions have been investigated in [7]. The Wronskians $w_{i,j}^n(t)$ are given by

$$w_{i,j}^n(t) = B_i^n(t) B_j^{n\prime}(t) - B_i^{n\prime}(t) B_j^n(t)$$

$$= (j - i) \frac{\binom{n}{i} \binom{n}{j}}{\binom{2n-2}{i+j-1}} B_{i+j-1}^{2n-2}(t). \qquad (15)$$

Obviously, $w_{i,i}^n(t) = 0$ and $w_{i,j}^n(t) = -w_{j,i}^n(t)$. And $w_{i,j}^n(t) \geq 0$ for $j > i$.

Figure 2 illustrates cubic Bernstein basis functions $B_0^3(t)$, $B_1^3(t)$, $B_2^3(t)$, $B_3^3(t)$ and the curves $c_{i,j}(t) = (B_i^3(t), B_j^3(t))$.

3.2 Wronskian of B-spline basis functions

When the curve $P(t)$ is a B-spline curve of degree d, the basis functions $b_i(u)$ are B-spline basis functions $N_{i,d}^T(u)$ with a knot sequence

$$
T = [t_0, t_1, \cdots, t_{n+d+1}]
$$
$$
= [\underbrace{t^0, \ldots, t^0}_{\tau_0 = d+1}, \underbrace{t^1, \ldots, t^1}_{\tau_1 \text{ times}}, \cdots, \underbrace{t^\nu, \ldots, t^\nu}_{\tau_\nu = d+1}]. \quad (16)
$$

The basis functions are calculated as

$$
N_{i,d}^T(u) = (u - t_i)\frac{N_{i,d-1}^T(u)}{t_{i+d} - t_i} + (t_{i+d+1} - u)\frac{N_{i+1,d-1}^T(u)}{t_{i+d+1} - t_{i+1}}, \quad (17)
$$

$$
N_{i,0}^T(u) = \begin{cases} 1 & \text{if } t_i \le u < t_{i+1}, \\ 0 & \text{otherwise}. \end{cases} \quad (18)
$$

As the derivatives of $N_{i,d}^T(u)$ are given by [4]

$$
{N_{i,d}^T}'(u) = d\left(\frac{N_{i,d-1}^T(u)}{t_{i+d} - t_i} - \frac{N_{i+1,d-1}^T(u)}{t_{i+1+d} - t_{i+1}}\right), \quad (19)
$$

the Wronskian $w_{i,j}(u)$ becomes

$$
w_{i,j}(u) = d\sum_{p=0}^1 \sum_{q=0}^1 (-1)^{p+q}(t_{j+q(d+1)} - t_{i+p(d+1)})
$$
$$
\times V_{i+p}(u)V_{j+q}(u), \quad (20)
$$

where

$$
V_i(u) = \frac{N_{i,d-1}^T(u)}{t_{i+d} - t_i} = \sum_{k=0}^n \frac{\delta_{k,i}}{t_{k+d} - t_k}N_{k,d-1}^T(u), \quad (21)
$$

and $\delta_{i,j}$ is the Kronecker delta

$$
\delta_{i,j} = \begin{cases} 1 & \text{if } i = j, \\ 0 & \text{otherwise}. \end{cases} \quad (22)
$$

There are some algorithms [5, 8] to compute the product of two spline functions $V_{i+p}(u)$ and $V_{j+q}(u)$.

Let $M_{i,j}(u)$ be the function of degree $2d-2$ defined as

$$
M_{i,j}(u) = V_i(u)V_j(u) = \sum_{k=0}^{n'} m_k N_{k,2d-2}^{T'}(u), \quad (23)
$$

with the knot sequence T'

$$
T' = [\hat{t}_0, \hat{t}_1, \cdots, \hat{t}_{n'+2d-1}] = [\underbrace{t^0, \ldots, t^0}_{\tau_0 = 2d-1}, \underbrace{t^1, \ldots, t^1}_{(\tau_1+d-1)\text{times}},
$$
$$
\cdots, \underbrace{t^i, \ldots, t^i}_{(\tau_i+d-1)\text{times}}, \cdots, \underbrace{t^\nu, \ldots, t^\nu}_{\tau_\nu = 2d-1}]. \quad (24)
$$

The B-spline coefficients m_k are obtained via polar form as

$$
m_k = m(\hat{u}_k, \cdots, \hat{u}_{k+2d-3})
$$
$$
= \sum \frac{v(u_{i_1}, \cdots, u_{i_{d-1}})v(u_{i_d}, \cdots, u_{i_{2d-2}})}{\binom{2d-2}{d-1}}, (25)
$$

where $m(u_1, \cdots, u_{2d-2})$ and $v(u_1, \cdots, u_{d-1})$ are the polar forms of $M_{i,j}(u)$ and $V_i(u)$, respectively. The summation is taken for all the combinations of $d - 1$ variables $\{u_{i_1}, \cdots, u_{i_{d-1}}\}$ chosen from the set $\{\hat{u}_k, \cdots, \hat{u}_{k+2d-3}\}$, no indices are equal, and the variables $\{u_{i_d}, \cdots, u_{i_{2d-2}}\}$ are the difference $\{\hat{u}_k, \cdots, \hat{u}_{k+2d-3}\} \setminus \{u_{i_1}, \cdots, u_{i_{d-1}}\}$.

Therefore, the Wronskians $w_{i,j}(u)$ for B-spline basis functions are expressed as

$$
w_{i,j}(u) = d\sum_{p=0}^1 \sum_{q=0}^1 (-1)^{p+q}(t_{j+q(d+1)} - t_{i+p(d+1)})
$$
$$
\times M_{i+p,j+q}(u). \quad (26)
$$

4 Signed Area defined by Bézier and B-spline Curves

4.1 Areas between Bézier curves and the origin

Since the definite integral of a Bernstein basis function is given by [2]

$$
\int_0^1 B_k^n(t)dt = \frac{1}{n+1}, \quad (27)
$$

the coefficients $a_{i,j}^n$ become

$$
a_{i,j}^n = \frac{1}{2}\int_0^1 w_{i,j}^n(t)dt = \frac{1}{2}\frac{j-i}{2n-1}\frac{\binom{n}{i}\binom{n}{j}}{\binom{2n-2}{i+j-1}}
$$
$$
= \frac{j-i}{2}\frac{2n}{\binom{2n}{n}}\frac{\binom{i+j}{i}}{i+j}\frac{\binom{n-j+n-i}{n-j}}{n-j+n-i}. \quad (28)
$$

The coefficients $a_{i,j}^n$ for Bézier curves have the following properties.

$$
a_{n-j,n-i}^n = a_{i,j}^n = -a_{j,i}^n = -a_{n-i,n-j}^n, \quad (29)
$$

$$
a_{i,n}^n = \frac{\binom{n-1+i}{i}}{\binom{2n}{n}} \quad (i < n). \quad (30)
$$

The followings are the coefficients $a_{i,j}^n$ for degrees from one to five.

$$
[a_{i,j}^1] = \frac{1}{\binom{2}{1}}\begin{bmatrix} 0 & 1 \\ -1 & 0 \end{bmatrix}, \quad (31)
$$

$$
[a_{i,j}^2] = \frac{1}{\binom{4}{2}}\begin{bmatrix} 0 & 2 & 1 \\ -2 & 0 & 2 \\ -1 & -2 & 0 \end{bmatrix}, \quad (32)
$$

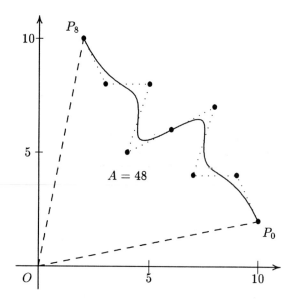

Figure 3: Area defined by a B-spline curve.

$$[a_{i,j}^3] = \frac{1}{\binom{6}{3}} \begin{bmatrix} 0 & 6 & 3 & 1 \\ -6 & 0 & 3 & 3 \\ -3 & -3 & 0 & 6 \\ -1 & -3 & -6 & 0 \end{bmatrix}, \qquad (33)$$

$$[a_{i,j}^4] = \frac{1}{\binom{8}{4}} \begin{bmatrix} 0 & 20 & 10 & 4 & 1 \\ -20 & 0 & 8 & 8 & 4 \\ -10 & -8 & 0 & 8 & 10 \\ -4 & -8 & -8 & 0 & 20 \\ -1 & -4 & -10 & -20 & 0 \end{bmatrix}, \qquad (34)$$

$$[a_{i,j}^5] = \frac{1}{\binom{10}{5}} \begin{bmatrix} 0 & 70 & 35 & 15 & 5 & 1 \\ -70 & 0 & 25 & 25 & 15 & 5 \\ -35 & -25 & 0 & 20 & 25 & 15 \\ -15 & -25 & -20 & 0 & 25 & 35 \\ -5 & -15 & -25 & -25 & 0 & 70 \\ -1 & -5 & -15 & -35 & -70 & 0 \end{bmatrix}. \qquad (35)$$

The coefficients $a_{i,j}^3$ are the areas between the curves $c_{i,j}$ and the origin, as illustrated in Figure 2.

The areas for linear, quadratic and cubic Bézier curves are expressed as follows.

$$A_1 = \frac{1}{2}(x_0 y_1 - x_1 y_0)$$
$$= \triangle(O, P_0, P_1) = -\triangle(O, P_1, P_0), \qquad (36)$$

$$A_2 = \frac{2}{3}\triangle(P_0, P_1, P_2) + \triangle(O, P_0, P_2), \qquad (37)$$

$$A_3 = \frac{3}{10}(\square(P_0, P_1, P_2, P_3) + \triangle(P_0, P_1, P_3)$$
$$+ \triangle(P_0, P_2, P_3)) + \triangle(O, P_0, P_3). \qquad (38)$$

4.2 Areas between B-spline curves and the origin

The definite integral of a B-spline basis function $N_{i,d}^K(u)$ of degree d with a knot sequence $K =$ $[\ldots, t_i \leq t_{i+1}, \ldots]$ is given by [6]

$$\int_{-\infty}^{\infty} N_{i,d}^K(u)\,du = \frac{1}{d+1}(t_{i+d+1} - t_i). \qquad (39)$$

Hence, the coefficients $a_{i,j}$ for B-spline basis functions become

$$a_{i,j} = \frac{1}{2}\int_{t_0}^{t^\nu} w_{i,j}(u)\,du \qquad (40)$$

$$= d \sum_{p=0}^{1} \sum_{q=0}^{1} (-1)^{p+q} \frac{t_{j+q(d+1)} - t_{i+p(d+1)}}{2} b_{i+p,j+q},$$

where

$$b_{i,j} = \int_{t_0}^{t^\nu} M_{i,j}(u)\,du = \sum_{k=0}^{n'} m_k \frac{\hat{t}_{k+2d-1} - \hat{t}_k}{2d-1}. \qquad (41)$$

For a B-spline curve of degree 3 with a knot sequence

$$T = [0,0,0,0,1,1,3,5,5,6,6,6,6], \qquad (42)$$

the coefficients $a_{i,j}$ are calculated as

$$[a_{i,j}] = \frac{1}{120} \begin{bmatrix} 0 & 36 & 22 & 2 & 0 & 0 & 0 & 0 & 0 \\ -36 & 0 & 30 & 6 & 0 & 0 & 0 & 0 & 0 \\ -22 & -30 & 0 & 43 & 8 & 1 & 0 & 0 & 0 \\ -2 & -6 & -43 & 0 & 31 & 19 & 1 & 0 & 0 \\ 0 & 0 & -8 & -31 & 0 & 31 & 8 & 0 & 0 \\ 0 & 0 & -1 & -19 & -31 & 0 & 43 & 6 & 2 \\ 0 & 0 & 0 & -1 & -8 & -43 & 0 & 30 & 22 \\ 0 & 0 & 0 & 0 & 0 & -6 & -30 & 0 & 36 \\ 0 & 0 & 0 & 0 & 0 & -2 & -22 & -36 & 0 \end{bmatrix}. \qquad (43)$$

The local supports of the B-spline basis functions yield the zeros in this matrix.

When the cubic B-spline curve with the knot sequence T in Figure 3 has the following control points

$$\{P_i\} = \{(10, 2), (9, 4), (7, 4), (8, 7), (6, 6),$$
$$(4, 5), (5, 8), (3, 8), (2, 10)\}, \qquad (44)$$

the area A between the curve and the origin is

$$A = \sum_{i,j} x_i y_j\, a_{i,j} = 48. \qquad (45)$$

As these control points are arranged symmetrically, the area A has the same value as the triangle $\triangle(O, P_0, P_8)$.

For a linear B-spline curve with the same control points as Equation (44) and a knot sequence

$$T' = [0,0,1,2,3,4,5,6,7,8,8], \qquad (46)$$

the coefficients $a_{i,j}$ are calculated as

$$[a_{i,j}] = \frac{1}{2} \begin{bmatrix} 0 & 1 & 0 & 0 & 0 & 0 & 0 & 0 & 0 \\ -1 & 0 & 1 & 0 & 0 & 0 & 0 & 0 & 0 \\ 0 & -1 & 0 & 1 & 0 & 0 & 0 & 0 & 0 \\ 0 & 0 & -1 & 0 & 1 & 0 & 0 & 0 & 0 \\ 0 & 0 & 0 & -1 & 0 & 1 & 0 & 0 & 0 \\ 0 & 0 & 0 & 0 & -1 & 0 & 1 & 0 & 0 \\ 0 & 0 & 0 & 0 & 0 & -1 & 0 & 1 & 0 \\ 0 & 0 & 0 & 0 & 0 & 0 & -1 & 0 & 1 \\ 0 & 0 & 0 & 0 & 0 & 0 & 0 & -1 & 0 \end{bmatrix}. \qquad (47)$$

As this B-spline curve is the polyline illustrated as dotted lines in Figure 3, the area is $A = 48$. This value is the same as the area of the polygon $\square(O, P_0, \cdots, P_8)$.

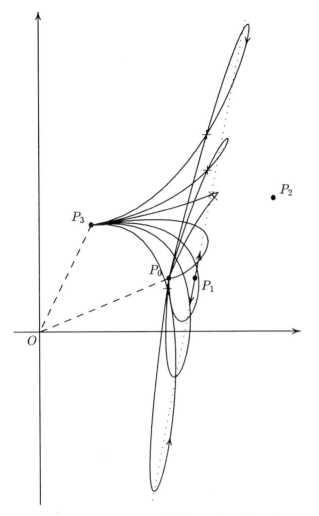

Figure 4: Area-preserving deformation of a Bézier cubic.

5 Area-Preserving Deformation

Since the coefficients $a_{i,j}$ depend only on the basis functions, they are applicable to compute the area for other spline curves with the same basis functions. For different control points $P'_i = (x'_i, y'_i)$ $(0 \leq k \leq n)$, the area A is also expressed as

$$A' = \sum_{i,j} x'_i y'_j \, a_{i,j} \,. \qquad (48)$$

Suppose that only a control point P_k is moved to

$$P'_k = P_k + (\Delta x_k, \, \Delta y_k) \,. \qquad (49)$$

The area changes by

$$A' - A = \Delta x_k \sum_{j=0}^{n} y_j \, a_{k,j} + \Delta y_k \sum_{i=0}^{n} x_i \, a_{i,k} \,. \qquad (50)$$

Thus, there is a direction for moving the control point P_k preserving the area. From $A' - A = 0$, the direction

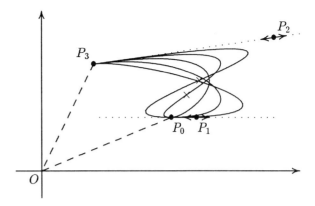

Figure 5: Area-preserving deformation of a Bézier cubic preserving the tangent lines at the endpoints.

becomes

$$\frac{\Delta y_k}{\Delta x_k} = -\frac{\sum_{j=0}^{n} y_j \, a_{k,j}}{\sum_{i=0}^{n} x_i \, a_{i,k}} \,. \qquad (51)$$

Figure 4 illustrates various area-preserving deformations of a Bézier cubic with the control points P_0, P_1, P_2, P_3 by moving the control point P_1 along the line with the direction.

We can also perform area-preserving deformation of the Bézier cubic by moving the inner control points P_1 and P_2. Suppose the control points move along the corresponding tangent line.

$$P'_1 = P_0 + (1+u)\overrightarrow{P_0 P_1} \quad P'_2 = P_3 + (1+v)\overrightarrow{P_3 P_2} \,. \quad (52)$$

This deformation also preserves the tangent line at the two endpoints. By solving the equation $A' = A$, we obtain the following relationship between the parameters u and v:

$$v = \frac{\triangle(P_0, P_1, P_2) + \triangle(P_0, P_1, P_3)}{\triangle(P_0, P_3, P_2)(1-u) + \triangle(P_1, P_3, P_2)(1+u)} u \,. \qquad (53)$$

The case of $v = 0$ happens, if

$$\triangle(P_0, P_1, P_2) + \triangle(P_0, P_1, P_3) = 0 \,. \qquad (54)$$

Equation (54) means that the line $\overline{P_0, P_1}$ bisects the line $\overline{P_2, P_3}$. In this case, there is no need to move the control point P_2.

Figure 5 illustrates various area-preserving deformations of a Bézier cubic by moving two inner control points P_1 and P_2 along the tangent lines at the endpoints.

In Figures 4 and 5, The symbol '+' indicates double points and the symbol '×' inflection points. A Bézier cubic may have a loop, as illustrated in Figure 4. Since the sector formula (4) represents the signed area, the area of the loop has the opposite sign. We can say that the area-preserving deformations can be performed with the loops for big moves of control points.

According to [1], we can obtain the parameters for the loops, cusps, inflection points of Bézier cubics as follows.

If two vectors $\overrightarrow{P_0P_1}$ and $\overrightarrow{P_2P_3}$ are not collinear (linearly dependent), $\overrightarrow{P_1P_2}$ can be represented as a linear combination of two vectors $\overrightarrow{P_0P_1}$ and $\overrightarrow{P_2P_3}$.

$$\overrightarrow{P_1P_2} = \rho\,\overrightarrow{P_0P_1} + \sigma\,\overrightarrow{P_2P_3} . \tag{55}$$

The values (ρ, σ) are expressed as

$$(\rho, \sigma) = \left(\frac{\overrightarrow{P_1P_2} \times \overrightarrow{P_2P_3}}{\overrightarrow{P_0P_1} \times \overrightarrow{P_2P_3}}, \frac{\overrightarrow{P_0P_1} \times \overrightarrow{P_1P_2}}{\overrightarrow{P_0P_1} \times \overrightarrow{P_2P_3}} \right) . \tag{56}$$

The parameters t_1 and t_2 for a double point $(P(t_1) = P(t_2),\ t_1 \neq t_2)$ are

$$t_{1,2} = \frac{1 - 2\sigma \pm \sqrt{3(4\rho\sigma - 1)}}{2(1 - \rho - \sigma)} . \tag{57}$$

The curve have two inflection points at t_3 and t_4.

$$t_{3,4} = \frac{1 - 2\sigma \pm \sqrt{1 - 4\rho\sigma}}{2(1 - \rho - \sigma)} . \tag{58}$$

If the radicals vanish, i.e., $4\rho\sigma - 1 = 0$, a cusp exists on the curve at t_5.

$$t_5 = \frac{1 - 2\sigma}{2(1 - \rho - \sigma)} . \tag{59}$$

Hence, a Bézier cubic has a loop, if both parameters t_1 and t_2 are in the interval $[0, 1]$. When a loop is detected on a Bézier cubic, the magnitude of the area is calculated by summating the absolute values of the signed areas for the curve segments on $[0, t_1]$, $[t_1, t_2]$ and $[t_2, 1]$.

Figure 6 illustrates the region satisfying the condition for a loop on Bézier cubics. The boundary curves of the region L are hyperbolas $4\rho\sigma - 1 = 0$, $\rho^2 - \rho + 1 - 3\rho\sigma = 0$ and $\sigma^2 - \sigma + 1 - 3\rho\sigma = 0$.

6   Conclusion

Formulas for calculating the signed area of the sectors between Bézier and B-spline curves and the origin have been presented. We can calculate the area of a region bounded by polynomial spline curve segments by applying the formulas to the segments on the boundary.

The formulas are expressed by combining the coordinates of the control points and coefficients calculated with the basis functions. The coefficients also represent the area between the curves defined by the basis functions and the origin. If the coefficients are calculated for a spline curve, they can be used for calculating the area of other curves with the same basis functions.

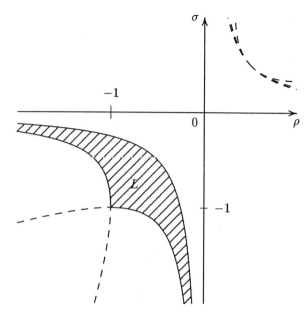

Figure 6: Bézier cubics have a loop, if $(\rho, \sigma) \in L$.

References

[1] W. Degen., "Some remarks on Bézier curves," *Computer Aided Geometric Design*, Vol. 5, pp. 259–268, 1988.

[2] R. T. Farouki and T. Rajan, "Algorithms for polynomials in Bernstein form," *Computer Aided Geometric Design*, Vol. 5, pp. 1–26, 1988.

[3] R. N. Goldman, "Area of planar polygons and volume of polyhedra," *Graphics Gems II*, J. Arvo (ed.), pp. 170–171, Academic Press, 1991.

[4] L. Piegl and W. Tiller, *The NURBS Book*, Springer-Verlag, 1995.

[5] L. Piegl and W. Tiller, "Algorithm for computing the product of two B-splines," *Curves and Surfaces with Applications in CAGD*, A. Le Méhauté, C. Rabut and L. L. Schumaker (eds.), pp. 337–344, Vanderbilt University Press, 1997.

[6] L. Schumaker, *Spline Functions: Basic Theory*, John Wiley and Sons, 1981.

[7] W. Sederberg and X. Wang, "Rational hodographs," *Computer Aided Geometric Design*, Vol. 4, pp. 333–335, 1987.

[8] K. Ueda, "Multiplication as a general operation for splines," *Curves and Surfaces in Geometric Design*, P.-J. Laurent, A. Le Méhauté, and L. L. Schumaker (eds.), pp. 475–482, A K Peters, 1994.

[9] K. Ueda, "Mean normal vector to a surface bounded by Bézier curves," *Computer Aided Geometric Design*, Vol. 13, pp. 441–451, 1996.

On Shape to Specifications Adequacy

Yvon Gardan, Christian Minich, Denis Pallez
Computer sciences laboratory
Metz University, France
{gardan,minich,pallez}@lrim.sciences.univ-metz.fr

Abstract

Computer Aided Design now aims to provide designers with a support during the early stages of design. The purpose is to translate the client's specifications into a shape as automatically as possible. However, the processing of a text in natural language is still out of reach. We then assume that the client's specifications are manually translated into intermediate specifications composed of intermediate constraints upon physical parameters. Our efforts concern the transformation of these intermediate specifications into a shape, precisely the way to compute whether a shape satisfies the intermediate specifications or not. We first study the case in which the shape is a single primitive solid; we shall also give elements to choose the instance that best fits the specifications. Then, we shall study the extension of the method to solids defined by a combination of primitive solids.

1. Introduction

Computer Aided Design now aims to provide designers with a support during the earlier stages of design. The purpose is to translate the client's specifications into a shape as automatically as possible. Studies we have listed in that field concern modelling of design methods or modelling of design products [1].

All the *methods* (value analysis, SADT, FAST, QFD...) express a function as a verb and complements. Thus, their automation implies a semantic processing of a text written in a natural language, which is still far beyond computer science capabilities. However, we retain the attempt of [2, 3] which aims at a system that is able, under some strong assumptions, to carry out a design without assistance: products are supposed to be described in term of rules and design methods in term of meta-rules. This supposes a very significant formalisation work, which has only been undertaken in very limited sectors. Analogy [4, 5, 6, 7] has also been the subject of an in-depth study, based in particular on artificial intelligence techniques. It encounters two main difficulties: detection of similarities between two products or two specifications and adaptation to the new product of previous design solutions.

The efforts in *product modelling* relate either to the data structure or to the treatments based on these structures. For a structure to be complete, it must contain the history, the shape and the behaviour of the product. The proposals found in the bibliography generally do not lead to such a structure. Exceptions are the FBS diagram [8, 9, 10], which really approaches this objective, and, to a lesser extent, other tools, which primarily work at a behavioural level. Consequently, simulation tools are right now operational: for example qualitative behaviour analysis [11, 12, 13, 14] or insertion of functional redundancies in order to improve reliability. An attempt to take subjective functions into account can also be mentioned. It consists in expressing subjective criteria as combinations of objective criteria [15].

As it is difficult to automate the design methods and as data structures are still inadequate, specifications to shape automatic translation remains generally out of reach, excepted in the field of routine designs (gear box, microprocessor, kitchen...). In such a context, shape and structure of the product are well known and it is possible to write a program that generates them from a small set of functional parameters.

Although it is economically less fundamental, we would like to come within a more innovative context, in which the designer has no definite idea of the shape or the structure of the product. As a complete automation is not possible yet, the complexity of the problem must be reduced: functional information can frequently be expressed as a set of constraints involving so called *physical parameters*, defined as quantifiable and measurable entities referring to the physical world. For instance, a table is convivial if it is convex (every guest faces the others), if its perimeter is greater than *Max_nb_persons* × *0.9 meter* (everybody has enough space), if the distance between two points does not exceed 5 meters (everybody can ear the others)... Thus, our simplifying assumption is that the client's specifications are translated *by the designer* into *intermediate specifications* composed of *intermediate constraints* upon physical parameters (for instance *perimeter > Max_nb_persons × 0.9*). The previous example shows that this offers the option of taking into account subjective functions, like conviviality or beauty, as suggested in [15]. Our efforts concern the transformation of these intermediate specifications into a shape. This raises several questions such as shape generation and shape quality calculus. This paper addresses the latter problem, precisely the way to compute whether a shape satisfies the intermediate specifications or not.

We shall first give some definitions. Then, we shall detail the method for checking whether a primitive solid satisfies the intermediate specifications and we shall propose some reflections on the way to perform the same operation on a complex solid.

2. Satisfaction degree

Let us recall that the client's specifications are supposed to be translated into a set of intermediate constraints, which represents the design intent in a computational format. An intermediate constraint can be more formally defined as a quadruple *<PP, Op, Exp, W>*. *PP* is a physical parameter. *Op* is one of the mathematical relations among $\{<, >, =, \neq ...\}$. *Exp* is a real arithmetical expression that may contain other physical parameters; its value is called the *wanted value*. *W* is the relative weight of the constraint in comparison with the other constraints of the intermediate specifications.

We define the Satisfaction Degree $SD_{ic}(s)$ of an intermediate constraint *ic* by a given shape *s* as a real number in the [0,1] interval. This number expresses the quality with which *s* satisfies the intermediate constraint *ic*. If $SD_{ic}(s)$ is near zero, the constraint is badly satisfied, if it is near one, the constraint is well satisfied. The method to compute $SD_{ic}(s)$ changes depending on whether *s* is a primitive solid or a complex object.

We define the Satisfaction Degree $SD_{ispec}(s)$ of the intermediate specifications *ispec* by a given shape *s* as a real number in the [0,1] interval. This number expresses the quality with which *s* satisfies the intermediate specifications *ispec*. As each constraint is affected a weight, the $SD_{ispec}(s)$ can be computed by the following formula, which simply is a weighted average of the constraints satisfaction degrees (*n* is the number of intermediate constraints):

$$SD_{ispec}(s) = \frac{\sum_{1 \leq i \leq n} SD_{ic_i}(s) \cdot W_{ic_i}}{\sum_{1 \leq i \leq n} W_{ic_i}}$$

Figure 1. Satisfaction degree of the specifications as a weighted average of intermediate constraints SDs

It can be noticed that this formula does not depend on the type of *s*. Therefore, it can be applied provided that the satisfaction degrees of the intermediate constraints are known.

We shall also call the computation of the $SD_{ispec}(s)$ the *estimation* of *s*.

It can be noticed that a formula similar to the one of Figure 1 is used in [15], to estimate the satisfaction degree of so-called functional constraints of a product whose structure and parameters are known. Consequently, their estimation method allows an automatic tuning of parameters but it is dedicated to a given object whereas our method is designed to be applied on any type of object. We shall see in the next chapter that this might provide the user with a support during the shape generation rather than during the shape optimisation.

3. Primitive solids

3.1. Estimation of a primitive solid

Let us assume we want to estimate the satisfaction degree of the specifications by a given primitive solid whose parameters values are known. For instance, we want to know whether a box, whose length, height and width respectively equal 10, 20 and 8, correctly satisfies the intermediate specifications. To distinguish these parameters from the intermediate parameters, the former are called *terminal parameters*.

The first step of the estimation consists in computing the physical parameters values from the terminal parameters. To perform this process, we need formulas or algorithms whose inputs are the terminal parameters and whose results are the physical parameters values. During the first designs, the user has to give these formulas. Little by little, the system knowledge will increase and it will be more and more possible to reuse existing formulas or to allow the user to combine them, which will save him from using terminal parameters. For example, suppose that the volume of a sphere is needed for a given design. There are three options:

- We already know how to compute the volume from the radius of a sphere...

- We just know how to compute the surface of the sphere: the user only has to give the formula that links the surface and the volume.
- No formula about the sphere is known; the user has to express the computation of the volume from the terminal parameters, that is to say the radius.

The computed value of the physical parameter is called *real value*. Once it is known, the satisfaction degree of the intermediate constraint (SD_{ICi}) is deduced from the gap between the wanted and the real values and from a curve that depends on the mathematical relation used in the constraint (Op).

The aspects of the curves are given in Figure 2.

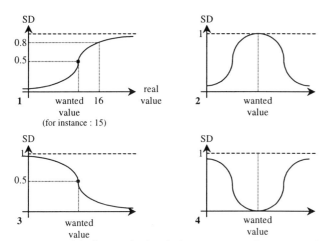

Figure 2. Mathematical relations curves (>, =, <, ≠) for SDs computation

Curve 1 is associated with relation ">". It is designed in such a way that the larger the real value is, the larger the satisfaction degree will be. Most probably, not all constraints can be ideally satisfied. That is why, curves are such that, when the constraint is not satisfied, the satisfaction degree does not necessarily equal zero. This justifies that, in the above example, the wanted value is the inflection point of the curve: it has been agreed that the wanted value corresponds to a 0.5 satisfaction degree. The designer experiment might lead him to associate another satisfaction degree with the wanted value. As an example, suppose the intermediate constraint is "surface > 15". If the real value is 16, the satisfaction degree will be around 0.8.

Curve 2 is associated with relation "=". It is designed in such a way that the nearer the real and the wanted value are, the larger the satisfaction degree will be. The shapes of other curves are motivated by similar reasonings (curve 3 corresponds to relation "<" and curve 4 to relation "≠").

Other curves might be used instead of those of Figure 2, provided that they have similar behaviours.

Once the satisfaction degrees of all intermediate constraints are known, the satisfaction degree of the specifications can be computed as indicated in chapter 2.

3.2. Selection of the best primitive solid

Naturally, the estimation must help the choice of the instance of a primitive that best fits the intermediate specifications. An intuitive approach might be to let every parameter vary on ℝ (eventually ℝ⁺), to estimate each corresponding instance and to memorise the best one. Obviously, this is computationally unrealistic. That is why the method we adopted consists in two steps:

- Narrowing the parameters variation intervals with the help of intermediate constraints. The principle can be illustrated by the following example: suppose that the intermediate constraints are "Surface > 16", "Surface < 20" and suppose that we are studying the sphere. The two constraints can be transformed into the following *terminal constraints*: "R > 2/√π" and "R < √(5/π)". The radius variation interval has thus been reduced to [2/√π, √(5/π)]. The translation of the intermediate constraints into terminal constraints is difficult because, in most cases, a physical parameter is a function of several terminal parameters. Formulas involved in these computations are the opposite of those that are used to estimate a primitive solid. Thus, we also think that, little by little, the software knowledge will increase and relieve the user of expressing those translations by himself.
- The Cartesian product of all the intervals represents the potential solutions space among which the best solution has to be chosen. Four approaches can be envisaged. One can first retry a systematic approach by an exhaustive discrete traversal. One can also think in a formal manner by looking for the extrema of $SD_{ispec}(s)$; as SD is an analytical function from ℝⁿ to ℝ (n is the number of terminal parameters), the zeros of its partial derivatives can be computed in order to obtain the maximum. However, to know which ones correspond to maxima, the Hessian matrix, and sometimes the Taylor's development, have to be computed. This raises many numerical problems. The third approach consists in using an iterative method, such as the Gradient. The main drawback is that it gives only local extrema. Finally, heuristics seem to offer a good compromise between performance and accuracy. Both simulated annealing and genetic algorithms seem adapted in our case. We give some elements to proof the feasibility. Classical problems of the simulated annealing are random modification

of the current solution, entropy calculus, initial and final values of the temperature. The modification can be performed by randomly selecting a terminal parameter and by randomly choosing the quantity to be added or subtracted to it (one just has to check that the parameter stays inside its interval). The entropy is the satisfaction degree of the specifications. The initial temperature must guarantee that all modifications are accepted at the beginning of the algorithm, that is to say $e^{-\Delta E / Init.Temperature}$ is near one. As ΔE at most equals one, it suffices to choose the initial temperature very superior to one. For similar reasons ($e^{-\Delta E / Final\ Temperature}$ near zero), the final temperature can be zero. Classical problems of genetic algorithms are solution coding, solutions crossover and mutations. A solution can be coded by simply enumerating the values of the terminal parameters. The crossover mechanism consists in randomly choosing values in the two parent solutions. Finally, to mutate a solution, one just has to change one or more parameters with random values.

Whichever the solutions space traversal method is, it will be necessary to check whether terminal parameter values n-uple (tpv_1, tpv_2, ..., tpv_n) belongs to the solutions space, for instance after a random modification of the n-uple. This operation raises difficulties because of the variation intervals dynamic aspect: when the value of one of the terminal parameters is set, it may happen that the variation intervals of other terminal parameters change. For example, suppose that one intermediate constraint is "perimeter < 20" and suppose we are looking for the rectangle that best fits the intermediate specifications. "perimeter < 20" implies "width + height < 10", so, for a given width w, the height varies in [0, 10-w]. Consequently, the variation interval of the height is dependent of the width value. Thus, to check whether a n-uple belongs to the solutions space, one has to check whether the terminal constraints, from which intervals are computed, are satisfied.

3.3. 2D implementation

We have implemented the methods described above to assist a designer with choosing the 2D-primitive shape (circle, box and triangle) that best fits specifications made of several intermediate constraints. This was done in C++ using a commercial Rapid Application Development tool. The approach used to traverse the solutions space is simply an exhaustive discrete search. For each candidate shape, the satisfaction degrees of specifications and of all intermediate constraints are dynamically displayed as status bars (Figure 3).

The dynamic and continuous evolution of the shape and of the corresponding SDs provides the end-user with a comfortable tool to visualise numerous solutions.

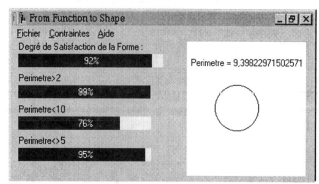

Figure 3. Software's screenshot of our C++ application

4. Complex shapes

Generally, parts satisfying the specifications are not single solids but combinations of primitive solids, called *complex shapes*, or assemblies of complex shapes. We do not address assemblies in this paper because it implies the use of mechanisms that increase the complexity of shape generation. Thus, automatic generation of the shape means automatic generation of a CSG tree. One way to approach this problem is to generate numerous trees and to select the best ones with the help of an estimation process. This chapter proposes some reflection axes about the estimation process of a complex shape described by a CSG Tree. As we assume the CSG tree is known, there exist two possibilities for estimating the complex shape: with or without incremental boundary evaluation.

In the first situation, the boundary representation of the complex solid is computed by recursively combining the sub trees of every node. Then, algorithms are needed to compute the real values of the physical parameters of the resulting solid. Once the values are known, the same reasoning as in chapter 3.1 can be applied to compute the intermediate constraints satisfaction degrees and the shape estimation. This sparks off two comments.

For the moment, the only solution we envisage to get the required algorithms is to ask the user or a computer scientist to program them. However, here again, it will probably be less and less necessary to solicit the user, as the knowledge of the system will increase. Besides, CAD software already propose many specialised functions (mass, surface, outflow... computations) that could probably be used. Finally, let us notice that no better solution is proposed even in the most recent knowledge based systems: when a user is up to add a rule in the base, the methods which query the model in order to get the values involved in the rule must be available. If they are not, they have to be programmed.

In addition, the need for a boundary representation is not necessarily a drawback. In current CAD software, two models are simultaneously maintained: a design history (which approximately looks like a CSG tree, although this is masked by recent formalisms such as form features) and an evaluated model, that is to say a boundary representation. Thus, the B-Rep is available and its use in the estimation process causes no extra computations. However, a current trend in CAD research aims to decrease the role of the B-Rep in favour of semantically higher level models. Thus, basing treatments on a B-Rep goes against this trend.

To estimate a complex shape without evaluating the CSG tree (chapter 3.1), one needs to deduce recursively the intermediate constraints satisfaction degrees from those of the leaves.

As the intermediate constraints SDs are known for the primitive solids at the leaves of the tree, a first option is to deduce, at a given node, the SD of every intermediate constraint from the SDs of its sons. We briefly envisaged this eventuality but it quickly appeared that it is unrealistic. Let us illustrate that with an example. Suppose that the specifications demand a stable object. A cube on the floor is very stable: when pushed, it does not roll. So, the satisfaction degrees of this particular constraint are very high, near one, for the cubes at the leaves of the following tree (Figure 4.a). However, according to their dimensions and positions, the resulting object may be stable (Figure 4.b) or unstable (Figure 4.c). Consequently, the knowledge of the sons' satisfaction degrees is not sufficient to compute the father's satisfaction degree.

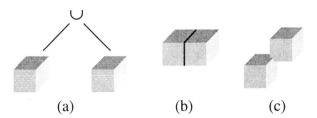

(a) (b) (c)

Figure 4. The combination of two stable simple shapes (a) may be stable (b) or unstable (c)

As the satisfaction degrees are calculated from physical parameters' values and as physical parameters of the leaves are calculable (chapter 3.2), another approach could be to recursively obtain the root's physical parameters with the help of its sons' physical parameters. However, all the attempts we made, concluded that it is

only possible to approximate the physical parameter very imprecisely. For instance, consider $A \cup B$, $A \cap B$ and $A - B$, where A and B are two primitive solids whose volumes, v_A and v_B, are known. The volume of the resulting object respectively varies in $[\max(v_A, v_B), v_A + v_B]$, $[0, \min(v_A, v_B)]$, $[0, v_A]$. This is the best approximation we can provide without evaluating the object, which would bring back to the very first method.

As a conclusion, we think that the use of a boundary representation is the only option that offers real prospects.

5. Conclusion and future works

This paper presents our studies of the possibilities to automatically check whether a shape satisfies the specifications.

Our opinion is that this operation can not be performed without a human support, whether the shape is simple (a primitive solid), or complex (combined object). However, it seems that the software will be more and more self-sufficient as its experience will grow, particularly for simple shapes.

Of course, these works aim to provide the designer with a support during the generation of a shape satisfying given specifications. For instance, the estimation function might be interfaced with a tool able to generate a large number of CSG trees in order to invalidate automatically all the unsatisfactory propositions.

6. Acknowledgements

We thank E. Perrin, Computer Aided Functional Design team at Metz University, for contributing to discussions that lead to this paper.

7. References

[1] C. Minich, and D. Pallez, "Vers des outils informatiques d'assistance aux phases amont de la conception – Etat de l'art", *Revue internationale de CFAO et d'informatique graphique*, Hermes eds., 14, 1999.

[2] H. Takeda, "Towards multi-aspect design support systems", *Technical Report NAIST-IS-TR94006*, Nara Institute of Science and Technology, Nara, Japan, February 1994.

[3] H. Takeda, and T. Nishida, "Integration of aspects in design processes", *Artificial Intelligence in Design*, Kluwer Academic Publishers, J. S. Gero and F. Sudweeks editors, 1994, pp. 309-326.

[4] A. K. Goel, "Design, Analogy and Creativity", *IEEE Expert Intelligent Systems & Their Applications*, 12(2), May/June 1997, pp. 42-48.

[5] K. Börner, "Structural similarity and adaptation", *Proc. Third European Workshop Case-Based Reasoning*, Springer-Verlag, New York, pp. 58-75.

[6] L. Qian, and J. S. Gero, "A Design Support System Using Analogy", *Proc. Second Int'l Conf AI in Design*, Kluwer

Academic publishers, Dordrecht, The Netherlands, 1992, pp. 795-813.

[7] S. Bhatta, A. Goel, "From design experiences to generic mechanisms: model-based learning in Analogical Design", *AI in Engineering Design*, Analysis and manufacturing, special issue on machine learning in design, 10, 1996, pp. 131-136.

[8] T. Tomiyama, Y. Umeda, and H. Yoshikawa, "A CAD for functional Design", *Annals of CIRP'93*, 1993, pp. 143-146.

[9] Y. Umeda, M. Ishii, M. Yoshioka, Y. Shimomura, and T. Tomiyama, "Supporting conceptual design based on the function-behaviour-state modeller", *Artificial Intelligence for Engineering Design*, Analysis and Manufacturing, 10, 1996, pp. 275-288.

[10] M. Ranta, M. Mäntylä, Y. Umeda, T. Tomiyama, "Integration of Functional and Feature-based product modelling – the IMS/GNOSIS experience", *Computer Aided Design*, 28(5), 1996, pp. 371-381.

[11] T. Kiriyama, T. Tomiyama, H. Yoshikawa, "The use of qualitative physics for integrated design object modelling", *Proceedings of Design Theory and Methodology*, ASME Press, L. A. Stauffer éd, 1991, pp. 53-60.

[12] Y. Umeda, T. Tomiyama, "Functional reasoning in design", *IEEE Expert Intelligent Systems & Their Applications*, 12(2), March - April 1997, pp. 42-48.

[13] O. Salomons, "Dynamic tolerance analysis using bondgraphs", *Proceedings DETC'98*, September, Atlanta, 1998.

[14] University of Twente, Netherlands, http://www.rt.el. utwente.nl/20sim/clp.htm

[15] Y. Shimomura, S. Tanigawa, H. Takeda, Y. Umeda, T. Tomiyama, "Functional evaluation based on function content", *Proceedings of ASME Design Engineering Technical Conference and Computers in Engineering Conference*, Irvine, California, 18-22 August 1996.

Augmented and Virtual Reality

Chair
Eric W. Tatham
The Open University, UK

Analysis and Design of Virtual Reality Applications in the WEB: a Case of Study

De Abreu A., Rodriguez O.
Laboratorio de Computación Gráfica.
Facultad de Ciencias.
Universidad Central de Venezuela UCV.
Apartado 47002. Los Chaguaramos 1041-A. Caracas-Venezuela
e-mail: [adabreu,omaira]@agata.ciens.ucv.ve

Matteo A.
Laboratorio Teoría y Tecnologías Orientadas a Objetos, Lenguajes y Sistemas. TOOLS.
Centro de Ingeniería de Software Y Sistemas. ISYS.
Facultad de Ciencias.
Universidad Central de Venezuela. UCV.
Apartado 48093. Los Chaguaramos 1041-A. Caracas-Venezuela
e-mail: amatteo@isys.ciens.ucv.ve

Abstract

The new coming era of the WEB represents a challenge in the development analysis of software systems, incorporating new technologies to access and present information, that combines 3D images, sounds, video, and text, in a way that the user gets involved in the interaction with it. This is known as non-inmersive Virtual Reality. Reusing software to solve such problems is then necessary. On the other hand, there are no other known specific methods or/and techniques for the development of applications on the WEB. In this article, we present an analysis and design of a WEB application,. a Virtual Reality Architecture Editor (EVA)[1], using the OOSE method for defining the system architecture, where the reused and developed parts are showed, along with their communication relationships.

1. Introduction

Virtual Reality has been present for more than a decade, but just recently it has begun to be used to present information in the WEB. The display of virtual scenes in the WEB, is possible using new technologies, languages and appropriated formats for their conception and exploration. There are Virtual Reality applications on the WEB [6] where the user interacts with objects in a virtual environment. These environments are worlds modeled integrating video, audio and 3D graphics, among others. Using modeling languages like VRML does the definition of such worlds or scenes possible.

On the other hand, the WEB´s vogue has established a new challenge of software development, which has to incorporate new technologies to get and display the information. These applications are characterized by the reuse of software components and the use of Java applets in the design. However there are no known specific methods and/or appropriate techniques for the WEB application design. Due to the features of these kind of

problems, we can think about using any object oriented method.

In this work, we develop an application for the WEB, "Editor Virtual de Arquitectura, (EVA)", using OOSE[8][3] method mainly for the analysis process in which we identify all the functionalities and actors, as well as, everything related to the system software architecture, in which we recognize the set of components and their communication relationships and we distinguish the reused components. The definition of software architecture is relevant for this kind of applications, since it is used to identify all the components to be developed, reused and how they communicate between them. Because we are dealing with WEB applications, the components to be developed correspond to the definition of a Java applet that are loaded and run in the WEB page. The browser is by itself a reused component, and in our case EVA, the tool "Cosmo Player" allows the scene's manipulation and exploration. This is treated also as a reused component.

322

2. Problem description and requirements

The system proposed here EVA, is created to enhance modeling and design of low level complexity housing, made with lecture purpose for the "Laboratorio de Técnicas Avanzadas en Diseño", Department of Architecture at UCV. EVA is a help tool that allows students to create and design in a two-dimensional space taking advantage of a tridimensional space where the design is modeled, making them possible to explore and manage it.

We identify three main funcionalities for the system:

- Design the house. Allows the user to create a simple housing model, using predefined elements such as: walls, windows, doors, fretwork.
- Furnish the house with virtual objects such as: chairs, tables, beds, cars, bell, phone, lights, virtual characters, etc., allows the user to model the inner and outer environment. In our case, the virtual objects and their behaviors, are also predefined.
- Explore and manipulate the virtual scene. Here the user has a 3D view of the 2D model he is designing, allowing him to navigate, interact and explore it. The 3D view is permanently updated according to the changes made in the 2D design.

The first two functionalities have to be integrated in the system, in such a way, that the user can do any kind of modification at any time.

3. Analysis Process.

Using the OOSE[8][3] method, we construct the requirements and the analysis models.

3.1. Requirements Model

Here we propose an interface prototype, creating the Problem Domain (optional), as well as, the Case Of Use model, in which we identify the actors and their functionalities.

Following are the Use-Case model and the interface prototype.

3.2 Use-Case model

3.2.1. Identifying actors and Use-Cases. For our problem, we identify only one actor that has the following functionalities:

- Housing design
- Housing exploration

However, we have to point out that the VRML browser, who also allows the connection with the Java applet, makes the interaction between the author and his model. Thereafter, the two main functionalities of EVA are viewed as extension of the browser functionalities. We claim that this singularity is characteristic of software applications for the WEB, and has to be included in the Use-Case model.

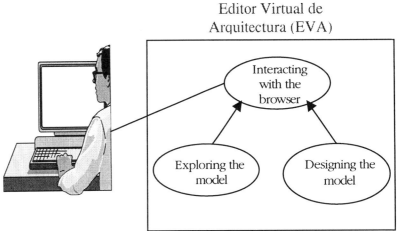

Figure 1. Main Use-Cases

3.2.2. Description and Use-Case purging. Following are the description of the identified Use-Cases:

Browser interaction: The user begins a working session invoking a WEB browser, hence all the functionalities associated to it, are available. EVA can be reached at the following WEB address: http://cuarzo.ciens.ucv.ve/

Housing modeling: Is considered as an abstract Use-Case, which is constituted by the Use-Cases: Model design and Model furnish.

Model Design: The actor, pressing the button associated to the 2D editor activates this functionality. Allowing him to build a 2D-model house.

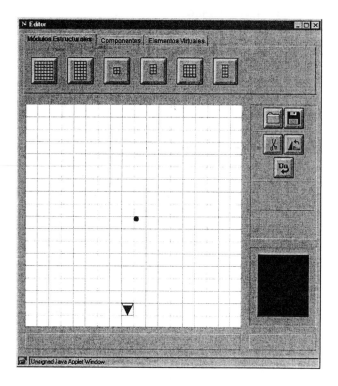

Figure 2. The 2D Editor

In the previous figure, we show the interface prototype that accomplishes this functionality. Four main work areas are identify in our editor:

Working area: A square grid whose basic unit is the Design Module (M), in our case 80x80 cm2.

Library area: Allows the user to a classified list of predefined objects to be inserted in the working area.

Edition area: Here we find all the functionalities proper to an editor such as: cut, undo, save, etc.

Legend area: Where the 3D picture corresponding to each architecture element, is shown.

Furnishing Model:

Allows the actor to build a 2D-house model. This Use-Case reuses the interface from Model Design adapted to the functionalities of the virtual objects available.

No restrictions are imposed to the order in which these Use-Cases must be applied, ie, they are considered independent in spite that the logical expected order to be is the furnishing of the house followed by the design.

Exploring the virtual scene:

This Use-Case is initialized through the interaction with the VRML browser window. Its capabilities, allows the user to interact and navigate a 3D virtual representation of the floor design previously build using the previous Use-Cases. The VRML browser provides the proper set of functionalities corresponding to the process of exploration and management of the 3D scene: walk, slide, examine, speed and sound adjustment, rotation, jump.

3.3. Analysis Model

Our strategy here relies on the paradigm of interface separated from the problem abstraction.

In our case, the analysis model showed in the previous figure corresponds to the development of the 2D editor. The entity objects conform the required objects in the housing furnishing and design. The interface objects, the most important are the HTML and VRML browser, which correspond to the reused components, of the application. On the other hand, we have the applet object that corresponds with the button that activates the 2D editor represented by the object FrameEditor. We define an intermediate control object between the interface and the entity objects that also accomplishes the communication between the 2D editor interface objects and 3D scene objects, keeping the two views updated.

Following we describe the main objects:

- **IGrid.** The object who represents the grid. Composed by IObjects.
- **IObject.** Are the basic building objects of the design.
- **IME.** Are IObjects that define what we call the "Structural Modules". They define a whole design ambient with different dimensions.
- **IM.** Is an IObject representing the design module. Windows (ITWindow), walls (ITWall), calados (ITFretwork), doors (ITDoor) and electrical elements (ITElectric) comprise them.
- **IFurniture.** Are IObjects that represent the furnishing virtual objects, such as: chairs (IChair), tables (ITable), viewpoints (IViewpoint), etc.

4. EVA´s Architecture

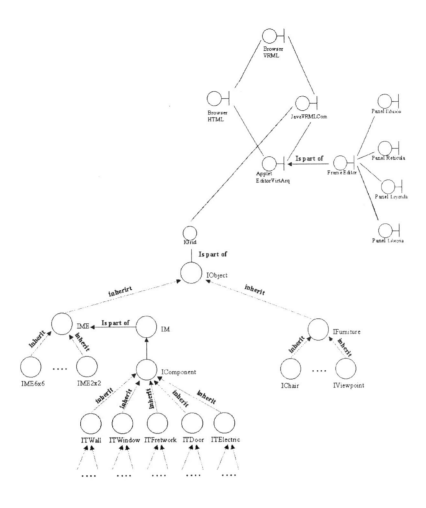

Figure 3. Analysis Model

Due to the special features of this problem, is very important to define all the development tools used, before establishing the architecture.

- Java 1.1 as the development language.
- An HTML browser to load and run the application. EVA resides in a WEB page that holds the applet, as well as the VRML scene.
- The Java applet represents the 2D editor.
- The VRML97 specification is used to build the predefined virtual objects and the whole 3D virtual scene.
- VRML browsers to display, manipulate and explore the 3D virtual scene that is currently created in the 2D editor.
- The Java API External Authoring Interface (EAI) is necessary to communicate the applet with the VRML browser.

In Figure 4 are shown the reused tools: the HTML

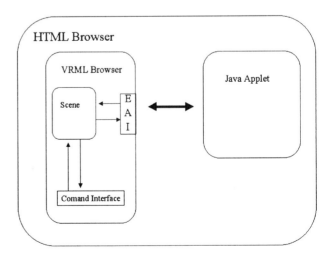

Figure 4. System Overview

browser and the VRML browser. The Java applet is the software component to be developed. A control class called JavaVRMLCom, where all invocations to the API classes are defined, accomplishes the communication between the VRML browser and the Java applet.

5. Applet Design

Figure 5 shows the Class Diagram for the 2D Editor, using OMT[9] notation. These classes are defined in the Java applet and have a direct correspondence with the Analysis Model objects.

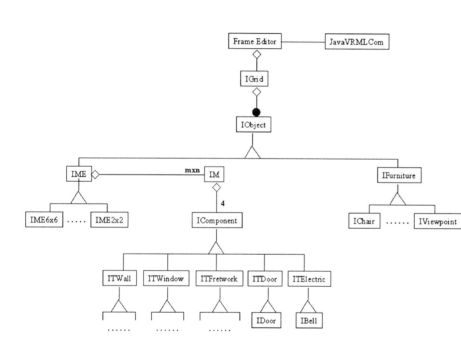

Figure 5.Class Diagram

The JavaVRMLCom class, correspond to the same object control defined in the Analysis Model. There, we define all the methods necessary to establish the communication between the applet and the VRML browser. The implementation of this class makes use of the API EAI to create the 3D virtual scene in the VRML browser, and permanently update it. The other classes are the ones defined to accomplish all the design requirements, and correspond to the entity objects defined in the analysis model.

6. Summary

A WEB application that incorporates Virtual Reality techniques is developed under the Object Oriented approach. The analysis process is eased using the OOSE method to define the different object types that comprise the model.

This kind of applications requires cutting edge technologies available as reusable components, and is important to establish the system architecture once we had ended the system analysis. This, clarifies communication between components to be developed and reused.

The WEB application development has their own features that are different from conventional applications. Our experience, shows that is possible to develop this kind of applications under a systematic object oriented approach.

Our application has been satisfactorily proved under Netscape Navigator 4.5 with the VRML plug-in Cosmo Player 2.1 on Windows 95/NT working environment.

Following there are two images corresponding to a simple design made with the 2D editor and the corresponding 3D model.

Acknowledgments: To Architect Gonzalo Velez Jahn for all his valuable suggestions for the architecture design.

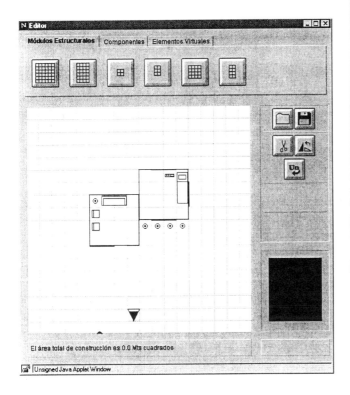
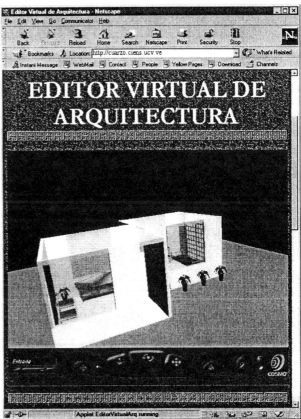

Figure 6. 2D and 3D view of EVA.

7. References

1. DE ABREU A., *Desarrollo de un prototipo de una aplicación WEB utilizando tecnologías de Realidad Virtual no inmersiva.* Laboratorio de Computación Gráfica. T.E.G. Escuela de Computación, UCV. 1999.

2. HECK M. MORELAND J., NADEAU D. *Inroduction to VRML97.* Siggraph97. Los Angeles-California, USA. 1997

3. DIAZ I., MATTEO A., *El método OOSE..* Technical Report No.22, Centro de Ingeniería de Software y Sistemas. UCV, 1997.

4. COSMO SOFTWARE. PLATINUM TECHNOLOGY, INC. *http://cosmosoftware.com/*

5. NETSCAPE COMMUNICATOR. *http://www.netscape.com/*

6. BLAXXUN INTERACTIVE. *http://www.blaxxun.com/*

7. JAVA ™ TECHNOLOGY. *http://www.java.sun.com/*

8. JACOBSON I., CHRISTERSON M., JONSSON P., ÖVERGAARD G. *Object-Oriented Software Engineering: A use-case driven approach.* Addison-Wesley Publishing Company. 1992.

9. RUMBAUGH J., BLAHA M., PREMELANI W., EDDY F., LORENSEN W. *Object Oriented Modeling and Design.* Prentice-Hall International Editions. 1991.

Pseudo-real-time Phenomenon in an Augmented Distributed Virtual Environment (ADVE) with Lag

HOR Li San, Tatsuhiro YONEKURA

Department of Computer & Information Sciences,
Faculty of Engineering,
Ibaraki University,
Hitachi City, 316-8511 JAPAN.
Tel. 81-294-38-5142
Fax. 81-294-38-5282
li_san@rocketmail.com, yonekura@cis.ibaraki.ac.jp

Abstract

This paper introduces the actualization of a new communication channel under a pseudo-real-time phenomenon, in an Augmented Distributed Virtual Environment (ADVE) framework through the implementation of a Prediction Feedback Loop (PFL), upon the existence of the unavoidable lag derived from the natural and artificial temporal factors. By implementing PFL, the ADVE framework is enriched with predictive characteristic where it is able to predict and foreshow information of a remotely controlled avatar (virtual body) in the ADVE. Based on the predictive results, interactions between a locally controlled avatar and a remotely controlled avatar in the ADVE can be carried out smoothly, effectively and strategically under an illusory real-time phenomenon without influence from the existence of lag. With this Pseudo-real-time Channel, we would like to bring forth a new era of effective man-to-man virtual communication over the network without inefficiency caused by the unavoidable lag, whether it is solvable or unsolvable.

Keywords

Pseudo-real-time, ADVE, PFL, Unavoidable Lag, Virtual Communication.

1. Introduction

In order to provide a new era of realistic man-to-man virtual communication channel beyond geographical boundary, studies and researches to optimize the immersion and presence effects in a Distributed Virtual Environment (DVE) have been actively carried out [1]~[4]. However, lag or latency is a crucial problem inherent in most DVEs, which decreases realism and degrades the achievement of immersion and presence effects [5][6]. Lag is referred to the asynchronous output between user's performance of movements and movements reflected in a DVE [5]. Any lag between actual movement and system response degrades the perception of a more real experience [7][8]. There have been many efforts to understand and overcome lag [5][6]. However, light speed's propagation delay contributes lag despite other artificial temporal factors like network latency, 3D graphics generation, etc. Obviously, this natural temporal factor is a constant factor that cannot be eliminated no matter how advanced are the implemented technology solutions.

In this paper, instead of working towards the reduction of lag from the technology enhancement approaches [5][9]~[11], we introduce a framework that works upon the existence of the unavoidable lag. If the framework could predict the transmitting data or the generating data before it is reflected in the virtual environment due to lag, the predictive data can be fully utilized to actualize a new channel of man-to-man virtual communication in a DVE to compensate the existence of lag. We named this new communication channel as Pseudo-real-time Channel. In addition to this, human natural adaptability would be naturally triggered under the Stimulus-Response behavioristic learning theory during the execution of *PFL (Prediction Feedback Loop)*. (The illustration of PFL will be carried out in Section 5.) Thus, pseudo-real-time illusory effective and strategic interactions are possible to be actualized.

The terminology of *pseudo-real-time* is derived from the illusory real-time environment that user could experience during system runtime upon PFL execution. In other words, this Pseudo-real-time Channel would appear to be as *real* as real-time to the user. In addition, as this framework utilizes real world perceptions upon the enhancement of technology, the terminology of *ADVE (Augmented Distributed Virtual Environment)* is also derived.

The ADVE is an avatar-based DVE that is enriched with the Visual, Acoustic, Tactile and Haptic (VATH) modalities, where user takes on the identity of an avatar, to interact with another avatar in a near-hallucinatory 3D world across the network. During this ADVE real-time virtual communication, the user is able to experience the four human beings' senses provided by the VATH modalities simultaneously with his long distant colleague through their respective avatar.

2.   Why prediction is essential?

In the Jet Propulsion Laboratory of Pasadena in California, a predictive display was developed to remotely control a robot's arm that resides thousands of miles away from the control station on the earth [12]. Obviously, this communication suffers a great deal from time delay. A high fidelity calibration technique is used to generate motion of the robot's arm off-line in the predictive display for the operator to preview. After satisfaction is achieved upon the preview, the operator will send his command to maneuver the robot's motion. In this context, prediction is an essential step for achieving successful communications between the earth and satellites or other planets that are influenced by time delay.

When we narrow down the communication scope to the earth, solving time delay problems is still one of the main challenges in the way of technology advancement. Since much of the lag seen by us today comes from light speed's propagation delay that is unsolvable, we foresee that prediction is an essential concept that could open up a new era of man-to-man virtual communication through the Pseudo-real-time Channel.

If it is possible to predict the in-coming data that is influenced by lag, we foresee the following advantages:

- Real-time communication between two mobile computers would not be affected by lag problems that keep on differing in real-time due to changing distance, as prediction is carried out in real-time with adjustments done according to lag influence.

- In the game context, predicting an opponent's situation would eventually become a motivation factor to players. Based on the predictive results, players can be motivated towards strategic thinking. Thus, this could bring forth a new educational achievement in the Intranet and the Internet world of computer games.

- In the context of the unavoidable lag whether it is solvable or unsolvable (i.e. network latency, computer frame generation rate, etc.), prediction

opens up a new field of study with regards to Human-Computer Interaction by providing humans a new way to adapt to the advancement of technology while compensating for the inefficiency of technology.

3.   Natural and artificial temporal factors

In the illustration thus far, the unavoidable lag is the core reason that brings forth the prediction issue. In our VATH modalities enriched ADVE framework, the following natural and artificial temporal factors give rise to lag problems:

- Data transmission delay caused by light speed and network infrastructure limitations.

- Synchronization between user-avatar and avatar-user during correlative interactions or cooperative working in the ADVE over the networks.

- Synchronization between user's input and avatar's response that is reflected in the ADVE.

- Synchronization of the basic architecture of an avatar that involves the generation of graphics frames, speech data buffer, haptic and tactile information (force feedback instances) buffers. In other words, synchronization of the effects of the avatar's VATH modalities in the ADVE.

4.   Derivation of Pseudo-real-time Channel

In order to explain the derivation of Pseudo-real-time Channel, current scenarios that are influenced by the existence of the unavoidable lag are analyzed. For ease of illustration of Pseudo-real-time Channel's fundamental concept, a geometrical model involving collisions between a locally controlled sphere and a remotely controlled sphere is considered (Figure 1). These spheres represent the simplest form of a locally controlled *Avatar A* and a remotely controlled *Avatar B* in the ADVE. Each of the local user and the remote user is given a full control over his avatar through a haptic device. Two assumptions were made in this model:

- No lag occurs from the direct haptic control of the user to the avatar's movements, which are reflected directly on the screen locally.

- Constant network latency occurs where α seconds is needed for data transmission from a local site to a remote site and vice versa.

4.1.   Asynchronous real-time scenario

Firstly, asynchronous real-time scenario in a peer-to-peer network model is analyzed. Based on the assumptions stated earlier, in this model that encounters network latency of αseconds, both of the reflected avatars on the screen currently are actually representing the states of the avatars at different moments of time as shown in Figure 1.

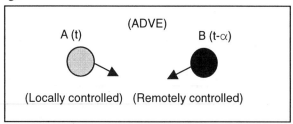

(ADVE)

A (t)   B (t-α)

(Locally controlled)   (Remotely controlled)

Fig.1 States of the avatars at site A at different moments of time due to lag.

The fact that αseconds is needed to send Avatar B's data across the network to the local terminal where Avatar A resides, has caused the outcome that the reflected Avatar B on the screen currently is actually Avatar B's data αseconds ago. In other words, the reflection of Avatar B's data on the screen would always be delayed in αseconds. Vice versa, a similar situation happens to Avatar A's data during its transmission to remote site B (Figure 2). In short, this means that Avatar A's state and Avatar B's state are always αseconds asynchronous.

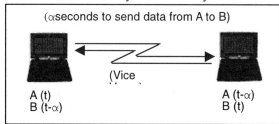

(αseconds to send data from A to B)

(Vice

A (t)   A (t-α)
B (t-α)   B (t)

Fig.2 Asynchronous real-time scenario in a peer-to-peer network model.

Thus, if these two avatars were to collide with each other in this asynchronous real-time scenario, it would be obviously an extremely difficult task to perform.

One of the solutions that humans could naturally apply due to the adaptive response, is to learn the pattern of movements of the remotely controlled avatar and then instinctively as well as strategically approach this opponent's avatar αseconds ahead of time. This illustrates the not-so-user-friendliness of the system, as humans need to react in a certain way to accommodate the inefficiency of the system in order to enable the occurrence of a collision.

4.2. Imperfect synchronous real-time scenario

In order to solve the above asynchronous dilemma from the technology point of view, a server is brought into the network model to manage the data flow and to synchronize the lag problems as in Figure 3.

The server would play a master role in maintaining all clients' states, updating the states according to actions taken by each client and notifying all clients of the relevant updated events. In short, all the transmitting data in the network would be routed through the server. With the data flow management and synchronization done by the server, the two avatars would be able to collide with each other now as the states reflected on the screen have been synchronized at the server site to be at the same moment in time.

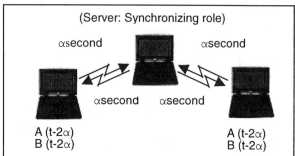

(Server: Synchronizing role)

αsecond   αsecond

αsecond   αsecond

A (t-2α)   A (t-2α)
B (t-2α)   B (t-2α)

Fig.3 Synchronous real-time scenario in a client-server network model.

However, this gives rise to waiting intervals at each client site before the arrival of their respective synchronized data, as round trips of transmission occur through the network. On top of this, network latency still exists and the load could be even heavier. Thus, besides the emotional irritation caused by the waiting intervals, it is still very difficult to set up a strategic approach towards the opponent's avatar, as its movement patterns are extremely difficult to trace due to the overall delay.

4.3. Pseudo-real-time scenario

From the above analysis, instead of the humans having to learn the movement patterns of the opponent's avatar, and then predicting the avatar's next position in order to collide with it, it would be ideal if we could assign this task to the system. In order to realize this, PFL that works under a pseudo-real-time phenomenon is implemented in our ADVE framework. Through PFL, the system is assigned to check out the lag influence, and then provide user with predictive data that is derived based on the previous information of the opponent's avatar as well as on the lag information.

5. Prediction Feedback Loop (PFL) design concept

The nature of Prediction Feedback Loop (PFL) lies in its capability of predicting remote opponents' information and providing feedback on the predictive results in a looping manner in real-time.

PFL is implemented based on a locally independent design concept at each client terminal. Thus, it can be implemented either on a peer-to-peer network model or a client-server network model. It also supports a multi-user simultaneously accessible ADVE as shown in Figure 4.

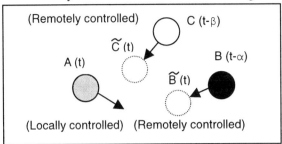

Fig.4 Predicting remotely controlled avatars' positions at time t.

In the above model, PFL is implemented at the local terminal where Avatar A resides. This loop is used to predict and foreshow graphically the possible next positions of Avatar B and Avatar C which are delayed in α and β seconds of time respectively (where $\alpha \neq \beta$). The predictive positions of Avatar B and Avatar C will be reflected on the screen as blur images at current time **t**, together with their real images at time **(t-α)** and time **(t-β)** respectively. The blur predictive images are denoted as $\widetilde{B}$ and $\widetilde{C}$. All the predictive data and the actual movement data will be kept in a database so that the pattern of movements can be analyzed based on this database.

Similarly, PFL is also implemented at site B and site C each as a local loop.

By utilizing the predictive results, these three avatars could strategically approach each other and thus collisions among these avatars are possible even with the existence of time lag of α seconds between site A and site B, and β seconds between site A and site C.

In addition, to enable a successful execution of PFL, a standard time, **t** as in Figure 4, is needed as a reference time to obtain the time lag between the participating sites. GMT time at Greenwich can be used for this standard time. Alternatively, the participating sites simply need to adjust their respective remote opponent's time according to their own local system clocks based on the time difference caused by the geographical distance between them.

5.1. Geometrical model based fundamental implementation of PFL

According to the nature of PFL, many high level methods that are capable of providing satisfied predictive results in real-time, can be utilized to implement PFL. The essential point in determining which implementation method to be used is to evaluate the prediction's purpose

and intention, which vary according to the predictive scenarios and depend on the nature of an ADVE. For instance, a *cooperative work based ADVE* and a *competitive game based ADVE* would obviously be having very different predictive scenarios with very different purposes and intentions.

In this paper, a very fundamental PFL implementation method, based on our previously illustrated geometrical model on the collisions of two spherical avatars is discussed.

5.1.1. The simplest case of PFL. First, the simplest case of PFL is analyzed, where both participating sites of an ADVE are assumed to be generating their frames at the same time at their respective local terminal. In addition, time lag is assumed to be constant. Based on these assumptions, we can trace the '*slip*' in frame generation cycle between the local and the remote avatar at each individual terminal, which results from the existence of lag. The *frame cycle* counts will start by initializing both avatars' frame cycles as 0, when a local system first detected in-coming data from a new remote site.

With reference to the model in Figure 5, **B'(n-3)** and **B'(n-2)** depict Avatar B's positions 3 frame cycles and 2 frame cycles ago respectively. All previous frame positions are kept in a database and will not be reflected on the screen. Meanwhile, **B(n-1)** is the position of Avatar B which is reflected on the screen currently. **B(n-1)** means that Avatar B is 1 frame cycle slipped (*behind*) in generation compared to Avatar A's frame. $\widetilde{B}(n)$ is the predictive position of Avatar B by PFL and it will be reflected as a blur image.

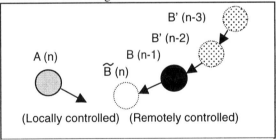

Fig.5 Avatars' positions at different frame cycles.

By utilizing the previous information of frame positions, velocities at **B'(n-2)** and **B(n-1)** are obtained at discrete time as follows:
When $\Delta t \rightarrow 0$, $\lim \Delta B / \Delta t \rightarrow \Delta B$.
Thus, $\quad$ **B'(n-2) - B'(n-3) = $V_{B'}$(n-2)**
and $\quad$ **B(n-1) - B'(n-2) = V_B(n-1)**.
When $\Delta t \rightarrow 0$, $\lim \Delta V / \Delta t \rightarrow \Delta V$.
Thus, acceleration at **B(n-1)** is obtained as follows:
$\quad$ **V_B(n-1) - $V_{B'}$(n-2) = a_B(n-1)**.
Next, constant acceleration is assumed, where:

$$\mathbf{a_{\widetilde{B}}(n) = a_B(n-1)}.$$

With this assumption, in a reverse manner, frame position of $\widetilde{\mathbf{B}}(\mathbf{n})$ is predicted as follows:

$$\mathbf{V_{\widetilde{B}}(n) - V_B(n-1) = a_{\widetilde{B}}(n) = a_B(n-1)}$$
$$\mathbf{\widetilde{B}(n) - B(n-1) = V_{\widetilde{B}}(n)}$$
$$\mathbf{\widetilde{B}(n) = B(n-1) + V_B(n-1) + a_B(n-1)}.$$

As a conclusion:

$$\boxed{\mathbf{\widetilde{B}(n) = B(n-1) + \alpha V_B(n-1) + 1/2\alpha^2 a_B(n-1)}} \quad - (1)$$

with ($\alpha = 1$) as the constant time lag between each frame generation cycle.

By using this method, Avatar B's position at frame cycle **n** can always be predicted even if its frame has slipped in generation for more than one frame cycle compared to Avatar A's frame.

5.1.2. A generalized case of PFL.
However, in a generalized case, two participating sites would most probably not be generating their frames at the same time at their respective local terminal. Thus, although both sites are simultaneously accessing the same ADVE, the reflection moment of both avatars' frames on each individual screen could somehow be very different due to network latency and different frame generation rates, as depicted in the relative time chart of Figure 6 below:

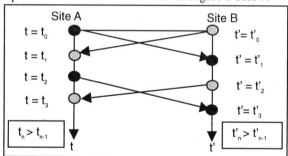

Fig.6 Relative time chart between A & B.

At each individual site, the time for its local avatar's frame to be generated (*generation time*) and the time for this frame to be reflected on the screen (*reflection time*) will be the same if the assumption of no lag occurs locally is made. However, the reflection time for a remote avatar on a local site will obviously be different from its generation time at its original site. This is due to the fact that the remote avatar's reflection time will depend on the local site's frame generation rate and the lag occurred during network transmission, whereas its generation time will only depend on its original site's frame generation rate.

Thus, during each frame generation of an avatar, a time stamp is essential to record the generation time. This generation time will be attached to the new generated frame when it is sent to a remote site, so that the time lag between the local generation time and the remote

reflection time can be obtained.

Figure 7 depicts the modified model of the previous simplest case model, where varying time lag is taken into consideration. In this modified model, $\widetilde{\mathbf{B}}(\mathbf{t_4})$ has to be predicted based on the reflection time (=generation time), **t** of Avatar A, with reference to the previous frame's generation times, **t'** of Avatar B.

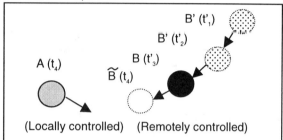

Fig.7 Avatars' positions attached with their respective generation time.

If constant velocity assumption is made:

$$\mathbf{V_{\widetilde{B}}(t_4) = V_B(t'_3)}.$$

Thus, $\quad \mathbf{\widetilde{B}(t_4) = B(t'_3) + (t_4 - t'_3) V_B(t'_3)}.$

If constant acceleration assumption is made, using the same method as for equation (1), equation (2) can be derived as below:

$$\boxed{\mathbf{\widetilde{B}(t_4) = B(t'_3) + \alpha V_B(t'_3) + 1/2\alpha^2 a_B(t'_3)}} \quad - (2)$$

with $\alpha = (t_4 - t'_3)$ as the time lag between Avatar B's generation time at site B and its reflection time at site A.

With regards to the actual collision, if a time lag of αseconds occurred, both users would be able to feel it after αseconds passed, when the predictive position coincides with the actual position and Avatar A is moved to approach this predictive position. Based on the law of inertia, the movement patterns of the remotely controlled avatar are able to be traced and predictable to a certain degree of accuracy. Thus, if a strategic approach is applied, collisions among these avatars in a lag influenced ADVE are possible.

5.2. Triggering of human natural adaptability

According to the above fundamental implementation, it is a challenging task for the user who controls Avatar A to wisely utilize the predictive results pertaining to Avatar B's next possible position. This determines his possibility of success in colliding with Avatar B.

Based on this *System Predicting→Human Observing→Human Trying→Human Finding Out* feedback loop nature, human learning behavior would be triggered. During the execution of PFL, the predictive result becomes a stimulus to the user and he would react by controlling his own avatar accordingly. According to the

Stimulus-Response behavioristic learning theory, humans will eventually learn the behavior of the framework that works under a pseudo-real-time phenomenon. When humans naturally adapt to this framework, the *realism* of this illusory real-time environment would appear to be as *real* as real-time to the user. Upon this, the realism would be increased if high accuracy of the predictive data were achieved.

5.3. Handling of the VATH Modalities in PFL

In the illustration thus far, each user is given a full control over his local avatar through a haptic device (*Haptic modality*). Upon this, the predictive result will be foreshown as a blur image together with the real images of the local and the remote avatars (*Visual modality*). However, in an ADVE that is enriched with the VATH modalities, besides haptic feel and visual information, when a collision takes place, both users should also be able to hear the collision impact (*Acoustic modality*) and feel the force feedback (*Tactile modality*) simultaneously.

Thus, the acoustic information and the force feedback instance magnitude should be generated and calculated relative to the local avatar's conditions, at each predictive position of the remote avatar and kept in advance in a database. At the moment a collision occurs between these two avatars, the information can be released at the same moment so that both users could experience the four VATH modalities simultaneously at their respective site.

6. Conclusion

According to our studies thus far, there has been research done on enhancing Augmented Reality systems through predictive tracking with the aid of inertial sensors [13]. However, in the context of distant man-to-man virtual communication, this paper is the first paper that utilizes prediction concept to bring forth a new fundamental communication phenomenon. Based on the theoretical analysis above, this new phenomenon through a Pseudo-real-time Channel is possible to be actualized upon the existence of the unavoidable lag. During the actualization of this new phenomenon, technology solutions are utilized to take over human natural instinctive responses in prediction. At the same time, human natural adaptability is triggered in return during runtime to accommodate this pseudo-real-time phenomenon so that this will further compensate the lag problem.

To evaluate from a broader perspective, we foresee that this new phenomenon has potential to go beyond the man-to-man virtual communication and impact on man-

to-man real-world communication, like teleconferencing in a mobile context. If this phenomenon is skillfully and wisely utilized, we believe that it will be a valuable contribution to the field of man-to-man distant telecommunication influenced by lag problems.

With regards to future works, the following issues are our concern for further enhancement:

- Issue related to the accuracy of predictive results.
- Issue related to how humans adapt to this pseudo-real-time phenomenon.

Acknowledgements
This research was partially supported by the SVBL (Satellite Venture Business Laboratory) of Ibaraki University, Japan.

References

[1] P.J., Metzger, "Adding Reality to the Virtual", IEEE VRAIS '93, pp.7-13, (1993).

[2] B.K., Choi, H.Y., Lee, "A Study on Multi-User 3D Game Using VR Technology", Proceedings of VSMM'96 Int. Conf., pp.389-394, (1996).

[3] M., Slater, V., Linakis, M., Usoh, R., Kooper, "Immersion, Presence and Performance in Virtual Environments: An Experiment with Tri-Dimensional Chess", Proceedings of VRST'96, pp.163-172, (1996).

[4] J., Vacca, "VRML Clearly Explained: Part 3: Distributed Virtual Environments", AP Professional, pp. 479-599, (1998).

[5] D.W., Kyger, P.S., Maybeck, "Reducing Lag in Virtual Displays Using Multiple Model Adaptive Estimation", IEEE Transactions on Aerospace and Electronic Systems, Vol. 34, No. 4, Oct 98, pp.1237-1248, (1998).

[6] Adelstein, B.D., Johnston, E.R., and Ellis, S., "Spatial sensor lag in virtual environment systems", Proceedings of the SPIE, 1833, (1993).

[7] Adam, J.A., "Virtual Reality is for Real", IEEE Spectrum, 30(10), pp.22-29, (1993).

[8] Ellis, S., "What are Virtual Environments?", IEEE Computer Graphics and Applications, 14(1), pp.17-22, (1994).

[9] V.N., Padmanabhan, J.C., Mogul, "Improving HTTP Latency", 2nd WWW Conference'94: Mosaic and the Web, Developers' Day: Technical Presentation, (1994). http://www.ncsa.uiuc.edu/SDG/IT94/Proceedings/Dday/mogul/HTTPLatency.html.

[10] M., Green, "A Framework for Real-time Rendering in Virtual Reality", Proceedings of VRST'96, pp.3-9, (1996).

[11] W., Liu, J., Li, "Distributed LoD Algorithm for Complex Virtual Environments", Proceedings of VRST'96, pp.21-25, (1996).

[12] W.S., Kim, A.K., Bejczy, "Predictive Displays for Remote Control under Communication Time Delay", VRAIS'93 Video Proceedings, IEEE Neural Network Council, (1993).

[13] R.T., Azuma, "Dissertation: Predictive Tracking for Augmented Reality", UNC Chapel Hill Dept. of Computer Science technical report TR95-007, 262 pages, (February 1995). http://www.cs.unc.edu/~azuma/d_abstract.html.

Molecular Dynamics Simulation and Visualization

Roman Ďurikovič

Department of Computer Software, The University of Aizu
Tsuruga, Ikki-machi, Aizu-Wakamatsu-shi, Fukushima, 965-80 Japan

Teruaki Motooka

Department of Materials science and Engineering, Kyushu University
6-10-1 Hakozaki, Fukuoka, 812-8581 Japan

Abstract

We have developed atomic-scale material models capable of melting, crystallization and amorphization. These models feature molecular dynamics governed by Langevin equations of motion in which particle interact through attractive covalent forces and short-range repulsion forces. Also, we present an interactive virtual visualization tool for the simulation of atomic scale material behavior. An application of this research is to understand the processes that can control the quality of a single-crystal Si grown from the melt.

1. Introduction

The quality of a single-crystal Si grown by Czochralski method [1] from melted silicon (see Fig. 1) is sensitive on the growth conditions such as crystal growth rates and temperature gradients at the liquid/crystal interface. Production of high quality crystal Si requires understanding of the growth mechanism on the atomic level. One of the experimental techniques is transmission electron microscope which gives direct images of atomic structures of crystals. However, preparation of samples for electron microscopy is a long process. In the approach described herein, the molecular dynamics simulation for large-scale systems (up to 10000 atoms) are used to model the crystal growth. Particles are objects that have mass, position, velocity, and respond to forces, they are easy objects to simulate. Despite their simplicity, they can be made to exhibit a wide range of interesting behavior. For example, the movement of atoms in materials can be simulated by particles with appropriate potential functions defined in the small neighborhood of

each particle. The developed computer system enable us modeling material behavior using the particle objects in an interactive 3D environment. Such environment can be used to facilitate the exploration of a structure in situations that are difficult or expensive to reproduce experimentally.

We calculate the position of the atoms in the material during the process and display atomic images of the crystal structure as a function of time. In addition, several diagnostic imaging techniques that aid the analysis of structure at atomic level: radial distribution function $g(r)$, bond angle distribution function $g(\theta)$, and static structure factors $S(k)$, were developed. This paper proposes the approach for modeling and visualization of large scale molecular models applied on the simulation of a single-crystal Si growth from molten silicon.

1.1. Related Work

There has been extensive research on physically based modeling and dynamic simulations for computer graphics. The basics of mass-spring systems and particle system dynamics including some implementation hints are well described in SIGGRAPH'94 tutorial [2]. Different approaches have been introduced to visually model the physical processes. The physically based models capable of heat conduction, thermoelasticity, melting, and fluid-like behavior in molten state were first described by Terzopoulos, *et al.* [3]. Their model is very simplified and lack of precise physical behavior on atomic level.

Greenspan [4] investigated various N-body systems as discrete models of solid, liquid and gaseous media. Over the years, much attention has been given in the physics and chemistry literature to the development of discrete liquid models involving aggregate molecular dynamics in

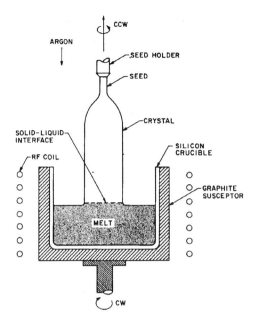

Figure 1. Czochralski crystal puller.

which the molecules are subject to various interaction potentials [5]. A basic technique is to model long-range attraction and short-range repulsion forces between pairs of particles according to potentials of the Lennard-Jones type, which lead to forces involving inverse powers of particle separation distance [6]. Recently Ishimaru, *et al.* [7] demonstrated that in addition to crystal silicon it is possible to simulate the amorphous and liquid state of pure silicon with this type of potential by different heating and freezing methods of melted silicon.

Small molecular models (up to 100 atoms) that may contain multiple types of atoms, can be created with a commercial quantum mechanics package called Gausian94 [8]. This package falls in to a group of *ab initio* methods when very accurate molecular orbital calculations are carried out for the entire structure with hydrogen termination. Unfortunately, no such system is available for larger molecular models.

Section 2 of this paper introduces the molecular dynamic approach to the simulation of material behavior. Here the equation of motion of a particle system and the total potential energy based on repulsive and attractive forces is defined. Next the numerical implementation using finite differences and stochastic forces is discussed. The modeling and visualization of simulated processes within a time interval is proposed in Section 3. Section 4 proposes the diagnostic techniques of simulated results consisting of multiple 2D graphs continually changing in time as the simulation proceeds. The last section demonstrates the modeling technique applied on the Czochralski crystallization process

from molten silicon.

2. Molecular Dynamics

The motion of the particle i is governed by a pair of the first-order ordinary differential equations (ODE)

$$
\begin{aligned}
m_i \dot{\mathbf{v}}_i(t) &= -m_i \gamma_i (\mathbf{v}_i(t) + \mathbf{v}_p) + F_i(\{\mathbf{x}(t)\}) + R_i(t) \\
\dot{\mathbf{x}}_i &= \mathbf{v}_i,
\end{aligned}
$$

where in our model, the explicit systematic force F_i between the N particles was derived from the total potential Eq. 2, stochastic force R_i was introduced to mimic the motion of solvent molecules on the solute, and $\mathbf{x}_i$, $\mathbf{v}_i$, m_i, and γ_i are the position, velocity, atomic mass and friction coefficient, respectively. In general, the force F_i may depend on the position of all particles, denoted by $\{\mathbf{x}(t)\}$. Concerning the nature of the stochastic force R_i it is assumed to be stationary, Markovian and Gaussian with zero mean and to have no correlation with initial velocities $\mathbf{v}_i(0)$ nor with the systematic force $F_i(0)$. The pulling speed $\mathbf{v}_p$ is assumed to be constant in time.

2.1. Total Potential Energy

A basic technique is to model attractive covalent and short-range repulsion forces between pairs of particles according to total potentials. The total potential energy of a system of N particles as proposed by Tersoff [6] is defined as a sum of interatomic potentials:

$$
\Phi = \sum_i^N E_i, \tag{2}
$$

$$
E_i = \frac{1}{2} \sum_{j \neq i}^N f_c(r_{ij})[V_R(r_{ij}) - b_{ij} V_A(r_{ij})],
$$

where $f_c(r_{ij})$ is a cutoff function controlling the influence of inter-atomic forces, written as

$$
f_c(r_{ij}) = \begin{cases} 1 & \text{if } r_{ij} < R_{ij} \\ \frac{1}{2} + \frac{1}{2}\cos[\pi \frac{r_{ij}-R_{ij}}{S_{ij}-R_{ij}}] & \text{if } R_{ij} < r_{ij} < S_{ij} \\ 0 & \text{if } r_{ij} > S_{ij}. \end{cases}
$$

The repulsive and attractive elements denoted by V_R and V_A, respectively depend on particle pairs, while the function b_{ij} includes particle triples in it's expression. We used the Tersoff definitions

$$
\begin{aligned}
V_R(r_{ij}) &= A_{ij} exp(-\lambda_{ij} r_{ij}), \\
V_A r_{ij} &= B_{ij} exp(-\mu_{ij} r_{ij}), \\
b_{ij} &= \chi_{ij}(1 + \beta_i^{n_i} \xi_{ij}^{n_i})^{-1/2n_i},
\end{aligned}
$$

$$\xi_{ij} = \sum_{k \neq i,j}^{N} f_c(r_{ij})g(\theta_{ijk}),$$

$$g(\theta_{ijk}) = 1 + c_i^2/d_i^2 - c_i^2/[d_i^2 + (h_i - \cos\theta_{ijk})^2],$$

where r_{ij} is internuclear distance between particles i and j, and θ_{ijk} is the bond angle between bonds ij and ik. Following reference [9] the double indexed constants are defined as $\lambda_{ij} = (\lambda_i + \lambda_j)/2$, $\mu_{ij} = (\mu_i + \mu_j)/2$, $A_{ij} = (A_i A_j)^{1/2}$, $B_{ij} = (B_i B_j)^{1/2}$, $R_{ij} = (R_i R_j)^{1/2}$, and $S_{ij} = (S_i S_j)^{1/2}$. All other parameters are constants reported by Tersoff [6] for silicon type of molecules, while their suitability and limitations were delineated by Halicionglu [9]. Even though, the Tersoff originally derived his potential for a crystal silicon, Ishimaru et al. [7] showed that the Tersoff empirical inter-atomic can be adapted for simulation of liquid and amorphous silicon as well. Thus, the potential shown in Eq. 2 is sufficient for our purpose to model the crystal growth form a liquid silicon consisting of three states of silicon. The assumption is made that no impurities are present in the silicon.

2.2. Implementations

Numerical integrations of equation of motion, Eq. 2, were performed under the constant volume within the cubic domain with periodic boundary conditions on side faces and a reflection plane on bottom. At each time step the collision between the particle and the reflection plane is calculated to prevent particle from escaping out of the volume. To simulate the dynamics of our models we provide the initial position $\mathbf{x}(t_0)$, $\mathbf{x}(t_{-1})$, and stochastic vector $X_{-1}(\Delta t)$, systematic force $F(t_{-1})$ of particle i for $i = 1, \ldots, N$. At each subsequent time step $t_0, t_1, \ldots, t_n, t_{n-1}, \ldots$, we evaluate the current velocities, current systematic force, current stochastic vector, and new positions using the explicit Gunsteren and Berendsed [10] stochastic approach. The integration method is of the third order and there is not necessity to assume that systematic force F_i is constant during time interval Δt, because the method includes higher order terms.

We use the units kJ mole^{-1} (energy), u (atomic mass), angstroms $\mathring{A}$ (10^{-10} m) (length), K (temperature), and time is in ps units. The integration time step Δt and friction coefficient γ were usually set to 0.002 ps and 5 ps^{-1} in our simulations.

3. Visualization

The data obtained from the molecular dynamic simulation can be visualized and processed by the diagnostic techniques. It is not possible at present to run the dynamic simulation in real time and to control the simulation and visualization parameters interactively. However, we can run

the molecular simulation for a given simulation parameters on a parallel workstation and calculate results for several discrete time steps. Finally, the stored solutions can be displayed as a 3D model changing its shape in time while a set of 2D diagnostic functions varying in time can help us to understand the undergoing structural changes.

Each atom in the molecular structure is characterized by five parameters: the atomic symbol, the van der Waals radius (a probability measure of the location of electrons), and x, y, z cartesian coordinates in angstroms $\mathring{A}$. As usual, atoms are represented as spheres, while bonds are drawn as thin cylinders. We note that the number of atoms is constant in time during our simulations. On the other hand, since the presence of a bond between two atoms is determined from automatically calculated threshold value, their appearance and disappearance are discontinuous in time. The view point and the objects in a scene are changing their positions, while the light sources are considered to be stationary.

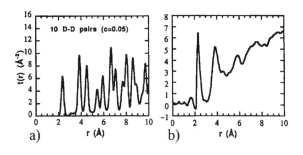

Figure 2. Radial distribution function for a) crystalline silicon and b) amorphous silicon.

4. Diagnostic Techniques

Taking just the direct view of the atoms as shown in Figure 4, it is difficult to determine where the structure is still crystalline but with some disorder. To analyze the different crystal structures in more detail, we plot a time varying radial distribution function $g(r)$, bond angle distribution function $g(\theta)$, and static structure factors $S(k)$.

The radial distribution $g(r)$ gives the probability of finding a pair of atoms a distance r apart, relative to the probability expected for a completely random distribution at the same density. It can be calculated by averaging the number of atoms a given distance away from each atom in the sample. The radial distribution function for a crystal differs from that for an amorphous and liquid sample. Figure 2 shows the plot of $g(r)$ for a crystalline and an amorphous sample. The significant distinguishing feature is the absence of the third peak from Fig. 2a in the amorphous sample. To compare the simulation data with the available data of neutron-diffraction measurements [7], the static structure factors $S(k)$ defined by Fourier transformation of $g(r)$ are used. In the bond angle distribution function $g(\theta)$, we count the number of bond angles for a given angle from each triple of atoms in the sample, see Fig. 3.

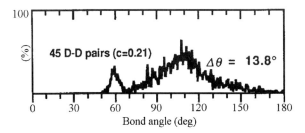

Figure 3. Bond distribution function for an amorphous silicon.

5. Results

In the first example 9216 Si atoms were initially placed on the diamond lattice sites within the volume $62 \times 62 \times 62$ $\mathring{A}^3$, *ie.* the tetrahedral prism. The entire volume was immersed in a heat bath with the fixed temperature distribution and pulled upwards in z direction for the simulation of crystal growth. In Fig. 4, the pulling speed and temperature gradient were set to $12 \, m/s$ and $15 \, K/A$, respectively. The singly subscripted parameters such as λ_i from Eq. 2 were set for a silicon molecule as follows: $A = 1830.8eV$, $B = 471.18eV$, $\lambda = 2.4799 \, \mathring{A}^{-1}$, $\mu = 1.7322 \, \mathring{A}^{-1}$, $\beta = 1.1 \times 10^{-6}$, $n = 0.78734$, $c = 1.0039 \times 10^5$, $d = 16.217$, $h = -0.59825$, $R = 2.7 \, \mathring{A}$, $S = 3.0 \, \mathring{A}$, $\chi = 1$.

The second example, Figure 5, demonstrates the effect of varying reference temperature. Initially, the cluster of two oxygen atoms placed into a regular hexagonal lattice of silicon atoms, Figures 5a, was heated at room and melting temperature shown in Figures 5b and Figures 5c, respectively. The high disorder observed at melting temperature is due to large stochastic forces applied to silicon atoms.

In the third example, Figure 6, we studied the oxygen and silicon interactions. Here, two oxygen and 37 Si atoms were used in quantum mechanics simulation package Gaussian94, while the visualization and post-simulation diagnostics were done by proposed system. Figure 6 shows the sequence of images from dynamic visualization.

The proposed system implemented on HP9000/800 workstation gives the user choice of displaying all diagnostic variables plotted against time. The program lets the user

orient his view arbitrarily in the 3D environment while observing the pre-calculated molecular dynamics simulations.

6. Conclusion

Applying techniques from physics-based modeling and molecular dynamics, we have illustrated an interactive virtual visualization tool for the simulation of material behavior at atomic level. Also, we have demonstrated the modeling technique of the crystallization process of liquid silicon for large-scale systems. Implementation of multiple types of atoms and their interactions in large-scale systems is under the current investigation.

7. Acknowledgment

The authors would like to thank K. Nishihira and M. Ishimaru for their collaboration during the course of this work. This research was sponsored by grants from the Japanese Society for the Promotion of Science Research for the Future Program in the Area of Atomic Scale Surface and Interface Dynamics under the project of "Dynamic Behaviour of Silicon Atoms, Lattice Defects and Impurities near Silicon Melt-crystal Interface".

References

[1] S.M. Sze. Semiconductor devices: Physics and technology. *John Wiley & Sons Press*,New York, 1985.

[2] A. Witkin (Ed.). An introduction to physically based modeling. *Computer Graphics (SIGGRAPH '94 Tutorials)*, Orlando, Florida, July, 1994.

[3] D. Terzopoulos and J. Platt and K. Fleischer. Heating and Melting deformable models. *The Journal of Visualizatoin and Computer Animation*, 2:68–73, 1991.

[4] D. Greenspan. Discrete models. *Addison-Wesley*, Reading, MA, 1973.

[5] H.J.C. Berendsen and W.F. van Gunsteren. Molecular dynamics simulations: techniques and approaches. In A.J. Barnes, W.J. Orville-Thomas and J. Yarwood (eds). Molecular liquids dynamics and interactions. *D. Reidel*, Dordrecht, Holland, 475–500, 1984.

[6] J. Tersoff. Modeling solid-state chemistry: Interatomic potentials for multicomponent systems. *Physical Review B*, 39(8):5566–5568, 1989.

[7] M. Ishimaru and S. Munetoh and T. Motooka. Generation of amorphous silicon structures by rapid quenching: A molecular-dynamics study. *Physical Review B*, 56(23):15133–15138, 1997.

[8] Gaussian 94 Revision E.2. *Gaussian, Inc.*, Pittsburgh, PA, 1995.

[9] T. Halicioglu. Comparative study on energy and structure-related properties for the (100) surface of β-SiC. *Physical Review B*, 51(11):7217–7223, 1995.

[10] W.F. van Gunsteren and H.J.C. Berendsen. Algorithms for brownian dynamics. *Molecular Physics*, 45(3):637–647, 1982.

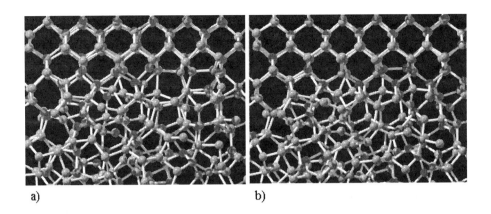

Figure 4. An example of atomic arrangements in crystallization processes after simulation time of a) 300 ps and b) 600 ps.

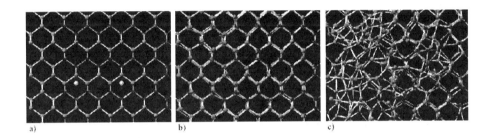

Figure 5. Varying temperature. a) Initial cluster of silicon atoms. b) Cluster after 600 ps at room temperature. c) The same initial cluster after 600 ps at melting temperature.

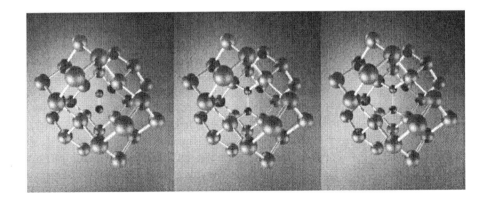

Figure 6. Oxygen and silicon interactions (SiO_2). Two oxygen atoms are located at the center.

Towards Interactive Finite Element Analysis
of Shell Structures in Virtual Reality

A. Liverani*, F. Kuester**, B. Hamann**

* DIEM – University of Bologna, Italy
a.liverani@mail.ingfo.unibo.it
** Center for Image Processing and Integrated Computing (CIPIC)
Department of Computer Science
University of California - Davis, CA 95616, USA
(kuester,hamann)@cs.ucdavis.edu

Abstract

A first step towards a semi-immersive Virtual Reality (VR) interface for Finite Element Analysis (FEA) is presented in this paper. During recent years, user interfaces of FEA solvers have matured from character-based command-line driven implementations into easy-to-use graphical user interfaces (GUIs). This new generation of GUIs provides access to intuitive and productive tools for the management and analysis of structural problems. Many pre- and post-processors have been implemented targeting the simplification of the man-machine interface in order to increase the ease of use and provide better visual analysis of FEA solver results. Nevertheless, none of these packages provides a real 3D-enabled interface. The main objective of this project is to join state-of-the-art visualization technology, VR devices, and FEA solvers into the integrated development environment VRFEA.

Keywords

Virtual Reality, Interactive Modeling, Finite Element Analysis, 3D Modeling, Simulation.

1. Introduction

Primarily driven by product quality, cost, and time-to-market considerations, most automotive and aerospace companies heavily invested into the development and implementation of new VR technology during the last five years. These newly created synthetic environments have matured into valuable tools in the areas of human factors and usability studies, manufacturing, and simulation-based design. Nevertheless, most of these applications use immersive or augmented VR technology primarily to visualize or interact with pre-defined data neglecting some of its powerful features in the area of content creation. As companies focus on streamlining productivity in the pursuit of global competitiveness, the migration to computer-aided design, computer-aided manufacturing and computer-aided engineering systems has established a new backbone of modern industrial product development. While most of these technological advances are of high benefit to the engineering and design community they still lack some of the important visual and haptic features crucial to efficient human computer interfaces that can be addressed using the available VR hardware.

1.1 Motivation

In classic FEA environments engineers usually spend 40% of their working time on 3D shape modeling, 30% on mesh generation (the definition of boundary conditions and simulation parameters), 20% on result analysis and review and only 10% on running the FEA solvers.

The observation that modeling, mesh generation and adjustment, specification of simulation parameters and result analysis tasks are responsible for 90% of the workload indicates that further technological advances are required. A significant number of the areas prone to improvement require the visualization of scientific data, and intuitive 3D-display technology could be successfully involved in a solution approach.

Furthermore, VR devices can aid the designer in content creation and design verification during the pre-processing and the evaluation and interpretation of results during the post-processing phase. The primary focus of this paper is on those tasks that can be performed in real-time. This paper is intended as a first step towards the development of a fully integrated modeling and simulation environment, combining VR and FEA.

The design goal was to provide a visualization front-end, which easily interfaces with either, the traditional command line driven FEA applications or newer plug-in based technology. Furthermore, the visualization component had to enable smooth transitions between standard on-screen and VR-enabled modeling tasks. Therefore, support for stereo output devices, additional VR specific input hardware such as spatial trackers and data gloves had to be provided besides the standard workstation specific display modes.

1.2 Related work

Recent experiments performed at Iowa University [1] have used VR approaches in FEA to evaluate "parameter sensitivity" and facilitate design. This means that VR is not really integrated into the FEA modeling and analysis procedure, but it is only used as a visualization tool to seek optimal design parameters.

Our environment, VRFEA, was designed to overcome the integration gaps between VR and FEA. In this environment the designer uses immersive VR tools to manage a FEA model, manipulate nodes or shells, create or adjust the mesh, specify boundary conditions, and visualize the results.

2. Setup

2.1 Hardware

VRFEA was designed for a new generation of stereo projection systems currently marketed under names like *ImmersiveWorkbench*, *Responsive Workbench* and *ImmersaDesk* [21,22]. We used the *ImmersiveWorkbench* from Fakespace which allows stereo projection of 3D computer-generated images onto an approximately 2m*1.5m wide projection area. A four-processor SGI Onyx2 InfiniteReality (225MHz, R10000 processor) system was used as the rendering and computation engine. The basic hardware setup is illustrated in Figure 1. The user is wearing shutter glasses with integrated head tracking for stereoscopic viewing and uses a set of pinch gloves combined with a stylus device for interaction with VRFEA. The spatial data-set describing the user's head

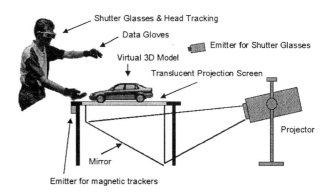

Figure 1: Hardware setup.

position and hand movements is fully incorporated into the environment. We briefly describe the input devices:

- **Stylus**. Using a fixed transmitter as reference, this pencil-like system accurately computes position (x, y and z coordinates) and orientation (yaw, pitch and roll) of a tiny receiver contained in the stylus. In addition, it provides an integrated button that can be used for picking actions.

- **Gloves.** The pinch system uses cloth gloves with electrical sensors in each fingertip. Contact between any two or more digits completes a conductive path, providing a variety of possible "pinch" gestures that can be associated with distinct actions. Additionally, an attached electromagnetic tracker captures the position of each glove.

2.2 Software

One of the governing development goals was to provide a platform-independent visualization front-end for FEA applications, which supports either plug-in technology or the traditional command line interface. In addition, a smooth transition between conventional and VR display modes had to be possible. To facilitate these requirements OpenInventor was selected as the implementation language of choice for the visualization component.

2.2.1 Open Inventor. Open Inventor is an object-oriented developer's toolkit that simplifies 3D graphics programming and developing high-performance interactive 3D programs. The rich Inventor set of pre-programmed building blocks defines a full-featured, extensible framework upon which entire applications can be developed.

It includes a wide variety of geometry, property, and group objects as well as manipulators for user interaction, and high-level viewers and editor components.

The underlying object hierarchy produces for each shape model change and motion an on-screen visualization. Additionally, OpenInventor establishes a file format standard for 3D data exchange that is the basis for the Virtual Reality Modeling Language (VRML).

2.2.2 Device Drivers under Inventor. A new set of device plug-ins was developed to provide OpenInventor with the real-time support for VR input devices, including the Fakespace pinch glove and the Polhemus Fastrack system. Furthermore, a new object selection method was introduced to bypass standard libraries for mouse-based object selection.

This modification was essential to enable real-time transition between keyboard-mouse and semi-immersive modeling metaphors. In fact, a generic event-based collision detection routine continuously checks for object collisions. Verified collisions trigger intuitive visual and audio feedback. These additions to the OpenInventor toolkit have substantially increased its VR potential.

3. Finite Element Code

3.1 Solver

The FE solver was implemented as a console-type application using ANSI C for portability reasons. Commands are passed to the solver through a command line interface (see Figure 2) and a generic file description language.

```
C:\TMP\FEA>fea.exe
NOME FILE INPUT :
     [ test ] alaf4
TIPO USCITA GRAFICA :
   0  =  IGES
   1  =  ALIDRAFT
     [ 0 ] 0

Lettura Dati.

MEMORIA ALLOCATA  = 136.52 K

   Soluzione sistema lineare F = Kt*u.

MEMORIA ALLOCATA  = 3564.56 K

------ C A L C O L O   E S E G U I T O ------

C:\TMP\FEA>
```

Figure 2: FE solver command line interface.

The file format supports geometry information in mesh format, node coordinates, a variety of element types, boundary conditions and modeling parameters such as forces or displacements applied to particular nodes.

An input file might look like this:

```
# NUM. MATERIALS
  1
# IND. MAT. FILE NAME
  0  MAT08.MAT

# NUM. NODI
  4
# IND.   X      Y       Z
0  0.00   0.00    0.00
1  1.00   0.00    0.00
2  1.00   1000.00    0.00
3  0.00   1000.00    0.00

# BEAM SHELL BRICK
   0    1    0
# BEAM ELEMENTS:

# SHELL ELEMENTS:
# ind  id_laminato
#    n0  n1  n2  n3
  0   0
         0   1   2   3

# NUM. CONSTRAINTS
  2
0  0  G
   6  1  2  3  4  5  6
1  3  G
   6  1  2  3  4  5  6

# NUM. LOADED NODES
  1
0  2
     0.000   0.000   0.000
     0.000   0.000   50.000

# NUM. GIVEN DISPLACEMENTS
  0
# GIVEN DISPLACEMENTS.
# id_nodo x  y   z
#      rx ry  rz
```

The FE model can be described with either solid 3D elements as bricks, with shell elements for thin parts or a combination thereof. A classic frontal method was implemented to solve linear and non linear equation systems. This solver demonstrated good performance, solving small meshes (around 200 nodes) in less than two seconds and large models (around 3000 nodes) in about one minute. The command line-based interface style was chosen to simulate and test the visual front-end for its suitability with off-the-shelf products.

3.2 Input and Output Files

VRFEA provides two core modules for pre-processing and post-processing that encapsulate the FE solver. Like most commercially available pre-processor FEA solvers, VRFEA writes an input file (described above) and passes it to the solver. The files created by the solver include node displacements, written in ASCII format. This is an example:

```
                 DISPLACEMENTS
node   Ux       Vy       Wz       Thx      Thy      Thz

  0 +0.000000E+00 +0.000000E+00 +0.000000E+00
     +0.000000E+00 +0.000000E+00 +0.000000E+00
  1 +0.000000E+00 +0.000000E+00 +0.000000E+00
     +0.000000E+00 +0.000000E+00 +0.000000E+00
  2 +0.000000E+00 +0.000000E+00 +0.000000E+00
     +0.000000E+00 +0.000000E+00 +0.000000E+00
  3 +0.000000E+00 +0.000000E+00 +0.000000E+00
     +0.000000E+00 +0.000000E+00 +0.000000E+00
```

Von Mises stresses on elements:

```
      sigma1          sigma2          tau12

  0   -8.129862e-01   1.793307e-01   1.418309e+00
  1    4.189166e+00   9.180581e-02   6.915451e+00
  2    7.480460e+00   3.414629e-02  -1.414779e+00
  3    2.482450e+00   1.211878e-01  -6.898216e+00
  4    1.519136e-17   4.326919e-17   3.223468e-17
  5   -2.482450e+00  -1.211878e-01   6.898216e+00
  6   -7.480460e+00  -3.414629e-02   1.414779e+00
  7   -4.189166e+00  -9.180581e-02  -6.915451e+00
  8    8.129862e-01  -1.793307e-01  -1.418309e+00
      .....
```

After the solver terminates, the results are passed to the post-processing stage of VRFEA. As mentioned earlier, information is passed through a file-based interface for compatibility reasons. Considering the real-time requirements for certain components, the use of multi-programming and shared memory has proven advantageous.

4. Static Simulations

The proof-of-concept implementation of VRFEA was tested by interactively applying specified node forces and node displacements.

The meshes for the given examples (Figures 3-5) were created with build-in VRFEA functionality.

Mesh generation was strongly simplified due to the chosen regular geometric design, which resulted in a mesh consisting of 150 nodes (magnified by colored spheres) and 126 shell elements (connecting the nodes). Constrained nodes are represented using red cubes, as shown in Figure 3.

4.1 "Forceless" Force Input

Following this new paradigm for integration among VR and FEA, the designer might be interested in testing and simulating the finger touch on a stereo deck or the strength of a drawer in a car console.

During the first implementation cycle, force feedback devices were not available and we had to define new metaphors for "*forceless-force-input*". This is the list of supported interaction modes:

- interactive node force displacement
- interactive node displacement
- force as implied by displacement
- force as a result of compressing a virtual medium
- force as implied by magnitude (distance between two points)
- force as implied by a visual queue (arrow)

Ultimately, the goal is to replace these concepts with actual force-feedback devices enabling the user to physically perceive model contents.

4.2 Interactive Node Force Application

The application of forces to mesh nodes may be considered a classical example of FEA. Standard 2D interfaces give a designer the option to select a node on the screen. VRFEA introduces a new interaction paradigm, a symbolic arrow, representing the force being applied.

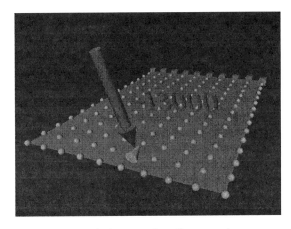

Figure 3: Increasing force value

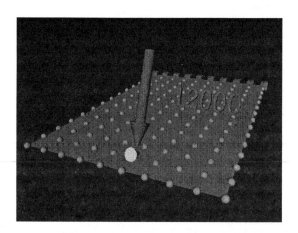

Figure 4: Decreasing force value.

The magnitude of these force vectors can be easily adjusted through associated gestures or actions provided by the stylus and glove interaction devices. If the stylus proxy is in the upside position, the force increases (Figure 2), otherwise it decreases (Figure 3).

However, this enhancement does not exclude the presence and use of multi-purpose menus, but it can dramatically reduce the frequency with which the menus have to be accessed and thus intuitive modeling efficiency is increased.

Object selection is based on a collision detection algorithm that continuously monitors the input device proxy in relation to the FE model. At any time the FE solver can be accessed to interactively update the model parameters. The surface is colored based on strain or displacement information obtained from the solver. For our test cases the solver latency was minimized to be lower than a three-second threshold.

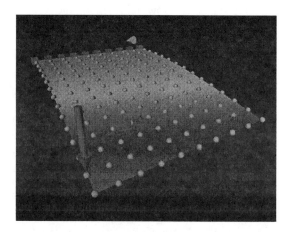

Figure 5: Color-coded results.

4.3 Interactive Node Displacement Application

To enable complete simulation in a VR environment, a very interesting FEA example could push VR and interface technology. In many test environments for ergonomic and usability studies, the designer needs to investigate the capabilities of the structure strength under displacements.

This test could easily be performed by simulating node displacement and computing the resulting surface deformation. To underlay the node displacements, a symmetric constraint set can be chosen (Figure 5).

Figure 6: Symmetric constraint set.

As in the previous example, nodes or shell elements can be selected. However, in this setting forces are applied implicitly through the displacements applied to the elements. Figure 6 shows such a displacement test and the results obtained from the solver (Figure 7).

Figure 7: Applying node displacement.

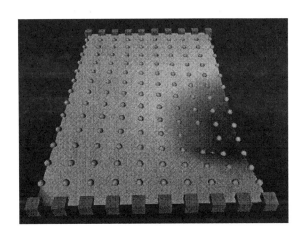

Figure 8: Color-coded results.

5. Conclusions

A new interaction method for FEA was introduced in this paper. While modern pre-processor and post-processor software for FEM/FEA primarily utilizes 2D interfaces, this interface prototype represents an essential step towards proving the benefits of VR to FE applications, and goes beyond visualization and navigation of results.

The use of 3D input devices and stereo rendering systems has the potential to transform how engineers interact with design environments enhancing model manipulation, examination and modification efficiency and product quality.

6. Future Work

So far, the current research focus has been on the integration of fully interactive 3D meshing techniques and the associated interactive meshing interface. With increasing system performance and the growing availability of a new generation of force-feedback devices we plan to develop an improved version of VRFEA in the near future.

7. Acknowledgements

This work was supported by the National Science Foundation under contract ACI 9624034 (CAREER Award), the Office of Naval Research under contract N00014-97-1-0222, the Army Research Office under contract ARO 36598-MA-RIP, the NASA Ames Research Center through an NRA award under contract NAG2-1216, the Lawrence Livermore National Laboratory through an ASCI ASAP Level-2 under contract W-7405- ENG-48 (and B335358, B347878), and the North Atlantic Treaty Organization (NATO) under contract CRG.971628 awarded to the University of California, Davis. We also acknowledge the support of Silicon Graphics, Inc., and thank the members of the Visualization Thrust at the Center for Image Processing and Integrated Computing (CIPIC) at the University of California, Davis.

8. References

[1] Tsung-Pin Yeh, Vance, Judy M.: "Combining MSC/Nastran, sensivity methods, and Virtual Reality to facilitate Interactive Design", MSC/Nastran Web site: http://www.macsch.com/tech/paper1/paper1.html

[2] Sastry, L, J. V. Ashby, D. R. S. Boyd, R. F. Fowler, C. Greenough, J. Jones, E. A. Turner-Smith and N. P. Weatherill, "Virtual Reality Techniques for Interactive Grid Repair", Numerical Grid Generation in Computational Field Simulations, Ed.

[3] J.F. Thompson, B. Soni, N. Weatherill, "Handbook of Grid Generation". CRC Press, 1999 (ISBN 0-8493-2687-7).

[4] Foley, J. D., Van Dam, A., Feiner, S. K. and Hughes, J. F., 1992, "Computer Graphics, Principles and Practice", Addison-Wesley Publishing second edition.

[5] Newman, W. M. and Sproull, R. F., "Principles of Interactive Computer Graphics", McGraw-Hill, 1979.

[6] Kalawsky, R.S., "The Science of Virtual Reality and Virtual Environments", Addison-Wesley, 1994, ISBN 0-201-63171-7.

[7] "HIT Lab Overview and Projects" Human Interface Technology Laboratory Seattle/WA/USA, Technical Report No. HITL-P-91-1, 1991.

[8] Hollerbach, J.M., Cohen, E.C., Thompson, W.B., and Jacobsen, S.C., "Rapid Virtual Prototyping of Mechanical Assemblies", Proc. 1996 NSF Design and Manufacturing Grantees Conf., (Albuquerque, NM), Jan. 2-5, 1996, pp. 477-478.

[9] Ballard, D., Brown, C.: "Computer Vision", Prentice Hall, 1982.

[10] Persiani, F., Liverani A.: "Virtual Reality CAD Interface", ADM Proceedings, Florence 17-19 Sept. 1997.

[11] Liang, J., Green, M.: "JDCAD: A Highly Interactive 3D Modeling System", Computers and Graphics, Vol. 18, No. 4, pp. 499 - 506, 1994.

[12] Butterworth, J., Davidson, A., Hench, S., Olano, T. M.: "3DM: A Three Dimensional Modeler Using a Head-Mounted Display", Proc.1992 Symposium on Interactive 3D Graphics, Cambridge, Massachusetts, pp. 135 - 138, March 29 - April 1 1992.

[14] Wang, Sidney W., Kaufman, Arie E., "Volume Sculpting" 1995, Symposium on Interactive 3D Graphics, Monterey CA USA, ACM Press, 1995.

[17] Williams, L. "3d paint" in: Computer Graphics, 24(2):225-233, March 1990.

[18] Murakami, T.: "Direct and intuitive input device for 3D shape design", DE-Vol. 83, 1995 Design Engineering Technical Conferences, Vol. 2, pp. 695-701, ASME, 1995.

[19] Sachs, E., Roberts, A., Stoops, D.: "3Draw: A Tool for Designing 3D Shapes", IEEE Computer Graphics and Applications, Vol.11, pp. 18-24, 1991.

[20] Sutherland, I. E.: "SKETCHPAD: a man-machine graphical communication system", MIT Lincoln Laboratory, Lexington, MA. Technical Report, TR-296, 1965.

[21] Krueger, W., Froehlich, B. "Visualization Blackboard: The Responsive Workbench", IEEE Computer Graphics and Applications, 14(3):12-15, May 1994.

[22] Rosenblum, L., Durbin, J., Doyle, Tate, D., "Projects in VR: Situational Awareness Using the Responsive Workbench. IEEE Computer Graphics and Applications 17(4):12-13, July/August 1997.

Visualization & Animation

Chair
Mark W. McK. Bannatyne
Purdue University, USA

Movie Maps

Heimo Müller, Ed Tan
Vrije Universiteit Amsterdam
e-mail: mue@smr.nl

Abstract

This paper presents methods for moving image sequence visualization and browsing based on algorithms from computer vision, information visualization and on a hierarchical model for content semantics. We introduce a new method, OM-Images, for the visualization of temporal changes in a moving image sequence. Together with interactive browsing techniques the visualization methods can be used for the exploration of a movie at different levels of abstraction. The proposed levels of abstraction are the physical, image, object or discourse level. The visualization is used to generate 1) static descriptions, which printed on paper yield a "movie book" and 2) interactive documents, e.g. web pages or special movie browsers. Finally, we give examples of a movie book of a feature length film.

1 Introduction

Starting from the question "How can we describe and visualize a movie?" we encountered only text oriented and simple visual techniques, e.g. keyframes, for the description and visualization of the rich information space embedded in a movie. In most cases descriptions of a movie are only beneficial for a user, who already has seen the movie, and neither suitable for first time viewing nor for visualization of the structure and semantics of a movie in a more than superficial way.

When we investigate a movie, we usually play the movie and optional capture descriptions for permanent access. In most cases the interaction is restricted to simple play controls (stop, pause, play, forward, rewind, etc.) and jump functionality if a non-linear media is used. This process can not be sped up very much (the only way is to play fast through the movie without sound information) nor can the linear ordering of the movie elements (shot, scenes) be altered. In order to extend the interactivity of movie browsing we use pre-computed descriptions and allow for interactive exploration depending on the narrative structure, sound, location, etc. of movie elements. Such detailed descriptions can be generated by human annotations, as for example done in the archives of all television broadcasters, or by an automatic system [1-4]. However, if the descriptions become very detailed we have to apply visualization methods to arrange the large

quantities of information and to explore the information space. In the following we describe a hierarchical model for the description of movies and methods for the visualization of movie descriptions in so called movie maps. Application areas for movie maps can be seen in

- film analysis – movie maps can visualize the internal structure of films and support the interactive exploration of a movie.
- post production – movie maps can be seen as a visual script, similar to a score or storyboard used in the final post production of music or animation movies.
- archiving and film information systems – movie maps can deal as a visual interface for browsing and search/retrieval applications.

2 Description Levels

We group descriptions into four levels: The physical level, the image level, the object level and the discourse level. We assume, that each level is self-contained and complete, that is, the set of all possible descriptions covers all movies hierarchically. That means that higher levels are based on the descriptions of lower levels.

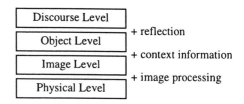

Figure 1 – Description Levels

2.1 Physical Level

At the physical level descriptions of a movie are given by attributes of the storage media. Examples for attributes are the storage location, owner, and depending on the storage media: film-format, aperture, film-stock, sound format, etc. for celluloid media and tape-format, color-depth, video-format, color-coding, etc. for electronic media.

Attributes can be grouped into location, media type, history (generation), commercial and process specific parameters of a physical representation.

In most cases descriptions at the physical level are only used in commercial applications, e.g. in an archive or in postproduction environments. For the visualization of a movie these descriptions are not very useful, and we will therefore not go into detail on this subject. However for a metadata model as MPEG-7 the physical level builds the basis of all movie annotations.

2.2 Image Level

At the image level a movie can be seen as a sequence of frames, either in analogue or digital form. Descriptions at the image level can be based on audiovisual features generated by image/audio processing methods, e.g. sonograms [5], histograms [6,7,8], shapes [9,10], textures [11], camera parameters and motion representations [12-16].

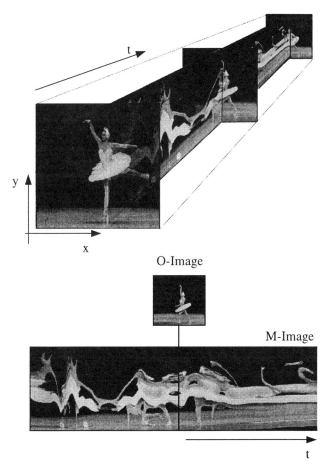

Figure 2 – OM Images

Image processing features have no "knowledge" about real world objects, e.g. there may be shape representations

to recognize round objects and a segmentation by the color values "white" and "black", nevertheless there is no representation of the concept of a football at the image level.

In addition keyframes can be selected as representation of a sub-sequence of a movie. We use an extension of the classical keyframe concept, the so called OM, Object(s) + Movement(s) representation. An OM representation consists of a O-image (defined by the plane of maximum image flow in the 3D image volume) and a M-image orthogonal to the O-image. If an O-image is parallel to the x,y plane it is equivalent to a classical keyframe and the M-Image is a time section image [17] parallel either to the x,t or y,t plane. See Figure 2.

2.3 Object Level

At the object level a movie is described by the objects it contains. We can extract content objects automatically, e.g. by a face detection algorithm, or manually by traditional film and video annotation procedures. Content objects descriptions can be grouped into "atomic descriptions" and "structuring objects".

- *Atomic descriptions* – map the appearance of an object and its attribute on the time line of the image sequence. In film analysis atomic descriptions would correspond to denotative annotations and the time line would correspond to the screen duration of a movie [18,19]. Each content object can be visualized in a movie map, see Figure 3, which can easily be modeled by a relational database.

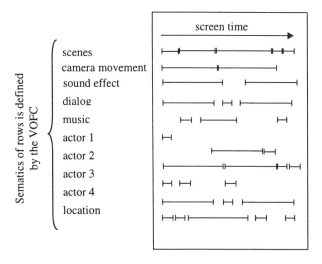

Figure 3 – A simple movie map (object layer)

We define the semantics of the rows by the so called Video Object Foundation Classes – VOFC. The overall class structure of the VOFC can be seen in Figure 4. VOFC describe the semantics of the content object by a class hierarchy holding attributes and methods for the automatic generation of descriptions.

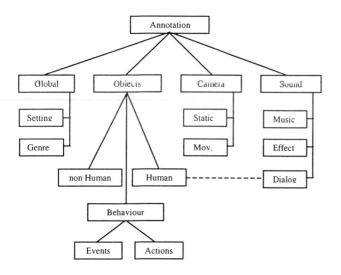

Figure 4 – Video Object Foundation Classes

- *Structuring Objects* – group and describe the hierarchical structure of content objects, e.g. grouping all shots together in which a certain person appears, or modeling the structure of a news program by clips and separators [20]. In film analysis the formal composition and the plot structure of a movie can be modeled with the help of structuring objects, see Figure 5.

2.4   Discourse Level

At the discourse level descriptions contain meta information about the movie, the nature of which depend on the particular form or genre. This means that the description of any particular sequence refers to the larger context of 1) the production (program, film, etc.) the sequence is a part of, 2) the form or genre to which the production belongs. For instance, the traditional description of a scene refers to the plot of an entire film ("last meeting of the Good and the Bad"), and to conventional events and objects in a genre ("final shoot out"). Discourse descriptions can be grouped into two classes (e.g. [21]):

- *Deep structure* - consists of propositions describing the complete contents including all logical relations (See the upright planes in Figure 5, each representing one discourse genre.) The nature of the predicates and arguments differs from one genre to another. Fictional, historical story, rhetorical argument and categorical exposition are four

examples of major genres. For instance, in fictional stories, the predicates are causal and chronological relations, and the arguments are fictional events and characters. In categorical expositions (e.g. documentaries, demonstration films), predicates are part-whole and order relations, and arguments are real world categories of interest (airplane, butterfly, actions in cardiac surgery).

- *Surface structure* - describes the way the deep structure is represented in the object level, in terms of atomic objects as well as of structuring objects. (See dotted lines in Figure 5). As a description of a mapping, an application of transformations, it should be distinguished from the object level description itself.

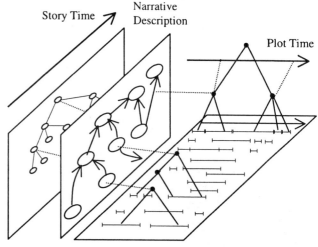

Figure 5 – A Movie Map with Structuring Objects and Narrative Descriptions

There is no one-to-one correspondence between the deep structure description (e.g. the complete story) and the object level description. The transformations inherent to surface structure description include (partial) deletion, summarization, embedding, restricting point of view, emphasizing, reordering and serialization. Profound knowledge exists as to the transformation of stories into film narratives, particularly as temporal and spatial aspects are concerned [20]. However, this knowledge is insufficient to render a complete mapping of story structures onto the object level. To complicate matters, phenomena such as irony and metaphor indicate that other, much more sophisticated transformations should be accounted for in the discourse structure description.

3 Movie Visualization

In order to support the navigation through a movie we visualize movie descriptions at various levels. Automatic video annotation algorithms produce, in the literature often called, "low-level" feature using computer vision algorithms. Low–level features are always descriptions at the image level. In addition "high-level" feature can be generated at the object and discourse level by AI methods (taking into account context and domain knowledge) and by human annotation.

New ways for using this rich information in interactive exploration of movies has attracted many research efforts. In most cases they only integrate descriptions at the image level and are restricted to short (up to several minutes) video clips.

Techniques used are Rframes [22], scene transition graphs [23] or clustering methods [24]. In this paper a generalized approach, including all levels of descriptions is studied, and used to build static and interactive visual representations of a movie. The requirements for a interactive browsing tools are the following:

- It should be possible to handle *large amounts of data* (more than 1 hour, typical 20 hours, up to several 100 hours) in an efficient way. A real world application (e.g. a video archive) deals with such quantities in its daily work. Such quantities request hierarchical ordering and abstraction mechanisms.

- It should provide *good browsing and sorting capabilities.* If the user doesn't know exactly what he is looking for, a visual *movie mining* functionality is required.

- It should *be intuitive* to operate either through a WEB interface or using the common place GUI look and feel.

- The *response time* should be below a (psychological) limit and the degree of *interactivity* should be high. If time consuming operations are performed, e.g. automatic annotation or shot detection, the user should receive feedback about the operation's progress.

We use OM-Images and sonograms at the image level and graphical representations (arrows, different layers, font weights) at the object and discourse level to visualize structuring objects. All image level descriptions are directly generated from an MPEG-2 representation of a movie.

4 An Example

In Figure 6 the first 8 pages of the Pulp Fiction movie book can be seen. Due to very dense information in the OM-frames these pages are originally printed on A3 paper using a 600 dpi color laser printer.

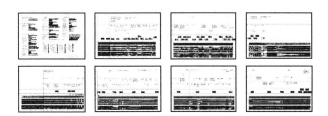

Figure 6 – Navigation page and visualization of the first 14 minutes of Pulp Fiction

The overview page – the table of content of a movie – shows the top level structuring elements of a movie scenes and their respective M-Images (a), the cast (b) and the plot- versus story time visualized by a temporal ordering of the scenes.

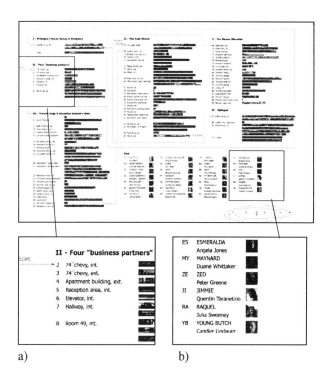

a)   b)

Figure 7 – The overview Page

Figure 8 shows the visualization of minutes 10 to 12 of the movie by O-Images and sonograms (a), the script of the movie in relation to the movie plot time (b) and 3 vertical and one horizontal M-Images (c).

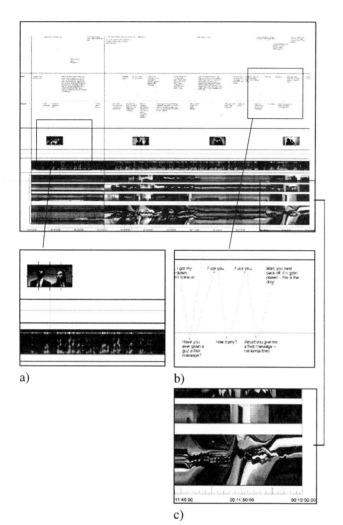

a)   b)

c)

Figure 8 – Minutes 10 to 12

In Figure 9 the user interface of an interactive movie browser (including a re-ordering functionality for virtual shots) is shown. This user interface is a design study and will be implemented by the VICAR project in the near future. Within the browser a movie is divided into *shots* (a sequence of images typically equivalent to a camera shot), *scenes* (a sequence of shots with a common theme, location, action, etc.) and *parts* (structuring elements inside movies). A movie is defined as a continuous stream of images. The ordering of shots, scenes and parts in the visualization of a movie can not be altered. In contrast to this a *virtual movie* (a movie without physical representation) is defined by a sequence of links static movie object. Within a *virtual movie* elements can be arbitrarily reordered and grouped. Virtual movies allow for different views to a subset of a movie and can be used for the organization of special collections or search results.

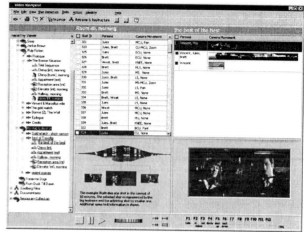

Figure 9 – An interactive Movie Browser

5 Summary and Future Work

As the use of movies in digital representations, e.g. MPEG-2 and the quality of automatic annotation tools are speedily increasing, browsing through huge content collection is a major problem. This development can be compared to the first steps in scientific visualization. In this paper we address the problem of movie description and visualization. We propose to structure descriptions in a hierarchical way:

- Physical Level – image sequences are described by a physical representation.

- Image Level – image sequences are described by the feature space of the used image processing algorithm.

- Object Level – image sequences are described by a denotative annotation (human or automatic generated) and structuring objects.

- Discourse Level, where the descriptions are at time only given in natural language describing the discourse content addressed by the sequence and its expression in the object level.

We describe the principle of movie maps at the object and discourse level, and present a new visualization method at the image level. Finally, we demonstrate the concepts behind a movie book of Pulp Fiction and show the user interface of a interactive image browser. Our future work will address hypermedia visualizations (hyper movies) and new human computer interaction techniques using high resolution displays (dynamic paper).

6 Acknowledgments

The work reported here was carried out under the Training and Mobility of Researcher (TMR) program of the EC. Our thanks are due to Marten den Uyl, and Herre Kuipers of Sentient Machine Research, Werner Haas and Peter Uray of Joanneum Research for their critical reviews and various discussions. Furthermore we like to thank to MIRAMAX for their support of the project.

7 References

[1]   Flickner J.P., Sawnhey H., Niblack W, et al, Query by image and video content: the QBIC system, IEEE Computer, 28, Spetember 1995 pp. 23-30.

[2]   Aigrain P., Zhang H.J., Petkovic D., Content-Based Representation and Retrieval of Visual Media – A State-of-the-Art Review, „Multimedia Tools and Applications 3(3), 1996, pp. 179-202.

[3]   Bolle R.M., Yeo B.-L., Yeung M.M. Video Query: Research directions, IBM Journal of Research and Development, Vol 42. No. 2 – Multimedia Systems.

[4]   Müller H., Haas W., Uray P., VICAR – An Automatic Video Annotation System, Proc. of EMMSEC 98, Bordeaux, Oct. 1998.

[5]   Minami K, Akutsu A, Hamada H., Video Handling with Music and Speech Detection, IEEE Multimedia July-September 1998, pp. 17-25.

[6]   Beigi M,, Benitez A., and Chang S.-F., MetaSEEk: A Content-Based Meta Search Engine for Images, SPIE Conference on Storage and Retrieval for Image and Video Database, Feb. 1998.

[7]   Lienhart R., Kuhmiinch C., Effelsberg. W. On the Detection and Recognition of Television Commercials, Proc. IEEE Conf. on Multimedia Computing and Systems, Ottawa, Canada, pp. 509-516, June 1997.

[8]   Zhang H.J., Tan C.Y., Smoliar S.W., Gong Y., Automatic Parsing and Indexing of News Video, Multimedia Systems, Vol. 2, No. 6, 1995, pp. 256-265.

[9]   Eakins J.P., Retrieval of trade mark images by shape feature, Proc of ELVIRA, 1994.

[10]   Herodotou N., Plataniotis K.N., Venetsanopoulus A.N., A Content-Bases Storage and Retrieval Scheme for Image and Video Databases, SPIE Vol. 3309, pp. 697-708.

[11]   Tamura H., Mori S., Textural Features Corresponding to Visual Perception, IEEE Trans. on Systems, Man and Cybernetics Vol. 8, No. 6, 1978.

[12]   Akutsu A., Tonomura Y., Hashimoto H., Ohba Y., Video Indexing using Motion Vectors, Proc, Visual Communications and Image Processing, SPIE. Vol. 1818, 1992, pp. 1522-1530.

[13]   Ardizzone E., Cascia M.La, Video Indexing using Optical Flow Field, Proc. of ICIP 96, vol 3, 1996, pp. 831-834.

[14]   Kato T., Database Architecture for Content Based Image Retrieval, Proc. of SPIE Conference on Image Storage and Retrieval Systems, Vol. 1662, 1992, pp. 112-123.

[15]   Nam J., Tewfik A.H., Motion-based Video Object Indexing using Multiresolution Analysis, SPIE Vol. 3309, pp. 688-696.

[16]   Sahouria E., Zakhor A., Motion Indexing of Video, Proc of ICIP 97, vol. 2, 1997, pp. 526-529.

[17]   Uray P., Müller H., Plaschzug W., Haas W.: Visualising Artefacts, Meta Information and Quality Parameters of Image Sequences, Proc. of the IS&T Conference on Visual Data Exploration and Analysis V, San Jose, pp. 145-152, 1998.

[18]   Bordwell D., Thompson K., Film art – an introduction, 5th ed. McGraw-Hill, 1997.

[19]   Faulstich, W., Einführung in die Filmanalyse. 2te Auflage. Tübingen: Narr, 1980.

[20]   Zhong D., Zhang H., and Chang S.-F., Clustering Methods for Video Browsing and Annotation, SPIE Conference on Storage and Retrieval for Image and Video Database, Feb. 1996.

[21]   van Dijk T.A., Macrostructures: An interdisciplinary study of global structures in discourse, interaction and cognition. Hillsdale NJ, L. Erlbaum, 1980.

[22]   Arman et al., Content-Based Browsing of Video Sequences, *Proceedings of ACM Multimedia 94.*

[23]   Yeung M. et al., Video Browsing using Clustering and Scene Transitions on Compressed Sequences, Multimedia Computing and Networking, San Jose, Feb. 1995.

Integration of High-End and Low-End Animation Tools: A Case Study of the Production Pathway for the Chicago Bulls Broadcast Animation

Carlos R. Morales
Purdue University
Crmorales@puk.indiana.edu

Abstract

The broadcast animation division of High Voltage Software was contracted by the Chicago Bulls Organization to complete an animated opening to be shown at the United Center and on television before each home game. A team of animators and compositors developed a production pathway based on the use of motion capture data to coordinate the use of high-end NURBS based animation and lower-end polygonal based animation tools, and compositing software.

The Problem

In August 1998, the Chicago Bulls Organization contracted High Voltage Software (HVS) to develop a 3D animated opening to be shown on the JumboTron at the United Center and on television before each home game. The Bulls Organization had an animation of a single Gouroud shaded bull running down a generic city completed in 1991 by Animation Station. They wanted to update the animation to more accurately reflect the current state of computer graphics.

Client Mandates

Over a series of meetings with the client, it was decided that the animation should include a series of 3D rendered bulls running from numerous places in the city toward the United Center. Along the way, the bulls would pass Chicago landmarks. Each landmark passed by the bulls was to "include enough detail so that the average Chicagoan could recognize it." [2]. The choice of landmarks was left up the HVS, except for the inclusion of the Art Institute. One shot was to include a bull stopping in front of one of the statues in front of the Art Institute where it would scare one of the lions. The deadline for the project was set for November 1, 1998.

The Solution

Personnel

HVS assigned a total of six people to the project. Three would form the core production team responsible for generating all of the graphic elements that would actually comprise the final animation. The core production team was comprised of one character animator, one effects/architectural animator, and one technical director/compositor. The author served as the technical director. The remaining personnel would form the support staff comprised of one storyboard artist, one art director, and one project administrator. Table 1 details the responsibility of each person.

Table 1. Production Personnel

Position	Responsibilities
Character Animator	Model and animate all organic elements to include the bull, and lion
Effects/Architectural Animator	Model inorganic structures to include buildings, street elements (garbage cans, traffic lights, etc.), and cars
Technical Director/Compositor	Solve technical problems pertaining to use and implementation of software and hardware tools, composite animation plates.
Storyboard Artist	Draw storyboards to reflect the client's vision
Art Director	Interact with client and develop the look of the project
Project Administrator	Track media elements, and time management

Project Planning

The art director and storyboard artist concluded that the entire city should be built using 3D software instead of using 3D bulls running through live video shots of the city. The look would be a hyper-realistic yellowish overcast similar to what film makers call the golden hour. The bulls were to be fully textured using bitmap images. Buildings and street elements would be left untextured and only given definition though the use of creative lighting and basic color. The length of the animation was to be 32 seconds and take place over a series of 18 shots [6]. A grayscale set of storyboards was prepared showing the sequence of the animation [figure 1] and a set of three color still images to depict the look and feel of the animation [figure 2]. Combined these two documents would serve as an objective reference to which the production team could look to for guidance.

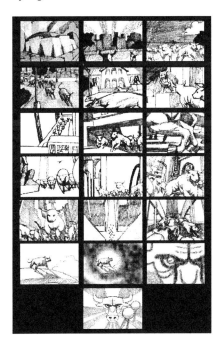

Figure 1. Sequential storyboards

Figure 2. Art storyboards

Production

While the art director and storyboard artist finalized the vision for the animation, the production staff worked on establishing a production pathway to meet the project needs. The production pathway would be developed by animating a sample scene. In the course of producing the sample scene the production team would select software and hardware that could deliver the look established by the storyboards, test new techniques, and start to create the production models. In short, the production of the sample scene would serve to establish the milestone schedule, map out the production pipeline, and also secure the final approval from the client to start production.

Production of the sample scene started on August 3, 1998. To maximize production time while maintaining creative control, the production team decided to render all of the scenes in multiple passes. Individual elements would be created in the package of choice by the expert in his respective area and composited together by the technical director. This approach would allow all of the members of the team to use the software most appropriate for his task and not have to compromise by using software that might be known by all of team members, but not the best for the task at hand. This arrangement would also allow the team to make changes without having to rerender all of the elements in a scene. If a particular bull looked too slow, too yellow, or not dark enough only that bull would have to be rerendered.

The character animator decided that only a high-end NURBS based animation package with support for expressions would be appropriate. He selected SoftImage 3D Extreme [3]. The architectural animator determined that a lower-end polygonal based package such as LightWave 3D would allow him to model, texture, and animate much faster than using SoftImage (Schutlz, 1999). The technical

director decided that After Effects 3.1 Production Bundle would be used for compositing. Organic models would be built and animated in SoftImage 3D, inorganic models in LightWave 3D, and everything put together in After Effects.

Preparing for Compositing

Once team members selected the tools they would be using for completing the sample scene, they focused their attention on making the necessary preparation to ensure a successful composite. To enable the production team to composite organic elements rendered in SoftImage with inorganic elements rendered in LightWave 3D, all of the objects in a scene would have to exist in both SoftImage and in LightWave at the same scale. Second, a texture that would receive and cast shadows, but not render would have to be developed. This would allow the bulls rendered in SoftImage to cast shadows on the streets and sidewalks rendered in LightWave. Finally, the movement of the camera and any lights would have to match exactly in both scenes.

The team decided to model everything using real measurements. To create a sense of power and strength for the bull, its scale was changed to approximately 4 times the size of a real bull. The modeling of the bull proceeded rapidly using standard NURBS modeling techniques. The bull was modeled in SoftImage using primarily loft surfaces and proportional modeling. Construction history and the "select by U/V" made it possible to make small changes to the model effortlessly [3]. The character animator finished the basic model of the bull in three days.

To prepare the model of the bull for animation, an Inverse Kinematics (IK) skeleton was built and assigned to an automatic global envelope. The weights of the generated envelope were then edited manually and nulls added to the end effector of the IK chains. With the body of the bull set up for IK animation, it was time to prepare the head of the bull for shape or morph target based animation.

The head of the bull was replicated multiple times and modeled to reflect different facial expressions. Each instance of the bull's head was then assigned to a null object that would control how much of that instance would be reflected in the original head. SoftImage's expressions and channel drivers were used to connect the null to the influence of the individual shapes on the target bull head. This made it possible to animate the bull's face by just moving the null objects [3]. Finally, textures for the bull's skin were generated using Metacreations Detailer and Adobe Photoshop and applied as a UV map. Figure 3 shows the final bull model with textures applied. The entire process, including modeling, texturing, and enveloping the bull took approximately one week. When tessellated for rendering the bull weighed in at approximately 2 million polygons.

Figure 3. Bull Model

Models of the city streets were created using LightWave's standard polygonal tool set. Photographs gathered by the project administrator were used as a guide in modeling the street elements. Because the placement of the camera in the scene had not been determined at this point, it was decided that the all of the details on the buildings would be modeled and no bump maps would be used. The Bloom and Gaffer plug-ins were then used to give the buildings the look designated in the storyboards. It took approximately 1.5 days to set up the street scene [7].

To allow for proper shadow interaction between the SoftImage and LightWave objects, a DXF model was made of a bull modeled in SoftImage. The bull was imported in LightWave and assigned the "unseen by camera" surface. This plug-in allows an object to cast a shadow onto the scene without it rendering [4]. The net effect was that by placing the dummy DXF bull object in the same position to where the bull would be rendered in SoftImage, it was possible to properly cast a shadow onto the LightWave background plate without showing the dummy bull. The same was accomplished in SoftImage by importing a dummy DXF version of the street under the bull and assigning it a "shadow object" shader [8]. This arrangement resulted in four unique layers rendered from the two packages [table 2].

Table 2. Rendered layers

Layer	Software Package	Content	Example
Foreground	LightWave 3D	Any street element that needed to be in front of the bulls. Alpha channel.	
Bulls	SoftImage 3D	Render of Bulls only. Alpha channel.	
Bull Shadows	SoftImage 3D	Shadow of bulls falling on dummy LightWave street elements. Shadows rendered into the alpha channel.	
Background + Foreground	LightWave 3D	Render of buildings, pavement, sidewalk, street signs. Both the background and foreground are included in this layer. No alpha channel necessary.	

The most significant problem in the production pipeline was figuring out how to match camera movements in SoftImage to camera movements in LightWave. The team first tried using a commercial product called PolyTrans 2.1, but it proved unsuccessful. It transferred geometry, but not animation [5]. The motion of the camera was not transferred. A viable alternative was to use motion capture. Calls to SoftImage and LightWave revealed that both packages import and export motion data, but the motion data was incompatible [8]. LightWave uses a proprietary format [table 3] while SI uses Biovision BVA [table 4].

An analysis of the LightWave motion data revealed that it closely resembled the Biovision BVA format [1]. By multiplying the Z axis values from the LightWave motion dump by negative one and reordering the file to include the proper the TAB delimiters and header it was

possible to format the LightWave motion dump into a BVA motion file. Further analysis showed that the SoftImage camera always reflects a rotation of 0,0,0 because it derives this quality by the location of null object to which the camera always faces. The camera object in LightWave carries the rotation qualities within the object. The technical director wrote a program to read in LightWave motion files, determine the location of the camera and the null object needed by SoftImage 3D, and write it out in Biovision BVA format. The program, called SoftImage to LightWave Converter (SIL), was written in Macromedia Director.

Table 3. Lightwave motion dump

```
0.0225 0.12 -1.0837 0 0 0 1 1 1
0.0232557 0.117897 -1.0526 0 0 0 1 1 1
0.024022 0.115758 -1.02118 0 0 0 1 1 1
```

Table 4. Biovision motion dump

Segment: TEST								
Frames: 3								
Frame Time: 0.033333								
XTRAN INCHES	YTRAN INCHES	ZTRAN INCHES	XROT	YROT	ZROT	XSCALE DEGREES	YSCALE DEGREES	ZSCALE DEGREES
0.0225	0.12	01.0837	0	0	0	1	1	1
0.0232557	0.117897	01.0526	0	0	0	1	1	1
0.024022	0.115758	01.02118	0	0	0	1	1	1
0.0247978	0.113586	00.989462	0	0	0	1	1	1

With the 3D elements matched, the production team was able to focus on rendering. SoftImage elements would be rendered using the Mental Ray renderer and LightWave elements using LightWave's internal renderer. The technical director decided to field render all elements for smoother motion at a resolution of 720 pixels by 486 pixel at D1 aspect ratio. Initial tests proved that while the field dominance could be set for SoftImage and LightWave, the method that both programs use to calculate field motion was incompatible. SoftImage rendered its fields to separate files and compressed the vertical size of the images to only contrain the the information for that field [8]. This generated pictures that were half the height of the corresponding LightWave pictures. LightWave interlaced its fields into one file [4]. The technical director decided that it would be best to render the scene at 60 frames per second and then conform it to 29.97 frames per second with the appropriate field dominance during compositing.

After rendering the 3D elements of the test scene, the production team directed its attention to compositing. The 3D elements had been completed in four days, including building the scene elements, matching the camera, and rendering the scene. The production team could use this figure as a guideline for how long the 3D portion of each scene would take to complete. But, before benchmarks could be set for the entire process and before the production pipeline could be finalized, the individual layers would have to be composited successfully.

Compositing

The integration of the discreet 3D rendered layers was accomplished by using Adobe After Effects 3.1 Production. Compositing consisted of interlacing the frames, color correcting the layers, masking and keying out the shadow areas, and finally applying camera shake. The main premise of the compositing phase was to put everything together while keeping all of the image files uncompressed.

Before the individual layers could be manipulated in After Effects, they had to be interlaced and conformed to proper NTSC video timing. The SoftImage fields could not be properly expanded in After Effects. The technical director wrote a script using AppleScript that would rename the SoftImage pictures into the needed naming convention, convert the SoftImage PICS into 32 bit Targa images, and resize each picture to the proper size. The resultant files could then be imported into After Effects where they could be conformed and interlaced to 29.97 frames per second lower-field dominant files. This was accomplished via the After Effect interpret footage option (After Effects, 1998).

With the footage properly interlaced, the technical director concentrated on color correcting the layers and adding effects. The materials rendered with Mental Ray had a different gamma and more contrast than those rendered in LightWave. After Effects levels were used to match the color qualities of the renders. The bull's shadow layer was added by keying the non-shadow elements in the layer via a Difference Key and softened via a gaussian blur. The layer with the bulls was then given motion blur and finally the entire composition was nested into a second composition where camera motion could be added via the wiggler plug-in to simulate the weight of the bulls as they ran past the camera. Finally, motion blur was added and the composition was output as an uncompressed QuickTime movie file at 720 pixels by 486 pixels at D1 aspect ratio lower field dominant. Figure 4 shows the composite of the layers shown in Figure 2.

Figure 4. Composited frame

Production Pipeline

The successful completion of the test scene finalized the production pathway for the rest of the project. Through the completion of the scene, the team had derived a production methodology which each team member could use a guiding reference for determining his responsibilities. Not only had they formed a procedural plan that dictated the ordinal order for the completion of the task by the team members, but they also generated a time schedule which could be used to orchestrate the rest of the production [see table 5]. This made it possible for the team to use an assembly line approach in completing the project, and to accurately parcel out the time devoted to each task. Compensating for tasks that would not have to be replicated for each scene, such as writing the SIL application or building the bull model, the team estimated that it would take approximately five days to complete a single scene. The only unaccounted event was the final edit, because it could not be completed until all of the scenes had been composited.

Table 5. Production pathway

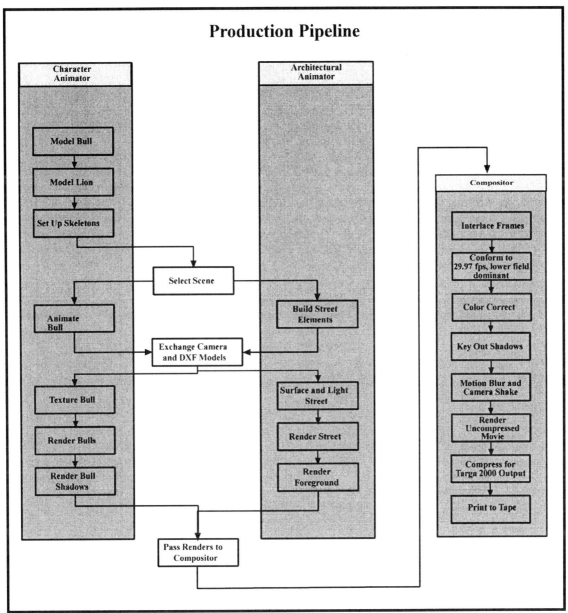

The Final Edit

Once all of the individual scenes had been completed and rendered as individual QuickTime files, the technical director focused on sequencing the clips into a final edit that could be printed to tape. The individual uncompressed QuickTime movies for each clip were imported into Adobe Premiere where they were sequenced using standard cuts and dissolves. Once properly sequenced, another uncompressed QuickTime movie was output at 720 pixels by 486 pixels at D1 aspect ratio, lower field dominant. The rationale for outputting a properly sequenced uncompressed movie was the ability to access an uncompromised movie without having to go back to the individual scenes.

The final uncompressed movie was then imported into a second Adobe Premiere project where it was output as a M-JPEG TARGA compressed movie that could be played out in real-time using one of the Targa 2000 PRO board at HVS. It was then printed to a Sony BVW-75 BetaCam SP deck. The tape was delivered to the Bulls Organization on October 28, 1998. On November 1, 1998, the animation was shown for the first time on WGN and on the JumboTron at the United Center.

Conclusion

By relying on multi-pass rendering, the HVS production team was able to exploit the best qualities offered by SoftImage and LightWave in the production of the Bulls animated opening. By concentrating on using the tools best for each task and then relying on compositing to integrate the results into a finished animation, the production team was able to bring the vision depicted on the storyboard to the screen.

The production model employed by the HVS production team brings two issues to surface. First, we must consider the selection of the two 3D animation packages selected by the animators in this project. The character animator selected SoftImage 3D Extreme, a package often hailed as being on of the top animation packages in the world and has a price tag to prove it. It has capabilities that few other programs can match. The architectural animator elected to use LightWave 3D, a very inexpensive package. When asked why he elected to use Brian Schultz said, "I could have used PowerAnimator, SoftImage, or Visualizer for animating the back plates, but putting price tags asides, LightWave was just better for what I needed to do with the amount of time that I had." [7]. This choice was made not because of a limited budget or limited resources, but instead because LightWave could best deliver inorganic elements needed by the architectural animator.

Second, we must consider the reliance on composting and the implications for the production pipeline employed by the team. Every scene contains elements completed by all members of the team. Each scene has bulls completed by the character animator, street elements by the architectural animator, and effects composited by the technical director. This level of interdependence on scene elements necessitated a very exact production pipeline as shown on table five. The 3D animators had to exchange camera positions before they could animate their scenes. The character animator needed DXF versions of the street elements produced by the architectural animator before he could render the shadow layers. The technical director could not composite anything until all of the layers had been properly rendered. It was imperative that all of the production members follow the production model developed while producing the test scene. If any of the steps in the pipeline model were skipped or not followed in order by any of the production members, the scenes would not composite correctly.

In the end, we can conclude that the HVS production team subordinated the selection of tools to the creation of the client's vision. By selecting tools that would best create the client's vision and then subscribing to a very strict production model, the production team was able to meet the client's content mandates.

References

[1] Biovision Incorporated, Biovision Motion Data Specifications. http://www.biovision.com, 1999.

[2] Fiore, R. Personal Interview. *Art Director at High Voltage Software.* Hoffman Estates: Illinois, 1999

[3] Jeffrey, E. Personal Interview. *Character Animator at High Voltage Software.* Hoffman Estates: Illinois, 1999.

[4] Newtek. LightWave 3D 5.5 Users Manual. Austin, Texas: Newtek, 1998.

[5] PolyTrans. Polytrans 2. Users Manual. Seattle, WA: Okino,1998.

[6] Russell, P. Personal Interview. *Storyboard Artist at High Voltage Software.* Hoffman Estates: Illinois, 1999.

[7] Schultz, B.. Personal Interview. *Architectural and Effects Animator at High Voltage Software.* Hoffman Estates: Illinois, 1999.

[8] SoftImage. SoftImage 3D 3.7 Extreme Users Manual. Seattle, WA: Microsoft Press, 1998.

[9] Whiteaker, J. Personal Interview. *Director of Creative Services at High Voltage Software.* Hoffman Estates: Illinois, 1999.

Utilizing Desktop Virtual Reality to Enhance Visualization: Applied Projects from the Department of Computer Graphics

James L. Mohler
Department of Computer Graphics
Purdue University

Abstract

Virtual reality technologies provide a unique method for enhancing user visualization of complex three-dimensional objects and environments. By experience and environmental interaction, users can more readily perceive the dimensional relationships of objects typically portrayed via static multiview or pictorial representations. Until recently, many of the VR technologies required significant computing power for adequate delivery and provided realism that is often less than actual. Alternatively, video-based VR technologies overcome the two major limitations of true three-dimensional VR technologies - computing horsepower and realism. The focus of this contribution is to provide background information on VR technology for the improvement of spatial abilities, describe the advantages of video-based VR technologies, and provide examples showing how video-based VR can be used to enhance visualization in education and training.

Keywords: visualization, virtual reality, QuickTime VR, interaction, emersion, and multimedia, industry training, education, projects.

Introduction

Spatial ability is a significant component of a variety of disciplines and is often paramount for success in those disciplines. Although researchers have defined spatial ability in various ways, there is agreement that spatial ability is vitally important to their respective disciplines. As much of the literature suggests, experts from seemingly unrelated fields share the commonality of spatial ability, as Bertoline [1] reported. He stated that spatial ability is important for success in biology [2], chemistry [3], mathematics [4], and science [5].

Others, such as Gardner [6, 7], go beyond linking spatial ability to discipline-based application only. Gardner proposed a multifaceted model of intelligence that suggested spatial abilities are one of seven major components. He defined spatial intelligence as the ability to think in pictures and images, the ability to perceive, transform, and recreate different aspects of the visual-spatial world. His definition also included sensitivity to visual details, and the ability to draw or sketch ideas graphically. Gardner's explanation continued by stating that key intelligences are not discontinuous, but interrelated. For example, spatial intelligence coincides with logical-mathematical, that is mathematical ability and the ability to reason.

Nevertheless, without spatial abilities students are often hindered in the learning environment and ultimately within their chosen field [8]. Increasingly, research supports the idea that spatial ability is a primary ability or domain of knowledge, parallel to mathematical or verbal skills.

Improving Spatial Ability

With the acknowledgement that spatial ability is important, it is meaningful to identify the primary implementations that have attempted to increase the spatial abilities of students. Research findings point toward several appropriate technologies that can be used, as well as the shortcomings of previous methods. The findings have also indicated a trend toward the increased use of computer technology in the advancement of spatial abilities.

Researchers have used numerous methods in an attempt to teach and further spatial abilities, each with varying levels of success. Traditional paper and pencil, 2D CAD, 3D CAD, 3D animation and computer games have all been used in an attempt to improve students spatial abilities. Although not an exhaustive list of approaches, an increase in the capabilities of the desktop computer has dramatically multiplied the various strategies that can be employed. The most notable of these evolutions have occurred within the last 10 years with the emergence of the PC. Many computer-based tools are well suited for visualization instruction and remediation. The desktop computer also provides an environment that allows for development and delivery of both static and dynamic media [9]. The computer can easily become an extension of the mind, allowing the student to view their cognitive processes. Frequently, the computer monitor becomes both a looking glass and a tutor for mental processes.

However, the complexity of some environments can add to the cognitive workload required of a student [10]. The mental focus should not be upon the digital tool. Rather, emphasis should be placed upon exercising visual abilities. The digital tools can become a hindrance to learning, particularly upon first exposure. Suitably designed digital tools must provide affordances and conceptual clues that allow the student some relationship to the real world so that they may easily operate within the environment [11]. When a computer is used, ultimately students must understand the environment and the methods for controlling that environment.

Several of the methods employed for visual ability improvement have led to important discoveries of mental capacities that comprise cognitive spatial abilities, as well as ways in which the student can improve those abilities. As technology has improved, students have become more able to readily externalize and exercise cognitive processes with the technology, as long as the computer and its interface do not interfere with the objectives for learning.

Regardless of implementation, all the methods strive to increase the student's capability to mentally construct a three-dimensional object, which is defined as visualization. Secondly orientation, or the relationship of the object to oneself, must also be cognitively realized. The combination of these two components forms the basis for spatial ability and the capacity for understanding and manipulating three-dimensional mental imagery [12].

Yet, implementation of a learning strategy must also consider learning styles. While one method may be appropriate for some learners, that same method may be completely inadequate for others. Large proportions of learners may fall into a category that excels with a particular style of instruction. Therefore, strategies must coincide, or at least accommodate, various styles of learning.

For example, Miller [13] noted the significant differences between visual and haptic learners and how the use of computer-generated models can assist learners who fall in either category of learning. Albeit, Miller noted that the results may have been affected by other variables. However, he recommended the use of advance technologies, if for nothing more than the motivational and interest aspects that it induces. A significant variable that contributes to learning is motivation. Advanced technologies can increase student motivation toward learning conceptual and applied information [14].

Virtual Reality & Spatial Visualization

One of the most promising technologies for increasing student spatial abilities is virtual reality (VR) technology. One of the detriments of other computer-based strategies is that the student is often distanced from the environment or objects. The real power of VR technology is that it allows people to expand their perception of the real-world in ways that were previously impossible [15]. As McLellan stated, VR is a cognitive tool that allows dynamic and immediate interaction. The interactivity inherent to VR is aimed at extending and enhancing human cognitive abilities. Thus, it provides a superb vehicle for enhancing and possibly improving spatial abilities.

Ross and Aukstakalnis [16] proposed several scenarios in which VR technologies could be used to increase visual abilities. Recommendations made are related to increasing a student's ability of visualization and orientation. It should be noted that orientation includes not only the static relationship, but also the dynamic relationship between the user and the environment. Rotation and translation as well as the controls for performing these actions on the viewer and object(s) are included within this aspect of spatial ability. As suggested, VR provides a superb vehicle for testing, enhancing, and possibly improving both visualization and orientation skills. However, more research is needed to qualify and quantify the impact of its use.

VR Classification

The perception of VR technology often portrayed by the media through movies and other sources reveals a photo realistic environment, flawless in its representation of reality. However, the desktop application of VR is far from the complete and perfect representation of the real world. All media is subject to three sets of constraints: cognitive, structural, and technical. With VR, the most significant set is the technical constraints.

Several technical limitations prevent the real-time display of completely realistic environments with total submersion on the desktop. Tremendous processing requirements, high data rates, and expensive display technologies limit the amount of realism that can be provided. Although considerable research in hardware and software development is taking place, technology has not advanced to a stage that can provide the real-world on the desktop. Yet, the purpose of VR is not to provide the complete and exact representation of the real world on the computer, although someday desktop-computing power, attainable by the masses, may allow it. Today, VR is about experience and interaction, not the simulation of true reality or creating the surreal.

To determine the level of reality of VR systems, several researchers are developing scales by which these systems can be measured and compared. Thurman and Mattoon [17] presented a model that classifies VR based on three dimensions: verity, integration, and interface. The verity dimension attempts to describe the level at which the environment or the objects represent true reality. The integration dimension describes how the user is integrated and/or represented in the environment, and the interface dimension describes how the user interacts with the environment.

Today, an environment that provides the maximum in all three dimensions has not been developed. However, several technologies show promise in reaching the maximum. Proprietary technologies and non-proprietary technologies, such as VRML, provide a means for creating virtual worlds. Yet, these technologies have significant technical limitations and are far from reaching the highest rating for verity, integration, or interface. Most of the proprietary programs do provide high quality virtual environments (high verity). Yet, they are often far more costly than most educational institutions can afford due to the processing power needed and the expense of input and output devices. This is particularly true where multi-workstation laboratory configurations are concerned. VRML, which is far more cost effective, provides a lack of realism (low verity) and requires significant bandwidth considerations for delivery. Additionally, the interface dimension of these tools is often difficult to use and control. Thus, the tool has a tendency to get in the way of developing spatial ability.

Although both these technologies provide true three-dimensional environments a third evolving technology, video-based VR, provides promise as it is significantly less expensive to create, easier to deliver, and provides photo realistic content. Due to the fact that it is a video-based technology, it is not based upon the real-time delivery of three-dimensional data. Rather, it is composed of snapshots of predefined views that give the illusion of navigation within a three-dimensional environment, or manipulation of a three-dimensional object.

Because video-based VR is based upon predefined views, educators who use it can control the path of motion through an environment, or the translation and rotation of an object. Educators have complete control over the pedagogical degrees of freedom within the illusionary three-dimensional environment. A significant detriment with other technologies is that students can quickly become disoriented because of the infinite freedom within the three-dimensional environment, that

is, the ability to manipulate objects and viewer independently. By affixing either object or environment in the VR clip, learners can more readily interact and understand the presented materials. Limitless navigation during learning can often defeat the educational objectives [10].

Video-based VR Technologies

The most widely used video-based VR technology is QuickTime VR (QTVR), which is an extension of Apple's QuickTime (QT) digital video file format. QTVR movies share the same cross-platform playback capability as the normal QT clips, which is a significant advantage to using them. The true difference between normal linear QT clips and QTVR clips is based on the way in which the file is created and digitally written. Both contain frame-differenced raster images that can be compressed using a variety of compression algorithms.

QTVR movies can provide both egocentric and exocentric content (albeit the two different types are created in different ways). Using Apple's terminology, egocentric movies are called panoramas and exocentric movies are termed object movies. Both of these QTVR clips can be created using a digital camera in a real environment, or they may both be digitally generated using three-dimensional models or scenes as a foundation.

In either scenario, the advantages that QTVR movies offer are numerous. Since QTVR movies are based upon rendered raster images, rather than live three-dimensional data, the processing requirements for true photo-realistic playback is quite low. In fact, processing requirements are no more than those required for 10 to 15 second linear, digital video clips. Additionally, due to the raster nature of QTVR files, the digital file size is much smaller, meaning that delivery over a network or even within a CD-ROM format is much more responsive to the learner or user.

Further, as QTVR is based upon the QT format, another advantage is the large base of users who already have the required software installed on their computers. As the demographics site MediaMatrix [18] indicates, QuickTime extensions are one of the top 50 software components owned and installed on business computers. Other strategies for VR implementation require special software programs, browsers, or plug-ins that are not as widely distributed. Indeed, many have special licensing for distribution on multiple machines or multiple platforms.

Applications for Visualization

Over the past four years, the Department of Computer Graphics at Purdue University has been actively developing education and training materials for a variety of commercial companies, as well as for its own students. Due to photo-realism, low bandwidth and data rate requirements, and the ease of creation and delivery, the department has implemented QTVR technology in a variety of these projects. Additionally, the department is successfully applying the technology to specific learning situations that concern the enhancement and improvement of visualization ability.

Bethlehem Steel Corporation SOP Program

The Bethlehem Steel Corporation (BSC) contracted the Department of Computer Graphics to assist them in creating computer based training materials for their Burns Harbor steel making facility. With a large retirement turnover approaching, and with the current materials being technologically out-of-date, BSC decided to take the opportunity to upgrade its existing training and documentation system to CD-ROM multimedia with eventual migration to distributed intranet materials. BSC envisioned a digital system that would utilize text, graphics, sound, narration, digital video, and animation to increase training efficiency, effectiveness and employee motivation.

One of the principle reasons for the transition from the existing text-based standard operating procedures (SOP) to multimedia-based SOPs was the difficulty that new employees had in visualizing the procedures, processes, and equipment described in previous training materials. BSC's existing system was comprised of a database containing systematic text instructions that could be searched, edited and read by employees. Although the text system seemed adequate for existing employees, new employees had continual difficulty understanding and putting into practice the information presented. The difficulty was not the content, but in visualization and interpretation of the content. With only text-based information, new employees found it difficult to understand the procedures without on-the-job instruction. It was hoped that the new multimedia system would help alleviate this problem due the graphical and animated content it would contain.

To overcome the difficulties associated with visualization of the processes, procedures, facility, and equipment, each SOP was portrayed using static and dynamic graphics, text, as well as vocal narration. VR

clips were integrated in several ways to help new and existing employees understand the content more efficiently as shown in Figure 1. One of the initial tasks was the development of a series of VR clips that showed every location within the plant. Learners could use both navigable ego- and exocentric views to better understand the layout of the facility.

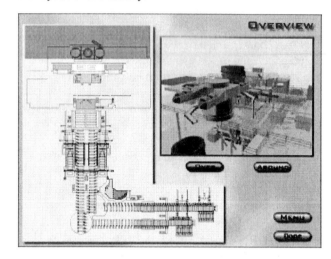

Figure 1. BSC employees can navigate the steel making facility using egocentric and exocentric viewpoints.

In addition to the VR clips that described the facility, VR was used in appropriate places to help the employees understand specific, critical processes and procedures, as shown in Figure 2. For example, a crucial task is the preparation of the casting machine. If the machine is not precisely prepared for casting, malfunction is often the result and frequently leads to the loss of money. In the

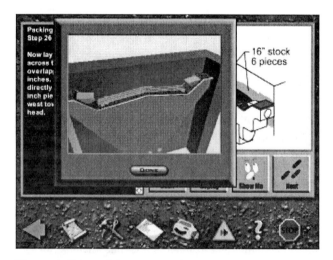

Figure 2. Proc edures and tasks may also be represented with QTVR clips to aid in visualization.

most severe instances, errors in preparation can lead to the loss of human life. The use of VR clips in these procedures has increased accuracy and reduced dangerous situations, such as steel breakouts, within the plant.

Material Science & Engineering

One of the difficulties in presenting scientific content is that often the concepts being portrayed are microscopic in detail. From biological cell structures to the structures of atoms, learner understanding of the content is often limited by the media that is being used to present it.

In an effort to enhance the understanding of material science concepts, McGraw-Hill publishers worked with the department to create an ancillary CD-ROM called *Materials in Focus* to accompany one of its material science texts. The CD-ROM was designed to provide interactive multimedia components that would enable students to better understand minute details and interactions on which the discipline focuses. Using QTVR technology, the CD-ROM provides the ability to navigate an NaCl molecule (see Figure 3), explore a diamond crystal, examine a zinc-blende crystal, as well as a wealth of other concepts.

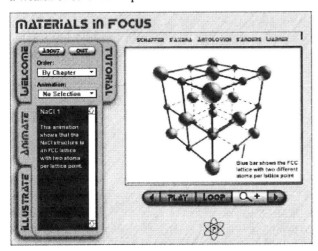

Figure 3. Navigation of an NaCl molecule.

In most instances the *Materials in Focus* is the first exposure that students have had with QTVR and VR technology. Using the video clips, students are able to build a cognitive model of the content. Students are able to not only visualize a structure, but also manipulate it and view it from a variety of locations. Relationships between particles, as well as an overall understanding of the composition, is more readily understood, as shown in Figure 4.

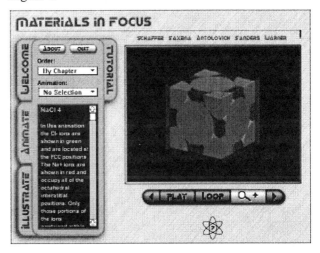

Figure 4. QTVR clips allow students to dynamically interact with compound structures giving them a better understanding of relationships and structures.

Purdue University's Virtual Visit

In the summer of 1998, the department was charged with creating an online resource for students, faculty, and visitors on Purdue's West Lafayette campus. The goal was to create an interactive Web site that would allow the user to view the campus, examine its buildings, and

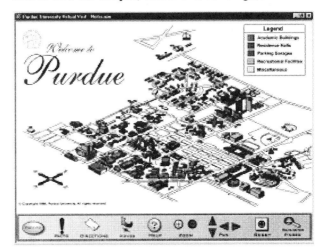

Figure 5. The Purdue University Virtual Visit provides a visit to campus via the WWW.

search for specific buildings. Additionally, the site was to provide interesting facts, directions, and other bits of information about the campus.

The final site, *The Purdue University Virtual Visit*, contains a wealth of textural and graphical information that allows almost anyone to browse the West Lafayette campus via the WWW. Figure 5 shows the interface for the Virtual Visit, which can be found at http://www.tech.purdue.edu/resources/map/.

One of the unique features of the Virtual Visit is the use of photo-based QTVR video clips. Throughout the map, the user can click on a VR location that opens a pop-up window where the user is presented with a QTVR clip from the chosen location, as shown in Figure 6. Both external and internal VR clips are provided, including those from the football, basketball and indoors athletic facilities.

Response from the Virtual Tour has exceeded input from any other project. Respondents have indicated that the site is one of the most unique they have found on the Internet. Plans for the site include virtual tours of buildings and special laboratories on campus as well as use as a stand-alone kiosk across campus that displays the Virtual Visit for those on site.

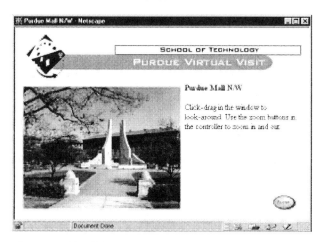

Figure 6. The QTVR clips provide a view of the actual campus.

Implications for Visualization Research

In addition to the applied projects, the department is also beginning to use QTVR clips as a basis for research on visualization. One proposed use includes the study of dynamic field dependence and field independence learning styles on visualization ability and improvement. By creating video clips that simulate static viewer and static object modes of manipulation, as shown in Figure 7, studies could be performed on users to see which mode of manipulation correlates to their mode of learning, if a correlation exists at all. Nonetheless, much

effort and research needs to be done in this area, particularly since the technology is now readily available for the desktop computer.

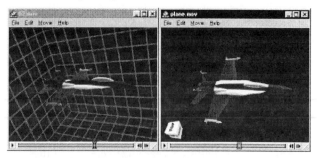

Figure 7. QTVR movies that simulate static viewer and static object modes of manipulation may be used in visualization research.

Conclusions

Although research results are still being gathered, at this point in the project QTVR appears to increase learner comprehension and understanding of complex environments and objects. Additionally motivation and learner interest increase using realistic, navigable VR environments. The low-cost of creation and playback, as well as the broad installed user base of QuickTime, makes video-based QTVR technology a reasonable choice for education and training materials.

Most importantly, video-based VR technologies are well suited where photo-realism is vital and imperative. Additionally, where data rate and bandwidth are a concern, video-based VR technologies, such as QTVR, provide an efficient and effective means of delivery via CD-ROM or the World Wide Web.

References

[1] Bertoline, G. (1988). The implications of cognitive neuroscience research on spatial abilities and graphics instruction. *Proceedings ICEGDG*, 1, Vienna, 28-34.

[2] Lord, T. (1985). Enhancing the visuo-spatial aptitude of students. *Journal of Research in Science Teaching*, 22, 5, pp. 395-405.

[3] Talley, L. (1973). The use of three-dimensional visualization as a moderator in th ehigher cognitive learning of concepts in college level chemistry. *Journal of Research in Science Teaching*, 12, 41-43.

[4] Maccoby, E. & Jacklin, C. (1974). *The Psychology of Sex Differences*. The Stanford Press.

[5] Small, M. & Morton, M. (1983). Spatial visualization training improves performance in organic chemistry. *Journal of College Science Teaching*, 12, 41-43.

[6] Gardner, H. (1984). *Frames of mind*. New York: Basic Books.

[7] Gardner, H. (1993). *Multiple intelligences: The theory in practice.* New York: Basic Books.

[8] Bertoline, G., Burton, T., & Wiley, S. (1992). Technical Graphics as a catalyst for developing visual literacy within general education. *Visual Communications: Bridging Across Cultures: Selected Readings from the 23rd Annual International Visual Literacy Association Annual Conference*, pp. 243-257.

[9] Wiebe, E. (1993). Visualization of three-dimensional form: A discussion of theoretical models of internal representation. *The Engineering Design Graphics Journal*, 57, 1, 18-28.

[10] Mohler, J. (1997). A macro-organizer for AutoCAD instruction. *The Engineering Design Graphics Journal*, 61, 1, 5-13.

[11] Gibson, J. (1986). *The ecological approach to visual perception.* Hillsdale, NJ: Lawrence Erlbaum Associates.

[12] McCuistion, P. (1990). Static vs. dynamic visuals in computer assisted instruction. *ASEE Annual Conference Proceedings*, pp. 143-147.

[13] Miller, C. (1992). Enhancing visual literacy of engineering students through the use of real and computer generated models. *Visual Communications: Bridging Across Cultures: Selected Readings from the 23rd Annual International Visual Literacy Association Annual Conference*, pp. 85-96.

[14] Bertoline, G.R., Miller, C.L., & Mohler, J.L. (1995). Using multimedia tools in the presentation of engineering graphics concepts. *Proceedings of the American Society for Engineering Education North Central Section Annual Meeting* (pp. 89-95).

[15] McLellan, H. (1998). Cognitive issues in virtual reality. *Journal of Visual Literacy*, 18, 2, 175-199.

[16] Ross, W. 7 Aukstakalnis, S. (1993). Virtual reality: Implications in engineering design graphics. *The Engineering Design Graphics Journal*, 57, 2, 5-12.

[17] Thurman, R. A. & Mattoon, J. (1994). Virtual reality: Toward fundamental improvements in simulation-based training. *Educational Technology*, 34, 8, 56-64.

[18] Media Metrix (1998). *Top Software Owned by Percent Reach* [On-line] http://www.mediametrix.com/interact_mm.html.

Session 2-9

Computer Aided Geometric Design

Chair

Robert A. Noble

The Robert Gordon University, UK

A Smooth Rational Spline for Visualizing Monotone Data

Muhammad Sarfraz

Department of Information and Computer Science

King Fahd University of Petroleum and Minerals

KFUPM # 1510, Dhahran 31261, Saudi Arabia

E-mail: sarfraz@kfupm.edu.sa

Abstract

A C^2 curve interpolation scheme for monotonic data has been developed. This scheme uses piecewise rational cubic functions. The two families of parameters, in the description of the rational interpolant, have been constrained to preserve the shape of the data. The monotone rational cubic spline scheme has a unique representation.

1. Introduction

Smooth curve representation, to visualize the scientific data, is of great significance in the area of Computer Graphics and in particular Computer Aided Design (CAD). Specially, when the data is arising from some complex function or from some scientific phenomena, it becomes crucial to incorporate the inherited features of the data. Moreover, smoothness is also one of the very important requirements for pleasing visual display. Ordinary spline schemes, although smoother, are not helpful for the interpolation of the shaped data. Severely misguided results, violating the inherited features of the data, are seen when undesired oscillations occur. For example, the curve in Figure 1 is not as may be desired by the user for a monotonically increasing data. The user would be interested to visualize it as displayed in Figure 6. Thus, unwanted oscillations which completely destroy the data features, are needed to be controlled.

The achievement of this paper is that a smoother C^2 scheme has been searched which provides an automatic procedure to obtain the derivative parameters instead of the approximation choices as in [8]. The imposition of C^2 constraints give rise to a linear system which is soluble using an efficient tridiagonal linear system solver.

The paper begins with a definition of the rational function in Section 2 where the description of rational cubic spline, which does not preserve the shape of a monotone data, is made. Although this rational spline was discussed in [15], but it was in the parametric context which was useful for the designing applications. This section reviews it for the scalar representation so that it can be utilized to preserve the scalar valued data. The monotonicity problem is discussed in Section 3 for the generation of a C^2 spline which can preserve the shape of a monotonic data. This section derives the constraints, on derivative parameters, which lead to a linear system of equations in Section 4 and seeks for the existence and uniqueness of their robust solution. The Section 4, together with some algorithmic details, also demonstrates the output of the scheme for various data sets in literature. The Section 5 concludes the paper.

2. Rationl Spline

Let (x_i, f_i), $i = 1, 2, ..., n$, be a given set of data points, where $x_1 < x_2 < .... < x_n$. Let

$$h_i = x_{i+1} - x_i, \quad \Delta_i = \frac{f_{i+1} - f_i}{h_i}, \quad i = 1, 2, ..., n-1. \quad (1)$$

Consider the following piecewise rational cubic function:

$$s(x) \equiv s_i(x) = \frac{P_i^*(\theta)}{Q_i^*(\theta)}, \quad (2)$$

$$\begin{aligned}
P_i^*(x) &= U_i(1-\theta)^3 + v_i V_i \theta (1-\theta)^2 \\
&\quad + w_i W_i \theta^2 (1-\theta) + Z_i \theta^3, \\
P_i^*(x) &= (1-\theta)^3 + v_i \theta (1-\theta)^2 + w_i \theta^2 (1-\theta) + \theta^3
\end{aligned}$$

where

$$\theta = \frac{x - x_i}{h_i}. \quad (3)$$

To make the rational function (2) C^1, one needs to impose the following interpolatory properties:

$$\left. \begin{aligned}
s(x_i) &= f_i, & s(x_{i+1}) &= f_{i+1} \\
s^{(1)}(x_i) &= d_i, & s^{(1)}(x_{i+1}) &= d_{i+1}
\end{aligned} \right\}, \quad (4)$$

which provide the following manipulations:

$$U_i = f_i, \qquad Z_i = f_{i+1} \atop V_i = f_i + \frac{h_i d_i}{v_i}, \qquad W_i = f_{i+1} - \frac{h_i d_{i+1}}{w_i} \right\}, \qquad (5)$$

where $s^{(1)}$ denotes derivative with respect to x and d_i denote derivative values given at the knots x_i. This leads the piecewise rational cubic (2) to the following piecewise Hermite interpolant $s \in C^1[x_1, x_n]$:

$$s(x) \equiv s_i(x) = \frac{P_i(\theta)}{Q_i(\theta)}, \qquad (6)$$

where

$$\begin{aligned}
P_i(\theta) &= f_i(1-\theta)^3 + v_i V_i \theta(1-\theta)^2 \\
&\quad + w_i W_i \theta(1-\theta)^2 + f_{i+1}\theta^3,
\end{aligned}$$

$$Q_i(\theta) = (1-\theta)^3 + v_i\theta(1-\theta)^2 + w_i\theta(1-\theta)^2 + \theta^3.$$

The parameters v_i's, w_i's, and the derivatives d_i's are to be chosen such that the monotonic shape is preserved by the interpolant (6). One can note that when $v_i = w_i = 3$, the rational function obviously becomes the standard cubic Hermite polynomial. Variation for the values of v_i's and w_i's control (tighten or loosen) the curve in different pieces of the curve. This behaviour can be seen in the following subsection:

2.1. Shape Control Analysis

The parameters v_i's and w_i's can be utilized properly to modify the shape of the curve according to the desire of the user. Their effectiveness, for the shape control at knot points, can be seen that if $v_i, w_{i-1} \to \infty$, then the curve is pulled towards the point f_i in the neighbourhood of the knot position x_i. This shape behavior can be observed by lookig at $s_i(x)$ in Equation (6). This form is similar to that of a Bernstein-Bezier formulation. One can observe that when $v_i, w_{i-1} \to \infty$, then V_i and $W_{i-1} \to f_i$.

The interval shape control behavior can be observed by rewriting $s_i(x)$ in Equation (6) to the following simplified form:

$$\begin{aligned}
s(x) &= f_i(1-\theta) + f_{i+1}\theta + \\
&\quad \frac{[(1-\theta)(d_i - \Delta_i) + \theta(\Delta_i - d_{i+1})]\, h_i\theta(1-\theta)}{Q_i(\theta)}.
\end{aligned}$$

When both v_i and $w_i \to \infty$, it is simple to see the convergence to the following linear interpolant:

$$s(x) = f_i(1-\theta) + f_{i+1}\theta. \qquad (7)$$

It should be noted that the shape control analysis is valid only if the bounded derivative values are assumed. A description of appropriate choices for such derivative values is made in the following subsection.

2.2. Determination of Derivatives

In most applications, the derivative parameters $\{d_i\}$ are not given and hence must be determined either from the given data (x_i, f_i), $i = 1, 2, \ldots, n$, or by some other means. In this article, they are computed exactly from the system of equations which arises after applying the splinning constraints.

Since, the smoothness of the interpolant (6) is C^1 and this article has been attempted to achieve higher degree of smoothness to C^2. For this, it is required to impose the second derivative constraints at the knot positions of the interpolant (6). After some simplications, the second derivatives at x_i and x_{i+1} respectively are as follows:

$$s^{(2)}(x_i) = \frac{1}{3h_i} [w_i\Delta_i - (v_i - 1)d_i - d_{i+1}], \qquad (8)$$

$$s^{(2)}(x_{i+1}) = \frac{1}{3h_i} [-v_i\Delta_i + (w_i - 1)d_{i+1} + d_i]. \qquad (9)$$

The C^2 constraints

$$s^{(2)}(x_{i+}) = s^{(2)}(x_{i-}), \ i = 2, 3, \ldots, n-1 \qquad (10)$$

then lead to the consistency equations:

$$\begin{aligned}
h_i d_{i-1} &+ [h_i(w_{i-1} - 1) + h_{i-1}(v_i - 1)]d_i + h_{i-1}d_{i+1} \\
&= h_i v_{i-1}\Delta_{i-1} + h_{i-1}w_i\Delta_i, \ i = 2, 3, \ldots n-1.
\end{aligned} \qquad (11)$$

For given appropriate end conditions d_1 and d_n, this system of equations is a tridiagonal linear system. This is also diagonally dominant for the following constraints (12) on the shape parameters:

$$v_i, w_i > 2, \ i = 1, 2, \ldots n-1. \qquad (12)$$

and hence has a unique solution for d_i's. As far as the computation method is concerned, it is much more economical to adopt the LU-decomposition method to solve the tridiagonal system. Therefore, we can conclude the above discussion in the following:

Theorem 1 *For $v, w_i \geq \alpha > 2, \forall i,$ the spline solution of the interpolant (6) exists and is unique.*

The parametric representation of this rational spline method has been discussed in detail in [15] for CAD applications. Therefore, the reader is referred to [15] for the detailed analysis and demonstration. Since this article is for scalar curves, therefore some demonstration of the above scheme, in the context of scaler curves, is given in the following subsection.

2.3. Demonstration

For the demonstration of this C^2 rational cubic spline curve scheme, we will choose the following choice of shape parameters:

$$v_i = 3 = w_i, \qquad (13)$$

and the derivatives will be computed from the system of equations (11) to generate the initial default curve. This initial default curve is actually same as a cubic spline curve. Further modification can be made by making changes into these parameters. The Figure 1 is the default curve to a monotonically increasing data taken at random. It can be seen that the ordinary spline curve does not gaurantee to preserve the shape. The Figures 2, 3, and 4 are for the demonstration of global shape control $v_i = w_i = 5, 25, 500, \forall i$, respectively. One can see that the increasing global values of the shape parameters gradually pull the curve towards the control polygon and hence the default curve moves towards the data preserved curve. But this way the curve is getting tightened everywhere which may be undesired. The curve in Figure 5 is for the shape parameter values $w_1 = 4, v_3 = 10$ and $w_3 = 25$. This curve seems satisfying the shape to be preseved in a reasonable way that it is looking visually pleasant. But this shape was achieved after making couple of experiments for different values of parameters which is really time consuming and not very accurate and, therefore, is not recommended for practical applications too.

3. Monotone Rational Spline

The rational spline method, described in the previous section, has deficiencies as far as shape preserving issue is concerned. For example, the rational cubic in Section 2 does not preserve the shape of the monotonic data (see Figure 1). Very clearly, this curve is not preserving the shape of the data. It is required to assign appropriate values to the shape parameters so that it generates a data preserved shape. Thus it looks as if ordinary spline schemes do not provide the desired shape features and hence some further treatment is required to achieve a shape preserving spline for monotonic data.

This article targets towards an automated generation of shape preserving curve. This requires an automated computation of suitable shape parameters and derivative values. To proceed for this strategy, some mathematical treatment is required which has been explained in the following paragraphs.

For simplicity of presentation, let us assume

monotonic increasing set of data so that

$$f_1 \leq f_1 \leq \ldots\ldots \leq f_n, \qquad (14)$$

or equivalently

$$\Delta_i \geq 0, \ i = 1, 2, \ldots\ldots, n - 1. \qquad (15)$$

(In a similar fashion one can deal with a monotonic decreasing data.) For a monotonic interpolant $s(x)$, it is then necessary that the derivative parameters should be such that

$$d_i \geq 0 \ (d_i \leq 0, \ \text{for monotonic decreasing data}),$$
$$i = 1, 2, \ldots\ldots n. \qquad (16)$$

Now $s(x)$ is monotonic increasing if and only if

$$s^{(1)}(x) \geq 0 \qquad (17)$$

for all $x \in [x_1, x_n]$. For $x \in [x_i, x_{i+1}]$ it can be shown , after some simplification, that

$$s^{(1)}(x) = \frac{\left[\sum_{j=1}^{6} A_{j,i} \theta^{j-1} (1-\theta)^{5-j} \right]}{[Q_i(x)]^2}, \qquad (18)$$

where

$$
\left.
\begin{aligned}
A_{1,i} &= d_i, \\
A_{2,i} &= 2w_i \left(\Delta_i - \frac{1}{w_i} d_{i+1} \right) + d_i, \\
A_{3,i} &= 3\Delta_i + 2w_i \left(\Delta_i - \frac{1}{w_i} d_{i+1} \right) \\
&\quad + v_i w_i \left(\Delta_i - \frac{1}{v_i} d_i - \frac{1}{w_i} d_{i+1} \right) \\
A_{4,i} &= 3\Delta_i + 2v_i \left(\Delta_i - \frac{1}{v_i} d_i \right) \\
&\quad + v_i w_i \left(\Delta_i - \frac{1}{v_i} d_i - \frac{1}{w_i} d_{i+1} \right) \\
A_{5,i} &= 2v_i \left(\Delta_i - \frac{1}{v_i} d_i \right) + d_{i+1}, \\
A_{6,i} &= d_{i+1}.
\end{aligned}
\right\} \qquad (19)
$$

Since the denominator in (18), being a squared quantity, is positive, therefore the sufficient conditions for monotonicity on $[x_i, x_{i+1}]$ are:

$$A_{j,i} \geq 0, \ j = 1, 2, \ldots\ldots, 6, \qquad (20)$$

where the necessary conditions

$$d_i \geq 0 \ \text{and} \ d_{i+1} \geq 0 \qquad (21)$$

are assumed. If $\Delta_i > 0$ (strict inequality) then following are the sufficient conditions for (20):

$$
\left.
\begin{aligned}
\Delta_i - \frac{1}{v_i} d_i &\geq 0 \\
\Delta_i - \frac{1}{w_i} d_{i+1} &\geq 0, \ \text{and} \\
\Delta_i - \frac{1}{v_i} d_i - \frac{1}{w_i} d_{i+1} &\geq 0.
\end{aligned}
\right\} . \qquad (22)
$$

374

which lead to the following constraints:

$$v_i = \frac{r_i d_i}{\Delta_i} , \quad w_i = \frac{q_i d_{i+1}}{\Delta_i} . \tag{23}$$

where r_i and q_i are positive quantities satisfying

$$\frac{1}{r_i} + \frac{1}{q_i} \leq 1. \tag{24}$$

This, together with (23) leads to the following sufficient conditions for the freedom over the choice of r_i and q_i:

$$r_i \geq 1 + \frac{d_{i+1}}{d_i} , \quad q_i \geq 1 + \frac{d_i}{d_{i+1}} . \tag{25}$$

One can make the choice of r_i and q_i to be the greatest lower bound as follows:

$$r_i = 1 + \frac{d_{i+1}}{d_i} , \quad q_i = 1 + \frac{d_i}{d_{i+1}} . \tag{26}$$

This choice satisfies (24) and it also provides visually very pleasant results, as can be seen in the demonstration Subsection 4.2. It should be noted that if $\Delta_i = 0$, then it is necessary to set $d_i = d_{i+1} = 0$, and thus

$$s(x) = f_i = f_{i+1} \tag{27}$$

is a constant on $[x_i, x_{i+1}]$. Hence the interpolant (6) is monotonic increasing together with the conditions (21), (23) and (26). For the case where the data is monotonic but not strictly monotonic (i.e., when some $\Delta_i = 0$) it would be necessary to divide the data into strictly monotonic parts. If we set $d_i = d_{i+1} = 0$ whenever $\Delta_i = 0$, then the resulting interpolant will be C^2 at break points. The above discussion can be summarized as:

Theorem 2 *Given the conditions (16) on the derivative parameters, (23) and (26) are the sufficient conditions for the interpolant (6) to be monotonic increasing.*

4. Practical Implementation

This section will discuss the computational aspects of the scheme and then practically demonstrate the results.

4.1. Determination of Derivatives

Some robust and automated method, for the determination of suitable derivative values, is one of the fundamental requirements of the scheme under discussion. To proceede for this strategy, let us substitute the sufficient monotonicity conditions (23) and (26) into (11). Some simplifications yield:

$$a_i d_{i-1} + (a_i + b_i)d_i + b_i d_{i+1} = c_i, \\ i = 2, 3, \ldots, n-1, \tag{28}$$

where

$$\left. \begin{array}{l} a_i = h_{i-1}\Delta_{i-1}, \\ b_i = h_i\Delta_i, \\ c_i = 2(h_{i-1} + h_i)\Delta_{i-1}\Delta_i, \end{array} \right\} \tag{29}$$

Given d_1 and d_n, The set of equations (28) gives a system of $n - 2$ linear equations for the unknowns $d_2, d_2, \ldots, d_{n-1}$. This is a diagonally dominant tridiagonal system and hence has a unique solution. One can note that, for monotonically increasing data, $a_i, b_i, c_i \geq 0, \forall i$. Hence , for the end conditions $d_1, d_n \geq 0$, the solution of (28) is non-negative. Thus we have the following:

Theorem 3 *Given the end conditions $d_1, d_n \geq 0$,the constraints (23) and (26) are sufficient to provide a unique spline which preserves the shape of a monotone increasing data.*

4.2. Demonstration

We will assume the end conditions as some suitable positive values and the rest of the derivative values are computed from the system of equations (28). The scheme has been implemented on the data set of Table 1. Figure ?? is the default rational cubic spline curve for the choice of parameters in (13), whereas the Figure ?? is its corresponding shape preserving spline curve for the automatic choice of parameters in (23) and (26). The pleasing visualization of the data set in Figure 6 is apparent from its counterpart rational cubic spline default curve (see Figure 1) as well as the spline curve controlled by hit and trial method (see Figure 5).

5. Concluding Remarks

A rational cubic interpolant, with two families of shape parameters, has been utilized to obtain C^2 monotonicity preserving interpolatory spline curves. The shape constraints are restricted on shape parameters to assure the shape preservation of the data. For the C^2 interpolant, the consistency equations on the derivative parameters have been derived. The solution to this system of linear equations exists and provides a unique solution. A robust solution, using the LU decomposition method, has been recommended. For an efficient implementation of the C^2 scheme, it has been taken into account that, in each of the interval, the curve scheme intelligently saves the higher degree arithmetic into a lower degree according to the nature of the slope.

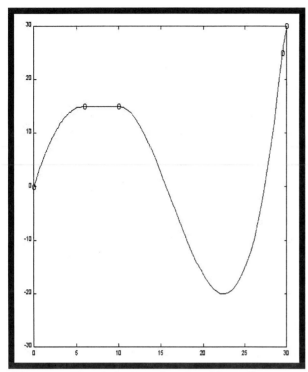

Figure 1. The default rational cubic spline curve to the data taken at random.

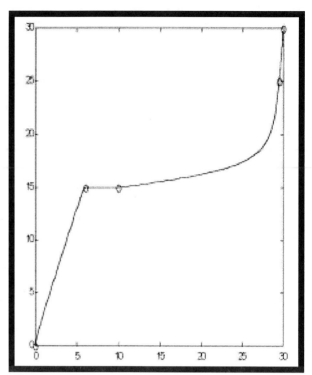

Figure 3. The rational cubic spline with global shape control having $v_i = 25 = w_i$, for all i.

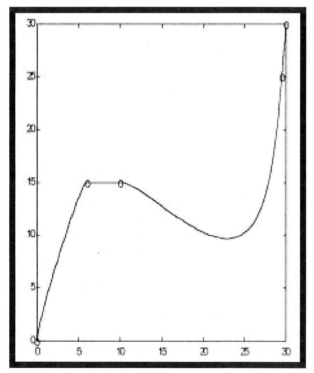

Figure 2. The rational cubic spline with global shape control having $v_i = 5 = w_i$, for all i.

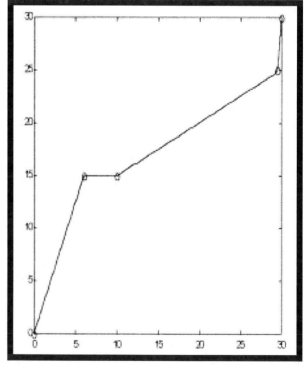

Figure 4. The rational cubic spline with global shape control having $v_i = 500 = w_i$, for all i.

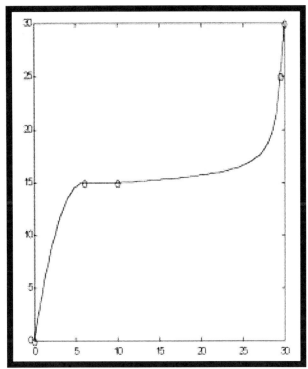

Figure 5. The rational cubic spline with various choices of shape parameters intervals.

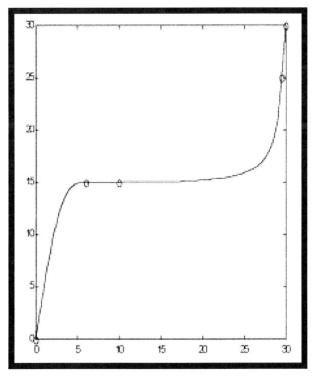

Figure 6. The rational cubic shape preserving spline curve to the data in Figure 1.

References

[1] D.F. McAllister and J.A. Roulier, (1981), An algorithm for computing a shape preserving osculatory quadratic spline, ACM Trans. Math. Software, 7, 331-347.

[2] E. Passow and J.A. Roulier, (1977), Monotone and convex spline interpolation. SIAM J. Num. Anal. 14, 904-909.

[3] F.N. Fritsch and R.E. Carlson, (1980), Monotone piecewise cubic interpolation, SIAM J. Num. Anal. 17, 238-246.

[4] J.A. Gregory, (1986), Shape preserving spline interpolation, Computer-Aided Design, 18(1), 53-57.

[5] F.N. Fritsch and J. Butland, (1984), A method for constructing local monotone piecewise cubic interpolants, SIAM J. Sc. Stat. Comput., 5, 303-304.

[6] L.L. Schumaker, (1983), On shape preserving quadratic spline interpolation, SIAM J. Num. Anal., 20, 854-864.

[7] K.W. Brodlie and S. Butt, (1991), Preserving convexity using piecewise cubic interpolation, Comput. & Graphics, 15, 15-23.

[8] M. Sarfraz, (1992), Convexity preserving piecewise rational interpolation for planar curves, Bull. Korean Math. Soc. 29(2), 193-200.

[9] M. Sarfraz, (1997), Preserving Monotone shape of the Data using Piecewise Rational Cubic Functions, Computers & Graphics, 21(1), pp. 5-14.

[10] K.W. Brodlie (1985), Methods for drawing curves, in : Fundamenal algorithm for Computer Graphics, ed. R.A. Earnshaw (Springer, Berlin, Heidelherg) pp. 303-323.

[11] A. DeVore and Z. Yan, (1986), Error analysis for piecewise quadratic curve fitting algorithms, Comp. Aided Geom. Design 3, pp. 205-215.

[12] K. Greiner, (1991), A survey on univariate data interpolation and approximation by splines of given shape, Math. Comp. Mod. 15, pp. 97-l06.

[13] P. Constantini, (1997), Boundary-Valued Shape Preserving Interpolating Splines, ACM Transactions on Mathematical Software, 23(2), pp. 229-251.

[14] A. Lahtinen, (1996), Monotone interpolation with application to estimation of taper curves, Annals of Numerical Math. 3, pp. 151-161.

[15] M. Sarfraz, (1992), Interpolatory Rational Cubic Spline with Biased, Point and Interval Tension, Computers & Graphics, 16(4), pp. 427-430.

Towards a Feature-Based Interactive System for Intelligent Font Design

FIAZ HUSSAIN

*Department of Computer and Information Sciences,
De Montfort University, Kents Hill Campus,
Hammerwood Gate, Milton Keynes, MK7 6HP,
England.*

email: fiaz@dmu.ac.uk

BORUT ZALIK

*Faculty of Electrical Engineering & Computer Science,
University of Maribor, Smetanova 17,
P.O. Box 224, SI-62000 Maribor,
Slovenia.*

email: zalik@uni-mb.si

Abstract

The desire to computerise and accurately represent contours of characters has seen an increased emphasis as more and more applications endeavour to seek benefits from the digital form. The latter lends itself to be exploited by fast processors and the resulting output to be displayed not just on electronic devices such as computer monitors and laser printers, but also on numerically controlled machines. These in practice are used to generate desired outlines on paper, metal, plastic or wood by means of cutting and engraving.

The process of computerising font outlines, however, embodies the common problems of domain change approximations and truncations. In the case under consideration, the capturing phase is best undertaken by means of mathematical splines, where a series of spline segments are connected together to form a computer model of the original. The digitisation phase of representing the modelled image on a finite resolution output device tends to be the more dominant concern. This is not just because of the transformation process (going from semi-continuous to discrete form), but also because the resulting image needs to embrace the distinct features of a font, has to be aesthetically acceptable, and requires to be in a form which is legible.

This paper attempts to address some of the concerns encountered by modern typographers. It reports on a development of an interactive system to facilitate a feature-based design approach. This uses geometric constraints to express spatial relationships within, and between, font features. These provide much of the instructions required by a rasterizer to ensure a satisfactory outcome. In addition, to aid flexibility and reusability, a font feature is not required to be constrained completely at the outset. Instead, the system prompts the user to confirm relations as and when necessary. Workings of the system and its respective architecture is illustrated through its handling of the Times Roman half-serif. The paper also looks at the way the system glues two

(or more) font features together. The discussion, throughout, is levelled at providing a practical understanding of the subject matter.

Keywords:
character, feature-based design, font, geometric constraints, typography.

1.0 Introduction

The attractions for using a spline model to capture outlines of figures, including those forming characters and symbols, has lead to its incorporation within and for a number of applications. The primary appeal being the flexibility and the semi-continuous representation of a given, continuous, outline that it exhibits. Though the usage of splines is maybe ideal for computer modelling a desired outline, its main shortcoming is that its form is incompatible with any attached peripheral display device. The latter works with a discrete format, whilst the former has a more continuous nature. This inevitably leads to problems when attempting to digitise spline models, especially so when a low finite resolution output device is used (see chapter 8 of [1], for example).

The work reported here concentrates on describing a system for creating, manipulating and representing outlines of fonts. The system employs geometric constraints to yield structural shapes and parts of a font. The approach is termed constraint-based and provides an interactive platform for typographic designers to undertake the design and development of characters. The process makes use of partially constrained font features to aid flexibility and to enhance their reusability. The work supports and is geared to assist the process of rasterisation, whereby the induced (either by the user or by the system) constraints can be used as instructions by a rasterizer.

The main purpose of this paper is to offer a working system for using constraints to model font characteristics. Through this, an illustration is used to show how the user interacts with the system to realise a half-serif, which is partially constrained and which, once complete, is available to be exploited and used as desired. This paper follows on from a companion submission entitled "Type Design with Flexible Constrained Font Characteristics"[2].

2.0 Generation of a Font Feature

This section provides an insight to the development of a font feature and in particular at the way a designer would interact with the system to generate a desired font feature. For purposes of illustration, it will be assumed that the user wishes to design a half-serif, similar to that shown in Figure 1.

The interface, as Figure 2 depicts, consists of a main window which is subdivided into four working windows. These sub-windows are headed: Features, Drawing, Constraints and Information. The Features window contains a list of all the structural units (font features) which have already been generated and are available to the user. The Drawing window allows the insertion of sketches and diagrammatic information. Effectively, this is the editing window. The window labelled Constraints lists the topological and geometrical information which has thus far emerged from the sketch in the Drawing window. The Information window gives a complete overview of all the constraints inserted, whether manually by the designer or automatically by the system, for the sketch.

Figure 2, also, shows the situation after the first line segment for the half-serif is inserted interactively by the user in the Drawing window. Insertion of this is via the mouse, where it is used to mark the two respective endpoints. Once the line segment is drawn, the system responds by creating an auxiliary line which lies upon and extends beyond the line segment just drawn. It also identifies and lists a set of constraints which describe the spatial relationships between these two lines. This process, in addition, removes the burden away from the user to insert necessary detail to achieve an appropriate constraint-based description.

In Figure 3, we can see the situation after a complete initial shape for the half-serif has been created. Note the fact that the required information relating to the topology and to the geometry of the sketch, together with its set of constraints, has been extracted automatically by the system. The user at this stage has the option of either storing the half-serif as a feature in the font-library, or to insert additional constraints.

To illustrate the way new constraints could be inserted, let us assume that the user would like to express the bottom line for the half-serif to be horizontally straight and that the left most line to be vertically straight. In order for this to occur, the user needs to embody two new constraints in the feature. These are available from a pool of constraints, as shown in Figure 4, and listed within the opened window. Additional constraints are simply picked, attached, and then stored. The process is guided by the system to aid usability. The way this would work in our case is as follows: To denote a line as horizontal, the user chooses the constraint *Hline* and then applies this option to those lines desired to have this property.

Once a new constraint has been inserted, the system attempts to solve it immediately, if possible. The result of the constraint solver is shown as soon as it is available. The user then has the option of either storing or removing the inserted constraint. Figure 4 shows the case after our desired (two) constraints have been inserted: *Hline* has been applied to the bottom line and *Vline* to the left most line of the half-serif. Note that the auxiliary geometry shown in the Drawing window is meant to aid the designer and can, of course, be toggled off when appropriate.

The outcome from the system constraining process can be tabulated in terms of the inserted constraints. Table 1 shows the set of constraints inserted till now. It should be realised that the majority of the constraints (marked by a "*" in Table 1) have been entirely generated by the system. The sequence of the constraints is itself arbitrary. It is the task of the constraint solver to generate such a sequence of constraints which leads to a solution.

These constraints are used to generate a constraint description graph, which in turn is used by the constraint solver.. Such a graph for our case is shown in Figure 5.

To generate the outline for the half-serif, additional topological and geometrical information is needed. Looking at Figure 5, it is not possible to determine whether, for example, points p_0 and p_1 are connected with a line segment which needs to be visible. On the other hand, points p_5 and p_6 also lie on a line, but they are not part of a visible description for the font. So, more information is required about the half-serif. This information has, in fact, has already been captured by the system (see information window in Figures 3, 4, and 5) and is in concise form given in Table 2.

*	$On(p_0, l_0)$	$Through(l_0, p_0)$
*	$On(p_1, l_0)$	$Through(l_0, p_1)$
*	$On(p_1, l_2)$	$Through(l_2, p_1)$
*	$On(p_4, l_2)$	$Through(l_2, p_4)$
	$HLine(l_0)$	
	$VLine(l_2)$	
*	$On(p_4, l_{15})$	$Through(l_{15}, p_4)$
*	$On(p_{18}, l_{15})$	$Through(l_{18}, p_{10})$
*	$On(p_{18}, l_{16})$	$Through(l_{16}, p_{18})$
*	$On(p_{19}, l_{16})$	$Through(l_{16}, p_{19})$
*	$On(p_{19}, l_{17})$	$Through(l_{17}, p_{19})$
*	$On(p_{20}, l_{17})$	$Through(l_{17}, p_{20})$

Table 1: Depicts the partial constraining scheme for the half-serif, constraints marked by "*" are produced automatically by the system.

edge	type of connection	control geometric data
el_0	line segment	p_0, p_1
el_2	line segment	p_1, p_4
eb_2	Bézier cubic curve	$p_4, p_{18}, p_{19}, p_{20}$

Table 2: Lists the geometrical and topological information for the half-serif.

As mentioned earlier, the approach presented here does not just provide a more flexible approach to designing characters and fonts, but also assists the process of digitisation. The additional information embodied within the constraining process are available for a rasterizer to fully utilise. In fact, Tables 2 and 3 are in a form which could be sufficient as input to such a process.

3.0 Gluing of font-features

A serif can be considered as a composed font feature consisting of two glued half-serifs. One of them is directly obtained from FFL and the second one is just mirrored around line l_4 (see Figure 1).

The mirroring does not have any influence on already given constraints neither on topological information. The situation shown to the user is depicted in Figure 6. Internally, its description consists of two joined BCDGs which are linked by a few new, manually given constraints. The following procedure consisting of two major steps identifies the tasks performed by the gluing algorithm:

In the first step, to bind two BCDGs, the user inserts interactively by a mouse, constraints which are shown in Table 3. The indexes shown in Table 3 are added just for the explanation purposes. The algorithm does not generate them neither they are shown to the user. Numbers in indexes in Table 3 correspond to the indexes in Figure 1, while characters L and R denote left and right half-serif.

At first, inserted constraints are stored in a so-called constraint interface - CI. In Figure 7 a schematic presentation of the first step of binding BCGDs is shown. For the purposes of clarity, predicate *Symmetric* is not drawn.

Coincidence(l_{1L}, l_{1R})	Coincidence(l_{4L}, l_{4R})
Coincidence(l_{6L}, l_{6R})	Coincidence(l_{5L}, l_{5R})
Symmetric(l_{3L}, l_{4L}/l_{4R}, l_{3R})	

Table 3 Constraints which glue BCDGs of two half-serifs

To optimise constraint propagation, both BCDGs are joined in the second step of the algorithm into a new unique BCDG and the constraint interface is gradually removed. This step is performed by the algorithm called a BCDG optimiser. It main tasks arc:

1. At first, tuning of the names of the used geometric elements is done. In this way, each BCDG node stores a geometric element with a unique name. The naming of the geometric elements is not critical because the user accesses them interactively by a locator (mouse).
2. The BCDG nodes which are connected by the predicate *Coincidence* are simply joined. For example, in Figure 7, BCDG nodes of the left and right-half serifs store line l_5 but in new situation only one line l_5 actually exists. Therefore, in one of the BCDGs, the node carrying line l_5 can be removed from the graph. All BCDG links, which was connected with removed BCDG node are now connected with remaining BCDG node storing line l_5.
3. The geometric entities, which are identical, but are not explicitly connected by the predicate *Coincidence,* are discovered and removed from the BCDG in the same way as it has been just described. For example, point p_1 is not mentioned in the constraints listed in Table 5.1, but it lies on lines l_1 and l_4 which are present in the Table 5.1.
4. The new topological information is generated.

One can ask why the constraint interface has been introduced if it is removed in the final stage. The main reason for its introduction is that it is very easy to erase just inserted font-feature if its BCDG is separated from the main BCDG. When the user is happy with the inserted font-feature, he/she starts the BCDG optimiser and from this moment, the font-feature cannot be extracted from the common shape any more.

4.0 Conclusions

This paper has given outline of a system for generating, editing and designing font features. The primary goal of the system is to support an interactive environment by using the principle of partially constraining any desired feature. To aid usability and limit user involvement, much of the cumbersome and tedious tasks of identifying and determining spatial relationships within and between font features is to be undertaken by the system. The employment of partial constraints also supports the reusability of such features. The design of a half-serif is taken as a sample to illustrate the various properties of the system.

One natural extension to the system would be to provide a "gluing" option for the designer. This will allow the linking of two or more features (such as a serif to a stem) to be undertaken. The work will involve the development of an appropriate user interface which supports an interactive environment.

5.0 References

[1] Font Technology (Methods and Tools), P Karow, Springer-Verlag, Berlin, 1994.

[2] Type Design with flexible constrained font characteristics, Proc: IEE Document & Image Processing and Multimedia, March 1999, London.

Acknowledgement

We would like to thank our students S Strah and S Kolmani, who helped to realise our ideas with programming. The system has been written in Borland C++ (Version 4.5) and runs on personal computers in MS Windows environment.

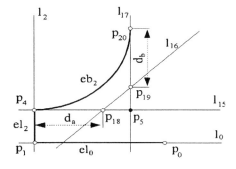

Figure 1: Depicts the geometric entities for the half-serif.

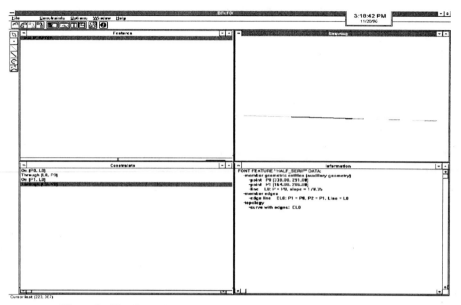

Figure 2: The Graphical User Interface (GUI) for the feature-based design system, showing the case where a line with endpoints p_0 and p_1 has been sketched in the Drawing window.

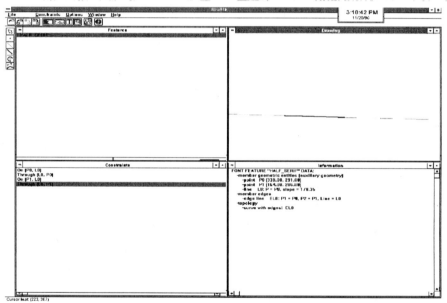

Figure 3: Depicts the sketch for the half-serif, together with the extracted information required for the constraining process.

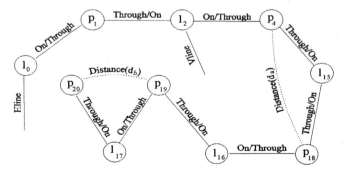

Figure 5: Constraint description graph for the partially constrained half-serif.

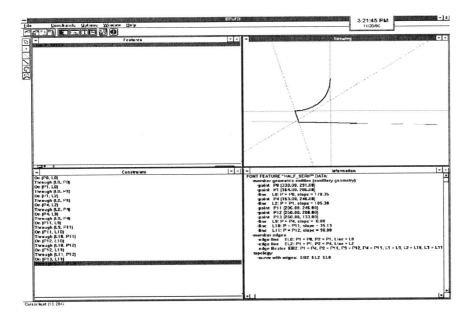

Figure 4: The half-serif after insertion of two additional constraints: *Hline* for the bottom line to make horizontal and *Vline* for the left most line to make vertical.

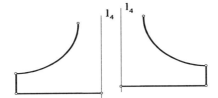

Figure 6 Initial steps in generating serif

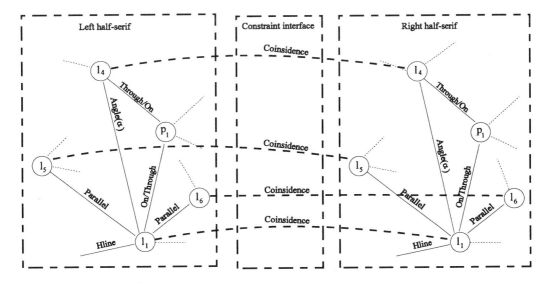

Figure 7 Schematic presentation of joining of BCDGs

Towards a Consistent Distributed Design:
a Multi-Agent Approach

Victor Taratoukhine, Kamal Bechkoum

Department of Computer & Information Sciences, De Montfort University, Hammerwood Gate,
Kents Hill, Milton Keynes MK7 6HP, U.K.
Vtaratoukhine@dmu.ac.uk, kbechkoum@dmu.ac.uk

Abstract

This paper reviews existing methods and techniques addressing the problem of mismatch control in distributed collaborative design. In order to contribute towards a more comprehensive solution a basis for a taxonomy of design mismatches is presented. The paper argues that a multi-agent approach is a more effective, and a promising, way forward towards a reliable automatic solution to the problem. An outline multi-agent architecture is proposed. The architecture assumes that the design knowledge is encapsulated within the different members of agent community. Agents are endowed with the capacity of negotiation with one another to ensure that any mismatches are detected and that a solution is proposed. The notions of proactiviness and social ability, which the agents need to exhibit, are central to this work.

1. Introduction

Research into the use of knowledge engineering in design has become widely accepted as a fast growing subfield of Artificial Intelligence (AI). Increasing numbers of researchers, and research groups, are active within this emerging subfield. From advocates of *"knowledge intensive"* CAD/CAM/CAE (eg. [1][2]) to promoters of broader *"intelligent CAD frameworks"* (eg. [3][4]) the common thread is the use of AI tools and techniques to provide automatic and semi-automatic solutions to the problem. These solutions aim at increasing the "intelligence" of existing CAD/CAM/CAE systems [9].

The AI technologies used are varied and include expert systems [5], genetic algorithms and evolution programming [6], neural networks [7], fuzzy logic [8] and multi-agent systems [4][10][11][12][13]. Hybrid methods combining more than one technology have also been used [14].

It is fair to say though, that design engineers are still skeptical about the ability (or inability) of current intelligent design-support systems. For example, even when endowed with some sort of intelligent behaviour, existing CAD/CAE systems cannot handle several types of inconsistencies that may occur during the design phase. The situation deteriorates if the system is dealing with CAD/CAE data that was generated as part of a distributed collaborative design process.

We re-inforce here the view that a multi-agent approach can tackle many of the problems posed by the centralisation of knowledge into a single Knowledge Base. A brief overview of related work is presented in Section 2. In Section 3, we revisit the problem in the light of currently proposed solutions. A key issue raised in this paper is that any solution is as good as the knowledge about the problem itself. In other words, if a particular type of mismatch is ignored the system cannot be expected to deal with that sort of mismatch when it occurs. This is why we attempted to define a basis for a taxonomy of design mismatches which is described in Section 4. The conceptual framework, based on a multi-agent architecture and a proposal for the organisation of the distributed knowledge base, knowledge representation paradigms, types and classes of knowledge is presented in Section 5. Cooperation and negotiation strategies presented in Section 6. Concluding notes and future work are described in Section 7.

2. Multi-agent alternatives

Due to the above mentioned difficulties, it seems reasonable to believe that a Distributed Artificial Intelligence framework, using a multi-agent architecture, is a natural alternative in dealing with the problem at hand. Work in this area is already gaining an increasing popularity.

LuaObr [4] is an original implementation of multi-agent systems in design, which supports event driven design processes. This work is based on the concept of *Extended Constraint Graphs.*

384

J. D'Ambrosio et. al. [10] have presented also an agent-based framework to support hierarchical concurrent engineering. Within the framework preferences and constraints of a design supervisor are distributed to design subordinates, who are expected to exploit their local expertise within the context provided by global design information.

M. Hale and J. Graid [11] have developed a distributed intelligent system for aircraft design based on conception of a design integration framework. An Intelligent Multi-disciplinary Aircraft Generation Environment (IMAGE) is discribed which uses state-of-the-art computing technologies.

R. Subbu et. al. [12] have described an information architecture called *Virtual Design Environment*. The approach utilises evoluntionary intelligent agents as program entities which generate and execute queries among distributed computing applications and design databases.

H. Frost and M. Cutkosky [13] have developed a multi-agent architecture, which makes the capability of manufacturing processes manifest to designers starting with earliest stages of geometry specification. The approach is being implemented using agents, written in object-oriented language, which exchange feature-based capability models.

None of the aforementioned applications of multi-agent systems is orientated towards dealing with the problem of detecting mismatches that may occur during the integration phase of distributed design.

K. Bechkoum [5] describes a Intelligent Mismatch Control System (IMCS) which has the potential to detect some types of mismatches. The IMCS implementation is an important step towards a more comprehensive solution but is far from being defects free. For example, the number and types of mismatches handled by the system is narrowed down to a few geometric mismatches.

The work presented here takes the IMCS' development one step forward. A new multi-agent architecture is proposed which gives the IMCS the ability to handle issues peculiar to the nature of distributed design. This multi-agent architecture will be at the heart of an intelligent distributed mismatch control system (IDMCS) that aims at ensuring that the overall design is consistent and acceptable to all.

Such systems can be categorised into three major classes of (by order of increased intelligence):

(1) Interpreters. Systems designed for interpreting the design situations. They utilise logical derivation sequences of the simplest form.

(2) Advisory Systems. Systems with enlarged knowledge base concerning the object of design. They analyse the situation obtained as a result of geometrical modelling and perform "k" lookahead of the user's action. They can answer "What if?" questions. When working with this type of systems designers will be able to improve (or get rid of) the mismatches manually, using their interpretation of the design situation.

(3) Prescriptive Systems. Systems with a capacity for controlling the mismatch detection and correctness process. They are capable of carrying out a series of modelling experiments, by themselves, to try several system models and optimise their structure or characteristics. Whilst doing so, and if a situation cannot be classified or a conflict cannot be resolved the decision making process is left to the user. In this type of systems semi-automatic and/or automatic mismatch control can be applied. The work described here falls under this class of systems.

3. Re-visiting the problem

The problem becomes that of creating a conceptual framework for building a knowledge-based mismatch control system. The framework is based on a community of agents which are capable of learning and/or adapting to changes in the environment.

In order to contribute towards a solution to the above problem the following steps were taken:
- define a taxonomy of distributed design mismatches.
- develop a Conceptual Framework for a multi-agent system that handles these mismatches. This should take into account:
- the design knowledge needed to be considered whithin each agent.
- the knowledge representation paradigm.
- communication and negotiation issues, including conflict resolution.

4. A taxonomy of mismatches in design

The problem of devising a fully-fledged taxonomy for design mismatches is a very complex one. This is because design is a multi-disciplinary task that involves several stages. These stages include input data analysis, conceptual design, basic structural design, detail design, production design, manufacturing processes analysis, and documentation (see [9]).

A broad classification based on geometrical mismatches is represented in [5]. Some of the important parameters to consider in the case of Design for Assembly (DFA), are presented in [15]. Our taxonomy uses some of these known parameters, but is especially oriented for implementation for mismatch detection during the integration phase of mechanical engineering design. The proposed taxonomy of mismatches is presented in Fig. 1.

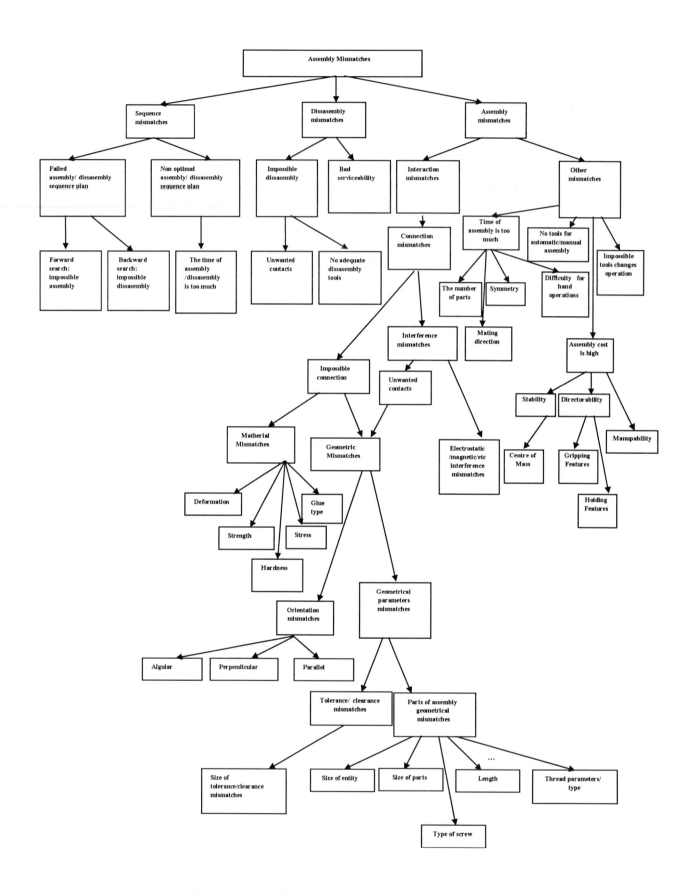

Figure 1. An initial taxonomy of design mismatches

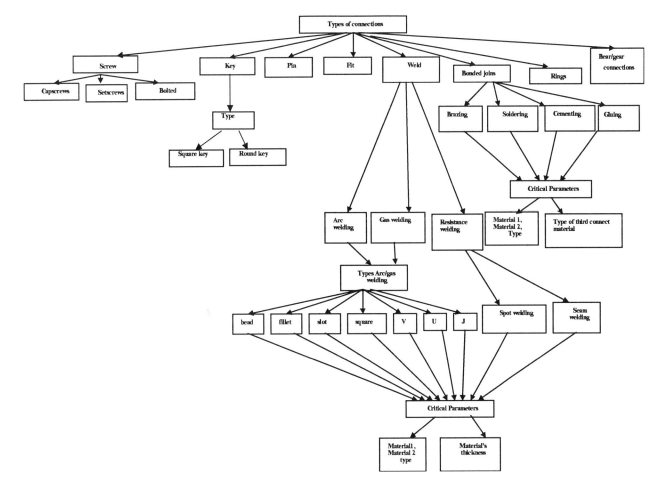

Figure 2. Types of connections

The types of possible connections are presented in Fig.2. It is making the capacity for new a class of design systems to impoving assembly mismatches at the earliest stage of the design.

It can be seen from Fig. 2, for example, weld connections require accordance between types of materials and material thickness, as well as, geometric parameters of material. The bolted connection requires parameters such as thread major diameter, minor diameter and pitch to be in accordance.

For the correct mismatch detection process we need to represent into our knowledge-base geometric information and information about materials from which parts are prepared.

This general summary has been used in the development of the conceptual framework for a multi-agent system that handles mismatches.

5. Conceptual framework

This section briefly reviews the agent framework and the components within, the distributed knowledge-base organisation.

5.1. Formal description of the multi-agent framework

The conceptual framework of the IDMCS is shown in Fig. 3. The architecture assumes that the design knowledge is encapsulated within the different members of agent community.

Conceptual framework (CF) may be formally presented formally as follows:

$$CF = \{AP_1, \dots, AP_t, \dots, AP_n\},$$

where AP_t is the tth Assembly Part, $t = 1, 2, \dots, n$.

$AP = \{DA_1, \dots, DA_i, \dots, DA_m, CA_1, \dots, CA_j, \dots, CA_k\}$,

where DA_i is the ith Design Agent (D-agent),
$i = 1, 2, \dots, m$,

CA_j is the jth Control Agent (C-agent),
$j = 1, 2, \dots, k$.

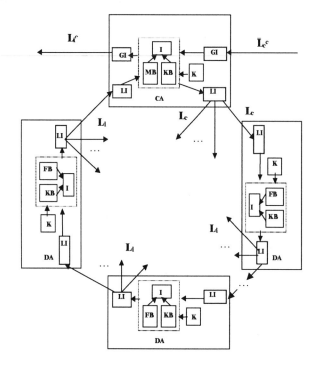

Figure 3. A multi-agent framework for mismatch control in distributed design

Each DA_i consists of eight elements:
FB - facts base, which including information about geometric characteristics of the part and material type. KB - knowledge-base. K - corrector block - which is adapted knowledge-base, as the result of communications with any other agents. I - interference engine. LI - local interface mechanism.

Each CA_j consists:
MB - metaknowledge base, knowledge-base of control agent, interference engine, corrector block, local and global interface mechanism (GI).

Communications is key ability of multi-agents systems. The proposed communication protocol (CP) for the above agents is as follows:

$CP = \{L_{c1}, \dots, L_{cm}; L_{i1}, \dots, L_{im}; L_{c}^{c}{}_1, \dots, L_{c}^{c}{}_k; L_{i}^{c}{}_1, \dots, L_{i}^{c}{}_k\}$,

where L_i - information language, which describes current situation into multi-agent system, L_c - control language, which includes imperative commands about adaptation fact base of design agent for mismatch improvement,

adaptation and modification D-agent's knowledge-base. L_i^{c} - information language, which describes current situation for control agents, L_c^{c} - control language, which adapt meta- and knowledge-base of C-agents.

5.2. Organisation of the distributed knowledge base

The organisation of the distributed knowledge-base is presented as follows:
FB of D-agent including frame facts containing information about parts geometric and material consistency.

Rules in KB and MB of D- and C-agents provide analysis of design situation using experts knowledge.

Each rule M_p, $p = 1, \dots, r$, is characterised by premise part, comprising the IF preconditional statements, and the consequent part (THEN part), comprising the inferred outputs.

KB of D-agents is represented by the following rules of productions: rules called **Receptors** for making an analysis of the design situation, rules called **Classifiers** for making classification of situations according to the necessity of control actions.

KB of C-agents consists: Receptors, Classifiers and **Effectors**.

Receptors are represented as:

IF < situation = ST > THEN < start C >,

where ST - set of mismatch situations,

$ST \in \{ST_1, ST_2, \dots, ST_p\}$,

C - classifier. Classifiers are devided into three types:

IF < ST > THEN < estimation >,

IF < ST > THEN < estimation and recommendation>,

IF < ST > THEN < start E >,

where E - is effectors. Effectors are divided into 2 sets:

$E = <E_{ext}, E_{int}>$,

E_{ext} is a set of rules for modification and adaptation of the FB and KB of D-agents and E_{int} - self-adaptation MB and KB of C-agents.

6. Cooperation and negotiation in a multi-agent framework

We represent conceptual framework as community of calendar [16] and reactive [2] agents. In our case D-agent is a reactive agent, which negotiate with other D-agents using design' schedule (assembly sequence) generating C-agent.

Agents exchange information using messages with syntax and semantics defined by communication protocol CP. The context of these messages can be defined by L_i and includes declarative and procedural knowledge.

Each D-agent is operated as independent entity and interactes asynchronously with other D-agents on peer-to-peer level and client server architecture (under the supervision of the C-agent).

D-agents are endowed with the capacity of negotiation with one another to ensure that any mismatches are detected and that a solution is proposed, but do not modify each other, because that is responsibility of C-agents.

C-agent receives the new information from D-agents using syntax of L_i, negotiate with other C-agents, using L_i^c and L_c^c, and updates the D-agents fact- and knowledge base using L_c, if mismatches occur.

7. Conclusion and future work

In this paper we have introduced a taxonomy of mismatches in design, have described a conceptual framework for building knowledge-based mismatch distributed control system which would be capable of detecting and resolving mismatches.

A proposal for negotiation protocol, which described the mechanisms of communication between agents, is also outlined.

The next step is a creation of initial prototype of IDMCS, which will liable us to evaluate the effectiveness of the proposed framework.

We hope that such systems will be another step toward a new generation of integrated intelligent design systems.

References

[1] T. Tomiyama, "Towards knowledge intensive intelligent CAD," JSME-ASME Workshop on Design, pp. 46-51, 1993.

[2] T. Tomiyama, T. Kiriyama, and Y. Umeda, "Towards knowledge intensive engineering," in Knowledge Building and Knowledge Sharing, IOS Press, pp. 308-316, 1994.

[3] V. Akman, P.J. ten Hagen, and T. Tomiyama, "A Fundamental and Theoretical Framework for an Intelligent CAD System," Computer Aided Design Journal, Vol. 22, pp. 352-367, 1990.

[4] J. Bento, and B. Feijo, "An Agent Based Paradigm for Building Intelligent CAD Systems," Artificial Intelligence in Engineering Journal, Vol. 11, pp. 231-244, 1997.

[5] K. Bechkoum, "Intelligent Electronic Mock-up for Concurrent Design," Expert Systems with Applications Journal, Vol. 12, pp. 21-36, 1997.

[6] J. S. Gero, "Adaptive Systems in Designing: New Analogies from Genetics and Developmental Biology," in Adaptive Computing in Design and Manufacture, I. Parmee (ed.), Springer, London, pp. 3-12, 1998.

[7] D. D. Daberkow, and D. N. Marvis, "New Approaches to Conceptual and Preminary Aircraft Design: A Comparative Assessment of a Neural Network Formulation and a Response Surface Methodology," Proceedings of World Aviation Congress and Exposition, Anaheim, CA, USA, Paper N. SAE-985509, 1998.

[8] I. V. Semoushin, V.V. Shishkin, and V. V. Taratoukhine, "Knowledge-based Network Simulation System," Proceedings of the 7th International Fuzzy Systems Association Congress, Czech Republic, Prague, pp. 532 – 537, 1997.

[9] C. McMahon, J. Browne, Computer-aided Design and Manufacture, Addison-Wesley Press, 1993.

[10] J. G. D'Ambrosio, T. Darr, and W.P. Birmingham, "Hierarchical Concurrent Engineering in a Multiagent Framework," Concurrent Engineering: Research and Applications Journal, Vol. 4, pp. 47-57, 1996.

[11] M. A. Hale, and J. I. Craig, "Preliminary Development of Agent Technologies for a Design Integration Framework," Proceedings of 5th Symposium on Multi-disciplinary Analysis and Optimisation, Panama City, FL, USA, September 7-9, 1994.

[12] R. Subbu, C. Hocaoglu, and A. Sanderson, "A Virtual Design Environment using Evolutionary Agents," Proceedings of the 1998 IEEE International Conference on Robotics & Automation, Belgium, pp. 247-253, 1998.

[13] H. R. Frost, and M. R. Cutkosky, "Design for Manufacturability via Agent Interaction," Proceedings of ASME Design for Manufacturing Conference, Irvine, CA, August 18-22, Paper N 96-DETC/DFM-1302, 1996.

[14] S. H. Kim, "An Automata-Theoretic Framework for Intelligent Systems," Robotics and Computer Integrated Manufacturing Journal, Vol. 5, pp. 43-51, 1989.

[15] S. Lee, G. Kim, and G. Bekey, "Combining Assembly Planning with Redesign: An Approach for More Effective DFA," Proceedings of the 1993 IEEE International Conference on Robotics and Automation, Vol. 3, pp. 319-325, 1993.

[16] J. Liu, and K. Sycara, "Distributed Meeting Scheduling," Proceedings of Sixteenth Annual Conference of the Cognitive Science Society, 13-16 August, Atlanta, USA, 1994.

Information Visualization

Chair
Carlos R. Morales
Purdue University, USA

An Empirical Study of Task Support in 3D Information Visualizations

Ulrika Wiss[1]

Effnet AB

Aurorum 2

S-977 75 Luleå, Sweden

e-mail: ulrika@effnet.com

David A. Carr[1]

Department of Computer and Information Science

Linköping University

S-581 83 Linköping, Sweden

e-mail: davca@ida.liu.se

Abstract

There is still little knowledge about what factors are important for the usability of a 3D user interface. We have performed a comparative study of three 3D information visualizations as a step towards a better understanding of this. The study involved 25 volunteer subjects, performing three different tasks with the Information Landscape, Cam Tree, and Information Cube. The results of the study indicate that the subjects were significantly faster with the Information Landscape when compared with both other visualizations. The Cam Tree was significantly faster than the Information Cube. Our observations during the study indicate that local and global overview are extremely important factors. We also observed that custom navigation is crucial in 3D user interfaces. Finally, the study raises the question: "For what types of tasks is a 3D user interface best suited?"

Keywords: 3D information visualization, usability study, empirical study, navigation, overview

1   Introduction

Lately, technological advances in computer graphics have made 3D information visualization feasible on personal computers. Meanwhile, the World-Wide Web has made a vast amount of information available to individuals. In parallel with these developments, a number of 3D information visualizations have been invented by both researchers and commercial software developers. But, the research community has still made very few comparative studies of these visualizations.

The study described in this paper aims to explore what factors are important for task support in 3D information visualization. Three 3D information visualizations were studied: the Cam Tree [10], the Information Cube [9] and the Information Landscape [1, 12]. These information visualizations all visualize hierarchical data. In our study, we chose to visualize a hierarchical file system, which is familiar to most computer users.

The three user tasks in our study were based on the seven high-level information visualization tasks as described by Shneiderman [11]: overview, zoom, filter, details-on-demand, relate, history and extract. When designing tasks for the study, we refined three of these tasks into lower-level subtasks relevant to the hierarchical file system domain. Based on the zoom task, we designed a *Search* task where subjects needed to zoom into the visualization to find directories. Based on the relate task, we designed a *Count* task where subjects counted the number of files in directories. And finally, we designed a *Compare* task based on Shneiderman's overview task, where users compared two directories and selected the largest one.

We first describe the three visualizations used in the study. The study setup, including tasks, data sets, subjects, and procedures follow. After this, we report on the statistical analysis of the results. These results are then discussed, and conclusions about important factors are drawn. Finally, we review some related work in the area and point out future work.

2   The Visualizations

In order to be able to compare task support between the visualizations, all three 3D information visualizations used in our study visualize the same type of data, hierarchies. The chosen visualizations are all different in the way they visualize the hierarchical data. The Information Landscape is a "2.5 D" visualization, meaning that the tree layout is restricted to a flat surface. The Cam Tree is more of a true 3D visualization,

---

[1]also, the Department of Computer Science, Luleå University of Technology, Luleå, Sweden

using all dimensions to lay out the tree. Differing from the two others, the Information Cube does not display the data in a traditional tree structure. It instead fully exploits the possibilities of 3D space by representing the hierarchy as nested cubes.

2.1 The Information Landscape

Our implementation of the Information Landscape is based on the File System Navigator (fsn) from Silicon Graphics and the Harmony Information Landscape. These two information visualizations are similar, basically differing only in how they are used by the surrounding application.

In the Information Landscape, internal nodes are represented as pedestal shapes standing on a flat surface with lines connecting pedestals to form a tree. Leaves are represented as box shapes standing on the pedestals. This makes the pedestal cross-section proportional to the number of leaf children. The height of the boxes encodes an attribute such as the size of the data element represented by the box. Being a "2.5 D" visualization, the pedestals are restricted to a flat surface in 3D space. Only the box height makes use of the third dimension. Figure 3 shows the Information Landscape in our implementation.

Interactions in the Information Landscape include selecting boxes or pedestals with the mouse and "flying" up to a viewpoint close to the selected element. Our implementation of the Information Landscape does not include this custom navigation feature.

2.2 The Cam Tree

The Cam Tree displays hierarchies as trees of rectangular shapes representing internal nodes and leaves, connected by lines. Each subtree is laid out as a cone with its root at the top of the cone and the children along the cone base. Rectangles and cones are semi-transparent in order to reduce problems with occlusion. Figures 2 and 5 show the Cam Tree in our implementation.

Interactions with the Cam Tree include rotation of the tree when a node or leaf has been selected with the mouse. This brings the path to the selected rectangle closest to the user and highlights the rectangles on that path. The tree can also be pruned via a control panel with buttons.

Our implementation of the Cam Tree did not include any independent rotation of sub-trees, nor any pruning operations. Also, the original design included the shadow of the tree placed underneath the tree. We did not implement the shadow since its importance was said to be small.

2.3 The Information Cube

The Information Cube uses semi-transparent, nested cubes to represent leaves or internal nodes. The parent-child relationships are represented by nesting child cubes inside their parent cubes, scaling cubes to enclose the contained cubes. Textual labels are displayed on cube surfaces. Color and degree of transparency indicate the currently selected cube. Figure 4 shows the Information Cube in our implementation.

The original system is designed for use with special virtual reality equipment. The output can either be displayed stereoscopically or monoscopically with head motion tracking. The input device allows a model of the user's hand to be displayed within the visualization for grabbing, rotating, and pointing.

Our implementation includes no virtual reality equipment or stereoscopic display techniques. Consequently, the model of the user's hand and the associated affordances are not present.

3 Study Setup

We designed three tasks based on Shneiderman's seven high-level information visualization tasks. The three tasks were all related to the file-system application domain and were expected to reveal different factors affecting the task support of a 3D information visualization.

Task 1, Search: The subjects were instructed to find two directories and click on them in the visualization. This task is based on Shneiderman's *Zoom* task, since we expected that subjects would need to zoom into the visualization to look for the directories, and then zoom to the directory in order to click on it. We thought performance on this task would be affected by the degree that the visualization supported a global context while zooming in on a directory. The expectation was that the Cam Tree would provide the best support, while the Information Cube and the Information Landscape would suffer from the lack of global context.

Task 2, Count: The subjects were instructed to count the number of files in each of the two directories they found in the previous task. This task is based on Shneiderman's *Relate* task, since users had to understand parent-child relationship in the visualizations. Here, we expected that performance would be affected by the way the visualization separates directories and files. The Information Landscape was expected to be the best, and the Cam Tree worst.

Task 3, Compare: The subjects were instructed to compare the two directories and select the one that contained most descendants. This task was based on

Level	Directories	Files
0	1	0
1	3	5
2	7	10
3	4	25
4	0	20

Table 1: Data set description

Shneiderman's *Overview* task. The subjects had to gain a local overview of each directory to discover how many children it contained and a global overview of the two directories to simultaneously compare them. The performance for this task was expected to be affected by the support for getting an overview of the number of children. Here, the Information Cube was thought to give the least support since children on lower levels are occluded.

We implemented a visualization generator as described in [15]. The visualization generator takes hierarchical data as input, and creates any of the three different 3D visualizations in VRML2.0 format. Our implementations did not include any of the custom interaction or navigation features found in the original implementations. Instead we relied entirely on the VRML browser's interface for navigation and interaction. We used CosmoPlayer2.0 from SGI for the study. It offers all the basic navigation functions such as: moving in all directions, rotating, undoing movements and moving to preset viewpoints. By eliminating all custom navigation, the three visualizations were used under similar conditions. We also hoped to get an indication of the importance of custom navigation.

We then generated six different data sets, representing files and directories in a hierarchical file system. All six data sets were some permutation of the description in Table 1. The two directories involved in the three tasks were both located on level 2 in the tree. Using these six data sets as input to the visualization generator, we created one Cam Tree, one Information Cube, and one Information Landscape with each data set.

The user interface for this study consisted of a number of WWW pages generated by CGI scripts. Each WWW page contained a visualization displayed in an embedded CosmoPlayer browser plus a Java applet. The applet gave instructions and recorded times and answers.

The 25 subjects for the study were recruited from the student body at Luleå University of Technology. Subject ages ranged from 19 to 35, with a median age of 22 years. Four were female. Three of the subjects stated that they had been using computers 1-3 years, six for 3-6 years and 16 for more than six years. Most subjects also used computers frequently; 19 for more than 10 hours per week and none less than one hour per week. When asked if they had ever used software with 3D graphics, seven answered no and 18 yes.

Each subject spent about 1–1.5 hours with the study, including about 20 minutes of practice tasks. The six data sets were randomly assigned so that no data set was seen twice by the subject. The order in which the visualizations were presented was also randomized, but the subjects always performed the tasks twice with one visualization before moving on to the next. During the study, time per task and error frequency was recorded. The study leader also made notes of the subjects' behavior and comments. If the subject did not finish a task within five minutes, the subject was instructed to move on to the next task. Subjects were at all times allowed to abort a task if they felt they could not perform it without guessing.

After finishing all the tasks, a questionnaire form was displayed for the subject. It contained background questions about the subject such as age and computer experience. The subjects were also asked to rate the visualizations. Each visualization was given a rating from 1 to 7 on four different scales as seen in Figure 1.

4 Statistical Analysis

Due to technical problems during the study, results from two of the subjects were removed from the analysis. For the remaining, an ANOVA for the task times and a Chi-Squared Test for the error frequencies was performed.

4.1 Analysis of Task Times

A total of 45 tasks were either timed-out or aborted by the user. All these were tasks using the Information Cube. Assigning a fixed time of 5 minutes to these tasks caused a skewed distribution of the data, not the near-normal distribution needed for the ANOVA. We therefore replaced this censored data with simulated data, using the following procedure:

1. From the non-censored data, randomly select the number of times needed.

2. Find the median of the non-censored data.

3. Add the median to each of the randomly selected times.

4. Replace the censored data with these times.

Table 2 shows mean times for all three tasks. For the Information Cube, both the mean including 5 minute values and the mean with the simulated data are shown. The simulated data was used in the

	Search	Count	Compare
Info Land	20.4	42.8	24.7
Cam Tree	67.7	88.7	46.4
Info Cube, censored	219.4	246.8	166.0
Info Cube, simulated	226.4	291.3	160.6
Simulated values	18	20	7

Table 2: Mean task times, seconds

MAIN EFFECTS	F-Ratio	P-Value
Search Task		
dataset	2.24	0.0560
subject	1.52	0.0844
visualization	202.78	0.0000
sequence	1.36	0.2467
Count Task		
dataset	1.23	0.3022
subject	3.66	0.0000
visualization	259.51	0.0000
sequence	1.17	0.3280
Compare Task		
dataset	4.69	0.0007
subject	2.05	0.0091
visualization	100.11	0.0000
sequence	3.83	0.0033

Table 3: ANOVA tables

ANOVA. As can be seen, only seven values needed to be simulated for the *Compare* task. The random sampling procedure resulted in some lower-range values that had a strong overall effect on the small number of simulated values and resulted in a lower simulated mean.

We found that the variance was considerably larger for the Information Cube than for the two other visualizations. The ANOVA requires stable variances. To achieve this, we transformed the values with a logarithm function.

ANOVA tables for the three tasks can be found in Table 3. To block out unwanted effects, the ANOVA included effects of the different *datasets* and individual *subjects*. We also included the *sequence* of the visualization in the analysis. The *visualization* effect is in that way cleared of any contribution from the other effects.

Looking at the "P-Value" column in the ANOVA tables, we see that the p-value for the *visualization* effect in all cases is well below .01. This means that we can say, with 99% confidence that there is a significant difference between the times to perform the tasks with the tree visualizations. We also performed confidence interval analysis on the data at the 95% level. This analysis confirmed that for all tasks, the mean times among the different visualizations are distinctly different. The mean time is lowest for the Information

	Info Land	Cam Tree	Info Cube
Search			
No Error	46	46	28
Error	0 (0/0/0)	0 (0/0/0)	18 (0/17/1)
Skipped	0	0	0
Count			
No Error	46	36	10
Error	0 (0/0/0)	10 (10/0/0)	35 (15/17/3)
Skipped	0	0	1
Compare			
No Error	46	44	33
Error	0 (0/0/0)	0 (0/0/0)	9 (2/4/3)
Skipped	0	2	4

Table 4: Error Frequency Table (erroneous answers / timeouts / aborts)

Landscape, higher for the Cam tree, and highest for the Information Cube.

We also see that the *subject* effect is significant for the *Count* and *Compare* tasks. These two tasks required a lot of navigation. Some subjects managed navigation well, while others had difficulties with the CosmoPlayer controls.

For the *Compare* task, effects of *dataset* and *sequence* are also significant. In four of our six datasets, one of the two directories contained no subdirectory. These datasets showed the lowest mean times. Many of the subjects did not need to count files and directories for these datasets, but instead immediately chose the directory without a subdirectory. The *sequence* effect is very interesting. The lowest means were for the second, fourth, and sixth visualizations. Therefore, there is a significant learning effect for this task. Our observations and the comments from the subjects suggest that they learned to remember the relative sizes of the directories from the *Count* task, and used this knowledge in the *Compare* task. The first time with each visualization subjects were not able to do this, but the second time they had grown more familiar with the visualization and could use this strategy to improve performance.

4.2 Analysis of Error Frequencies

As errors, we counted erroneous answers (not applicable for the *Search* task), aborts, and timeouts. Since the Chi-Square Test requires the expected frequencies for each cell to be at least 5, we summed up the three types of errors into one row. In Table 4, the number of erroneous answers, timeouts, and aborts are shown within parentheses next to the sum of errors. The table also contains a row labeled "Skipped". The numbers in this row represent tasks that were ac-

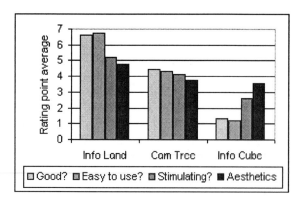

Figure 1: Subjects' ratings of the visualizations

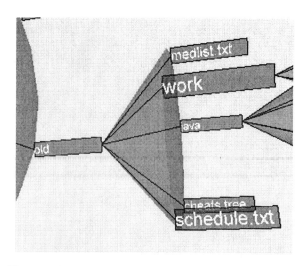

Figure 2: Separating files and directories in the Cam Tree

cidentally skipped by the subjects. For the *Compare* task, this row also includes four tasks for which subjects stated that they accidentally selected the wrong directory while navigating.

The Chi-Square Test was performed at the 99% level of confidence. For all three tasks, the Chi-Square Test showed that the error frequencies were indeed related to the visualization used to perform the task.

5 Discussion

So, were our initial expectations as described in Section 3 met? Overall, the answer is no. We can, however, see that some of the factors we anticipated did affect performance (Section 5.1).

But, as the statistical analysis of the results show, the Information Cube performed worst for all tasks, and the Information Landscape performed best. Looking at the subjects' ratings (Figure 1) we see that they were overall most satisfied with the Information Landscape, and least satisfied with the Information Cube. Our observations during the study also confirm this.

It seems factors that we had not taken into account, or had not expected to have such an influence, played an important role for the usability of the visualizations. Our results indicate that the most influential factor was *overview*. This can be further refined into *local* and *global* overview (Sections 5.2 and 5.3). Navigation also played an important role (Section 5.4).

5.1 Initial Expectations

For the *Search* task, we expected both the Information Landscape and the Information Cube to suffer due to lack of global context while zooming. This was however true only for the Information Cube. In the Information Landscape, subjects either did not need to zoom to find the directories, or they managed to find their way around the visualization without the global context.

Our initial expectation for the *Count* task was that the Cam Tree makes it difficult to separate files from directories. This is illustrated in Figure 2. The two rectangles labeled "work" and "java" are directories. The only indication of this is the cones attached to their right side. Looking at the error frequencies for the *Count* task, we note that this is the only task with errors using the Cam Tree. We believe that this indicates that our initial expectation was correct but that the effect of overview was more powerful.

For the *Compare* task, our initial expectation was that the Information Cube would perform worst since children on lower levels were occluded. It did indeed perform worst, but not more so than in the other two tasks. This indicates that both the expected lack of local overview and the lack of global overview affected task performance.

5.2 Local Overview

When examining a directory in detail, subjects had to use different strategies with the three visualizations. These strategies varied due to the degree to which the third dimension was used.

The Information Landscape is the "least" three dimensional of the visualizations. Here, a directory could often be examined without too much navigation. As a matter of fact, a majority of the subjects figured out that if they flew up above the Information Landscape and tilted down, the tree of directories and files virtually became a 2D visualization (Figure 3). This made counting files and directories faster and easier, since subjects did not need to move around in 3D space to look at objects from different angles.

The Information Cube is the "most" three dimensional of the visualizations. To examine a directory, subjects had to look into a directory cube from different angles to be able to see all the contained cubes. This was made even more difficult by the fact that adjacent cubes would block the subjects' line of sight at times (Figure 4). Several of the subjects explicitly requested the possibility to filter out all other cubes.

The Cam Tree's degree of usage for the third dimension lies between that of the Information Cube and that of the Information Landscape. Consequently, strategies to examine a directory varied. Subjects were at times able to get an overview of the contents of a directory from one single position, but just as often they needed to navigate around the tree to make sure they had seen everything in the subtree cone (Figure 5). Adjacent cones blocking the line-of-sight were not as big a problem. But when we informed subjects about the pruning function in the original design, most said that it would have made the tasks easier.

5.3 Global Overview

In addition to experiencing a lack of *local* overview when studying a directory in detail, subjects also suffered disorientation and lack of *global* overview when navigating. The nature of our tasks which involved two directories in a file system made it necessary for the subjects to navigate between directories while performing the tasks.

We observed that the subjects had big difficulties with this in the Information Cube. The lack of a global context caused them to frequently get lost and head back to the preset viewpoint outside the root cube, only to get lost again due to directory occlusion. Some subjects explicitly asked for an overview map so that they would be able to orient themselves.

Contrary to our expectations, subjects did not experience this loss of global context when using the Information Landscape. They always had a sense of "up" and "down" and could quickly find their way again on the few occasions they got lost. (We must, however, remember that the data sets used in our study were relatively small. 3D visualizations are often claimed to be useful for large data sets, so we cannot say whether this result would have been different with 100 times more data.)

In the Cam Tree, the horizontal orientation of the tree seemed to provide a similar aid in orientation.

5.4 Navigation

As previously mentioned, no custom navigation was available to the subjects in the study. The Cosmo-Player navigation controls were not easy to master for most of the subjects in spite of the practice tasks. It

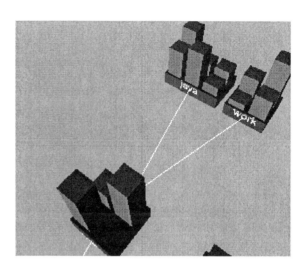

Figure 3: Local overview in the Information Landscape

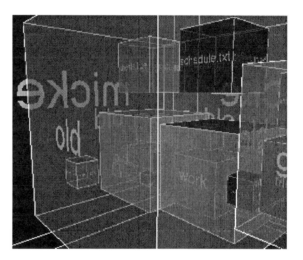

Figure 4: Local overview in the Information Cube

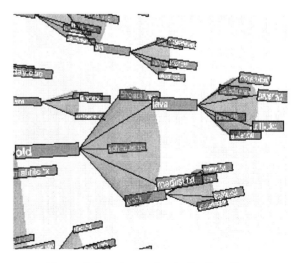

Figure 5: Local overview in the Cam Tree

is indeed possible that an efficient custom navigation might have improved the performance for those visualizations that required a lot of navigation to overcome the lack of global context.

After the study was finished, we informed the subjects about the navigation features offered by the original visualizations, and asked them if they thought it would have helped. For the Information Landscape, most thought that it was easy enough as it was. For the Information Cube, most thought it would be interesting to try the Virtual Reality equipment, but no one seemed convinced that this would help. Only for the Cam Tree did the subjects reply that features such as independent rotation of the cones and pruning the tree would have made a big difference.

5.5 Conclusion

To summarize, our observations show that the possibility to get a good local and global overview is the single most important factor in supporting the types of tasks that we studied. One way to overcome a lack of overview is, as suggested by some of our subjects, to provide an overview map of some kind.

Custom navigation might also be a partial solution to the problems, but it is not clear how this custom navigation should work. It is clear, however, that the closer we get to a "true 3D" visualization, the more important it is to have an efficient navigation method.

6 Related Work

Information visualization designs similar to the Cam Tree include hyperbolic-space displays [8] of directed graphs with cycles such as the WWW. The SeeNet3D information visualization application [4] visualizes global networks on a sphere and local networks on a map.

The Bead system [3] is similar to the Information Landscape. It displays bibliographic data with documents as cubes interconnected by triangles in a landscape-like space.

Nested designs, such as the Information Cube, are more uncommon. The n-Vision system [5] visualizes data with more than three dimensions. It uses nested 3D coordinate systems with axes. The Web Forager and the Web Book [2] adopt a metaphorical nesting. WWW pages are contained in books that in turn can be contained in book shelves in a 3D room.

Previous 3D user interface studies concentrate on the lower level cognitive aspects. One such study [6] suggests that users' understanding of a 3D structure improves when they can manipulate the structure. Yet

another [14] indicates that displaying data in three dimensions instead of two can make it easier for users to understand the data. Our study complements this approach by looking at higher level aspect – task support. Task support in 2D information visualizations has been studied (for example [13]), but task-oriented comparative studies of 3D information visualizations are still scarce.

7 Future Work

As can be expected, this study has raised more questions than it has answered. Foremost is the question of the actual usefulness of 3D user interfaces. We believe that for the types of tasks and data sets that we have used in this study, a 3D user interface is probably not preferable to a 2D user interface. But can 3D be useful for other types of tasks? For huge data sets? In order to make use of the possibilities offered to us by 3D user interfaces, these issues should be addressed. The results from the subjects' ratings of the visualizations point out an interesting angle (Figure 1). The ratings for *aesthetics* and *stimulation* were not so different between the visualizations. So perhaps, 3D user interfaces are most suitable in applications that are more about exploration and long-term learning, where stimulating, aesthetically pleasing interfaces can be expected to be important.

It is clear that navigation is crucial in 3D user interfaces. It is also clear that "one fits all" is not true – the navigation features must be adapted to the user interface at hand, and, more importantly, to the user tasks. Navigation in 3D and Virtual Reality is being researched, but the importance of tailoring the navigation to the application, tasks, and users, should be explored more.

8 Acknowledgments

We would like to thank the subjects for their participation in our study. Thanks also to Iva Tzankova, Quality Technology and Statistics, Luleå University of Technology, for guidance in the design and statistical analysis of the study. We also owe thanks to Brian Johnson for making his dissertation [7] available. It was helpful in designing and analyzing our study. Finally, we would like to thank Carl Rollo for his help in proofreading our drafts.

This work was partly performed under NUTEK grant number P10552-1.

References

[1] Keith Andrews. Visualizing Cyberspace: Information Visualization in the Harmony Internet Browser. In

Proceedings of Information Visualization, pages 97–104. IEEE, 1995.

[2] Stuart K Card, George G Robertson, and William York. The WebBook and the Web Forager: An Information Workspace for the World-Wide Web. In *Proceedings of CHI'96*, pages 111–117. ACM, 1996.

[3] Matthew Chalmers, Robert Ingram, and Christoph Pfranger. Adding Imageability Features to Information Displays. In *Proceedings of UIST'96*, pages 33–39. ACM, 1996.

[4] Kenneth C Cox, Stephen G Eick, and Taosong He. 3D Geographic Network Displays. *Sigmod Record*, 25(4):50–54, December 1996.

[5] Steven Feiner and Clifford Beshers. Worlds within Worlds: Metaphors for Exploring n-Dimensional Virtual Worlds. In *Proceedings of UIST'90*, pages 76–83. ACM, 1990.

[6] Geoffrey S Hubona, Gregory W Shirah, and David G Fout. 3D Object Recognition with Motion. In *Extended Abstracts of CHI'97*, pages 345–346. ACM, 1997.

[7] Brian Johnson. *Treemaps: Visualizing Hierarchical and Categorical Data*. PhD thesis, University of Maryland, USA, 1993.

[8] Tamara Munzner and Paul Burchard. Visualizing the Structure of the World Wide Web in 3D Hyperbolic Space. In *Proceedings of VRML '95*, pages 33–38. ACM, 1995.

[9] Jun Rekimoto and Mark Green. The Information Cube: Using Transparency in 3D Information Visualization. In *Proceedings of the Third Annual Workshop on Information Technologies & Systems (WITS'93)*, pages 125–132, 1993.

[10] George G Robertson, Jock D Mackinlay, and Stuart K Card. Cone Trees: Animated 3D Visualizations of Hierarchical Information. In *Proceedings of SIGCHI'91*, pages 189–194. ACM, 1991.

[11] Ben Shneiderman. The Eyes Have It: A Task by Data Type Taxonomy for Information Visualizations. In *Proceedings of 1996 IEEE Visual Languages*, pages 336–343. IEEE, 1996.

[12] J Tesler and S Strasnick. FSN: 3D Information Landscapes, 1992. Man page entry, Silicon Graphics, Inc.

[13] David Turo and Brian Johnson. Improving the Visualization of Hierarchies with Treemaps: Design Issues and Experimentation. In *Proceedings of Visualization '92*, pages 124–131, Boston, MA, October 1992.

[14] Colin Ware and Glenn Franck. Viewing a Graph in a Virtual Reality Display is Three Times as Good as a 2D Diagram. In *Proceedings of 1994 IEEE Visual Languages*, pages 182–183. IEEE, 1994.

[15] Ulrika Wiss, David Carr, and Håkan Jonsson. Evaluating Three-Dimensional Information Visualization Designs: A Case Study of Three Designs. In *Proceedings of 1998 IEEE Conference on Information Visualization, IV'98*, pages 137 – 144, London, England, July 1998. IEEE.

Visualizing World-Wide Web Search Engine Results

Sougata Mukherjea and Yoshinori Hara,
C&C Research Laboratories,
NEC USA Inc.,
San Jose, Ca, USA
E-mail: {sougata,hara}@ccrl.sj.nec.com

Abstract

Most of the popular WWW search engines show the documents that match the users' queries as pages of scrolled lists. If lots of information are retrieved this is not very user-friendly. Moreover, there is no mechanism to easily determine documents linked to the retrieved documents or keywords related to the query terms. This paper presents a system that allows the user to visualize various related information for the search results. We also introduce a focus+context visualization technique for the search space of WWW queries.

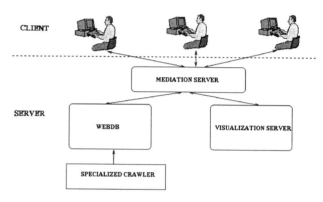

Figure 1. System Architecture

KEYWORDS: Query Result Visualization, World-Wide Web Search, Focus+Context Visualization.

1. Introduction

Although search engines are one of the best methods to retrieve information of interest from the World-Wide Web, most popular search engines only retrieve documents that match the user specified query terms. Sometimes the user may be interested in other related information. For example, they may be interested in the pages that are linked to the retrieved pages; they may also be interested in keywords that are related to the query terms.

Another problem with the search engines is that they show the results as pages of scrolled lists. With the explosive growth in the amount of information that is available on the World-Wide Web, many queries result in a large number of retrieved documents. It is very tedious for the users to go through pages of scrolled lists to find the relevant information.

This paper presents a system that allows the user to navigate through the result space of a World-Wide Web search to find the relevant information. The user can look at the documents connected by links to the retrieved documents.

They can also look at keywords relevant to the query terms. Visualization is used to present the results because it allows people to use perceptual rather than cognitive reasoning in carrying out tasks [19].

This paper also introduces a visualization technique, **Card-Vis**, that is useful to show the search space to the user. The technique is based on the metaphor of a pack of playing cards and uses the *focus+context* technique to handle a large amount of information. For the focus or the section of the information space that is of interest to the user, we show the details. The 3rd dimension is used to show a large amount of contextual information.

The next section gives an overview of our system. Section 3 introduces the visualization technique by showing how it can be used to visualize World-Wide Web search engine results. Section 4 presents related work. Finally section 5 is the conclusion.

2. System Overview

Our system is based on client and server mediation architecture similar to [7]. A mediation server facilitates the interaction between users and various service providers. The me-

```
<query_result>
    <query_term>.....</query_term>
          ......
    <document>
       <url>...</url>
       <title>...</title>
       <linkin>...</linkin>
          ....
       <linkout>...</linkout>
          ....
       <keyword>....</keyword>
          ....
    </document>
       ....
    <semantically_similar_kwd>
       <keyword>.....</keyword>
       <document_url>...</document_url>
             .....
    </semantically_similar_kwd>
       .....
    <syntactically_related_kwd>
       <keyword>.....</keyword>
       <document_url>...</document_url>
             .....
    </syntactically_related__kwd>
          .....
</query_result>
```

Figure 2. Query Result Format for Visualization

diation server forwards users' requests to the corresponding servers based on users' preferences and functional requirements. An overview of the system architecture is illustrated in Figure 1. The components of the system are presented in this section.

2.1. Specialized Crawler

A specialized crawler is used to gather information from the World-Wide Web. Unlike traditional crawlers used by the search engines whose role is to gather as much information as possible, our crawler only gathers pages related to the users' interests. For example, we can gather all Web pages relevant to Visualization or all pages related to Computer Science conferences.

2.2. WebDB

One essential server is the WebDB hypermedia database system [11] since it provides indexing of the gathered information and supports comprehensive database-like query functionalities. WebDB has two levels: a *logical* level consisting modules for logical Web document modeling and storage, the query language translator, and an XML document

generator; and a *physical* level consisting modules for internal class representations, object depository, query processing, and an internal query result class generator.

In WebDB, we view and model the Web as a labeled directed graph $G_{web} = (V_{web}, E_{web})$, where the vertices (V) denote the pages and the edges (E) denotes the hyperlinks between these pages. The vertices have information, including title, keywords, and other metadata. The edges are links from source pages to destination pages. We represent the document contents and Web structure using an object-oriented data model and implement *WebDB* on top of NEC PERCIO OODBMS.

When a document is passed to *WebDB* by the crawler, link and keyword information is extracted and maintained in the database. For each keyword in the databases, we perform keyword co-occurrence analysis to derive syntactically related keywords (e.g. car and Toyota) and consult an online lexical dictionary to derive semantically similar keywords (e.g. car and automobile). These relationships are maintained using pointers.

During querying, the system can traverse from the user specified keywords to related keywords and from the retrieved documents to linked documents easily. These information help the user to gain a better understanding of the search space. Instead of seeing the information in a series of HTML pages, the user can also visualize the data.

2.3. Visualization Engine

The visualization engine supports various languages for generating the visualizations. For example Java can be used and the resultant visualizations can be shown as an applet. We also allow the use of *Virtual Reality Markup Language (VRML)*, which can be shown in a VRML browser like SGI's CosmoPlayer.

To support various visualization functionalities, we define a protocol for data exchange between the visualization engine and *WebDB*. XML is used as the format in our implementation. The data exchange format is given in Figure 2. This allows the visualization engine to be integrated with other systems as long as they follow the same format.

With the augmented query results, the visualization engine has many options to display the query results based on users' preferences. For example, as shown in Figure 3, the user can visualize the neighborhood of any retrieved Web page. One of the retrieved pages for a specialized search engine for visualization was the homepage of the visualization group of the Lawrence Berkeley National Laboratory. The user can visualize the link neighborhood of (nodes linked to and from) the page as shown in Figure 3(a). The user can also determine pages that are semantically similar to this page.

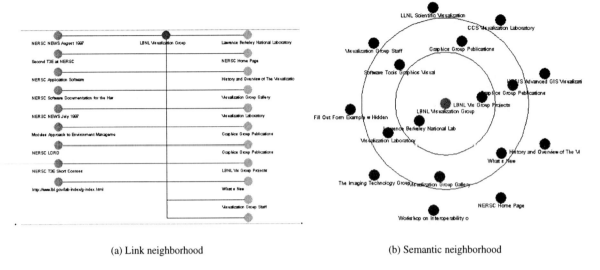

(a) Link neighborhood   (b) Semantic neighborhood

Figure 3. Showing the neighborhood of a Web page (Url *http://www-vis.lbl.gov*)

(Similarity is determined using the vector space model [18]). This semantic neighborhood can be shown in a **Bulls-Eye visualization** as shown in Figure 3(b). In this visualization the document of interest is at the center; the position of the other documents are determined by how similar they are to the main document. The next section introduces another visualization technique to show the entire search space.

3. Card Visualization

Sometimes the user is interested in getting an overview of the whole search space. The objective will be to show the structure of the retrieved Web pages as well as how these pages are relevant to the main keywords of the search space.

Considering the information space as a graph, we can first determine its *connected components*. Assuming that a link exists between two nodes if they are related, these connected components will have related nodes. A typical WWW search will result in many connected components. We have developed a visualization technique that is suitable for such an information space whose data organization is a group of disconnected graphs.

Figure 4 is an example of this visualization technique. It shows the results of a query to a database consisting of Computer Science conference Web pages indexed by WebDB. Each graph of the search space is shown in a card. One card is at the focus and shown at the top. The nodes and links comprising this graph are also shown. The nodes are shown as cubes and labeled by the HTML page titles. Moving the mouse over them shows their URLs at the status area of the VRML browser and clicking on them retrieves the cor-

responding URLs. The other graphs are shown in the context by arranging them in different planes in the 3rd dimension. The position in the 3rd dimension is determined by how relevant the nodes of the graph are to the original query terms. The titles of their main nodes are also shown. (The node with the maximum number of links is assumed to be the main node of a component).

The query terms are shown at the top as spheres. The other related keywords are also shown as cylinders. Their sizes indicate how closely they are related to the query terms. Initially one of the query terms as well as all the nodes which are relevant to the query term in the focus card are highlighted. The cards in the context are also highlighted if they have nodes relevant to the query term. Thus, in Figure 4 the query term *"web"* and nodes and graphs relevant to it are highlighted. The focus graph shows pages related with the WWW8 conference and the links between them.

The visualization allows two types of user interaction. (We use Javascript to program the interactions).

- The user can click on any of the related keywords. The nodes in the focus graph are highlighted if they are relevant; the other cards are also highlighted if they have relevant nodes.

- The user can click on any of the context cards to bring them into focus.

Thus in Figure 5 the user has clicked on the sphere for the keyword *database*; all the nodes and context cards relevant to the keyword were highlighted. The user has brought into focus a graph with pages related to the SIGMOD conference; note that a related conference (PODS) also belongs to this graph.

402

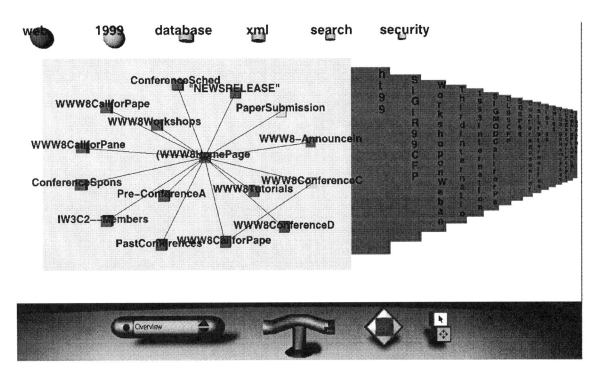

Figure 4. Visualizing the results of a query with the term "1999" and "web" to a WebDB database containing Computer Science conference Web pages. Initially, pages for the WWW8 conference is at the focus.

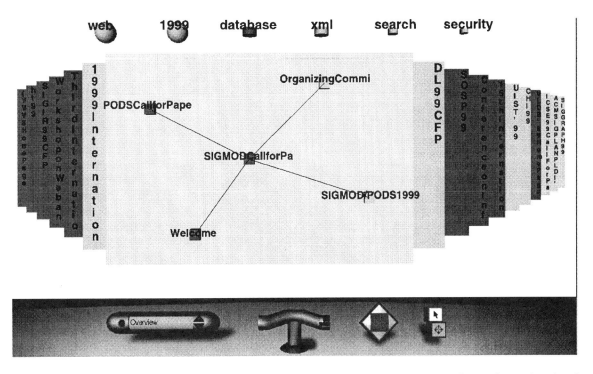

Figure 5. Visualization with *database* as the selected keyword. The user has also selected a database conference as the focus.

This visualization is based on the metaphor of how a player arranges a group of playing cards. One card is kept at the top and the other cards are arranged in such a manner that the main information (suit and color) of them are easily apparent. The user also has the ability of bringing any card to the top.

4. Related Work

4.1. Focus+Context Visualization

A popular approach for visualizing abstract information is to use focus+context techniques by which the information of interest to the user is shown in detail, smoothly integrated with other context information. By balancing local detail and global context, this technique can display information at multiple levels of abstraction simultaneously. An example of this technique is the fisheye-view concept [6]. The focus+context technique has been used to develop visualizations of different data structures. Examples include perspective walls [13] for visualizing linear data; document lens [17], a 3D visualization strategy for textual documents; table lens [16], a method for presenting tabular information and hyperbolic browser [10] for visualizing trees. A focus+context visualization for World-Wide Web nodes has also been developed [15]. In this paper we discuss a visualization technique that is suited for a collection of disconnected graphs.

4.2. Visualizing Web Sites

Several systems for visualizing WWW sites have been developed. Examples includes Navigational View Builder [14], Harmony Internet Browser [1], Narcissus [9] and WebCutter [12]. Since Web sites are large graphs and visualizing large graphs is difficult [3], these systems use various data simplification techniques like filtering and abstraction. The CardVis technique is not suited for visualizing large graphs. It is ideal for a collection of disconnected graphs and thus is a good technique to visualize Web search results.

4.3. Visualizing Search Results

Unique interfaces for viewing information retrieval results have been developed. Recent examples include SenseMaker [2] and Cat-a-Cone [8]. SenseMaker is an interface for information exploration across heterogeneous sources in a digital library. Cat-a-Cone is a 3D interface that integrates searching and browsing of very large category hierarchies with their associated text collections. Another interesting approach is the WebBook [4], which potentially allows the

results of the search to be organized and manipulated in various ways in a 3D space. These systems show the usefulness of visualization for better understanding of the results of search engines.

Visualization techniques for World-Wide Web search results are also being developed. For example, the WebQuery system [5] visualizes the results of a search query along with all pages that link to or are linked to by any page in the original result set. On the other hand, Alta Vista (*http://www.altavista.com*) shows the keywords related to the original query terms. However, the World-Wide Web has two aspects: the contents of the Web pages as well as the links connecting different Web pages. Therefore, an effective visualization should show the user both the content and the structural information.

5. Conclusion

We have presented a system that provides specialized search on the World-Wide Web. It allows the user various techniques to visualize and navigate through the search results as well as other related information. We believe that the combination of visualization and searching will make it easier for the user to retrieve relevant information.

The paper also introduced a focus+context visualization technique called CardVis which is very suitable to visualize Web search results which can be organized as a collection of disconnected graphs. The visualization presents the details of the structure and contents of the focus graph. Moreover, it provides the user with an idea about the other graphs in the information space. The user can also bring any graph into focus. Therefore, we believe that the visualization is quite useful to gain an understanding of the search space.

Future work is planned along various direction:

- We believe that the CardVis technique can be generalized for visualizing information that can be clustered based on two criteria of similarity. Cards representing the clusters for one criteria of similarity can be arranged in different planes in the 3rd dimension. One of these cards will be in the focus and at the top. The details of the focus card will be shown to the user. To enable the user to get an understanding of the contents of the other clusters, their labels should be displayed. The labels of the clusters for the second criteria of similarity will be shown at the top. If one of these clusters is selected, all nodes in the focus card that belong to this cluster will be highlighted. The other cards will be also highlighted if they have relevant nodes.

- If the information space is really big, the visualizations may be too cluttered to be useful. Therefore, we are exploring effective abstraction and filtering techniques.

- Usability studies are also essential to determine the actual usefulness of the system.

References

[1] K. Andrews. Visualizing Cyberspace: Information Visualization in the Harmony Internet Browser. In *Proceedings of the 1995 Information Visualization Symposium*, pages 97–104, Atlanta, GA, 1995.

[2] M.Q.W. Baldonado and T. Winograd. SenseMaker: An Information-Exploration Interface Supporting the Contextual Evolution of a User's Interest. In *Proceedings of the ACM SIGCHI '97 Conference on Human Factors in Computing Systems*, pages 11–18, Atlanta, Ga, March 1997.

[3] G.D. Battista, P. Eades, R. Tamassia, and I.G. Tollis. Algorithms for Drawing Graphs: an Annotated Bibliography. Technical report, Brown University, June 1993.

[4] S.K. Card, G.G. Robertson, and W. York. The Web-Book and the Web Forager: An Information Workspace for the World-Wide Web. In *Proceedings of the ACM SIGCHI '96 Conference on Human Factors in Computing Systems*, pages 112–117, Vancouver, Canada, April 1996.

[5] J. Carriere and R. Kazman. Searching and Visualizing the Web through Connectivity. In *Proceedings of the Sixth International World-Wide Web Conference*, pages 701–711, Santa Clara, CA, April 1997.

[6] G.W. Furnas. Generalized Fisheye Views. In *Proceedings of the ACM SIGCHI '86 Conference on Human Factors in Computing Systems*, pages 16–23, Boston, MA, April 1986.

[7] Ashish Gupta. Junglee: Integrating Data of All Shapes and Sizes. In *Proceedings of the 14th International Conference on Data Engineering*, Orlando, Florida, USA, February 1998.

[8] M.A. Hearst and K. Chandu. Cat-a-Cone: An Interactive Interface for Specifying Searches and Viewing Retrieval Results using a Large Category Hierarchy. In *Proceedings of the ACM SIGIR '97 Conference on Research and Development in Information Retrieval*, pages 246–255, Philadelphia, Pa, July 1997.

[9] R.J. Hendley, N.S. Drew, A.M. Wood, and R. Beale. Narcissus: Visualizing Information. In *Proceedings of the 1995 Information Visualization Symposium*, pages 90–96, Atlanta, GA, 1995.

[10] J. Lamping, R. Rao, and P. Pirolli. A Focus+Context Technique Based on Hyperbolic Geometry for Visualizing Large Hierarchies. In *Proceedings of the ACM SIGCHI '95 Conference on Human Factors in Computing Systems*, pages 401–408, Denver, CO, May 1995.

[11] W. Li and J Shim. Facilitating Complex Web Queries through Visual Interfaces and Query Relaxation. *Computer Networks and ISDN Systems. Special Issue on the Seventh International World-Wide Web Conference, Brisbane, Australia*, 30(1-7):149–159, April 1998.

[12] Y. Maarek and I.Z.B. Shaul. WebCutter: A System for Dynamic and Tailorable Site Mapping. In *Proceedings of the Sixth International World-Wide Web Conference*, pages 713–722, Santa Clara, CA, April 1997.

[13] J. D. Mackinlay, S.K. Card, and G.G. Robertson. Perspective Wall: Detail and Context Smoothly Integrated. In *Proceedings of the ACM SIGCHI '91 Conference on Human Factors in Computing Systems*, pages 173–179, New Orleans, LA, April 1991.

[14] S. Mukherjea and J.D. Foley. Visualizing the World-Wide Web with the Navigational View Builder. *Computer Networks and ISDN Systems. Special Issue on the Third International World-Wide Web Conference, Darmstadt, Germany*, 27(6):1075–1087, April 1995.

[15] S. Mukherjea and Y. Hara. Focus+Context Views of World-Wide Web Nodes. In *Proceedings of the Eight ACM Conference on Hypertext*, pages 187–196, Southampton, England, April 1997.

[16] R. Rao and S.K. Card. The Table Lens: Merging Graphical and Symbolic Representations in an Interactive Focus+Context Visualization for Tabular Information. In *Proceedings of the ACM SIGCHI '94 Conference on Human Factors in Computing Systems*, pages 318–322, Boston, MA, April 1994.

[17] G.G. Robertson and J.D. Mackinlay. The Document Lens. In *Proceedings of ACM Symposium on User Interface Software and Technology '93*, pages 101–108, Atlanta, GA, 1993.

[18] G. Salton and M.J. McGill. *Introduction to Modern Information Retrieval*. McGraw-Hill, 1983.

[19] K.J. Vincente and J. Rasmussen. The Ecology of Human Machine Systems: II. Mediating "Direct Perception" in Complex Domain. *Ecological Psychology*, 2:207–249, 1990.

Session 2-11

Digital Art

Chair
Carlos R. Morales
Purdue University, USA

Mirroring Medusa: *Counterveillance* in <u>ShootingBack</u>

Jieun Rhee

Department of Art Hisory, Boston University, 725 Commonwealth Ave. Boston, MA 02215
jnrhee@bu.edu

Abstract

In our society, apparati of electronic surveillance and satellite systems pervade almost every sector of our public and private lives. Information concerning individuals is controlled mostly by institutions, serving bureaucratic or corporate interest. This paper examines the possibilities of counter-surveillance in socio-cultural practices through Steve Mann's <u>ShootingBack</u>. In this 'meta-documentary,' Mann dares to shoot back at the power of institutions and capital by recording the very devices of surveillance (e.g., surveillance cameras) with his tiny TV camera NetCam, which is hidden in his eyeglasses and connected to his wearable computer. This 'shooting' usually provokes quarrels with the clerks or the security guards. NetCam transmits the whole situation to share simultaneously with others who have access to his website. Through this skirmish with authority, we can examine the structure of omnipresent, 'capillary' power and grope for the possibilities for counterveillance via World-Wide Web.

(I)t was Medusa's gaze that was endowed with the power of turning to stone all who came within its purview (....) Perseus contrived to steal this power for himself (....) This he accomplished by means of a ruse: using his shield as a mirror, he reflected the deadly gaze back upon itself, whereupon Medusa was immediately---or so the narrative proposes---petrified. Turned against itself, Medusa's power turns out to be her vulnerability, and Perseus's vulnerability, his strength.

(Craig Owens, "The Medusa Effect, or, The Specular Ruse")

In the society in which we live, technology can no longer be conceived as neutral. It *is* authority. The optimism of global communication and open distribution of information still sounds attractive, but information is controlled by institutions serving mainly bureaucratic or corporate interest. In our society, power is not centered around the physical existence of a monarch or a hierarchical structure of a court. Rather, it takes a "capillary form of existence" which permeates every sector of our public and private life [1]. Surveillance, in this context, is a strategy of power which controls society by observing the body of individuals. Imbricated with the network of surveillance, such as apparati of electronic surveillance and satellite systems, individuals are subject to the new panopticon, the omniscient, omnipresent god of advanced capitalism. In this network, the powerful gaze of the new panopticon not only regulates the possibility of violation of the norms that authorities pose, but also infiltrate the norms into individuals through the process of "internalization" [2]. In this paper, I would examine how individuals counteract, via socio-cultural practices, to the omnipresent surveillance, the vehicle of the "capillary" yet gigantic power. Steve Mann's 'meta-documentary' <u>ShootingBack</u> suggests several significant aspects of the issue of surveillance and *counterveillance*.

On the Aegis of Minerva

Steve Mann, a media artist and a professor in Electrical Engineering at the University of Toronto, dares to shoot back at the immeasurable power of institutions and capital by recording the very devices of surveillance (e.g., surveillance cameras in a department store) with his inventions which he aptly calls "rigs." He equips himself with a covert video recording system concealed in his eyeglasses and with an 'underwearable' computer inside his pants (fig. 1 and 2). A small handset device he carries controls every shooting process while he is on the go. The pictures taken along the way are directly transmitted to his World-Wide Web site via air waves. Any person who accesses Mann's webpages can see what Mann sees in the first-person point of view.[1]

Steve Mann goes into stores such as Seven-Eleven or WalMart and institutions where the photographing is implicitly or explicitly prohibited. He carries his *NetCam* and *WearComp* along with an outmoded potable camcorder. This bulky camcorder functions as a mere prop, while the real recording is actually being done by the *NetCam* in his eyeglasses. In most cases, security guards or the representatives of the institution try to stop him taking pictures of their security devices (usually the surveillance cameras). Interesting conversations, and often quarrels, ensue between Steve Mann and the employees when Mann persistently questions the authorities behind the surveillance camera who are presumably observing others while preventing others from watching them. During these live debates, Mann rests his hand-held camcorder, while the *NetCam* captures the whole situation and transmits the pictures to his website. This is Mann's "meta-documentary — a documentary about making a documentary about video surveillance," ShootingBack [3, 4].[2]

Mann interrupts corporate culture's authority by generating disturbance in its very locus of surveillance with his wearable *NetCam*. Armed with advanced technology, he holds up a mirror to the surveillant authority by spotting and recording the very devices of surveillance. The fact that we are being watched (in a department store or other institution) has been already naturalized as a part of our everyday lives. But the acknowledgment of us being watched through Mann's website reveals this process as suppressive and violating.

Surveillance has become a more and more important issue in terms of the tactics of power to increase the efficiency of its reign over the individual constituents of the society. According to Michel Foucault, the shift in the embodiment of power from a monarch or a court to a more subtle "capillary form of existence" brought an emphasis on the techniques of surveillance as an effective means of ruling [1, 5]. Power found the system of surveillance as a much more economic and safer way of control than the previous public exhibition of punishment, which had a lot of negative effects besides its high costs. From Jeremy Bentham's Panopticon [6] to Mark Poster's "superpanopticon" [7], the technique and rhetoric of surveillance have been extraordinarily elaborated. As Shoshana Zuboff rightly acknowledges, the subjects of surveillance often show "anticipatory conformity" proving that the standards of ruling are "internalized" in themselves [2, 8].

In this regard, critical discourses on surveillance have surged in the 1980s and 1990s. Early in 1973, James Rule worried about the nightmarish Orwellian society imbricated with the network of surveillance [9]. Anthony Giddens [10] and Gary Marx [11] delve into the Static surveillance. Giddens acknowledges two major loci of surveillance as bureaucratic administration and the capitalist workplace; together they work as "the twin process of surveillance" which reveal the historical intertwining of "the capitalist labor contract with the state monopoly of violence" [8, 10]. Marx's analysis of American undercover police is yet another insight of the panoptic shift, which he indicates as "diffusing into the society at large" [11]. On the other hand, Shoshana Zuboff seeks the parallel of authority as "spiritual basis of power" in the technology as "material basis of power." Here the core of the contemporary management technique, she argues, is panopticism. According to Zuboff, the omnipresent digital gaze of computerized information systems replaces the authority of supervisor and draws compliance from the subjects of the systems who have been already "internalized" into the norms of the systems by using them without much trouble [2]. Her use of the term "internalization" echoes Foucaulian "interiorisation" [1].[3] He explains the function of power as follows.

(...)power(...) is not that, which makes the difference between those who exclusively possess and retain it, and those who do not have it and submit to it. (....) Power is employed and exercised through a net-like organization. And not only do individuals circulate between its treads; they are always in the position of simultaneously undergoing and exercising this power. (...) In other words,

---

[1] It is interactive, of course. His wife can send a message to get some food when she sees the local market through the picture he is transmitting. The message appears on a tiny projection of a window which functions as a screen on his darkglasses's interior.

[2] See also Mann, " Smart Clothing: The Wearable Computer and WearCam", *Personal Technologies* (March 1997), and "Wearable Computing as means for Personal Empowerment", a keynote address for The First International Conference on Wearable Computing, ICWC-98 (May 12-13, 1998) Fairfax VA.

---

[3] The basis of Zuboff's assumption is the equal — or at least seemingly equal — access to the information for both the management and the workers. On the contrary, Foucault's analysis on "normalization" gives more subtle pictures of the scene.

individuals are the vehicles of power, not its points of application. (Foucault, Power/Knowledge, 1980, 98)

According to his interpretation, power does not flow only in one direction. The operation of power is not the one from the center to the periphery or from the top to the bottom. The individuals are not always passively submissive to the norms of power, but they are in fact the subjects who are practicing the norms in their everyday lives. This is what particularly empowers Foucaulian 'capillary power.' Since power is not centralized but permeated in every sector, every trajectory, and every field of life, its omnipresent "micro-mechanisms" bolster power's polymorphous structure with more intact operation on the respective bodies of individuals. And also, it is the beauty of this "capillary power" that it treats the individual as the bearer and practitioner of power via the process of "interiorisation" [1]. "Interiorisation," in Foucaulian view of panopticism, is allotting dispersed power to the individuals and making them participate in the power operation in the surveillance network as a respective "inspecting gaze." Here the individuals can be the overseers of each other; "each individual thus exercising this surveillance over, and against," oneself [1].

The power can flow both in centrifugal and centripetal ways; the sums of individuals' watching consist of institutional surveillance. The *counterveillance* that the remainder of this paper discusses founds its discourse on these reciprocal ways of power operation. If what we are dealing with is a capillary power in a specific locus of our everyday lives, individuals could possibly carry out their own skirmishes with this pervasive yet substantial power. Since the battle is fought on the capillary loci, the strategies should be set up for skirmishes fought at the individual level. In ShootingBack, Mann engages in this everyday skirmish with corporate authority.

Mann legitimately calls his documenting performance "reflectionism," a term which he borrows from the Situationist[4] concept of *detournement*, which is "re-situating ordinary everyday objects in a disorienting

fashion in order to challenge our pre-conceived notions and cultural biases" [3]. In ShootingBack, a hidden camera installed in a pair of eyeglasses becomes a weapon for disturbing the authorities' surveillance cameras. Mann defines the defense strategies of authorities' "video surveillance superhighway" as follows.

1. **Secrecy**: Cameras are often hidden in whole or in part. The security industry is itself also often not subject to open debate or peer-review;
2. **Rhetoric**: "Public safety," "loss prevention," or "For YOUR protection you are being videotaped;
3. **Constancy**: Department store clerks don't follow you around with camcorders; rather, video surveillance is present in a "matter of fact" manner, as part of the architecture's prosthetic territory;
4. **Appeal to a higher and unquestionable authority**: "I trust you and know you would never shoplift, but my manager installed the cameras; or, "We trust you, but our insurance company requires the cameras;"
5. **Criminalization of the critic**: "Why are you so paranoid — you're not trying to steal something are you?" [3]

The strategies for individual *counterveillance* mirror that of surveillance.

1. **Secrecy**: completely covert embodiments of the *WearComp/WearCam* invention have been created, and used in places where photography is strictly prohibited[...]
2. **Rhetoric**: the rhetoric of personal safety is used to mirror the rhetoric of public safety.
3. **Constancy**: the devices are wearable, rather than carried, so that either they cannot be discerned by others, or it cannot be determined whether they are in actual use or not at any given time. The devices are part of any prosthetic territory, e.g., clothing.
4. **Appeal to a higher and unquestionable authority**: various performances, such as *My Manager* use the principle of "subservient empowerment."
5. **Criminalization of the critic**: inferences pertaining to the possible criminal intent of those who question personal safety devices are made, e.g., possible violations of fire safety, such as fire exist being illegally chained shut or exists blocked [3].

So the shiny shield of Minerva — the *NetCam* — reflects the gaze of Medusa — the pervasive power of authority — back on herself. If the authorities explain to Mann that they are videotaping him for his own safety, Mann, then, will kindly show them their own images

---

[4] Situationists are originated in a small band of avant-garde artists and intellectuals who founded the magazine *Situationaliste Internationale* in 1957. From early 1960s, the Situationists increasingly applied their critique not only in culture but to all aspects of capitalist society. Guy Debord, the author of *Society of the Spectacle*, emerged as one of the most important Situationist theoreticians who influenced French society during the 1968 student rebellion. For Situationists, to transform the perception of the world is to change the structure of society. By liberating themselves, people change power relations and therefore transform society. See Guy Debord, *Society of the Spectacle*. Detroit: Black & Red, 1983.

being transmitted live at his website, of course, for their own safety. Medusa would be petrified. But is she?

WWW : "The Whole World is Watching?"

Steve Mann's agenda in ShootingBack is to "re-situate" the surveillance devices by integrating those tools with the body of the individual, "who might otherwise be completely powerless" before the daunting force of authority/surveillance [3]. He arms the individuals with the apparati of counter-surveillance, yet another name of the device of surveillance. These apparati function as 'equalizers' which suggest that "shopkeepers and customers alike, police and ordinary citizens alike, etc., must respect the possibility that they could be caught on camera" [12]. He also contrives the connection of these individuals via the World-Wide Web. Connected together wirelessly, the groups of individuals who wear the *WearCam*s, according to Mann, form a "personal safety network" -- what Mann calls the *SafetyNet* **"to reduce crime"**[13]. But isn't this rhetoric reminding us of the very slogan of public surveillance? Isn't the fear of criminals the infrastructure of static surveillance? [1].

As Foucault argues, each individual is watching others, while simultaneously being watched by uncertain others. "You have an apparatus of a total and circulating mistrust, because there is no absolute point. The perfected form of surveillance consists in a summation of malveillance" [1]. This is what Zuboff defines as "internalization of standard" [2]. Poster also acknowledges the same problem of the individuals' "self-constitution as subjects in the normalizing gaze" [7]. Then, is power soliciting individuals by allotting their share of the pleasure of observation for making the individuals as effective enforcement of its pervasive surveillance network?

As Clifford Shearing and Philip Stenning indicate, the situation is less like Orwell's nightmarish society under Big Brother, but rather like Huxley's Brave New World, where the control of the society is consensual. So the individuals in the society are "seduced into conformity by the pleasures offered by the drug, 'soma' rather than coerced into compliance by threat of Big Brother, just as people are toady seduced to conform by the pleasure of consuming the goods that corporate power has to offer" [14]. Information as commodities is attached to both the individuals and power with an umbilical cord of gold.

This problem of "internalization" or "interiorization" has been discussed at the beginning of this paper. This is a part of the "dialectics of control" that Giddens points out; all strategies of control "call forth counter-strategies

on the part of subordinates" [10]. In this context, the logic of *counterveillance* via surveillance relies on the same problem-solving solution, the assumption that "if technological advancement produces perceived problems, then some technological fix can be applied to overcome it" [8]. But in reality, the previous debates on the "personal safety," or privacy issues are delimited in those who are privileged to negotiate his or her own self-protection [8].

Going back to Steve Mann's ShootingBack, questions emerge. Is his use of technology truly subversive? Or is he inserting himself into this network of surveillance as yet another authority? How much of the information that he shows us is controlled by him? As a Ph.D. in Media Art at MIT, and a professor in Electrical Engineering at the University of Toronto, working in the lab of that institution funded by some gigantic multinational corporations, is Mann's technology 'independent' enough to keep its private agenda apart from any other corporate interest? What company funds the Media lab?   By posing such questions, we just begin to recognize the complexity of the given situation which shadows an optimistic view of the critical use of technology in socio-cultural and artistic practices. The pervasive power of capital encroaches on the criticality of any practice by historicizing it and packaging it as a 'cultural product.' These questions, I think, link up to the issues that I viewed as central in defining the human existence in the digitized surveillance era — power, knowledge, and the body. In this regard, the work of Steve Mann bears much attention in terms of cultural criticism.

Bibliography

1. Michel Foucault, *Power/Knowledge: Selected Interview & Other Writings 1972-1977*. 39-158, Ed. Colin Gordon.Trans. Colin Gordon et al. NewYork: Pantheon Books, 1980.
2. Shoshana Zuboff, *In the Age of the Smart Machine*. NewYork: Basic Books, 1988.
3. Steve Mann, "ShootingBack." *The Art of Detection: Surveillance in Society*. Ed. Jennifer Riddell. Exhibition catalogue at MIT List Visual Art Center. Cambridge: 1997.
4. Jennifer Riddell, ed. *The Art of Detection: Surveillance in Society*. Exhibition catalogue at MIT List Visual Art Center. Cambridge: 1997.
5. Michel Foucault, *Discipline & Punish*. 206-7, Trans. Alan Sheridan. New York: Vintage Books, 1977.
6. Jeremy Bentham, *Jeremy Bentham: Collected Works*. Ed. J. Bowring. London, 1843.
7. Mark Poster, *The Mode of Information*. Cambridge, UK: Polity Press, 1990.
8. David Lyon, *The Electoronic Eye: The Rise of Surveillance Society*. Minneapolis: University of Minnesota Press, 1994.

9. James Rule, *Private Lives, Public Surveillance*. London: Allen-Lane, 1973.

10. Anthony Giddens, *The Nation-State and Violence*. Cambridge, UK: Polity Press, 1985.

11. Gary T. Marx, *Undercover: Police Surveillance in America*. Berkeley: University of California Press, 1988.

12. Steve Mann, "Wearable Computing as means for Personal Empowerment." A keynote address for The First International Conference on Wearable Computing ICWC-98 Fairfax VA: 1998.

13. Steve Mann, " Smart Clothing: The Wearable Computer and WearCam." *Personal Technologies*. 1.1(1997).

14. Clifford Shearing, and Philip Stenning. "From the Panopticon to Disneyworld: The Development of Discipline." *Perspectives in Criminal Law*. Ed. E. Doob and E.L.Greenspan. Aurora: Canada Law Books, 1985.

"Merging Realities: Psychosocial Happenings--A World on Stage"

Tammy Knipp
Florida Atlantic University, Boca Raton, Florida

ABSTRACT

One of the virtues of our changing times is that new media has challenged us to rethink and reexamine our basic presumptions about reality and the reality that is virtually perceived.

From the perspective of an electronic media artist, I present a body of work (CASE STUDIES) of performative-like installations comprised of 3-D structures integrating video imagery with the reality of the physical, psychological, virtual, and social worlds. These structures are instigators for enticing "social happenings" whereby participants and viewers become subjects from an observational perspective, providing a simulated clinical "case study." With the influence of theoretical and scientific information in the constructs of mediated environments, perceptions of risk, danger, trust, and self identity(s) are challenged. Using a metaphor to that of a "world on stage," the works provide a visual, conceptual, and concrete model to illustrate "Progress from Theory to Practice."

Introduction:

With the impact of technology on our lives, it is becoming harder to distinguish between what is virtual, what is fantasy, and what is considered to be real. Is reality in a postmodern society becoming more like theater, a techno-driven happening whereby our perceptions and experiences are continuous states of illusion? In current times, perhaps illusions are redefining our sense of reality.

Metaphor: A World on Stage

In the theatrical arena if the concept of virtual reality (what is illusional) references a metaphor to that of a "world on stage," the immersed performers would come to experience psychosocial effects among the physical, the virtual, and the psychological realities. In effect, the biological and emotional faculties of the performers on stage would come to respond *unconditionally* to the mediated stimuli. Whether or not the stimuli of the environment (a world on

stage) would be factual (real) or illusional (virtual) is not the issue. The important element is the mediated perceptions on the part of the performers in that their psychosocial and biological responses to the stimuli communicate a sense of realism (or an implied truth). In other words, the world on stage may be a *truer representation* of a techno-driven reality--a reality from which we can not escape.

The Perspective of an Electronic Artist:

I am an electronic fine artist who uses new media to create virtual environments (happenings). The works I produce investigate the psychosocial effects in the constructs of techno-driven environments. I use technology to initiate a communal exchange of reactions among both viewers and participants, thus, providing a simulated clinical "case study" through an observational perspective. This method of collecting data from an observational view and constructing a phenomenological analysis is a practice employed in the field of existentialism (a discipline of psychology whereby the investigator establishes validity by describing and explicating a verbal report from observing the subject's behavior and perceptual experiences.)

In this essay, I reference two specific works of art (phenomenological reports): *CASE STUDY 107* and *CASE STUDY 309*. These works provide a visual, conceptual, and concrete model to explore *Progress from Theory to Practice*. Using a metaphor to that of a "world on stage," these case studies illustrate:

1. Methods for blurring, both literally and perceptually, the boundaries of multiple realities (i.e., the physical, the psychological, and the virtual).

2. Theoretical and scientific influences in the constructs of virtual, mediated environments whereby perceptions of trust, truth and self identity(s) are challenged.

Defining and Positioning Terms:

In 1989, the term virtual reality (VR) was coined by Jaron Lanier, a chief officer of a research company. Typically, VR (new media) references particular technological devices such as head-mount displays and motion-sensing gloves that produce electronically simulated environments.[1] From a computer scientist's perspective, VR is "to foster in the viewer a sense of presence: the viewer should forget that [he/] she is in fact wearing a computer interface."[2]

Author of the text *Virtual Reality*, Howard Rheingold provides an alternative view of VR, claiming that "the heart of VR is an experience - the experience of being in a virtual world or remote location."[3] Sharing a similar view, Jonathan Steuer in his article entitled "Defining Virtual Reality: Dimensions Determining Telepresence" argues the position of VR to be a "particular type of experience rather than as a collection of hardware."[4] These perspectives shift the focus of virtual reality from a particular hardware package to the perceptions of an individual in a mediated environment. It is from this position of mediated perceptions that I draw a parallel to a postmodern, techno-driven happening (a world on stage) whereby the boundaries of the psychological, the physical and the virtual realities merge.

A World on Stage: A Refashioned Reality

Theater and VR share a number of similar practices: creating fantasy and illusive environments; altering perceptions; and, in some respects, attempting to immerse the viewer. The typical objective of VR is to achieve "immediacy" whereby the presence of the medium is *forgotten, denied or hidden*. In the context of entertainment, our logical intuition perceives virtual experiences to be the art of divergence and illusion; thus, the altered perceptions can be rationally and logically explained. However, outside the realm of the arts, theater, and entertainment, if no mediation is perceptually detected, would the immersed fantasy or illusive experience be a "real" or "virtual phenomenon"?

I propose this question in support of studies conducted in the area of mental imagery. Experiments have been conducted whereby patients were asked to mentally visualize a described scene. Researchers discovered that the subject's blood flow increased to precisely those areas involved in that of the "actual viewing."[5] These studies imply that when the subjects "mentally imagine a visual scene, [their] eyes and brain act as if [they] were looking at the scene in reality, correlating mental imagery to perceptual process."[6] This same study suggests that the biological effects (enforcing a sense of realism) induced by the power of mental visualization, blur the boundaries between what is virtual and what is real. Perhaps, what once claimed to be an illusion has now come to be a "refashioned reality"--a world on stage.

Contemporary German philosopher Hans-Georg Gadamer is referenced as stating that a "work of art requires imaginative activity on the part of the observer."[7] I correlate "imaginative activity" with "mental imaging" whereby perceptual and experiential realisms are framed in a similar remote location to that of the cybernatural. Lisa Blackman, author and lecturer on media and communications, references author and theorist S. Cubitt as coining the term "cybernatural" and defining its discourse as when "virtual space is viewed as a 'third space'--a space existing beyond those divisions and limits that currently position subjects in the social world."[8] I would like to expand and broaden "cybernatural," as outlined by Cubitt, to include a position similar to that of a bird's-eye / mind's eye / mental imaging perspective. I consider this "third space" to be a fourth-dimensional remote location similar to the observational view inherent in the study of existentialism. The video / kinetic case studies I will be referencing, provide these remote, analytical perspectives and entice "imaginative activity" on the part of both the observer and participant. It is from these perspectives that the *Progress from Theory to Practice* is explored.

Psychosocial Realities: Level of Consciousness

There are three described realities outlined by Max Velmans, author and reader in psychology: the physical, the psychological, and the virtual.[9] My focus addresses

1. Jonathan Steuer, "Defining Virtual Reality: Dimensions Determining Telepresence," *Journal of Communication* 42, No. 4 (Fall 1992) p. 79.

2. David Jay Bolter and Richard Grusin, *Remediation: Understanding New Media* (Cambridge, Mass.: MIT Press, 1999) p. 22.

3. *Ibid.*

4. Jonathan Steuer, "Defining Virtual Reality: Dimensions Determining Telepresence," *Journal of Communication* 42, No. 4 (Fall 1992) p. 79.

5. Ann Marie Seward Barry, *Visual Intelligence: Perception, Image, and Manipulation in Visual Communication* (New York: State University of New York Press, 1997) p. 86.

6. *Ibid.*

7. Gordon Graham, *Philosophy of the Arts: An Introduction to Aesthetics* (London, New York: Routledge, 1998) p. 15.

8. Lisa Blackman, "Culture, Technology and Subjectivity," in J. Wood (ed.), *The Virtual Embodied* (London, New York: Routledge, 1998) p. 133.

9. Max Velmans, "Physical, Psychological and Virtual Realities," in J. Wood (ed.), *The Virtual Embodied* (London, New York: Routledge, 1998) p. 46.

the level of consciousness (or the lack of) regarding the perceived boundary framing these multilevel realities (the physical, the psychological, and the virtual).

With selective types of VR whereby a head-mount is worn, the obvious factor denoting the point of entrance and exit from the simulated, mediated environment is the physicality of the hardware itself. Cumbersome hardware of this nature provides a tangible, physical "thing" for claiming a reality check; the hardware acts as a reminder, a conscious presence for differentiating the two experiential worlds. A similar reality check is appropriated for the theatrical arena. For example, when a member of the audience steps on stage (equating a mediated environment) and assumes a role with the aid of a physical, tangible costume (equating a hardware component) and interacts with stage props (equating simulated 3-D computer-generated objects), several key elements provide a level of consciousness for the points of entrance and exit between the two realities. These metaphorically shared distinctions identify not only the characteristics of the media (VR and theater) but also define the boundaries and parameters framed by the two worlds and the environments each medium creates.

In the above cited essay, Blackman references virtual reality to be understood as "either providing the means to enable greater freedom and autonomy (a place where one can choose an identity and play away from the material constraints of repressive society) or, in a more dystopian fashion, as dissolving and fragmenting the 'whole person', leading to greater alienation and estrangement from the self and others."[10] The key phrase I wish to address here is: "A place where one can choose an identity and play." In the context of theater, the term "place" I equate with the stage; the term "play" I equate with roleplaying, the multiple roles an actor embodies. Philosopher Kendall Walton, who wrote *Mimesis as Make-Believe*, "develops and applies the idea that many art works are what he calls 'props' in a game of make-believe, and he finds the value of art rests in the value of playing this game" according to Gordon Graham.[11]

I expand the perspectives of both Blackman and Walton to include the psychosocial effects that could, or would, occur if the checkpoints between the realities (the physical,

the virtual, and the psychological) became inseparable, undefinable, or invisible. In other words, what if the conscious mind could no longer distinguish between which "identity and play" were to be performed in which reality; and what if the "props" or mediated / unmediated imagery shared the presence of all realities?

Case Studies: Models and Methods by Which Messages Shape Meaning

In the theatrical arena, omitting the perceptual barrier that separates the viewing audience from center stage promotes psychosocial interplay. A cultural anthropologist might say that without social interaction and human physical contact, we would lack social cognition and loose the content that shapes meaning--meaning that derives from body language and physiognomic characteristics based on *the interpretation of / interaction with others*.

Communication expert John L. Locke, author of *The De-voicing of Society: Why We Don't Talk to Each Other Anymore*, is credited with the notion that "human voice and gesture provide constant feedback [immediacy]."[12] Philosopher and author Paul Ekman echoes Locke, stating that "one important function of facial and other gestural expressions of emotion is to communicate one's inner states to oneself and others."[13]

As an electronic artist, I seek a forum whereby technology facilitates or perhaps instigates a "social happening" (a serendipity), encouraging elements of laughter and humor as humanistic models for interactivity and play. My works consist of 3-D video / kinetic sculpture installations entitled *CASE STUDY*, each of which is assigned an identifying number. As previously noted, these works provide a simulated clinical "case study"--an existential analysis.

Each *CASE STUDY* integrates diverse fields of study that draw from models of research in areas such as: cognitive styles of the haptic (touch) / kinetic (motion) learner; motivational, behavioral, and existential practices; perceptions of danger and risk hunger; social / kinetic language; the psychology of humor and play; and research in the area of selective optimum stimuli. *CASE STUDY 107* and *CASE STUDY 309* (see Figure 1 and Figure 3) exemplify the employment of these areas of research, as well as illustrate psychosocial happenings among the multiple realities.

10. Lisa Blackman, "Culture, Technology and Subjectivity," in J. Wood (ed.), *The Virtual Embodied* (London, New York: Routledge, 1998) p. 132.

11. Gordon Graham, *Philosophy of the Arts: An Introduction to Aesthetics* (London, New York: Routledge, 1998) p. 17.

12. Jeff Minerd, "The Decline of Conversation," *The Futurist* 33, No.2 (February 1999) p. 18.

13. Stephen Davies (ed.), *Art and Its Messages: Meaning, Morality, and Society* (Penn State Press, 1997) p. 40.

CASE STUDY 107:

CASE STUDY 107 (Figure 1) consists of two chairs bolted back-to-back, positioned directly under a suspended cinder block. With the aid of four pulleys attached to the ceiling, the cinder block is held in place by a 3/4-inch rope. The rope leads to two black boxes that encase 19-inch color video monitors. As illustrated in Figure 2, the objective is to create an optical illusion, making it appear as though the rope passes through to the underneath side of each black box. The physical weight and gravity of the suspended cinder block create an illusion (perception) of stress, tension and virtual danger--conversely, a "true" physical and emotional risk.

An eight-minute video segment displays a similar 3/4-inch rope, which gradually unravels. As each strand of rope breaks (video imagery), the cinder block overhead physically shakes. Simultaneously, the two chairs are jolted with an electronic vibration--a shock.

CASE STUDY 107 revealed the following observations:

1. *Diversion: Selective optimum stimuli*

The bystanders (the arena of viewers, or audience) appeared to believe that the people in the chairs were jumping out of their seats in fear that the cinder block overhead would fall. In actuality, the jolting chairs caused the unexpected stimulus-response. As in the art of theater, this tactic (optimum selective stimuli of diverting the expected with the unexpected) was used to maintain a level of novelty and arousal, as well as to alter expectations and perceptions of both participants and the audience. Through the combination of real and virtual reality, the immediacy provided each person the opportunity to encounter a peak (immersed) experience.

2. *Merging Multiple Realities: Center stage*

CASE STUDY 107 merged the perceptual boundaries of the physical, the psychological and the virtual reality. The arena of viewers took on the role of performers. Their participatory response gave additional meaning to the perception and interpretation of the mediated environment. The shared presence of "center stage" (center stage references a central location where the realities interact and merge) encompassed all of the individuals who were present.

If interactivity requires a center stage arena, people are more likely to interact if the invitation accommodates two or more participants (performers). The dialogue becomes, "I'll do it, if you do it." Additionally, participants feel less intimidated and self-conscious if the seating arrangement is positioned back-to-back, versus face-to-face. Creating appropriate personal space encourages participation while enhancing the virtual / real experience.

3. *Interfaces: Accessibility, timing, attention span, and mental visualization*

Chairs signify an invitation for seating. Metaphorically, the two chairs signify a hardware interface and the two participants in the chairs signify a software interface. The level of interactive accessibility in this piece was intuitively framed in that it did not include the technical complexity common in most VR systems. In other words, the participants were not required to read a set of instructions, point-and-click a hardware device, or be clothed with a cumbersome hardware-wired system.

Figure 1. *CASE STUDY 107,* 1997
Video/kinetic sculpture installation,
10'H x 12'W x 6'D

Figure 2. *CASE STUDY 107* (detail view), 1997

Pushing the envelope of patience and attention span in linear time, the eight-minute video segment appeared to be the breaking point in this piece. The video ended with a very thin thread virtually appearing to hold the weight of the cinder block. People proclaimed a disappointment the rope didn't break after waiting for the entire length of video segment. It seemed that the slightest possibility of danger was the motive for capturing and maintaining the attention span for the entire length of the "performance." This fascination supports Gadamer's argument in that a "work of art requires imaginative activity."[14] Interestingly, the observation of the viewers and participants seemed to included the imaginative activity and physical attraction to the element of apparent danger. In other words, it appeared the viewers were unconsciously drawn to the visual of the cinder block falling on the two participants sitting in the chairs, awaiting to see the experiential after-effects. Perhaps, this says something about our society--desires of risk with a fascination for danger.

The enticing traits of risk and danger employed in *CASE STUDY 107* engaged and merged the psychological, the physical, and the virtual reality, thus, challenging a sense of trust, truth, and realism on the part of both the observer and participant.

CASE STUDY 309:

Sharing similar characteristics with *CASE STUDY 107*, *CASE STUDY 309* (Figure 3) utilizes a personable language, such as kinesthesia (uniting physical sensations with sound and imagery). The installation consists of two identical structures, each measuring 12 feet high, 4 feet wide, and 4 feet deep. Once again, the invitation accommodates viewing for two participants, each having an individual zone. However, the viewing perspective (Figure 4) in this installation requires the participants to lie on their backs (a vulnerable position) on creepers and roll beneath a suspended two-foot square black box. The boxes (as in *CASE STUDY 107*) encase 19-inch video monitors. The objective is to synchronize the video imagery with that of physical kinetic sensations similar to *CASE STUDY 107*.

One of the towering structures depicts a video image of a cement brick falling in the direction of the reclined viewer. At the moment the brick breaks the glass (simulating the glass of the video screen), the black box (the 19-inch video monitor) physically shakes. Similarly, a video image displays an egg being dropped and removed by a vacuum cleaner, at which time an actual vacuum cleaner pulls the participant's hair from the headboard of the

creeper. Other synchronized visual-audio, kinetic elements are images of machinery parts that correspond to vibrating motions of head-and-body massage units.

CASE STUDY 309 revealed the following observations:

1. *Sensory Adaptation: Timing, attention span, accessibility and selective optimum stimuli*

Sensory adaptation refers to a "decrease in sensory response to a constant or unchanging stimulus."[15] As both stations (structures) were visually identical in construction, each provided different visuals corresponding to different

Figure 3.   *CASE STUDY 309,* 1998
Video/kinetic sculpture installation,
12'H x 4'W x 4'D.

Figure 4.   *CASE STUDY 309* (detail view), 1998

14. See Gordon Graham, *Philosophy of the Arts: An Introduction to Aesthetics* (London, New York: Routledge, 1998) p. 15.

15. Dennis Coon, *Essentials of Psychology*, 6th ed. (St. Paul, New York, Los Angeles, San Francisco: West Publishing Company, 1994) p. 180.

physical sensations. The structures were purposely designed to be identical as to challenge predictability (sensory adaptation) and to create a momentum of curiosity and interaction between the two stations.

Research indicates that an environment designed to minimize stimulus input is not something humans generally seek out.[16] Dr. Daniel Berlyne, a major figure in the study of motivation, references four valuable traits for research into stimulus selection: novelty, uncertainty, conflict, and complexity.[17] By altering the viewing perspective (a non-traditional approach to viewing a work of art), disorientation was a stimulus selection employed in *CASE STUDY 309*, a method of enhancing the realism. Disorientation is defined as overwhelming or conflicting stimuli that complicates the brain's correlation of information. The brain consequently sends false input to the various senses whereby the altered perceptions are, in turn, experienced as reality.[18]

The only way to view and experience *CASE STUDY 309* was to place oneself in a vulnerable position. This disoriented position involved an element of risk with plausible danger of the suspended video monitor falling. The reclining position also included emotional risks of embarrassment and social consciousness. More importantly, the enticing element which encouraged participation appeared to be that of curiosity and the element of (perceived) physical danger.

The kinetic experience (video segment) lasted 90 seconds. The attention span in a reclining position appeared to max between 60 to 90 seconds before the peak experience would have been lost to predictability (sensory adaptation). Timing, attention span, accessibility, and selective optimum stimuli were all important elements of consideration in these interactive electronic works of art.

2. *Risk Factor: The demarcation between virtual risk and real risk*

Galleries displaying *CASE STUDY 309* requested a signed release form from each participant stating the risks involved and declining liability if a mishap occurred. Obviously, this added another dimension to techno-driven virtual environments, and raises many concerns for the elec-tronic artist who creates social interactive works. By raising issues of belief and perceptions of trust, the demarcation between virtual risk and real risk (virtual reality and reality) breaks down.

3. *Merging Multiple Realities: Psychosocial, multilevel interactivity*

Similar to *CASE STUDY 107, CASE STUDY 309* displayed multiple levels of psychosocial interactions, blurring the perceptual boundaries of the physical, the psychological, and the virtual realities. Both the on-stage participants and the implied offstage audience shared the presence of center stage.

Referencing Gadamer's philosophy, the "mind" of the art work (*CASE STUDY 107 and 309*) and the "mind" of the audience must be mutually engaged in the creative activity--"the work's creativity needs its audience."[19] This view is shared by author and philosopher R. G. Collingwood: "'Art is not contemplation, it is action' and the function of the audience is 'not a merely receptive one, but collaborative'."[20] Collingwood rejects any "conception of audience as passive spectator."[21]

Synopsis:

In both *CASE STUDY 107 and 309*, the sculptural contraptions took a life form all their own. The structures became instigators for enticing and facilitating a "social happening"--borrowing the term "happening" from Allan Kaprow, artist and author of *Assemblage, Environments and Happenings*. Participants and viewers were unbeknownst "subjects" from an observational perspective, a view whereby human behavior, psychosocial responses, and social interaction could be analyzed in real time. Both case studies provided this analytical view (i.e., the cybernatural / an existential analysis) from which to observe the subjects in a mediated, techno-driven environment, one which also encompassed multicultural diversity.

Each case study invited participants and viewers to exchange roles. The direct experience actually caused participants to become an even more knowledgeable viewer. In other words, the haptic-kinetic experience began with a curious viewer, changing into an active participant, then

16. Lyle E. Bourne, Jr. and Bruce R. Ekstrand, *Psychology: Its Principles and Meanings,* 2nd ed. (Holt, Rinehart and Winston, 1976) p. 206.

17. D.E. Berlyne, *Conflict, Arousal, and Curiosity* (New York, Toronto, London: McGraw-Hill Book Co., 1960) p. 18.

18. Ronald D. Davis, *The Gift of Dyslexia* (Burlingame, CA: Ability Workshop Press, 1994) pp. 18-19.

19. Gordon Graham, *Philosophy of the Arts: An Introduction to Aesthetics* (London, New York: Routledge, 1998) p. 15.

20. *Ibid.*, p. 33.

21. *Ibid.*, p. 33.

returning to the role of a viewer. This secondary viewing leads to a more sophisticated observational role. It is from this "haptic-experiential perspective" that the most self-learned meaning is constructed. These many perspectives created an experiential embodiment (incarnation) of both body and mind.

In both case studies, the following elements were points of consideration for merging the constructs framed by each reality:

Somesthetic Senses:

Somesthetic is a combination of "soma," meaning body, and "esthetic," which means "to feel." Somesthetic senses include the skin (touch), kinesthetic (receptors in the physical body for detecting position and movement), and vestibular senses (receptors in the inner ear for maintaining balance).[22]

Research has discovered that "skin receptors produce at least five different sensations: light touch, pressure, pain, cold, and warmth. Altogether, the skin has about 200,000 nerve endings for temperature, 500,000 for touch and pressure, and 3 million for pain."[23] Because the body has more nerve endings for the sensation of pain, the key stimuli in both case studies was that of (implied) pain, engendered by elements of perceived risk and danger.

The interesting phenomena is the "sense of truth" and realism that results from creating an illusive virtual pain versus real physical pain. The physical body reacts and responds in a similar biological and physiological fashion, whether or not the pain is physical or perceptually experienced. The brain triggers the release of a chemical called beta-endorphin (similar to morphine) to combat pain.[24] Receptor sites for endorphins are located in the same area of the brain associated with pleasure, pain, and emotions.[25] Researchers have concluded that "there is reason to believe that pain and stress cause the release of endorphins. These in turn induce feelings of pleasure or euphoria similar to morphine intoxication."[26] I conclude the physical and emotional responses resulting from the (perceived / real) stress and tension in both case studies caused these receptor sites to release endorphins, thus producing a "peak expe-

rience." A peak experience, a term coined by Abraham Maslow, is defined as the cognition of being, an ecstatic moment, *an awareness of the body*.[27]

In *CASE STUDY 107 and 309*, peak experiences embodied the cognition(s) of the being(s) -- the physical, the psychological, and the virtual. The ability to produce peak experiences by enticing the receptor sites was an important factor. The stimulus-response heightened the level of awareness of the body, providing a sense of truth and realism on the part of the participants.

Haptic-ism:

My self-generated definition, or description, of hapticism is akin to the somatic in which we learn principally through the physical body itself. "Haptic" relates to touch; "ism" defines a system, theory, practice, or action. I refer to hapticism as experiential interactive art that utilizes kinetic methods to produce a reality virtually perceived by the haptic learner.

In investigating the haptic learner (that is, one who learns best by experience, utilizing and encompassing as many of the senses as possible), I have discovered the importance of including the element of touch in virtual environments. It is through touch that we define meaning, according to David Katz, a major figure in the study of the psychology of perception. Katz states: "From a perceptual viewpoint, we must give precedence to touch over all other senses because its perceptions have the most compelling character of reality. Touch plays a far greater role than do the other senses in the development of belief in the reality of the external world. . . . What has been touched is the true 'reality' that leads to perceptions."[28]

Play Behavior:

Both *CASE STUDY 107 and 309* challenged psychosocial issues such as social pretentiousness; embarrassment; insecurities; and emotional, guarded boundaries. Therefore, it was important to maintain a light-hearted perspective, engendered by play in these mediated environments. This element of play was induced and promoted by applying both visual and haptic / kinetic absurdities.

22. Dennis Coon, *Essentials of Psychology*, 6th ed. (St. Paul, New York, Los Angeles, San Francisco: West Publishing Company, 1994) p. 177

23. *Ibid.*, p. 178.

24. *Ibid.*, p. 183.

25. *Ibid.*, p. 183.

26. *Ibid.*, p. 183.

27. See Abraham H. Maslow, *The Farther Reaches of Human Nature* (New York: Penguin Group, 1971).

28. Lester Krueger, *The World of Touch* (New Jersey: Lawrence Erlbaum Associates, Publishers, 1989) p. 240.

According to Joseph Levy, a major figure in the study of play, humor, and laughter states: "Play is necessary to affirm our lives. When we slip into play, we slip into a self-experience where we can afford to 'let go' and respond to ourselves, to others, and to the environment in an unpredictable, personal way. Living in play means confirming our existence and celebrating life."[29]

Humor:

Just as absurdities promoted play in each case study, it was also important for play to promote the language of humor--the ability to laugh at oneself and with others.

Patricia Keith-Spiegel, a researcher in the psychology of humor, notes that there are four elements deemed by many theorists as necessary (though not sufficient) to appropriate conditions for the experience of humor and laughter:

- the element of surprise
- the element of shock
- the element of suddenness
- the element of unexpectedness[30]

With the use of bizarre video imagery, absurd kinetic devices, and tactics that imply risk and danger, I was able to produce these four elements in each case study. These elements enticed (triggered) the release of endorphins, and thus, created peak experiences for both the participant and the audience. It was observed that humor was the communal reaction as a result of the combination of stimulus and response, creating the appropriate conditions for social interactions. This observation of communal laughter reflects examples from anthropology, researched by Jacob Levine, claiming: "There is nothing so completely shared as laughter."[31] Konrad Lorenz, one of three recipients to share the Nobel prize for work on behavior, states: "Laughter produces, simultaneously, a strong fellow feeling among participants. . . . Heartily laughing together at the same thing forms an immediate bond."[32]

Risk Hunger:

An additional trait evident in both case studies was the element of risk. Immersed in a technoculture, we wrap ourselves in a cocoon of safety, comfort, and convenience to the degree that we have become bored. Ralph Keyes, author of "Chancing It: Why We Take Risks," claims that "we suffer from risk hunger." He suggests people need to take risks because our nervous systems and our bodies demand the stimulation, that a little danger is good for people. Taking risks brings us back to something primal and original, relieving us from the tedium of everyday life.[33] However, according to Keyes, the concept of risk, becomes confusing if we define risk as a fear of loss. If fear is amputated from danger then it becomes a Disney ride--a leisure activity. Many people aren't satisfied taking risks unless something of value is at stake.[34]

The definition of risk is subjective, as is peak experience. Paradoxically, what is most revealing may not be the risks people take, but the ones they don't take. For example, for some individuals, the prospect of being rejected by another poses a greater risk than engaging in an activity like bungee jumping. Could virtual environments promote an unemotional, risk-free society whereby the attachment for objects and virtual identities govern human interaction on the physical plane? Because of the emotional and psychological risks involved, will we become a culture that lacks a social / kinetic language that builds on intuition developed from the interpretation of gestures, expressions, and body languages communicated in the physical reality? Locke warns: "'De-voicing' may cause both Westerners and Easterners to become more isolated, distrustful, and unhappy."[35]

If technological devices and trends progressively move us away from social interaction in the physical sense, then we may risk losing touch with our own presence. Then again, our subconscious / conscious attraction to the "world on stage" may be the primary objective so as to avoid the emotional risk of being in touch with our own self-presence.

Conclusion:

Art critic and author Timothy Druckrey states: "The body is unquestionably the next frontier--the body, and then cognition."[36]

29. Joseph Levy, *Play Behavior* (Toronto: John Wiley & Sons, 1978) p. 1.

30. Jeffrey Goldstein and Paul McGhee, *The Psychology of Humor: Theoretical Perspectives & Empirical Issues* (New York, London: Academic Press, 1972) p. 9.

31. Jacob Levine, *Motivation in Humor* (New York: Atherton Press, 1969) p. 12.

32. *Ibid.*

33. Joe Surgarman, "Chancing It: This Thing Called Risk," *College Park* 8, No. 2 (Winter 1997) p. 16.

34. *Ibid.*, p. 17.

35. Jeff Minerd, "The Decline of Conversation," *The Futurist* 33, No. 2 (February 1999) p. 18.

36. Timothy Druckrey, "Introduction," in Grentchen Bender and Timothy Druckrey (eds.), *Culture on The Brink: Ideologies of Technology* (Seattle: Bay Press, 1994) p.9.

Throughout this essay, I have discussed the invitation of a "world on stage" to illustrate *Progress from Theory to Practice.* I have provided the description of artistic examples with scientific reasoning and applied tactics for merging multilevel realities, while enticing critical and provocative dialogue. Aside from a theoretical perspective, whichever reality in which we decide to engage, I suggest that we maintain one important element: our sense of humor--the ability to laugh at our multiple (mediated) selves and with the multiple selves of others.

Bibliographical References

1. Barry, Ann Marie Seward. *Visual Intelligence: Perception, Image, and Manipulation in Visual Communication.* New York: State University of New York Press, 1997.

2. Berlyne, D.E. *Conflict, Arousal, and Curiosity.* New York: McGraw-Hill Book Co., 1960.

3. Blackman, Lisa. "Culture, Technology and Subjectivity," in Wood, J. (ed.). *The Virtual Embodied.* London: Routledge, 1998.

4. Bolter, David Jay and Grusin, Richard. *Remediation: Understanding New Media,* Cambridge, Mass.: MIT Press 1999.

5. Bourne, Jr., Lyle E. and Ekstrand, Bruce R. *Psychology: Its Principles and Meanings,* 2nd. ed. New York: Holt, Rinehart and Winston, 1976.

6. Coon, Dennis. *Essentials of Psychology,* 6th ed. St. Paul, New York, Los Angeles, San Francisco: West Publishing Co., 1994.

7. Davis, Ronald D. *The Gift of Dyslexia.* Burlingame, CA: Ability Workshop Press, 1994.

8. Davies, Stephen (ed.). *Art and Its Messages: Meaning, Morality, and Society.* Penn State Press, 1997.

9. Druckrey, Timothy. "Introduction," in Bender, Grentchen and Druckrey, Timothy (eds.). *Culture on The Brink: Ideologies of Technology.* Seattle: Bay Press, 1994.

10. Goldstein, Jeffrey and McGhee, Paul. *The Psychology of Humor: Theoretical Perspectives & Empirical Issues.* New York, London: Academic Press, 1972.

11. Graham, Gordon. *Philosophy of the Arts: An Introduction to Aesthetics.* London, New York: Routledge, 1998.

12. Hall, Calvin S., Lindzey, Gardner., Loehlin, John C., and Manosevitz, Martin. *Introduction to Theories of Personality.* New York: John Wiley & Sons, 1985.

13. Hjelle, Larry A. and Ziegler, Daniel J. *Personality Theories,* 2nd. ed. New York: McGraw-Hill Book Company, 1981.

14. Krueger, Lester. *The World of Touch.* New Jersey: Lawrence Erlbaum Associates, 1989.

15. Levine, Jacob. *Motivation in Humor.* New York: Atherton Press, 1969.

16. Levy, Joseph. *Play Behavior.* Toronto: John Wiley & Sons, 1978.

17. Maslow, Abraham, H. *The Farther Reaches of Human Nature.* New York: Penguin Group, 1971.

18. Minerd, Jeff. "The Decline of Conversation," *The Futurist* 33:2 (February 1999) pp. 18-19.

19. Steuer, Jonathan. "Defining Virtual Reality: Dimensions Determining Telepresence," *Journal of Communication* 42:4 (Autumn 1992) pp. 73-91.

20. Surgarman, Joe. "Chancing It: This Thing Called Risk," *College Park* 8:2 (Winter 1997) pp. 12-19.

21. Velmans, Max. "Physical, Psychological and Virtual Realities," in Wood, J. (ed.). *The Virtual Embodied.* London, New York: Routledge, 1998.

22. Wilson, Colin. *The Essential Colin Wilson.* Berkeley, CA: Celestial Arts, 1986.

Session 2-12

Computer Aided Geometric Design

Chair
Muhammad Sarfraz
KFUPM, SA

A General Approach to Constraint Solving for Declarative Modeling Domain

Kwaiter Ghassan

Department of Computer Science
University of Paul Sabatier
118, route de Narbonne, 31062 Toulouse Cedex, France
E-mail: kwaiter@irit.com

Abstract

Research in declarative modeling started some years ago, and an important progress has been accomplished and different orientations have been studied. However, some fundamental problems are not exhaustively explored: the role of the constraint solvers in maintaining the scene, detecting the incoherence and the contradictions between constraints, reducing the number of generated solutions by dynamically adding new constraints, are not sufficiently distinct.

In this paper, our main contribution concerns the declarative modeling with constraints. We have developed a constraint solver called ORANOS that offers an extended model of constraint satisfaction problems. The solver supports two independent domains of artificial intelligence research: hierarchical constraints and dynamical constraints. The former offers efficient solving techniques for over-constrained problems; the latter allows development of interactive applications. These essential features allow the solver to extend the range of declarative modeling applications.

Keywords: Declarative Modeling, Constraint Satisfaction Problem, Dynamical Constraints, Hierarchical Constraints, and Intervals Propagation.

1. Introduction.

Today, the declarative modeling presents an interesting methodology and offers helpful means to support the designer in his modeling tasks. With this paradigm, the designer raisons about the objective to reach and not about the construction. In other words, the designer can describe a scene not in providing a numeric data, but by expressing the *features* defining the model characteristic in a high level of abstraction and imprecision. The modeler then looks for a set of *solutions* verifying the given description. Consequently, the underlying geometrical model of the scene is hidden from the designer and lets him concentrate on the essential aspects.

Research in declarative modeling started some ten years ago. The achieved works in this domain let us to distinguish a three main phases:

- The description phase: This phase allows the designer to describe scenes in a high level of abstraction. Currently, the existing modelers offer different tools of interaction. The scene can be described either by an interpreted language [19], or by dynamic and scrolling menus [15], or by an almost natural language [2].

- The generation phase: In this phase, the modeler solves the features and provides one or several solutions, if they exist. The model can be solved by a procedural approach [22], or by transforming the description either to a set of rules, which can be solved using a rule-based technique [24], or to a collection of constraints which can be solved by a constraint solver technique [7].

- The understanding phase: As the designer's description is generally vague, several or an infinity of solutions can be found. In order to overcome this drawback, the declarative modelers now offer specific tools allowing the designer to navigate in the solution space. One can distinguish refinement tools [3,4] and browsing tools [22]. The modelers suggest also a set of tools that help the designer to understand the solutions. One can classify four tools: presentation tools [9], exploration tools [23], highlighting tools [5,24] and comparison tools [21].

In this domain, an important progress has been accomplished and different orientations have been studied. The current works have been addressed either to the phase of description, or to some particular problems, regarding the reduction of number of tests during the generation and the management of the multiple solutions. However, several fundamental problems have been very little studied:

• The current declarative modelers use a procedural method to describe features. This approach obliges the designer to write detailed code fragments when the scene becomes more and more complex. However, the constraint method as means of description, and the role of the constraint solver to maintain the described models are not sufficiently distinct.

• The current declarative modelers don't offer any solution to deal with over-constrained problem produced by contradictions and inconstancies description. However, the role of the constraint solver to detect and solve the incoherence is not explored.

• The current declarative modelers are not enough interactive. The designer is not able to describe the scene dynamically and control the generated solutions numbers. Moreover, the utilization of the constraint solver to solve this type of problem by incrementally adding additional constraints has not been prospected.

We believe that the constraint solver has significant benefits when it is fully integrated into declarative modelers. Thus, the improvement of declarative modeling process must take into account, jointly with a rich designer interface, an efficient constraint solver module that must represent a central component in any truly declarative modeler. The constraint solver must be generic in order to extend the application domains though it must always find a solution to critical situation such as over-constrained problem. Furthermore, it must resatisfy dynamically the constraints whether new constraints are added or existing constraints are removed.

The goal of this paper is to show a complete view of our constraint solver ORANOS that answers to these requirements. Thus, some related concepts are not deeply explained but are referred to its references[1]. The rest of this paper is organized as follows: Section 2 introduces the constraint solver; section 3 presents its basic aspects; section 4 explains the ORANOS phases; section 5 gives a simple example clarifying the solver process; section 6 describes an implementation of

---

[1] ORANOS data structures, implementation code, and complexity are not presented in this paper. The author's dissertation [17] describes the constraint solver in more detail. The reader may contact also the author for information about implementation of ORANOS.

ORANOS in DEM'ONS declarative modeler; and finally section 7 presents the final conclusion.

2. ORANOS constraint solver.

The numeric constraint satisfaction problem NCSPs over continuous domains (NCSPs) [6, 12, 20] offers a general representation allowing to express and solve a vast range of combinatorial declarative problems. The formal definition of NCSPs is given by a set of numeric variables defined over continuous domains and a set of constraints that describes different numerical relations on the variables. The task of constraint satisfaction is to find the value assignments for the variables such that *all* constraints are satisfied.

However, this approach is still too restrictive and has two main limitations: It assumes that the set of constraints is static and completely given from the beginning, and that no constraint can be relaxed. The first limitation inhibits the designer's interaction and the second does not offer any answer to deal with over-constrained problem, while these aspects are indispensable in the declarative and interactive applications.

The ORANOS constraint solver, presented in this paper, offers an extended model of NCSPs: DHNCSPs (Numerical, Dynamical and Hierarchical CSP), which is based on two independent domains of artificial intelligence research: dynamical constraints and hierarchical constraints. The former allows development of interactive applications, whereas the latter offers an efficient solution for over-constrained problems. Moreover, although the dynamic and hierarchical aspects are extended upon numeric continuous constraint satisfaction problems, these aspects stay general and can be applied also on the numeric discreet constraint satisfaction problems.

3. Basic Aspects.

ORANOS extends the constraint satisfaction problems providing a new formal representation called DHNCSPs that defined by [14]:

$$HP = (V, D, C_p)$$

• a set of numeric variables $V=\{V_1,....V_n\}$.

• a set of domains $D=\{D_1,....D_n\}$, where $D_i=[a_i,b_i]$ is a closed interval of continuous numeric values.

• a set of constraints $C_p=\{C_{1p},....C_{np}\}$. Constraints could represent a linear and no linear equations, equality and inequality equations. Each constraint is attached by an arbitrary strength, indicating how strongly the designer wants particular constraints to be satisfied. A constraint is a conjunction of primitive constraints where each one has a set of methods that satisfies it.

For example, the primitive constraint $V_1 = V_2 + V_3$ has tree methods:

$$V_1 = V_2 + V_3, V_2 = V1 - V_3, \text{ and } V_3 = V_1 - V_2$$

Each method tightens the minimum and the maximum values of the output variable employing the minimum and the maximum values of the input variables:

$$V_1 \geq min_D(V_2) + min_D(V_3), V_1 \leq max_D(V_2) + max_D(V_3),$$
$$V_2 \geq min_D(V_1) - min_D(V_3), V_2 \leq max_D(V_1) - max_D(V_3),$$
$$V_3 \geq min_D(V_1) - min_D(V_2), V_3 \leq max_D(V_1) - max_D(V_2).$$

The constraints are seen as really declarative descriptions of relationships between variables without making commitment to how these relations are implemented computationally. This generalized view has several important practical applications. For example, in declarative modeling applications the same constraint description can be used for computing outputs variables from inputs variables but also in another direction, needed inputs variables from given outputs specifications. The method interpretation of the constraint can be determined dynamically depending on propagation variable process.

In addition, ORANOS supports constraint hierarchy theory[2] [1] to handle over-constraint problem. Thus, if conflict situation occurs, ORANOS leaves weaker constraints unsatisfied in order to satisfy stronger constraints. As a result, it divides HP into two independent DHNCSPs: HP' and HP''.

$$HP = (V, D, C_p), HP' = (V, D, C'_p), HP'' = (V, D, C''_p)$$

While the variables are still shared between HP' and HP'', the constraints now are divided into two disjointed sets of constraints C'_p and C''_p. The first one represents a set of satisfied constraints whereas the second represents a set of unsatisfied constraints.

$$C = C'_p \cup C''_p \text{ and } C'_p \cap C''_p = \varnothing$$

Before the designer's interaction, the solver is in *static state*. In this state, the variables are placed in Gen_Vars list, and a constraint is either satisfied and placed in SCL constraints list in decreasing order to its strength, or unsatisfied and situated in UCL constraints list.

When a designer's interaction occurs, the solver changes its state and passes to a *transition state*. In this state, some related constraints, according to their strengths, are retracted from both lists and placed in retracted constraints list RCL, and the task of the

constraint solver is to try to satisfy each of them. In this stage, the behavior of the solver is intrinsically important when retracted constraint is added to previously satisfied constraints.

Supporting designer's interaction, in naive way, by iteratively solve a sequence of retracted constraints is time consuming, since each time the solver is invoked with one of the constraint, it solves the problem from the beginning. Thus, incremental aspect must supported to rapidly pass the solver from the transition phase to a new static phase.

In literature, *time stamping technique* has been used in several constraint solvers, such as CLP (R) [13], to support incremental aspect. Unfortunately, this technique has a major limitation. It explicitly saves all the constraints when a manipulated constraint is being satisfied, and it restores the system when it backtracks to this constraint. Naively saving and restoring the entire constraints by pushing and popping them to and from a stack is expensive in both space and time because it charges the solver by extra information is not really necessary. Further, it does not take into account the fact that adding new constraints may change the domains of the variables of satisfied constraints.

In order to overcome this problem, the solver supports incremental aspect, to avoid restarting completely solving the system from initial variable domains, by employing *memorizing and restitution technique*. The solver saves only the variable domains before trying to satisfy a constraint and restores them when an inconsistency between this constraint and the other satisfied constraints is detected. Whenever a constraint is satisfied, the domains of concerned variables are tightened and are saved also in current satisfied constraint itself. These domains are restored later, if a satisfied constraint is removed, or retracted in order to satisfy unsatisfied constraints.

Next, the solver tries to satisfy all the constraints in RCL employing *interval propagation* algorithm. If manipulated constraint is satisfied, it is situated in SCL list. Otherwise, an inconsistency between the manipulated constraint and SCL constraints is detected and the constraint is placed in UCL list. When the process is terminated a new static state of SCL and UCL are recovered. Finally, the solver extends *Forward Checking* technique over continuous domain to generate solutions.

One can infer that the comportment of ORANOS is independently defined, apart from any specific declarative application. Moreover, the designer manages and controls the solutions, without taking into account the details of the implementation of the constraint solver. However, this behaviour is not completely determined, and is controlled by the designer through the use of constraint strength.

---

[2] The theory of constraint hierarchies has been implemented in several constraints solver based on local propagation technique [8, 25].

4. ORANOS Phases.

In ORANOS constraint solver, we can distinguish four main phases (Cf. Figure 1): the phase of the interaction, the transition phase, the refinement phase and the solution phase.

the other satisfied constraints. In any case, the solver retracts the constraint from its list and transmits it to transition phase.

4.2 The transition phase:

In this phase, ORANOS retracts from SCL and

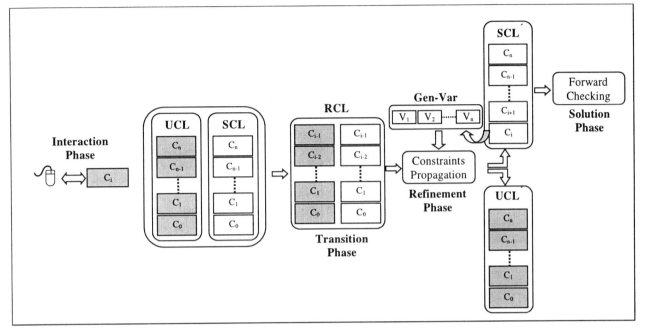

Figure 1: Architecture overview of the ORANOS constraint Solver.

4.1 The interaction phase:

ORANOS supports designer's interaction that wants to add, remove, or change the strength of a constraint.

• Adding the constraints dynamically offers many advantages: It frees the designer to provide at once a complete list of constraints, and lets him add constraints one by one according to his needs. It guides the designer toward the wished solution. It helps to restrict the generated solutions number. ORANOS accepts the newly constraint, and transmits it to transition phase.

• At a given time, an unsatisfied constraint becomes unnecessary, and the designer removes it to decrease the number of treated constraints when the number of constraints grows up. The designer can also remove a satisfied constraint to enlarge the solution number. In the first case, the constraint is simply removed from UCL list without invoking the next phases, whereas in the second case the solver passes to transition phase.

• The solver also offers to designer the possibility to control the generated solution by modifying the constraint strength. For example, an unsatisfied constraint could become satisfied either by increasing its strength or by weakening the strength of

UCL lists the constraints whose strength is inferior to the strength of the manipulated constraint in interaction phase, putting them in the RCL list in decreasing order according to their strengths. Heuristic strength ordering guarantees that no satisfied constraint will be retracted again to satisfy any subsequent constraint. Thus, each retracted constraint will be treated once. Before treating these constraints in the next phase, the solver needs to know the currents domains of the variables. In order to do so, it restores the variable domains from the weakest satisfied constraint stayed in SCL and updates the Gen_Vars list. Finally, the RCL list is passed to the refinement phase.

4.3 The refinement Phase:

In this phase, the solver attempts to satisfy all retracted constraints in the RCL with SCL constraints. ORANOS reaches its objective employing two algorithms:

• The solver uses interval propagation algorithm[3] to detect if HP' is still satisfied, when it tries to satisfy a retracted constraint from RCL, and at the same time, to transform the HP' into an equivalent HP'

---

[3] Interval propagation algorithm is derived from original algorithm presented by [27] and generalized by [6] in order to take into account the numeric constraints.

but one in which the domains of the variables are decreased. This algorithm is based on bound-consistency concept [20]. By definition, a variable V_l of HP' is bound-consistent iff :

$\forall C(V_1,...,V_k)$ a constraint of HP',
$\exists v_2,..., v_k \in D_0 \times ... \times D_k /C(a, v_2,..., v_k)$ is satisfied,
$\exists v_2,..., v_k \in D_0 \times ... \times D_k /C(b, v_2,..., v_k)$ is satisfied.
where $D_{vl}=[a,b]$.

Therefore, a HP' is satisfied if all the domains of the variables are bound-consistency. This concept provides efficient solutions for two fundamental problems:

- The reduced domains of constrained variables can be a union of disjointed intervals that are produced from the disjunctive constraints[4]. Disjunctive constraint destroys the convexity of the domains and produces a combinatorial problem. However, bound-consistency concept preserves the convexity and guarantees consistence conditions over the bounds of the domains.

- Constraint cycles can lead to the convergence problem that slows the solver considerably. The bound-consistency concept surmounts this problem by interrupting the propagation when the domains are not more sufficiently restricted. In this case, the concerned constraints are not anymore propagated.

Practically, ORANOS removes constraint from RCL and decomposes it to its primitive constraints. Then, it executes all the methods associated with each one. When a method is executed, the intervals for constrained variables are tightened and propagated through SCL constraints list, to eliminate values from the domains of other related variables, using interval propagation algorithm. If any of the domains of the variables become empty, then the evaluated HP' are unsatisfiable and an inconsistency between this constraint and SCL constraints list is detected. In this case, the previous evaluated variable domains are restored and the manipulated constraint is added to the UCL. Otherwise, if manipulated constraint is satisfied, it is added to the SCL list. The solver repeats this process for all the constraints until RCL is empty.

For example, let HP' be a set of satisfied constraints presented by:
- a set of variables $V = \{v_1, v_2\}$,

- a set of domains $D = \{D_{V1}=[0,100], D_{V2}=[0,100]\}$,

---

[4] The presence of disjunctive constraints depends on the domain of variables, where the same constraint can be disjunctive for certain domains but not disjunctive for others. For example, the constraint $y=x^2$ is non disjunctive for $D_x=[-2,2]$ and $D_y=[0,4]$, but is disjunctive for $D_x=[-2,2]$ and $D_y=[1,4]$. A complete survey of the disjunctive constraints is found in [12].

- a set of constraints $HP = \{C_{1strong} : V_1+V_2=2, C_{2medium} : v_2 \le v_1+1, C_{3weak} : v_2 \ge v_1\}$.

Interval propagation algorithm reduces the domains to be $\{D_{v1}=[0,2], D_{v2}=[0,2]\}$.

- The bound-consistency concept determines only a local consistency and interval propagation algorithm reaches a fixed point and stops. Generally, the fixed point doesn't allow to determine a global solution of constraints system. So, the solver achieves additional stronger filtering, based on 3-bound-consistency concept [20], which also preserves the convexity and reduces at the utmost the two bounds of the variables.

By definition, a variable V_l of HP' is 3-bound-consistent iff:

$$\begin{array}{ll} & HP'_1 = (HP' \cup \{V_l =a\}), \\ and & HP'_2 = (HP' \cup \{V_l =b\}), \\ where & D_{vl}=[a,b]. \end{array}$$

Therefore, a HP' is satisfied if all the domains of the variables are 3-bound-consistency.

This concept has been already implemented by successively adding additional constraints on each bound of the variables. However, this implementation presents a major inconvenient because it adds an excessive number of constraints and makes the system slow.

ORANOS supports 3-bound-consistency concept but it introduces efficient improvement allowing to overcome this drawback. First, the solver collects the constrained variables in HP' and puts them in temporary list in increasing according to their domain lengths. After that, ORANOS tries to restrict each variable domain by increasing its lower bound. It reduces the domain for manipulated variable, and collects the related satisfied constraints that share the manipulated variable, and propagates them using interval propagation filtering. After the propagation, if HP' stays consistent, the process will be iterated for the same variable but with a more restricted domain. On the contrary, if an inconsistency is detected, the examined domain will be removed and the process will be stopped in this direction. When the solver treats all the variables in the list, it repeats the same process, but in opposite direction considering the higher bounds of the variables.

Applying this filtering now on the previous example, allows to restrict the domains to $\{D_{v1}=[0.5,1], D_{v2}=[1,1.5]\}$ which presents a global solution of the constraints.

4.4 The solution Phase:

Thanks to refinement phase, the designer can reason on the range of variable domains that satisfy constraints globally and not on discrete solution. In practical situations the designer also needs to obtain one or multiple solutions. For example, instantiating the variables are necessary to visualize or place objects in declarative modeling applications.

Forward Checking [11] is really a hybrid of a tree-search algorithm and a filtering algorithm for classic CSP problem. ORANOS extends this technique for numeric continuous domains in order to instantiate the variables [18]. ORANOS sorts the variables in increasing order according to their domain lengths. When a variable is instantiated, interval propagation algorithm filters all the domains of the future variables in such a way that the remaining domains are still consistent with the current variable. If during this filtering process one of the domains of the future becomes inconsistent, a new value for the current variable must be tried. When the Forward Checking algorithm moves forward to instantiate the next variable it does not need to perform any consistency checks because all the remaining values in the domain are guaranteed to be consistent with the past variables.

However, declarative applications involve inaccurate data or partially defined parameters that make the problem generally under-constrained, and a very large number of solutions can be obtained (infinite solution in the case of continuous domains). Thus, ORANOS proposes one only solution. In any cases, the designer can ask the solver for other possible solutions or control the produced solution, either by changing the strength of existing constraints or by adding additional ones.

5. Example.

The given example has an objective to illustrate the basic aspects of ORANOS solver: generally, avoid breaking and dynamically. Considering the following variables: V_1, V_2, V_3 and V_4. Initially, we suppose that the variables have an initial domain initial $[-300,300]$ and SCL, RCL, and UCL are empty.

- First, the designer adds a weak constraint cn_1 composed of 4 primitive constraints: (V_1=5, V_2=5, V_3 =10 et V_4=200). ORANOS accepts this constraint and satisfies cn_1 and places it in SCL list, tightening the variable domains to be (D_{V1}=[5,5], D_{V2}=[5,5], D_{V3}=[10,10] and D_{V4}=[200,200]).

- Then, it adds a medium constraint cn_2 composed of one primitive constraint (V_1=50). The solver satisfies cn_2 according to constraint hierarchy theory. As a result, the constraint cn_2 is placed in SCL list, whereas the constraint cn_1 is retracted from SCL and placed in UCL. Thus, the tightened variable domains are now (D_{V1}=[50,50], D_{V2}=[-300,300], D_{V3}=[-300,300], and D_{V4}=[-300,300]).

- The designer adds a new required constraint cn_3 composed of two primitive constraints (V_1≥10 and V_2≥20) is added. So, the solver satisfies cn_3 and places it in SCL with cn_2, whereas cn_1 is still unsatisfied and

placed in UCL. The tightened variable domains now are (D_{V1}=[50,50], D_{V2}=[20,300], D_{V3}=[-300,300], and D_{V4}=[-300,300]).

- The designer adds a new required constraint cn_4 composed of two primitive constraints (V_1+ V_2= V_3 and V_3 +25= V_4) is added. So, the solver retracts cn_2 from SCL and places it with cn_4 in RCL. Then, it satisfies first cn_4 and cn_2 respectively and places them in SCL. According to its strength, cn_3 is still satisfied and will never be retracted. When cn_4 is satisfied, the variable domains become (D_{V1}=[10,255], D_{V2}=[20,265], D_{V3}=[30,275] and D_{V4}=[55,300]). When the solver tries to satisfy cn_2, the new reduced domain of V_1 propagates through the satisfied constraints in SCL. Thus, the tightened variable domains are modified again and have finally the values: (D_{V1}=[50,50], D_{V2}=[20,225], D_{V3}=[70,275] and D_{V4}=[95,300]). Obviously, cn_1 stays unsatisfied and placed in UCL.

- Adding a strong constraint cn_5 composed of one primitive constraint (V_4≤100) will retract cn_2 from SCL and places it with cn_5 in UCL. ORANOS satisfies first cn_5 propagating the tightened domains through cn_3 and cn_4; then it satisfies cn_2 and the tightened variable domains will be modified again and have finally the values: (D_{V1}=[50,50], D_{V2}=[20,25], D_{V3}=[70,75] and D_{V4}=[95,100]).

- Finally, the designer asks the solver to find a solution. ORANOS employs Forward Checking algorithm to generate the solution: V_1=50, V_2=20, V_3=70 and V_4=95.

6. Integration of ORANOS in DEM²ONS declarative modeler.

DEM²ONS declarative modeler (Declarative Multimodal MOdeliNg System) [10] represents an interesting declarative modeler for three-dimensional scenes. The conceptual design of DEM²ONS must support a wide class of applications (declarative placement, declarative animation, and mechanical assembly modeling,…).

Although the constraints are expressed in high level of abstraction, they are solved by *dynamic links* technique, which doesn't present a generic method and inhibits the modeler to maintain a large range of applications. For complex scene, it becomes much more difficult to keep track of all the relationships. Furthermore, it is limited for particular kinds of constraints and it doesn't offer any solution to deal with over-constrained problem and dynamic constraints.

In order to make DEM²ONS declarative modeler more efficient, an independent module that presents ORANOS constraint solver is integrated in the modeler. Therefore, the modeler now is composed of three main parts: a multimodal interface, the solver, and a 3D-scene modeler [16] (Cf. Figure 2):

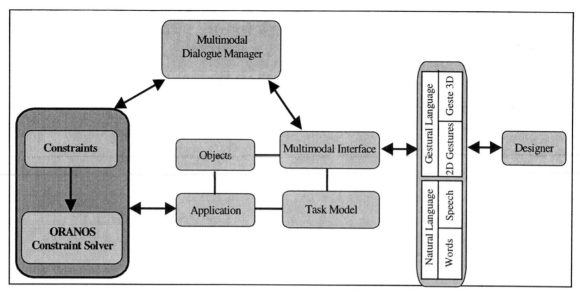

Figure 2. The new architecture of the DEM²ONS System.

- *Multimodal Interface:* The DEM²ONS multimodal interface allows the designer to easily describe a scene throughout multiple combined modalities, provided by several input devices. Designer's interaction is collected and treated by an *Event Managing module* to provide a single command sent to the constraint solver. DEM²ONS uses a *Task Model* module which defines a lot of application features (function specifications, object attributes, list of objects...). This model is used to provide information about the application to the generic modeler, if needed.

- *The 3D Scene Modeler:* The 3D constrained objects are instantiated from several abstract classes using object oriented techniques and are modeled and rendered by using the Inventor ToolKit [26]. Inventor supports several tasks. It offers a high level for the designer's interaction; it handles events and allows the system to manage pop-up menus and widgets. It also lets the designer explore the scene from multiple points of view.

- *ORANOS constraint solver:* In DEM²ONS, the constraints have a high significant role in the design process. The solver supports linear equality as well as inequality constraints. For example, it supports geometric constraints expressed by linear and non-linear equality equations such as distance constraint, parallel constraint and horizontal constraint; as well as topologic constraints that are expressed by linear inequality equations. Encapsulation object-oriented technique helps the solver to define various types of constraints, whereas inheritance mechanism aids it to deal with complex constraints.

The relations between the different modules of the modeler are strong and coherent. ORANOS handles the constraints passed from the multimodal interface, maintains the system, and transmits to DEM²ONS the new refined interval domains variables, as well as the

instantiated variables values in order to update the constrained object attributes.

Thanks to the ORANOS module, the utility of DEM²ONS is considerably enhanced and the ergonomic of the modeler is greatly improved. ORANOS provides the modeler a generic method to deal with different declarative applications. Moreover, the solver increases the interactivity of the modeler offering different tools of interaction allowing the designer to dynamically construct the model, and easily interact to modify the description or the results through the constraints. The solver also guarantees the continuous working of the modeler, even if all the constraints are not satisfied.

Currently, The modeler is employed to solve *declarative placement problem* [18]. For this problem, the modeler differences between three constraint types. *Internal constraints* are applied on one object and used to define its intrinsic properties such as its position, orientation, or fixed dimensions without any relation to other objects. These constraints are considered as required constraints, which are always satisfied. *External constraints* are preferential and are applied between objects. The modeler provides several types of spatial and geometric constraints such as: in front of, behind, against, on the left of, and a distance x of, in order to express relationships between objects. *Boolean constraints* react on the pragmatic level also well as on the geometric level of placement problem. A Boolean constraint can be imposed on the relevance of the objects in order to validate a declarative expression. It can be invoked also to examine the stabilization of the objects and manages the collisions between them. They have some common properties: they are implicit, required, and are not integrated in the solver but are managed by the modeler.

Each object refers to a particular class that describes its specific properties. Several properties and attributes are shared among the objects. On can

430

distinguish classic geometric attributes such as position, volume, and bounding box of the object, as well as functional and pragmatic properties such as orientation properties, and type property. These properties integrate knowledge about the usual function of objects in order to offer the closest solution for the designer dealing with semantic and the pragmatic constraints.

7. Conclusion.

In this paper, we have first outlined several works in declarative modeling domain to demonstrate the need of developing an efficient constraint solver to deal with the designer's requirements. Then, we have presented a complete presentation of ORANOS constraint solver: both the design principal and different phase's process. We have proved that constraint hierarchies and dynamical and incremental aspects are fundamental for any truly declarative modeler, by integrating ORANOS into DEM^{2}ONS declarative modeler.

References

[1]   Borning A., Benson B-F, Wilson M. *Constraint Hierarchies*. In Lisp and Symbolic Computation Journal, Vol. 5, 1992.

[2]   Caubet R., Djedi N., Gaildrat V., Rubio F., Pérennou G., Vigouroux N. *NOVAC: A drawing tool for blind people*. In Interface to real and virtual worlds, France, 1992.

[3]   Champciaux L. *Declarative Modelling: speeding up the generation*. In Proceedings of the International Conference on Imaging Science Systems and Technology, CISST'97, Las Vegas, June 30-July 3, 1997.

[4]   Chauvat D. Le projet VoluFormes: un exemple de modélisation déclarative avec contrôle spatial. Thèse de Doctorat, Université de Nantes, Décembre 1994.

[5]   Colin C. Towards a system for Exploring the Universe of polyhedral Shapes. In Eurographics'88, Nice, 1988.

[6]   Davis E. *Constraint Propagation with Interval Labels*. In Artificial Intelligence, Vol. 32, 1987.

[7]   Donikian S., Hégron G. *A Declarative Design Method for 3D Scene Sketch Modeling*. In Eurographics'93, Vol. 12 (33), 1993.

[8]   Freeman-Benson B., Maloney J. and Borning A. *An Incremental Constraint Solver*. Communications of the ACM, Vol. 33 (1), January 1990.

[9]   Gaildrat V., Caubet R., Rubio F. Conception d'un modeleur déclaratif de scènes tridimensionnelles pour la synthèse d'images. MICAD'93, Paris, 1993.

[10]   Gaildrat V., Caubet R., Rubio F. Declarative scene modelling with dynamic links and decision rules distributed among the objects. In ICCG'93, Bombay, February 1993.

[11]   Haralick R.M., Elliot G.L. *Increasing tree search efficiency for constraint satisfaction problems*. In Artificial Intelligence, Vol. 14, 1980.

[12]   Hyvönen E. Constraint reasoning based on interval arithmetic: the tolerance propagation approach. In Artificial Intelligence, Vol. 58, 1992.

[13]   Jaffar J., Michaylov, S., Stuckey P., Yap R. *The CLP (R) language and system*. ACM Transactions on Programming Languages and Systems, Vol. 14 (3), July 1992.

[14]   Kwaiter G., Gaildrat V. and Caubet R *Dynamic and Hierarchical Constraints Solver with Continuous Variables*. In Proceedings of the 6th French Conference on Logic Programming and Constraint Programming, Orléans, 26-28 May 1997.

[15]   Kwaiter G., Gaildrat V. and Caubet R. *DEM2ONS: A High Level Declarative Modeler for 3D Graphics Applications*. In Proceedings of the International Conference on Imaging Science Systems and Technology, CISST'97, Las Vegas, June 30-July 3, 1997.

[16]   Kwaiter G., Gaildrat V. and Caubet R. *Integrating an Incremental Constraint Solver With a High Declarative Modeler for 3D Graphics Applications*. In Practical Application of Constraint Technology Proceedings, PAPPACT'98, London UK, 25-27 March 1998.

[17]   Kwaiter G. Modelisation declarative de scenes: Etude et realisation de solveurs de contraintes. Thèse de Doctorat, Université Paul Sabatier, Toulouse, Décembre 1998.

[18]   Kwaiter G., Gaildrat V. and Caubet R. Controlling Objects Natural Behaviors with a 3D Declarative Modeler. In Proceeding of Computer Graphics International, CGI'98, Hanover, Germany, 24-26 June 1998.

[19]   Laakko T. and Mäntyla Martii. *Incremental constraint modelling in a feature modelling system*. Eurographics'96, Vol. 15 (3), 1996.

[20]   Lhomme O. *Consistency Techniques for Numeric CSPs*. In Proceeding of the 13th International Joint Conference on IA, 1993.

[21]   Lucas M. et Desmontils E. *Les modeleurs déclaratifs*. Revue internationale de CFAO et d'informatique graphique, Vol. 10 (6), 1995.

[22]   Martin P. and Martin D. *Declarative generation of a family of polyhedra*. In Graphicon'93, Saint Petersbourg, September 1993.

[23]   Mounier J.P. *Le projet UrbaForme: premiers pas*. Rapport interne IRIN, N. 117, Nantes 1996.

[24]   Plemenos D. Contribution à l'étude et au développement des techniques de modélisation, génération et visualisation de scènes: Le projet MultiFormes. Thèse de Doctorat d'état, Université de Nantes, Novembre 1991.

[25]   Sannella M. *SkyBlue : A multi-Way Local Propagation Constraint Solver for User Interface Construction*. ACM SIGGRAPH Symposium on User Interface Software and Technology Proceedings, California, November 1994.

[26]   Strauss S., Carey R. *An Object-Oriented 3D Graphics Toolkit*. In Computer Graphics, Vol. 26 (2), July 1992.

[27]   Waltz D. Understanding line drawings of scenes with shadows. The Psychology of Computer Vision, 1975.

Session 3-1

Graphics & Visualization Fundamentals

Chair

M.L.V. Pitteway

Brunel University, UK

Generating Synthetic Image Integrated With Real Images In Open Inventor

M. J. Abásolo, F. J. Perales

Graphics and Vision Unit. Department of Mathematics and Computer Science

Balearic Islands University

Baleares, España

Abstract

We describe a simple system for producing synthetic 3-D scenes integrated with real images captured with a camera, by using the graphic library Open Inventor. All the parts of the system are being described: real image capture, parameters measuring from the real scene, synthetic scene formation and coherent integration between the synthetic scene and the captured sequence. Finally we present some results of the proposed system.

Keywords: Real images, 3-D Modelling, Synthetic images, 3D-Scene, Camera views, Virtual world

1. INTRODUCTION

There are sophisticated methods for integrating virtual and real worlds to make an audiovisual program. [1][2][3][4] describe complex virtual studios that automatically produce images where real and synthetic 3-D objects are integrated. It obtain high quality results, but both a complete process of camera calibration and sophisticated hardware, such sensors that allows to know the state of the camera with accuracy, are necessaries.

We define a simple method for creating a 3-D scene which contains both synthetic objects and images that were captured with a camera from a real scene. There is no need of additional hardware more than a digital camera connected to a computer. The initial system that we propose for integrating real and synthetic objects doesn't want to be a professional tool for video producing. A possible application could be the construction of a prototype of a 3-D ambient with the added realism of a real scene as a backstage.

Section 2 describes the designed system and every step of the manual or semiautomatic process. Section 3 presents tests and results obtained.

2. DESCRIPTION OF THE INTEGRATION SYSTEM

Figure 1 shows a scheme of the integration process. Basically it consists of the following steps:

1. Create a real scene (or use an existent one).

2. Capture a sequence of images of the real scene with a digital camera.

3. Measure some needed parameters of the real scene and the camera.

4. Create 3-D synthetic scene with Open Inventor.

5. Import the images and create a "screen" in the 3-D synthetic scene for "watching" the images with Open Inventor.

6. Create a virtual camera with Open Inventor to visualise the 3-D complete scene correctly integrated.

Subsection 2.1 describes the creation of a real scene used in the tests done. Subsection 2.2 presents the capture of a sequence of images of the real scene, besides the format conversions needed to visualise it later. Subsection 2.3 describes the graphic library Open Inventor (Silicon Graphics) and the constructions needed to represent the 3-D "screen". Finally, subsection 2.4 describes the process of integration: measuring the needed parameters of the real scene, constructing the 3-D synthetic scene according the measures, and defining a virtual camera that allows visualising the 3-D scene and the sequence of images coherently integrated.

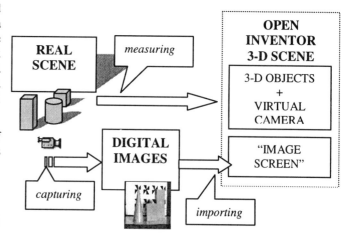

FIGURE 1. Scheme of the process

2.1. Creating a real scene

To integrate a 3-D scene and a sequence of images captured with a camera from a real scene, a reference in the real scene is needed. A point in the real scene is taken as the origin (0,0,0) and we have to know its position relative to the camera. We take another two points to determine the coordinate system. The position of the camera and every object are determined relative to this coordinate system.

As an example, a simple real scene is created: a cone A, a cube B and a rectangle parallelepiped C. The geometric objects are on an $(\mathbf{X},\mathbf{Z})$ horizontal plane. The origin (0,0,0) or reference point is the centre of the base of the cone A. Figure 2 a) shows the scene from the air. Figure 2 b) shows how the camera $\mathbf{c}$ is translated (tx,ty,tz) relative to the reference system and is rotated θ respect to $\mathbf{Y}$ axe, with $\mathbf{Y}$ perpendicular to the grid plane.

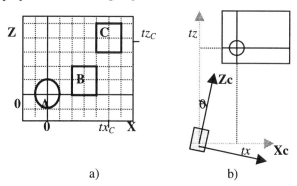

a)   b)

FIGURE 2. Example of a real scene

2.2. Capturing a sequence of images.

With a digital camera (Jai1510 Cosmicar) connected to a PC by a Matrox Meteor RGB card, we capture a sequence of images from the real scene described in the last subsection. The software used for the video capturing is Inspector 2.1. The technical aspects are not discussed here because are irrelevant in this description.

From the video capturing a video with AVI format is obtained. The video is decomposed in separate images files in a Open Inventor compatible format. This two steps are:

1- AVI-MPG conversion: Ulead MPEG Converter software is used to convert from AVI to MPEG format.

2- Image files generation from MPG format: MediaConverter software is used to decompose the MPEG video in the separate image files (i.e. in JPG format).

Figure 3 shows a captured image from the real scene of the example of section 2.1. (Figure 2).

FIGURE 3. Image from the real scene of Figure 2-a

2.3. 3-D Scene by using Open Inventor

2.3.1. Open Inventor

Open Inventor [5] is a library of objects and methods written in C++ that is based on Open GL, used to create 3D graphic applications.

The node is the basic unit for constructing a 3-D scene. Inventor objects include data base primitives such as shape nodes that represent geometric 3-D objects; properties nodes that represent qualitative characteristic of the scene; group nodes that are containers that group other nodes and as a consequence, create a hierarchical scene.

Nodes of a scene are structure in a graph. During *rendering* process, the scene graph is visited starting with the root node, in a left-right, and top-down way. The right (and down) nodes of the graph inherit the state set by the left (and top) nodes.

2.3.2. Image sequence visualization

The goal is to visualise the images resulted from the capturing process (section 2.2). A 3-D "image screen" is created by using Open Inventor. Three kinds of Open Inventor nodes are used: *SoCube, SoTexture, SoBlinker.*

SoCube

This class provides the shape for the "image screen". We construct a cube with minimal depth, i.e. *width x high x 1.*

SoTransformation

A derived of this base class is used to apply a geometric transformation to a shape node. To rotate an object a *SoRotationXYZ* node is used, and to translate it, a *SoTranslation* node is used instead. In this case, this nodes are used to set the exact position of the "screen".

SoTexture2

A node of this type contains a texture to be applied to an object. For every image of the video sequence a *SoTexture2* node is built and the image file is associated to it. The textures are applied to the "image screen" node to simulate the image "projection" over the screen. In the Open

Inventor scene graph the *SoTexture* node has to be on the left of the *SoCube* node that represents the "image screen", for the texture to be applied to this object.

SoBlinker

A node of this type has the property of *switching* between all its children nodes at a specified speed. To simulate the video projection over the screen, the *SoTexture2* node are grouped under a *SoBlinker* node that switches between the images.

The *speed* attribute represents the number of complete cycles per second (a cycle means visiting all the children nodes). The user specify a required projection speed or *frame rate* (i.e. 25 frames/sec) and with the length *n* of the image sequence, the *speed* attribute is determined as *frame rate / n*.

A *SoSeparator* node groups the textures node, the position nodes and the "screen node", in the correct order for the textures and position changes be applied to the last node. The subgraph is the following:

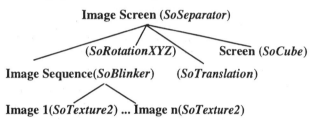

This graph represent a subgraph in the complete scene graph. The *SoSeparator* node isolates the effects of its children, that is the nodes inside this group don't affect upper or right in the complete scene graph.

2.3.3. 3-D synthetic objects creation

We create a synthetic scene by using the set of Open Inventor primitives of shape (i.e. *SoCube, SoCone, SoCylinder, SoSphere,* etc.). A specific material can be applied to the objects by the effects of a *SoMaterial* node.

For every synthetic object that we want to create, we build a *SoSeparator* node that groups *SoMaterial* and *SoTransformation* node together with the node that defines the shape. The subgraph is the following:

All the 3-D object defined are grouping under a *SoSeparator* node, for the synthetic objects set be isolated from the rest of the Inventor scene. The subgraph is the following:

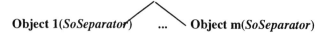

The overall goal is to integrate the synthetic 3-D objects set created and the real object reproduced in the image sequence. Both of the subgraphs defined for the 3-D synthetic objects and the image screen object respectively, are grouping under a *SoSeparator* node forming the integrated scene graph as follow:

Figure 4 shows the 3-D objects created and the screen object where the image sequence is "projected", in a Open Inventor scene examiner.

FIGURE 4. 3-D synthetic objects and image screen object

2.4. Correct integration between 3-D synthetic objects and a video sequence

The overall goal of the described process is to integrate the 3-D synthetic objects created and the image sequence projection of the real objects captured with the camera. A correct visual integration means a visualisation of the global scene that gives the illusion of having both the real objects of the images and the 3-D synthetic objects in the same 3-D scene.

2.4.1. Virtual camera definition

A virtual camera implemented in a graphic workstation, makes a bidimensional projection of a 3-D synthetic world. What the user visualises on the screen is always the projection of a synthetic scene according a virtual camera. Generally, the images are obtained from a perspective projection based on the *pinhole* camera model [6]. As Figure 5 shows, this model is characterised by an optic center **C** and a plane **P** where the images are projected. **Zc** is the camera optic axe, and is perpendicular to plane **P**. **P** is situated at a distance **f** called focal distance. A point p(x,y,z) referenced in the camera coordinate system is projected over the plane **P** in the point i(u,v,d).

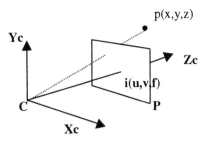

FIGURE 5. Virtual camera model

To define a virtual camera in Open Inventor, there exists a *SoPerspectiveCamera* node that emulates a real camera. This node produces a frame from all the objects that are after it in the scene graph. The complete scene graph is as follows:

The position of the virtual camera relative to the 3-D scene corresponds to the real camera position relative to the real scene. Theoretically, having a synthetic scene equivalent to the real one and the virtual camera positioned analogously to the real one (Figure 2 b) the final image is equivalent to the image obtained with the real camera from the real scene (Figure 3). Practically, there are errors caused by different sources, such as the fact that Open Inventor virtual camera model doesn't emulate accurately the real camera used. As it was said, the virtual camera follows the *pinhole* model, that due to the great simplicity doesn't introduce all the parameters intervening in forming an image in a real camera, classified as intrinsic and extrinsic. The intrinsic parameters are those related with the intrinsic behaviour of the camera, such as focal distance, geometric distortion, optical center translation, etc. The extrinsic parameters position the camera in the space. In the definition of a realistic camera, a complete calibration of both intrinsic and extrinsic parameters must be followed [7][8].

In the method described in this paper, it is not a goal to make an exact camera calibration. In contrast we follow the *pinhole* model to evaluate the quality of the visual results obtained with the simplest process.

The following lineal equations define the transformation from p(x,y,z) to i(u,v,f):

$$v / y = f / z \quad (1)$$

$$u / x = f / z \quad (2)$$

In the experiment, the final image is the result of the projections of both point of the 3-D objects of the synthetic scene and all the points of the image that is projected on the screen object. For all the elements to be coherently integrated, that is being coherent in scale and perspective, it

is needed to correctly position not only the virtual camera relative to the scene but relative to the screen object. The following subsection explains how to position the screen object to correctly integrate the scene.

2.4.2. Distance from the screen object to the synthetic scene

The screen object where the video sequence is projected emulates the plane **P.** As a consequence, the screen object must be centered in the optic axe and it must be parallel to the view plane. Besides, the scene must be between the virtual camera and the screen object, for the objects don't be hidden by the screen. In Figure 6, we can see that that distance **d** from the screen object to the optical center must be greater than the coordinate z of any point p(x,y,z) belonging to an object of the 3-D synthetic scene, for the virtual camera to project point p.

At this time, a point $p_r(x_r,y_r,z_r)$ of the reference object and the reference coordinate system are known. Applying equations (1) and (2),

$$v_r / y_r = f / z_r \quad (3)$$

$$u_r / x_r = f / z_r \quad (4)$$

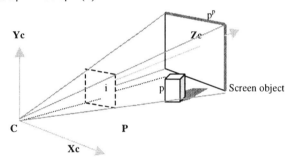

FIGURE 6. Screen object position

If we suppose **f** unknown some of the (u_r,v_r) coordinates have to be known. Point $i_r(u_r,v_r)$ belongs to the image and corresponds to p_r. Because we can manipulate the captured image it is easy to find the point $i_r(u_r,v_r)$. Note that this coordinate are in pixels. In (1) or (2) we can replace **f** with the result of (3) or (4), to obtain

$$v / y = v_r z_r / z\, y_r \quad (5)$$

$$u / x = u_r z_r / z\, x_r \quad (6)$$

The projection of the screen object vertices must coincide with vertices of the view plane of the camera. Applying equations (5) and (6) with point $p_p(x_p,y_p,d)$ unknown, because still screen object dimension and distance to the virtual camera are unknown, we obtain

$$v^p / y^p = v_r z_r / \mathbf{d}\, y_r \quad (7)$$

$$u^p / x^p = u_r z_r / \mathbf{d}\, x_r \quad (8)$$

Coordinates (u^p, v^p) are deduced from the image dimensions in pixels (*width, high*), with $u^p = width/2$ and v^p

=*high*/2. Because of that, we have only two variables in equation (5): distance **d** from the screen object to the camera and coordinate y^p. Analogously, in equation (6) we have the variables **d** and x^p.

Choosing any value **d** > z, for all p(x,y,z) that belongs to the synthetic scene, we obtain (x^p, y^p), that determines the size of the screen object. Determining only one dimension of the screen we can obtain the other one with the $P_{X/Y}$ proportion of the captured images, with $P_{X/Y}$ = *width / high*. This works well when the real camera doesn't produce any distortion between width and high dimensions. We can make a distortion testing by capturing a square positioned in a plane parallel to the view plane and centered in the optical axe of the real camera. We can then observe the distortion Dx/y in the resulting image, and use this factor to correct the proportion as $P'_{X/Y}$ =$P_{X/Y}$ / Dx/y.

3. EVALUATION OF RESULTS

The following tests were done:

1- The real scene of the example presented in section 2.1 is reproduced by using the primitives of Open Inventor. It implies the manual measuring of the real shapes and determining the relative position to the origin. (Figure 4)

2- Some of the 3-D objects are eliminated and new 3-D synthetic objects are added in the scene, resulting the scene showed in Figure 7 a).

a)

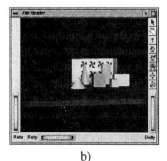

b)

FIGURE 7. Synthetic scene that includes new 3-D objects

First we evaluate subjectively the visual effect of the integrated scene. Figure 7 b) shows how the illusion of the integration between the real and synthetic object is obtained.

Given $p_r(x_r,y_r,z_r)$, we call $p^p_r(x^p_r,y^p_r,z^p_r)$ the point corresponding to the first in the screen object projected image. The integration is correct when the virtual camera projects p_r and p^p_r to the same point i^p_r $(u^p_r,v^p_r,\mathbf{f})$. A visual checking in the scene of test 1, is drawing the line that joins the camera center and the reference point $p_r(x_r,y_r,z_r)$, and then to observe the point where line cut the screen object. Figure 8 shows the error in three points taken as reference (cone highest extreme, corner of the cube and the parallelepiped). There are error sources from the manual phases and some assumptions of the method. From the manual process, the errors can be:

- Erroneous measuring of the dimension or position of a real object reproduced in the synthetic scene.

- Erroneous measuring of the camera position relative to the reference coordinate.

- Erroneous positioning of a new 3-D synthetic object in a non-free place, because uncertainty of the real scene.

- Erroneous determining the corresponding pixel to a reference point in the image.

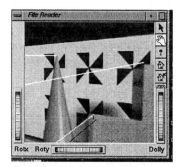

FIGURE 8. Error visualisation

There are other errors from the assumptions of an ideal camera model that doesn't correspond exactly with reality, such as:

- It is assumed a camera with an optical center that intersect the view plane at its center, but in practice there always exist a translation.

- It is assumed an ideal lens following *pinhole* model, but in practice, the lens is not ideal and not all the points are projected according to the same optical center C, and that is call geometric distortion.

4. CONCLUSSION

We present a simple system to produce 3-D synthetic scenes that integrate real image captured with a camera. Particularly we use the graphic library Open Inventor, but in the same manner we can use VRML or other 3-D tools.

This initial system doesn't want to be a professional tool for video production. We just present the evaluation of a very simple process, with no need of complex camera calibration and no additional specific hardware more than a computer and a digital camera. Quality of the result depends of the degree of visual coherence of the integration of 3-D synthetic objects and the images captured with the camera, and that is depending to the precision with which the manual measures are done.

Initially we consider simple scenes that include geometric objects that correspond to 3D primitives in Open Inventor. That is only to demonstrate the coherent visual integration between the images of the real scene and an exactly reproduced synthetic scene. In future applications, we hope extend the type of integrated objects. Besides, realism could be added with the inclusion of lights, shades, transparencies, reflections, etc. Given a method that integrate a synthetic scene with a sequence of images, it is possible to animate the synthetic objects while the video of the real images is projected. Another extension is to visualise the scene from different angles considering that the integration is correct when the scene is visualised with a camera corresponding to the real one. We can capture the real scene with different cameras to simulate the navigation of the scene.

5. REFERENCES

[1] S. Gibbs, C. Arapis, C. Breiteneder, V. Lalioti, S. Mostafawy, J. Speier. "Virtual Studios: An Overview". *IEEE Multimedia,* vol. 5, no. 1, pág. 18-35, 1998.

[2] M. Hayashi. "Image Compositing Based on Virtual Cameras". *IEEE Multimedia,* vol. 5, no. 1, pág. 36-48, 1998.

[3] L. Blondé, M. Buck, R. Galli, W. Niem, Y. Paker, W. Schmidt, G. Thomas. "A Virtual Studio for Live Broadcasting: The Mona Lisa Project". *IEEE Multimedia,* vol. 3, no. 2, pág.18-29, 1996

[4] A. Iborra, M. Lázaro, P. Campoy, R. Aracíl. "Sistema de integración automática de imágenes reales con imágenes sintéticas". *CEIG' 93,* Granada, June 1993.

[5] Wernecke, Josie. "The Inventor Mentor", Addison-Wesley Publishing Company, 1993

[6] Watt, Alan. "3D Computer Graphics", Addison-Wesley Publishing Company

[7] R. Tsai. "An Efficient and Accurate Camera Calibration Technique for 3D Machine Vision". *Proc. IEEE Computer Vision and Pattern Recognition,* p. 68-75, 1986.

[8] W. Grosky, L. Tamburino. "A Unified Approach to the Linear Camera Calibration Problem". *Pattern Analysis and Machine Intelligence,* vol. 12, no. 7, p. 663-671, 1990.

Author(s):

María José Abásolo, the CONICET (Argentina) fellow and postgraduate student of the Department of Mathematics and Computer Science, Balearic Islands University (Baleares, Spain).

E-mail: abasolo@ipc4.uib.es

Dr. Francisco Perales, the professor of the Department of Mathematics and Computer Science, Balearic Islands University (Baleares, Spain).

E-mail: paco@anim.uib.es

A Multimedia Learning Environment for Creative Engineering Design

Jing-Jing Fang*, Yao-Ching Huang**
Email: fangj@mail.ncku.edu.tw
Department of Mechanical Engineering
National Cheng Kung Unversity,
Tainan 70101,TAIWAN

Abstract

The purpose of the paper is to design an asynchronous on-line and off-line multimedia learning environment for the learners. The learners include those students in school and graduate people in work. It provides the learners an interesting and vivid environment for self study. The learners are able to systematically study the selected course whatever/whenever they like. The environment includes text, graphics, pictures, audio and video in order to provide the users an easy and comfortable learning environment. The body of the subjects is well-designed by both the software tools and hardware facilities, such as hypermedia hierarchy, motion pictures, Video on Demand (VOD) films, and the equipment for on-line interaction. The software is popularization and freely shares with other users in the net. Creative Engineering Design (CED) is selected as a pioneer in developing such an object-oriented lesson in the environment. The other object lesson, the cam follower interactive instruction system is also introduced in the paper.

Keywords: Multimedia Learning Environment, Creative Engineering Design, Video on Demand, Cam Follower.

1. Introduction

The traditional method for education is usually proceeded in a classroom, the instructor systematically presents his knowledge via the auxiliary tools, such as boards, projectors, sliders, textbooks, etc. However, students may not completely understand the essence of the course in class. They ought to work after class by the ways of reviewing their notes or references.

Nowadays, computer plays an important role in our modern life. It is unarguable that the use of computers

benefits of mankind. One of its applications in education becomes eminent achievement. Because it's easy with by human that wins popularity to any levels of ages in a family. By the flourished development of computer network, information communications become more and more frequent between people in a distance. Computers are then deeply involved in as the auxiliary tools in daily necessary. In short, education no longer limits students to learn in school, or focuses their study from books.

Based on the fundamental theory of mechanism and machine, configurations of mechanical devices are capable to be designed and then constructed. It is also one of the crucial subjects in mechanical engineering education. In the research, CED and disk cams are the selected subjects for asynchronous exhibitions in the multimedia learning environment. The products of the work are web pages, videotapes, and compact disks.

The object of the CED is devoted to present engineering creative techniques and a novel creative design methodology for the systematic generation of all possible design configurations of mechanical devices. With the authorization, the CED learning environment is constructed based on the contents of the books "Creative Design of Mechanical Devices" [1]. It is using in the classes of undergraduate, graduate and extended education school in mechanical engineers education for the purpose of providing the learners the capabilities of self studying, practicing and reviewing.

Cam is one of the widely applicable parts in machinery. Practical applications for cam mechanisms are numerous. One of the better-known applications is the timing system used in automotive engines. Starting from graphical cam definitions, the cam follower interactive instruction system can apply to design the desired motion curves in machinery.

---

*   Associate Professor
**   MSc Student

2. Multimedia Learning Environment

The use of several media simultaneously is named multimedia, which consists of the combinations of text, graphics, images, audio and video. The multimedia learning environment is separated into two types: one is synchrony, another is asynchrony [2].

2.1 Synchrony

Synchrony denotes teaching and learning is proceeded synchronously. Video and audio systems are utilized in the classrooms. Therefore, an instructor could give his talk during the same time in remote classrooms. Discussion between students and instructor is ongoing in real time via the system equipment. They, instructor and students may not meet each other face-to-face. We named the environment a Videoconference Classroom. The classroom can be located in any places where hardware environment is properly set up. Breaking space limitations and discussions in real time between lecturer and students are the advantages of synchronous learning. Moreover, the common source of content is distributed to learners at the same time in different places, that avoiding repetition work of the lecture. Although it has several advantages, steady and wide bandwidth network configuration is absolutely needed. However, the cost of the equipment using in this system is expensive, in addition, dozens people are involved in to guard the system in process straightly. Hence, synchronous system is not widely used in constructing the learning environment.

2.2 Asynchrony

Asynchrony denotes the teaching and learning is proceeded asynchronously. Based on the developed techniques of networking, asynchronous learning is split up into on-line and off-line status.

Off-line Learning

Computer-Aided Instruction (CAI) is a typical method of off-line learning [3]. In general, the content of CAI — text, graphs, pictures, audio and video are stored in a CD-ROM (Compact Disk Read Only Memory). Recent product a DVD-ROM (Digital Versatile Disk) is capable to store seven times more capacities than a CD. Therefore, these two kinds of disks are basic storage for off-line learning.

In general, interactive response on off-line state is faster than on-line state. Once the contents have been stored, editing is not allowable. Hence, it is suitable to construct the core courses that are well-developed fundamental curriculums, such as Mechanisms,

Kinematics, Dynamic Machinery, etc. Recently, many software development company designs the interactive multimedia instruction CD-ROM that provide the users to connect directly to network which is so called Internet. The usage of Internet accommodates the learner with various sources from the net.

On-line Learning

The content of on-line learning is built by the hypermedia technique, which is stored in the network computer server. Students can study or review the contents from the web site at anytime, whenever he/she likes. According to the ways of exhibition, there are two types of data sources. The first one is steady type. Based on text, graphs and pictures are combined into it as the auxiliary parts of the resources in order to provide the learners a complete concept. The second is mobility type. Videotapes are involved to shoot the motion pictures, associate texts, matched sounds, speaking and music. Because of easy making, fast transmitting, and undemandingness of network bandwidth, the former is common in on-line learning environment. However, it shorts of sense of reality that enables the learners a whole picture of the subject. On the other hand, the latter type enables the learners' sense of reality. Students would pay more attention on the subjects due to the colorful and diversified environment; hence the outcome is better than the former one. But, huge amount of data and slow transmission speed of the net are its weaknesses.

The content of on-line learning is shown in ways of homepage format that is transmitted via the cable nets. Contents are allowed to renew at anytime, therefore, it always remains up-to-date. Besides, it offers a space for public board for the latest announcements. Problem discussions and communications between students and students, or students and instructors would go through one or both ways of electronic mail and guest book.

3. Configurations of the Learning Environment

3.1 Hardware and System Architectures

In order to improve the outcomes of learning, the system comprises mainly web pages and VOD on the net. Computers are prerequisite equipment at the server ends, which are used as a tool for learners at the client ends to access World Wide Web, File Transfer Protocol and Video on Demand from the net.

Figure 1 illustrates the relationship between clients and servers. The net is one of the Internet, Intranet, or Extranet. The WWW server of our work is working under Windows NT 4.0(IIS 4.0) in a personal computer.

FrontPage 98 [4] is used as the tool of web page construction for the web pages. Operating system FreeBSD 2.2.6 and RealServer are employed in the VOD system. The server machine is set up and administrated in the Virtual Reality and Multimedia laboratory in the department.

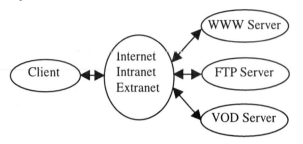

Fig.1 The relationship between clients and servers

3.2 Designed Processes

Figure 2 shows the processes of content creation on the Internet.

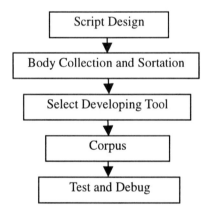

Fig. 2 Flowchart of web contents creation

Step 1. Script Design

It contains course conspectus and plans that are displayed in hierarchical order. In order to express the body logically, nodes or hyperlinks are arranged in its proper positions.

Step 2. Body Collection and Sortation

The bodies of the content are carefully tailored to related script. Combined the media such as text, video, pictures, action film, audio or graphs with associated textual description.

Step 3. Select Developing Tools

Evaluate the ongoing application browsers (Netscape Navigator or Internet Explorer), web pages creator (Netscape Composer, FrontPage 98, ... etc.), web languages (HTML, CGI, JAVA) and useful plug-in browsers.

Step 4. Corpus

The form of the web page should be self-consistent easy to read. Resolution of screen should be well set in advance, 640×480 or 800×600 are suggested options to give the readers a comfortable sight of view. The size of graphics and video film ought to be reproduced as small as it can be for avoiding network traffics.

Step 5. Test and Debug

Browse the web site with different web-browsers in order to avoid errors occurred in some particular browsers. After testing thoroughly and debug, the web site is open to the learners.

3.3 Video on Demand

Since the sprout of World Wide Web, quite a few scholars started their studies in synchronous and asynchronous distance learning through internet in order to develop a vivid and intriguing multimedia environment. Part of the researches is focus on the techniques of digitized compression and programming. Recently, many software companies make their efforts to develop network multimedia programs; one of them is the RealNetworks Software Corporation. Based on their free trial production, we combined the network browsers with the RealSystem to offer a function of Video On Demand. The components of RealSystem are shown in Figure 3.

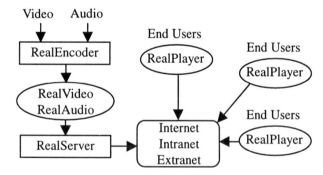

Fig. 3 The RealSystem Components

RealPlayer is a browser plug-in shareware, provides the function of real-time decompressing on network. Basically, such a video/audio file would occupy huge apace in memory. In general, the file is either downloaded from the server to the user's computer or opened to display on screen. Due to network bandwidth limitations, it takes time to open or download the huge-size file. By using RealPlayer, the file is loaded to machine buffer; the users can concurrently play and download. In addition, discontinuous phenomena in video playing would not occur.

The video files, named AVI files, are converted from

the media hardware such as VCR, V8 or VCD. It is distilled by a powerful image capture card installed in a PC. However, the size of AVI file is so large that can not directly play on the net. Therefore, we firstly transfer the AVI files into the RealVideo file format. The RealEncoder is then employed to compress the RealVideo files. All the compress files are stored in the video server (RealServer), therefore it can be immediately accessed through the net.

Based on different bandwidths used on the net, associated compress ratio is selected to make the RealVideo aforetime. Therefore, the right bandwidth is selected by the users to fit in their systems. The higher the bandwidth, the better the quality one can have.

3.4 Videotape

Apart from web site creation out of the contents, videotapes are also employed in order to enrich the contents. The bodies of the videotape may be a sequence of motion pictures of a subject, computer animation of action texts, or something related to the exhibited subject.

The software, Director 6.0 from Macromedia Inc. [5] and 3D Studio Max [6] from Autodesk Inc., are employed to program the animation pictures at the final script. Via the video capture card, the video proof are transferred into many pieces of AVI files. Then, Premiere 5.0 [7] (Adobe Inc.) is used to piece together the AVI files with the scripts of music and voices. After the video is revised completely, it is then stored to a VCD. The video files are stored in the RealServer, therefore, the learners could browse it whenever he/her likes.

4. Creativity Engineering Design Web Site

"Creativity Engineering Design" web course is using in the classes of undergraduate, graduate and extended education school in the mechanical engineers department for the purpose of providing the learners the capabilities of practicing and reviewing. The bodies consist of the following topics:

1. What is Design? — It describes the definitions of design. The processes of engineering design, mechanical design, machine design, and mechanism design are presented. The nature of creative design is also explained.

2. Engineering Design Methodology — It involves design process, stages of design, sources of necessity, problem statements, engineering models and rational engineering problem solving.

3. Characteristics of Design — Characteristics of creativity introduce terminology and its definitions, creative personality, barriers for creativity, enhancement of creativity and creative process.

4. Creative Techniques — Creative techniques have been

proven the most useful in stimulating engineers' production. The techniques employ attribute listing, morphological chart analysis, brainstorm and checklist method.

5. Creative Mechanism Design — Based on modification of existed devices, a creative design methodology is illustrated. Every possible topological structure of mechanical devices is derived.

6. Design Considerations — It includes functional considerations, standards and regulations, economic considerations, green considerations and engineering ethics.

7. Product Evaluation — Evaluation is the final proof of a successful design and usually involves the testing of a prototype in the laboratory. Testing is the determination of performance, workability, reliability, and durability for evaluating a product.

8. Design protections and Patents — It includes trademarks, copyrights, patents and research notebooks.

9. Engineering Communications — It includes report compose, verbal report and engineering proposal.

The course is now taking at the Department of Mechanical Engineering in National Cheng Kung University, TAIWAN. The original contents has been translated and revised for the purpose of studying among Chinese students. Figure 4 illustrates the head page of the Creative Engineering Design web site. The subject of the pages is divided into sequences of branches: introduction, contents, board, discussion, assignments, exhibitions, examinations and guest books. Students can choose either dynamic or statistic types to browse it. In the dynamic type, lectures were giving a talk with associate transparencies synchronized display on the screen as shown in Figure 5.

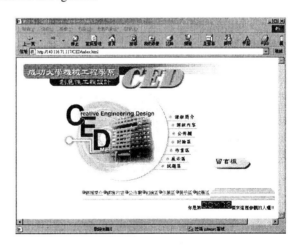

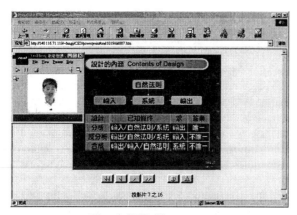

Fig. 4 CED Homepage

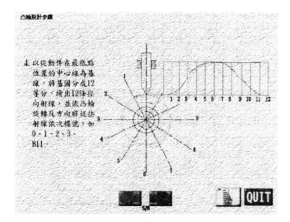

Fig. 5 Film with Transparency

At the end of the CED course, students ought to hand in a report titled a self-construct creation, such as a four-foot walking mechanism or a turnable four-foot power mechanism. Figure 6 illustrates the creations, which are exhibited at the end of the course and framed into the exhibition part in the web site.

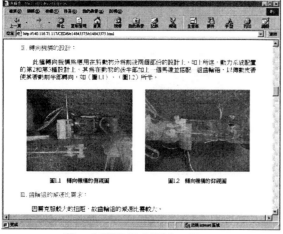

Fig. 6 CED Exhibition Room

5. Disk Cam-Follower Learning System

Cam-follower is widely used in machines in industry. It is also an obligatory subject of machinery in mechanical engineering education. Many textbooks on machinery are published for years. In recent years, many kinds of multimedia instruction software are available to provide the learners the other ways of learning interface. However, such instruction software involving machinery topics is not so many as general instruction software in market. Therefore, we create the multimedia instruction software — "Disk Cam Follower Learning System". The software combines text, graphics, audio, images, and video to provide the other kinds of learning interface for students. The process of software development includes script design, content preparation, programming, and testing. Based on the off-line developed software, Authorware 4.0 from Macromedia Inc., the final script is then plugged in under network browsers. Therefore, the learners are able to on-line interact with the instructor. In the meantime, the progress of the learners can be marked through the Internet.

Figure 7 illustrates the term definitions of a cam. Once the users locate mouse cursor on the term, it's definitions and descriptions will be showed up. The processes of profile design of a specific cam are demonstrated in Figure 8. Moreover, an external executable file "Motion Curves Design of Cam" programmed in C language is linked to the instruction software to facilitate the computational capabilities (see Figure 9).

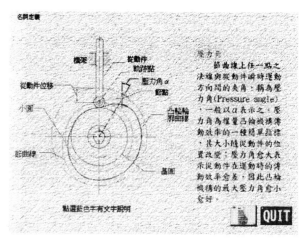

Fig. 7 Term Definitions of A Cam

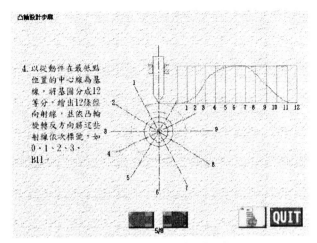

Fig. 8 Graphical Profile Design

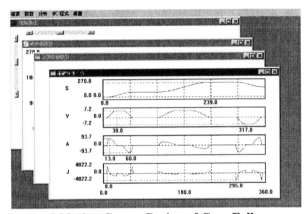

Fig. 9 Motion Curves Design of Cam-Follower

6. Conclusion

The multimedia learning interface is implemented by ways of either synchrony or asynchrony. In the paper, we present two types of asynchronous multimedia learning environments to utilize in the courses for mechanical engineering students. The multimedia web site of Creative Engineering Design course is using in the current study for both undergraduate and graduate students. It is a representation of asynchronous on-line learning environment. In order to enhance the learning effects the system involves two basic formats of web pages and video on demand. Under the acceptable bandwidths in Taiwan academic net (TANET), students can possible take the full course via the Internet.

The other instruction software of Cam-Follower System is also presented to represent the asynchronous off-line learning environment. The document is stored in the web server and learners can browse it through the net whatever he/she likes. Due to the complex calculations

for motion curves in the cam system, a linking of the executable file is used to facilitate fast computation.

The learning curves of the two asynchronous multimedia learning software in the paper are currently under estimation. The questionnaires have been collected from part of the learners, it is appreciated that the learning environments are proved useful for the students to provide a possible way for both preview and review the course contents. Information and latest news are spread easily and quickly. Moreover the techniques and the processes of developing the multimedia learning environment can be systematically transferred to the other courses using both in school and off school.

Acknowledgments

The authors wish to thank grant support from NII (National Information Infrastructure) Enterprise Promotion Association. We also acknowledge the members of Virtual Reality and Multimedia Laboratory in NCKU for their assistance in system hardware maintenance.

References

1. Yan, H.S., Creative Design of Mechanical Devices, Springer, 1998.
2. Chen, N.S., Integration of Synchronous and Asynchronous Distance Learning, Computer Center, Ministry of Education, Taipei, Taiwan, 1998.
3. Huang, Y.C., Fang, J.J., Yan, H.S., A Multimedia Instruction Software for Motion Curves Design and Applications of Disk Cam-Follower Systems, Proceedings of The First National Conference on the Design of Mechanisms and Machines, Tainan, TAIWAN, pp.213-218, 1998.
4. Li, Z.D., FrontPage 98 Secret, GOTOP Information Inc., Taipei, TAIWAN, 1997.
5. Wu Q.W., Multimedia Practice for Director 5.0, Unalis Corporation, Taipei, TAIWAN, 1997.
6. Autodesk Incorporated, 3D Studio MAX User Guide, 1996.
7. Adobe Systems Incorporated, Adobe Premiere 5.0 User Guide, 1997.

Data and Metadata for Finding and Reminding

James Gheel and Terry Anderson
School of Computing and Mathematics
University of Ulster, Jordanstown
Newtownabbey, Co. Antrim
Northern Ireland
jf.gheel@ulst.ac.uk; tj.anderson@ulst.ac.uk

Abstract

This paper discusses the benefits of using document metadata that exists as part of the document and which is also generated by its use, to assist users in retrieving the document and remembering what it contains. By extracting valuable descriptive information from a document, and analysing what a user does, such as the files they open, when they are used and for how long, a repository of information can be built up to help users with the tasks of finding and reminding. Since such a vast quantity of raw metadata can be acquired, visualisation is needed to elicit meaning from it.

Keywords: Metadata, visualisation, user activity, information navigation.

1. Introduction

In the service sector, productivity has not changed significantly in the last 15 years [2]. Many reasons are given, such as the extra time devoted to presentation quality, but the time spent searching for paper-based documents remains stubbornly high. New and improved ways of finding relevant information are vitally important so that we can organise and make sense of documents and information [18].

Research efforts, however, are still focused strongly on searching for information which is largely unknown to the user, Internet search engines being the most obvious example. Vital though finding new information is, often the key requirement is relocating documents and imperfectly remembered fragments of text or images. To the information worker, the task is to recall key documents and facts, assess their relevance, martial ideas, and summarise/synthesise key concepts usually from a comparatively small set of documents previously visited.

This paper reviews first how people remember and relocate documents and their contents. Then conventional physical and computer-based approaches are described and discussed, particularly to their support for our cognitive processes. Emerging approaches using various kinds of metadata are then considered. This allows the requirements for more effective strategies for finding and reminding technology [5] to be identified.

2. Strategies for remembering and relocating documents

How do we remember documents for retrieval?

If we have misplaced some physical object in the real world, we retrace our steps to try and relocate it. The things that are prominent in our memory are locations, the time of day, and other people and activities we were involved with, aside from the obvious physical characteristics of the object in question [9]. Similarly, a memory trace may relate a document to others we were using at the same time or with those of a similar topic of which we are aware [10]. The size and type of an electronic document are examples of other metadata that assist us in retrieving an association from long-term memory.

Traditional storage methods for physical documents have relied on filing cabinets and folders assisted by a reliable indexing mechanism created by the person storing the documents [8]. At a basic level, individual documents are typically arranged in alphabetical or chronological order, and grouped according to their function or domain. This simple but highly effective metaphor has been translated into electronic form. However, as more users amass large sets of online documents, it is becoming increasingly evident that this approach does not scale well. Just as it would be impossible to efficiently retrieve from thousands of files in hundreds of physical storage cabinets, it is similarly problematic on a computer where the physical element is also missing. We remember parts of a document and certain keywords; although this is often not discriminating enough to narrow a search to produce an acceptably small and manageable selection set. No matter if a document name has 8 characters or 50, it is still difficult to remember a document by its name and relate it to what we were working on.

In addition to remembering a document by keywords, section topics and various other important textual facets, our iconic memory paints a visual portrait of the document or parts of it [11]. For example, if a document contains images, these may be remembered more readily than parts of the text. If it contains a unique or unusual layout including a particular arrangement of typefaces and colour, this may be what is remembered the most.

Approaches to the problem

Books have withstood the test of time. The simple approach of information laid out in sections facilitated by contents and an index has become second nature for us to use. The benefits of a book's physical attributes are well known, enabling us to scan and browse pages with ease. A major drawback with something so physical and rigid is that there is usually only one sequential way to access the information. It is with no surprise that attempts have been made to mimic the representation of books in an electronic format [14]. The translation of information from printed material to an electronic format of any kind has left behind some important indicators for finding and reminding. The size of a book and the size of the text it contains reflect the amount of information it holds. The visible wear and tear shows how much a book has been used and may depict its popularity and usefulness.

Emanating from Vannevar Bush's prophetic insight into this problem [3], embedded hypertext links provide access to a given topic and allow more general topics to be broken down and navigated. The links are easily recognisable in a document by their colour, font and underlining. Connected topics form a sequence of links that can be mentally reformed if required at a later stage, assisted by the size of link, textual reference, position in document and page, and connection between previous and subsequent links.

Traditional office productivity software such as word processors, spreadsheet applications and presentation tools contain a list of the most recently accessed files, retrievable from the application's file menu. This is based on the principle that the file most likely to be required is one of the most recently used. It is also evident in Web browser history mechanisms, but is considered to be of limited value since neither usage patterns or multiple browsing sessions are taken into account [16]. Other applications such as graphics packages make use of a function known as 'memory buttons' [17], where the current state of an image or document under modification can be saved as an iconic representation. If the user wishes to return to a previous state, clicking on the graphical memory button will bring up the previous stage of development.

Modern information visualisation methods such as focus and context techniques enable a large quantity of related information to be interactively arranged in a small area. The hyperbolic browser [4] typically employs a 'fish bowl' method to distribute information that is structured hierarchically, for example files and folders, so that an item of interest (in focus) is shown with related items in the visual periphery (context). Designed for information that is hierarchical in nature, it is inapplicable for the increasing quantity of unstructured information available from disjoint sources over the Internet. Similarly, cone trees [12] rely on hierarchical structures for their operation. As a three-dimensional technique, an effective use of visual space is possible although some peripheral information is always obscured by information in the foreground.

WebBook and Web Forager create a 3-dimensional document-centric workspace [14]. The WebBook brings together collections of documents from the Web into an interactive 3d book and allows rapid interaction of objects at a higher level of aggregation than pages. Scaling of text is possible on the pages of the book, and the book can be exploded out to view all pages simultaneously using the Document Lens [13] focus and context method. The Web Forager provides access to multiple WebBook entities and has three main levels: the focus place, where a book is being directly accessed and manipulated; an immediate memory space, where pages and books are placed when in use but not immediately; and a tertiary place, where multiple books or pages can be placed for more long-term storage.

The reasoning behind both the WebBook and Web Forager is that users tend to interact repeatedly with small clusters of information, following the principle 'locality of reference'. There is little to suggest that a Web Book is less capable than any other visualisation system in providing access to information over a long period of time, and can grow accordingly when extra pages are introduced. It is uncertain though if Web Forager is as scalable when the number of Web Books becomes large, and whether the 3-dimensional workspace metaphor can cope when overloaded, to provide easy access to information.

Dynamic queries [1] can assist the retrieval of any type of information, even if it is not of a hierarchical nature. Mainly for filtering purposes, they possess the ability to reduce the subset of large document stores using multiple non-related fields. The granularity of the search and refining process is in the control of the user. Document keywords for example could be used as query fields, allowing documents on particular topics to be displayed and document patterns to be detected.

A Lifestream is a time-ordered stream of documents [7]. The tail of the stream contains documents from the past, while moving away from the tail and toward the present, the stream contains more recent documents such as papers in progress or the latest electronic mail received. Pictures, documents, voice mail, even applications may be stored in between. The head of the stream may be set to contain tasks that the user is required to perform in the future. Substreams can be derived from the main stream based on specific tasks and continue to collect new documents added to the Lifestream.

Locating information in a Lifestream is facilitated by the time-structured organisation of documents. Short-lived and working information is typically in the 'present' part of the stream. This is very similar to a location-based approach where the user returns to a common area to locate files. Users can quickly escape information overload by working in a substream that removes such interruptions or narrows their focus to the task at hand. They can quickly search for archived information through substreaming, or set up organisation categories by letting substreams persist. Reminding is an integral part of Lifestreams and is built into the semantics of the model. Users create documents in the future that alert them by arriving in the present.

3. A typology of metadata for digital documents

The techniques mentioned in the previous section make use of different types of metadata in varying quantities. Books for example have two levels. Internally, the

images, text size, font and section topics may help us remember the information in the long term. Externally, the size, shape, colour and title of the book help us to find it amongst a group of books in a bookcase. The primary goal of dynamic queries is to find information and exploit patterns, with little provision for reminding. The user of the query typically uses characteristics of the data and associated quantitative factors to narrow down a search.

The mode of use in Lifestreams revolves around a time ordering of documents to assist both finding and reminding. Other metadata types in Lifestreams are used to create substreams, perform searches and summarise streams. The remainder of this section considers the metadata types from the examples already mentioned, and suggests additional types and examples of metadata primarily in the context of Web documents. This leads to a typology of metadata for digital documents.

A document metadata typology

Documents contain metadata in addition to raw information. It is important to identify what constitutes metadata in a document and to further classify it, so that it can be properly utilised and effective visualisations can be created. A document on the Web, for example, contains much metadata both visible to the user when reading the document, and also by way of embedded tags that are not intended to be read directly as content. Furthermore, metadata exists that isn't immediately evident from the actual document contents.

Examples of visible metadata are the document's title, subject and section headings. These provide a direct representation of the document's topic and domain. Within the document, the author may include his name, company, keywords and an expiry date for reference purposes, all of which are not immediately visible. These metadata fields are also typically created by the author(s) of the document and can be considered as **manually determined**. In addition, the document has a location at which it is stored and can be retrieved from (a URL if on the Internet), size, security information, a number of images and a number of links. This can be considered as **automatically generated** metadata.

If a user of the Internet retrieves a document for viewing, a history of the usage of that document exists and forms valuable metadata in this respect. Such examples would be the number of times the document has been accessed and the date and time of the last access. If it has been accessed through a search engine, it may have been given a rating of relevance. Again these are automatically

	Manually Determined	*Automatically Generated*
Intrinsic	Title, Author, Keywords, Annotations, Category, Company name, Expiry date	URL, Size, No. of images, Set of contained images, No. of links, Creation date
Extrinsic	Citation, Comments, Highlighting	No. of accesses, Date/Time of last access, Visualisation of document in content, No. of local revisions, Date of last update

Table 1: A typology of metadata for digital documents

generated items of metadata. Should the user then make changes, or add extra comments to the document locally, these will form examples of manually determined metadata.

This leads to a further important distinction of metadata. In the first instance, metadata exists at the time of the document's creation by the author, i.e. **intrinsic metadata** that belongs as part of the document implicitly. In the second illustration, through usage and potential local modifications and additions, after a period of time **extrinsic metadata** is created that doesn't directly originate from the document. This has been summarised in table 1.

The intrinsic metadata are static elements, and never change unless the author specifically modifies the document to create a new version. Correspondingly, automatically generated extrinsic metadata is dynamic, and changes as the document is used and updated locally by a user. Manually determined extrinsic metadata contains a mixture of both static and dynamic types.

Metadata standards

The above-mentioned typology reflects metadata from the perspective of a user's actions and needs but has also drawn on other metadata classifications and frameworks. The Dublin Core Metadata Element Set is a simple 15-element classification developed to facilitate discovery of electronic resources. It is intended to be usable by non-cataloguers as well as by those with experience with formal resource description models. Most of the 15 elements have commonly understood semantics that represent what might be described as roughly equivalent to a catalogue card for electronic resources.

The classification presented by Boll et al. [15] is useful in that it covers various types of media other than text-only documents and takes into consideration those actions that may be performed to find and access the multimedia information. The classification is based on the following groupings: content-independent metadata, content dependent metadata, direct content-based metadata, content descriptive metadata, domain-independent metadata and domain-specific metadata. In practice, we have found this organisation difficult to use when placing metadata elements in the different categories.

Visually representing metadata

From the classification in Table 1, it becomes easier to understand what metadata is associated with a document and the various levels at which it exists. The result of this is a framework that can underpin visualisation techniques, dedicated to the perceptual characteristics of users during the management of electronic documents. It is the information personalisation for users that is important, as it is the user who seeks the information, retrieves the files and makes modifications. Therefore, appropriate visualisations need to reflect users' actions and intentions using existing and generated document metadata.

The authors have already experimented with web document formats in respect of metadata compilation and presentation. HTML and XML provide different degrees of metadata storage, the latter having a metadata description framework as part of its specification. With greater acceptance of XML in the future, the possibility of automatic conversion of HTML to XML, and the use of XML as a standard document format, the benefits of XML [6] should ensure that visualisations have the necessary supply of information required to make them effective.

One such example of a visualisation based on metadata would be an iconic representation of a file, as shown in Figure 1. The metadata is encoded into a suitable format for display on a pixel by pixel scale. Depending on the colour depth and appropriate legends or indicators, a combination of metadata elements can be incorporated into an individual icon, depicted as time-based histograms for document access and usage, bar charts for image and URL quantities, and pixellated scatter plots for keyword occurrences.

Figure 1. An example file icon based on metadata

4. Summary and conclusion

This paper has discussed document metadata and its implications for finding and reminding. Using information contained in a document that represents its purpose, origin, applicability and content, and also metadata generated by its use, visualisations can be formed to help information workers remember documents and their contents for effective use and retrieval.

We have discussed how users currently manipulate documents and information, and remember it for future use and retrieval from both a physical and electronic perspective. A typology for metadata was then presented, categorising metadata elements such as author, expiry date, size, URL, comments, time of last access and no. of accesses into four distinct categories: the metadata is either manually determined or automatically generated, either of which can be intrinsic or extrinsic to the document. This classification provides a framework on which suitable visualisations can be built for documents and information, to assist the complex and time consuming tasks of finding and reminding.

References

[1]   Shneiderman, Ben, *"Dynamic Queries for Visual Information Seeking"*, IEEE Software, pp. 70-77, November 1994.

[2]   Landauer, Thomas K., *"The Trouble With Computers : Usefulness, Usability, and Productivity"*, MIT Press, 1996

[3]   Bush, V., *"As We May Think"*, The Atlantic Monthly, July 1945, Volume 176, No. 1, pp 101-108.

[4]   Lamping, John, Rao, Ramana and Pirolli, Peter, *"A Focus+Context Technique Based on Hyperbolic Geometry for Visualising Large Hierarchies"*, Proceedings of the ACM CHI '95 Conference: Human Factors in Computing Systems, pp. 401 - 408. 1995.

[5]   Fertig, S., Freeman, E. and Gelernter, D., *"Finding and Reminding Reconsidered"*, SIGCHI Bulletin, Vol. 28, No. 1, January 1996.

[6]   Bosak, J., *"XML, Java, and the future of the Web"*, Sun Microsystems, Available from: http://sunsite.unc.edu/pub/sun-info/standards/xml/why/xmlapps.htm

[7]   Freeman, E. and Fertig, S., *"Lifestreams: Organizing your Electronic Life"*, AAAI Fall Symposium: AI Applications in Knowledge Navigation and Retrieval, November 1995, Cambridge, MA.

[8]   Norman, Donald A., *"Things that make us smart: defending human attributes in the age of the machine"*, 1993, Addison-Wesley

[9]   Lamming, M., Brown, P., Carter, K., Eldridge, M., Flynn, M., Louie, G., Robinson, P. and Sellen, A., *"The Design of a Human Memory Prosthesis"*, The Computer Journal, Vol. 37, No. 3, 1994, pp. 153-163

[10]   Baddeley, Alan, *"Human Memory: Theory and Practice"*, Psychology Press, 1997.

[11]   Nickerson, R. S., *"Short-term memory for complex meaningful visualisations: A demonstration of capacity"*, Canadian Journal of Psychology, Vol. 19, 1965, pp 1550-160

[12]   Robertson, G.G., S.K. Card, and J.D. Mackinlay, *"Information visualization using 3D interactive animation"*, Communications of the ACM, Vol. 36, No. 4, April 1993, pp 57-71

[13]   Robertson, G.G. and J.D. Mackinlay, *"The Document Lens"*, UIST '93, ACM Conference on User Interface Software and Technology, 1993, pp. 101-108

[14]   Card, S. K., Robertson, G. G., York, W., *"The WebBook and the Web Forager: An Information Workspace for the World-Wide Web"*, Proceedings of the ACM conference on Human Factors in Computing Systems, ACM: Vancouver, 1996, pp. 111-117

[15]   Boll, S., Klas, W. and Sheth, A., *"Overview on Using Metadata to Manage Multimedia Data"*, in Sheth and Klas, eds., Multimedia Data Management – using

metadata to integrate and apply digital media, McGraw-Hill 1998.

[16]   Tauscher, L. and Greenberg, S., *"How people revisit web pages: empirical findings and implications for the design of history systems"*, International Journal of Human-Computer Studies, 47, 1997, pp. 97-137

[17]   Tognazzini, B., "Tog on software design", Addison-Wesley, 1995

[18]   Card, S. K., *"Visualizing Retrieved Information: A Survey"*, CG & A, Vol. 16, No. 2, March 1996.

2D Texture Refinement Using Procedural Functions

E. Clua[1] , M. Dreux[2] and M. Gattass[3]

Pontifícia Universidade Católica do Rio de Janeiro – PUC-Rio

[1, 3] Computer Science Department

[2] Mechanical Engineering Department

[1] esteban@inf.puc-rio.br

[2] dreux@mec.puc-rio.br

[3] gattass@tecgraf.puc-rio.br

Abstract

In Computer Graphics, aliasing is a problem which is always present when discrete elements are mapped to continuous functions or vice-versa. Although there is no general solution for this kind of problem, there are many techniques that aim at reducing the effects of aliasing. This work first discusses how interpolation methods are usually applied in order to correct this problem and shows the limitations of those techniques. It is then presented another solution for this problem, that can be used together with the interpolation. It increases the texture details, making use of procedural functions.

Keywords: *Procedural functions, texture-mapping, interpolation.*

1 Introduction

During texture mapping, usually using an image, there are some problems related to the texture sampling due to the fact that a 2D discrete function is being mapped onto a 3D continuous surface.

In such cases there are aliasing artifacts caused by the image sampling. There are some antialiasing techniques that reduce this problem, since it is not possible to completely solve it. This problem can be stated as follows: given a set of points $P = \{ P_1, P_2, ..., P_i \}$, $i > 1$, belonging to a continuous 3D surface S, with all points within a sphere of radius ε, a discrete function f (e.g. an image mapping) returns the same result for all elements of P, producing jaggies. This problem increases when working with low-resolution mapping images.

A technique to reduce this problem makes use of interpolation methods. Several interpolation methods can be used, such as linear, spline, etc. This work also presents a new interpolation method that better suits the problem.

2 Interpolation

A texture function f to be mapped onto a surface has $U = (u_1, u_2, ..., u_i)$ as its input parameters, where i is the dimension of the domain of f, and in the case of a 2D image $i = 2$. The output value of f is the mapping value, e.g. the color. In the case of f being a discrete function within the domain, U has to be approximated to a valid number, e.g. only integer values. The linear interpolation averages the distance from a desired point to surrounding valid points, rather than simply using the output of the nearest valid point:

Let:

$$U_1 = (\lfloor u_1 \rfloor, \lfloor u_2 \rfloor, ..., \lfloor u_i \rfloor)$$
$$U_2 = (\lceil u_1 \rceil, \lfloor u_2 \rfloor, ..., \lfloor u_i \rfloor)$$
$$...$$
$$U_k = (\lceil u_1 \rceil, \lceil u_2 \rceil, ..., \lceil u_i \rceil)$$

and $m_1 = | U - U_1|$

$m_2 = | U - U_2|$

...

$m_k = | U - U_k|$

where $k = 2^I$.

Equation (1) is used in order to find the mapping of a given surface point U using linear interpolation:

$$C = f(U_1) \cdot \frac{m_1}{m_1 + m_2 + ... + m_k} +$$
$$f(U_2) \cdot \frac{m_2}{m_1 + m_2 + ... + m_k} + ... +$$
$$f(U_k) \cdot \frac{m_k}{m_1 + m_2 + ... + m_k}$$

$$(1)$$

where C is the interpolated result of the mapping function.

This work proposes an alternative method to evaluate C through a fractal interpolation. This technique introduces a noise generated by a fractal iteration of a given function. The previous equation would be modified to:

$$C = f(U_1) \cdot r(U_1) \cdot \frac{m_1}{m_1 + m_2 + ... + m_k} +$$
$$f(U_2) \cdot r(U_2) \cdot \frac{m_2}{m_1 + m_2 + ... + m_k} + ... +$$
$$f(U_k) \cdot r(U_k) \cdot \frac{m_k}{m_1 + m_2 + ... + m_k}$$

$$(2)$$

where r is a noise function with the following properties:

$$r(U_1) + r(U_2) + ... + r(U_k) = 1$$

and

$$0 \leq r(U) \leq 1$$

Although interpolation alone can reduce the jaggies of a mapped texture, the result consists of a blurred image, which in many situations does not improve the image quality. The proposed method combines patterns with the desired texture, including new data to the

original texture and refining the final image. These patterns can be other images or procedural functions.

The use of procedural functions eliminates the aliasing problems, since they are continuous and, hence, for each input point there is a unique output point. Nevertheless, the functions that can describe the procedural textures are restricted. There are some cases in which these functions do not work, e.g. it is impossible to find a function that might describe an artistic painting to be mapped onto a frame.

3 Basic Procedural Functions

This work makes use of the noise function, initially described by [3]. This function has some relevant characteristics for this work:

1) It is a repeatable pseudorandom function of its inputs. This means that every time it is called with the same parameters it returns the same output value.

2) It is continuous in a given interval of R^n, and band-limited in the frequency domain. This means that the function has no sudden changes, returning similar values for similar parameters.

3) Statistical invariance under rotation and translation.

Basically, these properties guarantee that a sequence of rendered images in an animation are consistent, not changing the patterns for a specific region. Because of the continuity, there will be a coherence between neighboring points when the refinement is applied.

By using the noise function it is possible to derive some useful functions that will also have the above described properties.

One of these functions is the *fractal Brownian motion* (fBm) [2], which is a fractal iteration of the noise function over a point. Initially, a table of coefficients is built. The coefficients are used to limit the result obtained in each fractal iteration. The values must decrease and be between 0 and 1, the first value being equal to 1. The following pseudo-code shows how this table can be constructed:

frequency = 1.0
i = 1
While (i < table length) do
    Table[i] = frequency^{-H}
Frequency = frequency x 2

Any function that varies between 0 and 1, and is decreasing is a candidate function. Different results are obtained by simply changing the *H* exponents. Therefore, the user should be allowed to interactively modify these parameter.

Once the table is initialized, the fractal iterations are performed using a chosen function applied to the surface points. For each iteration the partial result is stored, and the function is called again to the same point, but this time with a small spatial displacement. This work uses the noise function during the iterations.

For i = 1 to (Number of Fractal Iterations) do
result = result + Noise(point) * Table[i]
point = point * spatial displacement

The coefficient *Table* limits the value of each iteration, as shown in the above pseudo-code. The point spatial displacement means that a new point sampling is made with a spatial resolution higher than the previous one. A greater number of fractal iterations produces a better refinement of the pattern being built.

This work applies texture refinement for natural phenomena, such as water and landscapes. The fBm function, described above, produces excellent results for water, with a few number of iterations (2 or 3). As fBm is a homogeneous function - equal distribution through all the space - and isotropic - equal in all directions-, it does not present excellent results for general landscapes. So, for applications that deal with such features, best results are obtained with an fBm variation: the multi-fractal functions. They are similar to fBm but have a heterogeneous distribution. [1] describes such functions, providing also implementation details. (See color plate - Figure 3.)

4 Texture Refinement Using Procedural Functions

In order to use the method, it is necessary to choose the procedural function that is adequate to the set of textures to be refined. There are situations with excellent results, and cases in which the method should not be used. That choice could either be made by the program, automatically, or by the user. The automatic choice, in most cases, is not so precise, but sometimes it is strictly necessary. For instance, a landscape scene could have many different components such as rocks, earth, water,

etc, and several functions could be necessary to make the refinement for each component. Finding the appropriate functions is sometimes computationally expensive. An alternative solution is to search for a function, in a table, based only on the color of the pixel (blue could be a function for water, green for grass, and so on). Figure 3 from the color plate uses an adequate function for sand, and figure 5 was generated using a function for sand and another one for water.

As previously mentioned, the texture aliasing problem happens because, for a given set of surface points, the texture mapping value is the same. Since the domain of the used procedural functions is continuous, the returning values are not necessarily the same. So, for each point that is being visualized, the procedural function is called with the points coordinates as the input parameters. As each point of a continuous surface may only appear in a single pixel of the rendered image, different data can be included for each point of a surface that is receiving the same texture mapping value. Although the results may be different for each point at the surface, the function has to guarantee that close points will produce values that form the desired patterns. Once a value has been evaluated, by using a procedural function for a given point, it is necessary to blend it with the original texture.

It is important to remember that every time a function is called with the same parameters its return value is the same (see properties 1 and 3 of the noise function). However, if a surface is moving between frames, it is necessary to use local coordinates, otherwise the texture would have different results for the same surface point (to guarantee invariance under rotation and translation).

Blending

There are different ways to perform the blending. Ideally, the output value of the procedural function should be the final texture value. This is only the case in which the procedural function exactly describes the mapping texture. Suppose that a sand texture has to be mapped onto a surface. If there is a function than can simulate its appearance, the aliasing problem is completely eliminated. In most cases there is not such function, and it is necessary to combine a procedural function with the mapping texture. This blending could be achieved as follows:

$$T(P) = Texture(P) * (1 - coef) + f(P) * coef \qquad (3)$$

where *f* is the chosen procedural function, and *coef* is the blending coefficient, i.e., the percentage of procedural texture contribution.

It is also possible to include another procedural factor in order to achieve a non-uniform blending. This new factor allows the generation of non-uniform textures such as surfs, pieces of wood on a sandy soil, etc. The above equation would be modified to:

$$T(P) = Texture(P) * (1 - coef*f2(P)) + f(P) * coef*f2(P) \qquad (4)$$

where *f2* is the other procedural function applied to the blending.

The use of fractal interpolation during the blending process can produce impressive effects, especially when the textures represent noisy surfaces such as sand, water, marble, etc. (see color plates 3 and 5).

The general equation for the texture refinement, using the fractal interpolation for a given point *P*, is the following:

$$
\begin{aligned}
C = T(U_1) \cdot r(U_1) \cdot \frac{m_1}{m_1 + m_2 + ... + m_k} + \\
T(U_2) \cdot r(U_2) \cdot \frac{m_2}{m_1 + m_2 + ... + m_k} + ... + \\
T(U_k) \cdot r(U_k) \cdot \frac{m_k}{m_1 + m_2 + ... + m_k}
\end{aligned}
$$

$$(5)$$

where $T(U_1)$, $T(U_2)$, ..., $T(U_k)$ correspond to the results of the blending equation, with the values that surround the point *P*.

Optimization

The blending process sometimes becomes a lengthy task with calls to *f(P)*, *f2(P)*, and *r(U_l)*. Texture refinement can be optimized if these functions are pre-evaluated and stored in a table. On one hand, this optimization generates lower-quality images, especially for small tables, since there will be pattern repetitions.

On the other hand, it speeds up the rendering, as it consists of a simple look-up table. The table´s input parameters are the spatial coordinates of the desired point. The images shown in color plates 3 and 5 were generated making use of that optimization.

5 Conclusion and Future Research

This work has presented a new method for reducing aliasing problems in texture mapping. It has introduced procedurally-created patterns that are similar to the original texture, and has proposed a method for blending them. Some functions that simulate natural elements, such as water, sand, grass, etc., have been explored, but other patterns could also be used. This work has applied the method proposed to the color attribute only, but this study could be extended to other attributes (e.g. bump-mapping).

Acknowledgements

The authors are grateful to TeCGraf, at PUC-Rio, where this research was developed, and to Flávio Szenberg, who made all his previous work available to the authors. The first author would also like to thank CAPES, whose grant partially sponsored this work. Also thanks to Carolina Alfaro for the text review.

References

[1] Davis Ebert, F. Kenton Musgrave, Darwyn Peachey, Ken Perlin, Steve Worley. Texture and Modeling: A procedural Approach. Academic Press, 1994.

[2] F. Kenton Musgrave, Craig E. Kolb and Robert S. Mace. The synthesis and rendering of eroded fractal terrains. *Computer Graphics (SIGGRAPH '89 Proceedings)*, volume 23, pp. 41-50, July 1989.

[3] Ken Perlin. An image synthesizer. In B. A. Barsky, editor, *Computer Graphics (SIGGRAPH '85 Proceedings)*, volume 19, pp. 287-296, July 1985.

[4] Steve Worley. A Cellular Texture Basis Function *(SIGGRAPH '96)*, volume 30, pp 291-294, August 1996.

Color Plates

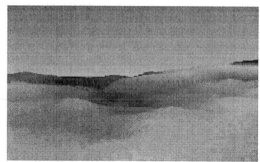

Figure 1- Original terrain, without interpolation and texture refinement.

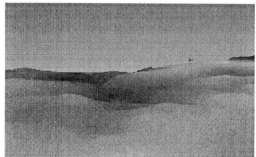

Figure 2- Terrain with fractal interpolation

Figure 3- Terrain with fractal interpolation and texture refinement, using multi-fractal functions.

Figure 4- Texture of a lake in a terrain with linear interpolation.

Figure 5- The same lake of figure 4, with fractal interpolation and texture refinement using fBm function.

Session 3-2

Augmented and Virtual Reality — Application

Chair
Eric W. Tatham
The Open University, UK

Visualization in Tunnelling – New Developments

G. Opriessnig and G. Beer[+]

Keywords: Visualization, Numerical Simulation, Tunnelling, Virtual Reality

Abstract

Within the Visualization project of the Austrian Joint Research Initiative (JRI) Numerical Simulation in Tunnelling (SiTu) the Tunnelling Visualization System (TVS) is being developed, to display information in tunnelling. The aim of the Project is to implement a user friendly visualization system, where the data can be displayed in a way, that tunnelling engineers can understand. Virtual Reality techniques are new in tunnelling and offer a lot of new possibilities. 3D-scalar-fields are visualised in a novel way. The data to be visualised are either results from numerical simulation or ones describing geological features. Such data have special properties, which have to be considered by the visualization system. This paper will present innovative techniques for this purpose.

Introduction

Without good visualization numerical simulation would be useless because tunnel engineers will not be satisfied with printed numbers. Good visualization is difficult since one must be able to display often complex three-dimensional visual information on a flat computer screen. The best way to do this is by immersing into the three-dimensional data using techniques of virtual reality. An important issue is that out of the large amount of data which is produced by a numerical simulation model we should display only what is important to the decision making process. For example for the tunnelling engineer displacements are best understood as 'trend-lines' which very effectively show the change in displacement magnitude and direction as the tunnel is excavated. With regards to stress values what may be of interest is not the absolute values of stress at various points but locations of maximum compressive or shear stress. Because this quantity changes in space one must find innovative techniques to display it. Basically the visualization should enable the engineer to see at 'a glance' where problem areas are.

The use of numerical simulation on site to assist the tunnel engineer in often very difficult decisions is not very wide spread. However, to be able to 'sell' this kind of technology to people working in tunnel construction one has to have very effective and easy to use software tools. Visualization of data plays an important role here. A Tunneling Visualization System (TVS) was developed from scratch with the benefit of experience from a previous system developed for

[+] SiTu-Research Initiative; Institute for Structural Analysis, Lessingstraße. 25/II, Technical University of Graz, Austria
opriessnig@ifb.tu-graz.ac.at

the mining industry [1]. The use of special tools for the development of software and modern object oriented programming techniques allowed the first prototype to be already presented 3 months after the start of the project. TVS makes it possible to perform a virtual walk through a tunnel which exists in computer memory only. During the virtual walk through the model the user may observe different results of numerical simulations and geological features. For example stresses become visible as clouds with variable densities depending on the stress value. To be able to perform the computational and graphical work in stereo in real time innovative methods had to be developed [2][6].

The data base

For numerical simulation the geometry of the model is described as a mesh. The mesh used (Fig. 1) has special properties which are different to the properties of wireframes, created for visualization. In visualization the standard element

is the triangle. This element type is not ideal for numerical simulation[3]. For this purpose different types of elements are used.

If a 3D calculation is done with finite elements, the three dimensional space is filled with brick elements. These elements are used for the calculation, but their geometry does not need to be drawn. Results of simulation inside these elements are of interest and only visible surfaces need to be displayed. If the tunnel advance is visualised, some elements become invisible, so this calculation must be redone for every excavation stage. To improve the smoothness of the surface, additional points on the element edges are calculated. This calculation is done, using the Newton interpolation algorithm. Usually elements are defined by their borders. To render surfaces, the midside node of the element has to be known. The position of this point can be calculated with the help of shape functions[3].

OpenGL has options to use different kinds of lighting effects. The characteristic of a light source can be modified in a wide range. Position, direction, opening angle, colour, attenuation factors

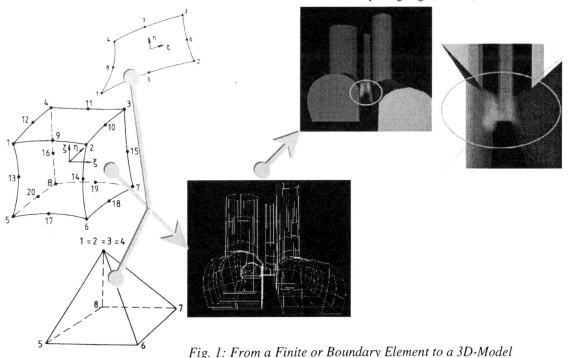

Fig. 1: From a Finite or Boundary Element to a 3D-Model

or the loss of intensity depending on the distance to the source may be varied. These adjustments are only effective if the normal vector of the model surface is known. If the model is drawn with triangles, this is no problem, because this vector can be easily found. Using the mesh from numerical simulation, the quadrilateral elements usually consist of four or eight points. Such elements do not have a planar surface, so a normal vector cannot be calculated explicitly. Making triangles out of each non triangular element will increase the necessary rendering effort. The Tunnelling Visualization Software defines the normal vector as perpendicular to both diagonals. This is not exact, but sufficient for good lighting effects.

Display simulation results

Simulation results have special properties, which have to be considered by the visualization tool. In some cases there are areas, where the values have peaks. These peaks sometimes do not have physical meaning but are caused by the

$$C = A * \left(\frac{Value - Min}{Max - Min} \right)^{(1*prog)}$$

C	contour-value
A	linear amplification factor
Max	maximum value of scale
Min	minimum value of scale
$prog$	progression factor

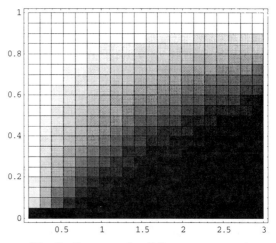

Fig. 2: Contours for different progression values

$$N_n = \frac{1}{2}(1-\xi^2)(1+\eta_n\eta); \quad n = 5,7$$ middle-points

$$N_n = \frac{1}{2}(1-\eta^2)(1+\xi_n\xi); \quad n = 6,8$$

$$N_1 = \frac{1}{4}(1-\xi)(1-\eta) - \frac{1}{2}N_5 - \frac{1}{2}N_8$$

$$N_2 = \frac{1}{4}(1+\xi)(1-\eta) - \frac{1}{2}N_5 - \frac{1}{2}N_6$$

$$N_3 = \frac{1}{4}(1+\xi)(1+\eta) - \frac{1}{2}N_6 - \frac{1}{2}N_7$$ edge-points

$$N_4 = \frac{1}{4}(1-\xi)(1+\eta) - \frac{1}{2}N_7 - \frac{1}{2}N_8$$

$$\vec{x} = \sum_{n=1}^{L} N_n(\xi, \eta) \vec{x}_n$$

Fig. 3: Shape functions of the quadratic serendipity element. They are used to convert local element-coordinates to global coordinates

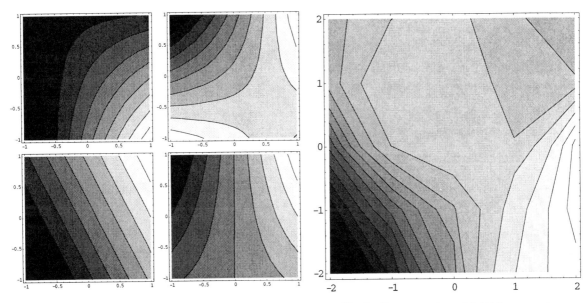

Fig. 4: Discontinuities in the contour-plot due to extrapolation from Gauss point in each element

Fig.5: Contour-plot with TVS-averaging

discretisation procedure [3][5]. They are important for error checking but for the purpose of the interpretation of the results by the tunnel engineer, these areas are not good, if the scaling is done automatically. The Tunnelling Visualization System offers the possibility to cut off such peaks. The user can define a maximum and minimum value, progression and amplification factor of the scaling curve. So the scaling can be modified for each purpose[4], e.g. to highlight peaks or troughs Figure 2 shows a density plot with different progression factors. The results of a finite element simulation usually are computed inside the element and not on the edges, where they would be necessary for drawing. Only displacements are calculated at these points. Stress values for example are known in the Gauss integration points. These points are internal points of an element. The geometry of an element is described by shape functions (Fig 3). With the help of these functions, it is possible to find the values at the edge points. If one point is part of more than one element, the extrapolated values for this node should be the

same for each element. If there is a large difference, this indicates, that the mesh is too coarse, and the results suspect and the size or the type of the elements need to be changed. Figure.4 shows an example of averaging

Solution

With a special procedure it is possible to smooth differences between elements For displaying three dimensional scalar fields as fog, an averaging algorithm was implemented. The Tunnelling Visualization Software uses the same algorithm for averaging and for calculating the density values for the fog[2]. This algorithm can be used, independent from the element type, which is very important for displaying results of numerical simulation. If the surface drawn consists of parts of brick elements, this kind of averaging has another advantage. Since Gauss integration points are inside an element, this means they are not part of the drawn surface. So the error decreases it the values are extrapolated for each element.

Algorithm

The value at a point or node is defined as an weighted average of all known values. These values usually are located in Gauss integration points. In the first step, the position of these points has to be found. The position is known in a local coordinate system, defined for each element. In this local system the coordinates η, ξ and ζ can have values from –1 to 1. The transformation from the local to global coordinates can be done, using the shape functions.

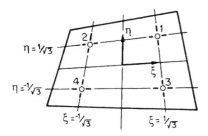

Fig. 6: Position of the Gauss integration points in a quadrilateral linear element

In many cases the Gauss integration points have the local coordinates $\pm\frac{1}{\sqrt{3}}$ (Fig. 6).

The shape functions of a quadrilateral linear element are:

$$N_1 = \frac{1}{4} * (1-\xi) * (1-\eta)$$

$$N_2 = \frac{1}{4} * (1+\xi) * (1-\eta)$$

$$N_3 = \frac{1}{4} * (1+\xi) * (1+\eta)$$

$$N_4 = \frac{1}{4} * (1-\xi) * (1+\eta)$$

To get the global coordinates for the four Gauss points the following transformation is necessary:

$$\begin{pmatrix} x_{GP1} \\ x_{GP2} \\ x_{GP3} \\ x_{GP4} \end{pmatrix} = \begin{pmatrix} N_{1GP1} & N_{2GP1} & N_{3GP1} & N_{4GP1} \\ N_{1GP2} & N_{2GP2} & N_{3GP2} & N_{4GP2} \\ N_{1GP3} & N_{2GP3} & N_{3GP3} & N_{4GP3} \\ N_{1GP4} & N_{2GP4} & N_{3GP4} & N_{4GP4} \end{pmatrix} * \begin{pmatrix} x_1 \\ x_2 \\ x_3 \\ x_4 \end{pmatrix}$$

x_{1-4} are the x-coordinates of the edge points. $x_{GP1-GP4}$ are the x-coordinates of the Gauss points

For the quadrilateral linear element the transformation matrix becomes to:

$$\begin{pmatrix} \frac{1}{6}*(2-\sqrt{3}) & \frac{1}{6} & \frac{1}{6}*(2+\sqrt{3}) & \frac{1}{6} \\ \frac{1}{6} & \frac{1}{6}*(2-\sqrt{3}) & \frac{1}{6} & \frac{1}{6}*(2+\sqrt{3}) \\ \frac{1}{6} & \frac{1}{6}*(2+\sqrt{3}) & \frac{1}{6} & \frac{1}{6}*(2-\sqrt{3}) \\ \frac{1}{6}*(2+\sqrt{3}) & \frac{1}{6} & \frac{1}{6}*(2-\sqrt{3}) & \frac{1}{6} \end{pmatrix}$$

The Transformation has to be done also for y and z. The influence of a Gauss integration point depends on the distance to the position of the wanted point.

$$f_{node} = \frac{\sum_{GP} f_{GP} * \frac{1}{(r_{GP-node})^2}}{\sum_{GP} \frac{1}{(r_{GP-node})^2}}$$

f_{node} is the value, computed for each node, f_{GP} the simulation result in a Gauss integration point. $r_{GP-node}$ is the distance between node and Gauss integration point. This calculation takes a very long time, but it has to be done only once. The resulting contours are a very good description for the physical properties of the model.

Conclusion

In many cases commercial visualization tools are designed to display phenomena, which can be described mathematically or with the help of statistical methods. Another large field in this area are products, designed for the car industry.

But in none of these fields, the special properties of numerical simulation results are considered in a way, that is appropriate for tunnelling. Computing performance becomes cheaper and cheaper, so the use of numerical simulation is becoming more widespread. Numerical Simulation in Tunnelling should be performed during the planning and construction phase. A good visualization is absolutely necessary, to sell this kind of technology. The features of the Tunnelling Visualization System, described in this paper are an important part of the visualization of numerical simulation results. They should help to increase the acceptance of these methods.

Acknowledgement

The work reported here was supported by the Austrian Science Found (Project Nr.: FWF-S08001-TEC)

References

[1] Beer, G. & Lang G. 1992. A graphical Post-processor for Computer-aided Design of Mine Excavations. Int. J. Rock Mech. Min. Sci. & Geomech. Abstr. Vol 29, No. 3, 307-322.

[2] Opriessnig, G. & Beer , G. 1998. Visualisation in Tunnelling Proceedings 1998 IEEE Conference on Information Visualization, 33-38.

[3] Beer, G. & Watson, J.O. 1992. Introduction to Finite and Boundary Element Methods for Engineers, J. Wiley, Chichester.

[4] Yuanxian Gu, Xiaosong Yang, Cangzhou Yuan, Yungpeng Li "Advanced Visualization Techniques for FEM-Computing-Scan-Buffer based direct Volume Rendereing for 3D irregular meshes" CIMNE, Barcelona Spain 1998

[5] Yingmei Lavin, Yuval Levy, Lambertus Hasselinkl, "Singularities in Nonuniform Tensor Fields" Stanford University

[6] Werner Haas, Harald F. Mayer, Georg H. Thallinger, "Visualisierung und Animation in der Geomechanik für Strömungs-, Transport-, und Spannungsberechnungen" Institut für Informationssysteme Joenneum Research Graz

A Prototype Hotel Browsing System Using Java3D

D. Ball and M. Mirmehdi
Department of Computer Science
University of Bristol
Bristol BS8 1UB, England

Abstract

Java3D is an application-centred approach to building 3D worlds. We use Java3D and VRML to design a prototype WWW-based 3D Hotel Browsing system. A Java3D scene graph viewer was implemented to interactively explore objects in a virtual universe using models generated by a commercial computer graphics suite and imported using a VRML file loader. A special collision prevention mechansim is also devised. This case study is reported here by reviewing the current aspects of the prototype system.

1. Introduction

A number of hotel companies, travel agents and other organisations currently have sites on the World Wide Web (WWW) where guests can get information about hotel accommodation. The aim of this project is to specify, design and implement a WWW application which will allow guests visiting such web sites to download 3D models of a hotel and take a virtual tour of the facilities available. For example, this may involve "walking" around a room or the sports centre of the establishment.

The number of hotels marketing themselves on the WWW is constantly increasing. A 3D hotel browser is one way in which a hotel company can stand out from its competitors on the Internet, and benefit its users at the same time. The current WWW hotel services exploit some advantages of the Internet, but provide little more information than a conventional printed brochure. This will only hold the users' attention for a short while. If, however, the user could interact with the WWW site by getting inside the hotel and walking around, then they are likely to be more interested, stay longer at the site, and remember what they have seen during their interesting (and fun) virtual tour.

There are many immediate benefits of this system. It could be adapted for use by Estate Agents to present houses for sale or rent, or to allow prospective students to view University campus accommodation. In fact, the pro-

totype system is a generic system and is called the Virtual Tour System (VTS), and while it is tailored towards hotel browsing, it is easily adaptable for other virtual tours.

Section 2 considers the tools used in this project. The prototype system is described in Section 3 along with some example images of the current state of development. Section 8 discusses the tasks remaining to complete the project in the near future.

2. The Tools

In this section we briefly review some (of the more important) software tools used in this project.

The Java3D Application Programmers Interface (API) [1] has been specified as a new extension to the core Java language which will support 3D computer graphics. Although this API has been finally specified, a full implementation is not yet available. The Computer Science Department at the University of Bristol was provided with a pre-alpha release of Java3D which has been used for this project. Some of the features currently supported by Java3D are: perspective or parallel projection, solid or wireframe rendering, flat shading engine of polygons, and multiple viewports (multiple views of the same scene) each with its own set of parameters, and full 3D frustum and screen level clipping.

Alias Wavefront [2] is a commercial graphics application which can be used for rendering photo-realistic 3D models. These models can be exported in a number of file formats which can then be loaded and used by other 3D viewers.

VRML (Virtual Reality Modelling Language) [3, 4] can be used to enable WWW browsers to download and display 3D models or virtual worlds. Models developed using Alias Wavefront are exported using the VRML file format.

It may well be possible to use other technologies, however we used the resources immediately available to us, and we believe it is the first time that VRML files are used in Java3D. In fact, VRML and Java3D are an ideal combination for this project as the Java3D scene graph matches very closely with the VRML structure.

3. System Overview

Naturally, robust design and performance issues are applicable here as in any software project. Also, human factors and general user requirements are imperative necessities. These were considered through liaison with the external industrial partner. The basic architecture of the prototype system involves three major components:

- Hotel Database - the hotel database contains all the information required for the hotel browser to generate virtual tours of featured hotels. This content comprises 3D model data and general hotel information. The database is located on a single Web server host. The database may contain references to external information sources on the same site or at other locations on the Internet.

- Hotel Browser - the hotel browser is a Web-based application which accesses information from the database via the WWW. It operates within a conventional Web browser, integrating the virtual tour capability with existing WWW hotel information services.

- Database Editor - the database editor provides a fully featured tool to create and edit all sections of the database. Through a graphical user interface it allows a skilled operator to build and modify hotel models and configure other database information including selection, insertion, deletion, and parameter editing. We will not consider the Editor any further in this paper.

The system will consist of a single database and any number of hotel browsers. A hotel browser will interact with its user through a Java3D interface running in a WWW browser. Figure 1 illustrates the three main components in the prototype system.

4. Hotel Database

The database provides a description of a closed hotel *universe* (Figure 2). It consists of a hierarchy of hotel description objects. There are four types of hotel objects: Hotel Group, Hotel, Room, and Feature. Each object has a number of properties and the following are common amongst them: *Name*, *Description*, and *References* (to related WWW Resources).

A Hotel Group object collects together one or more Hotel objects and has the aforementioned properties only. A Hotel Object collects together one or more modelled rooms from the same hotel. It has the following additional properties: *View Parameters* which should be defined to give the user the best view of the room models belonging to the hotel, and *Avatar Parameters* which should describe the size

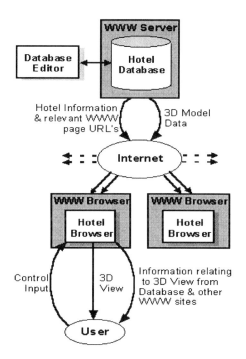

Figure 1. An overview of the Hotel Browser System.

of the avatar such that it is in proportion with the room models belonging to the hotel.

A Room object defines data to generate a 3D model of a hotel room or facility and groups together one or more features which are contained within that room. Additional properties include *3D Model Description Data* which can be used to construct a model for the user to view, *Location* to determine the physical position of the room within the hotel, *Room Bounding Region* which describes the physical volume in space occupied by the room, and *View Position* which defines a viewpoint within the room at which the virtual tour should start (this might typically be set at the doorway into the room). Figure 4 shows the definition of a typical double bedroom (specified using the Database Editor interface).

A Feature object defines a 3D model of a physical feature within a hotel room, such as a bed or a lamp-shade. The additional properties are similar to a Room object and provide 3D model description of the feature, its physical location in the room, and the preferred viewpoint for showing the feature to the user. Typically, moving the user to the view position will generate a 'close-up' of that feature.

The system user will submit control input through a user interface displayed in their WWW browser. These controls will enable the user to visualise the information stored in the hotel database. Figure 1 also provides a schematic view

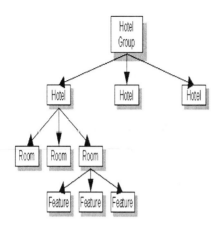

Figure 2. Hotel universe structure.

of the flow of data in the 3D Hotel Browser system.

5. Our Use of Java3D

This section briefly reviews some of those aspects of Java3D used in this application which are regularly referred to in the next sections of this paper. Central to Java3D, is the scene graph method for describing the content and behaviour of objects in a 3D universe. The scene-graph approach to describing a 3D universe is not new, or unique to Java3D. It has been used in various forms, perhaps most notably in VRML [3, 4]. A scene graph in Java3D is a directed acyclic graph [5]. The basic idea is that each object in the feature of the universe is described by a node, or small collection of nodes in the graph, sometimes called a group. The exact state of a feature (i.e. its location, orientation, size, etc.) is determined by the nodes traversed in the path from the root of the scene graph to the feature's node (or nodes). We use the Java3D scene graph for various purposes one of which is as part of a collision detection mechanism as described later below.

Java3D introduces a new View model which aims to ensure compatibility of applications across a wide range of visual hardware from simple desktop monitor screens to full virtual reality head-mounted displays. Conventional 3D APIs such as OpenGL utilise a camera-based view model where the programmer has ultimate control and must implement the exact position, orientation and other view properties in order to render a scene. Java3D by contrast separates the virtual property of the viewer's position in the Virtual Universe from physical display properties such as the number of screens, field of view or orientation of the viewer's head (for a head-mounted display). This is achieved within the context of a scene graph. A View Platform leaf node

is provided which can be added into the scene graph, perhaps below a Transform Group node to allow its position and orientation to be altered by the application. Physical information about the user and the display hardware are then accessed through special information objects. For more details on Java3D the reader is referred to [1].

6. Hotel Browser Application

The hotel browser consists of the View Display, Avatar Control Panel, Hotel List, Room List and Feature Lists components. It starts automatically when the user selects a link on the appropriate Web page. The application appears within the original Web browser window on the user's computer and loads a specific Hotel Group from the database according to the exact link selected by the user. The user will be given clear instructions at all times to assist them in using the browser.

The functions supported by the browser are the selection of a Hotel, selection of a Room, navigation between rooms in the View Display part of the browser, selection of a Feature for detailed viewing, etc.

One novel idea is to allow the user to select the type of features he/she requires (from the Features List) in order to define the sort of room they would like to stay in at that hotel. This means the room will be custom designed by the user and will be prepared by the hotel management in time for the user's arrival. Better still, this idea could be applied when users wish to specially arrange a conference or seminar room in the hotel.

6.1. Tour Simulation Behaviour

The user should be able to explore the hotel models in a manner similar to walking around a real hotel. This section briefly specifies the behaviour of the system.

The parameters used to specify the view rendered from a specific viewpoint in the hotel universe are the standard Graphics viewpoint geometry parameters: the user Field Of View Angle, the Front Plane, defined by a distance from the view point beyond which objects become visible, and the Back Plane, defined by a distance from the view point beyond which objects become invisible. Only objects in the visible region will be rendered and seen by the user.

The avatar description is used to determine how the user interacts with the scene. It comprises height, depth and width dimensions defining a bounding box approximation of a human body, and gravity simulation. This bounding box will be used to determine collisions between the avatar and objects in the universe. A step height parameter is used to determine the maximum height of objects above the base of the bounding box which the avatar can step up onto. The avatar and view parameters will be set on a per-hotel basis

466

according to the values specified for the current Hotel object which describes the hotel being viewed.

Java3D supports the animation of 3D objects and user interaction via the Behaviour leaf node. Behaviour nodes can be used to capture keyboard or mouse input from the user and manipulate (for example) the position of the View Platform. Java3D provides various features which can be combined with mouse events to support the picking of objects in a 3D scene. Other uses of Behaviour nodes include continually modifying a Transform Group node to animate part of a scene graph, altering the intensity of a light or starting a sound node. A basic approach to user interaction support through the Behaviour leaf node might be to implement a Behaviour node which has a reference to the View Platform Transform Group. This Behaviour would specify, for example, a key press as its initial wake up condition. When the user presses a key an event is generated which the Java3D scheduler passes to the Behaviour node to notify it that the wake up condition has been met. The Behaviour node can examine the event generated by the key press and alter the Transform Group matrix based on which key the user actually selected. To refine this solution further the Behaviour node might alter its wake up condition after a key has been pressed to be the disjunction of a key released event and the elapsing of a single frame. The next time the scheduler awakes the Behaviour node, it can examine the wake up condition satisfied. If a frame has elapsed then the Behaviour would repeat the last move made (still based on the key which the user last pressed). If, alternatively, a key released event was generated by the user then the Behaviour node ceases to alter the View Platform Transform Group, and return its wake up condition to waiting for the next key press. With this approach the user can hold down a key to instruct the Behaviour node to repeat the same operation, for example 'step forward', several times.

When this system of control was implemented in a test prototype two problems were highlighted. Firstly, binary (on/off) type inputs such as buttons and key presses were not found to be user friendly when trying to navigate through a 3D scene. This was due to the need in some cases to travel quickly, in large steps, and at other times to travel slowly. The naive control logic described above offers the user only one speed of action. Secondly, and more fundamentally, a property of the Behaviour scheduler came to light which is undesirable in this type of control system. When rendering more complex models a tendency emerged for the scheduler to 'lose' Java Advanced Window Toolkit (AWT) events. The result was that key released events would not be received by the Behaviour node and motion of the View Platform would therefore continue after user actually requested it to cease.

A solution was devised for this project which combines the use of the Java3D scheduler, a Behaviour node and the Java1.1 AWT event model used in 'conventional' Java window applications. User input events are detected using the implementations of the Java AWT event listener interfaces and custom developed user interface components. When the user activates one of these components a Behaviour node is notified directly by the component. This bypasses the Java3D scheduler as the Behaviour no longer needs to specify AWT events in its wake up conditions. When a component is activated the notified Behaviour node sets its wake up condition to be one elapsed frame. The Java3D scheduler will then wake the Behaviour every frame allowing it to move the View Platform according to the user's exact input.

6.2. View Platform Collision Prevention

A fundamental issue in interactive applications such as computer animation and virtual environments is collision detection [6, 7]. When navigating a virtual scene, it is reasonable for the user to expect that the View Platform cannot pass through a solid object. Java3D offers fairly comprehensive high-level support for collision detection in which each object may define a region known as its collision bounds. These collision regions may be described as simple box or sphere objects, or more complicated regions comprising a combination of simple objects. According to the Java3D specification, the Java3D renderer runs an infinite loop consisting of the following operations:

```
while(true) {

1. Process Input
2. If (Request To Exit) break
3. Perform Behaviours
4. Traverse Scene Graph and Render
   Visible Objects

}
```

What this brief description does not make clear is exactly where the occurrence of collisions is calculated. Various test applications written for the project suggest that the collision calculations are performed as part of step 1. This was deduced by the fact that if a Behaviour modifies part of the scene graph such that a collision between two nodes occurs, it is does not result in the interaction of any collision related Behaviour nodes until the current frame has been rendered. In practice this means that all collisions are rendered to the screen before they are reported. This property is not unreasonable given that if the actions of one Behaviour node were able to stimulate another in the same frame a dead-lock situation could occur where competing Behaviours prevent the renderer ever completing a frame.

Hence, since in Java3D all collisions are rendered to the screen before they are reported, we have designed a "1-step ahead" collision detection scheme to work alongside the Java3D mechanism. In the context of this application, we refer to this mechanism as Collision Prevention (rather than Collision Detection). Since the requirement is to give advanced warning that the viewer is *about* to intersect an object, collision prevention is a more appropriate action which implicitly deals with collision detection.

It is not possible in Java3D to specify visible geometry or collision bounds for a View Platform node. To enable proper collision prevention, a separate geometric representation of the View Platform must be added as a separate node to the View Platform's Transform Group (Figure 3). Collisions are then detected between this extra node, which will retain a constant position with respect to the View Platform. The "1-step ahead" scheme developed extends this strategy further by separating the collision bounded object completely from the View Platform, as shown in Figure 3.

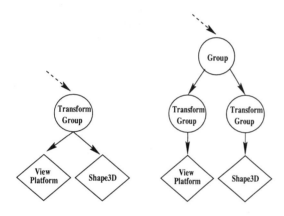

Figure 3. (a) Conventional scene graph, (b) Separating the transform of a View Platform and its associated geometry and collision bounds.

The View Behaviour node described in the previous section is extended to control the two Transform Group nodes now used. When user input generates a movement of the View Platform, the new transformation is first applied to the Transform Group of the collision bounded node while the View Platform transformation remains unchanged. The current frame is rendered and Java3D performs the collision calculations. If a collision is detected for the collision bounded node, then its transform is returned to that of the View Platform. However, if no collision occurs, the View Platform transform is set equal to that of the collision bounded node. In the latter case when more user input is received, the collision bounded node is moved on to the next transformation.

The result of this system is that movement of the View Platform lags one frame behind that of its associated collision bounds. If a collision occurs for a specific transfor-

mation the View Platform is prevented from moving to that position. Thus, Collision Prevention is achieved at the cost of a one frame delay in the response of the View Platform to the users commands.

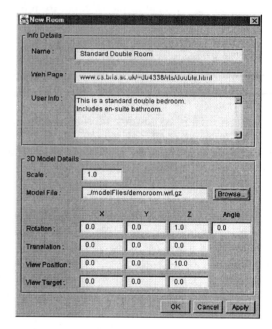

Figure 4. Definition of a new Room object.

Finally, in Figure 5 we show a snapshot of a hotel tour inside a room. The use of Java3D has enabled the key sections of the system to be independent of any 3D file format. It can be extended easily to support other file formats. The Hotel Browser is a good example of how simple HTML hypertext links can be used within an intuitive and interactive application user interface. In this case the distributed nature of the information on the internet is "hidden" and referenced from different features in a single hotel model.

7. Performance

At this stage in the development of Java3D much has been said about its performance with most observers claiming that it is exceptionally poor. The average duration of a frame render has been used as a rough benchmark in the development of this project, hence we measured the time in milliseconds between successive frames when the user moves the View Platform. By running the Editor application using the same hotel model and performing approximately the same manoeuvres it has been possible to compare the relative performance of different *dev08* and *Alpha01* implementations of Java3D. The results presented in Table 1 suggest that, while it is slow, performance improvements have been made in Java3D. The Just In-time Compiler (JIT) available for the JDK also provides a significant

Figure 5. A snapshot from a hotel tour inside a room.

JDK Version	Compiler	Java3D version	Time *ms*
JDK 1.1.5	Interpreter	dev08	2800
JDK 1.1.5	JIT	dev08	1490
JDK1.2 Beta3	Interpreter	Alpha01	1760
JDK1.2 Beta3	JIT	Alpha01	1270

Table 1. Performance comparison of various Java3D versions

performance improvement, however at the time of writing even the JDK1.1.5 JIT is specified as 'under development' and is not 100% stable. All the timings in milliseconds were recorded on a Pentium PC.

8. Conclusions & Future Work

In this case study, we have produced a full project plan including the final specification (not specified fully here) for a non-immersive VR application, namely a Hotel Browsing system. Some key aspects of this work are as follows.

The definitions are generic for other browsing applications; for example whether a system is required by an Estates Agent for viewing properties or a Car Dealership to demonstrate the inside of a vehicle, the principles described here will remain largely the same. Also, we have demonstrated a novel combination of Java3D and VRML. VRML was the ideal file format for this project as the Java3D scene graph matches very closely with the VRML structure. This correlation is likely to make it the preferred file format for many developers, although Java3D was designed to remain independent of any file format. Another novel method was the "1-step ahead" scheme. This was an intuitive necessity to comply with expected human movement in a virtual environment and had to be specifically designed to work around the Java3D provisions for collision detection. Finally, the user interfaces in this project were designed for (manipulation and visualisation of data by) non-VR experts.

All that remains is for the full system to be developed based on future funding. The full system will benefit from a greater range of Room types (to comprise the full hotel, i.e. corridors, seminar room, swimming pool, Bar, etc...) and a greater range of Feature objects. The future development of Java3D will heavily influence the technical aspects of this project.

Acknowledgements
The authors would like to thank Peter Gardner, Manager of Royal Swallow Hotel, Bristol, UK, for discussions and allowing us to measure rooms and other facilities in the hotel.

References

[1] Java3D. JavaSoft Java3D WWW Home Page. http://www.javasoft.com/products/java-media/3D.

[2] Alias Wavefront WWW Home Page. http://www.aw.sgi.com/.

[3] The VRML Consortium. The VRML Consortium WWW Home Page. http://www.vrml.org/.

[4] A. L. Ames, D. R. Nadeau, and J. L. Moreland. *The VRML 2.0 Sourcebook*. John Wiley & Sons, 1997.

[5] P.S. Strauss and R. Carey. An object-oriented 3d graphics toolkit. In *Proceedings of SIGGRAPH*, pages 341–349, 1992.

[6] K. Chung and W. Wang. Quick collision detection of polytopes in virtual environments. In *ACM Symposium on Virtual Reality Software and Technology*, pages 1–4, 1996.

[7] M. Lin and S. Gottschalk. Collision detection between geometric models: A survey. In *Proceedings of IMA Conference on Mathematics of Surfaces*, pages 33–52, 1998.

Visualization of Multi-scale Data Sets in Self-Organized Criticality Sandpile Model.

B. Hnat, S. C. Chapman

Space and Astrophysics Group, University of Warwick, UK

Abstract

To study the three-dimensional evolution of a CA model of a sandpile as a function of control parameters a computational steering approach has been used. Sandpile profiles are calculated in real time and displayed in three dimensions simultaneously with the evolution plots of state variables. This represents a generic problem of multi-scale structure in data sets derived from nonlinear systems. The software modules were developed in OpenGL^{TM} and the Glut^{TM} library and will ultimately be implemented in semi-immersive VR on ImmersaDesk^{TM}. To achieve sufficient speed in real time display, the full data set is represented graphically in a compact form.

1. INTRODUCTION

Most visualization techniques deal, to some extent, with handling of the large data sets. Algorithms such as visibility culling, triangle meshes or polygonal surface simplification are available to reduce the complexity of the graphical representation of the model [4, 3]. Many of those techniques, however, have serious limitations when used for multi-scale structures that require a close-up viewing at full resolution. Another problem that most visualization applications must overcome is real-time managing and rendering of the data. For application that perform data storage (CAD systems) some optimization/compression of the geometry can be performed to speed up future rendering. Computational steering methods, however, must respond to user's interrupts at a speed that makes any disk storage rather impractical in use.

Many complex physical systems generate data sets that are both large and multi-scale. A generic class of cellular automata (CA) used to simulate complex systems are avalanche or "sandpile" models. Multi-scale structures are a hallmark of complex nonlinear systems [6]. To study their

dynamics in space and time requires simultaneous display of structures differing in scale by several orders of magnitude. An additional challenge is that the bandwidth of the multi-scale sandpile implies large data sets. Our selection of a CA model for Self-Organized criticality [1] system, that is used as an example here, is quite arbitrary. The goal was to develop a tool for display and analysis of the multi-scale structures, that is, with generic features on different scales. To achieve that, one has to be able to select interesting regions of the structure and focus on its detailed topology. Selecting the region of interest can be a problem. For the sandpile problem considered here, the data set size is so large that simple static display of the entire structure is prohibitive. Under these circumstances an overview (a state variable, such as total energy) can be used to summarize the data.

In this paper we present some complex problems that arise when the large size of the data set is accompanied by its multi-scale character. For analysis of the full three-dimensional surface we need to retain all the information required for understanding a decimated data set without a priori knowledge of the region of interest. Here we discuss developing, in OpenGL^{TM}, rendering techniques for real-time display of the multi-scale data. Information of detailed structure in the sandpile has also been coded into the sound, which can be played simultaneously by the user to further enhance data analysis.

Since the future goal is to port the code to ImmersaDesk^{TM} tracked semi-immersive virtual reality system as a real-time computational steering application the benefits and drawbacks of the different implementations will be discussed in some detail.

1.1. TERMINOLOGY

Figure 1 shows two-dimensional (length vs. height) time slice of the sandpile surface. The sandpile *length* is descretized (slots), each part with one unit of length. The sand is always added to slot one, positioned at the origin

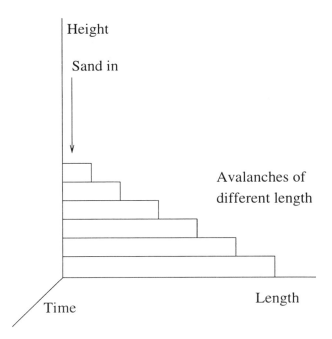

Figure 1. Timeslice of the sandpile evolution surface.

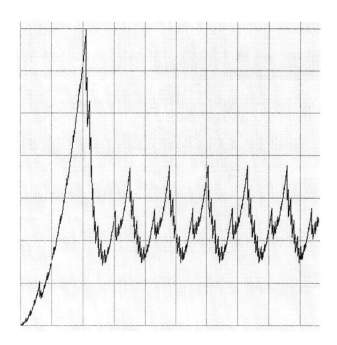

Figure 2. Time evolution of the state variable. Total energy of the system

of the graph. Dynamic rules applied to the model cause the distribution of the sand from one slot to another. These *avalanches* can move from left to right only. *Avalanche length* is defined as the number of slots involved in one slope relaxation process. The system has a single control parameter which determines the range of interaction of the CA (this range of interaction is referred to as *correlation length* here). The system is open at the end, allowing the sand to leave the system when boundary is reached.

2. STRUCTURE VISUALIZATION.

The easiest method of summarizing the evolution of a complex system is to use a state variable graph. The simplicity of the plot allows display of the entire evolution of the system. Figure 1 is a time evolution of the total energy of the CA system. Although simple, the graph can present researcher with very useful information. The existence and starting position of the equilibrium state is important physically. Multi-scale character of the system is also revealed. In the equilibrium state of the system the energy plot has clearly self-repeating and, for some values of control parameters, fractal pattern. Different scales of this oscillations allow us expect the existence of the similar features in the generated three-dimensional image.

Figure 3 presents the simplest technique for generating the surface of the sandpile profile in time. A wire frame was created using thickened lines and no lighting model was used. It quickly become apparent that one needs much advanced methods to visualize the topology of the model. A polygonal surface with OpenGL lighting model was used to generate the image on Figure 4. The three-dimensional surface can be rotated, translated and viewed in a close-up mode by the user.

Looking at Figure 4 multi-scale character of the structure is very obvious. The topology of the surface also varies strongly with a distance across the system and time. Over a short length range one can observe a plethora of short peaks oscillating in time. The structure contains complex patterns the user needs to extract. If we look on increasing length scales, larger, simpler "step-like" structures are apparent.

Such large dynamic range in the structures is hard to manage. Since different regions of the surface must be studied in a close-up mode we cannot use anyone simple optimization techniques for coarse graining of the entire surface. Different regions have to optimized differently based on the topology details they include. The simplest regions are the ones that create flat facets. Successive vertex removal can be used for these areas as described in [3]. Smooth surfaces should be estimated more carefully. Nor-

Figure 3. Sandpile height time evolution. Grid with no light

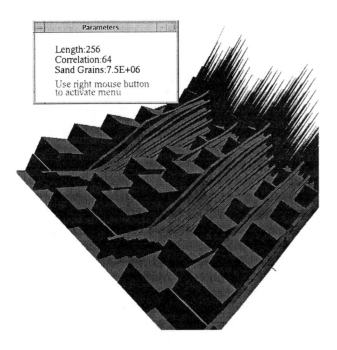

Figure 4. Sandpile height time evolution. Polygonal surface with lighting. The time scale is $7.5 \cdot 10^6$, y-axis varies from 0 to 256. Maximum height is 10^4.

Figure 5. Close-up view of the surface.

mal vector direction changes can be used to estimate the amount of information loss during the surface coarse grain process. No simplification is possible for the most rapidly changing areas (peaks). One could use a simple interpolation method to smooth the peaks for further close-up analysis [7]. We describe this simplification method and its impact on the size of the data set in the next chapter.

Ability to view the closed-up details of the surface presents yet another problem. In order to achieve sufficient speed for computational steering it is not feasible to use normal vector averaging. Since most of the surface contains flat facets this seems to be a reasonable approach. However, once the close-up view is in use, normals may have to be averaged for the smooth curves represented by polygons. Figure 5 shows a close-up of the curved structure on the surface.

The image on Figure 6 represent a special case in our studies. An exact analytical solution exists for a sandpile model with correlation equal to the length of the system (both parameters equal 256 in our case) and the surface is known to be fractal [2]. That allowed us to test the efficiency of our visualization techniques against the existing mathematical model.Figure 6 shows clearly the fractal character of the system - i.e., self repeating patterns in both

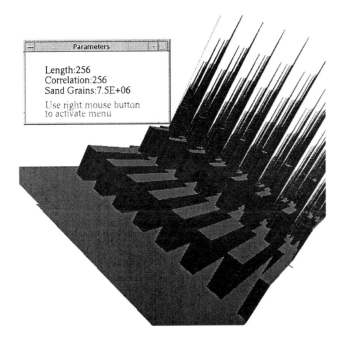

Figure 6. Fractal character of the surface revealed.

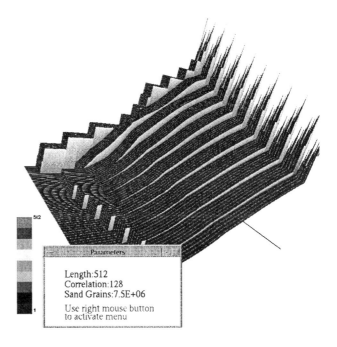

Figure 7. Color meshing of the avalanche length (shown as greyscale).

the length and time directions. Regions of fractal structures are revealed in all our images once correct visualization techniques are used.

2.1. COLOUR CODING AND SONIFICATION.

To encode more data elements into three-dimensional structure we also used color meshing to represent certain parameter. Figure 7 shows 250 records output with avalanche length encoded as a color mesh (greyscale here). Adding color increases already large amount of data per vertex, therefore we limited it to images of the small size (250 - 500 records). In our case color coding also required different algorithm for surface optimization. Coarse graining was run only along one direction (y-axis) since each polygon strip required different color.

Quantitative sonification was also used to enhance user's experience of the explored system. In our case we used sound to improve the analysis of the most complex areas of the surface. The frequency of the sound, its volume and duration are all based on the sequence of avalanche lengths in time. The choice of the parameter was based on the analytical solution presented in [2]. In this special case of the sandpile with correlation being equal to the length of the system, avalanche lengths are shown to only exist

with lengths 2^N cells (where N is an integer). For other values of the correlation length, avalanches cluster around values of 2^N. The avalanche lengths are hence approximately, always linear on the logarithmic scale and so are tones in the octave. Combined with a "close-up" view of the structure sonification is an additional tool for visualization of the multi-scale topology. We should mention, however, that the large disadvantage of sonification is that various parameters describing the sound can influence each other (i.e., the volume and the frequency of the sound) giving false perceptions of the changes within the system.

3. DATA SET REDUCTION AND SURFACE OPTIMIZATION

The computational steering method calls for the output data to be manipulated and recomputed with high speed. To accomplish both requirements, the disk access must be limited to minimum and all output data should be maintained in the memory.

The storage requirement for the presented problem may be quite stringent. For typical system length and correlation (256 length and 64 correlation were most commonly used) interesting behavior could be observed for amount of sand exceeding 10^6 grains. Smaller values of correlation need more sand grains to reach the equilibrium state. Table 1. presents input and output parameters of the system together with sizes of data sets before and after optimization process.

To achieve sufficient speed and memory usage, some simple techniques has been used. Examining closer the algorithm for our CA model one can deduce that after the relaxation the large part of the sandpile would form step-like areas. Such structures are compatible with the run length encoding to reduce the size of the data describing it. If the heights in the neighboring sites are the same, or lay within allowed difference, only one record is used to record the heights together with its start and end position. Efficiency of this procedure decreases with increasing complexity of the image - the surface includes less flat areas. For the correlation length equal to one-forth of the system's length, however, the impact is very significant. When the correlation equals the length of the system, the size of the output can be reduced by the factor of four.

The next step for data reduction exploits the continuity of the time function, related to the value of the sand grains. Instead of storing the absolute value of the sand grain we store a first instance (for the first relaxation) and then the difference for each record after the relaxation. The procedure can be written as:

$$z'(0) = z(0); z'(i) = z(i) - z(i-1). \quad (1)$$

Both methods allowed us to reduce the output size from about 500 MB per run to around 100 MB. Run length encoding of the height data sets also allowed us to simplify OpenGL^{TM} display routines. Surface coarse graining process was used to reduce the number of polygons drawn for the three-dimensional image. Data sets were first searched for large, flat surfaces that can be drawn as one polygon. Then remaining, smaller surfaces were created.

Corre-lation	Sand Grains	Size Before	Size After
1	$2.0 \cdot 10^7$	700 MB	250 MB
16	$1.0 \cdot 10^7$	500 MB	200 MB
32	$7.5 \cdot 10^6$	350 MB	150 MB
64	$5.0 \cdot 10^6$	275 MB	100 MB
128	$2.0 \cdot 10^6$	180 MB	80 MB
256	$1.0 \cdot 10^6$	160 MB	40 MB

Table 1. Data set size before and after optimization.

Surface coarse graining methods often introduce shading problems. The problem appears where the surface bends sharply and the polygons were used to describe a smooth surface, rather then facets. In our case however the large areas are flat facets and the curves are made of small polygons for which normal vectors do not have to be average, since run length encoding maintains the original accuracy of the calculations. Once "close-up" functionality is added to an application, allowing the user to view the three- dimensional graph in more detail, normal vectors need to be processed differently to avoid the problem. The standard procedure involves calculating normals for the polygonal facets, averaging them and then assigning them to a vertex that the neighboring facets have in common.

4. FURTHER DEVELOPMENT

The ultimate goal for this development process is to port the simulation into an ImmersaDesk^{TM} semi-immersive virtual reality environment. An eight processor Onyx2^{TM} will be used to calculate multiple instances of the sandpile running under different control parameters. Higher computational capability would allow us to view multiple surfaces and compare their structures. The number of records displayed in three dimensions could be increased also (currently maximum of 4000 records can be drawn).

Porting the code to a semi-immersive environment presents certain problems. The user interface must be modified to implment pop-up panels to allow the user to access parameters with a wand; as there is no keyboard access. Selection of the time interval of the data and the length interval of the sandpile, currently done through the state variable window, may be changed to a cube selection directly from the surface model. Apart from the changes associated with change of the environment new features will be added to existing application. Normal vector averaging combined with edge detection will be introduced to improve smooth surface close-up view. A linear interpolation algorithm is required to enhance most complex surface details in the areas where many rapid changes appear on a short length/time scale. Texture mapping should replace simple colour meshing technique to avoid the constrains that colour meshing puts on the surface simplification. Ability to generate cross sections of the surface will also be explored.

5. Acknowledgment

S. C. Chapman was supported by a PPARC Lecture Fellowship and B. Hnat was supported by HEFCE for this work.

References

[1] P. Bak, C. Tang and K. Weisenfeld, Phys. Rev. Lett. **118**, 381 (1987).

[2] P. Helander, S. C. Chapman, R. O. Dendy, G. Rowlands, and N. W. Watkins, in press at Phys. Rev.

[3] P. Lindstrom, G. Turk Proceedings of IV 98 Conference, San Francisco, 1998.

[4] M. M. Chow Proceedings of IV 98 Conference, San Francisco, 1998.

[5] H. J. Jensen, *Self-Organized Criticality, first edition*, (Cambridge University Press, Cambridge, 1998).

[6] M. F. Barnsley, R. L. Devaney, B. B. Mandelbrot, H. O. Peitgen, D. Saupe, R. F. Voss ,*The Science of Fractal Images*, (Springer-Verlag, NY, 1988)

[7] Alan Watt and Mark Watt ,*Advanced Animation and Rendering Techniques*, (Addison-Wesley, NY, 1998).

Distributed Information Sharing for Collaborative Systems (DISCS)

Anderson N, Abdalla H S

Department of Mechanical and Manufacturing Engineering
Faculty of Computer Sciences and Engineering
De Montfort University, Leicester, UK.

Email: nell@dmu.ac.uk / ha@dmu.ac.uk
http://www.eng.dmu.ac.uk/concurrent/

Abstract

With the advent of global competition, greater numbers of organisations require collaborations with others. Concurrent engineering can provide a highly effective framework for this collaboration. A Distributed Object Oriented Concurrent Engineering System (DISCS) focuses on the communication of data between the members of a distributed project team. Conceptually the communication is the enabling factor; technologically the use of the WWW and object oriented technologies. A portfolio of collaboration support tools facilitates practical mechanisms for information sharing within the distributed enterprise, communication / conferencing for project teams, configuration / version control and workflow structures. DISCS effectively facilitates the virtual team, currently within an engineering context.

Keywords

Concurrent Engineering, Object-Oriented Programming, Java, XML, STEP, Object-Oriented Database, Concept Mapping, VRML, Internet, WWW, Virtual Team.

Introduction

The purpose of DISCS is to enable distributed project teams who for which co-location is either very expensive or impossible to share the benefits experienced by co-located teams. The increase in collaborating organisations sharing expertise to stay competitive leaves a void where previous facilitating tools are minimal in function. Currently each tool only provides part of the solution; they lack the integrated completeness, which is a prime enabling factor. Projects such as MONET [1] and Cyberview [2], are where some of the founding concepts for DISCS are drawn. These only concentrate on the sharing of data such as CAD models. Assuming the sharing to be the enabling factor for the communication of a distributed project team. DISCS expands this to place retrieved data within a concept framework [3, pp. 132-138], hence giving each piece of data a context and increasing the coherence of the information. Thus improving the communication between members of the project team. This framework also assists the generation of new concepts not just their retrieval, tackling a conclusion of [4, p 11]; "Teams should encourage the sharing of new ideas, brainstorming to solve a problem."

The benefits which arrive from an improvement in the communication of a distributed concurrent engineering team are a reduction in costs, a reduction in time to market, an improvement in business processes throughout the product lifecycle, and an improvement in the final applicability to market for the product. The entire lifecycle is considered leading to these improvements.

The technologies chosen for the development of DISCS are VRML [5], STEP [6], Java [7], XML [8, 9], and an object oriented database [10]. These offer the potential for a highly portable system. Distributed access introduces a high likelihood of different platform usage throughout the

476

distribution. IT investment in platforms cannot be disregarded, in fact it should be exploited. An enabling tool must bridge this gap to be of any real world use. Another valid reason for their selection is the industries activity and support for them, they are each the current technology in their domain. Hence the functionality is still increasing allowing a closer integration of the components.

Previous Background Work

As previously mentioned DISCS overcomes what is considered the shortcomings of previous systems within this problem domain. It is the integration and portability of the sub system components, which increases the utility of such a system. Previous systems [11, 12, 2, 4, 1, 13] have a reduced integration of their component parts and a reduced portability. This results in a lack of a context for the information retrieved.

DISCS has relationships to projects, which in the past have provided only part of solution to the communication problem of the virtual team. However it also provides benefits identified as desirable in recent / currently undergoing projects such as CENTEX (Concurrent Engineering Needs & Technologies Experimentation).

MONET

Facilitates the creation and operation of the virtual team, via an application sharing mechanism. Technologically MONET [1] uses UNIX-BSD sockets and TCP/IP protocols to provide the communications infrastructure. Thus allowing X-Windows applications to be shared by the members of a virtual team such as CAD, art packages, and text windows. The information exchange possible in this manner is relatively limited. The scope of the system is restricted to a UNIX network; the portability is hence limited to within this operating domain. Control is achieved through floor control or chalk passing mechanisms.

CENTEX

CENTEX [13] is the evaluation of the impacts of the concurrent design process on product quality, costs and time to market. A new generation radio system is the target project to be evaluated. A combination of virtual co-simulation and workflow / process flow technologies are used to create an Integrated Collaborative Working Environment.

CYBERVIEW

Cyberview [2] was undertaken by the Department of Industrial Engineering at Seoul National University and the Department of Industrial Engineering at the University of Iowa. It is an enabling system for distributed concurrent engineering. It allows the distributed viewing of CAD models with some simple textual mark-up information. It is in essence a database of CAD models with the facility to view them over the Internet.

The proposed DISCS will provide a far greater access scope, instead of being limited to the UNIX network as in MONET, the access is provided via a connection to the Internet. This scope requires the platform portability of DISCS, which is not present within MONET. In previous work [11, 12, 2, 4, 1, 13] the connectivity between data created in the various applications has little semantic linking between them. DISCS allows a wide variety of connection possibilities directly within the information, at the strongest points of cognitive mapping.

CENTEX used the Mentor Graphics WorkXpert tool. After user feedback, WorkXpert was implemented with the introduction of a new graphical design process view based on a hierarchical representation. DISCS emulates both this structure and expands upon it to permit any linked structure of the data. Conceptual ideas can be mapped / linked into a process flow management display within DISCS, also linkable, hence increasing the entry points into the system. CENTEX identified a problem with the motivation of the team to adopt the new methods. DISCS tackles this in terms of simplicity of use, and cognitive understanding of the retrieved information.

Cyberview's mark-up information is of a limited scope, a short textual annotation is all that is permitted. There is no support for the initial phases of a concurrent engineering lifecycle. DISCS takes this much further with an assisting concept generation and viewing mechanism which can be linked into any part of the CAD model. This enables the initial phases of a concurrent engineering lifecycle. The design is then linked into the initial ideas, creating a cognitive map of the flow of concepts and designs within the minds of the team members, greatly increasing the understanding of the project among the team.

The Proposed System (DISCS)

Conceptual Overview

Through the linking of conceptual trains of thought to a variety of information mediums ranging from sound, video, images through to CAD data, the understanding of designs can be enhanced. Virtually every component in the system can be linked to another, hence providing a context with which the retrieved information can be interpreted. Another important aspect is the expansion of potential users. Currently a sound knowledge in computer systems is required to operate most facilitating tools. However with DISCS a cognitively understandable concept mapping system is used, derived from the Mind Mapping Technique [3]. This makes the understanding of the data second nature, the information and its relationships can be very easily visualised.

If the system is easier to use for the target user audience, it then allows a much greater flow of ideas into the system. The variety of team members can be expanded from the highly technically skilled group to form an IPD (Integrated Product Development) Team [11, p102]. This includes end product users, assembly teams, sales, marketing, i.e. categories of people whose input makes a big difference if captured early on in the product lifecycle. With the more usual "over the wall" [11, p102] approach this input would arrive at a much later stage when redesign is costly and thus possibly omitted, resulting in a substandard product. DISCS facilitates this early retrieval of data with a tool, which provides a cognitively applicable interface allowing the expansion of the possible user base.

The anonymity of many workers and a sense of lack of importance in larger corporations are often due to their lack of opportunities to contribute. This would also be assisted as a side effect of involving more people early on in the design stage of a project. The sense of ownership of the project would be higher increasing motivation aspects. The

insight from views other than high level management can easily be obtained; the value of this contribution should not be under estimated. The daily issues, which lack consideration at the initial stages then, represent barriers and problems later on in the lifecycle. These are now identified at a stage where their rectification is of a lower cost.

The benefits of the insight into a problem before construction, has been shown before for example on 3D models of pipe arrangements for chemical plants. Maintenance teams can be taken through the expected maintenance routine, virtually so that their input could be obtained. However 3D modelling although compared to a real world construction is extremely rapid, compared to an overview driven conceptual analysis it is not. Obviously detail cannot be considered at this level but the higher level thought which may not usually be visible to the rest of the team can be taken into account in the least amount of time. More detailed viewpoints such as the 3D models can then be linked into the system for review purposes. DISCS offer various planes of detail for information to be presented; this facilitates new team members with a system, which allows them to gain the essence of project quickly, but also allows them to delve into regions of greater detail if required.

Architectural Overview

The system is centred on the Internet protocol. This is the primary link between components. This protocol of communication was chosen for the target audience, which ranges from the global distributed collaboration of organisations, to the internal Internet solution within a multi-site company.

The system has five main interconnected sub-systems. At the heart of the system is an object oriented database, a concept creation / viewing tool, CAD model creation, VRML viewing of the CAD data, and a suite of supplementary communication tools. Figure 1. below shows the relationships between these components.

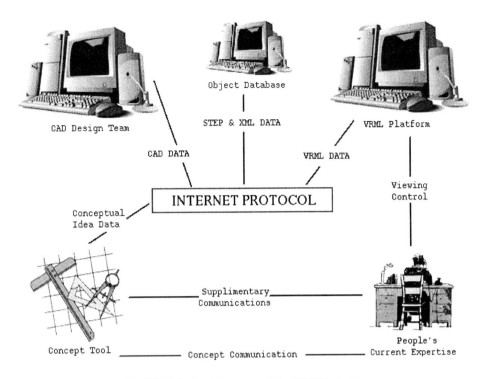

CAD Design Team

Object Database

STEP & XML DATA

VRML Platform

CAD DATA

VRML DATA

Viewing
Control

INTERNET PROTOCOL

Conceptual
Idea Data

Supplimentary
Communications

Concept Tool

Concept Communication

People's
Current Expertise

FIGURE 1: Architecture of the DISCS System

Database

The obvious database choice is between relational and object oriented, due to the complexity of CAD data plus the additional linking framework the choice was made to use an object oriented database. The security aspects can also be implemented in a more logical fashion with various levels of locking. This flexibility is well suited to the multi-user format the system will support.

The database essentially stores the CAD data to be shared with a host of linked in supplementary information in a wide variety of formats, from the concept maps produced within the concept map tool, through to images, video, audio, and even HTML documents. The possible information experience is limited only by the imagination of the creator.

Sharing of CAD models - VRML

Information at the conceptual level is essential for guiding a project in the correct direction during the early phases and providing an overview of the work required. This conceptual level can be used to browse through the model, an essential element for an information server [12].

However this is lacking the technical detail and hence communication of detail needed. The sharing of CAD models poses a problem for viewing. The translators which are required to translate between CAD formats increase in number exponentially. A model needs to be used as a medium; chosen for this task is STEP. CAD models are translated into STEP then into VRML. As the support for the STEP standard increases this will increase the future scope and possibilities for the system. STEP is a platform independent format aiding the portability aspect of the system.

The intended VR mechanism is through VRML. The source for the VRML worlds will be translated CAD models; VRML is the chosen technology for a variety of enabling factors [2]. The components are primarily being based on their adaptation to the distributed aspects of the system. I.e. for software the portability factors rank very highly. VRML through common web-browser support is highly portable. Various plug-ins can be downloaded for most browsers on most platforms. This support allows the CAD models to be viewed anywhere in the world where there is access to the Internet. VRML also allows the linking of nodes in a model to other URLs. These URLs can be other VRML models allowing the nesting of models. Concept maps can also be linked to, along with any other commonly found web documents, text, graphics, sound etc. Existing databases could be connected via an ODBC (Open Database Connectivity) connection / bridge. Allowing a change over from a legacy of stored models / file of a project.

VRML is also flexible enough to accommodate the various CAD formats once translated. Currently perceived as a purely desktop based viewer. There is no reason why specialist nodes / sites in the communicating team couldn't be set up to allow a more realistic and immersive experience in terms of virtual reality coves / caves. These allow the system to be used for after design applications. Instead of storing a lot of technical inaccessible data, the system is encouraging previously input data to be reused. The reality level of VRML is sufficient for the system to be used to provide a walk through of designs either for iterative modification and review or even to provide the first steps of training for future users of the product. This would be cheaper than building real world models / simulators, also somewhat more portable and modifiable.

VRML also allows the multi-participants existence in a single world. Again increasing the concurrency and the communication. If you want to show a person an aspect of the world for discussion the ability to follow someone around the world is invaluable. The use of more standard natural communication is suggested to accompany this sort of procedure. This approach can be termed the tour guide and can be used to help new team members become accustomed to the viewed product noting important features. A basic mannequin represents each user.

Other Components Overview

Translators

The system requires two points of translation from CAD data to STEP data, which can then be stored. Then for the viewing i.e. VRML this STEP data must be translated into VRML worlds. This is opposed to the more direct CAD format to format translation, which increases exponentially with each new configuration. For each CAD application a single translator to the STEP model is all that is required as the basis for conversion to VRML. Hence increasing the real world applicability and acceptance criteria.

STEP

STEP is an expanding technology, platform independent, with industry backing. Apart from the translation and transport medium within DISCS, the expansion of STEP compliant applications means that data stored in this way will be available to communicate this information during the next generation of systems. Product lifecycles often extend far beyond the operational life of the applications, systems software and hardware. Its important that a storage and translation medium should be able to from the outset bridge these changes when they occur rather than cause disruption upon change.

Conclusion

DISCS offers a wide range of benefits based on vastly improving communication between team members. This improvement in communication is derived through a linked repository of globally accessible information. Related information, concerning conceptual analysis, design, and workflow processes can all be retrieved from each other. This reinforces the understanding of the material retrieved and the hence the communication of ideas between team members. If the understanding of team members can all be increased an extra emphasis on involving a wide range of people at the earliest opportunity allows a variety of common problems to be communicated to the rest of the project team and dealt with at the point of lowest cost. A lifecycle of problems can be identified at the beginning stages, improving the number of change requests, marketing, assembly, testing, usability, through to ecological disposal of the product.

However DISCS offers the facilities to reuse this information, basic training can be performed via the VRML interface, maintenance teams can be given a run through of the expected servicing routine before they have to encounter it for real. Service manuals could be easily linked in to the repository of information used to build the product ensuring the accuracy of the data.

Unexpected changes to the project team later on in the lifecycle can be more suitably dealt with; the concept maps provide a clear overview of any product.

In conclusion DISCS offer the facilities to create information repositories that have real world value, throughout the entire concurrent engineering lifecycle, these information repositories offer benefits in terms of reduced costs, decreased turn around times, increased team-building qualities, a reduced time to market and an increase in applicability and quality. Hence improving both product and business processes.

Future Work

DISCS is an ongoing project and hence has various outlets for the expansion of other considerations. The virtual reality aspects can be taken to a higher level of realism, this would reflect the general improvements which could be made to a virtual world such as sound, nasal and haptic (tactile) feedback.

In terms of other domains, DISCS could replace the CAD model components with a software component viewing system, this could be initially textual expanding to a graphical representation. Hence reusing the linking possibilities within DISCS.

References

[1] SRINISVAS K., et al. *MONET: A multi-media System for Conferencing and Application Sharing in Distributed Systems*, CERC-TR-RN-91-009, CERC Technical Report Series, West Virginia University. Feb. 1992

[2] KIM C-Y., et al. Distributed Concurrent Engineering: Internet-Based Interactive 3-D Dynamic Browsing and Mark-up of STEP Data. *Concurrent Engineering: Research and Applications,* March 1998, vol. 6 (pt. 1). pp. 53-70.

[3] BUZAN, T. *The Mind Map Book.* 2nd ed. London, BBC Books, 1995.

[4] LONDONO F. et al. *Co-ordinating a Virtual Team*, Morgan Town West Virginia, CERC Concurrent Engineering Research Center Drawer 2000, West Virginia University. [No Date].

[5] Web 3D Consortium. *Web 3D Consortium.* [WWW]. Available from: http://www.vrml.org/ [Accessed March 1999].

[6] FOWLER, J. *STEP For Data Management Exchange and Sharing.* Twickenham, Technology Appraisals, 1995. pp. 53-67.

[7] FLANAGAN, D. *Java in a Nutshell.* 2nd ed. Sebastapol, O'Reilly & Associates, Inc., 1997.

[8] CONNOLLY D., et al. *The Evolution of Web Documents: The Ascent of XML.* World Wide Web Special Issue on XML, vol. 2 (pt. 4), Fall 1997. pp 119-128.

[9] REES, L. *A brief Introduction the Mysteries of the Extensible Mark-up Language.* [WWW, Printed October 28th 1998]. pp. 1-8.

[10] BARRY, D. *The Object Database Handbook.* United States of America , Wiley Computer Publishing, 1996. pp. 29-45.

[11] GAIENT A. Agility through Information Sharing: Results Achieved in a Production Setting. *Concurrent Engineering: Research and Applications*, June 1997, vol. 5 (pt. 2). pp. 101-111.

[12] JAGANNATHAN, V., et al. *Model Based Information Access.* In: *Proceedings of the Second Workshop on Enabling Technologies: Infrastructure for Collaborative Enterprise.* CERC-TM-93-007, IEEE Computer Press, April 1993. pp. 198-212.

[13] CENTEX, *Concurrent Engineering Needs & Technologies Experimentation.* [WWW]. Available from: http://esoce.pl.ecp.fr/ce-net/Information/cerelated/centex/Projectoverview.htm [Accessed 16th March 1999].

Session 3-3

Multimedia

Chair
Fiaz Hussain
De Montfort University, UK

Visual Metaphors to Enhance Hypermedia

Senaka Perera   Dave Hobbs   David Moore

d.perera@lmu.ac.uk   d.hobbs@lmu.ac.uk   d.moore@lmu.ac.uk

Virtual Learning Environments Group, Leeds Metropolitan University, UK

Abstract

This paper argues that whilst hypermedia systems potentially have a major role to play in education there is the danger that they tend to engender cognitive and navigational overhead in their users, which in turn detracts from their educational value. A potentially valuable means of ameliorating this difficulty is to use metaphors to aid the user as they interact with the system. The value of metaphors in overcoming the problems of cognitive overloading and navigational overhead is discussed and an experimental study proposed to investigate the design and deployment of suitable metaphors in this context.

1: Introduction

Hypermedia applications provide a non-sequential and flexible means of accessing information through navigation and exploration (Tomek et al 1991, Davies et al 1991). This linking capability makes hypermedia very powerful in terms of its ability to organise, store and present large amounts of complex information. Although there are many advantages in the use of hypermedia systems as described below, there also exist issues of cognitive overloading and navigational overhead for users interacting with such systems. This paper explores these issues in detail and proposes the use of metaphors as a possible mechanism to overcome them.

2: Educational Hypermedia Systems

The underlying structure of hypermedia provides for storage of information in atomic nodes in the form of different multimedia elements such as text, graphics, animation, audio and video, thereby allowing a multidimensional association of information (Davies et al 1991). The nodes are typically interconnected in a semantic network and each node's information is made available to the user via one or more links. A hypermedia application may initially be presented to the user in such a way that the user is shown a simple overview of the system before being able to drill down to more detail and greater complexity.

From an educational standpoint the principal attraction of hypermedia is that it lends itself naturally to non-sequential education since it encourages the free association apparently favoured by human thought. Hypermedia potentially provides both an object and a process of education (Norman 1994) - it provides the object in that it contains at the node level the content information to be presented to the student; it provides the process in that it also contains the dynamic links that lead from one node to another. Technology-based teaching based on hypermedia principles can now incorporate video clips, voice annotations attached to reference text, and digitised video (Marcus 1997, Jacobs 1992). It also affords the user the ability to interact with information in a non-sequential way, the user selecting their own path and navigating it at their own pace, acquiring knowledge by discovery and exploration (Norman 1994, Jacobs 1992).

On the other hand, however, hypermedia may often seem to users to be richer and more dynamic than expected (Norman 1994, and because of complex spatial relationships between these nodes, designers of hypermedia systems are faced with problems of *cognitive overloading* and *navigational overhead* (Tomek et al 1991, Davies et al 1991, Subramaniam and Tauf 1993). Cognitive overloading is encountered by users interacting with hypermedia applications due to the sheer quantity and association of information in such systems. Furthermore, users can become lost in a wealth of information, and also disoriented and unable to build mental models of the information space, thereby giving rise to navigational overhead that is partly attributable to cognitive overloading but also due arises out of the use of complex navigational patterns. The main causes of navigational overhead and cognitive overload have been variously identified as disorientation, inability to judge the amount of available information and the structure of that information, difficulty in locating the desired information, inability to retrace the path to a known region of the hyperspace, and general tendency to lose sense of position in the information space.

3: Issues in Hypermedia Design

The problems of cognitive overloading and navigational overhead have raised a number of issues in the development of hypermedia systems. Research is now beginning to focus on possible mechanisms for organising and controlling the complex association of information in a hypermedia system as well as enhancing and facilitating the navigational functions of searching and browsing. This in turn should then bring a greater coherence to hypermedia structure, allowing users to obtain information more easily without becoming lost, and facilitating their ability to build mental models of the system.

3.1: Cognitive Overloading

One of the causes of cognitive overloading is the inability of the user to obtain a rapid and intuitive understanding of the system functionality (Tomek et al 1991, Vannen 1993), leaving them confused as to the content and structure of information available. Empirical studies have shown that a reader's ability to understand and remember information depends on the degree of coherence of the reading matter; in analagous fashion, it is expected that coherence in hypermedia systems may reduce cognitive overloading. In psycholinguistics coherence is not regarded as an isolated text feature, but as the result of a cognitive

construction process (Van Djik & Kintsch 1983). A document is deemed coherent if a reader can derive a mental model from it that corresponds to facts and relations in a related world. This construction process is facilitated when the document is set out in a well-defined structure and provides rhetorical cues reflecting these structural properties (Thurin 1991). Since users of an educational environment frequently need to explore concepts, it is important that they should be able to build a mental model from what is presented to them. This in turn depends on presenting a coherent structure them user in the first place. All this should, it is argued, be striven for in an educational hypermedia system.

3.2: Navigational Overhead

Another issue that directly affects the construction of mental model is related to the limited capacity of human information processing. Every extra effort required in the course of processing a document reduces the mental resources available for comprehension. Thus, all additional activities create an extra workload that the user has to cope with. In hypermedia, these additional activities mainly concern the user's navigation, so users should be able readily to interact and navigate the information space. Navigational overhead arises from the process of interacting with the information, whether searching or browsing for what is required, whilst lacking an overview of the links and the nodes that are not directly linked to the active node (Tomek et al 1991, Charny 1987, Gordon et al 1989). This causes difficulty in locating the desired information, or retracing to a known region of the hyperspace. Empirical research shows that these additional activities may create navigational overhead by interrupting the train of thought (Gordon et al 1989, Monk, Walsh and Dix 1988, Subramaniam and Tauf 1993). It follows that navigation in an educational environment should be made as straightforward and require as little effort as possible in order to minimise this overhead.

4: The Metaphor as a Possible Organising Device

It is the contention of this paper that metaphors may provide a suitable means of addressing the issues of cognitive overloading and navigational overhead. Metaphors are seen as analogical models of entities and experiences existing outside the domain to which they are applied. Through them, knowledge in one already familiar domain becomes directly applicable to another, less familiar or unfamiliar domain. Appropriate metaphors built into the user interface may help the user rapidly to adopt a correct mental model of how the system works. (Nadeau 1996, Glowella 1995).

4.1: The Nature and Role of Metaphors

Metaphors are the fundamental concepts, terms and images by which and through which information is easily recognised and understood (Marcus 1997). Linguists assert that the way we think, what we experience, and what we do everyday frequently make recourse to metaphors (Lakoff and Johnson 1980). Often in communicating events and concepts lengthy descriptions and probably technical jargon are required. This often poses a problem to a novice user who does not understand such technical jargon. The use of metaphors may, therefore, help to overcome such problems through its ability to provide descriptions by reference to something with which the hearer is familiar.

Metaphors are very powerful devices for communicating even a complex, structured set of properties in shorthand that is easily understood. For example, if a person describes their job as a prison they communicate all properties of the superordinate category (prison) such as confining, unpleasant, difficult to escape from, and so on. The metaphor is more efficient and more precise than listing all the properties exhaustively, especially as the latter is rarely achievable. This becomes readily apparent in the sciences where it is quite common to use metaphors for conceptualising abstract concepts in terms of the apprehensible (Gentler, 1982). Metaphors are also commonly used to help users to construct an appropriate cognitive representation of computing systems in general (Carol and Thomas 1982) and user interfaces in particular (Carol, Mack and Kellogg 1988).

Some well-known examples of user interface metaphors are the *Desktop* metaphor common on Windows systems, the *Book* metaphor in which users see an open book on the screen with a table of contents and pages to turn showing how much of the book has been used, *Guided Tours* which enable students to 'take a bus' for a guided tour through the information space, and *Rooms* where 'opening a door' may exit the program or transport the user to a new area. Some other metaphors are *Library*, *Map*, *Whiteboard* or *Chalkboard*, and the physical *World*.

4.2: The Mechanics of Metaphors

As previously pointed out, metaphors can allow the knowledge in one already familiar domain to become directly applicable to another domain and encourage the user rapidly to adopt a correct mental model of how the system works. The inherent structure possessed by any the metaphor will transfer across and impose structure and landmarks on the hypermedia application domain. This may be supplemented by dynamic guidance that can dynamically guide a user to the information available in nodes that are not directly linked to the active node. It may be also used to enhance and facilitate the navigational tasks of searching, browsing and orientation. Indeed, a variety of metaphorical tools might be used for this purpose. Tools such as guided tours, narrated tours, guides, fisheye views, trails, and mirrors might all enhance and facilitate navigational tasks (Davies et al 1991). For example, guided tours could allow the user to catch a virtual bus and be given a tour around the information space (Hammond and Allison 1988). The 'guided discovery' approach is a valued tool in learning since it offers freedom to the learner whilst providing controlled guidance (Laurillard 1995); a judicial choice of metaphors may help a hypermedia system to be used in such an approach.

4.3: Application of Metaphors

There are different kinds of metaphors with different cognitive and conceptual properties (Stanford 1997). The use of metaphors in a particular application depends on their role within that application – for example, to make structure explicit, give a rapid overview, support navigation or support organisation (Drieberg 1994). For example, understanding a computer system of any complexity can be characterised as layers of different metaphors ranging from silicon gates and electrons to those that are used by the user at the interface (Hutchinson 1989). However, further research is needed to explore further the potential of diverse metaphors, their impact on communication and means of evaluating their effectiveness (Marcus 1997). It is unlikely in most applications that any single metaphor will be suitable for the whole system and for all users engaged in a wide variety of tasks (Davies et al 1991). Different metaphors may cover several, partly overlapping aspects of an information system such as presentation, structure and interactivity (Vannen 1993). It is important therefore in seeking to choose or generate appropriate metaphors for use firstly to recognise and identify the possible metaphor types.

4.4: Metaphor Types

Through their use of a single organising theme *composite metaphors* give a rapid overview of the system functionality. On the other hand, *spatial metaphors*, through the use of virtual buildings, rooms, cities, and landscapes can make structure more explicit, provide coherence and facilitate navigation. Maps and other spatial representations may additionally be used to reveal spatial structure and thus can facilitate navigation; guides and guided tours are particularly aimed at achieving the latter. Other metaphors, such as games, books, simulations, desks, and television are characterised by Marcus (1997) as visual-verbal communication and may be derived and used according to the needs of the tasks when the system is developed.

4.4.1: Composite metaphors

Composite metaphors are based on a single organising theme such as 'The world of Travel' or the 'Land of ancient Egypt'. The main purpose of the composite metaphor is to indicate to the user the type of metaphors used. Composite metaphors integrate well with other metaphors in terms of relating to the same source domain so that users do not become confused (Davies et al 1991, Drieberg 1994). A composite metaphor will provide an appropriate umbrella for other metaphors to be included; it should also allow for decomposition and better organisation of complex information. It is hypothesised within this research study that composite metaphors have the potential to present the user with a rapid overview of system functionality and of what they can expect when they interact with such systems.

For example, the study of ancient Egypt could make use of the composite metaphor with a single organising theme 'Museum of Ancient Egypt'. Users will then intuitively know to expect, for example, other familiar metaphors such as buildings and rooms, and know that the information about the civilisation, pyramids, and mummies is likely to be organised in the different rooms, floors or buildings as in a traditional museum. They will also expect to find maps, guides, and other navigational aids that can give the user an overall picture as to the content of the information available. The composite metaphor therefore embraces and integrates other metaphors according to the needs of the application and associated tasks. Other metaphors such as games, simulations, video-clips, books, and guides could also be included in the composite metaphor to enhance coherence, facilitate navigation, and further the discovery process. Equally, alternative composite metaphors such as cities and landscapes might

instead be chosen dependant on the particular needs of the application.

4.4.2: Spatial Metaphors

Spatial metaphors essentially try to make use of humans' abilities to use spatial environments to organise information and human skills in navigating such spaces (Dieberger 1994, Schawn 1996). In this way complex multimedia information may become more familiar when presented as a building, room, book, city or a landscape. (Vannen 1993, Vannen and Diesberger 1995, Schawn 1996). It is hypothesised that spatial metaphors seem to have the potential to enhance coherence in hypermedia systems by visually laying out information and organising related information in groups or hierarchies.

Spatial metaphors can be classified into two basic types, namely those depicting large-scale spatial areas and those showing small-scale areas (Schawn 1996). The large-scale area metaphor utilises the concept of a larger geographical site comprising a number of distinguishable places with different functionalities. Examples are a campus (with lecture halls, cafeterias, and libraries) or shopping mall (with different rooms for different functions, entrance halls, and so on). In the 'real world' the topography of large-scale areas primarily serves the function of providing convenient transitions between the different locations of the site. Similarly, the purpose of large-scale metaphors in interface design is to visualise the complex structure of hypermedia applications and to allow the user to switch easily between their different functional parts. The visual specification of their topological relationships allows the user to determine where they actually are, where the different places of the site are located and how they may be reached (Drieberg 1994, Schawn 1996). Similarly, a small-scale spatial metaphor could be used to carry out a certain specific function, such as the earlier example of 'opening a door' in a Rooms metaphor causing the user to transit to another area of the domain (Schawn 1996)

Interaction within these metaphors follows the modes of interaction in their originating environments (Vannen 1993). In the previous example of the Ancient Egypt museum composite metaphor, a film or a video clip about the development of different civilisations could be shown in a one room ('cinema') whilst another room ('studio') could display photographs; a third ('lecture theatre') could host a presentation by a human expert. Similarly, different activities related to pyramids such as walking through a pyramid, simulating the effect of building a pyramid, and so on could be organised in the 'pyramid gallery'.

Spatial metaphors could, in addition, enhance and facilitate navigation. Users intuitively identify navigation patterns in buildings, cities and landscapes. Furthermore, some characteristics of buildings and other places indicate their importance, purpose, and accessibility and these can help users decide which places they should visit to accomplish their goals (Schawn 1996). For example, important places are typically located at the centre of their site within direct reach of anywhere on the site. Specific architectural features allow further inferences to be made concerning purpose and functionality so that, for example, cafeterias look different from libraries. Such features can also indicate accessibility so that open doors or lit windows might, for example, indicate that they may currently be visited or accessed. Arrows, landmarks, different coloured areas, and sign-posting could all enhance and facilitate navigation. For example, a colour code could be used to differentiate the various areas of civilisations, pyramids, and mummies. Other metaphors such as maps, guides, guided tours and fish-eye views could also be used to facilitate navigation.

5: Objectives of the Research

The main focus of the current research in the VLE group at LMU is an empirical approach to identify the potential of metaphors as a mechanism to control and organise the association of information in large and complex hypermedia systems. Of initial interest is how effectively the single organising theme of composite metaphors helps users to obtain a rapid overview of the system functionalities and how successfully it helps prevent them becoming lost. Other avenues being explored include the extent to which spatial metaphors are able to group, organise and control information in a multidimensional hypermedia system, the extent which they can provide coherence to the hypermedia structure, and the extent to which they facilitate the user in building mental models so that they may easily switch between their different functional parts and accomplish their tasks.

The research will attempt to find out whether it is possible for architectural features within spatial metaphors to enhance and facilitate navigation by making it easy for users to identify their importance, purpose and accessibility, thereby allowing them more successfully to accomplish their goals. Given that cluttering the interface with irrelevant or non-functional visual details in order to achieve a greater sense of 'realism' can confuse users and

lead to errors (Dercyke et al 1995), a pertinent practical research question concerns the nature of the optimal mapping, as well as what type and styles of maps, guides, guided tours and other navigational metaphors could be used to facilitate and enhance navigation. A more psychological aspect of the investigation will hope to reveal the limitations of human perception that might cause metaphors to fail.

Questionnaires and interviews will be used to assess the ease to which users obtain a rapid overview of the system and its functionality, the effectiveness of spatial metaphors to organise information in terms of the users building suitable mental models, the success with which users identify the purpose, importance and accessibility from architecturally different buildings and rooms, and the effectiveness of maps, guides and guided tours.

6: Conclusions

Although it is believed that metaphors hold great potential value to teaching, there is little, if any, empirical research demonstrating the claimed benefits of metaphors and the usability of metaphor types such as the composite metaphor and the spatial metaphor (Smilowitz 1998, Drieberg 1994, Marcus 1997, Schawn 1995, Boyce 1996).

More research is therefore needed in these areas, and the intent of this research at LMU is to investigate different metaphors in terms of their effectiveness and efficiency in overcoming the issues related to cognitive overloading and navigational overhead. The prototype interfaces to be built involving a number of spatial and composite metaphors will be evaluated against a non-metaphorical environment with respect to their effectiveness in overcoming the problems associated with cognitive overloading and navigational overhead. It is anticipated that important guidance on the use and the generation of appropriate metaphors will result which will then be of direct value in building more useful and effective hypermedia learning systems in the future.

References

Boyce, D (1996), *Spatial Metaphors in user interfaces,* University of Wales Research Electronic Publication.

Carol J, Thomas JC (1982), Metaphors and the Cognitive representation of computing systems, in *IEE transaction on systems, man and Cybernetics*, SMC 12, 107-115.

Carol J, Mack R, Kellogg J (1988), Interface metaphors and user interface design, in *Handbook of Human ComputerInteraction*, ed Hallender M, Elsvier publishers, Holland, 67-85.

Charny G (1987), Comprehention of non linear text: The role of discourse cues and reading stratergies: in *Proceedings of the first ACM Conference in Hypertext*, 109-119, Chapel Hill, North Carolina.

Davies G, Maurer H, Preece J (1991), Presentation metaphors for a very large Hypermedia systems, in *Journal of Microcomputer applications*, 14, 105-106.

Dercyke A,Smith C, Hemery L.(1995), Metaphors and Interactions in virtual environments for open and distance education, in *Proceedings of ED-Media 95* Maurer H (ed), 181-186, AACE, Graz.

Dieberger A (1994), Spatial User interface metaphors in Hypermedia Systems, in *(Workshop) Proceedings of the European Conference on Hypermedia Technology*, Edinburgh, Scotland, 1-4.

Gentner D (1982), Are scientific analogies metaphors? in *Metaphor: Problems and Perspective*, Mialll DS (Ed), (pp 106-133), Harvester Press, Brighton, Sussex, England

Glowella U (1995), Metaphors for Hypermedia interfaces, in *Designing user Interfaces for Hypermedia* 1, 55-57.

Gordon.S, Gustavel J, Moore J, Hanky J (1989), The Effects of Hypertext on reader knowledge representation, *in Proceedings of Human Factor Society 32nd Annual Meeting.*, 296 – 300.

Hammond N, Allison L (1988), Travel around a learning support environment: Rambling. Orienteering or Touring, in *Proceedings of CHI 88*, 269 – 273.

Hutchinson E (1989) Metaphors For interface Design, in *The structure of Multimodel Dialogue,* Taylor MM et al. (eds), Amsterdam: North Holland, 1989, 11-28.

Jacobs G (1992), Hypermedia and discovery based Learning: Historical perspective, in *British Journal of Educational Technology*, Vol 23, 113-121

Lakoff and Johnson (1980), *Metaphors we live by*, University of Chicago press.

Laurillard D (1995), Multimedia and the changing experience of the learner, in *British Journal of Education Technology* 26, 179 – 189.

Marcus A (1997), Metaphor Design in User Interfaces: How to manage expectation, Surprise, Comprehension, and Delight Effectively, in *Proceedings of CHI 97,* Atlanta, Georgia, USA.

Monk A, Walsh P, Dix A (1988), A comparison of hypertext, scrolling and folding as mechanism for program browsing, in *People and computers*, Cambridge University Press.

Nadeau D (1996), User Interface metaphor in virtual reality using RML, in *Behaviour Research methods, Instruments and Computers* 28, 170-173.

Norman K (1994), Navigating educational space with Hypercourseware, in *Hypermedia* 6, 35-39.

Schawn S (1996), Communicating and learning in 'Virtual Seminars': The use of spatial metaphors in interface Design, German Institute for research on Distance Education, Electronic Publication.

Smilowitz (1998), *Do Metaphors Make Web Browsers Easier to Use?* Claris Corporation, Santa Clara, California, UAS, Research publication. Electronic Publication.

Thurin M (1991), What's ELIZA doing in the Chinese room? - Incoherent Hyperdocuments- and how to avoid them, *in Proceedings of the 3rd ACM conference on Hypertext (Hypertext 91),* 161-177.

Tomek I, Khan S, Muldner T, Nasser M, and Novak G (1991), Hypermedia Introduction and Survey, in *Journal of Microcomputer Applications* 14, 63-103.

Vannen K (1993), SHARE ME: Metaphor Based Authorial Tool for Multimedia, in *Proceedings of HCI 93*, Springer-Verlag, Vienna, Sept 1993.

Vannen K and Diesberger J (1995), Metaphor based user interfaces for hyperspace: Designing user interfaces for Hypermedia, in *Hypermedia,* 1, 68-77.

VanDijk TA, Kintsch W (1983), *Strategies of Discourse Comprehension*, Academic Press, Orlando.

Multimedia Information Systems in Education

Pat Jefferies and Fiaz Hussain,
De Montfort University
Department of Computer and Information Sciences,
Kents Hill Campus,
Hammerwood Gate,
Milton Keynes,
MK7 6HP,
England.

Email: pjefferi@dmu.ac.uk or fiaz@dmu.ac.uk

Abstract

Multimedia applications within the academic environment can be varied and include such things as: marketing of courses with an interactive prospectus; providing general administrative information (student handbooks, timetables, assignment schedules, module content, etc.); facilitating co-operative working using such things as computer conferencing or collaborative whiteboards; and for the purposes of computer-assisted-learning (CAL). In addition, multimedia can be used as an end in itself through students employing the embedded techniques in development of a spectrum of products.

The main purpose of this paper is to explore the lessons that might be learnt through the application of information systems research to the field of multimedia education. By adopting this approach, parallels might be drawn between the two application areas to highlight the convergence of underlying philosophies and methods in order to inform good practice. The paper aims to promote discussion of the various aspects involved in multimedia systems development within an educational environment.

Keywords: Multimedia Technology, Educational Applications, Information Systems

1.0 Introduction

In General Systems theory there are a number of different classifications which may be used to categorise systems. Such classifications include closed/open (determined by the interaction or otherwise of the system with its environment), and deterministic/probabilistic, (determined by the existence or absence of defined and predictable stimulus-response pairings). General systems theory further defines 'open' systems as being a set of components (e.g. an organised collection of people, machines, procedures, documents, data and any other entities) that interact with each other as well as with the environment to reach a predefined goal. This particular theory is illustrated in Figure 1 below.

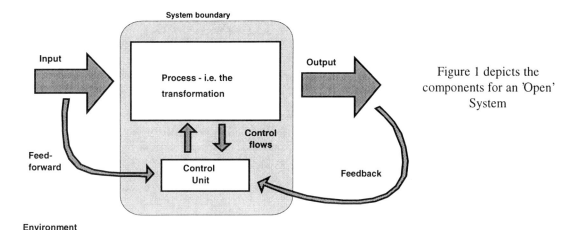

System boundary

Input

Process - i.e. the transformation

Output

Control flows

Feed-forward

Control Unit

Feedback

Environment

Figure 1 depicts the components for an 'Open' System

Thus, the model illustrated in Fig 1 may be seen, in simple terms, to be based on the idea that all 'open' systems operate within an environment and have a boundary within which controlled processes act upon identifiable inputs to produce required outputs. Systems thinking also implies that there are a series of inputs which can be direct or as a consequence of environmental influence; whereas the outputs will be determined by both the inputs and the processing itself. The central transformation is also controlled by an element of feed-forward and feedback which are themselves dependent upon the particular system under review. The above model, which depicts a single feed-back loop system, has, however, been found to be much too simplistic and deterministic a view to adequately illustrate complex, adaptive human systems which are perceived to consist of a 'web of non-linear feedback loops' (Stacey [10]).

However, if we consider education as a specific example of an 'open', probabilistic system then this may also be seen in terms of inputs, processes, outputs and interaction with the environment. Inputs to the system might be potential learners. The educational process may be one of learning and experiencing. Outputs will seemingly vary depending upon the perspective taken. The environment in this case is society in general and more particularly the government, business and the family. The curriculum or process itself is controlled by the academic institution (tutors, managers, resources, etc) and informed via the feed-forward and feedback loops from the learners.

This paper therefore seeks to explore some of the issues relating to the educational system in terms of information systems thinking and the role of multimedia as a facilitating technology. The paper

gives an introduction to the two systems (education and information) and then discusses identified similarities in approach to development of such systems and the relevance of multimedia. Such discussion is meant to stimulate further research into some of the issues involved.

2.0 The Education System

The education system in the United Kingdom has been evolving for a great deal of time and has, over the years, been significantly influenced by the work of a number of researchers and philosophers. At one stage the influence of B F Skinner (Skinner [9]) and other reductionist philosophers had a great deal of impact upon education in as much as learning and teaching took on a very structured, scientifically oriented approach. For example "Bobbitt argued for a scientific approach to planning school curricula by systematic analysis of those human activities which the curriculum was intended to develop. The activities to be focused on were those which made for efficiency in living as a healthy, gainfully employed citizen. Those activities, analysed in detail, would be the intended outcomes of the curriculum", (Taylor & Richards [12]). This, in simplistic terms, may be seen to reflect a deterministic view of a 'closed' system in which specific outcomes may be defined for appropriately developed processes to achieve. Further work by the behaviourist philosophers such as Basil Bernstein (Bernstein, [1]) added weight to such approaches through the identification of what were perceived to be desired, observable behaviours. Thus much of the early influences upon education stemmed from particular beliefs of what learners ought to learn which were, in turn, based upon very subjective ideals. It may also be seen that the perception that education's primary aim was to teach such ideals, led to the 'objectivist' or traditional model of learning. Such a model is based on the notion that the goal of learning is to understand, what is perceived to be, an objective reality. In addition, following the work of such behaviourists as Basil Bernstein, achievement of such learning was also deemed to be measurable through observable behaviour. This approach to assessment could also be perceived in terms of the simple, deterministic 'closed' systems model where learning is seen in simple stimulus-response terms reflected in the objectivist model of learning. However, latterly more liberal, divergent philosophies have had an influence and contributed towards the widespread adoption of a more student-centred curriculum which takes account of the more cognitive aspects of learning. Thus education may be seen as an area that has been significantly influenced over time by a number of ideologies which each encapsulate the views of different groups who, in turn, seek to impose their own views of the purpose of education upon the system itself. For example, "Scrimshaw distinguishes five major educational ideologies: (a) 'progressivism' which views education as a means of meeting individual needs and aspirations; (b) 'instrumentalism' which stresses the responsiveness of education to the requirements of the current socio-economic order; (c) 'reconstructionism' which conceives of education as an important way of moving society in desired directions; (d) 'classical humanism' where education serves the function of transmitting the cultural heritage and (e) 'liberal humanism' which acknowledges the importance of the intellectual disciplines for all pupils and seeks to help create a vision of common educational experience, (Taylor & Richards, [12]). If taking a 'Soft Systems' approach, (Checkland, [3]), in trying to conceptualise and model the education system according to these various ideologies it might be seen that we could define a variety of 'Root definitions' which reflected each of these perspectives. Building upon each 'Root definition' we might then be able to define appropriate inputs and outputs for meeting the given objectives. This may, however, again fall into too simplistic a trap in trying to define learning in terms of single-loop feedback systems which reflect the notions of single-loop, low-level, stimulus-response learning reminiscent of classical conditioning and the objectivist model.

3.0 Information Systems

Information Systems, in similar fashion to educational systems, were originally subject to a very structured, deterministic approach to development based on scientific reductionism and this is largely evidenced in such methodologies as Structured Systems Analysis & Design Methodology (SSADM). However, as with the area of education, researchers in the information systems field have long been advocating that account be taken of the more social nature of such development activity. To this end they have developed various other methodologies to take account of this fact. Examples of these can be seen in the work of Peter Checkland (Checkland, [3]) with the Soft Systems Methodology approach and of Frank Stowell & Daune West with their Client-Led Systems Design (Stowell & West, [11]). Further work has also been undertaken by Enid Mumford which proposes an ethical approach to systems development (Mumford, [6]). Enid Mumford also stresses the importance of aspects such as participation within systems development and quality of working life. These are, of course, only a selection of methodologies that incorporate recognition of the importance of the users in the information systems being developed. However, to take the Ethics approach, it might be that this may provide an appropriate framework for the development of learning and teaching systems. For example, with the emergent use of multimedia technology, education may be viewed as a socio-technical system and as such would, in Mumford's view, need to be developed with the participation of all of those involved. In this way specific, individualised learning outcomes might be specified. Appropriate assessment would then need to be arranged and a divergence of pathways towards achievement of these afforded to the learners. However, the fundamental problem with the education system is, it seems, the divergence of opinion as to who or what the outcomes of the system should be and consequently their requirements. Perhaps this is where the application of systems thinking may offer a way forward.

4.0 A Comparison of Systems development

In comparing the two areas (education and information systems) it may be argued that the underlying philosophies and development of Information Systems, have, to a large extent, mirrored those that have been evident in education. For example, initial methodologies in the field of both educational and information systems began with very deterministic, reductionist approaches. This has been clearly evidenced in the structured approaches adopted by both early SSADM in information systems and teaching and learning methods, based on the work by Skinner, (Skinner, [9]) and other educational philosophies, in education. More recently, however, it has become increasingly acknowledged that whilst such structured methods may offer a very logical, methodical, clearly defined and scientifically supportable approach to both educational and information systems development, the products of such activity seldom meet the requirements of the 'users'. Hence the almost weekly reports in the computing news of system failures and also the well documented reports of educational failures which have led to the introduction of the National Curriculum and other initiatives such as those which are addressing the teaching of basic literacy and numeracy.

However, in the area of information systems, analysts and designers have, for some time now, been attempting to develop methodologies which are not based quite so firmly in the area of science. Soft Systems Methodology has, for example, recommended consideration of aspects of human sociology in systems development as there has been a recognition of the subjectivity of the human beings necessarily involved.

Much of this can also be said of education. Early attempts at education reflected the scientific, reductionist approach to learning in which learning was seen as simple or single-loop learning where consequences of previous actions are used to amend subsequent actions. Later methodologies were, however, beginning to take much more account of the subjectivity of the learner in terms of both the concepts of learning and of the constructive aspects of knowledge itself. In information systems it has also been perceived that learning is a complex activity which involves more than one feedback loop. A second loop is perceived to occur "when the consequences of actions lead to a questioning of the mental model, the underlying assumptions, that have been driving the actions. That questioning may lead to the amendment of the mental model, the reframing of the problem or opportunity, before action is amended." (Stacey, [10]). Complex learning is thus perceived to involve both destruction and creation. Such perceptions of learning may be seen to have led to the more student-centred curriculum and models of learning that have been prevalent in recent times. Such models include the 'constructivist' model of learning (which is based on the individual making their own constructs of reality), the 'co-operative' model of learning (in which participation within a

group is critical to individuals achieving higher order learning of critical thinking and creativity), the 'cognitive information processing' model (which facilitates learner managed learning), and the 'sociocultural' model of learning (in which learners form their own, unbiased version of understanding that fits in with their own cultural and social background) (Iran-Nejad, et al, [5]; O'Loughlin, [7]). Each of these may be seen to fit in with the 'Soft Systems' view that all human systems are complex, adaptive systems which may be subject to such theories as complexity, chaos and self-organisation. Complex systems are also perceived to be subject to non-linear feedback loops which can be either negative or positive which can, in turn, lead to unexpected or counter-intuitive results.

Despite the fact that greater insights have been gained in systems thinking current trends within education are now seemingly deviating from the approach to systems development. With the imposition of the National curriculum into school education and other initiatives related to, what could, perhaps, be termed, 'payment by results' there seems to be encouragement for a more convergent approach to learning and teaching. This may then signal a return to, what could be seen as, a very much more deterministic approach to education from both the point of view of the teacher as well as the learner. Much of this has probably been encouraged through the increasing pressure to get all students to achieve specific learning outcomes by specific assessment points and through the publication of league tables. Students, for example, seem increasingly to perceive that education is simply a matter of learning a series of facts in order to jump the various 'hurdles' of assessment rather than development of the skills required for life-long learning and social contribution.

Teachers may also feel constrained by the pressures upon them to ensure that their students pass assessments - league tables and funding requirements are all likely to have exerted enormous pressures in this regard. Obviously, it might be acknowledged that there is a clear need to define specific learning outcomes and to have these assessed. However, many could argue that it would seem to constitute a serious backward step if all of the pathways to achieving such objectives were to return to the very constrained, determined routes reminiscent of the past.

This is, perhaps, where multimedia, and particularly use of the Internet, as a teaching resource may be able to facilitate a certain amount of 'tailorability' of the learning experience as such technology is concerned with representing a mixed mode of information (text, static images, sounds and video). The digital medium also provides the potential of a more flexible approach to learning than has hitherto been possible in terms of interactivity and availability.and thus may allow a divergence of approach yet a convergence of achieved outcomes. For example, students could be facilitated to asynchronously explore a variety of approaches using multimedia resources in order to achieve specified outcomes. Such students would, therefore, be able to 'tailor' their educational experience to their own particular needs which would very much accord with the views of the de-schoolers such as Ivan Illich (Illich, [4]). Illich even states that "the syntactic alternative to it" (*i.e. traditional education*) "is an educational network or web for the autonomous assembly of resources under the personal control of each learner", (Illich, [4]). Thus the idea of a learner managed/learner centred approach is not new but the technology ought not, it would seem, be used simply to 'package' courses to be delivered on an assembly-line basis but rather should be used to facilitate access to resources traditionally unavailable in the classroom and thus enhance the learning experience.

The problem is, however, that there needs to be an awareness that information technology is simply a tool which facilitates an organisation that uses it to achieve its strategic objectives and that the use of technology is not an end in itself. For example education needs to be wary of falling into the trap of following the 'IT vision' rather than the strategic vision which has been the downfall of many business organisations. One of the problems, however, is that the rapidly advancing technology and the manifold opportunities that it is beginning to afford educationalists is extremely seductive. For example, such ideas as learner managed learning, distance learning, life-long learning facilitated by multimedia information systems are gaining a great deal of impetus and support. Much of this impetus is stemming from a belief that technology can facilitate learning at any time and at any place and that enhanced learning experiences can be achieved with potentially significant (long term) reductions in cost. Such cost reductions are perceived to be possible through the provision of 'virtual' educational institutions which are aimed to cater for the any time, anywhere concept of learning.

However, regardless of whether or not savings in the provision of traditional campus education can be achieved, it would seem that the requirements of the learner ought to be weighed against how well and in what ways such multimedia information systems can support educational objectives. To a very large extent such issues are, it seems, becoming secondary in the 'race' to harness the potential of the multimedia technology which is far more accessible than would have been thought possible a few years ago. For example the recent initiative taken by the Dudley Council (West Midlands, England) is costing £43 million. This 10-year deal is putting Dudley "at the forefront of the government's efforts to connect the nation's schools via a national grid for learning by 2002" (D Sabbagh, [8]). It is thought that such an initiative will lead to many other councils following the example of Dudley. As reported in the same article "Bob Griffith, national secretary of local government IT managers' association Socitm, said 'The government is placing a lot of emphasis on a national grid. So interest in investing in educational IT is growing in importance to our members'" (D Sabbagh, [8]). Thus there are increasingly very powerful influences being brought to bear which will almost certainly hasten the rush to implement the technology. However, current evidence is showing that the benefits that might be hoped for haven't really been forthcoming and that the costs of producing effective on-line learning materials are high. For example numerous approaches have been taken to develop materials but with limited success in fulfilling the need for on-line learning resources. (Carswell & Murphy, [2])

It is therefore of concern that there are many questions which remain, to a large extent, unanswered and yet the push for technological change is gathering impetus at an ever increasing rate. Some example questions which might be posed are as follows:

- How might we guard against the seductiveness of the IT vision?
- How can technology help education achieve its strategic objectives?
- Have the various pedagogical, ethical and sociological issues been addressed?
- For example:
  - Which paradigm of learning can be supported by the technology?
  - Can knowledge and learning be conveniently packaged?
  - What will the impact of a lack of consultation with the learners, the teachers, the parents and other interested parties have post implementation?
  - What will be the impact on the learning/educational process?

- What are the real benefits of using IT for supporting learning - do we yet know what these really are?
- What impact will computer-mediated education have on society/business/family?
- Have issues such as language, age, gender and culture been taken into account?
- Have the issues of privacy and security been addressed?
- What are the cost and technology issues and how will this impact on implementation?

Until these and other concerns are thoroughly researched, it seems appropriate to exercise restraint in our acquiescence to the apparent technological imperative and the attendant allocation of large quantities of scarce resources.

5.0 Conclusions and Further Work

It can therefore be concluded, from this initial work, that further exploration needs to be undertaken into how 'successful' information systems can be developed and how organisational learning is being facilitated through the use of technology. Comparisons may then be made which may result in lessons learned from information systems development being able to inform the field of education.

There is, however, a great deal more research needed into issues such as determining; what lessons can we learn from current systems thinking that can inform how we deploy the technology, if education is perceived as being a socio-technical system can we facilitate greater participation of learners in its development through use of the technology?, who is the 'client' of the education system?; what are the objectives of the educational system?; what constitutes 'good' learning and how this can be achieved for all learners?; how may the new technologies which facilitate multimedia be exploited to maintain the divergence of opportunity whilst retaining the divergence of achievement? All of these and other issues are becoming increasingly important in the field of education and it seems that there is much work yet to be done to inform good practice.

7.0 References

1 Bernstein, B. (1977) "Class, Codes and Control, Volume 3, Towards a theory of educational transmissions. London: Routledge & Kegan Paul

2 Carswell, L & Murphy, M (1994) "Pragmatic Methodology for Educational Courseware Development, retrieved May, 1999 from: http://www.ulst.ac.uk/cticomp/carswell.html

3 Checkland, P.B. (1989) "Soft Systems Methodology" in: Rational Analysis for a Problematic World (ed. J. Rosenhead), Chichester: Wiley

4 Illich, I., (1974) "Deschooling Society", Open Forum

5 Iran-Nejad, A, McKeachie, W, Berliner, D.D., (1990) "The Multisource Nature of Learning: An Introduction". Review of Educational Research, 60 (4), pp 509-515

6 Mumford, E. (1996) "Ethical Tools for Ethical Change", Macmillan

7 O'Loughlin, M., (1992) "Rethinking Science Education: Beyond Piagetian Constructivisim Toward a Sociocultural Model of Teaching and Learning". Journal of Research in Science Teaching 29 (8), pp 791-820

8 Sabbagh, D. (1998), "UK Schools linked to national grid", Computing magazine, 8 October 1998, pg 10

9 Skinner, B.F. (1954) "The science of learning and the art of teaching" Harvard Educational Review

10 Stacey, R.D. (1996) "Strategic Management & Organisational Dynamics (2nd ed), Pitman Publishing

11 Stowell, F. & West, D. (1994) "Client-led Design", McGraw-Hill

12 Taylor, P.H. & Richards, C.M. (1987) "An Introduction to Curriculum Studies", Nfer-Nelson

Visualization of Economic Input-Output Data

Octavio Juarez Espinosa, Chris Hendrickson Ph.D., James H. Garrett Jr. Ph.D.

Civil and Environmental Engineering Department, Carnegie Mellon University, Pittsburgh, PA

Abstract

In this paper, visual techniques used to present economic input-output data are described. These techniques were created because the size of the data matrices and the screen limitations complicate data navigation. These techniques allow users to ask questions about detailed and global information. The techniques were designed based on the user tasks.

The graphic techniques are combined with direct manipulation techniques to improve the ease and efficiency with which users interact with the system. The software prototype uses 1992 US economic data.

1. Introduction

For many users, it is difficult to perform analysis of data used to support economic input-output analysis. This is particularly true for users who are not familiar with this data.

Both the size of the matrices and the limitations of the screen size used to display the information complicate the users ability to navigate the data set from the complete view to detailed information. This results in users using the input-output data without analyzing the data in detail. The quality of input-output analysis could be better if a user were more familiar with the data being used.

Input-output is a framework developed by Leontief in the late 1930's [2]. The purpose of input-output analysis is to study the interdependencies between industries in one regional economy. It is also used as an underlying model in some forms of environmental life-cycle assessment (LCA) [1].

Input-Output data includes sets of matrices which can not be displayed completely on the computer screen. Only matrix regions can be displayed on the screen.

Current interfaces for the input-output data use only text to display the information. The user interaction with the data is minimal. For example, a user can extract a row or a column of a matrix. Input-output data consists of the following four matrices: *make matrix, use matrix, total requirements* and *direct requirements matrix.*

This research contributes a new way of resolving this problem by doing visualization of input-output data. The visualization was created as part of an interface for users doing disaggregation of input-output data. Disaggregation is the breaking of an industrial sector into two or more rows and columns in each matrix. In order to perform this operation, users need to manipulate the *make* and *use* tables to regenerate the total requirements data. A visual presentation of the data matrix might improve the navigation and the understanding of the input-output data.

The design of the graphics and interaction techniques was based on the task analysis of users.

The input-output data is explained in more detail in the following sections.

2. Input-Output Data

The information contained in an input-output analysis includes flows of products from producers to consumers which are stored in matrices. The goods produced are outputs (sales) and the goods consumed are inputs (purchases) [2].

Data and models are available for many regions and most countries, at levels of detail from 20 to 500 sectors.

Matrices are used because the input-output model consists of a set of n equations and n unknowns. An example with two elements will be used in this section to explain the model.

The set of equations has the following form:

$$
\begin{aligned}
(X_1 &= z_{11} + z_{12} + Y_1) \\
(X_2 &= z_{21} + z_{22} + Y_2)
\end{aligned}
\tag{1}
$$

While elements z_{11} and z_{21} (column 1) represent the purchases made in sector 1, elements z_{11} and z_{12} (row 1) represent the sales of sector 1 to other sectors. X_1 represents the total output for sector 1 and Y_1 represents the final demand for sector 1. The matrix that describes the sectors transactions consists of sellers represented by rows and buyers represented by the columns.

The system of equations presented in (1) needs to be augmented with rows representing the value added, consisting of employee compensation, government services, interest payments, and land. The same system represented in (1) is augmented with extra columns representing the final demand that consists of household purchases, government purchases, private purchases, and sales abroad or exports.

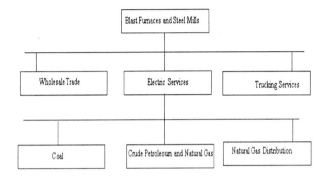

Figure 1: Direct and indirect suppliers to the steel industry

Equation (2) represents the relation between the total output represented by X and the final demand represented by Y. I is the identity matrix which contains 1's in the diagonal and 0's out of the diagonal, and A is the direct coefficient matrix that represents the interaction between industrial sectors.

$$ X = (I - A)^{-1} \cdot Y \qquad (2) $$

To obtain the total requirements matrix, represented by $(I - A)^{-1}$, the use matrix, the make matrix, and the direct requirements matrix are used. These matrices are described in the following paragraphs.

Figure 1 shows a section of the supply chain of the steel industry. The first level in the chain consists of the direct suppliers. The matrix of direct coefficients (A) only contains values for the first level of suppliers. The following chain levels are included in the total requirements matrix. The sectors in the levels higher than 1 are the indirect suppliers of a product.

The use matrix represents the interindustry activity and describes the commodity inputs to an industrial production process. This matrix includes the value added rows and the final demand columns.

The make matrix describes the commodities produced by industries. However, this matrix does not consider the interaction between industries.

The direct requirements matrix is computed based on the use matrix and the total output. The matrix coefficients are computed using equation (3).

$$ a_{ij} = z_{ij}' X \qquad (3) $$

Where z_{ij} is the quantity of commodity i used by industry j, X_j is the vector industry total output, and a_{ij} is the dollar value of commodity i needed to produce a dollar of industry j.

The total requirements matrix contains the direct and indirect interactions between industrial sectors and is equal to $(I - A)^{-1}$.

3. The User Tasks

Common tasks performed by users when using input-output data are described in this section. The tasks include questions about the following three levels of information: elementary level, intermediate level, and overall level. The elementary level deals with the matrix cells, the intermediate level works with information subsets such as rows and columns, and the overall level deals with the whole matrix.

3.1. Looking for the interaction of two sectors

To find the coefficient of interaction of two economic sectors, the user looks in the total requirements, direct requirements, or use matrices.

A user looks for a sector name in the rows and a sector name in the columns to obtain the coefficient in the intersection.

3.2. Labeling a data point

In this task, a user selects a point in the matrix to obtain the coefficient value. The two sectors that interact in that cell are obtained from the row and column labels. This is the inverse task to the previous one.

3.3. Magnifying a matrix area

In this task, a user wants to see in detail a region because he/she has identified an interesting pattern. To do that, a user changes the ranges and the scales used to plot the data.

3.4. Comparing two industries based on the commodities produced

In the make matrix, a user wants to create a comparative chart with the commodities produced for two industries. To create the chart, a user gets the two industries data from the matrix, sorts them, and creates the chart.

3.5. Comparing two sectors based on the coefficient values

Users want to compare two industrial sectors in the *use* matrix or in the *total requirements* matrix. The sectors compared are selected and displayed to see the similarities and differences between them.

3.6. Looking for patterns in the matrix

Users search for patterns of interaction between sectors. For example, in the total requirements matrix, the diagonal is a pattern with values larger than one.

3.7. Modifying values and recomputing the total requirements matrix

Users sometimes want to change values in some cells of the *use* and *make* tables to see the effects in the direct and total requirements.

3.8. Geographic visualization of economic activity

A user wants to see where the economic activity takes place. This information completes the picture captured by the input-output data.

4. Visualization Techniques

The matrices are completely displayed in a window using a pixel for each cell. By screen limitations, the information is encoded with color instead of writing the text for each cell.

While the matrix rendered is displayed in a window, regions of the matrix can be rendered in another window.

The values in the visualized matrix are divided into five categories. A color is assigned to each cell based on its category.

Figure 2 shows the *total requirements* matrix. The larger window contains the matrix while the window in the bottom contains detailed information. The left window defines the data to be visualized.

The numbers to the right of the matrix represent the ranges of values in the matrix. Users can update the values.

The detailed window, shown in Figure 2, displays an area of 7 by 7 cells with a label for the sector code.

4.1. Use Matrix

This *use* matrix for the US has 491 rows and 538 columns [3]. Figure 3 shows the use matrix that contains the interactions between industries. It is larger than the other matrices because it includes extra rows consisting of wages and salaries as well as profits. This matrix also includes extra columns for final demand, consisting of households, government, and others.

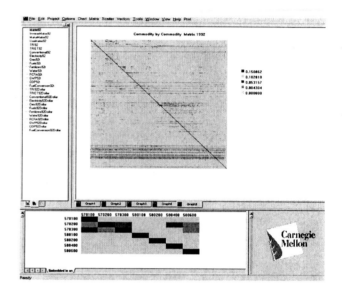

Figure 2: Visualization framework

4.2. Make Matrix

This matrix has 498 rows and 498 columns and represents information about commodities produced in 1992 by US industries [3].

Figure 4 shows that the diagonal has the highest values. Elements in the diagonal are primary products. The elements out of the diagonal represent secondary products. Figure 3 enables the user to see that an industry produces more than one commodity. However, only one of the commodities is considered to be a primary product.

4.3. Total Requirements Matrix

The *total requirements* matrix is shown in Figure 2. This matrix represents the interaction between industrial sectors. The *total requirements* matrix represents direct and indirect interactions.

Figure 2 shows patterns consisting of horizontal lines in the bottom of the matrix. These lines represent patterns of the sales of industrial sectors. The diagonal members are the highest values. Users can change the color map to see other patterns.

4.4. Direct Requirements Matrix

The *direct requirements* matrix is obtained from the *use and make* matrices.

The values are lower than the values in the total requirements matrix because the matrix values only include direct components.

Patterns similar to those observed in Figure 2 are observed in the *direct requirements* matrix.

4.5. Geographic Visualization

The economic data for 1992 includes geographic information [4].

An input-output estimation can be rendered in a map showing the economic impacts as can be seen Figure 5. The data is rendered at the state level and the information is presented for each industrial sector. Figure 5 maps the total value of shipments for one industrial sector.

5. Interaction Operations

The software prototype to visualize and manipulate these matrices provides operations to interact with the system. There are operations to interact with matrices and maps. Users modify the visualization by using the operations to better understand the encoded information.

5.1. Matrix Operations

The matrix operations allow users to ask questions at different levels of detail. These operations consist of changing the color map, labeling cells in the detail window, finding a point in the matrix, viewing the coefficients for a row or column, and reading a cell value.

Changing the Color Map. This operation allows users to ask questions about patterns in the matrix.

Some of the user choices consist of:

- select a different set of colors and different ranges for every category, and
- select only some of the range categories.

Labeling Cells in the Detail Window. It is not practical to label every cell in the matrix view because the screen size limits the number of labels displayed. To view the labels, users select a cell to display on the detail window.

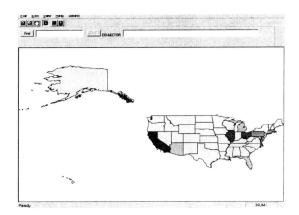

Figure 3: Geographic View of the data

Finding a Point in the Matrix. A user can search for a specific point in the matrix. To search for the point, a user types the names of two industrial sectors and the system displays the point with its neighbors labeled in the detail window.

Viewing the Coefficients for a Row or Column. A user can view the coefficients of an economic sector.

Figure 6 shows a chart with the coefficients of the matrix row. Also a user can compare two rows or two columns by creating several charts. While Figure 6 shows the total requirements coefficients for steel, Figure 7 represents the direct requirements coefficients. These two charts allows to see the difference between direct and total requirements.

Reading a Cell Value. A user is able to read the exact value of a cell displayed on the detail window. To display the names and the values attached to a particular cell, a user selects the cell rendered in the detail window. Then the information is displayed in a dialog box.

5.2. Map Operations

Maps are generated based on the value of the industrial sector the user wants to visualize. In addition, a user can move the map and zoom in particular regions. Also a user can move the map to focus attention on a very specific area.

The map operations consist of changing the industrial sector and viewing the state information.

Changing the Industrial Sector. The map can be modified by changing the name of the industrial sector to be displayed.

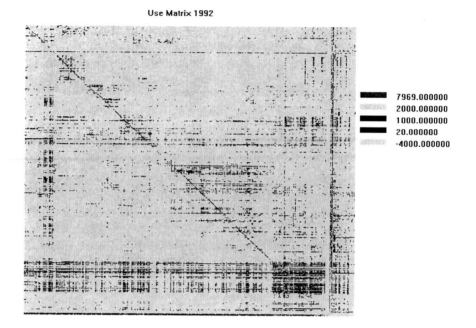

Use Matrix 1992

▬	7969.000000
▬	2000.000000
▬	1000.000000
▬	20.000000
▬	-4000.000000

Figure 4: Use Matrix

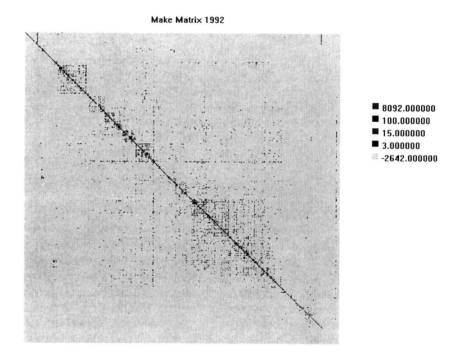

Make Matrix 1992

■	8092.000000
■	100.000000
■	15.000000
■	3.000000
▪	-2642.000000

Figure 5: Make Matrix

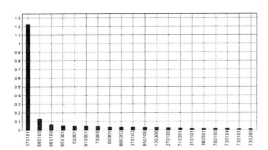

Figure 6: Total requirements coefficients for Blast Furnaces and Steel Mills

Viewing the State Information. The state information can be displayed by clicking on the right polygon.

6. Conclusions and Future Research

The visualization techniques used in this research were created based on user tasks and data characteristics. These techniques allow naive and experienced users to navigate through the data. While naive users can learn about input-output data by just using the mouse and selecting areas on the screen, experienced users can perform detailed analysis.

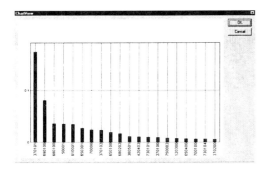

Figure 7: Direct requirements coefficients for Blast Furnaces and Steel Mills

The geographic view complements the input-output information and gives information about states that are directly impacted by the production of a product.

In the near future, usability testing will be conducted with users to refine the techniques used to visualize the input-output data.

These visualization techniques will be used as an interface for input-output data disaggregation. The main tasks to be performed with this interface consist of:

- Edit values in the matrix. Users modify values on the make and use tables and then recompute the *direct* and *total requirements* matrices.
- Visualize effects after the disaggregation of industrial sectors.

ACKNOWLEDGMENTS

We thank Carnegie Mellon's Green Design Industrial Consortium for the support received for this research.

We also thank the Department of Energy, Office of Energy research, EPA cooperative Agreement # CR825188-01-2 NSF/EPA Grant # BES-9873582 for the support received for this research.

We thank Julia Gardner Deems for her comments.

I. References

[1]   Hendrickson, C., S. Joshi and L.B. Lave, "Economic Input-Output Models for Environmental Life Cycle Analysis," Environmental Science & Technology, April, 1998.

[2]   Miller, R., Blair, P. "Input-Output Analysis: Foundations and Extensions," Prentice-Hall, Inc., 1985.

[3]   U.S. Department of Commerce, "1992 Benchmark I-O Six-Digit," Bureau of Economic Analysis, 1998.

[4]   U.S. Department of Commerce, "1992 Economic Census CD-ROM," CD-EC92-1J, 1998.

[5]   Bertin, J. "Graphics and Graphic Information Processing," Walter de Gruyter, 1981.

Three Dimensional Animation of Web Access Behavior Using Indirect Mapping

Noritaka OSAWA, Kikuo ASAI, Hitoshi OHNISHI

National Institute of Multimedia Education
2-12 Wakaba, Mihama-ku, Chiba 261-0014, JAPAN
{osawa,asai,ohnishi}@nime.ac.jp

Abstract

This paper proposes and discusses a 3-D animation method for helping us to comprehend the behavior of the Web accesses. The proposed method uses dynamic system modeling because human beings live in a dynamic world and they have been trained to comprehend the world since their birth. The method maps the Web access data to mass and forces in a dynamic system model, then simulates the model, and renders the results as graphical objects in the 3-D space. An animation tool using the proposed method has been developed. It is implemented with the Virtual Reality Modeling Language (VRML) and the Java programming language, and it works on a Web browser. The features and functions of the tool are described, and some snapshots of animations of a Web server log are presented.

1. Introduction

The Web has been widely used, and the size of Web servers has been usually enhanced. As the enlargement of the Web, it becomes more difficult to comprehend the accesses of the Web and to find dynamic relationships among documents. In other words, the understanding of the Web access behavior is a difficult task. In order to find users' interests, we need to understand the access behavior properly. It is not only the static analysis of the Web, but also the comprehension of the changes in the Web, which are important. The Web structure is usually irregular and does not have a corresponding physical structure, that is, it is abstract. Therefore changes in the Web are also abstract information.

In order to make abstract information easily understandable, visualization is effective in general. The bar graph and pie chart are simple examples of information visualization. As the processing performance and graphics performance of computers advances, it becomes easier to visualize a lot of data.

There are a lot of studies on information visualization[10], network visualization[2], and Web visualization [9]. In visualization, it is important to utilize human visual cognitive and perceptual abilities fully. It is not the main objective to put a lot of data onto a screen. That is to say, it is more important to show data in easily understandable forms than to show a lot of data simultaneously.

Most of usual visualization methods map data directly into attributes of graphical objects such as the positions, sizes, directions, colors etc. Figure 1 shows the visualization procedure using a direct mapping. However, it is not necessarily needed to map data into attributes of graphical objects directly. Sometimes it is effective to use an indirect mapping with an intermediate model.

Furthermore, many studies focus on static representation of structures. However, many systems such as the Web dynamically change their structures. Information flows in the structures also change. Dynamic representation has advantages to capture dynamic properties in the systems. Research on animation of dynamic changes in the Web accesses is insufficient.

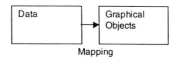

Figure 1: Visualization procedure using a direct mapping

Human beings live in a dynamic world and can easily recognize the movement or changes of bodies in a dynamic system. Human beings are sensitive to the movement, because they have been trained to comprehend a dynamic world since their birth. If we could not understand the dynamic world properly, it would be difficult to live in this world.

Therefore we have proposed an animation method using dynamic system modeling[12]. The method establishes correspondence between abstract data structures and dynamic system model structures, then maps data to parameters of the dynamic system model, simulates the dynamic system model, and then visualizes the simulation results. In brief, it uses an indirect mapping of data to graphical representation.

We have applied the method to visualization of trace data for performance debugging of parallel programs on a parallel computer[13][14]. Parallel computers have rather regular structures. On the other hand, hypertext systems such as the Web have irregular structures. Thus we should investigate animation of changes in irregular structures.

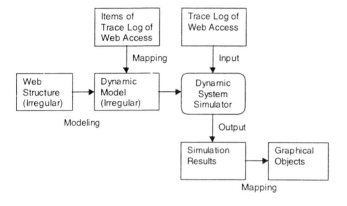

Figure 2: Animation procedure of the proposed method

This paper proposes and describes a new animation method for the Web dynamic access analysis[15]. The proposed method uses dynamic system simulation in order to exploit human cognitive and perceptual abilities. Figure 2 shows the animation procedure of the proposed method. This paper also reports on a prototype implementation of 3-D animation tool and the snapshots of animation generated by the tool. First, Section 2 explains related work and discusses the differences between the related work and our work. Next, Section 3 describes a prototype system for the Web access animation, and Section 4 shows snapshots of animations using the prototype system. Future work is stated in Section 5 and a summary is given in Section 6.

2. Related Work

This section discusses related work and the differences between the related work and our work.

There have been various studies on the topic of visualization using a dynamic system. For example, a spring model[8] and force-directed drawing[5] are well

known in static planar graph drawing. Moreover, these techniques have also been applied to static graph drawing in 3-D space. All of them are based on a stable solution of a dynamic system.

On the other hand, our method is based on dynamic simulation or solving equations of motion. Furthermore, our method maps log data into dynamic system parameters such as mass of objects and external forces. These features differentiate our work from static planar graph drawing using dynamic system modeling.

Dynamic system simulation is applied to visualization of the behavior of object-oriented systems[19]. However, it uses 2-D representation and its animation of links is different from ours.

As stated in Section 1, the usual visualization techniques[2][4][9][10][16][17] use direct mappings, which map data into graphical attributes such as size, color and orientation of the bodies and links. Although some techniques use a non-Euclidean space such as hyperbolic visualization[11], they are a kind of direct mapping.

Our method not only uses the mapping to graphical attributes but also uses dynamic system modeling and simulation so as to utilize fully human cognitive ability of dynamic system behaviors that are familiar to us. In other words, the method uses a kind of indirect mapping of data to graphical attributes as stated before.

3. A Prototype Tool for the Web Access Animation

We have developed a 3-D animation tool for visualizing the Web document structures and the changes of access requests to Web documents. It is programmed with the Virtual Reality Modeling Language (VRML)[18] and the Java programming language[6]. It works on a Web browser such as Microsoft InternetExplorer[22]. The tool consists of a Java applet, a VRML browser and a Web browser. A Java applet communicates with VRML objects through EAI (External Authoring Interface)[23]. Figure 3 shows the overall structure of the prototype tool.

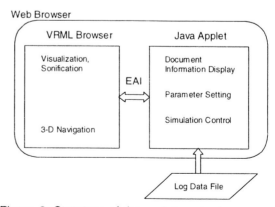

Figure 3: Structure of the prototype tool

3.1. Input

In this paper, a `referer`[1] log [20] in a Web server is used as input data. Each line in a `referer` log contains the information of an access request, that is, a referring URL and a referenced local URL. The following is a line of a `referer` log.

```
http://www.nime.ac.jp/~taro/bbs/bbs.cgi
?page=0 -> /icons/well-bg.jpg
```

`http://www.nime.ac.jp/~taro/bbs/bbs.cgi?page=0` is a referring URL, and `/icons/well-bg.jpg` is a referenced local URL. When the tool loads a line, a referring URL is converted to a local document path (`/~taro/bbs/bbs.cgi`). The local document path does not include a host part (`//www.nime.ac.jp`) nor a query part (`?page=0`). If the referring URL resides outside the server, the line is marked as an incoming request.

3.2. Modeling

A document on the Web is mapped to a body in a dynamic system. Access data to a document is mapped to forces of the corresponding body. In order to simplify explanation, we use a document and a body interchangeably unless confusion is caused.

The mass of a document is constant in this case. Repulsive force, elastic force, attractive force and frictional force are used in simulation. First, the repulsive force, which is inversely proportional to the square of distance between documents, is applied to separate documents in a stable state. Unless the repulsive force is applied, documents converge as intra-requests occur. Elastic force is exerted between a child and its parent. The attractive force (external force) of a referenced document towards a referring document is exerted. When a request occurs, the attractive force is applied for a fixed period of time. No force is exerted on a referring document. This asymmetry violates the law of action and reaction in physics, however, this setting shows imbalance of access amounts between documents. The imbalance helps us to recognize access directions of requests. The frictional force is proportional to the velocity of a document. If friction is not used but external forces are exerted, the energy of the system increases monotonically. Friction prevents the energy of the system from increasing indefinitely. Friction smoothes movement and reduces oscillation of a document. This makes it easy for us to recognize the movement and balance of documents in the system.

---

[1] `Referer` should be spelled as referrer but the file name is spelled as `referer`.

Equations of motion in the case of this modeling are given by the next formula.

$$\frac{d^2 \mathbf{x}_i}{dt^2} = R \sum_{\substack{j=1 \\ j \neq i}}^{N} \frac{\mathbf{x}_i - \mathbf{x}_j}{\left| \mathbf{x}_i - \mathbf{x}_j \right|^3} + k \sum_{\substack{j=1 \\ j \neq i}}^{N} \frac{\mathbf{x}_i - \mathbf{x}_j}{\left| \mathbf{x}_i - \mathbf{x}_j \right|} \left(L - \left| \mathbf{x}_i - \mathbf{x}_j \right| \right) + \sum_{\substack{j=1 \\ j \neq i}}^{N} \mathbf{F}_{ij}(t) - \beta \frac{d\mathbf{x}_i}{dt}$$

Terms on the right hand side are repulsive forces, elastic forces, attractive forces and frictional forces from the left in that order. $\mathbf{x}_i$ is a coordinate of document i. $\mathbf{F}_{ij}(t)$ represents external force exerted from document i to document j at time t. Let N be the total number of documents. R, k, L and β are constants. L is a natural distance between a child and its parent where no elastic force is exerted. $\left| \mathbf{x}_i - \mathbf{x}_j \right|$ represents the distance between $\mathbf{x}_i$ and $\mathbf{x}_j$

3.3. Mapping

In 3-D space, a document is represented by a sphere as shown in Figure 4. The directory structures of documents form a kind of cone tree[17]. Document structures are arranged hierarchically. A thin line shows a parent-child relationship between a directory and its subdirectory.

Not all of documents on the server are shown in 3-D space because unaccessed documents obscure the relationships of accessed documents. When a document is accessed for the first time, a sphere is dynamically created. The initial size of spheres is the same. The spheres will be called document spheres.

An intra-request between documents on the server is represented by a cone as an arrow-like shape. We will refer the arrow-like cone to an access arrow. No inter-requests are shown as a cone, that is, an incoming request is not shown. Incidentally, outgoing requests are not recorded in the `referer` log. Thus outgoing requests are not shown either.

A request increases the volume V_i of the referenced document i by a fixed amount γ. The request also increases the radius r_{ij} of an access arrow from document i to document j by a fixed quantity. The request does not affect the intermediate directories between the root and the referenced document.

The volume of a sphere decreases exponentially as time passes. In other words, the second order derivative of the volume is a negative constant. The radius of an access cone is reduced linearly. Hence, the volume of a document sphere and the radius of an access cone are given by the following formulae where no requests occur. v and ρ are constants.

$$\frac{d^2 V_i}{d t^2} = -v$$

$$\frac{d r_{ij}}{d t} = -\rho$$

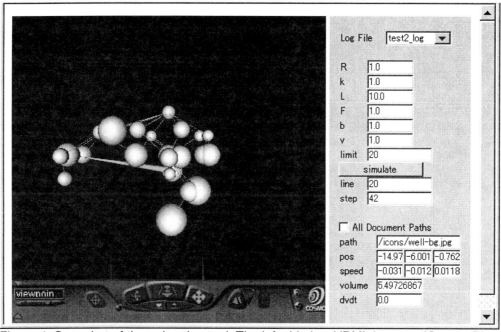

Figure 4: Snapshot of the animation tool. The left side is a VRML browser (Comso Player) plug-in. The right side is a Java applet for setting and control.

3.4. Implementation

We have implemented a prototype Web animation tool using the VRML and the Java programming language.

The prototype tool has been implemented on a Web browser. The tool also uses a VRML browser and a Java applet. The VRML browser and the applet communicate through VRML External Authoring Interface (EAI) [23]. The Web browser, VRML browser and a Java applet run in various environments. Thus our animation tool potentially works on various hardware and operating system platforms. That is to say, it is portable.

The animation tool loads an access log file, simulates a dynamic system, and then visualizes the simulation result. The VRML browser CosmoPlayer 2.1 [21] is used to give a 3-D view and to navigate the 3-D space. The Java applet loads an access log file, controls the simulation parameter settings, simulates the dynamic system based on the log file, and shows a selected document information. The Java applet at the right side in Figure 4 show and control simulation parameter settings. The applet shows an input log file name, simulation time step (step) and the number of lines processed (line). We can set the strength of repulsive force (R), the strength of elastic force (k), the strength of attractive force (F) and the strength of frictional force (b= β), the second order derivative of the volume

(v= v) on the applet. The applet can also show the local path of a document and its position, velocity and volume in numerical forms as shown in Figure 4. If one clicks a document on VRML browser, the information about it will be displayed on the Java applet.

4. Snapshots of Animation

This section gives some snapshots of animation. In the initial state, no document is shown as in Figure 5. As the log file is processed, documents are displayed. When a document is requested, the intermediate directories between the root and the document are also displayed as document spheres.

Figure 6 and Figure 7 show snapshots after 10 log lines are processed. The figures show that some documents have been frequently requested recently. Their spheres are large. Other documents that have not requested are displayed as small spheres since the volume of spheres decreases as the passage of time. In Figure 7, all document path strings are shown. This display is controlled by a check box labeled "All Document Paths" on the applet. If one wants to know the details of a document sphere, he/she can click the sphere to display them at bottom right of the applet as shown in Figure 4.

505

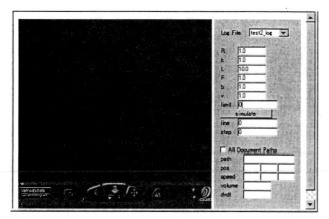

Figure 5: Initial state

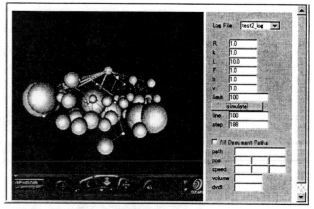

Figure 8: Snapshot after 100 lines are processed.

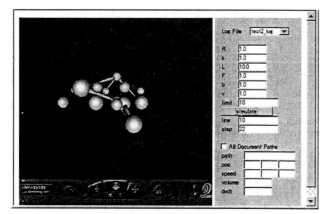

Figure 6: Snapshot after 10 lines are processed.

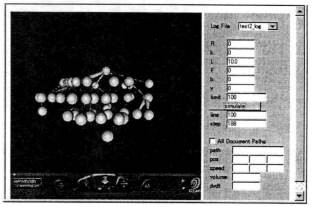

Figure 9: Snapshot after 100 lines are processed without dynamic system simulation.

Figure 8 and Figure 9 show snapshots with and without dynamic system simulation respectively after 100 lines are processed. Figure 9 is almost the same as a cone tree. By comparing Figure 8 with Figure 9, we can understand that dynamic system simulation results show effectively the recent access frequencies of documents and the relationships among documents.

Our method uses an indirect mapping and thus the initial values and history of external forces influence animation. Therefore we cannot understand the states at one time only by looking at a snapshot of our animation. However, our objective of animation does not aim at the understanding of the system only using a snapshot. Our method helps us to comprehend the system behaviors not with a static snapshot but with movement in animation.

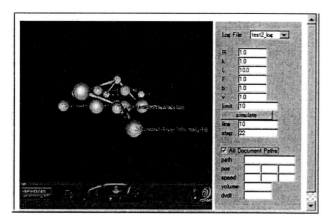

Figure 7: Snapshot with path display after 10 lines are processed.

5. Future work

We are now developing the system using Java3D because manipulation of VRML objects through EAI of the VRML browser is fairly slow. We are also developing a real-time animation tool. It collects log data, simulates the mapped dynamic system, and visualizes the simulation results in real-time. Moreover, we have a plan to apply the animation tool to more general information visualization.

We will extend our animation method to a virtual reality system. We have built an immersive virtual environment system[1] such as CAVE[3]. The immersive virtual reality system makes dynamic data tangible[7]. In addition to visualization and sonification, haptic display such as force feedback will also be utilized. We believe that immersive virtual reality helps us to comprehend the behaviors of the Web system more easily.

The dynamic system modeling in this paper is only an example. The mappings of data to the dynamic system parameters and graphical attributes are also examples. Other modelings and mappings are possible and should be investigated.

6. Summary

This paper has proposed and discussed a new animation method for comprehending the dynamic behavior of the Web. The method does not directly map an access log into graphical attributes but uses both dynamic system simulation and mapping so as to exploit human cognitive and perceptual abilities. Since we are familiar with the dynamic world and sensitive to changes in the dynamic world, the proposed method helps us to comprehend the dynamic changes on an irregular structure such as the Web. We have implemented a prototype animation tool using the proposed method and demonstrated the use of the tool and some snapshots of animation.

References

[1] Asai, Kikuo, Noritaka Osawa, and Yuji Y. Sugimoto, "Virtual Environment System on Distance Education," *Proc. of EUROMEDIA '99*, pp.242-246, 1999.

[2] Becker, Richard A., Stephen G. Eick, and Allan R. Wilks, "Visualizing Network Data," *IEEE Trans. on Visualization and Computer Graphics*, Vol.1, No.1, pp.16-28, March 1995.

[3] Cruz-Neira, Carolina, Daniel J. Sandin, Thomas A. DeFanti, Robert V. Kenyon, and John C. Hart, "The CAVE: audio visual experience automatic virtual environment", *Comm. ACM*, Vol.35, No.6, pp. 64 - 72, 1992.

[4] Daniel A. Reed, Keith A. Shields, Will H. Scullin, Luis F. Tavera and Christopher L. Elford, "Virtual Reality and Parallel Systems Performance Analysis," *IEEE Computer*, Vol.28, No.11, pp.57-64, Nov. 1995.

[5] Fruchterman, T. M. J. and E. M. Reingold, "Graph Drawing by Force-directed Placement," *Software - Practice and Experience*, Vol. 21, No. 11, pp. 1129-1164, 1991.

[6] Gosling, James, Bill Joy and Guy Steele, *"The Java Language Specification,"* Addison-Wesley, 1996.

[7] Ishii, Hiroshi and Brygg Ullmer, "Tangible bits: Towards seamless interfaces between people, bits and atoms," *Proc. of the 1997 Conference on Human Factors in Computing*

[8] Kamada, T., and S. Kawai, "Algorithms for drawing general undirected graphs," *Information Processing Letters*, Vol. 31, No. 1, pp. 7-15, 1989.

[9] Mukherjea, Sougata and Foley, James D., "Visualizing the world-wide web with the navigational view builder," *Computer Networks and ISDN Systems*, Vol. 27, No.6, pp.1075-1087, Apr. 1995. (Proceedings of the 3rd International World-Wide Web Conference) <http://www.igd.fhg.de/www/www95/proceedings/papers/44/mukh/mukh.html>

[10] Mukherjea, S., J.D.Foley, and S. Hudson, "Visualizing complex hypermedia networks through multiple hierarchical views," *Proc. of ACM Conf. on Human Factors in Computing Systems CHI-95*, pp.331-337, 1995.

[11] Munzner, Tamara, and Paul Burchard, "Visualizing the Structure of the World Wide Web in 3D Hyperbolic Space," *Proc. of ACM Symp. on Virtual Reality Modeling Language (VRML95)*, pp.33-38, 1995.

[12] Osawa, Noritaka and Toshitsugu Yuba, "Three Dimensional Animation for Performance Debugging Utilizing Human Cognitive Ability," *Proc. of IFIP INTERACT97*, pp.102-103, July 1997.

[13] Osawa, Noritaka, Hisaya Morita, and Toshitsugu Yuba, "Animation for Performance Debugging of Parallel Computing Systems," *Proc. of 2nd Annual Symp. on the Virtual Reality Modeling Language (VRML97)*, pp.101-107, 1997.

[14] Osawa, Noritaka, "An Enhanced 3-D Animation Tool for Performance Tuning of Parallel Programs Based on Dynamic Models," *Proc. of ACM 2nd SIGMETRICS Symposium on Parallel and Distributed Tools (SPDT98)*, pp.72-80, 1998.

[15] Osawa, Noritaka, and Hitoshi Ohnishi, "Three Dimensional Animation of Changes in Web Accesses Using Dynamic System Simulation," *8th World Wide Web Conference (WWW8)* (Poster) (to appear), 1999.

[16] Robertson, G.G., S.K.Card, and J.D. Mackinlay, "Information visualization using 3-D interactive animation," *Comm. ACM*, Vol.36, No.4, pp.57-71, 1993.

[17] Robertson, George, Jock Mackinlay, and Struart Card, "Cone Trees: Animated 3D Visualizations of Hierarchical Information," *Proc. of ACM SIGCHI Conf. on Human Factors in Computing Systems*, pp.189-194, April 1991.

[18] VRML Consortium, *The Virtual Reality Modeling Language*, International Standard ISO/IEC 14772-1:1997 <http://www.vrml.org/Specifications/VRML97/>

[19] Wim De Pauw, Richard Helm, Doug Kimelman, and John Vlissides, "Visualizing the Behavior of Object-Oriented Systems," *Proc. of 1993 Object-Oriented Programming Systems, Languages, and Applications (OOPSLA'93)*, pp.326-337, 1993.

[20] Apache HTTP Server Version 1.3 module mod_log_referer. http://www.apache.org/docs/mod/mod_log_referer.html, Apr. 1999.

[21] Cosmosoftware home page. http://www.cosmosoftware.com/, Apr. 1999.

[22] Microsoft Internet Explorer home page. http://www.microsoft.com/windows/ie/default.htm, Apr. 1999.

[23] External Authoring Interface Working Group home page, http://www.vrml.org/WorkingGroups/vrml-eai/, Apr. 1999.

Session 3-4

Digital Art

Chair

Tammy Knipp

Florida Atlantic University, USA

ULTIMA RATIO
A Visual Language for Argumentation *

Michael Schroeder[1], Daniela A. Plewe[2], and Andreas Raab[3]

[1] City University, London, UK, msch@soi.city.ac.uk
[2] Berlin, Germany, plewe@is.in-berlin.de
[3] University of Magdeburg, Germany, raab@isg.cs.uni-magdeburg.de

Abstract

In the third act of Shakespeare's Hamlet, the hero is unsure whether to kill Claudius - the assassin of Hamlet's father - or not. He argues that if he does kill him, Claudius who is praying at that very moment goes to heaven and if he does not kill him Hamlet's father is not revenged. A contradiction.

Ultima Ratio aims at formalization and visualization of argumentation for agents. An agent is constituted by a set of arguments and assumptions. Facing a particular world, the agent's believes may be inconsistent triggering a rational monologue to deal with the situation.

Formally, we define a framework for argumentation based on extended logic programming under well-founded semantics. The system serves as decision support and is capable of detecting and removing contradictions and deriving conclusions of the agent's arguments.

To demonstrate the structure and dynamics of the agent's argumentation, we visualise the process as dynamic construction of proof trees. The paper includes screenshots of the logical engine and the visualisation unit as exhibited at the computer arts exhibition Ars Electronica 98.

1. Introduction

The project Ultima Ratio aims at formalisation and visualisation of argumentation for agents. An agent is defined by a set of arguments and assumptions. Facing a particular world, the agent's beliefs may be inconsistent triggering a rational monologue to deal with the situation. In this paper, we give a theoretical account on how arguments attacking each other are used for conflict resolution and show the animated visualisation process. The paper contains screenshots of the system as exhibited at Ars Electronica. To see the screenshots in colour please visit the URL below. [1]

Our work is closely related to logic programming and formal argumentation [8, 10]. Intuitively, argumentation treats the evaluation of a logic program as an argumentation process, where a goal G holds if all arguments supporting G cannot be attacked anymore. Thus, logic programming is seen as a discourse involving attacking and counterattacking arguments.

Ultima Ratio is a system that relies on a formalism to represent ambivalence by arguments and to solve them by argumentation. Arguments are modeled by extended logic programs which provide two forms of negation, assumptions, integrity constraints, and contradiction removal. Using this expressive language, we implement human decision making and argumentation including features such as: don't believe in a statement if there is evidence to the contrary, don't rely on premises which are defeated, try to find inconsistencies and remove them by changing relevant assumptions. This methodological canon works on a knowledge base which contains logical representations of various conflicts occurring in classical literature. For Hamlet, for example, it is contradictory to have the goal to take revenge and not to take it. The argument that Claudius killed Hamlet's father supports Hamlet's goal. Subsequently, Hamlet killing Claudius would remove Hamlet's contradiction, if there was not another counter-argument: Claudius would go to heaven (which is too good for him) if killed while praying. Hamlet is caught in cascades of doubt.

Besides formal argumentation, Ultima Ratio aims at visualizing the process of argumentation in a form understandable by human beings even without basic knowledge about the foundations of formal logic. To achieve this goal, we use the construction of argumentation trees as visual metaphor for the process of argumentation. The tree's construction is a representation of an argument (the logic) and

---
*We'd like to thank Bela Bargeld and Joachim Böttger for helping with the visualisation, Uwe Küssner and Manfred Stede for the audio output and Dirk Weinreich, Tristan Thunnissen, Jens Eidinger, Martin Dahlhauser, Pik You Chan, Tilo Meisel of Softimage Operation for the video.

---
[1] www.soi.city.ac.uk/homes/msch/ultima/ars/screenshots.html

the execution event (the control flow) in the logic program. While visualizing the current state of execution of the logic program can and has been done by tree structures, our approaches mainly differs in the dynamics of the presentation. Rather than only changing attributes of the visualization (such as color of an argument) in a more or less static view, we generate an interactive animation of the whole process. The goal of this animation is to enable users to navigate through the argumentation *space* as well as the argumentation *process* without losing the overall view.

2. Formal Foundations of Argumentation

Argumentation is very useful metaphor to define the semantics of logic programs. Intuitively, argumentation semantics treats the evaluation of a logic program as an argumentation process, where a goal G holds if all arguments supporting G cannot be attacked anymore. Thus, logic programming is seen as a discourse involving attacking and counter-attacking arguments.

While argumentation in rhetoric comprises a variety of figures such as arguments by example, by analogy, by the consequences, a pari (arguing from similar propositions), a fortiori (arguing from an accepted conclusion to an even more evident one), a contrario (arguing from an accepted conclusion to the rejection of its contrary), and the argument of authority, logic programming can be described in terms of two figures: rebut and undercut [8]. The former classifies an argument that leads to a contradiction under the current believes and arguments, and the latter an argument that falsifies the premise of one of the current arguments.

2.1. Formalizing Argumentation in Literature

We represent arguments as extended logic programs.

Definition 1 *An extended logic program is a (possibly infinite) set of rules of the form $L_0 \leftarrow L_1, \ldots, L_l, not L_{l+1}, \ldots, not L_m$ $(0 \leq l \leq m)$ where each L_i is an objective literal $(0 \leq i \leq m)$. An objective literal is either an atom A or its explicit negation $\neg A$. Literals of the form not L are called default literals. A subset R of default literals which do not occur in the head of a rule is called revisables. The set of all objective literals is called the herbrand base $\mathcal{H}(P)$. A rule with head $L_0 = \bot$ is called integrity constraint. The symbol $\bot$ stands for falsity. A program P is inconsistent iff $P \models \bot$, otherwise it is consistent.*

While objective literals have a fixed truth values, default literals have a default truth value. For revisables this truth value may be changed. The limitation of revisability to default literals which do not occur as rule heads is adopted for

efficiency reasons, but without loss of generality. We want to guarantee that the truth value of revisables is independent of any rules. Thus we can change the truth value of a revisable whenever necessary without considering an expensive derivation of the default literal's truth value.

Consider the excerpt of the third scene in the third act of Shakespeare's Hamlet below:

1   *Hamlet. [approaches the entry to the lobby]*
    Now might I do it pat, now a'is a-praying-
2   And now I'll do't, *[he draws his sword]* and
    so a' goes to heaven,
3   And so am I revenged. That would be scanned:
4   A villain kills my father, and for that
5   I his sole son do this same villain send
6   To heaven...
7   Why, this is bait and salary, not revenge.

Hamlet is caught in a conflict. On the one hand he wants revenge for his father being murdered. On the other he knows that having revenge by killing Claudius, the murderer, is not possible since Claudius is praying at that very moment and would go to heaven which contradicts the goal of having revenge. The text can be formalised as follows:

a $praying(claudius).$
b $in\_heaven(X) \leftarrow kills(Y,X), praying(X).$
c $took\_revenge\_on(X,Y) \leftarrow kills(X,Y).$
d $killed(claudius, king).$
e $\neg took\_revenge\_on(X,Y) \leftarrow in\_heaven(Y).$
f $goal\_revenge(X,Y) \leftarrow close(X,Z),$
    $killed(Y,Z), not\ justified(killed(Y,Z)).$
g $close(hamlet, king).$
h $\bot \leftarrow goal\_revenge(X,Y), not\ took\_revenge\_on(X,Y).$
i $revisable(kills(hamlet, claudius), false).$

In line 1, Hamlet realizes that Claudius is praying. This is represented as a fact (a). In line 2, Hamlet continues that Claudius would go to heaven if killed while praying. Formally, this is an instantiation of the general rule (b). In line 3, Hamlet states that killing Claudius satisfies Hamlet's desire for revenge. Or more general (c). In line 4, Hamlet starts another line of thinking by mentioning the fact that Claudius killed Hamlet's father, the king (d). In line 7, Hamlet finds that he does not have revenge if he sends Claudius to heaven (e). Beside this direct translation of Hamlet's monologue to logic, we have to add further facts and rules which are mentioned throughout the scenes before or which are given implicitly. First of all, we need a rule to express when someone wants revenge (f). I.e. X wants to take revenge on Y if Y killed a person Z being close to X, and the killing is not justified. Left implicitly in the piece is the fact that Hamlet and his father are close to each other (g). To specify conflicting goals we use besides facts and rules integrity constraints. In this scene we state formally that it is contradictory to want to take revenge and not have it (h). Finally, we have to specify the assumptions Hamlet is willing to change to solve conflicts. For this scene, Hamlet adopts the default assumption of not killing Claudius. I.e. (i) states that Hamlet killing Claudius is assumed false initially, but may be changed in the course of argumentation.

To formalise human argumentation as shown in the previous example one has to detect first the assumptions the protagonist is willing to change. These assumptions are made revisable and are assigned to a default value. Secondly, the problem domain has to be modeled in terms of facts and rules. The two negations (*not* and $\neg$) are important for this modeling task. For example, *not justified(killed(X,Y))* expresses that a murder is not justified as long as there is no explicit proof for the contrary. In contrast, $\neg took\_revenge\_on(X,Y) \leftarrow in\_heaven(Y)$ states that there is explicit evidence that X did not take revenge on Y if Y ends up in heaven. Besides the three ingredients of revisable assumptions, facts, and rules, we have to define which conclusions are contradictory. Naturally, we say that, for example, *took_revenge_on(X,Y)* and its explicit negation $\neg took\_revenge\_on(X,Y)$ are contradictory, i.e. $\perp \leftarrow took\_revenge\_on(X,Y), \neg took\_revenge\_on(X,Y)$, but for convenience we are at liberty to define further conflicts such as, for example, $\perp \leftarrow goal\_revenge(X,Y), not\ took\_revenge\_on(X,Y)$.

Formally, we define an argument as follows:

Definition 2 *Let P be an extended logic program. An argument for a conclusion L is a finite sequence $A = [r_m, \dots r_n]$ of ground instances of rules $r_i \in P$ such that 1. for every $n \leq i \leq m$, for every objective literal L_j in the antecedent of r_i there is a $k < i$ such that L_j is the consequent of r_k. 2. L is the consequent of some rule of A; 3. No two distinct rules in the sequence have the same consequent. A sequence of a subset of rules in A being an argument is called subargument.*

Example 3 *An argument for the conclusion goal_revenge(hamlet, claudius) is the sequence:*
$$goal\_revenge(hamlet, claudius) \leftarrow$$
$$close(hamlet, king),$$
$$killed(claudius, king),$$
$$not\ justified(killed(claudius, king));$$
$$close(hamlet, king) \leftarrow true;$$
$$killed(claudius, king) \leftarrow true;$$

2.2. The Process of Argumentation

There are two ways of attacking an argument for a conclusion L. We may prove that the argument for L leads to a contradiction since there is also proof for $\neg L$. Such a counter-argument is called *rebut*. The second possibility

is to attack the premises of the argument for L. If L's argument is based on an assumption *not L'* we can attack the argument with a counter-argument for L'. Such an attack is called undercut.

Definition 4 *Let A_1 and A_2 be two arguments, then A_1 undercuts A_2 iff A_1 is an argument for L and A_2 is an argument with assumption not L, i.e. there is an $r : L_0 \leftarrow L_1, \dots, L_l, not\ L_{l+1}, \dots, not\ L_m \in A_2$ and a $l + 1 < j \leq m$ such that $L = L_j$. A_1 rebuts A_2 iff A_1 is an argument for L and A_2 is an argument for $\neg L$. A_1 attacks A_2 iff A_1 undercuts or rebuts A_2.*

Example 5 *The argument took_revenge_on(hamlet, claudius) $\leftarrow$ kills(hamlet, claudius) can be attacked by the rebut*
$$\neg took\_revenge\_on(hamlet, claudius) \leftarrow$$
$$in\_heaven(claudius);$$
$$in\_heaven(claudius) \leftarrow$$
$$kills(hamlet, claudius), praying(claudius);$$
$$praying(claudius) \leftarrow true.$$

Definition 6 *An argument is coherent if it does not contain subarguments attacking each other. A set Args of arguments is called conflict-free if no two arguments in Args attack each other.*

Definition 7 *Let A_1 and A_2 be two arguments, then A_1 defeats A_2 iff A_1 is empty and A_2 incoherent or A_1 undercuts A_2 or A_1 rebuts A_2 and A_2 does not undercut A_1. A_1 strictly defeats A_2 iff A_1 defeats A_2 but not vice versa. A_1 is acceptable wrt. a set Args of arguments iff each argument undercutting A_1 is strictly defeated by an argument in Args.*

Our notion of acceptability deviates from Prakken and Sartor's definition [8] where an argument A_1 is accepted if each *defeating* argument is accepted. Our notion is more credulous and leads to more intuitive results.

Example 8 *Consider the program $P = \{a \leftarrow not\ b; b \leftarrow not\ a; \neg a\}$, then $\neg a$ and $b \leftarrow not\ a$ are acceptable, whereas $a \leftarrow not\ b$ is not. For Prakken and Sartor's definition of acceptability there is no acceptable argument which contradicts the intuition of $\neg a$ being a fact.*

Definition 9 *Let P be an extended logic program and S be a subset of arguments of P, then $F_P(S) = \{A \mid A \text{ is acceptable wrt. } S\}$ is called characteristic function. A is justified iff A is in the least fixpoint of F_P. A is overruled iff A is attacked by a justified argument. A is defensible iff A is neither justified nor overruled.*

Argumentation is closely related to logic programming. It turns out that the above argumentation framework is eqivalent to WFSX [1], a semantics for extended logic programs. While the above fixpoint definition of justified, over-ruled, and defensible arguments is suitable to give a declarative semantics to argumentation, WFSX provides an efficient operational semantics with a top-down derivation procedure. In Ultima Ratio, we use this derivation procedure and annotate the proof on the fly. Additionally, we compute revisions, which remove conflicts between arguments by adapting the involved assumptions appropriately. To compute revisions we use REVISE 2.4 [3]. The derivation procedure and contradiction removal algorithm are extended to generate proof traces which are then used for visualisation.

Definition 10 *The traces are composed of the following speech-act-like tags:*
1. Derivation of default negated literals not L is accompanied with the tags propose_not(L) entering the definition of not L and accept_not(L) if the proof for L fails and reject_not(L) otherwise.
2. If a revisable L is encountered during the proof the tags revisable_assumed(L) and revisable_not_assumed(L) are generated depending on the current truth value of L
3. If a literal L is part of a loop the tag loop(L) is generated
4. If L is a fact then fact(L) is generated
5. If the proof involves rules for a goal L, then rule(L, Body) indicates the rule used in the proof and no_rule(L) that there is no rule. If a rule's body is proven rule_succeeds(L, Body) is generated and otherwise rule_fails(L, Body)
6. If a partial revision R is assumed then assume(R) is generated and if R turns out to be a solution assume_solution(R) otherwise assume_closed(R)

Having developed the argumentation theory we turn now to the functionality of the implemented system.

3. Visualizing Extended Logic Programs

Kowalski's phrase "Algorithm = Logic + Control" has some interesting implications for visualizing logic programs. *Logic*, interpreted as formulating premises and queries can be seen as static since it forms a well-founded *argumentation space* in which the actual proof for a given query is found. *Control* means the process of deriving a solution and is inherently dynamic since it requires inference, backtracking etc.

Previous work such as [4], [2] and [6] has primarily focused on visualizing the control flow in an AND/OR tree by displaying success of failure of rules and the associated unification process. While these approaches are well suited for debugging or analyzing the execution of a logic program they are not very "visually pleasing" and require a good portion of knowledge about the execution of logic programs. Also, the detection and removal of contradictions, a central point of extended logic can not be visualised easily by the techniques used so far.

In contrast, Ultima Ratio aims at visualizing the process of argumentation in a form understandable by human beings even without basic knowledge about the foundations of formal logic. To achieve this goal, we use the construction of proof trees. The construction is a representation of an argument (the logic) and the execution event (the control flow) in the logic program. While visualizing the current state of execution of the logic program can and has been done by tree structures, our approaches mainly differs in the dynamics of the presentation. Rather than only changing attributes of the visualization (such as color of an argument) in a more or less static view, we generate an interactive animation of the whole process. The goal of this animation is to enable users to navigate through the argumentation *space* as well as the argumentation *process*.

3.1. Argumentation Space

As has been mentioned above, a significant place to start the visualization with is the argumentation space. It is more or less the background for the reasoning taking place during the process of argumentation. This space, although containing sets of pre-defined (i.e. static) facts and rules, may be used in different contexts and therefore lead to different results. To emphasise this non-absolute behaviour, the visualization of an argumentation space is not static – it provides a dynamic background on which the actors (the synthetic agents) perform its "discussion".

Arguments, seen as sequences of rules, are arranged hierarchically to communicate the dependencies between the argument and its sub-arguments. For efficient use of screen real estate its layout is arranged in 3D, allowing to focus on the argument at hand while still having contextual information of the overall information flow. This type of visualization, also known as implicit distorting views [7], has been used to visualise complex nested structures by exploiting perspective transformations of 3D objects on 2D screens [5, 9].

3.2. Argumentation Process

Due to the limited number of execution events in Definition 10, visualising the dynamics of an argumentation process is done using a forest of trees for the different argumentation processes based on different assumtions and coloured nodes representing arguments' conclusions.

The tags in Definition 10 are visualised as follows:

- The tag *assume* indicates the generation of a new argumentation tree.

- Once the tree is fully processed *assume_closed* and *assume_solution* indicate a derivation of a conflict or not. This event is represented by two rotating, orange

Figure 1. Ultima Ratio's User Interface

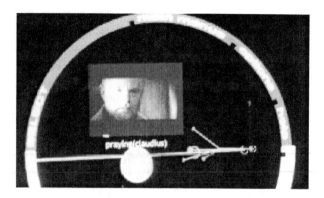

Figure 2. Cascades of Doubt: Should Hamlet take revenge on Claudius?

ellipses. If a conflict is derived (*assume_closed*) the ellipses intersect, otherwise they do not.

- The structure of the tree is determined by the tags *rule* creating internal nodes in the tree and *fact* creating the leaves of the argumentation tree. Initially, the tree is constructed rapidly moving from the root to the leaves. All nodes are left open and rotate indicating that it is not yet known whether they are valid or not.

- In the next phase the tree is traversed bottom-up and nodes are filled in yellow if they form a valid conclusion (*rule_succeds*) or blue otherwise (*rule_fails*, *no_rule*).

Interestingly, users favoured the visualisation combining a fast top-down traversal followed by a slow and detailed bottom-up traversal to pure top-down or bottom-up. This is very remarkable since this corresponds technically exactly to the magic-set algorithm used in deductive databases. This algorithm combines the advantages of top-down and bottom-up evaluation to improve performance and appears to capture closely human reasoning.

4. Ultima Ratio's Functionality

Figure 1 shows Ultima Ratio's graphical user interface whose form is derived from a compass. At the rim of the compass one can select menus which appear as a sphere. With a joystick the user rotates the sphere until the entry of choice is in the centre. Via the compass menu the user selects one of the following functions:

1. **Cascades of Doubt - Struggling Agents.** The user selects an agent according to the author's version. Currently the knowledge base contains Shakespearce's Hamlet, Ilsa

and Rick in Casablanca, Siegfried, Krimhild, Brunhild, Hagen and Etzel of the German saga Nibelungenlied, Euripides' Medea, Molière's Don Juan, the artist Duchamp and his readymades, Robocop, and Macchiavelli. The arguments for these agents are online.[2]

Consider Hamlet, for example. The argumentation process which is represented by a proof tree is visualised as a 3D tree. Premises which are not yet proven are represented by rotating circular rims. If they are successfully proven an orange disc moves to the rotating rim and fills it out (see Figure 2). If the proof failed the disc is blue. If the argumentation finally results in a conflict two rotating and intersecting ellipses appear at the conflicting nodes. If the potential conflict did not occur the ellipses do not intersect. The user can navigate in the argumentation space or switch to auto-pilot. For the auto-pilot, we combined top-down and bottom-up derivation. Technically, the system performs the proof top-down, but users felt more comfortable with a bottom-up proof starting with the facts and leading to a conflict in the end. We have combined both by the camera moving directly from the root of the proof tree to the leaves and then moving step by step bottom-up from the facts.

2. **Crossovers - Tracing Motifs.** Crossovers allow to trace motifs in the complete argumentation space. In the on-line knowledge base[3] one can see, for example, that the arguments for revenge occurring in Hamlet are also part of the Nibelungenlied and of the agent property "revengeful". Similarly, the topic of offences connects Don Juan to Medea. Visually, the tree structure of the arguments is shown and different regions in the 3D space correspond to different agents. The same argument occurring in different regions is connected by a bridge of grey cubes (see Figure 3) leading from one agent to another. Besides this 3D visu-

---

[2]http://www.soi.city.ac.uk/homes/msch/cgi/aec/kbwww/cod.html
[3]http://www.soi.city.ac.uk/homes/msch/cgi/aec/kbwww/co.html

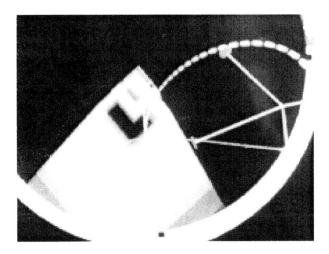

Figure 3. Crossovers: Hamlet and Krimhild share the revenge motif

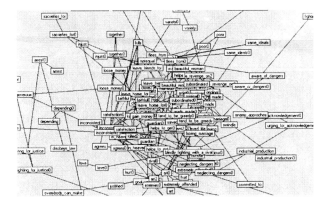

Figure 4. Crossovers in 2D

alisation, the above online knowledge base provides and an applet showing the dependencies of arguments

3. **War of Convictions - Arguments as Forces.** The war of conviction function focuses on conflicts in general, independent of their instances for particular agents and worlds. The online knowledge base[4] lists all conflicts and arguments together with cross-references showing on which arguments conflicts are based and how arguments support and attack each other.

4. **Reasoning Running Wild.** In contrast to the above logical modes, Ultima Ratio also provides a visual metaphor for reasoning running wild: The proof trees move very fast so that their structure is not graspable anymore, additionally the user's head tracker is switched on leading to a distorted view depending on the user's head movements.

[4]http://www.soi.city.ac.uk/homes/msch/cgi/aec/kbwww/woc.html

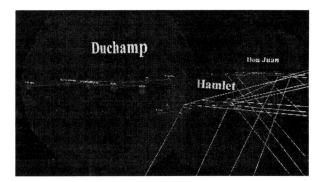

Figure 5. Crossovers in 3D

5. Conclusion

Ultima Ratio is a system for formal argumentation and its visualisation. Ultima Ratio allows to specify an agent and the world it is situated in as an extended logic program. Using argumentation, it is possible to detect and remove conflicts the agent is facing. Given the agent's arguments and a world it faces, Ultima Ratio unfolds a process of argumentation in which arguments and counter-arguments are exchanged to detect conflicts and remove them. The visualisation enables users to navigate through the argumentation space and the argumentation process which is constructed dynamically as the argumentation process evolves.

References

[1] J. J. Alferes and L. M. Pereira. *Reasoning with Logic Programming.* (LNAI 1111), Springer-Verlag, 1996.

[2] M. Brayshaw and M. Eisenstadt. A practical graphical tracer for prolog. *Intl. J. of Man-Machine Studies*, 35(5):597–631, 1991.

[3] C.V. Damásio, L.M. Pereira, and M. Schroeder. REVISE: Logic programming and diagnosis. In *Proc. of LPNMR97*. LNAI 1265, Springer–Verlag, 1997.

[4] A.D. Dewar and J.G. Cleary. Graphical display of complex information within a prolog debugger. *Intl. J. of Man-Machine Studies*, 25(5):503–521, 1986.

[5] J. D. Mackinlay, G. G. Robertson, and S. K. Card. The perspective wall: Detail and context smoothly integrated. In *Proc. of Conf. on Human Factors in Computing Systems*. ACM, 1991.

[6] E. Neufeld, A. Kusalik, and M. Dobrohoczki. Visual metaphors for understanding logic program execution. In *Proc. of Graphics Interface*, pages 114–120, May 1997.

[7] E. G. Noik. A space of presentation emphasis techniques for visualizing graphs. In *Proc. of Graphics Interface*, pages 225–234, May 1994.

[8] H. Prakken and G. Sartor. Argument-based extended logig programming with defeasible priorities. *J. of Applied Non-Classical Logics*, 7(1), 1997.

[9] G. G. Robertson, J. D. Mackinlay, and S. K. Card. Cone trees: Animated 3D visualizations of hierarchical information. In *Proc. of Conf. on Human Factors in Computing Systems*. ACM, 1991.

[10] M. Schroeder. An efficient argumentation framework for negotiating autonomous agents. In *Proc. of MAAMAW99*. Springer-Verlag, 1999.

Generation of Passion Images from "Tanka" Poems
based on the Synesthesia Phenomenon

Tsutomu Miyasato

ATR Media Integration & Communications Research Laboratories
2-2 Hikaridai, Seika-cho, Soraku-gun, Kyoto 619-0288, Japan
Tel. +81 774-95-1490, Fax.+81 774-95-1408, E-mail: miyasato@mic.atr.co.jp

Abstract

This paper describes an investigation of the generation of surrealistic spaces that aim to achieve a new communications environment in which people can mutually convey their thoughts, mental images, and passions. Passion images here can be compared with conceptual images in the analogy of "logos versus pathos." Our focus was on the phenomenon of synesthesia, and the results shown are of the testing of color image creation involving "tanka" (i.e., 31-syllable Japanese poems), aiming at the generation of images where some passions are reflected rather than concrete scenes imagined from word meanings. In addition, this paper proposes an application that judges the similarity of pieces of music, showing the possibility of making instant, subjective judgements without need for a performance.

1. Introduction

The authors are progressing with research on a technology to create new communication environments and methods to overcome present communications limitations by applying virtual reality, for the purpose of allowing people to mutually convey their thoughts, mental images, and emotions more effectively [1-2].

Human recognition and human communications are classified as being either logical or emotional. In this paper we explain an investigation on the generation of passion images focusing on the synesthesia phenomenon. Passion images here are compared with conceptual images [2] in the analogy of "logos vs. pathos."

2. Synesthesia Phenomenon

Expressions involving the sense of sight are often used to express sounds, in what is called "colored hearing." The painter Wassily Kandinsky was said to possess synesthesia [3]. It has been said that when he viewed some colors, these colors would also become audible. In addition, the French poet Arthur Rimbaud made a poem relating images (evoking vowels under the theme called "Voyelles") to colors [4].

Synesthesia, besides being reactions belonging to a system of senses in the case of stimulation being given to the receptors of the senses, denotes a phenomenon that causes reactions to senses belonging to a system originally excluding the above senses [5]. One example of this is the phenomenon of hearing a sound and feeling a color known as "colored hearing." Yellow is usually assigned to the sound of a child's voice.

3. Generation of Passion Images by Media Exchange

People possessing typical senses find it difficult to understand the phenomenon of synesthesia. We, who possess typical senses, are merely able to enjoy pictures as media while mixing their own past experiences generated by images for sight stimulation and acoustics effects for hearing stimulation. However, what kind of world do people with synesthesia perceive?

Imagining the world that people with synesthesia perceive, we investigated the generation of images. We focused on poems. Relationships are said to be strong among colors, sounds, and feelings. We then tested color image creation from the Japanese "tanka" poems of Ogura Hyakunin Isshu*, which were written with 31 Japanese syllables. However, this is not about the correspondence of simple sounds and colors, it is not like the flashback of concrete scenes like Fig.1 imagined from the meanings of the words of the poems. Our goal is to generate images so that passions are reflected.

We generated passion images from Japanese poems using the following steps.

Step 1: A table was created beforehand of the corresponding relationships between phonemes and colors. For ex-

---

* "Ogura Hyakunin Isshu" is an anthology of 100 poems by 100 different poets. The poems are all "tanka." "Tanka" consist of five lines with a total of 31 syllables in the syllabic pattern of 5-7-5-7-7. They originated in the thirteenth century.

ample, the vowel "i" is made to correspond to red, the vowel "a" is made to correspond to black, etc. In addition, for differences in the sounds of voiced consonants and so on, correspondences are made to differences in brightness. Here, the correspondence relationships between phonemes and colors have been determined by the senses of the authors themselves, because "there is no natural correspondence between colors and sounds" [6].

Step 2: The phonemes that compose 31-syllable Japanese poems were made to correspond to image elements, and a

Figure 1. Example of a scene imagined from a poem.

Image courtesy of Soseki (http://mall.ec.infoweb.ne.jp/korokan/ tanka/index.htm)

multidimensional image element array was constructed. In this paper, we took a two-dimensional array so that the image became rectangular, i.e., a square matrix. The image elements corresponding to the phonemes by the time series of the reading, were colored in the direction from the upper left to the right in the two-dimensional array. Here, in the case of image elements emerging without color information being given (unless the total number of image elements is the square count), the color white is allocated. After that, various types of image processing (of low-pass filtering and so on) were carried out and displayed.

In Fig. 2, two results are shown from carrying out the above-mentioned color image creation processing to the "tanka" poems by two poets from the Ogura Hyakunin Isshu.

The same method can be applied to music. For example, if a quarter musical note is the shortest musical note in a musical score, it can be made to correspond to image elements as the shortest part of the score. Even if there are differences in the scores, it is common for pieces of music to resemble each other. Any judgment on similarity therefore depends on human judgment. With color images, the comparative ability is high, and even people who can not read complex musical scores are able to feel the similarities without the need for a musical performance. Figure 3 shows an example of a picture converted from a musical score of a song titled "cosmos."

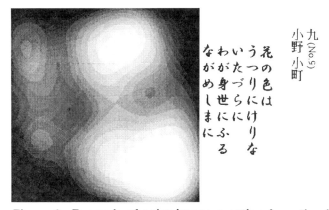 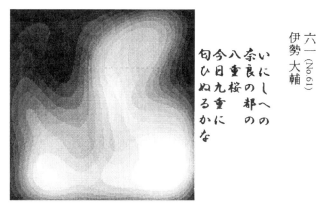

Figure 2. Example of color image creation from the Japanese "tanka" poems of Ogura Hyakunin Isshu.

No . 9 poem by Lady Ono no Komachi

Color of the flower
Has already faded away,
While in idle thoughts
My life passes vainly by,
As I watch the long rains fall.

No. 61 poem by Lady Ise no Osuke

Eight-fold cherry flowers
That at Nara--ancient seat
Of our state--have bloomed,
In our nine-fold palace court
Shed their sweet perfume today.

4. Conclusion

We explained our investigation on the generation of surrealistic images aiming at the achievement of a new communications environment for people. This time, color correspondence was performed with phoneme units involving "tanka," but we are also considering investigations on color correspondence with word units (such as seasonal words) and on the reflection of the peculiarities of every songbook or every poet focusing on the similarity of the method of expression.

References

[1] J. Satoh, H. Noma and T. Miyasato, T., "Emotional Virtual Environment", Iasted International Conference on Computer Graphics and Imaging (CGIM'98), pp. 245-248 (Jun 1998).

[2] H. Noma, Y. Sumi, T. Miyasato and K. Mase, "Thinking Support System via a Haptic Interface" [in Japanese], 13th Human Interface Symposium, pp. 1 - 16 (1998).

[3] F. Whitford , "Abstract Art Guide" [T. Kinoshita (translation in Japnanese], Bijutsu Publishing, (Oct. 1991).

[4] D. Horiguchi, "Rimbaud Anthology" [translated in Japanese], Shinchou Press, (Oct. 1951).

[5] T. Oyama, S. Imai, and T. Wake , "Sense and Perception Psychology Handbook" [in Japanese], Seishin Shobou Press, (Jan. 1994).

[6] K. Gelstern , "Color and Form, Chapter 9, Correspondence" [K. Abe (translation in Japanese)], Asakura Press, (July 1989).

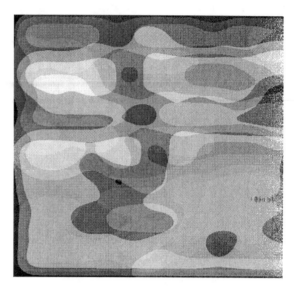

Figure 3. Example of a picture converted from a musical score of a song titled "cosmos" by Sada Masashi.

PosadaSpace: a Skeletal Fine Art Virtual Environment

by Mike Mosher <mikemosh@well.com>
and Tim McFadden <tim.mcfadden@thinkone.com>

Abstract:

The 1998 artwork PosadaSpace is a virtual world exhibited in a decorated computer kiosk. Mike Mosher and Tim McFadden built it around the historic cartoon imagery of Jose Guadalupe Posada (and some other Mexican art) to investigate the appeal and narrative power of simple 2D sprites in defining and populating an interactive 3D world.

I. Preface:

In the spring and summer of 1998, Mike Mosher and Tim McFadden created a fine arts VR kiosk artwork called PosadaSpace. Mike designed its environments and component JPEGs, and painted an external facade for its computer. Tim programmed the world in VRML and JavaScript, as well as programming three predetermined paths for the viewer. This work however was the fruition of discussions between the two-an artist and a software engineer-dating back to the First Conference on Cyberspace in Austin, TX, in April 1990.

II. Aesthetic issues:

Art can be said to be the subtle manipulation of limitations. Mike has long held that too many 3D worlds remain kitsch, overly-complicated, overdetermined and overdesigned, splendidly serving to demonstrate the capabilities of a computer's hardware and software but little else. These interactive 3D virtual worlds could best be constructed not by attempting a debatable "realism" of every detail, but by emphasis on selected onscreen objects (sprites) and diminution of detail on others. Lessons are to be learned from the early low-resolution videogames like "Tank Commander" circa 1980, where the interactive experience is probably enhanced rather than diminished by the economy of visual information on the screen. The viewer's attention is thus focused upon a clearly-designed center. With more limited visual information the eye also better follows movement of a sprite. Limited visual information may also aid the viewer in spatially locating oneself as the viewpoint moves. Smoothness of navigation may give the greatest experience of real-world veracity, not the detail of rendering of the objects depicted. Low-resolution depiction on screen may have additional performance benefits (1), and economy of rendering might free up processing power to be better applied to responsiveness and refresh rate.

For these reasons it was decided the team would create a 3D world containing 2D JPEGs, nearly-monochromatic cartoon figures standing like flat cut-outs. A visually appealing JPEG of a painting, drawing or photograph can be positioned vertically in a virtual world creates the metaphor of an environment with muralized walls.(2)

III. Content:

PosadaSpace used JPEGs of imagery drawn by José Guadelupe Posada (1852-1913), a hardworking illustrator for forty years of nearly 20,000 cheap, popular broadsides and handbills in Mexico City (3). He frequently used the motif of the *calavera*, or skeleton, to illustrate humorous social or political commentary. Skeletons were presented dressed in the garb of their owner's role when living-bishop, businessman, fashionable lady, Zapatista revolutionary, etc.-or carrying on activities such as reading, eating, bicycling etc. They are visually simple yet powerful and memorable, as the best cartoons and comics artwork must be. (4).

Posada was a significant inspiration for Diego Rivera and his generation of Mexican muralists and painters. Mike took the liberty of including Diego's wife the painter Frida Kahlo in the artwork, using Posada's busy skeletons and exaggerated figures as metaphor for the tensions within their marriage. Three tours through the PosadaSpace were designed in hopes in proximity they convey a certain evocative narration whose imagery links artists, love and death.

"PosadaSpace"
kiosk facade

acrylics on
masonite
4' x 2' x 1.5'

The painted, cut-out facade designed to surround the computer in which PosadaSpace is exhibited is intended to give the work a certain carnival-ride attraction (5). Yet it is also hides or masks the machine, for if the computer is to become more a servant of daily life and become absorbed within other appliances it should certainly do so within artworks as well. It is hoped that works like this then take their place as part of a continuum of complex narrative figurative artwork that includes the architectural frescoes of Michelangelo and Rivera, rather than inhabitant of a separate category "computer art".

IV.The Three Tours:

The first tour carries the viewer from an opening "gateway" with a portrait of Posada, the title and explanatory paragraph hovering in space to a "sculpture garden". The viewer moves between the sprites in a sort of star pattern, moving close to investigate each one. Two walls that share a vertex to form a corner are fairly ornate, one having Rivera's "Dream of a Sunday Aftertoon in Alameda Park" mural (which alludes to Posada's *calaveras*) mapped upon it, for a free-standing complex graphic image becomes a muralized wall within the architecture of cyberspace.

The second path moves from the gateway towards the sculpture garden, then veers sharply to the left where it moves towards what appears to be a gravestone or monument. The viewer then descends, the visible walls of the "elevator" proving to be Diego Rivera's mural of millionaires dining. Upon reaching the bottom, the viewer turns to see "Frida's Boudoir", her portrait upon a bed-like floating rectangular object. A bust of Russian revolutionary Leon Trotsky, murdered in exile in Mexico, stands beside it. Images from a "Mexican Art" disk of clip art, of several women drawn by Rivera, were positioned to serve as the walls of Frida's boudoir. This imagery alludes to the fact that Frida Kahlo had a love affair with Trotsky as well as with several women, and Diego had affairs with many women that he painted.

The third path takes the viewer to the frontiers, where four Posada images of crowds among buildings appear, finally shooting the wiewer upwards to view close-up the moon, a rotating sphere with a crazy face mapped upon it.

V. Engineering Issues:

Tim McFadden relished the opportunity of this project as a great way to learn the languages VRML and JavaScript. In something resembling a movie's director-cameraperson relationship, Mike designed the scenario's storyboard and look and feel of the project while Tim performed the coding. "For a programmer, it was a big thrill to be in control of moving bodies in color" said Tim.

Most of the VRML was hand coded, but for creating the navigation paths a table-driven curve generator was written in C. A table would specify start and endpoints, type of curve, rotation, and initial value for splines. The output of the C program would be loaded into MFVec3f arrays in a JavaScript node to be loaded sequentially into eventOut SFVec3f and SFRotation fields on clock ticks. The spline code came directly from William Press' *Numerical Recipes in C*.

VI. Process Issues:

Mike Mosher handed over to Tim McFadden specifications for PosadaSpace, including sketches of proposed positioning of the sprites and the trajectory of the viewer's paths through the world. Upon viewing the results notes on their modification would be presented in action item lists.

For an artist and a software engineer to work together efficiently meant a learning process towards a common language, so visual ideas which Mike would otherwise express evocatively yet imprecisely could be quantified for the most precise implementation by Tim. By assigning numerical values to the position of each sprite, Tim could build paths that most accurately resembled Mike's intentions, and then together they could refine them upon viewing of the results in thebrowser.

VII. Further Development:

The initial version of PosadaSpace was exhibited upon an Intergraph workstation in "The Art of Digital Technology", an exhibit curated by Barbara Allie and Barbara Rainforth held at the Santa Clara County Fair in August 1998. All visual development on PosadaSpace had to cease in mid-July prior to Mike's travels (6); coding, of course, continued up until the last possible minute. It was exhibited behind a painted facade of two skeletons kissing, with another skeleton on each side wing panel.

There were significant difficulties encountered with the browser, requiring positioning a strip of black tape on the screen and Tim clicking at precise moment to stop its rotation. It is also suspected the piece may have been down (frozen or shut off) a considerable amount of time during the exhibit.

Work has begun on refinement of the Tour paths, with the addition of one or more new Tours under consideration. The optimum goal would be to allow the user total freedom to wander, yet worlds built in this manner traditionally suffer the problem of the user flying out into empty space without sufficient visual clues that allow easy return, unless an invisible bounding box or sphere is in place.

Tim has begun to code PosadaSpace to swap high-resolution JPEGs for conventional ones when the viewer reaches a predetermined distance from a specific JPEG. A later version will use LOD (level of detail). This would give the illusion of near focus without big pixels' blockiness interfering with reading of the image.

Some of the animated movement within the world could not be implemented, due to the browser slowing down. In three instances the swapping of alternatives to specific sprites, so skeletons would appear to strum a guitar or stab a piece of meat with a fork. However the standing portrait of Posada by Rivera would momentarily momentarily swap with a version wearing a skeleton head, and a large moon face mapped upon a sphere above him would rotate.

The story of Indra's Net says that the universe is made of an infinite net at whose intersections are jewels, each jewel reflecting all the others. This image engaging him as a provocative paradigm of cyberspace, Tim hopes to continue the work within it begun in his essay "Notes on Cyberspace and the Ballistic Actors' Model" (7) both in writing and embodied in future collaborative art projects. Tim did not have access to a Java-compliant VRML browser early enough in the PosadaSpace project, but in the future hopes such projects will be networked and multi-user.

It is hoped by both Mike and Tim that continued development of VRML, and supportive technologies like MPEG-4, will support continued investigation by many more teams of artists and programmers, pursuing their personal investigations into design and content amidst the burgeoning potential of creative virtual worlds.

Notes:

(1) First proposed by Mike Mosher in "Objects in Mirror May Be Larger: On Designing Low-Rez Virtual Worlds" a poster installation at the Second Conference on Cyberspace, Santa Cruz CA, 1991.

(2) Mike's experience painting murals in San Francisco, and living in the mural-rich Mission neighborhood there 1981-84, inspires this investigation.

(3) Berdecio, Robert & Applebaum, Stanley, *Posada's Popular Mexican Prints* (Dover Publications, New York NY, 1972), Preface and Acknowlegements.

(4) When Tim wore a Posada *calavera* t-shirt to a breakfast meeting at Hobee's Restaurant, Mountain View, California in February 1998 Mike realized the appropriateness of Posada's simple, powerful imagery for their first virtual world.

(5) Two recent public sculptures in Mountain View are larger-than-life cut-out figures in metal by Joe Sam stand at the City Hall and at the Whisman Sports Center. Mike acknowleges the influence of works like this on PosadaSpace's "sculpture garden". Mike painted mural panels in 1990 for Laguna Honda Hospital, San Francisco, California, cut to the contours of the composition of multiple figures, and since 1992 has exhibited multimedia and hypertext software in kiosks whose screen is cut into shaped, painted facades.

(6) While in Memphis, Tennessee in August 1998, Mike organized and painted a collaborative mural panel "Transistor Healing Elvis", described in "Elvis Healed! A Report From His Conference" in BAD SUBJECTS #39 <http://eserver.org/BS/39/> .

(7) Published in Benedikt, Michael, *Cyberspace: First Steps* (MIT Press, Cambridge MA 1991).

Bibliography:

Anders, Peter, *Visualizing Cyberspace* (Macmilliian & Co., New York NY, 1999). Includes mention of PosadaSpace plus three screenshots on p. 44.

Bad Subjects Production Team, *Bad Subjects* (NYU Press, New York NY, 1998). Includes Mike Mosher's 1995 essay "Towards Community Art Machines" <http://eserver.org/BS/18/>.

Benedikt, Michael, *Cyberspace: First Steps* (MIT Press, Cambridge MA 1991). Includes Tim McFadden's essay "Notes on the Structure of Cyberspace and the Ballistic Actors Model".

Berdecio, Robert & Applebaum, Stanley, *Posada's Popular Mexican Prints* (Dover Publications, New York NY, 1972).

Carey, Rick and Bell, Gavin, *The Annotated VRML 2.0 Reference Manual* (Addison-Welsey Publishing Co., Reading, MA, 1997). Tim found this book especially a joy to read and use.

Press, William et. al., *Numerical Recipes in C* (Cambridge University Press, Cambridge UK, 1988).

Rothenstein, Julian, *J. G. Posada: Messenger of Mortality* (Moyer Bell Limited, Mt. Kisco, NY, 1989).

Mike Mosher <http://www.ylem.org/artists/mmosher/Opening.html> is an artist and an Adjunct Professor in the University of San Francisco Information Systems Program, Cupertino, CA. He has taught in the San Francisco State University Art Department, the SFSU Inter-Arts Center and the SFSU Multimedia Studies Program. His multi- media artwork has been exhibited at the Franklin Institute, Philadelphia, PA, at the Rochester Institute of Technology, and at Artists' Television Access, San Francisco.

Tim McFadden is a software engineer at ThinkOne, Brisbane, California, U.S.A., where he is currently networking MPEG-4. Please note that PosadaSpace is unrelated to any work done by Tim for ThinkOne, and does not in any way represent its efforts in VRML or MPEG-4. Tim is also working privately on a sonar cyberdeck, and will continue to upload fun art into cyberspace.

Collaborative Visualization:
New Advances in Documenting Virtual Reality with IGrams

Ellen Sandor, Janine Fron, Kristine Greiber, Fernando Orellana and Stephan Meyers

(art)^n Laboratory

847 W. Jackson Blvd., 6th Floor, Chicago, IL 60607 USA

artn@artn.com

Dana Plepys, Margaret Dolinsky, and Mohammed Dastagir Ali

Electronic Visualization Laboratory

University of Illinois at Chicago

851 S. Morgan St., Room 1120, Chicago, IL 60607 USA

dana@eecs.uic.edu

Abstract

(art)^n Laboratory and the Electronic Visualization Laboratory (EVL) at the University of Illinois at Chicago have collaborated on the development of the first real-time, stereoscopic hardcopy output of virtual reality applications - the ImmersaGram (IGram). The results of this new technology directly address a broad range of information visualization issues along a wide spectrum of disciplines from art, architecture, and science, to medicine, engineering and education.

Keywords: Virtual Reality, Art, Science, lenticular, PHSCologram, autostereography

1. Introduction

How can virtual reality applications be documented and shared outside the virtual environment without the use of expensive computer hardware, access to limited resources, simulators, etc.? What medium is available for artists/scientists to record their work in-progress to contemplate, assess and evolve without direct access to the virtual reality system? Is there a way to extend one's artistic expression beyond the virtual application itself? An underlying answer to these and many other questions is the IGram - a virtual reality snapshot.

Among the more principal and critical concerns has been the ability to capture a fleeting moment or state within a virtual reality experience. Video and photographic documentation of virtual reality participants and environments has yielded only marginal results; the interactive nature of the experience can be documented, though image quality is significantly compromised due to resolution loss, monoscopic display and difficult lighting circumstances. High-resolution digital slides or photographs can be created, but do not record the stereoscopic nature of the event, and cannot be generated in real-time. IGrams address these problems by providing a low cost, real-time method for printing three-dimensional virtual imagery to an 8"x10" or 11"x14" stereo transparency. Larger format 20"x24", and 20"x40" medium priced IGrams are viable with a Hewlett Packard Design Jet 2500CP. Other printing variations are optional and currently being explored.

2. Aesthetic background

IGrams are a direct outgrowth of (art)^n Laboratory's computer interleaving process, known as PHSColograms®. The results of computer interleaving provide an archival three-dimensional photograph from computer rendered content. PHSCologram is an acronym for photography, holography, sculpture and computer graphics. In search of new artistic paradigms, the PHSCologram founding artists synthesized the arts of sculpture, photography and computer visualization. PHSCologram are made from a series of 10-65 (or more) snapshots of a virtual environment that are photographed inside of the computer. This series of frames is then combined inside of the computer, output to film and viewed with a barrier screen or lenticular lens [1]. PHSCologram artistry traverses frontiers of science and medicine, as well as educational and historical documentation while remaining true to the fundamentals of fine aesthetics and new technology.

(art)ⁿ's body of work in PHSColograms created a unique dialogue between photography and sculpture in computer graphics and virtual reality [2]. The PHSCologram process draws on earlier advances in photography, including daguerreotypes, photogravures and gelatin silver prints. Rodin was among the first sculptors to use photogravures to publish his "Monument to Balzac" in the famous Camera Work quarterly [3].

Figure 1, *Balzac-The Open Sky*, 1911, Edward J. Steichen, photogravure, from The Sandor Family Collection

Brancusi and David Smith are also known for using photography to document their works. Brancusi's photographs show his vision of the artist in the studio; Smith's photographs reveal the artist in the landscape [4]. The documentation produced by these artists are strong works in their own right. It is (art)ⁿ's vision for IGrams to inspire a new aesthetic consciousness in virtual environments that encourages artists to explore photography and sculpture in their own work.

3. The IGram system

IGram development has addressed the desire to better document virtual reality environments created for EVL's CAVE™ virtual reality system [5]. The CAVE is a fully immersive 10'x10'x10' cubic room, where stereo images are projected onto three walls and the floor. A participant wears LCD shutter glasses, equipped with a tracking device to create the stereo effect and define the user's location within the environment. A three-dimensional 'wand' is used to navigate and interact with virtual objects within the space. IGrams are created within the CAVE system - virtually – while exploring and manipulating the three-dimensional space.

Any 'Performer-based' CAVE application can be used to capture IGrams. The three-dimensional scene is ported to the IGram utility and displayed in the CAVE, where the user manipulates (translates, rotates and scales) the scene within a virtual three-dimensional frame representative of the IGram (hardcopy) output area. The 'depth-of-field' is controlled by changing interleaving values/distances with the 'wand', which affects the stereo perspective projection. In this process, the CAVE itself is akin to a virtual camera, the virtual frame in 3-space - the camera's view-finder, and the wand - the lens/aperture controls.

Interleaving is the digital simulation of the photographic combing procedure. (art)ⁿ's autostereo-graphic process is a result of interleaved computer graphics based on the concept of binocular disparity. Following the virtual 'positioning' of a digital setting, individual images are captured at slightly different angles across the scene in a straight line from left to right. Each of the images is broken up into rows and columns of pixels. (art)ⁿ Laboratory's proprietary software combines these rows and columns of pixels, and arranges them into a single image. The image is output onto a piece of film or paper. The result is a blurred image on transparency film. A barrier screen is placed over this image to complete the 3-D effect. In the case of IGram production, once virtual "positioning" of the scene is complete, ten individual images are captured, interleaved and displayed full scale in the CAVE for technical and aesthetic evaluation before committing to final hardcopy output. When cropping and framing results are satisfactory, interleaved IGram images are sent to the Epson Photo EX color inkjet printer to transparency material and final processing.

4. Experiences

Early on in the development cycle of the IGram CAVE utility, virtual 'art' environments were selected as the initial focus [6]. Capturing the virtual art experience and extending the application beyond the walls of the CAVE environment was an obvious choice. A creative and aesthetically pleasing scene was selected for development, in order to assess whether or not the IGram could capture the essence of the virtual experience, preserve the sense of immersion, and act as an extension of the original artwork into the domain of virtual hardcopy.

Figure 2, *Blue Window Pane (with Man Ray detail),* Margaret Dolinsky and Dana Plepys, Electronic Visualization Laboratory, Stephan Meyers, Ellen Sandor, Janine Fron, Fernando Orellana and Nichole Maury, (art)[n] Laboratory: 1998, 8"x10" Vintage IGram, framed in a wooden lightbox

Results of early experiments were somewhat enlightening. Of concern was how to capture a vast space within a limited frame. Since virtual space can be infinite, objects within the scene can be located at great distances from each other. The ability to quickly move from place to place in virtual reality minimizes this distance, yet in trying to document the scene in time, does not necessarily yield visually appealing results. To address the spatial considerations, it became obvious additional control over the environment position and scale was required. These features are inherent to the IGram program, and are used to compose or select the most representative portion of the virtual scene for archival. A sequence or series of IGram 'snapshots', as in any 'photographic' medium, most readily documents states in time, as well as vast space not easily captured in a single image.

An unexpected discovery was that the artist could use an IGram as a creative development tool. Having an accessible hardcopy to analyze the interrelationship of objects and composition within a specific area of the scene is incredibly beneficial. Access to the virtual display environment can be limited to application review. Scenes are developed in a simulator on the workstation, then checked in the virtual display environment. Going back and forth between writing code to displaying the results can be somewhat disconcerting and indirect for the creative process. The artist's ability to 'study' the scene with some consistency and accessibility can be vastly improved by using the IGram as a working 'sketch' from which to develop and enhance the artwork when not at a workstation or in the virtual system.

5. Conclusion

The primary goal in developing the IGram hardcopy was to archive the virtual environment, while creating a derivative art form or document that can stand on its own merit, tell a story or evoke an emotion. Clearly, it was not developed strictly to document artistic and creative virtual reality applications, but the wide range of virtual reality application areas. In the case of scientific, engineering or medical applications, the IGram can reveal an important feature or aspect of a data set. For architecture/design applications, the IGram can be used for design review, client presentations, as well as recording 'stages' in the production cycle. As virtual reality applications evolve, the IGram will continue to play an important role in preserving and enhancing the exchange of information and recording of technology across a diverse and expanding audience base.

Author Stephan Meyers is presently a Senior Research Engineer at the Nokia Research Center in Tampere, Finland. (art)[n] Laboratory would like to thank Nokia Corporation for their support.

[1] S. Meyers, E. Sandor and J. Fron, PHSColograms and Rotated PHSColograms. *Computers & Graphics* **19.4** (July/August 1995): 513-522
[2] M. Neal, More then Science, More than Art. *Computer Graphics & Applications.* **8.6** (November 1988): 3-5
[3] E. Steichen, *Camera Works 34/35* (April/July 1922):7-11
[4] Pachner, J. *David Smith Photographs 1931-1965.* San Francisco: Fraenkel Gallery, New York: Matthew Marks Gallery & San Francisco: Fraenkel Gallery, 1998
[5] C. Cruz-Neira, D. J. Sandin, T. A.DeFanti, R. V. Kenyon, and J. C. Hart, The CAVE: Audio Visual Experience Automatic Virtual Environment, *Communications of the ACM* **35. 6** (June 1992): 65-72.
[6] M. Dolinsky, Creating art through virtual environments, *Computer Graphics* **31.4** (November 1997): 34-5

Session 3-5

Information Visualization

Chair

Jonathan C. Roberts

University of Kent at Canterbury, UK

Information Highlighting

Timothy Ostler
Anaphora Ltd.
anaphora@cogarch.com

Abstract

This paper reports on an empirical study in which, for the purposes of developing an automatic highlighting tool, 11 subjects were asked to highlight important passages in an 1111-word text. These results were cross-referenced with a range of word attributes in order to test hypotheses about the principles underlying highlighting decisions. With this data a combination of selection criteria was proposed that was able to predict probability of highlighting with a correlation of approximately 0.56, compared with an average correlation of 0.47 amongst the test subjects, and a figure of 0.30 for Word97's highlighting feature. The paper argues that the common factor behind the most successful hypotheses was that they are all signals denoting "new" as opposed to "given" information at the discourse level. Although based on a very limited sample this observation seems clear enough to make detecting such signals a promising candidate for further research.

1. Introduction

1.1 Highlighters as an established tool

The practice of using yellow fibre or felt pens to highlight text appears to have begun in the USA during the 1960s, but it was not until 1971 that Schwan-Stabilo of West Germany launched the first highlighter pen to use fluorescent ink.

Today highlighters are in widespread use, and there is an intuitive impression that for a student the process of highlighting (or other forms of visual cueing such as underlining or bars on the margin) and annotation itself plays a vital process in the revising process, perhaps by encoding or priming material that is then incorporated into long-term memory during revision. This view is supported by the findings of Hult et al. [2], who found that note-taking does indeed involve semantic encoding.

Highlighters are also used to mark up a text for the selective attention of another person and, because of its clear application to the problem of information overload, it is this function that was chosen to study with a view to developing TextLight, an automatic highlighting tool (this paper describes only a brief subset of the research: see the original paper for a study of the cognitive function of highlighting and more extensive examples [1]). To this end, an experiment was conducted to define suitable heuristics for text selection.

2. Previous work

2.1. Criteria for word selection

Herbert Dreyfus once asked if the ability to discriminate between the important and the unimportant was a fundamentally human cognitive operation ([3], reported in [4]). However, many genres have become formalised with tacit agreement on the conventions signalling different stages in a discourse. So while it may never be possible to tell what *seems* important for every person, arguably we can broadly distinguish what *is being presented as important.*

A weakness of all research into visually cued text has been the absence of formal rules governing *which* text should be cued. Here Foster's research of 1979 [5] is perhaps most apposite. 26 students and lecturers were given a 3400-word text and asked to underline sentences that they thought contained the key ideas the author was trying to put over. Foster asked his subjects to use sentences as the minimal unit for underlining.

The terms of the experiment were tightly drawn. In one condition, subjects were told not to underline more than 16 sentences. In the other, not more than eight.

In the first case the 213 selections spanned 80 sentences, with only nine sentences being selected by six

Subject	M1	F1	M2	F2	F3	F4	M3	F5	M4	M5	M6	Ave	Ave	Ave
Sex	M	F	M	F	F	F	M	F	M	M	M	F	MF
Total highlighted	50	291	132	396	306	167	283	257	204	97	341	166.8	283.4	231.8
Percentage highlighted	4.5	26.19	11.88	35.64	27.54	15.03	25.47	23.13	18.36	8.73	30.69	15.01	25.51	20.86
Correlation	0.28	0.48	0.42	0.67	0.47	0.34	0.63	0.32	0.43	0.35	0.41	0.43	0.45	0.43

Table 1. Test results with averages by sex and overallg

	Situation	Problem	Solution	Evaluation
Total highlighted	203	461	153	294
Percentage highlighted	18.27	41.49	13.77	26.46
Correlation	-0.19	-0.01	0.28	-0.05

Table 2. Problem-Solution model status vs. probability of highlighting

	Prox to Seg S	Prox to Para S	Present tense	1st ass (dseg)	1st ass (quote)	List status	Sol'n Status	Hybrid Hypoth
Total highlighted			600	185	108	42	153	398
Percentage highlighted			54.01	16.65	9.72	3.78	13.77	35.82
Correlation	0.33	0.16	0.21	0.44	0.23	0.17	0.28	0.56

Table 3. Alternative criteria vs. probability of highlighting

	Word97 Cond. 1	Word97 Cond. 2	Data Hammer	Subj ave M	Subj ave F	Subj ave MF	Best hypoth
Total highlighted	155	405	353	166.8	283.4	231.8	398
Percentage highlighted	13.95	35.82	31.77	15.01	25.51	20.86	35.82
Correlation	0.2	0.3	0.02	0.43	0.45	0.43	0.56

Table 4. Comparison of highlighting selection strategies

or more judges. In the second, 102 selections were distributed over 52 sentences, with only two being selected by six or more. Foster concluded that it would be difficult to identify sections of text for cueing.

In other experiments the information on word selection was more incidental and merely records what the experimenters chose to do with their test materials rather than what subjects were found to do in an experiment. Klare et al, [6] cued single words. Dearborn et al. [7] emphasised the one word carrying the "peak stress" in a sentence but did not describe how this word was selected. Crouse & Ildstein [8] and Fowler & Barker [9] cued statements or sentences. The most specific suggestions came from Hershberger & Terry [10], whose "core" content made up one third of the total text length and consisted of new key words, familiar key words, key statements, basic core statements, key examples and rephrasing of key statements.

How *much* text should be cued has also remained an open question. Foster [5] suggested that in a particularly dense text, more text might be considered to be "core" than "enrichment", leading to most of the text being highlighted and a figure-ground reversal making the enrichment and not the core most prominent. Crouse & Ildstein [8] suggested that the density of cued material influences its effect. Foster [5] commented that the optimal proportion of text to be highlighted had still not been established. Fowler & Barker [9] pointed to the large variance (4.2% to 32.1%) observed in the proportion of text highlighted by members of the test group who were asked to highlight for themselves. Asked to highlight passages of structural importance, Rickards & August's [11] test subjects all chose passages that Rickards & August considered relatively unimportant when they themselves highlighted the text.

2.2 Experiment

2.2.1. Procedure. 11 subjects — 6 male and 5 female — were provided with an 1111-word article from the Financial Times IT Supplement [13], brief instructions and a questionnaire. They were asked to imagine they were corporate librarians identifying the key points in an article for a board member. The questionnaire sought details about subjects' past experience of highlighting, their criteria for text selection, at what points during the process they made their selection, and other comments.

2.3.2. Performance metric. The article itself was input into a spreadsheet as a column spanning 1111 rows (one word per row). Along each row were entered the attributes associated with each word, which fell into 36 categories. For each word the probability that it lay within a highlighted passage was given a decimal figure between 0 and 1.

All other parameters were also rebased to give figures falling between 0 and 1. Some parameters, such as the part of speech of a particular word, already existed as Boolean values, treated here as 1 or 0. Other parameters, such as the proximity of words to the beginning of dicourse units such as sentences or paragraphs, were expressed as a decimal number between 1 and 0 (1 for the first word in the unit, 0.5 for the middle word and so on). In this way it was possible to calculate the correlation of any given parameter with the probability that a word fell within a highlighted group of words. The degree of correlation was calculated using Excel's CORREL() function.

2.3.3. Results. The results are given in Tables 1 to 5. They show a wide variance in terms of the number of words highlighted, from a minimum of 50 (4.5%) to a maximum of 396 (35.64%). There was also a marked difference between male and female subjects, the males averaging 15% and the females 25.5% In general there was little correlation between part of speech/syntactic role and probability of highlighting, but there was a noticeable association with longer words.

Although the experiment generated 39,996 data elements the results are open to question as serious experimental data especially as all this data was generated from only one text. Nevertheless this is an aspect of human reading activity that has been insufficiently studied in the past and the results are enough to suggest ample pointers to future research in this area.

Most importantly, it provided a basis for generating hypotheses about human highlighting decisions, and for testing those hypotheses. Comments by subjects indicated that none of them made their highlighting decisions before having read at least a paragraph. A large majority (70%) delayed highlighting until the whole passage had been read. This suggests that decisions were made at a discourse-analytical and not a strictly linguistic level.

The variance in the proportion of words highlighted was strikingly close to that observed in Fowler & Barker [9]: 4.5%-35.64% as against 4.2% to 32.1% in the earlier study. This offers a guide for where to set upper and lower limits in highlighting proportion for TextLight

.The form in which these results appear makes them hard to compare with Foster [5]. The average correlation between any one person's highlighting decisions and the scores for probability of given words being highlighted was 0.44. However, for any individual word the probability of being highlighted varied between 0 and 0.83, offering clear guidelines for assessing any trial selection criteria

3. Development of selection heuristics

3.1. Derived criteria

Correlation with the percentage proximity of each word to the beginning of the paragraph proved relatively strong at 0.16. More strikingly, correlation with the same measure as applied to discourse segments (parsed by hand) was 0.33. Parsing of the article into the constituent

parts of the Problem-Solution model was not a simple task because of the degree of recursive nesting. However, when this analysis was carried out (again by hand) there was a strong positive correlation with Solution and a slightly weaker negative correlation with Situation. Attempts were made to combine these and other criteria that seemed promising. However, some of these weakened in combination with other criteria.

The most successful combination was found to be the satisfaction of any one of four criteria:
1)   The word should be part of the first assertion in a discourse segment
2)   The word should be part of the first assertion in a quotation that was not an immediate continuation of a previous quotation.
3)   The word should be part of a list.
4)   Given an analysis of the text according to the "Problem-Solution" discourse structure, the word should be part of a passage in the "Solution" category.

The best hypothesis produced a 0.56 correlation with actual highlighting probability. Bearing in mind that the performance metric was governed by a list of probabilities that individual words would be highlighted, we should not expect any test subject to achieve a correlation of 1.00 with the consensus. In fact this figure varied between 0.28 and 0.63, with an average of 0.43. In other words, selecting text according to the specified criteria achieved a correlation with the consensus selection that was greater than all but one of the test subjects achieved, and considerably higher than the average.

The percentage of the article highlighted using these criteria was, at 35.82%, at the top of the range of percentages shown by the test subjects (perhaps coincidentally, this proportion was similar to the proportion allocated to "core" content by Hershberger & Terry [10]).

For the purposes of additional comparison the study text was passed through the program Data Hammer [12] at a specified percentage of the original article that was as close as practicable to that resulting from the best hypothesis. The retained words were charted alongside those retained by Word97's Auto-Summarization feature. They showed no significant correlation with the words highlighted by the experimental subjects. This demonstrates the difference between retained in a summary and those chosen for highlighting. In the former, unimportant words must be retained in order to give context; in the latter, they can be more or less ignored as they remain visible. Even so, the words highlighted by Word97's statistically-based feature as "key points" are indeed the same as those retained in the equivalent summary, and the correlation performance proved moderately positive, at 0.3.

Although the results achieved by the specified criteria derived from the experiment seem good, the rules observed are only secondary characteristics that depend upon identifying the markers denoting more basic discourse elements, namely the following:

1) Discourse segment boundaries
2)) Simple assertions
3) Lists
4) Passages that fall into the "solution" category

3.2. Identifying primary markers

3.2.1. Discourse segments. Because the test article was manually segmented the efficacy of one means of discourse segmentation rather than another is not strictly relevant. Nevertheless the identification of cohesive markers and their physical relationship to the passages to which they cohere offers fruitful possibilities for discourse segmentation in any attempt to create an automatic highlighter.

3.2.2. Simple assertions Paragraphs normally begin with a proposition, sometimes preceded or followed by a question or other linguistic feature that maintains cohesion makes the proposition's relevance to the preceding text clear. This feature is referred to as a coherence relation, and is analogous to clause relations that provide similar connection at the sentence level. The text that follows tends to fill out details and/or provide supporting evidence for the assertion.

Discourse segments most commonly coincide with the beginning of paragraphs, and so also normally begin with a proposition. The rule that was found to emulate subjects' highlighting choices at the beginning of segments most effectively was to select the segment's opening proposition in its simplest form, without any introductory coherence relation before it. Where one sentence is embedded inside another, as in: "Mr Courtot is keen to point out that **Topic is far more effective than the popular Internet search engines** because **it reads each document and therefore returns a more accurate answer to queries.**" (highlighted words in **bold**). the embedded sentence is selected, together with the causative clause supporting it.

3.2.3. Lists. What for the purposes of this exercise we refer to as lists comprise the first of six categories of prediction in expository text identified by Tadros [14]: enumeration, advance labelling, reporting, recapitulation, hypotheticality and question. Each category consists of a pair of members: a V member, which is predictive, and a D member that fulfils the prediction.

3.2.4. The "Solution" category. As yet, no unifying overall theory of discourse structure analysis exists, and it remains an imprecise science. The more a genre is subject to formal convention, however, the more likely it

is we can overlay this structure literally on a text.

It is outside the scope of this study to present a comprehensive list of the range of discourse structures. However, one particular schema recurs frequently across a range of genres. This is the "Situation-Problem-Solution-Evaluation" structure, usually referred to as the Problem-Solution structure. It is as characteristic of narrative structures (e.g. Boy meets girl—Boy loses girl—Boy regains girl—Boy & girl live happily ever after) as of feature articles (e.g. Dogs make great pets—However they can get fleas—Winalot have now launched a new anti-flea dog food—Owners all over Britain have declared it a success). News stories, however, tend to follow a somewhat different schema [18].

The structure can be nested recursively: for example, an account of a previously resolved problem may form part of the Situation; equally, if a Solution is evaluated negatively it becomes a new Problem. For example, if in the example above the final clause was "Owners all over Britain say that it's useless", there would be an expectation that this would be followed by "So Winalot have brought out a new formulation—This one is reported to work very well".

How do we recognise the elements of this structure? Hoey [15] demonstrates how it can often be recognised by means of lexical signalling cues, i.e. certain words or word roots tend to be associated with particular stages of a discourse. At the most basic level, the stage labels themselves may occur within the text, viz.

"Cars are a common way of getting from A to B. However, the congestion that they cause is a problem. The solution is to get people to use public transport. In this way everyone can get to work quickly."

Hoey argues that discourse structure is essentially evaluative. For instance, in the case of the sentence *"If thyristors are used to control the motor of an electric car, the vehicle moves smoothly but with poor efficiency at low speeds"* its status as a Problem is signalled by the negative evaluation "poor".This suggests that we may b categories simply by spotting cue words or phrases in a given passage.

Because in the experiment it was only the Solution category that was found to have a significant correlation with highlighting, we can afford to concentrate exclusively on words and phrases associated with this category.

Hoey cites two examples of such signals: the use of words to do with "solving", "developing" or "inventing", and the change of verb form into the present perfect tense. indicated by "have -ed". Once the response has been generally described, the form reverts to the simple non-past to denote that a new situation exists, which results from the application of the solution.

4. Discussion

4.1. "Given" and "new" information

Why were the best algorithms more effective than others? What indications did they convey for possible extensions to the specified criteria? An insight first expressed by members of the Prague School before the Second World War [16], is that information is composed of a mixture of "given" and "new" information.

From the experiment, there is clear evidence for an interpretation that the essential factor behind the choice of text to highlight is that they are all ways in which "new" information is signalled at the discourse level.

This hypothesis is supported by the frequency (80%) with which subjects stated that they were highlighting words that "marked significant stages in the narrative." The acceptance of the word "stage" implies a view that the text is organised as an ordered whole that moves successively from one topic to the next. As to the use of the word "important", it is this author's opinion that an idea's perceived importance is judged according to the extent to which it is:

a) new as opposed to given, and
b) matches a perceived gap in the structure of the reader's domain knowledge.

Another concept of importance in a discourse topic is given by Brown & Yule [16]: "A hypothesis underlying much of the work we shall report is that there is a specific connection between "discourse topic" and "discourse content". The former can be viewed as, in some sense, comprising the "important" elements of the latter.

An author will judge information to be important if he expects it to be new in the context of the intended audience's knowledge base. Meanwhile, when a person is highlighting on behalf of someone else, he has to make an informed judgement on which information might fall into this category as far as the ultimate reader is concerned.

Halliday [17] concluded that in spoken discourse, intonation is used to signal to the listener what the speaker understands to be new information. It does not take too great a leap to equate the process of highlighting a passage in written text with raising the pitch of one's voice to indicate new information. If we do, we can conclude that the large amount of research that has been carried out on intonation and prosody in speech will have much to contribute to what we might presume to call a "theory of highlighting."

We have seen how paragraphs usually begin with an assertion, preceded by a coherence relation to the foregoing text and followed by supporting information. In the case of discourse segments, the relation is less with the preceding paragraph and more with the overall strategic structure of the argument. In these terms, the assertion at the beginning of a paragraph can be considered as a supporting (and supported) structure for the assertion at the beginning of the discourse segment that contains it. Meanwhile this assertion operates as one of a small number of *primary* assertions that contain the major part of the "new" information in the document.

An assertion within a quotation is a special case. The quotation will not in most cases be the only thing the person being quoted said, but instead a passage assembled or selected by the author from a finite set of verbatim statements. Given this limited supply, quoted statements hold a special status that increases their apparent significance to the reader within a mass of text for which the author otherwise has an unlimited range of statements available.

The common highlighting of list elements is also consistent with the "new" information hypothesis, as lists typically act as a systematic and concentrated tabulation of what the author believes to be important (i.e. "new" and relevant) information. A speaker conveying the same information might very well emphasise this by counting the points off using the fingers of his hand.

Finally, the preference for highlighting Solution stages can also be viewed in terms of "new" information. In the typical Problem-Solution organisation, the Situation stage places the text meaningfully in relation to the author's model of the reader's knowledge base (this stage showed a strong negative correlation with highlighting). The Problem stage prepares the ground for the new piece of information imparted in the next stage. In terms of cohesive relations, it draws attention to a discordant factor in the previously reported Situation (that is, one particular aspect of the reader's assumed knowledge base). Thus prepared, the Solution presents itself as important new information that resolves, or partly resolves, the discordant aspect of the Situation represented by the Problem. Finally, the Evaluation defines the degree to which the Solution resolves the original Problem.

In this context, the Solution can be viewed as a climactic point of novelty in the Problem-Solution schema, thus justifying its status as "highlightable" text.

If it were possible to model the article as a histogram with sentences represented by columns plotted against a scale of new information content, we can imagine the highlighting process as being akin to slicing across the graph with a threshold value. Figuratively speaking, the highest peaks in a mountain range are selectively lit at sunrise.

4.2. Implications for "new" information as a criterion.

If we accept the idea that novelty of information is the fundamental criterion for highlighting text, it follows that:

a) The efficiency with which we shall be able to select text for highlighting will depend upon our ability to recognise signals indicating new information.

b) Any other signals commonly associated with new topics but not present in the experimental text are prime candidates for selection criteria.

Conversations with subjects suggested that the criteria adopted for each function and the typical highlighting procedure would have been very different in the case of quasi-revision, where decisions would have been made on a shorter-range basis. Arguably, this kind of highlighting produces highlighting that is more spontaneously applied and spanning fewer words.

We can hypothesise that this is so because a reader has a more detailed knowledge of what constitutes "new" information to himself than he has to a third party. Highlighting can therefore be done in real time (i.e. while reading as opposed to after having read the text) and with greater precision (e.g. at the word or clause level rather than the sentence or paragraph level).

The responsibility of interpreting an article for someone else eliminates this spontaneity. In the subject article, users not only perceived that it was "about" a specific product: they had also been informed that they were corporate librarians marking up a text for a board member. This scenario conjures up a range of frames and scripts. Two functions of the corporate librarian that subjects might have recalled or inferred are:

a) to keep management informed about the developing state of business knowledge, and

b) to inform management of new products that may be of value.

An alternative hypothesis is that the perceived novelty of information occurs at a number of levels. Within a sentence, particular words can be perceived as new. Within a paragraph, some sentences can be interpreted as new and others as contextual or supporting information. Meanwhile, within a discourse segment or discourse, still longer passages may be perceived as containing "new" information (see discussion of the Solution category above).

5. Conclusion

5.1. Highlighting as Information Visualization

TextLight [1], the software tool for which this research was carried out, is designed to detect certain attributes of a text's cognitive structure, encode them in visual, non-lexical form, and superimpose them on the corresponding text in the same physical location. In this sense, it can be viewed as a form of information visualization, exploiting the brain's capacity for processing visual data such as colour and shape to which it is optimally adapted. Like a geographical information system (GIS) it can reveal attributes of its data set that would otherwise be obscured, throwing the underlying structure into high relief.

However it does not pay to make the signals communicated via this additional channel too complex [11], and there seem to be no benefits for readers from using different colours for different categories of "new" information. For authors and text analysts, however, an extension of TextLight to identify attributes within text that are of interest to them would be as valuable to them as the colouring of objects on different layers is to architects.

Content-driven visual cues can be presented as a way of visualizing the logical or conceptual structure of a text. In this way, the brain's predisposition to visual understanding is exploited to enhance the understanding of text, or to guide the eye quickly to the most important passages.

This principle is widely demonstrated by the syntax-highlighting in text-editors for programmers. Here the need to visualize logical structure is acute, and programming languages offer a finite and precise set of words for editors to detect and colour. The most striking use of this principle is SeeSoft, one of a suite of text structure visualization tools developed by Stephen Eick at Lucent (formerly Bell) Laboratories. Software engineers typically operate at the scale of thousands of lines of code. With SeeSoft, each line of code is reduced to a line of single pixel thickness, coloured according to a range of user-specified criteria. Thousands of lines of code can be displayed on the screen at once, enabling a strategic grasp of the status of different parts of the program and their importance to the whole.

The same principle could be applied to help writers. Adding one or more layers of annotation to a text, based upon attributes such as readability or levels of completion would be like a knowledge discovery system for authors. Using it we could expect significant insights about the subject-matter to flow from being able to compare the occurrence of different parameters.

Such forms of visualization would help us to navigate a text "architecturally". In other words by having a clearer idea of a fragment's place in the overall cognitive structure of the document, we can more easily gauge its importance. Its degree of isolation from other highlighted text, or its location within a dense area of other highlighted sentences would give us an intuitive grasp of the structure of the entire document.

5.2. Future directions

The study of the selection of words for highlighting is an area that has previously been neglected — perhaps because the potential contribution of automatic highlighting has itself been ignored in the struggle against information overload. Yet as a class of information processing agent, highlighters possess several virtues. Their output is familiar to users. Highlighting has been shown to be helpful in content recall. Finally, it addresses the issue of confidence: unlike conventional summarization tools, highlighting acts not as a censor but as a guide, leaving non-selected text (and therefore the context) always in view.

6. References

[1] Ostler, T. "TextLight: Towards an Intelligent Text Browser". MSc. Dissertation, University of Westminster, 1998. URL: http://www.cogarch.com.

[2] Hult, R E., Jr., et al. "Different effects of note taking ability and lecture encoding structure on student learning." Paper presented at the Annual Meeting of the Eastern Educational Research Association, 1984.

[3] Dreyfus, Hubert & Stuart. "Making a Mind versus Modelling the Brain", in Graubard, Stephen R., (ed.) *The Artificial Intelligence Debate: False Starts, Real Foundations.* Cambridge: MIT Press, 1988.

[4] Crevier, D. *AI: The Tumultuous History of the Search for Artificial Intelligence.* Basic Books, New York, 1993:126.

[5] Foster, J.J. "The use of visual cues in text," in Kolers, P.A., Wrolstad, M.E., Bouma, H. (ed.) *Processing of visible language.* New York/London: Plenum Press, 1979: 189-204.

[6] Klare, G R, Mabry, J E & Gustafson, L M. "The relationship of patterning (underlining) to immediate retention and to acceptability of technical material". *Journal of Applied Psychology.* 39(1), 1955: 40-42.

[7] Dearborn, W.F., Johnston, P.W., & Carmichael, L, "Oral stress and meaning in printed material". *Science,* v.

110, 1949: 404.

[8] Crouse, J.H., & Idstein, P, "Effects of encoding cues on prose learning." *Journal of Educational Psychology,* 63, 1972: 309-313

[9] Fowler, R.L & Barker, A. S. "Effectiveness of highlighting for retention of text material". *Journal of Applied Psychology.* 39 (3) 1974: 358-364.

[10] Hershberger, W.A. & Terry, D.F. "Typographical cuing (sic) in conventional and programed (sic) texts". *Journal of Applied Psychology,* 49, 1965: 55-60

[11] Glucose Inc. URL: http//www.glucose.com/

[12] Rickards, J.P., & August, G. .J., "Generative underlining strategies in prose recall." *Journal of Educational Psychology,* 67, 1975: 860-865.

[13] Anon. "Coping with the Deluge of Data", in *Financial Times Information Technology Supplement,* 5 May 1997.

[14] Tadros, A."Predictive Categories in Expository Text", in *Advances in Written Text Analysis,* Coulthard, M. (ed.). Routledge London, 1994.
[18] van Dijk, Teun A. *News as Discourse.* Hillsdale: Lawrence Erlbaum Associates, 1988.

[15] Hoey, M. "Signalling in discourse: a Functional Analysis of a Common Discourse Pattern in Written and Spoken English." In Coulthard, M. (ed.) *Advances in Written Text Analysis,* London: Routledge 1994: 26-45.

[16] Brown, G. & Yule, G. *Discourse Analysis.* Cambridge University Press, Cambridge, 1983.

[17] Halliday, M.A.K. *A Course in Spoken English: Intonation.* Oxford: Oxford University Press, 1970

Environment piJ for Visual Programming in Java

Vladimir V. Prokhorov, Ph.D. in Math

Vadim A. Kosarev

Institute of Mathematics and Mechanics, Russian Academy of Sciences/Ural Branch

Abstract

Authoring tool $^{\pi}J$ (piJ) is based on original results in areas of visual languages and programming technology. It is developed 2 main versions: (a) a tool to program in Java (as stay-alone tool, as add-on for MS FrontPage, and as component of our MetaCalc environment), (b) add-on for MS FrontPage to develop fragments in JavaScript. The software supports chart versions of Java and JavaScript in Prokhorov's structured π-chart, flow-chart, and Nessie-Shneidermann structure grams. $^{\pi}J$ includes tools to convert a plain Java text to chart and back. The tool allows user to change textual representation of any structured part of a program to graphic one and back.. The tool realizes technology of extension/cutting of user language and technology of linking with external languages. A version of a tool supports programming of microprocessor Z8 in visual assembler. The tool can be used in software design, education, web design, supercomputing, and another areas

1: Introduction

There are wide known a number of "visual" authoring tools for programming in Java, such as Symantec Cafe™ by Symantec®, Visual J++™ by Microsoft®, Visual Age™ for Java by IBM®. The main feature of the tools is possibility to edit elements of graphic user interface in their natural visual representation. More, the tools support graphic representation of program structure for packages, classes, methods and variable-fields levels. The tools apply the visual representation to view, edit, and debug programs. Nevertheless, there is applied classic textual representation of algorithm in method descriptions in the tools. However, a graphic representation of the operator level of a program can be convenient in some areas. Representation of algorithm by a chart is useful in education, in structured representation of large modules, and in other cases.

Furthermore, there is a trouble related with necessity for user to have relatively high "starting level" of language knowledge to use traditional authoring tools, even if it is needed to create a simplest program. On the other hand, the traditional tools not allow to tune programming language on demands of specialist in concrete partial area of programming, to construct specialized language.

2: Main features of the authoring tool $^{\pi}J$

$^{\pi}J$ is an environment for development of professional software in MS Windows-98 or MS Windows NT basing on concepts of object-oriented programming. There are no any restrictions on complexity of programs developed in the tools.

$^{\pi}J$ can operate with two kinds of program file formats. On the one hand, the tool allows to open and save text file with program in plain Java. On the other hand, the tool allows to save and open program file as structured container-storage. The file-container can include text of the program in plain Java, additional information for graphic formatting, compiled modules, icons, embedded elements of a program, menus, documentation, colors, metrics, and another settings, etc.

The tool operates together with Java Development Kit by Sun Microsystems and uses compiler, debugger and libraries of the JDK. However, the tool displays messages of JDK about errors in terms of graphical program.

Some characteristics of the above mentioned authoring tools and $^{\pi}J$ are compared in the following table.

The current version 1.3 of the tool is created in Borland C++ ver. 5.0 for MS Windows--98 and MS Windows NT and in Java.

	Visual Age (IBM)	Visual J++ (Microsoft)	$^\pi J$
Supported language:			
• Java	✓	✓	✓
• JavaScript	—	—	✓
Graphical representation of program structure:			
• packages level	✓	—	—
• classes level	✓	✓	✓
• methods and variables-fields level	✓	✓	✓
• operators level	—	—	✓
Possibility to edit a program with graphical representation of structure			
• packages level	✓	—	—
• classes level	✓	✓	✓
• methods and variables-fields level	—	—	✓
• operators level	—	—	✓
Debugging using graphical interface	✓	✓	✓ *
Representation of classes inheritance structure	✓	✓	✓
Import of visual resources	—	✓	—
Visual editing of interface elements	✓	✓	✓
Possibility to adapt user language for concrete area of application	—	—	✓
Possibility to incorporate supercomputer resources and external languages	—	—	✓

* — the feature under construction.

This is a screenshot of $^\pi J$:

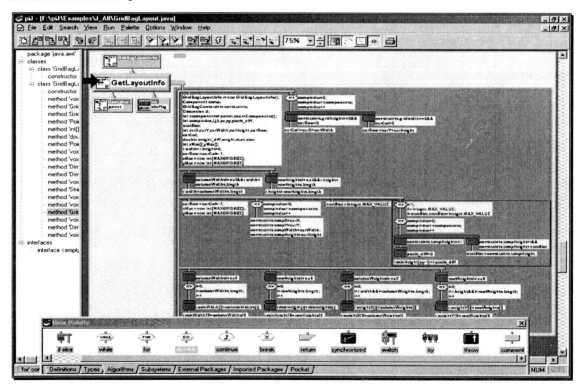

The main elements of $^{\pi}J$ window:

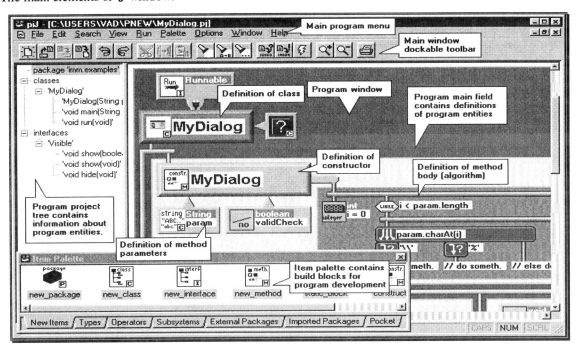

3: Visual programming of algorithms in $^{\pi}J$

The main distinctive feature of the tool is possibility to use graphical representation of algorithm in program method's description. The tool allows to show a program parts as plain text in JAVA and graphically:

- as structured π-chart [1, 2],
- as structured flow-chart, and
- as Nessie-Shneidermann's structure gram.

The form of representation can be free changed in any time by tabs on the left bottom part of program window. $^{\pi}J$ allows converting programs in plain (textual) Java to chart form, and from chart form to plain text.

The following screenshots shows these representations of the same simple program fragment.

This is a screenshot for "structured π-chart" mode:

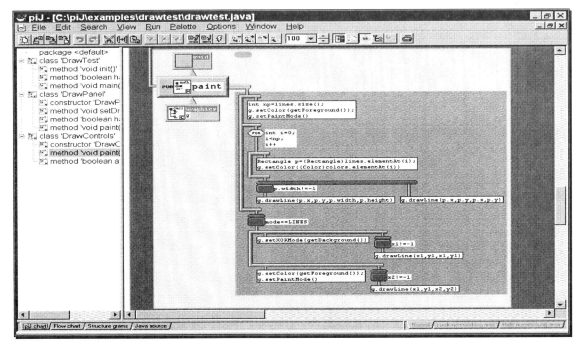

Structured flow-chart:

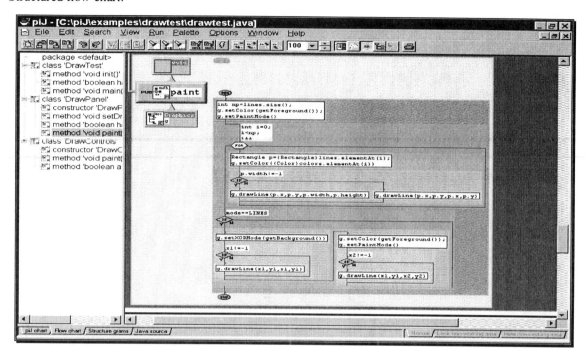

Nessie-Shneidermann's structure gram:

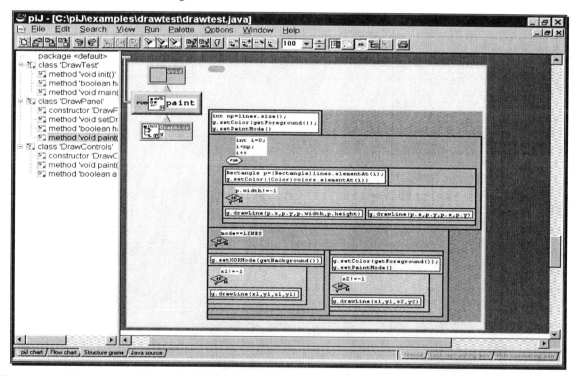

Here is used innovative additional form of program structure impression for flow chart and for Nessie-Shneidermann's structure gram (the feature is switched off for screenshot for π-chart mode). The form uses intensity of background color of fragments to reflect different level of hierarchy.

4: Mixing of graphical and text representation of program

The tool allows user to select, what parts of a program should be looked as chart and what parts should be looked as text. User can change graphical or text look of any structured part of program independently, to make the program look much convenient. Moreover, the software allows mixing chart and textual representations of different parts of a program and change look of a fragment from text to chart and back. That is some parts of a program can be represented as charts, but others can be represented textually. A chart may include textual fragments, however textual fragment can not include a chart yet.

User may set number of top levels of program hierarchy, which should be represented graphically, then bottom levels will be represented as plain text.

One more command allows to represent elements (methods, classes, variables, etc.) of textual parts as icons.

The following screenshots illustrate change of graphical representation of program fragments (shown on the last screenshots) to textual one:

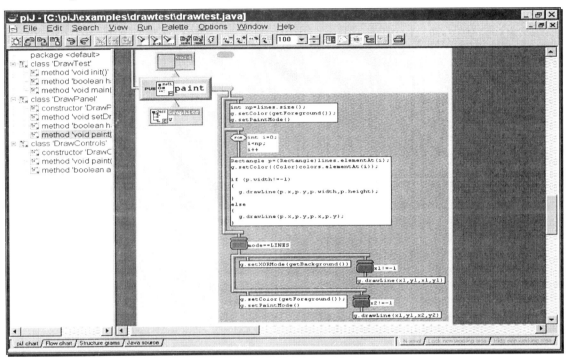

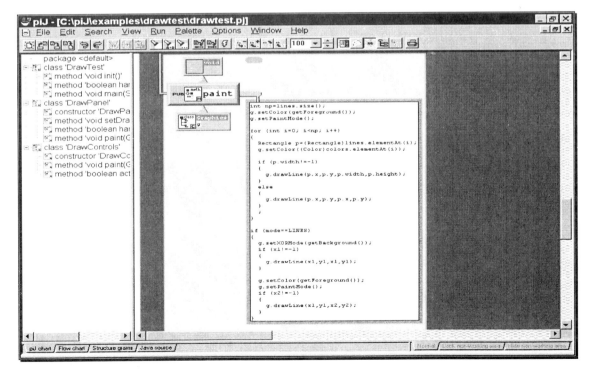

5: Working area

One of innovative features realized in $^{\pi}J$ is operating with "working area". User can set any structured part of a program as working area. Then the working area is bounded by a frame.

Setting of working area allows to achieve the following features:

- Use of remarkable frame as bookmark for visual navigation in a program.
- Use of the command "Go to working area" for quick navigation by jump to bookmark.
- Make part of a program outside working area be locked for any changes.
- Make part of a program outside working area be invisible.

Mode of non-working area representation is selected by tabs in right bottom side of program window. Change of modes can be protected by password.

The following screenshot corresponds to "normal" mode of working area representation:

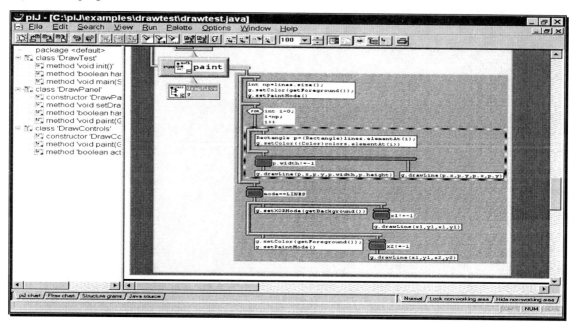

This is a screenshot for "lock non-working area" mode:

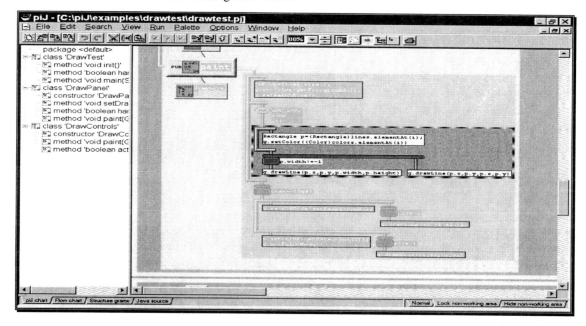

540

In the "lock non-working area" mode, program area outside working area is locked for any change. The mode can be protected by password, then user can't change elements outside non-working area without authorization

Non-working area is visualized in low-contrasted gray scale.

This is a screenshot for "hide non-working area" mode:

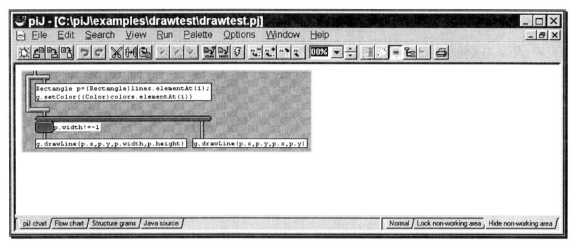

The "hide non-working area" mode can be protected by password, then user can't change elements outside non-working area without authorization.

Note, that the tool remembers what mode of representation of working area was used, and old program is opened in the same mode as when the program was saved.

6: Favorites

The instrument palette of the tool includes tab "Template Items" (or "favorites"), which includes hierarchically organized icons of some classes, methods, and variables of developing program. The elements of the tab can be dragged by mouse to program window to be inserted to the created program chart.

To set/remove a program unit to/from the tab it is necessary to check/uncheck a flag in the header of the unit description in the program. Structure of the icons in the tab is corresponding to structure of descriptions in the program (classes in the tab looks like folders for meth-

ods). Note, that the tab can include references on external libraries of classes too.

The content of the tab "favorites" of the elements palette is saved with the program in the program file container.

7: Templates

The tool allows to use any program as template to start new project.

This is very powerful feature, because file-container of program includes not only source of the program, but structured list of favorites, description of working area and mode of the working area representation, some settings of the tool, etc.

Such a way, a template can includes description of specialized language with operators, included to "favorites" tab of the elements palette. The following screenshot shows the palette with turtle control elements and a simplest program in graphical Java with the turtle control elements:

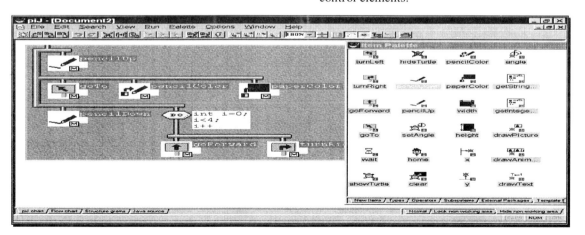

The descriptions (particularly, references to library items) can be hide for end user, being outside of the working area. User can operates in working area, which is preset for the template, not seeing something outside the working area, however the user can use elements included in the favorites palette.

So, the tool can include a set of programs-templates, that forms specialized environments for partial classes of problems.

The feature allows so simplify the programming, that common-used as simplest program printing "Hello, world" consists of 1 operator.

One example is a template that includes library for Logo-like turtle control. The template allows create object-oriented programs for number of turtles in Java-based extension by children. Web site http://vpro.convex.ru/igor (http://igorpro.hypermart.net) includes some applets developed by 10 years old kid after some hours of introduction to $^\pi J$. Another example is a template that includes main tools for designer of web-sites.

One more example is template with collection of tools, supporting computing (such as modules for differential equation modeling or solution of convex optimization problems) using supercomputers.

8: Subsystems

$^\pi J$ supports multilanguage technology [3, 4] and allows user to define language "subsystems" to assign external elements to sublanguage program elements. A subsystem is defined by software which should activate for the program element for various stages of work: creation of such an element, editing, compiling, execution, deleting, copying, printing, etc.

An example of a subsystem is the one allowing to incorporate supercomputer resources in Java program. Note, that multilanguage multicomputer distributed program seems like one program in the tool. The following screenshot shows a program fragment that includes plug-ins in C++ and Pascal, and window of "CPP" subsystem properties:

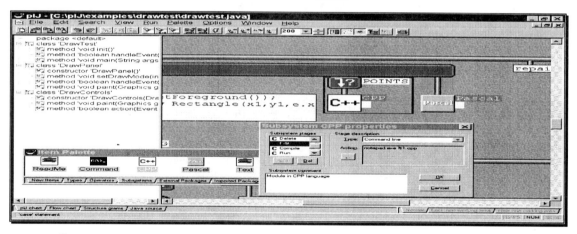

Moreover, $^\pi J$ includes the following features related with component π-model [3, 4]:

- support of Java applet creation as plug-in for HTML page (it is developed for MS FrontPage);
- support of programming in JavaScript as plug-in for HTML page (it is developed for MS FrontPage);
- can be applied as component of our MetaCalc tool for visual functional programming.

A version of a tool supports programming of microprocessor Z8 in visual assembly language.

The tool can be used in education, in web design, in supercomputing.

The author, developer and manager of the project is V. Prokhorov, programming is fulfilled by V. Kosarev. The paper authors would like to thank A. Yakovlev, D. Toropov, M. Prokhorova, and L. Volkanin for participation in the project.

References

[1] Prokhorov, V. Pi-charts: the language for graphical representation of algorithms and syntactical descriptions. Cybernetics and Systems Analysis, 1992, №2, p.93-107 (ISSN 1060-0396)

[2] Prokhorov, V. On representation of syntax definitions. In: J. G. Chen, ed. *Expert Systems Applications and Artificial Intelligence. Technology Transfer Series.* IITT International, Gournay-Sur-Marne, 1995, p.53-58 (ISBN 2-90766931-1).

[3] Prokhorov, V. PYTHAGORAS: multienvironment software. In: B. Blumenthal, J. Gornostaev, and C. Unger, Eds. Human-Computer Interaction. Lecture Notes in Computer Science 1015. Springer Verlag, Berlin, 1995, p.135-148 (ISBN 3-540-60614-9).

[4] Prokhorov, V. On the microcontext approach to construction of knowledge representation languages and human-computer interaction. *Journal of Computer and Systems Sciences International*, 1997, №5, p.5-16 (ISSN 1064-2307).

Teleoperation and Java3D Visualization of a Robot Manipulator over the World Wide Web

Igor R. Belousov [1], JiaCheng Tan [2], Gordon J. Clapworthy [2]

[1] *Keldysh Institute of Applied Mathematics, Russian Academy of Sciences, Moscow, Russia*
[2] *Depart. of Computer & Information Sciences, De Montfort University, Milton Keynes, U.K.*
ibelousov@dmu.ac.uk, jtan@dmu.ac.uk, gc@dmu.ac.uk

Abstract

A system for WWW-based remote robot tele-operation is presented in this paper. It addresses important problems of Internet telerobotics such as "how do we make the system reliable?", "how do we make the system fast?", and, finally, "how do we make the system open and portable?". The recent open technologies Java and Java3D are used for developing the system. Key features of the system are (1) the Java3D-based "live" virtual representation of the real robot and its environment, and (2) the use of a powerful tool for the remote programming of the robot. Possible applications of the teleoperation tools developed and methods within VR are also briefly discussed.

1. Introduction

WWW-based remote teleoperation is an interesting and promising field of investigation in robotics, VR and visualization. Applications of these investigations in areas such as space and underwater robotics, remote manufacturing, operator training, remote education and entertainment are of great importance. A detailed overview of the methods applied in this area is presented by Brady & Tarn [1].

In the last few years, many systems for WWW-based robot control have been developed. The list of active systems providing free access through Web browsers is presented on the NASA Telerobotics Web-page [2]. Some disadvantages of these systems are: slow reaction of the system to the operator's input, the fact that they contain poor visualization tools, and the lack of capability of programming the robot remotely.

The goals that we pursued while developing our system were inspired by the desire to create an efficient teleoperation system, that would be fast, easy to control,

and open, i.e. capable of running on a variety of computer platforms.

One of the main problems to be overcome while developing such a system is how to achieve fast, near real-time, response to the operator's actions when faced with a relatively slow rate of WWW connection (usually within 0.1-3.0 KB/sec). Transmission of video data with TV images of the robot and its environment is important, but it is usually subject to delays, which greatly complicates the teleoperation task.

To overcome this problem, 3D visualization of the robot and its working environment has to be implemented to provide the operator with a "live" virtual representation of the scene instead of the delayed TV images.

One such approach is the *immersion* of the graphic robot model into TV images transmitted from the remote work site. Calibrated Synthetic Views were used at JPL to provide the operator with a 3D model of the robot over the TV image, Bejczy [3]. The same technique was used for augmented telerobotic control in the University of Toronto, Rastogi et al [4]. The main advantages of the method are that minimum knowledge of the remote site is required, and the TV images are not updated except for some changes of the camera view.

But in such an interface, the graphic robot model may be available only as a tool for *simulation* of the remote robot and the tasks, *preliminary planning* of the operations, their graphical previewing and further *autonomous* repetition by the robot. The manipulation process with the *real robot* is not visually available to the operator who sees only the final status of the robot and the work site between control sessions.

We propose here another approach, which allows the operator to see a "live" virtual representation of the current state of *real robot* and the environment. A fast Java3D model of the robot arm and its working environment was developed to provide a rapid reaction of the system to the operator's actions. Nevertheless, two TV images of the robot work space are also transmitted to the operator's control environment to allow him to verify that the robot is operating as required.

The operator's control environment also contains a sophisticated graphic control panel and, of great importance, a tool for *remote robot programming*. The latter gives the operator the useful possibility of programming such complicated robot actions as pick-and-place operations and assembly, **within the control environment**, during the **current** control session. This significantly simplifies the problem of remote robot control and could also be useful for controlling objects in a general VR environment.

We applied these tools and methods while developing the system for remote control of a PUMA 560 industrial robot over the World Wide Web. All components are realised with open technologies, Java and Java3D, to allow the system to be accessible through any standard Web browser with Java support, such as Netscape Communicator or MS Internet Explorer.

The following section of the paper describes the system architecture and the control processes during the operation of the system. Section 3 presents methods of 3D visualization of the robot and its working environment. Other parts of the robot control environment – the graphic control panel and the module for remote robot programming – are described in Sections 4 and 5. Section 6 contains a description of the experimental setup, current experiments and directions of further experiments and investigations. Section 7 concludes the paper, reflecting on the key features and novel aspects of the system developed.

2. System architecture & control processes

There are two main parts in our system – the *client* and the *server*. The client runs at the remote, or user, site, while the server runs at the robot location (Fig. 1).

The system is capable of operating in two control regimes – *on-line* and *off-line*. In the *on-line* regime, the operator remotely controls the real robot, while in the *off-line* mode, he controls the virtual robot, i.e. a 3D graphical model of the robot. In the latter mode, work is performed fully on the client part of the system, which is useful for preliminary testing of the operation prior to operating with the real equipment.

The *client* part of the system – the *robot control environment* (RCE) – is a set of interface tools located in the robot control web page. It consists of the following parts, running as *independent applets*:

- the robot visualization module
- "live" video images of the robot
- the robot control panel
- the module for remote robot programming

It is important that the applets are *independent* as this significantly simplifies the development of a complicated control environment such as RCE.

The *robot visualization module* provides the operator with the current coordinates of the real (on-line control) or virtual (off-line control) robot, and a 3D picture of the robot and its working environment. It is implemented with a Java3D API (see Section 3 for further details).

To be more confident while working in the on-line regime, the operator should have the possibility of seeing *"live" video images* of the real robot. The RCE contains two such images, captured by TV cameras, one of which is located above the robot working area, and the other in front of the robot.

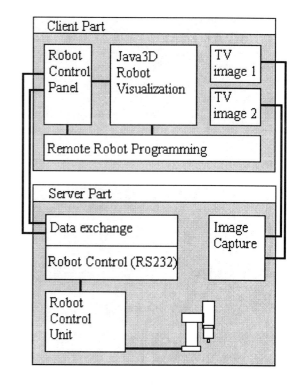

Figure 1. System architecture

The *robot control panel* (RCP) allows the user to define the desired motion of the remote robot, to set the control regime (on-line or off-line) and to see the current robot state (see Section 4).

The *robot remote programming module* is organised as an interpreter of the commands of the Robot control language (Rcl). The operator can perform both individual commands and arbitrary sets of them (i.e. programs). This provides a very powerful tool for developing scenarios of robot activity (such as assembly, object capturing, etc.), for testing with the 3D robot model in the off-line regime, and for performing tasks on-line with the real robot. Section 5 describes the Rcl commands and their use for remote robot control and operations with objects in VR.

The *server part* of the system contains the following modules:

- a module for capturing TV images
- the robot control unit
- the robot control and client/server interconnection module

For *capturing TV images*, a special application was developed. It works as an independent process in the server computer at the same time as the main server application. The *robot control unit* is a standard hardware module, supplied with the PUMA 560. To control the robot from PC, this control unit was connected to the computer via the RS-232 interface. *Communication* with the client part of the system and *robot control* is implemented by the Java-based server application. The "sockets" mechanism was used for client/server data exchange, and the Java Communication API was used for serial port programming.

The main processes of the active system in the on-line regime are as follows.

The first is the independent process of TV-image transfer. The server application saves images on hard disk, and the applet at the remote site visualizes them several times per second (the rate is dependent upon the communication rate between the client and server parts of the system).

The second process, the transmission of the robot current state and coordinates (the angles of the joints, and the position and orientation of the robot grip) is activated by the RCP applet several times per second. After receiving the coordinates, the applet activates a Visualization applet, which displays a 3D model of the current state of the robot and its environment.

The third type of process is activated when the user pushes a button to move the robot or to change its speed. The corresponding input parameters are transmitted to the server application to control the robot.

3. Java3D robot visualization

3.1. Choosing the implementation technique

PUMA robots are well-defined 6-DOF robots and are in common use in many application areas. The graphical counterpart has been successfully modelled in both Open GL and C++, Dafe [5]. In our application, the Java3D API was chosen to implement the visual interface.

At the outset, Java3D and VRML were both candidate tools. Trial programs were written in both languages to test some functions that were to be implemented in the user interface.

In the implementation of the 3D world, there was little to choose between them. If anything, the use of VRML appeared to be more straightforward. For example,

sophisticated VRML models of several robots with powerful user interfaces for testing teleoperation tasks were developed in the Institute for Robotics and System Dynamics of the German Aerospace Center, [6]. In the behaviour-control domain, the behaviour of an object in a VRML world can be realized, in principle, through script nodes and event routing, Brutzmann [7]. However, in implementation, Web browsers and plug-ins often impose restrictions on script languages. Moreover, behind the 3D visual display of the control interface, there is intensive real-time computation of robot inverse kinematics and dynamics, so it is not efficient to implement these in script languages.

By comparison, Java3D leaves the user more freedom. In constructing and animating the 3D world, we can retain its scene graph structure to make the program run in retained mode or, alternately, choose to use it just as an extension to AWT. We can run the program as an applet within a Web browser for easy access by an Internet user and we also can run it as a stand-alone application.

Another important factor for choosing Java3D is that, besides 3D graphics, the other components of the control interface can be implemented using the standard Java language.

3.2. Model of the virtual robot

The geometrical structure of the PUMA robot is relatively simple – it has an open-loop structure and can easily be defined by a Java3D scene graph. Actually, the whole graphic structure consists of seven cylinders, two prism links and a floor object, as shown in Fig. 2. To use as little data as possible, and to speed up the rendering

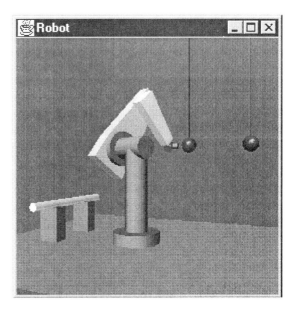

Figure 2. Java3D model of the robot.

rate, the 3D geometry of the prism links of the PUMA is created by defining a QuadArray object within a Shape3D node. The floor is also a QuadArray object, on which texture can be mapped, if desired.

The model was tested on a PC (Pentium 200, 32MB RAM, 16Bits graphics card). The image sizes were 350×350 pixels. If we chose ViewPlatform (position and orientation of the virtual camera) as above, the rendering rate was approximately 11 frames per second.

The rendering rate depends upon both the image size and the chosen ViewPlatform. The nearer the location of the virtual camera is to the robot, the more time is needed to produce the image. The rendering time also depends upon the angle between the direction of the camera view and the floor. The larger the angle, the more time is needed for rendering.

Manipulation actions have no significant influence on the rendering rate, which implies that the kinematic calculations form a relatively minor part of the whole computation.

3.3. Robot visualization

To provide a rapid system reaction to the operator's actions in on-line control mode, we use a Java3D model of the robot and its working environment to represent the current state of real ones. Small data parcels with the current robot coordinates (6 joint and 6 Cartesian coordinates) are transmitted to the visualization module several times per second and the drawing program is invoked to visualize the robot and objects of the working environment in the current location.

This technique accelerates the system response and provides the operator with a synthesised view of the **real** robot and the working environment. To smooth the motion of the 3D model between the positions received, we use the path-planner module at the local (operator's) site. This module calculates interim points in accordance with the current motion regime – along a straight line or along an interpolated trajectory in joint space.

To extend the control possibilities in the off-line regime, a Recorder Applet was created to function as a robot motion player. It records as many key points along the trajectory of the robot grip as necessary for the operator. It regards consecutive points with the same coordinates as one effective point on the trajectory. At any stage of the planning process, the operator can assess the planned path by using the play function of the recorder and viewing the motion of the virtual robot. This facility is extremely useful for the operator to plan, view, and edit the desired trajectory before submitting the control commands to the real robot.

4. Robot control panel

The robot control panel allows the user to define the desired motion of the remote robot, to select the control regime, and to see current state of the robot (Fig. 3).

Interface elements on the left side of the RCP allow the user to choose the speed of the robot, the robot grip state (open/closed) and the motion space ("World" – the base reference frame (RF), "Tool" – the robot grip RF, "Joint" – joint space). The push buttons on the right side provide the possibility of controlling the robot in either Cartesian or joint space. In Cartesian space, it is possible to move the robot grip along the X, Y, Z axes (in both directions) and to rotate the grip around these axes. In joint space, the user can perform direct control of each joint.

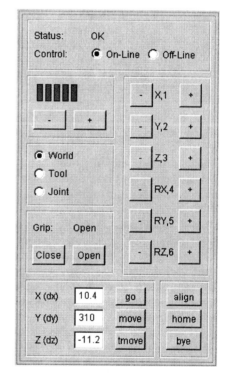

Figure 3. Robot control panel

Interface elements at the bottom of the RCP allow the robot grip to be aligned along the axes of the base RF, and the desired location of the robot grip to be directly defined (absolute, in the base RF, or relative) and for it to be moved to that point.

5. Robot remote programming

When we consider the problem of robot control (remote or direct), it is not usually sufficient to use only graphic control interfaces (like RCP) or input devices (joysticks, haptic devices, data gloves, etc.) to solve all the control problems. For example, if we consider robot assembly, welding or another complicated tasks, it is useful to have the possibility *to program robot actions* instead of obliging the operator *to repeat manually* tedious actions over a long period. Hence, we need to use a language which provides this possibility, i.e. a robot control language. The same consideration applies also to controlling objects in VR, since the developer of a VR environment may have to provide complicated behaviours for both passive objects and actively-controlled objects in the VR "world".

Further, if we are controlling the robot remotely (or controlling the object in VR), we need a tool that allows the commands of such a control language to be performed *during the session*, in real time. This requires a high level language, in which commands are interpreted rather than compiled. For this purpose Rcl (Robot control language) was developed; a detailed description of Rcl commands and variables is presented by Belousov [8]. Here we describe only the main possibilities of the language.

There are three types of Rcl commands:

- motion commands
- commands for setting robot location
- servicing commands

Motion commands allow the user to move the robot to predefined points, to translate the grip, or rotate it about any axis, in base or grip reference frames. For example,

- "**go A**" moves the robot to the predefined point A
- "**move 10 20 0**" translates the robot grip along the X and Y axes by 10 mm and 20 mm respectively
- "**trot z 30**" rotates the robot grip by 30 degrees around the Z axis of the grip RF.

Robot location commands allow points in the robot working space to be defined and operated on. For example,

- "**setp B 100 300 200 10 20 30**" defines a new point B with Cartesian coordinates (100, 300, 200) and Euler angles, defining the grip orientation, of (10, 20, 30) degrees, respectively;
- "**shift B 0 0 100**" increases the Z coordinate of the point B by 100 mm.

Servicing commands allow the user to open and close the grip, to calibrate the robot, to draw the current robot joints and Cartesian coordinates, etc.

Rcl was realised using Tcl/Tk (Tool command language/Toolkit), an interpreted scripting language developed at the University of California at Berkeley, Ousterhout [9]. All Tcl standard commands are interpreted inside the Tcl-shell; that is very important – it is an embeddable language. New commands of Rcl were developed that could be evaluated (interpreted) within the Tcl-shell together with Tcl standard commands. So we

have the possibility to develop and to perform complicated programs for robot control, using both Rcl commands, and all the capabilities of the Tcl/Tk scripts (including control flows, procedures, access to the Input/Output system, etc.). The Tcl/Java version of Rcl has now been realized using the Jacl package. The Tcl-shell is embedded in an applet, and all Rcl commands and their combinations can be performed within any Web browser which has Java support.

6. Current experiments and future work

Several experiments on remote robot programming over the WWW have been conducted. During the experiments, the robot was located at the Keldysh Institute of Applied Mathematics (Moscow, Russia), while the operator controlled the robot from De Montfort University (Milton Keynes, U.K.).

We used the following hardware on the robot (server) site: industrial robot manipulator PUMA 560 with 6 revolving joints, robot control unit Sphere-36, two TV cameras with frame-grabbers and a PC Pentium-166 with the Windows 95 operating system (Fig. 4). Web server Web Site 1.1 was running on the server site. The operator software was running on a PC Pentium-150 with Windows NT 4.0, with browser Netscape Communicator.

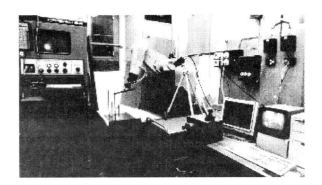

Figure 4. Robot PUMA & working environment

An initial series of experiments was conducted to verify the basic possibilities of the system, its reliability and its time characteristics.

It was revealed that successful robot control based on TV-image information is impossible under the existing communication rate between the server and client sites (0.1 KB/sec). Despite the fact that the TV images were quite small (resolution 192×144 pixels) and were compressed to JPEG format with ultimate file size about 1 KB, nearly 20 seconds were needed to receive every portion of the TV data. Thus, the only way to provide suitable control conditions for the operator was by using the 3D model of the robot and the environment. It allowed the suppression of time delays and provided quite fast response of the system to the operator's actions.

The next experiment was connected with solving a concrete control task. We suspended two tennis balls on threads in the robot work area. The goal of the experiment was to use the robot grip to strike one ball so that it would collide with the other. The experiment was performed successfully, verifying the correctness of the chosen approaches for system development. A more complicated experiment a pick and place operation with a tubular element – is currently under preparation.

Future investigations and development of the systems will address three main problems.

The first is connected with improvements to the 3D visualization module. These may include exhibiting the interactive behaviour between the virtual robot and virtual objects and the use of a stereoscopic display to obtain depth information.

The second is preparation of experiments on the capture of, and interaction with, moving objects. These are very challenging tasks, which will demand further improvements of the system reactivity, based on the use of prediction methods to suppress time delays [10, 11].

The third goal is the further development of the module for remote investigation of robot-manipulator kinematics and dynamics. The most attractive part of this module should be the possibility of investigating the motion and control of this synthesised object, not only in the 3D graphic environment, but also by observing its real motion on TV images. This will be represented by the real robot, located at the remote site (see Belousov et al [12] for a detailed description of this approach).

7. Conclusion

An efficient system for remote robot control over the World Wide Web has been developed. Firstly, and most importantly, the system provides *rapid response* to the operator's actions because of both the minimisation of data exchange and the use of the Java3D virtual robot representation with a local path planner, as opposed to commonly-used TV images. Secondly, the system provides the operator with a *powerful and comfortable control environment*, comprising a graphic interface and a language for remote robot programming. Thirdly, the system has been realised with the use of *open technologies*, Java and Java3D, and is thus capable of working on a variety of computer platforms.

Experiments on WWW-based remote control of a PUMA manipulator have been conducted. The robot was located at the Keldysh Institute of Applied Mathematics, and was controlled by the operator situated at De Montfort University. Experiments confirmed the reliability and efficiency of the system.

Acknowledgements

This work was performed at the Keldysh Institute of Applied Mathematics and De Montfort University. The authors would like to thank colleagues from the Keldysh Institute of Applied Mathematics: Prof. Victor Sazonov for his kind assistance in preparing the robot control experiments, and Dr. Andrey Boguslavskiy and Dr. Sergey Sokolov for developing the software for capturing the TV images.

References

[1] K. Brady and T.-J.Tarn, "Internet-based Remote Teleoperation", *IEEE International Conference on Robotics & Automation ICRA'98*, Leuven (Belgium), May 1998, pp.65-70.

[2] NASA Space Telerobotics Program, http://rainer.oact.hq. nasa.gov/telerobotics_page/telerobotics.shtm.

[3] A. K. Bejczy, "Virtual Reality in Telerobotics", *7th International Conference on Advanced Robotics ICAR'95*, Saint Feliu de Guixols (Spain), Sept 1995.

[4] A.Rastogi, P.Milgram and J.Grodski, "Augmented Telerobotic Control: a Visual Interface for Unstructured Environments", *KBS/Robotics Conference*, October 1995.

[5] O. Dafe, "Off-line Robot Programming & Simulation", http://www.cs.uiowa.edu/reu/summer95/Ovo-Dafe/ovo/ovo.html

[6] The Telerobotics Activities in the Institute of Robotics and System Dynamics (German Aerospace Center), http://www.robotic.dlr.de/TELEROBOTICS.

[7] D.Brutzman, "The Virtual Reality Modelling Language and Java", http://www.stl.nps.navy.mil/~brutzman/vrml/vrmljava.ps.

[8] Belousov I., "Rcl/Rci: Multiplatform Tcl/Tk-based Robot Control Language and Robot Control Interface", *International Conference on Adaptive Robots and General System Logical Theory*, St.-Petersburg (Russia), July 1998.

[9] Ousterhout J., *Tcl and the Tk Toolkit*, Addison Wesley, 1994.

[10] Okhotsimsky D., Platonov A., Belousov I. et al., "Vision System for Automatic Capturing a Moving Object by the Robot Manipulator", *International Conference on Intelligent Robotics IROS'97*, Grenoble (France), Sept 1997, pp. 1073-1079.

[11] Okhotsimsky D., Platonov A., Belousov I. et al., "Real-Time Hand-Eye System: Interaction with Moving Objects", *IEEE International Conference on Robotics & Automation ICRA'98*, Leuven (Belgium), May 1998, pp.1683-1688.

[12] Belousov I., Kartashev V. and Okhotsimsky D., "Real-Time Simulation of Space Robots on the Virtual Robotic Testbed", *7th International Conference on Advanced Robotics ICAR'95*, Sant Feliu de Guixols (Spain), Sept 1995, pp. 195-200.

Session 3-6

Virtual Reality in Construction

Chair

Aouad Ghassan

University of Salford, UK

Usability of Associated GIS and VRML Urban Models.

Nada Brkljac, John Counsell,
Faculty of the Built Environment
University of the West of England, Bristol. Frenchay Campus,
Coldharbour Lane, Bristol, BS16 1QY, U.K.

Abstract

This paper appraises the role of Virtual reality modelling language (VRML) based 3D computer based Urban and Heritage models in assisting professional collaboration on common tasks and engaging the participation of the general public in decision making. The University of the West of England (UWE) have created such models of both a significant area of central Bristol and for the Tower of London. The model and associated information can be interactively viewed through low-cost WWW browsers and updated on-line.

The model is held to be a useful analogue for linking available information in more accessible form. Use of an underlying Geographic Information System (GIS) allows other information to be readily associated with elements within the models. The costs of creation and ownership of traditional and Digital Models are compared with those of GIS generated models. Developments are discussed to improve and ease collaborative creation and use of such models.

1: Introduction

The graphical interface offered by WWW browsers enhances previous computer aided design (CAD) based models of buildings and landscape. As a multimedia tool it enables multiple different representations of real-world objects to be viewed on screen at once and explored interactively by its recipients without the overhead costs of an expensive CAD system and the skills needed to use it. As a development of hyperlinks it enables a broader range of connections to be freely formed between these different representations and associations made between graphical and non-graphical attributes (Figure 1).

Vector geometry has been used traditionally in CAD and GIS alike both because it accords more with maps and drawings and is a compact means of data storage that yet can also serve to locate bitmap images. VRML is the currently available WWW technology that enables vector geometry to be deployed. The same WWW browser plug-ins support both 2D graphics and 3D models. 2D graphic representations of buildings and landscapes may be defined as more abstract and symbolic models than 3D. 2D representations therefore require more accordance with formalised draughting conventions to enable common understanding and interpretation. 3D models tend to accord more closely with 'real' buildings in their setting and hence are more immediately communicated to a wider audience less versed in graphical conventions.

The Bristol Harbourside model is linked to photographs, planning brief, newspaper articles on the

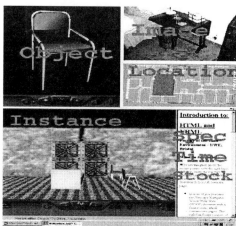

Figure 1 - *Frames with associated information. incorporating multiple WWW pages, Object relates to class, instances to linked locations of the object.*

area and data in the public domain. The Tower model is being linked to material that in contrast is in the management domain, although also to material which would be of interest to visitors to the Tower. Currently such material is held in disparate forms and locations which make it difficult for professionals to obtain an intergrated view or communicate it without simplification.

2: Developing 3D data exchange standards

currently 2D graphics still account for approximately 85% of all construction data exchanged between organisations and across disparate software systems within such organisations. Hence there has been a major development effort put towards developing an ISO Standard for 2D-information exchange, although a 3D form is also under development. Of the remaining 15%, which is 3D, a large proportion is either what is termed 'visualisation' or animated simulation or specialised examples such as structural steel framework. Although both Standards are based upon STEP and include metadata which VRML as a standard does not yet support, VRML browsers are being developed in conjunction as an easy means of viewing the graphical data held. [Haas WR. 1998]. VRML has already been prototyped and valued as a particularly effective means of accessing and integrating construction information in general, using an underlying object oriented database. It has been described as a more natural way of interfacing with construction information as the user can visually identify the objects of interest and retrieve information about them. [Aouad et al. 1998].

Figure 2 - *Photo-Realistic View from 3D CAD As-existing Model of Tower Environs*

3: Recent Development at UWE

While much WWW based narrative is currently 2D or text dominated, UWE have been exploring the use of 3D Digital Models for enhancing current descriptions of an area of central Bristol and for the Tower of London and its surroundings. The modelling of both areas was

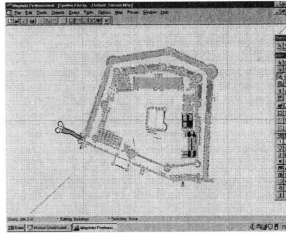

Figure 3 - *View of Tower Model in GIS form, using Pavan & Mapinfo*

initially carried out between 1996 and 1997 using 3D CAD tools. The resulting models were of use in generating single illustrative images of proposed change, in providing views that might otherwise require a helicopter to obtain, and in generating photorealistic video sequences with which to compare the proposed with the existing (Figure 2). At the time both models were too large with too high a polygon count to easily view in VR on high-end Silicon Graphics installations. For instance the Tower Environs model consisted of an as-existing and an as-proposed vector geometry model each of about 90 Megabytes and over 300 Megabytes of associated digital bitmaps. The proprietary 3D file format could not be readily associated with other information.

During the last few months the source data has been re-entered into a Geographic Information System (GIS), a 2D map-based spatial information system (Figure 3). A succession of beta releases of VRML authoring software have been used to generate VRML from the database in the form of a 3D Model related to WWW pages of associated information. The resulting models are not quite as complex or as detailed as their predecessors, but can be interactively experienced, and that experience can be scripted. The Tower Model in VRML is currently less than 10 Megabytes of data including bitmaps, although more of the environs and more detail remain to be added.

At its simplest this model connects pages of HTML, with text, images and graphs, to the appropriate parts of the geometry of the buildings and landscape in the area expressed in VRML.

Further development of the current model is intended to provide narrative in the form of a guided tour of the area enhanced by sound clips. Use of an underlying GIS as the mechanism from which the VRML and WWW data is published makes it possible for questions to be posed on demand and for selected buildings and landscape to be either brightly lit or enhanced by false colour to demonstrate the answer. This would involve using the GIS as an on-demand server. Work is currently under way to implement database queries using Structured Query Language from the VRML model & browser to the spatial database in the GIS. The facility for updating the model as a consequence of an external event has already been implemented.

The quality of data available at a resolution capable of WWW transmission limits credible viewpoints and detail to distance rather than close up. Environments without visible activity tend to appear sterile. Yet while for example animated people and traffic are technically possible their successful orchestration in 3D landscapes has so far been found to be beyond the scope of currently available tools. Some animation has been achieved in development of the original CAD based model but depends on uniform slopes or a misleadingly flat site. Close up detail and credibility may be improved in the VRML model by the insertion of digital images or digital movie clips triggered by context and projected between the Avatar and the general scene.

4: Change over Time & What If Scenarios

Some of the buildings in the Bristol Model are of significant local or national historic importance (Figure 4). The VRML model of this substantial urban area shows the buildings in their current context, derived from maps, digital terrain models (DTM), digital images of street frontages, aerial photographs of roofscapes and calculations of building height.

A similar exercise based upon old prints and maps could enable travel back to experience interpretations of

Figure 4 - *Photo-realistic View of 3D CAD Model of Bristol Harbourside, Bristol Cathedral mid-top-right.*

the past. Continuing to keep the inventory of information about the site up to date in the longer term takes that inventory beyond the snapshot of a single moment and will make it possible to travel back in recent time. Time-lapse photography across a site has been used as a form of narrative in film. Similarly diurnal or seasonal change has been used to convey the passage of time. Such techniques may be used within the VRML model to map predicted change. The specific visible moment can be interactively linked to a dynamic graph to indicate the current point on

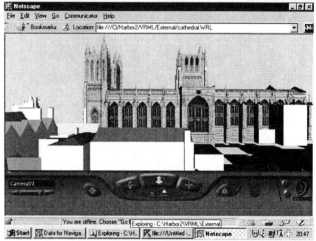

Figure 5 - *View of Bristol Cathedral exported from 3DS to VRML using Street's original 19th Century Elevational Drawings for elevational detail and tracery.*

a time-line or to select a different moment to which to jump (Figure 5).

GIS are often used now to model what-if scenarios of different possible future outcomes. The close relationship possible between GIS and VRML models permits these to be illustrated more realistically. Hence UWE are exploring the use of the same Harbourside model for enhanced public participation in decision making about future development. One similar current use of the Harbourside model is to act as part of the briefing documentation for a multi-disciplinary design project based on a site within the area engaging over 40 groups of 6-7 students drawn from different disciplines acting as design teams. A particularly weak element in previous years in the student work has been 3D realisation and understanding of the importance of townscape and the impact of their proposals on the context. The process is being evaluated to determine if use of the VRML model leads to improvement.

5: Professional Use of Data about the Tower

There is a substantial amount of information held by Historic Royal Palaces and other agencies about the Tower of London and its surroundings in addition to that which can be derived from firsthand experience. Data about the Tower of London is currently either held in archives, or digitally in databases. Most of this data serves the needs of the professional staff.

Thompson gives two basic aims for the preserver, 'to secure what remains and to render what he secures intelligible, both to himself and to the onlooker that he is going to invite to the site... intelligibility is the foundation of the whole operation of preservation and display.' ' Study of the relationship between written sources and visible remains is like the reciprocating action of a piston'. [Thompson MW. 1981]. At the Tower the results of Primary Interpretative research are summarised by professional staff to provide the Secondary Interpretation experienced by the visitors. Because most of the data was not accessible in a single unifying format and much was still held on paper the causal link between primary evidence and interpretation was generally broken in the material supplied to the visitor. Hence there was no traceable audit trail back from the secondary interpretative material to the primary sources.

Visitor Interpretation in the sense of conservation education includes a documentary record of the process of Professional Interpretative use, to provide case studies or a detective story. Visitor Interpretation in the sense of edification involves simplifying and reworking the above material to bring out and highlight specific moments that catch the attention. Much of this information would be more accessible if it was held in digital form and manipulable through a single easy to use interface. The Museum of London Archaeological Service for example use a spatial database to hold a stratigraphic model of finds, to look for patterns and discover whether they vary over time and space, for instance to identify when finds from a notably earlier era are in a later deposit. [MOLAS. 1995]. Four major functions have been described as currently using information held about the Tower, those of Curatorial Artefacts, Project Specific, Building Works, and Historical Authenticity.

The curatorial function is that of holding a record of the artefacts for security purposes. Where the items are on loan an additional requirement is to manage insurance cover. Other uses of data under this heading are for research, and for identifying and defining specific curatorial projects.

The project-specific function is to be able define the historical development of the buildings prior to undertaking any work, to identify the potential for archaeological investigation and the need for any preliminary investigative work. There is also a need to define what is preserved and to provide interpretation to the general public. Most current research consists of typewritten reports not held digitally.

The building works function is to maintain a property history, to inform the process of building work, and to assist in planning maintenance works. While the set piece and staterooms are seen as largely unchanging, there is a continual demand for alteration and modification within the ancillary accommodation to meet changes in use and in accepted standards. Such ancillary accommodation consists of offices, apartments, and the approximately 155 Casemates at the Tower.

The authenticity function is to be able to review change over time with old prints and photographs. Old accounts also assist in ensuring historical accuracy such as the number of daffodil bulbs ordered for the privy garden, which was helpful in defining the scope of its restoration.

Most of the above needs may be defined as professional, and by definition professionals may be expected to invest sufficient time to gain an in depth understanding. Meeting the fleeting needs of the one-time non-specialist visitor may be seen as more demanding. Yet solutions which ease access for non-specialists may also be used to reduce the barriers that professionals face in their shared group work use of Information and Communications Technologies (ICT).

6: A unified digital archive of information

Part of the research by UWE has been to determine the extent to which a unified digital archive of information might serve the various needs which staff at the Tower have expressed. A VRML model has been developed to explore the extent to which such a model can provide and enhance a common means for all to access such information. The specific goal is to assist in assessing the significance and the vulnerability of elements of the cultural heritage sites. This will aid more informed planning to conserve that significance, providing a basis for managing and recording the process and monitoring its effectiveness. Explaining the significance of elements of the site is also central to Visitor Interpretation. "Site Significance, which is synonymous with the American term 'Park Value' helps to answer the question: why was this area... considered worthy of special protection or provisions and why is it 'special'?" [HMSO. 1975]. Recording and explaining the process underlies the more in depth interpretation that is conservation education.

7: Collaborative group work

'Post-it' notes and redlining techniques have been widely used in group-work using computer aided drafting. With the advent of ISDN and video conferencing white boarding has become possible, which may be seen as the interactive application of post-its and redlining. The significant elements of the Tower itself, as with most heritage sites, are intended to be as unchanging as practicable. (Although its context is continuously threatened with change.) Batch processing and distribution of copies of the Tower model using VRML is therefore likely to be acceptable without over-frequent reconciliation. The model is not intended and is unlikely to be an acceptable substitute for on site firsthand inspection and meetings. Yet many management discussions take place and decisions are often made while not at the spot to which they apply. In these circumstances the Tower model may prove a central component of an improved white-boarding system where the model is held locally in each instance but the animation of viewpoints and highlighting of points of interest is exchanged interactively.

Peters states that the camera is the user's viewpoint, it only becomes 'significative' when it is shown to explain information to others. [Peters JM. 1981]. One important aspect of being able to explain or tell a story remotely while using VRML is a facility with which to take control of someone else's browser and show them the view that you wish them to see. In VR generally there have been various attempts to insert a virtual guide into the scene, but even on expensive high-end systems these have so far seemed statue like and lacking in animation. Until these problems can be overcome palettes of tools such as laser-pointers are needed for the Avatar to deploy. In this manner the avatar becomes a mediator between the local user and the scene being viewed. The Avatar is not only a representation of the local user in the scene being viewed, it ought also to be a tool with which to take a look through the eyes of the remote user. The Avatar may in effect be used in the guise of a 'Spectacle de Son et Lumière.'

VRML substitutes for some of the other illustrative means previously used to provide effective interpretation. VRML also adds abilities to do things that have not necessarily been practicable before. The research at UWE indicates that VRML can now be used both as a backbone with which to link other media through the window of a WWW browser and also as an embracing environment within which various media can be set. Some interpretation benefits specifically from modelling in 3D, other interpretation benefits from the immediacy and interactivity of VR, such as interactive white-boarding. The interpretation that is appropriate to visitors may also be useful to managers, for example removing the buildings to look at the landscape beneath, which is a particular benefit offered by computer modelling. Such clarity of view of the point of interest is important, requiring a facility with which for example to switch on trees, switch off trees, or render both trees and intervening buildings translucent.

8: Costs of Ownership

Long-term usability of such models remains an issue. A close link is needed between the model building tools and the means by which the data is acquired, in order to maintain the model and keep it up to date. In the absence of effective scanning or remote sensing techniques from which to automatically generate models there is a need for efficient survey. Collation and integration of survey data from various sources including digital images can be assisted by use of a Spatial or Geographic Information System.

With conventional physical or even digital models the costs of both recording and explaining are high. Traditional architectural physical models can cost several hundred thousand pounds to create depending on their level of detail. The resources required to keep them up to date are commensurate. This has been the basis for justifying the cost of Digital Models. Although cheaper the as existing and as proposed Tower of London 3D Studio based Models created at UWE cost almost one hundred thousand pounds. Arguably a significant proportion of the cost was because the data available was not in suitable form for such modelling. However few organisations have the good fortune to be able to both create completely new surveys of cultural heritage sites and at the same time gain feed back from the modelling process to re-specify the nature and the content of the survey data. In addition to provide the resources and expert knowledge necessary to keep such a model containing some 90 complex building forms up to date in conventional CAD or 3D modelling programmes is as daunting as for the physical relief model.

Other development at UWE has been a project in which a group of 30 students are collaborating in groupwork to create a 3D model of the UWE Campus including terrain on a 1 metre grid. The students have limited previous experience of CAD and are from a variety of disciplines. This model is based entirely on data owned by UWE to avoid the copyright problems that currently impede publication of such models on the WWW. The data therefore includes 3D stereo-graphic aerial photos, digital elevational photos, digital building plans and site survey drawings. It is significant that it has been necessary to deploy a range of different software packages to accomplish the whole task of data entry and preparation since no one package is adequate. The student experience in collaborating in this manner is being evaluated.

In the longer term much of the data currently being collated from a variety of sources will be available through remote data capture such as the Lidar aerial survey system being deployed by the DoE which has a claimed accuracy within a few centimetres. The same flight is also being used to scan and coordinate colour information.

The recent re-entry of the original source data for both Tower and Harbourside into GIS form has provided a comparison of time and resources with that of the original more specialist CAD work. Development through successive Beta versions of the software has not permitted an exact comparison but it would now take between one third and one sixth of the time to create a 1:1250 map tile based model compared to the original 11 man-months involved in the original Harbourside 3DS model. Evidently such a model is simpler than the complex 3D forms in the original but substitutes effectively for over 90% of that original and would provide a useful context in which to add a CAD modelled remainder as a close-up level of detail.

9: Suggested order of work for Urban Models

The 3D CAD based Tower Model generates Video, which is directorial and sequential, and produces highly credible ray-traced or radiosity rendered and shadow casting images for embedment in documents. The VRML model on the other hand produces a much enhanced multi-media synthesis of hyper-linked parts of modelled reality, text, video, database and so on, where the model forms the backbone. Both enable views not easily seen for reasons of cost of access, or even safety of access. VRML can be used to affordably storyboard the 3D CAD modelling. The 3D CAD model is too slow to use to effectively story-board a VR experience, (between 15 and 30 minutes depending on field of view to generate a ray-traced photo-realistic image on a Pentium 133 Mhz.). VRML can also be used to build the initial stages of a model subsequently developed further and more flexibly in 3D CAD. Taking VRML output from the 3D CAD model into VRML however is difficult because the direct translators at present produce high polygon count and over-detailed indexed face-sets rather than optimised geometric primitives. Both file-sizes and detail are too great. A sensible order of work has thus emerged. This commences with initial data capture, then GIS collation, then VRML generation, then proceeds to identify those specific parts which lack credible detail following generation from VRML. These parts are modelled specifically and then pieced into the VRML model. The final outcome may be either imported to form the basis of a 3D CAD based model used to produce highly detailed photo-realistic images or remain in simpler form in VRML to create an interactive VR experience.

10: Conclusion

Current digital descriptions of building projects tend to comprise a complex mix of 2D graphics, text and schedules with 3D 'visualisation'. VRML alone cannot readily incorporate these diverse media, but a WWW browser using Frames can mix VRML with other media. A linked under-lying spatial information system allows the flexible extract of selected data using GIS tools that range from simple 'cookie cutting' to complex spatial analysis.

2D GIS Systems are increasingly used in management of the built environment, although often in the restricted guise of specialist facilities management systems. Compared to the overall task of data capture in digital form and its validation it is relatively little extra work to encode height data and add digital photographic elevations. Little more is necessary to generate a 3D VRML model that can act as an easy to use integrating interface to the diverse non-graphical data held.

Once the model has been created it offers the potential of off-site collaborative group work and also an effective context in which the visual impact of proposed changes can be evaluated. Narrative use of the model for visitor interpretation or virtual tourism would be enhanced by improved simulation of crowds and activity in VRML. Collaborative work would be assisted by the ability to remotely direct attention through a common viewpoint and to flag points of interest.

The cost of creation of the Harbourside and Tower Models in GIS generated VRML has already been found to be substantially less than that of previous CAD based modelling. Group work using students to create a shared model has shown that the skill level is reduced and that collaborative update of the model is greatly eased. In addition the GIS may be described as a VRML authoring system which enables minor changes to the model such as additional hyper links or viewpoints to be added and re-published in moments.

Acknowledgements

This work has been partly funded through the National Creative Technology Initiative of the ESRC in the UK.

References

HMSO 1975. 'Guide to Countryside Interpretation Part 1, Principles of Countryside Interpretation and Interpretative Planning', published by HMSO.
MOLAS. 1995. The Museum of London Archaeological Service Annual Report for 1994.
Thompson MW, 1981, 'Ruins, their preservation and display', British Museum Press.
Peters JM. 1981, 'Pictorial Signs and the Language of Film'.
Haas, WR, 'STEP and its implementation in Factory Design, the STEP-CDS Initiative' in proceedings of the 1998 EC Product & Process Modelling Conference, BRE, Garston Wood, UK'.
Aouad G, Child T, Brandon P, Sarshar M, 1998. 'Linking Construction Information through VR using an Object Oriented Environment' in proceedings of the 1998 14th Annual Conference of the Association of Researchers in Construction Management.

Supporting the Life-Cycle of Multimedia and Visualization Using Distributed Performance Support Systems

Dr N. Bouchlaghem
Loughborough University
N.M.Bouchlaghem@lboro.ac.uk

Dr N.Beacham
Loughborough University
N.Beacham@lboro.ac.uk

Mr W.Sher
Loughborough University
W.D.Sher@lboro.ac.uk

Abstract

UK Higher Education Institutions have invested significantly in the implementation of multimedia and visualization material in teaching, learning and assessment of civil and building engineering - with mixed results. This paper focuses on the use and life cycle of digital imagery and visualization material, which is embedded within multimedia teaching aids to improve student understanding. It describes ways in which these materials are developed and used in the civil and building engineering curriculum and, in particular, how distributed performance support systems can be applied to make more effective use of digital imagery and visualization material. Following this, the paper then describes how a distributed performance support system approach to education is being adopted at Loughborough University as part of the CAL-Visual project. After highlighting the main aims and objectives of the project, the paper concludes by discussing some of the issues encountered during the design and implementation of a distributed performance support system.

1. Introduction

In the construction sector, students learning about construction technology need to visualize materials and components and have an appreciation of the total constructional form of a building. The traditional lecturing environment cannot replace the benefits to be gained from access to construction sites and completed buildings. However, such traditional approaches are characterized by problems of cost, safety, availability of and access to a variety of suitable construction sites, and time. Such is the importance of using images to support and enhance students' understanding of building design and construction that this issue has been recognized by accrediting bodies as an important part of the learning process. The Chartered Institute of Building (CIOB) also actively supports initiatives that promote such methods.

In order to address the problems highlighted above, many educational organizations have turned to C&IT, and in particular multimedia, computer-based learning (CBL), computer-assisted assessment (CAA) with the intention of introducing some of the experiences gained from construction sites into the classroom. Amongst the many methods in which visual material (in the form of multimedia) have been utilized to better educate civil engineering students, have been discussed by Aminmansour [1], Echeverry [2], Chinowsky [3], Riley and Pace [4] and Finkelstein [5].

Many CBL packages tend to be complete and autonomous pieces of course material containing clear learning objectives and used to support or supplant lectures. In contrast, multimedia teaching aids are small, discrete tools used to help tutors convey complex material within lectures, such as the form cycle for self-climbing form system described by Riley and Pace [1].

Riley and Pace [1] advocate the use of multimedia teaching aids by arguing that, *'once they are developed, they have the potential to decrease the preparation time and classroom time needed to effectively convey course material to students'.* Furthermore, these teaching aids can be used to form the foundations of a CBL and CAA package. In doing so, using teaching aids in this way can also reduce the time and cost of developing CBL and CAA packages.

Unlike CBL and CAA packages, which tend to dictate how a course will be implemented and delivered, multimedia teaching aids do not contain rigid learning objectives. Teaching aids not only allow tutors to embed them into their course without having to adapt the course's structure, but also use conventional computer tools and techniques familiar to tutors to create and deliver them. For example, many tutors create their presentations using Microsoft

PowerPoint. PowerPoint is particularly effective at creating teaching aids, because it is easy to embed various forms of digital visual material. Furthermore, because the use of MTAs is an evolutionary approach to traditional teaching and learning, resistance to change is reduced.

Barker [6] has also investigated the development and delivery of multimedia teaching aids using an 'electronic course delivery' approach to present course material. A fundamental difference in this case is that Barker [6] describes a methodology for creating, organizing and delivering these multimedia teaching aids from two perspectives: a staff perspective and a student perspective. An important part of this methodology has been the development of a distributed performance support system to facilitate the creating, organizing and delivery of multimedia teaching aids. Distributed performance support systems and their ability to facilitate the implementation and use of visual material in MTAs by staff and students are discussed in detail in the following section.

2. What is a DPSS?

In their day to day activities, civil engineering tutors and students, are often required to perform a wide range of different tasks and jobs. These tasks vary quite considerably in their complexity. The successful execution of many of the more complex tasks often requires the use of some sort of tool, aiding facility or performance support system (PSS). The basic rationale underlying the use of a PSS is that individuals or groups of people (working together on a common project) are provided with appropriate tools and techniques to support the tasks that they have to perform. According to Barker and Hudson [7], four major objectives of a performance support system are: (1) to achieve increases in productivity; (2) to improve the overall quality of task/job execution; (3) to improve the overall quality of the environments in which people work; and (4), from a human perspective, to reduce the complexity of the processes involved in executing a task.

Simple examples of performance support tools include: a typewriter, a telephone, a bicycle and an automobile. Increasingly, computer-based resources are being used to implement performance support systems. An electronic performance support system (EPSS) is therefore a facility which uses various types of computer technology to realize each of the four previously listed objectives within a given working environment or problem solving domain. Software packages such as word-processing systems and spreadsheets provide a good example of computer-based performance support systems.

Naturally, a fundamental requirement of an EPSS is that it should increase users' on-the-job performance within a given task domain. This usually involves improving skill levels, reducing task complexity and/or providing appropriate training. These requirements can be achieved in two basic ways. First, through the provision of 'automation aids'; and, second, by providing various mechanisms to support 'on-the-job', 'just-in-time' (JIT) training which will enable users of any given system to 'learn as they do'.

Many of the early developments in EPSS have been described by Gery [8], McGraw [9], Varnadoe and Barron [10], Raybould [11], Banerji [12] and Barker [13]. Currently, there are two important directions of development for EPSS facilities. First, the creation of integrated toolsets that are able to meet the performance support needs of particular application domains (Barker and Hudson, [7]; Hudson, [14]); and second, a growing requirement to facilitate group working at a distance through the incorporation of network technology and the principles of distributed computing environments (Beacham, [15]; Barker, Richards, Banerji, [16]). Indeed, the advent of relatively low-cost network technologies and the widespread availability of facilities such as the Internet and the World Wide Web has meant that performance support systems can now become highly distributed in nature - that is, different components can reside (or be replicated) at, and be accessed from, different geographical locations.

As far as this paper is concerned, we therefore regard a distributed performance support system as an integrated and globally accessible collection of electronic aids, tools and data that can be used (as and when required) at particular points of need (within a workgroup or an organization) in order to improve human performance within a given task domain.

3. An electronic course delivery approach

The main method of delivering teaching and learning materials within many university organizations is through lectures and tutorials. Although more technological methods of teaching and learning have been implemented, one evolutionary approach as already mention above is electronic course delivery. Both Banerji [12] and Barker [6] have highlighted the benefits of using electronic course delivery within the School of Computing and Mathematics, at the University of Teesside. Electronic course delivery is based on two basic perspectives: lecturer and student.

The relationship between these is illustrated in figure 1.

To improve access to the components, this model has to be mapped onto a suitable organizational

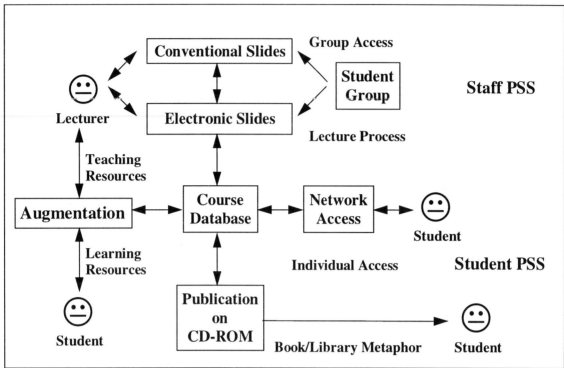

Figure 1. A performance support system for staff and students

The lecturer's perspective involves the creation of both traditional and electronic slides. These slides can be created: (a) totally from new; (b) by changing existing slides; or (c) by copying extracts from existing slides. Once a sequence of electronic slides has been created a lecturer can print them onto overhead transparencies, or publish them on a CD-ROM or network. Further augmentation can be embedded in order to improve the slide's ability to transfer knowledge.

The students' perspective involves accessing learning materials and associated learning resources. This can be done in three ways: (1) through the delivery of lectures; (2) using a computer network; and (3) by means of a CD-ROM. Unlike the traditional model specified by Banerji [12], this revised model highlights the need for students to augment their own material (electronic and non-electronic) to the course database - for example through the use of a discussion group. This allows tutors to monitor the progress of important issues which have arisen in a discussion group and to be able to include quotations from them in a future sequence of electronic slides (Irving, Higgins and Safayeni, [17]).

structure. In order for a distributed performance support system to be realized, it has to be mapped onto an intranet/Internet structure, similar to that illustrated in figure 2.

Because of a DPSS's future importance as a tool for facilitating 'learning-by-doing', and sharing teaching and learning material, the remainder of this paper describes and discusses the evolution and future potential utility of distributed performance support systems within civil and building engineering. The design and construction of a distributed performance support facility as part of the project CAL-Visual is described and an outline is given of some the ways in which we are intending to use it. An attempt is currently being made to measure the potential utility of the system from the perspective of supporting its end-users' use of MTAs, CBL and CAA packages.

4. DPSS within CAL-Visual

CAL-Visual is a research project being undertaken by a consortium of universities within the UK to investigate how experiences on a construction site can be brought into the classroom using computer-based imagery and visualization materials. The project is part of the Teaching and Learning Technology Programme (TLTP) initiative funded by Higher Education Funding Council for England (HEFCE).

tools the person is using. Third, the overall system needs to be accessible, portable, inexpensive, platform-independent and able to facilitate sharing of visual resources, 'on-the-job' support and 'just-in-time'

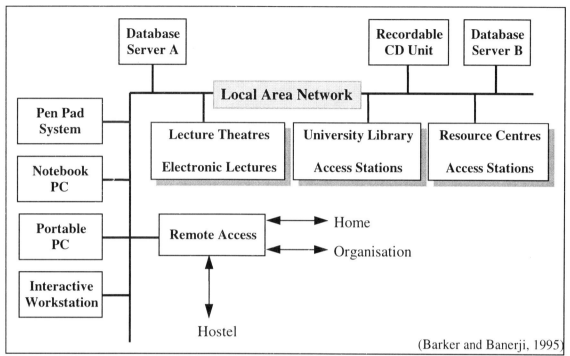

Figure 2. Internet/intranet structure underlying a DPSS

The CAL-Visual project's main aim is to implement the use of computer imagery to support the teaching, learning and assessment of subject areas where visualization of objects and processes play an important role. As already mentioned above images are usually readily available in slide or paper form and used in an uncoordinated manner. This project is developing a digital based framework for an efficient use of existing and new imagery to aid teaching and learning technology, hence offering time and cost benefits to the process.

The rationale for using a DPSS approach to CAL-Visual is threefold. First, the aims of the project highlight the need for an integrated repository of digital, visual material which is cross referenced and can be used to embed visual resources within external teaching and learning aids - similar to the ECD approach described above. Second, the framework specified to accommodate existing visual materials, tools, learning resources and pedagogic methods needs to provide access to resources, such as support aids that give assistance to tutors who wish to embed visual material into a presentation, regardless of the specific

training.

In order to realize the development of the DPSS, an infrastructure similar to that shown in figure 2 has been used. For the purpose of evaluation the CBL and CAA modules are to be made available on the department's intranet and the MTAs are to be published on CD-ROM in order to contend with the bandwidth requirements. The design and implementation of the DPSS within the CAL-Visual project is described in the following section.

4.1. Design and implementation of CAL-Visual

Since choosing to develop a DPSS, we have created the framework for organizing digital, visual material, as shown in figure 3. This repository of visual material has formed the foundations upon which to create a searchable resource (in the form of a web-based database), three integrated CBL modules, a CAA module and the development of a suite of electronic lectures containing MTAs. Furthermore, it is proposed to include 'on-the-job' support and 'just-in-time' training for tutors who require assistance embedding such visual material within their electronic lectures. A detailed description of the design and implementation of the framework, database and additional system components is given in this section.

illustrate building defects and simulate how such defects are caused. Finally, the framework assists students in visualizing graphical information from the perspective of various topics, such as building material, defects, technology, design and production.

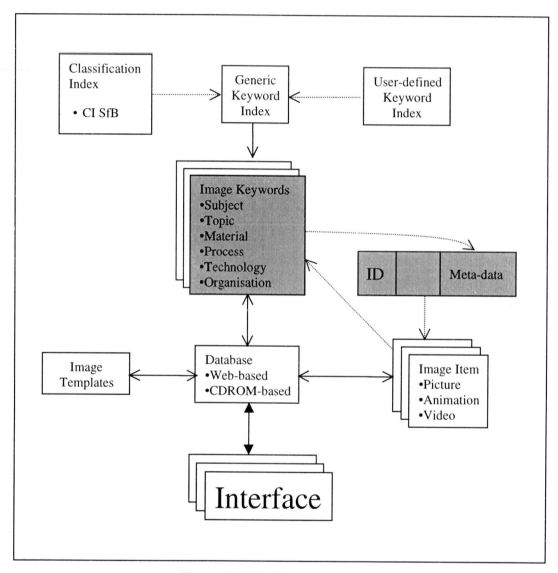

Figure 3. CAL-Visual framework

The framework assists in students' understanding of complex concepts by providing graphical material which can be used to illustrate: objects, materials, activities, processes, relationships, principles and guidelines. In the case of using this framework within the building and construction curriculum, the framework helps students to visualize different types of building materials, construction activities and processes undertaken on site. It can be used to

4.2. Detailed framework description

The framework development (shown in figure 3) began by investigating a number of classifications systems for the indexing of visual material. It was then decided to use a keyword system based on the CI SfB classification augmented with user-defined keywords to form a generic index. Each set of keywords associated with a visual object is to be augmented with administrative information to form the meta-data. A number of indexes have also been created using the visual material and meta-data which arrange the visual material into a number of key subjects. The entering of meta-data is discussed later in this section.

This framework is also used as the foundation for the design and implementation of a web-based database which is to store the visual material and its meta-data. Once the meta-data and visual material is entered into a web-based database the database can be automatically

4.3. System components

The system contains a number of integrated components (figure 4) in order to provide staff and students with different pathways in which to access the visual material. Starting with the underlying web-based database, a retrieval system is the main form of access to the visual material. In doing so, the retrieval system provides two methods of browsing the database. The first is in the form of an Internet hybrid search engine and the second is in the form of a virtual reality

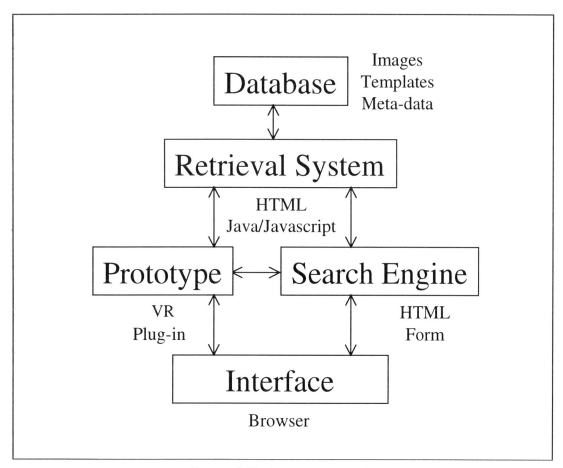

Figure 4. System components

published along with its indexes. In order to publish the database as a web site, on the Internet, intranet or CDROM (using the infrastructure given in figure 2), each image will be stored in an HTML page template. Once the database is published as a web site, staff and students can use a number of DPSS components to access the visual material through an integrated user interface.

environment. Both of these pathways are accessible through a standard web browser. Each of these components is described in detail below, beginning with the design of the database.

4.4. Database design

One of the project's objectives is to produce a set of CD-ROMs that contains platform-independent visual information. The rationale for publishing the database in a web-based form on CD-ROM was to produce a product that is maintenance free and able to be transported to a server-based configuration if

The actual solution has involved using a combination of the options given above. A Microsoft Access database has been created in order to facilitate the entering of meta-data and publishing the

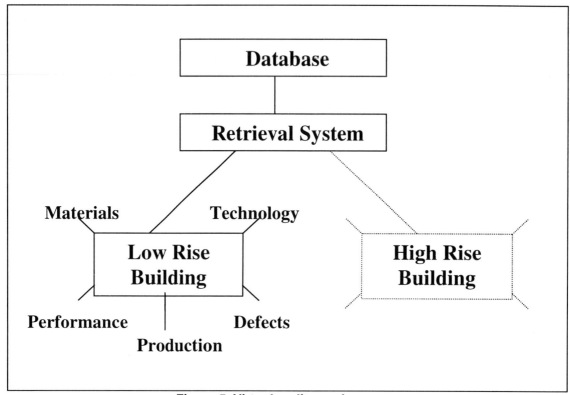

Figure 5. Virtual reality environment

required. This flexibility will also enable the database to be adaptable to the needs of both end-users and institutions.

information in the form of a web site. A retrieval system has then been developed using Web-based technologies. There is due to the issue of retrieving

Table 1. Fields for marking up visual material

Fields	Description	Format	Example
Image ID	Reference number (see left of images)	[ImgXXXX.jpg]	Img0001.jpg
Title	Summary of image	[String]	An outer wall
Author/Owner	Creator or holder of image	[Surname, Initials.]	Beacham, N.
Date Created	Date when image taken or put in database	[dd/mm/yyyy]	01/01/1998
Processes/ Description	Detail description of image including any processes being performed	[String]	Building a wall
Keywords	A list of comma delimited words and phases describing materials, labour, technology, defects, components, tools, systems, plant, manufacture and so on.	[keyword, keyword, etc.]	wall, bricks, cement, window, window ledge
Image Type	Text, Drawing, Graphic, Photo, Animation, Simulation, Emulation	[Type 1, Type 2, etc.]	Drawing, Photo

this web-based information, regardless of whether it exists on a CD-ROM or a server.

4.5. The virtual reality environment

Although the textual user interface is considered to be the main access point for searching for visual material, the other form of access will be through a number of virtual reality models. Each model will form a navigational aid and will be developed as an alternative interface for the retrieval of images from the database. These models will represent a type of building through which the user can navigate and access the information in the database (figure 5).

system to search the database for particular images based upon some form of criteria. For consistency, the marking up of each image is based on the fields shown in table 1. Table 1 lists a number of fields that should accompany each image before they can be entered into the database. The table also acts as a support aid to help end-users mark up images. The table describes each of the fields and the format the field is to take. Following this is an example showing how an image of an outer wall could be marked up. For efficiency a Microsoft Access form has been produced for entering this information (figure 6).

A comprehensive list of keywords relating to the CI SFB classification (mentioned above) is used to describe each image. This list of keywords is also

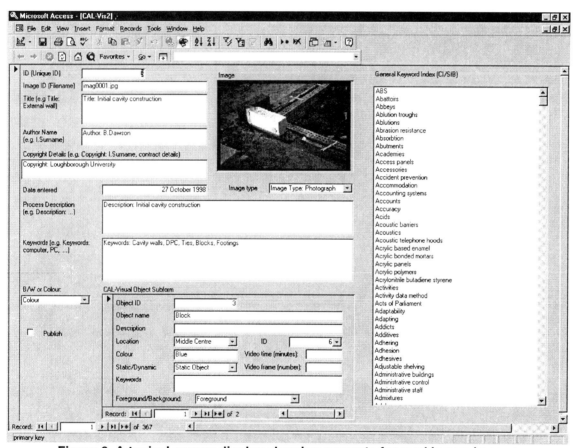

Figure 6. A typical screen display showing prompts for marking up images

4.6. Marking up images

Before any image can be entered into the database and accessed through the retrieval system, each image must be described in a textual form (otherwise known as marking up). This will allow the hybrid retrieval

displayed in the Access form along side the input fields and used by end-users as a reference aid. Whenever a keyword is used to identify part of an image, which is not in the index, it is also added to the list. To accompany this list there will be a need for a tool and support aid which can help end-users mark-up their images.

As well as the keywords field, each image will have five other fields: image ID, title, date entered, author/owner, copyright details and process/description (table 1). Each of these additional fields will be used for the purpose of managing and publishing the resources. They will also be displayed as a complementary aid when end-users are searching for specific materials.

Finally, it was decided to physically storing the actual images within a single directory. This would make finding the retrieval system's task of finding specific images easier – as long as they were identified within the database - and make a the web-based database easier to develop, publish and maintain.

5. Conclusion

The paper discussed the potential of using distributed performance support systems as a tool for facilitating the development, and organization of Multimedia Teaching Aids and, in particular, delivering them using electronic course delivery and electronic open-access student information service.

Based upon the principles of Distributed Performance Support Systems and their implementation into mainstream education, the paper discusses the rationale for using such systems to facilitate the implementation of computer based visualization in the teaching of construction technology. Following this the design and implementation of a DPSS based methodology within the CAL Visual project is presented. The project is nearing the completion of the design and implementation phase, the final stage of the work will include a detailed evaluation to measure the effectiveness of embedding visual material within a construction technology curriculum using the CAL Visual system.

6. References

[1] Aminmansour, A., (1996). Utilizing Information Technologies to better Educate Engineers of Tomorrow, *Computing in Civil Engineering*, Proceedings of the Third Congress held in conjunction with A/E/C Systems '96, June 17-19, 1996, Anaheim, California, 965-971, Editors: Jorge Vanegas and Paul Chinowsky, Published by the ASCE (New York).

[2] Echeverry, D., (1996). Multimedia-based Instruction of Building Construction, *Computing in Civil Engineering*, Proceedings of the Third Congress held in conjunction with A/E/C Systems '96, June 17-19, 1996, Anaheim, California,

972-977, Editors: Jorge Vanegas and Paul Chinowsky, Published by the ASCE (New York).

[3] Chinowsky, P.S., (1997). Introducing Multimedia Cases into Construction Education, *Computing in Civil Engineering*, Proceedings of the Fourth Congress held in conjunction with A/E/C Systems '97, June 16-18, 1997, Philadelphia, Pennsylvania, 122-128, Editors: Teresa M. Adams, Published by the ASCE (New York).

[4] Riley, D. and Pace, C., (1997). Improving Teaching Efficiency with Multimedia Teaching Aids, *Computing in Civil Engineering*, Proceedings of the Fourth Congress held in conjunction with A/E/C Systems '97, June 16-18, 1997, Philadelphia, Pennsylvania, 129-135, Editors: Teresa M. Adams, Published by the ASCE (New York).

[5] Finkelstein, J., (1998). 3D Multimedia Datascapes: The SSV Program, *In the proceedings of the International Conference on Information Visualisation*, July 29-31, 1998, London, UK, 280-285.

[6] Barker, P.G., (1996). Living Books and Dynamic Electronic Libraries, *Electronic Library*, 14(6), 491-502, December.

[7] Barker, P.G. and Hudson, S.R.G., (1998). An Evolving Model for Multimedia Performance Support Systems, 60-73, *Trends in Communication: Part 4 Interface Technology - Enhancing the Quality of Life*, edited by H. van Oostendorp and A.G. Arnold, Boom Publishers, The Netherlands.

[8] Gery, G.J., (1991). *Electronic Performance Support Systems - How and Why to Remake the Workplace Through the Strategic Application of Technology*, Weingarten Publications, Boston, MA 02111, USA.

[9] McGraw, K.L., (1994). Performance Support Systems: Integrating AI, Hypermedia and CBT to Enhance User Performance, *Journal of Artificial Intelligence in Education*, 5(1), 3-26.

[10] Varnadoe, S. and Barron, A., (1994). Designing Electronic Performance Support Systems, *Journal of Interactive Instruction Development*, 6(3), 12-17.

[11] Raybould, B., (1995). Performance Support Engineering: An Emerging Development Methodology for Enabling Organisational Learning, *Performance Improvement Quarterly*, Special Issue on Electronic Performance Support Systems, 8(1), 7-22.

[12] Banerji, A.K., (1995). Designing Electronic Performance Support Systems, *PhD Thesis*, HCI Laboratory, University of Teesside, UK.

[13] Barker, P.G., (1995). Emerging Principles of Performance Support, *Online Information*, 14(1), 407-416.

[14] Hudson, S.R.G., (1998). Multimedia Performance Support Systems, *Draft PhD Thesis*, School of Computing and Mathematics, University of Teesside, Middlesbrough, UK.

[15] Beacham, N.A., (1998). Distributed Performance Support Systems, *PhD Thesis*, Interactive Systems Research Group, Human-Computer Interaction Laboratory, School of Computing and Mathematics, University of Teesside, Middlesbrough, UK.

[16] Barker, P.G., Richards, S. and Banerji, A., (1994). Intelligent Approaches to Performance Support, *ALT-J - Journal of the Association of Learning Technology*, 2(1) 63-69.

[17] Irving, R.H., Higgins, C.A. and Safayeni, F.R., (1986). Computerised performance monitoring systems: use and abuse, *Communications of the ACM*, 29(8), 794-801.

Case-based Analysis for Virtual Model Application in AEC industry

Ogata Seigo
Kumamoto University
2-39-1 Kurokami, Kumamoto 860-8555, Japan
TEL:096-342-3536,FAX:096-342-3507
E-Mail:980d9719@eng3.stud.kumamoto-u.ac.jp

Kobayashi Ichiro, Dr. of Eng.
Kumamoto University
2-39-1 Kurokami, Kumamoto 860-8555, Japan
E-Mail:ponts@gpo.kumamoto-u.ac.jp

Hoshino Yuji
Kumamoto University
2-39-1 Kurokami, Kumamoto 860-8555, Japan
E-Mail:hoshino@gpo.kumamoto-u.ac.jp

Fukuchi Yoshihiko, Ph.D
Konoike Construction Co., Ltd.
3-6-1 Kitakyuhoji-machi, Chuo-ku, Osaka 541-0057, Japan
TEL:06-244-3674,FAX:06-244-3632
E-Mail: yfukuchi@alum.mit.edu

Abstract

This paper introduces the efficient application of Virtual Reality (VR) technologies in the Architecture, Engineering and Construction (AEC) industry, where conventional plastic models are mainly used, which is called Physical Mock Up (PMU). An idea of Virtual Model (VM) is introduced in the paper.

The VM consists of digital models added by digital information about the project, such as CAD drawings, digital maps of periphery, scanned aerial photos, on-site digital pictures and documents.

The paper investigates three principal points as follows; (1) whether presentation of the VM is as efficient as the PMU in terms of its power of expression, (2) whether digital information of the VM is useful to discuss views, ideas and interests about the construction project, (3) whether the VM is practical enough to use in the AEC industry. Pilot trials of the VM in actual construction projects are illustrated in the paper. Those are an on-going land readjustment project in Osaka and a large-scale soil borrowing project in Wakayama, Japan.

***Keyword**: Virtual Model, Physical Mock Up, Presentation Use, Study Use*

1. Introduction

Consensus making among clients, designers and the local community is important for the construction project. On the planning and designing stages, the designers presented their work to the clients or the local community by using PMU (Physical Mock Up) which is the conventional plastic model. The presentation through the PMU is the usual method of information.

This paper introduces the VM (Virtual Model) as a tool to achieve consensus instead of the PMU. Herein, the VM is defined as the three-dimensional model attached the digital information about the construction project such as CAD drawings, digital maps of periphery, scanned aerial photographs, on-site digital photos and documents.

In this paper, the authors investigate three principal issues as follows; (1) the presentation of the VM is as efficient as the PMU in terms of its power of expression, (2) the digital information of the VM is useful to exchange views, ideas and interests about the construction project, (3) the VM is practical enough to use in the AEC industry.

2. Proposal of Virtual Model (VM)

The VM introduced in this paper, is one of the functional roles of Virtual Reality (VR) technology. Because VR technology can not exactly reproduce reality, it tries to practically reproduce it. The most important criteria in VR technology is the ability to simulate reality sensibly and accurately. The three basic characteristics involved in VR technology are[1], [2]:

(1) PRESENCE: to exist in the virtual space,
(2) INTERACTION: to share communication between the user and the computer,
(3) AUTONOMY: to own originality and autonomy in virtual space.

However, the utilization of these characteristics together in the construction field are unsuitable on the desk-top personal computers because the limitation of hardware and software application[3].

Therefore, the authors have been demonstrated the possibility of an effective application of VR technology assuming consensus and presentation in the construction project[4], [5]. This paper believes that its necessary to give priority to easy understanding of the construction project contents than only give three-dimensional reality to the model made by computer. The main condition is to reproduce the three-dimensional model on the virtual space in a certain degree smoothly. The three-dimensional model should be good enough to be freely and easily inspected for the construction project participants.

For this reason, the authors attached digital information such as CAD drawings, digital maps of periphery, scanned aerial photos, on-site digital pictures and documents about the construction project to the VM. Integrating these digital information may provide easy understanding of the project outline and reproduces reality practically, even if it does not exactly represent reality. The VM is made by VRT from Superscape, a UK based software vender. A desk-top personal computer used as hardware[6].

The goal is to provide the simple and efficient use of the VR technology in the construction field. Synthesizing three-dimensional model through digital information this paper proposes a VR easily to inspect and to understand the contents of the construction project.

3. Preparation and the advantage of Virtual Model (VM)

In the past, Physical Mock Up (PMU) were used as a tool for consensus making procedures among construction project members. The VM is confirmed as a practical tool to provide the information about the construction project. The differences can be compared in the VM (Figure 1) and the PMU (Figure 2) are

Figure 1. The PMU

Figure 2. The VM

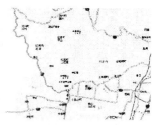
Figure 3. Integration of Map

Figure 4. Integration of Document

Figure 5. The result of Integration

produced. The VM reproduces exactly the PMU in the virtual space. The VM created three-dimensionally by computer presents four main characteristics as follows;

(1) Interactive movement

The VM can interactively moved by using the interactive function of the VR technology, setting up different viewpoints in the virtual space. The User can freely move and change the viewpoint in the VM space anytime and use it like a video. Another, the VM provide flexibility to visualize the model on a large or small scale in conditions that a naked eye could not observed in the usual PMU. The VM provides many viewpoints requested from the users that are hard to be observed from the inside of the PMU. Therefore, the user can observe in detail at the whole construction project through the VM space.

(2) Integration with digital data

The three-dimensional models in the VM space can be attached at the digital information such as CAD drawings, digital maps of periphery, scanned aerial photographs, on-site digital photos and documents. VM

represents the concrete information about the construction project. Moreover, the VM have the ability to provide easy understanding information. This section illustrated two example as follows;

(a) Example 1: Maps (Figure 3)

To integrate information about mapping on the outskirts of the construction project zone to the project participants, VM provide general information such as relationship of geography, methods of traffic, map draw scale and so on. Also, one model is arranged the landmarks of the mountain periphery using the map as a base. Thus, the user are able to look at the mountain through a viewpoint from inside of the park by interactive movement.

(b) Example 2: Documents (Figure 4)

The three-dimensional models in the VM space which are explained by documents, are understood by viewing explanation. The Figure 4 illustrates how the VM recognizes the simple triangular cone object is "Mt. Kinpo", for example. Moreover, it is easy to communicate and unify of consensus among the participants on the construction project. The explanation documents in the VM space are viewed

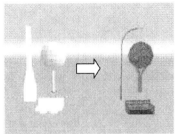

Figure 6. Replacement of the models

Figure 7. Attachment of textures

Figure 8. Use on WWW

anywhere.

Figure 5 illustrates the results of all the digital information collected and integrated. In this way, the VM was taken the periphery information (aerial photographs, site photographs, maps) and used as a extent visual space. So far, its proved that the traditional PMU is difficult to visualize. In the other hand the VM is very clear to visualize and help participants of the project to understand the outline of the construction process. The VM allowed designers and engineers to view the entire site in detail and to simulate construction activities according to proposed construction plans. The VM have effective and practical digital information uses in the construction field than the conventional models and drawings.

(3) Control by script

The three-dimensional structural models in the VM space can be easily turned on and off, moved or erased. The models in the VM space are easily moved and erased compared to the PMU. Also, in the VM the shape and color of the objects can be changed, so the user can examine the landscape of the area and compare the plans of arrangement before and after construction status.

(a) Replacement of the structure models

The VM can be exchanged the model for another one. Figure 6 shows the sample of a simple model object tree been replaced by the detail model one. Also, the structure models can be added or updated without erase existing structures. The user can examine and compare several optional plans using replacement methods of the three-dimensional models. The VM established the library of these structure models.

(b) Attachment of textures

The three-dimensional models in the VM can attached textures such as photos, pictures and so on. Attachment of textures give more reality to the object models (figure 7, for example).

(c) Turned on/off of the three-dimensional models

The three-dimensional models, which are controlled by script, can be turned on / off with a mouse click in the VM space.

The control by script gave reality to the VM space. Although the VM have enough reality to provide easily understanding of the construction project. The VM which has surplus reality prevented creation of the user from entertaining. The optimum method of information presentation is the presentation by using the VM which has both proper reality and interactive movement.

(4) Use on the World Wide Web (WWW)

The VRT data can be downloaded and viewed within the Internet browsers on the computer. The VM data can be changed from normal file format (*.vrt) into archive file format (*.svr) The file size comes to one-fifth of the original one. The user can download the plug-in software (Superscape Viscape 5.0) from the

Superscape Web Site[7]. Figure 8 shows the example of the VM used on the WWW. The VM is shared and viewed by unspecified people. With the maturation of information and communication technologies the concept that distributed VM facilities are delivered over the Internet. For Collaborative work, VM provides the possibility for several users to participate in the same project.

4. Case studies

4.1. Readjustment Project[8], [9]

4.1.1. Overview

A major US-based recreational facility is being constructed in the middle of a heavily industrialized bay area in Osaka. This project is the division of an area which is about 156.2ha. The estimated completion is from August 1995 to March 2002, and its cost is about 640 million dollars.

It is the main concern for clients and developers of the park itself and the land readjustment project in the vicinity whether the scenery from or around the park is pleasantly match to the actual environment. The project is in the phase of the preparation of land and the design-build contracts of the park have been ordered.

4.1.2 Results of Application

Konoike Construction Co., Ltd. took the presentation to the clients of the industrial park and to the 19 enterprises which have their factories or real estates around the construction site (figure 9, for example). As a result of the presentation, the authors got several answers. From the list of activities for marketing by the VM, the principal advantages by using it are illustrated as follows; (1) high appraisal of using at PC level (9 enterprises), (2) there is value of investigation/they want to use it (6 enterprises), (3) easy to understand/interest (8 enterprises). In these, it is said that the VM is very efficiency for the use of the presentation of construction project in designing stage.

Figure 9. Readjustment Project

Figure 10. Soil Borrowing Project

4.2. A Large-Scale Soil Borrowing Project[10]

4.2.1. Overview

Because construction process in fact is a large scale and great quantity of area is involved, it seemed to be impossible to plan and examine carefully by using two-dimensional drawings or PMU. The VM allowed designers and engineers to view the entire construction site surroundings in detail, and to construct temporary construction facilities according to proposed plan.

4.2.2. The VM for Construction Project

The VM was chosen for the project (figure 10). Entire landscape of the area consists of maps, aerial photographs, and three-dimensional objects such as the soil borrowing site. The overall goal is the VM that provides relevant people with the vision of suggested new facilities in the context of the already existing environment while they are freely moving about in the scene and can turn them on and off at any given time.

570

4.3. Discussion

In those applications, the authors described that the method of information through the VM has two forms of application. They are presentation and study. Either presentation or study will depend on the exactly purpose of use. Over Internet any person is able to exchange an opinion about the project. Therefore, they can freely look at the entire landscape of the construction project through the VM space. Also, the constructor can easily examine the project by using a desk-top PC. As a result, any person can use VM efficiently in accord of its purpose of application.

5. Conclusion

This paper has described the utility value of VM as a tool to achieve consensus instead of using PMU and usual drawings. As a result, it confirm that VM is efficiently used by providing facilities of information in the point of helping to understand the outline of a construction project, there is more value than the conventional models and drawings. Further, for the good of the construction participants it is very suitable to discuss about the construction project. In other words, it is said that the VM is necessary to achieve consensus. And, the VM will be able to cope with the accountability on the public. The authors are personally thinking of going to propose a more effective way of VM application in the future researches.

Acknowledgement

This research was supported by the Grant-in-Aid for Scientific Research (c) by the Ministry of Education, Science, Sports and Culture, Government of Japan, under Grant No.09650591.

References

[1] Hirose Michitaka,, "VIRTUAL REALITY" , OHMUSYA, Japan, 1995, in Japanese.

[2] Zeltzer D, "Autonomy, Interaction and Presence" ,PRESENSE, USA, Vol.1, No.1, pp.127-132, 1992.

[3] Kato Hiroshi et al, "The digital information technology implemented in Automobile industry", JAMAGAZINE, JAMA, Tokyo, Japan, Vol.31, pp.3-19, February, 1997, in Japanese.

[4] Ogata, Seigou et al., "Smooth Consensus Making by using Real Time Animation", *Seibu Chapter Proc. of Annual Conference of Civil Engineers*, JSCE, Tokyo, Japan, pp.930-931, March, 1998, in Japanese.

[5] Koboyashi, Ichiro et al., "Application of VR as a tool to achieve consensus on Construction Project", *Proc. 52th Annual Conference of Civil Engineers*, JSCE, Tokyo, Japan, pp.88-89, 1997, in Japanese.

[6] Seigou Ogata et al, "Application of Virtual Model to Achieve Consensus for Construction Project", *First International Conference on New Information Technologies for Decision Making in Civil Engineering Vol.2*, Montreal, Canada, pp.1217-1226, 1998.

[7] Superscape Web Site: http://www.superscape.com

[8] Fukuchi, Yoshihiko et al., "CG Animation for Collaborative Integrated Communications for Construction Management", *Journal of Symposium on Civil Engineering Information Processing System*, JSCE, Tokyo, Japan, pp.149-156, October, 1997, in Japanese.

[9] Ogata Seigo et al., "Application of Virtual Model to Achieve Consensus for Construction Project", *Journal of Symposium on Civil Engineering Information Processing System*, JSCE, Tokyo, Japan, pp.88-95, October, 1998, in Japanese.

[10] Seigou Ogata et al, "CONSENSUS MAKING WITH VIRTUAL MODEL FOR CONSTRUCTION PROJECT", *THE EIGHTH INTERNATIONAL CONFERENCE ON ARTIFICIAL REALITY AND TELE-EXISTENCE*, VRSJ, Tokyo, Japan, pp188-195, 1998, 12.

Fast 3D Visualization of Road Product Models

Andrej Tibaut, Branko Kaučič[1], Danijel Rebolj[2]
Civil Engineering Informatics Lab
Faculty of Civil Engineering, University of Maribor, Slovenia
andrej.tibaut@uni-mb.si

Abstract

Due to its monolithic nature, 3D visualization software integrated with legacy engineering applications contain every possible feature you might use – whether or not a user really wants them. With the advent of distributed objects and interpreted platform-independent languages such as Java and VRML it is possible to develop cross-platform portable 3D visualization software as components that work in an ease-to-use manner. Adopting these advances, fast 3D visualization can considerably simplify the job of maintaining the life cycle of a road integrated within an agreed road product model.

This paper aims to introduce new levels of support to engineers throughout the integrated product life cycle by dealing with issues such as fast platform-independent 3D visualization and product modelling using roads as an example.

1. Introduction

Since the term visualization (see [McCormick 1987]) has found its place in the computing dictionary it has brought substantial benefits to the areas where the visual perception and graphical human-machine interaction accounts for better understanding of problem domain.

The historical trend in the field of 3D visualization of a road has been: to help designers and other experts to evaluate the design and compare different variants on a visual basis and to present the newly designed road to many different groups of interested non-experts. In both cases there is a need for immediate and efficient visual information that can be easily understood and manipulated.

With the fast development of hardware and graphic software, high quality computer visualization of planned or existing building objects was made possible. Also, in the field of roads, specialised software for road design, apart from the usual 2D design drawings, includes more or less realistic, static or dynamic, 3D visualization of the designed object. 3D visualization can be very widely applied. Let us look at some of the possibilities:

1. a simultaneous 3D visualization during the design stage provides engineers with 3D view of a product,
2. virtual drive-on simulation sums up impressions about the road quality,
3. fly-over simulation surveys the harmony of road and terrain.

According to the arrangement of required data for generation of the 3D geometric model, two general cases may occur:

1. design software contains only basic data to which the missing data required for visualization must be added,
2. all the required data for visualization is included, in the proper form, already in the program.

An important characteristic of the first case is unconnected data structures, which are subordinated to the procedure of conventional road design. This is particularly true with the upgrades of the different universal CAD software, where extra-specialized functions for road design are included, and which are above all directed to the composition of drawings – designs. From the point of view of 3D visualization, the deficiencies of the software in the first case are obvious: not only that steps towards a 3D-road presentation require considerable extra effort, but they are also non-trivial.

In the second case automatic visualization can be discussed, because after the design is complete all that is required for visualization is, literally, the touch of a button. However, the automatic generation of the 3D model is possible only with software, which at least possesses a suitable integral road model – a data structure therefore, in which the road axis, the elements of the crossection, and the terrain are all linked together. There is much less software, that contains an

---

[1] branko.kaucic@uni-mb.si, Laboratory for Computer Graphics and Artificial Intelligence

[2] rebolj@uni-mb.si

integral road model, and even the software that does is mostly specialised for photorealistic survey. A huge amount of extra data is therefore required for visualization. In each case the software modules for 3D visualization (or at least for the generation of the 3D graphic model, which can be written into one of the more or less standard graphic formats) are inseparable parts of the road design software packages. However, dynamic 3D visualization is often needed elsewhere as well – not only for those who are directly involved in the design of the road geometry. It is also interesting for investors, analysts and jurists, who are included in the purchase of the land, for ecologists and last of all for the general public, who are more and more involved in the decision-making process, and for whom an objective and above all understandable information is required.

What is needed therefore, is open and independent visualization software, which can be easily used by everyone who will have access to appropriate data about a road.

Our research group has for the last few years been focusing on the integration of computer-supported processes of the life cycle of building objects – especially roads. We have designed an open and integrated product model of a road. For the last couple of years we have been constantly refining model's elegant internal structure by reverse-engineering it through several various software components that we have implemented. The present model's structure has been most influenced by the software component, which automatically generates a 3D graphic road model. The latest version of the component has been developed in Java. It transforms the model of a road into a VRML representation, which can then be presented on the WWW. The VRML representation of a road is suitable for distributed environments where virtual teams are often brought together for a project and then break apart on completion.

The product model and 3D visualization will be described further in the rest of the paper.

2. Product models versus legacy information models

Design and engineering companies want to integrate their engineering process around a product model. One reason for this is because engineering applications have unusually complex information models. These information models are complex because engineering applications manipulate simulations of the real world. Integration around product model can enable concurrent engineering – a process where multiple engineers work on different facets of a product concurrently.

Often, the information models exist only as program language structures taken from a primary application, usually a CAD system. However, without a well-defined model, subsequent applications must be modified whenever the primary application changes. To date, the models for areas such as CAD geometry have been the geometric models of popular CAD systems such as AutoCAD, CATIA, Pro/Engineer, and Unigraphics [Loffredo 1998]. Because the models are structurally and semantically rich, developers can only afford to build tools around these successful models.

In practice, only small, highly focused, applications are ever developed by anyone other than the primary application vendor. The resulting situation is that only special-purpose applications, controlled by CAD vendors, are used to describe complex engineering products. Also, mainstream CAD applications are monolithic and vertically subordinated which in consequence doesn't leave much space to other applications that could improve segments of a market.

Industry has begun to address this problem by developing standard engineering information models.

The ISO-10303 Standard for the Exchange of Product Data (STEP) contains formal descriptions of the information used by the engineering activities in a product lifecycle [Helpenstein 1993, ISO 1994a]. It provides users with the ability to express and exchange digitally useful product information from design to analysis, including manufacture, quality control testing, inspection, product support functions, and even product demolition. In order to do this STEP must cover geometry, topology, tolerances, relationships, attributes, assemblies, configuration and more. To accomplish this ambitious goal, STEP has been divided into multi-part standard. The STEP parts cover general areas, such testing procedures, file formats, and programming interfaces, as well as industry-specific information. STEP is extendable. Industry experts use tools to detail the exact set of information required to describe products of that industry. The Application Protocols form the bulk of the standard, and are the basis for STEP product data exchange. Application protocols are available for mechanical and electrical products, and are under construction for composite materials, sheet metal dies, automotive design and manufacturing, and others. Over time, many industries will develop their own application protocols.

Another specification for industry information models is known as Industry Foundation Classes (IFC) and supported through the International Alliance for Interoperability (IAI). The IFC aims to serve as a basis for project information sharing in the AEC (architecture, engineering, construction, and facilities-management) industry. The information sharing is world-wide, throughout the project life cycle, and across all disciplines and technical applications.

The IAI with its IFC 1.5 released in 1997 is rather new and yet to come. Much more work has been done in product modelling within the STEP community.

For the vast majority of known software used in road construction, badly linked or unconnected data structures are greatly significant. Out there is a software on the market which relies on an underlying road model in form of integrated data structures where the basic elements, like the road axis, crossection elements and terrain are mutually linked. But such road models are usually not interoperable with other software. This means that the program can not export its model to other software without considerable loss of information. This is very common with software where standard like IGES, CGM or DXF are used for description of geometrical data. A good example of commercial road design software where the underlying road model is not open is Plateia, an AutoCAD based software package developed by CGS Software (http://www.cgs.si). Plateia, which has been widely accepted by engineers, supports the procedure of conventional road design through features that surround an in-house road model - a collection of scattered data files. This makes Plateia not interoperable with other software that support the follow-up phases (planning, building, usage, maintenance) of the road lifecycle. This accounts for yet another vertically integrated road design software.

New standards in the field of information exchange offer greater possibilities for more integral external descriptions of building construction models – including roads. We could for example integrate axis elements with crossections to form a more compact model, with the standard for the semantic description of the graphical layers [Björk 1996]. However, the description of complex constructions with the help of layers has other disadvantages. It is unsuitable when we wish to derive one model from another, in order to produce a different view of a building construction, because direct integration of particular data in different layers does not exist as such.

STEP, as the more universal standard, has been gaining in popularity within the AEC community because it goes considerably further than just transmitting two-dimensional drawings (as does the IGES). It transmits complete product models. STEP is slowly, yet rather successfully getting importance, especially for use in very complex projects [Hardwick 1997]. One of the early projects that aimed to develop product model for highways started around 1990 at Rijkswaterstaat and TNO in Holland. After several years of unsuccessful attempts to propose the resulted Road Model Kernel [Willems 1990] as an ISO/STEP application the project was shut down due to model's complex data requirements that existing road design applications couldn't provide. In 1994 new project with more limited scope was derived from the previous one. It deals with integration of road shape modelling (RMSK - Road Model Shape Kernel) and product modelling [Willems 1998].

The largest project concerning road product modelling is running in Sweden. Swedish National Road Administration wants to see its STEP based Road Network Model [http://www.eurostep.com/] as an international standard.

3. MCT - a step to road product model, yet without STEP

While facing the emerging need for the integration of computer supported processes of the life cycle of building constructions, roads in particular, our research group CGI initiated the project for development of an open and simple road product model. The project is expected to shift the current road construction practice from the "human-only understanding of drawing" towards the more meaningful product data structures that define the semantic context of geometry data.

The development of the road model can be followed through [Rebolj 1993], [Tibaut 1994], [Rebolj 1995], [Rebolj 1996], [Rebolj 1997a]). The road body model (MCT), as we named it, serves as a starting-point for an improvement of data exchange among existing road design software that supports different phases of the road life cycle.

The linking element in the model structure is the *Project*, which includes the main information about the road project, as well as the essential attributes for the rest of the structural parts (Figure 1). The whole model is defined in such a way that it enables addition-to and modification-of the individual segments, without affecting other sections of the structure.

The *Corridor* is a simple structure, which defines the possible borders within which a road may be located. It is important in the early phase of a road life cycle, when the most suitable road corridor is selected and the first approximation of the road axis is elaborated. The corridor is again used in the road geometry definition phase (road design), since it determines the design area. After the geometry of the road is defined, the corridor represents the external borders of the observed area.

The road is a geographical feature, therefore the *Corridor* and the *Road geometry* can be seen as thematic components of a geographic information system (GIS). Furthermore, other spatial data in the form of geographic themes (or layers) are required in several phases of the road life cycle. For this reason, a link to *Geographic themes* is provided in the model.

The details of the model description are evident from the external representation of the model – the metafile of the road (Figure 2), which serves as a data translator between applications involved in the road life cycle. The first step in our approach was a simple metafile, called mCT (road body metafile). We have implemented interfaces for import/export of mCT between software packages that are being used in many planning and consulting bureau's and are included in the road life cycle. mCT has a hierarchical structure and is stored as a text file. Its components are described in the form of sections, subsections, etc. Different sections always begin with the section name, which can be found in the square brackets, and end with a new section or with the end of a file. The metafile can comprise only several sections, depending on the project phase and the choice of the user.

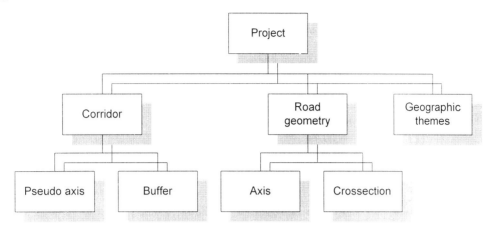

Figure 1. Main structure of the road product model

It seems to be best, if the model is designed and described with the help of a standard like STEP ([Bakkeren 1994]), but at this stage our in-house description proved itself to be more easy to implement than complex STEP interfaces [Rebolj 1997a].

Besides visualization, the road model, explicitly described with the mCT, can also be applied to sight distance evaluation [Easa 1996], noise analysis, calculation of substance emissions and their dispersion [Rebolj 1997b].

4. Fast 3D visualization

The road geometry in digital form is obtained from any road design package that implements the appropriate mCT translator. The road design applications that apply the mCT translator are Plateia and Cador.

Generation of the 3D graphic model is the key component of the visualization program. The basic algorithm provides for the connection of corresponding elements in adjacent crossections along the road axis. That is how the spatial surfaces, which form the road body are created. The algorithm is constructed in such a way, that it springs up from the road axis and connects elements that undoubtedly belong together – e.g. pavement, gutter, etc. In situation, where every single element in the two adjacent crossections has its counterpart, the solution is simple. If for some reason (for example, end of gutter) the corresponding element is missing in one of two adjacent crossections, the program searches for the best element

match in another crossection according to the distance from the axis and side of the road (left or right). It then tries to link two elements of different types, according to the distance from the axis. The algorithm generates 3D road surface - collection of arbitrary patches composed of triangular and quadrangular facets ([Tibaut 1994]).

The connection between the two adjacent crossections can be whether rectilinear or parallel to the road axis (curved). With the rectilinear connection all that is required for 3D body generation is the cros-section data (Figure 2, section [CROSSECTIONS]), in the second case we also need the axis element data (Figure 2, section [AXIS]). The rectilinear connections give adequate visualization quality, if the distances between the crossections are short enough (typical < 20m). In both cases, the model is more precise where the connections are in accordance with the axis. However, the generation of 3D graphic model with curved connections can be problematic. If the spatial curved surfaces are to be used for the presentation, more complex graphic systems must be employed. However, this does not fulfil the criteria of ease and speed of visualization. If, on the other hand, the interpolation of flat surfaces, which are dispersed between the existing crossections on the road axis are used and they are connected with straight lines, we encounter the problem of increased time and memory requirements. In the present software version the plain rectilinear connections between the crossections are used.

5. RoadVi

First implementation of the visualization software RoadVi dates back to 1994 [Tibaut 1994]. We used RAD tools from MS Visual Studio package (Visual C++, VB) and Micro systems' 3d Graphic Tools library for the graphic support.

The features we have included in the visualization software make possible:

- automatic generation of 3D graphic model,
- camera and light position,
- "drive-on", following the road pavement at a chosen height,
- "fly-over", following the chosen trajectory,
- simple shading,
- export of the 3D graphic road model to the VRML format.

```
[PROJECT]
'comments
    [NAME]
        ProjectName(text)
    [DESCRIPTION]
        ProjectDescription(text)
    [SCHEDULE]
        Start_date(date)  Actual_date(date)
    [WINDOW]
        Y_min  Y_max  X_min  X_max
[THEMES]
        Path  Name  Type
[CORRIDOR]
    [PSEUDOAXIS]
        X  Y
    [BUFFER]
        X  Y
[AXIS]
    [HORIZONTAL]
        X_start  Y_start  X_end  Y_end  Radius  A  Length
    [VERTICAL]
        L_start  Z_start  L_end  Z_end  Radius  Length
[CROSSECTIONS]
    [POSITION]
        Number  L  X  Y  Z
    [TERRAIN]
        X'  Y'
    [ELEMENTS]
        [POINTS]
            Id  X'  Y'
        [CONNECTIONS]
            Id_startpoint  Id_endpoint  Element_Type(text)  GLOBAL | LOCAL
[CROSSECTION ELEMENT TYPES]
        Element_Type(text)  Class(text)  Description(text)
(eof)
```

[ ]	beginning of the section
⇑	repetition is allowed
X,Y,Z	world co-ordinates
X', Y'	local (crossection) co-ordinates
L	axis co-ordinat (station)
italic	variables (words in parenthesis denote variable types)
|	or (eg. GLOBAL | LOCAL means GLOBAL or LOCAL, but not both)

Figure 2. Definition of the road metafile MCT.

The MS Windows based implementation of RoadVi was integrated into the Road life-cycle environment (RO) [Rebolj 1996] - a software frame for applications that employ the road model MCT for different purposes. Figure 4 and 5 show 3D wire-framed and rendered road surface, respectively. Both pictures were generated in RoadVi. The camera was positioned at the crossection number 41. The corresponding road geometry data were obtained from a road design project in Austria and consisted of 82 crossections along the road axis. The generated 3D road surface contained 2739 facets spanned over 3050 vertices. Generation of the rendered 3D road surface on an average PC (Pentium 133 MHz), took only about 5 seconds.

The camera and target position (view direction) can be defined with a crossection number or with global coordinates.

Drive-on feature increments the camera position along the road axis so that one can visually evaluate the symmetry and harmony of road. Sequence of pictures can then be processed and stored as an animation.

6. VR-Vi

Among RoadVi features there is a translator for VRML. The translator facilitates export to a neutral ASCII file format (Figure 3) which can be imported by another application called VR-Vi that we have developed in Java. Vr-Vi is a multi-thread Java based application developed with JavaSoft's JDK 1.2. It uses only JDK provided packages and is therefore fully platform independent. The standardization of the platform independent programming language Java offers great opportunity to create highly dynamic visualization software.

The Vr-Vi features generation of the VRML 2.0 (Virtual Reality Modelling Language) representation of a road which gives our road model the potential to

576

expand its online interactivity. At this development stage RoadVi exports road geometry to the neutral file format which shows the Figure 5. This file is then imported by VR-Vi and serves for generation of VRML model.

```
#Info
#Author TEXT
#Date TEXT
#Comment TEXT

#Intern
#N
InternID,InternName,Red,Green,Blue,TextureFileName

#Extern
ExternID,FileName,PositionX,PositionY,PositionZ

#Animations
CameraX,CameraY,CameraZ,TargetX,TargetY,TargetZ,Roll

#Lights
LightX,LightY,LightZ,Radius

#Point
PositionX,PositionY,PositionZ

#Faces
#Range
PointID1,PointID2,PointID3,...,PointIDN,InternID
```

Figure 3. RoadVi's export format

With the VRML the road model is now easily accesible to end-users.

There's not nearly as much excitement about VRML today, as there was a year ago [Rist 1998]. However, a popular way to use VRML now is within a frame in an HTML document. Users can manipulate it with VRML browsers. Although, this year SGI terminated the development of its popular Cosmo Player [Karpinski 1998], other VRML browsers do exist – most notably WorldView that is now also distributed as part of Windows 98 and Internet Explorer.

A good news for the future of VRML is that Sun Microsystems has joined the VRML Consortium to promote the compatibility and interoperability of its Java 3D API technology and the ISO VRML 97 (VRML 2.0). VRML became a standard for the encapsulation, delivery, and playback of interactive 3D graphics on the Internet or intranets. Java 3D is a general-purpose, scene-level 3D graphics API extension to the Java language.

Figure 6 shows the same road in VRML (it can be obtained from our Web site at http://kamen.uni-mb.si/cgi). It was generated with the Java version of RoadVi. In this version we made our road visualization software independent from operating

system and as such much more universal. VRML representation enables the designers to publish the new road variants on the Internet so that investors can control progress of the project. What is required for the visualization in this case, is the VRML viewer, which is already included in some Internet browsers or can be downloaded from the Internet at any time. lot features can now be visually recognized from the picture, generated in the office. It is expected that this might speed up the process of land acquisition. Such application wouldn't be possible without an open road model.

The Slovene Ministry of traffic and communications and the Ministry of science and technology financially support development of the MCT and the visualization software. Therefore the described software is freely available to all interested parties in the road life cycle.

8. Conclusion

With our road visualization software many excellent 3D graphic pictures and animations have already been made. The essential advantage of our work is the generation of the 3D road model, originating, entirely automatically, in the integrated road product model. The multi purpose use of the model and its standardization are therefore important. In the future, we will use standards like STEP for road description.

Java implementation of the visualization software RoadVi will shape the future of its development because it eliminates problems with code distribution, versioning and more. An obvious research direction is to use Java applets for visualization. Using Java applets, visualization code doesn't actually even need to be installed on a user's machine. Instead, code can be loaded dynamically to users as required. In theory, an n-tiered web application written in Java eliminates the problems of code distribution and versioning. Each time users would hit our visualization Web site, they received a new version of applet for road visualization.

Further more, the VRML translation of the road product model's geometry data is facilitated.

If Java 3D API and VRML become synergistic this would accelerate the deployment of 3D content on the Web. In spite of this compatibility, VRML support is an important feature.

Product modelling and 3D visualization - little things perhaps but the sum is greater than the parts.

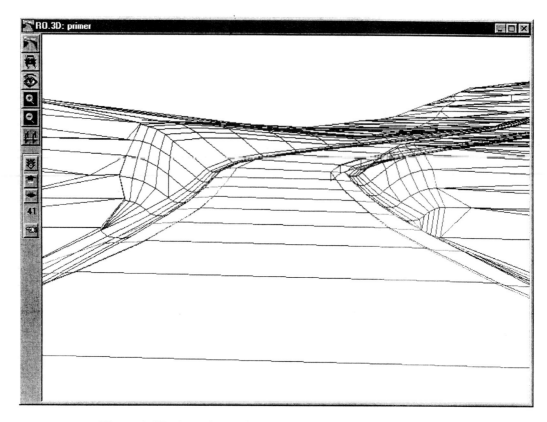

Figure 4. 3D view of the wire-framed road generated in RoadVi

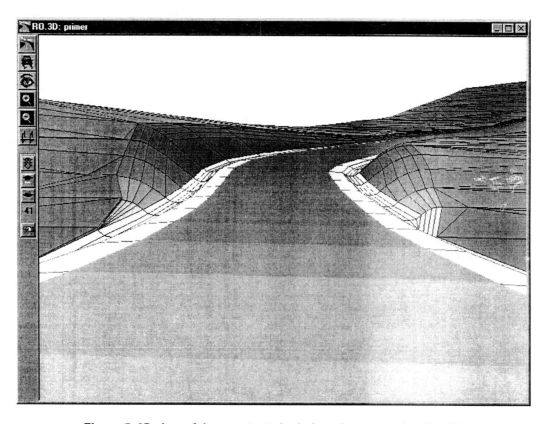

Figure 5. 3D view of the constant shaded road generated in RoadVi

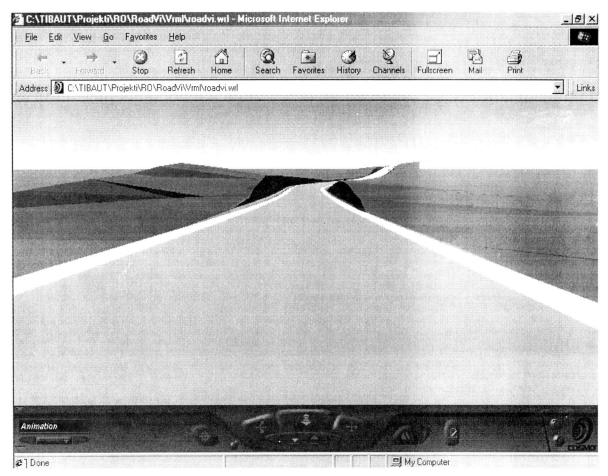

Figure 6. VRML representation of the road generated in Java version of RoadVi

9. References

[Bakkeren 1994]

> Bakkeren. W.J.C. *Integrating Structural Design and Analysis through Product Modeling. Proceedings of CIB W78 Workshop on Computer Integrated Construction,* Helsinki. Finland. 1994.

[Björk 1996]

> Björk. B.. K. Löwnertz. A. Kiviniemi. *ISO 13567 - The proposed international standard for structuring layers in computer aided building design. Construction on the information highway.* University of Ljubljana. 1996. pp. 77-88.

[Easa 1996]

> Easa. Said M.. Abd El Halim, Hassan Yasser. *Sight distance evaluation on complex highway vertical alignments.* Canadian Journal of Civil Engineering. Vol. 23. No. 3. June 1996, pp 577-586.

[Eckel 1998]

> Eckel. Bruce. *Thinking in Java.* ISBN: 0136597238. 1152 pages. Prentice Hall. 1998

[Hardwick 1997]

> Hardwick. M.. D. L. Spooner, T. Rando. and K.C. Morris. *Data protocols for the industrial virtual enterprise.* IEEE internet computing. Vol. 1, No. 1. January - February 1997, pp 20-29.

[Hartman 1996]

> Hartman, J., and J. Wernecke. *The VRML 2.0 Handbook.* Addison-Wesley. Reading. Mass., 1996.

[Helpenstein 1993]

> Helpenstein J. Helmut: CAD Geometry Data Exchange using STEP. Springer-Verlag. ISBN 3-540-56902-2. 1993

[ISO 1994]

> International standard ISO 10303-1 Part 1: Overview and fundamental principles. 1st Edition 1994-12-15

[Karpinski 1998]

> Karpinski. Richard. *Software unit closing clouds VRML's future.* Internetweek. 07/13/98. Issue 723, p14, 1/6p

[Loffredo 1998]

> Loffredo. David. *Efficient Database Implementation of EXPRESS Information Models.* PhD Thesis. Rensselaer Polytechnic Institute. Troy. New York. May 1998.

[McCormick 1987]

> B. H. McCormick and T. A. DeFanti and M. D. Brown. "Visualization in Scientific Computing". *Computer Graphics.* Nov. 1987. Vol. 21. No. 6

[Rebolj 1993]

> Rebolj. D. *Computerunterstützter integrierter Straßenentwurf in einer objekt orientierten Umgebung.* Verlag für die Technische Universität Graz. Graz. 1993.

[Rebolj 1995]

Rebolj, D. Integrated road design and evaluation environment. *Computing in civil and building engineering.* A. A. Balkema. Rotterdam, 1995, pp. II/1001-1006.

[Rebolj 1996]

Rebolj, D. *Integrated information system supporting road design, evaluation, and construction..* Computing & information technology for architecture, engineering & construction. CI-Premier, Singapore, 1996, pp. 281-288.

[Rebolj 1997a]

Rebolj, D. A product model of a road. *IKM - Internationales Kolloquium über Anwendungen der Informatik und Mathematik in Architektur und Bauwesen.* Bauhaus - Universität Weimar, 1997. digital proceedings on CD-ROM.

[Rebolj 1997b]

Rebolj, D., P. J. Sturm, and S. Hausberger. *Dynamic estimation and visualization of road traffic related air pollution.* Proceedings of the Power Engineering Expert Meeting, Univerza v Mariboru, 1997, pp. C/201-210.

[Rist 1998]

Rist, Oliver. *VRML: Not gone and not forgotten, either.* Internetweek, 01/12/98 Issue 697, p29, 2/5p, 1c

[Tibaut 1994]

Tibaut, A., D. Rebolj. *Visualisierung des Straßenkörpermodells.* Proceedings of Internationales Kolloquium über Anwendungen der Informatik und der Mathematik in Architektur und Bauwesen, held in Weimar, Germany, p. 151-156, 3, 1994.

[Willems 1990]

Willems, P.H. *Road Model Kernel.* TNO Building and Construction Research, B-89-831, March 1990.

[Willems 1998]

Willems, P.H.. *Conceptual Modelling of Structure and Shape of Complex Civil Engineering Projects.* PhD Thesis, Delft University Technology, September 1998.

Session 3-7

Applied Visualization

Chair
Rivka Oxman
Technion, Israel

A Prototype System for Cooperative Architecture Design

Yuhua Luo[*], Ricardo Galli[*], Antonio Carlos Almeida[**], Miguel Dias[***]

*University of Balearic Islands, Palma de Mallorca, Spain
** Instituto de Telecomunicaçoes, Instituto Superior Tecnico, Lisbon, Portugal
***ADETTI, ISCTE, Lisbon, Portugal
Email: dmilyu0@clust.uib.es

Abstract

The paper presents a prototype system for cooperative architecture design. The system includes a multi-site cooperative 3D editor and a cooperative and communication support platform. By using the prototype system, the users are able to load a design scene, modify its properties and save the result cooperatively. The on-line basic cooperative, interactive editing functionality on the designed objects via the communication network has been achieved.

Keywords: Cooperative Design, CSCW, interactive 3D graphics, architecture design.

1. Introduction

The architecture design and the construction industry as a whole is highly data extensive. Many different technical specialties have to work tightly together for a single project. A lot of redundancy, reproduction and error can occur because of the lack of integrated information technology support. However, due to the high volume of data to be transferred, the limitation in the network capacity, the lack of standards for data exchange, real time multi-site cooperative architecture design has not yet come to reality. The ultimate objective of the work presented here is to integrate the CAD technology with the virtual reality and high performance network technology to provide a solution to such problems.

In the current architectural production process, there are many iterations necessary to complete the design. This iteration process is mainly between the main architectural design, the design of structural engineering and other specialties. The main design has to be decomposed for different engineers and specialists to design their projects. These projects have to be integrated later to form the global project. This iteration process repeats many times during different project phases. During all iterations, a large amount of errors can occur. These errors are usually unrecognized until the construction phases, which is extremely costly. It causes a great amount of financial and other difficulties in today's architectural production. The most important reason of the occurrence of all these errors is the lack of efficient cooperative work during the above iterations.

The system we present here is called the M3D[1] prototype system. This is the first attempt to provide an on-line higher level cooperative working tool for an architecture design team. Its capability of supporting the cooperative work not only includes the cooperative visualization, but also, and more important, the on-line modification of CAD objects. This means that the team members can stay at their own location but participate in a virtual design conference remotely. They can visualize the design work and modify the design on line when necessary.

The M3D prototype system includes two major parts: an editor and a cooperative support platform. The editor provides basic editing operations of the design work in 3D. The cooperative support platform governs an on-line cooperative working session. The system has a layered structure. It uses low bandwidth and low cost communication network. It provides Internet and ISDN connections. The prototype system has been implemented on both PC and SGI platforms. Open Inventor tool kit and C++ have been used for implementation of the system.

Section 2 introduces the architecture of the system. Section 3 explains the cooperative editor. Section 4 gives a close look at the conference and cooperative support platform. Conclusions and future work are described in Section 5.

2. General architecture

The M3D prototype system is composed of a set of different applications that is replicated in each workstation on each site. Currently, the application is only the editor [6]. A set of such workstations are connected together through the network to form the system. See Figure 2.1 for the general configuration of the system.

---

[1] M3D stands for Multi-site Cooperative 3D Design System for Architecture. See http://www.m3d.org/ for more information

The system uses a fully distributed, layered architecture [1][2]. There are two major layers in the prototype system on top of the communication network:

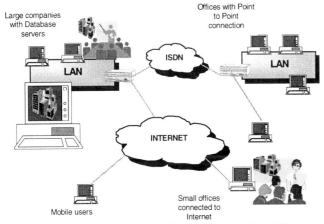

Figure 2.1 The general configuration of the M3D

the Application layer and the Cooperative support layer (see Figure 2.2). The cooperative support layer is application and network independent. By the distributed architecture, all the hosts in the system that run a collaborative session have the same set of resources and replicas of the applications.

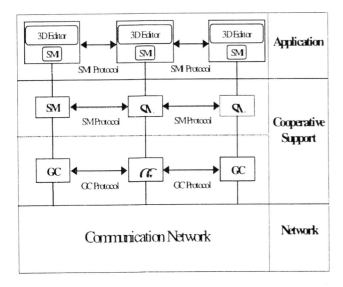

Figure 2.2 The layered structure of the M3D prototype system

The current application, the 3D editor, is located at the Application Layer. An application layer protocol, the Session Manager Interface protocol (SMI protocol), has also been implemented at this level [5][7]. The Cooperative Support Layer includes a session manager

module (SM) and a group communication (GC) module of which itself is also a layered structure.

The application layer holds a set of 3D cooperative design tools, currently the 3D editor. The architectural design usually contains massive amount of data. To reach the speed of cooperative interactive modification, we have to choose a workable strategy. Our major strategy is to send as less data as possible via the network. By this strategy, we decide only to send the modification data and recreate the events locally. The replicated structure is the base to realize this strategy.

In order to send the modifications of the scene to the peer application replicas during a running working session, an application layer protocol, the **SMI** protocol, has been designed and implemented at this level. This protocol is an essential element to support the full multi-user interactions in a shared 3D virtual world. There is a submodule in charge of the communication with the lower layer called SMI module (Session Manager Interface module). It encapsulates the SMI protocol information into a lower layer protocol.

A Joint Editing Supporting Platform (JESP) [1] has been adopted for this layer. It includes a session control module (**SM**) and a group communication module (**GC**). The group communication module itself is also a layered structure. The SM module is responsible for the tasks required by a cooperative working session such as service multiplexing, data consistency control, member admission. The GC module provides the point to point or point to multi-point communication.

At the lower layers in the architecture, there is the network protocol and the physical network. Currently the standard TCP-UDP/IP suite protocol is used. There is no restriction on the physical network. It can be an Ethernet or a PPP/ISDN network.

The advantage of using a layered structure is that the layers are independent. Changes at one layer do not affect the other layers. This can give the system a more general-purpose characteristic. It can be easily tailored for other similar applications and adopt the rapid technology development of the communication network.

3. The Editor

The 3D Editor is the central tool for on-line cooperative design working sessions. The editor has to meet the highest requirement of on-line cooperative design from distance. There are important technical requirements for this tool:

- Editing capability
- Interactive response
- Concurrency control

The implemented functions in the M3D prototype system are described below.

Editing capability

The major function of the 3D Editor is the capability of editing an architectural design. It has two modes: on-line cooperative editing mode and the off-line editing mode.

The on-line editing mode is for the chief architect or project leaders to chair a cooperative working session, especially for integration of design work from different specialists. During such a working session, the participants should be able to discuss specific design problems and make modifications on line using the on-line mode. On the other hand, an off-line mode can be used to prepare an on-line discussion of the global design.

The major functions of the 3D editor are divided into several groups. They are operations and management for a scene, for objects, for scene environments, and viewing management, etc.

The first group of functions is for operating and managing a scene. A scene here is in VRML terms, which refers to a larger scale and independent design work usually corresponding to a global design in the building construction.

The functions include opening, saving a scene, displaying the scene structure and making a query on the objects of the scene etc.

There are different options for saving a file. It may be a whole scene or a part of it. The display options include showing the tree structure of a scene, the object class etc. This is very useful for dealing with inputs from different kinds of CAD software. They normally have different ways to decompose a scene. The basic visualization options of a scene are also included in this group.

The second function group provides a set of operations on the objects within a scene. Object here is a small unit in the design. It is usually an element in the building such as a column, a wall, etc. It can also be any group of geometric elements that has been defined as an object.

By using this group of functions, one can insert, delete, and modify an object. The modification of an object includes modifying its geometry, its properties such as color, roughness, texture etc.

There is an important operation on the objects, the selection. Since the 3D editor is a cooperative, multi-user, multi-site editing tool, we have to distinguish if an object is selected locally or remotely. The selection also serves as a locking operation. Once an object is selected, it is locked by a participant in the working session. It can not be selected by others until the object is released.

Another group of functions concerns the manipulation of environment properties of the scene. These properties are not part of the scene nor the objects, for example, the lighting, rendering parameter etc. One can locate a particular type of lights to see the lighting effect in the designed building. Rendering parameters can also be defined to give different quality of the rendered 3D scene. They will help to perceive the design work better in the virtual 3D environment.

The group of functions that provides viewing assistance to the user has the options to add text and change the window environment etc. Virtual camera manipulation is within this group. When a window is created, there is a virtual camera associated with it. There will be more functions available in the future development.

Interactive response

Since interactive cooperative design of a 3D virtual world usually involves a great amount of data to be manipulated and visualized, to minimize the network traffic becomes vital. This affects the feasibility of the whole system. If one participant modifies an object and it takes a long time for other participants to visualize it, or even worse, the change never appears on another participant's screen, the cooperative design will become completely impossible. Therefore, the interactive response time is a crucial requirement that the editor must meet.

Our solution to meet this crucial requirement is twofold. On one hand, we implement a totally replicated in-memory database on each site. On the other hand, messages with small size are sent via the network to represent the user modification.

The reason to have the replicated database is due to the high read-to-update ratio when rendering the 3D objects. It is also because of the high memory read throughput required for rendering a complex design. We call this replicated in-memory database, the *persistent database*.

Sending the small size messages is the major strategy to meet the crucial requirement, the interactive response time. The SMI protocol mentioned above is especially designed for this purpose. This protocol specifies the structure of the messages to code the *user events* and to capture the changed data. This means to create relatively small size messages for each event and recreate the remote events locally. Small messages will take relatively shorter time to reach the remote sites. To recreate the event locally does not depend on the network traffic, so that the remote users can have a quicker response.

Concurrency control

Concurrency control is another critical requirement to the editor because it supports the cooperative editing. This problem arises when more than two members in the working session modifying the same object at the same time. This is a typical problem of concurrency control.

By the definition of the SMI prototype, local copies of the database on other remote workstations are updated only if they receive the *update* message. To maintain the consistency of the local copies of the database we must avoid possible conflicts that can appear when two or more users intend to modify the same *region* of the scene. The major solution we choose is to apply the locking policies and transaction-oriented operations. These policies are based on techniques of distributed data processing [3][4][8].

The most frequent user operations are camera movements and object modification. For camera movement, there is no need to assure any mutual exclusion or packet ordering. However, for object editing it is extremely important to assure mutual exclusion. To avoid latencies that can disturb the user interaction, the following approach is taken:

We allow a user to modify an object only after the object is selected by this user. The selection of an object involves the "locking" of the VRML subtree under the selected node in the scene graph.

In addition, an object can be selected only if no other members in the working session have previously selected any part of the subtree that the object belongs to. To achieve this condition, if a user makes a selection attempt, the editor on his machine must communicate with the other peer editors about this operation through the SMI protocol.

In case of conflicts, our policy is that just one of the members can acquire the right. If two or more applications try to lock intersecting subtrees, the timestamp scheme can be used to resolve the conflict. The sender of the packet with a global minor timestamp is selected as the "temporally owner" of the scene subtree. Although this can be a very time expensive task, we can avoid further delays when users edit the scene. We may reduce the computation time by exploiting the total and causal packet ordering QoS.

The 3D editor in the M3D prototype system can been seen in figure Figure 4.1.

4. The Conference and Cooperative Support

The M3D prototype system is an on-line cooperative working tool for an architecture design team. To achieve the interactive speed during a cooperative working session that covers a wide geographical area, a strong support for conferencing and cooperative working control is necessary. A cooperative and communication support module has been developed in M3D prototype for this purpose.

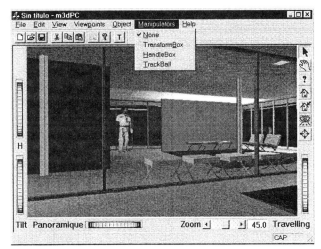

Figure 4.1 : The 3D editor in the M3D prototype system

The main objective of the module is to enable the users to share one or more applications as transparently as possible [2]. It intends to emulate a full joint meeting environment with full connectivity and interaction in spite of geographic restriction.

The module has been designed to be transparent to the users. The users are kept away from the networking and session control details. It has also been designed to keep the distributed applications independent of the underlying networking process.

The structure of the cooperative and communication support module can be seen in Figure 4.2. It also shows the interaction between the entities in the module.

There are three replicates of the same module indicated in the figure. Each of them represents a remote location. The minimum number of sites to hold a conference for a working session is two. On each site there are two groups of entities. The first group is the *Joint Editing Service Platform New Generation* (JESP NG) which is in charge of session control and communication. It has two layered entities: the Session Manager (SM) and the Group Communication (GC) entity. The second group is the *meta-conferencing control platform* which deals with the external control over running collaborative sessions. It has two entities: the GUI (Graphic User Interface) and the GD (Group Daemon). The following explains them in more detail.

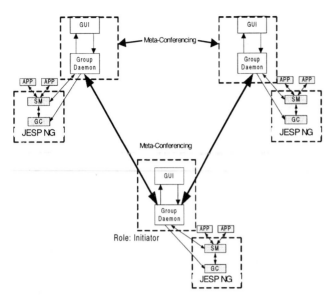

Figure 4.2. The structure of the cooperative and communication support module

The JESP NG service platform

The services provided by the JESP NG are available to the applications through a common service interface. The set of communication services hides the network configuration from the applications. The session control mechanisms provides the applications the necessary functions in the cooperative environment. The platform ensures the possibility of the co-existence of a set of applications on top of a common service interface. It provides a dynamic application environment to the users.

The platform was designed to support synchronous and asynchronous interactions among the users, although special emphasis is given to the synchronous interaction here. The platform supports the simultaneous operation of a group of users spread over multiple remote locations. It intends to avoid significant latencies. This becomes a critical point when the number of users and the distance among them increases. In addition, it supplies fault-tolerance mechanisms for error and failure recovering.

The communication and session control mechanisms are organized in a layered structure, as depicted in Figure 4.3. The SM entity is responsible for session control tasks and the GC entity is responsible for point-to-multipoint communication functions. These two entities are the building blocks of the support platform. The application environment layer includes several distributed applications. They act as clients requesting services from the platform through *Service Access Points* (SAPs).

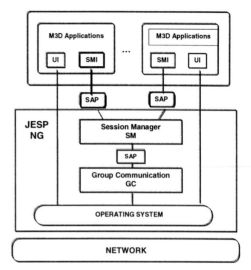

Figure 4.3 The local structure

On each site there is one instance of the structure shown in Figure 4.3. Session control is achieved by a distributed protocol executed among the SM entities. These entities have the same set of capabilities. Some specific attributes may be given to just one of the session managers in order to perform special tasks. For example, the permission functions may be given to the SM of initiator site of the conference.

Each distributed application makes use of a specific protocol to exchange messages. Most of the messages contain *user events* produced through one or more input devices at the user interface. These local events are encapsulated in messages and sent to the other sites through a service request made to the SM entity. The application layer contains two I/O logical entities located at the application layer environment. One of them is the *User Interface* (UI). It is the interface to all the devices that collect the local user events of a particular application. Examples of such devices are mouse devices, keyboards, audio and video codecs etc. Normally, the capture of these events is associated with the Operating System procedures or, at a different level, controlled by some Window System. The platform is not aware of the UI entities.

The second I/O logical entity associated with the JESP platform at the application layer is the *Session Manager Interface* (SMI) as mentioned before. It structures the communication between the application layer and the SM layer. In particular, the SMI is responsible for service requests to the SM layer for a particular application. These requests are either to transfer messages among the application replicas or to invoke some session control tasks.

Meta-Conferencing Control

The meta-conferencing control in the prototype system is external to the co-operative platform. We have designed a distributed meta-conferencing system because the whole system is based on a multi-site distributed architecture. The objective is to provide external control over running collaborative sessions such as starting and stopping them. Other meta-conferencing operations include JESP NG platform initialization, error reporting and recovery, joining and withdrawal of users, cancelling of shared applications and obtaining general session information.

The meta-conferencing system used to control the conferencing platform and applications has two entities running on each site. They are the **GD** and **GUI**. The main role of the Group Daemon is to manage all the processes related to the conference (platform processes and applications). This entity is able to invoke, cancel and communicate with those processes. On the other hand, the main role of the GUI is to serve as the conferencing interface with the users. It is the visible part of the meta-conferencing system.

To establish a conference, one of the sites has to be the **initiator**. The initiator starts the session configuration which is dynamic during the session. New users may be admitted into the running sessions. During the first iteration, at least two members should exist (on different machines).

Starting a session requires an interaction between a given user and his process interface (**GUI**) which interacts directly with the respective (**GD**). After specifying the initial configuration (with a minimum of two members) the **GD** entity starts connections in a star configuration with the other **GDs** running on the other hosts. This star configuration will persist during the session and will serve to control the conference.

The processes **SM** and **GC** will be started afterwards. Each one of the **GDs** that accepted the invitations will automatically start their local structure of the cooperative work platform (composed by processes **GC** and **SM**). Each non-initiator **GD** will notify the initiator **GD** of the success of the launching processes **SM** and **GC**. The last set of processes **SM/GC** is launched on the initiator machine. After this point, the collaborative platform may start its own protocols independently of the conference management components **GUI** and **GD**.

Nevertheless, the initiator **GD** is responsible to broadcast the names of the applications to the other **GD** components. After this, each **GD** will start a new process for each required application, on each machine. See Figure 4.4 for the local interaction processes.

Each application copy then knows its role within the session. It may be an initiator or a non-initiator application replica. This role will determine who will start the application protocol after the establishment of the application environment. This protocol is executed by means of **SMI** messages as described is section 3.

In summary, the Meta-Conference supports all the functionality to:

- Initialize the JESP NG CSCW platform
- Report and recover from error conditions
- Report status messages
- Launch distributed applications such as the 3D Editor

There are more functionalities that will be available after further development, such as: interfacing with the audio/video conference facility, file transfer, etc.

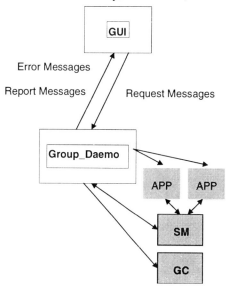

Figure 4.4: Local interactions

5. Conclusions and future work

The paper presents a prototype system for cooperative architecture design. The system is currently functioning on two development sites in Spain and Portugal. By using the prototype system, the users are able to load a design scene, modify its properties and save the result. Basic cooperative, interactive editing on the designed objects is already achieved via the communication networks.

Further development is undergoing towards a more complete system. Some important features such as the inconsistency and interference detection, storing and retrieving database information etc. will be further investigated to suit the day-to-day use of the architectural production process.

We sincerely hope that the further development based on this prototype system will contribute to a significant change of the traditional architecture design process. We expect that by using such a system and a new business process it supports, the occurrence of errors can be minimized. The construction cost and time can therefore be reduced.

Acknowledgment

This work is supported by the Esprit project No. 26287 M3D funding and the Spanish CICYT project funding TIC-98-1530-CE and Tel. 96-0544. The authors would like to thank Sergio Alves, David Sanchez, Marco Moita, Renato Marques and many other people that participated in the implementation of the prototype system.

References

[1] A. Almeida and C. A. Belo. "Support for Multimedia Cooperative Sessions over Distributed Environments." *Proc. Mediacomm'95*, Society for Computer Simulation, Southampton, April 1995.

[2] A. Almeida et al., Definition, Test and Management of Network Model, Esprit project Deliverable DL 1.4, April, 1999.

[3] Hagit Attiya, Jennifer L. Welch. "Sequential consistency versus linearizability." *Transactions on Computer Systems* Vol. 12, No. 2 (May 1994), Pages 91-122.

[4] R. Galli, P. Palmer, M. Mascaro, M. Dias, Y. Luo. "A Cooperative 3D Design System." *Proceedings of CEIG97*, Barcelona, Spain, June, 1997.

[5] Y. Luo, R. Galli, M. Mascaro, P. Palmer, F. J. Riera, C. Ferrer, S. F. Alves, Real Time Multi-User Interaction with 3D Graphics via Communication Network, Proceedings of IEEE 1998 Conference on Information Visualization, pp. 60-68, July 1998, London.

[6] Y. Luo et al. M3D Technical Specifications, ed. R. Galli, Esprit Project Deliverable DL 1.2, April, 1999.

[7] Y. Luo, R.Galli, M. Mascaro, P. Palmer, Cooperative Design for 3D Virtual Scenes, Proceedings of the Third IEEE International Foundation on Cooperative Information Systems Conference on Cooperative Information Systems (CoopIS'98), pp. 373-381, August 1998, New York, U.S.A.

[8] Nancy Lynch. *Distributed Algorithms*. Morgan Kaufman Publishers, Inc. ISBN 1-55860-348-8. 1997.

Visualisation in construction - Trends and future directions

Ghassan Aouad

Research Centre for the Built and Human Environment, University of Salford, UK

ABSTRACT

It is widely recognised that construction is an information intensive and complex industry. Traditional computational techniques have failed our industry because of the shear number of information interfaces and complex relationships. Modern visual technologies can resolve many of the aforementioned problems by providing construction professional with 3 dimensional information interfaces that allow them to use the visual model (3D, VR, etc) as the medium for communication, interaction, and integration.

This lecture looks at trends and predictions within the construction sector for technologies such as visualisation through CAD and VR. It then presents an improved model for information interfacing through VR capabilities. The information interface model is a web-based one developed to provide opportunities for many construction professionals across the supply chain using open technologies such as the Internet. This lecture will demonstrate that information visualisation is of importance and can be used by every participant within the construction sector including clients, contractors, cost estimators, project planners, and others. Finally, this lecture will conclude with a series of live demos resulting from state of the art research on information visualisation and interfaces being conducted at the University of Salford in the UK. Salford is bringing together visualisation, object oriented and web-technologies to solve the problems associated with construction information integration and communication. This lecture will provide an overview of this research that will help many interested parties understand how these technologies can work together.

Trends in information visualisation in construction

Ghassan Aouad. BSc, MSc, PhD.

Research Centre for the Built and Human Environment

University of Salford

e-mail g.aouad@surveying.salford.ac.uk

Abstract

It is widely recognised that construction is an information intensive and complex industry. Traditional computational techniques have failed our industry because of the shear number of information interfaces and complex relationships. Modern visual technologies can resolve many of the aforementioned problems by providing construction professionals with 3 dimensional information interfaces that allow them to use the visual model (3D, VR, etc) as the medium for communication, interaction, and integration.

This paper looks at trends and predictions within the construction sector for technologies such as visualisation through CAD and VR. It then presents an improved model for information interfacing through VR capabilities. The information interface model is a web-based one developed to provide opportunities for many construction professionals across the supply chain using open technologies such as the Internet. This paper will demonstrate that information visualisation is of importance and can be used by every participant within the construction sector including clients, contractors, cost estimators, project planners, and others. Finally, this paper will conclude with a series of screen snap shots resulting from state of the art research on information visualisation and interfaces being conducted at the University of Salford in the UK. Salford is bringing together visualisation, object oriented and web technologies to solve the problems associated with construction information integration and communication. This paper will provide an overview of this research which will help many interested parties understand how these technologies can work together.

Keywords: Virtual Reality, Trends, VRML, User Interface, Visualisation, Project Databases, construction.

1. Introduction

Recent research into learning styles demonstrate that the need for an imagery/visual type of interface can no longer be ignored. Research has shown that some people tend to learn in a visual, preferably 3D environment. It is therefore crucial to consider information visualisation in construction, at least from a learning perspective. Research at Salford demonstrated that construction professionals prefer 3D/VR types of models for user interface to traditional records/instances in databases. This paper demonstrates how the web/VRML and object technologies can work together to provide good information interfaces in construction. Technologies are now available which can be used to this end. The Internet and its facilities should be exploited for the benefits of better management and retrieval of construction information. The VRML (Virtual Reality Modelling Language) which is a web-based standard will be explored as a means of remotely interrogating information stored within an integrated database.

This paper aims to show trends in information visualisation in construction using CAD/VR technologies. It also includes some practical examples of how the industry is moving in that direction.

2. Previous work

The benefits of using VR as the technology for visualisation and interactions have been highlighted by many researchers in the construction sector [1, 2, 4, 10, 13, 15]. Some useful web sites are included in the references [5, 6, 7, 8, 9]. Most of these references address the issue of information visualisation and recommend VR/3D as the medium for visualisation and interfacing.

3. Trends in Visualisation

Research at Salford has shown that the use of VR and CAD for visualisation and interfacing purposes is on an upward trend. UK funded projects in this area have increased in the last few years. The data was collected from various sources in the UK. It is evident that CAD and VR research goes hand in hand as they are to a large extent inter-related. Figures 1 and 2 show trends in VR and CAD respectively.

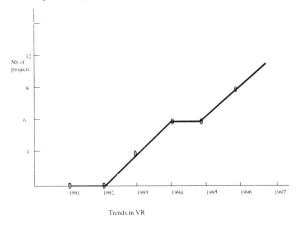

Trends in VR

Figure 1 Trends in VR research in construction

Figure 1 shows that research into VR in construction started to pick up since 1992. Most of this research is still at the experimental phase.

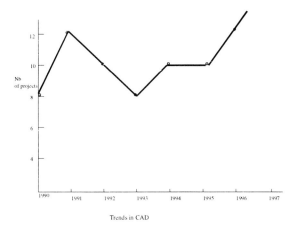

Trends in CAD

Figure 2 Trends in CAD research in construction

Figure 2 shows that CAD has been an active research area in the last 10 years. This is attributed to the fact that research into integrated systems is centered around the use of a CAD model. The last few years have seen a sift towards 3D type of research.

4. The need for a VR interface

Research undertaken at the University of Salford has shown how VR can be used as an interface to a complex system. The system is called "OSCON". (Open Systems for CONstruction). The system was developed using a VRML (Virtual Reality Modelling Language) interface to an integrated object oriented database, which supports the design, planning and estimating of buildings. The database uses the Object Store software, from which the information can be retrieved and stored. The user can interact with a Virtual Reality (VR) model without having to understand the background programming of the system. The user queries the database using the VR model to obtain information on elements of a proposed design of a building. Information available to the user includes texture, cost and time of elements within the building. As VRML is a World-Wide-Web (WWW) programming standard the information can be passed to other construction professionals relatively easily using the Internet. Figure3 below is a diagram showing the architecture of the system.

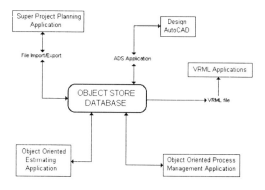

Figure 3 The architecture of the OSCON system

The model has been implemented and a graphical representation is shown below. The 3D capabilities provided by AutoCAD and VRML have been crucial to the development of the integrated system.

AutoCAD has been used to displaay 3D information of the intended design. All design parameter are stored in the database, but attched to objects shown in the CAD system. The user can manipulate design information using the interface provided within AutoCAD. However, VRML has been used as a sole interface. The user can display information in this environment without being able to change any of the parameters. This has been a requirement of the system in order to provide better control. The applications shown in Fifure 3 are distributed while conforming to the same data model. The use of client-server technology has enabled this to be implemented with a great suceess.

5. A scenario for a visual distributed construction environment

The visualisation and interfacing capabilities of the system are provided by AutoCAD and VRML as shown in Figure 4. The user is provided with a suite of integrated applications which support the design and time and cost planning of buildings. The AutoCAD design interface is used to generate the design layout of the building. The user interacts with AutoCAD as the graphical display environment. In reality, the design information is instantiated in the integrated object oriented database and displayed in AutoCAD. The design information is then used in generating quantities which are used by the time and cost planning prototype software. The VRML application is used to show the building in 3D and to retrieve information about specific objects in terms of cost, time, etc. The parameters of design objects could be changed in the object oriented database and the implications on cost and time are displayed within the VRML environment. This is one example of how design can be changed in the database by modifying its specifications and VR is used as the medium to show the such implications. For a better description of the numerous functions supported by the OSCON database, the reader is referred to Aouad et al [3].

This direct interaction with a VR environment has many advantages over the use of a CAD package. In traditional CAD systems, the design is relatively static which makes changes costly and time consuming as new images are re-generated from sequences of fixed frames [11]. In a VR environment, changes are handled efficiently by the technology. The ultimate benefit is the ability to create walkthroughs which can facilitate collaboration between clients, designers, contractors and suppliers. This is the main objective of the OSCON database and it is strongly believed that VR is the medium for communication and convergence. This approach is ideal for creating virtual organisations that communicate via an integrated database. This will allow companies to use their legacy applications, but the data shared between them is stored in the database to provide integrity and consistency. The interface is provided by VR to allow for 3D visual representation of data. This is a novel approach that will be adopted by

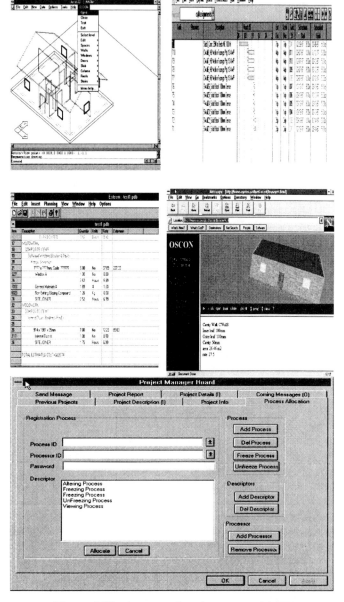

Figure 4 The integrated environment with VR as an interface.

innovative organisations striving for efficient ways of managing and storing data [15].

Figure 5 shows how companies can work together in a distributed environment while relying on CAD and VR capabilities to provide for better visualisation of construction information.

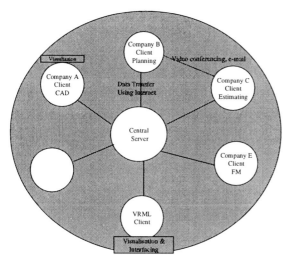

Figure 5 The Virtual Organisation

6. Industry involvement

The work presented here is being exploited by some construction firms which can help them through an experimentation phase. The VRML prototype has been demonstrated to major construction firms in the UK (ten companies). The overall feedback from the demonstrations was promising and encouraging. The users have indicated their favouritism for VR as an interface. The visualisation capabilities provided by the system has been a major driver for the aforementioned companies who started the experimentation phase. This 3D-based visual interfacing is promising as research in the learning area has shown that a learning style based on visual capabilities will be ideal for many companies in the construction sector.

7. Conclusions

This paper presented trends and capabilities within the are of information visualisation in construction. The tend is upwards and a lot of companies will be investing in these promising technologies. This paper also presented a VRML

prototype which will be used as an interface for a project integrated database (OSCON). This prototype is a web-based application which can be run from any web site. This will allow for construction information to be readily communicated between head offices and construction sites and any other locations and provide better visualisation and interfacing. This will ensure that information is communicated in a much better format with a lot more user-friendly visualisation capabilities. This paper has demonstrated that a VRML can be used as an interface to a complex object oriented database. This interface has more navigation capabilities. The user will ultimately find it simpler to navigate in a VR environment rather than browsing through thousands of records in a crude database environment.

8. References

1. Alshawi, M & Faraj, I. Integrating CAD and VR in construction. Proceedings of the Information Technology Awareness Workshop. January 1995, University of Salford.

2. Ames, A et al. The VRML source book, John Wiley and sons, 1996.

3. Marir.F, Aouad.G, Cooper. G. OSCONCAD: a model based CAD system integrated with computer-related construction applications, ITcon the electronic journal,1998, http://itcon.org

4. Griffin, M. Applications of VR in architecture and design. Proceedings of the Information Technology Awareness Workshop. January 1995, University of Salford.

5.http://www.construct.rdg.ac.uk/ITProjects/proje12 3.htm(Ashworth: linking Kappa, AutoCAd and WTK)

6.http://www.strath.ac.uk/Departments/CivEng/vcsr g.html (Retik visual scheduling)

7.http://www.construct.rdg.ac.uk/ITsearch/Projects/ project12.html(James Powell: visualisation)

8.http://wquoll.maneng.nott.ac.uk/Research/virart/i ndustry/maintran.html(Nottingham,maintenance training: VIRART)

9.http://wquoll.maneng.nott.ac.uk/Research/virart/i ndustry/rp.html(Nottingham,Rapid prototyping: VIRART)

10. Hubbold, R and Stone, R. Virtual reality as a design tool in Rolls Royce. Proceedings of the

Information Technology Awareness Workshop. January 1995, University of Salford.

11. Larijani, L.C. The virtual reality primer. McGraw-Hill, USA, 1994.

12. Lorch, R. Animation in communication. Proceedings of the Information Technology Awareness Workshop. January 1995, University of Salford.

13. Penn, A et al. Intelligent architecture: rapid prototyping for architecture and planning.

Proceedings of the Information Technology Awareness Workshop. January 1995, University of Salford.

14. Retik, A & Hay, R. Visual simulation using VR. Arcom 10th conference, Vol 12, 1994. pp 537-546.

15. Whyte, J, Bouchlagem D & Thorpe, T (1998). The Promise and Problems of Implementing Virtual Reality in Construction Prcatice. Proceedings, CIB W78, Sweden, 1998.

Author Index

Notes

Notes

**IEEE
COMPUTER
SOCIETY**

Press Activities Board

IEEE Computer Society Publications

The world-renowned IEEE Computer Society publishes, promotes, and distributes a wide variety of authoritative computer science and engineering texts. These books are available from most retail outlets. Visit the Online Catalog, *http://computer.org*, for a list of products.

IEEE Computer Society Proceedings

The IEEE Computer Society also produces and actively promotes the proceedings of more than 141 acclaimed international conferences each year in multimedia formats that include hard and softcover books, CD-ROMs, videos, and on-line publications.

For information on the IEEE Computer Society proceedings, send e-mail to cs.books@computer.org or write to Proceedings, IEEE Computer Society, P.O. Box 3014, 10662 Los Vaqueros Circle, Los Alamitos, CA 90720-1314. Telephone +1 714-821-8380. FAX +1 714-761-1784.

Additional information regarding the Computer Society, conferences and proceedings, CD-ROMs, videos, and books can also be accessed from our web site at *http://computer.org/cspress*

1/29/99